CRISIS INTERVENTION HANDBOOK

Third Edition

CRISIS INTERVENTION HANDBOOK

Assessment, Treatment, and Research

THIRD EDITION

Edited by

Albert R. Roberts, Ph.D.

OXFORD
UNIVERSITY PRESS

2005

OXFORD
UNIVERSITY PRESS

Oxford University Press, Inc., publishes works that further
Oxford University's objective of excellence
in research, scholarship, and education.

Oxford New York
Auckland Cape Town Dar es Salaam Hong Kong Karachi
Kuala Lumpur Madrid Melbourne Mexico City Nairobi
New Delhi Shanghai Taipei Toronto

With offices in
Argentina Austria Brazil Chile Czech Republic France Greece
Guatemala Hungary Italy Japan Poland Portugal Singapore
South Korea Switzerland Thailand Turkey Ukraine Vietnam

Published by Oxford University Press, Inc.,
198 Madison Avenue, New York, New York 10016

www.oup.com

Library of Congress Cataloging-in-Publication Data
Crisis intervention handbook : assessment, treatment,
and research / edited by Albert R. Roberts. — 3rd ed.
p. cm.
Includes bibliographical references and index.
ISBN-13 978-0-19-517991-0
ISBN 0-19-517991-9
1. Crisis intervention (Mental health services)—Handbooks, manuals, etc.
2. Community mental health services—Handbooks, manuals, etc.
I. Roberts, Albert R.
RC480.6.C744 2005
362.2′2—dc22 2005010137

Chapters 4, 6, 7, 11, 13, and 14 are reproduced from the journal *Brief Treatment and Crisis Intervention* by permission of Oxford University Press.

9 8 7 6 5 4 3

Printed in the United States of America
on acid-free paper

Acknowledgments

I want to express my sincere gratitude to the authors who contributed their expertise and original chapters to this book. I am also appreciative of the anonymous reviewers' important insights and technical suggestions.

Grateful acknowledgment goes to my exceptional editor, Joan Bossert (Editorial Director, Academic Books at Oxford University Press) for her deep commitment to this third edition and her editorial wisdom and care for detail. This book also owes a debt to the late Lilian Schein, longtime director of the Behavioral Science and Nursing Book Clubs. Ms. Schein helped me plan the first edition and taught me to appreciate interdisciplinary clinical practice.

My wife Beverly deserves special thanks and appreciation for thoroughly editing and proofreading several chapters and co-authoring chapter 19. Most important, Beverly's patience with me for the lost weekends and for the overflowing numbers of books, files, and papers in several rooms of our house went way beyond the call of duty of a marital partner. I am delighted and appreciative of the excellent illustrations drawn by my sister-in-law, Carole S. Roberts.

I dedicate this book to my late parents, Evelyn and Harry Roberts, who gave me unconditional love, emotional strength, and encouragement. They instilled within me a deep conviction to pursue knowledge, overcome adversity, and thrive to set realistic short-term and long-term goals; to aid and support vulnerable groups; and to persevere in all my occupational and family endeavors. I am forever devoted and appreciative of everything they did for me and my brother during our childhood and adolescence.

Both of them demonstrated superior inner strength after being diagnosed with cancer. At a time when women had only a 10% chance of a two- to five-year survival from breast cancer and mastectomy, my mother lived sixteen years. During his two years with the intense pain of prostate cancer, my father rarely complained and bravely persevered. Their quiet fighting spirit, courage, and resilience serve to make them role models for all persons in medical and psychological crisis.

I also dedicate this book to Dr. Viktor Frankl, psychiatrist, author of *Man's Search for Meaning*, and founder of logotherapy. When I was a young adult, his book helped me cope, survive, and master depression in the aftermath of my parents' deaths. His work continues to sustain and motivate many others.

NATIONAL INTERNET RESOURCES AND 24-HOUR CRISIS INTERVENTION HOTLINES

The National Suicide Prevention Lifeline is a 24-hour, toll-free suicide prevention hotline. Persons in crisis can call 1-800-273-8255 and be connected to one of the 115 crisis centers in the NSPI Network located in the city and state nearest to the caller's location. The national hotline network is administered through the Mental Health Association of New York City and is funded by Substance Abuse and Mental Health Services Administration's Center for Mental Health Services of the U.S. Department of Health and Human Services.

The National Disaster Technical Assistance Center of the Substance Abuse and Mental Health Services Administration (SAMHSA) in Bethesda, Maryland, provides resources and expertise to assist states, territories, and local communities that are preparing for or responding to the mental health needs of natural and man-made community disasters. Website: http://www.mentalhealth.samhsa.gov/dtac or phone: 1-800-308-3515.

The International Crisis Intervention Network was developed in 2001 and its overriding goal is to provide the latest information on evidence-based crisis intervention protocols, disaster mental health protocols, trauma treatment models, suicide prevention center directories, and domestic violence intervention resources as well as the latest books and peer-reviewed journal article abstracts on crisis intervention. Website: http://www.crisisinterventionnetwork.com

The National Domestic Violence Toll-Free Hotline provides crisis telephone counseling and referral to a network of emergency shelters and support groups for survivors of intimate partner violence. In addition to the hotline, the website contains information on teen and dating violence, domestic violence in the workplace, information for victims and survivors of domestic violence, and information for abusers. Website: http://www.ndvh.org or phone: 1-800-799-SAFE (7233).

Foreword

Unlike the usual stresses and conflicts that are a part of everyday life at home and at work, acute crisis episodes frequently overwhelm our traditional coping skills and result in dysfunctional behavior, "going to pieces," intense fears, and a highly anxious state, also known as a state of disequilibrium. This handbook focuses on acute crisis episodes and psychiatric emergencies and the step-by-step crisis intervention strategies used by crisis counselors. Each chapter focuses on a different major crisis-precipitating event, such as turbulent divorces, adolescent suicides, airplane crashes and fatalities of family members, date rape on the college campus, shootings in the public schools, battering of women and their children, polydrug abuse, HIV-positive women, patients in intensive care units, and survivors of community disasters and mass terrorist attacks. This book includes many illuminating case studies that illustrate how best to intervene in the aftermath of a crisis episode or traumatic event.

The acute and situational crises experienced by millions of individuals and families has been escalating in intensity and frequency. Crisis intervention programs and strategies can limit the debilitating impact of acute crisis episodes as they maximize opportunities for crisis stabilization and resolution.

It is a remarkable thing when crisis clinicians, counselors, and researchers from different disciplines collaborate on a major mental health and public health problem. Some practitioners have been concerned about psychiatric disorders, others about life-threatening illnesses, and some others about developmental crises. But, all mental health practitioners and graduate students have an overriding concern about the impact of community-wide disasters, especially mass terrorist attacks and how to rapidly assess and provide crisis intervention services. What sets this pathfinding and seminal book apart from others on crisis intervention is both the systematic application of Roberts's 7-Stage Crisis Intervention Protocol, the introduction of the Assessment, Crisis Intervention, and Trauma (ACT) Treatment Model, and the copious use of compelling and thought-provoking case illustrations on 60 different types of the most prevalent acute crisis episodes in society today. Disaster mental health teams have proliferated in these important few years since the September 11 terrorist bombings of the World Trade Center and the Pentagon. Many of the 15 brand new chapters seize on the opportunity to empower, support, and build on the inner strengths of millions of individuals by describing the process and therapeutic techniques of evidence-based crisis intervention. This is the most practical time-limited treatment book I have read in the past 10 years. It is timely, focused, straightforward, comprehensive, empowering, highly readable, and extremely valuable.

Dr. Roberts has always been an innovator and clinical research professor in the forefront of futuristic treatment planning. In 1999, Professor Roberts completed his six-level continuum on the duration and severity of domestic violence based on 501 cases. Now at the end of 2004, Professor Roberts has updated and expanded the second edition of his authoritative handbook. The *Crisis Intervention Handbook* is a masterful sourcebook of practical significance, bridging crisis theory and assessment to evidence-based practice. This book provides well-written, detailed, up-to-date, thorough, and practical best practices. I predict that this authoritative volume will become the classic definitive work on crisis intervention for the important years ahead.

As editor of this volume, Dr. Roberts has selected as the chapter authors an outstanding cast of 50 internationally recognized experts in the rapid assessment and treatment of crisis episodes. Each chapter provides the reader with a comprehensive and practical application of Roberts's seven-stage crisis intervention model to the key components of acute and situational crises. This third edition of 32 specially designed chapters includes 14 brand new chapters and 18 thoroughly revised chapters. This is the first handbook on crisis intervention to incorporate into each chapter a section on resilience, protective factors, and the strengths perspective. Also, 15 of the chapters each apply two or more case studies to the seven stages in Roberts' Crisis Intervention Model.

This all-inclusive resource provides everything mental health clinicians, crisis counselors, healthcare specialists, crisis intervenors, and trained volunteers need to know about crisis intervention. This book is a stunning achievement and landmark work.

Ann Wolbert Burgess, RN, CS, D.N.Sc., FAAN., DACFE
Professor of Psychiatric-Mental Health Nursing
School of Nursing, Boston College

Contents

Part III: Crisis Assessment and Intervention Models with Children and Youth

Part IV: Crisis Intervention and Crisis Prevention With Victims of Violence

Part V: Crisis Assessment and Crisis Intervention in Health-Related and Mental Health–Related Crises

Part VI: Evidence-Based Practice and Research

Contributors

EDITOR

Albert R. Roberts, Ph.D., B.C.E.T.S., D.A.B.F.E., is Professor of Criminal Justice and Social Work in the Faculty of Arts and Sciences, Livingston College Campus at Rutgers, The State University of New Jersey in Piscataway. Dr. Roberts was awarded his doctorate in 1978 from the School of Social Work and Community Planning at the University of Maryland in Baltimore. Dr. Roberts served as Director of Faculty and Curriculum Development for the Administration of Justice Department from September 2001 through 2004. He is a Diplomate with the American College of Forensic Examiners and has been certified as an expert witness by the Illinois State Courts in Chicago. He was an Associate Professor and Chairman of Planning and Management Curriculum at the Indiana University School of Social Work from 1984 through 1989. He is the founding Editor-in-Chief of the *Brief Treatment and Crisis Intervention* quarterly journal (Oxford University Press) and serves on the advisory board to Encyclopedia Americana as well as on the editorial boards of seven professional journals. Dr. Roberts is a member of the Board of Scientific and Professional Advisors and a Board Certified Expert in Traumatic Stress for the American Academy of Experts in Traumatic Stress. Dr. Roberts is the founding and current editor of the 42-volume Springer Series on Social Work (1980 to present) and is the author, co-author, or editor of over 200 scholarly publications, including numerous peer-reviewed journal articles and book chapters, and 26 books. Dr. Roberts's most recent book, *Ending Intimate Abuse: Practical Guidance and Survival Strategies* (Oxford University Press), was published in March 2005 and was co-authored by his wife, Beverly Schenkman Roberts.

Dr. Roberts has 30 years of full-time teaching experience at the undergraduate and graduate levels in both criminal justice and social work. He has conducted eight different national organizational surveys over the past 30 years and has been project director or principal investigator on research projects in Maryland, New York, Indiana, and New Jersey. In 2002, Dr. Roberts completed the first national organizational survey of 39 statewide domestic violence coalitions under the auspices of the National Network to End Domestic Violence (NNEDV) in Washington, D.C. His recent books include *Evidence-Based Practice Manual: Research and Outcome Measures in Health and Human Services* (co-edited by Kenneth R. Yeager, Oxford University Press, 2004); and *Social Workers' Desk Reference* (co-edited by Gilbert J. Greene, Oxford, 2002). *Social Workers' Desk Reference* has won three national awards from the Association of American Publishers, the American Library Association User's Reference Division, and *Choice*. Dr. Roberts has been listed in *Who's Who in America* since 1992.

Contributors

Gary Behrman, Ph.D.
Research Associate
School of Social Work
State University of New York
Albany, New York

Alan L. Berman, Ph.D.
Executive Director
American Association of Suicidology
Bethesda, Maryland
Professor Emeritus of Psychology
American University
Washington, D.C.

Linda L. Black, Ph.D.
Associate Professor
Department of Educational Psychology, Counseling, and Special Education
Northern Illinois University
DeKalb, Illinois

Mary Boes, D.S.W., M.P.H.
Associate Professor
Department of Social Work
University of Northern Iowa
Cedar Falls, Iowa

Ann Wolbert Burgess, R.N., D.N.Sc., F.A.A.N.
Professor of Psychiatric-Mental Health Nursing
School of Nursing
Boston College
Boston, Massachussetts
Forensic Mental Health Editor for the journal
Brief Treatment and Crisis Intervention

Ellis Copeland, Ph.D.
Professor of School Psychology
Division of Professional Psychology
University of Northern Colorado
Greeley, Colorado

Sophia R. Dziegielewski, Ph.D.
Professor and Director
School of Social Work
University of Cincinnati
Cincinnati, Ohio

Yvonne M. Eaton, M.S.W.
Clinical Supervisor
Safe Harbor Behavioral Healthcare
Clinical Director
Erie County Critical Incident Stress Management Team
Erie, Pennsylvania

George S. Every, Jr. Ph.D., FAPM., CTS
Co-founder, International Critical Incident Stress Foundation, Inc.
Ellicott City, Maryland
Adjunct Professor of Psychology
Johns Hopkins University and
Loyola University
Baltimore, Maryland

Donald K. Granvold, Ph.D.
Professor and Associate Dean
School of Social Work
University of Texas at Arlington
Arlington, Texas

Gilbert J. Greene, Ph.D.
Professor
College of Social Work
Ohio State University
Columbus, Ohio

Thomas K Gregoire, Ph.D.
Associate Professor
College of Social Work
Ohio State University
Columbus, Ohio

Dianne F. Harrison, Ph.D.
Associate Vice-President of Academic Affairs
Professor and Dean Emerita of Social Work
Florida State University
Tallahassee, Florida

Vincent Henry, Ph.D.
Associate Professor and Director
Homeland Security Training Institute
Southampton College of Long Island University
Southampton, New York

Ann M. Ingala, M.A.
Division of Professional Psychology
University of Northern Colorado
Greeley, Colorado

David A. Jobes, Ph.D.
Professor
Department of Psychology
Catholic University of America
Washington, D.C.
Former President, American Association of Suicidology

Eric D. Johnson, Ph.D.
Assistant Professor and Director
Family Therapy Graduate Programs
Drexel University
Philadelphia, Pennsylvania

Rachel Kaul, M.S.W.
Director
Disaster and Emergency Services

Maryland Department of Health and Mental Hygiene
Baltimore, Maryland
Former Coordinator
Pentagon Employee Assistance Program
Washington, D.C.

James F. Klein, Ph.D. Candidate
Counseling Psychology
University of Northern Illinois
DeKalb, Illinois

Karen Knox, Ph.D.
Associate Professor and Director
Field Placements
School of Social Work
Southwest Texas State University
San Marcos, Texas

Jeffrey M. Lating, Ph.D.
Professor and Director
Doctoral Program in Psychology
Loyola University of Baltimore
Baltimore, Maryland

Mo-Yee Lee, Ph.D.
Professor of Social Work
Ohio State University
Columbus,Ohio
Visiting Research Professor
University of Hong Kong
Hong Kong, China

Sarah J. Lewis, Ph.D.
Associate Professor
School of Social Work
Barry University
Miami, Florida

Jan Ligon, Ph.D.
Associate Professor
Department of Social Work
College of Health and Human Sciences
Georgia State University
Atlanta, Georgia

Gordon MacNeil, Ph.D.
Associate Professor
School of Social Work
The University of Alabama
Tuscaloosa, Alabama

Catherine E. Martin, Ph.D.
Department of Psychology
Catholic University of America
Washington, D.C.

Joseph McBride, M.S.W.
Critical Incident Stress Debriefing Trainer
New Jersey Chapter of NASW
Clinical Social Worker
Lawrenceville, New Jersey

Virginia McDermott, R.N.
Medical-Surgical Nurse
Cardiac Care Unit
Allen Memorial Hospital
Waterloo, Iowa

Linda G. Mills, Ph.D., J.D.
Professor of Social Work and Affiliated Professor of Law
Vice-Provost for Student Services
New York University
New York, New York

Jeffrey T. Mitchell, Ph.D.
Co-founder, International Critical Incident Stress Foundation
Ellicott City, Maryland
Associate Professor
Emergency Services Department
University of Maryland at Baltimore County
Baltimore County, Maryland

Scott Newgass, M.S.W.
Clinical Instructor in Social Work
Yale Child Study Institute
Coordinator
Regional School Crisis Prevention and Response Program
New Haven, Connecticut

M. Sean O'Halloran, Ph.D.
Professor of Counseling Psychology and Clinic Director
Psychological Services Clinic
Division of Professional Psychology
University of Northern Colorado
Greeley, Colorado

Allen J Ottens, Ph.D.
Associate Professor
Department of Educational Psychology, Counseling and Special Education
Northern Illinois University
Dekalb, Illinois

Cheryl Regehr, Ph.D.
Professor of Social Work and Director, Centre for Applied Social Research
University of Toronto
Former Clinical Director
Critical Incident Stress Team at Pearson International Airport
Toronto, Canada
Research Commentaries Editor of the
Brief Treatment and Crisis Intervention journal

William J. Reid, D.S.W. (Deceased)
Professor Emeritus of Social Work
State University of New York at Albany and
The University of Chicago
School of Social Service Administration

Judy Rheinsheld, M.S.W.
Scioto Paint Valley Mental Health Center
Fayette County Clinic
Washington Court House, Ohio

Albert R. Roberts, Ph.D., D.A.B.F.E.
Professor of Criminal Justice and Social Work
Faculty of Arts and Science
Rutgers University, Livingston College Campus
Piscataway, New Jersey
Editor-in-Chief of the
Brief Treatment and Crisis Intervention journal

Beverly Schenkman Roberts, M.Ed.
Health Advocate and Director
Mainstreaming Medical Care Program
The Arc of New Jersey
North Brunswick, New Jersey

Donna Kirkpatrick Pinson, Ph.D. Candidate
Counseling Psychology
University of Northern Illinois
DeKalb, Illinois

Gerald T. Powers, Ph.D.
Professor Emeritus
School of Social Work
Indiana University
Indianapolis, Indiana

David Schonfeld, M.D.
Professor of Pediatrics and Child Study
Department of Pediatrics and Institute for Child Study
Yale University School of Medicine
Yale-New Haven Hospital
Director
Regional School Crisis Prevention and Response Program
New Haven, Connecticut

Amy L. Shewbert, B.A.
Research Assistant
Psychological Management Services
Lubbock, Texas

Norman M. Shulman, Ed.D.
Clinical Assistant Professor
Department of Neuropsychiatry and Behavioral Science
Texas Tech University School of Medicine
Licensed Psychologist
Psychological Management Services
Lubbock, Texas

Jonathan Singer, M.S.W.
Doctoral Candidate and Instructor
School of Social Work
University of Pittsburgh
Pittsburgh, Pennsylvania

Chris Stewart, Ph.D.
Assistant Professor
School of Social Work
University of Pittsburgh
Pittsburgh, Pennsylvania

Kristy Sumner, M.S.W.
Ph.D. Candidate
College of Public Affairs and Health Sciences
University of Central Florida
Orlando, Florida

Rhonda Trask, M.S.W.
Clinical Social Worker
Newark, Ohio

Victor Welzant, Psy.D.
Director of Training
International Critical Incident Stress Foundation
Ellicott City, Maryland

Kenneth R. Yeager, Ph.D.
Director of Quality Assurance and
Assistant Professor of Psychiatry,
Department of Psychiatry
School of Medicine
Ohio State University Medical Center
Columbus, Ohio

Introduction

The first edition of this book (published in 1990) and the second (published in 2000) were major successes, and the editor has kept the same framework with the five original sections. However, this new edition is basically a new book, with 15 brand-new chapters and an additional section on disaster mental health and crisis intervention. The remaining original chapters were thoroughly updated and revised by the original authors.

Since the publication of the first edition, crisis intervention practices and programs have changed considerably. Professional and public interest in crisis intervention, crisis response teams, crisis management, and crisis stabilization has grown tremendously in the past decade, partially due, no doubt, to the prevalence of acute crisis events impacting on the lives of the general public. The focus of this book is on crisis intervention services for persons who are victims of natural disasters; school-based and home-based violence; violent crimes, such as homicide, aggravated assault, sexual assault, domestic violence, and date rape among college students; and personal or family crises, such as the death of a loved one, incest, life-threatening medical conditions, divorce, suicide and suicide attempts, and drug abuse.

Suicide prevention programs and other 24-hour crisis hotlines provide valuable assistance to callers who are contemplating suicide and related self-destructive acts. These telephone hotlines are operational nationwide, usually staffed by trained graduate students and volunteers. The programs that are accredited by the American Association of Suicidology require all crisis hotline workers to complete a minimum of 40 hours of training and 20 hours of supervised hotline experience.

Hundreds of thousands of persons in distress turn to health care, family counseling, and domestic violence and mental health facilities throughout the United States for help in resolving crisis situations. Many crises are triggered by a life-threatening event, such as acute cardiac arrest, attempted murder, criminal homicide, motor vehicle crashes, child custody battles, drug overdoses, psychiatric emergencies, sexual assaults, woman battering, suicide, and/or community disasters. Crisis events and situations can often be critical turning points in a person's life. They can serve as a challenge and opportunity for rapid problem resolution and growth, or as a debilitating event leading to sudden disequilibrium, failed coping, and dysfunctional behavior patterns. In addition, given the limitations imposed on crisis interveners and clinicians by the requirements of managed care groups, the use of brief treatment has become more widespread.

INDIVIDUAL VERSUS GROUP CRISIS INTERVENTION

There is debate in the field of crisis intervention among competing professional groups. The primary debate stems from each professional group's somewhat different crisis intervention model, and the groups' different training and educational requirements for certification. The nature of the debate is complicated by the fact that in the professional literature read by the involved professional groups and organizations, crisis intervention has been defined in different ways, including different concepts and parameters of intervention. *This handbook applies a unifying model of crisis intervention while building on the strengths of each model.*

At the core of the debate among professionals in the crisis intervention field is the definition and scope of the assistance provided by professionals *immediately* after the crisis event has occurred, and the definition and scope of the assistance provided by professionals in the short-term period (several weeks) following the crisis event. Also key to the debate is the level of training and expertise of the professionals who provide the *immediate* assistance. This issue is further compounded by the fact that there are two overarching categories of crisis events: *private events* that impact individuals or families (e.g., a suicide attempt, an HIV diagnosis, divorce, woman battering, or the untimely death of a close family member), and *public events* that impact groups of individuals (e.g., a shooting at a school or in the workplace, a devastating tornado, or an airplane crash). A complicating factor in the latter category is the involvement and intrusion of the news media at a time when the affected individuals may want to be left alone to deal with the crisis situation. This handbook will address and clarify these issues.

Some authorities have mistakenly defined *crisis intervention* as grief counseling, hostage negotiations, or observing and collecting evidence at the crime scene of a domestic violence incident. Other authorities define crisis intervention to include disaster relief work and emergency medical services performed by paramedics, firefighters, emergency medical technicians (EMTs), airport security officers, flight attendants, and airline baggage handlers, as well as trained volunteers. Other authorities contend that crisis intervention is synonymous with the work of crisis response teams consisting of trained mental health professionals, victim advocates, law enforcement specialists, and clergy (2-day training and follow-up debriefings by the trainers from the National Organization for Victim Assistance [NOVA]). Finally, the third and largest group of authorities (including the editor of this book) have operationally defined crisis intervention as immediate, short-term, and applied through rapid assessment protocols; bolstering coping methods, psychosocial adaptation, solution-focused, timely crisis resolution. In general, the expectation is that the crisis intervenor (also referred to as the crisis clinician, crisis counselor, psychologist, or social worker) has completed a graduate degree in clinical, community, or school psychology; guidance and counseling; pastoral counseling; psychiatric–mental health nursing; or social work. As part of the master's or doctoral program, the mental health professional has acquired basic counseling, crisis intervention, and clinical practice training and skills, as well as field practicum experience.

In chapter 1, and subsequent chapters, the authors focus on the extensive step-by-step, eclectic model of crisis intervention (interchangeable with the term *crisis counseling*). There is much confusion among the general public regarding the definition of crisis intervention among mental health professionals in the aftermath of traumatic events, such as mass shootings in the schools, airplane disasters, and murders in the workplace. Frontline crisis workers and emergency services personnel are well trained and effective in rescuing survivors and defusing potentially disastrous situations. The average citizen is not aware of the vital work of crisis clinicians after the work of first responders/frontline crisis workers is completed. Because of a strong code of ethics and confidentiality safeguards, it would be a violation for social workers and psychologists to issue press releases or engage in interviews with journalists. Chapter 9, by Everly, Lating, and Mitchell, focuses on Critical Incident Stress Debriefing for emergency services personnel, firefighters, and police officers after individuals in the disaster receive medical attention and are stabilized. Jeff Mitchell and George Everly are the founders of the International Critical Incident Stress Foundation, and critical incident stress and trauma debriefing teams.

The controversy in this field developed as a result of rigid adherence to one model or approach rather than using an eclectic perspective that recognizes and accepts the most effective components of each model. *This is the first comprehensive handbook that prepares the crisis intervenor for rapid assessment and timely crisis intervention in the twenty-first century.* Emotional and psychological first aid (also known as critical incident debriefing, frontline first response, and crisis stabilization) can be effectively administered by trained volunteers, including emergency service workers. *However, crisis intervention or crisis counseling is much more extensive than critical incident debriefing and crisis stabilization, usually requiring considerably more time (usually 4 to 6 weeks) and graduate-level courses in a mental health discipline.* Since crisis intervention is a multidisciplinary field, the editor is more concerned with the graduate courses and training seminars completed, and the skills of the crisis intervenor, than with the particular academic discipline with which the crisis clinician is identified.

There are two primary phases to crisis intervention. The initial phase occurs either immediately after the acute crisis episode or disaster has occurred or within 48 hours of the event. This phase is generally referred to as defusing the crisis and securing safety, crisis stabilization, emotional first aid, or crisis management. This phase is usually standard operating procedure for statewide crisis response teams (who have been trained by the American Psychological Association disaster task force, the International Critical Incident Stress Foundation, and/or the American Red Cross), law enforcement agencies, hospitals and medical centers, and correctional agencies.

The specific nature of the intervention varies depending on the type of crisis event that has occurred. An example is the need for crisis intervention brought on by violence in the workplace, in which a disgruntled employee returns to his former place of business and shoots his former supervisors and/or coworkers. In this scenario, the initial intervention revolves around providing emergency medical services for the shooting victims, as well as crisis stabilization for the victims and coworkers, particularly those who were at the scene and witnessed the shooting. The first activity of the crisis team is to meet with the key people who are in charge at the site where the crisis event occurred to establish the plan of action. Next, the crisis team assembles the victims and observers to the crisis event (who have been medically stabilized) to provide a debriefing and to clarify the facts surrounding the event (e.g., has the shooter been taken into custody? has a telephone hotline been set up for family members who want to know what is happening?); identify postcrisis problems; provide an overview of what to expect emotionally in the aftermath of the crisis event; and describe where victims and observers can go for individual counseling and support. The team also facilitates individual and group discussions to help the parties involved to ventilate and process the event. Finally, the crisis team communicates with the supervisors to help them understand how to identify and facilitate their employees' recovery by referral to a licensed mental health professional.

Although the crisis team approach described here is the recommended response to an institutional or natural disaster, it is not always available and depends on the readiness and proactive stance of the community in which one lives and works. Every community should have access to trained crisis intervenors, either locally or through a consulting contract with a crisis team from a nearby city. The most commonly used models for group crisis intervention—emotional first aid, crisis and disaster management—were developed by Jeff Mitchell, George Everly, David Schonfeld, and Scott Newgass. These two models will be applied in chapters 8, 9, 21, and 26.

The most popular model for individual crisis intervention is generally known as *crisis intervention* or *crisis counseling*, which takes place during the days and weeks immediately after the crisis event. This phase or type of crisis intervention is commonly utilized by clinical social workers and psychologists in group private practices, crisis intervention units of community mental health centers, child and family counseling centers, and hospital settings. Various practice models have been developed to assist clinicians in working with persons in crisis including the three-step model (assessment, boiling down the problem, coping alternatives). This book will consistently utilize the Roberts seven-stage crisis intervention model, which is applied as an intervention framework for providing crisis counseling. This thorough and sequential model can facilitate early identification of crisis precipitants, active listening, problem solving, effective coping skills, inner strengths and protective factors, and effective crisis resolution.The Roberts seven-stage model consists of the following:

1. Assess lethality and mental health status.
2. Establish rapport and engage the client.
3. Identify major problems.
4. Deal with feelings.
5. Explore alternative coping methods and partial solutions.
6. Develop an action plan.
7. Develop a termination and follow-up protocol.

This handbook was written for frontline crisis workers, graduate students, and clinicians who work with individuals, families, and communities in crisis. Crisis theory and practice principles cut across several professions, including counseling, social work, psychology, psychiatric nursing, psychiatry, law enforcement, and victim assistance. Therefore, an interdisciplinary approach has been used in compiling and editing this book. This volume is a collaborative work, with original chapters written by prominent clinical social workers, health social workers, clinical nurse specialists, clinical psychologists, counseling psychologists, community psychologists, and victim advocates. Each practice chapter (chapters 5 through 30) begins with one to three case studies or vignettes, followed by sections that present an introduction; the scope of the problem; and the research literature related to resilience and protective factors for specific high-risk groups (e.g., depressed adolescents, incest survivors, stressed-out college students, battered women, chemically dependent individuals). The main part of each chapter includes a framework for the practice of crisis intervention with a specific target group. Several detailed cases and case commentaries are included in each chapter to demonstrate the steps in the operation of the seven-stage crisis intervention model. Also highlighted in each chapter are clinical issues, controversies, roles, and skills. Many of the chapters conclude with summaries and predictions for the future use of crisis intervention with a particular target group, such as callers to a 24-hour mobile crisis unit, college students in crisis, women with AIDS, adolescent suicide attemptors, victims of violent crimes, victims of community disasters, and substance abusers.

Although the primary focus of this book is crisis intervention in the United States, some of the chapters do include a discussion of suicide and family crises and community disasters in other countries. Chapter 2 (by Roberts) reviews studies on the effectiveness of suicide prevention centers in Canada, England, and Japan, as well as the United States. Suicide prevention by e-mail has been shown to be effective through the network of Samaritans mutual aid in Australia, England, and Hong Kong. Chapters 1 and 2 also includes information on crisis intervention studies conducted with groups of clients in Switzerland, Canada, and the United States who had psychiatric emergencies.

In Chapter 9, Everly, Mitchell, and Lating, the founders of Critical Incident Stress Management (CISM), apply their group crisis intervention model to community disasters—for example, the bombing of the U.S. Embassy in Nairobi; a nationwide crisis intervention system for postwar Kuwait; and crisis intervention services for families of victims of the TWA 800 air disaster that occurred over Long Island, New York.

In Chapters 21 and 22 there is a discussion of school shootings, potentially violent situations, and crisis prevention, as well as group crisis intervention models in the aftermath of school fatalities in the United States. Chapter 9 focuses on a statewide school crisis prevention team and crisis response program that has helped thousands of children and adolescents during the past decade. These chapters contain valuable information for mental health professionals worldwide, by providing detailed information on how to plan and implement individual crisis intervention, schoolwide notification systems, classroom interventions, training and support for schoolteachers and guidance counselors, and crisis intervention in resource rooms. No nation is immune from the shootings at schools and at work that have received extensive attention in the media. An example of a horrendous act of violence, in what could have been viewed as an unlikely location for mass murder, occurred in Sterling, Scotland on March 13, 1996. A disgruntled former school custodian, angry because he had been fired, returned to the elementary school where he had worked, killing a teacher and 16 children and injuring many other children before turning the gun on himself. The police and emergency services staff brought the injured victims to the three infirmaries (hospitals) in the area. In the aftermath of this horrific school disaster, no crisis intervention teams were available to provide assistance to the grieving family members and the recovering victims.

Recognizing the necessity of having mental health professionals mobilized to respond quickly if a disaster occurred in their local community, the American Red Cross in the 1990s developed cooperative agreements with the American Counseling Association, the American Psychological Association, and the National Association of Social Workers in order to facilitate the development of mental health and crisis response teams to provide immediate intervention. As a result, within 24 hours of a major disaster in the United States (such as a plane crash of tornado) community crisis response teams are on the scene, providing crisis intervention services.

Historically, in each decade there have been a number of fatal terrorists attacks that result in acute crisis episodes and psychological trauma to survivors and secondary victims in different parts of the world. The following is a sample of some of the worst events in the past four decades:

- On September 5, 1972, Palestinian terrorists attacked Olympic Village in Munich, Germany, 11 Israeli Olympic athletes, one policemen, and five of the terrorists were killed, and the remaining 3 terrorists were captured;
- On November 23, 1985, Palestinian terrorists hijacked an Egypt Airliner in the Middle East and forced the pilot to fly them to Malta—when Egyptian Commandoes tried to rescue all of the passengers, 59 people were killed;
- On December 21, 1988, Pan Am 103 was bombed over Lockerbie, Scotland, and as a result 259 people were killed by Libyan terrorists;
- April 19, 1995, the Federal Building in Oklahoma City was bombed with a 4,000 pound fertilizer bomb and 168 people were killed, including 19 children, and more than 500 people were injured;
- On August 7, 1998, U.S. Embassies in Nairobi, Kenya, and Tanzania were bombed by terrorists—291 people were killed in Nairobi, including 12 U.S. citizens, and more than 5,000 people were seriously injured, while 11 people were killed and 77 injured at the U.S. Embassy at Tanzania;
- On September 11, 2001, 19 Islamic terrorist suicide bombers highjacked four large passenger airliners killing almost 3,000 people by crashing the planes into New York City's World Trade Center Twin Towers, the Pentagon in Virginia and a field in Shanksville, Pennsylvania;
- On March 11, 2004, the terrorist bombing of train in Madrid, Spain, kills 190 passengers and injures 1800 others;
- and on September 4, 2004, a school is taken over in Beslan, Russia, and more than 340 children and adults are killed.

We cannot predict the psychological impact of future mass terrorist attacks. However, the best method of preparing ourselves as mental health professionals is to develop the skills necessary for rapid acute lethality and clinical assessment, as well as training in evidence-based crisis intervention protocols, multicomponent critical incident stress management, trauma treatment methods, and other disaster mental health interventions (for detailed information and the latest protocols see chapters 5 through 14 of this book).

This volume is intended to be a key resource for professionals who are called upon to intervene with individuals and groups in crisis. There is a very strong interest in the application of crisis theory and crisis intervention techniques among professionals practicing in school, family, health, mental health, victim assistance, and group private practice settings. This book has been designed primarily for frontline crisis workers (e.g., clinical psychologists and social workers at outpatient mental health centers, psychiatric–mental health nurses, social work case managers, and clinicians skilled in crisis management after a community disaster), clinicians in managed care settings, and graduate students who need to know the latest steps and methods for intervening effectively with persons in acute crisis. This book will also be useful as the primary text in courses such as crisis intervention, crisis counseling, crisis intervention and brief treatment, social work practice II, and mental health practice, and as the supplementary text in health social work, introduction to human services, psychiatric nursing, and community psychology.

I

OVERVIEW

CRISIS HOTLINE
I'VE WORKED FOR THE COMPANY 20 YEARS AND THEY GOT RID OF ME. LIFE IS NOT WORTH LIVING ANYMORE !!
DON'T GIVE UP HOPE. WE HAVE HELPED ALOT OF PEOPLE WITH THE SAME PROBLEM. THERE ARE SEVERAL WAYS TO GET A NEW JOB. LET'S TALK.

1

Bridging the Past and Present to the Future of Crisis Intervention and Crisis Management

ALBERT R. ROBERTS

This book is an interdisciplinary handbook, specially written by a team of 50 esteemed crisis and trauma experts, to prepare crisis workers, crisis counselors, crisis therapists, emergency services workers, clergy, and graduate students for rapid lethality assessments, timely crisis intervention, and trauma treatment in the 21st century. It is the third edition of the *Crisis Intervention Handbook: Assessment, Treatment, and Research.*

The landscape of crisis intervention practices and services was forever altered on September 11, 2001, with the mass terrorist disasters at the World Trade Center Twin Towers in New York City, the Pentagon in Arlington, Virginia, and United Airlines Flight 93, which crashed in Shanksville, Pennsylvania. As a result of this catastrophic terrorist attack, 2,973 lives were lost—the largest loss of life of U.S. citizens, firefighters (343 fatalities, FDNY), and police (23 fatalities, NYPD) on one day in our history. The impact of this attack spread far beyond New York and Washington, D.C. All over the country crisis intervention procedures were reviewed and updated.

This edition contains 14 new chapters and a new section on disaster mental health and frontline crisis intervention strategies. The other 18 chapters in sections 1 and 3 through 6 have been revised and updated for this edition.

We live in an era in which sudden and unpredictable crisis and traumatic events have become the familiar subjects of everyday news. Millions of people are struck by potentially crisis-inducing events that they are not able to resolve on their own. They need immediate help from mental health professionals, crisis intervention workers, or their significant others. The up-to-date chapters in this book include thought-provoking case illustrations of acute crisis episodes, with a step-by-step crisis intervention protocol applied to each of the 50 case histories discussed.

The prevalence of social, psychological, criminal justice, and public health problems has increased dramatically in recent years. Most notable are these potentially crisis-inducing or trauma-provoking events:

Violent crimes (e.g., hostage situations, assaults, terrorist bombings, bioterrorism threats, domestic violence, muggings, sniper or drive-by shootings, sexual assaults, murder and attempted murders, violence in schools and the workplace, mass murders).

Traumatic stressors or crisis-prone situations (e.g., becoming divorced or separated from one's spouse, losing one's job, being hospitalized for a sudden heart attack, being diagnosed with cancer, being diagnosed with a sexually transmitted disease, having emergency surgery, watching a close family member die, sustaining serious injuries in a car accident, experiencing a near fatal encounter).

The onset or reoccurrence of mental illness (e.g., schizophrenia, schizoaffective disorder, bipolar disorder, personality disorders, obsessive compulsive disorder, phobias, panic disorder, posttraumatic stress disorder, major depression).

Natural disasters (e.g., hurricanes, floods, tornadoes, earthquakes, volcanic eruptions).

Accidents (e.g., airplane crashes, train crashes, multiple motor vehicle and truck crashes, bus crashes, ferry boat crashes).

Transitional or developmental stressors or events (e.g., moving to a new city, changing schools in the middle of the year, divorce, unwanted pregnancy, having a baby with a disability, becoming physically disabled and placed in a nursing home).

The increase in terrorist threats as reported by the Federal Bureau of Investigation and the Office of Homeland Security has made many Americans anxious and panicky, hypervigilant, and intensely fearful that the next mass terrorist attack will result in the death of one of their loved ones. In addition to generalized fears about future terrorist attacks, there are numerous other scenarios that are potential triggers for a crisis:

The homicide rate in the United States is the highest of all countries except Colombia and South Africa, and for the year 2000, it was the second leading cause of death for individuals age 15 to 24.

Approximately one out of every five children and youths in the United States exhibit signs and symptoms of a psychiatric disorder each year.

Domestic violence is prevalent throughout the United States, with an estimated 8.7 million cases annually.

The National Institute of Mental Health reports that more than 30,500 people die annually from suicide, 80 people die each day of the year.

The U.S. Department of Health and Human Services reports that more than 3,200 new cases of cancer are diagnosed each day of the year.

The U.S. Public Health Service reports that 140 patients with AIDS die each day of the year.

Motor vehicle accidents alone kill 118 people each day of the year.

All of these life-threatening or fatal events can produce acute crisis episodes and posttraumatic stress disorder (PTSD). Therefore, it is critically important for all mental health and public health professionals to provide early responses in the form of lethality assessments, crisis intervention, and trauma treatment (see Chapter 6 in this volume for an overview of the seven new chapters in Section 2 on disaster mental health strategies and for a discussion of first responders' and frontline crisis workers' application of the ACT model: Assessment, Crisis Intervention, and Trauma Treatment).

The high physical and psychological costs of traumatic events, such as the ones listed above, are all too familiar to mental health and health care professionals. Chapter 7 presents a detailed discussion of the different weapons of mass destruction, how first responders should prepare for and respond to terrorist threats, and the vital work of the New York City Disaster Coalition of over 300 licensed clinicians who have provided free and confidential treatment to survivors and their families post-September 11. Chapter 8 examines the disaster mental health and crisis intervention strategies used with survivors at the Pentagon for the past three years.

Crisis intervention can lead to early resolution of acute stress disorders or crisis episodes, while providing a turning point so that the individual is strengthened by the experience. Crisis and traumatic events can provide a danger or warning signal, or an opportunity to sharply reduce emotional pain and vulnerability. The ultimate goal of crisis intervention is to bolster available coping methods or help individuals reestablish coping and problem-solving abilities while helping them to take concrete steps toward managing their feelings and developing an action plan. Crisis intervention can reinforce strengths and protective factors for those who feel overwhelmed by a traumatic event. In addition, it aims to reduce lethality and potentially harmful situations and provides referrals to community agencies.

When two people experience the same traumatic event, one may cope in a positive way and experience a manageable amount of stress, while the other person may experience a crisis state because of inadequate coping skills and a lack of crisis counseling. Two key factors in determining whether or not a person who experiences multiple stressors escalates into a crisis state are the individual's perception of the situation or event and the individual's ability to utilize traditional coping skills. Roberts and Dziegielewski (1995) have noted that crisis precipitants have different levels of intensity and duration, and likewise, there are wide variations in different individuals' ability to cope. Some people are able to cope effectively and mobilize their inner strengths, despite their perceptions that the stressor or crisis precipitant is intense. However, many other individuals need to learn new resources and coping skills through skillful crisis intervention (Roberts, 1990, 2000). Professionals often confuse the meaning and operational definition of stressful life events, acute stress disorder, acute crisis episodes, and PTSD. Chapter 4 differentiates and clearly defines the differences between the four terms, and also presents a new paradigm with four different case studies: a person under stress, a person experiencing acute stress disorder, a person encountering an acute crisis episode, and a person suffering from PTSD. In Chapter 5, the six levels of the stress-crisis-trauma continuum are described, with case illustrations and treatment recommendations.

Counselors, social workers, psychiatric nurses, psychiatrists, psychologists, and emergency services personnel are working collaboratively to provide a new vision and clinical insights into crisis intervention and crisis response teams. Crisis intervention has become the most widely used time-limited treatment modality in the world. As a result of the crisis intervention and critical incident stress management movement, millions of persons in crisis situations have been helped in a cost-efficient and timely manner. Chapter 9, written by the founders of critical incident stress management (CISM), has a thorough and up-to-date discussion of the components and effectiveness of group crisis intervention and debriefing by first responders.

While it is vital to ensure that emergency responders have services available to help mitigate the consequences of disaster, emergency workers do not suffer alone. Families of responders cope with long absences and fears for their loved one's safety during the disaster event. They feel the aftershock as the emergency responder returns home having faced trauma and devastation. Chapter 10 reviews the impact of emergency service work on families and suggests means for contributing to their health and well-being.

This work can be used by students and professionals in all the health and human service professions to further their understanding of crisis and its reduction and as a base for crisis intervention practice to increase their skills.

CASE SCENARIOS

Some crisis situations are personal, such as the death of a loved one or being the victim of a rape, a robbery, or a severe battering incident; others are triggered by a sudden, community-wide traumatic event, such as an airplane crash, flood, hurricane, terrorist attack, or tornado. Both individual and community-wide traumatic events can cause widespread crisis for dozens, hundreds, or even many thousands of people.

Secondary Victims in the Aftermath of the World Trade Center Terrorist Attack on September 11, 2001

Shelley is a 20-year-old college junior whose uncle was one of the 343 brave NYFD firefighters who died trying to rescue people trapped in the carnage of the Twin Towers at the World Trade Center on the morning of September 11. Shelley was very close to her uncle and grew up two blocks away from him and his family on Staten Island. Shelley's mother was the sister of her deceased uncle. Uncle Frank had three kids, two at colleges in North Carolina and Massachusetts, and a third, Samantha, who was only 10 years old at the time. Samantha's father used to take her to work with him in the morning, where she would have breakfast with the other firefighters, and then her dad would drop her off at school, which was near the firehouse in Staten Island. Shelley was very supportive of her own mother, her widowed aunt, and her 10-year-old cousin and did her best to help with their immediate concrete and crisis needs.

Since returning to NYU in lower Manhattan, Shelley has had difficulty concentrating, has nightmares and gets only a few hours sleep each night, and is anxious about her grades and graduation. Shelley speaks to her mother or aunt almost every day after her classes. She also attended her Uncle Frank's funeral and wake, as well as two memorial services. In addition, Shelley and other members of her immediate family watched the television coverage repeatedly after the terrorist attacks. Shelley seems to be overwhelmed emotionally by her grief-stricken aunt and young cousin as well as the intrusive thoughts and nightmares she has of the television images of the collapse of the Twin Towers and the aftermath of the rescue efforts. Some days she cuts all classes and completely withdraws and isolates herself in her dorm room.

Shelley goes to the university counseling center on referral from her academic advisor. However, she is very quiet and withdrawn due to her depressed mood and crisis reactions.

Sudden Death of a Spouse and Child

Joe begins to barbecue the hamburgers for tonight's dinner. His wife and their two daughters are expected home in about 20 minutes. His older daughter had a track meet, and his wife and younger daughter went to watch her. The phone rings, and Joe is informed by a police officer that his wife and older daughter have been killed by a drunken driver who sped through a red light and smashed into their car two blocks from their house. His life will never be the same.

Deaths and Injuries Related to Plane Crash

At 9:00 A.M. one morning, the pilot of a malfunctioning air force attack jet tried unsuccessfully to make an emergency landing at Indianapolis International Airport. The out-of-control jet clipped the top of a nearby bank building, then rammed into the lobby of a Ramada Inn and exploded, killing 10 people and injuring several others. This tragic accident resulted in hundreds of persons in crisis: those injured in the explosion, the family members of the dead and injured, the guests and surviving employees at the hotel who witnessed the horror, and the employees and customers at the bank building that was struck by the plane, even though no one at the bank was physically hurt.

Woman Battering

Judy B., a 27-year-old surgical nurse, was a survivor of wife battering. She and Ray had been married for 6 years, and they had two children. As Ray's drinking increased, so did his beatings. The final straw was a violent attack in which Ray punched Judy many times in her face. The day following this last assault, after looking at her swollen face in the mirror, Judy went to a gun store and purchased a handgun. As she drove home looking at the gun by her side, she finally decided to seek help. She called the battered women's shelter hot line and said, "I'm afraid that I'm going to kill my husband."

Forcible Rape

Mary R. was a 22-year-old college senior when she was raped. At 11 P.M. one evening Mary had just left the health sciences library at the university and was walking the three long blocks to the parking lot where her car was parked. She recalls her reactions a week later: "I was sort of in shock and numb. It was a terrifying, painful, and degrading experience. It was something you don't expect to happen. But it could have been much worse. He held a knife to my throat while raping me. I thought he was going to kill me afterward. I'm glad to be alive."

Robbery

John A., a 24-year-old blind male, was a victim of robbery. John was returning to his apartment in the Bronx following an afternoon appointment with his physician when he was robbed. John recalled what took place: "A guy came up to me and pressed the cold barrel of his gun on my neck. He said if I don't give him what I got he would shoot me and the dog. I gave him the $21 I had. Nobody helped me. Everybody's afraid to intervene. They're afraid because they know the guy will get off or be put on probation and may come after them.

About a week after the robbery, I woke up sweating and had a serious asthma attack. I was hospitalized for a week. Now I try not to visit friends or my cousin in Manhattan. I go out a lot less. I stay home and listen to the radio or TV most of the time."

Broken Romance, Depression, and Alcoholism

Liz, a 21-year-old college senior, is very depressed. She and her fiancé have just broken up, and she feels unable to cope. She cries most of the day, feels agitated, and isn't sleeping or eating normally. Since the beginning of the relationship a year ago, Liz has become socially isolated. Her family strongly dislikes her fiancé, and her fiancé discouraged her from spending time with her friends. Liz now doubts that she will find a job upon graduation in 3 months and is considering moving home. She comes from a large family, with parents who are very much involved with the other children. Thoughts of moving back home and losing her independence, as well as the broken romance and the lack of a support system, have immobilized Liz, who has cut all her classes for the past week. She has not talked with friends or family about the breakup, and she is "holed up" in her room in the dormitory, drinking herself into a stupor and refusing to eat or leave the building even for a walk.

Shelley, Joe, Judy, Mary, John, and Liz are experiencing crisis reactions in the aftermath of highly stressful hazardous events. The initial crisis reaction in the aftermath of the sudden death of a loved one or being the victim of a violent crime is usually a series of physiological and emotional reactions. Some common reactions and symptoms after traumatic and crisis events include overwhelming feelings of anxiety, despair, and hopelessness, guilt, intense fears, grief over sudden losses, confusion, difficulty concentrating, powerlessness, irritability, intrusive imagery, flashbacks, extreme suspiciousness of others, shame, disorientation, loss of appetite, binge drinking, sleep disturbances, helplessness, terror, exhaustion, losses or lapses of religious beliefs, and/or shattered assumptions about personal safety. Persons experiencing traumatic events or an accumulation of stressful life events usually attempt to understand and reduce their symptoms, to regain control of their environment, and to reach out to their support system (e.g., a significant other). Sometimes the person's internal and external coping methods are successful, and an acute crisis episode is averted; at other times vulnerable individuals and groups fail in their attempts to cope, and crisis episodes escalate.

Chapters 1 through 5 of this book link crisis theory to practice. The emphasis in the first five chapters is placed on the application of individual and group crisis intervention paradigms and models to facilitating crisis resolution. Chapter 1 links the past to the present state-of-the-art knowledge of conceptualizing crisis theory, crisis reactions, and crisis intervention practices. Chapter 2 focuses on how-to conduct lethality/danger assessments and apply each of the seven stages of the crisis intervention model to 3 individuals with different degrees of suicide ideation presenting to a crisis center or psychiatric screening unit. Chapter 3 integrates Roberts's seven-stage crisis intervention model with solution-based therapy and a strengths perspective. Chapter 4 delineates and examines a stress, crisis, PTSD Classification Paradigm which provides guidelines for practitioners to effectively assess the severity of initial event, diagnostic symptoms, and treatment planning options. Chapter 5 develops a continuum of stress and crisis episodes ranging from low-level somatic distress to cumulative and catastrophic acute crisis episodes.

Chapters 6, 12, 15, through 30 apply Roberts's seven-stage model of crisis assessment and intervention to particular high-risk groups and situations such as the following:

- persons experiencing the loss of a loved one at the World Trade Center and the Pentagon on September 11th
- early adolescents who have experienced a significant loss
- adolescents and adults with suicidal ideation and plans
- child and adolescent psychiatric emergencies
- crises on the college campus
- battered women in crisis
- crisis related to separation, divorce, and child custody
- HIV-positive women in crisis
- persons in medical crisis presenting at the emergency room
- persons presenting with life-threatening injuries at a hospital emergency room
- persons experiencing psychiatric crises and coming to the local mental health center or emergency room
- a series of crises experienced by substance abusers
- people experiencing mental health–related crises and being helped by a frontline 24-hour mobile crisis team
- persons in crisis as a result of the burden of caring for a terminally ill or disabled parent

This is the first comprehensive handbook to consistently apply a comprehensive seven-stage crisis intervention model to a wide range of clients in acute crisis.

SCOPE OF THE PROBLEM AND PREVALENCE ESTIMATES

We live in an era in which traumatic events and acute crisis episodes have become far too prevalent. Each year, millions of people are confronted with traumatic crisis-producing events that they cannot resolve on their own, and they often turn for help to 24-hour telephone crisis hotlines; crisis units of community mental health centers; and outpatient, hospital-based programs.

During the past two decades, thousands of crisis intervention programs have been established throughout the United States and Canada. There are over 1,400 grassroots crisis centers and crisis units affiliated with the American Association of Suicidology or a local community mental health center. Altogether there are also over 11,000 victim assistance programs, rape crisis programs, child sexual and physical abuse intervention programs, police-based crisis intervention programs, and battered women's shelters and hotlines. In addition, crisis services are provided at thousands of local hospital emergency rooms, hospital-based trauma centers and emergency psychiatric services, suicide prevention centers, and pastoral counseling services.

Crisis centers and hotlines provide information, crisis assessments, intervention, and referrals for callers with such problems as depression, suicide ideation, psychiatric emergencies, chemical dependency, AIDS, sexual dysfunction, woman battering, and crime victimization. Because of their 24-hour availability, they can provide immediate, though temporary, assistance. Some crisis victims do not have a caring friend or relative to whom they can turn; they often benefit from an empathetic, active listener. Even when significant others are available to aid the person in crisis, hotlines provide a valuable service by linking the caller to appropriate community resources.

The large number of documented calls to crisis hotlines—an estimated 4.3 million calls annually—indicates the importance of these programs (Roberts & Camasso, 1994). The first national organizational survey of crisis units and centers yielded a response from 107 programs (Roberts, 1995). The researcher's summary findings indicated that a total of 578,793 crisis callers were handled by the crisis centers and programs in the 1-year period directly prior to receipt of the mailed questionnaire, or an annual average of 5,409 callers per crisis intervention program. In 1990, 796 crisis intervention units and programs (affiliated with a community mental health center) were in operation throughout the United States, and the annual average number of callers received by each program was 5,409. As a result of multiplying the average number of callers by the number of programs, Roberts (1995) estimated the annual number of callers to be sightly over 4.3 million. If we broaden our estimate to all national and local 24-hour crisis lines, including those for crime victims, survivors of terrorist attacks, battered women, sexual assault victims, troubled employees, adolescent runaways, and child abuse victims, as well as the crisis intervention units at mental health centers, the total estimate would be approximately 35 to 45 million crisis callers per year.

CRISIS REACTIONS AND CRISIS INTERVENTION

A *crisis* can be defined as a period of psychological disequilibrium, experienced as a result of a hazardous event or situation that constitutes a significant problem that cannot be remedied by using familiar coping strategies. A crisis occurs when a person faces an obstacle to important life goals that generally seems insurmountable through the use of customary habits and coping patterns. The goal of crisis intervention is to resolve the most pressing problem within a 1- to 12-week period using focused and directed interventions aimed at helping the client develop new adaptive coping methods.

Crisis reaction refers to the acute stage, which usually occurs soon after the hazardous event (e.g., sexual assault, battering, suicide attempt). During this phase, the person's acute reaction may take various forms, including helplessness, confusion, anxiety, shock, disbelief, and anger. Low self-esteem and serious depression are often produced by the crisis state. The person in crisis may appear to be incoherent, disorganized, agitated, and volatile or calm, subdued, withdrawn, and apathetic. It is during this period that the individual is often most willing to seek help, and crisis intervention is usually more effective at this time (Golan, 1978).

Crisis intervention can provide a challenge, an opportunity, and a turning point within the individual's life. According to Roberts and Dziegielewski (1995), crisis clinicians have been encouraged to examine psychological and situational crises in terms of "both danger and opportunity" (p. 16). The aftermath of a crisis episode can result in either a highly positive or a highly negative change. Immediate and structured crisis intervention guided by Roberts's seven-stage model facilitates crisis resolution, cognitive mastery, and personal growth, rather than psychological harm.

A divorce, a robbery, a broken engagement, being the victim of a domestic assault, and being the close relative of a person killed in an automobile accident or a plane crash are all highly stressful occurrences that can result in an active crisis state. The persons involved may exhibit denial, intense anxiety, and confusion; they may express anger and fear, or grief and loss, but they can all survive. Crisis intervention can reduce immediate danger and fear, as well as provide support, hope, and alternative ways of coping and growing.

Persons in acute crisis have had similar reactions to traumatic events, from initial feelings of disruption and disorganization to the eventual readjustment of the self. During the impact phase, survivors of victimization and other crisis-producing events often feel numb, disoriented, shattered, fearful, vulnerable, helpless, and lonely. The survivors may seek help, consolation, and advice from friends or professionals within several hours or days after the traumatic or stressful life event.

Helping a person in crisis—whether it be in the aftermath of a violent crime, a suicide attempt, a drug overdose, a life-threatening illness, a natural disaster, a divorce, a broken romance, or an automobile crash—requires exceptional sensitivity, active listening skills, and empathy on the part of the crisis intervenor. If a hotline worker, crisis counselor, social worker, or psychologist is able to establish rapport with the person in crisis soon after the acute crisis episode, many hours of later treatment may be averted.

DEFINING A CRISIS AND CRISIS CONCEPTS

Crisis may be viewed in various ways, but most definitions emphasize that it can be a turning point in a person's life. According to Bard and Ellison (1974), crisis is "a subjective reaction to a stressful life experience, one so affecting the stability of the individual that the ability to cope or function may be seriously compromised" (p. 68).

It has been established that a crisis can develop when an event, or a series of events, takes place in a person's life and the result is a hazardous situation. However, it is important to note that the crisis is not the situation itself (e.g., being victimized); rather, it is the person's *perception of and response to* the situation (Parad, 1971, p. 197).

The most important precipitant of a crisis is a stressful or hazardous event. But two other conditions are also necessary to have a crisis state: (a) the individual's perception that the stressful event will lead to considerable upset and/or disruption; and (b) the individual's inability to resolve the disruption by previously used coping methods (see the Glossary p. 513).

Crisis intervention refers to a therapist entering into the life situation of an individual or family to alleviate the impact of a crisis to help mobilize the resources of those directly affected (Parad, 1965).

In conceptualizing crisis theory, Parad and Caplan (1960) examine the fact that "crises have a peak or sudden turning point"; as the individual reaches this peak, tension increases and stimulates the mobilization of previously hidden strengths and capacities. They urge timely intervention to help individuals cope successfully with a crisis situation. Caplan (1961)states that "a relatively minor force, acting for a relatively short time, can switch the balance to one side or another, to the side of mental health or the side of mental ill health" (p. 293).

There is a general consensus among clinical social workers, counselors, psychologists, and emergency services workers that the following characterize a person in crisis:

1. Perceiving a precipitating event as being meaningful and threatening
2. Appearing unable to modify or lessen the impact of stressful events with traditional coping methods
3. Experiencing increased fear, tension, and/or confusion
4. Exhibiting a high level of subjective discomfort
5. Proceeding rapidly to an active state of crisis—a state of disequilibrium

The term *crisis* as it has been described here is applicable to most of the clients of the social workers, psychologists, emergency service workers, disaster mental health workers, and professional counselors who prepared chapters for this handbook. The definition of a crisis stated previously is particularly applicable to persons in acute crisis because these individuals usually seek help only after they have experienced a hazardous event and are in a vulnerable state, have failed to cope and lessen the crisis through customary coping methods, and want outside help.

Foundation Assumptions and the Crisis Theory Framework

The conceptual framework for crisis intervention practice presented in this handbook incorporates the basic principles of crisis theory. The crisis intervention specialization is built on a basic knowledge of crisis theory and practice. Crisis theory includes a cluster of principles upon which crisis clinicians and researchers usually agree. In this book the prominent authorities on crisis intervention demonstrate the application of the crisis intervention process and practices to special groups at high risk of crisis. But first it will be helpful to summarize the foundation principles of crisis theory and to place them in a step-by-step crisis management framework.

Basic Tenets of Crisis Theory

As mentioned earlier, a crisis state is a temporary upset, accompanied by some confusion and disorganization, and characterized by a person's inability to cope with a specific situation through the use of traditional problem-solving methods. According to Naomi Golan (1978), the heart of crisis theory and practice rests in a series of basic statements:

> Crisis situations can occur episodically during "the normal life span of individuals, families, groups, communities and nation." They are often initiated by a hazardous event. This may be a catastrophic event or a series of successive stressful blows which rapidly build up a cumulative effect. (p. 8)
>
> The impact of the hazardous event disturbs the individual's homeostatic balance and puts him in a vulnerable state. (p. 8)
>
> If the problem continues and cannot be resolved, avoided, or redefined, tension rises to a peak, and a precipitating factor can bring about a turning point, during which self-righting devices no longer operate and the individual enters a state of a disequilibrium . . . (an) active crisis. (p. 8)

Duration of the Crisis

Persons cannot remain indefinitely in a state of psychological turmoil and survive. Caplan (1964) noted, and other clinical supervisors have concurred, that in a typical crisis state equilibrium will be restored in 4 to 6 weeks.

However, the designation of 4 to 6 weeks has been confusing. Several authors note that crisis resolution can take from several weeks to several months. To clarify the confusion concerning this period, it is useful to explain the difference between restoring equilibrium and crisis resolution.

Disequilibrium, which is characterized by confusing emotions, somatic complaints, and erratic behavior, is reduced considerably within the first 6 weeks of crisis intervention. The severe emotional discomfort experienced by the person in crisis propels him or her toward action that will result in reducing the subjective discomfort. *Thus, equilibrium is restored*, and the disorganization is time limited.

Viney (1976) aptly describes *crisis resolution* as restoration of equilibrium, as well as cognitive mastery of the situation and the development of new coping methods. Fairchild (1986) refers to crisis resolution as an adaptive consequence of a crisis in which the person grows from the crisis experience through the discovery of new coping skills and resources to employ in the future. In this handbook, crisis intervention is viewed as the process of working through the crisis event so that the person is assisted in exploring the traumatic experience and his or her reaction to it. Emphasis is also placed on helping the individual do the following:

Make behavioral changes and interpersonal adjustments.
Mobilize internal and external resources and supports.
Reduce unpleasant or disturbing affects related to the crisis.
Integrate the event and its aftermath into the individual's other life experiences and markers.

The goal of effective crisis resolution is to remove vulnerabilities from the individual's past and bolster him or her with an increased repertoire of new coping skills to serve as a buffer against similar stressful situations in the future.

HISTORICAL DEVELOPMENT

As far back as 400 B.C., physicians have stressed the significance of crisis as a hazardous life event. Hippocrates himself defined a crisis as a sudden state that gravely endangers life. But the development of a cohesive theory of crisis and approaches to crisis management had to await the twentieth century. The movement to help people in crisis began in 1906 with the establishment of the first suicide prevention center, the National Save-a-Life League in New York City. However, contemporary crisis intervention theory and practice were not formally elaborated until the 1940s, primarily by Erich Lindemann and Gerald Caplan.

Lindemann and his associates at Massachusetts General Hospital introduced the concepts of crisis intervention and time-limited treatment in 1943 in the aftermath of Boston's worst nightclub fire, at the Coconut Grove, in which 493 people perished. Lindemann (1944) and colleagues based the crisis theory they developed on their observations of the acute and delayed reactions of survivors and grief-stricken relatives of victims. Their clinical work focused on the psychological symptoms of the survivors and on preventing unresolved grief among relatives of the persons who had died. They found that many individuals experiencing acute grief often had five related reactions:

1. Somatic distress
2. Preoccupation with the image of the deceased
3. Guilt
4. Hostile reactions
5. Loss of patterns of conduct

Furthermore, Lindemann and colleagues concluded that the duration of a grief reaction appears to be dependent on the success with which the bereaved person does his or her mourning and "grief work." In general, this grief work involves achieving emancipation from the deceased, readjusting to the changes in the environment from which the loved one is missing, and developing new relationships. We learned from Lindemann that people need to be encouraged to permit themselves to have a period of mourning and eventual acceptance of the loss and adjustment to life without the parent, child, spouse, or sibling. If the normal process of grieving is delayed, negative outcomes of crises will develop. Lindemann's work was soon adapted to interventions with World War II veterans suffering from "combat neurosis" and bereaved family members.

Gerald Caplan, who was affiliated with Massachusetts General Hospital and the Harvard School of Public Health, expanded Lindemann's pioneering work in the 1940s and 1950s. Caplan studied various developmental crisis reactions, as in premature births, infancy, childhood, and adolescence, and accidental crises such as illness and death. He was the first psychiatrist to relate the concept of homeostasis to crisis intervention and to describe the stages of a crisis. According to Caplan (1961), a crisis is an upset of a steady state in which the individual encounters an obstacle (usually an obstacle to significant life goals) that cannot be overcome through traditional problem-solving activities. For each individual, a reasonably constant balance or steady state exists between affective and cognitive experience. When this homeostatic balance or stability in psychological functioning is threatened by physiological, psychological, or social forces, the individual engages in problem-solving methods designed to restore the balance. However, in a crisis situation, the person in distress faces a problem that seems to have no solution. Thus homeostatic balance is disrupted, or an upset of a steady state ensues.

Caplan (1964) explains this concept further by stating that the problem is one in which the individual faces "stimuli which signal danger to a fundamental need satisfaction . . . and the circumstances are such that habitual problem-solving methods are unsuccessful within the time span of past expectations of success" (p. 39).

Caplan also described four stages of a crisis reaction. The first stage is the initial rise of tension that comes from the emotionally hazardous crisis-precipitating event. The second stage is characterized by an increased level of tension and disruption to daily living because the individual is unable to resolve the crisis quickly. As the person attempts and fails to resolve the crisis through emergency problem-solving mechanisms, tension increases to such an intense level that the individual may go into a depression. The person going through the final stage of Caplan's model may experience either a mental collapse or a breakdown, or may partly resolve the crisis by using new coping methods. J. S. Tyhurst (1957) studied transition states—migration, retirement, civilian disaster, and so on—in the lives of persons experiencing sudden changes. Based on his field studies on individual patterns of responses to community disaster, Tyhurst identified three overlapping phases, each with its own manifestations of stress and attempts at reducing it:

1. A period of impact
2. A period of recoil
3. A posttraumatic period of recovery

Tyhurst recommended stage-specific intervention. He concluded that persons in transitional crisis states should not be removed from their life situation, and that intervention should focus on bolstering the network of relationships.

In addition to building on the pioneering work of Lindemann and Caplan, Lydia Rapoport was one of the first practitioners to write about the linkage of modalities such as ego psychology, learning theory, and traditional social casework (Rapoport, 1967). In Rapoport's first article on crisis theory (1962), she defined a crisis as "an upset of a steady state" (p. 212) that places the individual in a hazardous condition. She pointed out that a crisis situation results in a problem that can be perceived as a threat, a loss, or a challenge. She then stated that there are usually three interrelated factors that create a state of crisis:

1. A hazardous event
2. A threat to life goals
3. An inability to respond with adequate coping mechanisms

In their early works, Lindemann and Caplan briefly mentioned that a hazardous event produces a crisis, but it was Rapoport (1967) who most thoroughly described the nature of this crisis-precipitating event. She clearly conceptualized the content of crisis intervention practice, particularly the initial or study phase (assessment). She began by pointing out that in order to help persons in crisis, the client must have rapid access to the crisis worker. She stated: “A little help, rationally directed and purposefully focused at a strategic time, is more effective than more extensive help given at a period of less emotional accessibility” (Rapoport, 1967, p. 38).

This point was echoed by Naomi Golan (1978), who concluded that during the state of active crisis, when usual coping methods have proved inadequate and the individual and his or her family are suffering from pain and discomfort, a person is frequently more amenable to suggestions and change. Clearly, intensive, brief, appropriately focused treatment when the client is motivated can produce more effective change than long-term treatment when motivation and emotional accessibility are lacking.

Rapoport (1967) asserted that during the initial interview, the first task of the practitioner is to develop a preliminary diagnosis of the presenting problem. It is most critical during this first interview that the crisis therapist convey a sense of hope and optimism to the client concerning successful crisis resolution. Rapoport suggested that this sense of hope and enthusiasm can be properly conveyed to the client when the interview focuses on mutual exploration and problem solving, along with clearly delineated goals and tasks. The underlying message is that client and therapist will be working together to resolve the crisis.

Seeking Help

In the late 1960s the suicide prevention movement took hold, and suicide prevention centers were established across the United States. From the outset, the initial request for help was generally made via a telephone hotline, a practice that continues to the present day. Aided by funding from the National Institute of Mental Health's Center for Studies of Suicide Prevention, these centers grew from 28 in 1966 to almost 200 by 1972. They built on Caplan's crisis theory and the work of Edwin Schneidman and Norman Farberow at the Los Angeles Suicide Prevention Center (Roberts, 1975, 1979).

An enormous boost to the development of crisis intervention programs and units came about as a result of the community mental health movement. The availability of 24-hour crisis intervention and emergency services was considered a major component of any comprehensive community mental health center (CMHC). As a prerequisite to receiving federal funding under the Community Mental Health Centers Act of 1963, CMHCs were required to include an emergency services component in their system plan. During the 1970s the number of CMHCs that contained crisis intervention units grew rapidly, more than doubling from 376 centers in 1969 to 796 as of 1980 (Foley & Sharfstein, 1983).

What motivates people in crisis to seek help? Ripple, Alexander, and Polemis (1964) suggest that a balance of discomfort and hope is necessary to motivate a distressed person to seek help. *Hope* as defined by Stotland (1969) is the perceived possibility of attaining a goal.

The crisis clinician knows that coping patterns differ for each of us. The crisis clinician also knows that for an individual to suffer and survive a crisis (such as losing a loved one, living through an earthquake or a tornado, attempting suicide, or being sexually assaulted), he or she must have a conscious purpose to live and grow. Each individual in crisis must define his or her own purpose. Persons in crisis need to ventilate, to be accepted, and to receive support, assistance, and encouragement to discover the paths to crisis resolution.

It is useful for the client to understand the specific personal meaning of the event and how it conflicts with his or her expectations, life goals, and belief system. Thoughts, feelings, and beliefs usually flow out freely when a client in crisis talks. The crisis clinician should listen carefully and note any cognitive errors or distortions (overgeneralizing, catastrophizing) or irrational beliefs. The clinician should avoid prematurely stating rational beliefs or reality-based cognitions for the client. Instead, the he or she should help the client to recognize discrepancies, distortions, and irrational beliefs. This is best accomplished through carefully worded questions such as "How do you view yourself now that you realize that everyone with less than 5 years' seniority got laid off?" or "Have you ever asked your doctor whether he thinks you will die from cancer at a young age or what your actual risk of getting cancer is?"

CRISIS INTERVENTION MODELS AND STRATEGIES

Several systematic practice models and techniques have been developed for crisis intervention work. The crisis intervention model applied in this book builds on and synthesizes those developed by Caplan (1964), Golan (1978), Parad (1965), Roberts (1991, 1998), and Roberts and Dziegielewski (1995). All of these practice models and techniques focus on resolving immediate problems and emotional conflicts through a minimum number of contacts. Crisis-oriented treatment is time limited and goal directed, in contrast to long-term psychotherapy, which can take several years to complete.

Crisis intervenors should "adopt a role which is active and directive without taking problem ownership" away from the individual in crisis prematurely (Fairchild, 1986, p. 6). The skilled crisis intervenor should display acceptance and hopefulness in order to communicate to persons in crisis that their intense emotional turmoil and threatening situations are not hopeless, and that, in fact, they (like others in similar situations before them) will survive the crisis successfully and become better prepared for potentially hazardous life events in the future.

In order to become an effective crisis intervenor, it is important to gauge the stages and completeness of the intervention. The following seven-stage paradigm should be viewed as a guide, not as a rigid process, since with some clients stages may overlap.

Roberts's (1991) seven-stage model of crisis intervention (Figure 1.1) has been utilized for helping persons in acute psychological crisis, acute situational crises, and acute stress disorders. The seven stages are as follows:

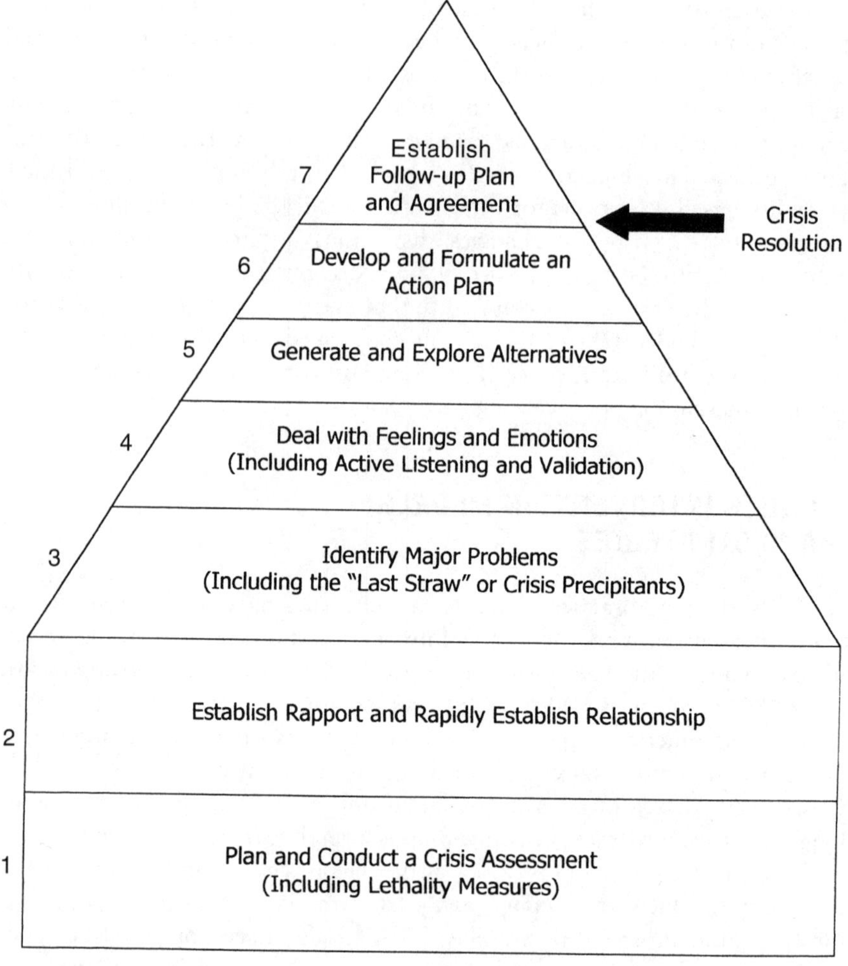

Figure 1.1 Roberts's Seven-Stage Crisis Intervention Model

1. Plan and conduct a thorough assessment (including lethality, dangerousness to self or others, and immediate psychosocial needs).
2. Make psychological contact, establish rapport, and rapidly establish the relationship (conveying genuine respect for the client, acceptance, reassurance, and a nonjudgmental attitude).
3. Examine the dimensions of the problem in order to define it (including the last straw or precipitating event).
4. Encourage an exploration of feelings and emotions.
5. Generate, explore, and assess past coping attempts.
6. Restore cognitive functioning through implementation of action plan.
7. Follow up and leave the door open for booster sessions 3 and/or 6 months later.

1. *Plan and conduct a thorough psychosocial and lethality assessment.* In many cases, stages 1 and 2 occur at the same time. However, first and foremost, basic information needs to be obtained in order to determine whether the caller is in imminent danger. Crisis clinicians are trained to perform an ongoing, rapid risk assessment with all clients in crisis. Crisis counselors, psychologists, and social workers encounter a full range of self-destructive individuals in crisis, including those who have taken potentially lethal drug overdoses, depressed and lonely callers who have attempted suicide, and impulsive acting-out adolescents threatening to injure someone. In cases of imminent danger, emergency medical or police intervention is often necessary. All suicide prevention and other 24-hour crisis hotlines have access to paramedics and emergency medical technicians, poison control centers, the police, and the emergency rescue squad. It is critically important for the crisis intervenor to be in close contact with the crisis caller before, during, and after medical stabilization and discharge.

In many other crisis situations, there is some potential for danger and harm. As a result of potential danger to crisis callers with a history of reckless driving, binge drinking, chemical dependency, bi-polar disorder, explosive anger, passive aggressive behavior, schizophrenia, and/or preoccupation with suicidal thoughts or fantasies, it is imperative that crisis intervenors use stages 1 through 7 of Roberts's model as a guide to crisis intervention.

Assessments of *imminent danger and potential lethality* should examine the following factors:

- Determine whether the crisis caller needs medical attention (e.g., drug overdose, suicide attempt, or domestic violence).
- Is the crisis caller thinking about killing herself or himself? (Are these general thoughts, or does the caller have a specific suicide plan or pact, with the location, time, and method specified?)
- Determine whether the caller is a victim of domestic violence, sexual assault, and/or other violent crime. If the caller is a victim, ask whether the batterer is nearby or likely to return soon.

- Determine whether any children are in danger.
- Does the victim need emergency transportation to the hospital or a shelter?
- Is the crisis caller under the influence of alcohol or drugs?
- Is the caller about to injure herself or himself (e.g., self-injurious behaviors or self-mutilations)?
- Inquire whether there are any violent individuals living in the residence (e.g., assaultive boarders or perpetrators of elder abuse or sibling abuse).

If time permits, the risk assessment should include the following (recognize that a client who is in imminent danger needs to go immediately to a safe place):

- In domestic violence situations, determine the nature of the caller's previous efforts to protect herself or her children, in order to determine her ability to protect herself.
- In order to fully assess the perpetrator's threat in cases of domestic violence, inquire into the batterer's criminal history, physical abuse history, substance abuse history, destruction of property, impulsive acts, history of mental disorders, previous psychiatric diagnosis, previous suicide threats or gestures, stalking behavior, and erratic employment or long periods of unemployment.
- If the caller is a victim of a violent crime, is there a history of prior visits to the hospital emergency room for physical abuse, drug overdose, or suicide attempts?
- Are there any guns or rifles in the home?
- Has anyone recently used a weapon against the caller?
- Has the caller received any terroristic threats, including death threats?
- Determine whether the caller is suffering from major depression, intense anxiety, phobic reactions, agitation, paranoid delusions, acute stress disorder, adjustment disorder, personality disorder, post tramatic stress disorder (PTSD), and/or sleep disturbances.

2. *Make psychological contact and rapidly establish the relationship.* This second stage involves the initial contact between the crisis intervenor and the potential client. The main task for the clinician at this point is to establish rapport by conveying genuine respect for and acceptance of the client. The client also often needs reassurance that he or she can be helped and that this is the appropriate place to receive such help. For example, sufferers of obsessive-compulsive disorders (OCDs) and phobias, such as agoraphobia, often believe that they will never get better. This is often the case when they have been misdiagnosed with a psychosis or personality disorder by a crisis clinician who has never seen patients with OCD or agoraphobia. If the crisis clinician has helped many other clients suffering from agoraphobia, he or she should describe the situation of a previous client who at one

point could not even leave his room for a 4-month period and now is married and successfully working 5 days a week outside of his home.

3. *Examine the dimensions of the problem in order to define it.* It is useful to try to identify the following: (a) the "last straw," or the precipitating event that led the client to seek help; (b) previous coping methods; and (c) dangerousness or lethality. Crisis counselors should explore these dimensions through specific open-ended questions. The focus must be on *now* and *how* rather than *then* and *why*. For example, key questions would be: "What situation or event led you to seek help at this time?" and "When did this event take place?"

4. *Encourage an exploration of feelings and emotions.* This step is closely related to examining and defining the dimensions of the problem, particularly the precipitating event. It is presented here as a separate step because some therapists overlook it in their attempt to make rapid assessment and find the precipitating event. It is extremely therapeutic for a client to ventilate and express feelings and emotions in an accepting, supportive, private, and nonjudgmental setting.

The primary technique for identifying a client's feelings and emotions is through *active listening*. This involves the crisis intervenor listening in an empathic and supportive way to both the client's reflection of what happened and how the client feels about the crisis event.

5. *Explore and assess past coping attempts.* Most youths and adults have developed several coping mechanisms—some adaptive, some less adaptive, and some inadequate—as responses to the crisis event. Basically, an emotionally hazardous event becomes an emotional crisis when the "usual homeostatic, direct problem-solving mechanisms do not work" (Caplan, 1964, p. 39). Thus, attempts to cope fail. One of the major foci of crisis intervention involves identifying and modifying the client's coping behaviors at both the preconscious and the conscious level. It is important for the crisis intervenor to attempt to bring to the conscious level the client's coping responses that now operate just below the surface, at the preconscious level, and then to educate the client in modifying maladaptive coping behaviors. Specifically, it is useful to ask the client how certain situations are handled, such as feelings of intense anger, loss of a loved one (a child or spouse), disappointment, or failure.

Solution-based therapy should be integrated into crisis intervention at this stage. This method emphasizes working with client strengths. The client is viewed as being very resourceful and having untapped resources or latent inner coping skills from which to draw upon. This approach utilizes specifically explicated clinical techniques (e.g., the miracle question, the partial miracle question, the scaling technique) appropriate for crisis intervention practice. Solution-focused therapy and the strengths perspective view the client as resilient. The resilient person generally has sufficiently high self-esteem, a social support network, and the necessary problem-solving skills to bounce back, cope with, and thrive in the aftermath of stressful life events or traumatic events.

Integrating strengths and solution-focused approaches involves jogging clients' memories so they recall the last time everything seemed to be going well, and they were in a good mood rather than depressed and/or successfully dealt with a previous crisis in their lives. These are some examples of components in a solution focused approach:

- How would you have coped with the divorce or death of your parents when you were in a good mood?
- Write a letter to your parents, letting them know that you are setting a specific goal for yourself in order to make them proud of the values and ambition they instilled within you.
- If your deceased parents are in heaven looking down on you, what could you do to make them proud?

See chapters 3, 14, 17, and 25 for thorough applications of crisis intervention and brief solution-focused therapy with traumatized children and youth as well as suicidal, abused, unemployed, and drug-addicted clients.

It is important to help the client to generate and explore alternatives and previously untried coping methods or partial solutions. If possible, this involves collaboration between the client and the crisis intervenor to generate alternatives. It is also important at this stage to explore the consequences and client's feelings about each alternative. Most clients have some notion of what should be done to cope with the crisis situation, but they may well need assistance from the crisis clinician in order to define and conceptualize more adaptive coping responses. In cases where the client has little or no introspection or personal insights, the clinician needs to take the initiative and suggest more adaptive coping methods. Defining and conceptualizing more adaptive coping behaviors can be a highly productive component in helping the client resolve the crisis situation.

6. *Restore cognitive functioning through implementation of an action plan.* The basic premise underlying a cognitive approach to crisis resolution is that the ways in which external events and a person's cognitions of the events turn into personal crisis are based on cognitive factors. The crisis clinician who uses a cognitive approach helps the client focus on why a specific event leads to a crisis state (e.g., it violates a person's expectancies) and, simultaneously, what the client can do to effectively master the experience and be able to cope with similar events should they occur in the future. Cognitive mastery involves three phases. First, the client needs to obtain a realistic understanding of what happened and what led to the crisis. In order to move beyond the crisis and get on with life, the client must understand what happened, why it happened, who was involved, and the final outcome (e.g., being locked out of one's house, a suicide attempt, death of an adolescent, a divorce, a child being battered).

Second, it is useful for the client to understand the event's specific meaning: how it conflicts with his or her expectations, life goals, and belief system. Thoughts and belief statements usually flow freely when a client in crisis talks. The crisis intervenor should listen carefully and note any cognitive errors or distortions (overgeneralizing, catastrophizing) or irrational beliefs. The clinician should avoid prematurely stating the rational beliefs or reality-based cognitions for the client. Instead, the clinician should help the client discover distortions and irrational beliefs. This can be facilitated through carefully worded questions such as "Do you still want to move out of state now that you know that the person who raped you and brutally killed his previous two victims will be executed today in the electric chair?" or "Have you ever asked your doctor whether he thinks you will die from a heart attack at a young age?"

The third and final part of cognitive mastery involves restructuring, rebuilding, or replacing irrational beliefs and erroneous cognitions with rational beliefs and new cognitions. This may involve providing new information through cognitive restructuring, homework assignments, or referral to others who have lived through and mastered a similar crisis (e.g., a support group for widows, for rape victims, or for students who have been confronted with school violence).

7. *Follow up.* At the final session the client should be told that if at any time he or she needs to come back for another session, the door will be open and the clinician will be available. Sometimes clients cancel their second, third, or fourth appointment prior to resolving the crisis. For example, a client who was raped at knifepoint is up half the night prior to her appointment with her clinician. She mistakenly thinks her nightmares and insomnia are caused by the clinician. In actuality, she has not come to grips with her vulnerabilities and fears that the rapist will return. The clinician, knowing that victims of violent crimes often go into crisis at the anniversary of the crime—exactly 1 month or 1 year after the victimization—informs the client that she would like to see her again, and that as soon as she calls she will be given an emergency appointment the same day.

CRISIS INTERVENTION UNITS AND 24-HOUR HOTLINES

Where can persons in crisis turn for help? How do they find the phone number of the crisis intervention program in their area? Police officers, hospital emergency room staff, crisis workers, and psychiatric screeners are available 24 hours a day, 7 days a week. In fact, on weekends and at night they are often the only help available. The police or an information operator can give a person in crisis the name of a local hotline, a community crisis center, the crisis intervention unit at the local community mental health center, a rape crisis center, a battered women's shelter, or a family crisis intervention program that provides home-based crisis services. In addition, many large cities have information and referral networks funded by the United Way, the Community Service Society, or the American Red Cross. These information and referral (I and R) services give crisis callers the phone numbers of community agencies in their localities. Unfortunately, because of limited resources, some of these information and crisis lines are available only from 8:30 A.M. to 5:00 P.M.

The information and referral services throughout the United States, which number in excess of 30,000, operate under different organizational auspices, including traditional social service agencies, community mental health centers, public libraries, police departments, shopping malls, women's centers, travelers' aid centers, youth crisis centers, and area agencies on aging (Levinson, 2004). The goal of information and referral networks is to facilitate access to services and to overcome the many barriers that obstruct entry to needed resources (Levinson, 2003, p. 7). According to the United Way of America, "I and R is a service which informs, guides, directs and links people in need to the appropriate human service which alleviates or eliminates the need" (1980, p. 3).

Some information and referral networks are generic and provide information to the public on all community services, including crisis centers. Others are more specialized and focus on meeting the needs of callers such as those who are depressed and have suicide ideation, children and youths in crisis, women in crisis, survivors of violent crimes, runaways and homeless youths, or the elderly.

The *primary objective* of a crisis intervention program is to intervene at the earliest possible stage. Thus, given the immediacy and rapid response rate of telephone crisis counseling and referrals, 24-hour crisis lines generally meet their objective (Waters and Finn, 1995). With the development of crisis centers nationwide, there has been a considerable increase in the use of the telephone as a method of rapid crisis assessment and management. The 24-hour telephone crisis service maximizes the immediacy and availability of crisis intervention. It also provides anonymity to the caller while allowing the intervenor to assess the risk of suicide and imminent danger. The telephone crisis intervenor is trained to establish rapport with the caller, conduct a brief assessment, provide a sympathetic ear, help develop a crisis management plan, and/or refer the caller to an appropriate treatment program or service. In most cases effective crisis resolution can be facilitated by suicide prevention hotlines as long as they provide referral and follow-up services.

Waters and Finn (1995) have identified and discussed the goals of 13 types of crisis hotlines for special and high-risk groups:

- Career-oriented and job information hotlines
- Employee assistance hotlines
- Information and referral hotline for dementia caregivers

- Kidline
- Media call-ins
- Police emergency calls (911)
- Substance abuse crisis lines
- Suicide prevention hotlines
- Teen lines
- Telephone reassurance programs for the elderly
- Telephone crisis treatment for agoraphobia
- University-based counseling hotlines
- 24-hour availability for telephone therapy with one of the 300 licensed family therapists, psychologists, or social workers on call

Suicide Prevention and Crisis Centers

Suicide prevention services began in London England, in 1906 when the Salvation Army opened an antisuicide bureau aimed at helping persons who had attempted suicide. At about the same time, the Reverend Harry M. Warren (a minister and pastoral counselor) opened the National Save-a-Life League in New York City. Over the years the league's 24-hour hotline has been answered by full-time staff, by trained volunteers, and, in a few instances, by consulting psychiatrists who have served on the agency's board of directors.

In the 1960s and early 1970s, federal funding was made available as a result of the Community Mental Health Centers Act of 1963 and by the National Institute of Mental Health (NIMH). Between 1968 and 1972, almost 200 suicide prevention centers were established (Roberts, 1979, p. 398). In the United States and Canada that number now has increased more than sevenfold. See chapters 2, 5, 6, 15, and 16 for detailed examinations of crisis intervention and follow-up treatment of depressed children, youth, and adults, and of persons with suicide ideation and prior suicide attempts.

At about the same time that 24-hour suicide prevention centers were developing and expanding, crisis units of community mental health centers were also being established throughout the United States. The overriding goal of both types of crisis intervention programs was rapid assessment and early intervention for potentially suicidal callers. There was an emphasis in the late 1960s and throughout the 1970s on 24-hour telephone crisis intervention, outreach to clients in the community, and, on a more limited scale, 24-hour mobile crisis units, which were part of the community mental health centers. See chapters 23, 26, and 27 for a detailed examination of three 24-hour mobile crisis intervention units currently saving numerous lives in the communities of Erie, Pennsylvania, Atlanta, Georgia, and Piscataway, New Jersey.

National Domestic Violence Hotline

A 24-hour, toll-free, national domestic violence hotline became operational in February 1996. Operated by the Texas Council on Family Violence in Austin, this crisis phone line provides immediate crisis assessment and intervention, as well as referrals to emergency services and shelters throughout the United States. The national hotline received an initial $1-million-dollar grant from the U.S. Department of Health and Human Services, and its annual budget is $1.2 million per year.

In January 1997 the Center for Social Work Research at the School of Social Work of the University of Texas at Austin completed the first evaluation study of the National Domestic Violence Hotline (NDVH; McRoy, Danis, and Lewis, 1997). The high frequency of incoming calls to the NDVH—61,677 calls during its first 6 months of operation—is an important initial indicator of success. The volume of calls far exceeded expectations.

The hotline has an electronic phone-tracking system that monitors the number of incoming calls, the average length of calls, the busiest call times, and the number of calls received from all the different area codes. The NDVH also has an internal database consisting of the information logs the hotline workers complete on each caller.

The national hotline averaged 300 calls per day, with the highest volume days handling more than 2,000 calls. Calls are distributed throughout the United States, with all 50 states represented. The highest and the lowest use states, based on phone bills, are as shown in Table 1-1.

Another important measure of effectiveness is the extent to which hotline workers linked domestic violence callers in crisis to community resources such as an emergency shelter. During the first 6 months of operation, 89% of the 24,441 referrals were made to shelters for battered women. In addition, 80% of the shelters receiving referrals from the national hotline have

Table 1.1 Volume of Calls From the 15 States With the Highest and Lowest Utilization

States	Number
Highest Use	
1. California	8,645
2. Texas	7,151
3. New York	4,433
4. Florida	2,873
5. Pennsylvania	2,353
6. Ohio	2,268
7. New Jersey	2,223
Lowest Use	
1. Virgin Islands	21
2. Puerto Rico	91
3. North Dakota	104
4. Vermont	107
5. South Dakota	120
6. Alaska	132
7. Wyoming	150
8. Rhode Island	150

indicated that they operate their own local 24-hour hotline (Lewis, Danis, and McRoy, 1997).

There seem to be two primary reasons for the high visibility and large number of calls. First and foremost, the national hotline is highly visible due to public service announcements made in conjunction with television movies on domestic violence and other major media campaigns. Second, the hotline provides immediate information for women who plan to move or are in transit to another state to escape from the batterer, and thus most likely are unfamiliar with shelters and transitional housing in a different area.

It is important to point out that the phone bill by design protects callers' anonymity. No information provided by phone records can be connected to identifiable information on actual callers.

In-depth interviews were conducted with all hotline workers to determine what they considered the most important crisis intervention technique they provided to callers. The three most important crisis services or techniques were actively listening, making referrals, and being empathetic with callers (Lewis, Danis, and McRoy, 1997, p. c13).

Child Abuse Hotlines and Referral Networks

Childhelp USA operates a national tollfree (1-800-4-A-Child) child abuse hotline dedicated to the prevention of physical and emotional abuse of children. It is staffed 24 hours a day with professional crisis counselors and serves the United States, Canada, U.S. Virgin Islands, and Puerto Rico. Between its inception in 1982 and the end of 1999, it had received more than 2 million calls. It utilizes a database of 55,000 resources.

A number of states, cities, and counties have developed hotlines for reporting suspected cases of child abuse and neglect. Early case finding and rapid investigation and intervention can lead to resolving crisis situations and preventing further child maltreatment. Many communities have also developed parental stress hotline services, which provide immediate intervention for potentially abusive parents who are at risk of injuring their child. These crisis intervention hotlines offer supportive reassurance, advice, and nonjudgmental listening from trained volunteers. The hotlines are usually available on a toll-free basis, 24 hours a day, 7 days a week.

Respite centers or crisis nurseries are available in most large cities to provide parents in crisis with temporary relief from child care. For example, New York City's Foundling Hospital has a crisis nursery where parents can take their children and leave them overnight when they fear they may lose control and inflict injury.

Rape Crisis Programs

Programs for rape crisis have been developed by medical centers, community mental health centers, women's counseling centers, crisis clinics, and police departments. Social workers at rape crisis organizations provide crisis intervention, advocacy, support, education, and referral to community resources. Crisis intervention generally involves an initial visit or accompaniment from a social worker, crisis counselor, or nurse while the victim is being examined in the hospital emergency room. Although follow-up is often handled through telephone counseling, in-person counseling sessions may take place when the victim is in distress. In several parts of the country, rape crisis programs have begun support groups for sexual assault victims. See chapter 11 for a comprehensive review of assessment and crisis intervention strategies for rape and incest survivors.

Battered Women's Shelters and Hotlines

A number of state legislatures have enacted legislation that provides special grants, contracts, and city/county general revenue funding for hotlines and shelters for victims of domestic violence. There are crisis intervention services for battered women and their children in every state and major metropolitan area in the country. The primary focus of these services is to ensure the women's safety, but many shelters have evolved into much more than just a place for safe lodging. Crisis intervention for battered women generally entails a 24-hour telephone hotline, safe and secure emergency shelter (the average length of stay being 3 to 4 weeks), an underground network of volunteer homes and shelters, and welfare and court advocacy by student interns and other volunteers (Roberts, 1998). Shelters also provide peer counseling, support groups, information on women's legal rights, and referral to social service agencies.

In some communities, emergency services for battered women have been expanded to include parenting education workshops, assistance in finding housing, employment counseling and job placement for the women, and group counseling for batterers. In the all-too-often neglected area of assessment and treatment for the children of battered women, a small but growing number of shelters provides either group counseling or referral to mental health centers, as needed. For a more complete discussion of crisis intervention practices with battered women and their children, see chapter 19.

Case Example

The Victim Services Agency in New York has a 24-hour crime victim and domestic violence hotline, staffed by 68 counselors and 20 volunteers, that responded to approximately 71,000 callers in 1998. The following is a case illustration of a battered woman who required many calls, hours of commitment from the crisis worker, and case coordination to resolve her life-threatening situational crisis.

Jasmine

An emergency call was received at 8:00 one morning from Jasmine, the 15-year-old daughter of Serita, who begged the crisis worker to help her mom, frantically explaining, "My mom's live-in boyfriend is going to kill her." The crisis worker reported that the daughter described previous incidents of violence perpetrated by the boyfriend. Jasmine described a serious argument that had erupted at 6:00 that morning, with loud yelling from the boyfriend, who threatened to kill Serita with the gun he had recently obtained, while pointing it directly at her.

The crisis worker tried to build rapport with the terrified girl, asking where her mother was and whether she could be reached by phone. Jasmine replied that her mother had escaped temporarily to a neighbor's apartment as soon as the boyfriend stormed out of the apartment following a visit from the police, which had occurred a few minutes before Jasmine made her phone call to the Victim Services Agency.

Jasmine gave the worker the neighbor's phone number, and the worker called Serita there. The neighbor had called the police at 6:45 A.M. because of the yelling and fighting in the nearby apartment. The boyfriend had previously told Serita that if anyone ever called the police, he would kill her. After the police were called by the neighbor, Serita knew that her boyfriend's violent temper would become even worse. She was terrified to go to a local battered women's shelter, fearing that he would track her down and kill her.

Serita had a sister living in Georgia, who was willing to take her and Jasmine in on a temporary basis. The advantage of staying with her sister was that Serita had never talked to her boyfriend about where her sister lived, telling him just that it was "down South," and had never mentioned her sister's last name, which was different from Serita's. She believed he would never be able to find her if she traveled so far away from New York.

The worker needed to quickly coordinate plans with Travelers' Aid to provide a bus ticket for Serita and her daughter to travel to Georgia that evening. Serita obtained an Order of Protection, and the police took the batterer's keys to the apartment. For a period of time during the afternoon, the batterer watched the apartment from across the street.

A taxi cab (which had a special arrangement with Victim Services) was called to take Serita and Jasmine to Travelers' Aid to pick up the bus ticket for her trip to Georgia. The driver needed to wait until the boyfriend left the area before arriving at the apartment. The crisis worker felt that secrecy was necessary to avoid the inevitable confrontation that would have ensued if the boyfriend had seen Serita leaving the apartment with all her luggage.

Serita's escape from the batterer was handled flawlessly; she reached

Georgia, with the batterer unaware of her plans or her intended destination. Serita and Jasmine stayed with Serita's sister until her Section 8 housing paperwork was transferred from New York to Georgia.

Chapter 3, by Gilbert Greene, Mo-Yee-Lee, Rhonda Trask, and Judy Rheinscheld demonstrates through case illustrations how to tap into and bolster clients' strengths in crisis intervention. The chapter demonstrates how to integrate Roberts's seven-stage crisis intervention model with solution-focused treatment in a stepwise manner. The crisis clinician utilizing this integrated strengths approach serves as a catalyst and facilitator for clients discovering their own resources and coping skills. Greene et al. systematically bolster their clients by emphasizing the person's resilience, inner strengths, and ability to bounce back and continue to grow emotionally. This highly practical overview chapter aptly applies the strengths-based approach to a diverse range of clients in crisis situations.

I firmly believe that crisis intervention which focuses on the client's inner strengths and resilience, and that seeks partial and full solutions will become the short-term treatment of choice during the first quarter of the twenty-first century.

SUMMARY

It is clear, in reviewing current progress in applying time-limited crisis intervention approaches to persons in acute crisis, that we have come a long way in the past decade. Crisis intervention is provided by several hundred voluntary crisis centers and crisis lines; by most of the 790 community mental health centers and their satellite programs; and by the majority of the 11,000 victim assistance, child abuse, sexual assault, and battered women's programs available throughout the country. In addition, crisis services are provided at thousands of local hospital emergency rooms, hospital-based emergency psychiatric services, suicide prevention centers, crisis nurseries, local United Way–funded information lines, and pastoral counseling services. The crisis services that have proliferated in recent years are often directed toward particular groups, such as rape victims, battered women, adolescent suicide attemptors, victims of school violence as well as students who were in the building but were not directly harmed, separated and divorced individuals, abusive parents, and victims of disasters. The increased development of crisis services and units reflects a growing awareness among public health and mental health administrators of the critical need for community crisis services.

This handbook provides an up-to-date, comprehensive examination of the crisis model and its application to persons suffering from an acute crisis. Most social workers, clinical psychologists, marital and family therapists, and counselors agree that crisis theory and the crisis intervention approach provide an extremely useful focus for handling all types of acute crisis. Almost every distressed person who calls or visits a community mental health center, victim assistance program, rape crisis unit or program, battered women's shelter, substance abuse treatment program, or suicide prevention program can be viewed as being in some form of crisis. By providing rapid assessments and timely responses, clinicians can formulate effective and economically feasible plans for time-limited crisis intervention.

REFERENCES

Aguilera, D. C., & Messick, J. M. (1982). *Crisis intervention: Theory and methodology.* St. Louis, MO: C. V. Mosby.

Bard, M., & Ellison, K. (1974, May). Crisis intervention and investigation of forcible rape. *The Police Chief, 41,* 68–73.

Bellak, L., & Siegel, H. (1983). *Handbook of intensive brief and emergency psychotherapy.* Larchmont, NY: CRS.

Burns, D. D. (1980). *Feeling good.* New York: New American Library.

Caplan, G. (1961). *An approach to community mental health.* New York: Grune and Stratton.

Caplan, G. (1964). *Principles of preventive psychiatry.* New York: Basic Books.

Fairchild, T. N. (1986). *Crisis intervention strategies for school-based helpers.* Springfield, IL: Charles C. Thomas.

Foley, H. A., & Sharfstein, S. S. (1983). *Madness and Government: Who Cares for the Mentally Ill?* Washington, D.C.: American Psychiatric Press.

Golan, N. (1978). *Treatment in crisis situations.* New York: Free Press.

Halpern, H. A. (1973). Crisis theory: A definitional study. *Community Mental Health Journal, 9,* 342–349.

Kadushin, A., & Martin, J. A. (1988). *Child welfare services* (4th ed.). New York: Macmillan.

Levinson, R. (April 30, 2004). Personal communication.

Levinson, R. W. (2003). *Information and referral networks.* 2nd edition New York: Springer.

Lewis, C. M., Danis, F., and McRoy, R. (1997). *Evaluation of the National Domestic Violence Hotline.* Austin: University of Texas at Austin, Center for Social Work Research.

Lindemann, E. (1944). Symptomatology and management of acute grief. *American Journal of Psychiatry, 101,* 141–148.

Meichenbaum, D., & Jaremko, M. E. (1983). *Stress reduction and prevention.* New York: Plenum.

Parad, H. J. (1965). *Crisis intervention: Selected readings.* New York: Family Service Association of America.

Parad, H. J. (1971). Crisis Intervention. In R. Morris (Ed.), *Encyclopedia of social work* (Vo1. 1, pp. 196–202). New York: National Association of Social Workers.

Parad, H. J., & Caplan, G. (1960). A framework for studying families in crisis. *Social Work, 5*(3), 3–15.

Rapoport, L. (1962). The state of crisis: Some theoretical considerations. *Social Service Review, 36,* 211–217.

Rapoport, L. (1967). Crisis-Oriented Short-Term Casework, *Social Service Review* 41, 31–43.

Ripple, L., Alexander, E., & Polemis, B. (1964). *Motivation, capacity, and opportunity.* Chicago: University of Chicago Press.

Roberts, A. R. (1975). *Self-Destructive Behavior.* Springfield, IL: Charles C. Thomas.

Roberts, A. R. (1979). Organization of suicide prevention agencies. In L. D. Hankoff & B. Einsidler (Eds.), *Suicide: Theory and clinical aspects* (pp. 391–399). Littleton, MA: PSG Publishing.

Roberts, A. R. (1984). *Battered women and their families.* New York: Springer.

Roberts, A. R. (1991). Conceptualizing crisis theory and the crisis intervention model. In A. R. Roberts (Ed.), *Contemporary perspectives on crisis intervention and prevention* (pp. 3–17). Englewood Cliffs, NJ: Prentice-Hall.

Roberts, A. R. (1995). Crisis intervention units and centers in the united states: A national survey. In A. R. Roberts (Ed.), *Crisis intervention and time-limited cognitive treatment* (pp. 54–70). Thousand Oaks, CA: Sage.

Roberts, A. R. (1998). *Battered women and their families: Intervention strategies and treatment programs* (2nd ed.). New York: Springer.

Roberts, A. R. (2000). An overview of crisis theory and crisis intervention. In A. Roberts (ed.) *Crisis intervention handbook*, 2nd edition (pp. 3–30). New York: Oxford.

Roberts, A. R., & M. Camasso (1994). Staff turnover at crisis intervention units and programs: A national survey. *Crisis Intervention and Time-Limited Treatment, 1*(1), 1–9.

Roberts, A. R., & S. F. Dziegielewski. (1995). Foundation skills and applications of crisis intervention and cognitive therapy. In A. R. Roberts (Ed.), *Crisis intervention and time-limited cognitive treatment* (pp. 3–27). Thousand Oaks, CA: Sage.

Slaby, A. E. (1985). Crisis-oriented therapy. In Frank R. Lipton & Stephen M. Goldfinger (Eds.), *Emergency psychiatry at the crossroads* (pp. 21–34). San Francisco: Jossey-Bass.

Stotland, E. (1969). *The psychology of hope.* San Francisco: Jossey-Bass.

Tyhurst, J. S. (1957). The role of transition states—including disasters—in mental illness. In *Symposium on preventive and social psychiatry* (pp. 1–23). Washington, DC: Walter Reed Army Institute of Research.

United Way of America. (1980). *Information and referral: Programmed resource and training course.* Alexandria, VA: Author.

Viney, L. L. (1976). The concept of crisis: A tool for clinical psychologists. *Bulletin of the British Psychological Society, 29,* 387–395.

Waters, J., & Finn, E. (1995). Handling client crises effectively on the telephone. In A. R. Roberts (Ed.), *Crisis intervention and time-limited cognitive treatment* (pp. 251–189). Thousand Oaks, CA: Sage.

2

Lethality Assessment and Crisis Intervention With Persons Presenting With Suicidal Ideation

ALBERT R. ROBERTS
KENNETH R. YEAGER

Every 17 minutes someone in this country commits suicide. This equates to 83 suicides each and every day throughout the United States. Crisis counselors and psychiatric screeners must make assessments, often under daunting conditions, that may determine life and death for thousands of people making calls to hotlines and appearing at emergency rooms across the country. Below we recount three actual cases. How would you assess their situations, and how should the crisis intervention worker respond?

Case 1 Synopsis: Maryann

Maryann has barricaded herself in her bedroom for the past 24 hours. She has called her cousin to offer him her favorite CDs. She has ripped the phone out of the wall and thrown it into the hallway. Her mother can hear her sobbing. Knowing she has just broken up with her boyfriend and had taken an overdose of sleeping pills eight months ago in a similar situation, Maryann's mother is worried. Making matters worse, Maryann lost her father within the past year. Maryann's mother calls the crisis intervention hotline.

Case 2 Synopsis: Jeanette, call me "Jet"

Jeanette, who preferred to be called Jet, is a 27-year-old female who has suffered a traumatic event in conjunction with her cocaine dependence. Jeanette presented to the treatment facility following an episode of physical and sexual abuse while under the influence of cocaine. While she was in treatment, Jet's withdrawal symptoms combined with her resistance to participate in programming led to her being considered noncompliant and resistant to treatment. Perceptions of Jet's treatment needs varied widely among staff. Unfortunately, her agitation led to an altercation with staff, resulting in an episode of restraint. In the process of restraining Jet, she was retraumatized by the staff, forced onto a bed in the restraint room by two male staff in a manner similar to the physical and sexual abuse experienced prior to her admission to the inpatient psychiatric facility.

Case 3 Synopsis: Harvey

Harvey, a successful dentist, age 50, has been suffering with bipolar disorder for 16 years. He entered a substance abuse treatment facility for alcohol dependence and was successfully undergoing treatment when he began exhibiting signs of major depressive disorder. Harvey confessed to his business partner that he planned to shoot himself. Staff reported that Harvey had a plan to hang himself. Consequently, he was transferred to an inpatient psychiatric facility for stabilization. Harvey was remorseful and worked diligently on his treatment plan. He agreed not to harm himself and made plans for the future. He was returned to the substance abuse treatment facility, then to a halfway house, where, after two weeks, he was given a temporary leave to return home.

Were these three people in immediate danger of committing suicide? How will the crisis counselors or psychiatric screeners decide the severity of the crisis and the most beneficial treatment? In this chapter we consider these important clinical issues and methods of suicide risk assessment. We review evidence-based findings concerning signs of acute suicidal behavior and present Roberts's seven-stage crisis intervention model, the most effective model for intervening quickly on behalf of persons with suicidal ideation. Readers will follow the process of each of the seven stages in the crisis intervention framework as it was applied to each of these three individuals. Finally, you will find, perhaps to your surprise, what eventually happened to Maryann, Jet, and Harvey.

SCOPE OF THE PROBLEM

Suicide and suicide attempts are a major social and public health problem in the United States. The scope of the problem is evidenced by national data indicating that over 30,500 individuals kill themselves annually; approximately 765,000 individuals attempt suicide each year; and 1 out of every 59 people in the United States is a suicide survivor, a close family member, or friend (Alan L. Berman, Executive Director, American Association of Suicidology, personal communication, 2003; Jobes, Berman,& Martin, 2000; Westefeld et al., 2000).

On a busy night in the emergency room waiting area, a young psychiatric resident receives a page from the answering service. A patient recently discharged from the inpatient unit asks a question: "I'm feeling funny. Could this be the medication?" The resident reads the page and accurately prioritizes to address the actively psychotic patient in the emergency waiting room. Twenty minutes later, another page from the same patient, pleading: I'm feeling funny . . . I need to speak with someone right now." The resident continues to work up the four patients in acute distress in the emergency room. Another 20 minutes pass. The resident receives yet another page from the same patient: "I'm going to kill myself if I don't hear from someone in the next 10 minutes." With the acute issues addressed, the resident returns the patient's call. She asks the patient: "Are you currently suicidal?" The patient responds: "No, I knew that saying I was going to kill myself would get your attention . . . I was tired of waiting for you to call back." Tired and frustrated, the psychiatric resident reprimands the patient: "The threat of suicide is not an appropriate way to have a question answered." To which the patient responds in frustration:

> You have no idea what I go through on a day-to-day basis and how often I consider taking my life, you don't know what I go through . . . The effectiveness of the medication you are prescribing is disappointing at best and the side effects are terrible. Three times this year you have hospitalized me when I'm trying my best by taking the medication you have prescribed. I just needed someone to talk to and you act as if I mean absolutely nothing.

The patient is admitted to the emergency department seven hours later, having taken all of her prescribed antipsychotic medication.

Patients are facing remarkable barriers to treatment. Given the nature of their illness, persons with mental illness are challenged to access services. Community mental health centers as well as private psychiatric clinics are experiencing remarkable waiting lists for services. Desperate and in an effort to have their voices heard, people at times take drastic steps to make a plea for services. The goal of mental health professionals is to assure that each individual voice is heard. No plea for service should go unanswered. However, dollars for services are shrinking. Mental health professionals are stretched beyond reasonable limits, and direct line staff are frequently reacting to the constraints of the treatment delivery system. This chapter presents a clear framework for providing effective crisis intervention within the current constraints of today's mental health practice environments.

CRISIS INTERVENTION

Crisis intervention is a difficult task and is especially difficult to do well. As the acuity of mental health consumers increases and the service delivery system buckles under the increasing pressure of those seeking services, specific and efficacious interventions and guidelines are clearly needed to keep the process flowing. Growing evidence indicates that the risk factors for suicide include a precipitating event such as multiple stressors or a traumatic event, major depression, increased substance abuse, deterioration in social or occupational functions, hopelessness, and verbal expressions of suicidal ideation (Weishaar, 2004). For some individuals, dealing with ambivalence (simultaneous thoughts of self-harm and thoughts of immediate gratification and satisfaction) is a day-to-day event. For others, the thought of suicide mistakenly appears to be an immediate fix to an emotionally painful or acutely embarrassing situation that seems insurmountable.

For the chemically dependent individual suicide may be the easy way out of a cycle of use and withdrawal. Every person brought to local hospital emergency rooms or psychiatric screening centers is different. The scenarios are as endless and diverse as the population served. Therefore, it may be helpful to begin with a working definition of crisis:

> Crisis: An acute disruption of psychological homeostasis in which one's usual coping mechanisms fail and there exists evidence of distress and functional impairment. The subjective reaction to a stressful life experience that compromises the individual's stability and ability to cope or function. The main cause of a crisis is an intensely stressful, traumatic, or hazardous event, but two other conditions are also necessary: (1) the individual's perception of the event as the cause of considerable upset and/or disruption; and (2) the individual's inability to resolve the disruption by previously used coping mechanisms. Crisis also refers to "an upset in the steady state." It often has five components: a hazardous or traumatic event, a vulnerable state, a precipitating factor, an active crisis state, and the resolution of the crisis. (Roberts, 2002, p. 516)

This definition is particularly applicable to persons in acute crisis because these individuals usually seek help only after they have experienced a hazardous or traumatic event and are in a vulnerable state, have failed to cope and lessen the crisis through customary coping methods, lack family or community social supports, and want outside help. Acute psychological or situational crisis episodes may be viewed in various ways, but the definition we are using emphasizes that a crisis can be a turning point in a person's life.

Crisis intervention generally occurs when a counselor or behavioral clinician enters into the life situation of an individual or family to alleviate the impact of a crisis episode by facilitating and mobilizing the resources of those directly affected. Rapid assessment and timely intervention on the part of crisis counselors, social workers, psychologists, or psychiatrists is of paramount importance.

Crisis intervenors should be active and directive while displaying a nonjudgmental, accepting, hopeful, and positive attitude. Crisis intervenors need to help clients to identify protective factors, inner strengths, psychological hardiness, and resiliency factors that can be utilized for ego bolstering. Effective crisis intervenors are able to gauge the seven stages of crisis intervention, while being flexible and realizing that several stages of intervention may overlap. Crisis intervention should culminate with a restoration of cognitive functioning, crisis resolution, and cognitive mastery (Roberts, 2000; see Figure 2.1).

Practitioners addressing crisis frequently know the best approach to take; however, being in a stressful situation, they may revert to behaviors that are less than effective in treating the population presenting for crisis intervention. Therefore, we have included a quick reference list of Do's and Don'ts

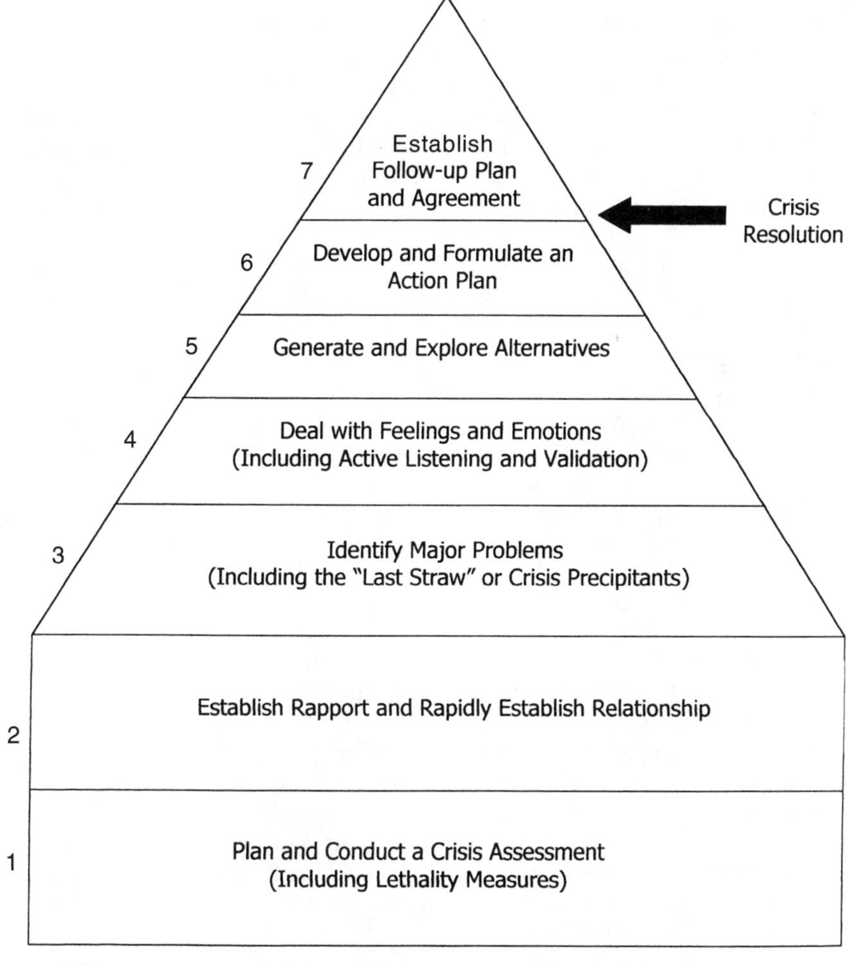

Figure 2.1 Roberts's Seven-Stage Crisis Intervention Model

for crisis workers. Though they seem obvious, it is important to keep them close as a reminder of effective tools or approaches to crisis intervention.

Do's

- Treat every caller with respect: Speak and listen to the caller as you would like to be spoken and listened to.
- Help the caller to feel he or she did the right thing by calling. "I'm glad that you called."
- Assess in your own mind whether the call is an emergency:
    - Is the caller safe?
    - Is someone or something in immediate danger?
    - If so, act appropriately.
- Except in an emergency, at the beginning of the call concentrate on the caller's feelings and not on the situation.
- Make the caller feel heard. Be empathetic. "It sounds like you're feeling disappointed with your boyfriend."
- Allow the caller to vent his or her feelings.
- Be aware of your own feelings and how they may interfere with your handling of the call. For example, if you are having strong feelings about a divorce in your own life, you need to remind yourself to exclude these feelings when talking with a caller who is having problems with a divorce.
- Recognize that although you might feel you are not doing enough, just listening and "being there" may be extremely helpful and all that is necessary.
- If not obvious, ask what made the caller ask for help at this time.
- Help the caller to generate choices and make decisions.
- Help the caller establish a relationship with the agency rather than with you as an individual. You may not always be available when the caller is in need of help, but the agency can be.
- When ending a call, find out what the caller's plans are, what comes next, what tomorrow looks like. Offer to make a follow-up call.

Don'ts

- Do not minimize the caller's feelings. Do not say, "How can you feel that way? It's not as bad as you are imagining."
- Do not be judgmental, place blame, or take sides. There are usually more than enough people in the caller's life who fill these roles.
- Remain neutral, allowing the caller to solve his or her own problems.
- Do not preach, moralize, or diagnose.
- Do not offer solutions or tell the caller what you think he or she should do. Do not hide suggestions or statements in the form of questions, such as "Do you think it would be better to stay there and feel awful or go and talk it over with him?"
- Do not give compliments beyond reflecting the strengths illustrated in the caller's story.

- Do not ask the caller why he or she felt or behaved a certain way. The caller may not know why, respond defensively, or both.
- Do not share your thoughts or theories with the caller. Share only your concern about the caller's well-being.
- Do not reveal to the caller whether another person has used the service.
- Do not have unrealistic expectations about what can be accomplished during a single call. If the caller's problems have developed over time, realizations and change will probably also take time.

SUICIDE ASSESSMENT MEASURES, TOOLS, AND GUIDELINES

The critical first step in applying Roberts's seven-stage crisis intervention model (R-SSCIM) is conducting a lethality and biopsychosocial risk assessment. This involves a relatively quick assessment of the number and duration of risk factors, including imminent danger and availability of lethal weapons, verbalization of suicide or homicide risk, need for immediate medical attention, positive and negative coping strategies, lack of family or social supports, active psychiatric diagnosis, and current drug or alcohol use (Eaton & Roberts, 2002; Roberts, 2000; see also Eaton, this volume).

If possible, a medical assessment should include a brief summary of the presenting problem, any ongoing medical conditions, and current medications (names, dosages, and time of last dose). According to Roberts and Yeager (2004), if, during a suicide risk assessment, the person exhibits any of the following factors, then it would seem prudent for an ambulance to be called; if the patient is already at the emergency room, he or she should be further evaluated by a psychiatric screener, psychiatric mental health nurse, or psychiatric resident and hospitalized in a psychiatric inpatient unit for 48 to 120 hours of observation and evaluation (see Table 2.1):

- Patient expresses suicidal ideation.
- Patient has a suicide plan.
- Patient has access to lethal means and exhibits poor judgment.
- Patient is agitated and exhibits imminent danger to self or others.
- Psychotic patient exhibits command hallucinations related to harming self or others.
- Patient is intoxicated or high on illegal drugs and acting in an impulsive manner.
- Family member reports on patient's suicidal thoughts.

TRIAGE ASSESSMENT

First responders, also known as crisis response team members or frontline crisis intervention workers, are called on to conduct an immediate debriefing

Table 2.1

Immediate safety risk, ONE

___ *DSM-IV-TR* Diagnosis
___ ***Command hallucinations with direction to harm self/others.***
___ ***Suicide/homicide attempt.***
___ ***Suicide/homicide ideation, ONE***
 ___ Specific plan
 ___ Nonspecific plan with means and no deterrents
 ___ Intent/potential to harm others

___ ***DSM-IV-TR diagnosis with associated symptoms and active substance abuse w/in past 24 hours, ONE***
 ___ Suicide attempt within past year
 ___ Hx.of high lethality/intent in past 6 mos.
 ___ Current refusal to disclose plan
 ___ Self-mutilation ***and*** increase in intensity pattern
 ___ Psychiatric medication noncompliance/intensified symptoms characteristic of *DSM-IV-TR* diagnostic code ___ ___ ___ . ___ ___
 ___ Comorbid medical condition acute or debilitating illness
___ ***Delirium ONE***
 ___ Unable to focus/sustain attention
 ___ Change in cognition
 ___ Misinterpretations/illusions/hallucinations

If any <u>one</u> criterion are met STOP…<u>Admit to Inpatient.</u>
If one criterion is not met continue to next section.

Potential safety risk, ONE

___ *DSM-IV-TR* Diagnosis, ___ ___ ___. ___ ___
and ***ONE***
 ___ Somatic symptoms
 ___ Behavioral symptoms
 ___ Psychological symptoms

___ Suicidal/homicidal ideation, ***ONE***
 ___ Nonspecific plan
 ___ Refusal to disclose plan
 ___ Hx. of high lethality/intent past year
 ___ Active substance abuse w/in past 24 hrs./ failed toxicology screen
 ___ Substance dependence w/o withdrawal potential
 ___ Acute/debilitating medical condition with acceptable lab values/medical stability currently
 ___ Self-mutilation

Continued Action Required: Select ONE from the Level of Care Indicators below

- **Severe impairment**
- **Moderate impairment**
- **Mild impairment**

INPATIENT

Patient, ONE
___GAF < 30
___Unable/refuses to comply with treatment
___Hx of inpatient admission w/in past 3 yrs.
___Expected to comply with negotiation

ADLs, ONE
___Nonambulatory
___Unable to attend to hygiene
___Unable to nourish self
___Unable to perform daily tasks/activities

Relationships, ONE
___Socially withdrawn
___Nonverbal
___Sexually inappropriate/abusive
___Physical abuse
___Terminated significant relationship(s)
___Restraining order/hx. of domestic dispute

Role Performance, ONE
___Absent > 5 days (work)/10 days (school)
___Suspended/terminated/quit/expelled
___Self-employed and unable to maintain business
___Unemployed and unable to seek work
___Unable to care for/neglect of dependent children/elders
___Exposes dependent children/elders to physical abuse/sexual abuse
___Removal from current living situation by authorities

Support System, ONE
___Unavailable
___Unable to ensure safety
___Intentional sabotage of treatment
___Ongoing contact with perpetrator of abuse

PARTIAL HOSPITALIZATION/IOP

Patient agrees with treatment, ONE
___GAF 30 or below
___Inconsistently compliant with treatment
___Hx. of inpatient admission w/in past 3 yrs.
___ Expected to comply with continued negotiation

ADLs, ONE
___Ambulatory only with assistance
___Maintains hygiene with frequent reminders
___Declining unreliable nutritional status
___Declining ability to perform daily tasks

Relationships, ONE
___ Moderate conflict with significant others
___ Increasing verbal hostility/threatening
___ Socially isolated/alienated
___ Easily frustrated and exhibiting reckless or
___ Impulsive behavior or angry outbursts

Role Performance
___ Absent > 3–4 days from work/> 5–9 days from school
___ Self-employed with significantly decreased productivity
___ Unemployed and job seeking 1–3 days/wk
___ Formal warning/mandated employee assistance/counseling
___ Ongoing academic difficulty/significant decreased productivity
___ Medical LOA due to psychiatric/substance abuse problem
___ Deterioration in care of children/elders
___ Threatened removal of children/elders

Support System, ONE
___Available weekends/nights only
___Occasional visits/phone contact
___Questionably competent/unable to manage symptoms

OUTPATIENT

Patient Agrees with treatment
___GAF 30–50
___ Patient is expected to comply with tx.

ADLs mild deterioration, ONE
___ Ambulation
___ Hygiene
___ Nutrition
___Daily tasks/activities

Relationship, ONE
___ Significant other suggests/demands treatment
___ Increasing social isolation
___ Occasional arguments/avoidance of contact
___ Occasional verbal hostility

Role Performance, ONE
___ Absent 1–2 days from work/1–4 days from school
___ Unemployed and job seeking > 4 days/wk
___ Mild decrease in productivity at work/school
___ Informal warning about performance at work/school
___ Mild decrease in care for dependent children
___ Complaints registered with child/elder services/authorities

Support System Consistent, supportive, competent, ONE
___Available 24 hrs./day
___Available weekends/nights only
___Occasional visits/phone contact
___Able to manage intensity of symptoms

under less than stable circumstances. Sometimes they may have to delay the crisis assessment until the patient has been stabilized and supported; in other disaster responses, an assessment can be completed simultaneously with the debriefing. According to many first responders, ideally A (assessment) precedes C (crisis intervention), but in the midst of a disaster or acute crisis, this linear order is not always possible (see Chapter 6 in this book for a detailed discussion of the ACT integrative model).

In the immediate aftermath of a community disaster, the first type of assessment by disaster mental health specialists should be psychiatric triage. A triage or screening tool can be useful in gathering and recording information about the initial contact between a person experiencing crisis or trauma reactions and the mental health specialist. The triage form should include essential demographic information (name, address, phone number, e-mail address, etc.), perception of the magnitude of the traumatic event, coping methods, any presenting problem(s), safety issues, previous traumatic experiences, social support network, drug and alcohol use, preexisting psychiatric conditions, suicide risk, and homicide risk (Eaton & Roberts, 2002). Several hundred articles have examined emergency medical triage, but very few publications have discussed emergency psychiatric triage (Liese, 1995, pp. 48–49; Roberts, 2002;). Triage has been defined as the medical "process of assigning patients to appropriate treatments depending on their medical conditions and available medical resources" (Liese, 1995, p. 48). Medical triage was first used in the military to respond quickly to the medical needs of soldiers wounded in war. Triage involves assigning physically ill or injured patients to different levels of care, ranging from "emergent" (i.e., immediate treatment required) to "nonemergent" (i.e., no medical treatment required).

Psychiatric or psychological triage assessment refers to the immediate decision-making process in which the mental health worker determines lethality and referral to one of the following alternatives:

- Emergency inpatient psychiatric hospitalization.
- Outpatient treatment facility or private therapist.
- Support group or social service agency.
- No referral needed.

The ACT intervention model refers to triage assessment, crisis intervention, and trauma treatment and referral to appropriate community resources. Concerning triage assessment, emergency psychiatric response should take place when the rapid assessment indicates that the individual is a danger to self or others and is exhibiting intense and acute psychiatric symptoms. These survivors generally require short-term hospitalization and psychopharmacotherapy to protect themselves from self-harm (e.g., suicide attempts and self-injurious behavior) or harm to other persons (e.g., murder and attempted murder). The small number of individuals needing emergency psychiatric treatment are generally diagnosed with moderate- to high-potential lethality (e.g., suicidal ideation and/or homicidal thoughts) and acute mental disorder. In the small percentage of cases where emergency psychiatric treatment is indicated, these persons are usually suffering from an accumulation of several previous traumatic events (Burgess & Roberts, 2000).

Concerning the other categories of psychiatric triage, many individuals may be in a precrisis stage due to ineffective coping skills, a weak support system, or ambivalence about seeking mental health assistance. These same individuals may have no psychiatric symptoms and no suicide risk. However, because of the catastrophic nature of the September 11 disaster, persons who had suddenly lost a loved one and had no previous experience coping with sudden death were particularly vulnerable to acute crisis or traumatic stress.

Another type of triage assessment used almost exclusively by crisis intervention and suicide prevention programs is the Intervention Priority Scale, developed by the 24-hour mobile crisis intervention services of Community Integration, Inc. of Erie, Pennsylvania. This scale should be utilized by other programs throughout North America. The Intervention Priority Scale allows a number from I to IV based on clinical criteria to be assigned at the time the triage information is collected. Each number on the scale corresponds to an outside time limit considered to be safe for crisis response. Examples of a priority I situation include requests for immediate assistance by police and emergency services personnel, suicide attempts in progress, suicidal or homicidal individuals with the means currently available, and individuals experiencing command hallucinations of a violent nature. Examples of a priority II crisis include individuals who are able to contract for safety or who have reliable supports present, individuals experiencing hallucinations or delusions, and individuals who are unable to meet basic human needs. Examples of a priority III crisis include individuals with fleeting suicidal ideation or major depression and no feasible suicide plan, and individuals suffering from mood disturbances. Examples of a priority IV crisis include individuals who have no thought to harm self or others, who present no psychiatric symptoms, and who are not experiencing any other situational crises (Eaton & Ertl, 2000; Eaton & Roberts, 2002).

In Gregory Brown's (2002) final grant report to the National Institute of Mental Health, he reviews and evaluates the psychometric properties of a number of the most commonly used suicide assessment measures. We recommend that every crisis counselor, psychiatric screener, medical social worker, psychiatric mental health nurse, and psychiatrist be trained in the use of these suicide assessment measures:

- Beck Hopelessness Scale
- Beck Depression Inventory
- Beck Scale for Suicide Ideation

- Firestone Assessment of Self-Destructive Thoughts
- Modified Scale for Suicide Ideation
- Linehan Reasons for Living Scale
- Self-Monitoring Suicide Ideation Scale
- Scale for Suicide Ideation at Worst Point
- Lifetime Parasuicidal Count
- SADS Person Scale
- Suicide Potential Lethality Scale

The National Mental Health Association has developed the following useful warning signs of someone considering suicide:

- Verbal suicide threats such as "You'd be better off without me around."
- Expressions of hopelessness and helplessness.
- Personality changes.
- Depression.
- Daring or risk-taking behavior.
- Previous suicide attempts.
- Giving away prized possessions.
- Lack of interest in future plans.
- Gun ownership among the poor.

Two of the most useful evidence-based measures of suicide risk are the Beck Hopelessness Scale (BHS) and the Scale for Suicide Ideation–Worst (SSI-W). The latter 19-item scale is an interviewer-administered rating scale that seems to accurately measure the magnitude of a patient's specific beliefs, behaviors, attitudes, and plans to commit suicide during the specific time period when he or she is at the highest risk of suicide. More specifically, interviewers asked patients to recall the approximate time frame and day when they had the most intense and strongest desire to kill themselves. Patients were then asked to keep this worst experience in mind while they answered and were rated on 19 items related to their wish to die, duration and frequency of suicide ideation, number of deterrents, actual amount of preparation for a contemplated attempt, and the desire to make an active or passive suicide attempt (Beck, Brown, & Steer, 1997).

Retrospective longitudinal research of suicide ideation at its most severe point or worst point in time seems to be a valid predictor of eventual suicide among psychiatric outpatients within an average of four years from the initial assessment interview. This important study by Beck and associates (1999) was based on a large sample of 3,701 outpatients who sought psychiatric treatment at the University of Pennsylvania between 1979 and 1994. After follow-up on all patients four years after completion of treatment, it was found that only 30 of the former patients, or fewer than 1%, had committed suicide. All 3,701 patients were assessed on three scales: Current Suicide Ideation (SSI-C), SSI-W, and BHS. With regard to the findings related to the SSI-W: "Patients who scored in the higher risk category of SSI-W had a 14 times higher odds of committing suicide than patients who scored in the lower risk category" (p. 7). With regard to the BHS, patients who scored in the highest category for hopelessness had a 6 times higher odds of committing suicide than patients who scored in the lower-risk category.

One implication of the longitudinal study is that patients who present at outpatient clinics and community mental health centers may not be experiencing as much suicide ideation or hopelessness as they did in past days, weeks, or months. Therefore, it is critically important to determine suicide ideation at the worst point in time: when the person in crisis called a 24-hour crisis hotline, when the person asked a significant other to drive him or her to the hospital, or when the person arrived at the emergency room. It is also imperative to monitor risk of suicide at regular intervals throughout treatment.

Two Cautionary Notes Regarding Suicide Lethality Assessment

Unfortunately, two of the most frequently cited risk factors of high suicide intent—a history of one or more prior suicide attempts and a current suicide plan—are often misunderstood. It has been obvious to most clinicians and suicidologists that either having a history of a prior suicide attempt or having a specific suicide plan should result in a prediction of high suicide risk. However, it is critically important for crisis counselors and psychiatric screeners to be made aware that the research demonstrates that the absence of a prior suicide attempt should not be taken as an indication that the crisis caller will not commit suicide or make a very serious lethal attempt (Clark, 1998; Fawcett et al., 1990; Kleespies & Dettmer, 2000; Maris, 1992). Reviews of the suicide risk assessment literature indicate that 60% to 70% of suicide completers complete suicide on their first attempt and "had no known history of prior attempts" (Kleespies & Dettmer, 2000).

The second cautionary note relates to the fact that some patients may well be ambivalent about suicide, untrusting of the clinician or psychiatric screener, ashamed, or guarded and unwilling to share suicidal thoughts with a stranger such as a crisis clinician or psychiatric screener. In other cases, the suicidal individual may have a concrete and specific plan with location and lethal method of suicide but be unwilling to share his or her thoughts with anyone. Psychiatric screeners, intake workers, crisis counselors, psychiatric residents, and emergency room nurses and social workers should be vigilant and cautious in suicide risk assessments, and should never assume that a crisis caller or patient is not at suicide risk because he or she reports no suicidal thoughts, wishes, or plans. Fawcett and associates (1990) in their research found that a small group of depressed patients who committed suicide within one year of clinical suicide assessment were more likely to be those

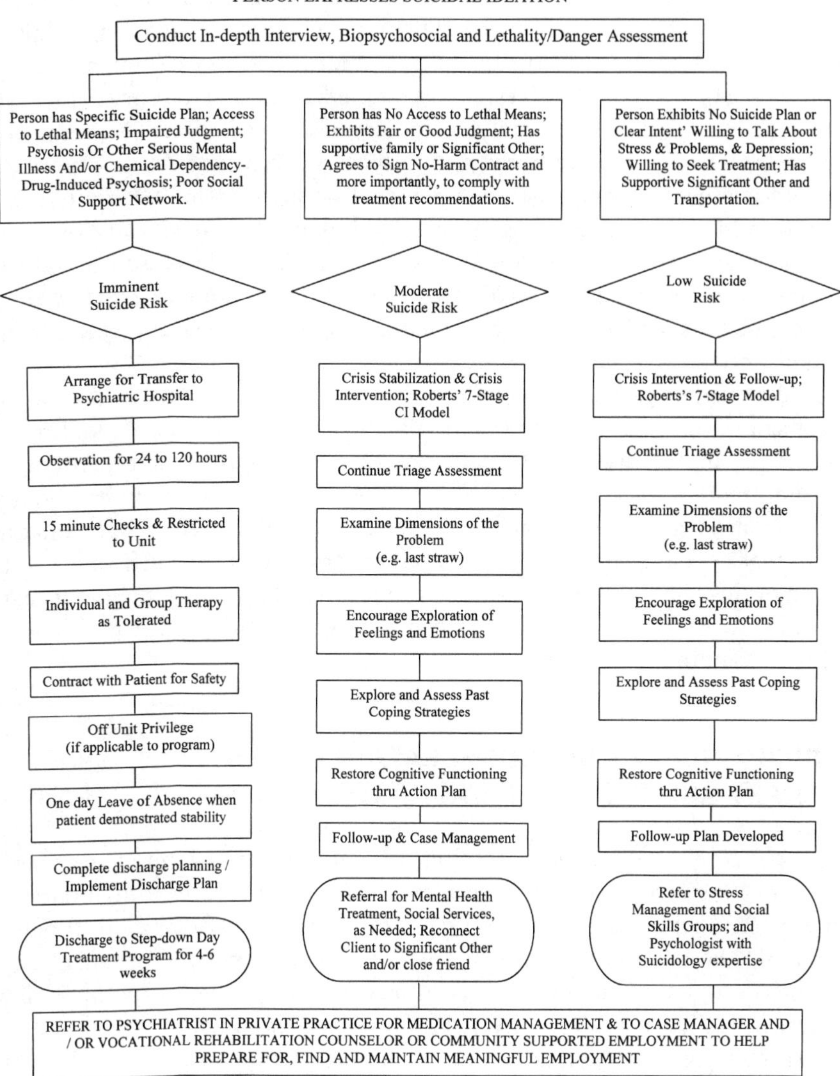

Figure 2.2 Person expresses suicidal ideation

3. Help the caller in crisis to develop a plan of action that links him or her to community health care and mental health agencies. The most frequent outcome of depressed or suicidal callers is that they are transported to psychiatric screening and intake, a behavioral health care facility, hospital, or addiction treatment program.

The crisis intervention worker assumes full responsibility for the case when he or she answers the phone. The caller cannot be rushed and handled patients who said they had no suicidal thoughts or ideas. In sharp contra: the large group of depressed patients who were still alive five years after initi: assessment shared their suicidal thoughts and ideas with the clinician.

With regard to suicide risk estimates and lethality assessments, Rudd anc Joiner (1998) have pointed out that individuals in the severe or imminent suicide risk category have predisposing factors, such as a long history of substance abuse, a family history of a parent or sibling who committed suicide, or a history of child physical or sexual abuse; multiple acute risk factors, such as a recent job loss due to substance abuse, depressed mood, or specific suicide plan with a lethal method available; and a lack of protective factors, such as a significant other or close family members and medication compliance.

In the current care environment, practitioners are required to determine imminent, moderate, and low suicide risk. In doing so, the individual practitioner is required to assign the patient to the most appropriate level of care. The implementation of Roberts's SSCIM provides appropriate interventions for resolution of moderate and low suicidal ideation immediately on the individual's seeking assistance. If the appropriate clinical pathway is followed during the initial assessment, application of the seven-stage model can provide insight in a nonthreatening manner to assist the patient in development of cognitive stabilization.

DISCUSSION OF SUICIDE IDEATION FLOW CHART AND INTERVENTION PROTOCOL

The operation of a crisis intervention program and time-limited treatment program for persons with suicide ideation is shown by the flow chart in Figure 2.2. This provides a general description of the different clinical pathways and the functions of mobile crisis intervention programs, emergency psychiatric units, inpatient treatment units, partial hospital programs, day treatment facilities, and other referral sources in the community.

Crisis intervention and suicide prevention programs usually maintain a 24-hour telephone crisis service. This service provides a lifeline as well as an entry point to behavioral health care for persons with major depression or suicidal thoughts and ideation. When the crisis worker answers the cry for help, his or her primary duty is to initiate crisis intervention, beginning with rapid lethality and triage assessment and establishing rapport. In essence, crisis intervention and suicide prevention include certain primary steps in an attempt to prevent suicide:

1. Conduct a rapid lethality and biopsychosocial assessment.
2. Attempt to establish rapport, and at the same time communicate a willingness to help the caller in crisis.

simply by a referral to another agency. Crisis workers should follow the case until complete transfer of responsibility has been accomplished by some other agency assuming responsibility. The crisis worker should complete the state-mandated mental health and psychiatric screening report, which makes an initial determination as to whether or not the person is a danger to self or others. This report should be given to the ambulance driver and faxed to the intake worker on duty at the receiving psychiatric unit or hospital. In other cases where the risk of suicide is low and a close family member or significant other can take responsibility for the person in crisis, the client and the family member need telephone numbers to call in the case of an emergency. The ultimate goal of all crisis and suicide prevention services is to relieve intense emotional pain and acute crisis episodes while helping the caller to find positive ways to cope with life.

Imperative for all crisis clinicians is the ability to establish rapport with the person in crisis by listening in a patient, hopeful, self-assured, interested, and knowledgeable manner. The skilled crisis worker communicates that the person has done the right thing by calling and, furthermore, that the crisis worker is able to help. An empathetic ear is provided to the crisis caller to relieve his or her intense stress by active listening. The crisis worker should relate to the caller in a confidential, spontaneous, and noninstitutionalized manner (Roberts, 2000; Yeager & Gregiore, 2000).

After listening to the story of the person in crisis and asking several key questions, the crisis worker makes a determination as to whether or not the caller has a high, moderate, or low suicide risk.

If the caller has a lethal method (e.g., a firearm) readily available and a specific plan for suicide, or has previously attempted suicide, he or she is considered to have a high suicide risk. Callers frequently evaluated as low suicide risk still need help, but they are primarily depressed and sometimes expressing ambivalent thoughts about what it's like to be in heaven versus hell. They have not yet planned the specific details of suicide or shared a concrete plan with the crisis counselor. As discussed earlier, if the caller has predisposing factors (e.g., a possible copycat suicide, such as a teenager whose high school classmate committed suicide in the past year, or who has a parent or sibling who committed suicide), he or she may be at moderate to high risk of suicide. Other callers may be persons seeking information for themselves or a family member, social callers with personal problems such as loneliness or sexual dysfunction, or callers needing emergency medical attention.

With regard to inpatient versus outpatient psychiatric treatment, the most important determinant should be imminent danger and lethal means to suicide. It is also extremely important for crisis clinicians and intake psychiatric screeners to make a multiaxial differential diagnosis, which determines acute or chronic psychosocial stressors, dysfunctional relationships, decreased self-esteem or hopelessness, severe or unremitting anxiety, living alone without social support, intimate partner violence, personality disorders (particularly borderline personality disorders), major depressive disorders, bipolar disorders, and comorbidity (American Psychiatric Association, 2003). Making accurate assessments and predicting short-term risk of suicide (one to three days) has been found to be much more reliable than predicting long-term risk (Simon, 1992). For example, a 65-year-old widower has some symptoms of major depressive disorder and sometimes smokes marijuana; he may be a long-term risk of suicide. Therefore, he should be asked every month or two if he has been thinking of suicide. Risk will increase when this man learns that he has liver cancer as a result of 30 years of alcohol abuse. He should then be assessed with a full clinical interview for an escalation of depressive thoughts and drug addiction as well as any suicidal thoughts or plans. Another serious clue to increased suicidal risk is when a person has no social support network, poor judgment and poor impulse control, and adamantly refuses to sign a contract for safety.

CASE STUDIES AND APPLICATION OF R-SSCIM

Maryann

Maryann's mother reports that her 17-year-old daughter is barricaded in her bedroom and last night ripped the phone out of the wall and threw it into the hallway. Maryann has not eaten for 24 hours. Her boyfriend broke up with her, and her mother has heard her crying for many hours. Maryann refuses to speak with her mother. The mother is very worried because eight months earlier, Maryann had ingested a lot of sleeping pills and been rushed to the ER when she was distraught about the breakup with her previous boyfriend. A few hours ago, Maryann called her favorite first cousin and told him that she was giving him all of her favorite CDs. Maryann's father passed away 12 months ago from cirrhosis of the liver. She was very close to her father. The mother calls the psychiatric screening and crisis intervention hotline at one of New Jersey's large medical centers and indicates that she thinks her daughter is depressed and possibly suicidal.

Suicide Risk Assessment

After reading Maryann's case synopsis and reviewing the suicide risk assessment flow chart (Figure 2.2), would your preliminary rapid assessment rate Maryann as at low, moderate, or high suicide risk?

It is important to keep in mind that while many persons at high risk of suicide have expressed or exhibited a specific suicide plan and availability of a lethal method (e.g., firearms or hanging), there are exceptions. There is a relatively small group of individuals who do not talk to anyone before making a lethal suicide attempt, but do give clear clues of imminent suicide risk. For example, a college student fails a course for the first time and can't sleep, although he has never had a problem sleeping and has been an honor student for the past three years. Or a young adult who never expressed paranoid delusions has now expressed irrational fears that a violent gang with 100 members is after him and will try to kill him tonight. These delusions are an outgrowth of a drug-induced psychosis. *Psychiatric screeners, crisis workers, counselors, social workers, family members, and close friends should be made aware of the fact that a critical clue to suicidal ideation and suicide attempts is a drastic change in behavior patterns, daily routine, or actions* (e.g., barricading oneself in a room for 24 hours and refusing to come out to eat or go to the bathroom, giving away prized possessions, having paranoid delusions or command hallucinations for the first time, talking about how wonderful it would be to go to Heaven to be with one's recently deceased and loving father).

The psychiatric screener crisis worker who answered the phone determines that this call seems to be at moderate to high risk of lethality and that she needs to immediately go to Maryann's home. The preliminary lethality assessment is based on the following seven high-risk factors:

1. This is the first time that Maryann has ever barricaded herself in her room.
2. She seems to be depressed, evidenced by not eating for 24 hours and crying for many hours.
3. She had a previous suicide attempt only eight months ago.
4. She recently gave away prized possessions.
5. Her father, to whom she was close, died only 12 months ago.
6. She refuses to communicate with anyone.
7. She broke the phone (property damage).

You are the crisis worker, and you are dispatched to the home. The following application focuses on what you should say and do when you arrive. We describe this crisis situation with specific details, statements, and questions on ways to apply each of the seven stages in the R-SSCIM. First, it is important to be aware that Stages 1 and 2 often take place simultaneously. However, in the case of life-threatening and high-risk suicide ideation, child abuse, sexual assault, or domestic violence, the emphasis is on rapid crisis, lethality, and triage assessment.

Stage 1: Assess Lethality

The crisis worker needs to obtain background information quickly from the mother (rapid collateral assessment).

Ask the mother if the daughter has been taking Acutane for acne. Then ask the mother if Maryann was ever prescribed any antidepressant medication.

If yes, does she know if Maryann has been taking her medication, and what it is, and who prescribed it?

Was it prescribed by a family doctor or a psychiatrist?
Does Maryann currently have access to her medications or any other drugs?
Ask the mother if anything has changed in the past 20–30 minutes (since her phone call) in her daughter's situation.
Next, give the mother something to do so she is not in the way (e.g., ask her to call the ex-boyfriend or best girlfriend to obtain background data, especially whether Maryann has recently taken any illegal drugs).
Assess Maryann's danger to herself and others (suicidal or homicidal thoughts), as well as substance abuse history and preexisting mental disorders.
Ask questions about symptoms, traumatic events, stressful life events, future plans, suicidal ideation, previous suicide attempts, mental illness.
Ask about upcoming special events or birthday celebrations that the youth in crisis may be looking forward to, or recollections of happy events or celebrations in the past that may be repeated in the future (special events can instill hope for the future).
Determine if youth needs immediate medical attention if there are drugs, sleeping pills, or weapons in her room.

Rapid Triage Assessment:

1. The individual is a danger to herself or others and is exhibiting intense and acute psychiatric symptoms. These survivors generally require short-term emergency hospitalization and psychopharmacotherapy to protect themselves from self-harm or harm to other persons (Priority I: Emergency medical treatment, ambulance or rescue transport, and psychiatric screening center).
2. The individual is in a precrisis stage due to ineffective coping skills, a weak support system, or ambivalence about seeking the help of a therapist. These individuals may have mild or no psychiatric symptoms or suicide risk. They may need one to three sessions of crisis counseling and referral to a support group.
3. The third type of client may have called a suicide prevention program or a 24-hour mobile crisis intervention unit for information because he or she is sad, anxious, lonely, or depressed.

It is important to make a determination of whether the person in crisis needs the mobile crisis intervention team to respond quickly to the home or other place in the community. The caller may have just attempted suicide or is planning to attempt suicide shortly, or may be experiencing command hallucinations of a violent nature (Priority I). The caller may be experiencing delusions and may be unable to leave the house (Priority II), or may be suffering from mood disturbance or depression and fleeting suicidal ideation, with no specific suicidal plan (Priority III, probably in need of an appointment with a caring counselor or therapist).

Stage 2: Establish Rapport

It is very important to introduce yourself and speak in a calm and neutral manner.

Crisis workers should do their best to make a psychological connection to the 17-year-old in a precrisis or acute crisis situation.

Part of establishing rapport and putting the person at ease involves being nonjudgmental, listening actively, and demonstrating empathy.

Establish a bridge, bond, or connection by asking Maryann what CDs or posters she likes.

"Do you have any posters on your wall right now?"

"Do you have a favorite TV show?"

"Do you have a favorite recording artist?"

An alternative approach is brief self-disclosure. For example: "When I was 17 years old my boyfriend broke up with me. I think I understand the emotional pain and sadness you are going through. I thought I loved my boyfriend very much. In fact, he was my first love. He broke up with me for another girl and I was very sad, just like you. But, about two months after the breakup, I met someone else and we had a very enjoyable long-term relationship."

Ask Maryann what her favorite deserts or candy are.

It is important to understand that many adolescents are impulsive and impatient, may have escape fantasies, and be very sensitive and temperamental. So don't lecture, preach, or moralize. Make concise statements, be caring, display keen interest, and do not make disparaging or insulting statements of any kind.

Stages 3 and 4 sometimes take place simultaneously.

Stage 3: Identify the major problem, including crisis precipitants or triggering incidents

Ask questions to determine the final straw or precipitating event that led Maryann into her current situation.

Focus on the problem or problems and prioritize and focus on the worst problem first.

Listen carefully for symptoms and clues of suicidal thoughts and intent.

Make a direct inquiry about suicidal plans and about nonverbal gestures or other communications (e.g., diaries, poems, journals, school essays, paintings or drawings).

Because most adolescent suicides are impulsive and unplanned, it is important to determine whether the youth has easy access to a lethal weapon or drugs (including sleeping pills, methamphetamines, or barbituates).

Stage 4: Deal with feelings and emotions and provide support

Deal with the client's immediate feelings or fears.

Allow Maryann to tell her story and why she seems to be feeling so bad.
Provide preliminary empathy to the impact of Maryann's breakup with her boyfriend.
Use active listening skills (e.g., paraphrasing, reflection of feelings, summarizing, reassurance, compliments, advice giving, reframing, and probes).
Normalize the client's experiences.
Validate and identify her emotions.
Examine past coping methods.
Encourage ventilation of mental and physical feelings.

Stage 5: Explore possible alternatives
First, reestablish balance and homeostasis, also known as equilibrium:
Ask Mary Ann what has helped in the past. For example, what did she do to cope with the loss and grief of losing a loved family member after her father passed away?
Integrate solution-based therapy (e.g., full or partial Miracle question).
Ask her about bright spots from her past (e.g., hobbies, birthday celebrations, sports successes, academic successes, vacations).
Mutually explore and suggest new coping options and alternatives.
It is important for the crisis worker to jog the client's memories so she can verbalize the last time everything seemed to be going well and she was in a good mood. Help the client find untapped resources.

Stage 6: Help client develop and formulate an action plan.
Provide client with a specific phone number of a therapist.

Stage 7: Follow-up phone call, in-person appointment for booster session, or home visit
Let Maryann know that she can call you, and give her your beeper number. Let her know that the beeper is for an emergency.
Depending on the crisis worker's assessment when leaving the home, it would be useful to schedule a follow-up with the therapist to whom Maryann is being referred, so that there is a team approach.
Follow-up also may include a booster session with the crisis worker scheduled for one week or 30 days later.

Jeanette

Jeanette introduced herself in the session by saying "My name is Jeanette, but everyone calls me Jet." She is a 27-year-old female who presented to the hospital emergency department seeking treatment for a severe laceration above her right eye. In the process of triaging Jet, an astute medical student questioned if the cut was the result of physical abuse. Jet became tearful and reported that she had been beaten and sexually assaulted by two men while "semiconscious" at a house where there was "a party going on." Jet reported, "I was really high and almost passed out, when these two guys came in the room. I was too messed up to fight, it just happened. One of them was rough, he kept hitting me . . . but I couldn't stop him, I was just too high to protect myself." As the assessment progressed, Jet reported current suicidal ideation as well as a past history of suicide attempts and substance abuse, including smoking cocaine and taking crystal methamphetamine for the past three years. Jet reports smoking $300 to $800 worth of cocaine, as available. Jet also drinks daily, reporting a tolerance of nearly two bottles of wine per day. During the admission, Jet reported that she feels there is no hope and that she would like to "end it all." She reported to staff that she knew acetaminophen in a large enough dose would "do the trick." She reported a plan of picking up two large bottles on the way home, taking the drug with "downers," and just not waking up. This report led to voluntary admission to the inpatient psychiatric unit for psychiatric stabilization and detoxification.

Following admission to the inpatient unit, Jet slept for nearly 24 hours. On the third day of treatment (at approximately 9:00 A.M.), Jet began to experience mood swings. At this time, she yelled at the nursing staff when she did not receive Motrin for the headache she was experiencing. As the day progressed, Jet experienced a variety of moods ranging from relief to paralyzing anxiety. By noon she had experienced a confrontation with each nurse on duty. Jet reported severe cravings and feelings of uncertainty of her well-being and in general her ability to maintain abstinence. By 2:00 Jet was reported by staff to be participating in treatment groups and integrating well into the community. However, with the change of shift came a change of staff and new personality conflicts.

Jet was immediately confronted by the evening charge nurse for being late to treatment activities; there was a second confrontation regarding attendance of the evening AA meeting. Finally, at 10:00 P.M., Jet and the nurse were at the nursing station screaming at one another. Jet had requested a cup of coffee, and the charge nurse refused, stating, "Speed freaks don't need a stimulant." At this, Jet lunged at the charge nurse. She was immediately restrained by two male staff and given Haldol and Ativan. The effect of this medication was similar to her feelings while being physically abused. Jet reports believing the two male staff were going to rape her. She began to fight, and the harder she fought, the worse her experience became. By 10:30 Jet was in five-point restraints, screaming and sobbing while reliving the trauma that led to her admission to the psychiatric and detoxification unit.

R-SSCIM Application

Stage 1: Plan and Conduct a Crisis and Lethality Assessment

Stage 1 of the seven-stage crisis intervention model began with the night nurse speaking calmly with Jet and working to bring her to a rational state where she could begin to assess the nature of the reaction Jet was displaying while restrained. The nurse accurately assessed that the restraints were a large portion of the issue. Despite conflict between staff regarding Jet's actions, the night nurse began reducing Jet's distress by removing one restraint at a time, assuring Jet that others would be removed as she demonstrated her ability to cooperate.

Stage 2: Establish Rapport and Rapidly Establish Relationship

As Jet demonstrated her willingness to cooperate, the night nurse began the process of rapidly establishing rapport with Jet, as outlined in the seven-stage model. Establishing rapport began with a smile and soft conversation. A cold compress was placed on Jet's forehead, while another was used to wipe her face and arms. These simple acts of kindness would set the stage for further investigation, treatment, and stabilization.

While establishing a relationship appears simple, it is frequently difficult to do well given the time constraints experienced in crisis stabilization. For example, in this case, the team was aware that Jet was experiencing withdrawal and mood swings characteristic of cocaine dependence. For this reason, the night nurse began the process of assessing the physical distress related to withdrawal and began to approach Jet in a manner to address the physical and emotional aspect of her illness.

Stage 3: Identify Major Problems (Including the Last Straw or Precipitants)

It is interesting how each staff responded to Jet as she progressed through the first day of treatment. Jet was labeled by staff as "depressed," "a danger to self and others," "noncompliant," and "drug seeking." As the team reviewed the case they began to assume preferred philosophical and theoretical perspectives regarding this case and Jet's response to treatment. None considered the potential of retraumatization until the night nurse began to identify key components of the case.

While talking with Jet, the nurse utilized probing questions and active listening to facilitate Jet's expression of the "last straw" leading to her restraint. The probing questions were specifically designed to examine the dimensions of the problem in order to further define the problem. Jet reported:

> I began to remember the assault. When I was being assaulted, I was high, so the impact wasn't that bad . . . but when those two big male staff held me down it all came rushing back in. I was there again. I kept trying to tell myself this wasn't real. But it was very real. I wasn't able to convince myself that they weren't going to hurt me . . . That's probably because they were hurting me. Not the same way, but it was the same in my mind at

the time. I just remember not being able to move while they had their way with me.

Stage 4: Deal With Feelings and Emotions

Dealing with the feelings and emotions that Jet experienced as a result of the retraumatization became a critical portion of the crisis intervention process. Having explored the dimensions of the problems as outlined by Jet, the crisis team once again utilized the strength of the positive rapport with the night nurse to address the feelings and emotions associated with this case. The crisis intervenor was able to offer assuring comments designed to reframe Jet's cognitive distortions while at the same time validating accurate perceptions. The intervenor first explored concepts of fact as opposed to Jet's perceptions by asking clarifying questions:

Intervenor: Jet, you said the abuse was all your fault. What exactly do you feel you were doing wrong?

Jet: I put myself in the position of being abused and shouldn't have . . . I shouldn't have used so much, I shouldn't have been at that party.

Intervenor: No one deserves to experience what you have experienced, not at the party and not here in the hospital. What can we do today to begin to deal with this?

Jet: Can you really help me to get sober? If you can, I'd like that . . . I don't ever want to be there again.

Intervenor: I agree, that's a great start, and we can help with that, but you realize that at some point we will have to address the other issues?

Jet: (tearful) Yes.

Stage 5: Generate and Explore Alternatives

In this stage, Jet worked with the team to develop a plan for her ongoing problem-solving process. She and the social worker, having sorted through facts and perceptions, made a list of actions for Jet to engage in to facilitate psychiatric stabilization and to establish a program of recovery. Jet agreed that she would begin an antidepressant (SSRI) and that she would work with her social worker to address issues related to her abuse. Finally, Jet began to actively participate as a member of the Women's Cocaine Anonymous Group.

Stage 6: Develop and Formulate an Action Plan

Jet realized that she would need to establish a self-directed program of recovery. As time progressed, she was demonstrating clear thinking. She was able to formulate plans designed to distance herself from situations that led to her vulnerability, thus reducing fears that were previously driving her actions. Jet requested to speak with the second shift charge nurse, the medical director, and staff involved in the restraint episode to discuss her experiences on the night she was restrained. She provided a powerful description of how staff had in fact engaged in actions that retraumatized her. In essence, Jet demonstrated restoration of cognitive functioning through the development of a self-directed plan of action.

Stage 7: Establish Follow-up Plan and Agreement

Given the moderate expression of suicidal ideation and the development of a plan of action designed to examine and explore the events leading to Jet's crisis admission and restraint episode, the staff now revisited Jet's case to determine the next most appropriate actions. With her plan in hand, Jet reported feeling stable enough to return to her home environment. Staff readministered the depression scale and hopelessness scale given at the beginning of crisis intervention. The depression scale had improved remarkably, as had the hopelessness scale. More important, Jet was able to verbalize seeing a way out by being an active participant in her recovery plan. The plan consisted of three to six weeks of partial hospitalization to provide her with the necessary support and opportunity to implement her plan of action and to monitor her functioning as she progressed through the potentially stressful events contained in the plan of action.

Jet progressed well through her plan of action. She attended and actively participated in the partial hospitalization program. She attended a minimum of three 12-step support groups per week. During this time, she participated in group and individual sessions designed to increase her overall functionality.

One year later, Jet continues in her program of recovery. She is now the chairperson of the women's group that she attended on the first night of her admission. She is completing the first year of nursing school and plans to take a master's degree as a psychiatric nurse practitioner.

Harvey

Harvey is an extremely successful dentist practicing in a midwestern city suburb. He is married with three children, ages 12, 15, and 18. Although extremely successful, Harvey has struggled with bipolar disorder since age 33; he is currently 50. Harvey was referred to a substance abuse treatment facility for alcohol dependence. This referral came following three successive complaints to the state medical board stating that he smelled of alcohol. Harvey admitted his abuse of alcohol and that in fact on the days of each complaint he had drinks during lunch prior to returning to his practice in the afternoon.

Harvey had successfully completed detoxification and was in the second week of his treatment when he demonstrated symptoms of major depressive disorder, severe. He expressed extreme feelings of despair and depressed mood nearly every day, loss of interest in almost all activities of the day, psychomotor agitation, fatigue, hypersomnia, and excessive guilt about being "sick." By the end of the second week, he expressed suicidal ideation, including a plan to kill himself with a gun, which he had access to while on a therapeutic leave from the facility. This information was shared in a conversation with his business partner, who immediately called the treating facility to alert them to this issue.

The staff intervened, completing the first stage of Roberts's seven-stage model. In completing the lethality assessment, staff revealed a second, more pressing concern. This was that Harvey's actual plan was to hang himself in the bathroom of the halfway house that evening. As a result, Harvey was transferred to an inpatient psychiatric facility for a brief period of stabilization.

During this time, Harvey expressed remorse for his actions, stating, "I would never kill myself." He reported to staff that he had far too much to live for and simply would not waste his life. Harvey worked diligently on his treatment plan, participated in group and individual sessions, and completed goal work related to specific areas of needs, including family therapy and addiction treatment.

With regard to suicidal ideation, Harvey spoke openly in session with his family that he would not harm himself. He agreed to have his gun collection removed from the house and spoke openly of future plans. After four days, Harvey returned to the addiction treatment facility. He was admitted to the halfway house program. Following two weeks in the halfway house, Harvey was granted a leave of absence.

Harvey's flight arrived in his hometown at 6:00 P.M. At 8:00, Harvey's wife contacted the treatment facility expressing concern that he had not returned home. At 10:00 that evening Harvey's body was discovered at his office, the apparent victim of death by asphyxiation. He was found in a chair with nitrous oxide on full without sufficient oxygen to support life. Although questions were raised related to the possibility of accidental death, the autopsy indicated the presence of sufficient lethal amounts of barbiturates in the system to facilitate overdose if asphyxiation had not occurred.

R-SSCIM Application

In the case of Harvey, review of the clinical practice indicated that staff had completed all necessary steps to provide a treatment plan to protect the patient from self-harm. The psychiatric facility had followed the American Psychiatric Association's approved practice guideline for the management of depressive disorder. Family conferences had been completed. Harvey and family members agreed to have all of his guns removed from the house, and an additional safety sweep removed potentially mood-altering substances from the home environment.

It was believed that Harvey did not have a key to his office, that the key had been surrendered to his wife on his admission to the addiction treatment center. Further, it was not clear to peers or family how or where Harvey had gained access to mood-altering substances. Discussions with Harvey's roommates provided no insight into potential risk for self-harm. Furthermore, everyone believed that Harvey was doing exceptionally well in his treatment.

Investigations were launched by the treating facility in an attempt to determine if there had been any discrepancies in Harvey's treatment that could have contributed to this event. Review of the case indicated that on numerous occasions there was clearly completed assessment of suicidal ideation. On each occasion, the patient denied suicidal ideation. In the record, numerous notes indicated discussion of his remorse for suicidal ideation and of his efforts to resolve issues that might lead to future suicidal ideation. Harvey was compliant with the treatment milieu, including group and individual sessions and medication, and was involved in family therapy.

The patient's discharge conference from the psychiatric facility summarized all progress made, including efforts to remove risk factors from the home. This documentation was compared with the halfway house documentation and demonstrated remarkable similarities in progress notes, which also described the patient's progress in management of his depressive symptoms and resolution of suicidal ideation. While relieved that the case had apparently not been mismanaged, concerns remained given the reality of the loss of this patient.

In assessment of the case, some raised the question of whether it was possible that the patient could have made a decision to commit suicide but have chosen not to share this information with anyone. Was it possible for the patient to hide this from staff? Literature review found that Beck et al. (1993) had indicated that dealing with suicide by identifying intent only as a global concept is an oversimplification. Suicidal ideation and suicidal acts are complex patterns of behavior requiring increasingly thorough analyses for better understanding. Furthermore, it is indicated that the decision to communicate suicidal ideation, plan, and intent is an extremely personal decision. Although many will discuss suicidal ideation prior to the attempt, some choose to communicate after the event with a note, and still others choose not to communicate at all.

In revisiting the subject, Beck et al. (1973, 1993) conclude the following with regard to communication of suicidal ideation:

There is no clear evidence that verbal communication, final acts, and previous suicide attempts are justifiably labeled together as ways of communicating suicidal intent.

Prior verbalization of suicidal ideation or intent bears little relationship to the extent of the wish to die experienced at the time of the suicide attempt.

Talking or not talking about suicidal plans may be a manifestation of personal style rather than an index of despair or hidden motives.

It was believed, but of course not confirmed by those investigating the case, that the patient had indeed developed and carried out the plan without communication of his intent. In reality, this left staff of both facilities feeling helpless in their ability to predict potential for self-harm in this case.

CONCLUSION

Due to the increasing demand that mental health professionals be able to work within time-limited and resource-limited environments with increasingly complex populations, straightforward, realistic approaches to crisis intervention are critically needed.

Our goal in this chapter has been to provide a realistic framework for crisis intervention, examining potential clinical pathways for patients presenting across the continuum of care need. Mental health practitioners working in crisis intervention and stabilization environments should consistently consider assessment strategies, the utility of instruments to assess and reassess patient status, amount of time available, patient burden, cost, and potential outcome of chosen interventions. Application of best practices based on evidence-based reviews and use of systematic approaches such as the R-SSCIM will assist practitioners by providing a stable framework for addressing crisis in a continuously changing care environment. It is the challenge of all mental health practitioners to develop their skills in rapid assessment and risk and rescue strategies, building on the strengths of the patient as outlined by the seven-stage model.

REFERENCES

American Psychiatric Association, Steering Committee on Practice Guidelines. (2003). *Practice guideline for the assessment and treatment of patients with suicidal behavior*. Washington, DC: American Psychiatric Association.

Beck, Aaron T., & Lester, D. (1976). Components of suicidal intent in completed and attempted suicides. *Journal of Psychology: Interdisciplinary & Applied*, 92(1), 35–38.

Beck, A. T., Brown, G., & Steer, R. (1997). Psychometric characteristics of the scale for suicide ideation with psychiatric outpatients. *Behavior Research and Therapy, 11,* 1039–1046.

Beck, A. T., Brown, G., Steer, R., Dahlsgaard, K., & Grisham, J. (1999). Suicide ideation at its worst point: A predictor of eventual suicide in psychiatric outpatients. *Suicide and Life-Threatening Behavior, 29*(1), 1–9.

Beck, A. T., Steer, R. A., Beck, J. S., & Newman, C. F. (1993). Hopelessness, depression, suicidal ideation, and clinical diagnosis of depression. *Suicide and Life-Threatening Behavior, 23,* 139–145.

Brown, G. (2002). *A review of suicide assessment measures for intervention research with adults and older adults.* Unpublished manuscript. Department of Psychiatry. University of Pennsylvania.

Burgess, A. W., & Roberts, A. R. (2000). Crisis intervention for persons diagnosed with clinical disorders based on the stress-crisis continuum. In A. R. Roberts (Ed.), *Crisis intervention handbook: Assessment, treatment, and research* (2nd ed., pp. 56–76). New York: Oxford University Press.

Clark, D. (1998). The evaluation and management of the suicidal patient. In P. M. Kleespies (Ed.). *Emergencies in mental health practice* (pp. 379–397). New York: Guilford Press.

Eaton, Y., & Ertl, B. (2000). The comprehensive crisis intervention model of Community Integration, Inc. crisis services. In A. R. Roberts (Ed.), *Crisis intervention handbook: Assessment, treatment and research* (2nd ed.) (pp. 373–387). New York: Oxford University Press.

Eaton, Y., & Roberts, A. R. (2002). Frontline crisis intervention: Step-by-step practice guidelines with case applications. In A. R. Roberts & G. J. Greene (Eds)., *Social workers' desk reference* (pp. 89–96). New York: Oxford University Press.

Fawcett, J., Scheftner, W., Fogg, L., Clark, D. C., Young, M. A., Hedeker, D., & Gibbons, R. (1990). Time-related predictors of suicide in major affective disorder. *American Journal of Pyschiatry, 147,* 1189–1194.

Jobes, D. A., Berman, A. L., & Martin, C. (2000). Adolescent suicidality and crisis intervention. In A. R. Roberts (Ed.). *Crisis intervention handbook: Assessment, treatment, and research* (2nd ed. pp. 131–151). New York: Oxford University Press.

Kleespies, P. M., & Dettmer, E. L. (2000). An evidence-based approach to evaluating and managing suicidal emergencies. *Journal of Clinical Psychology, 56*(9), 1109–1130.

Kovacs, M., Beck, A. T., & Weissman, A. (1976). The communication of suicidal intent: A reexamination. *Archives of General Psychiatry, 33*(2), 198–201.

Leise, B. S. (1995). Integrating crisis intervention, cognitive therapy and triage. In A. R. Roberts (Ed.). *Crisis intervention and time-limited cognitive treatment* (pp. 28–51). Thousand Oaks, CA: Sage Publications.

Maris, R. W., Berman, A. L., Maltsberger, J. T., & Yufit, R. I. (Eds.). (1992). *Assessment and prediction of suicide.* New York: Guilford Press.

Roberts, A. R. (Ed.). (2000). *Crisis intervention handbook: Assessment, treatment, and research* (pp. 513–529). New York: Oxford University Press.

Roberts, A. R. (2002). Assessment, crisis intervention and trauma treatment: The integrative ACT intervention model. *Brief treatment and crisis intervention,* 2(1),1–21.

Roberts, A. R., Yeager, K. R., & Streiner, D. L. (2004). Evidence-based practice with comorbid substance abuse, mental illness and suicidality: Can the evidence be found? *Brief Treatment and Crisis Intervention,* 4(2), 123–136.

Rudd, M., &Joiner, T. (1998). The assessment, management, and treatment of suicidality: Toward clinically informed and balanced standards of care. *Clinical Psychology: Science and Practice, 5,* 135–150.

Simon, R. I. (1992). *Psychiatry and law for clinicians.* Washington, D.C.: American Psychiatric Press.

U.S. Department of Health and Human Services. (2001). *National strategy for suicide prevention: Goals and objectives for action.* Rockville, MD: Author.

Weishaar, M. E. (2004). A cognitive-behavioral approach to suicide risk reduction in crisis intervention. In A. R. Roberts & K. Yeager (Eds.), *Evidence-based practice manual: Research and outcome measures in health and human services* (pp. 749–757). New York: Oxford University Press.

Westefeld, J. S., Range, I. M., Rogers, J. R., Maples, M. R., Bromley, J. I., & Alcorn, J. (2000). Suicide: An overview. *The Counseling Psychologist, 28,* 445–510.

Yeager, K. R., & Gregoire, T. K. (2000). Crisis intervention application of brief solution-focused therapy in addictions. In A. R. Roberts (Ed.), *Crisis intervention handbook: Assessment, treatment and research* (2nd ed., pp. 275–306). New York: Oxford University Press.

Yeager, K. R., & Roberts, A. R. (2004). Mental illness, substance dependence and suicidality: Secondary data analysis. In A. R. Roberts & K. R. Yeager (Eds.), *Evidence-based practice manual: Research and outcome measures in health and human services* (pp. 70–75). New York: Oxford University Press.

3

How to Work With Clients' Strengths in Crisis Intervention: A Solution-Focused Approach

GILBERT J. GREENE
MO-YEE LEE
RHONDA TRASK
JUDY RHEINSCHELD

Through a review of literature, theory, and case examples, this chapter will address the following:

- How to use solution-focused therapy in working with the strengths of clients in crisis
- How to structure a solution-focused/strengths-based approach to crisis intervention in a stepwise manner
- How to consistently engage clients in "change talk" and not stay stuck in "problem talk"
- How to co-construct with clients outcome goals that include a future without the presenting problem
- How to develop homework tasks that are consistent with enhancing client strengths

According to Roberts (1991), a crisis is "a period of psychological disequilibrium, experienced as a result of a hazardous event or situation that constitutes a significant problem that cannot be remedied by using familiar coping strategies" (p. 4). Crisis intervention tends to view the precipitating event as overwhelming the client's usual coping skills (strengths); consequently, these coping skills are inadequate to meet the challenge of the precipitating event. The Chinese translation of the word *crisis* consists of two separate characters that literally mean "danger" and "opportunity." Crisis intervention views the provision of services to clients in crisis as an "opportunity" for clients to learn new coping skills. In fact, the literature has consistently stressed that clients need to develop new resources and coping skills in order for crisis intervention to be successful (Eaton & Roberts, 2002; Roberts and Dziegielewski, 1995; Roberts, 1996; Kanel, 1999). The emphasis throughout the crisis intervention literature has overwhelmingly been on how to help clients develop new coping skills.

People in crisis also have the "opportunity" to further identify, mobilize, and enhance the strengths (coping skills) they already have. Some scholars have stated that crisis intervenors should also identify and work with clients' personal strengths (Parad & Parad, 1990; Puryear, 1979; Roberts, 1991); however, the crisis intervention literature lacks a clear explication of how to specifically operationalize doing this. One possible source for information on how to operationalize working with clients' strengths in crisis intervention is the *strengths perspective* (Rapp, 1998; Saleeby, 1992, 1997).

The strengths perspective views clients as having the resources and coping skills for successfully handling crisis situations but they are not using them, are underusing them, or are not aware that they are using them (Saleebey, 2002). The job of the clinician using this approach is to help clients tap into the resources within themselves (Saleebey, 2002). A clinician, therefore, does not change people but serves as a catalyst for clients discovering and using their own resources to accomplish their goals (Saleeby, 2002). General guidelines for the clinical use of the strengths perspective have been discussed in the literature (Cowger & Snively, 2002; Rapp, 1998, 2002); however, a more specific operationalization of its use in conducting and facilitating the therapeutic conversations that make up clinical practice generally and crisis intervention specifically is lacking.

One approach to clinical practice that emphasizes working with client strengths is *solution-focused therapy*, which has been developing since the 1970s and emphasizes working only with client strengths (DeJong, 2002; de Shazer, 1985; de Shazer et al., 1986), This approach provides specifically defined clinician behaviors that are very appropriate for operationalizing a strengths perspective in the practice of crisis intervention. Like the strengths perspective, solution-focused therapy views clients as being very resourceful and assumes they have all they need to solve their problems (Walter & Peller, 1992). The use of solution-focused therapy for operationalizing the strengths perspective has been discussed in the literature (DeJong & Miller, 1995). There has been some discussion in the literature of using solution-focused therapy in crisis intervention (Berg & Miller, 1992b; Berg, 1994; Brown, Shiang, & Bongar, 2003; DeJong & Berg, 2002; Lipchik, 2002; Wiger & Harowski, 2003).

Both the strengths perspective (Rapp, 1998; Saleeby, 2002) and solution-focused therapy (Selekman, 1997) view clients as resilient. *Resilience* has been defined as a person's ability not only to cope with, survive, and bounce back from difficult and traumatic experiences and situations but also to continue to grow and develop psychologically and emotionally (Walsh, 1998). However, in the crisis intervention literature, the emphasis has consistently been on helping people return only to their precrisis level of functioning (Fraser, 1998); such a perspective is not completely consistent with client resilience. Fraser (1998) proposes that clinicians should consistently view a crisis as a catalyst for clients experiencing growth and development beyond a precrisis level of functioning. The literature does not contain a discussion of operationalizing working with clients' strengths and powers of resilience in the provision of crisis intervention services. The purpose of this chapter is to present such an operationalization so that clients in crisis have the opportunity not only to develop new coping skills but also to identify, mobilize, and enhance those strengths and coping skills they already have but may have forgotten or may be underutilizing.

CRISIS INTERVENTION AND SOLUTION-FOCUSED THERAPY

Crisis Intervention

A crisis can result from situational stressors, transitional changes, or disasters (Parad & Parad, 1990). The degree to which an event is experienced as a crisis depends on how the person perceives it; a crisis for one person may not be a crisis for another (Roberts & Dziegielewski, 1995). A crisis occurs when a precipitating event disrupts an individual's or a family's usual ways of functioning, resulting in their experiencing a sense of disequilibrium (Roberts, 1991; Parad & Parad, 1990). When in this state, people experience a variety of strong feelings, such as vulnerability, anxiety, powerlessness, and hopelessness (Parad & Parad, 1990). At this point a person may resort to increasing the use of his or her usual coping strategies or trying some new strategies in a trial-and-error manner to attempt to deal with the crisis situation (Ewing, 1990). If these additional efforts are unsuccessful, the person experiences increasing tension and is at risk for major disorganization of his or her functioning (Caplan, 1964).

After 4 to 6 weeks, clients will, with or without treatment, experience either a return to their previous equilibrium or a new equilibrium that may leave them coping better or worse than prior to the crisis (Parad & Parad, 1990). The primary purpose of crisis intervention is to accelerate the return to equilibrium and at least prevent individuals from stabilizing at a new, regressed level of equilibrium. There are various models of crisis intervention. One of the most complete models is the seven-stage approach developed by Roberts (1991): (1) assess lethality and safety needs; (2) establish rapport and communication; (3) identify the major problems; (4) deal with feelings and provide support; (5) explore possible alternatives; (6) assist in formulating an action plan; and (7) follow up.

A central idea in crisis intervention is that because of their disequilibrium and emotional distress, clients will take steps that they otherwise might have resisted prior to the crisis and in the process develop new coping skills (Ewing, 1990; Parad & Parad, 1990; Roberts, 1991). Client change in crisis intervention is accomplished by various in-session and between-session activities. One clinician activity in the session involves challenging the client's negative self-talk or irrational beliefs by the use of "carefully worded questions" (Roberts, 1991, p. 8). The purpose of such questions is to get the client to replace the negative, irrational self-talk with positive, rational self-talk. The clinician also works with the client to identify alternative courses of action for successfully dealing with the crisis. After various alternatives have been identified, the clinician and the client develop an action plan for implementing them. An action plan involves carrying out specific *tasks*, "primarily by the client, but also by the worker and significant others, designed to solve specific problems in the current life situation, to modify previous inadequate or inappropriate ways of functioning, and to learn new coping patterns" (Golan, 1986, p. 323). Tasks are specific actions that must be performed in order for the client to achieve his or her treatment goal (reestablish equilibrium; Fortune, 1985; Golan, 1986; Levy & Shelton, 1990). Most tasks are performed by the client between sessions in the form of "homework assignments," but some are done within the treatment situation. Successfully performing therapeutic tasks should result in the client feeling, thinking, or behaving in new and different ways. In crisis intervention, clinicians should "encourage clients to think of alternative ideas, coping methods, and solutions" (Roberts, 1991, p. 12). However, when they are under the stress of helping clients deal with the crisis, clinicians are often tempted to jump in quickly to offer solutions and advice.

A clinician who offers advice to and generates solutions for a client may quicken crisis resolution but does not foster client empowerment. Clients often do not respond as quickly as clinicians would like. However, clients are more likely to generate their own solutions, and thus feel empowered, if clinicians show patience. Perhaps clinicians would be less likely to "rescue" (Friesen & Casella, 1982) clients and more likely to reinforce client strengths, even in a crisis, if they had a specific model to guide them in such situations. One therapeutic model that lends itself to working with client strengths in crisis situations is solution-focused therapy.

Solution-Focused Therapy

Solution-focused therapy views change as inevitable and continuous (Kral & Kowalski, 1989). This approach presumes that there are fluctuations in the client's presenting problem such that it does not remain constant in severity;

at times the problem is either not present or at least is less frequent or intense than at other times (Berg & Miller, 1992b). The task of a clinician using a solution-focused approach is to work collaboratively with the client to identify what she or he is already doing that contributes to the diminishing of the problem. Solution-focused therapy, therefore, emphasizes identifying and amplifying clients' strengths and resources used in solving or reducing the frequency and/or intensity of the presenting problem. This therapeutic approach assumes that clients ultimately possess the resources and capabilities to resolve their problems (de Shazer, 1985). Solution-focused therapy, therefore, is a nonpathologizing approach to working with clients.

In solution-focused therapy the emphasis is on finding solutions rather than solving problems. The solution-focused therapist is a catalyst for the client, enlarging and increasing the frequency of solution patterns rather than decreasing problem patterns; the focus is on "what is happening when things are going well" instead of "what is happening when the problem is present." Solution-focused therapy's emphasis on strengths and solutions helps build the expectation that change is going to happen (de Shazer et al., 1986). According to de Shazer et al. (1986), the more the therapeutic discourse concerns alternate futures and solutions, the more clients expect change to occur. The clinician's focus is on asking clients questions that achieve solutions through encouraging "change talk" (Weiner-Davis, 1993) or "solution talk" as opposed to "problem talk" (Walter & Peller, 1992). Change talk involves clients identifying either positive changes that have occurred in the problem or exceptions to the problem, or their no longer viewing the situation as problematic (Weiner-Davis, 1993). Gingerich, de Shazer, and Weiner-Davis (1988) found that when clinicians intentionally engage in change talk, clients are more than four times as likely to discuss change in their next speaking turn. This is in keeping with an assumption of solution-focused therapy that a small change is all that is necessary to elicit a larger change (O'Hanlon & Weiner-Davis, 1989; Walter & Peller, 1992), thus resulting in a positive self-fulfilling prophecy instead of a negative one.

Solution-focused therapy assumes that clients really do want to change rather than seeing them as resistant. Clients not changing is viewed as their way of letting the clinician know how to help them. Asking the client to do more of what he or she is already capable of doing can strengthen the therapeutic relationship because the clinician is not asking the client to do something unfamiliar (Molnar & de Shazer, 1987); the client is likely to get the message that he or she is okay and is not deficient or in need of "fixing." According to Berg and Jaya (1993), when clinicians focus on working with clients and respecting their way of solving problems, the clients will offer clinicians many opportunities to learn from them. Adaptation to the way clients see their situation not only is respectful but also promotes cooperation in therapy. It is the clinician's responsibility to be sensitive to the client's worldview and try to fit with it as closely as possible.

Solution-focused therapy is appropriate for use with clients in crisis because it is known to produce quick and dramatic changes. Solution-focused therapy is also especially useful with clients in crisis because the therapist usually begins in the present and focuses on joining and understanding the client's view of the problem. After the problem is defined as concretely and specifically as possible, the clinician moves the focus to discussion of solutions. A basic tenet of solution-focused therapy is that one does not need to know the cause or function of a problem in order to resolve it (O'Hanlon & Weiner-Davis, 1989). This is consistent with crisis intervention, in which a clinician does not have to know everything about the client's problem and the goal in order to successfully provide crisis intervention as soon as possible (Gilliland & James, 1993).

A SOLUTION-FOCUSED APPROACH TO CRISIS INTERVENTION

The structure of a solution-focused approach to crisis intervention, which has some overlap with Roberts's model of crisis intervention, described earlier, is the following: (1) join with the client; (2) elicit the client's definition of the problem; (3) elicit the client's desired outcome goal; (4) identify solutions; (5) develop and implement an action plan; (6) conduct termination and follow-up. The solution-focused crisis worker assesses lethality and safety needs from the very first contact with the client. Assessing lethality and safety needs, however, is not listed as a separate step here because it is done in the course of joining, defining problems, and identifying goals and solutions. The solution-focused crisis worker relies heavily on the use of questions during the interview to identify and amplify client strengths, successes, and solutions. In this regard, the primary intervention is the use of questions.

Step 1: Joining

According to Berg (1994), joining involves "what the worker needs to do in the engagement phase in order to establish a positive working relationship" (p. 51). Joining is comparable to Roberts's stages 2 and 4. For joining to occur, the crisis clinician must use a number of skills, including empathy (identifying and reflecting the client's feelings), support, acceptance, tracking, matching and mirroring nonverbal communication, and using the client's language. Joining is done throughout the crisis intervention work but is especially important in the beginning. To facilitate joining, Berg recommends that the clinician should avoid confronting clients and provoking defensiveness, avoid getting into debates and arguments with clients, and when appropriate take a "one-down position" and see the client as the "expert" on her or his situation (p. 53).

In this phase the crisis worker also should immediately begin assessing the extent to which the client is a threat to him- or herself or to others or is being threatened by others. Such an assessment is certainly an initial focus and should continue throughout the crisis work. Ensuring client safety is analogous to stage 1 (assessing lethality) of Roberts's model of crisis intervention (1996). In the solution-focused crisis intervention model discussed here, assessing lethality, which includes ensuring client safety, is viewed not as a separate step but as a theme continuing throughout the crisis work; the crisis worker performs these activities as the crisis work unfolds.

Step 2: Defining Problems

Although the approach described in this chapter emphasizes "solutions," the first interview usually begins with the client describing the problem(s) that precipitated seeking crisis services. At this point the client may want to talk about the problematic situation and the accompanying painful feelings. The crisis worker can begin the interview by asking, "What kinds of concerns are you having now for you to want to see someone like myself?" Instead of using the word *problem,* the crisis worker may want to use *concern* or *issue* as a way to normalize the crisis event the client is experiencing. In this way, the crisis worker moves away from pathologizing the crisis and conveys the message that such an event can be a part of life, although mostly unexpected, that calls for extra effort to find a solution. A question many therapists use when beginning a first interview, which should not be used, is: "What brings you here today?" This question can reinforce a sense of external locus of control, which most clients already are experiencing (Frank, 1982). Since all clinical work should be empowering to clients (reinforcing an internal locus of control), clinicians should choose their words carefully.

When the client mentions a number of problems, the crisis worker should ask the client to prioritize them. This prioritizing could be done by the worker saying the following: "You have mentioned several problems you are having now. I find it very helpful to work on one problem at a time, whenever possible. Which of the problems you just mentioned do you want to focus on first in our work together?" It is important for problems to be defined as specifically (concretely and behaviorally) as possible in terms of who, what, when, where, how, and how often. Once the worker thinks the client has defined the problem as specifically as possible for now, the worker should ask the client to define his or her goal(s). Some clients, however, have a greater desire to ventilate and may still want to keep focused on problem talk. When this occurs, it is best to not push clients to define goals and solution talk until they are ready.

Step 3: Setting Goals

In solution-focused therapy, setting goals receives more emphasis than defining problems (de Shazer, 1985). A goal describes a desired future state for the client in terms of how she or he will be feeling, thinking, and behaving differently. Like problems, goals should be set by the client and defined as specifically as possible (de Shazer, 1988). Clients are much more likely to cooperate (not resist) in the clinical situation when the focus of the work is on their goals rather than those set by the clinician (Berg & Gallagher, 1991).

Often when clients are asked what their goal is, they might say something like: "I want to stop being depressed" or "I want to get rid of my depression." Goals, however, should be stated in the positive rather than the negative, such as, "What do you want to be feeling instead?" or "How do you want to be feeling differently?" (Walter & Peller, 1992). Goal setting involves clients representing to themselves a future reality that does not contain the presenting problem. The more they describe in detail how they want to be feeling, thinking, and behaving differently in the future, the more real these become (Walter & Peller, 1992).

The Miracle Question and the Dream Question

Sometimes clients have trouble setting a goal with sufficient specificity. A clinician can use the *miracle question* or the *dream question* to facilitate such specificity. An example of the miracle question is the following:

> Suppose that after our meeting today you go home and go to bed. While you are sleeping a miracle happens and your problem is suddenly solved, like magic. The problem is gone. Because you were sleeping, you don't know that a miracle happened, but when you wake up tomorrow morning, you will be different. How will you know a miracle has happened? What will be the first small sign that tells you that a miracle has happened and the problem is resolved? (Berg & Miller, 1992a, p. 359)

The *dream question,* which is an adaptation of the miracle question, is illustrated in the following:

> Suppose that tonight while you are sleeping you have a dream. In this dream you discover the answers and resources you need to solve the problem that you are concerned about right now. When you wake up tomorrow, you may or may not remember your dream, but you do notice you are different. As you go about starting your day, how will you know that you discovered or developed the skills and resources necessary to solve your problem? What will be the first small bit of evidence that you did this? (Greene, Lee, Mentzer, Pinnell, & Niles, 1998; Lee, Greene, Mentzer, Pinnell, & Niles, 2001)

The miracle question was adapted for use in the following cases.

Domestic Violence

An anonymous woman called, and her voice was barely audible. She sounded exhausted, lethargic, hopeless, and depressed. She began the call by saying she lives with a man who is very abusive. He beat her up yesterday, claiming he must discipline her. He makes her write out her mistakes on paper 100 times, and then she must write him a formal apology promising not to do it again. When he goes to work, he locks all doors, windows, and cupboards and the refrigerator. He allows her to eat only one meal a day and withholds that if she is being punished.

Worker: Suppose that while you are sleeping tonight a miracle happens and your problem is suddenly solved. Like magic the problem is gone. Because you were sleeping, you don't know that a miracle happened, but when you wake up tomorrow, you will be different. How will you know a miracle happened? What will be the first small sign that tells you that a miracle has happened and the problem is resolved?

Client: He would be out of the house, and I would be here safe.

Worker: What would your being safe look like?

Client: I would be free to go about the house as I please and do what I want to do. I might even leave the house and walk to the store.

Worker: What would you do at the store once you were there?

Client: I might call my sister and talk to her, which I haven't done in months.

Worker: What would you talk to her about?

Client: I'd probably tell her what a no-good SOB Bill is, and then she would help me figure out how to get out of the house for good.

Worker: What would need to happen for even a small part of this miracle to happen?

Client: Well, I'd have to have a plan. A plan that would let me sneak out of the house when Bill is at work.

Worker: Have you ever done this before? (questions on past successes)

Client: Yes, a long time ago.

Worker: How did you do that at that time?

Relationship Questions

Based on a systems perspective, individuals never exist alone. Besides asking clients to establish concrete, precise indicators of change for themselves through the use of miracle questions, it is also helpful to ask what their significant others think or might think about their problematic situation and progress (Berg, 1994). Establishing multiple indicators of change helps clients develop a clearer vision of a desired future appropriate to their real-life context. Examples are: "What would your mother (or husband, friend, sister, etc.) notice that's different about you if they didn't know that a miracle had occurred?"

Harrassment

An anonymous woman called feeling hopeless, helpless, and angry. She is a lesbian who is being harassed and discriminated against by coworkers because of her lesbianism. She feels trapped because she enjoys her work and does not want to leave, but she is also sick of the harassment. Recently, someone has begun following her and driving by her house all night. She believes it is a coworker but has no proof. The client reports feeling extremely fearful and has no idea what to do.

Worker: Suppose that while you are sleeping tonight a miracle happens and your problem is suddenly solved, like magic. The problem is gone. Because you were sleeping, you don't know that a miracle happened, but when you wake up tomorrow, you will be different. How will you know a miracle happened? What will be the first small sign that tells you that a miracle has happened and the problem is resolved?

Client: I would be able to wake up, not in fear, and I would be able to go to work, enjoy my work and my coworkers, and I would be treated like any other normal decent human being, without being treated like some freak with the plague.

Worker: That's a big miracle! What will be the first small sign that tells you a miracle has happened? (Focus on small, concrete behavior instead of the big, grandiose solutions)

Client: Well, first, I'll wake up with no fear.

Worker: What would your partner notice about you if you wake up with no fear?

Client: Well, she'll probably feel that I am more relaxed . . . umm, probably less tense.

Worker: What will she notice you doing when you are more relaxed when you wake up in the morning?

Client: Umm, I'll be in a good mood, maybe joke around a little bit, and get both of us a good breakfast (a smile on her face). Isn't that nice?

Worker: What would it take for you to start acting as if you wake up with no fear?

Client: I would need to know I was safe.

Worker: What would you need to do in order to feel safe?

Client: I would probably need to get the police involved. And maybe I could tighten up my security, you know, buy a deadbolt lock and a saber-toothed tiger (ha-ha!).

Worker: See, you have some great ideas to help yourself! (Compliment) What will you do first? (Assisting client to develop a concrete plan to make her feel safe)

Step 4: Identifying Solutions

After the client describes in detail a future without the problem(s), the crisis worker uses exception questions, coping questions, and questions about past successes to assist the client to identify solutions that are conducive to realizing the envisioned future. At the same time, the crisis worker uses scaling questions to help the client quantify and evaluate his or her situation and progress.

Scaling Questions

Scaling questions allow for quantifying the client's problem and goal, which can be helpful not only in evaluating the client's situation and progress but also is an intervention itself (Greene, 1989). Scaling questions ask the client to rank the problem and goal on a scale of 1 to 10, with 1 as the worst the problem could possibly be and 10 as the most desirable outcome. The clinician usually begins each meeting by asking the client where he or she is on the 1 to 10 scale of the problem/goal continuum. When clients rank themselves higher on the scale in subsequent meetings, even slightly, the clinician asks what she or he has been doing to make this happen (Berg, 1994). This is a way to help the client notice what has been helpful, which may otherwise go unnoticed. The following case illustrates the use of scaling questions.

Grief and Loss

A woman called saying she needed to talk. Her father died yesterday. The client is upset but goes on to say that her main problem is the fact that her divorce will be final any day. She was married for 3 years and has two children under the age of 3. Her husband left her with the children and has moved in with another woman. The client says she does not know how she will make it.

Worker: I'm amazed that you've kept yourself going for the past 6 months.

Client: Yeah, me too. I guess things have been worse.

Worker: They've been worse than even now?

Client: Yeah, when he first left I was at an all-time low.

Worker: If I were to ask you to rate the way you're handling this situation on a scale of 1 to 10, with 1 being 6 months ago and 10 being where you want to get to, where would you say you're at today?

Client: I'd say I'm at a 3 or 4.

Worker: Wow, that's pretty impressive given what you've been through. How have you gotten yourself from a 1 to a 4?

Client: Well, I decided I've got to keep myself going for the kids. I've been taking classes to get my GED, even though I'm not very good at math.

Worker: Your kids give you energy to move on and to start planning for your future.

Client: Yes, I think so.

Worker: What would need to happen in order for you to move from a 4 to a 5? (Using the scaling question to help the client identify solutions)

Client: Well, I haven't thought about that. . . . Maybe if I get support from my own family . . . like if they baby-sit my babies when I am preparing for the exam.

Worker: Who in your family can possibly baby-sit your children? (Be specific)

Client: Maybe my sisters.

Worker: How will they know that you need their help?

Client: Well, maybe I need to talk to them. . . . We have pretty good relationships with each other.

Exception Questions

When clients first see a crisis clinician, they usually start talking about their crisis situation and their corresponding feelings (the presenting problem). In keeping with solution-focused therapy's assumption that there are fluctuations in how the client experiences the problem, the clinician asks questions to learn when the problem does not exist or at least is less frequent or intense. In regard to this Kral and Kowalski (1989) state: "The therapist's job is not to initiate change, but to punctuate the differences between the complaint pattern and the pattern of the exceptions (change) thereby making explicit the 'naturally' occurring variations which are in the direction of the desired solution" (p. 73). The assumption is that during these times the client is usually doing something to make things better, and the clinician asks further questions to discover what the client is doing. After "doing more of what works" comes "do more of the same," making the exception the rule (Kral & Kowalski, 1989). The next case provides an illustration of identifying exceptions.

Maintaining Sobriety

Jane is extremely disappointed by and ashamed of her recent fall from sobriety. She has been sober for 19 months but yesterday got into a big argument with her ex-husband and spent the evening in a bar getting drunk.

Worker: You were able to stay sober for 19 months?

Client: Yeah, but what good is it? I wasn't sober last night!

Worker: It sounds like you felt drinking would be a way for you to deal with the stress of your ex-husband?

Client: Yeah, that's usually when I always got my drunkest, when he and I would get into one of those fights.

Worker: How many times during the last 19 months did you argue with your ex-husband and not drink?

Client: Well, there have been a few times.

Worker: How did you manage to not drink during those times?

Client: Well, one thing that kept me from drinking is going to my AA meetings. I really count on those people for support.

Worker: How did you know to go to an AA meeting when you had these arguments with your ex and you did not drink?

Client: I just told myself if I don't go to a meeting and talk to someone I'm going to drink. And I got myself away from him.

Worker: That's very smart thinking on your part. Is this something you're willing to do again in the future?

Client: Well, I think I can, especially with the help of the program.

Past Successes

Sometimes clients initially have difficulty identifying exceptions to their presenting problem in their current lives or their recent past. When this situation occurs, the clinician can ask about times in the past when the client successfully handled the same or similar situations and how she or he was able to do so (Berg & Gallagher, 1991). In regard to the presenting problem, the clinician can even ask the client about exceptions that occurred years earlier. If the client cannot come up with any exceptions, the clinician can ask about an exception to similar problems in the past. The idea is to find out what solutions have worked in the past and to apply them to the current crisis situation. The following case illustrates the use of identifying past successes.

A Suicidal Client

The anonymous client was a 58-year-old woman who reported feeling depressed and suicidal. She began having these feelings at Christmas, when an argument developed between her sister and mother. The client stated that she had spent several years and much effort trying to mend these relationships, and she now fears it has all been for nothing. The argument also brought up the many issues of her childhood, and now she finds it necessary to deal with these issues again. The client says she is so depressed that she is contemplating suicide.

Worker: Have you ever felt suicidal in the past?

Client: Yes, about 25 years ago.

Worker: Did you make a suicide attempt then?

Client: No, somehow I got out of it.

Worker: How did you do that?

Client: A doctor put me on antidepressants for a while. I also keep busy walking and exercising. Talking to friends also was very helpful.

Worker: How did you keep from thinking about those family problems?

Client: I just kept occupied.

Worker: Are you doing any of those things now that you did then?

Client: No, but I guess I could.

Worker: What is one small thing you could start with?

Coping Questions

Oftentimes clients in crisis will state that nothing is going right, that they can find nothing positive in their lives, and that they are unable to identify any exceptions, either present or past. Such clients can feel hopeless about themselves and their future (Berg & Miller, 1992b). The crisis worker needs to recognize such negativity as a sign of great desperation and a signal for empathetic help. In such a situation, the client could perceive the clinician's focus on the positive as being artificial and imposing. The coping question can be quite effective with these clients in crisis who see little possibility for positive changes (Berg & Miller, 1992b). Coping questions can be an impetus for clients feeling a sense of empowerment because they start to become aware of resources they did not know they had or had forgotten (Berg, 1994). The following example illustrates the use of coping questions.

The Desperate Single Mom

Loraine was a 26-year-old unemployed single mother with a 7-year-old, "impossible" boy, Teddy. According to Loraine, she had never been able to handle Teddy, who never listened and destroyed almost everything. Recently, Teddy set fire at the apartment and inappropriately touched a 5-year-old girl. Loraine claimed that she had a very bad relationship with Teddy, had not talked to him for a long time, and was on the verge of giving up. Loraine was very depressed and became agitated when the worker tried to get her to think about positive changes in the mother-child relationship, which seemed to be impossible to Loraine. The worker used the coping questions instead.

Worker: If I ask you to rank your relationship with Teddy on a scale of 1 to 10, with 1 as the worst scenario both of you can get to and 10 as the best possible relationship that both of you can have, how would you rank your relationship with Teddy now?

Client: I have to say it would be in the minus range.

Worker: Sounds like the situation is really bad. I just wonder what have you been doing to keep it from getting worse? You know, the situation can be much worse; how do you keep it from getting any worse?

Client: I do pay attention to him sometimes. I don't ignore him totally, even though sometimes I feel so depressed and overwhelmed it's all I can do to pay attention to what's going on with me.

Worker: So how are you able to do that—to take care of Teddy some of the time even though you are feeling so bad you don't feel like it?

Client: I just do it. I am his mother, and I do have responsibility for him. I really don't know how I do it. I let things go for a while, but eventually I just tell myself I've got to take care of Teddy, since no one else can. I know I should be doing a better job of being a mother, but right now I feel like I can barely take care of myself.

Worker: That's really something that you are able at times to get yourself to do what you have to do for Teddy even though you don't feel like it. Using the same 1 to 10 scale, with 1 meaning you don't want to take care of him at all and 10 meaning that you would do whatever you have to in order to take care of Teddy and keep him from getting into trouble, how would you rank yourself?

Client: I would say around 7.

Worker: That's pretty high. When was the last time you were able to take care of Teddy and keep him from getting into trouble? (Exception questions)

Compliments

Many clients seeing a clinician for the first time expect to be judged and criticized, and they may be prepared to defend themselves (Wall, Kleckner, Amendt, & duRee Bryant, 1989). Complimenting clients is a way to enhance their cooperation rather than elicit defensiveness and resistance. Compliments do not have to be directly related to the presenting problem but can be related to whatever the client is doing that is good for him or her, that he or she is good at or aspires to (Berg & Gallagher, 1991, p. 101). Such compliments, therefore, are feedback to clients about strengths, successes, or exceptions. Clients are usually surprised, relieved, and pleased when they receive praise from the clinician. A consequence of therapeutic compliments is that clients are usually more willing to search for, identify, and amplify solution patterns. The following provides an example of using compliments.

Relationship Issues

Betty was hysterical when she called and asked for advice. She is a single mother of four children. Betty must work full-time to support her children and often feels guilty about the time she spends away from them. Betty's guilty feelings intensified today when she came home from work to find her 7-year-old daughter and 9-year-old son involved in "sexual play." She is feeling very inadequate as a parent.

Worker: Wow, this must feel terribly overwhelming for you. I want to commend you on your strength and courage in calling here today.

Client: Well, I don't know how strong I am. Look what a mess my kids are in. And it's all my fault. If I didn't have to work so much, this probably wouldn't be happening.

Worker: What have you said to your children about your working?

Client: They know I work to feed 'em, clothe 'em, and keep this shack over their heads.

Worker: That is a lot of responsibility: working, raising four children as a single parent, keeping food on the table, clothing on the children, and a home together. It takes a lot of energy, skill, and motivation to do that. I really admire you for being able to do all that.

Complimenting clients is helpful at any time during the interview but especially toward the end of a session as a preface to giving clients homework assignments or tasks. However, clients in crisis often are overwhelmed by their problematic situations and tend to be pessimistic. The crisis worker has to be careful not to overcompliment, which the client may perceive as superficial and insincere. Compliments should be based on what clients have actually done or mentioned in the interview.

Step 5: Develop and Implement an Action Plan

Tasks or homework assignments are also used in solution-focused therapy but in different ways than in other crisis intervention models. As mentioned earlier, solution-focused therapy assumes clients are already doing to some extent or are capable of doing whatever is needed for problem resolution and goal attainment. Therefore, tasks in solution-focused therapy involve the client identifying solutions and/or doing more of them (Walter & Peller, 1992). Tasks are based on thoughts, feelings, and behaviors that the client has used in the past or is using in the present (Molnar & de Shazer, 1987). The following are some commonly used solution-focused tasks.

Formula First Session Task

> Between now and next the time we meet, we[I] would like you to observe, so that you can describe to us[me] next time, what happens in your [*pick one*: family, life, marriage, relationship] that you want to continue to have happen. (de Shazer, 1985, p. 137)

Clients in crisis situations often feel that nothing is going right for them and that they are losing control of their lives. This task helps refocus clients' attention to something they are doing *well* rather than problems or failures. This change of focus can lead to clients realizing that there still is something working in their lives, and thus they can have some sense of control of their life situation (Berg, 1994).

The name of this task comes from its successful use at the end of the first session with a wide variety of clients regardless of presenting problem (de Shazer et al., 1986). The formula first session task is especially useful with clients who present vaguely defined problems and are not responsive to the clinician's attempt to define them more concretely and specifically. In one follow-up survey on the use of the formula first session task, 89% of clients reported at the next session that they noticed things they wanted to continue, and 92% of these clients said that at least one was something "new or different" (de Shazer et al., 1986, p. 217).

Keep Track of Current Successes

> Identify the ways you are able to keep doing _____ (behaviors which are exceptions to the problem behavior). (Molnar & de Shazer, 1987, p. 356)
>
> *or*
>
> Pay attention to and keep track of what you do to overcome the temptation or urge to . . . (perform the symptom or some behavior associated with the problem). (Berg & Gallagher, 1991, p. 101; Molnar & de Shazer, 1987, p. 356)

The purpose of this task is to help clients focus on what skills and abilities they have and use them to improve their situation. The more specific and detailed the clients are in making these descriptions, the more likely they are in anchoring such behaviors into their behavioral repertoire. Furthermore, the more they notice the connections between their behavior and positive outcomes, the more likely they are to have a sense of control over their problematic situation.

Prediction Task

Oftentimes the client experiences the problem as outside her or his control. The client is able to identify exceptions but believes that she or he has no control over these occurrences. In the prediction task the client is asked to predict or rate something, e.g., "First thing each morning rate the possibility of ______ (an exception behavior) happening before noon" (Molnar & de Shazer, 1987, p. 356). The purpose of this task is to help clients realize that the exception behaviors may be much more within their control than they think. By asking a client to keep a careful record of what he or she predicted and how the day actually turned out will produce important insights into the client's ability to make what appears to be a random or spontaneous exception into a deliberate one (Berg, 1994). The crisis worker can then encourage the client to do more of such deliberate exception and ultimately making the exception into the rule.

Pretend the Miracle Has Happened

This task asks the client to pick a day when he or she is to pretend that a miracle has happened and the problem or crisis that brought him or her for help is solved. The worker should encourage the client to do everything that he or she would do if the miracle had happened and to keep track of what he or she notices that is different about himself or herself and how other people react to him or her (Berg, 1994). The purpose of this strategy is for clients to have a reason to have good feelings and successes in a way they otherwise would not. Clients do not need to wait for a miracle to happen before they can experience good feelings, thoughts, and behaviors that are associated with a problem-free situation. This task allows clients to learn that they can turn a desired "fantasy" into a reality.

Solution-focused tasks have been shown to be effective in a wide variety of problem situations. The important issue for the worker, however, is to find a good fit between the client's circumstances and strengths and the task assignment. The worker has to judge whether the task appears to make sense to the client and the client's readiness to engage in the specific task assignments.

Step 6: Termination and Follow-Up

A person in a crisis situation usually experiences significant disequilibrium. Crisis intervention attempts to prevent a person from stabilizing at a regressed level of functioning and preferably helps a person reestablish equilibrium with increased coping abilities. An important criterion for termination is for the client to return to the previous level of functioning, if not a higher one, rather than having all of his or her problems solved. In this regard, a solution-focused approach shares a philosophy with crisis intervention with respect to termination. A solution-focused approach perceives that life is full of problems to be solved, and it is simply not realistic for clients to solve all their problems before terminating the case. Instead, specific goal achievement is identified as the criterion for termination. Therefore, at termination, the worker assists clients to review their specific goals, assess their readiness for termination, and anticipate possible future setbacks. Scaling questions are frequently used in the process. The following examples illustrate the process.

The Doubtful Single Father

John was a 37-year-old single father with a 9-year-old son, Justin, who has been diagnosed as having attention deficit hyperactivity disorder. The father has learning difficulties of his own and did not finish high school. John is separated from Susan, Justin's mother, who has some serious "mental problems" and "poor parenting skills." Justin chose to live with his father. In addition to the separation and the stresses of single parenting, John's mother died recently and he became very depressed. Two months ago he got drunk, and the apartment caught on fire, apparently because of a lighted cigarette. Luckily, no one got hurt. The Children Services Department got involved because of suspected child neglect. John had six sessions of crisis intervention and made tremendous improvement. Although John was still lacking confidence in his parenting, both John and the worker thought termination was in order at this time.

Worker: John, suppose when we first started meeting, your ability to take care of Justin was at 1 and where you wanted your parenting ability to be was at 10. Where would you say you are at today between 1 and 10? (Evaluating progress)

Client: I would say I am at maybe 6 or 7.

Worker: That's a lot of progress. Looking back, what have you done to help yourself to be an adequate parent?

Client: Well, I keep telling myself that I don't want to mess up the life of my son. Later on when I thought about it, I didn't dare to think about what would happen if I'd set the apartment on fire.

Worker: So, you remind yourself a lot that you don't want that to happen again. What else have you been doing that's helpful?

Client: Hey, the list that we came up with helps me a lot (client referred to a checklist that the worker developed with him about things that he should do regarding adequate parenting). I put it on the fridge so I can see it every day.

Worker: I'm glad to hear that. What else have you been doing with Justin that's helpful? (Try to get a behavioral description of the interaction between father and son)

Client: With Justin. . . . Oh, I guess I do more things with him. He really likes it.

Worker: You know, you have made terrific progress since we started. I just wonder on a scale of 1 to 10, with 10 meaning you have every confidence that you will keep up with your progress and 1 meaning you have no confidence at all to maintain the changes, where would you put yourself between 1 and 10 today? (Evaluating confidence to maintain the changes)

Client: I don't know, maybe 5. Sometimes I have doubts about whether the situation would go back again.

Worker: So, you're a little bit uncertain. What would it take for you to move from a 5 to a 6?

Client: Maybe I just have to keep doing what I've been doing. Well, it's good to have someone reminding me, I guess.

Worker: Who may be a good person to remind you?

Client: Let me think. My sister is really concerned about Justin and me. She would probably like to help if I ask her.

Worker: How easy would it be for you to talk to her about this?

Client: Very easy; there should be no problem.

Worker: I want to ask you a slightly different but very important question. What would be the earliest sign to you that you are starting to go backward? What would your sister notice about you that would tell her that you are beginning to slip?

The primary task at termination is for clients to evaluate and consolidate their progress. It is important for clients to know what is working for them so they can connect their own action to the successful outcomes. In this way, life is no longer a series of crises that are out of their control. They can actively participate in creating solutions and enhance their skills and competencies as a result of the experience. The emphasis is no longer on deficits; instead, clients' strengths are recognized and celebrated. The use of the compliment is especially important for clients who have successfully coped with a crisis. A general guideline is for clients to own and take full credit for their successes.

Besides evaluating and celebrating positive progress, it is important to assist clients to go beyond current successes and develop indicators that will tell them when they may need help in the future. A solution-focused approach views problems as both normal and inherent in human living. Therefore, helping clients to ameliorate all their problems is less realistic than helping clients to recognize times when they will need help again and/or giving them the skills for dealing with new problematic situations when they occur.

Sometime after termination of crisis intervention, the crisis worker, whenever possible, should contact the client to see how well she or he is doing (Roberts, 1991, 1996). The length of time between termination and follow-up will vary, but follow-up usually should occur within 1 month (Roberts, 1991, 1996). At termination the worker should inform the client that he or she will want to make a follow-up contact and seek permission to do so. Such a contact can help support and consolidate the client's continued successes, solutions, and strengths. In addition, during a follow-up contact the worker can make a referral for longer term clinical work if the client requests it. Most therapeutic approaches do not make follow-up an explicit component, and solution-focused therapy is no exception. The authors of this chapter, however, agree with Roberts in this regard.

SUMMARY AND CONCLUSION

Although crisis intervention and solution-focused therapy come from distinct therapeutic traditions, they do have commonalities. For instance, crisis intervention perceives most crises as self-limiting in that the state of disequilibrium usually lasts 4 to 6 weeks (Parad & Parad, 1990). Consequently, crisis work tends to be immediate, short-term, and intense. A solution-focused approach also emphasizes a rapid and brief response to clients' help-seeking effort.

Although a solution-focused approach assumes clients already have resources and strengths and that the purpose of intervention is to help clients successfully deal with their presenting problem(s) by utilizing what they bring with them to the treatment situation, it does not deny that at times a more direct approach may be necessary. A solution-focused approach encourages clients to look for exceptions to the problem and do more of the exception-maintaining patterns. A crisis event, however, may be so novel that new coping and problem-solving skills are needed. In a solution-focused approach, if no exceptions can be found, clients are encouraged to do something different. In fact, one of the basic tenets of solution-focused therapy is "If it works, do more of it. If it doesn't work, don't do it again, do something else" (de Shazer et al., 1986, p. 212). In addition, even a solution-oriented crisis worker may need to actively provide concrete services, practical support, information, and other interventions that will help alleviate clients' immediate disequilibrium in their life situation—actions that are not emphasized in a typical solution-focused approach. The authors of this chapter, however, encourage crisis workers, whenever possible, to not use a direct approach too quickly before trying a solution-focused approach. A more direct approach may quickly resolve the presenting crisis but may not leave the client with a greater sense of strength, competence, and empowerment.

Experience, skilled judgment, flexibility, and individualized treatment may best describe the wisdom required in using a solution-focused approach to crisis intervention. For many years now, the crisis intervention literature has recognized the "opportunity" inherent in a crisis situation: A person can experience notable personal growth if the situation is handled successfully (Caplan, 1964). This chapter adopts a strengths perspective operationalized by the use of solution-focused therapy integrated with crisis intervention. It is assumed that clients, in spite of their crisis situation, come with a diverse repertoire of strengths and skills that they are not currently noticing. In solution-focused crisis intervention, clients are assisted in discovering and amplifying their strengths and resources—an intervention approach that envisions clients' new learning and strengths through the passage of life. This approach provides clinicians with a systematic way to work with clients' strengths and resilience to help them handle crises and experience personal growth and development.

There are numerous reports in the literature of successfully using solution-focused therapy with clients in crisis and difficult situations such as those who are suicidal (Sharry, Darmody, & Madden, 2002; Softas-Nall & Francis, 1998), have a serious mental disability (Hagen & Mitchell, 2001; Rhodes & Jakes, 2002; Rowan & O'Hanlon, 1999; Schott & Conyers, 2003), are physically disabled (Johnson & Webster, 2002), have experienced trauma (O'Hanlon & Bertolino, 1998), child abuse or neglect (Berg & Kelly, 2002), domestic violence (Lee, Sebold, & Uken, 2002, 2003), and self-harm (Selekman, 2002). The authors believe that a solution-focused approach to crisis intervention is the treatment of choice in the majority of crisis situations. Currently, there are no well-designed studies documenting the effectiveness of a solution-focused/strengths-based approach to crisis intervention. However, one of the authors in a previous job at a crisis hotline documented that shortly after introducing solution-focused techniques to the staff, the time spent on the telephone with chronic callers decreased from 1,000 minutes to 200 minutes in a 1-month period. Only future research can shed light on what this dramatic decrease means and whether it can be attributed to the use of a solution-focused approach.

ACKNOWLEDGMENTS Portions of this chapter are adapted from G. J. Greene, M. Y. Lee, R. Trask, & J. Rheinscheld (1996), Client strengths and crisis intervention: A solution-focused approach. *Crisis Intervention and Time-Limited Treatment, 3,* 43–63.

REFERENCES

Berg, I. K. (1994). *Family based services: A solution-focused approach.* New York: Norton.

Berg, I. K., & Gallagher, D. (1991). Solution focused brief treatment with adolescent substance abusers.

In T. C. Todd & M. D. Selekman (Eds.), *Family therapy approaches with adolescent substance abusers* (pp. 93–111). Boston: Allyn and Bacon.

Berg, I. K., & Jaya, A. (1993). Different and same: Family therapy with Asian-American families. *Journal of Marital and Family Therapy, 19,* 31–38.

Berg, I. K., & Kelly, S. (2000). *Building solutions in child protective services.* New York: W. W. Norton & Co.

Berg, I. K., & Miller, S. D. (1992a, June). Working with Asian American clients: One person at a time. *Families in Society,* 356–363.

Berg, I. K., & Miller, S. D. (1992b). *Working with the problem drinker: A solution-focused approach.* New York: Norton.

Brown, L. M., Shiang, J., & Bongar, B. (2003). Crisis intervention. In G. Stricker & T. A. Widiger (Eds.), *Handbook of psychology: Clinical psychology, vol. 8.* (pp. 431–453). New York: John Wiley & Sons.

Caplan, G. (1964). *Principles of preventive psychiatry.* New York: Basic Books.

Cowger, C. D., & Snively, C. A. (2002). Assessing client strengths. In A. R. Roberts & G. J. Greene (Eds.), *Social workers' desk reference* (pp. 221–225). New York: Oxford University Press.

Dattilio, F. M., & Freeman, A. (1994). *Cognitive-behavioral strategies in crisis intervention.* New York: Guilford.

DeJong, P. (2002). Solution-focused therapy. In A. R. Roberts & G. J. Greene (Eds.), *Social workers' desk reference* (pp. 112–116). New York: Oxford University Press.

DeJong, P., & Berg, I. K. (2002). *Interviewing for solutions* (2nd ed.). Pacific Grove, CA: Brooks/Cole.

DeJong, P., & Miller, S. D. (1995). How to interview for client strengths. *Social Work, 40,* 729–736.

de Shazer, S. (1985). *Keys to solution in brief therapy.* New York: Norton.

de Shazer, S. (1988). *Clues: Investigating solutions in brief therapy.* New York: Norton.

de Shazer, S., Berg, I. K., Lipchik, E. Nunnally, E., Molnar, A., Gingerich, W., & Weiner-Davis, M. (1986). Brief therapy: Focused solution development. *Family Process, 25,* 207–221.

Eaton, Y. M., & Roberts, A. R. (2002). Frontline Crisis Intervention: Step-by-step practice guidelines with case examples. In A. R. Roberts & G. J. Greene (Eds.), *Social workers' desk reference* (pp. 89–96). New York: Oxford University Press.

Ewing, C. P. (1990). Crisis intervention as brief psychotherapy. In R. A. Wells & V. J. Giannetti (Eds.), *Handbook of the brief psychotherapies* (pp. 277–294). New York: Plenum.

Fisch, R., Weakland, J. H., & Segal, L. (1982). *The tactics of change: Doing therapy briefly.* San Francisco: Jossey-Bass.

Fortune, A. E. (1985). The task-centered model. In A. E. Fortune (Ed.), *Task-centered practice with families and groups* (pp. 1–30). New York: Springer.

Frank, J. D. (1982). Therapeutic components shared by all psychotherapies. In J. H. Harvey & M. M. Parks (Eds.), *Psychotherapy research and behavior change* (pp. 5–38). Washington, DC: American Psychological Association.

Fraser, J. S. (1998). A catalyst model: Guidelines for doing crisis intervention and brief therapy from a process view. *Crisis Intervention and Time-Limited Treatment, 4,* 159–177.

Friesen, V. I., & Casella, N. T. (1982). The rescuing therapist: A duplication of the pathogenic family system.

American Journal of Family Therapy, 10, 57–61.

Gilliland, B. E., & James, R. K. (1993). *Crisis intervention strategies* (2nd ed.). Pacific Grove, CA: Brooks/Cole.

Gingerich, W., de Shazer, S., & Weiner-Davis, M. (1988). Constructing change: A research view of interviewing. In E. Lipchik (Ed.), *Interviewing* (pp. 21–32). Rockville, MD: Aspen.

Golan, N. (1986). Crisis theory. In F. J. Turner (Ed.), *Social work treatment: Interlocking theoretical approaches* (pp. 296–340). New York: Free Press.

Greene, G. J. (1989). Using the written contract for evaluating and enhancing practice effectiveness. *Journal of Independent Social Work, 4,* 135–155.

Greene, G. J., Lee, M. Y., Mentzer, R. A., Pinnell, S. R., & Niles, D. (1998). Miracles, dreams, and empowerment: A brief therapy practice note. *Families in Society, 79,* 395–399.

Hagen, B. F., & Mitchell, D. L. (2001). Might within the madness: Solution-focused therapy and thought-disordered clients. *Archives of Psychiatric Nursing, 15*(2), 86–93.

Hoff, L. E. (1995). *People in crisis: Understanding and helping* (4th ed.). San Francisco: Jossey-Bass.

Johnson, C., & Webster, D. (2002). *Recrafting a life: Solutions for chronic pain and illness.* New York: Brunner-Routledge.

Kanel, K. (1999). *A guide to crisis intervention.* Pacific Grove, CA: Brooks/Cole.

Kiser, D. J., Piercy, F. P., & Lipchik, E. (1993). The integration of emotion in solution-focused therapy. *Journal of Marital and Family Therapy, 19,* 233–242.

Kral, R., & Kowalski, K. (1989). After the miracle: The second stage in solution focused therapy. *Journal of Strategic and Systemic Therapies, 8,* 73–76.

Lee, M. Y., Greene, G. J., Mentzer, R. A., Pinnell, S., & Niles, N. (2001). Solution-focused brief therapy and the treatment of depression: A pilot study. *Journal of Brief Therapy, 1*(1), 33–49.

Lee, M. Y., Sebold, J., & Uken, A. (2002). Brief solution-focused group treatment with domestic violence offenders: Listening to the narratives of participants and their partners. *Journal of Brief Therapy, 2*(1), 3–26.

Lee, M. Y., Sebold, J., & Uken, A. (2003). *Solution-focused treatment of domestic violence offenders: Accountability for change.* New York: Oxford University Press.

Levy, R. L., & Shelton, J. L. (1990). Tasks in brief therapy. In R. A. Wells & V. J. Gianetti (Eds.), *Handbook of the brief therapies* (pp. 145–163). New York: Plenum.

Lipchik, E. (2002). *Beyond technique in solution-focused therapy.* NY: The Guilford Press.

Molnar, A., & de Shazer, S. (1987). Solution focused therapy: Toward the identification of therapeutic tasks. *Journal of Marital and Family Therapy, 5,* 349–358.

O'Hanlon, B., & Bertolino, B. (1998). *Even from a broken web: Brief, respectful solution-oriented therapy for sexual abuse and trauma.* New York: John Wiley & Sons.

O'Hanlon, W. H., & Weiner-Davis, M. (1989). *In search of solutions: A new direction in psychotherapy.* New York: Norton.

Parad, H. J., & Parad, L. G. (1990). Crisis intervention: An introductory overview. In H. J. Parad & L. G. Parad (Eds.), *Crisis intervention book 2: The practitioner's sourcebook for brief therapy* (pp. 3–68). Milwaukee, WI: Family Service America.

Puryear, D. A. (1979). *Helping people in crisis.* San Francisco: Jossey-Bass.

Rapoport, L. (1970). Crisis intervention as a mode of brief treatment. In R. W. Roberts & Robert H. Nee (Eds.), *Theories of social casework* (pp. 265–312). Chicago: University of Chicago Press.

Rapp, C. A. (1992). The strengths perspective of case management with persons suffering from severe mental illness. In D. Saleebey (Ed.), *The strengths perspective in social work practice* (pp. 45–58). New York: Longman.

Rapp, C. A. (1998). *The strengths model: Case management with people suffering from severe and persistent mental illness.* New York: Oxford University Press.

Rapp, C. A. (2002). A strengths approach to case management with clients with severe mental disabilities. In A. R. Roberts & G. J. Greene (Eds.), *Social workers' desk reference* (pp. 486–491). New York: Oxford University Press.

Rhodes, J., & Jakes, S. (2002). Using solution-focused therapy during a psychotic crisis: A case study. *Clinical Psychology and Psychotherapy, 9,* 139–148.

Roberts, A. R. (1990). Overview of crisis theory and crisis intervention. In A. R. Roberts (Ed.), *Crisis intervention handbook: Assessment, treatment and research* (pp. 3–16). Belmont, CA: Wadsworth.

Roberts, A. R. (1991). Conceptualizing crisis theory and the crisis intervention model. In A. R. Roberts (Ed.), *Contemporary perspectives on crisis intervention and prevention* (pp. 3–17). Englewood Cliffs, NJ: Prentice-Hall.

Roberts, A. R. (1996). Epidemiology and definitions of acute crisis in American society. In A. R. Roberts (Ed.), *Crisis management and brief treatment: Theory, technique, and applications* (pp. 16–33). Chicago: Nelson-Hall.

Roberts, A. R., & Dziegielewski, S. F. (1995). Foundation skills and applications of crisis intervention and cognitive therapy. In A. R. Roberts (Ed.), *Crisis intervention and time-limited cognitive treatment* (pp. 3–27). Thousand Oaks, CA: Sage.

Rowan, T., & O'Hanlon, B. (1999). *Solution-oriented therapy for chronic and severe mental illness.* New York: John Wiley & Sons.

Saleeby, D. (Ed.). (1992). *The strengths perspective in social work practice.* New York: Longman.

Saleeby, D. (Ed.). (2002). *The strengths perspective in social work practice* (3rd ed.). New York: Longman.

Schott, S. A., & Conyers, L. M. (2003). A solution-focused approach to psychiatric rehabilitation. *Psychiatric Rehabilitation Journal, 27*(1), 43–50.

Selekman, M. D. (1997). *Solution-focused therapy with children: Harnessing family strengths for systemic change.* New York: Guilford.

Selekman, M. D. (2002). *Living on the Razor's Edge: Solution-oriented brief family therapy with self-harming adolescents.* New York: W. W. Norton & Co.

Sharry, J., Darmody, M., & Madden, B. (2002). A solution-focused approach to working with clients who are suicidal. *British Journal of Guidance & Counseling, 30*(4), 383–399.

Softas-Nall, B. C., & Francis, P. C. (1998). A solution-focused approach to a family with a suicidal member. *The Family Journal, 6*(3), 227–230.

Wall, M. D., Kleckner, T., Amendt, J. H., & duRee Bryant, R. (1989). Therapeutic compliments: Setting the stage for successful therapy. *Journal of Marital and Family Therapy, 15,* 159–167.

Walsh, F. (1998). *Strengthening family resilience*. New York: Guilford.

Walter, J. L., & Peller, J. E. (1992). *Becoming solution-focused in brief therapy*. New York: Brunner/Mazel.

Weiner-Davis, M. (1993). Pro-constructed realities. In S. Gilligan & R. Price (Eds.), *Therapeutic conversations* (pp. 149–160). New York: Norton.

Wiger, D. E., & Harowski, K. J. (2003). *Essentials of crisis counseling and intervention*. New York: John Wiley & Sons.

4

Differentiating Among Stress, Acute Stress Disorder, Acute Crisis Episodes, Trauma, and PTSD: Paradigm and Treatment Goals

KENNETH R. YEAGER
ALBERT R. ROBERTS

Why focus on the distinguishing components among stressors, acute stress disorders, acute crisis episodes, and Posttraumatic Stress Disorder (PTSD)? Can clear operational definitions and specific case illustrations clarify the parameters and differences among these four clinical concepts? What types of treatment goals are effective in treating the persons encountering the four events and disorders? What are the components of a diagnostic stress-crisis-trauma-PTSD paradigm? This chapter answers these vital questions. In addition, we thoroughly examine the clinical issues and controversies, diagnostic indicators, and treatment goals necessary for advancing mental health assessment, crisis intervention, and trauma treatment. We aim to enhance theory building, assessment, and practice skills in behavioral health and public health and medical settings.

There are few human conditions that are so diversely described as stress, crisis, and trauma. Many report that stress helps them to work productively and meet multiple deadlines; others report on the stressful burden of managing a professional career, parenting children, and caring for aging parents, launching the individual into a downward spiral that culminates in physical and emotional consequences of tremendous proportion. Then there is the term "crisis," which some people use when they are having a bad day, as in "one crisis after another." In sharp contrast to stress and crisis perceptions, trauma reactions are frequently precipitated by a random, sudden, and arbitrary traumatic event, such as a natural disaster, terrorism and mass murder, violent sexual assault, or sniper or drive-by killings (Roberts, 2002). One reason for the overuse of the words stress, crisis, and trauma is a lack of understanding of the true definitions and parameters of each term. Frequently in the academic literature, the definitions are overlapping.

Individuals do not respond to stress in the same manner. Responses are unique and often determined by each individual's personality and character, temperament, other stressors that day, protective factors and coping skills, adaptability to change and unexpected events, support system, and the intensity and duration of the stressor. Therefore, what is simple stress for one individual may result in the onset of a crisis episode or traumatic reaction for another (Corcoran & Roberts, 2000). At times, this confusion leads to denial or underestimation of stress and related conditions and a buildup of multiple stressors without effectively adapting and coping.

This chapter delineates and presents for discussion a trimodal approach to addressing stress, crisis, trauma, and PTSD. We define and compare each term, outlining similarities contributing to confusion among mental health professionals. Case examples will demonstrate methodology to accurately delineate and discuss the degree and severity of the issue facing each individual, applying the solution-focused approach, crisis intervention, and a strengths perspective.

DEFINING TERMS AND HISTORICAL OVERVIEW

> *Stress:* Any stimulus, internal state, situation, or event with an observable individual reaction, usually in the form of positively adapting or negatively adapting to a new or different situation in one's environment. The concept generally refers to the nature of an experience, resulting from the person interacting in the context of their his or her environment, through either physiological overarousal or underarousal, with an outcome of psychological or physiological distress (bad stress outcome) or eustress (good stress outcome). Stressors range from minor to major and can be positive or negative events. Generally, stressors are life events such as daily annoyances, pressures at home or on the job, marital discord and conflicts, emergencies, motor vehicle accidents, illness, and injury. Positive stressful life events and transitions include birth of a child, a graduation ceremony, a family vacation, and a job promotion.

Mason (1975) developed one of the most inclusive operational definitions of stress, stressors, and stressful experiences. Mason delineated a conceptual framework and application of three different definitions of stress to unravel some of the confusion with general usage of the concept. Stress may be caused by (1) an internal state of the organism, also known as strain based on both the physiological and psychological reactions; (2) an external event or stressor, such as combat trauma and natural disasters; major life events, such as marriage, divorce, and being laid off; noxious environmental stressors, such as air pollution and overcrowding; or role strain, such as a bad marriage; or (3) an experience that arises from a transaction between a person and his or her environment, particularly where there is a mismatch or poor fit between the individual's resources and the perceived challenge, threat, or need (Mason, 1975).

Hans Selye (1956) concluded from his influential physiological research, "Stress is part of life. It is a natural by-product of all our activities. . . . The secret of life is the successful adjustment to ever-changing stress" (pp. 299–300). According to Selye's general adaptation syndrome, there are generally three stages in the human body's reaction to extreme stress. First is the alarm reaction, in which the body stirs its defense mechanisms—the glands, hormones, and nervous system—into action. Second is the adaptation stage, when the body fights back (e.g., the arteries can harden when the heart is under pressure). Third is the exhaustion stage, when the body's defenses seem to be unable to cope, and the individual becomes seriously ill and may die (Selye, 1956). Selye concludes that the best way to survive and thrive is to adapt and respond in positive ways to the stress of life.

Stressors frequently are characterized as ranging from minor to major and as negative or positive stimuli or events. They are inclusive of daily problems. Sometimes they appear as pressure; at other times, stressors are described as disturbing annoyances. Events such as intense marital strife/discord, physical illness of family members and friends, hospitalization of family members, caring for children and loved ones, accidents, emergencies, being responsible for a special needs child or terminally ill aging parent, job pressure to perform, financial difficulties, and even moving across town or severe weather can present as stressors. The challenges that are framed by stress, both positive and negative, provide defining structures for meaning in our day-to-day lives. The complete absence of stress can lead to boredom and lack of meaning in one's life. Too much stress, or a pile-up of multiple stressors without effective coping, frequently can have a detrimental impact on an individual's physical and mental health.

Some careers, such as rescue work, emergency service work, surgical and emergency medicine, and law enforcement, are known to be highly stressful and physically demanding. In these high-stress jobs, people may thrive, be continually reenergized, and experience occupational growth, or they may encounter vicarious traumatization. Dr. Hans Selye, a Nobel Laureate and founder of the International Institute of Stress in Montreal, in an interview with *Modern Maturity* magazine (Wixen, 1978) stated that he thrives on and enjoys considerable satisfaction from an extremely demanding schedule. Directly prior to the interview, Dr. Selye had spoken at a major medical conference in Europe, slept four hours, then traveled 2,500 miles to Houston and his next interview and conference speaking engagement. The next day he flew to Montreal and two days later began a nine-day speaking tour throughout Scandinavia. Dr. Selye never tries to avoid stress; instead, he indicated that stress gives him pleasure and a great degree of satisfaction (Wixen, 1978). In contrast, Regehr's (2001) recent article focuses on vicarious traumatization of the hidden victims of disaster and emergency rescue work and the positive and negative effects of group crisis intervention and critical incident stress debriefings with worker stress reactions and the symptoms of PTSD. Regehr systematically reviews the strengths and limitations of crisis debriefing groups.

When intensely stressful life events and well-documented physiological events are placed in motion, these physiological responses to stressors are best described as a chain of biochemical reactions that have the potential to impact all major organ systems. Stress begins in the brain. Reaction to perceived stressful or emergency events triggers what Walter Cannon (1927) described as the fight or flight response. In response to neurochemical messages, a complex chain reaction is triggered, impacting specifically serotonin, norepinephrine, and dopamine. Adrenal glands release adrenaline and other hormones. The immediate physiological response is an increased heart rate and blood pressure, dilated pupils, and a heightened sense of alertness. These responses are linked to the survival mechanism of the human and have been present since the beginning of humankind (Chrousos & Gold, 1992; Haddy & Clover, 2001; McEwen, 1995).

Many have attempted to answer the question of the impact of stress. Simply put, how much stress is too much? There appears to be no definitive answer, as the same amount and type of stress may lead to negative consequences for one individual and have little to no impact on another. Thomas Holmes and Richard Rahe (1967) constructed a social readjustment rating scale after asking hundreds of people from a variety of backgrounds their response to changing life events and to rank the relative degree of adjustment necessary to address these life-change units (LCUs). For example, a child leaving for college = 28 LCUs; job promotion = 31 LCUs; marital separation = 56 LCUs; and death of a spouse = 100 LCUs. An accumulation of 200 or more LCUs in a single year increases the incidence of psychosomatic disorders.

Dohrenwend and Dohrenwend (1974) trace the relationship between stressful life events and physical illnesses as well as psychiatric disorders. Their review of the research indicates that a pile-up of certain types of stressful life events is correlated with depression, heart disease, and attempted suicide. There is some research evidence that specific types of stressful life events, such as marriage, marked trouble with your boss, being incarcerated, and death of a spouse, can play a significant role in the causation of several psychosomatic and psychiatric disorders (Dohrenwend & Dohrenwend, 1974). However, it should be noted that Dohrenwend and Dohrenwend document the methodological flaws and sampling biases in many of the early studies and aptly recommend greater use of prospective designs and controlled studies and development of reliable and measurable attributes of stressful life events and environmentally anchored measures.

> *Specific psychic stress:* May be defined as a specific personality response or an unconscious conflict that causes a homeostatic disequilibria contributing to the development of psychosomatic disorder. (Kaplan & Sadock, 1998, p. 826)

The changes that the body experiences in response to stress have long been thought to present a remarkable health threat. Franz Alexander (1950) hypothesized that unconscious conflicts are associated with certain psychosomatic disorders. For example, Friedman and Rosenman (1959) identified the high-strung, so-called Type A personality as a stress response that predisposes a person to coronary disease. Clinical studies continue to confirm the connection between stress and vulnerability to illness, for instance, in decreased resistance to infection. There is remarkable evidence that persons under intense stress for long periods of time are more susceptible to the common cold. Recent research demonstrated some of the impact of stress on the immune system's ability to fight illness. One such study demonstrated that women who scored highest on psychological stress scales had a shortage of cytokines, a set of proteins produced by the immune system to aid in the healing process. Despite recent advances, medical researchers are unable to explain the highly individualized response to stress. Many conclude that environmental factors combined with genetic makeup and innate coping skills are the best determinants of an individual's personal reaction to stress (Powell & Matthews, 2002).

> *Crisis:* An acute disruption of psychological homeostasis in which one's usual coping mechanisms fail and there exists evidence of distress and functional impairment. The subjective reaction to a stressful life experience that compromises the individual's stability and ability to cope or function. The main cause of a crisis is an intensely stressful, traumatic, or hazardous event, but two other conditions are also necessary: (1) the individual's perception of the event as the cause of considerable upset and/or disruption; and (2) the individual's inability to resolve the disruption by previously used coping mechanisms. Crisis also refers to "an upset in the steady state." It often has five components: a hazardous or traumatic event, a vulnerable state, a precipitating factor, an active crisis state, and the resolution of the crisis. (Roberts, 2002, p. 1)

This definition of crisis is particularly applicable to persons in acute crisis because these individuals usually seek help only after they have experienced a hazardous or traumatic event and are in a vulnerable state, have failed to lessen the crisis through customary coping methods, lack family or community social supports, and want outside help. Acute psychological or situational crisis episodes may be viewed in various ways, but the definition we are using emphasizes that a crisis can be a turning point in a person's life. Crisis intervention occurs when a counselor, behavioral clinician, or therapist enters into the life situation of an individual or family to alleviate the impact of a crisis episode by facilitating and mobilizing the resources of those directly affected. Rapid assessment and timely intervention on the part of crisis counselors, social workers, psychologists, or child psychiatrists is of paramount importance. Crisis intervenors should be active and directive while displaying a nonjudgmental, accepting, hopeful, and positive attitude. Crisis intervenors need to help crisis clients to identify protective factors, inner strengths, psychological hardiness, or resiliency factors that can be utilized for ego bolstering. Effective crisis intervenors are able to gauge the seven stages of crisis intervention, while being flexible and realizing that several stages of intervention may overlap. Crisis intervention should culminate in a restoration of cognitive functioning, crisis resolution, and cognitive mastery (Roberts, 2000a).

> *Acute Stress Disorder:* The development of characteristic anxiety, dissociative and other symptoms that occurs within one month after exposure to an extreme traumatic stressor. As a response to the traumatic event, the individual develops dissociative symptoms. Individuals with Acute Stress Disorder may have a decrease in emotional responsiveness, often finding it difficult or impossible to experience pleasure in previously enjoyable activities, and frequently feel guilty about pursuing usual life tasks. (American Psychiatric Association [APA], 2000)

Beyond a physiological response to stress, a sudden remarkable stressor (e.g., physical violence or threatened physical violence) can provoke more that a flight-or-fight response, triggering a psychiatric illness referred to as Acute Stress Disorder. A combined grouping of dissociative and anxiety symptoms with the avoidance of reminders of the traumatic event characterize this anxiety disorder. Dissociative symptoms are frequently present and include emotional detachment, temporary loss of memory, derealization, and depersonalization. Potential anxiety-based symptoms associated with Acute Stress Disorder may include but are not limited to irritability, confused and disordered thoughts, sleep disturbance, and being easily startled. The emergence of symptoms occurs within one month of a traumatic event. Associated features in the diagnostic criteria are symptoms that significantly interfere with normal social or vocational functioning. Symptoms associated with Acute Stress Disorder last between two days and four weeks. This disorder is a relatively new diagnostic category. It was introduced in 1994 in an effort to differentiate time-limited reaction to trauma and to provide clear delineation between brief stress reactions from extended reactions to trauma from PTSD (APA, 2000).

> *Trauma:* Psychological trauma refers to human reactions to traumatic stress, violent crimes, infectious disease outbreaks, and other dangerous and life-threatening events. For psychological trauma to occur, the individual's adaptive pathways become shut off as a result of overexposure to stress hormones. Persistent hyperarousal mechanisms related to the traumatic event continually reoccur and are amplified by traumatic recollections stored in the brain. The victims of trauma find themselves rapidly alternating their mental states between relatively calm and peaceful states to states of intense anxiety, agitation, anger, hypervigilance, and extreme arousal. (Roberts, 2002a, pp. 2–3)

Psychological trauma, or the human trauma response, can take place soon after observing or being the victim of a traumatic stressor or event. This is usually the case in Acute Stress Disorder. However, many times, individuals have a delayed reaction to a traumatic event, and this delay of several weeks to several months usually surfaces in the form of symptoms of psychological trauma such as avoidance of familiar surroundings, intense fears, sudden breaking of appointments, social isolation, trance-like states, sleep disturbances and repeated nightmares, depressive episodes, and hyperarousal.

According to Terr (1994), there are two types of trauma among children. Type I refers to victims who have experienced and suffered from a single traumatic event, such as the 26 Chowchilla, California, children who were kidnapped in 1976 and buried alive in their school bus for almost 27 hours. Type II trauma refers to experiencing multiple traumatic events, such as ongoing and recurring incest, child abuse, or family violence. The exception is an extremely horrific single traumatic occurrence that is marked by multiple homicides and includes dehumanizing sights (e.g., dismembered bodies), piercing sounds, and strong odors (fire and smoke).

The American Academy of Experts in Traumatic Stress (ATSM) is a multidisciplinary network of professionals dedicated to formulating and extending the use of traumatic stress reduction protocols with emergency responders (e.g., police, fire, EMS, nurses, disaster response personnel, psychologists, social workers, funeral directors, and clergy). Dr. Mark D. Lerner, a clinical psychologist and president of ATSM, and Dr. Raymond D. Shelton, Director of Emergency Medical Training at the Nassau County (New York) Police Training Academy and director of professional development for ATSM, provide the following guidance for addressing psychological trauma quickly during traumatic events:

> All crisis intervention and trauma treatment specialists are in agreement that before intervening, a full assessment of the situation and the individual must take place. By reaching people early, during traumatic exposure, we may ultimately prevent acute traumatic stress reactions from becoming chronic stress disorders. The first three steps of Acute Traumatic Stress Management (ATSM) are: (1) assess for danger/safety for self and others;

(2) consider the type and extent of property damage and/or physical injury and the way the injury was sustained (e.g., a terroristic explosion); and (3) evaluate the level of responsiveness—is the individual alert, in pain, aware of what has occurred, or in emotional shock or under the influence of drugs? (Lerner & Shelton, 2001, pp. 31–32)

Personal impact in the aftermath of potentially stressful and crisis-producing events can be measured by:

- *Spatial dimensions:* The closer the person is to the center of the tragedy, the greater the stress. Similarly, the closer the person's relationship is to the homicide victim, the greater the likelihood of entering into a crisis state.
- *Subjective crime clock:* The greater the duration (estimated length of time exposed and estimated length of exposure to sensory experiences, e.g., an odor of gasoline combined with the smell of a fire) that an individual is affected by the community disaster, violent crime, or other tragedy, the greater the stress.
- *Reoccurrence* (perceived): The greater the perceived likelihood that the tragedy will happen again, the greater the likelihood of intense fears, which contribute to an active crisis state on the part of the survivor (Young, 1995).

Posttraumatic Stress Disorder: A set of typical symptoms that develop after a person sees, is involved in, or hears of "an extreme traumatic stressor." PTSD is an acute, chronic, delayed, debilitating, and complex mental disorder. It includes altered awareness, detachment, dissociative states, ego fragmentation, personality changes, paranoid ideation, trigger events, and vivid intrusive traumatic recollections. PTSD is often comorbid with major depression, dysthymia, alcohol or substance abuse, and generalized anxiety disorder. The person reacts to this experience with fear and helplessness, sleep disturbances, hyperarousal and hypervigilance, persistently reliving the event through graphic and magnified horrific flashbacks and intrusive thoughts, and unsuccessful attempts to avoid being reminded of it. The symptoms must last for more than a month and must significantly affect important areas of life. (APA, 2000)

Some stressors are so severe that almost anyone is susceptible to the overwhelming effects of the experience. PTSD can arise from war experiences, torture, natural disasters, terrorism, rape, assault, or serious accidents. A recent example reflective of this is the random sniper shootings in Rockville, Maryland, and Virginia. In today's society, television is spreading individual reaction to traumatic stressors. Examples of this can be seen daily when persons cast their eyes to the sky in fear as a jet flies over or stoop low beside their car while pumping gasoline. The complete impact of vicarious stressors as delivered through multimedia bombardment is not examined in this chapter; however, this subject warrants further examination.

The history of PTSD begins with Jacob DaCosta's 1871 paper "On Irritable Heart," describing the symptoms of stress witnessed in Civil War soldiers. The disorder was referred to as "traumatic neurosis," resulting from the strong influence of psychoanalysis. This was replaced by the term "shell shock" during World War I, as psychiatrists hypothesized this was the impact of brain trauma resulting from the percussion blows of exploding bombshells. It was not until 1941, when the survivors of the Coconut Grove nightclub fire began to demonstrate symptoms of nervousness, nightmares, and graphic recollections of the tragedy, that the definition was expanded to include operational fatigue, delayed grief, and combat neurosis. It was not until the return of Vietnam War veterans that the notion of posttraumatic disorder emerged in its current context. Throughout the history of this disorder one inescapable fact has been present: The appearance of the disorder was roughly correlated with the severity of the disorder, with the most severe stressors resulting in the emergence of characteristic symptomatology in 75% of the victims.

The critical feature of PTSD is the development of characteristic symptoms following exposure to an extreme traumatic stressor involving direct personal experience of an event of direct or threatened death or severe injury, threat to one's physical integrity or that of another person, or being witness to an unexpected violent death, serious harm, or threat of injury to self or another. Criteria in the *Diagnostic and Statistical Manual of Mental Disorders* (*DSM-IV-TR;* APA, 2000) specify that the presence of symptoms of hyperarousal, avoidance, and reexperiencing of the trauma must have been present for more than one month. Patients who have experienced symptoms for less than one month should be diagnosed as having Acute Stress Disorder. The *DSM-IV-TR* provides clinicians the opportunity to specify acute (symptoms less than three months) or chronic (symptoms lasting longer than three months). There is also provision for delayed onset if the appearance of symptoms occurs six months or more after the stressful event.

The need for a consolidated approach to individual and group psychological crisis intervention appears to be significant. Breslau et al. (1991) indicated that 89.6% of adults may experience a traumatic event over the course of their lifetime. Previous thought has linked the risk of exposure to trauma to specific occupational groups, including the military, firefighting, and law enforcement. However, recent events have expanded this scope to include educators, emergency medical personnel, and even innocent bystanders, as demonstrated following the terrorist attack in New York City. Previously, Everly and Mitchell (1999) indicated that conditional risk of developing a stress disorder for the general population was in excess of 9%, with high-risk population potential ranging from 10% to 30%. It is too soon to measure the direct impact of recent events on the general population; however, it is certain that many more persons are experiencing significant exposure to risk for stress, acute stress, crisis, and posttraumatic stress.

The need for prompt intervention cannot be underestimated. Over a decade ago, Swanson and Carbon (1989) began writing on the need for prompt intervention in cases of stress, crisis, and trauma for the APA's task force on the treatment of psychiatric disorders. Concurrently, Roberts' seven-stage model of crisis intervention emerged, urging a systematic and eclectic approach to crisis intervention. There is an emergent need and strong argument for providing immediate aid and forming a treatment alliance with psychological trauma victims. The question is not whether to provide emergency psychological services, but how to frame the interactions and diagnoses in a manner that provides accurate and consistent individualized care approaches.

A CLINICAL FRAMEWORK

It is not difficult to understand the confusion experienced by practitioners surrounding the terms stress, trauma, and crisis. These terms are used to describe not only the event or situation, but also the individualized response to the event and, at times, the diagnosis associated with the individual's response to the event. It is important to differentiate the severity of event from patients' perception and their unique abilities to cope with the event. In doing so, the clinician will have a clearer picture of the appropriate diagnostic framework criteria and categories to be applied.

To utilize the diagram below in Figure 4.1, the practitioner must first examine the severity of the event and its potential impact on the individual's response when accounting for individual personality and character, temperament, other stressors that day, protective factors and coping skills, adaptability to change and unexpected events, support system, and the intensity and duration of the stressor. Once the nature of the initial event is clearly understood, the practitioner can construct an accurate depiction of the individual's condition. Note: Accurate differentiation among stress, crisis, Acute Stress Disorder, and PTSD should be accomplished through a multimeasurement, multidisciplinary approach: completion of an informational interview, examination of the social environment, application of scale measurement, and consultation with medical practitioners. This process leads to a greater understanding of the factors impacting the individual. Determinations made through this process are approximations, seeking to construct a framework to serve as a foundation for treatment planning and care delivery. This process is not a diagnostic criterion, nor is it intended to replace *DSM-IV-TR* classification.

What follows are a series of case examples that differentiate among stress, crisis, Acute Stress Disorder, and PTSD. Special emphasis is placed on the event, the individual's response to the event, the application of appropriate diagnostic criteria when warranted, resiliency factors, and treatment planning.

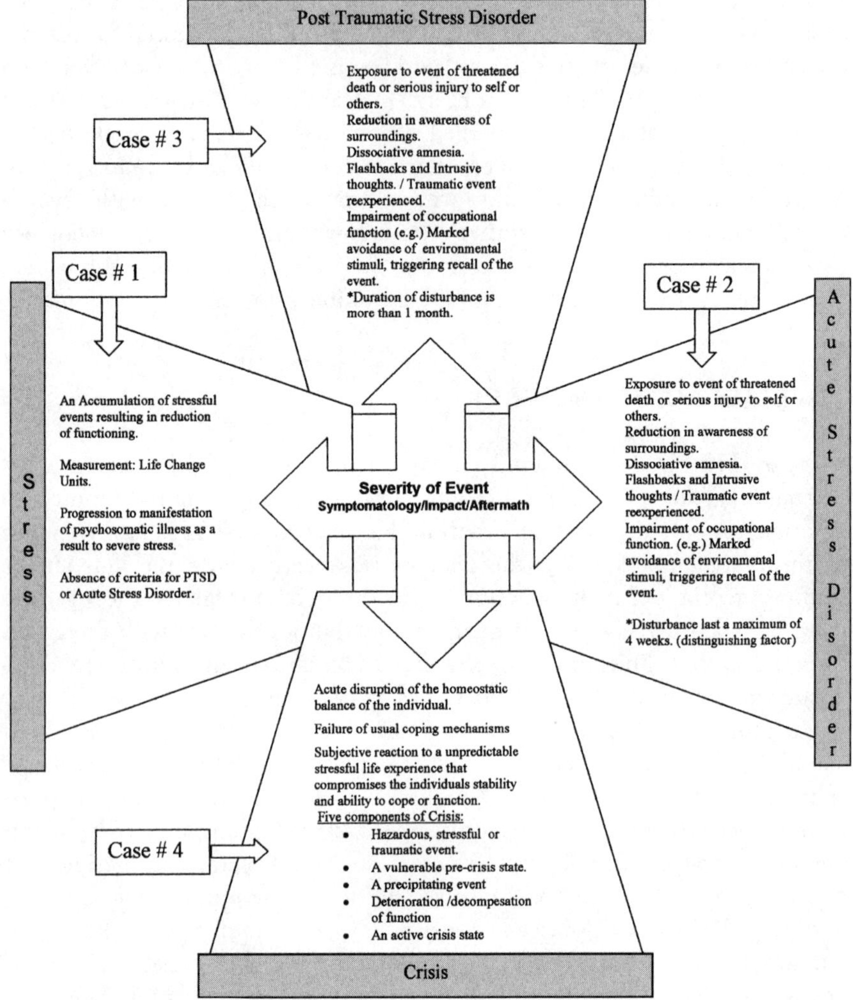

Figure 4.1 Stress, Crisis, Acute Stress Disorder, and PTSD Classification Paradigm

CASE ILLUSTRATIONS

Case Example 1

Kevin is a manager in a large insurance corporation. He was brought in during a point of transition in the organization, replacing a manager who was less than effective but well-liked. Kevin has held this position for two years. He has consistently found himself in the middle of critical and sensitive issues between department staff and administration. At this point in his life, Kevin is responsible for the care of his elderly frail mother, who was diagnosed with terminal cancer three months previously. He is a single parent with three children, of whom the eldest has recently left for college. Kevin is experiencing financial difficulties and may be facing foreclosure on his house. He presents for counseling to address job stress, as he is fearful the company is looking at demotion or termination from his position. On the positive side, Kevin reports that he has become involved in a significant new relationship, but he fears that this will end when "the wheels come off in his employment."

Case Example 2

Jill is a nurse manager with 27 years of experience in critical care working in the transplant unit of a large metropolitan medical center. Two days prior to seeking assistance, her last living and favorite uncle was admitted to the medical center following a mild heart attack. Jill reports that on the first day of her uncle's hospitalization, she assured him and his wife that they were in "the right place." Knowing the medical staff, Jill arranged for her uncle to be seen by the very best cardiologist and a group of nurses whom she personally knew and felt would do excellent work. Jill left the unit that day feeling very good about her work. When she returned to work the next day, she checked in on her uncle. A unit assistant told Jill that he had been moved to a critical care pod and that his condition had worsened over the last shift. Jill approached the critical care pod as her uncle experienced a major cardiac event. She remained present throughout the code, assisting the residents, cardiologist, and anesthesiologist. Unfortunately, her uncle did not survive the event. Still, Jill remained focused. She accompanied the cardiologist as he informed family of the unanticipated outcome. Jill contacted pastoral care to provide a private area for her aunt and cousins to grieve their loss. She was present until all arrangements had been made and her family had left the medical center. Realizing she could not work, Jill took the nearest stairwell to her unit to explain her absence. She was unable to proceed and was found by staff sitting on the stairs tearful and overwhelmed by the experience. Since that time she has relived the experience of the code, reporting vivid recollections of the death of her favorite uncle and the faces of her family members.

Case Example 3

Thomas is a firefighter with Engine House 1 in a large metropolitan area who presents following the loss of three peers in a warehouse fire in the garment district. Tom recounts that the fire was intense: "This is the most intense fire I had ever seen. The smoke was extremely thick and very toxic. As time progressed, the heat was overwhelming." Tom notes that he and three peers were on the third floor of the warehouse when he heard a large explosion. "I knew it was bad. When you hear anything above the roar of the fire it's got to be very big and very dangerous." At the time of the explosion Tom had moved away from the team to secure equipment for advancement and to direct the reinforcement team. He reports, "After the explosion I turned around to see where my buddies were, but I didn't see 'em. . . . At first I thought it was the smoke, so I moved closer. . . . Then I saw what really happened. . . . The floor had given way, it just fell out from under them. Two of my buddies were on the next floor down, I could hear them screaming, they was in the middle of the fire, there wasn't anything I could do for them. I just sat there and watched them thrash, kick, scream, and die. I didn't see Vince at first, then I saw him. He was hanging on a pipe about four feet below me. I reached down for him. I had a chance . . . but when he reached up for my hand, all I grabbed was his glove . . . I still see his face as he fell. After I got out I realized his glove was still in my hand. . . . What I realized is . . . Oh my God . . . the flesh of his hand was still in the glove. I hadn't missed, there just wasn't nothin' there to grab. Now I know what that look on his face was about. . . . I can't seem to shake it. . . . I haven't had a decent night's sleep for about six months. . . . I was doing all I could to help. . . . It haunts me. Sometimes it's not even a dream. I'm just thinking and there it is, boom . . . right in my face, like I'm living it all over again. I'm just not sure how much more of this I can take. I don't know how I got out . . . worse yet, I don't know why."

Case Example 4

William is a 54-year-old information technology director for a large manufacturing firm. While working in the plant one afternoon, William was struck by a large piece of equipment that was being moved via overhead crane; this resulted in a closed-head trauma. Once he was physically stabilized, the true effects of William's injuries became apparent. William experienced moderate cognitive impairment, affecting his ability to concentrate and to consistently complete logical problem solving. The head trauma had also impacted William's ability to ambulate. It became apparent that his rehabilitation was going to be not only difficult and lengthy, but he would be challenged to learn to walk again. To further complicate matters, William was plagued by chronic pain in the form of migraine headaches, which would present without warning, often lasting for days. William is the sole support for his family and found that he had no short-term disability and that his long-term disability was only 60% of his income. He was faced with not only remarkable health issues, but also remarkable financial stressors. William's wife and family were extremely supportive and actively participated in each phase of his rehabilitation. William was connected with a social worker to begin the process of establishing social, emotional, and vocational rehabilitation.

Clearly conceptualizing each of the cases provides the opportunity for examination of the defining factors of stress, crisis, Acute Stress Disorder, and PTSD. Figure 4.2 provides a roadmap for practitioners to process the nature of an individual's presenting problems and precipitating event and serves as a springboard for intervention based on the ACT intervention model (Roberts, 2002).

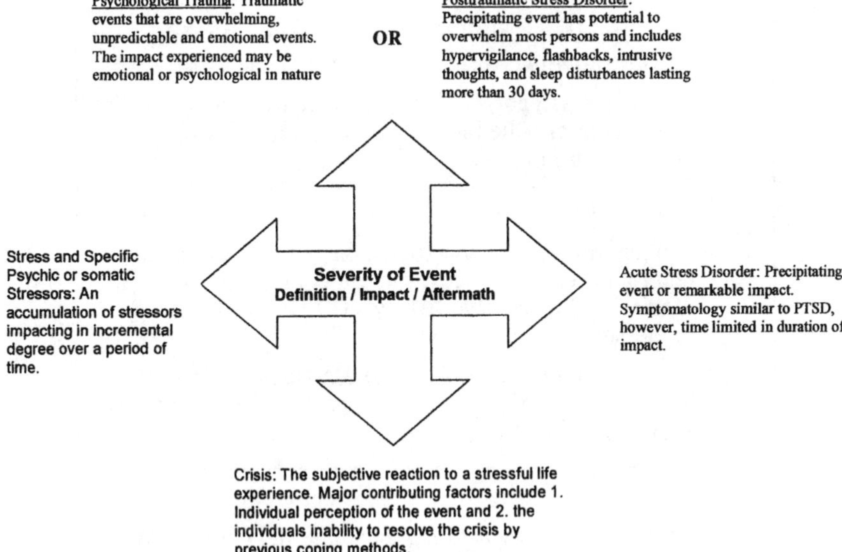

Figure 4.2 Five-Way Diagram of Trigger or Precipitating Event and Outcome

With the onset of crisis, stress, and trauma, the single common event is an episode that challenges or threatens the individual and his or her perception of the world. Based on the severity of the event and the individual's perception of the acute stressor, situational stressor, or accumulation of stressors, each person will progress in his or her response to the trigger/ precipitating event.

THE ACT INTERVENTION MODEL

A: The A in the ACT intervention model refers to *assessment* of the presenting problem. This is inclusive of (1) triage assessment, emergency psychiatric response based on crisis assessment and appraisal of immediate medical needs; and (2) trauma assessment, including the biopsychosocial and cultural assessment protocols.

C: The C in the ACT intervention model refers to *connecting* to support groups, the delivery of social services, critical incident stress debriefing, and crisis intervention.

T: The T in the ACT intervention model refers to *traumatic* reactions, sequelae, and posttraumatic stress disorders (see figure 4.3).

Immediate assessment of risk to self or others (e.g., suicide attempts, self-injurious behavior, and assessment of the individual's ability to care for self)

A	• Assessment/appraisal of immediate medical needs, threats to public safety and property damage • Triage assessment, crisis assessment, trauma assessment and the biopsychosocial and cultural assessment protocols
C	• Connecting to support groups, the delivery of disaster relief and social services, and critical incident stress debriefing (Mitchell & Everly's CISD model) implemented • Crisis intervention (Robert's seven-stage model) implemented, through strengths perspective and coping attempts bolstered
T	• Traumatic stress reactions, sequelae, and post-traumatic stress disorders (PTSDs) • Ten step acute trauma and stress management protocol (Lerner & Shelton), trauma treatment plans and recovery strategies implemented

Figure 4.3 ACT Model

or harm to others (e.g., potential for aggression toward others, attempted murder, murder) is the first step or A of the ACT model. Individuals presenting with homicidal or suicidal ideation or the demonstrated inability to care for self will require a brief hospitalization to become stabilized. The primary objective of assessment is to provide data to better understand the nature of the event and the individual's perception of and response to the event, extent of support system, effectiveness of coping mechanisms, and perceptions regarding willingness to seek assistance. Intake forms and rapid assessment instruments should be utilized to gather sufficiently accurate information to assist with the decision-making process. It is important to note that although the assessment is of the individual, the practitioner should always consider the person's immediate environment, including seeking information about supportive interpersonal relationships (Roberts & Lewis, 2001, 2002). Accurate assessment will lead to accurate diagnosis of the individual's condition and in turn will facilitate treatment interventions that are understandable, measurable, and accomplishable for the client.

The C in the ACT model addresses crisis intervention and connection to services. Although practitioners have training in a variety of theoretical approaches, this training is not easily applied to the nature of cases seen in actual practice in an emergency or crisis setting. The criteria for admission to inpatient psychiatric treatment require that patients be homicidal, suicidal, or unable to care for themselves. Although this is a very simplistic view of admission criteria, those working in psychiatry are acutely aware of the accuracy of these brief and overarching admission criteria. When trying to apply a clear, concise approach to crisis intervention regardless of diagnostic category or where the individual presents on the continuum of care need, practitioners are finding that traditional theoretical paradigms are not as effective as clear protocols. Roberts's (1991, 2000) seven-stage crisis intervention model provides practitioners with such a framework (see Figure 4.4).

The T in the ACT model refers to trauma assessment and treatment.

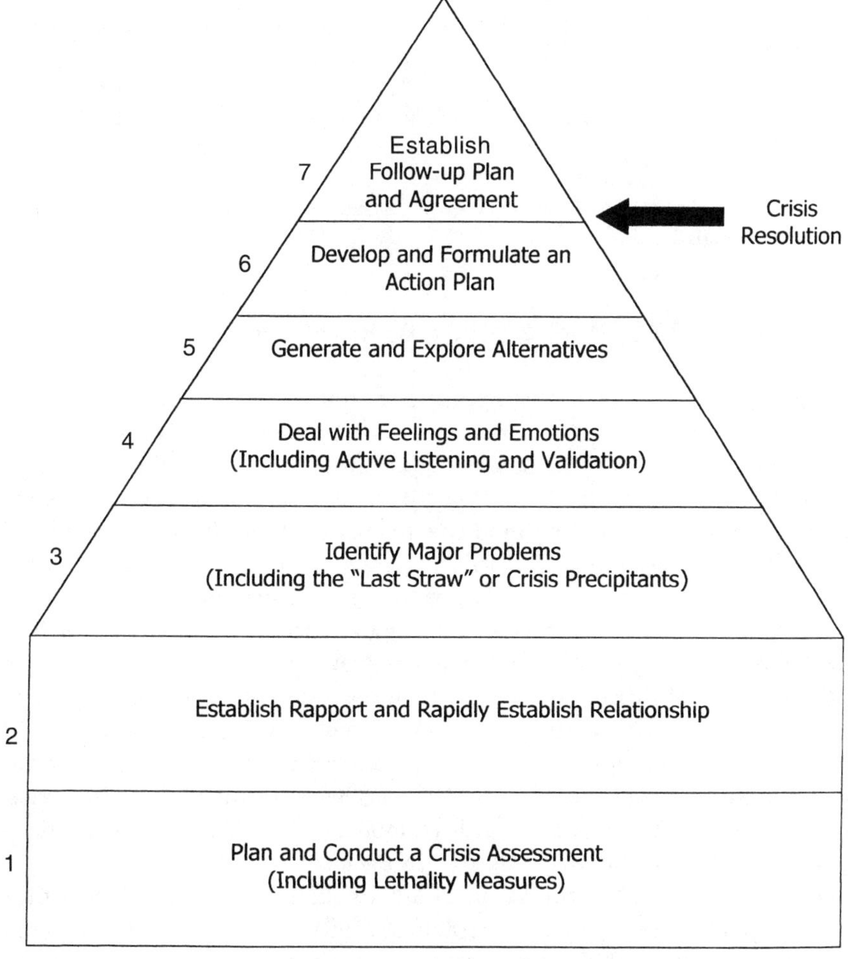

Figure 4.4 Roberts's Seven-Stage Crisis Intervention Model

Traumatic events are overwhelming and highly emotionally charged experiences that remarkably impact the individual's ability to maintain psychological/psychiatric stability. Long-term exposure to a series of traumatic events (e.g., domestic violence) may lead to deterioration of psychological well-being. Furthermore, it is important to note that of those who experience traumatic events, only 3% to 5% develop PTSD.

Lerner and Shelton (2001) have developed a model of intervention that they believe is effective in intervening with traumatic stress and psychological trauma survivors to prevent escalation into PTSD:

1. Assess for danger/safety for self and others.
2. Consider the physical and perceptual mechanism of injury.
3. Evaluate the level of responsiveness.
4. Address medical needs.
5. Observe and identify each individual's signs of traumatic stress.
6. Introduce yourself, state your title and role, and begin to develop a connection.
7. Ground the individual by allowing him or her to tell his or her story.
8. Provide support through active and empathic listening.
9. Normalize, validate, and educate.
10. Bring the person to the present, describe future events, and provide referrals.

CRITICAL INCIDENT STRESS DEBRIEFING

Critical incident stress debriefing has been found to be useful in the aftermath of floods, hurricanes, tornadoes, and large fires. Crisis response and crisis intervention work is demanding and highly stressful. Frontline crisis intervention workers may be exposed to gruesome and life-threatening events. Eaton and Ertl (2000) indicate that incidents such as completed suicides, dead bodies, and threats to or assaults on crisis workers warrant the use of critical incident stress management (CISM) techniques. Keeping workers safe and ensuring that they can find satisfaction in their work as well as in their personal lives requires that they receive support in managing their own stress. CISM can play an important part in providing that support to workers in crisis intervention programs. It includes a wide variety of techniques and interventions for individuals exposed to life-threatening or traumatic events (Mitchell & Everly, 1993). There are more than 300 crisis response teams utilizing a standardized model of CISM services internationally, as listed by the International Critical Incident Stress Foundation (Everly, Lating, & Mitchell, 2000). The utilization of CISM techniques allows workers the opportunity to discuss the traumatic event, promotes group cohesion, and educates workers on stress reactions and coping techniques (Eaton & Roberts, 2002).

For a detailed discussion of the stress-crisis-trauma flow chart, with resilience and hardiness protective factors built in, see Judith A. Waters's article. She also documents the perspectives of the most prominent clinical and research psychologists related to stress theory and trauma perspectives in the aftermath of September 11. Approximately 30 years ago, William Reid and Laura Epstein of the University of Chicago developed the first empirically tested time-limited social work treatment model: task-centered practice. As a result, we were delighted that Gary Behrmann and William Reid (2002), wrote a special article for this issue which integrates task-centered practice with crisis intervention based on their work in New York. For those individuals planning a training workshop on crisis intervention, we suggest you review Maureen Underwood and John Kalafat's crisis intervention curriculum and evaluation in this issue. The latter article, written by a clinical social worker and a clinical psychologist, is representative of the multidisciplinary team approach that the journal's mission encourages.

APPLICATION OF ACT MODEL AND SEVEN-STAGE CRISIS INTERVENTION MODEL

Case Example 1

Kevin presents with an accumulation of stress factors (Figure 4.5). On the LCU rating of common stressors, he has a cumulative stress score of 270. His psychosomatic symptoms are beginning to emerge as headaches and remarkable weight loss, accompanied by fleeting feelings of anxiety and hopelessness. Following assessment of Kevin's situation, crisis intervention consisted of addressing the issues that he prioritized in the first session. These were addressed as follows:

Problem: Job stress.
Goal: Increased understanding of personal reaction to stress.
Methods:

1. List stressful situations experienced in order of severity (Stage 3 of Roberts's seven-stage model).
2. Consider alternatives to stress that have worked (Stage 5 of Roberts's seven-stage model).
3. List alternative actions for given stressful situations (Stage 6 of Roberts's seven-stage model).
4. Keep a log of activities and how these have impacted your stress level.

Initially, Kevin was reluctant to complete this task. In fact, his first list consisted of looking at the employment ads on a daily basis and finding a new position. It was noted that this would be helpful, but would not resolve

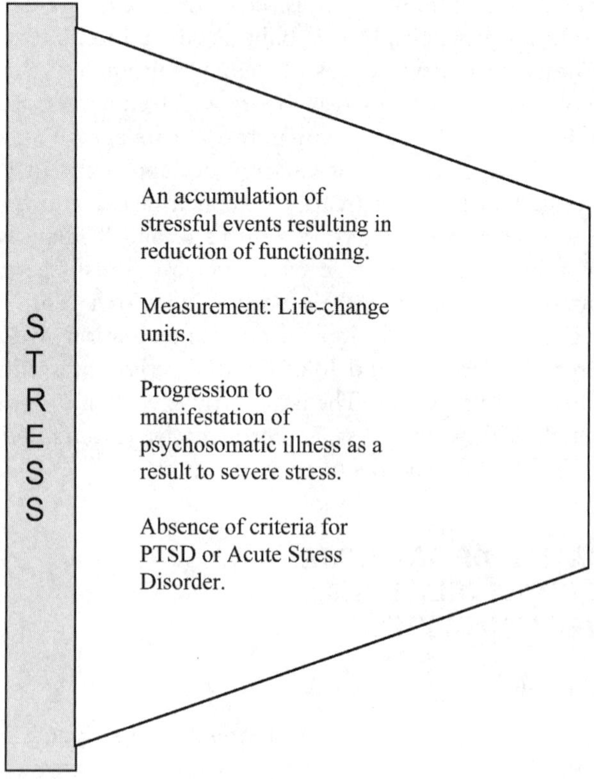

STRESS
An accumulation of stressful events resulting in reduction of functioning.
Measurement: Life-change units.
Progression to manifestation of psychosomatic illness as a result to severe stress.
Absence of criteria for PTSD or Acute Stress Disorder.

Figure 4.5

all of the problems Kevin was faced with. In subsequent sessions, Kevin did complete a list of stressors that encompassed each identified in the initial assessment. He acknowledged that he needed to take better care of himself. His list of activities included cutting back on caffeinated beverages and alcoholic beverages, improving his diet by staying away from fatty and fried foods, taking a walk each day on his lunch break, and making time after work to do something fun with his family and friends rather than focusing on the stressful daily events and how to "fix" them.

Kevin experienced an accumulation of stressors that were transitioning him into a state of specific psychic stress that was impacting his personal health. Following accurate assessment, Kevin was able to work through the seven-stage crisis intervention model to address the stressors in his life. In Kevin's log was a statement that demonstrated his understanding of the impact of stress on his life: "I now understand that it is not my job or those around me that is causing my problems, it's all about what I do with what is given to me. If I focus on every little issue I will never be able to see my way out of the hole I am continually digging!"

The T in the ACT model was combined with the seventh step of Roberts's model, follow-up. Kevin indicated that the pending loss of his mother would be a remarkably difficult time for him. He was able to process his concerns about this with his group. He shared that of all of his problems this was the final remaining issue. In the closing session, Kevin shared a plan specifying who he will utilize for support and the actions he will take following the loss of his mother. He was reassured that should there be a need to come for additional sessions, there would be openings for him. Kevin agreed to do so if necessary.

Case Autopsy

Kevin attended a total of six one-hour sessions. These sessions were based on a solution-focused approach combined with Roberts's seven-stage crisis intervention model. In each session clear goals were outlined. Homework sessions focused on specific actions to be taken based on collaborative interaction between Kevin and his therapist. Kevin did not change jobs. Rather, he chose to maintain his focus on completing the day-to-day tasks and removing himself from the office politics. He ran his division strictly by the book and documented every action according to company policy. The therapist capitalized on the strengths of Kevin's family and their willingness to make changes to address pending issues. Kevin developed a plan to sell the home he was living in, as his family no longer required such a large house. After speaking with his children, Kevin purchased a smaller house with a pool and a recreation room in the basement. He reports that this has been an excellent compromise for him and his children. Kevin was able to remove the majority of his financial stressors following the sale of his home. He was careful to remove himself from office politics, and while he was walking at lunch one day his boss was terminated. Kevin reports working to build a more positive rapport with his staff. In addition, Kevin displayed a number of resilience factors: supportive significant others or family, willingness to assess need for change, ability to enact changes, financial equity in his home to utilize for reduction of financial stressors, and consistent and steady full-time employment with good health benefits.

Case Example 2

The unanticipated death of Jill's favorite uncle precipitated a situational crisis (Figure 4.6). Jill was quite skilled in dealing with stressful situations; however, this situation was more than the typical stressor faced in her work environment. Assessment of this case included application of the Beck Anxiety Scale. Jill's score reflected significant anxiety associated with this experience. Assessment of competencies of nursing practice indicated minimal impact; however, emotionally, Jill was not prepared to return to her work.

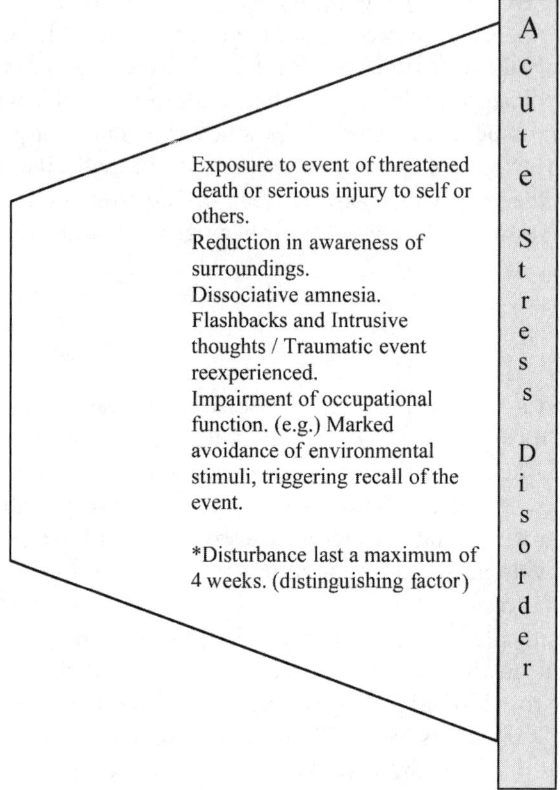

Figure 4.6

There are many strong arguments for providing acute psychological counsel and forming a therapeutic rapport as early as possible following a traumatic event (Roberts, 2000b). Slaikeu (1984) argued that rapid intervention is essential to successful resolution of crisis. McGee (1974) cites "Hansel's Law," indicating that the successful outcome for individuals addressing traumatic events increases directly as a function of the outcome's proximity in both time and place to the crisis event.

In Jill's case, the C and T of the ACT model took the form of brief, solution-focused intervention combined with Roberts's seven-stage crisis intervention model. This intervention was instituted within 48 hours of the trauma event. The intrevention occurred in the department of psychiatry associated with the hospital facility, thus providing proximity to the event. Jill's therapist provided support and assured her that the sessions would not be shared with her immediate supervisor and that they would work together as a team to develop her ongoing plan of care. Jill felt treatment in the institution of her employment was appropriate. These actions served to rapidly establish the therapeutic relationship between Jill and her therapist (Stage 2 of Roberts's seven-stage model).

The function of the debriefing was to "psychologically de-escalate" Jill, permitting the opportunity for her to explore and express feelings of guilt and her perception that she had not provided all of the assistance possible for her uncle (Stage 4 of Roberts's seven-stage model). As the debriefing continued, a pattern emerged of Jill's believing that she had a greater level of responsibility for her uncle's death than was warranted. Jill was experiencing remarkable difficulties sleeping and maintaining concentration, which ultimately resulted in significant distress in social and occupational functioning. Also, Jill was isolated from her primary support system, her family, as she felt that her failure to do all she could for her uncle made it impossible for her to seek assistance from them. Interventions associated with Jill's case utilized an integrated multicomponent approach, as debriefing as a stand-alone therapy has not been found to be as successful as a multicomponent approach. Jill worked with her therapist to develop and formulate her treatment plan (Stage 6 Roberts's seven-stage model). Interventions included:

1. Individual therapy sessions twice per week. Jill was encouraged to discuss the event and her subsequent reactions to the event.
2. Psychoeducational interventions to increase her awareness of a variety of coping mechanisms (e.g., relaxation techniques).
3. Pharmacotherapy, including the use of tricyclic medication (Elavil) and mild doses of sedatives as needed for sleep.
4. A family conference to provide education and to permit cathartic ventilation in a manner that empowered family members to provide constructive support in the face of a demanding crisis situation.
5. Because Jill reported having strong spiritual beliefs, pastoral intervention was utilized.

Jill responded almost immediately to the support of her family, indicating that she felt for the first time since the event that she was not alone. Within a week, Jill felt it was no longer necessary to utilize the sedative medication prescribed; however, she remained compliant to the prescribed tricyclic medication. By the end of the second week of therapy, Jill asked to return to her unit and visit her friends. Soon after this visit, she related her belief in her ability to return to the workforce. Three weeks to the day after the traumatic event, Jill returned to work. It is important to note that Jill's experience met the diagnostic criteria for Acute Stress Disorder (Figure 4.6), specifically the time component. Her disturbance occurred within four weeks of the event and persisted for approximately three weeks, which is within the maximum four-week duration (APA, 2000).

Case Autopsy

Although Jill was no stranger to stressful experiences in the hospital setting, she was not prepared for the emotional trauma associated with the loss of her uncle in her work environment. Jill related during therapy that the resident reported to her later that he felt it strange that she was on critical care unit; however, with the current nursing shortage, he assumed that Jill was covering an additional shift. In fact, none of the crisis team responding to the code had been aware that this was a relative. It was not until the cardiologist arrived that team members were aware of the true nature of the event. Jill reports that the cardiologist asked her in the hall while going to speak with the family if she was "all right." To this day, she is uncertain of her response.

Jill attended six follow-up sessions over a 4-month period and has not experienced significant symptoms associated with the traumatic event. By the final session, she had discontinued the tricyclic medication. The resilience factors she exhibited were pre-incident training and preparation, strong family support, support in her work environment, rapid response of debriefing and initiation of crisis intervention, spiritual beliefs, and cognitive abilities to apply multicomponent approach.

Case Example 3

Assessment of Tom indicated that he had been experiencing numerous diagnostic criteria for Acute Posttraumatic Stress Disorder (Figure 4.7). Symptoms identified during the initial assessment included intense feelings of helplessness and horror associated with the event. Tom also reported recurrent distressing recollections of the event, specifically, images of his friend's face and the realization of why his friend was unable to hold on during his rescue efforts. Tom described intense feelings suggesting the presence of flashbacks relating to the episode and that he had been experiencing recurrent distressful dreams of the event that were uncharacteristically realistic. He also reported feeling estranged from his peer group. There was a remarkable tendency toward isolation and reduction of participation in significant activities. Most important, Tom began to avoid thoughts, feelings, and conversations associated with the traumatic event. Finally, Tom was experiencing sleep disturbance, including insomnia and early morning wakening, and difficulty concentrating and had demonstrated in the course of the assessment interview an exaggerated startle response.

As time progressed, Tom's condition began to deteriorate, until he reached the point of suicidal ideation. He stated, "I can't deal with the torture of reliving this event every day. I don't understand why I had to survive. I should be dead." In this case, the C in the ACT model required admission to an inpatient psychiatric facility to facilitate psychiatric stabilization in a

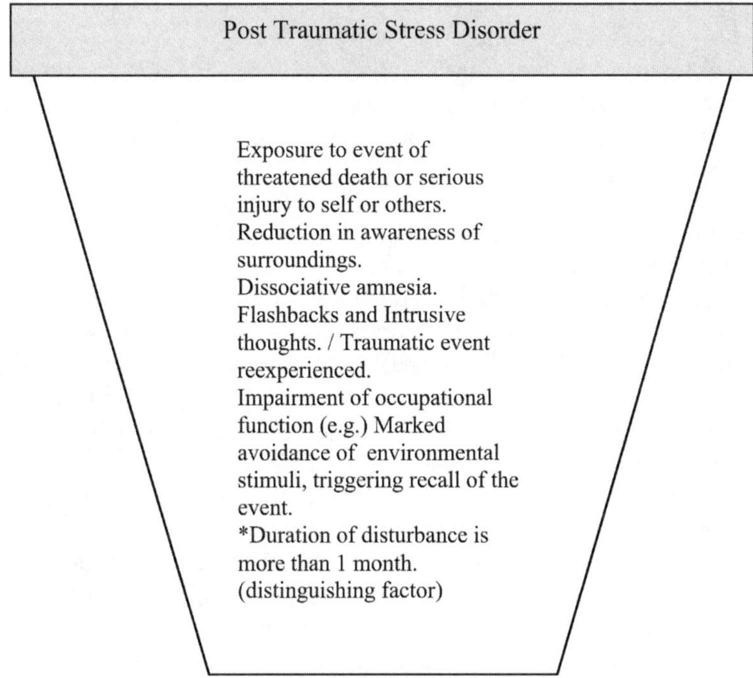

Figure 4.7

safe environment. Pharmacotherapy for Tom consisted of a selective serotonin reuptake inhibitor (SSRI) and Triazodone to assist with sleep.

Tom struggled to become involved in group therapy. He experienced remarkable difficulty relating to his peers on the unit. This was further complicated by the events of September 11, 2001, which occurred on the tenth day of Tom's treatment. On two separate occasions, Tom experienced violent physical outbreaks after watching televised accounts of this tragedy. On a third occasion, Tom was triggered by the unit fire alarm. This event was so severe that the crisis team was involved, and Tom was placed in seclusion to minimize stimuli. Zyprexa and Ativan were administered to minimize Tom's agitation.

Tom worked with the multidisciplinary treatment team to develop an integrated treatment plan. This was a slow process, initially focusing on integration into the community.

Problem: Lack of participation in programming.
Goal: Increased involvement in programming.
Methods:

1. Tom will meet with Mary Ann Jones, LISW, each morning and pick three groups to participate in each day.

2. Tom will talk with Mary Ann Jones at the end of the day and relate how these groups helped.
3. Tom will eat dinner in the community room with at least two peers.
4. Tom will limit his time watching the television to 1 hour per day.
5. Tom will sleep at least 8 hours per evening, utilizing medication as needed for sleep.

The focus of the initial goal was to establish relationships with his peers and the staff (Stage 2 of Roberts's seven-stage crisis intervention model). As time progressed, Tom found art therapy and music therapy to be helpful in relaxing him and improving his interactions on the unit. He became more active in group therapy and was challenged to identify his major problems (Stage 3 of Roberts's seven-stage model). Tom shared that trusting again would be difficult. He began by sharing the recurrent thoughts and dreams, first in the form of questions, then in more detail. Within three weeks he was beginning to deal with the feelings and emotions associated with the traumatic event.

Tom transitioned into the partial hospitalization program. One day while in group, he regressed as a result of an ambulance entering the Emergency Department with lights and sirens on. However, he was able to utilize the group to explore alternatives to his natural response to isolate and relive his trauma. He contracted to stay with two peers throughout the remainder of the day and to participate in art therapy, as he felt this would be relaxing. Tom was able to build on his strengths and to utilize a solution-focused approach to develop a plan that functioned for that day.

Case Autopsy

Tom's treatment has been lengthy. He continues to follow up in the outpatient clinic twice monthly for therapy and medication management. He has not been able to return to his work or the now empty site of the warehouse fire. Tom's treatment plan continues to be solution-focused, primarily dealing with environmental triggers. He has applied for vocational rehabilitation and is interested in education in computers. Tom occasionally attends a community-based support group for persons with PTSD; however, he acknowledges his ambivalence regarding the effectiveness of this group. Tom continues on medication and reports better results with Risperdal than previously experienced with the SSRI. His resilience factors include a strong will to survive, willingness to learn, and discovery of the ability to express emotion through art, crafts, and music.

Case Example 4

In the case of William, a series of neurocognitive testing indicated severe closed-head trauma. William was facing life-changing and life-long adjustments secondary to his crisis event (Figure 4.8). Remarkably, he was open and willing to do whatever was necessary. Once medically stable, William was transferred to a long-term residential physical rehabilitation facility. Assessment indicated the need for physical strengthening and rehabilitation to establish optimal functioning capacity.

William and his family met with the team, consisting of a physician, neurologist, physical therapist, and social worker. William connected best with the social worker. Building on this strength, the treatment team selected the social worker to review and develop treatment planning with William. Initially, the treatment plan addressed physical strengthening and integration into a physical rehabilitation program. However, as time progressed, all team members became involved in assessment and reassessment of functioning. For example, two weeks into rehabilitation, William decided the process was too painful, that he could not go on. Rather than engaging in arguments with him, the team took the approach of establishing a treatment plan based on William's transitioning into an extended care facility rather than returning to his home as he intended. The physician, physical therapist, and social worker met with William to discuss the nature of his extended care placement and the need to refocus attention on transition planning rather than on rehabilitation (Stage 5 Roberts's seven-stage model).

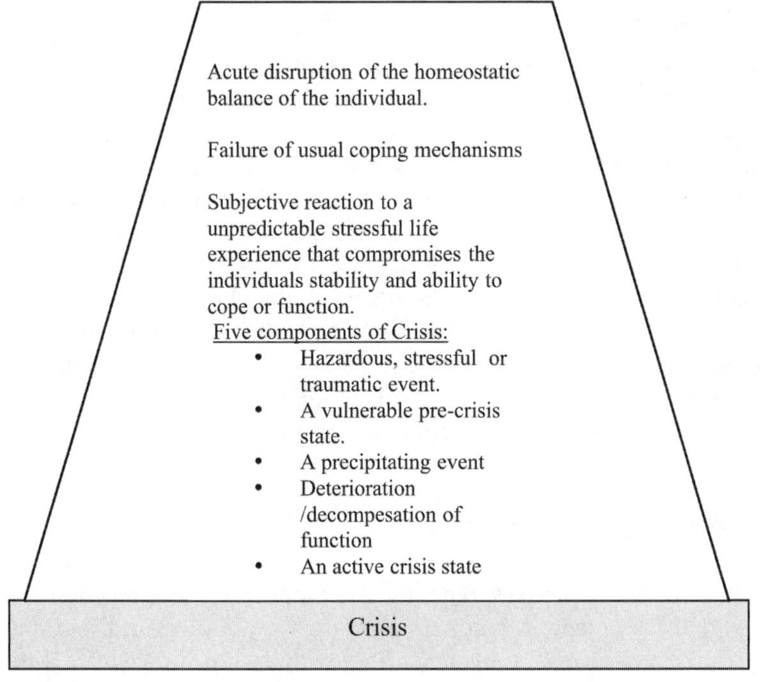

Acute disruption of the homeostatic balance of the individual.
Failure of usual coping mechanisms
Subjective reaction to a unpredictable stressful life experience that compromises the individuals stability and ability to cope or function.
Five components of Crisis:
• Hazardous, stressful or traumatic event.
• A vulnerable pre-crisis state.
• A precipitating event
• Deterioration /decompesation of function
• An active crisis state
Crisis

Figure 4.8

This shift in planning evoked a remarkably emotional response. The team made time for William and listened to his complaints of their lack of caring, validated this feeling, and proceeded to rewrite his treatment plan to move in a more aggressive manner toward strength training and rehabilitation (Stage 6 Roberts's seven-stage model). In solution-focused therapy, setting goals receives more emphasis than defining problems (de Shazer, 1985). In William's case, goal setting was based on a desired future state: how he perceived he would be acting, thinking, and feeling differently once the goal was accomplished. Without exception, William demonstrated willingness to work with the team and his family to successfully complete his rehabilitation (Yeager & Gregiore, 2000).

Resolving financial stressors was a remarkable issue in this case. Initially, William's wife assumed the responsibility for this process. However, the social worker arranged for a case conference with William's employer, William, his wife, and his attorney. Setting the process into motion led to a quick and fair settlement rather than a prolonged court hearing. Prior to this conference, William was asked with his family to establish concrete, precise indicators of changes for themselves. This process led to the ability to clearly articulate what their needs were and what concessions the family would be willing to make to facilitate the change process.

Case Autopsy

William was able to return to his home. Today he is able to walk with the assistance of support devices. He and his family are living a modest life. William is receiving disability from his company based on agreements made in the rehabilitation facility. In this case, crisis intervention and solution-focused therapy integrated commonalities focusing on time-limited, intense interventions. Resistance was avoided through the presentation of alternative realities. William made his choice to continue in rehabilitation, as this supported his perception of where he would like to be once discharged from the facility. He demonstrated the following resilience factors: utilization of multidisciplinary team approach, clear focus of ongoing living plans, supportive family, integrated treatment planning, utilization of problem-solving approach to address financial issues, and family cooperation.

CONCLUSION

In each of the case examples, the critical components for completion of diagnosis and development of treatment planning were addressed. Diagrams outlining characteristic symptoms associated with each disorder were also provided for an integrated overview of the critical factors associated with accurate classification. More important, this chapter provided a paradigm to clarify critical components and operational definitions and demonstrated a method to examine parameters and differences both within and among stress, crisis, Acute Stress Disorder, and PTSD.

REFERENCES

Alexander, F. (1950). *Psychosomatic medicine.* New York: Norton.

American Psychiatric Association. (2002). *Diagnostic and statistical manual of mental disorders* (4th ed., text revision). Washington, DC: Author.

Breslau, N., Davis, G. C., Andreski, P., & Peterson, E. (1991). Traumatic events and posttraumatic disorder in urban population young adults. *Archives of General Psychiatry, 48,* 216–222.

Cannon, W. B. (1927). A laboratory course in physiology. Cambridge, MA: Harvard University Press.

Chrousos, G. P., & Gold, P. W. (1992). The concepts of stress and stress system disorders: Overview of physical and behavioral homeostasis. *Journal of the American Medical Association, 267,* 1244–1252.

Corcoran J., & Roberts, A. R. (2000). Research on crisis intervention and recommendations for further research. In A. R. Roberts (Ed.), *Crisis intervention handbook: Assessment, treatment and research* (2nd ed., pp. 453–486). New York: Oxford University Press.

Dohrenwend, B. S., & Dohrenwend, B. P. (Eds.). (1974). *Stressful life events: Their nature and effects.* New York: Wiley.

de Shazer, S. (1985). *Keys to solution in brief therapy.* New York: Norton.

Eaton, Y., & Ertl, B. (2000). The Comprehensive Crisis Intervention Model of Community Integration, Inc. Crisis Services. In A. R. Roberts (Ed.), *Crisis intervention handbook: Assessment, treatment, and research* (2nd ed., pp. 373–387). New York: Oxford University Press.

Eaton, Y., & Roberts, A. R. (2002). Frontline Crisis Intervention: Step-by-Step Practice Guidelines with Case Applications. In A. R. Roberts and G. J. Greene (Eds). *Social Workers' Desk Reference* (pp. 89–96). New York: Oxford University Press.

Everly, G. S., & Mitchell, J. T. (1999). *Critical incident stress management: A new era and standard of care in crisis intervention* (2nd ed.). Ellicott City, MD: Chevron.

Everly, G., Lating, J., Mitchell, J. (2000). Innovation in group crisis intervention: Critical incident stress debriefing and critical incident stress management. In A. Roberts (Eds.) *Crisis intervention handbook: Assessment, treatment, and research* (2nd ed., pp. 77–97). New York: Oxford University Press.

Friedman, M., & Rosenman, R. (1972). "Alteration of Type A behavior and its effect on cardiac recurrences in post myocardial infarct patients. *Advances in Mind-Body Medicine, 17*(1), 12.

Haddy, R. I., & Clover, R. D. (2001). The biological processes in psychological stress. *Journal of Collaborative Family Healthcare, 19*(3), 291–299.

Holmes, T. H., & Rahe, R. H. (1967). Social adjustment rating scale. *Journal of Psychosomatic Research, 11*, 213–218.

Kaplan, H. I., & Sadock, B. J. (1998). *Synopsis of psychiatry: Behavioral sciences, clinical psychiatry* (8th ed.). New York: Lippincott Williams & Wilkins.

Lerner, M. D., & Shelton, R. D. (2001). *Acute traumatic stress management: Addressing emergent psychological needs during traumatic events.* Commack, NY: American Academy of Experts in Traumatic Stress.

Lewis, S., & Roberts, A. R. (2002). Crisis assessment tools: The good, the bad and the available. *Brief Treatment and Crisis Intervention, 1*, 17–28.

Lewis, S., & Roberts, A. R. (2002). Crisis assessment tools. In A. R. Roberts & G. J. Greene (Eds.), *Social workers' desk reference* (pp. 208–212). New York: Oxford University Press.

Mason, J. W. (1975). A historical view of the stress field. *Journal of Human Stress, 1*, 6–27.

McEwen, B. S. (1995). Stressful experience, brain and emotions: Developmental, genetic and hormonal influences. In M. S. Gazzanga (Ed.), *The cognitive neurosciences* (pp. 1117–1138). Cambridge, MA: MIT Press.

McGee R. K. (1974). *Crisis intervention in the community.* Baltimore: University Park Press.

Mitchell, J., & Everly, G. (1993). *Critical Incident Stress Debriefing: An operations manual for the prevention of traumatic stress among emergency services and disaster workers.* Ellicott City, MD: Chevron.

Powell, L. H., & Matthews, K. A. (2002). New directions in understanding the link between stress and health in women. *International Journal of Behavioral Medicine, 9*(3), 173.

Regehr, C. (2001). Crisis debriefing groups for emergency responders: Reviewing the evidence. *Brief Treatment and Crisis Intervention, 1*(2), 87–100.

Roberts, A. R. (1990). An overview of crisis theory and crisis intervention. In A. R. Roberts (Ed.), *Crisis intervention handbook* (pp. 3–16). Belmont, CA: Wadsworth.

Roberts, A. (1991). *Contemporary perspectives on crisis intervention and prevention.* Englewood Cliffs, NJ: Prentice-Hall.

Roberts, A. R. (Ed.). (1995). *Crisis intervention and time-limited cognitive treatment.* Thousand Oaks, CA: Sage.

Roberts, A. R. (Ed.). (2000a). *Crisis intervention handbook: Assessment, treatment, and research* (2nd ed.). New York: Oxford University Press.

Roberts, A. R. (2000b). An overview of crisis theory and crisis intervention. In A. R. Roberts (Ed.), *Crisis intervention handbook: Assessment, treatment, and research* (2nd ed., pp. 3–30). New York: Oxford University Press.

Roberts, A. R. (2002). Assessment, crisis intervention and trauma treatment: The integrative ACT intervention model. *Brief Treatment and Crisis Intervention, 2*, 10.

Selye, H. (1956). *The stress of life.* New York: McGraw-Hill.

Slaikeu, K. A. (1984). *Crisis intervention: A handbook for practice and research*. Needham Heights, MA: Allyn & Bacon.

Swanson, W. C., & Carbon, J. B. (1989). Crisis intervention: Theory and technique. In *Taskforce report of the American Psychiatric Association: Treatments of psychiatric disorders*. Washington, DC: American Psychiatric Association Press.

Terr, L. (1994). Unchained memories: *True stories of traumatic memories, lost and found*. New York: Basic Books.

Wixen, H. (1978, October–November). Lesson in living. *Modern Maturity*, 8–10.

Yeager, K. R., & Gregiore, T. K. (2000). Crisis intervention application for brief solution-focused therapy in addictions. In A. R. Roberts (Ed.), *Crisis intervention handbook: Assessment, treatment and research* (2nd ed., pp. 275–306). New York: Oxford University Press.

Young M.A. (1995). Crisis response teams in the aftermath of disasters. In A. R. Roberts (Ed.), *Crisis intervention and time limited cognitive treatment* (pp. 151–187). Thousand Oaks, CA: Sage.

5

Crisis Intervention for Persons Diagnosed With Clinical Disorders Based on the Stress-Crisis Continuum

ANN WOLBERT BURGESS
ALBERT R. ROBERTS

All mental health professionals, including crisis clinicians, will benefit from applying our seven-level stress-crisis continuum. By determining the level and category that the person in crisis presents with, clinicians will be in an optimal position to determine whether crisis intervention, cognitive-behavioral therapy, medication, inpatient hospitalization, or other treatment modalities are appropriate. This chapter delineates and discusses a stress-crisis continuum consisting of seven levels to be used in conjunction with persons diagnosed with clinical disorders. Burgess and Roberts's first two levels are identified as somatic distress–crisis and transitional stress–crisis. In both, the stress symptomatology is usually reduced with brief crisis intervention and primary mental health care treatment. Levels 3, 4, and 5 seem to have occurred with increasing frequency during the 1990s. Individuals suffering from level 3 (traumatic stress–crisis) benefit from individual and group crisis-oriented therapy; level 4 (family crises) benefits from case management, and crisis treatment with forensic intervention; level 5 (mentally ill persons in crisis) benefits from crisis intervention, case monitoring, and day treatment; level 6 (psychiatric emergencies) benefits from crisis stabilization, hospitalization, and/or legal intervention; and level 7 (catastrophic traumatic stress crises) involves multiple successive traumatic events in combination with level 4, 5, or 6 stressor and requires crisis stabilization, grief counseling, social support, and symptom resolution. A rapid escalation of level 7 clients took place in the months and years right after the September 11, 2001, mass terrorist attacks. The application of Burgess and Roberts's stress-crisis continuum can optimize treatment planning, symptom reduction, and cost-effective outcomes in the context of a managed care health system.

Managed care is emerging as the dominant model of care as we begin the twenty-first century, and mental health practice is envisioned as a system based on principles of management and competition. Feldman (1992) asserts that managed mental health care systems have a great potential to save insurance carriers money by reducing inpatient stays and purchasing therapists' treatment more cost-effectively. Lazarus (1995) points out that an important component in preparing for practice in an era of managed competition is a continuum-of-care model that matches treatment modality with severity of symptoms.

If it is true that history repeats itself, writes Arthur Lazarus (1994), then it is no accident that some managed mental health care programs of the 1990s resemble community mental health practice in the 1960s and 1970s. Prevention, outreach, team care, and case management are crucial to the operation of managed care programs, just as they were to community mental health. Treatment protocols indicate a resurgence of group and family therapy with individual counseling, strongly resembling that provided in community mental health centers: brief, symptom focused, and crisis oriented (Lazarus, 1994).

As we enter the twenty-first century, legislators, policy makers, and health care administrators have an intensified interest in issues related to the quality of patient care, patterns of utilization of services, costs, and benefits. Every day, millions of individuals and families experience acute crisis episodes. These individuals are not able to resolve their crises on their own; as a result, many seek help from a mental health professional in their community.

We believe that to compete in the managed mental health care arena, crisis intervention will be a critical component. To practice crisis intervention requires a theoretical conceptualization of the stress-crisis continuum, the assessment and classification of levels of stress-crisis, and an empirical basis to the interventions.

Patricia Kelley confronts the challenge of the managed care world and narrative constructivist psychotherapy (1998). She notes that as managed care pushes for time-limited treatment, DSM-IV diagnosis, concrete problem definition, specific goals, and preapproved treatment plans based on evidence-based outcome models, the constructivist therapies seem at odds with the approach. Such therapies are based on a world that is nonlinear, denies the possibility of objectivity, and holds multiple views of reality with no fixed truths. Kelley argues for optimism and outlines ways to improve the fit between narrative therapy and managed care.

This chapter presents a classification paradigm for assessing emotional stress and acute crisis episodes in terms of seven levels that fall along a stress-crisis continuum. This classification is an adaptation and expansion of

Baldwin's (1978) crisis classification. The seven levels are somatic distress, transitional stress, traumatic stress–crisis, family crises, serious mental illness, psychiatric emergencies, and catastrophic/cumulative crises (see Baldwin's Table 2.1). With advancement from level 1 to level 7, the internal conflicts of the client become more serious and chronic.

For example, the closing case in this chapter illustrates cumulative levels of ongoing stress and crises that interact with a somatic distress and traumatic event: the diagnosis of HIV. The woman was an adopted child (transitional stress), and her sexual identity (transitional stress) was also an issue for her over the years. Much of her substance abuse and suicidal intent (psychiatric emergency) numbed her confusion over developmental issues, including her employment disruption (transition stress) and physical assaults with female partners (transitional stress–crisis). The male patient assault (traumatic stress–crisis) precipitated her involvement in the legal system (transitional stress). Her HIV-positive status (somatic and traumatic event) remains her most immediate precursor to a series of acute crisis episodes.

Each of the seven types of crisis is presented with defining characteristics and suggested treatment modalities consistent with the managed mental health care objective of cost-effective and time-efficient clinical care. Cost-effectiveness measures of managed mental health and substance abuse services should be based on clearly delineated and measurable parameters. For example, what specific behavioral measures will indicate functional improvement of client groups receiving "x" number of crisis intervention sessions? Equally important from the insurance company's perspective is whether a client's improvement is predictable and within the guaranteed claim allowance or, ideally below, current claim costs.

THEORETICAL FRAMEWORK

The clearest framework for the description of a psychological/biological stress continuum is the model reported by the Institute of Medicine study of stress and human health (Elliot & Eisdorfer, 1982). There are three primary elements in the model, the activators/stressors, the reactions, and the consequences, which can be referred to as the "x-y-z sequence" (Elliot & Eisdorfer, 1982). Activators/stressors, which are the focus of this typology, may be internal or external events or conditions—such as depressive symptoms, a serious illness, death of a family member, violent crime victimization, child abuse, recurring psychosis, or a suicide attempt—that are sufficiently intense to evoke some change in the individual. Reactions include both biological and psychosocial responses to the activator/stressor. Consequences are the prolonged and cumulative effects of the reactions, such as physical and/or mental distress. The model attends to individual differences and variations throughout the sequence through its conceptualization of mediators, which are the filters and modifiers in the sequence (Elliot & Eisdorfer, 1982). Added to the model are interventions designed to reduce stress and symptomatology between reactions and consequences. This model suggests a dynamic, interactive process across the stress continuum between an individual and the environment (Lowery, 1987, p. 42).

Burgess and Roberts's (1995) stress-crisis continuum is an eclectic classification developed in 1995 and expanded from earlier models (Baldwin, 1978; Elliot & Eisdorfer, 1982).

LEVEL 1: SOMATIC DISTRESS

Case Example

Mrs. Gardner, a 30-year-old widow, was admitted to a psychiatric unit with numerous physical complaints, including urinary incontinence, nausea, generalized pain, and dizziness. The patient was about to be married for the second time and experienced severe symptoms while writing wedding invitations. Her fiancé's brother had been killed suddenly in an automobile accident while working at his job on the railroad several weeks before the patient's admission. This death was similar to that of the patient's first husband, who was killed in an automobile accident 1 year after their marriage. As a child, the patient had enuresis frequently until age 7. Although the diagnosis of multiple sclerosis was ruled out at this admission, this diagnosis might still show up in later years.

Initially, Mrs. Gardner showed no distress over her symptoms. She was able to give up the catheter when other patients exerted negative reinforcement for this behavior. After this milieu intervention, Mrs. Gardner was able to control her own urine. She concurrently began to talk to the psychiatric nurse about her fear of losing her fiancé as she had lost her first husband, which was causing her to fear another marriage. The nurse helped the patient connect this dynamic understanding to the multiple somatic symptoms she experienced prior to admission, especially the urinary incontinence. Mrs. Gardner was discharged with no recurrence of the symptoms. She and her second husband continued attending couples counseling on an outpatient basis after their marriage.

Such crises are defined by somatic distress resulting from (a) a biomedical disease and/or (b) minor psychiatric symptoms. The mental health issue may or may not be clearly identified. Examples of this type of crisis precipitant include biomedical diagnoses such as cancer, stroke, diabetes, and lupus, as well as minor psychiatric states such as somatization, depression, and phobia or anxiety. The patient's response to this level of stress-crisis is generally anxiety and/or depressive symptoms. The etiology of the crisis is biomedical, that is, there is generally an immune system suppression, a physical health disequilibrium, or, in minor psychiatric symptomatology, an unresolved dynamic issue.

Primary care providers generally see this type of somatic stress–crisis. Physical health symptoms bring the patient to a physician or nurse-practitioner. A physical examination with laboratory testing can generally identify patients with a clear medical diagnosis. Those patients without a biomedical diagnosis may move into the first group at a later time with additional physical symptoms.

Patients without a confirmed medical diagnosis may report physical complaints ranging from a specific set of pain symptoms related to the head, back, abdomen, joints, or chest, or pain during menstruation or intercourse; gastrointestinal symptoms such as bloating, nausea, vomiting; sexual symptoms; and pseudoneurological symptoms such as body weakness, loss of sensation, fatigue, and impaired concentration (American Psychiatric Association, 1994). In the case example, Mrs. Gardner had serious physical symptoms that were connected, in part, to an unresolved grief issue.

Both patients with and without a medical diagnosis can respond with minor psychiatric symptoms of anxiety and depression. Mechanic (1994) argues for a close connection between physical and mental health care in an integrated system in order to address the common comorbidities between physical and mental disorders. That is, a medical diagnosis of cancer or diabetes can easily increase a person's stress level leading to the development of depressive symptoms.

Research

Approximately half of all mental health care is provided by the general medical sector (Regier, Narrow, Rae et al., 1993). Studies indicate that utilization of primary care ambulatory services increases with patients who present with physical symptoms with underlying psychosocial issues. These studies suggest that 40 to 60% of all visits involve symptoms for which no biomedical disease can be detected (Barsky, 1981; Van der Gaag & Van de Ven, 1978). Bodily symptoms or negative mood may result from stress and/or psychosocial problems.

The prevalence of depressive symptomatology in primary care patients ranges from 3.4 to 5.4% (Hoeper, Nyez, Cleary et al. 1979; Barrott, Barrott, Oxman et al., 1988) compared with 4% for major depressive disorder (Blacker, Clare, & Thomas, 1979). Perez-Stable and colleagues (1990) found depression prevalent not only in medical patients but especially in the disadvantaged public sector.

Untreated minor psychiatric symptoms can be costly for a primary care facility. When patients with negative laboratory results complain of vague somatic symptoms, they may be referred to as *somatizers*. Miranda and colleagues (1991) examined the prediction from Mechanic's (1994) attribution theory of somatization that somatizers who are under stress will overuse ambulatory medical services. As hypothesized, life stress interacted with somatization in predicting number of medical visits; somatizers who were under stress made more visits to the clinics than did nonsomatizers or somatizers who were not under stress. Although stress affected somatizers most, stress was predictive of increased medical utilization for all patients. These results suggest that psychological services intended to reduce overutilization of outpatient medical services might be best focused on stress reduction and be most beneficial to somatizers and persons with negative mood states.

The etiology of stress and medical illness is being studied in the stress/immune response research (Lowery, 1987). One program of research that addresses the stress-illness linkages by examining central arousal, immune changes, and clinical outcomes, albeit with different populations, is the work of Levy and colleagues. In a series of studies Levy et al. (1987, 1990) found that breast cancer patients who were rated as less well adjusted to their illness, that is, expressing more distress, had lower levels of natural killer (NK) cell activity than did patients who were less distressed. Moreover, lower NK activity was associated with cancer spread to the axillary lymph nodes. In a sample of healthy individuals (Levy et al., 1991), younger subjects (18 to 29 years of age) who reported more perceived stress were more likely to have lower NK activity and lower levels of plasma beta endorphins, and reported more infectious morbidity.

Intervention

Patients with a defined medical illness will be treated with medical and nursing protocols appropriate to the illness. For patients without a clear medical diagnosis, the intervention strategy is symptom reduction, which requires the use of brief self-report assessment tools to first detect psychiatric symptomatology that is distressing but does not meet criteria for the *Diagnostic and Statistical Manual* (American Psychiatric Association, 1994, DSM-IV). The early treatment of psychiatric symptomatology has been shown to reduce symptoms and interrupt the progression to major psychiatric disorder (Miranda & Munoz, 1994).

An intervention of choice in level 1 somatic distress–crisis is education. Teaching patients about their illness, symptoms, and subsequent health care has long been a priority in health care practice. The method of teaching may be self-tutorial, as in watching videotapes or reading written materials, or individually taught by a nurse or health care provider or through a group method of learning. One teaching method, described by Miranda and Munoz (1994), reports on an 8-week cognitive-behavioral course that was intended to teach patients to control negative moods. The course was similar to cognitive-behavioral therapy.

LEVEL 2: TRANSITIONAL STRESS CRISIS

Case Example

Mary, age 8, is the only child of parents who have been married 12 years. The mother indicated that it took 4 years to get pregnant with Mary. The pregnancy was complicated by a 69-pound weight gain, chronic indigestion, and a blood sugar level of 160 (the mother was told she had gestational diabetes). Mary was born at term; forceps were used because she was in the occiput-posterior head presentation (described by the mother as "sunny-side up"); the delivery was complicated by shoulder dystocia. Mary was large for gestational age, with a birth weight of 10 pounds 13 ounces. At less than 24 hours of age, Mary had a generalized tonic-clonic seizure that lasted about 10 minutes. She continued to have intermittent seizures and was treated with Valium and phenobarbital. She became seizure free, and blood workups were negative. Skull films were negative except for bilateral hematomas from the forceps. Mary was continued on phenobarbital until 8 months of age. She was off anticonvulsants from 8 months until 15 months of age. Mary also had a heart murmur.

At age 8, neuropsychological testing revealed "a pattern of deficits consistent with right hemisphere atrophy and subsequent attention deficit disorder (ADD) with mild hyperactivity." Mary's primary ADD symptoms included visual distraction, slower processing speed, perceptual-motor disorganization, and impulsive response pattern. Both parent and teacher checklists reflect a high level of attentional problems, distractibility, impulsive behavior, and moderate behavior problems in both the home and the school settings. Mary's self-esteem is high; however, her ADD symptoms create considerable learning problems, and she is at continued risk for underachievement in the classroom. Her functioning was legally determined to be a result of neonatal head trauma.

Such crises reflect stressful events that are generally anticipated and reflect life transitions over which the child or adult may or may not have substantial control. Defining characteristics of transitional stresses are that there is disruption of the anticipated developmental event or role. The stressor is generally identified; the event is developmental in nature in that many people experience it. The transition is anticipated, and time is available to prepare for the changes that occur.

Transition stresses include normative events around parenthood such as infertility or premature birth; childhood such as birth injury, hyperactivity, or illness; adolescence such as teen pregnancy or school problems; adulthood such as work disruption or chronic illness; and legal issues such as litigation. The individual's response is the development of personality trait rigidity and loss of personal flexibility. The etiology of the crisis is the failure to master developmental tasks.

The case example describes a medical problem in a normative life event of childbirth. The transition stress results from interruption and delay in the normal neurobiological development of infancy into childhood. Mary's hyperactivity and academic problems are linked to a birth injury, something she and her mother had no control over. Additionally, this injury has the capacity to compromise mastery of the developmental tasks of childhood, adolescence, and adulthood.

Erikson (1963) attributed a central or nuclear conflict to each of the eight developmental life issues. His theory further states that a relatively successful resolution of the basic conflicts associated with each level of development provides an important foundation for successful progression to the next stage. Whatever the resolution of these conflicts—mastery or failure—the result significantly influences personality development. Thus, in transitional stress, there is the potential to fail to master a developmental task.

J. S. Tyhurst (1957) studied transition states—migration and retirement—in the lives of persons experiencing sudden change during civilian disaster. Based on his field studies on individual patterns of responses to community disaster, Tyhurst identified three overlapping phases, each with its own manifestations of stress and attempts at reducing it: a period of impact, a period of recoil, and a posttraumatic period of recovery.

Intervention

There are several useful interventions for transitional stress. The primary task of the crisis counselor during time-limited individual sessions is to educate the patient to an understanding of the changes that have taken or will take place and to explore any psychodynamic implications of these changes. Support is provided as needed, and anticipatory guidance is used to help the individual plan an adaptive coping response to problems that have resulted from the transition. Crisis intervention techniques are used if the event occurs without anticipatory information.

A second intervention is the use of group approaches. Following the brief individual therapy, the client is referred to self-help groups specific to the transition issue (e.g., parents without partners, parents of children with chronic illness). Self-help groups assist those experiencing a similar life transition (e.g., preretirement groups, childbirth preparation groups, group approaches to college orientation).

LEVEL 3: TRAUMATIC STRESS CRISIS

Case Example

Carol had been on maternity leave for 2 months and needed to return to work. She was a single parent who also had a 4-year-old boy and a 7-year-old girl, and she depended on the income she made as an assistant manager at a local restaurant, where she had worked for the past 5 years. Carol placed an ad for a baby-sitter in the newspaper. A woman called about the ad, set up an appointment, and the next day came to the house for an interview. Carol could not be there, so she had her mother come to the house to talk with the woman. The woman introduced herself to Carol's mother, who was holding the month-old baby. She seemed like a pleasant, competent woman and was well dressed. She said she didn't need the money but wanted to spend her time doing something she enjoyed. She said she had two teenage children of her own but missed taking care of an infant. Carol's mother wanted to see how she held a baby, so she handed the baby to the woman. At that moment the telephone rang, and Carol's mother went to the other room to answer it. As soon as she was out of sight, the woman left the house and drove off with the baby. When Carol's mother returned to the room, no one was there. She ran to the door just as the woman was driving away.

Carol's mother immediately called the police, who arrived within 5 minutes. Carol arrived shortly after and was told of her baby's kidnapping. She was devastated and at first blamed her mother. After this incident, Carol's mother began having nightmares and couldn't sleep. Carol, who could barely function, had to send the other children to their father's house to live temporarily.

The news media were immediately involved, and 4 days later the baby was recovered through a tip to a hotline. The abductor's husband's work associates had visited the baby and were suspicious when they noted it did not look like a newborn. They had heard the media announcement about the kidnapping and called the hot line. The abductor was a master's-prepared psychotherapist who had faked a pregnancy as a way to halt divorce proceedings. She pled guilty and spent 1 year in a psychiatric hospital plus 4 years on probation.

Such crises are precipitated by strong, externally imposed stresses. They involve experiencing, witnessing, or learning about a sudden, unexpected, and uncontrollable life-threatening event that overwhelms the individual. Other examples of traumatic crises include crime-related victimization of personal assault, rape, and sexual assault, arson, or hostage taking; victimization by natural disaster; being the victim of a serious vehicular accident or plane crash; sudden death of a partner or family member; accidents with physical dismemberment; and receiving a life-threatening medical diagnosis such as cancer. One of the most recent traumatic stress–crises events was the right-wing terrorist truck bombing of the federal office building in Oklahoma City in which 82 men, women, and children died. The trauma, stress, and crisis reactions of the hundreds of survivors and family members of the deceased will be remembered for years. The community was totally united, and hundreds of caring citizens came to the aid and support of the survivors. In addition, the FBI quickly mobilized and apprehended the two terrorists responsible for the bombing.

The individual's response in the midst of a disaster or traumatic event is intense fear, helplessness, and behavior disorganization. Usual coping behaviors are rendered ineffective due to the sudden, unanticipated nature of the stress. There may be a refractory period during which the person experiences emotional paralysis and coping behaviors cannot be mobilized.

In the case example, the infant's grandmother directly experienced the abduction by offering the infant to the abductor to hold and then leaving the room to answer a telephone call. The infant's mother experienced the trauma by learning about the abduction when she returned home. The women were unable to process the information about the trauma, and thus the dysfunctional symptoms developed. Until the infant was returned, the mother and grandmother were unable to cope with daily activities.

Research

Lindemann and his associates at Massachusetts General Hospital introduced the concepts of crisis intervention and time-limited treatment in 1943 in the aftermath of Boston's worst nightclub fire, at the Coconut Grove, in which 493 people perished. Lindemann (1944) and colleagues based their crisis theory on their observations of the acute and delayed reactions of survivors and grief-stricken relatives of victims. Their clinical work focused on the psychological symptoms of the survivors and on preventing unresolved grief among relatives of the persons who had died. They found that many individuals experiencing acute grief often had five related reactions: somatic distress, preoccupation with the image of the deceased, guilt, hostile reactions, and loss of patterns of conduct.

Furthermore, Lindemann and colleagues concluded that the duration of a grief reaction appears to be dependent on the success with which the bereaved person does his or her mourning and "grief work." In general, this grief work refers to achieving emancipation from the deceased, readjusting to the changes in the environment from which the loved one is missing, and developing new relationships. People need to be encouraged to permit themselves to have a period of mourning and eventual acceptance of the loss and adjustment to life without the deceased. If the normal process of grieving is delayed, negative outcomes will develop.

In the 1970s, the trauma of rape was introduced into the literature through the term "rape trauma syndrome" (Burgess & Holmstrom, 1974). Rape trauma consists of an acute phase of disorganization followed by a longterm phase of reorganization. A wide range of somatic, cognitive, psychological, and social symptoms are noted in both phases.

The trauma suffered by the victim affects her family, her social network, and the community. Recovery from rape is complex and influenced by many factors, including prior life stress, style of attack, relationship of victim and offender, number of assailants, pre-existing psychiatric disorders, the amount of violence or the sexual acts demanded, and postrape factors of institutional response to the victim, social network response, and subsequent victimization. Clinicians should consider all these factors in assessing and identifying victims who are at high risk for slow recovery from rape and who will remain vulnerable to many life stresses for a long time.

The pioneering work of Charles R. Figley and members of the Consortium on Veteran Studies (Figley, 1978) provides insight into the level 3 crisis of war combat. Figley suggests that combat includes four major elements that make it highly traumatic: a high degree of dangerousness, a sense of helplessness in preventing death, a sense of destruction and disruption, in both lives and property, and a sense of loss. Moreover, the long-term emotional adjustment to combat follows four stages: recovery, avoidance, reconsideration, and adjustment.

Intervention

Crisis reaction refers to the acute stage, which usually occurs soon after the hazardous event and includes the neurobiology of trauma. During this phase, the person's acute reaction may take various forms, including helplessness, confusion, anxiety, shock, disbelief, and anger. Low self-esteem and serious depression are often produced by the crisis state. The person in crisis may appear to be incoherent, disorganized, agitated, and volatile or calm, subdued, withdrawn, and apathetic. It is during this period that the individual is often most willing to seek help, and crisis intervention is usually most effective at this time (Golan, 1978).

Tyhurst recommended a stage-specific intervention. He concluded that persons in a traumatic crisis state should not be removed from their life situation, and intervention should focus on bolstering the network of relationships.

Cognitive-behavioral therapy to assist in the information processing of trauma (Burgess & Hartman, 1997) is a treatment recommended for rape-related posttraumatic stress disorder and depression. Also termed *cognitive processing therapy* (Resick & Mechanic, 1995), this treatment is time-limited and effective. Other modalities to consider include pharmacotherapy with antianxiety medication to help with the longterm physiological symptoms of posttraumatic stress disorder. In addition and/or following individual trauma work, patients are referred for stress reduction/relaxation treatment, crisis or self-help groups, and psychoeducation groups.

Strategic solution-focused therapy (Quick, 1998) combines the principles and techniques of strategic therapy and solution-focused therapy. In this approach, the therapist clarifies problems, elaborates solutions, identifies and evaluates attempted solutions, and designs interventions that include validation, compliment, and suggestion components. The pragmatic principle of doing what works and changing what is not working is the goal for both the client and the therapist. See chapter 3 for detailed information.

A promising therapeutic technique designed by Francine Shapiro, eye movement desensitization and reprocessing (EMDR), incorporates key aspects of many of the major therapeutic modalities. The basic underlying principles derive from an information-processing model that aims to directly access and process dysfunctional perceptions that were stored in memory at the time of the traumatic event. The state-dependent perceptions are considered primary to the development of posttraumatic stress symptoms. Additional, rigid thoughts are assumed to be caused by earlier life experiences that are dysfunctionally stored. The primary goal of EMDR is to release clients from the nonadaptive bonds of the past, thereby providing them with the ability to make positive and flexible choices in the present. Current research on EMDR substantiates its ability to rapidly and effectively process the targeted event and attendant traumatic information. The eight phases of treatment are considered necessary to resolve the trauma (Shapiro, 1998).

LEVEL 4: FAMILY CRISIS

Case Example

Meredith, age 23, first met Willis, age 29, when he came to the apartment she shared with a roommate hairdresser, to have a haircut. According to Willis, they felt an instant chemistry, and they began dating. From the beginning they isolated themselves from others, and when Meredith and her roommate parted, Willis asked Meredith to move in with him. Meredith ignored a nagging internal warning that this was not a good decision. For example, on their first date, Willis showed Meredith, a mental health counselor, his psychiatric record. She later said his diagnosis should have been a red flag to her: borderline personality disorder with antisocial, dependent, and passive-aggressive features. He also had a history of a drinking problem.

Willis believed he had found his future marriage partner; Meredith did not. After several months, she met another man she wanted to date and told Willis, whose reaction was worse than she imagined. He became depressed and began cutting himself and leaving blood on tissues around the apartment and writing "I love you" in blood on the wall. He begged her not to leave.

As Meredith began dating her new boyfriend, Willis obtained his address and telephone number. He began to write threatening letters. The boyfriend ended the relationship by leaving town. Willis continued to mail Meredith notes and greeting cards, pleading with her and then berating her. Detectives told Willis they could not arrest him, since his letters had been written before the new state stalking law took effect. They suggested he enter a psychiatric hospital.

Meredith left town, but within months Willis located her. She found a balloon and get-well card taped to her car and noticed two holes in the front windows of her apartment. When police arrested Willis, they found a stun gun, rope, latex gloves, duct tape, and a pocketknife in his car. He pled no contest to his 16-month obsession with his ex-girlfriend.

Some emotional crises result from attempts to deal with primary interpersonal situations that develop within the family or social network (e.g., relational dysfunction). These relate back to developmental tasks and level 2 transitional crisis. If unresolved, the family crises reflect a struggle with a deeper, but usually circumscribed, developmental issue that has not been resolved adaptively in the past and that represents an attempt to attain emotional maturity. These crises usually involve developmental issues such as dependency, value conflicts, sexual identity, emotional intimacy, power issues, or attaining self-discipline. Often a repeated pattern of specific relationship difficulties occurs over time in those presenting with this type of crisis (Baldwin, 1978). The crisis may be directed internally or externally, as in chronic abuse.

Examples of family crises include child abuse, the use of children in pornography, parental abductions, adolescent runaways, battering and rape, homelessness, and domestic homicide. The individual's response to this level of crisis is chronic fear, an inability to protect the self and others, and a type of learned helplessness. The etiology of the crisis relates to the neurobiology of chronic trauma. There is often undisclosed relationship abuse and divided family loyalty.

In the case example, the potential dangerousness of the male partner, Willis, is clearly noted. His psychiatric diagnosis of personality disorder suggests an unresolved developmental power issue as noted by his stalking.

Research

It is important to note that every type of emotional crisis involves an interaction of an external stressor and a vulnerability of the individual. However, it is in level 4 crisis that there is a shift from a primarily external locus of stress that produces the crisis to an internal locus determined by the psychodynamics of the individual and/or preexisting psychopathology that becomes manifest in problem situations. Child abuse and battering within a domestic violence context are prime examples of family crises. Both are interpersonal situations that exist around long-term relationships. See chapter 20 for a review of the research on child abuse and crisis intervention.

Intervention

In family violence, the goals of intervention in level 4 crises are to help individuals restabilize their lives, strengthen their interpersonal relationships, and deter psychiatric symptomatology. First the crisis state, if there is one, must be resolved. All abuse must cease, and children and adults must be safe. The survivors must adapt to immediate losses and changes created by the disclosure of abuse and the protective response by others. The dysfunction in the family system must be addressed.

Roberts's (1995, 1996) seven-step crisis intervention model is implemented. This model offers an integrated problem-solving approach to crisis resolution. The steps include assessing lethality and safety needs; establishing rapport and communication; identifying the major problems; dealing with feelings and providing support; exploring possible alternatives; assisting in formulating an action plan; and conducting follow-up.

Recovery services are to aid survivors in resolving the long-term issues. Stress reduction interventions are of two types: (a) those designed to help the individual prevent or manage stress, and (b) those aimed at eliminating or reducing the potency of the stressor. Techniques to consider include physical activity to discharge repressed energy; nutrition therapy to enhance physiological recovery; spiritual support for persons who value religious beliefs to promote a sense of integrity with the natural world; relaxation to counter hypervigilance; pleasure activities to promote a sense of fun and humor; and expressive activities such as reading, art, and music.

A variety of psychoeducational and therapeutic interventions have been developed to change perpetrator behavior, many of which have produced an actual decrease in violent or exploitive behavior. Generally, interventions include components designed to increase the knowledge and skills of the perpetrator with regard to anger control, mediation, communication, and family roles. See chapter 8 on domestic violence interventions.

Group models are often helpful. For example, narrative theory provides a useful framework for brief group treatment of persons in crisis because it proposes that understanding of experience is gained through social discourse. Groups offer persons in crisis a new context for attributing meaning to critical events (Laube, 1998).

LEVEL 5: SERIOUS MENTAL ILLNESS

Case Example

Mrs. Dee, age 32, was referred to the mental health clinic by her case manager. When she arrived, clinging to her were her four children: Doddy (age 2), Bryant (age 3), Katie (age 5), and Sally (age 6). The children were unkempt and waiflike. Mrs. Dee, chain-smoking cigarettes, stated that she wanted some Valium for her nerves. Mrs. Dee lives in the project with her husband, Jim. She and her family (namely, three sisters, a younger brother, father, and mother) have been known to the multiservice health center for more than 15 years. Mrs. Dee, upon questioning, revealed that she felt things were just getting to be too much this morning, and she decided to call her case manager. Although she did not describe herself as depressed, questioning revealed that she was hearing voices telling her not to eat because the food was poisoned. She had lost 20 pounds in the last month, and her sleeping was erratic because she felt the neighbors were able to see through her walls. She, as well as the children, looked emaciated. Although the children clung to their mother, she seemed to ignore them.

Three months earlier, Mrs. Dee had had a hysterectomy. She was upset with the home care she received after the surgery. She had been promised homemaker services, but when the homemakers came to the apartment, they quit the next day, which she attributed to the fact that they were Black and she was White Irish. A month later she got into a row with her father, who was an alcoholic. Her husband, who was out of work, was at home most of the day or out playing baseball. During this time, her three sisters were in and out of her apartment, as was her brother. All her siblings were on drugs or were drinking. Two sisters had children and presently the state was stepping in to remove the children from their mothers because of neglect and multiple injuries that could not be accounted for.

Shortly after her return home from the hospital after the hysterectomy, Mrs. Dee slashed her wrists. She was taken to an emergency ward, where her wrists were stitched. She refused to talk to a psychiatrist. Homemaker help was sent to her house, but she refused to let the homemaker enter her house. She did develop a relationship with a nurse, and she recounted a life full of struggle. Her first child was born when she was 16. She married 2 years later and had another child, followed by a divorce, then marriage to her present husband and two more children. She had difficulty with her husband, who often beat her. During this time a social worker came to the house, and eventually all these children were placed in a home and later were given up for adoption. Thus, Mrs. Dee forbade any investigation into the records at this time for fear her present four children would be taken away. She claimed that she had been abused by the authorities and that her children were removed from her against her will. The current stressor of the hysterectomy and its unresolved meaning reactivated underlying psychotic symptoms and heightened the multiproblem nature of this family.

Such crises reflect serious mental illness in which preexisting problems have been instrumental in precipitating the crisis. Or the situation may involve a state in which the severity of the illness significantly impairs or complicates adaptive resolution. There is often an unidentified dynamic issue.

Other examples of serious mental illness include diagnoses of psychosis, dementia, bipolar depression, and schizophrenia. The patient response will be disorganized thinking and behavior. The etiology is neurobiological.

The case example indicates that Mrs. Dee was experiencing perceptual difficulties and paranoid thinking. An unresolved issue for her was related to the hysterectomy and the psychological meaning of the end to her childbearing.

Intervention

The clinician needs to be able to diagnose the mental illness and adapt the intervention approach to include appreciation of the personality or characterological aspects of the patient. Persons with long-term and recurring severe mental illness require a mix of traditional medical and long-term treatments that are helpful in sustaining their function and role. Roberts's (1991, 1995, 1996) crisis intervention model may be used to reduce symptoms in an acute crisis.

The crisis therapist responds primarily in terms of the present problem of the patient, with an emphasis on problem-solving skills and environmental manipulation. The therapist gives support but is careful not to produce or reinforce dependency or regression by allowing the therapeutic process to become diffuse. The therapist acknowledges the deeper problems of the client and assesses them to the degree possible within the crisis intervention context, but does not attempt to resolve problems representing deep emotional conflict. Through the process of crisis intervention, the patient is helped to stabilize functioning to the fullest extent possible and is prepared for referral for other services once the process has been completed.

Case monitoring and management are indicated, as well as an assessment for inpatient hospitalization or sheltered care. Medication will be needed for psychotic thinking. Continuity of care is critical with this level of crisis and is generally accomplished through the case manager. Other services should include referral for vocational training and group work.

LEVEL 6: PSYCHIATRIC EMERGENCIES

Case Example

Mr. Mars, age 65, was admitted to a psychiatric unit following a suicide attempt. According to his history, he had two older sisters and several older half siblings. His mother, who had glaucoma, died in her 90s of a cause unknown to the patient; his father died at age 66 of prostate cancer. Mr. Mars described himself as the "bully" in his family and felt distanced from siblings and parents.

Mr. Mars enlisted in the Marine Corps after high school and served in World War II combat. After the war, he returned home and worked 20 years as a truck driver, then for 8 years as a prison guard. He and his wife had no children. Prior to his diagnosis of diabetes, he drank beer regularly and enjoyed the company of his tavern friends. He had many interests prior to his work retirement, belonging to community groups, the Marine Corps League, and the VFW, and he was chairman of his church picnic.

Mr. Mars was first hospitalized at age 48 with complaints of inability to sleep, no interest in work, suicide ideation, thoughts of wanting to hurt his wife, a peculiar preoccupation with numbers, lack of appetite, and weight loss. His recent diagnosis was diabetes mellitus, which was seen as a precipitant to the depression. He was diagnosed with psychotic depressive reaction and treated with Elavil, Trilafon, and group therapy and discharged after 6 weeks. Mr. Mars continued outpatient counseling and pharmacotherapy for a year. Counseling notes indicate he discussed his contemplated suicide at the time of hospitalization, displayed no insight into his condition, regretted not having children, always worked hard, had little communication with his wife, talked on a very superficial level, and had passive aggressive behavior (e.g., waiting weeks to get even for a perceived wrong).

Mr. Mars's history of medical problems included diabetes, high blood pressure, and glaucoma. He had a transurethral resection of the prostate for a benign condition. His second psychiatric hospitalization occurred following the laceration of his left wrist and arm, which required surgical correction. On admission, he stated, "I wanted to end it all . . . too many things in too little time." That evening he had eaten dinner around 6 P.M. and had a graham cracker snack at 10 P.M. While his wife was at choir practice, he cut his arm several times with a razor blade and "held it over the bathtub hoping to pass out and die." When nothing happened, he cut his arm several more times. He said that after retiring he "couldn't enjoy it like I wanted; I'm stuck in the house and bored." His stated goals for hospitalization were to "straighten out, get better and get the hell out of here."

Mrs. Mars stated her husband did not give her any indication he was depressed or was thinking of harming himself. She had gone to choir practice, and when she returned found her husband over the bathtub with several deep lacerations; she called the ambulance. Mrs. Mars described her husband as selfish and self-serving, showing no consideration for others. She said they argued frequently and that he did not talk about his feelings. They had been married 40 years. Mrs. Mars reported that when they argued, her husband would hold a grudge and not talk to her for days.

Psychiatric emergencies involve crisis situations in which general functioning has been severely impaired. The individual is rendered incompetent, unable to assume personal responsibility, and unable to exert control over feelings and actions that he or she experiences. *There is threat or actual harm to self and/or others.*

Examples of psychiatric emergencies include drug overdose, suicide attempts, stalking, personal assault, rape, and homicide. The individual presents with a loss of personal control. The patient's level of consciousness and orientation, rationality, rage, and anxiety all affect the level of cooperation he or she may give to the immediate assessment of the need for emergency intervention.

The etiology of these crises focuses the self-abusive component to suicide attempts and drug overdoses. Aggression toward others suggests a need for dominance, control, and sexualized aggression.

The case example illustrates serious suicidal intent on the part of Mr.

Mars. Of interest is the denial by Mrs. Mars of any warning signs. By history it was learned that Mr. Mars was trying to dispense some of his money to a favorite niece when Mrs. Mars interceded. While in the hospital, he tried to run away from a group activity and into a river. Three weeks after admission, he successfully hung himself in a bathroom at 12:30 A.M., between 30-minute unit checks.

Intervention

The clinician needs to be confident in his or her skills at managing a client's out-of-control behavior and/or must have adequate assistance available (see chapter 26). When an emergency presents itself, with appropriate cooperation, questions need to be raised and answered regarding the location of the patient, exactly what the patient has done, and the availability of significant others. In the case of a suicide attempt, the clinician's immediate task, to assess the lethality of the act, is greatly aided by published lethality scales. Where medical-biological danger has been determined to exist or where sufficient data for that determination are not available, emergency medical attention is required. Dangerous and volatile situations should be handled by police and local rescue squads, who can provide rapid transportation to a hospital emergency room. Rapid medical evaluation is an essential first step in resolving a current and future suicidal crisis (Jobes & Berman, 1996).

Psychiatric emergencies are the most difficult type of crisis to manage because there may be incomplete information about the situation, the patient may be disruptive or minimally helpful, and there is an immediacy in understanding the situation in depth in order to initiate effective treatment. Patient assessment is greatly facilitated when informants with some knowledge of the precipitating events accompany the patient; in many instances they can be helpful in planning appropriate psychological and medical services (see chapters 15 and 23–27).

The basic intervention strategy for level 6 psychiatric crisis involves the following components: (a) rapidly assessing the patient's psychological and medical condition; (b) clarifying the situation that produced or led to the patient's condition; (c) mobilizing all mental health and/or medical resources necessary to effectively treat the patient; and (d) arranging for follow-up or coordination of services to ensure continuity of treatment as appropriate. It is in this type of psychiatric emergency that the skills of the crisis therapist are tested to the limit because he or she must be able to work effectively and quickly in highly charged situations and to intervene where there may be life-threatening implications of the patient's condition (Burgess & Baldwin, 1981; Burgess & Roberts, 1995).

Police or emergency medical technicians are often called to transport the patient to a hospital or jail. Medication, restraint, and/or legal intervention are all indicated for psychiatric emergencies.

LEVEL 7: CATASTROPHIC CRISIS

Case Example

A young bisexual woman in her mid-30s was admitted to a psychiatric hospital following a serious suicide attempt. A number of stressful events had occurred over a 3-month period. She began drinking heavily when her partner moved out of her apartment; she had a car accident during a snowstorm; later her car was stolen, and she began "drinking around the clock." She could not control herself and took a leave of absence from her computer analyst job. She was hospitalized briefly at the local psychiatric hospital. Three weeks after that hospitalization, one evening she was drinking with a man she met at a bar. He drove her home, and they continued drinking in her apartment. The man wanted sex, but she refused, and he forced the situation. After he left the apartment she called a friend to take her to a local hospital, where a rape examination revealed vaginal lacerations. On returning home, the woman continued drinking and, while intoxicated, slashed her wrist with a broken glass. She again called her friend, who took her back to the hospital, where she received 10 sutures; later she was transferred to the psychiatric hospital.

The next day the woman requested discharge against medical advice. She returned to her apartment and went on an extended drinking bout for another 6 weeks, during which she was also very suicidal. About the time she brought a legal suit against one of the male patients and the psychiatric hospital for simple assault, blood tests revealed that she was HIV-positive.

Level 7 has two or more level 3 traumatic crises in combination with level 4, 5, or 6 stressors. Classifying an individual into one of the preceding levels of crisis is dependent upon the nature, duration, and intensity of the stressful life event(s) and one's perception of being unable to cope and lessen the crisis. Sometimes a crisis is temporary and quickly resolved; at other times it can be life-threatening and extremely difficult to accept and resolve (e.g., having AIDS or a multiple personality disorder, or losing all family members due to a disaster).

In summary, the lack of an up-to-date classification model for determining levels of emotional crises has resulted in a significant gap to advancing the development of crisis theory. The revised and expanded Baldwin (1978) crisis typology is presented to increase communication between therapists and other crisis care providers in clinical assessment, treatment planning, and continuity of health care within a managed care context.

REFERENCES

American Psychiatric Association. (1994). *Diagnostic and statistical-manual of mental disorders* (4th ed.). Washington, DC: Author.

Baldwin, B. A. (1978). A paradigm for the classification of emotional crises: Implications for crisis intervention. *American Journal of Orthopsychiatry, 48,* 538–551.

Barrott, J. E., Barrott, J. A., Oxman,

T. et al. (1988). The prevalence of psychiatric disorders in primary care practice. *Archives of General Psychiatry, 44,* 1100–1108.

Barsky, A. J. (1981). Hidden reasons some patients visit doctors. *Annals of Internal Medicine, 94,* 492.

Burgess, A. W., & Baldwin, B. A. (1981). *Crisis intervention theory and practice.* Englewood Cliffs, NJ: Prentice-Hall.

Burgess, A. W., & Hartman, C. R. (1997). Victims of sexual assault. In A. W. Burgess (Ed.), *Psychiatric nursing: Promoting mental health* (pp. 425–437). Stamford, CT: Appleton & Lange.

Burgess, A. W., & Holmstrom, L. L. (1974). Rape trauma syndrome. *American Journal of Psychiatry, 131,* 981–986.

Burgess, A. W., & Roberts, A. R. (1995). The stress-crisis continuum. *Crisis Intervention and Time-Limited Treatment,* 2(1), 31–47.

Caplan, G. (1961). *An approach to community mental health.* New York. Grune & Stratton.

Caplan, G. (1964). *Principles of preventive psychiatry.* New York: Basic Books.

Elkin, J., Shea, T., Watkins, J., et al. (1989). National Institutes of Mental Health treatment of depression collaborative research program: General effectiveness of treatment. *Archives of General Psychiatry, 46,* 971–982.

Elliott, G. R., & Eisdorfer, C. (1982). *Stress and human health.* New York: Springer.

Enthoven, A. C. (1993). The history and principles of managed competition. *Health Affairs, 12* (suppl.), 24–28.

Escobar, J. I., Rubio-Stipec, M., Canino, G., & Karno, M. (1989). Somatic symptoms index (SSI): A new abridged somatization construct. *Journal of Nervous and Mental Disease, 177,* 140–146.

Feldman, S. (1972). *Managed mental health services.* Springfield, IL: Charles C. Thomas.

Figley, C. (1978). *Stress disorders among Vietnam veterans: Theory, research and treatment implications.* New York: Brunner/Mazel.

Golan, N. (1978). *Treatment in crisis situations.* New York: Free Press.

Hoeper, E. W., Nyez, G. R., Cleary, P. D., et al. (1979). Estimated prevalence of research diagnostic criteria mental disorders in primary medical care. *International Journal of Mental Health, 8,* 6–13.

Hollon, S. D., DeRubeis, R. J., Evans, M. D., et al. (1992). Cognitive therapy and pharmacotherapy for depression singly and in combination. *Archives of General Psychiatry, 49,* 774–781.

Jobes, D. A., & Berman A. L. (1996). Crisis assessment and time-limited intervention with high risk suicidal youth. In A. R. Roberts (Ed.), *Crisis management and brief treatment: Theory, practice and research* (pp. 53–69). Chicago: Nelson-Hall.

Kelley, P. (1998). Narrative therapy in a managed care world. *Crisis Intervention and Time-Limited Intervention, 4,* 113–123.

Laube, J. J. (1998). Crisis-oriented narrative group therapy. *Crisis Intervention and Time-Limited Treatment, 4,* 215–226.

Lazarus, A. (1994). Managed care: Lessons from community mental health. *Hospital and Community Psychiatry, 45*(4), 30–31.

Lazarus, A. (1995). Preparing for practice in an era of managed competition. *Psychiatric Services, 46*(2), 184–185.

Levy, S. M., Herberman, R. B., Whiteside, T., et al. (1990). Perceived social support and tumor estrogen/progesterone receptor status as predictors of natural killer cell activity in breast cancer cell patients. *Psychosomatic Medicine, 52*, 73–85.

Levy, S. M., Herberman, R. B., & Winkelstein, A. (1987). Natural killer cell activity in primary breast cancer patients: Social and behavioral predictors. Paper presented at the Annual Meeting of the American Society of Clinical Oncology.

Lindemann, E. (1944). Symptomotology and management of acute grief. *American Journal of Psychiatry, 101*, 141–148.

Lowery, B. (1987). Stress research: Some theoretical and methodological issues. *Image, 19*(1), 42–46.

Mechanic, D. (1994). Integrating mental health into a general health care system. *Hospital and Community Psychiatry, 45*, 893–897.

Miranda, J., & Munoz, R. (1994). Intervention for minor depression in primary care patients. *Psychosomatic Medicine, 56*, 136–142.

Miranda, J., Perez-Stable, E., Munoz, R. F., Hargreaves W., & Henke C. J. (1991). Somatization, psychiatric disorder, and stress in utilization of ambulatory medical services. *Health Psychology, 10*(1), 46–51.

Perez-Stable, E., Miranda, J., Munoz R. F., et al. (1990). Depression in medical outpatients: Underrecognition and misdiagnosis. *Archives of Internal Medicine, 150*, 1083–1088.

Quick, E. K. (1998). Strategic solution focused therapy: Doing what works in crisis intervention. *Crisis Intervention and Time-Limited Intervention, 4*, 197–214.

Regier D. A., Narrow W. E., Rae, D. S., et al. (1993). The de facto US mental and addictive disorders service system: Epidemiologic Catchment Area prospective 1-year prevalence rates of disorders and services. *Archives of General Psychiatry, 50*, 85–94.

Resick, P., & Mechanic, M. (1995). Cogitive processing therapy with rape victims. In A. R. Roberts (Ed.), *Crisis intervention and time-limited cognitive treatment* (pp. 182–198). Thousand Oaks, CA: Sage.

Roberts, A. R., (Ed.). (1991). *Contemporary perspectives on crisis intervention and prevention.* Englewood Cliffs, NJ: Prentice-Hall.

Roberts, A. R., (Ed.). (1995). *Crisis intervention and time-limited cognitive treatment.* Thousand Oaks, CA: Sage.

Roberts, A. R. (1996). The epidemiology of acute crisis in American society. In A. R. Roberts (Ed.), *Crisis management and brief treatment* (pp. 13–28). Chicago: Nelson-Hall.

Shapiro, F. (1998). Eye movement desensitization and reprocessing (EMDR): Accelerated information processing and affect-driven constructions. *Crisis Intervention and Time-Limited Interventions, 4*, 145–157.

Tyhurst J. S. (1957). The role of transition states—including disasters—in mental illness. In *Symposium on social and preventive psychiatry*. Washington, DC: Walter Reed Army Institute of Research.

Van der Gaag, J., & Van de Ven, W. (1978). The demand for primary health care. *Medical Care, 16*, 299.

II

DISASTER MENTAL HEALTH AND CRISIS INTERVENTION AND TRAUMA TREATMENT

6

The ACT Model: Assessment, Crisis Intervention, and Trauma Treatment in the Aftermath of Community Disaster and Terrorism Attacks

ALBERT R. ROBERTS

Mental health professionals woke up on September 12, 2001, to find themselves, for the most part, ill-equipped to deal with the many thousands of persons encountering psychological trauma and acute crisis episodes as a result of the horrendous murder of 2,973 people on that fateful day of September 11. Although those in the health professions were anxious to help the thousands of survivors who were experiencing shock, fear, somatic stress, trauma, anxiety, and grief in varying degrees, few if any comprehensive models for assessment, crisis intervention, or trauma treatment were in current practice. Moreover, we have now come to understand that the ongoing intense stress and fear of a nation living under the threat of likely additional terrorist attacks makes the need for crisis-oriented intervention plans imperative for all communities across the nation.

This chapter presents a conceptual three-stage framework and intervention model that should be useful in helping mental health professionals provide acute crisis and trauma treatment services. The assessment, crisis intervention, and trauma treatment model (ACT) may be thought of as a sequential set of assessments and intervention strategies. This model integrates various assessment and triage protocols with three primary crisis-oriented intervention strategies: the seven-stage crisis intervention model, critical incident stress management (CISM), and the 10-step acute traumatic stress management protocol. In addition, this chapter introduces and briefly highlights the other six practical and empirically based papers that appear in this section of the book, whose focus is on how mental health disaster management skills and crisis-oriented intervention strategies were implemented in the aftermath of the September 11, 2001, terroristic mass disaster at the World Trade Center and the Pentagon.

OVERVIEW

This section of the third edition of the *Crisis Intervention Handbook* was prepared to provide administrators, clinicians, crisis counselors, trainers, researchers, and mental health consultants with the latest theories and best crisis intervention strategies and trauma treatment practices currently available. To assist all clinicians whose clients may be in a precrisis or crisis state, 10 experts in crisis intervention or trauma treatment were invited to write or cowrite chapters for this section of the *Handbook*.

As has been widely reported, the horrific events of September 11, 2001, resulted in the loss of approximately 2,973 lives in the World Trade Center; this includes 343 Fire Department of New York fatalities, 37 Port Authority police, 23 members of the New York Police Department, 125 persons in the Pentagon, and over 300 on four hijacked airliners (National Commission on Terrorist Attacks upon the United States, 2004, p. 311). The suddenness and extreme severity of the terrorist attack, combined with the fear of additional terrorist actions that may lie ahead, serves as a wake-up call for all mental health professionals as we expand and coordinate interagency crisis response teams, crisis intervention programs, and trauma treatment resources. This chapter presents an overarching theoretical framework and intervention model that may be useful in helping mental health professionals provide crisis and trauma services.

This overview chapter is built on the premise that it is useful for counselors, psychologists, nurses, and social workers to have a conceptual framework, also known as a planning and intervention model, to improve the delivery of services for persons in a precrisis or traumatic state. The second premise is that mental health professionals need an organizing framework to determine sequentially which assessment and intervention strategies to use first, second, and third. Thus, I developed a three-part conceptual framework as a foundation model to initiate, implement, evaluate, and modify a well-coordinated crisis intervention and trauma treatment program in the aftermath of the September 11 catastrophes.

Terrorist acts of mass destruction are sudden, unexpected, dangerous, and life-threatening, affecting large groups of people and overwhelming to human adaptation and our basic coping skills. Unfortunately, as long as there are terrorists, senseless murders of innocent persons and destruction of property are likely to continue. Therefore, it is imperative that all emergency services personnel and crisis workers be trained to respond immediately and appropriately. In the aftermath of catastrophic terrorist tragedies, people experience different symptoms, including surprise, shock, denial, numbness, fear, anger, adrenal surges, caring for others, attachment and bonding, isolation, loneliness, arousal, attentiveness, vigilance, irritability, sadness, and exhaustion. Many individuals, particularly those not living within 50 miles of the disaster sites and not losing a loved one, will generally adapt relatively quickly and return to their regular work schedules and routines of daily living. However, in the deep recesses of their minds is the knowledge that they may be the next victims. But for many of the survivors and those individuals living close to the disaster site and without personal resources and social supports, acute stress, crisis, and trauma reactions could be prevalent. In view of the most horrific and barbaric mass murders in U.S. history it has become critically important for all informed citizens to know the difference between acute stress, normal grief, acute crisis episodes, trauma reactions, and Posttraumatic Stress Disorder (PTSD). This overview chapter and the chapters by George Everly, Jeff Lating, and Jeff Mitchell; Vincent Henry; Joshua Miller; Sophia Dziegielewski and Kristy Sumner; William Reid and Gary Behrmann; and Rachel Kaul and Victor Welzantt examine the different definitions of acute stress, crisis, and psychological trauma as well as disaster mental health, critical incident stress management, and crisis intervention strategies.

Vincent Henry (currently a professor of criminal justice) was a first responder to the World Trade Center attacks and the rescue and recovery activities. In the weeks directly following the September 11 attacks and near the end of his 21-year career as an NYPD police officer and detective, he served as the commanding officer of a sniper unit on top of St. Vincent's Hospital in lower Manhattan protecting injured survivors and watching for terrorists. His chapter provides an overview of specific types of weapons of mass destruction and the type of response protocols utilized by police, fire, emergency medical services, and disaster mental health coalitions. He examines some of the psychological crises and traumas experienced by first responders to terrorist attacks and describes a successful clinical service consisting of more than 300 specially trained clinical volunteers, the New York Disaster Counseling Coalition. This counseling and psychotherapy group provides confidential and free treatment services to all first responders and their family members who request services. The volunteer clinicians have offices throughout the New York Metropolitan area, northern New Jersey, southern Connecticut, and parts of Pennsylvania.

Professors Mitchell and Everly are internationally known as the founders of the group crisis intervention model CISM, which includes the group crisis intervention protocol critical incident stress debriefing (CISD). It was certainly timely for them to update their chapter for this edition and take into account the adverse impact of mass disaster terrorism as the leading cause of posttraumatic distress. George Everly, Jeffrey Mitchell, and Jeffrey Lating aptly focus on how to implement CISD as a screening, triage, group discussion, and psychoeducational method. The goal of this intervention is to reduce acute distress and acute crisis episodes. The authors then focus on the 10 core elements of CISM as a multicomponent crisis intervention system and its recent applications to mass disasters, military venues, and terrorist-related situations. They also discuss a recent meta-analysis that demonstrated the effectiveness of crisis intervention with medical and surgical patients.

The poignant chapter by Linda Mills depicts the experiences and reactions of her 5-year-old son, through her eyes, when they were uprooted from their apartment and his school, which were in close proximity to the World Trade Center site. Professor Mills's chapter is compelling and heart-wrenching because she writes about the horror that she and her family experienced and its impact on her young child.

Rachel Kaul, a former emergency room social worker and American Red Cross disaster mental health responder, describes the disaster mental health strategies applied to the various populations affected by the Pentagon attack. Following her work as a disaster mental health responder, she worked as the coordinator of Trauma and Emergency Services at the Pentagon employee assistant program, assisting workers and family members with trauma reduction and recovery for over two years. Now, as the Maryland coordinator of emergency services, and in collaboration with Dr. Victor Welzant of the International Critical Incident Stress Foundation and Sheppard Pratt Health Services, she underscores the critical need for implementing crisis management and disaster mental health strategies as well as self-care techniques among all disaster mental health responders and for employing best practice approaches in the process.

Sophia Dziegielewski and Kristy Sumner's timely chapter focuses on the nature and extent of bioterrorism threats in the United States and an application of the seven-stage crisis intervention model to reduce fear, stress, crisis, and trauma among the survivors of bioterrorist attacks. Joshua Miller provides a thorough description of the emergency mental health system responses that he witnessed at the World Trade Center and the responses of the survivors of the tragedy. Professor Miller was inspired by the resiliency of the survivors, their capacity to use this tragedy to reevaluate their lives, cherish their relationships, and strengthen their social bonds with family, friends, and colleagues. This section ends with a chapter by Joseph McBride and Eric Johnson that clarifies the differences between grief counseling and crisis intervention and then examines the ways crisis intervention strategies have been effectively applied with survivors of mass terrorist murders.

According to Lenore Terr (1994), a professor of psychiatry, there are two types of trauma among children. Type I refers to child victims who have experienced a single traumatic event, such as the 26 children from Chowchilla, California, who were kidnapped in 1976 and buried alive in their school bus for almost 27 hours. Type II trauma refers to child victims who have experienced multiple traumatic events such as ongoing incest or child abuse. Research has demonstrated that most children experiencing a single isolated traumatic event had detailed memories of the event but no dissociation, personality disorders, or memory loss. In sharp contrast, child survivors experiencing multiple or repetitious incest and/or child sexual abuse trauma (Type II trauma) exhibited dissociative disorders (also known as multiple personality disorders) or Borderline Personality Disorder (BPD), recurring trance-like states, depression, suicidal ideation and/or suicide attempts, sleep disturbances, and, to a lesser degree, self-mutilation and PTSD (Terr, 1994; Valentine, 2000). The age of the incest victim frequently mediates the coping strategies of adult survivors who face crisis and trauma. Research has indicated that when the childhood incest was prolonged and severe, an adult diagnosis of BPD, Dissociative Disorder, Panic Disorder, alcohol abuse or dependency, and/or PTSD occurs with greater frequency (Valentine, 2000). The exception to the low incidence of long-lasting mental disorders among victims of a Type I trauma is an extremely horrific single traumatic occurrence which is marked by multiple homicides and includes dehumanizing sights (e.g. dismembered bodies), piercing sounds, and strong odors (fire and smoke). The long-lasting psychological impact of the September 11 mass disasters will not be known for at least another decade, at which time prospective and retrospective longitudinal research studies will be completed.

The American Academy of Experts in Traumatic Stress (ATSM) is a multidisciplinary network of professionals dedicated to formulating and extending the use of traumatic stress reduction protocols with emergency responders (e.g., police, fire, EMS, nurses, disaster response personnel, psychologists, social workers, funeral directors, and clergy). Dr. Mark D. Lerner, a clinical psychologist and president of ATSM, and Dr. Raymond D. Shelton, director of Emergency Medical Training at the Nassau County (New Jersey) Police Training Academy and director of professional development for ATSM, provide the following guidance for addressing psychological trauma quickly during traumatic events:

> All crisis intervention and trauma treatment specialists are in agreement that before intervening, a full assessment of the situation and the individual must take place. By reaching people early, during traumatic exposure, we may ultimately prevent acute traumatic stress reactions from becoming chronic stress disorders. The first three steps of Acute Traumatic Stress Management (ATSM) are: (1) assess for danger/safety for self and others; (2) consider the type and extent of property damage and/or physical injury and the way the injury was sustained (e.g., a terroristic explosion); and (3) evaluate the level of responsiveness—is the individual alert, in pain, aware

of what has occurred, or in emotional shock or under the influence of drugs? (Lerner & Shelton, 2001, pp. 31–32)

Personal impact in the aftermath of potentially stressful and crisis-producing events can be measured by:

- *Spatial dimensions:* The closer the person is to the center of the tragedy, the greater the stress. Similarly, the closer the person's relationship is to the homicide victim, the greater the likelihood of entering into a crisis state.
- *Subjective crime clock:* The greater the duration (estimated length of time exposed and estimated length of exposure to sensory experiences, e.g., an odor of gasoline combined with the smell of a fire) that an individual is affected by the community disaster, violent crime, or other tragedy, the greater the stress.
- *Reoccurrence* (perceived): The greater the perceived likelihood that the tragedy will happen again, the greater the likelihood of intense fears, which contribute to an active crisis state on the part of the survivor (Young, 1995).

NEED FOR EDUCATIONAL CURRICULUM, UNIVERSITY-BASED CERTIFICATE PROGRAMS, AND TRAINING IN CRISIS INTERVENTION AND TRAUMA TREATMENT IN THE AFTERMATH OF DISASTERS

An unprecedented outpouring of offers to provide counseling to help survivors cope with grief from the loss of loved ones resulted from the events of September 11. Mental health professionals reached out to assist thousands of people who survived the tragedy by escaping from the Pentagon, the World Trade Center, and nearby office buildings amid falling debris and thick black smoke. Many in the media and the general public have assumed that *all* clinicians have the proper training and experience to provide crisis counseling to persons traumatized by these events.

Despite the recognition of the urgent need for more comprehensive crisis intervention course and workshop offerings, as of July 2004, the level of training among the vast majority of social workers, psychologists, and counselors in crisis intervention work has been somewhat limited. For example, despite the heightened awareness in communities throughout the United States of the looming threat of another mass terrorist attack and the interest of university administrators and faculty on university and department curriculum committees, it has taken the author almost three years to get approval for a new 21-credit certificate program in crisis management and criminal justice practices. It was finally offered in September 2004 at Rutgers University's off-campus center in Monmouth County, New Jersey, thanks to the commitment of Vice President Raymond Caprio. This only came about as a result of my reconnecting with Caprio, who is interested in innovations and responding to community needs. There is a dearth of certificate programs and training opportunities at graduate schools in the human service professions. The overwhelming majority of graduate programs in social work, clinical psychology, and counseling do not require even one course in crisis intervention. The most deficient curricula are in the 147 Masters of Social Work (MSW) accredited programs throughout the United States. Only a handful of these large educational programs offer a one-semester course in crisis intervention. Even the small number of programs that offer required course content related to crisis intervention and trauma treatment usually limit the content to just one to three (two- or three-hour sessions) classes as partial fulfillment of a three-credit course on social work practice. I predict that this lack of education and skill building will change in the important years ahead. For example, Elaine Congress, professor and associate dean at the Graduate School of Social Services of Fordham University in Manhattan, has indicated to me that the curriculum committee at her school is developing a new crisis intervention course and one-day workshops. Some training for practitioners on crisis intervention (usually two to five days) is provided by such organizations as the National Organization for Victim Assistance, the American Red Cross, and the Crisis Prevention Institute.

As helping professionals in the aftermath of the mass destruction caused by the terrorist attacks of September 11, 2001, we all wanted to rush to action. However, I am calling for all mental health professionals to pause and assess. If we don't assess, we are likely to engage in well-intentioned but misguided and potentially harmful action. For example, a therapist with no training in crisis intervention or trauma treatment may encourage a survivor to make impulsive changes such as breaking his or her lease on an apartment in lower Manhattan and moving to New Jersey, where the lengthy commute to work will be very stressful and expensive.

As mental health professionals, what are the things we should assess, and which methods should we use to conduct assessments in the aftermath of a mass disaster? The answer to this question provides the focus of the next section.

THE ACT INTERVENTION MODEL OF CRISIS AND TRAUMA ASSESSMENT AND TREATMENT

Somatic stress, crisis, and psychological trauma frequently take place in the wake of unnatural, man-made disasters such as the terrorist mass murders of September 11, 2001. Most individuals have little or no preparation for traumatic events. The catastrophic nature of the World Trade Center and Pentagon disasters has impacted and threatened the safety of many U.S. citizens. The important first step in determining the psychosocial needs of all survivors and their families and the grieving family members of the murder victims is assessment. Thus, the focus of this section is to examine the A, *assessment,* component of the newly developed ACT intervention model for acute crisis and trauma treatment (Figure 6.1). First, I briefly identify psychiatric triage assessment and the different types of assessment protocols. Second, I identify and discuss the components of a crisis assessment. Third, I enumerate and review the dimensions of the biopsychosocial and cultural assessment. Finally, I briefly list the different types of rapid assessment instruments and scales used in mental health, crisis, and trauma assessments.

Triage Assessment

First responders, or crisis response team members, also known as frontline crisis intervention workers, are called on to conduct an immediate debriefing under less than stable circumstances and sometimes have to delay the crisis

A
- Assessment/appraisal of immediate medical needs, threats to public safety and property damage
- Triage assessment, crisis assessment, trauma assessment and the biopsychosocial and cultural assessment protocols

C
- Connecting to support groups, the delivery of disaster relief and social services, and critical incident stress debriefing (Mitchell & Everly's CISD model) implemented
- Crisis intervention (Robert's seven-stage model) implemented, through strengths perspective and coping attempts bolstered

T
- Traumatic stress reactions, sequelae, and post-traumatic stress disorders (PTSDs)
- Ten step acute trauma and stress management protocol (Lerner & Shelton), trauma treatment plans and recovery strategies implemented

Figure 6.1 ACT Model

assessment to right after immediate stabilization and support. With other disaster responses, an assessment can be completed simultaneously with the debriefing. According to many of the crisis intervention specialists whom I have trained, ideally A (assessment) precedes C (crisis intervention), but in the rough and tumble of the disaster or acute crisis, it is not always that linear.

In the immediate aftermath of a community disaster, the first type of assessment by disaster mental health specialists should be psychiatric triage. A triage/screening tool can be useful in gathering and recording information about the initial contact between a person experiencing crisis or trauma reactions and the mental health specialist. The triage form should include essential demographic information (name, address, phone number, e-mail address, etc.), perception of the magnitude of the traumatic event, coping methods, any presenting problems, safety issues, previous traumatic experiences, social support network, drug and alcohol use, preexisting psychiatric conditions, suicide risk, and homicide risk (Eaton & Roberts, 2002). Several hundred articles have examined emergency medical triage, but very few publications have discussed emergency psychiatric triage (Liese, 1995, pp. 48–49). Triage has been defined as the medical "process of assigning patients to appropriate treatments depending on their medical conditions and available medical resources" (p. 48). Medical triage was first used in the military to respond quickly to the medical needs of our wounded soldiers. Triage involves assigning physically ill or injured patients to different levels of care, ranging from "emergent" (i.e., immediate treatment required) to "nonemergent" (i.e., no medical treatment required).

Psychiatric or psychological triage assessment refers to the immediate decision-making process in which the mental health worker determines lethality and referral to one of the following alternatives:

Emergency inpatient hospitalization.
Outpatient treatment facility or private therapist.
Support group or social service agency.
No referral needed.

The A in my ACT intervention model refers to triage, crisis, and trauma assessments and referral to appropriate community resources. With regard to triage assessment, emergency psychiatric response should take place when the rapid assessment indicates that the individual is a danger to self or others and is exhibiting intense and acute psychiatric symptoms. These survivors generally require short-term hospitalization and psychopharmacotherapy to protect themselves from self-harm (e.g., suicide attempts and self-injurious behavior) or harm to other persons (e.g., murder and attempted murder). The small number of individuals needing emergency psychiatric treatment generally are diagnosed with moderate- to high-potential lethality (e.g., suicidal ideation and/or homicidal thoughts) and acute mental disorders. In the small percentage of cases where emergency psychiatric treatment is indicated, these persons usually are suffering from an accumulation of several previous traumatic events (Burgess & Roberts, 2000).

With regard to the other categories of psychiatric triage, many individuals may be in a precrisis stage due to ineffective coping skills, a weak support system, or ambivalence about seeking mental health assistance. These same individuals may have no psychiatric symptoms and no suicide risk. However, because of the catastrophic nature of the September 11 disaster, persons who have suddenly lost a loved one and have no previous experience coping with sudden death may be particularly vulnerable to acute crisis or traumatic stress. Therefore, it is imperative that all mental health professionals become knowledgeable about timely crisis and trauma assessments.

Another type of triage assessment used almost exclusively by crisis intervention and suicide prevention programs will now be addressed. Specifically, the 24-hour mobile crisis intervention services of Community Integration, Inc. of Erie, Pennsylvania, developed an Intervention Priority Scale that should be utilized by other programs throughout North America. This Intervention Priority Scale allows a number from I to IV to be assigned at the time the triage information is collected, based on clinical criteria. Each number on the scale corresponds to an outside time limit considered to be safe for crisis response. Examples of a Priority I assessment include requests for immediate assistance by police and emergency services personnel, suicide attempts in progress, suicidal or homicidal individuals with the means currently available, and individuals experiencing command hallucinations of a violent nature. Examples of a Priority II situation include individuals who are able to contract for safety or who have reliable supports present, individuals experiencing hallucinations or delusions, or individuals who are unable to meet basic human needs. Examples of a Priority III situation include individuals with fleeting suicidal ideation or major depression and no feasible suicide plan, or individuals suffering from mood disturbances. Priority IV assessments are those cases where there is no thought to harm self or others, no psychiatric symptoms are present, and no other situational crises exist (Eaton & Ertl, 2000; Eaton & Roberts, 2002).

Crisis Assessment

The primary role of the crisis counselor and other clinical staff in conducting an assessment is to gather information that can help to resolve the crisis. Intake forms and rapid assessment instruments help the crisis clinician or mental health counselor to make better-informed decisions on the type and duration of treatment recommended. Although crisis assessment is oriented to the individual, it must always include an assessment of the person's immediate environment and interpersonal relationships. As Gitterman (2002) eloquently points out in *The Life Model:*

> The purpose of social work is improving the level of fit between people and their environments, especially between people's needs and their environmental resources. . . . [The professional function of social work is] to help people mobilize and draw on personal and environmental resources for effective coping to alleviate life stressors and the associated stress. (p. 106)

Crisis assessment will facilitate treatment planning and decision making. The ultimate goal of crisis assessment is, first, to provide a systematic method of organizing client information related to personal characteristics, parameters of the crisis episode, and the intensity and duration of the crisis, and, second, utilizing these data to develop effective treatment plans. In the words of Lewis and Roberts (2001):

> Most intake workers have failed to distinguish between stressful life events, traumatic events, coping skills and other mediators of a crisis, and an active crisis state. Most crisis episodes are preceded by one or more stressful, hazardous, and/or traumatic events. However, not all stressed or traumatized individuals move into a crisis state. Every day thousands of individuals completely avert a crisis, while many other thousands of individuals quickly escalate into a crisis state. (p. 20)

Thus, it is extremely important to assess and measure whether a person is in a crisis state so that individual treatment goals and an appropriate crisis intervention protocol can be implemented. (For a detailed discussion of crisis-specific measurement tools and crisis-oriented rapid assessment instruments, see Lewis & Roberts, 2001.)

According to Eaton and Roberts (2002), there are eight fundamental questions that the crisis worker should ask the client when conducting a suicide risk assessment, for example, "Are you having thoughts of self harm?"; "Have you done anything to intentionally hurt yourself?"; and "Do you feel there is hope that things can improve?" Eaton and Roberts also delineate nine questions for measuring homicide/violence risk, such as "Have you made any preparations to hurt others?" (p. 92).

Biopsychosocial and Cultural Assessments

There are different methods of assessment designed to measure clients' situation, stress level, presenting problems, and acute crisis episode: monitoring and observing, client logs, semistructured interviews, individualized rating scales, goal attainment scales, behavioral observations, self-reports, cognitive measures, and diagnostic systems and codes (LeCroy & Okamoto, 2002; Pike, 2002).

Vandiver and Corcoran (2002) aptly identify and discuss the biopsychosocial-cultural model of assessment as the first step in the clinical interview aimed at providing the necessary information to "establish treatment goals and an effective treatment plan" (p. 297). It is important for individual assessments to gather information on the following:

1. Current health status (e.g., hypertension) and past health status (e.g., diabetes) or injuries (e.g., brain injury); current medication use and health and lifestyle behaviors (e.g., fitness exercises, nutrition, sleep patterns, substance abuse).
2. The psychological status of the client, including mental status, appearance and behavior, speech and language, thought process and content, mood and affect, cognitive functioning, concentration, memory, and insight and general intelligence. An additional critical area of assessment is the determination of suicidal or homicidal risk and possible need for an immediate referral.
3. The sociocultural experiences and cultural background of the client, including ethnicity, language, assimilation, acculturation, spiritual beliefs, environmental connections (e.g., community ties, neighborhood, economic conditions, availability of food and shelter), social networks and relationships (e.g., family, friends, coworkers). (Vandiver & Corcoran, 2001, p. 298)

The assessment process should provide a step-by-step method for exploring, identifying, describing, measuring, classifying, diagnosing, and coding health or mental health problems, environmental conditions, resilience and protective factors, positive lifestyle behaviors, and level of functioning. Austrian (2002) delineates the 10 basic components of a biopsychosocial assessment:

1. Demographic data.
2. Current and previous agency contacts.
3. Medical, psychiatric, and substance abuse history.
4. Brief history of client and significant others.
5. Summary of client's current situation.
6. Presenting request.
7. Presenting problem as defined by client and counselor.
8. Contract agreed on by client and counselor.
9. Intervention plan.
10. Intervention goals.

Some of the most popular assessment tools include:

The *Diagnostic and Statistical Manual-IV-TR* (*DSM-IV-TR;* American Psychiatric Association, 2000; Munson, 2002; Williams, 2002).

Rapid assessment instruments such as the Brief Symptom Inventory, the Beck Depression Inventory, the Derogatis Symptom Checklist SCL-90, the Reasons for Living Scale, and the Impact of Events scale (see J. Corcoran & Boyer-Quick, 2002; K. Corcoran & Fischer, 2000).

Person-in-Environment system (Karls, 2002).

Goal attainment scales (Pike, 2002).

CRISIS INTERVENTION STRATEGIES

It is imperative for all communities throughout the United States and Canada to have a multidisciplinary and comprehensive crisis response and crisis intervention plan ready for systematic implementation and mobilizations in the aftermath of a major disaster. Crisis intervention models and techniques provide guidelines for practitioners to resolve clients' presenting problems, stress and psychological trauma, and emotional conflicts with a minimum number of contacts. Crisis-oriented treatment is time-limited and goal-directed, in contrast to long-term psychotherapy, which can take one to three years to complete (Roberts, 2000).

Roberts's Seven-Stage Crisis Intervention Model

Although counselors, psychologists, and social workers have been trained in a variety of theoretical models, very little graduate coursework has prepared them with a crisis intervention protocol and guidelines to follow in dealing with crises. Roberts's (1991, 2000) seven-stage crisis intervention model begins to provide practitioners with this useful framework.

Case Example

The 24-hour crisis intervention unit of a New Jersey mental health center received a call from the mother of a 22-year-old college senior whose father (who worked on the 95th floor of the World Trade Center) was killed on September 11. The college student had barricaded himself in his bedroom. His mother indicated that she had overheard a phone conversation between her depressed son, Jonathan, and his cousin. Jonathan told his 19-year-old female cousin that he needed her to come over immediately because he was giving her his Super Nintendo set and all of his games. The mother was concerned about possible suicidal behavior because her son had never given away any of his prized possessions before. In addition, during the past two weeks he was eating very little, sleeping 12 to 15 hours each day, refusing to return to college, and mentioning that Heaven would be a nice place to live. His mom also overhead him asking his cousin if she thought there were basketball hoops in Heaven so that he and his father could play basketball again.

Roberts's (1996) seven-stage crisis intervention model (Figure 6.2) was initiated.

Stage 1: Assess lethality. The mother phoning crisis services had some information about the current mental status of the client. She indicated that she could hear her son speak very softly in a muffled voice through the

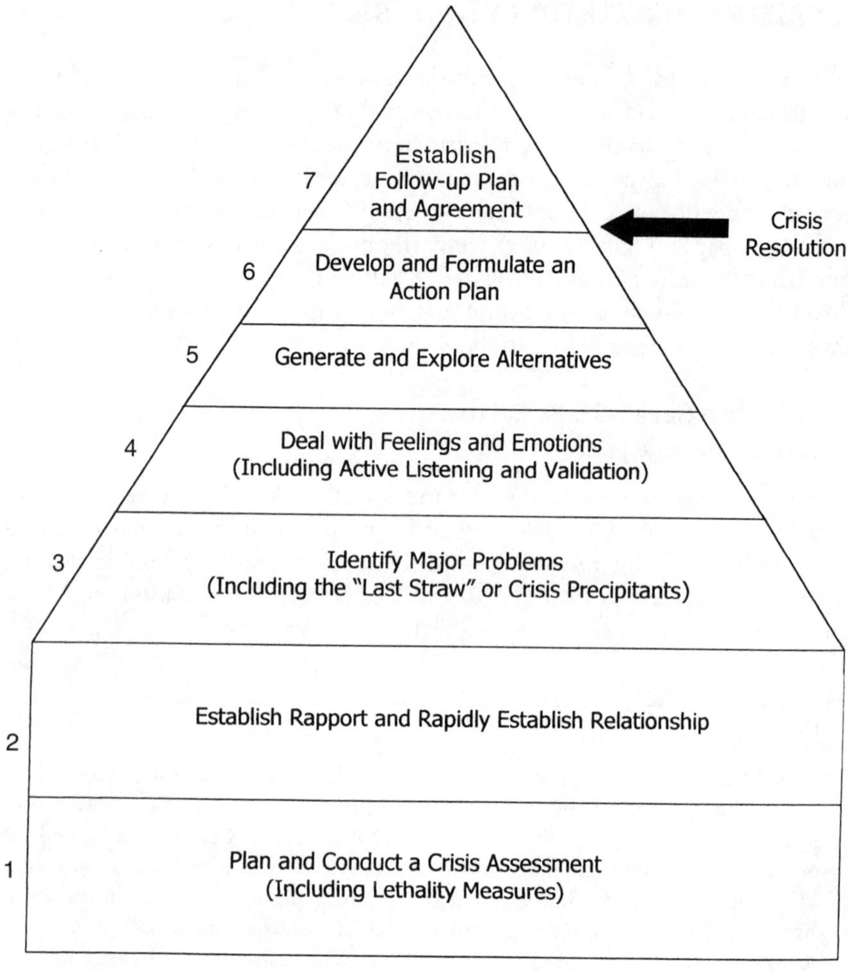

Figure 6.2 Roberts's Seven-Stage Crisis Intervention Model

locked and barricaded bedroom door. The mother further indicated that her son has stayed in his bedroom for about 12 hours since he telephoned his cousin and put his CDs and Super Nintendo game on the front porch. Crisis services immediately dispatched a worker to the residence.

Stage 2: Establish rapport. Understanding and support were two essential skills utilized by the crisis worker to establish a working relationship with the client. Immediately requesting him to open his bedroom door would not have been a helpful intervention. Workers need to begin where the client is. Through attentive listening, paraphrasing, and the use of open-ended questions, the worker eventually got Jonathan to agree to let him in his room so they could hear each other better.

Stage 3: Identify problems. Luckily, Jonathan had not yet done anything to harm himself, but he was contemplating suicide. He had a vague plan of overdosing, but no available method. He expressed his major problem as the sudden death of his dad.

Stage 4: Deal with feelings. The crisis worker allowed Jonathan to tell his story about why he was feeling so bad. The worker was able to validate and identify Jonathan's emotions. They then began to explore together more effective ways of coping with his upsetting feelings.

Stage 5: Explore alternatives. Various options were discussed, including inpatient and outpatient mental health services. The client allowed his mother to join the worker and himself during this stage. The mother provided a lot of support and encouragement to the client as well. At this stage, Jonathan indicated that he was feeling better and would not "do anything stupid."

Stage 6: Develop an action plan. Jonathan, his mother, and the crisis worker decided on the following action plan:

1. A contract for safety was signed by the client (this is a written agreement that the client agrees to call crisis services for help before he will act on any thought to harm himself or others).
2. A release of information was obtained by the worker to contact an outpatient provider.
3. An outpatient provider was contacted and the client received an appointment for the next afternoon.
4. The mother hid all medications on the recommendation of crisis services.
5. Both Jonathan and his mother were given a crisis card to call if any additional concerns or issues arose.

Stage 7: Follow-up. A follow-up phone call was made to the residence the next evening. Jonathan's mother indicated that he was in good spirits that day and had attended his first appointment with the therapist. Jonathan told the crisis worker that he was doing great, he thought his therapist was "really cool," and he had plans to "go bowling with friends on Saturday."

Effective crisis intervenors should be active, directive, focused, and hopeful. It is critically important that the crisis worker gauge the stages and completeness of the intervention. Roberts's seven- stage crisis intervention paradigm "should be viewed as a guide, not as a rigid process, since with some clients stages may overlap. Roberts' . . . model of crisis intervention has been utilized for helping persons in acute psychological crisis, acute situational crises, and acute stress disorders" (Roberts, 2000, p. 15). The seven stages of crisis intervention combined with a strengths perspective will now be discussed.

Roberts's Model From a Strengths Perspective

Stage 1

Plan and conduct a thorough biopsychosocial and crisis assessment. This involves a quick assessment of risk and dangerousness, including suicide and homicide/violence risk assessment, need for medical attention, positive and negative coping strategies, and current drug or alcohol use (Eaton & Ertl, 2000; Roberts, 2000). If possible, a medical assessment should include a brief summary of the presenting problem, any medical conditions, current medications (names, dosages, and most recent dose), and allergies. This medical information is essential to relay to emergency medical responders attempting to treat problems such as overdoses.

A drug or alcohol assessment should include information about drugs used, amount used, when last use, and any withdrawal symptoms the client is experiencing. Any knowledge of Angel Dust, methamphetamine, or PCP ingestion should always precipitate a team crisis response with the police, due to the likelihood of violent and bizarre behavior.

The initial crisis assessment should examine resilience and protective factors, internal and external coping methods and resources, and the degree of extended family and informal support network. Many individuals in a precrisis or crisis situation socially isolate themselves and are unaware of and lack insight into which persons would be most supportive in their efforts at crisis resolution and recovery. The crisis clinician can facilitate and bolster clients' resilience by encouraging them to telephone or write a letter to persons who may well support their efforts at recovery. Seeking advice on how best to cope with a crisis related to self-destructive patterns such as polydrug abuse, binge drinking, self-injurious behavior, or depression can lead to overwhelming support, suggestions, advice, and encouragement from one's support network (Yeager & Gregoire, 2000).

Stage 2

Rapidly establish rapport and the therapeutic relationship (this often occurs simultaneously with Stage 1). Conveying respect and acceptance are key steps in this stage. Crisis workers must meet the clients where they are; for example, if the client begins a conversation talking about his dog or parakeet, this is where we should begin (Roberts, 2000). We must display a neutral and nonjudgmental attitude as well, ensuring that our personal opinions and values are not apparent or stated. Poise, maintaining a calm demeanor, and appearing to be in control are essential skills in crisis work (Belkin, 1984).

Stage 3

Identify the issues pertinent to the client and any precipitants to the client's crisis contact. Use open-ended questions in asking clients to explain and describe their problem and to tell their story in their own words (Roberts, 2000). This provides the crisis worker with valuable insights into the nature of the presenting problem. It is important for clients to feel that the worker is truly interested in them and understands them; this also helps build rapport and trust. Also helpful during both Stages 2 and 3 is using the questions of solution-focused therapy (SFT) in identifying clients' strengths and resources, which includes discerning their effective past coping skills (Greene, Lee, Trask, & Rheinscheld, 2000; also see Yeager & Gregoire, 2000). Some of the SFT questions that would be helpful are:

- Exception question (identifying times when the problematic situation is not present or is just a little bit better and what is different about those times compared to the present crisis situation).
- Coping question.
- Questions for identifying past success.

Identifying client strengths and resources should also help in developing rapport and trust, as clients tend to develop comfort more quickly with someone who is not focusing only on their short-comings (deficits, dysfunction, and failures; Greene et al., 2000).

Stage 4

Deal with feelings and emotions by effectively using active listening skills. Show the client that you are listening to what they are saying by responding with encouraging phrases, such as "Uh huh" and "Oh." This type of verbal feedback is especially important when providing telephone intervention. Additional skills include reflection, paraphrasing, and emotion labeling (Bolton, 1984). Reflection involves restating the words, feelings, and ideas of the client; paraphrasing involves restating the meaning of the client's words in the worker's own language; and emotion labeling involves the worker summarizing the emotions that seem to underlie the client's message, for example, "You sound very angry" (Eaton & Roberts, 2002).

Stage 5

Generate and explore alternatives by identifying the strengths of the client as well as previous successful coping mechanisms. Ideally, the ability of the worker and the client to work collaboratively during this stage should yield the widest array of potential resources and alternatives. According to Roberts (2000), the person in crisis is viewed as resourceful, resilient

> and having untapped resources or latent inner coping skills from which to draw upon. . . . Integrating strengths and solution-focused approaches involves jogging clients' memories so they recall the last time everything seemed to be going well, and they were in a good mood rather than depressed and/or successfully dealt with a previous crisis in their lives. (p. 19)

Aguilera and Messick (1982) state that the ability to be creative and flexible, adapting ideas to individual situations, is a key skill in effective workers.

Stage 6

Implement the action plan. The crisis worker should assist the client in the least restrictive manner, enabling the client to feel empowered. Important steps in this stage include identifying persons and referral sources to be contacted and providing coping mechanisms (Roberts & Roberts, 2000). Crisis workers at Community Integration, Inc. Crisis Services utilize carbon forms to record the plan developed by worker and client. This is a useful mechanism to provide clients with phone numbers and specifics of the plan to follow, and also provides the necessary documentation for other crisis workers to know what to encourage and reinforce on subsequent contacts with the client (Eaton & Ertl, 2000).

Stage 7

Establish a follow-up plan and agreement. Crisis workers should follow up with the client after the initial intervention to ensure that the crisis has been resolved and to determine the postcrisis status of the client and the situation. This can be accomplished via telephone or face-to-face contact. In a team setting, when someone other than the original crisis worker will be conducting follow-ups, the utilization of a dry erase board can be a good organizational tool. At a glance, all workers can view the list of cases needing follow-up, when follow-up was requested, and items to address during follow-up contact. Of course, documentation in the client's chart would be more detailed and specific (Eaton & Roberts, 2002).

Critical Incident Stress Debriefing

Critical incident stress debriefing has been found to be useful in the aftermath of floods, hurricanes, tornadoes, and large fires. Crisis response and crisis intervention work is demanding and highly stressful. Frontline crisis intervention workers may be exposed to gruesome and life-threatening events. Eaton and Ertl (2000) indicate that incidents such as completed suicides, dead bodies, and threats or assaults on crisis workers warrant the use of CISM techniques. Keeping workers safe and ensuring they can find satisfaction in their work as well as in their personal lives requires that they receive support in managing their own stress. CISM can play an important part in providing that support to workers in crisis intervention programs. It includes a wide variety of techniques and interventions for individuals exposed to life-threatening or traumatic events (Mitchell & Everly, 1993). There are more than 300 crisis response teams utilizing a standardized model of CISM services internationally, as listed by the International Critical Incident Stress Foundation (Everly, Lating, & Mitchell, 2000). The utilization of CISM techniques allows workers the opportunity to discuss the traumatic event, promotes group cohesion, and educates workers on stress reactions and coping techniques (Eaton & Roberts, 2002).

Approximately 30 years ago, William Reid and Laura Epstein of the University of Chicago developed the first empirically tested time-limited social work treatment model: task-centered practice. As a result, I was delighted that Gary Behrmann and the late William Reid wrote a chapter for this book that integrates task-centered practice with crisis intervention based on their work in New York.

CRISIS VERSUS TRAUMA REACTIONS

For the most part, individuals function in their daily lives in a state of emotional balance. Occasionally, intensely stressful life events will stretch a person's sense of well-being and equilibrium. However, even stressful life events are frequently predictable within a person's ordinary routines, and he or she is able to mobilize effective coping methods to handle the stress. In sharp contrast, traumatic events lift people out of their usual realm of equilibrium and make it difficult to reestablish a sense of balance or equilibrium. Trauma reactions are often precipitated by a sudden, random, and arbitrary traumatic event. The most common types of trauma-inducing stressors are violent crimes, terrorism, and natural disasters (Young, 1995).

Trauma Assessment and Treatment

Traumatic events refer to overwhelming, unpredictable, and emotionally shocking experiences. The potentially traumatizing event may be a large-scale disaster, such as an earthquake, Hurricane Bonnie's devastastation in southern Florida, and the bombing of the Oklahoma City Federal Office Building. These were all disasters that occurred at one point in time. Traumas may also build up from a series of traumatic events that may repeat themselves many times over months and years, such as domestic violence, incest, hurricanes, floods, tornadoes, and war. The impact of the traumatic event(s) may be physical and psychological. Nevertheless, it is important to note that the majority of individuals who are exposed to a traumatic event experience psychological trauma symptoms, but never develop PTSD.

Working with survivors and secondary victims of mass murders poses special issues and problems for mental health professionals. Specialized knowledge, skills, and training should be required. For example, clients suffering from PTSD may need emergency appointments with little notice, or they may need to see their trauma therapist the morning after a night of intense nightmares and flashbacks. As a result of upsetting memories and insomnia after the nightmares, clients may have angry outbursts in the clinician's office. In addition, mental health practitioners working in outpatient and inpatient settings need to recognize that for some survivors of disaster-induced trauma, stress and grief reactions will last for 10 to 60 days and then totally subside. For others, there may be delayed acute crisis reactions at the one-month and one-year anniversaries of the disastrous event. Still others will develop full-blown PTSD, evidenced by their chronic intrusive thoughts, avoidance behavior, flashbacks, nightmares, and hypervigilance, which may persist for years. The traumatic memories keep intruding during the day and in the middle of the night until they become unbearable.

Research has indicated that the effects of community disasters on levels of psychological distress, transient stress reactions, Acute Stress Disorder, generalized anxiety disorder, death anxiety, and PTSD vary from one study to the next (Blair, 2000; Chantarujikapong et al., 2001; Cheung-Chung, Chung, & Easthope, 2000; Ford, 1999; Fukada, Morimoto, Mure, & Maruyama, 2000; Regehr, 2001). PTSD and high levels of psychological distress seem to be dependent on pre- and postwar factors, age, gender, personal resources and living arrangements, and quality of life after the traumatic event. Lev-wiesel's (2000) retrospective study of 170 Holocaust survivors 55 years posttrauma found that the most significant mediating factor in preventing PTSD was the child survivor's living arrangements at the end of the war. The study findings indicate that the most traumatic stress and PTSD was experienced by the child survivors placed in foster homes, and the lowest traumatic stress was found in the survivors who were sheltered by the partisans and/or hid in the woods (Lev-weisel, 2000). With regard to the influence of age and gender on the severity of depressive symptoms among 1,015 adults one year after the Armenian earthquake, the following was found: "Persons between the ages of 31–55 reported significantly higher depressive ratings than individuals who were 17–30," and women had much higher scores on the Beck Depression Inventory than the men in the study (Toukmanian, Jadaa, & Lawless, 2000). Research demonstrates that resilience, personal resources, and social supports are important variables in mediating and mitigating against the development of PTSD (Fukuda et al., 2000; Gold, Engdahl, Eberly, Blake, Page, et al., 2000; Lev-wiesel, 2000). In addition, while depressive symptomatology seems to be comorbid with PTSD, in studies of prisoners of war, higher educational levels and social support was associated with lower depressive symptoms and trauma (Gold et al., 2000; Solomon, Mikulciner, & Avitzur, 1989).

Several studies have examined whether there is an association between trauma exposure during traumatic events and death anxiety after witnessing or experiencing life-threatening or near-death encounters associated with a plane crash. For example, Cheung-Chung et al. (2000) found that in the aftermath of the Coventry (England) airline crash, in which the plane crashed near 150 private homes (no residents were killed, although multiple fires spread throughout the neighborhood as a result of the crash), 40% of the witnesses had instrusive thoughts, 30% found that other things kept making them think about the disaster, 36% had trouble falling or staying asleep, and 33% had pictures of the disaster popping into their minds. In sharp contrast, 70% reported that they either rarely or never had any dreams about the crash. With regard to death anxiety or fear of death, close to one in three persons (29%) expressed fears or anxiety about death. This study indicates the different responses of residents witnessing an aircraft disaster. Unfortunately, these types of studies rarely conduct a psychiatric or biopsychosocial history to determine the relationship of preexisting psychiatric disorders or physical illnesses on the development of partial or full-blown PTSD.

Posttraumatic stress reactions are a pattern of conscious and subconscious expressions of behavior and emotional responses related to handling recollections of the environmental stressors of the traumatic or catastrophic event and the immediate aftermath. First and foremost, public safety must be maintained. In other words, police, firefighters, and emergency services personnel should make sure that all survivors are transported to a safe place and that there is no further danger at the disaster site. Only after all survivors are in a safe place should group CISD, group grief counseling, and mental health referrals begin. In the weeks and months postdisaster, mental health professionals and crisis intervenors need to be ready to conduct crisis and trauma assessments. Only mental health professionals experienced in crisis and trauma work should conduct the assessments and interventions. Rushed assessments by inexperienced professionals or volunteers and use of standardized mental health intake rating forms have resulted in the false labeling of clients with posttraumatic stress reactions as having personality disorders (Briere & Runtz, 1989; Koss et al., 1994; Walker, 1991).

Kroll (1993) clearly delineates the differences between normative responses and adapting to traumatic events compared to the development of long-lasting PTSD symptoms. Kroll aptly suggests an addition to the *DSM-IV* V-code: simply adding "uncomplicated posttraumatic stress responses." This would help to differentiate between normal human responses to traumatic events and PTSD. It is critically important that every response to human tragedy and communitywide disaster not be labeled or classified as a mental disorder. Because of the catastrophic nature of the September 11 mass murders, the American Psychiatric Association diagnostic classification of PTSD may eventually need to be changed, particularly extending the time line of 30 days in the definition.

In the months following a community disaster, trauma therapists should be available and on-call for follow-up work. Once the traumatized person is referred to an experienced trauma therapist, the following should take place:

1. A comprehensive biopsychosocial, crisis, and trauma assessment should be completed.
2. Specific treatment goals and a treatment plan should be developed.
3. An agreed number of sessions, formal or informal contract, should be determined.
4. Both directive and nondirective counseling techniques should be utilized, as well as eye movement desensitization and reprocessing (EMDR), traumatic incident recording, deep breathing, systematic muscle relaxation, encouraging hobbies, or other trauma intervention techniques.
5. An open-door policy should be maintained so that clients can return periodically for booster sessions or follow-up treatment when needed.

Acute Stress Management

The American Academy of Experts in Traumatic Stress is an interdisciplinary network of professionals providing emergency responses and timely intervention for survivors of traumatic events. Drs. Mark D. Lerner and Raymond D. Shelton (2001) have written a monograph that includes their detailed traumatic stress response protocol. As a member of the Board of Scientific and Professional Advisors of the American Academy of Experts in Traumatic Stress, I support the Academy's systematic and practical interventions and recently developed training workshops. The following summary of Lerner and Shelton's 10 stages of acute stress management provides useful guideposts for all first responders (i.e., emergency service personnel, crisis response team members, and disaster mental health workers) in the direct aftermath of a community disaster:

1. Assess for danger/safety for self and others.
2. Consider the physical and perceptual mechanism of injury.
3. Evaluate the level of responsiveness.
4. Address medical needs.
5. Observe and identify each individual's signs of traumatic stress.
6. Introduce yourself, state your title and role, and begin to develop a connection.
7. Ground the individual by allowing him or her to tell his or her story.
8. Provide support through active and empathic listening.
9. Normalize, validate, and educate.
10. Bring the person to the present, describe future events, and provide referrals.

Eye Movement Desensitization and Reprocessing

Another trauma treatment model that has had some degree of success, although it is viewed as controversial by many practitioners, is EMDR. The EMDR time-limited eight-stage treatment method is utilized after a therapeutic bond has been established with the patient. There is a growing amount of evidence that EMDR is effective with patients who have had one specific traumatic experience when the treatment is implemented by an experienced therapist with extensive formal training in EMDR. The EMDR protocol includes eight phases with specific steps in each phase (Shapiro, 1995). EMDR integrates cognitive-behavioral strategies, such as desensitization, imaginal exposure, and cognitive restructuring, and systematic bilateral stimulation and relaxation techniques. There have been a number of studies, including a meta-analysis, documenting the efficacy of EMDR in treating PTSD. It has shown significant positive effects when compared with other treatment modalities or pharmacotherapy for PTSD and other trauma-induced problems (Rubin, 2002; Van Etten & Taylor, 1998). Rubin has reviewed controlled randomized studies that found positive effects, particularly with regard to reducing trauma symptoms in children who were suffering from a single trauma and/or loss of a loved one. (See Karen Knox's 2002 article for a relevant case application of EMDR with a young adult family member who lost a loved one in the World Trade Center terrorist disaster.) It should be noted that the research has shown that EMDR has not been effective in reducing psychiatric sequelae of agoraphobia, social phobia, and generalized anxiety disorder (Rubin, 2002).

Crisis Worker Self-Care

One cannot discuss working with populations affected by crisis and trauma without discussing the crisis counselor or social worker as well. An overlooked element of crisis work is the responsibility of the mental health professional to engage in appropriate self-care. Rachel Kaul's (this volume) first-person account of her two years of work providing crisis counseling and psychological first aid to victims and first responders after the attack on the Pentagon emphasizes this important feature of effective response to disasters. Inattention to elements of self-care can result in fatigue and in traumatic stress reactions on the part of the crisis clinician that can compromise his or her ability to provide mental health care for others.

CONCLUSION

The attack of September 11, 2001, resulted in huge personal, psychological, and financial traumas. Such community disasters can overload our traditional coping methods. This is particularly evident among the thousands of citizens who worked in or lived near the World Trade Center or Pentagon prior to September 11. Mental health professionals and emergency responders are always ready and eager to aid persons in crisis. However, prior to September 11, no one had anticipated that the United States would be victimized in an assault of the magnitude that occurred; therefore, the health care and mental health organizations were not prepared with an interagency coordinated disaster mental health response. With the increased threat of terrorist activity in the future, in the United States and throughout the world, mental health educators and practitioners must develop the following: training and certification programs for crisis intervenors and trauma specialists; systematic and empirically tested procedures and protocols for crisis response, crisis intervention, and trauma treatment in the event of a future mass disaster or terrorist attack; and coordinated interagency disaster mental health teams on-call and ready for rapid deployment to community disasters in their respective regions.

Behavioral clinicians, mental health counselors, and social workers are increasingly being expected to respond quickly and efficiently to individuals and groups who are in need of crisis intervention and time-limited, trauma-focused treatment. This overview presented the ACT conceptual model to help communities respond to survivors of disasters and prepare for the future. Concerns about the growing threat of violence in corporations, manufacturing facilities, hospitals, and educational institutions are resulting in organizational pressure being placed on practitioners to be skilled in effectively assessing risks and unmet needs and providing rapid intervention. Roberts's (1991, 2000) seven-stage crisis intervention model provides clinicians with a useful framework to follow. Lerner and Shelton's (2001) 10-step trauma assessment and intervention model also provides a useful framework to facilitate the recovery of survivors of traumatic events. These conceptual models will assist practitioners in facilitating effective crisis resolution and trauma reduction.

A number of studies and a meta-analysis have demonstrated that certain population groups benefit from crisis intervention programs. Females in the 15–24 and the 55–64 age groups benefited the most from suicide prevention and crisis intervention programs (J. Corcoran & Roberts, 2000). The research on the effectiveness of crisis intervention programs with people presenting with psychiatric emergencies also shows positive outcomes; however, those clients with preexisting severe personality disorders usually benefited from crisis intervention only when it was augmented with short-term inpatient treatment followed by twice-a-week outpatient treatment and medication management (J. Corcoran & Roberts, 2000). The research on the effectiveness of crisis intervention after the September 11 terrorist attack has yet to be completed. Therefore, it is recommend that future studies should be strengthened by including standardized crisis assessments at pretest, posttest, and follow-ups, along with determining preexisting psychiatric conditions. In addition, whenever possible, matched naturally occurring comparison groups or quasi-control groups (no crisis intervention) should be created. Most important, longitudinal follow-up studies, whether through face-to-face or telephone contact, should be administered at uniform periods (e.g., 1 month, 3 months, 6 months, 12 months, 24 months, 36 months, 5 years, and 10 years post–initial crisis intervention). Independent evaluators or researchers or university-based researchers should be hired or contracted with by crisis intervention units of local community mental health centers, victim assistance programs, and outpatient hospital clinics.

In the next five to 10 years we will begin to learn the results of longitudinal research on the psychological impact of the September 11 terrorist disasters on children, adolescents, and adults. Therefore, it is important for disaster mental health researchers and criminologists to start planning and implementing studies now. Because of the vulnerability of U.S. citizens to terrorist attacks, federal, state, and local training and educational curricula development activities should be given priority now, so that mental health professionals are better prepared to meet the mental health needs of our citizens in the event of future terrorist disasters.

REFERENCES

Aguilera, D., & Messick, J. (1982). *Crisis intervention: Theory and methodology* (4th ed.). St. Louis: Mosby.

Austrian, S. (2002). Biopsychosocial assessment. In A. R. Roberts & G. J. Greene (Eds.), *Social workers' desk reference* (pp. 204–208). New York: Oxford University Press.

Barker, R. (1999). *The social work dictionary* (4th ed.). Washington, DC: NASW Press.

Belkin, G. (1984). *Introduction to counseling* (2nd ed.). Dubuque, IA: William C. Brown.

Blair, R. (2000). Risk factors associated with PTSD and major depression among Cambodian refugees in Utah. *Health & Social Work, 25,* 23–30.

Bolton, R. (1984). *People skills.* Englewood Cliffs, NJ: Prentice-Hall.

Burgess, A. W., & Roberts, A. R. (2000). Crisis intervention for persons diagnosed with clinical disorders based on the stress-crisis continuum. In A. R. Roberts (Ed.), *Crisis intervention handbook: Assessment, treatment, and research* (2nd ed., pp. 56–76). New York: Oxford University Press.

Chantarujikapong, S. I., Scherrer, J. F., Xian, H., Eisen, S. A., Lyons, M. J., Goldberg, J., et al. (2001). A twin study of generalized anxiety disorder symptoms, panic disorder symptoms and post-traumatic stress disorder in men. *Psychiatry Research, 103,* 133–145.

Cheung-Chung, M. C., Chung, C., & Easthope, Y. (2000). Traumatic stress and death anxiety among community residents exposed to an aircraft crash. *Death Studies, 24,* 689–704.

Corcoran, J., & Roberts, A. R.

(2000). Research on crisis intervention and recommendations for future research. In A. R. Roberts (Ed.), *Crisis intervention handbook: Assessment, treatment, and research* (2nd ed., pp. 453–486). New York: Oxford University Press.

Corcoran, K., & Boyer-Quick, J. (2002). How clinicians can effectively use assessment tools to evidence medical necessity and throughout the treatment process. In A. R. Roberts & G. J. Greene (Eds.), *Social workers' desk reference* (pp. 198–204). New York: Oxford University Press.

Corcoran, K., & Fischer, J. (2000). *Measures for clinical practice: A sourcebook* (Vols. 1 and 2, 3rd ed.). New York: Free Press.

Eaton, Y., & Ertl, B. (2000). The comprehensive crisis intervention model of Community Integration, Inc. Crisis Services. In A. R. Roberts (Ed.), *Crisis intervention handbook: Assessment, treatment, and research* (2nd ed., pp. 373–387). New York: Oxford University Press.

Eaton, Y., & Roberts, A. R. (2002). Frontline crisis intervention: Step-by-step practice guidelines with case applications. In A. R. Roberts & G. J. Greene (Eds.), *Social workers' desk reference* (pp. 89–96). New York: Oxford University Press.

Everly, G., Lating, J., & Mitchell, J. (2000). Innovation in group crisis intervention: Critical incident stress debriefing and critical incident stress management. In A. R. Roberts (Ed.), *Crisis intervention handbook: Assessment, treatment, and research* (2nd ed., pp. 77–97). New York: Oxford University Press.

Ford, J. D. (1999). Disorders of extreme stress following war-zone military trauma: Associated features of post-traumatic stress disorder (PTSD) or comorbid but distinct syndromes? Retrieved from http://www.trauma-pages.com/ford99.htm.

Fukuda, S., Morimoto, K., Mure, K., & Maruyama, S. (2000). Effect of the Hanshin-Awaji earthquake on posttraumatic stress, lifestyle changes, and cortisol levels of victims. *Archives of Environmental Health, 55,* 121–125.

Gitterman, A. (2002). The life model. In A. R. Roberts & G. J. Greene (Eds.), *Social workers' desk reference* (pp. 105–107). New York: Oxford University Press.

Gold, P. B., Engdahl, B. E., Eberly, R. E., Blake, R. J., Page, W. F., & Frueh, B. C. (2000). Trauma exposure, resilience, social support, and PTSD construct validity among former prisoners of war. *Social Psychiatry & Psychiatric Epidemiology, 35,* 36–42.

Greene, G. J., Lee, M. L., Trask, R., & Rheinscheld, J. (2000). How to work with clients' strengths in crisis intervention: A solution-focused approach. In A. R. Roberts (Ed.), *Crisis intervention handbook: Assessment, treatment, and research* (2nd ed., pp. 31–55). New York: Oxford University Press.

Greenstone, J., & Leviton, S. (1993). *Elements of crisis intervention: Crises and how to respond to them.* Pacific Grove, CA: Brooks/Cole.

Hersh, J. (1985). Interviewing college students in crisis. *Journal of Counseling and Development, 63,* 286–289.

Karls, J. M. (2002). Person-in-environment system: Its essence and applications. In A. R. Roberts & G. J. Greene (Eds.), *Social workers' desk reference* (pp. 194–198). New York: Oxford University Press.

LeCroy, C., & Okamoto, S. (2002). Guidelines for selecting and using assessment tools with children. In A. R. Roberts & G. J. Greene (Eds.), *Social workers' desk reference* (pp. 213–216). New York: Oxford University Press.

Leise, B. S. (1995). Integrating crisis intervention, cognitive therapy and triage. In A. R. Roberts (Ed.), *Crisis intervention and time-limited cognitive treatment* (pp. 28–51). Thousand Oaks, CA: Sage.

Lev-wiesel, R. (2000). Posttraumatic stress disorder symptoms, psychological distress, personal resources, and quality of life. *Family Process, 39,* 445–460.

Lewis, S., & Roberts, A. R. (2001). Crisis assessment tools. In A. R. Roberts & G. J. Greene (Eds.), *Social workers' desk reference* (pp. 208–212). New York: Oxford University Press.

Mitchell, J., & Everly, G. (1993). *Critical incident stress debriefing: An operations manual for the prevention of traumatic stress among emergency services and disaster workers.* Ellicott City, MD: Chevron.

Moursund, J. (1993). *The process of counseling and therapy* (3rd ed.). Englewood Cliffs, NJ: Prentice-Hall.

Munson, C. (2002). Guidelines for the *Diagnostic and Statistical Manual* (*DSM-IV-TR*) multiaxial system diagnosis. In A. R. Roberts & G. J. Greene (Eds.), *Social workers' desk reference* (pp. 181–189). New York: Oxford University Press.

National Commission on Terrorist Attacks upon the United States. (2004). *The 9/11 Commission report* (authorized ed.). New York: Norton.

Parad, H. (1965). *Crisis intervention: Selected readings.* New York: Family Service Association of America.

Pike, C. K. (2002). Developing client-focused measures. In A. R. Roberts & G. J. Greene (Eds.), *Social workers' desk reference* (pp. 189–193). New York: Oxford University Press.

Roberts, A. R. (1991). Conceptualizing crisis theory and the crisis intervention model. In A. R. Roberts (Ed.), *Contemporary perspectives on crisis intervention and prevention* (pp. 3–17). Englewood Cliffs, NJ: Prentice-Hall.

Roberts, A. R. (1996). Epidemiology and definitions of acute crisis episodes. In A. R. Roberts (Ed.), *Crisis management and brief treatment.* Chicago: Nelson-Hall.

Roberts, A. R. (2000). An overview of crisis theory and crisis intervention. In A. R. Roberts (Ed.), *Crisis intervention handbook: Assessment, treatment, and research* (2nd ed., pp. 3–30). New York: Oxford University Press.

Roberts, A. R., & Roberts, B. S. (2000). A comprehensive model for crisis intervention with battered women and their children. In A. R. Roberts (Ed.), *Crisis intervention handbook: Assessment, treatment, and research* (2nd ed., pp. 177–207). New York: Oxford University Press.

Rubin, A. (2002). Eye movement desensitization and reprocessing. In A. R. Roberts & G. J. Greene (Eds.), *Social workers' desk reference* (pp. 412–417). New York: Oxford University Press.

Shapiro, F. (1995). *Eye movement desensitization and reprocessing: Ba-*

sic principles, protocols, and procedures. New York: Guilford Press.

Solomon, Z., Mikulciner, M., & Avitzur, E. (1989). Coping, locus of control, social support, and combat-related posttraumatic stress disorder: A prospective study. *Journal of Personality and Social Psycholology, 55,* 279–285.

Terr, L. (1994). *Unchained memories: True stories of traumatic memories, lost and found.* New York: Basic Books.

Toukmanian, S. G., Jadaa, D., & Lawless, D. (2000). A cross-cultural study of depression in the aftermath of a natural disaster. *Anxiety, Stress, and Coping, 13,* 289–307.

Valentine, P. (2000). An application of crisis intervention to situational crises frequently experienced by adult survivors of incest. In A. R. Roberts (Ed.), *Crisis intervention handbook: Assessment, treatment, and research* (2nd ed., pp. 250–271). New York: Oxford University Press.

Vandiver, V. L., & Corcoran, K. (2002). Guidelines for establishing treatment goals and treatment plans with Axis I disorders: Sample treatment plan for generalized anxiety disorder. In A. R. Roberts & G. J. Greene (Eds.), *Social workers' desk reference* (pp. 297–304). New York: Oxford University Press.

Van Etten, M., & Taylor, S. (1998). Comparative efficacy of treatments for post-traumatic stress disorder: A meta-analysis. *Clinical Psychology and Psychotherapy, 5,* 126–145.

Waters, J. A., & Finn, E. (1995). Handling client crises effectively on the telephone. In A. R. Roberts (Ed.), *Crisis intervention and time-limited cognitive treatment* (pp. 251–289). Thousand Oaks, CA: Sage.

Williams, J. B. W. (2002). Using the *Diagnostic and Statistical Manual for Mental Disorders,* 4th ed., text revision (*DSM-IV-TR*). In A. R. Roberts & G. J. Greene (Eds.), *Social workers' desk reference* (pp. 171–180). New York: Oxford University Press.

Yeager, K. R., & Gregoire, T. K. (2000). Crisis intervention application of brief solution-focused therapy in addictions. In A. R. Roberts (Ed.), *Crisis intervention handbook: Assessment, treatment, and research* (2nd ed., pp. 275–306). New York: Oxford University Press.

Young, M. A. (1995). Crisis response teams in the aftermath of disasters. In A. R. Roberts (Ed.), *Crisis intervention and time-limited cognitive treatment* (pp. 151–187). Thousand Oaks, CA: Sage.

Zealberg, J., Santos, A., & Fisher, R. (1993). Benefits of mobile crisis programs. *Hospital and Community Psychiatry, 44,* 16–17.

7

Crisis Intervention and First Responders to Events Involving Terrorism and Weapons of Mass Destruction

VINCENT E. HENRY

July Fourth was a beautiful day in Veterans Memorial Park, and Central City Police Officers Pedro (Pete) Bernal and Dennis O'Loughlin were happy to be assigned to the Park Car that day. The thousand-acre park was full of people strolling, cycling, and rollerblading, a band was playing at the gazebo, and families spread their picnic blankets on the lawns and barbecued at the small beach at the edge of MacArthur Lake. "It doesn't get much better than this," Officer Bernal said to his partner as they cruised slowly past the playground filled with laughing children, "and it sure beats answering jobs all day in Sector Charlie. It's too bad every day can't be as nice and relaxed as today. A day like today makes you glad to be alive. Good country, America."

"It sure is. What should we do for lunch?" O'Loughlin replied, savoring the aromas of various ethnic foods emanating from all the pushcarts in the park. "It's almost one o'clock and I'm starving." After some discussion, they settled on a Cuban sandwich for Dennis and two hot dogs with mustard, relish, onions, and sauerkraut for Pedro. The call came just as they were getting back in their cruiser.

"Park Car One on the air?"

"Park Car One. Go ahead, Central."

"Park One, we have multiple aided calls in the vicinity of the gazebo on the Great Lawn. Callers state several people are having seizures. An ambulance is on the way. Please check and advise."

Dennis and Pete looked at each other. Both were experienced and well-trained cops, and the implications of the call were readily apparent to them. Just this week the precinct's intelligence liaison officer, Lieutenant Kennedy, had briefed the outgoing roll call to be especially on guard for potential terrorist events during the holiday weekend. Based on information received at the weekly regional Terrorstat meeting, Kennedy related that credible but unspecified threats—"intelligence chatter"—had been received by the FBI and passed on to local agencies. Although the information was not specific, and although the nation and the city remained at Threat Condition Yellow, officers should be especially attentive when responding to unusual events.

"Ten-four, Central. Please try the callback numbers and determine the number of victims and if there are any other symptoms. Have the ambulance stand by at the south entrance to the park and have Park Two stand by near the Boathouse until we check and advise."

Dennis and Pete regretfully put aside their food, started up their cruiser, and headed slowly toward the Great Lawn. They had been partners for almost 10 years and were experienced enough to know that they should not rush in to a situation like this, but instead respond carefully and gather as much information as possible on their way to the scene. A great many things had changed in police work during their 10 years as partners, not the least of which was the strategic and tactical approach they now took to calls that might involve a possible terrorist act. The terrorist attacks on the World Trade Center and the Pentagon five years ago required cops across the nation to adopt a new and very different orientation to the way they worked, and the possibility that even the most mundane and seemingly ordinary call for service might have some terrorist connection was always in the back of their minds. So far, Central City had escaped the realities of terrorism, but Bernal and O'Loughlin and their entire department were well prepared and well trained to handle terrorist incidents.

Perhaps because Bernal and O'Loughlin were so well trained and so well prepared, they were also terribly frightened by the prospect of a terrorist attack, especially one involving weapons of mass destruction. Everyone, it seems, was affected by the September 11 terrorist attacks, and in that respect these police officers were no different: like many others, they were riveted by media accounts of the event, and for days and weeks afterward they followed the frightening and terrible events closely in the news. As police officers, though, Bernal and O'Loughlin had a particularly strong interest in the September 11 attacks. Because they were experienced cops, they could very easily relate to the challenges and struggles faced by the police, fire, and other rescue personnel who responded to the World Trade Center or the Pentagon, and felt great empathy for them. As experienced cops, they could well understand the extent of the human tragedy resulting from the terrorist attacks: the anguish of thousands of families torn apart, the sorrow of thousands of friends of those who lost their lives, the pain and suffering of all of those who were injured, the economic impact on those who lost their jobs and whose families lost a source of income. Bernal and O'Loughlin understood all this, and because they understood it so well—and because they were such good cops—they prepared themselves thoroughly for the possibility of such an event in their city. Their department provided excellent training, but like many other cops, they sought out additional knowledge and additional skills that might become important if a terrorist attack occurred.

Bernal and O'Loughlin knew a great deal about terrorism and weapons of mass destruction, and what they knew frightened them. They were frightened now, but they could not afford to let their fear become immobilizing: they had a job to do, responsibilities to fulfill. The public needed protection, and it was their role as police officers to provide that protection. Beyond the cognitive knowledge and skills they'd developed, the two cops had prepared themselves physically, emotionally, and psychologically for this day. Later, they'd both talk about how frightened they were, but their overall preparation had steeled them emotionally and psychologically and they were able to put their fear aside to fulfill both the public's expectations of them and their own expectations of themselves. Both would later say that although they were afraid, they were also quite focused on the task required of them and their fear had a somewhat distant or abstract quality to it. There was a job to do, and they refused to permit the substantial fear they felt to prevent them from doing what needed to be done.

Despite the warmth of the day, they rolled up the cruiser's windows and turned off the air conditioner; if the situation turned out the way they hoped it wouldn't, at least they would be partially protected from airborne contaminants drawn in through the ventilation system. Pete rummaged in the gear bags on the cruiser's back seat, pulling out two pairs of binoculars, a small radiation detector, and a copy of the department's field guide to hazardous materials and weapons of mass destruction.

On the way to the scene, they carefully watched the holiday crowds for anything unusual or out of the ordinary. No one they passed appeared to be ill, and no one seemed to be in a particular hurry to leave the area. Dennis stopped the cruiser at the edge of the woods surrounding the Great Lawn, about a quarter mile from the gazebo.

Pete scanned the area with the binoculars, first looking at the commotion near the gazebo and then scanning the trees at the edge of the lawn. Dennis also scanned the scene with his binoculars. The band had stopped playing and highly excited people were milling around, trampling the picnic blankets and turning over barbecue grills. Some civilians lay prone or rolled on the ground as others tired to administer aid, while others gathered their children and tried to flee the chaotic scene. Some fell to the ground as they ran, and others fell to their knees to vomit. Dennis and Pete could hear frenzied shouting, and several civilians, spotting the cruiser, ran toward the cops.

"No birds. I don't see any birds in the trees. And there's a mist or cloud hanging over the area. It could be barbecue smoke, but I don't know. There's a dog having some kind of seizure, too. What have you got?" Dennis said to his partner. "Rats. Look at the rats crossing the road. The rats are running away. The wind is blowing toward the west, spreading the cloud. Move the car up the hill to the east roadway, but don't get any closer to the gazebo. I think I see dead pigeons at the verge of the woods. I get nothing on the radiation detector for now, but we may be too far away."

The first civilian, a highly distraught man with a flushed face, streaming tears, and vomit on his shirt, reached the cruiser and shouted frantically at the cops to help. Pete and Dennis both knew that time, distance, and shielding were the keys to their self-preservation, just as they both knew that they would become a liability if they became contaminated or affected by whatever substance was making these people sick. Time, distance, and shielding were the keys to their survival as well as the survival of the victims. Pete used the loudspeaker to order the man to back off from the police car: the civilian could potentially be a vector to spread whatever chemical or biological agent was afflicting the crowd, and the two cops would be of no help to anyone if they became affected by it. They'd later say that one of the hardest things about the situation was avoiding the urge to rush in to immediately render aid; it is, after all, the natural tendency of cops and rescue workers to run toward trouble in order to help. But the very fact that they lived to say it was evidence that they acted wisely and according to the way they'd been trained.

Still, they'd later be troubled by an amorphous sense of guilt, an irrational form of guilt, because in reality they'd performed superbly in every respect. The nagging thoughts remained, though: perhaps they could have done more. Perhaps more lives could have been saved if only they had done something differently. If only . . . The guilt was just one lasting outcome of their experience, however. The horrible images and associations connected with their experiences on that day and on the days and weeks that followed would stay with them, always near the forefront of consciousness and seemingly ready to reemerge at the slightest provocation. One of the most difficult things was that no one, other than those who were also at the park that day, really seemed to understand how different the world had become. No one seemed to understand what they'd seen and felt and smelled and touched, how it changed their world. They, along with the others who responded, were lauded as heroes, a label that was at first intoxicating but which they quickly came to resent. It made them angry that no one else seemed to understand them, or that nothing would ever be the same.

Pete communicated with the man using the loudspeaker, learning more about what had gone on near the gazebo as the first victims fell ill and taking notes about the symptoms. He learned there was a faint odor, like the smell of newly cut grass, at the time the first people fell ill.

Dennis picked up the radio and spoke calmly. "Park Car One to Central. Be advised we have a likely mass chemical or biological event on the Great Lawn. Numerous civilians down. There is a crowd of several hundred people, and we'll be moving them away from the scene to the east side of the park near the boathouse. Notify the Emergency Response Unit. Notify Midtown Hospital, Saint Mary's, and all the other hospitals to expect casualties. Notify the patrol supervisor that we'll set up a temporary emergency headquarters in the Parks Department office north of the Lawn pending his arrival. Notify the chief and the Fire Department. Have all available PD units respond to seal the park exits and perimeter, and have a unit respond to the Broadway bus station to prevent further contamination from people leaving the park. Have the ambulances respond to the boathouse area to set up an aid station. Central, caution the responding units not to approach the gazebo or the Great Lawn itself until we have further information about the contaminant and its effects. Also, caution the responding units to be aware of secondary devices or events. Here are the symptoms, Central . . . "

The threat of terrorist events involving weapons of mass destruction is real, and the futuristic scenario described above is not at all far-fetched.

The September 11, 2001, terrorist attacks on the World Trade Center and the Pentagon changed the United States forever, ushering in a host of new and unprecedented realities for the American people, for the intelligence and national security communities, for medical personnel, for private security entities, and perhaps especially for the police, fire, and emergency medical personnel. In particular, police, fire, and emergency medical service personnel, the agencies and individuals most likely to be the first responders to possible terrorist attacks, now face compelling demands to adopt new strategies and tactics, to undertake new training, and to view their roles and their work in an entirely different way. As first responders, police, fire, and emergency medical service personnel are our first line of defense in case of terrorist attack, but the enormity and complexity of the challenges they face make it abundantly clear that they alone cannot bear the responsibility for ensuring our safety. Although first responders play an absolutely critical role in homeland security and domestic preparedness, and although a great deal of attention and resources have already been focused on them to counter the terrorist threat, much more needs to be done. Perhaps most important, the realistic potential that American people, towns, and cities may again come under attack from terrorists demands that significant systemic changes occur throughout the range of public agencies and private entities charged with the responsibility for ensuring public safety. We must develop and implement a broader, more coordinated, more cohesive, and more focused approach to terrorism and to weapons of mass destruction (WMD), and that approach must involve new relationships between and among all of these public agencies and private entities.

The actions necessary to bring about all these changes are extensive, and they lie well beyond the scope of this chapter to fully describe or explore. This chapter focuses more narrowly on the issue of WMDs in the hands of terrorist groups, on the danger they pose to the American people and our nation as a whole, and on the steps necessary to create a more viable system to counter the threat. The importance of adequate preparation for future terrorist acts involving WMDs is illuminated by the virtual consensus among knowledgeable experts that these future acts are a practical inevitability. It is not a matter of whether such incidents will occur, but when they will occur (Lynch, 2002; Shenon & Stout, 2002).

In the first section of this chapter I define WMDs in general and provide an overview of specific types of WMDs as a way of understanding the nature of the threat they pose. I then examine, in a general way, the type of response protocols police, fire, emergency medical service, and other agencies have employed in relation to a mass terrorist attack, highlighting some of the problems and issues that are likely to emerge. I then explore some of the psychological consequences likely to become manifest among first responders to terrorist and WMD events, finally describing an innovative and successful approach to providing first responders with the type and quality of clinical services they may need.

Largely because the author had a professional involvement as a first responder to the World Trade Center attacks and the rescue and recovery activities that ensued, this chapter draws many examples and insights from the September 11 terrorist attacks in New York City. The events surrounding the World Trade Center attacks serve as a useful model from which a variety of guiding principles and insights can be distilled, including insights into the range and quality of psychological consequences likely to affect first responders to terrorist events.

WEAPONS OF MASS DESTRUCTION: AN OVERVIEW

Weapons of mass destruction are devices, biological organisms, or chemical substances that, when successfully detonated or dispersed, are readily capable of causing massive casualties. WMDs have been defined in various ways. The Department of Defense (Henneberry, 2001), for example, defines WMDs as "weapons that are capable of a high order of destruction and/or of being used in such a manner as to destroy large numbers of people." The definition goes on to note that these can include nuclear, chemical, biological, and radiological weapons. For legal purposes, Title 18 of the U.S. Code (18 USC 113B) includes various types of firearms and other weapons in its definition of WMDs, but it goes on to include "any weapon designed or intended to cause death or serious bodily injury through the release, dissemination, or impact of toxic or poisonous chemicals, or their precursors; any weapon involving a disease organism; or any weapon that is designed to release radiation or radioactivity at a level dangerous to human life."

The Federal Emergency Management Agency (FEMA, 2001) defines WMDs as "any weapon that is designed or intended to cause death or serious bodily injury through the release, dissemination, or impact of toxic or poisonous chemicals; disease organisms; radiation or radioactivity; or explosion or fire." The FEMA definition goes on to point out that WMDs are distinguished from other types of terrorist tools because they may not be immediately obvious, because it may be difficult to determine when and where they have been released, and because of the danger they pose to first responders and medical personnel. Although a great deal of research has taken place on battlefield exposure to WMDs, scientists have a more limited understanding of how they might affect civilian populations.

Examples of WMDs include nuclear devices (ranging from nuclear bombs to smaller and more easily constructed "dirty bombs" that spread deadly radiation in a relatively small area), biological devices (such as anthrax, smallpox, and other deadly toxins), and chemical agents (such as nerve agents and gaseous poisons). These three categories of weapons are often referred to collectively as NBC (nuclear, biological, and chemical) weapons. It should also be recognized that the hijacked airliners used in the September 11 terrorist attacks on the Pentagon and the World Trade Center clearly conform to the FEMA definition of a WMD: they were high-powered explosive devices loaded with highly flammable fuel that caused a tremendous number of casualties, they were not immediately obvious as weapons, and they posed an exceptionally high degree of danger to first responders and medical personnel as well as to the general public.

Biological and Chemical Agents in Warfare and Terrorism

Chemical and biological agents have been used in warfare between nations for many years, and they have been extremely effective weapons in terms of causing casualties and death as well as in spreading fear and panic among an enemy's soldiers. More recently, they have become the weapons of choice for terrorists and extremist groups for essentially the same reasons, as well as the fact that they are rather easily manufactured and deployed. The first modern wartime use of chemical weapons of war occurred during World War I, when German forces used chlorine gas against Allied forces in April 1915 during the Second Battle of Ypres. British forces retaliated in September of that year, firing artillery shells containing chlorine gas against the German forces at Loos. Poison gas was a fairly successful but nevertheless imperfect battlefield weapon: French and Algerian troops fled in a panic when they confronted chlorine gas at Ypres, but shifting winds during the British action at Loos also caused numerous casualties among the British forces employing them (Duffy, 2002). The fact that the spread and effect of poison gases and some biological agents can be so easily affected by wind and other environmental factors makes them particularly unpredictable and especially dangerous to first responders, to rescue personnel, and to civilians in densely populated urban areas.

The development of the use of poison gases continued throughout World War I. Phosgene gas was used by both sides in the conflict, and it was seen as an improved weapon because it caused less choking and coughing than chlorine gas and was therefore more likely to be inhaled. Phosgene also had a delayed effect in which soldiers might suddenly die up to 48 hours after their exposure. Mustard gas, an almost odorless chemical, was developed by Germany and first used against Russian troops at Riga in 1917. The strategic advantages of mustard gas (also known as Yperite) included inflicting painful blisters, the fact that it was more difficult to protect against than chlorine or phosgene, and the fact that it could remain potent in the soil for weeks, making it dangerous to recapture contaminated trenches or territory (Duffy, 2002). The use of chlorine, phosgene, and mustard gas continued throughout World War I, inflicting a terrible casualty rate. According to one estimate, there were almost 1,240,000 casualties from poison gas during World War I, including more than 90,000 deaths. Russia alone suffered nearly 420,000 gas casualties (Duffy, 2002).

The decades following World War I saw continued development of poison gases as well as some use on the battlefield. During the 1920s, British forces used chemical weapons against Kurdish rebels in Iraq, and the 1930s saw the use of mustard gas by Italy during its conquest of Ethiopia and the use of chemical weapons by Japan in its invasion of China. The first nerve agent, Tabun, was developed in Germany in 1938.

In the United States, the first known attempt by a terrorist or extremist group to use biological agents against the civilian population occurred in 1972, when members of a right-wing group known as the Order of the Rising Sun were found to possess more than 30 kilograms of typhoid bacteria. The group intended to spread typhoid through the water supply systems of several major midwestern cities (Sachs, 2002, p. 3).

Another bioterrorism event occurred in the United States in 1984, when members of a religious cult known as Rajneeshee infected an estimated 751 people in Oregon with Salmonella bacteria (Torok et al., 1995). Cult members grew the bacteria from cultures they purchased from a medical supply company and disseminated the bacteria by spraying it on restaurant salad bars. Their goal was to influence the results of an upcoming local election by making a large number of voters too sick to vote on election day (McDade & Franz, 1988; Sachs, 2002, pp. 4–5). Investigators considered the possibility of bioterrorism when the outbreak occurred, but the possibility was deemed unlikely and the source of the contamination only became apparent when the FBI investigated the cult for other criminal violations. This incident highlighted the difficulties of distinguishing a bioterrorist attack from a naturally occurring infectious disease outbreak (McDade & Franz, 1988).

The series of anthrax attacks that took place across the United States in 2001 were a type of terrorist attack, spreading tremendous alarm and fear throughout the population. In these incidents, anthrax spores were distributed, perhaps at random, through the U.S. Postal Service to individuals, corporations, and political figures, and at least 10 cases of anthrax infection were documented by health officials (Jernigan et al., 2001; Traeger et al., 2001).

Former Iraqi dictator Saddam Hussein used both chemical weapons (nerve agents) and biological weapons (anthrax) on Iranian forces during the 1980–1988 war between Iran and Iraq, and he also used cyanide against Iraqi Kurds in 1987 and 1988. In 1995, members of the Aum Shinrikyo (or Supreme Truth) cult dispersed deadly Sarin gas on the Tokyo subway system, killing a dozen people and injuring more than 5,500 others.

Aum Shinrikyo's 1995 Tokyo subway attack, which represents the first known use of poison gas or other WMD by terrorists, had a tremendous impact on Japan and on Japanese society because it spread such fear and alarm among members of the public. The Japanese people, like the rest of the world community, were not well prepared for the possibility that a fairly small religious cult would carry out such an attack, nor were they prepared for the possibility that a fairly small religious cult *could* carry out this type of attack. The fact that such a small group marshaled the resources necessary to kill and injure large numbers of people and spread panic across an entire nation had repercussions throughout the world, demonstrating how easily terrorists or extremist groups can manufacture and disseminate deadly WMDs.

Aum Shinrikyo was a doomsday cult centered around leader Shoko Asahara's apocalyptic philosophy and his twisted notion that only the true believers belonging to the cult would be saved once the world ended. Asahara's goal in undertaking the attack was to hasten the end of the world. The cult, which accumulated immense wealth from its members, recruited young scientists as cult members and put them to work producing biological and chemical weapons. It also began to stockpile hundreds of tons of deadly chemicals and acquired a helicopter to help distribute the gas over densely populated Japanese cities (Kristoff, 1995; Lifton, 1999).

Sarin, an exceptionally toxic nerve agent that is several hundred times more toxic than cyanide, was first developed by Nazi scientists in the 1930s. Also known as GB, Sarin is a fairly complex chemical compound that can take either liquid or gaseous form, and although its manufacture requires a fairly high level of skill, training, and knowledge of chemistry, it is made from common chemicals that are readily available to the public. Once cult members manufactured a quantity of Sarin, it was a rather simple thing to disseminate it: liquid Sarin was sealed in paint cans and other containers that cult members carried into subway stations in shopping bags. They simply put down the bags, casually punctured the containers with the tips of their umbrellas, and walked away while the liquid evaporated into a gas and spread through the area. Experts concur that the 1995 subway attack was simply a test, a dry run in anticipation of and preparation for a much larger and much more deadly attack. Experts also concur that many more lives would have been lost and many more would have been injured if Aum Shinrikyo had been able to manufacture a purer form of Sarin or distribute it more effectively (Kristoff, 1995; Lifton, 1999).

Perhaps one of the most frightening aspects of Aum Shinrikyo's attack on the subway system was the relative ease with which the group obtained the necessary precursor chemicals to manufacture large quantities of deadly Sarin. There are many other biological and chemical agents that are relatively easy to obtain, manufacture, and disseminate, making them very attractive to terrorist organizations. Depending on the particular chemical or biological agent involved, a relatively small and easily transportable amount of the substance can spread throughout an area and contaminate or infect people coming in contact with it. Especially when toxic biological substances with a prolonged incubation period are involved, signs of illness may not be immediately apparent. Individuals infected with the toxic substance may act as a vector, spreading the substance to others with whom they have contact. As it might be days or weeks before the first infected individuals become ill, they can spread the infection to literally hundreds or thousands of other people, many of whom will in turn become vectors spreading the disease.

A chemical event is likely to immediately produce dozens of victims, and first responders who lack adequate personal protection equipment may also become victims. All exposed victims must be decontaminated before leaving the scene, because hospital emergency rooms will not accept the victims of a biological or chemical incident until they have been properly decontaminated.

Chemical agents can enter the body in various ways. Some agents are disseminated as aerosols or gases and enter the body through the respiratory tract, while others are disseminated in a liquid form and enter the body through contact with the skin. Because the eyes and mucous membranes are particularly sensitive to many toxic agents, irritated eyes and nasal passages often indicate exposure. While other chemical agents can be ingested via contaminated food or liquid, inhalation and skin contact are the primary hazard for victims and emergency responders.

There are three basic categories of chemical agents: nerve agents, blister or vesicant agents, and choking agents.

Nerve Agents

Nerve agents, which include the substances Tabun (GA), Soman (GD), Sarin (GB), and methylphosphonothioic acid (VX), are an especially toxic class of chemical weapon that act on the body by interrupting the central nervous system to prevent the transmission of nerve impulses, resulting in twitches and spasms. Other symptoms of exposure to nerve agents typically include dilation of pupils (pinpoint pupils), runny nose and lacrimation (tearing of eyes), salivation (drooling), difficulty breathing, muscle twitches and spasms, involuntary defecation or urination, nausea and vomiting.

Depending on their purity, nerve agents generally take the form of colorless liquids, although some may have a slight yellowish tinge if impurities are present. Tabun and Sarin may have a slightly fruity odor, Soman may have a slight odor of camphor, and VX smells like sulfur. Nerve agents evaporate fairly quickly and can be absorbed into the body either through inhalation or absorption through the skin. Nerve agents vary a bit in terms of their toxicity and the amount of exposure necessary to bring on symptoms or cause death, but all are exceptionally deadly at exceptionally low dosages. Exposure to a fatal dose of a nerve agent, if untreated, will typically cause death in a matter of minutes. The typical treatment for nerve agents is an injection of atropine.

Blister or Vesicant Agents

Blister or vesicant agents act by producing burns or blisters on the skin or any other body part they come in contact with, and they can be fatal. They act quickly on the eyes, lungs, skin, and mucous membranes, inflicting severe damage on the lungs and respiratory tract when inhaled and resulting in vomiting and diarrhea when ingested.

Blister agents include mustard gas (also known as Yperite or sulfur mustard), nitrogen mustard (HN), Lewisite (L), and phosgene oxime (CX). Mustard gas and Lewisite are particularly dangerous because they produce severe injuries for which there is no known antidote or therapy; a single drop of liquid mustard on the skin can cause serious damage and itching in only a few minutes, and exposure to even a slight amount of mustard in its gaseous state can cause painful blistering, tearing, and lesions of the eyes. Depending on weather conditions as well as the extent and duration of exposure, the effects of mustard gas can be delayed for up to a day. Several hours after the exposure, respiratory effects become apparent in the form of severe burning pain in the throat, trachea, and lungs. Although most mustard gas victims survive, severe pulmonary edema or swelling of the lungs may result in death. The only effective form of protection against mustard gas is the use of a full-body protective suit (Level I protection) and the use of a gas mask or respirator.

Lewisite, which is typically colorless and odorless in its liquid state but as a gas may emit the faint scent of geraniums, causes symptoms that are generally similar to mustard gas but also includes a decrease in both blood pressure and body temperature. Inhalation of Lewisite in high concentrations can lead to death in a few minutes, and the antidote (Dimercaprol) for skin blistering must be applied before the actual blistering begins to take place.

Phosgene oxime (CX) can exist as a white powder or, when mixed with water or other solvents, in a liquid state. Contact with phosgene oxime is extremely painful, and it quickly irritates the skin, the respiratory system, and the eyes, leading to lesions of the eye, blindness, and respiratory edema. Contact with the skin immediately produces an area of white surrounded by reddened skin and swelling. Because phosgene oxime is heavier than air, it can remain in low-lying areas for quite some time, and so it poses a particular danger for rescue workers. Phosgene oxime has a sharp and penetrating odor.

Choking Agents

These agents enter the body via the respiratory tract and often cause severe pulmonary edema. Because these agents are most effectively deployed as gases, they are typically stored and transported in bottles or cylinders prior to being disseminated into the air. As their name implies, choking agents quickly attack and cause severe damage to the lungs and respiratory system, and they can cause pulmonary edema and death. Choking agents include phosgene (CG), diphosgene (DP), and chlorine (CL) in liquid or gaseous form. It should be noted that phosgene (CG) and phosgene oxime (CX) are chemically different substances that have different properties and different symptoms. Symptoms include severe coughing, choking, nausea, lacrimation, difficulty breathing, and vomiting. The initial symptoms may subside for a period of up to a day, but the symptoms typically return when pulmonary edema takes place and individuals exposed to choking agents may go into shock as their blood pressure and heart rate drop precipitously.

Biological Agents

Biological agents share some common characteristics with chemical agents, but important differences distinguish this class of WMDs from chemical agents. Whereas chemical agents typically produce symptoms relatively quickly, biological agents may not produce symptoms for periods of up to several weeks. There may be no early warning signs to a bioterrorist event, and first responders may not easily or immediately recognize that they have been exposed. In contrast to the three classes of chemical agents, biological agents do not typically produce immediate symptoms on the skin or in respiratory system. Many biological agents are living organisms—bacteria or viruses; they cannot be detected by any of our senses, and the scientific devices used to detect and identify them are complex and difficult to use. Detection generally occurs only after an incubation period has elapsed and the infected person becomes ill.

Biological agents, which include anthrax, tularemia, cholera, plague, botulism, and smallpox, can be disseminated through a population in several ways. Although some biotoxins (such as anthrax) may be spread through contact with the skin (either through direct contact or through cuts and lacerations), in terms of WMDs and the terrorist goals of causing widespread casualties, the most effective means of dissemination are to aerosolize the biological agent into a fine mist or powder that is inhaled or to contaminate food or water that members of the public will ingest.

There are three classes of biological agents: bacteria, viruses, and toxins. Bacteria and viruses are living organisms that require a host organism in order to survive and reproduce. After entering the body (usually through inhalation or ingestion), the organism establishes itself within the host, begins to replicate, and produces poisonous toxins that cause severe and often fatal illnesses.

The difficulties involved in detecting and diagnosing biological WMD attacks can be especially pronounced when the biological agents result in a slowly developing community health crisis or an epidemic of some sort. Because a prolonged incubation period often precedes the appearance of symptoms, bioterrorist attacks may be difficult to trace back to their source and may not be easily recognized as part of a terrorist act. The difficulties involved in detecting and diagnosing cases of anthrax infection across the nation in the fall of 2001 are an example. While a more focused direct attack, such as the rapid release of a large quantity of fast-acting biological toxin in an office building or mass transportation center, would probably be recognized and dealt with more quickly, both forms of attack can have a potent psychological impact on the public as well as on first responders. Beyond the deaths and illnesses that may occur, such attacks suit the needs and objectives of terrorists because they can generate substantial fear and public alarm.

Terrorism and the Use of Nuclear Material

Although the likelihood is small that a terrorist organization could obtain or manufacture a high-grade nuclear device capable of destroying a large area, much less transport it to the United States and detonate it, there is a much greater potential for terrorists to construct an improvised nuclear device (IND) or dirty bomb. Such an improvised weapon would nevertheless have a devastating physical and psychological impact by spreading radioactive contamination throughout a densely populated urban area.

A dirty bomb is essentially a conventional explosive device surrounded by radioactive materials that, on detonation, spreads radioactive material within a relatively small fallout zone. Depending on the size of the device and the type and amount of radioactive material involved, the immediate area surrounding the detonation might be uninhabitable for a long time, and those directly exposed to the radioactive fallout are likely to suffer radiation sickness. The possibility also exists that exposed victims might eventually develop cancer, leukemia, or other diseases related to radiation exposure.

The possibility that INDs or dirty bombs might be detonated in urban areas is particularly alarming, because the materials required for such devices can be obtained fairly easily, because large amounts of radioactive material are not required for an effective device, and because radiation cannot be detected by human senses. A seemingly "ordinary" small explosion in or near a large crowd of people could spread nuclear contaminants through the crowd, with no immediately apparent symptoms. The low-grade nuclear materials required to construct such a device are used, transported, and stored in various locations, including hospitals and medical facilities, research laboratories, and industrial manufacturing facilities across the nation. Although these materials are more carefully guarded today than they were in the past, it is probably not beyond the capacity of a determined terrorist organization to obtain them.

FIRST RESPONDER SAFETY: TIME, DISTANCE, AND SHIELDING

Generally speaking, the police and emergency workers who might be called on to respond initially to a nuclear, biological, or chemical event are not adequately trained to deal effectively with those events. This is not to say that most police and emergency workers lack *any* training in this area, but rather that they lack the highly specific training and special expertise required to recognize and deal with many of the complex and unique threats posed by such events. At present, many also lack the special tools, gear, and protective equipment these events may require. Patrol officers, firefighters, and emergency medical service personnel who initially respond to an event involving WMDs should not be expected to undertake the specific duties and responsibilities that are better performed by well-equipped and more highly trained specialists. Their primary role should be to recognize the threat, to minimize additional exposure to chemical or biological agents, to ensure the safety of victims, to safeguard the scene, and to report their findings to those more competent to deal with these issues. Another primary responsibility is to minimize their own contact with the chemical or biological agent and to provide as much information as possible to ensure the safety and the effectiveness of other responding units. First responders who rush in to a WMD event not only risk death or serious injury from secondary devices that may have been placed at or near the scene precisely to disable or kill rescuers, but they may also become a significant liability to other victims as well as to other responders if they become contaminated themselves. The first responder who rushes in and becomes a victim may exacerbate the overall problem, consuming precious time and resources.

As Gordon M. Sachs (2002, pp. vii–viii) points out, responders must make some tough choices and difficult decisions:

> The first instinct for emergency responders at any incident is always to rush in and save as many people as possible; however, in a terrorist-related incident there are many factors to consider. Can the victims be saved? Will responders become targets? Was an agent of some type released? If it was, will responders have the means to detect it? Will their gear provide adequate protection? These are but a few of the questions that we must become accustomed to asking when responding to terrorist-related incidents. There is no reason to allow civilians to suffer needlessly; neither can there be any reason to send responders haphazardly into unknown and dangerous environments.

There are four types or levels of protective gear used by emergency workers during WMD events. *Level A* protection is a chemical-resistant suit that entirely encapsulates the emergency worker, and it includes a self-contained breathing apparatus (SCBA) or an independent air supply so that workers are not exposed to fumes, biological agents, or other toxic substances that may be present in the environment. This level of protection provides maximum respiratory and skin protection and is typically used when the situation involves a high potential for liquid splashes or vapor hazards or when the chemical agent is unidentified. Generally speaking, this level of protection is used by highly trained specialists who enter the "hot zone," or the area closest to the WMD's point of dispersal.

Level B protection is a chemical-resistant suit and gloves that does not entirely encapsulate the rescue worker, but it does include SCBA or an independent air supply. This type of gear provides a high level of respiratory protection but less protection against liquids and gases that may affect the skin or be absorbed through the skin. This type of gear provides the minimum amount of protection one should use in the hot zone, and is not recommended for prolonged exposure or use in the hot zone.

Level C protection is provided by hooded chemical-resistant clothing and gloves and is equipped with an air-purifying respirator or gas mask. It is generally utilized when there is minimal or no hazard posed by the potential for liquid splashes or direct contact.

Level D protection is the type most police, fire, and emergency medical workers typically have available to them: their uniforms and clothing. This type of protective gear provides minimal protection from chemical, biological, or nuclear hazards and should not be worn in or near the hot zone.

Perhaps the most important tools available to ensure the safety of first responders, though, have nothing to do with equipment or gear. They are the concepts of *time, distance,* and *shielding,* which, when properly applied, can be the key to the first responder's self-preservation. In terms of *time,* emergency responders should keep the time they spend in the vicinity of the incident to an absolute minimum. Minimizing the time spent in proximity to a nuclear, biological, or chemical substance generally reduces one's chance of illness or injury because it minimizes one's exposure to the toxic substance. If emergency workers absolutely need to approach the scene to rescue someone or to inspect it more closely, they should not remain there a moment longer than necessary. They should also be aware that if they do approach the scene they may inadvertently become a vector to spread the substance, and they should take appropriate steps to decontaminate as quickly as possible. First responders who come in proximity to the scene should promptly notify their supervisors and medical personnel to ensure a proper decontamination, and until decontamination occurs they should avoid contact with others.

Similarly, emergency workers should maintain a safe and appropriate *distance* from the hazard, and they should try to move uphill from the source if possible. In terms of distance, emergency responders must also bear in mind that many substances can be spread by wind currents, and they should consider the direction and velocity of the wind in determining a safe location. There are various charts and tables available to first responders to help them determine the proper interval of safety between them and a particular type, source, and quantity of toxic substance. Police, fire, and emergency workers should prepare themselves for the possibility of a WMD attack by obtaining these tables and consulting them before approaching the scene. For example, the *North American Emergency Response Guide,* developed jointly by the U.S. Department of Transportation, Transport Canada, and the Secretariat of Communications and Transportation of Mexico for use by first responders to transportation incidents involving hazardous materials, permits users to quickly identify the type of substance involved in the incident and to protect both themselves and the public during the initial response phase.

First responders should also bear in mind that these charts and tables provide general guidelines, and that qualified experts who subsequently arrive at the scene are likely to evaluate the situation and adjust the distances of the hot, warm, and cold zones. In establishing the initial zones, first responders should remain flexible and, if necessary, they should err on the side of safety to extend the distance. In terms of distance, first responders should also bear in mind that secondary devices or booby traps designed to injure and disable rescuers may be in the area, and they should proceed cautiously. The secondary devices might be as powerful or perhaps more powerful than the primary device.

Shielding refers to any object that can be used to protect the first responder from a specific hazard, and can include buildings, vehicles, and any personal protective equipment available. The type of shielding responders should use is determined by a number of factors, including weather, the physical environment, the geography, and the topography of the area; buildings in urban areas may, for example, provide shielding (as well as a better vantage point) that is not available in a rural area, where a hill or elevation may fulfill the same functions. Simply rolling up the windows of a police car, turning off the air conditioner, and putting on gloves can provide some degree of safety and protection to police officers approaching the scene of a potentially toxic event. If an officer's department does not furnish personal protective gear (as it should), it may be advisable to purchase an inexpensive and lightweight Tyvek jumpsuit for one's gear bag.

The most critical concerns for first responders must be their own safety and protection, and they must avoid the compelling urge to rush into a situation to render help. It can be a very difficult thing for a dedicated police officer, firefighter, or emergency medical worker not to rush in and not to render aid to someone in need, but training and common sense must prevail. As noted above, the rescuer who becomes a victim exacerbates and complicates the situation other responders must confront.

THE PRIVATE SECTOR'S ROLE

The problems associated with preventing, deterring, responding to, and investigating terrorist attacks involving WMDs are enormously difficult and complex, and they require solutions that are equally complex. We must recognize that the threat posed by a terrorist WMD attack involves much more than simply developing effective first-response capabilities and that an actual attack will have resounding impact and repercussions throughout the local (and possibly the national) economy, the health care system, the corporate and business communities, public utilities, and government operations at every level. We must also recognize that depending on the type, the quality, and the extent of a WMD attack, literally hundreds of public agencies and private sector entities may be called on to participate in initial response, in rescue and recovery, and in ongoing rebuilding efforts. We need look no further than the World Trade Center attacks in New York to realize that literally hundreds of organizations become involved in the overall recovery effort. While police, fire, and emergency medical personnel handled most of the first-responder duties in the first minutes and hours following the attack, they were very quickly joined at the scene by personnel from a host of other organizations. These organizations included the American Red Cross and other relief organizations, the telephone, gas, and electric utilities operating in New York City, federal law enforcement agencies (the FBI, BATF, Secret Service, and U.S. Customs, to name a few), law enforcement from other states and jurisdictions (the New York State Police, the New Jersey State Police, and practically every local municipality in the region immediately dispatched officers to the scene), FEMA, every branch of the U.S. military, the National Guard, and a raft of others. Personnel from all these organizations quickly converged on the scene, and although they were willing and to a large extent able to help out, the lack of central direction and focus created enormous confusion and duplication of efforts. Without for a moment reducing the commitment and bravery displayed by these individuals, the area that became known as Ground Zero quickly degenerated to a state of near chaos as everyone tried to pitch in and help.

Immediately after the attack, hospital emergency rooms within a 100-mile radius of New York City were mobilized and put on alert. Medical personnel were called in to hospitals and medical facilities, and medical personnel in private practices showed up to volunteer at hospitals. Private ambulance services were mobilized for the transport of casualties, and buses from the city's Transit Authority were commandeered to bring police and other rescuers to the scene. Corporate facilities, office buildings, and college campuses went into a high-security mode, often deploying their security personnel to evacuate and lock down their facilities. The city's transportation infrastructure—public transportation, subways and buses, bridges and tunnels, roads and highways—quickly became overwhelmed by the effort to evacuate tens of thousands of people from Lower Manhattan.

Communications systems were overwhelmed. Most cell phone service throughout Lower Manhattan ended when the Towers fell and cellular repeaters were destroyed, and a main switching station for the city's hard-wire telephone system flooded and interrupted most service in the area. As noted above, there was little or no interoperability between the police and fire radio communication systems to begin with, and the loss of radio repeaters made radio communications even more difficult.

In the days following the attack, help poured in from across the nation in the form of personnel, equipment, food, and medical supplies, and a complex logistical system of depots and distribution points had to be established and implemented. The work went on 24 hours a day for months, and workers required food, medical attention, and places to rest and recuperate between shifts. Heavy construction equipment was rushed to New York to aid in the removal of debris, and thousands of construction workers were deployed to make the area safe. The rescue and recovery phase of operations continued for several weeks in the futile hope that additional survivors would be located, and fires burned at the World Trade Center site for 99 days. The fires and smoke, along with the airborne hazardous materials they contained, prompted public health officials to monitor air quality throughout the Lower Manhattan area. As bodies and body parts were recovered, they were removed to a medical examiner's facility for DNA testing in hope of identifying the dead and bringing closure to surviving family and friends. Canine rescue teams were brought in to aid in the search for victims, and the animals required extensive and specialized veterinary care. Psychologists, psychiatrists, and mental health workers arrived to provide crisis intervention and therapy for those traumatized by the event, and a special center for family and friends of victims was established to help them deal with their loss and with the legal, financial, and personal consequences.

Even before the rescue and recovery phase ended, the process of removing millions of tons of debris via truck and barge to a site on Staten Island commenced. The debris would be sifted by hand by NYPD detectives and other law enforcement officers to locate body parts as well as any personal effects or crime scene evidence that might be recovered, and all recovered items had to be logged, vouchered, and forwarded to the morgue or to temporary storage facilities. Complicating the entire operation was the fact that the World Trade Center site became the world's largest and most difficult crime scene, and all the precautions ordinarily undertaken to discover and preserve evidence were put in place. Providing security for the site was a monumental effort.

The list of actions and activities that took place in the aftermath of this horrific and devastating attack goes on and on, and without belaboring the point further, it should suffice to say that this was the largest and most complicated enterprise ever undertaken as the result of a terrorist WMD attack. Tens of thousands of individuals, hundreds of public agencies, and dozens of private sector entities played a role in the initial response, in the rescue and recovery, or in the removal operations phases.

THE TRAUMATIC IMPACT ON FIRST RESPONDERS

The psychological repercussions of the September 11 terrorist attacks were far-ranging and consequential, as individuals across the nation and around the world felt the traumatic impact of the events and their aftermath. Indeed, the consequences and repercussions of the terrorist attacks continue to resonate in public discourse, in the political sphere, and in our individual and collective social and psychological worlds. Without minimizing the traumatic impact the attacks had on any individual or group, it should be pointed out that as individuals and as a group, first responders to the World Trade Center, many of whom witnessed the devastation firsthand, encountered profound sensory images of death and destruction, and were in close proximity to the alien landscape of Ground Zero for protracted period, were certainly among the most traumatized. These first responders are, in Robert Jay Lifton's (1980) definition, survivors: they have come in close physical and psychological contact with death but remained alive, and their post-exposure lives and experiences can be understood in terms of Lifton's (1967, 1974, 1980, 1983) "psychology of survival" perspective. The psychology of survival is a natural, adaptive, and universal human psychological response to an entirely unnatural experience involving profound death trauma, and as an adaptive and protective response it permits the individual to physically and psychologically survive the traumatic experience (Lifton 1967, 1974, 1980, 1983).

First responders to the World Trade Center attacks clearly manifest the five themes and features of Lifton's psychology of survival, a psychological perspective that was developed from extensive studies of other death-immersed groups. Among the groups Lifton studied were survivors of the Hiroshima atomic bombing (1967, 1970) and of natural disasters (Lifton & Olsen, 1976) and Vietnam veterans (1973). The perspective was also developed and refined in studies of Nazi doctors and the medicalization of killing (1986), the psychology of genocide (1986, 1990), the threat of nuclear extinction (1982, 1987, 1990), and the process of "thought reform" in the development of cults (1963). Given the breadth and scope of Lifton's research on traumatized individuals and groups and the fact that it has been successfully applied in the area of police psychology (Henry, 1995, 2001, 2004a, 2004b), his model seems particularly appropriate to understand the experience of first responders to terrorist events. The post–September 11 lives of first responders are characterized by lasting features of psychic numbing, death guilt, suspicion of various forms of nurturance they perceive as counterfeit, a lasting death imprint or indelible psychic image of death trauma, and a powerful quest to make coherent meaning of their absurd and painful experience (Henry, 2001, 2004a, 2004b).

Many first responders, particularly the police officers, firefighters, and emergency medical service personnel who were physically present during the actual attack as well as those involved in the rescue and recovery efforts following the Towers' collapse, were deeply traumatized by their experience. In the days and weeks following the attacks, those who worked at Ground Zero experienced a complete immersion in profound sensory images of death and destruction, and many experienced a deep and penetrating grief for lost friends, peers, and coworkers. Although each individual experienced and interpreted the event differently, many or most first responders encountered the traumatic sights and smells of death on a massive and unprecedented scale. Many experienced the trauma of body handling as they dug through the rubble in search of survivors and, ultimately, victims. They experienced, probably to a far greater extent than the average person physically distant from the site, an overarching sense of fear that a subsequent attack would imperil their safety. They were exposed to choking clouds of smoke rising from the rubble, and many understood or supposed that the noxious fumes they breathed contained all sorts of carcinogenic and poisonous chemical compounds likely to affect their future health. Many rescuers worked seemingly endless hours in and around the pile of rubble, and along with the stress and the lack of sufficient sleep and food their physical exertion led quickly to an overall exhaustion. Many were physically and emotionally isolated from their families as they worked almost continuously for weeks on end. Their isolation and absence in a time of great public fear often engendered resentment and anger among family members who perceived their absence as evidence that the first responder's priorities placed professional duties above family responsibilities. This introduced tremendous (and often enduring) strains to their most intimate relationships—the very relationships that are critical in providing the kind of ongoing sustenance and support traumatized individuals require. The specific (and quite complex) dimensions and features of the trauma experienced by first responders have been described at length elsewhere, as have many of the social and psychological outcomes and repercussions of that traumatic exposure (Henry, 2004a, 2004b).

It seems unnecessary to belabor the point further in the context of this chapter. It should be pointed out, however, that in addition to manifesting the features of survivor psychology, many first responders to the World Trade Center attacks as well as to the attacks on the Pentagon and the crash site in Pennsylvania can be expected to eventually manifest the symptoms of posttraumatic stress disorder (PTSD) or other traumatic syndromes. To a greater or lesser extent, all the first responders to these events carry the psychological baggage of having been immersed in this profound imagery of death and destruction. Although many continue to experience psychological difficulties, there remain few adequate sources of treatment available to them. Where resources are available, many first responders are resistant to accessing and utilizing them.

Generally speaking, members of the police and firefighter occupational cultures have traditionally been reluctant to seek assistance or treatment for the psychological difficulties they may encounter as a result of their work. While this widely recognized dynamic is often simplistically attributed to the "macho" features of their tight-knit and insular cultures, cultures that are often characterized as suspicious of outsiders and that place great value on ideals of personal courage and stoic self-sufficiency, it must be recognized that the reality of organizational life in police and fire agencies can also operate synergistically with these cultural features to actively discourage members from acknowledging difficulties and seeking help for them. This seems especially true of police agencies, whose formal and informal policies may in fact operate to effectively penalize officers who seek help. At the very least, policies can easily create the perception that negative career consequences will accrue to officers who come forward to admit they are having psychological difficulties.

It must be recognized that although many police, fire, and emergency medical service agencies provide employee assistance programs or other counseling services to their members, the advent of these services is a relatively recent phenomenon and they are not central to the agencies' larger organizational goals. Perhaps especially in the context of police agencies, a larger overriding organizational goal is that of liability abatement, and this goal impacts the provision of psychological services in important ways. Stated succinctly, officers who step forward to acknowledge their psychological difficulties pose a distinct problem for police agencies in terms of liability: by acknowledging difficulties, they implicitly increase the agency's potential liability if those officers subsequently become involved in, for example, an incident involving physical or deadly physical force. The legal issue of the officer's fitness for duty will inevitably arise in these and other cases, and the agency will have to prove that it performed due diligence in evaluating the officer before he or she was returned to full enforcement duties. Agencies that encourage members to come forward with their problems concomitantly increase their potential liability for the on- or off-duty actions those members take or fail to take.

Perhaps especially in police agencies (where liability may be greater), members acknowledging difficulties may find themselves removed from active duty, stripped of their weapons and enforcement powers, and relegated to desk duty for a prolonged period pending treatment, fitness evaluation, and administrative resolution of their case. Such reassignment becomes public knowledge throughout the member's workgroup and inevitably involves both a stigma and a significant loss of privacy. Because such reassignment involves an undoing of the officer's professional identity and a loss of the symbols of office, it may actually exacerbate his or her troubles. Further compounding the problem is the fact that many police officers, firefighters, and emergency medical service personnel have little trust in the abilities of agency therapists or in their assurances of confidentiality. These therapists are, after all, in the agency's employ, and the inherent potential for a conflict of interest may be magnified in the perspective of an already mistrustful officer. As members of tight-knit and insular occupational cultures whose features are not well understood by "outsiders," they often have little faith in the capacity of civilian therapists to understand the unique realities of their occupational and social worlds, the depth and dimension of the trauma and human suffering they frequently witness, the physical and emotional hazards they regularly face, or the particular worldview that sets them apart from the larger culture. Many police officers, firefighters, and emergency medical service personnel are understandably suspicious of the bureaucracies and distrustful of their agencies' employee assistance policies, and many simply do not seek help for fear they will be stigmatized, penalized, or misunderstood (see, generally, Henry, 2001, 2004a, 2004b).

An upshot of this complex dynamic is that although many police officers, firefighters, and emergency medical service personnel who participated in rescue and recovery efforts at Ground Zero were traumatized by their experience, they resist any impulse to acknowledge and seek help for their troubles. The empirical question of precisely how many first responders demonstrate clinical symptoms of traumatic disorders remains uncertain and may not be known for some time, but some early research indicates the number is substantial (Centers for Disease Control and Prevention, 2002; Galea et al., 2002; Goode, 2001; Schuster, 2001). Given their overall reluctance to seek help and the fact that stress-related symptoms often emerge long after the traumatic exposure, the dimension of traumatic syndromes among rescue workers may not be known for years, if ever. But although a clear causal link to the effects of trauma related to September 11 cannot be entirely established, anecdotal evidence documents a dramatic increase in the number and severity of drug- and alcohol-related incidents (both on and off duty) among FDNY firefighters (see, e.g., Celona, 2004; Hu, 2004).

THE NEW YORK DISASTER COUNSELING COALITION

Fortunately for first responders in New York City, there exists an organization that provides an array of necessary psychological services to police, firefighters, emergency medical service personnel, and their families, an organization whose structure, goals, and orientation offer a viable and attractive alternative to agency-based resources and helps to overcome a great deal of the traditional reluctance to seek assistance. The New York Disaster Counseling Coalition (NYDCC) was founded on September 12, 2001, by a group of concerned clinicians and psychotherapists who recognized the traumatic impact the World Trade Center attacks would have on first responders and their families. They also recognized and, in terms of formulating NYDCC's structure, policies, and operational protocols, accounted for many of the organizational and cultural impediments that deter first responders from officially seeking help.

The NYDCC, chartered as a nonprofit organization, has since grown into a network of almost 300 fully licensed, fully insured, fully credentialed clinicians with terminal degrees in their respective fields. These clinicians, representing a broad array of specializations and treatment approaches, including psychologists, psychiatrists, and clinical social workers, have committed to voluntarily provide a minimum of one hour of treatment services each week to a first responder or his or her family member who is affected by the September 11 attacks. Importantly, the commitment these mental health professionals make to their first responder and family member clients is open-ended and reflects the motto of NYDCC: they agree to provide their services "for as long as it takes." Depending on the individual circumstances of each referral, treatment for a first responder client or family member may consist of a few sessions, or it may continue for years. At no time, however, will the first responder or family member client be charged a fee of any kind. Consistent with the canons of ethical practice and availing law, principles of client-clinician confidentiality apply, and clinicians will not notify the client's agency that he or she is receiving treatment.

The NYDCC model is unique in the nation, and its highly innovative and effective approach clearly addresses the specific needs of the first responder community. NYDCC's operational protocols are designed to assure confidentiality and privacy. Following a brief telephone intake interview (conducted by a trained psychotherapist) aimed at evaluating the scope and dimensions of the particular issues the client is facing, he or she is provided with the names and contact information for three volunteer clinicians with appropriate credentials or areas of specialization in the client's local area of residence. Almost 300 volunteer clinicians are members of the NYDCC referral network, and their offices are widely distributed throughout the New York metropolitan area and a region that includes northern New Jersey, southern Connecticut, and parts of Pennsylvania. Consistent with NYDCC's pledge of complete confidentiality, no personally identifying data are recorded during the intake interview. The information retained at NYDCC is collected solely for statistical purposes and consists of the caller's agency, age, gender, and county of residence. While the individual clinicians typically maintain their own confidential clinical treatment notes, they do not submit health insurance reimbursement claims and there is no paper trail that might be traced back to the client.

As a nonprofit entity, the NYDCC is entirely supported by contributions and funding from philanthropic foundations. All the volunteer therapists in the NYDCC referral network are thoroughly vetted and must submit proof of licensure and malpractice insurance as well as a curriculum vitae and two professional reference letters from colleagues who have known them for a minimum of two years. NYDCC staff regularly update records proving licensure and valid malpractice insurance, and the volunteers have the opportunity to attend an array of ongoing training sessions to help them understand and treat the unique constellation of difficulties first responders confront. These sessions have addressed such topics as understanding the occupational cultures of police and firefighters, domestic violence in law enforcement families, the socialization and training of police, and a number of other issues affecting members of the first responder community and their families. Given the number of participating mental health professionals volunteering one hour each week and the number of clients referred, NYDCC estimates it provides the equivalent of more than $1.4 million in treatment services each year to first responders and their families. The cost-effectiveness of the NYDCC model is clearly evident in the fact that this figure represents approximately six times NYDCC's total operating costs, including rent, utilities, the salaries of two employees, and all outreach expenses.

One of the supreme ironies affecting the provision of services to all of those affected by the September 11 attacks is that federal, state, and private funding sources originally devoted to psychological treatment have largely been depleted, and sufficient additional funds have not been allocated. One part of this irony arises from the fact that the psychological features resulting from traumatic exposure often do not begin to manifest themselves until years after the traumatic event, and this appears to be particularly true among first responders. Whether due to delayed manifestation of symptoms, to resistance to seek treatment on the part of first responders, or to some combination of both, NYDCC referral statistics reveal steadily increasing rates and numbers of referrals for clinical services among first responders and their families with the passage of time. As this chapter is being written, nearly three years have elapsed since the September 11 attacks, and NYDCC's referral numbers and rates continue to increase each month. Although there is clearly a continued and expanding need for its services, the not-for-profit NYDCC finds it increasingly difficult to access funding to provide those necessary and very cost-effective services. Another ironic element is that NYDCC (and any other not-for-profit or volunteer entities that do not charge a fee for services) is ineligible under current federal rules to receive funding under Project Liberty and FEMA mental health counseling grant programs. If NYDCC clinicians charged their full fees for treatment services and submitted health insurance claims, that is, if they created the very paper trail that makes first responders reluctant to access those services, the organization would be eligible for federal support. Current regulations do not permit volunteer organizations to receive these funds.

Beyond providing free, high-quality, and confidential mental health services to first responders and their families, NYDCC has also undertaken a range of initiatives aimed at supporting police, firefighters, and emergency medical service personnel (and their families) and remediating the stress resulting from the physical and emotional dangers they deal with on a daily basis. These initiatives include a series of seminars designed to educate retiring first responders about their pension benefits, employment opportunities, and life after retirement, seminars whose success gave rise to a Retirement Services Division within NYDCC. The Retirement Services Division consists of retired first responders who are available to confer with prospective retirees about these and other issues and to fulfill an important peer support function. Grant funding also permitted NYDCC to conduct several weekend-long seminars to help nearly 200 first responders and their spouses or significant others to develop more resilient relationships.

Another NYDCC initiative is the "DCC in a Box" Replication Project, an effort under way to formally memorialize the experience of NYDCC and record the lessons learned in developing from a concept first conceived in the immediate aftermath of September 11 to a fully functioning entity that provides free and confidential clinical treatment services to hundreds of first responders and their families. The goal of the Replication Project is to make these nuts-and-bolts lessons available to other cities so that similar disaster counseling coalitions can be created prior to a disaster, ready to quickly mobilize the necessary personnel and resources in the event of an attack. Clearly, the NYDCC represents a unique and viable model to provide first responders and their families with the broad range of clinical and other services they require as the result of their traumatic exposures. The model is based on an altruistic appreciation for the needs and concerns of first responders, and it is an exceptionally cost-effective model that accounts for and overcomes many of the factors that inhibit police officers, firefighters, and emergency medical services personnel from going to their agencies for help.

CONCLUSION

The new realities of terrorism and WMDs demand a new set of policies, practices, and relationships among and between a host of entities and institutions charged with the responsibility to ensure public safety. As illustrated by the experiences and lessons of the September 11 attacks on the World Trade Center and the Pentagon, police, fire, and emergency medical services face unprecedented challenges in the future, and similar challenges confront virtually every institution in the United States.

This chapter outlined some of the issues, problems, and threats posed by the specter of terrorism and terrorists' use of WMDs, and it identified the compelling need for highly coordinated response and recovery planning that integrates resources, skills, personnel, and capabilities of a range of public sector agencies and private sector organizations. No plan can pretend to be perfect, there are simply too many unforeseen issues and exigencies that arise in specific events, and the planning must therefore be crafted for flexibility and adaptability. This involves nothing less than a new mind-set that accepts, accounts for, and takes up the challenges posed by the realities of our world.

Recent history reveals the extent and dimension of the threat posed by WMDs, their availability to terrorists and extremist groups, and the massive casualties they can inflict on public safety personnel and members of the public. These threats are not likely to subside, and in fact may increase. There is a pressing need for more and better training for the first responders to such events so that they can recognize events involving WMDs and so that they can operate safely to minimize deaths, injuries, and damage. Similarly, there is a pressing need for more and better equipment to help first responders achieve their goals. But here again we see the need for a new mind-set among emergency workers, a mind-set of safety and preparedness that infiltrates all their duties and activities. Beyond the essential role played by first responders, the issues of better training, better equipment, and better coordination apply as well to the broad array of secondary responders and institutions who will be called on once the immediate crisis has passed.

Terrorism and the use of WMDs pose a particularly significant threat to first responders: the police officers, firefighters, and emergency medical service personnel who are our first line of defense against such attacks and are typically among the first individuals and groups to enter the sites where attacks have taken place. By the nature of their work, first responders to terrorist and WMD events are exposed to a range of traumatic experiences, and many inevitably suffer the lasting physical, social, and psychological consequences of that exposure.

For a variety of complex and interrelated reasons, first responders who experience psychological difficulties are typically reluctant to seek help from their agencies' employee assistance programs. First responders are often distrustful of their agencies' motivations in offering help, they are often suspicious of an inherent conflict of interest they perceive among therapists employed by their agency, and they often lack faith that their problems will be treated with sensitivity and confidentiality. Many believe that by coming forward to acknowledge a difficulty and to seek help for it they place their reputation and their career in jeopardy. As a result, first responders as a group are generally reluctant to seek the kind of help they often need.

The New York Disaster Counseling Coalition provides an innovative model for treatment that overcomes many or all of the factors contributing to first responders' resistance. Created in recognition of the fact that many first responders to the World Trade Center attacks would suffer lasting psychological consequences and cognizant of the factors that encourage resistance, the NYDCC's referral and treatment protocols illuminate the kind of organization first responders need. The NYDCC model, which can easily be adapted and implemented in other venues in preparation for terrorist attacks or other forms of trauma-producing disasters, is a highly cost-effective means of providing high-quality psychological services to first responders and their families. The realities of our world are such that organizations like the NYDCC and the crisis intervention and relief services they provide must become part of an integrated and intelligent national response to the threat of terrorism and WMDs.

REFERENCES

Celona, L. (2004, August 16). 28th firefighter booze bust. *New York Post,* p. 7.

Centers for Disease Control and Prevention. (2002a, September 11). Injuries and illnesses among New York City Fire Department rescue workers after responding to the World Trade Center attacks. *Morbidity and Mortality Weekly Report, 51* (Special Issue).

Centers for Disease Control and Prevention. (2002b, September 11). Psychological and emotional effects of the September 11 attacks on the World Trade Center: Connecticut, New Jersey and New York, 2001. *Morbidity and Mortality Weekly Report, 51*(35), 784–786.

Centers for Disease Control and Prevention. (2002c, September 11). Impact of September 11 attacks on workers in the vicinity of the World Trade Center: New York City. *Morbidity and Mortality Weekly Report, 51*(35), 781–783.

Centers for Disease Control and Prevention. (2002d, January 11). Rapid assessment of injuries among survivors of the terrorist attack on the World Trade Center: New York City, September 2001. *Morbidity and Mortality Weekly Report, 51*(1), 1–5.

Duffy, M. (2002, May 5). Weapons of war: Poison gas. Available online: http://www.firstworldwar.com/weaponry/gas.htm.

Federal Emergency Management Agency. (2002, July). *Managing the emergency consequences of terrorist incidents: Interim planning guide for state and local governments.* Washington, DC: Author. Available online: http://www.fema.gov/txt/onp/managingemerconseq.txt.

Galea, S., et al. (2002). Psychological sequelae of the September 11 terrorist attacks in New York City. *New England Journal of Medicine, 346*(13), 982–987.

Goode, E. (2001, September 25). Therapists hear survivors' refrain: "If only." *New York Times,* p. F1.

Henneberry, O. (2001, December 5). *Bioterrorism information resources.* Paper presented at the New Jersey Hospital Association's Conference, "Thinking the Unthinkable: Biochemical Terrorism and Disasters: Information Resources for Medical Librarians," Princeton, NJ. Available online: http://www.njha.com/ep/pdf/biocdchandout.

Henry, V. E. (2001). *The police officer as survivor: The psychological impact of exposure to death in contemporary urban policing.* Unpublished doctoral dissertation, Graduate School and University Center of the City University of New York.

Henry, V. E. (2004a). *Death work: Police, trauma, and the psychology of survival.* New York: Oxford University Press.

Henry, V. E. (2004b). Police, the World Trade Center attacks and the psychology of survival: Implications for clinical practice. [Special issue: Dialogues on Terror: Patients and Their Psychoanalysts, Part 2]. *Psychoanalysis and Psychotherapy.*

Hu, W. (2004, February 29). Firefighter in crash took cocaine, city says. *New York Times,* p. B1.

Jernigan, J. A., Stephens, D. S., Ashford, D. A., Omenaca, C., Topiel, M. S., Galbraith, M., members of the Anthrax Bioterrorism Investigation Team, et al. (2001, November–December). Bioterrorism-related inhalational anthrax: The first 10 cases reported in the United States. *Emerging Infectious Diseases, 7*(6). Available online: http://www.cdc.gov/ncidod/eid/v017n06/jernigan.html.

Kristof, N. D. (1995, March 25). Police find more chemicals tied to sect. *New York Times.*

Lifton, R. J. (1967). *Death in life: Survivors of Hiroshima.* New York: Basic Books.

Lifton, R. J. (1970). *History and human survival.* New York: Random House.

Lifton, R. J. (1973). *Home from the war. Vietnam veterans: Neither victims nor executioners.* New York: Basic Books.

Lifton, R. J. (1974). The sense of immortality: On death and the continuity of life. In R. J. Lifton & E. Olson (Eds.), *Explorations in psychohistory: The Wellfleet papers* (pp. 271–287). New York: Simon and Schuster.

Lifton, R. J. (1976). *The life of the*

self: Toward a new psychology. New York: Simon and Schuster.

Lifton, R. J. (1980). The concept of the survivor. In J. E. Dimsdale (Ed.), *Survivors, victims, and perpetrators: Essays on the Nazi Holocaust* (pp. 113–126). New York: Hemisphere.

Lifton, R. J. (1983). *The broken connection: On death and the continuity of life.* New York: Basic Books. (Original work published 1979)

Lifton, R. J. (1986). *The Nazi doctors: Medical killing and the psychology of genocide.* New York: Basic Books.

Lifton, R. J. (1999). *Destroying the world to save it: Aum Shinrikyo, apocalyptic violence, and the new global terrorism.* New York: Henry Holt.

Lifton, R. J.,& Strozier, C. B. (2001, September 16). The fragile city: "We were exposed and raw." *New York Times,* pp. 14–17.

Lynch, C. (2002, January 24). U.N. monitors warn of Afghan missiles; Panel says Taliban, Al Qaeda remnants may pose conventional, chemical threat. *Washington Post.*

McDade, J. E., & Franz, D. (1988, July–September). Bioterrorism as a public health threat. *Emerging Infectious Diseases, 4*(3). Available online: http://www.cdc.gov/ncidod/eid/v014n03/mcdade.htm.

Sachs, G. M. (2003). *Terrorism emergency response: A handbook for responders.* Upper Saddle River, NJ: Prentice-Hall.

Schuster, M. A., Stein, B. D., Jaycox, L. H., Collins, R. L., Marshall, G. N., Elliott, M. N., et al. (2001, November 15). A national survey of stress reactions after the September 11, 2001, terrorist attacks. *New England Journal of Medicine, 345*(20), 1507–1512.

Shenon, P.,& Stout, D. (2002, May 21). Rumsfeld says terrorists will use weapons of mass destruction. *New York Times,* p. A1.

Torok, T. J., Tauxe, R. V., Wise, R. P., Livengood, J. R., Sokolow, R., Mauvais, S., et al. (1997, August 6). A large community outbreak of salmonellosis caused by intentional contamination of restaurant salad bars. *Journal of the American Medical Association, 278*(5), 389–395.

Traeger, M. S., Wiersma, S. T., Rosenstein, N. E., Malecki, J. M., Shepard, C. W. Raghunathan, P. L., Florida Investigation Team, et al. (2002, October). First case of bioterrorism-related inhalational anthrax in the United States, Palm Beach, Florida, 2001. *Emerging Infectious Diseases, 8*(10). Available online: http://www.cdc.gov/ncidod/EID/v018n010/02–0354.htm.

8

Disaster Mental Health: A Discussion of Best Practices as Applied After the Pentagon Attack

RACHEL E. KAUL
VICTOR WELZANT

On the morning of September 11, 2001, American Airlines Flight 77 took off from Dulles Airport bound for L.A. with two pilots, four flight attendants, and 58 passengers on board. Included among the passengers were five terrorists, who hijacked the aircraft and, at 9:38 A.M., deliberately crashed into the west side of the Pentagon, between corridors 4 and 5. Hundreds of military and civilian personnel struggled to reach safety through flames, choking black smoke, and debris. Many encountered closed fire doors that were difficult to open, bomb-proof glass windows that could not be broken, and narrow stairways blocked with people impeding escape. In other sections of the building, workers were ordered to evacuate. Upon exiting the building, rumors of a second plane heading for the Pentagon quickly circulated, adding to the confusion and fear of those gathered. Many civilian and military personnel made heroic attempts to assist injured colleagues or those remaining trapped inside the burning building. In spite of these efforts, by noon it appeared unlikely that anyone else would be rescued alive. Early death counts were speculated to be as high as 800, but, in total, 184 innocent lives were taken, including those on board the airplane, and at least 350 were injured that day. The five terrorists also perished.

By late afternoon, teams of military, local, and federal response and law enforcement agencies had set up operations surrounding the damaged segment of the Pentagon. A perimeter was secured and attempts to fight the still raging fire and begin further rescue and recovery operations were organized.

Disaster mental health volunteers from a variety of sources, including the American Red Cross, Department of Defense, and community mental health organizations, were enlisted to monitor the operation site and be on hand to assist personnel experiencing psychological distress. Mental health workers would be on site for the duration of the recovery operation, providing coverage 24 hours a day.

In the days following the attack, mental health professionals working inside the Pentagon with work groups and individuals were in high demand. Disaster mental health volunteers were requested to assist those working inside the building to augment services being provided. In addition, mental health professionals familiar with disaster were placed in the health care clinic to assist the military and employee assistance program staff meet the psychological needs of this diverse population.

A family assistance center was established swiftly after the attack. Families of those who had perished gathered at a nearby hotel, where briefings were held twice daily to apprise them of the status of the recovery and identification efforts. Agencies providing financial and tangible resources were also on site, such as the American Red Cross, the Social Security Administration, and the Uniformed Services Organization, in addition to providers of mental health and emotional support. Disaster mental health volunteers worked with family members and also with those staffing the center, strongly affected by their interactions with the grieving families day after day. At this location, and as time passed, the needs of those staffing and utilizing the family assistance center became more complex, and informal psychological first aid was not always sufficient to address concerns. Enhanced crisis intervention techniques were often required to assist people in understanding and accessing supportive resources and tangible needs.

Disaster mental health has become a significant focus for many engaged in the field of crisis intervention, particularly since September 11, 2001. Although mental health providers have long been responding to natural and man-made disasters, the complexity of the responses at the Pentagon, and in New York and Pennsylvania, created a desire to examine best practice approaches to disaster mental health. Recent consensus in the field indicates that multiple intervention strategies applied to different populations and in a phasic way creates a foundation that is essential to best practice.

Due to the often overwhelming and ongoing nature of disasters and the recovery efforts they necessitate, building competency in a variety of intervention techniques and prioritizing assessment and education is essential for effective response. Experts agree that most people will recover from the effects of a disaster with little or no formal psychological intervention (Norris, Friedman, Watson, Byrne, Diaz, et al., 2002). Providing well-planned and targeted psychological first aid may help many access coping skills and resources more quickly and may also allow disaster mental health providers to identify populations or individuals at greater risk for developing distressing psychosocial issues. In doing so, these individuals may be linked with the resources they need to ensure better outcomes. Different populations benefit from a variety of approaches applied at different stages of disaster response and recovery. In this chapter, these concepts are explored from a general perspective and then highlighted further in the context of the Pentagon disaster mental health response. The primary populations discussed are emergency responders and volunteers at the disaster site, civilians and workers inside the building following the attack, and staff and family members at the Family Assistance Center in the weeks following the attack.

DISASTER MENTAL HEALTH: A REVIEW OF THE EARLY INTERVENTION LITERATURE

Following significant crisis, there is a wide range of nonpathological stress responses that may be evidenced by those exposed (Caplan, 1964; Litz, 2004; Myers, 1994; North et al., 2002). In many situations, these expected reactions have led to both a professional concern and an outpouring of support for those impacted by crisis events. A strong and compelling desire to help those suffering the effects of disasters, criminal victimization, terrorism, and other adverse events is common among human service professionals. Many disaster relief programs, crime victim services, crisis hotlines, and disaster mental health initiatives were born from this strong desire to assist in the recovery of those affected by crises. Additionally, the public mental health reforms of the 1960s and 1970s led to a renewed interest in the provision of crisis intervention and brief crisis therapy for those in acute distress (Roberts, 2000).

Despite decades of development and increasing sophistication, the field of crisis intervention has recently been challenged to provide more rigorous, empirically based validation of crisis intervention strategies (Foa, Keane, & Friedman, 2000; National Institute of Mental Health [NIMH], 2002). A recent review of early interventions for mass violence incidents concluded that there are "few randomized controlled trials of psychological interventions following mass violence" and that the scientific community has an "ethical duty to conduct scientifically valid research to improve assessment, early intervention, and treatment of persons exposed to mass violence" (NIMH, 2002, p. 11). Concern has been raised that some early intervention models have even been shown to have minimal or even adverse effects in certain populations (Bisson & Deahl, 1994; McNally, Bryant, & Ehlers, 2003). This confluence of professional concerns is counterbalanced by the clinical experience of practitioners and the consistently positive reports of those receiving early intervention following traumatic events (Chemtob, Tomas, Law, & Cremniter, 1997; Dyregrov, 1998; Robinson & Mitchell, 1993). Many interventionists and researchers would agree that a strong desire to help, if not grounded in empirical and practical foundations, might lead to interventions that prove ineffective or potentially harmful despite good intentions. Training, informed by practical experience and grounded in scientific research, may be the optimal blend to prevent adverse effects of early intervention (Deahl, Srinivansan, Jones, Neblett, & Jolly, 2001).

The "lessons learned" of effective intervention have been transmitted through a variety of methods, including case studies, program descriptions, professional supervision, consultation, and empirical study (Everly & Mitchell, 1999; Lindeman, 1944; Roberts, 2000). The events of September 11, 2001, led to a renewed interest in effective early intervention following crisis events and have spearheaded efforts to reach consensus on best practices. In examining efforts undertaken by experienced disaster mental health practitioners after the Pentagon attack, these best practice guidelines are presented in detail below.

PRINCIPLES OF EARLY INTERVENTION AND PSYCHOLOGICAL FIRST AID

Early intervention has been defined as occurring within the first four weeks following a traumatic event. A key principle of early intervention is to expect normal recovery for the majority of those exposed (NIMH, 2002). Although there are predictable and transient stress reactions in many individuals following trauma (North et al., 1999; Shalev & Ursano, in press), there is also a natural pattern of recovery that is evidenced by most, even in the absence of formal intervention (Horowitz, 2001). This in no way invalidates the need for support, practical assistance, and assessment of individuals, groups, and organizations. Rather, it recognizes the inherent resilience of individuals and communities and supports natural recovery mechanisms in specific populations.

Effective early intervention is based on careful assessment of individuals, groups, and systems. This assessment recognizes that intervention is best applied when there are indications that coping is being overly challenged, as demonstrated by evidence of distress or an inability to function effectively to meet one's immediate needs and challenges (Caplan, 1964; Everly, 2001). Assessment also prevents unwarranted application of intervention strategies based on assumptions of providers.

Another guiding principle for those responding to the psychological needs created by disaster is that crisis intervention, like disaster, is phasic (Myers & Zunin, 1990). Disasters may have relatively predictable phases of response with differing psychological needs as events unfold over time. Careful assessment allows interventions to be matched to the needs of each response phase for individuals and groups at any given time. Phasic intervention requires flexibility in the application of any crisis intervention strategy or model. Crisis intervention programs are best organized as multicomponent systems, with the ability to provide psychological triage, assessment, individual crisis intervention, small and large group intervention, referral, follow-up, and organizational consultation (Everly and Langleib, 2003).

APPLICATION OF EARLY INTERVENTION

Early intervention first strives to meet basic needs of survivors and workers such as survival, safety, security, food, fluids, and shelter. Other needs may include communication with family, friends, and community, the need for orientation to disaster services, and additional sources of social support. As basic needs are met, ongoing assessment helps to determine what resources and level of intervention are necessary. Much of the early intervention in the initial phases of a disaster is done individually and informally (Myers, 1994). As the disaster unfolds over time, more in-depth intervention models may become necessary as survivors are faced with the additional stressors of disaster recovery. Survivors and responders are challenged by overwhelming and complex tasks, such as interacting with relief agencies, addressing insurance issues, rebuilding homes, and mourning losses. Later interventions may focus on groups of individuals and may begin to reconnect natural support networks and identify those in need of further assistance (Norwood, Ursano, & Fullerton, 2000).

Providing outreach and information is an integral task of early intervention (Ursano, Fullerton, & Norwood, 1995). The focus may be on normalizing stress reactions or on providing information about referral resources for additional mental health assistance or about disaster relief resources, such as shelter locations, assistance centers, and procedures for applying for tangible resources. Outreach provides an opportunity to further assess individuals and communities and to link individuals with available resources. Training is another application of early intervention that can enhance an organization's or community's ability to cope with adversity. Training programs undertaken in the workplace or among intact community groups can focus on stress and trauma management, worker self-care, building resilience, or helping parents meet children's needs during a disaster. From this point of view, training is an intervention in itself and offers the opportunity to screen and refer, as well as to educate and support.

PHASES OF DISASTER AND DISASTER RESPONSE

The phases of disaster and operations are important to consider when planning intervention strategy. Disaster response and recovery typically occur in several phases. Many disasters are preceded by a Warning or Threat Phase. The disaster event itself is known as the Impact Phase. This is followed swiftly by the Heroic or Rescue Phase, during which efforts to resolve the immediate and most destructive effects of the event are the main priority. The Honeymoon Phase occurs in the weeks following, and it is during this period that formal systems are created to provide assistance and support. As federal, state, and volunteer resources begin to scale back services or prepare to discontinue their role in the disaster recovery altogether, workers and survivors often enter a Disillusionment Phase, with the reality of the losses sustained and the challenges ahead taking on greater focus. Communities and workers then transition into the Reconstruction or Recovery Phase, during which those impacted by the disaster begin the long and often painful process of attempting to restore their lives to predisaster circumstances. Each phase correlates with different needs both by survivors of the event and those working to address and resolve the conditions brought about by the event (DeWolfe, 2000).

EMERGENCY RESPONDERS

First responders require varying levels of intervention depending on the phase of disaster during which the mental health worker interacts with them. During the Heroic Phase, responders and the community affected rise to the occasion, pulling together to meet the demands brought on by a crisis event. The psychological needs during this time are primarily met by reestablishing a sense of safety and security. During the Honeymoon Phase, when rescue or recovery operations have been established and coordinated, a common sense of purpose usually mitigates the accompanying distress of a disaster, particularly for responders. As the work continues, however, and the impact and losses of the disaster become more apparent, many workers enter a Disillusionment Phase, where tempers grow short and a sense of hopelessness may compromise the ability to remain optimistic or hopeful about the recovery mission. It is at this phase that disaster mental health workers may be most useful to first responders.

Helping responders on scene access their own social supports and providing them with useful solutions to reactions that may be interfering with their efforts can assist them in maintaining safety and effectiveness. This can be accomplished by a disaster mental health worker asking questions that focus specifically on the nature of the reactions responders are experiencing and on the coping strategies they are already utilizing or have utilized in the past. Intense emotional processing of the disaster event or of recovery operations is not encouraged, unless the responder initiates this kind of dialogue. On some occasions, typically during more protracted or particularly distressing operations, more formal intervention and referral may be indicated. The safety and well-being of others on scene can be better ensured if personnel with appropriate training in psychological rapid assessment and referral are on hand to take appropriate action steps with an acutely distressed individual (Watson, Friedman, Gibson, Ritchie, Ruzek, et al., in press).

Large group interventions, particularly during the Heroic and Honeymoon Phases, that provide information about traumatic stress and its effects and suggestions to cope with any troubling or adverse reactions are often utilized in many first responder populations as a way of preventing or mitigating psychological distress. These large group interventions are typically provided at the end of a shift and are brief in nature and predominantly informational and educational. Emotional and psychological processing is generally not encouraged, as workers may be expected to return to a scene after a few hours' rest, or they may not be psychologically ready to process the event and their experiences. These types of interventions are best provided by mental health workers familiar with first responder culture or by trained peers who are supported by clinical guidance from mental health professionals familiar with disaster and trauma.

The final stage of disaster response is the Reconstruction or Recovery Phase. For first responders, it is during this phase that they return to normal duties and attempt to make meaning of the event and resulting operation. Small group interventions that allow homogeneous work groups to discuss their experiences and responses may be indicated at this time. Many first responder groups have systems or utilize program models such as critical incident stress management (Mitchell & Everly, 2001) to allow for a range of supportive intervention. Small process groups within these programs allow responders to normalize any lingering or adverse reactions they may be experiencing, explore strategies for mitigating them, and identify reactions requiring a more intensive level of intervention. In certain circumstances, work groups involved in disaster site operations will require more formal small group intervention, such as a critical incident stress debriefing or one-on-one assistance. A thorough assessment and screening of individuals should be a priority prior to initiating more intensive group processing, as there may be a risk of secondary traumatization among those exposed to different traumatic stimuli. Most theorists recommend that these kinds of group interventions be voluntary to further ensure the overall psychological safety of the group (Bisson, McFarlane, & Rose, 2000).

THE DISASTER SITE: DAY 1–DAY 10

In the first few days following the Pentagon attack, disaster mental health workers were dispatched to the site and to respite areas established throughout the operations area to monitor personnel on scene and to provide appropriate support. Public safety, law enforcement, military, federal, and volunteer agency personnel together faced the grueling task of searching for and recovering the remains of all who had been killed in the terrorist attack. Operations were under way 24 hours a day, seven days a week. First responder teams from neighboring regions and states arrived to assist, and a camp was established to meet the needs of those working on site.

Disaster mental health workers were an integral part of the response efforts. The primary focus of these workers was to meet the basic needs of those involved in the many aspects of the recovery and firefighting operation. While on site, disaster mental health personnel focused initially on meeting physical and tangible needs. Passing out water, Gatorade, food, dry clothing, sunscreen, and other supplies helped mental health workers build rapport and establish trust among first responders, who are often wary of psychological intervention. In addition, responders were better able to maintain their ability to meet the extreme physical demands placed on them.

Psychological first aid, in the form of brief and informal conversations, allowed mental health personnel to assess basic levels of functioning among the site workers and ensure their safety and well-being. In addition, it allowed these practitioners to consider effective ongoing intervention strategy in this setting. It was important that inexperienced disaster mental health personnel exercise caution about asking probing questions that might lead to overt emotional catharsis. Responders tasked with the challenge of stabilizing the building, which burned for more than a week, and for recovering remains, were, by necessity, psychologically defended and wary of emotional conversations. They were primarily concerned with remaining operational and able to function effectively. Few were in need of structured, formal crisis intervention. However, a brief opportunity to ventilate with a mental health worker about what they were experiencing was often remarked on later as helpful and important to those engaged in the difficult recovery and stabilization mission. Disaster mental health workers also provided psychoeducation or suggested concrete strategies for addressing sleep disturbance or the occasional overwhelming emotional concerns of the first responders staffing the scene.

Hundreds of community volunteers were also on scene, serving food and organizing supplies to support the recovery effort. Mental health workers monitored this population as well for signs and symptoms of distress that could impact anyone's ability to function. On-site workers experienced mild to significant cognitive disorganization and emotional distress, and many commented on a sense of hopelessness or fear about the future. The adverse conditions of the site itself made the work physically challenging as well. The smells emanating from the burning building, extreme changes in temperature, long work hours, constantly changing personnel, and mud, dust, and debris caused physical and psychological strain. Mental health personnel, exposed to these same stressors, reassured those on site by educating them about the expected nature of these kinds of reactions. Handouts were readily available providing guidance about managing traumatic stress and facilitating self-care. People were encouraged daily to talk about their responses to one another and to rely on each other for support. Mental health workers also provided information about resources for further emotional or tangible support to everyone with whom they interacted.

As the recovery operation began to wind down and the focus shifted to repairing the building, disaster mental health workers were requested to assist with support services being provided to the military and civilian workers inside the Pentagon. First responders on site began accessing and mobilizing their usual mechanisms of support, including their employee assistance programs and their crisis response or critical incident stress management teams. The population inside the building had particular needs. They had returned to work on September 12, the day after the attack, and had walked back into a building to work while slain colleagues still burned inside of it. For the most part, work groups pulled together to provide one another with the support and courage they would need to continue the functions of the Department of Defense. Even so, in the days and weeks that followed, many individuals accessed psychological services and many work groups requested support. Services were available through the on-site employee assistance program (the Pentagon Employee Referral Service), the DiLorenzo Healthcare Clinic located inside the building, and military mental health and extended chaplain services established at the Pentagon after the attack. In addition to the resources available, disaster mental health workers arrived to augment and support existing services.

THE COMMUNITY

For the community directly impacted by a disaster, the Impact and Heroic Phases can be particularly traumatic. People are often forced, by necessity, into new or unfamiliar roles and may be exposed to gruesome or upsetting sights, sounds, and smells. The intense desire to survive and to assist others usually results in a sense of determination that will initially protect survivors from the shock, helplessness, and fear that may follow. Generally, disaster mental health workers interacting with community members at this stage focus on tangible needs and on connecting people with the resources or social supports they need to feel safe and secure.

As the Honeymoon Phase develops, disaster mental health workers rely on interventions that assist impacted individuals to access the resources required for recovery. Mental health workers often meet with local and faith-based community members and leaders to ascertain the level of distress in evidence among those impacted so that appropriate intervention may be planned and provided. Most supportive work is done one-on-one in disaster recovery centers or other venues providing a range of services. However, when a large and somewhat cohesive community is affected by a disaster, large and small group interventions may be indicated.

It is generally recommended that large groups of a heterogeneous nature be informational with a brief question-and-answer period, but otherwise include minimal discussion (Everly, 2003). This prevents the risk of secondary traumatization among people who may have experienced different levels of exposure. Most are primarily in need of concrete information about the disaster and any resulting rescue and recovery operations. Any informational briefing should include, in addition, education about traumatic stress and coping strategies. Handouts that further describe common reactions to crisis and disaster as well as handouts targeted to parents or caregivers of people with special needs are also helpful. Printed material should also be available in a variety of languages to meet the needs of diverse community groups.

Small group interventions may also be utilized for those primarily and secondarily impacted by a disaster. Groups of eight to 20 participants that allow for emotional ventilation and strengthen group cohesiveness may be conducted by experienced disaster mental health practitioners days or weeks after the event. A key feature of these groups is that members share a similar level of exposure to events related to the disaster. Intact work groups or community groups with comparable types of exposure to the disaster often find comfort in hearing each other's reactions and gain new insight into their own emotions. Furthermore, during these groups, mental health workers are well-placed to assess the individuals involved and target those who may be in need of further assistance or higher levels of care.

There are numerous group models utilized during and following crisis and disaster. Formal training in the approaches developed by the International Critical Incident Stress Foundation, the National Organization for Victims Assistance, the American Red Cross, and others, paired with a current understanding of best practice guidelines and recommendations, is important for anyone engaging in disaster mental health. In general, during a small process group, the first question asked addresses the facts of the event. By beginning with a question such as "Can you briefly describe what happened?" or "How did you hear about the event?" facilitators encourage people to remain fairly cognitive as they describe events that preceded the resulting distress or emotional reactions. Next, the group facilitator may ask "What kinds of reactions have you been experiencing since the event?" to elicit the signs and symptoms that will help group members realize the universality of many of their responses. This also allows mental health practitioners to evaluate the need for referral and further services among the individuals present. An important question to include as the group process develops is "What have you been doing to cope with these reactions?" This allows group members to shift to a strengths perspective as they begin to recount and to hear about strategies and mechanisms for self-care from one another. Group facilitators will generally begin to conclude the processing by providing additional education and teaching about stress, stress management, and resources. Handouts with phone numbers and referral sources are provided as well. It is advisable to have at least two people facilitate any small group, and one of these should be a mental health professional experienced in disaster and disaster response. Upon completion of the group process, participants who wish to are encouraged to talk one-on-one with facilitators so they may discuss any individual or personal concerns that were not adequately addressed by the group intervention. Any small group process should be followed a day or two later by a phone call or visit from a facilitator to key participants. In this way, providers can best ensure that they have done everything possible to meet the needs of all who attended.

One-on-one services following disaster are often provided by establishing outreach programs. Mental health practitioners go to the communities or worksites of the populations affected, bringing educational materials and engaging in informal conversation with whomever they happen to meet. In this way, the needs of the larger community are swiftly identified. Large group presentations targeting specific topics of concern may be planned or support groups established for populations with special needs arranged. Educational and training programs initiated by behavioral health and employee assistance programs following a disaster frequently target traumatic stress and educate participants on signs and symptoms that may be better addressed with professional assessment and treatment (Kaul, 2003). This type of intervention may be particularly beneficial during the Disillusionment and Reconstruction Phases, when many of the sources of support immediately following the disaster have begun to be dismantled.

THE PENTAGON WORKERS: DAY 11–DAY 20

Disaster mental health volunteers responded to requests from work groups and providers inside the Pentagon in greater numbers as the needs of those working the crash site decreased. The Pentagon population consists of approximately 50% military and 50% civilian workers. Work groups in the building experienced a wide range of exposure and response to the terrifying events of September 11. Some lost colleagues, friends, and even family members in the attack. Others felt their own lives in peril as they escaped from flames and falling debris. Many participated in heroic and difficult rescue attempts. Some individuals initially had little notion of what had occurred, and it was not until they were ordered to evacuate to the parking areas and saw the thick cloud of black smoke blocking out the sky that they realized a tragic event had occurred. Because of the rumors of a second airplane headed toward the building, many people became fearful for their lives only after leaving the building. Workers fled their offices, leaving purses, house keys, car keys, cell phones, and money inside. Once outside, many found they had no idea of what to do next or how to get home. Some were unable to contact loved ones for many hours to assure them they were safe. Feelings of shock and dismay gave way to anxiety about returning to work in the Pentagon, as a second attack was anticipated. The complex and intentional nature of the event, in addition to the fact that most workers returned to the scene of the attack the very next day, created a difficult task for mental health and disaster mental health providers.

Most individuals were seen by support mechanisms in place within the Pentagon. Disaster mental health volunteers were requested in the weeks following the attack to provide group interventions that would reach the greatest number of people rapidly and effectively. Large group briefings were held by Pentagon leadership to inform the community about the recovery operations and about additional and enhanced security measures being developed and implemented to ensure everyone's safety. Disaster mental health workers conducted small group interventions with work groups throughout the building that sought to address the emotional and psychological concerns in evidence.

Careful assessment prior to intervention application was considered a priority. Each work group, although intact, was made up of diverse individuals and a broad range of exposure to the event was common. Because of this, small process groups focused on the reactions people were experiencing at the time of the intervention, and little discussion about the events of September 11 were elicited. Groups were encouraged to understand their distress as expected and to view their ability to come to work or to access resources as indicative of great strength and courage. Lists of resources were developed and presented, and an important element in most of these groups was that mental health professionals created a positive perception of seeking psychological support and assistance if so indicated. During follow-up conversations conducted by providers, many of those interviewed stated that they found the chance to hear how their colleagues and friends were coping comforting and they appreciated the reassurance gained by having mental health professionals well versed in disaster response and recovery guiding the discussion. In addition, individuals who had never before accessed mental health resources stated that they were more inclined to do so after attending a well-facilitated group intervention.

Military and civilian outreach and education programs were designed and implemented in the weeks and months after September 11, 2001. Some of these programs continue today, and individuals who still struggle with recovering are identified and assisted. Although these programs do not fall under the purview of early intervention, they resulted from the guidance and direction provided by professionals committed to effective disaster mental health response and who understood that the need for ongoing support and assessment for the Pentagon community would continue long past the conclusion of formal disaster response efforts.

FAMILY MEMBERS

As the internal providers were establishing comprehensive, ongoing programming, services were also being provided to the families and loved ones of those who were killed in the attack. For the most part, tangible and emotional resources were available to survivors of the deceased at the Department of Defense's Family Assistance Center, established in the early aftermath of the attack. Counselors and disaster mental health providers were on hand to assist family members and friends to cope with the grief and uncertainty the ongoing recovery and identification efforts created.

The surviving loved ones of those who perish in a disaster are acutely impacted. For most, their lives are forever changed and the needs they present to caregivers are extreme. Grief and shock are often compounded by conditions that require significant delays in body recovery and identification. The normal processes by which people begin to grieve and gain support may be unavailable for days, weeks, or even months. For family geographically removed from the deceased, travel, unfamiliar surroundings, and separation from community support add to the isolation and despair. This is often tempered by the fact that following disasters resulting in multiple fatalities, service centers are established to bring grieving families together and allow them to support one another during the recovery operation.

Many services may be made available to surviving loved ones in one primary location. Agencies providing tangible resources, such as reimbursement for travel, lodging, or food, as well as victims' assistance or relief organizations are there to help. Family members receive guidance about the complicated documentation related to insurance and benefits and learn of resources that may assist them as they begin the process of learning to cope with their losses. Disaster mental health workers often find this population extremely challenging to assist. Informal intervention may not be sufficient to truly facilitate access to resources and support. In addition, disaster mental health workers are relied on, in these service centers, to monitor the stress and coping of the other workers staffing them. In this type of setting, the primary focus of the provider will be working with people one-on-one or with a family group. It is useful to utilize a model of crisis intervention to organize one's approach to addressing the complex needs found in each of these crucial populations.

Several models for individual crisis intervention exist that many practitioners and disaster mental health providers rely on. The SAFER-R model, developed by Everly (Everly & Mitchell, 1999), guides a clinician through a series of objectives to facilitate an individual's restoration to adaptive functioning or referral to a higher level of care. This is accomplished by:

S: Stabilizing the individual and acute adverse stress reactions.

A: Acknowledging the crisis event as well as the fact that the reactions experienced are due to the event and not due to personal weakness.

F: Facilitating understanding of the event and reactions to it.

E: Encouraging adaptive coping techniques.

R: Restoring functioning or referring.

Assessment for danger and lethality is conducted through every part of the process and appropriate action taken whenever a threat to self or others is identified.

Roberts's seven-stage crisis intervention model (Roberts, 2000) is also useful when working with a population experiencing complex and acute emotional reactions to an event. The seven stages articulated in the model are:

1. Assessment of lethality and safety.
2. Establishment of rapport and communication.
3. Identification of major problems.
4. Dealing with feelings and provision of support.
5. Exploration of possible alternatives.
6. Formulation of an action plan.
7. Provision of follow-up.

The application of these stages may not always follow this order, but the objectives are important regardless of the order in which they are achieved. Due to the intense and complicated issues faced by grieving families after a disaster, a strong grasp of tangible resources and psychological tools is essential for a disaster mental health worker. Utilizing a model will assist workers in formulating effective action plans that will aid survivors in restoring their ability to cope or access other resources they might require (Roberts, 2000).

Group interventions may also be utilized in family service centers. When a recovery operation is under way, family members desire frequent reports about the status of the operation and any new information that has been learned. Informational briefings may occur two or three times a day following a disaster. Mental health providers should be included to present information about the expected reactions and responses many of those gathered may be experiencing. In addition, surviving loved ones can be informed or reminded about the importance of social support or about the psychological resources available to them.

Formal small group intervention may be organized by advocacy or support groups. In general, families will gravitate toward each other naturally and will find others with whom they can share their loss and grief. When contemplating a small process group for family members, practitioners experienced in grief and loss counseling should be relied on.

For volunteers and staff in family support centers, stress levels generally increase after the initial Heroic Phase transitions to the Honeymoon Phase. These workers may enter the Disillusionment Phase earlier than workers at other venues, due to the extreme emotion they are exposed to at every shift every day. Disaster mental health practitioners provide other workers with opportunities to ventilate their emotions and to reinforce their value in the overall disaster response. The needs of those left behind by the deceased can seem insurmountable to workers interacting directly with them and many will meet people with whom they closely identify. Mental health providers can remind workers to take steps to meet their own self-care requirements and provide them with a compassionate and understanding ear.

All disaster response personnel should be provided with information on reactions they may experience after disaster response efforts are concluded. Many disaster responders, including those in the mental health field, find returning to their everyday lives extremely challenging and lonely. After witnessing so much loss and sadness, many feel reluctant to admit that they need assistance to cope effectively themselves. Workers are encouraged to maintain contact and connections with others who responded to the disaster and to reach out for support and reassurance.

As recovery and identification operations wind down, it is common practice to hold a memorial service for all those who perished during the disaster, before families who live elsewhere leave town. This final event often correlates closely with the closure of the family assistance center as well, and disaster mental health workers are available to provide for any emotional needs that arise. Families and workers are often doubly impacted during this time as they prepare to take leave of one another in addition to continue to grieve their losses. Disaster mental health workers should reiterate any plans formulated by those whom they have assisted and ensure that survivors and workers understand the resources available to them and how to access them.

The intentionality of the Pentagon attack as well as the shocking, unexpected nature of it resulted in a broad range of needs for those who survived the deceased. Many local and out-of-town families utilized the Family Assistance Center on a daily basis. They received updates twice daily on the recovery operations, applied for benefits and assistance, and received psychological and emotional guidance and support. Staff at this facility worked tirelessly to resolve complicated and heart-wrenching issues every day. Disaster mental health workers became more and more important as the days and weeks went by to stabilize and assist everyone there.

THE FAMILY AND WORKERS AT THE FAMILY ASSISTANCE CENTER: DAY 21–DAY 31

The Family Assistance Center for the families of those killed at the Pentagon was established at a local hotel and several floors were given over to its operations. Media and anyone not directly connected with response activities were denied access to the second floor, where the majority of services were collected. American Red Cross case workers were housed on additional floors and families signed in daily to consult with a caseworker about existing or emerging needs. Federal and volunteer agencies and other assistance groups provided literature, teddy bears for children, guidance about benefits, and counseling.

In the first week of the center's operation, disaster mental health volunteers initially provided supportive, reflective counseling and assisted family members in understanding resources. By the third week of the response, however, many survivors felt their shock give way to frustration and anger at their lack of control resulting from the situation. Identification of remains was a long process, from their perspective, and many worried they would be denied even the possibility of returning home with remains of their loved ones. Many different resources were available to surviving loved ones from a variety of sources. Navigating multiple and unfamiliar application systems was time-consuming and further taxed the patience and emotional reserves of families.

The workers responsible for guiding family members through the intricate systems in place also grew fatigued and stressed. Many responders and staff had been away from their homes and families for weeks and were also living in hotels or barracks, away from their normal mechanisms of self-care. Disaster mental health workers began spending more time with those staffing the center as the Disillusionment Phase began for many in the third week.

Most mental health providers found that longer and more structured intervention was needed to meet the demands apparent in those utilizing and working in the Family Assistance Center. Mental health responders monitored individuals more frequently to determine that agreed upon action plans or recommended resources were proving effective. Practitioners with specialized knowledge of children, grief, or military culture were called in to address concerns and questions related to these issues. Families were encouraged to bring photographs, letters, and other objects of meaning and to create a temporary memorial at the Family Assistance Center as a way of expressing and sharing their loss.

Staff at the Family Assistance Center were encouraged to spend time with one another at the end of each shift to process the events of the day and to reflect on the strategies they found most helpful in coping. It was not uncommon for disaster mental health staff to make recommendations regarding shift length and days off for staff who had been working this site for weeks. A general recommendation, adhered to by many relief and response agencies, is that each shift not exceed 12 hours and no one staff person work more than six days in a row. As is also common, however, these guidelines were often difficult to enforce. Workers committed to providing all they could for the families they met at times worked beyond points of personal exhaustion. Many workers lost their voice or developed minor illnesses during the response, and yet no one wanted to quit. Disaster mental health personnel worked with staff to develop ways to allow them to meet the needs of the families and continue to remain physically and psychologically healthy.

An important aspect of working in the Family Assistance Center was collaboration among a large number of federal, local, volunteer, and private agencies. Information and resources were shared and services provided to all who were seeking them, regardless of status or affiliation. Mental health workers swiftly learned what different agencies and organizations could provide to allow for appropriate referral.

The memorial service for the victims of the Pentagon attack was held on October 11, 2001. Families were escorted by military and civilian counselors and disaster mental health volunteers to the building where the terrible event had occurred. In a service attended by the president and other dignitaries, those who had been lost were remembered. Following this event, most families elected to return home, some with and some without positively identified remains of lost loved ones.Tearful goodbyes were exchanged between families, workers, and the Pentagon community. The next day, the bulk of the Family Assistance Center was dismantled. A limited number of services remained available at an alternate location for people with further needs. Community and military outreach programs took on the role of providing for the ongoing mental health needs of surviving family and friends. The Family Assistance Center staff accessed resources for emotional support in their own communities and workplaces. The community created within the Family Assistance Center and the support it provided, however, remained a prominent memory in the minds of all those who experienced it.

SELF-CARE FOR PROVIDERS

Compassion fatigue and secondary traumatization have been described by Charles Figley (1995) as important considerations for professionals who work closely with traumatized and grieving people. Disaster mental health providers, particularly those working for an extended period of time with populations affected by this kind of event, will find the work is as personally taxing as it is meaningful. The intensity of emotion surrounding disaster and the complex needs of large numbers of people can take a toll on the personal resources of a mental health provider. In some instances, the mental health worker is directly impacted by the tragedy by having been at the scene itself, as were many of the Pentagon mental health providers, or by having suffered a personal loss due to the event. Some mental health professionals may feel unprepared or lack training and experience to effectively address the intense needs of the people they are hoping to assist.

Providing for the needs of the caregivers must be a priority from the earliest possible phase of a crisis. One-on-one support for mental health providers may be offered through supervision by peers during the disaster response. This allows the mental health worker an opportunity to process some of the things he or she has seen and heard. Small group interventions can be conducted specifically for caregivers to encourage them to be mindful of their need for self-care throughout their work with others. Some mental health workers may need to be encouraged to take a break or an unplanned day off to bolster their own energy and emotional reserves. Others may require psychological services to better understand their experiences and personal reactions. Caregivers must be aware that disaster response work, though meaningful and exciting, is extremely stressful, and they will need to develop ways to ensure their own physical and psychological health (Figley, 1995).

The flexibility and breadth of experience required to assist individuals affected by disaster may also seem daunting to mental health practitioners new to disaster response. Confidence and ability can be built by taking formal training and by participating in drills and exercises in communities and workplaces. An important quality for any disaster mental health worker to possess is a tolerance for ambiguity and a problem-solving approach to obstacles and challenges. Experience and supervision are also essential components for disaster mental health workers to have in place when mobilized to respond to an emergency. Most disaster mental health workers say they find the value of the work far outweighs the stress and challenge associated with it. Proper training and support can minimize the adverse effects of working in the disaster response realm.

CONSIDERATIONS FOR FURTHER RESEARCH

As noted above, much of our knowledge base regarding early intervention following trauma originated in the collective experience of practitioners in the field. More recently, a focus on empirical evaluation of early intervention has been viewed as necessary to prevent adverse effects, for survivors and responders, and ensure the best care possible for everyone touched by a disaster event. Research in disaster mental health is difficult for many logistical reasons. However, creative research designs may allow fundamental questions to be answered concerning effectiveness. One question raised in discussions of the effectiveness of early interventions is which outcome measures most closely assess the value of early intervention. Traditional research in this area has focused on measures of psychiatric symptoms and the ability of early intervention to prevent psychopathology (McNally, Bryant, & Ehlers, 2003). This may be problematic, as the goals of early intervention emphasize additional and equally valid outcomes such as reduction of distress, enhanced coping, reconnection with one's social support system, education, and increased willingness to access further care when indicated. One future direction of research should be to identify more relevant variables and address measurement of these outcomes. Additionally, research to focus on the identification of early indicators of long-term difficulties could be helpful in allowing more effective secondary prevention efforts. Early intervention with diverse populations has suffered from a paucity of research, as have studies to address the effectiveness of predisaster training on enhancing outcomes following adverse events. Much of the recent focus on resilience following trauma may yield fruitful findings that will inform more effective practice (Bonanno, 2004). In the meantime, disaster mental health approaches firmly based in crisis intervention theory and guided by best practice recommendations and cautions may provide individuals and communities impacted by disasters with invaluable benefit and support in times of extreme need.

REFERENCES

Bisson, J. I., & Deahl, M. P. (1994). Psychological debriefing and prevention of post-traumatic stress: More research is needed. *British Journal of Psychiatry, 165*, 717–720.

Bonanno, G. A. (2004). Loss, trauma and human resilience: Have we underestimated the human capacity to thrive after extremely adverse events? *American Psychologist, 59*(1), 20–28.

Caplan, G. (1964). *Principles of preventive psychiatry*. New York: Basic Books.

Chemtob, C., Tomas, S., Law, W., & Cremniter, D. (1997). Post disaster psychosocial intervention. *American Journal of Psychiatry, 134*, 415–417.

Deahl, M. P., Srinivasan, M., Jones, N., Neblett, C, & Jolly, A. (2001). Evaluating psychological debriefing: Are we measuring the right outcomes? *Journal of Traumatic Stress, 14*, 527–529.

DeWolfe, D. (2000). *Training manual for mental health and human service workers in major disasters* (2nd ed.). (DHHS Publication No. ADM 90–538).

Dyregrov, A. (1998). Psychological debriefing: An effective method. *Traumatologye, 4*(2), Article 1.

Everly, G. S., Jr. (2000). Crisis management briefings (CMB): Large group crisis intervention in response to terrorism, disasters, and violence. *International Journal of Emergency Mental Health, 2*(1), 53–57.

Everly, G. S., Jr. (2001) Thoughts on early intervention. *International Journal of Emergency Mental Health, 3*(4), 207–210.

Everly, G. S., Jr., & Langlieb, A. (2003). The evolving nature of disaster mental health services. *International Journal of Emergency Mental Health, 5*(3), 113–120.

Everly, G. S., Jr., & Mitchell, J. T. (1999). *Critical incident stress management: A new era and standard of care in crisis intervention.* Ellicott City, MD: Chevron.

Figley, C. R. (Ed.). (1995). *Compassion fatigue: Coping with secondary traumatic stress disorder in those who treat the traumatized.* New York: Brunner/Mazel.

Foa, E. B., Keane, T. M., & Friedman, M. J. (Eds.). (2000). *Effective treatments for PTSD: Practice guidelines from the International Society for Traumatic Stress studies.* New York: Guilford Press.

Horowitz, M. (2001). *Stress response syndromes* (4th ed). New York: Aronson.

Kaul, R. E. (2003). Workplace interventions. In M. Lattanzi-Licht & K. J. Doka (Eds.), *Living with grief, coping with public tragedy.* Washington, DC: Hospice Foundation of America.

Lindemann E. (1944). Symptomatology and management of acute grief. *American Journal of Psychiatry, 101,* 141–148.

Litz, B. (2004). *Early intervention for trauma and traumatic loss.* New York: Guilford Press.

McNally, R. J., Bryant, R, A., & Ehlers, A. (2003). Does early psychological intervention promote recovery from posttraumatic stress? *Psychological Science in the Public Interest, 4*(2), 45–79.

Mitchell, J. T., & Everly, G. S., Jr. (2001). *Critical incident stress debriefing.* Ellicott City, MD: Chevron.

Myers, D. (1994). *Disaster response and recovery: A handbook for mental health professionals.* Rockville, MD: Center for Mental Health Services.

Myers, D., & Zunin, L. (1990). Unpublished training materials. California Department of Mental Health.

National Institute of Mental Health. (2002). *Mental health and mass violence: Evidence-based early psychological intervention for victims/survivors of mass violence. A workshop to reach consensus on best practices.* NIH Publication No. 02–5138, Washington, DC: U.S. Government Printing Office.

Norris, F. H., Friedman, M. J., Watson, P. J., Byrne, C. M., Diaz, E., & Kaniasty, K. Z. (2002). 60,000 disaster victims speak: Part I, an empirical review of the empirical literature, 1981–2001. *Psychiatry, 65*(3), 207–239.

North, C. S., Nixon, S. J., Shariat, S., Mallonee, S., McMillen, J. C., Spitznagel, E. L., et al. (1999). Psychiatric disorders among survivors of the Oklahoma City bombing. *Journal of the Americal Medical Association, 282*(8), 755–762.

North, C. S., et al. (2002). Coping, functioning, and adjustment of rescue workers after the Oklahoma City bombing. *International Society for Traumatic Stress Studies, 15,* 171–175.

Norwood, A., Ursano, R., & Fullerton, C. (2000). Disaster psychiatry: Principles and practices. *Psychiatric Quarterly, 71*(3), 207–227.

Roberts, A. (Ed.). (2000). *Crisis intervention handbook: Assessment, treatment, and research* (2nd ed.). New York: Oxford University Press.

Robinson, R. C., & Mitchell, J. T. (1993). Evaluation of psychological debriefings. *Journal of Traumatic Stress, 6*(3), 367–382.

Shalev, A. Y., & Ursano, R. J. (in press). Mapping the multidimensional picture of acute responses to traumatic stress. In U. Schneider (Ed.), *Early intervention for psychological trauma.* Oxford: Oxford University Press.

Ursano, R. J., Fullerton, C. S., & Norwood, A. E. (1995). Psychiatric dimensions of disaster: Patient care, community consultation, and preventive medicine. *Harvard Review of Psychiatry 3*(4), 196–209.

Watson, P., Friedman, M., Gibson, L., Ritchie, Ruzek, & Norris. (in press). Early intervention for trauma related problems. *Annual Review of Psychiatry.*

9

Innovations in Group Crisis Intervention

GEORGE S. EVERLY, JR.
JEFFREY M. LATING
JEFFREY T. MITCHELL

As this chapter is being written we find the world enmeshed in a war on terrorism. Because terrorism represents a form of psychological warfare, there has been considerable interest in the contribution that the mental health professions may make to this new era in world history. Preceding the interest engendered by terrorism, however, the mental health professions were responding to the perceived psychological needs of mass disaster victims. New data sets have emerged suggesting that posttraumatic distress is a significant mental health concern in military personnel returning from Iraq (Hoge et al., 2004; Friedman, 2004). Furthermore, longitudinal data on the terrorism of September 11, 2001, suggests that the adverse impact of mass disaster terrorism may persist so as to represent a significant public health challenge (Stein et al., 2004). The convergence of these two perspectives has led many to seek to innovate and refine emergent psychological intervention. In this chapter, we shall look at an innovation in the psychological phenomenology of posttraumatic stress, and we shall further examine the potential contributions of group process to the field of crisis intervention.

HISTORICAL BACKGROUND

Crises are affecting an ever-increasing number of businesses, schools, and communities, and mass disasters are becoming virtually epidemic. For example, the lifetime prevalence for trauma exposure has been estimated to be about 60% for males and about 51% for females in the United States (Kessler, Sonnega, Bromet, Hughes, & Nelson, 1995); the prevalence for trauma exposure for children and adolescents has been estimated to be about 40% (see Ford, Ruzek, and Niles, 1996); and the lifetime prevalence of criminal victimization as assessed among female HMO patients has been estimated to be 57% (Koss, Woodruff, & Koss, 1991).

As a result of these disturbing trends, formalized crisis intervention programs have been recommended and instituted in larger numbers than ever before (see chapter 1). For example, in 1989 the International Critical Incident Stress Foundation (ICISF) formalized an international network of crisis response teams that utilize a standardized group crisis intervention model and share access to centralized international coordination. This network now consists of over 300 crisis response teams with approximately 10,000 trained crisis team members worldwide. The ICISF network, which represents the largest crisis intervention system of its kind in the world, gained United Nations affiliation in 1997.

In 1992, the American Red Cross initiated its disaster mental health network, which as of 1999 had approximately 2,000 active disaster mental health personnel throughout the United States. In 1996, the Occupational Safety and Health Administration (OSHA, 1996) recommended that health care and social service organizations implement a comprehensive program of medical and psychological support services for employees who experience or witness violence at the workplace. Similarly, OSHA (1998) later recommended that such postincident response programs, including postincident debriefing and counseling, also be made available to the employees of late-night retail establishments. In addition, OSHA has specifically noted that an emerging trend in crisis response is the utilization of comprehensive, multicomponent Critical Incident Stress Management (CISM) programs in order to "provide a range or continuum of care tailored to the individual victim or the organization's needs" (OSHA, 1998, p. 8). Crisis intervention programs are not confined to civilian populations; they have been implemented by the United States military as well. The U.S. Air Force has mandated that crisis response teams be trained and available at every U.S. Air Force base to respond to any psychological crises that might arise. Similarly, the U.S. Coast Guard Policies and Procedures (COMDTINST 1754.3) has mandated that multicomponent crisis intervention programs be established in each geographic region for which the U.S. Coast Guard has responsibility.

In the wake of September 11, 2001, there has been great interest focused upon early psychological intervention, often referred to as crisis intervention (Caplan, 1964), psychological first aid, emergency mental health, or emotional first aid (Neil, Oney, DiFonso, Thacker, & Reichart, 1974). Conceptually, a parallel may be drawn between physical health and mental health, such that "as physical first aid is to surgery, crisis intervention is to psychotherapy." As the goals of physical first aid are

1. stabilization of physiological functioning,
2. mitigation of physiological dysfunction/distress,
3. return of acute adaptive physiological functioning, and/or
4. facilitation of access to the next level of care;

the goals of crisis intervention are

1. stabilization of psychological functioning through meeting basic physical needs, then addressing the most basic of psychological needs,
2. mitigation of psychological dysfunction/distress,
3. return of acute adaptive psychological functioning, and/or
4. facilitation of access to the next level of care.

The current practice of crisis intervention is founded upon a corpus of well-controlled empirical support. Langesley, Machotka, & Flomenhaft (1971) used random assignment (RCT) of 300 patients to inpatient treatment vs. family crisis intervention. Results indicated crisis intervention was superior to inpatient treatment for preventing subsequent psychiatric hospitalizations. Decker & Stubblebine (1972) followed 540 psychiatric patients for 2.5 years subsequent to an initial psychiatric hospitalization. Traditional follow-up treatment was compared to crisis intervention services. Results supported the superiority of the crisis intervention services in preventing subsequent hospitalizations. Bunn & Clarke (1979), in a randomized controlled design with 30 individuals who had accompanied relatives to the hospital after a serious injury, found 20 minutes of supportive crisis counseling superior to no intervention in reducing anxiety. Finally, Bordow & Porritt (1979) employed a three-group RCT of individual crisis intervention with hospitalized motor vehicle accident victims. Results were indicative of a dose response relationship between intervention level and the reduction of reported distress. A recent meta-analytic review of crisis intervention with medical and surgical patients revealed support for the ability of such intervention to mitigate acute psychological distress (Stapleton, 2004). Closer scrutiny revealed that specialized training, multiple sessions, and multiple intervention components all served to positively influence clinical outcome.

A TWO-FACTOR MODEL OF ACUTE CRISIS

Before introducing the aforementioned methods of group crisis intervention, let us begin with a brief introduction to the nature of the acute crisis response. The conceptual exploration and potential theoretical integration of the acute crisis response is not a new endeavor. More than 100 years ago, the psychologist Pierre Janet formulated a systematic therapeutic approach to posttraumatic psychopathology that recognized the various stages and evolutions of posttraumatic stress reactions. Janet contended that the cognitive appraisal of the traumatic event combined with emotional reactivity determined the degree, nature, and severity of psychological impact. In a later integrated conceptual delineation, Kardiner (1941) described posttraumatic stress as a physioneurosis, a term that encompasses the intricate connections of biological and psychological substrates. Almost 40 years after Kardiner's psychophysiological formulation of posttraumatic stress, the American Psychiatric Association (APA, 1980) operationalized posttraumatic stress disorder (PTSD) under the rubric of an anxiety disorder, combining more basic physiological constituents with higher order cognitive and affective processes. The APA criteria (APA, 1980, 1987, 1994) conceptualized PTSD within three symptom clusters that occur following exposure to a traumatic event. These symptom clusters are (a) intrusive psychological reexperiencing of the traumatic event; (b) psychological numbing to, or reduced involvement with, the external environment; and (c) autonomic nervous system (ANS) hyperreactivity and/or hyperfunction (although recent data suggest that the physiological arousal is not limited to the ANS).

Everly (1995) has posited that these symptom clusters may be blended into a two-factor "neurocognitive" phenomenological core. The two factors are:

1. A *neurological hypersensitivity*, which results in a pathognomonic proclivity for *neurologic arousal* (Everly, 1990; van der Kolk, 1988) existing within the limbic circuitry and primarily affecting amygdaloid and hippocampal cells (Everly, 1995).
2. A *psychological hypersensitivity* in the form of intrusive cognitive recollection of some uniquely meaningful aspect of the trauma. This psychological hypersensitivity may be viewed as some form of violation or contradiction of the individual's worldview (or Weltanschauung) regarding safety, security, or sense of self. Moreover, the individual is unable to assimilate the traumatic event into his or her idiosyncratic worldview (Bowlby, 1969; Everly, 1995; Janoff-Bulman, 1992; Lifton, 1988; Wilson, 1989).

Factor 1: Neurological Hypersensitivity

We will now briefly review each of these factors. As mentioned previously, Kardiner's (1941) term *physioneurosis* captured the inextricable combination of biological and psychological phenomena. More specifically, he purported five consistent clinical features of posttrauma syndromes:

1. Exaggerated startle reflex and irritability
2. Atypical dream experiences
3. A propensity for explosive and aggressive reactions
4. Psychic fixation upon the trauma
5. Constriction of personality functioning

Reviewing Kardiner's criteria, as well as DSM criteria, it is apparent that the core physiological mechanisms of a trauma reaction involve arousal of the central nervous system (CNS), the autonomic nervous system (ANS), and sundry neuroendocrine effector mechanisms (Everly, 1995). Moreover, van der Kolk (1988) views PTSD as a pathological inability to modulate arousal, which is also consistent with Kardiner's original perspective. Therefore, PTSD may represent CNS neurological hypersensitivity (in the form of "ergotropic tuning" or preferential sympathetic nervous system responsiveness) and hyperfunction (in the form of hypertonus, reactive hyperphasic amplitude, or both). Robert Post (1985, 1986; Post & Ballenger, 1981) has proposed the term *behavioral sensitization* to reflect the condition in which extreme stress, including psychosocial stressors, may render the neurological tissues of the limbic system hypersensitive to subsequent excitation. Post (1992) has since postulated that psychosocial stressors may be capable of creating a form of neurological sensitization that may be encoded at the level of gene expression. Thus, an individual suffering from posttraumatic stress may experience neurological hypersensitivity in the following forms:

1. Altered neuronal structural and intraneuronal function such as an augmentation of excitatory postsynaptic receptors and/or a decrease in inhibitory receptors (see Gray, 1982; Joy, 1985; Nutt, 1989; Perry, Southwick, & Giller, 1990; Post & Ballenger, 1981).
2. An augmentation of available excitatory neurotransmitters, such as norepinephrine (Davidson & Baum, 1986; Murburs, McFall, & Veith, 1990; Krystal et al., 1989); dopamine (Kalivas & Duffy, 1989); and glutamate (McGeer & McGeer, 1988; Palkovits, Lang, Patthy, & Elekes, 1986).
3. A decrease in inhibitory neurochemicals, such as gamma-aminobutyric acid (GABA; Biggio, 1983; Drugan et al., 1989; Gray, 1982; Krnjevic, 1983; van Gelder, 1986).

Excessive stimulation of CNS mechanisms may, in extreme cases, result in a well-documented phenomenon known as *excitatory toxicity.* In essence, excitatory toxicity entails massive release of excitatory neurotransmitters (primarily glutamate, but likely norepinephrine, aspartate, dopamine, and others as well), which in high enough concentrations may become "excitotoxins" capable of damaging or possibly destroying the neural substrates they serve. Neural excitatory toxicity within hippocampal, septal, and corpus callosum cells may account for some of the memory and concentration dysfunctions (Everly & Horton, 1989), aggressive behavior, and diminished family or social interaction or bonding, as well as posttrauma alexithymia (Henry, 1993). In fact, recent data have suggested reduced hippocampal volume in individuals with combat-related PTSD and in individuals with PTSD related to childhood physical and sexual abuse (Bremner et al., 1995; Bremner et al., 1997). As noted previously, overarousal in PTSD is not limited to the CNS; neuroendocrine hyperactivity (elevated circulating catecholamine levels) is considered a core feature of PTSD (Davidson & Baum, 1986; Mason et al., 1986). The data are, however, less conclusive regarding endocrine involvement of the hypothalamic-anterior pituitary-adrenal cortical (HPAC) axis (Davidson & Baum, 1986; Mason et al., 1986; Pitman & Orr, 1990; Rahe et al., 1990; Schaeffer & Baum, 1984).

Factor 2: Psychological Hypersensitivity

As mentioned earlier, the essence of a traumatic reaction from a psychological perspective is likely predicated on the violation of the individual's worldview as it pertains to safety or security, as well as the person's inability to assimilate the traumatic event into his or her perception of the self and/or the world. Janoff-Bulman (1988) described certain core assumptions about how people view the world and themselves with regard to invulnerability. More specifically, these assumptions are (a) that the world is benevolent (i.e., people are inherently good, and good things happen); (b) that events in the world are meaningful (i.e., events make sense); and (c) that the self is positive and worthy (i.e., good things happen to good people). Naturally, a traumatic event seriously threatens these core assumptions, and from the cognitive as well as existential perspectives, treatment consists of reestablishing an organized, integrated set of assumptions.

Other noted scholars have also addressed the psychological hypersensitivity associated with PTSD. For example, developmentalist John Bowlby (1969) noted that individuals need to create working models of the environment (called the *environmental model*) and of one's self (i.e., one's resources, proficiencies, etc., called the *organismic model*). Attainment of life's goals, including safety and security, requires continual and functional interaction between the models.

Robert Lifton (1988) has written extensively about survivors of trauma and their struggles to master and assimilate traumatic events into some meaningful context. One of his 10 formulated principles relevant to the study of psychological trauma specifically addresses the importance of meaning. According to Lifton (1988), "without addressing this idea of meaning . . . we cannot understand post-traumatic stress disorder" (p. 10).

Abraham Maslow's (1954) proposed hierarchy of human needs (physiological needs, safety, affiliation, self-esteem, and self-actualization) posits that the foundation of motivation is the need to satisfy basic physiological needs (e.g., food, water). He defined safety as freedom from fear, having security, protection, and the need for structure and order. The remainder of the hierarchy involves the need to belong and be loved, the need for self-esteem, and finally becoming self-actualized. Maslow maintained that one cannot progress to a higher level in the hierarchy until one has satisfied the need at the preceding level, which leads to some individuals "getting stuck" and spending a lifetime pursing a rudimentary need. As we know, trauma is the antithesis of order, protection, and security. No matter which higher order Maslovian need level one has reached prior to being traumatized, the trauma serves to return the individual back to a quest for safety. Therefore, concepts such as personal growth are suppressed until the safety need can once again be satisfied.

Existentialist Viktor Frankl (1959) argued that the failure to discover meaning and a sense of responsibility in one's life is the core of psychopathology. As Frankl explained in his exposition of logotherapy, he who loses the "why" to live may lose the "how" as well. Indeed, trauma may have a devastating impact because it produces a violation or contradiction to both the meaning and the sense of responsibility that one may have previously found in life. Frankl did, however, adhere to Nietzsche's famous motto, "That which does not kill me, makes me stronger." This statement helps to provide an optimistic cognitive foundation to help in reintegrating one's worldview or Weltanschauung.

CRITICAL INCIDENT STRESS DEBRIEFING

The "modern era" of crisis intervention has existed since the mid-1940s, built upon the work of Lindemann (1944) and the subsequent work of Caplan (1964), according to Roberts (in chapter 1 of this volume). Since that time, crisis intervention has become "a proven approach to helping people in the pain of an emotional crisis" (Swanson & Carbon, 1989, p. 2520).

For the most part, the history of crisis intervention has been built upon individual applications, that is, one-on-one applications. However, as crisis interventions were applied to large-scale crises and mass disasters, the need for more efficient tactics became clear. The tactic of *group* crisis intervention, which had its roots in the military and later the emergency services, emerged as an innovation to the field. One model of group crisis intervention was developed by Jeffrey T. Mitchell (1983), who built upon the historical tenets of crisis intervention combined with the insights gained through group therapeutic applications (Yalom, 1970). Mitchell formulated a specific model of group crisis intervention referred to as Critical Incident Stress Debriefing (CISD; Mitchell & Everly, 1996). A review of relevant literature reveals the CISD model of group crisis intervention to be an effective tactic (Arendt & Elklit, 2001; Everly & Boyle, 1999; Everly & Mitchell, 1999; Everly, Boyle, & Lating, 1999; Ritchie, 2002).

CISD is designed to mitigate the psychological impact of a traumatic event and accelerate recovery from acute symptoms of distress that may arise in the immediate wake of a crisis or a traumatic event. A very important component of CISD is identifying individuals who may require professional mental health follow-up after the event. The formal CISD process is a seven-phase group meeting or discussion in which individuals who have been affected by a traumatic event are given the chance to talk about their thoughts and emotions in a controlled and rational manner. The debriefing process has been carefully structured to flow in a nonthreatening manner from the cognitively oriented process of human experience through a more emotionally oriented experience, and then back to an educative, cognitive process.

As a true innovation, the use of the CISD has clearly expanded beyond its original intention. The CISD intervention is intended to serve as a screening/triage, group discussion, and psychoeducational mechanism.

It is further hoped that it will reduce acute distress. There is no evidence that it can prevent PTSD. Further, it should be utilized only with homogeneous groups that have been exposed to the same degree of trauma. Thus, the CISD will be a limited intervention used most commonly with the military and emergency response personnel. Some civilian use may be appropriate, if a homogeneous group. It is important to note that despite having both psychological and educative elements, the debriefing process should not be considered psychotherapy. We will now briefly review the formal stages of the CISD process, which usually takes 1 to 3 hours to complete. The CISD intervention may be done 1 to 10 days after emergency service applications and 1 to 4 weeks after mass disasters depending upon suitability and receptivity. CISD is a "ritual of closure." Its timing should reflect its nature.

Introduction Phase

The introduction to the CISD is absolutely critical for success; it sets the tone for the subsequent phases. If the introduction is mishandled, it is likely that the remainder of the debriefing will be awkward and difficult. The following are several objectives that should be achieved during the introduction:

- Explain the purpose of the meeting.
- Explain and give an overview of the process.
- Motivate the participants.
- Assure confidentiality.
- Explain the guidelines (e.g., no tape recorders or notes, talk only for yourself).
- Point out the team members.
- Answer questions or concerns.

The concept that drives the introduction is the attempt to anticipate logistical and psychological barriers to the group discussion and to establish guidelines to minimize or eliminate them.

Fact Phase

Typically, the most natural thing for a distressed individual to discuss is a description of the facts of an incident. Facts are, in essence, a collection of impersonal items. A discussion of facts is not likely to engender the type of distress that a more personal discussion of feelings would. To assist participants in talking about an incident in the fact phase, the leader of the debriefing may say something like this:

> The CISD team wasn't present during the incident. We only know some bits and pieces of what happened. It would be helpful to our understanding if you would tell us *who you are, what your role was during the incident, and, briefly, what happened from your perspective.* It doesn't matter if what you experienced is different from what everyone else experienced. You all had an important part to play in the situation, and it would help everyone to have a big picture constructed by putting all your pieces of the incident together. If you choose not to speak, that is OK; just shake your head, and we will pass over you. For the sake of organization, we will start on my left [or right] and proceed around the room. Again, what we need to know from you is (a) who you are, (b) what was your job or involvement during the incident, and (c) what happened from your perspective?

The group participants will then begin to tell their stories. The exact order of telling the story is irrelevant; the last to arrive at the scene might be the first to speak. As others present their pieces, ideally the story comes together. The concept that drives the fact phase is the notion, as Sir Francis Bacon stated, that "information is power."

Thought Phase

The thought phase begins when the CISD team leader asks each of the participants to express their *first thoughts* or *most prominent thought* concerning the traumatic event. This phase serves as a transition between the impersonal outside facts and that which is becoming more internal, close, and personal. It is quite difficult to respond to questions about thoughts without some discarding of emotion entering the discussion. CISD teams should expect this leakage of emotion as a natural by-product of the debriefing process. Emotional comments during the thought phase should be considered a sign that the process is working and on schedule.

Reaction Phase

The reaction phase is typically the most emotionally powerful of all phases. However, if the introduction, fact, and thought phases have been performed well, then the reaction phase will flow easily and naturally. The CISD team will typically experience a quieting of their interactions with the group during this phase. In fact, most of the talking during this stage is done by the participants. The discussion at this point is freewheeling. Whoever wants to speak may do so; there is no longer a specified order to the discussion (i.e., systematically going around the room) as during the fact and thought phases. The questions that trigger most of the discussion in the reaction phase are:

- What was the worst thing about this situation for you personally?
- If you could erase one part of the situation, what part would you choose to erase?"
- What aspect of the situation causes you the most pain?

The concept that drives this phase is that of cathartic ventilation with a potential for emotional abreaction.

Symptom Phase

This phase serves as another transition. The objective is to begin to move the group back from the emotionally laden content of the reaction phase toward more cognitively oriented material. Stopping the debriefing at this juncture would leave people in a charged emotional state, which could possibly be distressing. A debriefing is always continued to the end to complete the process and to restore people to the cognitive level.

The symptom phase is initiated when the team asks the participants to describe any cognitive, physical, emotional, or behavioral experiences they may have encountered at the scene of the incident, as well as symptoms that followed subsequently. The concept that drives this phase is consensual normalization and attacking the myth of unique weakness or vulnerability.

Teaching Phase

The teaching phase evolves naturally after the symptoms phase. It begins by acknowledging several of the symptoms just described in the symptom phase and reaffirming to the group that those symptoms are normal, typical, or predictable after the type of incident they experienced. Other team members forewarn the group about possible symptoms they might develop in the future. The team may then spend time providing stress management strategies such as instructions on diet, exercise, rest, talking to one's family, and a range of other topics. The teaching phase is very cognitive in its approach. It is designed to bring the participants further away from the emotional content they had worked through in the reaction phase.

Reentry Phase

This is the last, and possibly the most important, phase of the formal debriefing. It is used to clarify issues, answer questions, make summary statements, and accelerate homeostasis, sometimes thought of as psychological closure. The participants in the debriefing will need to do the following:

1. Introduce any new material they wish to discuss.
2. Review old material already discussed.
3. Ask any questions.
4. Discuss anything they wish that would help them bring closure to the debriefing.

The debriefing team will need to do the following:

1. Answer any questions posed.
2. Inform and reassure as needed.
3. Provide appropriate handouts.
4. Provide referral sources as appropriate for psychological assessment, therapy, and so on.
5. Make summary comments.

The summary comments made by the CISD team are usually words of respect, encouragement, appreciation, support, and direction. Every CISD team member should make a summary statement in the last few minutes of the debriefing, but the essence of this phase is the identification of homogenizing themes that may be used to facilitate closure and provide a psychological uplift.

CRITICAL INCIDENT STRESS MANAGEMENT: A STRATEGIC INTERVENTION SYSTEM

One of the earliest of the integrated multi-component psychological crisis intervention systems that has gained wide-spread utilization is Critical Incident Stress Management (CISM). The American Red Cross, the National Organization for Victims Assistance (NOVA), and the Salvation Army also utilize their own integrated multi-component crisis intervention systems. Early on, the British Psychological Society (1990) suggested that crisis intervention would likely be ineffective unless provided as a multi-component system. Historically, there has been some confusion as to the actual nature and evolution of the CISM approach to crisis intervention vis-à-vis the frequently utilized small group crisis intervention known as Critical Incident Stress Debriefing (CISD), as well as numerous other crisis interventions generically referred to as "debriefing." A brief review of the evolution of CISM may prove useful in understanding the evolution of the field of emergency/disaster mental health, additionally it may serve to correct possible misconceptions and inappropriate expectations for the entire field.

CISM represents, both strategically and tactically, an integrated multifaceted approach to crisis intervention. Consistent with Theodore Millon's (Millon, Grossman, Meagher, Millon, & Everly, 1999) concepts of *potentiating pairings* (using interacting combinations of interventions so as to achieve an enhancing clinical effect), *catalytic sequences* (sequentially combining tactical interventions in their most clinically useful ways), and the *polythetic nature* of the CISM approach (selecting the tactical interventions as determined by the specific needs of each crisis situation), specific crisis interventions within the CISM formulation are to be combined and sequenced in such a manner so as to yield the most efficient and effective crisis intervention possible. The various combinations and permutations that are actually utilized within the CISM model will be determined by the specific needs of each critical incident or traumatic event, as they uniquely arise (Everly & Mitchell, 1999). The current integrated, multi-component nature of CISM was not commonly practiced, nor was it fully developed in its formative years. Excessive reliance was placed upon one specific small group crisis intervention component of the overall CISM formulation. An over-utilization of the Criticial Incident Stress Debriefing (CISD) intervention seemed clearly in evidence. Such an over-utilization of CISD was not to be unexpected, however.

Let us now review the core components of the CISM model (Mitchell & Everly, 2001; Everly & Mitchell, 1999). This list of components has been significantly modified from a tactical perspective and has been strategically expanded since originally introduced. The expansion of CISM has been a direct result of its utilization beyond its original role serving emergency services personnel subsequent to well circumscribed critical incidents and its more recent applications to mass disasters, military venues, and terrorist-related situations. It may be argued that such tactical modification and strategic expansion represents the avoidance of stagnation and is an imperative dynamic for a healthy system. The ten extant core CISM elements are listed below.

1. Strategic planning and assessment
2. Precrisis preparation. This includes stress management education, mental preparedness training, stress resistance, and crisis mitigation training for both individuals and organizations.
3. Disaster or large-scale incidents, as well as school and community support programs, including demobilizations, informational briefings, and "town meetings."
4. Defusing. This is a three-phase, structured small-group discussion provided within hours of a crisis for purposes of assessment, triaging, and acute symptom mitigation.
5. Critical Incident Stress Debriefing (CISD) refers to (Mitchell & Everly, 2001), a seven-phase, structured group discussion, usually provided 1 to 10 days after an acute crisis and 3 to 4 weeks after the disaster in mass disasters. It is designed to mitigate acute symptoms, assess the need for follow-up, and, if possible, provide a sense of postcrisis psychological closure.
6. One-on-one crisis intervention/counseling or psychological support throughout the full range of the crisis spectrum (this is the most widely

used of the CISM interventions). Typically, this form of intervention consists of one to three contacts with an individual who is in crisis. Each contact may last anywhere from 15 minutes to 2 hours, depending on the nature and severity of the crisis.

7. Family crisis intervention, as well as organizational consultation.
8. Organizational and community consultation
9. Pastoral Crisis Intervention—the integration of psychological crisis intervention with pastoral support.
10. Follow-up and referral mechanisms for assessment and treatment, if necessary.

Specific guidelines for these interventions, summarized in Table 9.1, can be found in Everly and Mitchell (1999) and Mitchell and Everly (2001).

Just as one would never attempt to play a round of golf with only one golf club, one would not attempt the complex task of intervention within a crisis or disaster with only one crisis intervention technology. Because crisis intervention, generically, and CISM, specifically, represent a subspecialty within behavioral health, one should not attempt application without adequate and specific training (see Koss & Shiang, 1994). CISM is not psychotherapy, nor a substitute for psychotherapy. CISM is a form of psychological "first aid."

APPLICATION OF MODELS TO CASE STUDIES

To understand how the comprehensive and integrative CISM model works from a temporal perspective, the following case examples will provide intervention recommendations that may be offered during the precrisis phase, the acute crisis phase, and the postcrisis phase.

Case 1

The line of thunderstorms happened suddenly and seemed remarkably isolated. The 65 children and 38 staff at the relatively secluded Willow Park Day Care Center never saw it coming. The thunderstorms spawned several tornadoes of mainly low magnitude in the surrounding vicinity. The tornado near the day care center was the most powerful, with winds of close to 200 miles per hour. When it touched ground, it demolished the roof of the building while most of the children were napping. The collapsed roof immediately killed 14 of the children, and three of the staff, and left 7 other children trapped in the rubble for 8 to 12 hours while two shifts of emergency workers, as well as excavation experts from the next town, worked feverishly to rescue them. Despite the best efforts of the rescue workers, two of the trapped children suffered massive injuries and died.

Table 9.1 Critical Incident Stress Management (CISM): A Strategic Approach to Multi-component Intervention Systems (Adapted from: Everly and Mitchell, 1999; revised 2004)

Intervention	Timing	Activation	Goal	Format
1. Strategic planning	Pre-Crisis/Pre-Disaster	Crisis or Disaster Anticipation	Assessment. To develop a phase sensitive integrated multi-component intervention/response system	Individuals/Groups/ Organizations
2. Pre-crisis/pre-disaster preparation	Pre-crisis/Pre-disaster phase	Crisis or disaster anticipation	To foster resiliency Set expectations Improve coping Stress management	Individual Group Organizations
3. Demobilizations, respite centers & staff consultation (rescuer & recovery)	Shift disengagement	Event driven	To inform and consult, allow psychological decompression and physical restoration	Large groups/Organizations
4. Crisis Management Briefing (CMB) (civilians, schools, business)	Anytime post-crisis		Stress management	
5. Defusing	Post-crisis (within 12 hours)	Usually symptom driven	Symptom mitigation Possible closure Triage	Small groups

6. Critical Incident Stress Debriefing (CISD)	Post-crisis (1–10 days; 3–4 weeks mass disasters)	Usually symptom driven, can be event driven	Facilitate psychological closure Symptom mitigation Triage	Small groups
7. Individual crisis intervention 1:1	Anytime Anywhere	Symptom driven	Symptom mitigation. Return to function, if possible. Referral, if needed.	Individuals
8. Family CISM		Either symptom driven or event driven	Foster support & communications Symptom mitigation Closure, if possible Referral, if needed	Families/Organizations
9. Community and organizational consultation	Anytime			
10. Pastoral crisis intervention	Anytime	Usually symptom driven	To mitigate a "crisis of faith" and use spiritual tools to assist in recovery.	Individuals/Families/Groups
11. Follow-up/Referral	Anytime	Usually symptom driven	Assess mental status. Access higher level of care; if needed.	Individual/Family

From: Everly, G. & Mitchell, J. (1999). Critical Incident Stress Management (CISM): A New Era and Standard of Care in Crisis Intervention. Ellicott City, MD: Chevron Publishing. Revised January 2004

For this tragic event, CISM services would likely be offered to both the emergency service (EMS) workers and to the civilians. Upon being informed of the incident, a CISM team would be dispatched to the scene.

EMS Workers

It is hoped that the EMS workers would have received an introduction to the appropriate expectations about acute stress disorder and its management as part of their precrisis professional preparation. However, even with ample psychological preparedness, few EMS workers are actually prepared for the horrific psychological devastation that occurs when a group of children perishes. When the CISM team arrives at the scene, its initial duties would include not intruding on the rescue efforts but providing support to the operation as requested. The CISM team members may provide acute one-on-one support for those with clear evidence of functional impairment during the rescue efforts. Several models of one-on-one interventions may be employed (Everly & Mitchell, 1999; Roberts, 1991, 1996). Given the nature and severity of this trauma, for the workers completing their initial shift (and with the prospect of returning to the scene the next day), a demobilization area should be established where the workers can decompress and receive information for 10 to 20 minutes. A 30-minute defusing intervention may then be done to help mitigate the effects of acute trauma if deemed necessary. Approximately 1 week after the acute rescue assignment (when the out-of town rescuers are back home), debriefings would be conducted with those involved in the operation to assist them in normalizing their reactions, to put the incident in perspective, and to challenge irrational beliefs. A separate debriefing would be conducted with those from out of town who have since returned home. Also, the CISM team would want to make consultations with families available for those in need. It is also very important that follow-up services such as employee assistance programs (EAPs) or community mental health referrals are made available for those workers for whom the crisis intervention services described here are insufficient.

Civilians

For the civilians involved in the disaster, such as the day care staff or relatives of the victims, one-on-one interventions, family support, and follow-up referrals to mental health professionals are likely to be the most relevant CISM components. "Town meetings" and crisis management briefings (Everly & Mitchell, 1999) can be held for civilians and the community at large. Within a few days of the event, social support services may be offered. A week to 10 days after the completion of the event, the CISD may be utilized for the civilians most severely impacted. Chaplaining and pastoral crisis intervention services would be available.

Case 2

It was 9:58 A.M. on a morning in May, seemingly no different than most days in this small midwestern town. However, appearances can be deceiving. Two blocks away from the town's second-largest insurance building, 35-year-old David G., a recently unemployed auto and truck mechanic, sat passively in his car, contemplating what the next several hours would bring. He had fleeting, emotional thoughts about his mother, who passed away suddenly less than 2 months ago. He had described her to others as his only "true friend." He also continued to seethe about the rejection he encountered 2 days ago, when his girlfriend of 3 years, 28-year-old Angela, told him that she no longer wanted to see him. David, who did not have a history of violence, warned her following the breakup that he would not allow her to embarrass him and ruin his life. She refused to take his calls since the breakup, but David had decided that he would be heard. When his watch signaled 10:00 A.M., David slowly, yet purposefully, approached the building.

What happened next could only be described as a nightmarish blur. When David was questioned by the receptionist in the empty lobby regarding the purpose of his visit, he calmly removed the 9-millimeter pistol he had concealed under his jacket and shot her twice in the chest, killing her instantly. Seemingly void of emotion, he proceeded onto the elevator and then to Angela's crowded work area, where he located her talking to several of her colleagues while they were on a break. Unfortunately, she did not notice him until he was less than 10 feet away. Without uttering a word, David shot Angela three times, also killing her instantly. He then placed the weapon under his chin and with a single pull of the trigger ended this grisly, shocking, and tragic ordeal.

A highly efficient and well-organized EAP or in-house crisis team that may be part of a human resources department would likely provide initial support services. This, for example, may include two counselors trained in CISM who may be dispatched and who arrive at the scene within 2 to 4 hours after the shooting.

EMS Workers

This type of event, albeit devastating in its own right, typically does not result in inordinate functional impairment on the part of seasoned EMS personnel, who have received extensive psychological preparedness precrisis training. The CISD intervention and possible follow-up referrals should, however, be available for EMS workers who may experience functional difficulty with this event. Given the 2- to 4-hour time lag before the arrival of the counselors, any support service that the EMS workers need would come from resources connected with their respective organizations.

Civilians

In this type of crisis, interventions for the employees will be critical. The CISM counselors will likely begin by making themselves available for one-on-one interventions with those who were most directly involved in the incident and for those most clearly decompensated. Given the magnitude of this type of event within a company, a defusing may be done, and a CISD should be scheduled within a week's time. Moreover, in this type of incident in a relatively large company, it is important to have a group informational briefing that allows for dissemination of accurate information about the events and alleviation of concerns about security and safety for affected employees. Included within this briefing should be guidelines on how individuals may access "local" professionals who may be used for follow-up should individuals and/or families have further concerns about the incident. Indeed, follow-up services will be vitally important in this type of event.

As is clear from these examples, CISM covers the crisis spectrum, from preincident training to postincident follow-up. Every crisis is unique. Therefore, although it may not be feasible, or at times even efficacious, to provide the interventions exactly as described here, these suggestions allow the reader to have a better applied sense of CISM. Take, for example, the second case study. Should this insurance company be considered negligent for not having provided precrisis training for its employees? Clearly, in a high-risk industry, such as banking, the issue of negligence might be raised; however, should this be the case for businesses such as insurance companies? We would like to think not; however, incidents like the World Trade Center bombing, the Oklahoma City bombing, and the recent rash of school shootings may lead us to reconsider our response to this question.

CONCLUSIONS AND A CAUTIONARY NOTE

1. It is imperative that crisis intervention, especially disaster mental health interventions, follow the basic principles and hierarchy of needs, that is, meeting basic needs first. More specifically, needs for food, water, shelter, alleviation of pain, reunification with family members, and the provision of a sense of safety and security should all precede the utilization of psychologically oriented crisis interventions.
2. As compulsory participation in disaster mental health intervention is likely to be perceived negatively, participation in any psychologically oriented disaster intervention activities should be voluntary accompanied by some form of relevant informed consent when intervention goes beyond simple information or educational briefings.
3. Group disaster intervention poses a risk for iatrogenic harm if it introduces traumatogenetic material to group members who would not otherwise

be exposed to such material. To reduce this risk, it is suggested that small disaster intervention groups be made up of naturally occurring cohorts and/ or homogeneous groups with regard to trauma exposure and toxicity. The formation of small heterogeneous crisis intervention debriefings should not be endorsed.

4. It has been proposed that health education about signs and symptoms of distress may actually psychogenically create such symptoms in highly suggestible persons. It is hard to accept this notion of potential mass hysteria so as to "keep information from people for their own good." Nevertheless, it may be argued that the manner in which the information is presented may have a significant effect upon subsequent hysterical symptomatology. Such information should be presented as basic health education–related information designed to empower the recipients of such information to assume more, not less, control in responding to adversity, when such seems appropriate.

5. The notion of the value of cathartic ventilation has been challenged to the degree that concern has been expressed that cathartic ventilation may become a pathogenic abreactive process. To reduce this risk, it might be suggested that assessment and triage are essential elements of effective disaster mental health intervention wherein psychologically vulnerable or brittle persons (highly aroused, morbidly depressed, highly guilt-ridden individuals, the intensely bereaved, dissociating individuals, those experiencing psychotic symptomatology, those physically injured or in pain) not be included in group intervention, rather, they should be approached individually and more appropriate interventions should be utilized. Furthermore, whether individually or in groups, deep probing techniques, psychotherapeutic interpretation, and paradoxical intention should clearly be avoided.

6. Concern has been expressed that disaster intervention techniques should never consist of univariate standalone interventions. Rather, crisis intervention should consist of a phase sensitive, multi-variate intervention system. Critical Incident Stress Management (CISM) represents one such system. Consistent with the notion of integrative psychotherapy, crisis intervention should be integrative, that is, crisis intervention should be conceived of as a configurational system of strategies and tactics in which each intervention technique is selected not only for its efficacy in resolving singular clinical and preclinical features but also for its contribution to the overall constellation of intervention procedures in their task of responding to the unique demands of any given circumstance (adapted from Millon, 2003). Potential crisis interventions may include:

a. Assessment and triage
b. Strategic planning
c. Psychoeducation and anticipatory guidance
d. Liaison, advocacy, and reunification, or building, of familial and social support networks

e. Individual clinical intervention
f. Small group intervention
g. Large group intervention, e.g., "town meetings" and respite sectors for emergency response personnel
h. Follow-up and referral

7. So that disaster mental health intervention is not conceived of as a substitute for more formal psychotherapeutic and/or psychiatric interventions, crisis intervention is conceived of as but one point on a continuum of care which certainly includes psychotherapy. The natural corollary of this conceptualization is that successful crisis intervention, similar to successful physical first aid, may actually consist of simply facilitating access to the next and more appropriate level of care.

8. Unfortunately there is a misconception that evidence exists to suggest that CISD/CISM has proven harmful to its recipients (e.g., see Snelgrove, 1998). The investigations that are frequently cited to suggest such an adverse effect simply did not use the CISD or CISM system as prescribed (Dyregrov, 1998), a fact that often is unreported or overlooked (Friedman, Foa, & Charney, 2003; Wessely & Deahl, 2003; Rose et al., 2002).

A careful review of literature in the area of crisis intervention reveals a body of literature fraught with inconsistent terminology (Everly & Mitchell, 1999); inconsistent standards for training and practice (Dyregrov, 1998; Koss and Shiang, 1994; Mitchell & Everly, 2001); poorly defined and poorly controlled outcome investigations (Everly, Flannery, & Mitchell, 2000; Dyregrov, 1998; Everly & Mitchell, 1999; Mitchell & Everly, 2001); and even the possibility of "political" or guild issues (Dyregrov, 1998)—all of which apparently serve to hinder a more rapid refinement of the field. Nevertheless, the specific effectiveness of CISD and/or CISM programs has been empirically validated through thoughtful qualitative analyses, controlled investigations, and even meta-analyses (Everly, Boyle, & Lating, 1999; Everly & Boyle, 1999; Flannery, 1998; Mitchell & Everly, 2001; Everly & Mitchell, 1999; Mitchell & Everly, in press; Everly, Flannery, & Mitchell, 2000; Dyregrov, 1997). Unfortunately, this fact is often overlooked (e.g., see Rose & Bisson, 1998; Snelgrove, 1998). Flannery and his colleagues have applied the CISM model to violence in the workplace with strikingly beneficial results (Flannery, 1998). His Assaulted Staff Action Program (ASAP) stands as the gold standard for violence-oriented crisis intervention programs and has been validated through well-controlled empirical investigations (Flannery, 2001).

In sum, no one CISM intervention is designed to stand alone, not even the widely used CISD. Efforts to implement and evaluate CISM must be programmatic, not unidimensional (Mitchell & Everly, in press). While the CISM approach to crisis intervention is continuing to evolve, as should any worthwhile endeavor, current investigations have clearly demonstrated its value as a tool to reduce human suffering. Future research should focus upon how the CISM process can be made even more effective to those in crisis.

REFERENCES

American Psychiatric Association. (1980). *Diagnostic and statistical manual of mental disorders* (3rd ed.). Washington, DC: Author.

American Psychiatric Association. (1987). *Diagnostic and statistical manual of mental disorders* (3rd ed., rev.). Washington, DC: Author.

American Psychiatric Association. (1994). *Diagnostic and statistical manual of mental disorders* (4th ed.). Washington, DC: Author.

Biggio, G. (1983). The action of stress, beta carbornes, diazepam, Ro15-1788 on GABA receptors in the rat brain. In G. Biggio & E. Costa (Eds.), *Benzodiazepine recognition and site ligands* (pp. 105–119). New York: Raven.

Bisson, J., & Deahl, M. (1994). Psychological debriefing and preventing post traumatic stress. *British Journal of Psychiatry, 165*, 717–720.

Bowlby, J. (1969). *Attachment and loss: Vol. 1. Attachment.* New York: Basic Books.

Bremner, J. D., Randall, P., Scott, T. N., Bronen, R. A., Seibyl, J. P., Southwick, S. M., Delaney, R. C., McCarty, G., Charney, D. S., & Innis, R. B. (1995). MRI-based measurements of hippocampal volume in combat-related posttraumatic stress disorder. *American Journal of Psychiatry, 152,* 973–981.

Bremner, J. D., Randall, P., Vermetten, E., Staib, L., Bronen, R. A., Mazuré, C., Capelli, S., McCarthy, G., Innis, R. B., & Charney, D. S. (1997). Magnetic resonance imaging–based measurement of hippocampal volume in posttraumatic stress disorder related to childhood physical and sexual abuse: A preliminary report. *Biological Psychiatry, 41,* 23–32.

British Psychological Working Party. (1990). *Psychological aspects of disaster.* Leicester: British Psychological Society.

Caplan, G. (1964). *Principles of preventive psychiatry.* New York: Basic Books.

Davidson, L., & Baum, A. (1986). Chronic stress and post-traumatic stress disorders. *Journal of Consulting and Clinical Psychology, 54,* 303–308.

Drugan, R. C., Murrow, A. L., Weizman, R. et al. (1989). Stress-induced behavioral depression associated with a decrease in GABA receptor–mediated chloride ion influx and brain benzodiazepine receptor occupancy. *Brain Research, 487,* 45–51.

Dyregrov, A. (1997). The process of psychological debriefing. *Journal of Traumatic Stress, 10,* 589–604.

Dyregrov, A. (1998). Psychological debriefing: An effective method? *Traumatologye, 4*(2), Article 1.

Everly, G. S. (1990). Post-traumatic stress disorder as a "disorder of arousal." *Psychology and Health: An International Journal, 4,* 135–145.

Everly, G. S., & Boyle, S. (1999). Effectiveness of Critical Incident

Stress Debriefing (CISD): A meta-analysis. *International Journal of Emergency Mental Health, 1*(3), 165–168.

Everly, G. S., Boyle, S., & Lating, J. (1999). The effectiveness of psychological debriefings in vicarious trauma: A meta-analysis. *Stress Medicine, 15*, 229–233.

Everly, G. S., Jr., Flannery, R. B., Jr., & Eyler, V. (2002). Critical incident stress management: A statistical review of the literature. *Psychiatric Quarterly, 73*, 171–182.

Everly, G. S., Jr., Flannery, R. B., Jr., & Mitchell, J. (2000). Critical incident stress management: A review of the literature. *Aggression and Violent Behavior, 5*, 23–40.

Everly, G. S., Flannery, R., & Mitchell, J. (in press). CISM: A review of literature. *Aggression and Violent Behavior: A Review Journal.*

Everly, G. S., & Horton, A. M. (1989). Neuropsychology of PTSD. *Perceptual and Motor Skills, 68,* 807–810.

Everly, G. S., & Mitchell, J. T. (1997). *Critical Incident Stress Management (CISM): A new era and standard of care in crisis intervention.* Ellicott City, MD: Chevron.

Ford, J. D., Ruzek, J., & Niles, B. (1996). Identifying and treating VA medical care patients with undetected sequelae of psychological trauma and post-traumatic stress disorder. *NCP Clinical Quarterly, 6,* 77–82.

Flannery, R. B. (1998). *The Assaulted Staff Action Program: Coping with the psychological aftermath of violence.* Ellicott City, MD: Chevron.

Flannery, R. B., Jr. (2001). Assaulted Staff Action Program (ASAP): Ten years of empirical support for Critical Incident Stress Management (CISM). *International Journal of Emergency Mental Health, 3,* 5–10.

Flannery, R. B., Jr., Hanson, M., & Penk, W. (1994). Risk factors for psychiatric inpatient assaults on staff. *The Journal of Mental Health Administration, 21,* 24–31.

Flannery, R. B., Jr., Hanson, M., Penk, W., Flannery, G., & Gallagher, C. (1995). The Assaulted Staff Action Program: An approach to coping with the aftermath of violence in the workplace. In L. Murphy, J. Hurrell, S. Sauter, and G. Keita (Eds.). *Job stress interventions* (pp. 199–212). Washington, D.C.: APA Press.

Frankl, V. (1959). *Man's search for meaning.* Boston: Beacon.

Friedman, M. J. (2004). Acknowledging the psychiatric costs of war. *New England Journal of Medicine, 351,* 75–77.

Friedman, M., Foa, E., & Charney, D. (2003). Toward evidence-based early intervention for acutely traumatized adults and children. *Biological Psychiatry, 53,* 765–768.

Gray, J. (1982). *The neuropsychology of anxiety.* New York: Oxford University Press.

Henry, J. P. (1993, February). *Alexithymia and PTSD.* Paper presented to the Fifth Montreux Congress on stress, Montreux, Switzerland.

Hoge, C. W., Castro, C., Messer, S., McGurk, D., Cotting, D., & Koffman, R. (2004). Combat duty in Iraq and Afghanistan, mental health problems, and barriers to care. *New England Journal of Medicine, 351,* 13–22.

Institute of Medicine. (2003). *Preparing for the psychological consequences of terrorism.* Washington, DC: National Academies Press.

Janoff-Bulman, R. (1988). Victims of

violence. In S. Fisher & J. Reason (Eds.), *Handbook of life stress, cognition and health* (pp. 101–113). New York: Wiley.

Janoff-Bulman, R. (1992). *Shattered assumptions.* New York: Jason Aronson.

Joy, R. (1985). The effects of neurotoxicants on kindling and kindled seizures. *Fundamental and Applied Toxicology, 5,* 41–65.

Kalivas, P. W., & Duffy, P. (1989). Similar effects of cocaine and stress on mesocorticolimbic dopamine neurotransmission in the rat. *Biological Psychiatry, 25,* 913–928.

Kardiner, A. (1941). *The traumatic neuroses of war.* New York: Hoeber.

Kessler, R. C., Sonnega, A., Bromet, E., Hughes, M., & Nelson, C. (1995). Posttraumatic stress disorder in the National Comorbidity Survey. *Archives of General Psychiatry, 52,* 1048–1060.

Koss, M., & Shiang, J. (1994). Research on brief psychotherapy. In A. Bergin & S. Garfield (Eds.), *Handbook of psychotherapy and behavior change* (pp. 664–700). New York: Wiley.

Koss, M. P., Woodruff, W., & Koss, P. G. (1991). Criminal victimization among primary care medical patients. *Behavioral Sciences and the Law, 9,* 45–46.

Krnjevic, K. (1983). GABA-mediated inhibitory mechanisms in relation to epileptic discharges. In H. Jasper & N. van Gelder (Eds.), *Basic mechanisms of neuronal hyperexcitability* (pp. 249–263). New York: Liss.

Krystal, J. H., Kosten, T. R., Southwick, S., et al. (1989). Neurobiological aspects of PTSD. *Behavior Therapy, 20,* 177–198.

Langsley, D., Machotka, P., & Flomenhaft, K. (1971). Avoiding mental health admission: A follow-up. *American Journal of Psychiatry, 127,* 1391–1394.

Lifton, R. J. (1988). Understanding the traumatized self. In J. P. Wilson, Z. Harel, & B. Kahana (Eds.), *Human adaptation to extreme stress* (pp. 7–31). New York: Plenum.

Lindemann, E. (1944). Symptomatology and management of acute grief. *American Journal of Psychiatry, 101,* 141–148.

Maslow, A. H. (1954). *Motivation and personality.* New York: Harper.

Mason, J. W., et al. (1986). Urinary free cortisol in PTSD. *Journal of Nervous and Mental Disorders, 174,* 145–149.

McGeer, E., & McGeer, P. (1988). Excitotoxins and animal models of disease. In C. Galli, L. Manzo, & P. Spencer (Eds.), *Recent advances in nervous system toxicology* (pp. 107–131). New York: Plenum.

McNally, R., Bryant, R., & Ehlers, A. (2003). Does early psychological intervention promote recovery from posttraumatic stress? *Psychological Science in the Public Interest, 4,* 45–79.

Millon, T., Grossman, S., Meagher, S., Millon, C., & Everly, G. (1999). *Personality-guided therapy.* New York: Wiley.

Mitchell, J. T. (1983). When disaster strikes . . . The critical incident stress debriefing process. *Journal of Emergency Medical Services, 8*(1), 36–39.

Mitchell, J. T., & Everly, G. S. (2001). *Critical Incident Stress Debriefing: An operations manual.* Ellicott City, MD: Chevron.

Mitchell, J. T., & Everly, G. S.

(1999). Critical Incident Stress Management: A new era in crisis intervention. *Traumatic Stress Points,* Fall, vol. 1, no. 1, 6–7, 10–11.

Mitchell, J. T., & Everly, G. S. (in press). CISM and CISD: Evolution, effects and outcomes. In B. Raphael & J. Wilson (Eds.), *Psychological debriefing.* Cambridge: Cambridge University Press.

Murburs, M., McFall, M., & Veith, R. (1990). Catecholamines, stress and PTSD. In E. Giller (Ed.), *Biological assessment and treatment of post-traumatic stress disorder* (pp. 29–64). Washington, DC: American Psychiatric Press.

National Institute of Mental Health. (2002). *Mental health and mass violence.* Washington, DC: Author.

Nutt, D. (1989). Altered central a-2 adrenoreceptor sensitivity in panic disorder. *Archives of General Psychiatry, 46,* 165–169.

OSHA. (1996). *Guidelines for preventing workplace violence for healthcare and social service workers.* OSHA 3148-1996. Washington, DC: U.S. Department of Labor.

OSHA. (1998). *Recommendations for workplace violence prevention programs in late-night retail establishments.* OSHA 3153-1998. Washington, DC: U.S. Department of Labor.

Palkovits, M., Lang, T., Patthy, A., & Elekes, L. (1986). Distribution and stress-induced increase of glutamate and aspartate levels in discrete brain nuclei of rats. *Brain Research, 373,* 252–257.

Perry, B. D., Southwick, S. M., & Giller, E. L. (1990). Adrenergic receptor regulation in post-traumatic stress disorder. In E. Giller (Ed.), *Biological assessment and treatment of post-traumatic stress disorder* (pp. 87–114). Washington, DC: American Psychiatric Press.

Pitman, R. K., & Orr, S. P. (1990). Twenty-four hour urinary cortisol and catecholamine excretion in combat-related post-traumatic stress disorder. *Biological Psychiatry, 27,* 245–247.

Post, R. (1985). Stress, sensitization, kindling, and conditioning. *Behavioral and Brain Sciences, 8,* 372–373.

Post, R. (1986). Does limbic system dysfunction play a role in affective illness? In B. Doane & K. Livingston (Eds.), *The limbic system.* New York: Raven.

Post, R. (1992). Transduction of psychological stress into the neurobiology of recurrent affective disorders. *American Journal of Psychiatry, 149,* 999–1010.

Post, R., & Ballenger, J. (1981). Kindling models for progressive development of psychopathology. In H. Van Pragg (Ed.), *Handbook of biological psychiatry* (pp. 609–651). New York: Marcel Dekker.

Rahe, R. H., Karson, S., Howard, N. S., Rubin, R. T., et al. (1990). Psychological and physiological assessments on American hostages freed from captivity in Iran. *Psychosomatic Medicine, 52,* 1–16.

Roberts, A. R. (1991). Conceptualizing crisis theory and the crisis intervention model. In A. R. Roberts (Ed.), *Contemporary perspectives on crisis intervention and prevention* (pp. 3–17). Englewood Cliffs, NJ: Prentice-Hall.

Roberts, A. R. (1996). Epidemiology and definitions of acute crisis in American society. In A. R. Roberts (Ed.), *Crisis management and brief treatment* (pp. 16–33). Belmont, CA: Wadsworth.

Rose, S., & Bisson J. (1998). Brief early psychological interventions following a trauma: A systematic review of the literature. *Journal of Traumatic Stress*, 11, 698–710.

Schaeffer, M. A., & Baum, A. (1984). Adrenal cortical response to stress at Three Mile Island. *Psychosomatic Medicine, 46*, 227–237.

Snelgrove, T. (1998). Debriefing under fire. *Trauma Lines, 3*(2), 3–11.

Stein, B., Elliott, M., Jaycoxx, L., Collins, R., Berry, S., Klein, D., & Schuster, M. (2004). A longitudinal study of the psychological consequences of the September 11, 2001 terrorist attacks: Reactions, impairment, and help-seeking. *Psychiatry, 67*, 105–117.

Swanson, W. C., & Carbon, J. B. (1989). Crisis intervention theory and technique. In *The Task Force Report of the American Psychiatric Association Treatments of Psychiatric Disorders* (pp. 2520–2531). Washington, DC: APA Press.

van der Kolk, B. (1988). The trauma spectrum. *Journal of Traumatic Stress, 1*, 273–290.

van Gelder, N. M. (1986). The hyperexcited brain: Glutamic acid release and failure of inhibition. In R. Schwarz & Y. Ben-Ari (Eds.), *Excitatory amino acids and epilepsy* (pp. 331–347). New York: Plenum.

Wessely, S., Rose, S., & Bisson, J. (1998). A systematic review of brief psychological interventions (debriefing) for the treatment of immediate trauma related symptoms and the prevention of post traumatic stress disorder (Cochrane Review). *Cochrane Library*, Issue 3, Oxford, UK: Update Software.

Wilson, J. P. (1989). *Trauma, transformation, and healing*. New York: Brunner/Mazel.

Yalom, I. (1970). *Theory and practice of group psychotherapy*. New York: Basic Books.

10

Crisis Support for Families of Emergency Responders

CHERYL REGEHR

One cold winter night police, fire, and ambulance arrived in a snow-covered neighborhood following the frantic call from a mother that her baby was burned. The house had the appearance of despair and the cold February wind ripped through broken windows. As emergency crews entered the home, they realized that the home had no heat source and that a pungent smell filled the building. In the kitchen, they discovered the charred remains of a baby who had been placed on an open oven door to warm and, when left unattended, had been flung into the oven as the door hinge slammed shut.

The wife of a responder described the impact of this type of event on their family in the days that followed: "It's almost like a bomb going off. It hit him and just like an aftershock, hit all of us."

On September 2, 1998, Swissair 111 on a regular flight between New York and Geneva crashed into the ocean off the east coast of Nova Scotia, Canada, with its 229 passengers and crew. Word of the disaster spread quickly through the small towns surrounding the scene and people entered the water in small vessels searching for survivors, though none was to be found. In the subsequent days, weeks, and then months, the scenic tourist spot of Peggy's Cove became headquarters for an international investigation. Military and civilian personnel launched massive efforts to recover the remains of the dead from open waters and the nearby beaches that continued for almost one year. The long, exhausting hours of work and weeks away from home for military and emergency service personnel resulted in naming the event "Operation Perseverance."

The public's awareness that emergency responders are exposed to violence and danger well beyond most of our own experiences was never clearer than in the aftermath of 9/11. In this single, horrifying event, 343 firefighters and 75 police officers lost their lives in the line of duty. Thousands of other emergency responders worked tirelessly to assist the 2,261 people who were injured and seemingly endlessly to recover the bodies of the 2,801 people who were killed. Miles away at the Pentagon in Washington and Shanksville, Pennsylvania, where AA flight 93 crashed, a similar story unfolded as 228 people were killed and 76 were injured (September 11 News.com, 2004). Yet, risks to emergency responders exist not only during catastrophic but relatively rare events, rather, risks occur on a relatively frequent basis. for instance, 56% of volunteer firefighters in New South Wales reported that their safety had been seriously threatened at some time, 26% in the prior year (Marmar, Weiss, Metzler, Delucchi, Best, et al., 1999). Seventy percent of paramedics in an urban sample had been assaulted on the job, and 56% reported experiencing events on the job which they believed could have resulted in their own death (Regehr, Goldberg, & Hughes, 2002). In addition to personal danger, emergency responders are regularly exposed to the suffering and death of others. One study of paramedics reported that over 80% of those in a large urban area had experienced each of the following events: the death of a patient while in their care, the death of a child, events involving multiple causalties, and events involving violence perpetrated by one individual against another (Regehr, Goldberg, & Hughes, 2002). In a sample of 165 firefighters in Australia, 78% indicated that they had been exposed to at least one critical incident at work, including the death of a colleague, injury on duty, mass casualties, or the death of a child (Regehr, Hill, & Glancy, 2000). Over 40% of 103 firefighters studied in Canada report being exposed to each of the following events: violence against others, multiple casualties, and the death of a child; approximately 30% of firefighters report experiencing the death of a person in their care (Regehr & Bober, 2004).

Although in many ways, the training and personality styles of emergency responders prepare them to deal with high-drama situations, nevertheless, this exposure has an impact on their emotional and psychological well-being. McFarlane (1988) observed that 32% of firefighters in Australia reported significant levels of symptoms on the General Health Questionnaire (GHQ) four months after a huge brushfire, and 30% continued to have significant levels of symptoms at 29 months. Other firefighter cross-sectional design studies report rates of distress in the high or severe range on the Impact of Event Scale (IES) of 26% (Bryant & Harvey, 1996) and 24.6% (Regehr & Bober, 2004), suggesting that at any given time, approximately 25% of firefighters currently on the job are experiencing significant trauma symptoms. Similarly, sectional design studies have demonstrated that at any given time, approximately 25% to 33% of paramedics have trauma symptoms in the high or severe range, which is considered consistent with a diagnosis of posttraumatic stress disorder (PTSD; Alexander & Klein, 2001; Regehr, Goldberg, & Hughes, 2002).

In addition to traumatic exposure, emergency service work poses other stressors. Studies of emergency responders point to the difficulties presented by the everyday hassles of shift work, unpredictably long hours, organizational politics, and lack of opportunities for promotion. Several large-scale studies of police officers in England, Australia, Canada, and the United States have concluded that more than events such as dealing with victims of serious accidents, being attacked by aggressive offenders, or dealing with protesters, the police organization with its rules, procedures, communication paths, bureaucratic hierarchy, and management style was the greatest source of job stress (Brown & Campbell, 1990; Burke, 1993; Buunk & Peeters, 1994; Coman & Evans, 1991; Hart, Wearing, & Headley, 1995). Similarly, ambulance workers involved in body recovery duties following mass disasters in England identified that poor relationships with management, not being valued for their skills, and shift work were the major stressors they encountered (Thompson, 1993).

The support of family is paramount to reducing the impact of highly stressful work on emergency responders. In research conducted on emergency service personnel, social support of others including family and friends was significantly negatively correlated with scores on both trauma symptom scales and depression scales (King, King, Fairbank, Keane, & Adams, 1997; Leffler & Dembert, 1998; Regehr, Hemsworth, & Hill, 2001; Weiss, Marmar, Metzler, & Ronfeldt, 1995). Further, those who had higher levels of family support were less likely to take mental health stress leaves from work following a traumatic event (Regehr, Goldberg, Glancy, & Knott, 2002).

Yet, family members are not immune from the stresses encountered by their loved ones who place themselves in the line of fire. They, too, are affected by the impact of shift work and unpredictably long hours. They suffer from organizational politics and lack of opportunities for promotion, which would bring more financial resources to the family, along with more regular living and work schedules. They feel the secondary effects of traumatic events through exposure to traumatic material described by their family member and reported in the media. They also experience the trauma on an emotional level, through witnessing and coping with the trauma reactions of the emergency responder. This trauma exposure frequently results in fears and trauma symptoms in family.

The family is not a bottomless resource. Unless the needs of family members are attended to, their ability to support will wither away. While studies on divorce rates among emergency responders differ regarding whether they are higher than those in the general public, anecdotal evidence suggests that many senior responders are on their second and third marriages. Responders encountered in both research and clinical experience talk at length about the stresses that the job places on spouses and other family members (Regehr & Bober, 2004).

This chapter identifies the particular stressors encountered by families of emergency responders and suggests both means of prevention and specific approaches to dealing with crisis situations that follow traumatic exposures of emergency responders.

MARRIED TO THE JOB

The lives of emergency responders, and consequently their families, are fraught with uncertainty and tension. The job competes with the family for time and attention. Shift work in and of itself forces families to accommodate to missed social events and missed children's sports games and concerts. The regular six o'clock dinner of the TV family does not exist in these households. Emergency responders are called on to work special details or extra shifts. Emergency incidents requiring considerable time and paperwork never occur at the beginning of a shift. Further, emergency responders, particularly those in policing, describe how family vacation plans can be disrupted by a big case or impending trial (Regehr & Bober, 2004). As a result, the spouse of an emergency responder may have to make sacrifices in his or her own career to accommodate the needs of the responder's career and the competing demands of family (Kannady, 1993). Children of emergency responders may feel isolated and abandoned by the absent parent, and there is some evidence that they look exclusively to the other parent (usually the mother) for support (Maslach & Jackson, 1979). As one officer in our study explained, "My wife says she raised the kids, and she did. I wasn't out every night, but it certainly was a few nights a week. I'd mostly be home on weekends, but there's always an excuse: I'm going to do this, do that" (Regehr, Dimitropoulos, Bright, George & Henderson, in press).

Other factors also interfere with family life. During a long and complex case in policing, a sense of competition can arise between the spouse and the actors in the case. For officers in sexual assault squads or special victims units, victims may have access to the officer at all hours of the day and night, and when they call to discuss how they are managing, calls can appear to the spouse to be very personal and intimate. For officers working undercover, other challenges arise. One officer talked about the difficulty in readjusting to regular family life after a major undercover drug case: "At 10 or 11 at night, I would go out and walk for three hours. It used to drive my wife crazy. 'Where are you going? What are you doing?' I just couldn't sleep. It took me months to get back to routine and to sleeping well."

In addition, the organizational environment can create barriers between the responder and his or her family. To protect themselves from the dangers of the job, emergency service workers develop strong ties with colleagues. This cohesiveness and solidarity results in a rigid boundary between the members of the emergency organization and others, including not only the public, but also members of other organizations. Emergency workers maintain this professional boundary not only when on the job; frequently, social activities and social relationships become limited to others in the same profession. This boundary may limit the spouse's sense of connection and accessibility to the loved one and leave him or her feeling like another outsider (Borum & Philpot, 1993).

An additional problem for families is the public scrutiny that they encounter at times. Especially for families living in smaller communities, everyone knows who the emergency responders are. There may be higher expectations for the behavior of the "cop's kid" and higher visibility for misbehavior. Families can be subject to comments of neighbors when a rescue went badly or a scandal erupts in an organization and all members of the service become tainted. Responders have reported that families have been subject to accusations of racism or incompetence as a result of media reports. One officer who was involved in a trial heavily covered in the media described the impact on his family: "Some days I'd come home and my daughter would be crying, and she'd say nothing is wrong. Then you'd find out, 'The kids at school are teasing me, that you are a drug dealer.' And I sat down with her and explained what was happening."

The everyday job of an emergency responder is frequently fraught with minor hassles and conflicts. Emergency service organizations tend to be highly structured and organized and allow for little flexibility. This can breed anger and resentment among responders. Much citizen contact involves unlawful or abusive behavior or people complaining. While this may be most obvious in the work of police officers, our study of paramedics revealed that 70% had been victims of violence on the job (Regehr, Goldberg, & Hughes, 2002). This can result in emotional exhaustion, a chronic state of physical and emotional depletion resulting from excessive work demands and continuous hassles. Anger, impatience, cynicism, and other negative feelings are frequently expressed at home.

Researchers have demonstrated how job-related stresses experienced in a variety of working environments can be transmitted to other family members once the individual returns home. In general, findings suggest that job stress dampens the quality of marital interactions and causes the other spouse to feel more negatively toward the relationship (Larson & Almeida, 1999; Thompson & Bolger, 1999). One study of police officers, for instance, found that emotional exhaustion and negative affective states of police officers are associated with their spouses' reports of family conflict (Burke, 1993). Another study utilizing physiological measures discovered that on days officers reported higher levels of stress, both the officers and their wives showed greater levels of autonomic arousal during conversations (Roberts & Levenson, 2001). A particularly interesting finding in this study involved cardiovascular and somatic measures. Although greater vascular activity is generally associated with greater somatic or physical activity, Roberts and Levenson found that officers and wives showed greater cardiovascular activity but lower levels of body movement on high-stress days. They hypothesized that lower levels of activity may reflect a freeze-type response associated with intense fear or readiness. In police work, this type of vigilance and defensiveness is required to facilitate the quick response required during an incident. The authors propose that on high-stress days, officers maintain this stance at home and wives similarly take on a defensive stance.

TRAUMA CONTAGION

Trauma contagion, or secondary trauma, is often experienced by emergency responders who witness the pain and suffering of others. However, the traumatic experience does not stop there, but continues to ripple outward to encompass other family members. Several research studies have looked at the impact on mental health therapists of working with victims and of repeatedly hearing violent imagery about the atrocities that one human commits against another. It has been found that such exposure can result in experiences of terror, rage, and despair and symptoms of PTSD, including intrusion, avoidance, dissociation, and sleep disturbance on the part of therapists merely by hearing the stories told by clients (Chrestman, 1995; Figley, 1995; Kassam-Adams, 1995). In a related area, it was found that researchers doing chart reviews of child maltreatment cases began experiencing symptoms of trauma. Steps had to be taken to protect them from exposure to the traumatic stimuli by limiting their time spent reading the material (Kinard, 1996). If mental health professionals and researchers with specialized training and a support network of other professionals experience this distress, how much greater will the impact be on family members who lack this training and support and who actually love the person who was traumatized?

Family members hear stories of events through direct discussions with their loved one, through overhearing discussions with others, and through reading about events in the paper or seeing them on the television news. Casual conversations among emergency responders tend to involve recollections of gruesome details, jokes about dangerous behaviors of perpetrators and victims toward responders, and dangerous near-death situations in which responders are involved. Material brought home to work on may include gruesome pictures or written reports about the events of an incident. After repeated exposure to graphic imagery of death and destruction, these images may begin intruding on the waking fantasies and dreams of other individuals, such as the family member of a responder (Herman, 1992; Horowitz, 1976; McCann & Pearlman, 1990). It is difficult to shake the image of a child mangled and trapped in the wheel well of a bus, even if you did not see it with your own eyes. Dreams may incorporate one's own child in such a horrific situation.

Another issue for families is dealing with symptoms of the emergency responder who has been exposed. Dealing with anger and irritability, sleeplessness, and avoidance of social interactions, all of which may be symptoms of trauma, can be taxing for family members. A body of literature looks at the impact of posttraumatic stress experienced by one person on other members of the family. For instance, a study of Bosnian refugee couples found that PTSD symptomatology was the best predictor of marital functioning (Spasojevic, Heffer, & Snyder, 2000). That is, higher rates of trauma symptoms in one family member were related to poorer marital adjustment. Similarly, several studies have focused on the stresses experienced by wives of Vietnam veterans as a result of trying to cope with their husband's PTSD symptoms (Verboski & Ryan, 1988). In addition to having intrusion symptoms such as flashbacks, nightmares, and sleep disturbances, there is considerable evidence, from both community-based and laboratory studies, that veterans with PTSD have higher levels of anger and hostility and more difficulty managing their anger than do veterans without PTSD and men in the general population (Calhoun, Bechkham, Feldman, Barefoot, Haney, et al., 2002; McFall, Wright, Donovan, & Raskind, 1999). Veterans with PTSD are also found to have less effective coping mechanisms and problem-solving skills (Nezu & Carnevale, 1987). Consequently, veterans with PTSD have been found to have more severe marital problems, parenting problems, and violent behavior in the family (Davidson & Mellor, 2000; Jordan et al., 1992). It is not surprising that these reactions have an impact on family members. Wives of veterans with PTSD report feelings of isolation and loneliness, confusion, being overwhelmed, and having a sense of no control over their lives. Similar studies have not been conducted on the relationship between anger and PTSD in emergency responders, but some research has raised concerns about higher rates of violence in police families than in the general population (Lott, 1995).

Of perhaps greatest concern is the impact of parental PTSD on children. The major focus of this research has been children of Holocaust survivors. Symptoms experienced by offspring of Holocaust survivors include depression, mistrust, aggression, hyperalertness, emotional numbing and isolation, and some symptoms directly related to their parents' experiences, such as nightmares of the Holocaust (Sigal, Silver, Rakoff, & Ellin, 1973; Solomon, Kotler, & Mikulincer, 1998; Yehuda, Schmeidler, Wainberg, Binder-Brynes, & Duvdevani, 1998). These individuals have also been found to be less resilient to traumatic events in their own lives and to have higher levels of trauma related to such events as the diagnosis of cancer (Baider, Peretz, Hadani,

Perry, Avarmov, et al., 2000) and being exposed to combat (Solomon et al., 1988). Other research has focused on the children of Vietnam veterans. In their study of 1,200 veterans, Jordan and colleagues (1992) found that children of veterans with PTSD were more likely to have behavioral problems, with one-third of the group having one child with problems in the clinical range. Further, a similarity between the behavior of fathers with PTSD (especially violent behavior) and their children has been reported (Harkness, 1993; Solomon, Waysman, & Levy, 1992).

Almost no attention has been paid to the impact of this type of secondary trauma on the families of emergency responders. In a recent qualitative study, spouses of emergency responders described responses that the responders had to specific traumatic events (Regehr, in press). These included a variety of symptoms consistent with PTSD, such as withdrawal: "He's not just withdrawing from me, he's withdrawing from our children as well. It's affecting us." Intrusion symptoms included nightmares: "He will cry out in his sleep. . . . He still has nightmares." Arousal symptoms at times continued long after the event: "Things that happened a couple of years ago and all of a sudden now its affecting him. All of a sudden, he will become very emotional. He'll get all teary eyed"; "She flies into a rage." In addition, a number of respondents pointed to depressive symptoms: "He feels hopeless, hopeless." In one case, the family member reported that the paramedic spouse had suicidal ideation: "He wishes he died that night and this would all be over." Reactions described by respondents also included longer-term effects related to persistent exposure to trauma, suffering, and stress. Some of these reactions were physical and included chronic sleep deprivation and stress-related somatic conditions. Other reactions were related to temperament and personality changes.

One study investigated the impact of the 1995 Oklahoma City bombing on partners of firefighters. That event resulted in the deaths of 168 people, including 19 children and one nurse responder. Rescue and recovery efforts lasted 16 days and involved long hours and unsafe working conditions. Pfefferbaum, North, Bunch, Wilson, and Schorr (2002) interviewed 27 women who were wives of involved firefighters. They found that 50% of the women reported PTSD symptoms. In addition, 37% reported permanent changes in their marital relationship and 7% reported temporary changes in the relationship related to the bombing.

SAFETY FEARS

Immediately after the 2003 crash of the space shuttle *Columbia*, NASA astronaut Col. Chris Hadfield was interviewed by the press and asked how he prepared his family for the possibility of disaster and trauma. He answered:

> I don't dwell on it. I try to understand the risk as clearly as possible because it is life or death for us. It's different for my wife and children. They have to live with the consequences. My kids know their dad is in a risky profession. My wife and I have been married for 21 years and we discussed the possibility years ago. We get life insurance. It's just part of the relationship. ("Columbia Remembered," 2003, p. 15)

While risk may indeed "just be part of the relationship," it nevertheless has an impact on spouses and families. Each time an emergency responder dies in the line of duty, every family of every responder is reminded of the risks. They identify with the grieving spouse and children on the front page of the paper. They fear that one day the flag will be passed to them. At times, these fears are realized. One study focused on the impact of duty-related death on the surviving children of a dead officer. Williams (1999) describes how these children must deal with not only their own reactions and fears, but also those of people around them. The media attention to the deaths creates images that are etched in the child's mind. These children similarly have fears of losing the other parent, fears of their own death, fears of going to sleep (especially if the death occurred at night), and fears of being unprotected.

Fears for safety spill over from fears for the safety of the police officer, paramedic, or firefighter into concerns for other family members. Emergency responders and their families are well aware of the fragility of life and the danger in everyday activities. Exposure to trauma and suffering challenges an individual's beliefs about the safety of those they love, and they may consequently become hypervigilant about potentially dangerous situations (Chrestman, 1995; McCann & Pearlman, 1990; Resick & Schnicke, 1993; Stout & Thomas, 1991). While emergency responders may minimize the risk to themselves and control the potential risk through adherence to training and safety standards, they are acutely aware that they are powerless to protect family members from all risks. It is not uncommon for emergency responders to report extreme fears for the safety of their children and strategies to protect them that are beyond that of other families. One firefighter described coming home and removing all the hangers from the closet after seeing a child fatally injured by one. He recalls that his wife did not even question why. Another firefighter described cutting his children's food into microscopic pieces so that they would not choke. A police officer noted that his son had never been on a team that he did not coach. While these strategies seem reasonable in the minds of responders who have witnessed the effects of disaster and violence, they may seem to be overcontrolling in the minds of family members who are having their activities restricted. It is important for responders to work with their families to assess risk and to ensure that family members do not become resentful. This is one arena where emergency workers must work to keep the impact of their traumatic experiences from impinging too heavily on family life.

HOW DO YOU HUG A MAN OF STEEL?

There is no question that the demands of the job and the exposure to tragic and dangerous events have an impact on the families of emergency responders, but the influence of the organizational culture on the responder and coping strategies employed by the responder also affect family members. The role of an emergency responder often shifts from mediating civilian disputes to enforcing safety standards and laws, restraining individuals from harming themselves or others, and reviving and rescuing people. Each of these roles requires skills and traits not required in most occupations. These skills include taking control, springing into action, remaining detached, making quick and decisive decisions, and questioning everything. Southworth (1990), a former police officer, notes that the traits and dispositions that make a good emergency responder often do not make a good spouse or parent. He states that not only are emergency responders unaware that they are transferring their professional disposition onto family situations, but when they are aware, they often believe that it is appropriate. Examples of this are limiting behaviors due to safety concerns, issuing orders rather than negotiating family solutions, and investigating whether teenage children are using drugs or alcohol. These problems become particularly pronounced when responders have teenagers who no longer wish to follow rules they see as arbitrarily imposed (Maslach & Jackson, 1979).

Not only are the skills and traits necessary for the job a potential risk for healthy and happy family interactions, but so are the coping strategies employed by emergency responders. Emotional numbing is one of the strategies used by emergency responders to cope with stressful events. As discussed in previous chapters, this approach includes avoiding experiencing the emotional impact of tragic events by consciously minimizing emotions and focusing on the cognitive aspect of the job. Feelings about the event are avoided and efforts are made to avoid seeing the victims in the context of their lives, as this increases the risk of emotional distress in the emergency responder. Although this strategy may reduce the risk of traumatic stress symptoms, it does not come without costs: "The downside of my way of dealing with things is the personal side. You start blocking out personal feelings about anything and everyone because you don't want to carry the baggage home with you, but you can't turn it off completely when you go home."

This strategy of emotional numbing has consequences for the responders and for their families. Family members may perceive the police officer, firefighter, or paramedic as emotionally distant and unfeeling. Research has suggested that numbing associated with traumatic stress reactions is significantly associated with negative feelings of family members toward the relationship. In particular, disinterest, detachment, and emotional unavailability that characterize emotional numbing may diminish a parent's ability and willingness to seek out, engage in, and enjoy interactions with children, leading to poorer quality relationships (Ruscio, Weathers, King, & King, 2002).

ASSISTING FAMILIES THROUGH PREVENTION

The first step in providing crisis support for families is prevention. This means ensuring that systems are in place to assist families to develop healthy lifestyles and strategies so that crisis events do not further tax an already suffering system. Some organizations are beginning to provide preventive education for family members, usually aimed at the families of new recruits. Education and prevention programs working with families can incorporate the following suggestions:

1. Accommodate shift work: Families of responders suggest that it is useful to leave lights on at night to welcome home the person on the late shift and reduce the feelings of isolation; get an alarm system if they feel frightened to be alone; communicate through alternative means such as notes, e-mail, and pagers; plan activities with children that allow time with the parent who works shifts; develop a system of rain checks for unforeseen occurrences; and be flexible in the planning of important family events by holding them on alternative dates.
2. Establish decompression routines: Each person has ways that work best for him or her to create a space between work and home. Families need to discuss individual needs and family approaches to lessen the impact of work stress on the family.
3. Acknowledge personal reactions to events and separate them from responses to family situations: It is important to be aware that although individuals may feel they are hiding their distress related to either everyday hassles or traumatic events, very often family members are aware and affected. When experiencing stress or trauma at work, individuals need to work at not reacting immediately (often therefore overreacting) to situations at home, whether the misbehavior of a child, a safety concern, or an annoying behavior of a spouse.
4. Plan responses to questions and comments from others: Children and spouses of emergency responders will be questioned about their loved one's work. Negative comments about all police, firefighters, or paramedics will be directed at family members, with the implication that they are somehow

responsible. Following a major or highly publicized event, they will be sought out for the "insider's view." Families should plan responses to common comments or questions and give enough information to children to make them proud of the work their parent does.

5. Establish a system of supports: As one spouse of an emergency responder stated, "You have a team, we don't." In addition to developing supports of friends and family who can help out in times of disrupted schedules, it is also important to ensure that family members are aware of employee assistance and member assistance programs in the responders' organization where they can turn for information, advice, or support.

CRISIS PROGRAMS FOR FAMILIES

While trauma-related services have increasingly gained acceptance in emergency service organizations, families are often left out of these programs. Crisis response programs for families should therefore include the following elements:

1. Contact and assistance when a responder is injured: In the event of injury, families should be contacted in person by a crisis support person and driven to the most appropriate location to see their loved one. Provisions need to be made regarding child care and meals during this time. Informal supports can be mobilized. After the immediate crisis period, when health and safety are the primary concern, information must be given regarding disability and illness protection and job security. Support regarding the implications of changed family routines and with the emotional response of the emergency worker and fears of the spouse and children must be offered seamlessly from the immediate assistance.

2. Assistance during a critical event: An emergency number should be established that families can call to inquire about the current status of a large-scale event that they hear about on the news. At these times, they will be unable to contact their loved one and will fear for his or her safety. When the report goes out that a firefighter was killed or injured, they should not have to wait several hours until their own loved one can reach a phone to ensure that it was not him or her.

3. Assistance following a critical event: Family members must be included as part of the emergency service team and must be considered when initial contacts are made following traumatic events. Teams regularly make calls to responders offering assistance; these same calls must be made to family members. Support groups for family members following large-scale disasters should be designed and offered.

4. Ongoing assistance: Employee assistance programs are generally well established in emergency organizations. However, informal supports may

not be in place. In the past, many of the challenges experienced by families of responders were ameliorated by the social supports available within the emergency community and within the emergency organization. The changing face of the modern emergency service has had a significant impact on family supports, however. Larger, more complex organizations do not allow for the natural social supports that developed when services were more integrated with the community. The challenge, therefore, is to develop and implement programs that encourage mutual aid and social support among families to ensure that this valuable resource does not become depleted.

CONCLUSION

The families of emergency responders are arguably the most important resource not only of responders but also of emergency service organizations. Family members provide a buffer in times of emotional trauma, they accommodate the needs of responders so that responders can work disruptive schedules and long hours, and they provide a counterbalance to a job where individuals are confronted almost exclusively with the negative side of human nature. Yet, families are often the forgotten victims of workplace stress and trauma. Family members deal with trauma contagion, they are confronted with attitudes and behaviors of the responder emanating from the exposures on the job, and they fear for the safety of their loved one. If organizations do not expand their notion of membership to include families and intervention programs do not incorporate family needs, we run the risk of undermining the most important resource of any individual, and therefore of any organization.

REFERENCES

Alexander, D., & Klein, S. (2001). Ambulance personnel and critical incidents: The impact of accident and emergency work on mental health. *British Journal of Psychiatry, 178*(1), 76–81.

Baider, L. Peretz, T., Hadani, P., Perry, S., Avarmov, R., & De-Nour, A. (2000). Transmission of response to trauma? Second generation Holocaust survivor's reactions to cancer. *American Journal of Psychiatry, 157*(6), 904–910.

Borum, R., & Philpot, C. (1993). Therapy with law enforcement couples: Clinical management of the high-risk life-style. *American Journal of Family Therapy, 21*(2), 122–135.

Brown, J. M., & Campbell, E. A. (1990). Sources of occupational stress in police. *Work and Stress, 4*(4), 305–318.

Bryant, R., & Harvey, A. (1996). Posttraumatic stress reactions in volunteer firefighters. *Journal of Traumatic Stress, 9*, 51–62.

Burke, R. (1993). Work-family stress,

conflict, coping and burnout in police officers. *Stress Medicine, 9,* 171–180.

Buunk, B., & Peeters, M. (1994). Stress at work, social support, and companionship: Towards an event-contingent recording approach. *Work and Stress, 8*(2), 177–190.

Calhoun, P., Bechkham, J., Feldman, M., Barefoot, J., Haney, T., & Bosworth, H. (2002). Partner's ratings of combat veteran's anger. *Journal of Traumatic Stress, 15*(2), 133–136.

Chrestman, K. R. (1995). Secondary exposure to trauma and self-reported distress among therapists. In B. H. Stamm (Ed.), *Secondary traumatic stress: Self-care issues for clinicians, researchers, and educators* (pp. 29–36). Lutherville, MD: Sidran Press.

Columbia remembered. (2003, February 17). *Macleans,* p. 15.

Coman, G., & Evans, B. (1991). Stressors facing Australian police in the 1990s. *Police Studies International Review of Police Development, 14*(4), 153–165.

Davidson, A., & Mellor, D. (2000). The adjustment of children of Australian Vietnam veterans: Is there evidence for the transgenerational transmission of the effects of war-related trauma? *Australian and New Zealand Journal of Psychiatry, 35,* 345–351.

Figley, C. R. (1995). *Compassion fatigue: Coping with secondary traumatic stress in those who treat the traumatized.* New York: Brunner/Mazel.

Harkness, L. (1993). Transgenerational transmission of war-related trauma. In J. Wilson & B. Raphael (Eds.), *International handbook of traumatic stress syndromes* (pp 635–643). New York: Plennum.

Hart, P., Wearing, A., & Headley, B. (1995). Police stress and well-being: Integrating personality, coping, and daily work experiences. *Journal of Occupational and Organizational Psychology, 68,* 133–136.

Herman, J. L. (1992). *Trauma and recovery.* New York: Basic Books.

Horowitz, M. (1976). *Stress response syndromes.* New York: Jason Aronson.

Jordan, K., Marmar, C., Fairbank, J., Schlenger, W., Kulka, R., Hough, R., et al. (1992). Problems in families of male Vietnam veterans with posttraumatic stress disorder. *Journal of Consulting and Clinical Psychology, 60*(6), 916–926.

Kannady, G. (1993). Developing stress resistant police families. *The Police Chief, 60*(8), 92–95.

Kassam-Adams, N. (1995). The risks of treating sexual trauma: Stress and secondary trauma in psychotherapists. In B. H. Stamm (Ed.), *Secondary traumatic stress: Self-care issues for clinicians, researchers, and educators* (pp. 37–50). Lutherville, MD: Sidran Press.

Kinard, E. (1996). Conducting research on child maltreatment: Effects on researchers. *Violence and Victims, 11*(1), 65–69.

King, L., King, D., Fairbank, J., Keane, T., & Adams, G. (1997). Resilience-recovery factors in post-traumatic stress disorder among female and male Vietnam veterans: Hardiness, postwar social support, and additional stressful life events. *Journal of Personality and Social Psychology, 74*(2), 420–434.

Larson, R., & Almeida, D. (1999). Emotional transmission in the daily lives of families: A new paradigm for studying family process. *Journal of Marriage and the Family, 61,* 5–20.

Leffler, C., & Dembert, M. (1998). Posttraumatic stress symptoms among U.S. Navy divers recovering TWA Flight 800. *Journal of Nervous and Mental Disorders, 186*(9), 574–577.

Lott, L. (1995). Deadly secrets: Violence in the police family. *FBI Law Enforcement Bulletin, 64*(11), 12–16.

Marmar, C., Weiss, D., Metzler, T., Delucchi, K., Best, S., & Wentworth, K. (1999). Longitudinal course and predictors of continuing distress following critical incident exposure in emergency services personnel. *Journal of Nervous and Mental Disorders, 187*(1), 15–22.

Maslach, C., & Jackson, S. (1979). Burned out cops and their families. *Psychology Today, 12*(12), 59–62.

McCann, I. L., & Pearlman, L. A. (1990). Vicarious traumatization: A framework for understanding the psychological effects of working with victims. *Journal of Traumatic Stress, 3*(1), 131–149.

McFall, M., Wright, P., Donovan, D., & Raskind, M. (1999). Multidimensional assessment of anger in Vietnam veterans with post-traumatic stress disorder. *Comprehensive Psychiatry, 40,* 216–220.

McFarlane, A. (1988). The etiology of post-traumatic stress disorder following a natural disaster. *British Journal of Psychiatry, 152,* 116–121.

Nezu, A., & Carnevale, G. (1987). Interpersonal problem solving and coping reactions of Vietnam veterans with posttraumatic stress disorder. *Journal of Abnormal Psychology, 96*(2), 155–157.

Pfefferbaum, B., North, C., Bunch, K., Wilson, T., & Schorr, J. (2002). The impact of the 1995 Oklahoma City bombing on partners of firefighters. *Journal of Urban Health, 79,* 364–372.

Regehr, C. (in press) Bringing home the trauma: Spouses of paramedics. *Journal of Loss and Trauma.*

Regehr, C., & Bober, T. (2004). *In the line of fire: Trauma in the emergency services.* New York: Oxford University Press.

Regehr, C., Dimitropoulos, G., Bright, E., George, S. & Henderson, J. (in press) Behind the Brotherhood: Rewards and Challenges for Families of Firefighters. *Family Relations.*

Regehr, C., Goldberg, G., Glancy, G., & Knott, T. (2002) Post-traumatic stress and disability in paramedics. *Canadian Journal of Psychiatry, 47*(10), 953–958.

Regehr, C., Goldberg, G., & Hughes, J. (2002). Exposure to human tragedy, empathy and trauma in ambulance paramedics. *American Journal of Orthopsychiatry, 72*(4), 505–513.

Regehr, C., Hemsworth, D., & Hill, J. (2001). Individual predictors of traumatic response: A structural equation model. *Canadian Journal of Psychiatry, 46,* 74–79.

Regehr, C., Hill, J., & Glancy, G. (2000). Individual predictors of traumatic reactions in firefighters. *Journal of Nervous and Mental Disorders, 188*(6), 333–339.

Resick, P., & Schnicke, M. (1993). *Cognitive processing therapy for rape victims: A treatment manual.* Newbury Park, CA: Sage.

Roberts, N., & Levenson, R. (2001). The remains of the workday: Impact of job stress and exhaustion on marital interactions in police couples. *Journal of Marriage and the Family, 63,* 1052–1067.

Ruscio, A., Weathers, F., King, L., &

King, D. (2002). Male war-zone veterans' perceived relationships with their children: The importance of emotional numbing. *Journal of Traumatic Stress, 15*(5), 351–357.

September 11 News. (2004). Retrieved from www.september11news.com. Retrieved October 31, 2004.

Sigal, J., Silver, S., Rakoff, F., & Ellin, B. (1973). Some second generation effects of survival of the Nazi persecution. *American Journal of Orthopsychiatry, 43,* 320–327.

Solomon, Z., Kotler, M., & Mikulincer, M. (1988). Combat-related post-traumatic stress disorder among second-generation Holocaust survivors: Preliminary findings. *American Journal of Psychiatry, 145*(7), 865–868.

Solomon Z., Waysman, M., & Levy, G. (1992). From front line to home: A study of secondary traumatization. *Family Process, 31,* 289–302.

Southworth, R. (1990). Taking the job home. *FBI Law Enforcement Bulletin, 59*(11), 19–23.

Spasojevic, J., Heffer, R., & Snyder, D. (2000). Effects of posttraumatic stress and acculturation on marital functioning in Bosnian refugee couples. *Journal of Traumatic Stress, 13*(2), 205–217.

Stout, K. D., & Thomas, S. (1991). Fear and dangerousness in shelter work with battered women. *Affilia, 6*(2), 74–86.

Thompson, J. (1993). Psychological impact of body recovery duties. *Journal of the Royal Society of Medicine, 86,* 628–629.

Thomson, A., & Bolger, N. (1999). Emotional transmission in couples under stress. *Journal of Marriage and the Family, 61,* 38–48.

Verboski, S., & Ryan, D. (1988). Female partners of Vietnam veterans: Stress by proximity. *Issues in Mental Health Nursing, 9,* 95–104.

Weiss, D., Marmar, C., Metzler, T., & Ronfeldt, H. (1995). Predicting symptomatic distress in emergency services personnel. *Journal of Consulting and Clinical Psychology, 63,* 361–368.

Williams, M. (1999). Impact of duty-related death on officers' children: Concepts of death, trauma reactions and treatment. In J. Violanti & D. Paton (Eds.), *Police trauma: The psychological aftermath of civilian combat* (pp. 159–174). Springfield, IL: Charles Thomas.

Yehuda, R., Schmeidler, J., Wainberg, M., Binder-Brynes, K., & Duvdevani, T. (1998). Vulnerability to posttraumatic stress disorder in adult offspring of Holocaust survivors. *American Journal of Psychiatry, 115,* 1163–1171.

11

An Examination of the U.S. Response to Bioterrorism: Handling the Threat and Aftermath Through Crisis Intervention

SOPHIA F. DZIEGIELEWSKI
KRISTY SUMNER

The United States has never seen terrorist attacks such as that experienced on September 11, 2001. Following the attacks, many individuals have struggled with how to best address the vulnerabilities of American society relating to terrorist activity. This chapter identifies several issues that have affected the previous open nature of the American lifestyle with impending threats of biological warfare. This turbulent environmental context has caused the American people to experience a level of stress and fear never before experienced.

The purpose of this chapter is to present a brief overview of U.S. policy on terrorism, stressing the application of Roberts's seven-stage model of crisis intervention as one means to address the growing fears of the American public. All helping professionals, regardless of whether they work directly with a crisis survivor, need to be aware of basic crisis intervention techniques. Application of this model is stressed as one way to provide education in this area while highlighting how to best help individuals cope when faced with the continual threat of a new type of war. Recommendations for therapeutic content are made within the current time-limited practice setting.

The United States, along with the rest of the world, was shocked and stunned when the terrorist attacks of September 11, 2001, unfolded. Following the attacks, debates relating to terrorist activity within the United States and the vulnerabilities inherent in American society emerged. The issues of extensive borders and the relative ease with which immigrants can disappear into American society, and the global and open nature of lifestyles Americans have come to depend on, leave the society susceptible to terrorist threats and attacks. Furthermore, the threat of biological warfare and fears of a new type of war abound. This has caused the American people to experience a level of stress never before experienced. This chapter discusses the need for a proactive joining of law enforcement, government agencies, and professional practitioners to assess potential threats within the United States and address the growing fears of Americans in regard to safety and security.

TERRORISM AND THE UNITED STATES

Terrorism is defined by the Department of Defense as "the calculated use of violence or the threat of violence to inoculate fear; intended to coerce or to intimidate governments or societies in the pursuit of goals that are generally political, religious or ideological" (Terrorism Research Center, 2000). Terrorism is a crime that targets innocent and unsuspecting victims, and its purpose is to heighten public anxiety. Although acts of terrorism may seem random, they are planned by the perpetrators, whose main objective is to publicize their attacks. The growing threat of terrorism and terrorist activity is expanding across the United States, and success in combating it will require agencies to implement proactive approaches and strategies (Terrorism Research Center, 2000):

> It is time to recognize certain events that are currently occurring in society as potential forewarning. Disregarding them may result in tragic consequences. History clearly shows that those law enforcement agencies caught behind the operational curve of [terrorist] campaigns have a harder time controlling them and reducing their societal disruption than those that are properly prepared. (McVey, 1997, p. 7)

Terrorism Trends

The current trends in terrorism and terrorist activity make the need for a proactive approach critical:

1. Terrorism is becoming the war strategy of the future.
2. Terrorists are becoming more sophisticated and proficient at using technology.
3. The targets of terrorists' attacks will advance from buildings and airplanes to chemical plants, citywide water systems and utility companies, economic systems, and countries.
4. Traditional weapons will become obsolete against technologically advanced terrorists.
5. The United States will continue to be a target of terrorism. (Bowman, 1994; Levy & Sidel, 2003)

Since the 1980s, the United States has had a policy relating to counterterrorism; however, it is largely reactive in nature and lacks preemptive capabilities. This four-pillar policy states that (1) the United States makes no concessions to terrorists and strikes no deals; (2) the United States uses a "full-court press" to isolate terrorists and to apply pressure on state sponsors of terrorism to force them to change their behavior; (3) rules of law are followed to bring terrorists to justice; and (4) the United States seeks international support to increase counterterrorism capabilities (Badolato, 2001).

U.S. Vulnerabilities

Examining the vulnerabilities inherent in the United States further supports the need for a preemptive approach to combating terrorists and terrorism. First, the United States has extensive borders that are extremely easy to penetrate. Millions of legal and illegal immigrants enter the country each year. Second, the security measures at airports and other ports of entry are poor, and resources are stretched thin; in most cases, undertrained and ill equipped personnel secure ports of entry. Third, the structure of law enforcement in the United States can also be seen as a vulnerability because federal, state, and local agencies often lack communication between them, and, in cases where jurisdictions and charters overlap, friction between the agencies often occurs. Finally, the infrastructure of the United States has been centralized, allowing for large concentrations of people to inhabit relatively small areas. These large population areas capture the attention of terrorists because they allow for a larger casualty rate and a more public arena for attacks (Terrorism Research Center, 2000).

Since the September 11 terrorist attacks, government and law enforcement agencies have begun to implement strategies to counter these vulnerabilities; however, the openness of U.S. borders, which is the most critical area in need of change, is the most difficult vulnerability to effectively control. The current influx of immigrants highlights the necessity of an effective system that can scan and monitor those individuals entering the United States.

Problems Contributing to Increased Terrorism

In the United States in 1991, there were 455 million entries by immigrants and international travelers via air, land, and sea. By 1993, that number had increased to 483 million entries, and that trend in numbers is growing. The massive amount of entries is problematic in that there is no effective national system that screens those individuals coming into the United States. The infrastructure necessary to efficiently process this increasing movement has not kept pace with its growth, resulting in an easing of the barriers that formally kept ineligible travelers such as criminals, terrorists, and economic migrants out. In 1995 alone, at the ports of entry to the United States, the

4,000 immigration inspectors intercepted almost 800,000 persons who were ineligible for admission. There is no estimate available as to the number of those who got past them (Hays, 1996).

Today, the estimated number of illegal immigrants in the United States is roughly 5 million, with an estimated increase of about 275,000 per year. Those who enter legally at various ports of entry and then overstay their visas and disappear into society today represent the bulk of illegal immigrants. It is possible for illegal immigrants to disappear, move, or use different names, making location and deportation extremely inefficient. Of the 83,793 deportation orders issued to illegal immigrants who were not in prison in 1995, 32,246, or 44.5%, were issued for immigrants who could not be found (McDonald, 1997).

BIOTERRORISM: THREATS OF ANTHRAX AND SMALLPOX

Bioterrorism is defined as "the overt or covert dispensing of disease pathogens by individuals, groups, or governments for the expressed purpose of causing harm for ideological, political, or financial gain" (Texas Department of Health, 2001). Further, biological weapons are defined as "any infectious agent such as a bacteria or virus, when used intentionally to inflict harm upon others" (Texas Department of Health, 2001). Since the September 11 attacks, the fear of bioterrorism has escalated in the United States. The recent cases of anthrax infections has exposed America's vulnerabilities to biological agents and has highlighted the need for greater security measures to protect against bioterrorism attacks.

Bioterrorism Possibilities

According to the Centers for Disease Control and Prevention (CDC, 2001), biological agents can create a risk to national security because they are easily disseminated. Furthermore, bioterrorism can lead to high mortality, impacting public health systems and causing panic and social disruption, leading to special action and funding to increase public preparedness (Scardaville & Spencer, 2001). Bioterrorism mirrors conventional terrorism in that it is designed to affect a large number of people, it can be implemented with little or no warning, and it instills panic and fear in the population. However, there are several other aspects of bioterrorism that must be examined. First, the vast number of methods that can be used to spread biological agents into an environment is a concern. Airborne dissemination, pharmaceutical contamination, food or drink contamination, injection or direct contact, and water contamination are all methods that can be used by terrorists attempting to unleash biological agents (Backgrounder, 2001; Levy & Sidel, 2003). Other considerations include the vast number of biological agents that exist that could be used in a bioterrorism attack, the ability of terrorists to acquire such biological agents, and the massive casualties that could result if a bioterrorism attack occurs.

Anthrax and Smallpox

The biological agent that has gained primary attention since the September 11 attacks is anthrax, which was spread through contaminated letters at several U.S. Postal Centers to postal workers and the offices of two U.S. senators (Levy & Sidel, 2003). According to the CDC (2001; Levy & Sidel, 2003), anthrax is an infectious disease that is caused by the spore-forming bacterium *Becillus anthracis,* also known as anthrax spores. Humans can contract anthrax through inhalation and through breaks in the skin; it is not contagious. If contracted through inhalation, the incubation period is generally two to five days, and the symptoms mirror those of the flu: fever, muscle aches, nausea, and cough. More serious symptoms include difficulty breathing, high fever, and shock. Inhalation anthrax is almost always fatal once symptoms appear. If contracted through the skin, the incubation period is generally one to two days. Symptoms of skin exposure to anthrax begin as a small, itchy bump followed by a rash. Left untreated, the lesions fill with fluid and eventually turn black as the tissue begins to die. About 20% of untreated cases of infection through the skin result in death (Eisenburg, 2001, p. 44). Although potentially fatal, anthrax can be treated effectively through antibiotics if treatment is initiated early (CDC, 2001).

A second biological agent that has gained attention as a possible bioterrorism tool is smallpox. According to the American Medical Association (CDC, 2001), when used as a biological weapon, smallpox represents a serious threat because of its fatality rate of 30% or more among unvaccinated persons. Smallpox has long been feared as the most devastating of all infectious diseases, and its potential for devastation today is far greater than at any previous time. Routine vaccination throughout the United States ceased more than 25 years ago. In a now highly susceptible, mobile population, smallpox would be able to spread widely and rapidly throughout this country and the world (CDC, 2001).

According to the CDC, smallpox is a virus that has an incubation period of 12 days following exposure. Initial symptoms include high fever, fatigue, and head and back aches that are then followed by a rash on the face, arms, and legs. The rash progresses into lesions that become pus-filled, turn into scabs, and then eventually fall off. Smallpox is highly contagious and is spread by infected saliva droplets. While many patients with smallpox recover, death occurs in up to 30% of cases. There is no proven treatment for smallpox; however, a vaccine can lessen the severity of or prevent illness if given within four days of exposure (CDC, 2001).

IS THE UNITED STATES PREPARED FOR A BIOTERRORISM ATTACK?

On June 22–23, 2001, the Johns Hopkins Center for Civilian Biodefense Studies, in conjunction with the Center for Strategic and International Studies, the ANSER Institute for Homeland Security, and the Oklahoma National Memorial Institute for the Prevention of Terrorism, held an exercise at Andrews Air Force Base in Washington, D.C. named "Dark Winter." The first such exercise of its kind, Dark Winter was constructed as a series of mock National Security Council meetings in reaction to a fictional, covert smallpox attack in the United States (O'Toole & Inglesby, 2001).

The result of the drill highlighted several areas of concern with regard to governmental preparedness against bioterrorism attacks. First, there was a basic lack of understanding by leaders on the subject of bioterrorism. Second, early responses to the mock attack were slow to determine how many persons were exposed and how many trained medical personal would be needed. Also, the drill highlighted that the U.S. health care system lacks the ability to deal with mass casualties, and there is a shortage of necessary vaccines and medicines. Finally, the Dark Winter drill highlighted that conflicts between different levels of federal and state government and uncertainty in authority hampered responses (*The Economist,* 2001, pp. 29–30).

Due to the results of the drill and the September 11 attacks, lawmakers are trying to increase funding for various agencies to counter bioterrorism and its effects. In an effort to increase support, the fiscal 2002 spending bill for the departments of Labor, Health and Human Services, and Education (HR 3061-H Rept 107–229) included $393 million for measures to defend against biological or chemical attacks, an increase of $100 million in this area. Furthermore, the 2002 Senate bill (S 1536-S Rept 107–84) allocated $338 million and the House and Senate Armed Services Committees also greatly expanded biological defense and research efforts. The House's fiscal 2002 defense authorization bill (HR 2586-H Rept 107–194) funded chemical and biological defense procurement at $361.7 million. The House bill cut the administration's request for chemical and biological weapons research and development by $5 million to $502.7 million, but it increased spending for the Defense Advanced Research Projects Agency's biological warfare defense program by $10 million to $150 million. The Senate's defense authorization bill (S 1416-S Rept 107–62) included similar increases for chemical and biological weapons programs as part of an overall boost of more than $600 million to deal with "nontraditional threats" such as terrorism and cyber attacks. The Senate bill also directed the Defense Department to build a new facility to produce vaccines against anthrax and other biological agents (McCutcheon, 2001).

Psychological Implications

A central aspect of terrorism that should be examined is the psychological effect on the American people caused by acts of terrorism. Research on natural and human-caused disasters suggest that psychological reactions to terrorism are more intense and more prolonged than psychological reactions following natural types of disaster (Myers & Oaks, 2001). Terrorist attacks, by their very nature, are designed to instill fear, anxiety, and uncertainty in a population.

There are several characteristics of terrorism that can increase the magnitude and severity of psychological effects. First, terrorist attacks occur without warning, which produces a disruption to society and people's way of life. A lack of warning also prevents individuals from taking protective action, both physical and psychological. Terrorist attacks become more horrifying for individuals because there is usually a sudden change in reality and surroundings. For example, the New York City skyline changed in a matter of hours when the World Trade Center buildings collapsed and only a pile of smoking debris was left. Another psychological effect of terrorism is the threat to personal safety and security for both citizens and responders. Areas that were previously believed to be safe suddenly become unsafe, and this feeling of insecurity can be maintained in an individual for an extended period of time. Acts of terrorism can also be traumatic in the scope of their destruction: the exposure by citizens, survivors, and responders to gruesome situations; the emotional anger caused by the intentional human causalities; and the degree of uncertainty, lack of control, and social disruption that a society is exposed to (Myers & Oaks, 2001).

The September 11 attacks were different from other terrorist acts because of the magnitude and suddenness of the tragedy; the vast loss of life on American soil; the ability of citizens to follow the events of the attack through extensive media coverage; and the method of using airplanes, considered to be a common and safe mode of transportation, as a means of destruction (Dyer, 2001).

While every person who experiences a traumatic event responds to that event in different ways, there are many feelings and reactions that are common in the aftermath of a tragedy. These include sadness, anger, rage, fear, numbness, stress, feelings of helplessness, feeling jumpy or jittery, moodiness or irritability, change in appetite, difficulty sleeping, experiencing nightmares, avoidance of situations that are reminders of the trauma, problems concentrating, and guilt because of survival or lack of harm during the event (Dyer, 2001).

According to the National Center for Post Traumatic Stress Disorder (2001), there are several steps that individuals can take in the wake of a disaster to reduce symptoms of stress and to readjust to some sense of normalcy. First, following a tragedy, an individual should find a quiet place to relax and attempt to sleep at least briefly. Next, individuals need to reestablish priorities so that a sense of purpose and hope can be regained. Using the natural support of others such as friends, family, coworkers, and other survivors is necessary to establish a sense of togetherness and to help in the reduction of stress. Individuals should also try to engage in positive activities that can serve as a distraction from traumatic memories of or reactions to the event. Finally, a person should seek out the advice of a doctor or counselor for help in treating symptoms of depression or posttraumatic stress disorder (PTSD; National Center for Post Traumatic Stress Disorder, 2001).

APPLICATION OF ROBERTS'S SEVEN-STAGE CRISIS INTERVENTION MODEL AS AN ACUTE POSTTRAUMATIC INTERVENTION

Effective intervention with survivors of trauma precipitated by a crisis of this nature requires a careful assessment of individual, family, and environmental factors. According to Roberts (1991, 1992), a crisis by definition is short term and overwhelming, and the response will involve an emotionally taxing change. In a terrorist attack, the crisis event has caused a senseless disruption in the individual's normal and stable state. It makes sense that the individual's usual methods of coping will not work and a quiet place must be established allowing the individual to think and regroup.

According to Roberts (1991), there are seven stages of working through crisis:

1. Assessing lethality and safety needs.
2. Establishing rapport and communication.
3. Identifying the major problems.
4. Dealing with feelings and providing support.
5. Exploring possible alternatives.
6. Formulating an action plan.
7. Providing follow-up.

This model and support for development of the subsequent stages of adjustment can help the individual to begin to prepare for the long journey of recovery to follow. Assisting the individual in crisis as early as possible to begin this process can help create a better, healthier adjustment for all involved. In addition, as helping professionals, it is important to remember that both pleasure and pain remain a necessary part of growth, change, and adaption. Individuals who have suffered a crisis need to be allowed to experience both pleasure and pain and to realize that both emotions can coexist as well as wax and wane throughout the healing process.

In applying this model, the following assumptions are made: (1) all strategy will follow a "here and now" orientation; (2) most interventions provided should be given as close to the actual crisis event as possible (Raphael & Dobson, 2001; Simon, 1999); (3) the intervention period will be both intensive and time-limited (typically six to 12 meetings; Roberts, 1991); (4) the adult survivor's behavior is viewed as an understandable (rather than a pathological) reaction to stress (Roberts & Dziegielewski, 1995); (5) the crisis counselor will assume an active and directive role assisting the survivor in the adjustment process; and (6) all intervention efforts are designed to increase the survivor's remobilization and return to the previous level of functioning (Dziegielewski & Resnick, 1996).

Stage 1: Assessing Lethality

The unpredictability of terrorist attacks and the fear of further attacks make recovery from this type of acute trauma particularly problematic. Also, other events that happen in the environment are more likely to be emotionally linked to terrorist activity, regardless of actual cause, making it even more difficult for the survivor to progress past the active danger phase toward assuring safety. Listed below are some of the hazardous events or circumstances that can be linked to the recognition or reliving of terrorist traumatic events. Again, these events, although they may be unrelated to terrorist activity, can still trigger anxious responses from individuals.

1. Growing public awareness of the prevalence of the traumatic event or similar traumatic events (i.e., an accidental plane crash with subsequent loss of human life or incidents related to bioterrorism in the environment).
2. Acknowledgment by a loved one or someone that the client respects that he or she has also been a victim.
3. A seemingly unrelated act of violence against the individual or loved one, such as rape or sexual assault.
4. The changing of family or relationship support issues.
5. The sights, sounds, or smells that trigger events from the client's past (these can be highly specific to individuals and the trauma experienced).

Thus, when dealing with trauma, the sensitivity thresholds and the memories as to cues associated with the individual's interpretation process can vary (Wilson, Freidman, & Lindy, 2001).

Immediate Danger

With the seriousness and unpredictability related to terrorist acts, any intervention efforts will require careful assessment of suicidal ideation. In addition, the potential for initial and subsequent hospitalization and medication to help deal with serious episodes of anxious or depressed feelings surrounding the crisis event may also be required. Although no individual wants to experience pain, some professionals believe that some degree of pain is needed to facilitate the healing process. Therefore, medications should be used only with individuals with the most severe cases or as adjuncts to intervention, rather than as a crutch to simply avoid dealing with uncomfortable feelings (Dziegielewski & Leon, 2001).

When addressing the potential for suicidal behavior, questions to elicit signs and symptoms of suicidal ideation or intent should be direct in nature. The client should be asked about feelings of depression, anxiety, difficulties in eating or sleeping, psychological numbing, self-mutilation, flashbacks, panic attacks or panic-like feelings, and increased substance use. After carefully identifying the degree of loss experienced by the individual and based on the age and the circumstances of the trauma experienced, the individual's living situation needs to be assessed. Helping the client to identify members of his or her support system will not only help to assure that the client is not still in danger, it will also remind the client of the level and types of support that remain immediately accessible.

The first few contacts the crisis worker has with the individual in crisis should be individualized, structured, and goal-oriented to assist the individual to move past the traumatic event. It is critical for the crisis counselor to help the individual to generate understanding that what happened in regard to the traumatic event was beyond his or her personal control.

In these initial meetings (meetings 1–3), the goal of the therapeutic intervention is to recognize the hazardous event and help the survivor to acknowledge what has actually happened. In addition, when dealing specifically with terrorism, the individual needs to be made aware that other, seemingly unrelated events may also trigger a similar panic-like response. Once the individual is aware that panic symptoms may reoccur, specific preparation needs to be made to handle these occurrences and the feelings they elicit. Because the survivor of trauma is currently being subjected to periods of stress that disturb his or her sense of equilibrium, counselors should attempt to restore homeostatic balance.

Individuals should also be made aware that a crisis situation can be so overwhelming that the survivor may choose to focus on events other than the crisis event. For crisis counselors, it is essential to help the survivor get to the root of the problem (i.e., the event that precipitated the crisis or the reason for the visit). During these initial meetings, the survivor becomes aware and acknowledges the fact that the crisis or trauma has occurred. Once this is realized, the survivor enters into a vulnerable state (Roberts & Dziegielewski, 1995). The impact of this traumatic event is so horrific that it disturbs the survivor and his or her ability to utilize traditional problem-solving and coping methods. When these usual methods are found to be ineffective, tension and anxiety continue to rise, and the individual becomes unable to function effectively.

In the initial meetings, the assessment of both past and present coping behaviors of the survivor are important; however, the focus of intervention clearly must remain on the here and now. The crisis counselor must make every effort to stay away from past or unresolved issues unless they relate directly to the handling of the traumatic event.

Stage 2: Establishing Rapport and Communication

Many times, the devastating events that surround the immediate and unforeseeable loss of a loved one leave survivors feeling as though family and friends have abandoned them, or that they are being punished for something they did. Crisis counselors need to be prepared for the possibility that these types of unrealistic interpretations may result in the survivor's feeling overwhelming guilt. Feelings of self-blame may impair the individual's capacity for trust, and this may be reflected in negative self-image and poor self-esteem. A low self-image and poor self-esteem may increase the individual's fear of further victimization. Many times, survivors of trauma question their own vulnerability and know that revictimization remains a possibility. This makes the role of the counselor in establishing rapport with the client essential.

When possible, the crisis counselor should progress slowly and try to let the survivor set the pace of all attempts at intervention,as he or she may have a history of being coerced and forcing confrontation on issues may not be helpful. Allowing the survivor to set the pace creates a trusting atmosphere that gives the message "The event has ended, you have survived, and you will not be hurt here." Survivors often need to be reminded that their symptoms are a healthy response to an unhealthy environment (Dziegielewski & Resnick, 1996). They need to recognize that they have survived heinous circumstances and continue to live and cope. Trauma victims may require a positive future orientation, with an understanding that they can overcome current problems and arrive at a happy, satisfactory tomorrow (Dolan, 1991). Restoring a feeling of hope that change can occur is crucial to the survivor's well-being.

Perhaps more than anything else, throughout each of the meetings, these survivors need unconditional support and positive regard. These factors are especially crucial to the working relationship because a history of lack of support, blaming, and breach of loyalty are common. The therapeutic relationship is a vehicle for continued growth and development of coping skills and the ability to move beyond the traumatic event (Briere, 1992).

Stage 3: Identify the Major Problems

Terrorist attacks can be multifaceted, and once the major problems relevant to the particular event are identified and addressed, the concept of how to best provide support becomes essential. Once a survivor has been given individual attention, he or she may be ready for group participation. In crisis work, emphasis always needs to be placed on teaching relaxation techniques, encouraging physical exercise, and creating an atmosphere where the survivor gains an understanding that self-care is at the root of all healing, providing the basis for future coping and stabilizing efforts.

In these next few meetings (meetings 3–6), the crisis counselor needs to assume a very active role. First, the major problems to be dealt with and addressed must be identified. These problems must be related directly to how responses and actions will affect the present situation. Education in regard to the effects and consequences of terrorism are discussed. Discussing the event can be very painful for the individual; simply reacknowledging what happened can push the individual into a state of active crisis marked by disequilibrium, disorganization, and immobility (e.g., the last straw). Although this process may be painful, once the survivor enters full acknowledgment, new energy for problem solving will be generated. This challenge stimulates a moderate degree of anxiety plus a kindling of hope and expectation. The actual state of disequilibrium can vary, but it is not uncommon for individuals who have suffered severe trauma to remain that way for four to eight weeks or until some type of adaptive or maladaptive solution is found.

Stage 4: Dealing With Feelings and Providing Support

The energy generated from the survivor's personal feelings, experiences, and perceptions steer the therapeutic process (Briere, 1992). It is critical that the counselor demonstrate empathy and an anchored understanding of the survivor's worldview. The symptoms the survivor is experiencing are to be viewed as functional and as a means of avoiding further abuse and pain. Even severe symptoms such as dissociative reactions should be viewed as a constructive method of removing oneself from a harmful situation and exploring alternative coping mechanisms. Survivors' experiences should be normalized so that they can recognize that being a victim is not their fault. Reframing symptoms are coping techniques that can be helpful. In this stage (meetings 6–8), the survivor begins to reintegrate and gradually becomes ready to reach a new state of equilibrium. Each particular crisis situation (i.e., type and duration of incest, rape, etc.) may follow a sequence of stages, which can generally be predicted and mapped out. One positive result from generating the crisis state in stage 3 is that in treatment, after reaching active crisis survivors seem particularly amenable to help.

Once the crisis situation has been acknowledged, distorted ideas and perceptions regarding what has happened need to be corrected and information updated so that clients can better understand what they have experienced. Victims eventually need to confront their pain and anger so that they can develop better strategies for coping. Increased awareness helps survivors to face and experience contradictory emotions (anger/love, fear/rage, dampening emotion/intensifying emotion) without the conditioned response of escape (Briere, 1992). Throughout this process there must be recognition of the client's continued courage in facing and dealing with these issues.

Stage 5: Exploring Possible Alternatives

Moving forward requires traveling through a mourning process (generally in meetings 8–10). Sadness and grief at the loss needs to be experienced. Grief expressions surrounding betrayal and lack of protection permit the victim to open to an entire spectrum of feelings that have been numbed. Now, acceptance, letting go, and making peace with the past begins.

Stage 6: Formulating an Action Plan

Here the crisis worker must be very active in helping the survivor to establish how the goals of the therapeutic intervention will be completed. Practice, modeling, and other techniques such as behavioral rehearsal, role-play, and writing down one's feelings and an action plan become essential in addressing intervention planning. Often, survivors have come to the realization that they are not at fault or to blame. What their role was and what part they played become more clear and self-fault less pronounced. The survivors begin to acknowledge that they did not have the power to help themselves or to change things. Often, however, these realizations are coupled with anger at the helplessness they feel at not being able to control what has happened to them. The role of the mental health professional becomes essential here in helping clients to look at the long-range consequences of acting on their anger and in planning an appropriate course of action. The main goal of these last few sessions (meetings 10–12) is to help individuals reintegrate the information learned and processed into a homeostatic balance that allows them to function adequately once again. Referrals for additional therapy should be considered and discussed at this time (i.e., additional individual therapy, group therapy, couples therapy, family therapy).

Stage 7: Follow-up Measures

Follow-up is very important for intervention in general, but is almost always neglected. In the successful therapeutic exchange, significant changes have been made in the survivor in regard to his or her previous level of functioning and coping. Measures to determine whether these results have remained consistent are essential. Often, follow-up can be as simple as a phone call to discuss how things are going. Follow-up within one month of termination of the sessions is important. It may also be helpful to suggest debriefing or intervention to help the survivor reach a higher level of adjustment (Raphael & Dobson, 2001). It is important not to push individuals before they are ready; sometimes a survivor needs the time to self-recover, and once this is done, will open up to further intervention.

Other measures of follow-up are available but require more advanced planning. A pretest-posttest design can be added by simply using a standardized scale at the beginning of treatment and later at the end (Dziegielewski & Powers, 2000). Scales to measure the signs and symptoms of psychological trauma are readily available. (See Corcoran and Fischer, 1994, for a thorough listing of measurement scales that can be used in the behavioral sciences.)

Finally, it is important to realize that when dealing with this type of stress reaction, the determination of the course and type of intervention will always rest with the survivor. At follow-up, many survivors may need additional therapeutic help, yet be unable to express the request for a debriefing session, whereas others, after having initially adapted to the crisis and learned to function and cope, may find that they want more. After all, supporting the survivor as he or she progresses through the crisis period remains the ultimate goal of any helping intervention. Whether the survivor requests additional services or not, the crisis counselor should be prepared to help the client become aware of the options available for continued therapy and emotional growth. If additional intervention is requested, referrals for group therapy with other survivors of similar trauma, individual growth-directed therapy, couples therapy to include a significant other, and family therapy should be considered.

FUTURE DIRECTIONS

The tragic events of September 11, 2001, changed the United States forever. Terrorism in its various forms has exposed, on a national scale, the need for tighter security at the nation's borders as well as continued efforts to ensure protection from biological warfare (Levy & Sidel, 2003). Questions remain: How were the hijackers of September 11 able to get past airport security even though many of them were on an FBI watch list (McGeary & Van Biema, 2001, p. 29)? And, with threats of terrorism against the United States on the rise, how can Americans once again feel safe? Whether directly exposed to terrorist activity or not, the fear of terrorism can affect everyone.

With so many people being directly affected by terrorism and many more suffering the by-products of living in an unpredictable environment, the issue of crisis counseling to address stress and coping has gained significant attention. This increased attention has led to a rapid increase in many theoretical, empirical, and applied studies, books for the general public, and professional journals devoted to research in this field (Monat & Lazarus, 1991; Wilson et al., 2001). Recent events have led some researchers to claim that coping with trauma and stress has become a sociocultural phenomenon, which might result in higher self-reported stress levels due to the proliferation of information about stress in the popular culture.

Historically, three types of stress have been identified: systemic or physiological, psychological, and social (Levy & Sidel, 2003). However, the recent experiences of terrorism and the ways to cope with the resulting trauma and stress remain diverse. Levels of stress that these survivors experience, the sources of stress, stress related to self-esteem and self-perception, stress and coping skills, and how to best handle stressful situations are just a few of the many issues that need to be researched further. The violence caused by the recent turn of events starting with the incident on September 11, 2001, remains unprecedented in U.S. history. The American people have traditionally been expected to adjust to new social environments, maintain good personal and occupational standing, and face pressures related to supporting friends and family. Survivors of trauma need to continue to develop new roles and modify old ones in response to the developmental tasks faced. When an individual is pressured by these multiple demands, it can lead to role strain, role overload, and role ambiguity, which often result in intense feelings of stress. More attention needs to be given to understanding crisis and the responses that will occur initially and those that will continue to resurface after the initial phase of the trauma has passed. The threats of terrorist attacks can have considerable psychological effects, from immediate responses to those that are prolonged or delayed in nature (DiGiovanni, 1999). Also, more information is needed regarding the most effective time to address a stressful event (Raphael & Dobson, 2001). Coping and stress management techniques can help individuals return to a previous level of functioning, where healthy individuals who have been exposed to extreme trauma can receive the health and support needed.

NOTE

Adapted from S. Dziegielewski and K. Sumner. (2002). An examination of the American response to terrorism. *Brief Treatment and Crisis Intervention, 2*(4), 287–300. Reprinted by permission of the publisher, Oxford University Press, and the editor-in-chief of the journal, Dr. Albert R. Roberts.

REFERENCES

Badolata, E. (2001). How to combat terrorism: Review of United States terrorism policy. *World and I, 16*(8), 50–54.

Bowman, S. (1994). *When the eagle screams.* New York: Birch Lane Press.

Brady, T. (1998). The IDENT system: Putting "Structure to the chaos of the border." *National Institute of Justice Journal, 1237,* 21–25.

Briere, J. N. (1992). *Child abuse trauma: Theory and treatment of the lasting effects.* Newbury Park, CA: Sage.

Centers for Disease Control and Prevention. 2001. Facts about anthrax and bioterrorism are available online at www.cdc.gov/documents.

Coleman, S. (2000). Biometrics. *FBI Law Enforcement Bulletin, 69*(6), 9–20.

Corcoran, K., & Fischer, J. (1994). *Measures for clinical practice: A source book* (2nd ed.). New York: Free Press.

DiGiovanni, C. J. (1999). Domestic terrorism with chemical or biological agents: Psychiatric aspects. *American Journal of Psychiatry, 156*(10), 1500–1505.

Dolan, Y. M. (1991). *Resolving sexual abuse.* New York: Norton.

Dyer, K. (2001). What is different about this incident? Available online at www.kirstimd.com/911_health.htm. March 15, 2001.

Dziegielewski, S. F., & Leon, A. M. (2001). *Social work practice and psychopharmacology.* New York: Springer.

Dziegielewski, S. F., & Powers, G. T. (2000). Procedures for evaluating time-limited crisis intervention. In A. R. Roberts (Ed.), *Crisis intervention handbook* (2nd ed.) (pp. 487–506). New York: Oxford University Press.

Dziegielewski, S. F., & Resnick, C. (1996). Crisis assessment and intervention with adult survivors of incest. In A. R. Roberts (Ed.), *Crisis management and brief treatment: Theory, technique, and applications* (pp. 83–102). Chicago: Nelson Hall.

The Economist (2001). Avoiding dark winter, *361*(8245), 29–30.

Eisenburg, D. (2001). How safe can we get? *Time, 158*(13), 85–91.

Hays, R. (1996). INS passenger accelerated service system. Retrieved August 1, 2002. http://www.biometrics.org/ REPORT/INSPASS.html.

Levy, B. S. & Sidel, V. W. (2003). *Terrorism and public health.* New York: Oxford University Press.

Liu, S., & Silverman, M. (2001). A practical guide to biometric security technology. Available online: http:// www.computer.org/itpro/homepage/Jan_Feb/security3.htm. Retrieved August 1, 2002.

McCutcheon, C. (2001). From "What-ifs" to reality. *Congressional Quarterly Weekly, 59*(40), 2463–2464.

McDonald, W. (1997). Crime and illegal immigration: Emerging, local, state, and federal partnerships. *National Institute of Justice Journal, 1237*, 21–25.

McGeary, J., & Van Biena, D. (2001). The new breed of terrorist. *Time, 158*(13), 29–39.

McVey, P. (1997). *Terrorism and local law enforcement.* Springfield, IL: Charles C. Thomas.

Monat, L. & Lazarus, A. (1991). *Stress and coping.* New York: Columbia University Press.

Moss, S. E., & Lawrence, K. G. (1997). The effects of priming on the self-reporting of perceived stressors and strains. *Journal of Organizational Behavior 18*, 393–403.

Myers, D. & Oaks, N. (2001). *Weapons of mass destruction and terrorism.* Presented at the Weapons of Mass Destruction/Terrorism Orientation Pilot Program, August 5, 2004.

National Center for Post Traumatic Stress Disorder. (2001). Self-care and self-help following disaster. www.ncptsd.org/facts/disasters.html. Retrieved August 1, 2002.

O'Toole, T. & Inglesby, T. (2001). Shining a light on dark winter. Johns Hopkins Center for Civilian

Bio-defense studies. Available online at www.hopkins_biodefense.org. Retrieved November 30, 2001.

Raphael, B., & Dobson, M. (2001). Acute posttraumatic interventions. In J. P. Wilson, M. J. Friedman, & J. D. Lindy (Eds.), *Treating psychological trauma and stress* (pp. 139–157). New York: Guilford Press.

Roberts, A. R. (1991). *Contemporary perspectives on crisis intervention and prevention.* Englewood Cliffs, NJ: Prentice Hall.

Roberts, A. R., & Dziegielewski, S. F. (1995). Foundations and applications of crisis intervention and time-limited cognitive therapy. In A. R. Roberts (Ed.), *Crisis intervention and time-limited cognitive treatment* (pp. 13–27). Newbury Park, CA: Sage.

Simon, J. D. (1999). Nuclear, biological, and chemical terrorism: Understanding the threat and designing responses. *International Journal of Emergency Mental Health, 1*(2), 81–89.

Terrorism Research Center. (2000). Combating terrorism. In *U.S. Army field manual.* Available online: www.terrorism.com.index.html.

Texas Department of Health. (2001). Bioterrorism FAQs (online). Available at www.tdh.state.tx.us/bioterrorism/default.htm. Retrieved October 30, 2001.

Wilson, J. P., Friedman, M. J., & Lindy, J. D. (2001). Treatment goals for PTSD. In J. P. Wilson, M. J. Friedman, & J. D. Lindy (Eds.), *Treating psychological trauma and stress* (pp. 3–27). New York: Guilford Press.

12

Crisis Intervention, Grief Therapy, and the Loss of Life

JOSEPH McBRIDE
ERIC D. JOHNSON

Of the many forms of loss that may occasion crisis intervention, the loss of a significant person, whether family member or friend, is both extremely common and intensely personal. The fact that we have all witnessed the reaction to death in others does little to prepare us for the experience of loss that we feel on these occasions. It is, therefore, important for the crisis intervention practitioner to be aware of the extent of variation in reaction that may be idiosyncratically displayed on these occasions. This phenomenon was dramatically demonstrated in the wake of September 11, 2001, when the experience of personal loss, witness to tragedy, and corporate experience of violation combined to produce extreme reactions in the family and friends of those lost. This chapter explores the nature of loss in the case of death, as well as compounding factors, such as tragedy and witness, along a number of dimensions. We focus on both media-influenced public losses, like 9/11, and private personal losses.

THEORETICAL CONSIDERATIONS

Before proceeding to a discussion of the handling of crisis intervention, it is important to explore the theoretical basis of understanding crisis theory and grief theory. Rueben Hill (1949), in an early seminal article on family stress and coping, identified the ABCX model of adjustment to a crisis situation, consisting of (A) the objective event; (B) the personal, family, and community resources available to deal with the event; (C) the interpretation or appraisal of the victim(s); leading to (X) the assessment of the level of crisis experienced. Several authors have subsequently defined specific aspects of the experience. Parad and Parad (1990) focus on crisis as an upset in a steady state, a disruption or breakdown in the normal or usual pattern of functioning. In an acute crisis, this disequilibrium is of recent origin. While the event may be viewed objectively by an observer, the pain or discomfort of a crisis may be assessed only subjectively as perceived by the victim. Similarly, Roberts (1991; 2000) discusses crisis as a period of psychological disequilibrium, experienced as a result of a hazardous situation. This event constitutes a significant problem that cannot be remedied by using familiar coping strategies. The crisis occurs when a person faces an obstacle to life goals that seems insurmountable through the use of customary habits or coping patterns, requiring the invocation of coping mechanisms that may not have been previously utilized.

Fleming and Belanger (2002, p. 311) address the issue of the connection between trauma and grief: "The call has been made to bridge the largely artificial gap between the fields of traumatology and thanatology." They point out the similarities between the trauma of sexual abuse and that of loss through death. The search for meaning and the reconstruction of the shattered assumptive world are central to the adaptation to both death and trauma. Almost all trauma involves loss on some level, though not all grief involves trauma. Regehr and Sussman (2004) suggest that there is an interaction effect that needs to be considered in treatment, citing the research that indicates that reactions are more prolonged and distressing when trauma and grief occur together.

The grief literature offers many views on the timing of grief, building on the influential work of Bowlby (1980). The concept of a time line has been introduced to facilitate an understanding of the victim's response during a crisis situation (Humphrey & Zimpfer, 1996; Wortman, Cohen-Silver, & Kessler, 1993). However, although a heuristically useful method to describe the process of grief, the limitations of a purely linear focus have also been addressed in the grief literature (Archer, 1999). Stroebe and Schut (1999) offer a dual-process model that is both practical and efficient in its description of the varying nature of the grief response over time. This theory emphasizes the intensity of the grief experience at the time of the loss.

Given the limitations expressed concerning the time line, it can be useful to conceptualize the period of bereavement as comprising three distinct but overlapping phases, identified as "shock," "disorganization," and "reorganization" (Humphrey & Zimpfer, 1996; Tames, 1977). In the shock phase, disbelief, numbness, and crying are often evident and may persist for weeks to months. Daily activities may be done in a mechanistic fashion. Although this aspect of grief may be described as a negative experience, its adaptive function serves to insulate the bereaved from an overwhelming emotional experience. The immediate response from others is to increase closeness after the death (McBride & Sims, 2001).

When the death is due to trauma, the intensity of this phase can be increased. The suddenness and violence of the experience can often put the bereaved in a seriously compromised state, both medically and emotionally (Parkes, 1998; Regehr & Sussman 2004). It is here that intervention from the practitioner and the family is crucial in aiding coping. Proper handling of this intense grief experience has been shown to impact the long-term outcome for the bereaved. An example of this impact can be seen in the case of Pan Am Flight 103, which was blown up over Lockerbee, Scotland, on December 21, 1988. The first author has a fifteen-year relationship with many families in this group. Numerous families claimed that they were mishandled by both the airline and the State Department at the time of the event and were not given clear information or instructions on what to do during the crisis. This lack of direction and support at the time of the bombing led to a passionate response of anger and rage in many of the family members and had a negative impact on their grief. (Imagine, for example, how it felt to be called by a State Department employee several days after the bombing to inform you that your loved one was dead, a fact that had been painfully clear for those several days.)

One significant difference between crisis theory and grief theory is the timing of the intervention. In crisis theory, the intervention is short term and frequently takes place over a 6- to 8-week period. In grief theory, this is only the beginning of the process; grief therapy may well extend for months into years. Because the initial crisis intervention often takes place during what has been described as the shock phase of the grief experience, the client is in the least favorable position to benefit from psychotherapy. Therefore, the interventions described in many crisis intervention models that focus on the practical aspects and task orientation model make sound clinical sense for the grief-stricken individual (Burgess & Roberts, 2000; Everly, Lating, & Mitchell, 2000; Green, Lee, Trask, & Rheinscheld, 2000). In essence, the grieving person whose crisis involves the loss of life needs to have many practical matters dealt with, as well as the provision of a supportive environment. This focus can also be critical in preventing posttraumatic stress disorder.

The loss of life shares many elements with other types of crisis situations, but may differ in significant elements. For one thing, there is an objective, irretrievable loss. This differs from situations is which the loss is understandable only from the subjective viewpoint of the victim (e.g., rejection of a relationship by a significant other); an "ambiguous loss," wherein the physical presence of a loved one may be in doubt (e.g., prisoner of war); or a chronically recurring partial loss (e.g., repeated strokes, chronic mental illness; Boss, 2004). In the case of death, the survivor has to come to terms with the idea that a life has been ended permanently, and plans for future action will require a new paradigm of thinking.

APPLICATION OF ROBERTS'S SEVEN-STAGE CRISIS INTERVENTION MODEL

Roberts's (2000) seven-stage model for crisis intervention can be effectively utilized in situations of loss of life. In this discussion, we focus on some of the unique aspects of its application to the grieving process specific to death.

Plan and Conduct a Crisis Assessment

In approaching the assessment of crisis in the aftermath of death, the three critical elements of objective event, general and specific coping resources, and interpretation of the event need to be given consideration. In particular, it is important to assess for the following:

Relationship of the lost person to the person in crisis: The practitioner needs to identify whether this is a primary relationship (i.e., the loss of this person directly affects the survival of the survivor), a secondary relationship (the loss does not affect physical survival, but is of importance for emotional or psychological support), or a tertiary relationship (the loss is not an immediate loved one, but affects the survivor's sense of self or well-being). For example, many people were traumatized by observing the events of 9/11 through the media, even though they personally knew no one who died. Similarly, people may be affected by the loss of a young person of their acquaintance, more because it calls existential issues into question than the personal loss of the particular person.

Nature of the loss (e.g., anticipated, gradual, sudden, tragic): Acute crises do not allow the survivor to do "anticipatory grieving" and are likely to be experienced as more traumatic. However, even in situations where the loss is anticipated, the moment of death is often still a shock, as it eliminates fantasies of miraculous recovery and confronts the survivor with the harsh reality of permanent loss. As one young man said: "I always knew there would be a day when my mother would die. I just never thought the day would come."

Whether the loss was witnessed by or reported to the person in crisis: Witnessing a death adds a layer of trauma onto the experience of loss. Thus, people who have the misfortune of witnessing a death may need crisis intervention, even if the person involved was not personally important to them. If the person was also of psychological importance, the loss has been significantly compounded. Many families of 9/11 victims were exposed to the death of their loved ones several hundred times during the first week, due to extensive media coverage.

In the case of tragedy, details of the event may have been repressed because they are psychologically overloading. While they may not surface as requiring attention in crisis intervention, they may become a major focus in ongoing grief therapy, as they flush out not only the experience of terror, but the experience of shame over the impotence to prevent the terror, and of guilt over being a survivor.

Cumulative effect of this loss on other losses by the person in crisis: While the immediate loss of the person who died may be significant for the physical or psychological survival of the person in crisis, it is often the case that this loss adds to a burden of other kinds of losses experienced by the survivor, which may potentiate the experience of loss and the expression of grief. In some cases, a secondary or tertiary loss may feel like a primary loss due to this cumulative trauma effect. For example, many people in therapy at the time of 9/11 reacted at a higher intensity to media reports because it highlighted other losses in their lives, as well as their apparent impotence to prevent loss in general.

Shared experience of loss with others (family members, community): A sense of the shared suffering of others, both in one's immediate social network and among those who have experienced a similar loss, is often a great comfort to people. The survivor who feels alone in the aftermath of the loss, therefore, is in a seriously compromised position, and is likely to experience the loss in a more powerful way. This person may be at high risk of suicidal behavior, attempting to "join" the lost person and avoid having to deal with an imagined overwhelming aftermath.

In conducting the crisis assessment, the practitioner needs to assess, not only the presence of these several risk factors, but the likely synergistic effect that a combination of higher-risk components will have on the survivor's understanding of the event.

Establish Rapport and Rapidly Establish a Relationship

People in need of crisis intervention in response to a death may respond in idiosyncratic ways. It is important for the practitioner not to assume a particular reaction, and not to assume the meaning of the reaction. For example, at one time the second author had the job of telling inmates in a state penitentiary that a close family member had died. When informed of his mother's death, one inmate began laughing hysterically. It took some conversation to determine whether he was actually happy at the news of her death or was expressing grief in an idiosyncratic manner.

Because the practitioner has to establish rapport quickly, usually without the benefit of knowing much about the relationship between the deceased and the survivor, it is best to ask general questions that allow the survivor to elaborate. "Tell me about your father" is an example of this. This enables the survivor to address elements of the relationship that may have been meaningful or difficult, or elements of the event of death that may be more immediately traumatic. Similarly, a question frequently asked in critical incident debriefing, "What is the hardest part of this for you?," allows the survivor to include the practitioner in his or her subjective experience of loss or fear.

It is also during this critical time that the practitioner focuses on the immediate nature of the event and forgoes otherwise customary joining techniques, such as questions about other aspects of the survivor's life.

Identify Major Problems

The loss of life, like many other crises, emphasizes the inability to control fate and the sense of impotence that accompanies it. This is the stage of crisis intervention in which the knowledge gained in Stage 1 is employed, particularly noting the level of risk factors, compounding factors, and the survivor's subjective sense about them.

Because loss of life is often symbolic (especially in secondary and tertiary loss situations), it may be necessary for the practitioner to investigate beyond the "facts" of the case, to understand why the loss has particular power at this particular time. For example, one young woman had a severe anxiety reaction following the funeral of a coworker's husband. As she had only a passing relationship with the man, this was puzzling to the crisis intervention practitioner, until it became known that her own brother had died in a motorcycle accident less than a year prior, and her reaction had to do with unresolved loss and inability to understand and control death.

Both authors' experience with several 9/11 families pointed out that the major issue at the time of the event was the lack of knowledge—and often the lack of a body. The families knew the outcome but could not be certain that their intense reactions were justified without concrete proof. The task of the practitioner is to facilitate both the practical aspect of obtaining reliable information about the deceased and the supportive intervention to aid the family in accepting the inevitable. Without this help, some family members went for weeks fantasizing that some hospital in New York City was going to call them with information about their loved one.

Deal with Feelings and Emotions

The loss of life frequently invokes the issue of the "unfairness" of life, as well as feelings of personal (narcissistic) loss, which may alternately be expressed as hurt (I have been abandoned) or anger (How dare you abandon me). Consequently, the crisis intervention practitioner should be prepared for powerfully expressed feelings. It is important to note that feelings operate on a different plane than cognitions, and therefore are often not amenable to cognitive, rational interventions. As an example, the expression of rage, frequently misunderstood as extreme anger, is more about one's impotence to control the universe than about the object of the anger. The expression of rage behaviors, from the child's temper tantrum to the adult's destructive rampage, is often met with the rational response, "Well, that didn't solve anything, did it?" This response, though frequent, is totally meaningless, because the rage behavior was not intended to *solve a problem.* In fact, it is intended to demonstrate that the person in crisis is unable to solve the problem. The more useful response in this context is active listening and validation of the feelings. Problem solution can wait until a later time. At this stage, the often powerful expression of feelings, including fear, hurt, and anger, need to be released. This is often a difficult personal experience for the crisis intervention practitioner, as he or she may be turned into the proxy for an "unfair" world.

Another dynamic that frequently shows up at this stage is an obsessive preoccupation with "if only" (e.g., If only I had said "I love you" before he left; If only I hadn't given her the keys to the car). This is based on the assumption that the survivor could somehow have prevented the death if only more vigilance had been paid, or would feel less anguish if certain actions had been done. These thoughts and actions make sense only if the survivor anticipated the death, but as this is rarely the case, the survivor ruminates on an issue that cannot be positively resolved, thus provoking much self-blame and anger.

It is also important for the crisis intervention practitioner to ask about substance use, as survivors are likely to increase their use of prescription drugs and alcohol to mute feelings or to aid in getting to sleep. There may be complicating features of this coping mechanism that are interfering with social relationships, ability to continue work, or the ability to be available for children or others affected by the death.

Most grief work requires an ability to deal with these intense feelings of loss (McBride & Sims, 2001). Practitioners may find themselves overwhelmed by this intensity and may need support and supervision from other professionals to maintain balance, particularly in the context of dealing with a succession of people in a high state of crisis.

Generate and Explore Alternatives

After the survivor has had an opportunity to vent feelings (including those that may be apparently contradictory) in a supportive environment, the result should be an emotional calming. This allows for movement to the next stage, which is to begin brainstorming about alternative actions. At this stage, people frequently limit their options or assume that they have only one option. The job of the crisis intervention practitioner at this stage is to help open up possibilities, including the advantages and disadvantages of each. For example, it may help some people to develop finality on the death by seeing the body. For others, this vision may overpower their remembered experience of the person (particularly if the body has deteriorated due to a disease, or has been mutilated in a tragedy). Similarly, getting details of the death may provide some understanding that is helpful to a survivor; other survivors might find that that level of detailed information provides them with an overload. It is important for survivors to consider the alternatives and to imagine their possible positive and negative reactions.

The need for the survivor to collect information regarding the accident or crisis that led to the death can be of importance during the grief process and is often overlooked by the crisis intervention practitioner. In the first author's experience, bereaved persons will often develop a strong "need to know" what has occurred that led to the death. However, at the time of the crisis, due to the stress, they may not be in the best position to know what questions to ask. In this area, the practitioner can help by aiding someone significant to the bereaved to accomplish this task.

Develop and Formulate an Action Plan

It is important that the survivor be in an emotionally calm state before attempting to formulate an action plan. If, for example, the plan is formulated at a point of anger, the action plan might take the form of revenge on a real or imagined person responsible for the death, rather than an action plan formed to respect and honor the memory of the deceased. It may also be necessary for survivors to make a decision about taking action based on what action will leave them feeling "less bad." This relates to the exploration of alternatives discussed in the previous stage. For example, survivors may feel that although it will be difficult for them to see the body, not having an opportunity for a "last goodbye" may be more difficult to live with. In addition to respect for the deceased, the action plan may involve responding to other components of problem or loss buildup, including complications that may involve the responses of other survivors, police, media—or even professional helpers. For this reason, the identification of a point person, someone close to the bereaved but with enough distance to be calmer and more objective, may be helpful in taking action on collecting information, handling the media, and dealing with other details (hospital, police, funeral arrangements) immediately following the death.

Establish Follow-up Plan and Agreement

It is important to view the resolution of the immediate crisis following a death as a step in the resolution of grief rather than an end in itself. At the point that the crisis intervention practitioner completes Stage 6, it is wise to refer the survivor on to someone specialized in extended grief work, particularly if the loss is complicated by the other factors described in this chapter. In an extension of Reuben Hill's (1949) model of stress and coping, Hamilton McCubbin (H. I. McCubbin & Patterson, 1983; M. A. McCubbin & McCubbin, 1993) developed the Double ABCX model, which focuses on long-term adaptation rather than short-term adjustment. McCubbin and associates have focused on the buildup of events, resources, and interpretation that result from reactions to the event and subsequent complications. Whereas the focus of crisis intervention is on the immediate adjustment, the focus of grief work is on the long-term adaptation to death. Margaret Stroebe and her colleagues (Stroebe, Stroebe, & Hansson, 1993), in reviewing the literature on the grief process, suggested that a typical grief experience would be about two years. Other authors have suggested that this would be increased in the case of a sudden or tragic death (Parkes, 1998). Therefore, resolution of the immediate crisis of the death event is usually only the beginning for the bereaved. As there is often a lag in time between the experience of the death and the beginning of therapy (McBride & Sims, 2001), crisis intervention could be a useful adjunct by serving two purposes: (1) to help stabilize an initial psychological disequilibrium, and (2) to provide the groundwork for the more extensive grief work that will be necessary to address complicated bereavement.

CASE EXAMPLE

To further illustrate the application of these concepts, an extended case example is provided (names and identifying details have been modified to protect confidentiality).

Beth is a 44-year-old housewife with three children, a daughter (14) and two sons (12 and 8). Her husband was a well-paid vice president in an investment firm located in the World Trade Towers. On September 11, 2001, his office took a direct hit, and he was killed. She was seen for crisis intervention within a week, accompanied by a neighbor. At that time, no part of his body had been found, but within a few days, she was informed that part of his body was recovered, suggesting that he was in some other part of the building at the time of impact.

Beth presented in a highly agitated emotional state, with alternating feelings of disbelief, anger, and fear for the future. She did not appear to be at risk of suicide and was mentally able to continue with daily functioning, but was extremely volatile emotionally. The loss of her husband did not threaten her immediate economic survival, but she had been very dependent on him psychologically and questioned her ability to manage the needs of her children. Although financially secure in the immediate future, she also worried about her children's economic future and how they would manage without a father. In light of the acute tragic nature of her husband's death, she had no opportunity for anticipatory grieving and seemed uncertain about what "correct" grieving should be. The confusion surrounding the events of 9/11 further made her anxious, and she was irritated by media attention, needing someone to run interference for her (including bringing her to the crisis intervention practitioner). Although she had a shared experience with others, at the point of intake she did not have any close friends who had lost a family member in the WTC.

Beth presented with a great deal of anger and challenged the therapist with questions like "What will therapy do for me?" and "Will talking about this bring my husband back?" On the other hand, she clearly wanted (and needed) to talk, and after ranting for a while, agreed to bring in her children and extended family members as well.

As with other families of 9/11 victims, decisions about immediate family functioning were complicated by logistic issues of clearing debris, searching for bodies (or parts), setting up response stations, filing death claims, and more. Beth was confronted with the practical concerns of providing DNA to assist in search efforts and preoccupied with trying to recover body parts. In addition, media presentations (and recapitulations) were emotionally overwhelming for her and the children, and media attention distracted them from attending to their own needs and to their relationships with each other. Tension in the family ran high.

Beth's intense emotionality lasted for several weeks and took a roller-coaster course, in which she would rage at the children or the crisis intervention practitioner, while at other times being quietly grateful that she was getting support. She would also alternate between periods of uncontrollable crying and anxiety and moments of confidence and humor. It was important for the crisis practitioner not to take these ragings personally and to recognize the cathartic importance of allowing the expression of these powerful emotions, even though they sometimes appeared to be personally directed.

A significant issue at the stage of identifying alternatives came in the planning of death services. Although it was important for Beth to have a funeral once the body parts of her husband had been recovered, the older two children refused to attend. It was important for each family member to explore his or her own reasons for the handling of the event and how each wished to remember the deceased. In the end, members of the extended family came to town and supported Beth in having a private family funeral, and she and all the children, as well as extended family members, attended a public memorial ceremony at their church. The extended family and community handled some of the practical planning issues as well as dealing with the media, allowing Beth and her children to focus on their personal relationships with each other and with their own friends.

One of the major advantages of crisis intervention for Beth and her children was the recognition and validation of their highly charged (and often contradictory) emotional reactions and the understanding that what they were experiencing was "normal" to a crisis situation. This allowed them to feel sufficiently relieved to recognize the importance of ongoing therapy for themselves individually and as a family unit. Although the immediacy of the crisis had passed, they recognized that there would be major repercussions for months as they adjusted to the transition forced on them.

REFERENCES

Archer, J. (1999). *The nature of grief: The evolutions and psychology of reactions to loss.* New York: Routledge.

Boss, P. (2004). Ambiguous loss research, theory, and practice: Reflections after 9/11. *Journal of Marriage and the Family, 66,* 551–566.

Bowlby, J. (1980). *Attachment and loss: Loss, sadness and depression* (Vol. 3). New York: Basic.

Burgess, A. W., & Roberts, A. R. (2000). Crisis intervention for persons diagnosed with clinical disorders based on the stress-crisis continuum. In A. R. Roberts (Ed.), *Crisis intervention handbook: Assessment, treatment, and research* (2nd ed., pp. 56–76). New York: Oxford University Press.

Everly, G. S., Lating, J. M., & Mitchell, J. T. (2000). Innovations in group crisis intervention: Critical incident debriefing (CISD) and critical incident stress management (CISM). In A. R. Roberts (Ed.), *Crisis intervention handbook: Assessment, treatment, and research* (2nd ed., pp. 77–97). New York: Oxford University Press.

Fleming, S. J., & Belanger, S. K. (2002). Trauma, grief, and surviving childhood sexual abuse. In R. A. Neimeyer (Ed.), *Meaning reconstruction and the experience of loss.* Washington, DC: American Psychological Association.

Green, G. J., Lee, M. Y., Trask, R., & Rheinscheld, J. (2000). How to work with clients' strengths in crisis intervention: A solution-focused approach. In A. R. Roberts (Ed.), *Crisis intervention handbook: Assessment, treatment, and research* (2nd ed., pp. 31–55). New York: Oxford University Press.

Hill, R. (1949). *Families under stress.* New York: Harper & Row.

Humphrey, G. M., & Zimpfer, D. G. (1996). *Counselling for grief and bereavement.* London: Sage.

McBride, J., & Sims, S. (2001). Death in the family: Adapting a family systems framework to the grief process. *American Journal of Family Therapy, 29,* 59–73.

McCubbin, H. I., & Patterson, J. M. (1983). The family stress process: The double ABCX model of adjustment and adaptation. In H. I. McCubbin, M. B. Sussman, & J. M. Patterson (Eds.), *Social stress and the family* (pp. 7–38). New York: Haworth.

McCubbin, M. A., & McCubbin, H. I. (1993). Family coping with health crises: The resiliency model of family stress, adjustment, and adaptation. In C. Danielson, B. Hamel-Bissell, & P. Winstead-Fry (Eds.), *Families, health, and illness.* New York: Mosby.

Parad, H., & Parad, L. (1990). Crisis intervention: An introductory overview. In H. Parad & L. Parad (Eds.), *Crisis intervention book 2: The practitioner's sourcebook for brief therapy* (pp. 3–66). Milwaukee: Family Service Association of America.

Parkes, C. M. (1998). *Bereavement: Studies of grief in adult life* (3rd ed.). London: Penguin.

Regehr, C., & Sussman, T. (2004). Intersections between grief and trauma: Toward an empirically based model for treating traumatic grief. *Brief Treatment and Crisis Intervention, 4*(3), 289–309.

Roberts, A. R. (2000). An overview of crisis theory and crisis intervention. In A. R. Roberts (Ed.), *Crisis intervention handbook: Assessment, treatment, and research* (2nd ed., pp. 3–30). New York: Oxford University Press.

Shuchter, S. R., & Zisook, S. (1993). The course of normal grief. In M. S. Stroebe, W. Stroebe, M., & Schut, H. (1999). The dual process model of coping with bereavement: Rationale and description. *Death Studies, 23,* 197–294.

Stroebe, M., Stroebe, W., & Hansson, R. O. (1993). Bereavement research and theory. In M. S. Stroebe, W. Stroebe, & R. O. Hansson (Eds.), *Handbook of bereavement: Theory, research, and intervention.* New York: Cambridge University Press.

Tames, R. (1977). *Living with an empty chair.* Amherst, MA: Mandela.

Worden, J. W. (2002). *Grief counseling and grief therapy: A handbook for the mental health practitioner* (3rd ed.). New York: Springer.

Wortman, C. B., Cohen-Silver, R., & Kessler, R. C. (1993). The meaning of loss and adjustment to bereavement. In M. S. Stroebe, W. Stroebe, & R. O. Hansson (Eds.), *Handbook of bereavement: Theory, research, and intervention.* New York: Cambridge University Press.

13

Posttrauma Intervention: Basic Tasks

GARY BEHRMAN
WILLIAM J. REID

This chapter presents a task-based group treatment approach to posttrauma intervention. When persons are traumatized, much of what they assume about themselves, others, and the purposes of their lives are disrupted and lose connectedness. The model is designed to help individuals and the community of which they are a part recreate these connections in meaningful, creative, and responsible ways, which may result in change on informative, reformative, or transformative levels. The model makes use of nine basic tasks in which the practitioner, individuals, and community are active participants: welcoming, reflecting, reframing, educating, grieving, amplifying, integrating, empowering, and terminating/revisiting.

Trauma occurs when an experience is perceived as life-threatening and overwhelms normal coping skills. As we know, trauma on a large scale was one of the aftermaths of the horrific events that occurred on September 11, 2001. In this chapter, we present an approach to posttrauma intervention used in Behrman's work with employees of the New York City Adult Protection Services (APS) who were witness to the World Trade Center disaster at various levels of exposure. The model draws on prior work on posttrauma intervention (Everly & Mitchell, 1999) and the task-centered practice model developed by the second author (Reid, 1992, 1997, 2000; Reid & Epstein, 1972). It is also informed by Behrman's experience and reflections as a licensed clinical social worker trained in critical incident stress debriefings. Although the approach is cast as a social work model, it can also be used by practitioners from other helping professions.

BASIC ASSUMPTIONS

When persons are traumatized, much of what they assume about themselves, others, and the purposes of their lives are disrupted and lose connectedness. The concept of *connections* is integral to this posttrauma intervention model: "Connections are the many different kinds of communicative, productive, and organizational relationships among people in socially, historically, and discursively constituted media of language, work, and power, all of which must be understood dynamically and relationally" (Kemmis & McTaggart, 2000, p. 579). What are needed to maintain and reconstruct those meaningful connections between oneself and one's community are both the presence of inspirational persons in the community and effective tasks designed by oneself. There is a "reaching out and a reaching in" (p. 579). Together, the individual and the community help recreate these connections in meaningful, creative, and responsible ways, which may result in change on an informative, reformative, or transformative level.

On the informational level, this model "allows the formation of some new meaning and the recapturing of old meanings about the experience and encourages people to begin to create a vision about what might be and take some steps to achieve it" (Saleeby, 1994, p. 357). Creating new meanings that help us understand an experience in a new way leads to informative change. It does not necessary involve a change in behavior or identity. This level of change demands that we look beyond what is easily accounted for and examine what does not fit into our conceptions of the world (Sermabeikian, 1994). Applying this knowledge through tasks will subsequently lead to reformed ways of behaving. This change is then reformative: we have new behaviors that enable us to achieve our desired goals. Transformative change incorporates informative and reformative change but goes beyond them. Our identity as a person is changed, and subsequently how we think, feel, and behave are transformed. We bring a new self into every situation, and this transformed self creates possibilities and relationships that previously were inconceivable.

Individual and community rebuilding after a traumatic event is reciprocal. As individuals recover, they help to restore a sense of community. A regenerating community enables individuals to regain their sense of belonging. Critical to this process are tasks undertaken by the individuals, the community, and the social worker.

THE MODEL AND AN ILLUSTRATIVE APPLICATION

In its present form, the model is designed for simultaneous work with individuals and the community of which they are a part. It is organized around nine basic tasks aimed to further recovery from trauma. The social worker, individual client, and the community all share in these tasks. The social worker may act as initiator and facilitator, but for the tasks to be effective the client and the community must be active participants. The task concept serves to underscore the importance of the actions of the client and the community both during and following the intervention.

All tasks are initiated and worked on in group sessions. With the exception of the first and last (Welcoming and Terminating/Revisiting), all tasks can and should be pursued by the client/community between sessions. For this purpose, use can be made of well-developed, empirically tested methods used in the task-centered practice model (Reid, 1992, 2000: Reid & Fortune, 2002). In this chapter, we focus on tasks within the session.

The illustration involves Behrman's work with employees of the New York City APS referred to above. As individuals, they can be seen as clients; as a collective, they may be thought of as the APS community. In other applications, a community might be a school or a neighborhood.

Welcoming

This task involves building rapport, developing trust, and creating a psychologically safe environment in which to accomplish all the other tasks. The social worker communicates to others that he or she is emotionally and socially available and will perform his or her responsibilities with sensitivity, respect for diversity, and professional competence. The client/community must in turn be willing to trust the social worker and be receptive to his or her engagement efforts. Unless these tasks are successfully accomplished, remaining tasks are in jeopardy.

Welcoming can be accomplished through introductions, storytelling, icebreakers, or expressions of care and concern for the client and community. At APS, this task began with storytelling, informing the group a little bit about myself (Behrman), and inquiring about them and their role at APS, explaining why I was qualified to lead this group, honoring their work, and explaining how privileged I felt to be with them. I was very clear about why I was there and that there were no hidden agendas. We were there to create a healthy community in which all APS workers can maintain and enhance their knowledge, coping skills, and meaningful connections. I also spent some time before the debriefing walking among them and getting to know their names, where they were born, and what their work responsibilities were.

It was important to me that this debriefing be framed as a community experience, while acknowledging the cultural, religious, and racial differences among the individual participants. Also, the groups were large, with 60 or more members. Thus, striving for healthy outcomes not just for individuals but also for the community seemed appropriate. Another element of the welcoming task is to discuss the ground rules for the upcoming process: what is said will held in confidence; it is not necessary to speak; one should speak only for oneself; all comments should be directed to the group; everyone should stay for the entire session; the purpose of this intervention is not to evaluate who did what or how well.

At the APS debriefing, it was important to speak first with state officials and the local supervisors about the locations of the offices in relation to the World Trade Center, how many people work in the offices, where we would be meeting, and how much time would be given to each session. I discovered that we would be meeting in a work area and that there would be distractions and disruptions. I was also informed that 50% of the workers were recent immigrants from all over the world, which posed a challenge given our lack of knowledge of the role of race and ethnicity in traumatic experience (Borden, 2000). Finally, I learned that only a few of the caseworkers were social workers.

Reflecting

The purpose of this task, shared by the social worker and the client/community, is to reflect on the core principles that will shape the rebuilding proycess. What values guide the client/community's conception of health following the trauma? How had these beliefs shaped behaviors and relationships prior to this traumatic event? These questions will set the stage for the formulation of goals and tasks. Ideally, they will build community identification and a genuine connection between the social worker and the client/community.

Being a reflective practitioner (Schon, 1983) is useful in implementing this task. When the social worker and clients identify together what their underlying principles are, a level of trust and safety should result that will enable them to work together as a team in creating their tasks for healing. Thus, practitioners are called on to develop what Berman (1981) termed "participating consciousness," and what Polanyi (1962, p. viii) described as a "passionate participation of the knower in the act of knowing." Waite (1939) spoke of this task when he remarked, "What the client is responding to is not merely the spoken word but the total impression the worker's personality makes. If we want clients to give us their confidence, we have to become people who inspire confidence" (p. 186).

At the APS offices, there was immense cultural, age, religious, and racial diversity, as noted. The most obvious bonding core principle was their work and their clients. So we talked about the agency's mission and how their own personal and religious beliefs support that mission. There followed a discourse about why they chose to work with vulnerable neglected and abused adults, and why this was meaningful. During the task, we continued the process of meaning making and naming the principles that unite them as a practice community. Among the principles expressed were commitment to service, respect for each other and their clients, and the dignity and value of everyone in the room.

Framing

This task entails framing the traumatic event in meaningful language that makes sense to individuals and the community. The goal is to understand what happened so that distorted information about the event can be reduced and the facts surrounding the event can be clearly communicated. This lowers the risk for rumors disconnecting people from each other.

The task is framed around telling the story of what happened and can be facilitated with these questions: How did the traumatic event happen? Who was involved? Where and when did it occur? During this task, the social worker should refrain from asking why the event happened. Often, this will result in blaming someone or something for the trauma, and the process may be thrown offtrack. With the APS workers, this task was accomplished both in the large group and in small breakout groups. If the latter method is chosen, it is important to have competent facilitators who can keep the discourse focused on the task.

Educating

In the context of the present model, to educate is to create knowledge that will help restore the health of the individuals and their community: "The process of education and self-education among participants makes critical enlightenment possible" (Kemmis & McTaggart, 2000, p. 598). Educating by the social worker facilitates the client/community's complementary task of self-education or learning, the task that must be achieved if the social worker's efforts are to be of any value.

Basic information is provided by the social worker that enables the participants to distinguish between stress and trauma. That is, stress is a reaction to environmental stimuli within the ordinary range of human experience, whereas trauma is perceived as a life-threatening event, one that overwhelms usual coping strategies. The effects of trauma, such as numbness and fatigue, irritability, and fear, may be persistent. This serves as a "heads up" that can help prepare one for unexpected emotions, behaviors, and cognitions. Loss of focus (increasing risk for accidents), bursts of anger and irritability, headaches and backaches, upset stomachs, and nightmares are all common features of posttrauma experiences. Normalizing these experiences and listening for what may be unique is critical. Also, educating clients regarding some of the potential emotional reactions that may accompany a posttraumatic event, such as denial (numbing), sadness, anger, and blaming, is important. By sharing reactions to the traumatic event, individuals begin to see that there are both similarities and unique responses and that they can learn from one another, a process that helps restore a sense of community.

During this task, the key question for the social worker to ask is: "What is different for you physically, emotionally, socially?" Creating a discourse while educating enhances the group's responsibility for describing their symptoms and for developing knowledge about them. Here we are not informing them about what they have just experienced, nor are we telling them what they will be experiencing following a trauma; rather, we are asking them to reveal what their experience has been thus far. Responses by the social worker to this task should be in terms that participants use in their everyday lives, rather than medical, academic, or professional language. The social worker explains that reactions to a traumatic event may vary, that many different types of responses are to be expected, and that these responses differ from stress reactions. Explanations are given as to why trauma affects us the way it does. Also, we inform participants about sensory experiences or environments that will trigger a sense of reliving the trauma and alert them to these phenomena. Some basic steps in lowering the intensity of the triggers are provided, which include normalizing the experience and identifying what sensory experience might trigger a reexperiencing of the trauma. Is it a smell, sight, sound, taste, or touch? Once this is identified, we acknowledge where the trigger came from and take several deep breaths until the sensory experience dissipates.

The APS workers were very forthcoming about what was different with them physically, emotionally, and socially. We compiled an extensive list of symptoms, which served the purpose of instilling within the group a sense of communal suffering as survivors of the trauma. We then discussed ways of coping with the symptoms, which laid the groundwork for tasks that clients could undertake outside the session (see "Empowering" below).

Grieving

The fifth task is to name what meaningful connections with self and others have been threatened or permanently lost. Trauma creates an immense sense of loss, so beginning the grieving process with the client/community is a very valuable task. Discussing different ways of grieving that are sensitive to culture, religion, and gender is incorporated into this task.

Sometimes, when working with a community, it is helpful to meet with community representatives to begin this task. Whether working with individuals or communities, this task will identify what has been individually or communally lost. For example, individual identities were threatened or lost following the bombing of the World Trade Center. APS employees articulated this during the opening debriefing, when they described their experience of self since the bombing. A woman with two children who lost her husband in the bombing no longer saw herself as a wife and mother in an intact family and struggled with her new identity as a widow with children, all dependent on her extended family. Another said, "Who am I following this trauma? I thought I was a pacifist, but now I am not sure."

This task of the client or community is to assess what is changed or lost in their sense of self. The social worker facilitates this task with sensitivity and patience, respecting what the client or community has identified as a disconnection from self and not to minimize what has been named. This task is a process that is never completed, but will change and perhaps enlarge as the client/community's losses emerge after the trauma. The social worker and the group name what has been lost. A recording device, such as a flip chart, may be useful. Participants begin to see new connections and common experiences, which not only normalizes their posttrauma reactions but also engages them in community building.

The second part of this task is asking what has been lost with others. Where have unexpected disconnections appeared with families, coworkers, or communities? When I asked about disconnections from others during the debriefing with the APS workers, a recent citizen of the United States, who emigrated here from the Middle East, said that people on the street questioned his citizenship and his right to be in New York City. He no longer felt connected to his community and his alienation was mixed with fear and anxiety for his and his family's safety.

The third part of this task is exploring what meaning in their lives has been threatened or lost. These disconnections might appear initially as depression, with such comments as "I don't enjoy my work any more," "My hobbies have fallen to the sidelines," "I don't want to attend family functions." These are symptoms of a loss of meaning and need to be identified as such. Helping people to maintain and recreate meaning in their lives is a critical task in crisis work. With the APS workers, the social worker facilitated this task by asking the group what loss of meaning frightened them the most. Responses varied from not finding it meaningful to live in such a large city to doubting their previously held religious beliefs. This communal discourse around the loss of meaning can begin the process of rebuilding a more supportive community. One way that people recreate their connections with others is through such discourse, which enables them to identify what they can expect from themselves, others, and their environment (Bruner, 1990). This is critical when rebuilding trust after a traumatic event. The social worker assists clients in revisiting those "taken-for-granted meanings and reformulating them into constructions that are improved, matured, expanded and elaborated, and that enhance their conscious experiencing of the world" (Guba & Lincoln, 1986, p. 546). The goal is to create tasks that will enhance behaviors that lead to health.

Amplifying

Amplifying a person's or group's emotional and cognitive experience of the trauma means recreating elements of the traumatic experience in a safe environment to facilitate expressions of thoughts and feelings about it. Amplifying requires a competency of the social worker that lowers the risk of this task retraumatizing the participants. Without competent training in crisis intervention theory and skills, this task can potentially be more harmful than helpful. For many persons who have been traumatized, the numbing stage, which prevents the person from fully experiencing the trauma on an emotional and cognitive level, is initially a healthy mechanism. Without this automatic response many of those experiencing trauma would not be able to carry out activities of daily living. This coping strategy becomes unhealthy when the numbing stage persists. Much later, when the person begins "thawing" and begins to relive the intensity of the trauma, he or she may resort to self-medication techniques that keep the traumatic experience from surfacing. This can be manifested in legal and illegal substance abuse, workaholic and compulsive shopping behaviors, sexual rituals, and other strategies that either distract or numb the person enough so that the trauma never surfaces. It may be critical at some time during the recovery phase for the person or group to create a safe place where amplification can be experienced and related tasks completed. Sometimes, people and groups do not have the baseline health, resources, and support to do these tasks.

Amplifying is not recommended during the early weeks following the trauma, and hence it was not used in work with the APS employees reported on here. The task can be used only after a full assessment is done by a competent practitioner trained in trauma work who is able to provide the safety and resources for a person or group to revisit the emotional and cognitive arena of trauma.

The goal is to help participants understand and move through the experience in a purposeful and therapeutic manner. Amplifying is not a task that can be completed in one setting. The amount of time spent on it will depend on the intensity of the traumatic event, its perceived threat to life and safety, and the prior health of the persons traumatized.

If it had been done with the APS employees, amplifying might have made use of videotapes of the destruction of the World Trade Center as a way of recreating the traumatic event. This might have been accompanied by asking participants to recall the sounds, smells, and tastes they might have experienced during the event. For example, at a debriefing session, one participant spontaneously recalled that her most vivid sensation was the taste of soot in her mouth. Memories of this kind can help recreate the event in a safe environment. Successfully navigating through these sensory experiences with the help of a social worker can rob triggers of their ability to create disruptions. Between sessions, the client may, under the social worker's guidance, continue the process through self-exposure to stimuli associated with the traumatic event.

Integrating

Existential questions eventually arise following a traumatic event: How does this trauma connect to my overall life? Is it possible to be transformed by this experience, or is the only consequence tragedy and destruction? The natural strategy is for persons to compartmentalize the traumatic event with the belief that the trauma will not disrupt their health. We often hear, "Don't think about it, forget that it ever happened, get on with your life!" These sincere suggestions are attempts to compartmentalize the experience rather than integrate it. If this were the healthiest option, we would never have such organizations as Mothers Against Drunk Drivers. Following the trauma of her daughter's death at the hands of a drunk driver, a woman integrated the experience to forge a new identity as a national leader and advocate for stricter laws against drinking and driving. Who will be transformed following the World Trade Center trauma?

The goal is to create new possibilities for transformative ways of living following the trauma. Through discourse, the social worker and clients begin the work of transformation in narratives that depict how trauma transformed the lives of ordinary people. Telling these stories with sensitivity and without setting up unrealistic expectations that everyone should take on a new identity is critical. Creative ways of inspiring hope and courage are employed. Just raising the question "Is it possible for this tragedy to transform us individually and as a community?" creates a whole discourse and many potentials.

Empowering

Thus far, activities with the group in the session raised various possibilities for the participants' continued task work outside the session. Empowering involves identifying from among these possibilities the most effective and efficient tasks that will facilitate the maintenance and enhancement of healthy outcomes following trauma. It also involves planning ways to obtain the resources necessary to successfully complete these tasks, deciding on methods of task accomplishment, and considering obstacles that may interfere with task attainment.

One approach to facilitating empowerment is Kormanik's (1999) Four-S model: self, situation, strategy, support. What resources exist within the self? What is the individual's current situation? Are there important resource deficits, such as lack of an adequate income? What past strategies worked or were inadequate when the person/community previously experienced trauma or highly stressful situations? What new strategies did he or she learn from others? What supports are currently operative in the person's life and what new supports are available that he or she may not be aware of?

With the APS workers, it was important to ask "What do you now need? What are your priorities? What is most important for you in regaining or maintaining health?" What is critical is that the pressing needs of the individual and community are addressed and that tasks will be responsive to these needs.

Community tasks can be identified and planned with all participants together. The APS employees identified tasks that could be undertaken in groups, such as ongoing team-building meetings, potlucks, and volunteering for service in the city. Also, they agreed to post large sheets of paper in public areas where employees could list tasks they found helpful. Obstacles to tasks were considered. For example, some task possibilities involved obtaining mental health services, but it was not clear how APS employees might obtain these services. Suggestions for securing them were developed.

For more individualized tasks, small breakout groups can be used. At APS, six New York City Department of Mental Health professionals led small groups. The focus was on the following goal: Now that we have educated each other about how trauma impacts us physically, emotionally, and socially, and we have named what is lost in your lives, it is important that we identify what tasks can be developed to address these losses and how these tasks can be carried out. If small group leaders are not available, the practitioner can circulate among groups or use can be made of consulting pairs. Individual tasks that were identified and developed included carrying out volunteer, religious, leisure, and physical activities, eating nutritious meals, and doing relaxation exercises.

Terminating and Revisiting

The purpose of terminating is to summarize what has been covered and what has been learned. Attention is given to what has just been created together and how this experience has been helpful. The primary goal is to mark the transition from this structured experience to a fluid one. Care of self and others is emphasized, and the sharing that occurred in the group can be carried on outside this experience.

The social worker takes the emotional temperature of the group by checking on how the participants are feeling now. Any follow-up sessions are announced and the group is reminded of long-term resources that were identified. How their participation has helped one another is discussed. The session is closed with some type of ritual that reflects the group's cohesiveness in a genuine and appropriate manner. The social worker remains available to individuals after the session. Refreshments were served at the APS session, which provided an opportunity for conversation and relaxation.

Many things can change within days and weeks for persons who have been traumatized. It is important to revisit the individuals/community within several weeks or, earlier if warranted, and ask "What is different since we last met? What new needs have surfaced? What tasks have been effective in maintaining and recreating health? Do any tasks need to be altered or discarded and replaced with new ones? Are there problems of isolation and lack of connectedness?" Finally, long-term tasks for maintaining health can be reinforced and further developed at this time.

CONCLUSION

The model just presented can be applied to any group that has undergone a traumatic experience. It attempts, through tasks, to recreate lost connections affecting self and community and to enable participants to achieve changes at whatever levels may be possible. The model is still evolving. Directions for further work include further development of ways to translate tasks worked on in group sessions to healing actions that can be carried out in the participants' life situations and of achieving better articulation between tasks at individual and community levels.

NOTE

Adapted from Volume 2, No. 1 of *Brief Treatment and Crisis Intervention.* Special Issue on Crisis Response Protocols and Crisis Intervention in the Aftermath of the Sept. 11th Mass Terrorist Attacks on the Pentagon and World Trade Center. Reprinted with permission of the publisher of the journal, Oxford University Press, and the editor-in-chief of the journal, Dr. Albert R. Roberts.

REFERENCES

Berman, M. (1981). *The reenchantment of the world.* Ithaca, NY: Cornell University Press.

Borden, W. (2000). The relational paradigm in contemporary psychoanalysis: Toward a psychodynamically informed social work perspective. *Social Service Review, 74,* 352–379.

Bruner, J. (1990). *Acts of meaning.* Cambridge, MA: Harvard University Press.

Everly, G. S., & Mitchell, J. T. (1999). *Critical incident stress management: A new era and standard of care in crisis intervention* (3rd ed.). Chevron Publishing.

Everly, G., & Mitchell, J. (1999). *Critical incident stress management* (2nd ed.). Ellicott City, MD: Chevron.

Guba, E., & Lincoln, Y. (1986). Research, evaluation, and policy analysis: Heuristics for disciplined inquiry. *Policy Studies Review, 5*(3), 546–551.

Guba & Lincoln, 1989

Kemmis, S., & McTaggart, R. (2000) Participatory action research. In N. Denzin & Y. Lincoln (Eds.), *Handbook of qualitative research* (2nd ed., pp. 567–605). Thousand Oaks, CA: Sage.

Kormanik, M. B. (1999). The cycle of awareness development: A cognitive and psychosocial theory of adult development. In K. P. Kuchinke (Ed.), *Proceedings of the 1999 Academy of Human Resources Management Conference* (Vol. 2, pp. 634–640). Baton Rouge, LA: Academy of Human Resource Management.

Polanyi, M. (1962). *Personal knowledge.* Chicago: University of Chicago Press.

Reid, W. J. (1992). *Task strategies: An empirical approach to social work practice.* New York: Columbia University Press.

Reid, W. J. (1997). Research on task-centered practice. *Social Work Research, 21*(3), 132–137.

Reid, W. J. (2000). *The task planner.* New York: Columbia University Press.

Reid, W. J., & Epstein, L. (1972). *Task-centered casework.* New York: Columbia University Press.

Reid, W. J., & Fortune, A. E. (2002). The task-centered model. In A. R. Roberts & G. Greene (Eds.), *Social workers' desk reference* (pp. 101–105). New York: Oxford University Press.

Saleeby, D. (1994). Culture, theory, and narrative: The intersection of meaning in practice. *Social Work, 39*(4), 351–359.

Schon, D. (1983). *The reflective practitioner: How professionals think in action.* New York: Basic Books.

Sermabeikian, P. (1994). Our clients, ourselves: The spiritual perspective and social work practice. *Social Work, 39*(2), 178–182.

Waite, F. T. (1939). A little matter of self-respect. In F. Lowry (Ed.), *Readings in social case work, 1920–1938: Selected reprints for the case work practitioner* (pp. 184–186). New York: Columbia University Press.

III

CRISIS ASSESSMENT AND INTERVENTION MODELS WITH CHILDREN AND YOUTH

14

What He Knew Before It All Changed: A Narrative From Ground Zero

LINDA G. MILLS

Linda Mills lives in downtown Manhattan in the neighborhood known as Tribeca. Her loft, located on Murray Street, is just three blocks from where the World Trade Center once stood. Peter Goodrich, her husband, is a professor at Cardozo School of Law. Their son, Ronnie Mills Goodrich, now 8, started kindergarten at Public School 234 on September 6, 2001. The school is located three blocks from where the North Tower fell. Linda and her family were displaced for 6 weeks following the attack on the World Trade Center. Ronnie's school was relocated twice. P.S. 234 was not reoccupied until 4 months after 9/11.

SEPTEMBER 5, 2001

3:12 A.M.

Ronnie enters our room sleepy-eyed, searching for the warmth of his parents' bodies. We oblige, but not without its impact on our sleep. I am awake. It is the day before Ronnie's first day of kindergarten and we are conscious of his fear. It will get better, I say, just give him a few days.

8:30 A.M.

I put everything in my red bag. I walk to the Twin Towers and enter at the Border's bookstore located three short blocks from our apartment. I browse, as I always do, when I enter this important neighborhood landmark. The "new nonfiction" offers nothing "new" to the frequent shopper. I carry on down the escalator and through the shopping concourse. I fleetingly glance at the Gap window, the Banana Republic display, the sign for the Thomas Pink store to come. I enter the World Trade Center tower and notice a few people taking the express elevator to the Windows on the World restaurant. I remember with fondness the evening we spent there when my husband's friends came to visit from Britain.

The Marriott Hotel entrance located across from the World Trade Center elevator bank embraces me. I feel cared for by this remarkable place that provides solace and comfort to the city-worn. I nod as I walk past the bellhops who are standing by. I make my way to the hotel elevator. It always takes too long to get to the 21st floor, I remark to myself. When I finally arrive at my destination, I and a few other adventurous souls enter the designated health club elevator. I hand the receptionist my Fitness Company card and make my way to the dressing room. With bathing suit and cap on, I enter the cold water. Twenty minutes later I am in the steam room. I take in the warm air, shower off the sweat, and blow dry my hair straight. I am ready to start my day.

SEPTEMBER 6, 2001

8:45 A.M.

The day has finally arrived. Ronnie dresses without resistance. He is a mixture of excited and scared. We are aware of the difficulty Ronnie has separating from his parents; we want it to be smooth. We have spent much of the summer talking about P.S. 234. We reassure him that if he needs to, he can cry.

As we enter the school building on Greenwich—a fantastic tribute to modern education and to its ranking as one of New York City's finest public schools—we find Ronnie's name on the class roster. We are relieved by the news that his class will include his two closest friends from preschool. We are now confident that the transition—leaving Ronnie behind—will be smooth.

As we make our way to "Abby's class," Peter and I are struck by the meaning of this event. Ronnie is in school with his peers, but also with kids twice his age. His biggest fear, "the bullies," is not unwarranted. We reassure him through our glances.

Abby is the perfect kindergarten teacher. She moves from erect to her knees with ease; her speech is sufficiently slow to be understood by all ages and infirmities. We hesitate, but trust that Ronnie is in good hands. When he is ready, he pushes each of us out the door, a ritual he perfected at preschool. No tears on Ronnie's part. Once he isn't looking, I let myself go.

SEPTEMBER 7, 2001

11:30 A.M.

We pick Ronnie up after his second day of school. It is an early day today. Next week Ronnie will start the afterschool program and our lives will return to normal. We are anxious for these developments; Peter and I are both finishing books with deadlines and every lost hour makes a difference.

SEPTEMBER 10, 2001

8:30 A.M.

Today is Ronnie's first long day at school. "Do I really have to go to afterschool, Mommy?" he asks as he holds his ears plugged with his fingers. He knows the answer to his question; he just doesn't want to hear it. Just at that moment the phone rings. It is Caty, our downstairs neighbor. "Linda, how about if I pick Ronnie up at 2:40 and bring him home with Nick?" Nick is Ronnie's best friend. "Okay," I say hesitatingly. I am aware that my own desire to routinize Ronnie's life need not conflict with his desire to play with his best friend. I tell Ronnie that he and Nick will have a play date and he won't have to go to afterschool. "Yay," he shouts. "Okay," I tell him, "but tomorrow you will go to afterschool."

SEPTEMBER 11, 2001

6:30 A.M.

I really need to swim, I tell Peter as we start to stir. The idea fades as I get my morning coffee. I am too exhausted to exercise. Instead, I tell Peter that I will take Ronnie to school. Peter agrees to come along.

8:30 A.M.

When we get to the lobby of our building, I realize that we are leaving without Ronnie's sweater. I mistakenly ask my "I want all my options open" son if he thinks he needs one. "Yes," he says emphatically. By the time we are outside, I realize it isn't cold at all. "I still want a jacket," he insists. Peter runs upstairs to get it and I carry it along to P.S. 234, Ronnie in hand.

8:43 A.M.

As we enter the schoolyard, I am given a leaflet encouraging me to vote for Mark Green for mayor. I am annoyed that I have one more thing to carry. We search for the "Abby's class" sign that differentiates Ronnie's group from all the others. The sign is posted on the far brick wall and we make our way across the playground. Ronnie surveys the other kids. You know he is looking for bullies.

Like the days before, Ronnie runs as he gets closer to the collection of kids called "Abby's class." He spots Yohji and Sebastian and joins their imaginary game. They start horsing around. As Abby tries to gather all the kids together, I encourage Ronnie to take Yohji's hand. Eventually, the little people make their way into the building and Peter and I are left standing in the schoolyard with the mothers of Ronnie's friends. We chat aimlessly for a moment about how cute it all is and how we need to "get on with our day."

8:47 A.M.

Our leisurely anxiety is interrupted with the familiar but all too proximate sound of a jet. It is so close above our heads that it seems it is aimed for our very group. In the few seconds we are given to reflect, we become paralyzed with anticipation. Peter, 6 feet 4 inches tall, sees above the school building. I watch him look up, but I don't follow his gaze. Instead, I search his eyes for meaning. This summer we had heard planes at his mother's house in the English countryside. I listen. The plane is braking. The plane is stopping overhead. I listen harder. "No," I think. "This can't be." I do not look up. I search Peter's eyes again. I whisper to myself, "This doesn't happen in America." Somewhere inside me I know what this is. The screeching changes. The plane is no longer braking. The plane is accelerating. The engine is struggling to regain its speed. And then we hear a boom. The ground beneath us shakes like the earthquakes I grew up with in California.

"We need to find Ronnie," I scream. Peter is dazed but follows me anyway. I run up the stairs, as do the few dozen other mothers who just witnessed the event by sight or sound. Tears and measured hysteria engulf each of us as we search the unfamiliar building for our children. When I finally arrive at Ronnie's classroom, Peter is a few feet behind me. I run inside. No kids. My eyes are immediately drawn to the large picture window. Red smoke is billowing from the tower. Flames, smoke, glass. I am searching for my breath, repeating the words "no, no" over and over again. "That's what I saw," Peter said. I melt into his arms.

A few seconds later, I gather myself again. "Got to find Ronnie." "Is there a bomb shelter in this school?" I scream. "No," I hear a parent say. How does she know? I wonder. We had one in my elementary school. Up and down the stairs three times, I go looking for the person most precious to us in the world. He is nowhere.

Peter gets me to calm down. "He is here, Linda," Peter says, "we will find him." When I see Abby leading a group of kids up the stairs, my heart sinks. "Where's Ronnie? Where's Ronnie?" I am hollering, trying to control myself. "Right here, Mommy," I hear. He runs from the pack and I hug him with my shaking body.

There is some confusion about what we should do next. One parent, the wife of an NYU English professor, organizes the kids into a group for story time. The kids and parents slowly congregate on the hallway benches for a ritual they know well. "The dog . . . " her voice trails off.

8:52 A.M.

"We need to leave here, Peter," I am saying. "This isn't over and I don't feel safe." Peter is still dazed. When I reflect on my words, I am not exactly sure why I am saying them. An announcement comes overhead: "If you are the parent of a child, we think it is best to take your child home." I encourage us to walk quickly. "Come on," I am urging my small family along. The familiar faces of parents we hardly know line the hallways of the school. Some are chattering; others are wandering aimlessly. I am scared shitless.

We go outside the schoolyard when Angie, Yohji's mother, says she needs to be at work for a 9:00 meeting. "We would be happy to take Yohji for the day," I say, knowing that our plans to write today have been interrupted. "Great," she says, with some relief. Angie is an artist. A beautiful and creative woman, someone I have known from some distance as the parent of one of Ronnie's precious friends.

"Angie, I need to say something," choosing my words carefully. "I don't think you need to go to your meeting. This day will be remembered as one of the most significant days in American history. I think if you skip your meeting your office will understand."

Thirty seconds after these words trailed from my mouth we hear another boom. Again it feels like the earthquakes I have felt so many times before. This time I look up. A big black cloud of smoke emanates from the top of the other tower. The smoke is tinged with shimmering glass and a papery substance. It is beautiful in its way except that it is overhead and descending toward us. We start to run so as not to be overcome by it. Peter picks up Ronnie and we, with hundreds of other parents and children, run down Greenwich Street as fast as we can. It is organized in its way. We are all running together.

By the time we get to the Traveler's Insurance building 10 blocks away, I am exhausted. My stomach is tense; I have held it without air for several minutes. We are meeting people now who had been a safe distance from the explosions. They are different, much calmer. We look back with only the slightest interest in the fires. These are the first of many differences we will notice between those who experienced it firsthand, and those who watched it from afar. There is a fruit stand where I buy a banana.

9:16 A.M.

About three blocks later, and what feels like a safer distance from the black cloud, we ask two women standing on the street whether we can use their phone. They are obvious Tribeca-ites and I think they will take pity on us. But no cell phones are working, and so one woman escorts us to her loft. Angie calls her office to apologize for missing the meeting.

A moment later, I am connected to Los Angeles. It is dawn in the City of Angels. I am aware that I don't want to alarm my 80-year-old father. "Dad," I say in measured tone. "Yes," he replies in a sleepy voice. "You will see something terrible on television. I just want you to know that we are all fine. We watched a plane go into the World Trade Center, but we escaped. Ronnie is with us." I tell him I will call him again from our next destination. "Okay," he says in his groggy and naïve state. I call my friend Ed, who has an apartment in the Dakota building on West 72nd Street. "Can you help us out with some place to spend the day?" The Dakota building, so far north of downtown, is named for its mountainous distance. The answering machine that picks up does not respond. I am aware that I have no family here in New York City, that I have no second home. We have no other place to go.

We continue moving despite our exhaustion. We walk, away from everything we know and love. In our wandering state, we decide that NYU is probably a safe destination. Nothing seems safe, but of all the places to target, would you hit NYU? We decide against Cardozo Law School, where Peter is a professor, because of its connection to a Jewish university. We enter NYU's School of Social Work, where we learn that a tower has collapsed and the Pentagon has been hit.

3:45 P.M.

My office phone works only intermittently. Angie cannot get through to her husband's cell phone. He is on a business trip and will have no idea if his wife and child are safe. The television images often include P.S. 234. If Koji is watching, he will know that the school is still standing.

Ronnie and Yohji enjoy the freedom we offer them. They throw cars up and down the grand staircase of the Social Work School building and make pictures on the computer. They play PowerRangers.com and find the PowerpuffGirl Web site. They seem oblivious to our state of high alert.

We start to realize that we are not going to be able to return home tonight and that we might not ever be able to return home. We have $200 in our pockets. No credit card, no checkbook, no cell phone. I am wearing my slippers. I ran out to take our son to school; I hadn't prepared for evacuation.

I call Carol Gardner, personal assistant to John Sexton, NYU's incoming president. She offers me a guestroom in the townhouse of two law professors. I am touched by their generosity. I prefer a hotel stay. I call my dad for his credit card number. It isn't much use. No hotel rooms are available. Over the next hour, several offers of places to stay trickle in. We settle on either the Garlands' apartment or the Dakota building. We know the Garlands have two wonderful kids and we think this will be a comfort to Ronnie.

5:30 P.M.

We arrive at the Garlands' apartment, a few blocks from my office. The family isn't home. On entering the building I realize that I will probably feel more comfortable in my own space. Every noise, every plane, every movement reminds me of the unthinkable that has happened and how the unthinkable happened to us. We leave the Garlands a note of thanks and reenter the empty streets to look for a taxi uptown. Nothing is running in the city and I don't have the strength to walk 60 blocks to the Dakota. We return to the Garlands' apartment just as they are coming in. We settle into their guestroom den.

8:30 P.M.

David Garland makes us chicken nuggets. I enjoy them immensely. My husband, being English, always finds comfort in fried foods. Tonight I understand why.

10:00 P.M.

We go to bed, television blaring. We don't sleep a wink. Every real and imaginary sound is a plane overhead, screeching, accelerating, boom.

SEPTEMBER 12, 2001

8:00 A.M.

Ronnie wakes up refreshed. We make our way out into the world in the same clothes we were wearing the day before. We have to get back to our home soon. Ronnie is already restless for his room, for his toys. I want clean underwear. What would our insurance cover? Was our apartment standing?

10:00 A.M.

We start our search for a sympathetic department store. Daffy's will take our money, but they are unwilling to let us charge something on my father's credit card. Peter buys a few T-shirts, but I refuse to spend our precious cash in a store that isn't more understanding of our situation.

We make our way to the local K-mart. I am by this time on a razor's edge. I ask the manager what he can do for us. Yes, he would take a credit card number. He understands our predicament. After we shop I return for his assistance. "Oh," he said, he will need to call the credit card company. I break down crying. I call the Visa company myself. Between sobs I explain our predicament. They will accept our credit card number. They agree to send us a new card when the FedEx service is resumed.

2:00 P.M.

We call Ronnie's babysitter, Aja. "Could you watch Ronnie for a couple of hours while we try to get into our apartment?" "Sure," she says, she would love to see Ronnie.

3:00 P.M.

We walk toward Aja's NYU dorm, where she is a resident assistant. We realize that we need equipment if we are serious about going downtown. We need masks—the smoke and stench in the Village is terrible, what would it be like at Ground Zero?—and I needed more than just slippers. We stop at a friend's house and borrow a pair of sneakers.

After we drop Ronnie off at Aja's dorm, we start to walk downtown. At this point, there is no car traffic from the Village to the World Trade Center site, and so we are on foot. We will walk a total of 14 miles.

As we make our way toward Canal Street, it becomes clear that we will have to do a lot of persuading. All we have on us is Peter's Cardozo Law School identification and a World Trade Center Fitness Company card. The Fitness Company card links us to the World Trade Center neighborhood; at least that's what we believe. I have nothing with me but my emotion.

Peter and I debate the best way to get us into the neighborhood. I will do the talking, we agree, as Peter is British. We are uncertain how the cops will react to his accent, yet Peter has our only identification. One stop after another we get through the road blocks. When we arrive at Chambers Street, three blocks from our apartment and six blocks from the specter of the World Trade Center, we meet Officer Bob. He obviously takes pity on us and persuades his supervisor to let him escort us into our building.

There is no electricity, and so with Bob's flashlight, we walk up the stairs to the fourth floor. "How are we going to get our stuff out?" I wonder quietly. We enter our apartment and the sun fills us with sadness. "Great kitchen," Officer Bob says, "my wife would kill for it." "She can have it," I say almost seriously. We rush around to gather our things into the two suitcases we think we can wheel. Computer, cell phone, credit cards, identification. Everything we need to function. We are in and out in 15 minutes. I am crying by the time we finish. "Thanks, Officer Bob," I say. "I can't tell you what you have done for us."

12:00 midnight

I am retching over the toilet. My stomach has finally had it, and so have my nerves. I am throwing up the garlic pasta we ate for dinner. I resolve to find a hotel room in the morning.

SEPTEMBER 13, 2001

The Doubletree Hotel on 43rd Street offers the comfort of two rooms and the excitement of PlayStation for Ronnie. Ronnie loves hotels, and so we pack our few things and make our way to our new home. The room is fine and we can arrange child care for Ronnie and his two school friends. There is a playroom. We can pretend everything is normal.

SEPTEMBER 20, 2001

8:30 A.M.

Ronnie goes to school today for the first time since the attack. He is nervous but reassured to know that Yohji will also attend this new school. After much confusion and wrangling, the school district has arranged for P.S. 234 kids to attend P.S. 41. P.S. 41 is located near NYU and Cardozo and so we are both relieved. We arrive this morning to a schoolyard full of children. I see familiar faces. I am relieved to see the reporters who are interested in our children's well-being. When I see the sign for Abby's class, I burst into tears. I am looking away so that Ronnie doesn't see my reaction to his new first day of school. So long as Yohji is there, Ronnie is happy to go.

We make our way up the narrow staircase to Room 206. There are already 60 kids in this small room and Ronnie's class of 21 more kids enters it. I see the anxious, teary-eyed faces of the other mothers and I am comforted that their reactions parallel mine.

2:00 P.M.

The Doubletree Hotel has served us well. But despite our gratitude, the food is sufficiently bad and the space sufficiently small that we begin to think it is unworkable. Our neighbors are renting apartments for a month or two. We start the search for the next move. On Deborah Podgen's suggestion, Judy Mishne calls me to say that she has a friend who has an empty apartment on 56th Street. Do we want to stay there?

I am reluctant. Peter is clear. He is too large for a small hotel room. "Okay," I agree, "let's move."

SEPTEMBER 23, 2001

8:00 P.M.

Our neighbors arrive for a meeting at our borrowed apartment on the Upper East Side. There are five condominium owners at 37 Murray Street. Melvin and Helen, the condo's sponsors, agree to come and put people's minds to rest. They come despite the fact that their best friend, Herman Sandler, died 12 days before on the 104th floor of the World Trade Center. Two of the women in our building are pregnant. They are beaming. We share "what happened" stories and the evening provides the first comfort of our ordeal. We are among friends who understand. And we can feel a semblance of normalcy returning.

SEPTEMBER 27, 2001

9:30 A.M.

Melvin and Helen invite us to Long Island. Their house, they say, will be empty. We are torn between staying in the city and never coming back. We reluctantly agree to go.

10:30 A.M.

The phone rings again, Melvin and Helen calling back. "Linda, one of the plane's engines landed on a terrace on the top floor of the building. The piece tore the roof open. The rain penetrated the fifth floor apartment and probably yours," Melvin shouts into the phone. "We won't know if there is damage until the building is cleared for reentry. The FBI is investigating." "Thanks," I say, a bit dazed by what I am hearing.

4:15 P.M.

To our surprise, the Building Department announces that the north side of Murray Street can reoccupy. We feel mixed about the news. We desperately want to return to what we know, even if it has changed. It's got to be better than living out of a suitcase. I arrange for the hazardous waste cleaners to come the next day.

SEPTEMBER 28, 2001

8:00 A.M.

I inspect the apartment in daylight for the first time since the attack. The rain damage is significant but contained. I survey the damage from the roof.

A large piece of the fuselage sits atop my building. Just landed there on a 2 × 6 ft. terrace. I am grateful that it is plane and not body.

9:30 A.M.

The cleaning crew works hard without masks. I worry about them. They tell me that it will take three full days to clean the mess, six people working full time. The boss of the cleaning crew, Joe, calls me to say that he has been prevented from entering the "frozen zone." I tell him that I will meet him at Broadway and Park Place.

I go to where Joe is waiting. When I walk him to Murray Street, the police officer informs me that I need an escort to enter my street. "What?" I say, infuriated. "I am moving back in." "Sorry, lady," he says, "strict orders. I can't let you through." I sneak through an entrance the cops aren't monitoring.

1:00 P.M.

Peter arrives. We discuss how the apartment is a shell of itself. It is a military zone, a police headquarters. It is a bombsite and a graveyard. We decide that Long Island is just what we need.

2:15 P.M.

We pick up a rental car and arrive at Ronnie's school early. Abby is teaching the kids to think about concepts: above, beyond, underneath. They are taking this lesson in a janitor's closet, 21 kids in a room no larger than 3 × 6 feet. The kids are totally engaged in the story. They are totally oblivious to the tragedy.

3:00 P.M.

We drive to Southhampton, uncertain what we will find there. In the dark, we miss the driveway entrance. We finally find the gravel road and feel blessed by our good fortune. We enter the estate with some trepidation. This is the most beautiful house we have ever seen. There is a heated swimming pool, an empty beach. There are full-time housekeeping services. Despite our good fortune, nothing seems to penetrate the darkness of our mood.

OCTOBER 1, 2001

8:30 A.M.

As we return to the city Monday morning, we are struck by the changes. Trucks and cars are stopped for inspection. Cabs wait to enter the bridge. We barely get Ronnie to school on time.

2:00 P.M.

We learn that the asbestos levels in our apartment are okay. The dust will be kept to a minimum by keeping our windows shut. We can move back in if we want to. We hold our breath and take the plunge.

OCTOBER 2, 2001

1:30 P.M.

We see Steven through the window at his salon, Lapin Paoli. Steven rents the apartment we own next door. He sleeps there in the evenings and Peter works there in the days. Steven's presence helps defray the outrageous mortgage bill we pay each month. Steven is especially thrilled to see me. He thought I was dead. He had heard that some woman had been killed on Murray Street. His business, a thriving and beautiful hair salon, is nonexistent. His customers, which include the likes of Judge Judy, are refusing to come downtown. He can't afford to keep paying rent on our apartment. We are not surprised by his decision to move out.

OCTOBER 21, 2001

I am 44 years old today. It is Sunday and we are in our apartment after 6 weeks of hotel rooms, friends' guest beds, and weekend stays in the Hamptons. Murray Street is cut off from the rest of the world, divided by a blue painted wooden horse and a few wooden police officers. No residents have returned here, save us and the neighbors in our building. When we enter the frozen zone on West Broadway, we bear witness to the skin of the World Trade Center.

I feel both privileged to live at the site of the nation's greatest tragedy and burdened by the questions I am asked upon entry. I am privileged because our street serves as the thoroughfare for trucks hauling the 1.2 million tons of debris from the World Trade Center disaster site. The 24/7 activity turns out to be our source of inspiration. We are particularly impressed with the truck wash that involves four men in yellow slicker suits hosing down every vehicle that leaves the site. We are saddened by the occasional ambulance: a body or two is removed several times a week. We are comforted that somebody knows that the remains of a loved one have been recovered.

I am conflicted that the privilege should, on the one hand, be extended to everyone, and, on the other, be reserved for those of us who experienced the most direct hit. I understand why the families of the dead return to the WTC site over and over via boat and truck routes. As they should do. The healing occurs in this hallowed space. I want to offer it to everyone; I want to protect it for myself.

NOVEMBER 1, 2001

Some people return to look; I return to live. Every day I wonder if I am making the right decision. The *Daily News* reports that we are living in a toxic wasteland. My son is coughing. I wake with a sore throat. Yet I remain determined.

From my work on domestic violence, I know that people deal with trauma differently, so why should this be different? Some run and hide forever. Others will return more slowly. Still others think that the only way to heal is to face the demon head on. How to approach the trauma is a question that haunts each and every parent at P.S. 234, including me.

Some parents think that we should never return to P.S. 234: it is the site of America's greatest atrocity and should never be faced. Others think that we should return only after new construction at the WTC site is complete. Only a few others, like me, think our children's mental health is best served by returning to the lives we once knew.

When I ask Ronnie what he thinks, he is full of hope: "I want to go back to P.S. 234, Mommy. I want to walk to school so I can learn more." When I ask him about what happened, he is full of optimism: "I feel bad about the people in the building, the people who died, but I think a hundred people got out. . . . I want them to develop a World Trade Center that is real high so only a little tiny part falls off, instead of half. . . . I feel it is special to live here, Mommy, because there's a gate so if a part of the building falls down it will land on the gate and none of the people will die." And sometimes he is full of surprises: "I thought all the planes were dead," he tells Peter when he notices a plane in the sky six weeks after the event. "I thought all the planes crashed into the World Trade Center." I realize that my son is not so oblivious as I may think.

Encouraging my son's trauma narrative is not something I was conscious of before 9/11. Before 9/11, I encouraged my son to talk about his difference from a kid who was born with very short arms. Before 9/11, I encouraged my son to ask me why I was sad when I was crying. Before 9/11, I encouraged my son to explore how it felt when his best friend, Nick, rejected him. Now I just encourage him to do what he feels: "I'm just a kid, Mom," he says. "I just want to be a kid."

Michel Cohen, the pediatrician in the neighborhood, has observed that he has not seen an increase in asthma or rashes in children; he has, on the other hand, witnessed several anxious parents. Ronnie and all the children at P.S. 234 are both the source of our freedom from fear and the reason we feel terrified. To manage this tension is to provide a child who experienced such trauma the life he desperately needs: a semblance of what he knew before it all changed.

SEPTEMBER 11, 2004

Each year, at the anniversary of the attack, I sit back and take stock. Where have we been? Where are we going? Our lives will never be the same. At the same time, little has changed. I sit in my Tribeca loft preparing this piece for publication. I hear the sound of cars and trucks—no longer hauling debris. I hear my son's familiar cry, "Mom, can I have some cereal?"

Since 9/11, my scholarly work has changed. It is more urgent; I am more confident. When your life is threatened, it becomes all the more precious. I work harder than ever and I make every moment worth it.

The work I have done since 9/11—the Project Liberty "resilience" grant, and now the Homeland Security First Responder study—reflects the lessons I have learned from firsthand experience. The resilience of 9/11's first responders, the Tribeca community, and especially the children who live here is the most distinct feature of what remains. Like a bough from a windblown tree, we have all bounced back rather than broken in the storm.

We must learn more about this innate resilience. I recognize these days that mental health experts have only a peripheral role to play in helping people recover from terrorist attacks. The possibility of recovery is within each of us, and the question is only how best to facilitate it. Recovery comes in unexpected ways: through dialogue, peer support groups, and the reliving of 9/11 and the community's resilient response. Developing new models that focus less on professional, top-down approaches and more on the inherent mental health and resilience in the community is the direction that my scholarly efforts will take.

Nobody teaches me the power of resilience more than my own son. Although he still worries every time we board a plane, and reflects every once in a while on what he experienced that fateful day, he has "bounced back." The events of 9/11 did not break his spirit or damage him forever. Rather, through our persistent efforts as parents to stay attuned to his needs (and not to our fears), his little spirit bent but did not break. As a result, Ronnie, more than ever, sways with the wind.

NOTE

From the School of Social Work and the School of Law at New York University. Contact author: Linda G. Mills, Professor, New York University, 70 Washington Square South, Bobst Library, New York, NY 10012–1091. E-mail: linda.mills@nyu.edu.

15

Child and Adolescent Psychiatric Emergencies: Mobile Crisis Response

JONATHAN SINGER

CASE STUDIES

Nikki

On Tuesday morning, Mr. Anderson, a school counselor at a local elementary school, called the Child and Adolescent Psychiatric Emergency (CAPE) team to request a suicide assessment. Nikki, an 8-year-old female, had drawn a picture of herself with knives cutting large pieces out of her body; blood was spurting everywhere and a man was standing to the side laughing. The counselor reported that Nikki was well-known in the principal's office because of her frequent outbursts and fights with other children. According to Mr. Anderson, there were two previous incidents that caused concern for Nikki's well-being.

The first crisis occurred three months earlier. Mr. Anderson reports that during recess, Nikki was screaming at her classmates and stomping on the ground and refused to comply with the teacher's requests. Nikki reportedly picked up a rock and threw it at one of her classmates, grazing the student's shoulder. The school responded as follows: Nikki was restrained by school administrators and removed from the playground. Her classmates were taken back to the classroom, and the wounded student received first aid. The parents of both Nikki and the wounded classmate were called. School administrators had separate conversations with both parents. The school counselor was brought in to the classroom to debrief with the students. The zero-tolerance policy at Nikki's school required her to be temporarily expelled to the alternative elementary school. Although by law the school is not allowed to recommend mental health services to the parents, the school counselor mentioned that many children with anger problems benefit from counseling and provided the phone number for some local service providers. After a disruptive first week at the alternative school, Nikki's behavior improved somewhat due to individualized attention, structured classes, a no-talking policy, and weekly visits with the on-campus psychologist. Upon Nikki's return to her home school, the counselor again visited the classroom and provided a presentation to the students on what it means to be a friend. Nikki's behavior was somewhat difficult that first day, but the remainder of the week was without incident.

The second crisis occurred 2 weeks prior to the current crisis. Nikki reportedly refused to come in for recess. Her behavior escalated rapidly, going from arguing, to yelling, to stomping her feet on the ground, to biting her arm. At the first sign of self-injurious behavior, Nikki's teacher called for backup and restrained Nikki. During the restraint, Nikki smashed the back of her head into her teacher's face, bruising the teacher's jaw and enraging Nikki even more. Nikki was in restraints for approximately 10 minutes before her mother arrived. According to Mr. Anderson, Nikki's mother was "furious" with Nikki and screamed at her to "quit actin' a fool." Nikki's behavior de-escalated rapidly. She was suspended for two days and taken home. The school followed similar protocol for dealing with Nikki's classmates: the school counselor provided an in-service presentation, the teacher discussed the importance of listening to teachers, and Nikki's mother was again reminded that some children receive therapy services for this type of behavior.

Today's crisis appeared to be different from the previous two in that Nikki was not acting inappropriately. After confirming that Nikki's parent had been contacted and was on the way, a crisis worker drove out to the school to do a crisis and suicide assessment.

Later in the chapter we will describe an application of Roberts's seven-stage model of crisis intervention, including issues of rapport building, compliance with medication, relapse, and developmental issues.

Rolando

At 8:55 P.M. the phone rang in the offices of the CAPE team. "Don't answer it," I said to my coworker, Kim, "the on-call shift starts in five minutes. If you pick up, we might be here for hours. Let the on-call person take it." Kim reminded me that she was the on-call worker for the night. I agreed to stick around and help out if needed. Kim had done the same for me many times; that was part of the deal working as a team. The call was from Lupe, a mother who was well-known to the CAPE team staff. Her 16-year-old son, Rolando, had been diagnosed with schizophrenia after his first hospitalization two years earlier. Tonight would begin the family's third involvement with mobile crisis services.

The two previous hospitalizations were very similar to each other. Prior to each hospitalization, Rolando stopped taking his medication, decompensated, threatened to kill his brother, and was brought to the hospital by the mental health deputies from the sheriff's department. Because of funding restrictions, Rolando stayed six days for his first hospitalization and four days for the second. Both times he was admitted to the adolescent unit, placed in an observation room for 24 hours, and screened for suicide every 15 minutes. After 24 hours without indicating harm to himself or others, he was placed in a private room with 15-minute checks. He participated in group therapy on the fourth, fifth, and sixth days.

According to hospital records, Rolando described an increase in auditory and tactile hallucinations starting at age 13. He reported that they started to bother him when he was 14, but he knew they were not real and therefore he did not tell anyone. His tactile hallucinations were relatively infrequent, but when present consisted of feeling small insects trapped under his skin. The voices (outside of his head, neither male nor female, unrecognizable) told him to kill his brother. Occasionally he would hear people laughing at him. He reported difficulty concentrating in class, getting into fights with classmates, and being easily overwhelmed. After the sixth day at the hospital, despite continued reports of hearing voices, he was discharged to the CAPE team and the psychiatric care of the agency's psychiatrist.

Tonight Lupe reported that Rolando and his 13-year-old brother were arguing and pushing each other. Lupe was afraid that the violence might escalate. For the past two days Rolando has been tormented by command hallucinations telling him to kill his brother. Rolando and Hector got into a fistfight on the previous night. Today Rolando stayed home from school. Lupe threatened to call the police if Rolando did not return to school tomorrow. Rolando trashed his room and told Lupe that he hoped she died. Soon after that Hector threw a pillow at Rolando and told him to shut up. According to the client record, two to three times a year Rolando becomes actively psychotic and attempts to kill his brother. It sounded like tonight was turning into another one of those nights, but potentially worse. According to Lupe, Rolando was accusing everyone in the house of trying to kill him. Lupe reported that she did not remember Rolando ever being convinced of his paranoia before.

Rolando's case provides an opportunity to illustrate Roberts's seven-stage model of crisis intervention (2000) and Myer's Triage Assessment Model (2001). The case study will illustrate and discuss treatment in a hospital setting and in the home. The case will also address challenges and rewards of working with highly conflictual families. Solution-focused techniques will be integrated with family-centered treatment. Finally, cultural issues will be presented and integrated into the case study.

Brandon

On Sunday afternoon, the 24-hour crisis hotline received a call from staff at the local youth shelter. After gathering the information and determining that 911 did not need to be called, the hotline worker paged the on-call crisis worker. A 15-year-old male named Brandon had checked in to the shelter early this morning. Prior to falling asleep he told the staff that if they called the police, he would run away and did not care if he lived or died.

Although he has never run away before, he has more experience on the street than off. Brandon and his mother were homeless until Brandon was 11 years old. When she could, she would wait tables and meet men who would take them in. Some of these men raped Brandon. Due to their nomadic lifestyle, Brandon attended 40 schools before dropping out in the eighth grade. He was often popular in school, but never sustained friendships as a result of frequent moves.

Shelter staff reported that Brandon had a bus ticket from California, which is approximately a 30-hour, four-day bus trip to the shelter. The shelter supervisor stated that homeless youth were allowed to stay 24 hours before the police were called, unless parental consent could be obtained. The supervisor was concerned for Brandon's mental and emotional well-being and requested a suicide assessment.

The CAPE team and the youth shelter had a symbiotic relationship. The CAPE team would provide crisis assessments for youth at the shelter who were suicidal or psychotic. In return, the shelter provided respite for youth who presented at the CAPE team in crisis primarily due to conflict in the home. If the child was between the ages of 14 and 17, a low risk for suicide outside of the home but high risk for suicide in the home, the shelter would agree to provide temporary respite (up to a week) with signed parental consent. The shelter accessed CAPE services approximately twice a month and CAPE used the shelter three to four times a year. The collaboration between the two agencies created a safety net for adolescents who were not appropriate for hospitalization, but whose family lacked the coping skills to prevent an escalation of violence. The respite enabled the CAPE team to provide crisis intervention to the family and adolescent in the shelter.

The case example of Brandon illustrates the complexity of working with a homeless adolescent. In the case application we will explore more about the experience of homeless youth, rapport building, problem-solving, and strengths-based crisis intervention. Although the details of Brandon's crisis differ from Rolando's and Nikki's, all three of these cases illustrate the need for crisis assessment to happen quickly. Despite their varied circumstances and personalities, effective treatment in each of these cases follows Roberts's seven-stage model of crisis intervention. From the start of the process, the crisis worker needs to keep in mind that the road to health does not end with crisis intervention. There must also be a transition and aftercare plan.

Following the model is complex and difficult, but if you follow guidelines and protocols, you are in a better position to be effective.

This chapter focuses on crisis situations that, given their potential for harm, require mobile crisis outreach for children and adolescents. The approach involves case studies that follow Roberts's (2000) seven-stage model of crisis intervention. For the youth in the case studies, failure to provide timely crisis intervention could result in death. Because this is a textbook, no one dies. But not all youth in crisis are fortunate enough to be case examples in a handbook on crisis intervention. The case studies reported in the chapter are real; they are based on actual crises from the author's caseload. From 1996 to 1999 the author provided services to approximately 250 children and families per year and averaged five crisis assessments per week. The cases are presented to illustrate the experience of mobile crisis outreach. The interventions are more clinical than academic.Dialogue is used liberally to take the intervention off the page and into the field. When possible, the exact phrasing and rationale for a particular technique or intervention are provided.

Roberts (2000a) defines crisis as "a period of psychological disequilibrium, experienced as a result of a hazardous event or situation that constitutes a significant problem that cannot be remedied by using familiar coping strategies" (p. 7). Most children have their first contact with mental health services during a crisis (Burns, Hoagwood, & Mrazek, 1999). The presence of a previously documented serious mental illness makes crisis intervention more complicated. The worker must have a clear understanding of the way the diagnosis manifests in youth in general and, when possible, how it manifests in that particular youth. Once this is understood, the crisis worker must provide a realistic resolution to the crisis. Greene, Lee, Trask, and Rheinscheld (2000), in their chapter on solution-focused crisis intervention, frame crisis as an opportunity for growth. Effective crisis resolution can have as its goal to leave the client in a *better* place than prior to the onset of the crisis. But what if precrisis functioning was barely functioning at all? What if, prior to the precipitating event, the client experienced hallucinations, delusions of grandeur, low-lethality suicidal ideation, or homicidal ideation? These are the questions crisis intervention workers need to answer.

In this chapter, we look at mobile crisis intervention with the 20% of youth who have a serious mental illness, defined as any emotional, behavioral, or mental disorder that severely disrupts the youth's daily functioning at home, school, or in the community (Center for Mental Health Services, 2001). The chapter moves from an overview of the structure of mobile crisis intervention to a discussion of the scope of the problem and a review of the most recent literature on community-based services for youth in crisis. Following a brief explanation of Roberts's (2000) seven-stage model of crisis intervention and Myer's (2001) triage assessment model, three case studies are used to illustrate the application of the models. This chapter does not focus on youth who present in crisis due to environmental (e.g., hurricane, terrorist attack) or developmental (e.g., puberty, isolation vs. group identity) factors.

AGENCY CONSIDERATIONS

In Austin, Texas, mobile crisis services are provided through the local community mental health agency, where the author was employed between 1996 and 2002. Although various model programs exist (e.g., Eaton & Ertl, 2000), the organization and structure of mobile crisis services will change depending on state and local requirements. In Austin, children were eligible for services if they were under the age of 18 and either had no insurance or received Medicaid or CHIP. Children covered under private insurance were referred to their insurance provider. A child was said to be in crisis if he or she was suicidal, homicidal, or actively psychotic.

In Austin, mobile crisis services for children and adolescents had regular contact with a number of different agencies. Some were service recipients, others were services providers, and some agencies were both recipients and providers. Recipient agencies included the local homeless shelter for youth, the school system, and the juvenile detention facility. Provider agencies were law enforcement and emergency medical assistance. Developing a working relationship with law enforcement is mandatory whenever involuntary hospitalizations are part of the job. Both the Austin Police Department and the Travis County Sheriff's Department had mental health units staffed by officers who were specifically trained in mental health issues. Hospitals both received and provided services: they provided most-restrictive environments for clients who were unable to be safe in the community, and they received services through a special agreement. In the latter, agency workers would provide cotherapy with the hospital staff, attend discharge staffings, and coordinate services between the hospital and the client's family.

Within the agency, the two programs that worked most closely together were the Child and Adolescent Psychiatric Emergency (CAPE) team and the Family Preservation Program (FPP). After the CAPE team provided intensive crisis stabilization services, FPP would provide slightly less intensive community-based family-centered services. FPP workers would provide services wherever the client and family would most benefit: homes, schools, juvenile detention facilities, or hospitals. M. R. Evans et al. (2003) report success using an intensive in-home crisis service similar to the FPP. They report that over 75% of children enrolled in their programs were maintained in the community. This is significant because, by definition, children entering FPP programs are at risk for removal from the home. Because the purpose of the mobile crisis unit was to provide crisis intervention with the intention of keeping children out of the hospital and in their homes, the availability of a local family preservation program provided a logical referral along the continuum of care.

CONTINUUM OF CARE

A discussion of outpatient crisis services for youth would not be complete without introducing the idea of a *continuum of care.* Clients with mental illness received levels of care ranging from least restrictive (outpatient services such as those discussed in this chapter) to most restrictive (hospitals and residential treatment centers; Schoenwald et al., 2000; Wilmshurst, 2002). If the purpose of crisis intervention is to restore functioning, then there must be services beyond crisis intervention to maintain that functioning. For children and families in crisis, a single session of crisis intervention will not result in long-term change. Longer-term services are needed to address the dynamics that produced the crisis. Table 15.1 provides an example of the continuum of care available to children and families in Austin, Texas.

SCOPE OF THE PROBLEM

According to the U.S. Surgeon General's report on children's mental health (U.S. Public Health Service, 2001), 20% of children receive mental health services. Of these, 11% have significant functional impairment, and 5% have extreme functional impairment. The number of youth who access mobile crisis services in a given year is unknown.

One of the cornerstones of crisis theory is that crisis is universal. Anyone can be in a situation that overwhelms his or her usual coping strategy. Yet, while the experience of crisis might be universal, the approach to crisis intervention with people who have a mental illness requires modifications to address the symptomology. During the crisis assessment, crisis workers need to evaluate the precrisis mental health of the youth so that appropriate modifications to the crisis intervention can be made. Accurate assessment guides treatment planning; misdiagnosis can "pose serious consequences for the course of treatment" (Springer, 2002, p. 217). Children with serious mental illness have reduced coping strategies and are therefore more susceptible to crisis. This susceptibility leaves them open to the types of "serious consequences" referred to by Springer. Familiarity with the most common psychiatric disorders will better prepare crisis workers to address the subtle but important differences involved in working with children and adolescents with a preexisting psychiatric disorder. What follows is a brief review of the epidemiology and presentation of depressive and psychotic disorders, two disorders that play a part in the lives of the children in the case studies. For a more thorough discussion of these disorders, the reader is encouraged to consult a current abnormal psychology textbook.

Table 15.1 Continuum of Care at Children's Mental Health Services in Austin, Texas

Program	Population	Services	Duration	
CAPE Team (Child and Adolescent Psychiatric Emergency)	Children who were suicidal, homicidal, or actively psychotic	Crisis intervention, IT*, FT**, service coordination. Office- and community-based	As many hours per day as needed, up to 30 days	Most Intensive
FPP (Family Preservation Program)	Children who were engaged in activities that put them at risk for removal from their home or school	Crisis intervention, IT, FT, service coordination. Community-based	6–8 hours per week, up to 120 days	
DPRS Program (Department of Protective and Regulatory Services)	Children with open cases with the DPRS due to confirmed cases of parental neglect or abuse	Provided traditional office-based therapy and skills training to children; protective parenting classes to parents; made recommendations for or against reunification	1–2 two hours per week, up to 2 years	
DayGlo	Children with *DSM-IV* diagnoses.	IT, FT, GT***. Office-based	1 hour per week, up to 3 years	
Zilker Park Program	Children with *DSM-IV* diagnoses.	Outdoor, experiential therapy program for children 7–11	4 hours per week, 6 months to 3 years	Least Intensive
Intake	Children under 18, except for those presenting in crisis	Intake assessment, diagnosis, referral to appropriate program	Up to 2 hours	
Service Coordination	Children and families participating in the DPRS, DayGlo, or Zilker Park program. CAPE and FPP provide service coordination	Coordinate medication checks, pschiatric evaluations, connect with community resources, including rent assistance, utilities, food	1–2 hours per month for the duration of services	
Medication Services	All children with biologically based diagnoses	Medication checks, pschiatric evaluations	As long as needed	

*IT: Individual Treatment
**FT: Family Treatment
***GT: Group Treatment

Depressive Disorders

At any point in time, approximately 2% of children and 2% to 5% of adolescents will meet the American Psychiatric Association's (1994) *Diagnostic and Statistical Manual of Mental Disorders* (*DSM-IV*) criteria for a depressive disorder (Lewinsohn & Clarke, 1999). Lewinsohn, Rohde, Klein, and Seeley (1999) report that the cumulative prevalence of major depressive disorder in children up to age 18 is 28% (19% for boys and 35% for girls). Rates of comorbidity (the presence of more than one disorder) among children and adolescents are also significant. Birmaher et al. (1996) estimate that 40% to 70% of children with a major depressive disorder have a comorbid psychiatric disorder, and 20% have three or more disorders.

What depression looks like, how to assess for it, and how to intervene is better understood in adults than in younger clients. Depression in adolescence is distinguished by delusions and sleeping too much (American Psychiatric Association, 1994). Depression in preadolescents is characterized by more anxiety, frustration, or somatic complaints than in adolescents or adults (Birmaher et al., 1996; Allen-Meares et al., 2004).The nature of depression in preschool children, rates of occurrence, and assessment procedures is not well understood (Allen-Meares et al., 2004). The prevalence of depressive disorders among children and adolescents and the changing nature of the disorders' presentation over time complicates the already challenging task of assessment and intervention during a crisis.

Psychotic Disorders

Psychotic disorders in children and adolescents can be divided into two main groups: schizophrenia and bipolar disorder. There are distinct differences between the two; however, Fonagy, Target, Cotrell, Phillips, and Zarrina (2002) report that when children present with psychotic symptomology of bipolar disorder, they are incorrectly diagnosed as schizophrenic. The authors attribute this to the greater presence of psychotic rather than affective symptoms at the time of diagnosis. Morrison and Anders (2001) suggest another challenge in assessing schizophrenia in children and adolescents: the likelihood that only precursor symptoms are present. "The actual prevalence of psychosis in general, and Schizophrenia in particular, in children and adolescents has not been well determined" (p. 296).

Treatment of schizophrenia requires a multimodal approach, including case management, crisis intervention, skills training, neuroleptic medication, educational support, social support, and family therapy (Fonagy et al., 2002). In a review of psychosocial treatments for children and adolescents with schizophrenia, Fonagy and colleagues found only one controlled trial (Rund et al., 1994, cited in Fonagy et al., 2002). Although the results report a significant reduction in hospital admission rates, the study was criticized for its size and methodology. In the absence of empirical data, guidelines to clinical intervention for youth diagnosed with schizophrenia are derived from studies with adults or anecdotal evidence from specialized practitioners. For children diagnosed with bipolar disorder, Fonagy et al. write, "Current best practice suggests a variety of other psychosocial interventions aimed at reducing social disruption, enabling developmental tasks to be seen through, supporting education, and reducing distress" (p. 260). In this chapter, the acute psychotic episode is synonymous with a crisis state (although the reverse is not true). The necessity for medication as a primary means of crisis stabilization differentiates an acute psychotic episode from the traditional definition of a crisis state.

Family Influence

Treatment of children rarely happens without involving the family (biological or adoptive). The influence of parents needs to be taken into consideration when evaluating the child. Parents with mental illness are more likely than parents without mental illness to have children who develop emotional and behavioral problems (Comprehensive Community Mental Health Services for Children and Their Families Program, 1998). There is a documented genetic component to psychiatric disorders (Biederman et al., 2001), but the child's home environment has a greater impact than genetics on children's developmental and emotional growth and well-being (Silverman, 1989). Parental behavior along with how the partner/marital relationship functions significantly affects a child's well-being. Mothers who are depressed or schizophrenic use parenting behaviors that result in poorer attachment (Radke-Yarrow et al., 1995) and developmental delays in language, attention, and social competence among infants and toddlers (Goodman & Brumley, 1990). However, despite these risks, the majority of children of parents with mental illness are resilient and appear to "avoid" significant problems (Beardslee & Poderofsky, 1988).

Traditional treatment approaches have presumed that the relationship between parental mental illness and child outcomes was unidirectional: parental mental illness affected the child, but not vice versa. Recent research suggests that the effects are better understood as bidirectional and transactional, rather than unidirectional (Goodman & Gotlib, 1999). Cognitive, behavioral, and emotional characteristics of children affect parents' symptoms and behaviors, and parents' symptoms and behaviors affect children (Hammen, Burge, & Adrian, 1991). Providing treatment to the family as the identified unit of care can result in improved family functioning (Cox, Puckering, Pound, & Mills, 1987; Hammen, Burge, & Stansbury, 1990; Keitner & Miller, 1990).

LITERATURE REVIEW ON COMMUNITY-BASED SERVICES FOR YOUTH IN CRISIS

Literature on child and adolescent psychiatric emergencies tends not to evaluate intervention techniques for children and adolescents in crisis.[1] Specifically, I found no research that addressed the treatment issues discussed in this chapter. However, there are empirical studies that focus on the population (children and adolescents), the experience (psychiatric crisis, emergency services), the intervention (crisis), and the location (community and home). There were several evaluations of programs for children and adolescents in crisis.

Several randomized controlled studies examined the efficacy of community-based treatments as alternatives to hospitalization for children who presented with suicidal, homicidal, or psychotic symptoms (Evans, Boothroyd, & Armstrong, 1997; Greenfield, Hechtman, & Tremblay, 1995; Gutstein, Rudd, Graham, & Rayha, 1988; Henggeler et al., 1999). The treatment approaches among these studies of high-risk youth were similar. All studies used a multidisciplinary approach, provided assessments within 24 hours, and focused on family goals. The purpose of each program was to avert hospitalization and reduce at-risk behaviors. All programs demonstrated effectiveness in reducing problems in functioning and as a result were successful in reducing admissions to the hospital or residential facilities. In some of these studies, outcomes were examined (Evans et al., 2001; Evans et al., 2003; Schoenwald et al., 2000). While decreases in at-risk behaviors were noted, discussion about the successes of the programs focused on the money saved by diverted hospitalizations. Attempts to provide community-based best practices for children who are in crisis are limited by the data reported by the studies.

Wilmshurst (2002) compared the effectiveness of a three-month, five-day-a-week residential program with a community-based family preservation program for children with emotional and behavioral disorders. The treatment approaches for the two programs differed considerably. The five-day residential program staff included a psychologist, a psychiatrist, and a family therapist, who provided individual therapy and twice-monthly family therapy using a solution-focused approach. The family preservation program staff provided intensive in-home support up to 12 hours a week over a 12-week period. Treatment outcomes at discharge (three months) and one year revealed a significant reduction in symptoms for participants in the family preservation and an increase in symptoms for participants in the five-day residential program. The authors conclude that maintaining children in the community with their families rather than removing them and placing them with a cohort of similarly emotionally disturbed children contributed to the difference in outcome measures. This is important because it validates the effectiveness of community-based services for youth.

Though there are some studies that provide support for community-based services for children and adolescents in crisis, only one study has provided treatment recommendations that could be used by crisis workers in the field. Evans et al. (2001) generated four profiles "to determine which interventions worked best for which children, irrespective of program assignment" (p. 38). The four profiles were: (1) young boys with disruptive behavior; (2) children with psychotic-related disorders and functional impairments; (3) adolescents with mood disorders and comorbid substance abuse; and (4) children with adjustment disorders and suicidal tendencies. The authors identified clinical implications for three of the four profiles. Children with psychotic-related symptoms (profile 2) would benefit from participation in longer-term programs to address poor self-concept. Parents of adolescents with a mental health disorder (profile 3) would benefit in improving their sense of self-efficacy. Children in profile 4 would benefit from services to develop their sense of competence.

Profiles providing clear clinical guidelines for treatment of youth at risk would be a welcome addition to the literature. Each of the programs discussed included treatment approaches that reduced symptomology, but the emphasis was on savings on hospital costs rather than which treatment approaches were the most efficacious and why they worked. The savings from the hospital bills would be well served to fund research identifying best practices for crisis workers who provide community-based services to youth in crisis. Until then, the best treatments for youth will continue to be anecdotal.

RESILIENCE AND PROTECTIVE FACTORS

There are many definitions of "resilience" and "protective factors." Masten, Best, and Garmezy (1990) define resilience as "the process of, capacity for, or outcome of successful adaptation despite challenging or threatening circumstances" (p. 425). They identify three circumstances that can demonstrate resilience: (1) overcoming the odds, (2) sustained competence under adversity, and (3) recovery from trauma. Luthar (1993) uses the phrase "protective factors" to identify factors that are present in high-risk children who exhibit positive rather than negative adjustment. Cummings, Davies, and Campbell (2000) cite Garmezy's (1985) three-part framework of protective factors:

> (1) *dispositional attributes within the child,* including temperament, personality traits, gender, coping styles, locus of control and self-esteem; (2) *family characteristics,* including family cohesion and warmth, positive parent-child relationships, and harmonious inter-parental relations; and (3) *domains of extrafamilial contexts,* including the availability of a positive adult figure (e.g. teacher), positive school experiences academically and socially, and safe, supportive neighborhoods. (p. 143)

One of the challenges in discussing crisis intervention is the translation of abstract concepts like resilience and protective factors into operational definitions. Put another way, how do we know resilience and protective factors when we see them? In this chapter, resilience and protective factors are identified and discussed in the context of the crisis intervention. Although this organizational approach might be frustrating to academics, it reflects the process and experience of the crisis worker and client.

CLINICAL PRESENTATION: ISSUES, CONTROVERSIES, ROLES, AND SKILLS

It is important that service providers are individually consistent and consistent among each other in crisis intervention. Clearly defined protocols reduce individual error and improve continuity of services over time (e.g., during a shift change or with the use of relief workers). Roberts (2002) developed an integrated intervention model called ACT, standing for assessment, crisis intervention, and trauma treatment. One of the protocols recommended in the first part of the model is a four-level Intervention Priority Scale developed by Community Integration, Inc. The level of intensity and lethality decreases as the priority number increases. "Each number on the scale corresponds to an outside time limit considered to be safe for crisis response" (p. 7).

Working with youth requires an understanding of child development. There are many different theories of development (Erikson, Piaget, Kohlberg, etc.), all of which are based on "normal" children. The following are ways in which normal adolescent development may influence a crisis situation (Hillman, 2002; Jobes, Berman, & Martin, 2000). Adolescents tend to be more impulsive than adults. This puts them at a higher risk for harm (to self and others). Adolescents often develop their identity through imitating others. Peer influence is significant. This can be beneficial or problematic, depending on the peer group the child is involved with. A unique theory of development is needed for children with serious mental illness.

Roberts's Seven-Stage Model

Roberts's (2000) seven-stage model provides an excellent framework within which to provide crisis intervention. A client in crisis is unable to think, feel, or act in ways that resolve the crisis. Four benefits to using Roberts's model are: (1) it provides a structure within which to organize data; (2) it serves the practitioner as a reminder of important areas to cover; (3) practitioners can spend their time and energy making decisions about techniques, strategies, and skills they will use; and (4) it can be validated and critiqued for efficacy. Myer's (2001) triage assessment model can be used as an adjunctive framework for assessment. A brief description of the model is included below.

Myer's Triage Assessment Model

Myer's (2001; Myer, Williams, Ottens, & Schmidt, 1992) triage assessment model focuses on three functional domains: affective (emotional), cognitive (thinking), and behavioral (actions). Each domain is assessed and rated on a 10-point scale, where 1 = no impairment and 10 = severe impairment. The three scores are added together to provide an overall severity rating. The higher the rating, the more impaired the client. In the affective domain, the crisis worker assesses the client's emotional reaction to the crisis based on three pairs of emotions: anger/hostility, anxiety/fear, and sadness/melancholy. If more than one pair of emotions is present, the crisis worker rates the emotions as primary, secondary, and tertiary. Accurate assessment of the primary emotion and the severity of impairment are invaluable in successful application of Roberts's fourth stage: dealing with feelings and providing support. For the cognitive domain, the crisis worker assesses the client's perception of how the crisis has affected, is affecting, or will affect his or her physical, psychological, social, and moral/spiritual life. For the behavioral domain, the crisis worker assesses the client's behavioral reaction to the crisis. Myer (2001) asserts that clients will use one of three behaviors: approach, avoidance, or immobility. Each can move the client toward or away from successful crisis resolution. "Approach behaviors are either overt or covert attempts to resolve the crisis. Avoidance behaviors ignore, evade, or escape the crisis event. Immobility refers to behaviors that are nonproductive, disorganized, or self-defeating attempts to cope with the crisis" (p. 30).

The following examples illustrate application of Roberts's seven-stage model with children and adolescents in crisis.

CASE STUDY 1: NIKKI

Stage 1: Assessing Lethality

When assessing for lethality, a crisis worker gathers data to determine whether the person in crisis is at risk for harm. Failure to assess for lethality is both a legal liability and a failure to provide a professional service (Bongar, 2002). Accurate assessment of lethality provides the crisis worker with a solid base from which to move forward with the crisis intervention. A professional assessment instills a sense of confidence in the client. There are three parts of the lethality assessment, although they are not sequential and, depending on the situation, not equally weighted. The assessment of self-harm is also known as a suicide assessment. The crisis worker must determine if there is *ideation* (thoughts about killing oneself), *intent* (desire to kill oneself), and *plan* (when and how to kill oneself, including the means). Ironically, during the assessment of self-harm, the crisis worker must be careful to avoid using the words "harm" and "hurt" when assessing for suicide. The difference between "I want to hurt myself" and "I want to kill myself" is significant. One suggests the infliction of pain to a sustained life; the other suggests the infliction of pain to end a life. The crisis worker who asks "Have you had thoughts of hurting yourself?" might elicit the verbalized "no" and the nonverbalized "I have no intention of hurting any more than I already do. I want to end my pain and I plan on ending it by killing myself." The crisis worker could instead ask, "During all that has happened in the past 24 hours, have you found yourself thinking that you would be better off dead?" In situations where rapport would be lost with the immediate questioning of suicide (e.g., assessment of grief), it is appropriate to ease into the suicide assessment. The following brief example demonstrates one way of moving from "harm" to "kill":

Crisis Worker: Have you had thoughts of hurting yourself?

Client: Yes.

Crisis Worker: Have you thought of committing suicide?

Client: Yes.

Crisis Worker: When did you first think of killing yourself?

Client: This morning.

Precise questions result in accurate data. This facilitates determining whether the possibility of self-harm exists.

Outpatient crisis units for children play a vital role in the community. As a mobile crisis unit, the CAPE team traveled to schools on a regular basis. In a recent study on school counselor preparedness to handle crises, Allen, Burt, and colleagues (2002) concluded that most school counselors feel "less than 'adequately prepared' to deal with crisis situations" (p. 4). Mobile crisis units can ensure that youth get the clinical attention they need during a crisis.

Working with children requires the crisis worker to use simple language and concepts:

Crisis Worker: Hi Nikki, my name is Jonathan. You know what I do all day? I talk with kids who say they are thinking of killing themselves. Some kids want to hurt or kill someone else. Others kids hear or see things that nobody else can hear or see.

Nikki: I ain't crazy like that.

Crisis Worker: Oh. So maybe I'm in the wrong place. How embarrassing (smile). Why do you think I'm here, then?

Nikki: (smiles) Because I drew that picture.

Crisis Worker: You know, Nikki, I think you're absolutely right about that. Before you tell me about the picture, I want to let you know that you can tell me almost anything and I won't tell anyone else. They will be just between you and me. There are some things I have to tell your mom, or Mr. Anderson. Can you guess what they are?

The caseworker's tone is playful, but the content is serious. By turning the review of confidentiality ("There are some things I have to tell your mom") into a game, the caseworker demonstrates to Nikki that he is speaking her language, the language of play (Gil, 1991). Because play is the major form of treatment for children under the age of 12, a bag of art supplies (large paper, markers, crayons, colored pencils) is an invaluable tool for the mobile crisis worker. The caseworker takes out some sheets of construction paper and markers. Nikki and the caseworker draw pictures as they talk.

Nikki reported that she had thoughts of killing herself while drawing the picture in the classroom, but did not have them at that moment. Her plan was to stab herself to death with a knife from her kitchen, as she had depicted in the drawing. She was unclear when she might kill herself: "Maybe I'll do it after Shante's birthday party [next month]." While suicidal ideation must be taken seriously, Nikki's time frame (next month) provided an important window of opportunity for intervention. She denied homicidal ideation and stated that she did not hear voices or see things that weren't there. Nikki met criteria for low risk for suicide.

The assessment of lethality in a family requires the assessment of both the parent and the child. Rudd, Joiner, and Rajab (2001) recommend evaluating the parents' ability to fulfill essential functions (e.g., provision of resources, maintenance of a safe and nonabusive home) and parenting functions (e.g., limit setting, healthy communication, and positive role modeling). The overall risk for harm will go up or down depending on the evaluation of the parent.

Although the assessment of lethality has not finished, the next part of the intervention, the initial meeting with Nikki's mom, Mrs. D, is best described under Stage 2.

Stage 2: Establishing Rapport and Communication

Rapport is a short way of saying that the practitioner and the client have developed "a state of understanding and comfort" between one another (Kanel, 2003, p. 30). Developing rapport might have started during Stage 1, as the client began to feel safer in his or her external environment. Rapport building continues throughout the intervention process. During the initial rapport-building stage, the crisis worker assures the client that he or she made the right decision by seeking help and that the crisis worker will provide some assistance to the problem. Kanel (p. 31) identifies five basic attending skills that are used in developing rapport in crisis situations: attending behavior (eye contact, warmth, body posture, vocal style, verbal following, and overall empathy); questioning (open- and closed-ended); paraphrasing (restatement, clarifying); reflection of feelings (painful, positive, ambivalent, nonverbal); and summarization (tying together the precipitating event, the subjective distress, and other cognitive elements). These attending skills can be used throughout the crisis intervention process. The following is the beginning of a 30-minute interview.

Crisis Worker: Mrs. D? I'm glad you could come to the school so quickly.

Mrs. D: (frowning) Uh, yeah. That's all right. What did she do now?

Crisis Worker: It sounds like you are not surprised that you were called to the school.

Mrs. D: (angry) Do I look surprised? The office people don't even have to look up my phone number.

Crisis Worker: What usually happens once you get up here?

Mrs. D: Do you have kids?

Crisis Worker: No, I don't.

Mrs. D: Well if you did, you wouldn't be asking foolish questions.

Crisis Worker: Sometimes we have to ask questions that seem foolish, Mrs. D. What usually happens when you get here?

Mrs. D: The principal gets all up in my face about teaching her manners.

Crisis Worker: And when you get home?

Mrs. D: (smiling) Nothing. It is all over by then. I'm not going to let her behavior ruin my day.

The interview with Mrs. D. suggested a number of things. First, rapport building will be crucial in engaging her in treatment. Second, as per Rudd, Joiner, and Rajab (2001), she was partially fulfilling essential functions, but not parenting functions. Specifically, she had been aware of Nikki's suicidal ideation for a couple of years but had never pursued treatment. She reported that "limit setting doesn't work." At the end of the interview, the caseworker had doubts about Mrs. D's ability to keep Nikki safe or to provide an environment that was relatively free of emotional triggers. In any situation where lethality is an issue, consultation with a supervisor is advised. Because the mom's evaluation raised the risk of lethality, the caseworker contacted his supervisor, who recommended that the family come in for an emergency evaluation with the psychiatrist. Mrs. D reluctantly agreed to travel with the caseworker back to the offices.

Stage 3: Identifying Major Problems

Nikki and her mother met the caseworker in the CAPE team office to complete a more thorough psychosocial assessment in preparation for the appointment with the psychiatrist. A useful technique in family assessment is to speak with each member separately and then together as a family. Another CAPE team worker stayed with Nikki while the caseworker and Mrs. D identified the major problems in their family. Mrs. D reported that she is a client of Adult Mental Health for bipolar disorder. According to her, Nikki's rage and anger was the biggest problem. As a result of her ongoing tantrums, the landlord served them an eviction notice before they left for school today.

Mrs. D: Right in front of Nikki he says that *she* has 30 days to stop breaking things and disturbing the neighbors or else she's going to have to find a new place to sleep. I was *so* angry with her. I told her she'd better get her act together and not get us kicked out.

Crisis Worker: It sounds like both you and the landlord were angry with Nikki. When you said that she'd better get her act together, did you let her know what exactly you meant by that and what her consequences would be if she didn't?

Mrs. D: (change in tone) Well, you know, she knows that I just mean not to be so loud and bothering the neighbors. I don't really give consequences.

The biggest problem emerging was Mrs. D's anger and how Nikki's internalizing of the anger resulted in suicidal ideation. There are two dynamics that emerge in suicidal children with parents with mental illness. The first is when a child becomes overwhelmed by the parent's anger; she sees suicide as a solution to her pain. The second dynamic is when the parent is on the verge of going into crisis and will be unable to take care of the child: the child goes into a crisis state, forcing the parent to "get her act together" and care for the child. More assessment and contact with the family was needed to determine if either dynamic was at play. These dynamics are examples of bidirectional family influence.

Mrs. D also shared information about Nikki's behavior at home. According to her, Nikki would go through rapid cycles of feeling happy and being violent and rageful (like this morning). Mrs. D stated that she did not think Nikki was bipolar, because Nikki's behavior was very different from her own experience of bipolar disorder.

The caseworker met with Nikki and determined that the precipitating event was the landlord's signing the eviction notice. When a precipitating event is so specific it is valuable to spend time in Stage 4: dealing with feelings, processing the thoughts and feelings that were triggered by the event. To continue identifying problems, the family agreed to speak with the psychiatrist about Nikki's anger and her suicidal ideation. The psychiatrist reviewed the intake assessment and determined that Nikki met criteria for bipolar disorder. She did not believe that Nikki posed a threat to herself at that time and therefore did not meet criteria for hospitalization. A safety plan was written down and a copy was given to Mrs. D. The family was instructed to contact 911 in case of an imminent threat to safety, or the 24-hour hotline if Nikki felt suicidal. The caseworker agreed to call the family that night to check in. The psychiatrist prescribed a mood stabilizer and twice-weekly therapy with a CAPE team caseworker. Because Mrs. D takes the bus to work, the caseworker agreed to meet after school at their house.

Stage 4: Dealing With Feelings and Providing Support

The plan was to discuss Nikki's suicidal ideation, explore feelings, and provide psychoeducation about bipolar disorder. Regular assessment of suicidal ideation is vital during a suicidal crisis. The caseworker is advised to ask the basic questions at every session: "Have you had thoughts of killing yourself today? If so, how and when? How important is it that you succeed?" Proper documentation of this routine assessment will provide excellent continuity of care when the case is transferred, as well as reduce the risk of a law suit in the event of a completed suicide (see Bongar, 2002).

There is a simple yet elegant tool for helping individuals and families better identify emotions. The "How Are You Feeling Today?" chart illustrates dozens of common emotions. A laminated version can be used for circling emotions with a dry-erase marker and for playing checkers. In a game of "Feelings" checkers, checkers are placed on the feeling faces. As players move to a new feeling they (1) identify the emotion; (2) talk about a time when they had that emotion; or (3) discuss a situation in which they think they might have that feeling. With children Nikki's age, a popular variation is requiring players to imitate the feeling face they land on.

During school visits, Nikki and the caseworker discussed bipolar disorder and explored emotions. For the first two weeks of services, however, Mrs. D refused to allow the caseworker to come into the house for the prearranged appointments. She also declined the caseworker's offer to meet at the school.

By the end of the second week there was no indication that either Mrs. D or Nikki was taking her medication. Mrs. D refused to sign a release of information so that Nikki's caseworker could coordinate services with Mrs. D's caseworker. In a more traditional therapy model, it is standard practice to ultimately refuse to provide services if the client is legally preventing the therapist from adequately doing his or her job. Services to crisis clients preclude the option of refusing services.

Stage 5: Exploring Possible Alternatives

During a typical Stage 5, clients explore alternatives to the problem. Because Mrs. D was refusing to participate in services, the caseworker decided to explore possible solutions for engaging the family. There is one reframe that, on occasion, has been successful in developing a therapeutic alliance with nonparticipating parents. The following dialogue illustrates the concept of "It's not you, it's them."

Crisis Worker: I'm wondering if you've noticed a change in Nikki's behavior.

Mrs. D: I wish, but no.

Crisis Worker: I've been thinking about this a lot. My job is to help you two develop some new coping skills and I'm failing you. As far as I can tell, things are as bad now as they were when I first met you.

Mrs. D: (skeptical) Mmm hmm.

Crisis Worker: Tell me if this is true: your parenting style would work really well with a different kid.

Mrs. D: My 10-year-old nephew listens to me; I don't see why she don't.

Crisis Worker: Exactly. So here's my thought. Your parenting is not the problem. The problem is that Nikki's behavior requires a different approach to parenting.

Mrs. D: Well, ain't that the truth.

Crisis Worker: I'm wondering if you can remember a time when you did something different that made a difference in the way you got along?

Mrs. D: One night I was so tired, instead of yellin' at her to sit down, I just let her run around the apartment. We didn't fight once that night.

There are a number of components that make this a successful intervention. The first is the caseworker's taking responsibility for the family's problems. It is as if he is temporarily holding a heavy bag that the family has lugged around for years. The second component is externalizing the problem: "It's not you, it's them." The third component is the use of the exception question. This helped Mrs. D to step back into the role of successful mother, even if for but a minute.

After this dialogue, Mrs. D opened her doors to treatment again. Nikki started taking her meds regularly and the caseworker brought over the Feelings checkerboard. The school reported that Nikki's behavior became more stable in the classroom. Due to the family's progress, the caseworker discussed transferring the family to FPP for home-based services.

Four weeks after the initial call, the weekend on-call worker was paged to Mrs. D's house. Nikki had cut herself with a dull cutting knife. She was transported to the emergency room. She was released with the recommendation that she "get some sleep." After consulting with the agency's on-call psychiatrist, the recommendation was made that she remain in the city, but that she live temporarily with her grandmother, with whom she has a wonderful relationship.

The caseworker implemented Stages 1 and 2 again. In Stage 3, he and Nikki explored the precipitating event for the recent suicide attempt. According to Nikki, on the day she tried to kill herself she had seen the landlord put a piece of paper under her mom's door. She assumed it was the eviction notice they had been threatened with four weeks earlier. It is very important to be aware of anniversary or trigger dates. The caseworker missed it, but Nikki remembered.

Because Nikki was temporarily living with her grandmother, the caseworker had an opportunity to gather new information about the family, including confirmation of Mrs. D's drug addiction and history of prostitution. With the new information, the caseworker invited Mrs. D to join the discussion about family problems, possible solutions, and the formulation of a new action plan.

Stage 6: Formulating an Action Plan

The action plan for the family after the second round of the seven-stage model included:

1. Weekly house meetings to discuss family issues and watch a movie together.
2. Taking medication regularly as directed.
3. Regular appointments for Mrs. D with her psychiatrist.
4. Regular attendance at NA meetings.
5. Transition to the Family Preservation Program.

Stage 7: Follow-up

The traditional term for the end of services with a client is "termination" (Hepworth, Rooney, & Larsen, 2001). For the brief but intense nature of crisis intervention, which almost always results in the client's moving on to another service, the term "transition" is a better fit. At the end of the second month, the caseworker met the family and their new FPP therapist for a transition session. The family discussed what they had learned during the course of the services. The caseworker shared his impressions of the family's strengths. Nikki had made no suicidal statements since the second crisis. She was no longer considered a risk to herself or others. The family was told that they could always contact crisis services in the future if they needed to.

The complexities of this case were easier to navigate because of Roberts's framework.

CASE STUDY 2: ROLANDO

Stage 1: Assessing Lethality

Assessment of harm to self was illustrated in the first case example. The second area of lethality is the assessment of harm to others: What is the likelihood that the client will hurt someone (including the crisis worker)? Whereas the suicidal client turns on himself or herself to deal with overwhelming hurt, anger, fear, and frustration, the homicidal client turns on others. As with the suicide assessment, the crisis worker should assess for ideation, intent, and plan to harm others. Except for the rare occasion when the client clearly verbalizes homicidal ideation, the crisis worker needs to listen for cues to possible violent behavior. Is the client blaming others for the current situation? Is he or she talking about "getting back" at someone for what has happened? Does the client have a history of violence against others? (If law enforcement knows the client by name, there is a good chance that there is a history of violence.) The crisis worker should check the surroundings for weapons (knives or guns) or possible weapons (heavy ashtrays, broken bottles, scraps of wood). Once the crisis worker has enough information to assess the client's response, he or she needs to ask specific questions about whether or not the client has thoughts of, intention of, and plan for harming others. The accurate assessment of lethality will simplify the decision for what to do next: move to Roberts's second stage (building rapport) or remove the person (leaving the building).

According to Roberts (2000), most initial contact in a crisis happens over the phone. As a crisis worker, the author found a number of specific benefits to providing crisis intervention over the phone, including the ability to complete assessments and read from a list of questions. Two of the most important benefits of phone counseling are illustrated in Rolando's case: being able to write notes without distracting the client and having simultaneous phone access to other service providers, including supervisors, psychiatrists, and the police.

The assessment of lethality is urgent in Rolando's situation. Lupe's stated reason for contacting the CAPE team was that she was fearful that Rolando would harm his brother. His medical records indicate a history of violence. For maximum safety of everyone involved (crisis workers included), we continued our intervention over the phone. In the following dialogue, Kim uses strengths-based language, open- and closed-ended questions to gather descriptions and specific information, and reflection of feeling to maintain rapport.

Crisis Worker: Lupe, what are you doing to keep yourself safe right now?

Lupe: (voice trembling) I took the phone into the bathroom.

Crisis Worker: I'm glad you're safe. Where are Rolando and his brother right now?

Lupe: Yellin' at each other in the other room.

Crisis Worker: Does Rolando have access to any knives or other weapons?

Lupe: The knives have been locked up since the last time. I don't think there is anything else in the house.

Crisis Worker: I'm glad to hear that. You take your family's safety seriously. What started all of this?

Lupe: I don't know. I think Hector was teasing Rolando. I'm kinda worried; Rolando's been acting real funny today, though.

Crisis Worker: You're worried about the way Rolando has been acting. Has he been taking his medication? Can you check his bottle? You're in the bathroom, right?

Lupe: *Ay no!* Kim, it looks like he hasn't taken his meds in at least a week. *¿Que vamos a hacer* [What are we going to do]? I'm afraid to leave the bathroom.

Crisis Worker: *No te preocupas* [Don't worry]. I hear the fear in your voice. You've been doing great so far tonight. I see no reason why that will change.

One of the challenges of crisis intervention is that, at any given time, the intervention can go in a number of directions. Without Roberts's framework to remind us that we have not finished our assessment of lethality, we might focus on Lupe's escalating anxiety and proceed with exploring emotions and providing support (Stage 4). Rather than ignore Lupe's experience, we use it to further our assessment of lethality. Lupe's statements provide us with valuable data about her own assessment of safety and her parental authority in the situation. Crises in families require an assessment of the child's safety as well as the parent's capacity and ability to protect (Rudd, Joiner, & Rajab, 2001).

Myer's (2001) triage assessment model assists in assessing Lupe's capacity to function. Her primary emotion is anxiety or fear, based on her use of the word "fear." Given the potential for violence in the situation, her affect is appropriate to the situation, with a brief escalation of emotions. On the affective severity scale she rates a 3 out of 10. Her cognitive domain is future-oriented and focused on safety: "What are we *going* to do?" She believes something terrible will happen because Rolando is not taking his medications. She demonstrates some difficulties with problem solving and making decisions. Her fears about the future are not without basis. On the cognitive severity scale she rates a 5 out of 10. Behaviorally she is immobile: she is unable to leave the bathroom to address the situation. Her behavior is exacerbating the situation; the longer she stays in the bathroom, the more chance there is that violence could occur. On the behavioral severity scale she rates an 8 out of 10. Myer's model helps us to interpret the data. By identifying the most severely impaired domain, we can prioritize our interventions. Based on our assessment, we determine that Lupe cannot be considered a protective factor in the current crisis.

Rapid response is a hallmark of crisis intervention. Like Kim, crisis workers need to be able to think on their feet. Recognizing Lupe's crisis state, Kim writes a note to me: "Should we call the police?" I write, "Ask Lupe if she's comfortable with the police coming. If so, tell her I'd like to speak with Rolando." Involving Lupe in the decision to call the police addressed her cognitive domain: we affirmed her authority as a parent and provided her the opportunity to make a decision. Asking her to leave the bathroom and hand the phone to Rolando addresses her immobility. There are three purposes in talking to Rolando. The first is to remove him from the offending environment (his brother and the living room). The second is to gather more information about his mental state, to involve him in the intervention, and to determine if he can contract for safety. Third, if Rolando is assessed to be a danger to others, he will not be in the living room when the police arrive.

I assessed Rolando's current functioning and mental status. He confirmed that he had stopped taking his meds, had been sleeping poorly, and had no appetite. He denied use of alcohol or other drugs. He reported that he had no thoughts of killing himself and stated that he would only hurt his brother, not kill him. He refused to contract for safety. The dialogue that follows indicated that the situation was not safe and it was appropriate for Kim to call the police.

Rolando: Hector won't stop talking about me. All the time, yo. He and his friends are always saying things about me behind my back. He needs to stop, dogg.

Crisis Worker: How do you know they are talking about you?

Rolando: I know. What, you don't believe me? (laughs, then becomes angry) I know what you're thinking. I know what they're all thinking. Even when they don't speak out loud I hear them.

Crisis Worker: I can understand how you'd be angry if you thought your brother and his friends were talking about you. If you're willing, I'm going to help you so that he doesn't talk about you anymore. Are we cool?

Rolando presents with delusions of reference, thought broadcasting, and paranoia, all clear indications of psychosis. The extent to which his paranoia is based on actual events or delusional thinking is unclear; medical records note that Hector takes pleasure in teasing Rolando for being "crazy." Rolando's presentation of psychosis, his stated intention to harm his brother, and his prior history of violence when not taking medication place him at a high potential for lethality. Using the Community Integration, Inc. Intervention Priority Scale (Roberts, 2002), we rate the call a Priority I because of the threat of imminent violence. Priority I requires the mobilization of emergency services to stabilize the situation. I write a note to Kim to page the on-call psychiatrist for a consultation and call the police. The psychiatrist confirmed that children will start to decompensate after a week or two of being off their meds. The psychiatrist recommended hospitalization to stabilize Rolando on his medications, stating that the last time he was hospitalized it took approximately a week for the antipsychotics to reduce both negative and positive symptoms associated with his psychosis. The police agreed to meet us at the house. Police involvement is crucial for three reasons: (1) police increase the safety for the family and the crisis workers; (2) the State of Texas requires children 16 years old and older to sign themselves in and out of treatment;[2] to follow through with the psychiatrist's recommendations, an emergency commitment by the police officer would be required; (3) police can safely transport the client to the hospital.

Rolando stays on the phone with us as we travel to his house. With the police present, he agrees to be transported to the hospital. The psychiatrist on call admits him to the adolescent unit and starts him on his meds. At Rolando's request and with the permission of the hospital, I agree to return for visits.

Stage 2: Establishing Rapport and Communication

The second stage in Roberts's seven-stage model is establishing rapport and communication. CAPE team workers had established rapport with Rolando and his family over the course of their involvement with the team two years earlier, after Rolando's first hospitalization. During the first meeting at the hospital since Rolando has been stabilized on his meds, the family shared with the caseworkers some of the elements that facilitated rapport building. The first two comments speak to the value of language and the importance of cultural competence in developing a working relationship (Clark, 2002; Fernandez et al., 2004):

Rolando: Man, you know what's cool? You [addressing the CAPE team caseworker] speak Spanish with my mom. None of the staff at the hospital can do that.

Lupe: Yeah, that's really nice. *¿Sabes que* [Do you know what]? I also like that you have *personalismo* [a warm and familiar way of relating to people].

Rolando: The best thing, dogg, is that you don't mind when I talk about some of the crazy thoughts I have. I know my world ain't like yours, but you cool with that.

Crisis Worker: I appreciate you saying all of those things. What's true is that one of your strengths as individuals and a family is that you have a great capacity to trust others.

Rolando's reference to his "world" is a common way for people with psychotic disorders to identify their experience (Fonagy et al., 2002). The caseworker's willingness to discuss Rolando's "crazy thoughts" is more important in developing and maintaining rapport than it is in providing relief from his auditory hallucinations.

The caseworker continued to provide cotherapy with the hospital staff for another week, at which time Rolando was discharged back to the community. He was no longer suffering from hallucinations or delusions. His focus was improved and he appeared more relaxed. Because his psychotic symptomology was managed, Rolando was able to address the psychodynamic issues that preceded the crisis.

Stages 3 and 4: Identifying Major Problems and Dealing With Feelings

The higher the level of family conflict, the more important it is to deal with feelings while identifying major problems. The identification of the precipitating event can bring up feelings as family members try to blame each other for the crisis. The crisis worker can use strengths-based techniques to normalize feelings and reconceptualize individual blame as group responsibility.

The following dialogue illustrates the use of strengths-based language as the crisis worker facilitates a conversation among the three family members:

Crisis Worker: Who would like to share their thoughts as to what kicked off this last round of stress?

Lupe: If Rolando would just take his medicine, this wouldn't keep happening.

Rolando: Mom, you say it like this was all my fault. What about Hector?

Hector: What about me? I didn't do anything.

Crisis Worker: One of the amazing things about families is that everyone can be in the same room, see and hear the same things, and have completely different memories of it. None of them are wrong, they are just different. Rather than talk about what happened before Lupe called the office last week, perhaps we can talk about what the family has been doing to keep things going well these past seven months.

Hoff (2001, p. 159) cautions crisis workers to avoid identifying one family member as the problem. She recommends identifying the entire family as the client. In this case, the client is no longer Rolando and the problem is no longer Rolando's schizophrenia. It is now a systemic issue with the whole family. This does not mean that Rolando's contribution to the family crisis should not be ignored. Hoff states, "Often an individual in crisis may precipitate a family crisis" (p. 137). The discussion of major problems allowed each member of the family to take responsibility for his or her role in the crisis. The caseworker's responsibility was to ensure that people felt safe. A safe environment is an environment where family members acknowledge each other's share, take responsibility in front of others, praise each other, and agree to work toward solutions.

Mediating conflict is important in maintaining a safe environment. When working with people with a diagnosis of schizophrenia, maintaining a calm and emotionally safe environment is crucial. "A fundamental defect of schizophrenic patients' brains is their frequent inability to sort, interpret, and respond like normal brains" (Torrey, 1988, p. 28). Stress makes symptoms of schizophrenia worse (Herz & Marder, 2002). In other words, the more activity in the house, the easier for Rolando's brain to have difficulty filtering the stimuli. The crisis worker worked with the family to create a safe environment for Rolando.

Family art therapy is an expressive therapy that is well suited for families with a child who has schizophrenia (Kwiatkowska, 2001). Although expressive therapies are difficult to evaluate using best-practices criteria, the components of art therapy (focused kinesthetic work expressing ideas) address the treatment goals of schizophrenia: developing social skills to reduce family conflict and increasing client participation in family activities. For a person with schizophrenia, creative or representational drawing can be a normalizing activity. The caseworker asked family members to draw a picture of (1) the family, (2) how they are feeling right now, (3) how they were feeling the night of the crisis, and (4) how they would like to feel. The caseworker set up ground rules for discussing the activity. According to Lupe, this was the first time in months that the family had laughed together; drawing is one of the few activities where criticism is seen as laughable (e.g., "Dude, you call that a sun? It looks Mom's *barbacoa.*"). While Rolando had a much more difficult time creating a recognizable picture of the family, his drawings of feelings were remarkable. His brother and mother had difficulty representing abstract concepts as well as he did. Rolando's pride in his accomplishments was a stepping stone to increased self-confidence.

Stage 5: Exploring Possible Alternatives

The family identified one precipitating factor and three main problems they would like to work on. The precipitating factor was Rolando's yelling at his mom to say that Hector had hidden his medication. When the family processed the precipitating factor, they were able to see the part that each played in the crisis. As an alternative to blaming, arguing, and escalating emotions, the family stated they would like to improve relationships between family members, reduce conflict between the brothers, and reduce the stimulation in the house. Korkeila et al. (2004) report a positive correlation between optimism in adulthood and reports of positive parent-child relationships. The clinical importance of working with families to develop positive parent-child relationships cannot be overemphasized. The development of optimism begins with a strong parent-child relationship. In addition to the family's suggestions, the caseworker recommended a fourth goal. Although this is not typical in traditional outpatient therapy, taking an active approach is appropriate in crisis intervention. The goal was to eliminate threats to family members. The caseworker explained that there could be no progress on the other goals until the family believed that they would all be safe. The family agreed to the goals.

The caseworker met with Rolando individually. The purpose was not to single him out as a problem, but to provide extra support given that he was transitioning from a most restrictive to a least restrictive environment. He discussed his frustration at having no close friends. Rather than having a long discussion about the issue, which can be challenging for people with problems processing information, the caseworker helped Rolando draw a sociogram. The sociogram is a genogram (McGoldrick, Gerson, & Shellenberger, 1999) that represents a person's social rather than familial world. Through the exercise, Rolando was able to identify friends with whom he could spend more time. Addressing social concerns is significant for people with schizophrenia. Youth with serious mental illness often need concentrated efforts to help them participate in social activities that are crucial for their psychosocial development.

Stage 6: Formulating an Action Plan

One challenge to crisis work with families is the programmatic limitation of 30 days per family. One of the goals of this family was to strengthen relationships. The caseworker recognized that to support that goal, the family would benefit most from longer-term services. The solution came in the form of a referral to the Family Preservation Program. Similar to the crisis unit, FPP is mobile and provides services in people's homes. The difference is that the FPP services are somewhat less intensive (twice a week compared to daily), but they are more long term. FPP provided individual and family therapy to address the ongoing concerns of the family.

Solution-focused therapy is well suited for Stage 6. One of the classic solution-focused techniques for setting goals is the miracle question (Berg & Miller, 1992):

> Suppose that after our meeting today you . . . go to bed. While you are sleeping a miracle happens and your problem is solved, like magic. The problem is gone. Because you were sleeping, you don't know that a miracle happened, but when you wake up tomorrow morning, you will be different. How will you know a miracle has happened? What will be the first small sign that tells you that a miracle has happened and that the problem is resolved? (p. 359)

The responses were as follows:

Lupe: I wouldn't have to yell, "*Mijo,* get out of bed. You're going to be late to school."

Rolando: Hector and I wouldn't yell at each other.

Crisis Worker: Instead of yelling, what do imagine doing differently?

Rolando: I don't know. Say nothing?

Hector: Rolando would be nice to me like he used to be.

The final step in the action plan was to have Lupe join the local chapter of the National Alliance for the Mentally Ill (NAMI). NAMI provides social support and has an educational function that can reduce stress and increase knowledge of disorders. Fonagy et al. (2002) note that best practices in the treatment of schizophrenia is family education about the illness.

Stage 7: Follow-up

The final stage of Roberts's model is follow-up. The final two sessions were very important in bringing closure to the crisis. The penultimate session reviewed the progress made by the family. The following dialogue illustrates termination work with the family:

Crisis Worker: What was one of the most important things you learned about yourself and the family as a result of this experience?

Lupe: My house is much more calm if I am calm. I never knew how important I was. I know that sounds silly, but it is true.

Rolando: I'm the most important person in the family! Nah, just kidding, dogg. For real, my brother is a nice guy.

Hector: When Rolando takes his meds and Mom goes to her meetings, I don't get so mad. I don't know why, but I just don't.

Crisis Worker: It sounds like all of you have learned a great deal in the last four weeks. I have one more question for you: Let's say you met a family that was going through the same things as you were going through when you first started CAPE services. What advice would have for them?

Rolando: I would tell them to take their meds. That's real important.

Lupe: I would tell the mom to do whatever she could to have the family involved with crisis services.

Hector: I'd tell them not to get in this situation in the first place. (everyone laughs)

The family was successful at meeting their goals and the goals of the program. There were no incidences of violence for the duration of the services. Lupe was able to build a new support network. Rolando stabilized on his meds and successfully increased his social circle. Hector demonstrated improved functioning at school as well as at home. When we met with the FPP, the goal was to maintain Rolando in the community by engaging the family in communication skills training and cognitive behavioral therapy. The crisis that had been so powerful and vivid four weeks earlier was a foundation on which the family had built a new way of interacting and being together as a family.

CASE STUDY 3: BRANDON

Stages 1 and 2: Assessing Lethality and Establishing Rapport

The third area of lethality is the assessment of whether the client is in danger of being harmed by those around him or her. The crisis worker can think about the connection between Stages 1 and 2 in the following way: in Stage 1, the crisis worker helps clients believe that their external world is safe (safe from harm to self or others or harm by others); in Stage 2, a feeling of safety is established between the crisis worker and the client. Once both external and interpersonal safety has been established, the crisis worker and client can work through the remaining stages to reestablish the client's internal safety. As with all of Roberts's stages, the assessment of lethality should be revisited if the crisis worker believes that the client's initial reports have changed or were not accurate to begin with.

Traveling to the shelter, the crisis worker wondered what threats to harm might be present with Brandon. In the United States, between 16% and 50% of homeless youth have attempted suicide (Votta & Manion, 2004). Mortality rates are reported to be 12 to 40 times greater than in the general population (Roy, Boivin, Haley, & Lemire, 1998; Shaw & Dorling, 1998, cited in Kidd, 2003). Rates of sexual and physical abuse rage from 35% to 45% (Votta & Manion, 2004). Violence toward homeless youth is also greater than for nonhomeless youth (Kidd, 2003). The possibilities for lethality with Brandon were great.

The need to establish rapport quickly is important when working with a homeless teenager. Most youth leave home because of a problem with the adult caretaker. There is a built-in distrust of adults and authority. Lambie (2004) suggests that adolescents' distrust of adults is often expressed by displays of defiance and hostility when first meeting counselors. A strengths perspective reframes their defiance as a protective factor: living on the street requires a healthy skepticism. Rapport building with adolescents is simplified when the crisis worker is familiar with adolescent culture (movies, music, stars, hobbies, etc.). Humor is similarly important. The crisis worker considered all of these factors as he drove up to the shelter.

In this initial meeting's dialogue, the crisis worker is careful to let the client know he is not going to be biased against him for being a kid:

Crisis Worker: Hey Brandon, my name is Jonathan. I work with kids who want to kill themselves, kill other people, or who are actively psychotic. Am I in the right place? (smile)

Brandon: I didn't ask you to come.

Crisis Worker: Yeah, the shelter supervisor called and said you threatened to run if the police were called and that you didn't care if you lived or died.

Brandon: Man, I hate it when adults talk for me.

Crisis Worker: You and me both. Tell me if this sounds about right. Adults think they have to be in charge, so they are always telling kids how to live. People like me have to listen to adults talk about how kids don't act right, when the adults were the ones who told the kids how to act in the first place.

Brandon: (holding back a smile).

Crisis Worker: I'd much rather hear your side of the story. Since I'm here, why don't you tell what's going on.

In this dialogue, the crisis worker uses a technique the author conceptualizes as "shooting bullets," where the crisis worker addresses (or shoots down) objections before they arise. In this situation, the objection would be "Why should I talk to you? You're an adult and you just don't understand."

There are some basic rules for working with adolescents in crisis and traditional counseling:

1. Let them know you are willing to listen, without interruption, to their story.
2. Reflect and restate more than question.
3. Empathize with their situation.
4. Provide them opportunities to take responsibility in the session and in their life.
5. Be honest when you think they are telling you what they think you want to hear. (Peterson, 1995)

After using basic attentive skills and explaining confidentiality, the crisis worker performed a suicide assessment. Brandon expressed passive suicidal ideation: "Life would be so much better if I woke up dead." He had no intent and no plan. He did have dozens of old scars on his arms and legs. When asked about them, he said that he used to cut on himself. As discussed in the first case study, suicide is an attempt to end intolerable pain. Adolescents who engage in cutting or other self-injurious behavior (SIB) cut on themselves to elicit pain (Selekman, 2002). SIB should be taken as an indicator of severe emotional and cognitive distress. Taken to the extreme (e.g., deep cuts), SIB can lead to death.

Crisis Worker: Is there anyone you are planning on harming?

Brandon: Not here.

Crisis Worker: Tell me more.

In this situation, restatement would have sounded too fake. Instead, the response conveys three things: (1) the ball is in his court; (2) the crisis worker is interested; and (3) there is no judgment or fear about discussing the topic. Brandon explains that he would "do anything" to make his mom's boyfriend suffer. He reports ongoing abuse and humiliation; he left California because of an incident with the boyfriend. Brandon was determined to not be at risk for killing himself, harming others, or being harmed by others. If the discussion of returning to California came up, the issue of lethality would need to be revisited.

Stage 3: Identifying Major Problems

The crisis worker is interested in finding the precipitating event, or the straw that broke the camel's back. The crisis worker who is not used to the immediacy of crisis response might be uncomfortable eschewing the past for the present. It is the present, however, that will provide the necessary data with which to resolve the crisis. The client, by virtue of being in crisis, is in a state of disequilibrium and will likely have a difficult time deciding what are the most important problems to address.

With Brandon, identifying the precipitating event required a careful review of recent events in his life. Because homeless youth experience so many challenges to their basic functioning (physical and sexual abuse, prostitution, chemical dependency, street violence, hunger, etc.), the tendency is to assume that anything in their daily experience could be the precipitating event. It is important to remember that precipitating events directly precede the crisis. Still, it was a challenge identifying the precipitating event because Brandon was reluctant to talk about why he left California. Listen as the crisis worker uses the "I don't know" technique (G. Maddox, personal communication, April 4, 1997) to maintain rapport and break through the resistance:

Crisis Worker: What happened that made you want to leave?

Brandon: Dunno.

Crisis Worker: Is it that you really don't know, or you just don't want to tell me? If you don't know, I can help you figure it out. On the other hand, if you don't want to tell me, let me know. I respect you and wouldn't ask you to tell me anything you are not comfortable with. I just ask that you respect me by being honest.

Brandon: Okay. I don't want to tell you.

In fact, the caseworker never learned what the exact precipitating event was. The important thing is that Brandon knew what the precipitating event was. We explored the severity of the event using negative scaling questions. This variation of the solution-focused technique of scaling questions is useful when discussing something horrible. In the author's experience, teenagers, in general, respond well to these questions.

Crisis Worker: On a scale from –1 to –10, with –1 being bad to –10 being the worst ever, what would you rate the event?

Brandon: –7.

Crisis Worker: Wow. What would be a –10?

Brandon: If he kills my mom.

Crisis Worker: (lengthy silence, looking at Brandon) That would be a –10, wouldn't it?

Brandon explained that he was not sure if his mother was in danger or not. The caseworker explained that he was under no legal obligation to warn.[3] Brandon stated with more confidence that he was pretty sure his mom was safe. For many homeless youth, returning to their home places them in greater danger than if they remain on the street (Kidd, 2003). One example of Brandon's resilience is his decision to leave a dangerous situation. Many street kids can be seen as survivors who took their future into their own hands.

Exploration of the precipitating event led up to a discussion of current problems. These primarily involved meeting his basic needs: food, shelter, and clothing. Now that problems had been identified and rapport was firmly established, we were in a good position to begin addressing feelings.

Stage 4: Dealing With Feelings and Providing Support

Roberts's model does not contain a stage for dealing with cognitive and behavioral elements of a crisis. Myer's (2002) triage assessment model is a useful tool to ensure that the crisis worker is getting a thorough assessment.

Crisis Worker: Brandon, we've been talking for almost two hours and I can't tell how you feel. Are you happy, scared, angry, sad, or something in between?

Brandon: I'll tell you how I feel. I feel like I can't go home anymore. My mom is probably disowning me because I'm not there to keep him from turning her against me. I don't have any friends. Not that it matters. I'm outta here soon.

Crisis Worker: You sound sad and angry.

Brandon: What? Are you on crack? I never even said those things. Dude, have you been listening to me? What kind of shrink are you?

Crisis Worker: (oops look on face) Hmmm. I kinda blew that one, didn't I?

Brandon: Now that's funny.

There are a number of important components to this dialogue. The first is that Brandon made a common mistake; he used the word "feel" when he was describing a thought rather than a feeling. Words that follow "I feel" should be physical sensations or emotions. The phrase "I feel like . . ." is a clue that the client is about to provide insight into his cognitive domain.

The second component is that Brandon provided valuable information with which to assess his behavioral and cognitive domain with Myer's (2001) triage assessment model. When he said, "I'm outta here soon," he suggested a pattern of behavior that he had demonstrated before. Leaving California was a clear behavioral example of what Myer calls "approach": Brandon behaves in ways that he believes will ameliorate the crisis. He provided a great deal of information about his cognitive state. He believes that he *lost* his home when he left (past). He believes that he *will* lose his relationship with his mom (future). He has no friends (present).

The final area for assessment is emotions. Although there are no specific verbal clues to his emotional state, Brandon provided a number of visual clues. Since the start of the assessment, he had clenched his jaw and squeezed his hand into a fist. While talking about his mom's boyfriend his face became red and his breathing quickened. These visual cues, in conjunction with his statement about wanting to hurt the boyfriend, are good indications that he has a great deal of anger. His ability to control his anger might be a protective factor in an environment where anger is responded to with violence.

The third component is that the caseworker failed to respect Brandon's distrust of displaying emotions. The use of self-deprecating humor avoided a significant loss of rapport.

Providing validation is made easier once data have been gathered from the triage assessment model. In the following dialogue, the caseworker validates and supports Brandon. In doing so, he opens the door to exploring possible alternatives (Roberts's Stage 5).

Crisis Worker: One of the things I'm really impressed by, Brandon, is your approach to solving problems: You get yourself out of a bad situation in California. You found the shelter in Austin and you agreed to talk with me. All of those things are real strengths.

Brandon: (silent, eyes moving around nervously).

Crisis Worker: (recognizing Brandon's discomfort with praise, reframes the silence) I also appreciate you letting me say some of these things without interruption. That's a skill that not many people have.

Brandon: Thanks.

Crisis Worker: I also know that you are concerned about having to leave the shelter. I have the same questions you do: Where will I go? Will I be safe? How will I survive? *If* you are willing, I'd be happy to talk about some possible solutions to these problems.

Brandon: Okay.

Used Myer's triage assessment model provides the caseworker with data about Brandon's functioning. At the end of the intervention, the caseworker assesses Brandon again. Although the details are somewhat different, Brandon has shifted slightly in his affective impairment; he jokes with the caseworker that he will be sad to leave Austin. Without using the assessment tool, it would be easy for a crisis worker to overlook a comment like that and miss the significance of that shift.

Stage 5: Exploring Possible Alternatives

During this stage, it is important to explore past successes. In their chapter on solution-focused crisis intervention, Greene, Lee, Trask, and Rheinscheld (2000) discuss five solution-focused techniques that are appropriate in this stage: scaling questions, exception questions, past success, coping questions, and compliments. According to Kidd (2003), coping styles of homeless youth can be divided into "emotion-focused" or "problem-focused." Emotion-focused coping refers to coping with the outcome of the stressor, such as reducing anxiety by pretending that a problem does not exist. Problem-focused coping is regarded as more effective and involves taking steps to reduce or eliminate the stressor itself (e.g., checking into a substance abuse clinic; Kidd, 2003, p. 241). One of the challenges, then, for crisis workers in the fifth stage is getting homeless youth to focus on their problems.

Even if we cannot name the steps in the process, most adults know how to problem-solve. Many youth have not yet learned these steps. The author found it useful to write out the problem-solving steps on a piece of paper. Clients in crisis have difficulty remembering and focusing; this is particularly true with homeless youth. Having the steps on a piece of paper that they can take with them reduces the number of things they need to remember. It also provides a structured activity during the session.

The following dialogue illustrates the psychoeducational process of teaching the problem-solving method. Notice the use of the solution-focused technique of past successes.

Crisis Worker: Now that we have identified the problem as "I don't have a place to live," we brainstorm solutions. Tell me whatever comes to mind, as strange as they might sound, and we'll write them down. When we're done, we'll go back and evaluate which alternative would be the best solution.

Brandon: You could give me a thousand dollars. My mom could get rid of her boyfriend and come get me. The shelter could let me stay. I could hitchhike to the next town and stay in their shelter until they kick me out. . . . I can't think of any others.

Crisis Worker: I'm impressed with how quickly you came up with that list. You mentioned that you and your mom were homeless when you were a kid. Tell me about a time when you and your mom got off the streets.

Brandon: A couple of times Mom and I went and stayed at her cousin's house.

Crisis Worker: Great! So another alternative is to contact your relatives and see if you could stay with them.

Brandon's behavioral coping style, approach, is reflected by his choice of possibilities. Approach is not always a healthy behavioral coping style (e.g., if he actively sought out drugs or alcohol), but in Brandon's situation, he is making healthy choices. If a client is sufficiently cognitively impaired, the crisis worker will have to be more active in providing alternatives. Stage 5 can be an exciting and rewarding stage if the previous stages have been adequately addressed. If the crisis worker has difficulty engaging the client in exploring alternatives, it will be necessary to either reexamine the problem or address affect, cognitions, or behaviors that get in the way of looking forward.

Stage 6: Formulating an Action Plan

The creation of an action plan based on the alternatives generated in Stage 5 is a two-part process. First, support the client to develop specific actions based on the alternatives. Second, ensure that the steps are realistic, measurable, and have built-in support. The question "How will you know when you have achieved your goal?" is useful in evaluating the action steps. The following is Brandon's action plan:

1. *Problem:* I have no where to live.
   Solution: Call Aunt Fancy in North Carolina by tomorrow afternoon and ask if I can stay with her.
   Support: The caseworker will stop by tomorrow to see if I've made the call.
2. *Problem:* Mom doesn't know where I am.
   Solution: Write a letter this afternoon and tell her I'm safe.
   Support: Shelter staff will give me stamps and envelopes. They will collect my letter tomorrow morning and mail it for me.
3. *Strength:* I am good at solving my problems.
   Plan: When I get stuck I will sit down with a pen and paper and write out all the possible alternatives to my problem.
   Support: If I'm on the street, I'll call the runaway hotline.

Brandon's action plan addressed his immediate concerns and delineated one of his coping strategies.

It was important to have regular contact with Brandon. The caseworker and Brandon decided that daily visits were appropriate until his aunt sent for him. The shelter staff agreed that he could stay there until his mom contacted the shelter.

Stage 7: Follow-up

The last stage of Roberts's model is follow-up. In all clinical relationships, closure is important. It is a time when the crisis worker can provide final feedback about progress and the client can provide feedback about what has changed in his or her life. For many clients, formal closure is one of the few times when a close relationship has had a formal ending. The process of getting closure allows the client to look forward without regret or a sense of loss. The experience is just as valid a therapeutic tool as any implemented in the previous six stages.

Brandon's history suggested that he had never had closure with any relationship. To ensure that closure would happen, the caseworker taught Brandon the meaning of closure. He was informed of the questions that would be asked of him during the last session and was prompted to think of things to say to the caseworker.

When the letter arrived from North Carolina with a bus ticket, Brandon was ready for closure. He and the caseworker reviewed their services and Brandon stated that he was very happy with his progress but sad to leave.

SUMMARY AND CONCLUSION

This chapter looked at the use of mobile crisis response with children and adolescents. Because the empirical information is so sparse, it may be useful to think of this chapter as a guide to the issues and factors that need to be addressed in crisis intervention with children and adolescents. Roberts's seven-stage crisis intervention model and Myer's triage assessment model were discussed and examples of their use were provided. Examples of effective solution-focused techniques were integrated into the interventions. We discussed the complicating factor of mental illness in the treatment of children and adolescents. Examples of crisis intervention over the phone, in schools, at home, in the hospital, and in a homeless shelter were presented. The breadth of topics precluded an in-depth discussion of any one issue. When possible, sources for further study were provided.

If you find yourself overwhelmed by the amount of information presented, we encourage you to take a deep breath. Part of learning how to deal with crises involves increasing your own coping skills as a professional. Be yourself. Stay current with the literature. Seek supervision whenever possible. Allow yourself to take in the amazing gift of watching persons in crisis rediscover themselves.

The need for crisis intervention course work at the undergraduate and graduate levels is more important than ever before. Roberts (2002) reports that "only a handful [of the 137 Masters of Social Work programs] . . . offer a one-semester course in crisis intervention" (p. 4). Why stop at a single afternoon presentation on crisis intervention by a group of graduate students? The breadth of crises faced by children and adolescents requires a breadth of training that does not exist in graduate schools. Myer (2001) put it best when he said that the only client a mental health provider is sure to work with is a client in crisis. At the same time, training crisis workers in how to respond to children and adolescents in crisis is an empty gesture if there is nowhere for the kids to go and nowhere for the graduates to work. Haugh (2003) reports a decrease in outpatient crisis mental health facilities for children.

While mental health services exist for adults and children separately, there are very few programs that conceptualize and implement intervention in a family-centered context (Hinden et al., 2002). Nicholson et al. (2001) identified 18 programs in the United States that focus specifically on providing services to families in which a parent has a mental illness. The authors concluded that "family-centered, strengths-based values and practices may be the central key ingredients to program success and improved outcomes for parents and children" (p. 13). In this day of managed care, the need for streamlined services and effective protocols is more important than ever. Addressing the crisis and the underlying serious mental illness (SMI) will reduce the crisis-inducing symptoms, thereby reducing the reliance of the family on the social services system, increasing the time available to work with other families and freeing the clients to live their own life. To this end, future research should include efficacy studies of treatment interventions where the focus is on treatment and not the amount saved in diverted hospitalizations. Crisis workers know when a specific intervention has been successful based on a feeling, an energy between themselves and their client. What we don't know, however, is whether that feel-good moment increases the long-term happiness, productivity, or overall satisfaction of the client. In a provocative challenge to current models of crisis intervention, Rogers and Soyka (2004) assert, "Our structured and mechanistic models for assessment and intervention with suicidal clients inadvertently contribute to their continued suicidality" (p. 9). Without knowledge of the effectiveness of our interventions, could not the same be said for crisis intervention in general?

NOTES

1. In July and August 2004, an EBSCO search of PsychINFO, Medline, ERIC, Academic Search Premier, and Psychology and Behavioral Sciences Collection, using a combination of key words (crisis, intervention, psychiatric, emergency, child, adolescent, family, pediatric, home-based, family preservation program, services, evidence-based, empirical, therapy, intervention, techniques, mobile, and community), resulted in hundreds of articles, none of which specifically addressed the treatment issues discussed in this chapter.

2. In September 2003, the laws in Texas changed. Minors up to age 18 could be admitted or released from an in-patient setting only with permission from their legal guardian or a judge's order.

3. In 1999 the Texas Supreme Court, in *Thapar v. Zezulka,* ruled that mental health providers in Texas do not have a duty to warn in cases of harm to others.

REFERENCES

Allen, M. H., Burt, K., Bryan, E., Carter, D., Orsi, R., & Durkan, L. (2002). School counselors' preparation for and participation in crisis intervention. *Professional School Counseling, 6*(2), 96–103.

Allen-Meares, P., Colarossi, L., Oyserman, D., & DeRoos, Y. (2003). Assessing depression in childhood and adolescence: A guide for social work practice. *Child and Adolescent Social Work Journal, 20*(1), 5–20.

American Psychiatric Association. (1994). *Diagnostic and statistic manual of mental disorders* (4th ed.). Washington, DC: Author.

Beardslee, W. R., & Podorefsky, D. (1988). Resilient adolescents whose parents have serious affective and other psychiatric disorders: Importance of self-understanding and relationships. *American Journal of Psychiatry, 145*(1), 63–69.

Berg, I. K., & Miller, S. D. (1992). *Working with the problem drinker: A solution-focused approach.* New York: Norton.

Biederman, J., Faraone, S. V., Hirshfield-Becker, D. R., Friedman, D., Robin, J. A. & Rosenbaum J. F. (2001). Patterns of psychopathology and dysfunction in high-risk children of parents with panic disorder and major depression. *American Journal of Psychiatry, 158*(1), 49–57.

Birmaher, B., Ryan, N. D., Williamson, D., Brent., D. A., Kaufman, J., Dahl, R. E., et al. (1996). Childhood and adolescent depression: A review of the past 10 years. Part I. *Journal of the American Academy of Child and Adolescent Psychiatry, 35,* 1427–1439.

Bongar, B. (2002). *The suicidal patient: Clinical and legal standards of care* (2nd ed.). Washington, DC: American Psychological Association.

Brennan & Walker, 2001

Burns, B., Hoagwood, K., & Mrazek, P. (1999). Effective treatment for mental disorders in children and adolescents. *Clinical Child and Family Psychology Review,* 2(4), 199–252.

Center for Mental Health Services. (2001). Knowledge exchange network: Childrens' and adolescents' mental health. Retrieved online on August 2, 2004 at http://www.mentalhealth.org/publications/allpubs/CA-0004/default.asp.

Clark, Lauren. (2002). Mexican-origin mothers. *Western Journal of Nursing Research,* 24(2), 159–180.

Center for Mental Health Services. (1999). *Annual Report to Congress on the Evaluation of the Comprehensive Communtiy Mental Health Services for Children and Their Families Program, 1999.* Atlanta, GA: ORC Macro.

Comprehensive Community Mental Health Services for Children and Their Families Program, 1998

Cox, A. D., Puckering, C., Pound, A., & Millis, M. (1987). The impact of maternal depression in young children. *Journal of Child Psychology and Psychiatry,* 28(6), 917–928.

Cummings, E. M., Davies, P. T., & Campbell, B. S. (2000). *Developmental psychopathology and family process: Theory, research, and clinical implications.* New York: Guilford Press.

Eaton, Y. M., & Ertl, B. (2000). The comprehensive crisis intervention model of Community Integration, Inc. Crisis Services. In A. R. Roberts (Ed.), *Crisis intervention handbook* (pp. 31–55). New York: Oxford University Press.

Evans, M. E., Boothroyd, R. A., & Armstrong, M. I. (1997). Development and implementation of an experimental study of the effectiveness of intensive in-home crisis services for children and their families. *Journal of Emotional and Behavioral Disorders,* 5(2), 93–105.

Evans, M. E., Boothroyd, R. M. I., Greenbaum, P. E., Brown, E. C., Armstrong, M. I., & Kippinger, A. D. (2001). Outcomes associated with clinical profiles of children in psychiatric crisis enrolled in intensive, in-home interventions. *Mental Health Services Research,* 3(1), 35–44.

Evans, M. R., Boothroyd, R. A., Armstrong, M. I., Greenbaum, P. E., Brown, E. C., & Kippinger, A. D (2003). An experimental study of the effectiveness of intensive in-home crisis services for children and their families: Program outcomes. *Journal of Emotional and Behavioral Disorders,* 11(2), 92–102, 121.

Fernandez, A., Schillinger D., Grumbach K., Rosenthal, A., Stewart, A. L., Wang, F., et al. (2004). Physician language ability and cultural competence: An exploratory study of communication with Spanish-speaking patients. *Journal of General Internal Medicine,* 19(2), 167–174.

Fonagy, P., Target, M., Cotrell, D., Phillips. J., & Zarrina, K. (2002). *What works for whom? A critical review of treatments for children and adolescents.* New York: Guilford Press.

Garmezy, N. (1985). Stress-resistant children: The search for protective factors. In J. E. Stevenson (Ed.), *Recent research in developmental psychopathology* (pp. 213–233). Oxford: Pergamon Press.

Gil, E. (1991). *The healing power of play: Working with abused children.* New York: Guilford Press.

Goodman, S. H., & Brumley, H. E. (1990). Schizophrenic and depressed mothers: Relational deficits in parenting. *Developmental Psychology, 26*(1), 31–39.

Goodman, S. H., & Gotlib, I. H. (1999). Risk for psychopathology in the children of depressed mothers: A developmental model for understanding mechanisms of transmission. *Psychological Review, 106*(3), 458–490.

Greene, G., Lee, M., Trask, R., & Rheinscheld, J. (2000). How to work with clients' strengths in crisis intervention: A solution-focused approach. In A. R. Roberts (Ed.), *Crisis intervention handbook* (pp. 31–55). New York: Oxford University Press.

Greenfield, B., Hechtman, L., & Tremblay, C. (1995). Short-term efficacy of interventions by a youth crisis team. *Canadian Journal of Psychiatry, 40*(6), 320–324.

Gutstein, S. E., Rudd, M. D., Graham, J. C., & Rayha, L. L. (1988). Systemic crisis intervention as a response to adolescent crisis: An outcome study. *Family Process, 27*(2), 201–211.

Hammen, C., Burge, D., & Adrian, C. (1991). Timing of mother and child depression in a longitudinal study of children at risk. *Journal of Consulting and Clinical Psychology, 59*(2), 341–345.

Hammen, C., Burge, D., & Stansbury, K. (1990). Relationship of mother and child variables to child outcomes in a high-risk sample: A causal modeling analysis. *Developmental Psychology, 26*(1), 24–30.

Haugh, R. (2003). A crisis in adolescent psych. *Hospitals and Health Networks, 77*(1), 38–41.

Henggeler, S., Rowland, M., Randall, J., Ward, D., Pickrel, S., Cunningham, P., et al. (1999). Home-based multisystemic therapy as an alternative to the hospitalization of youths in psychiatric crisis: Clinical outcomes. *Journal of the American Academy of Child and Adolescent Psychiatry, 38*(11), 1331–1339.

Hepworth, D. K., Rooney, R. H., & Larsen, J. (2001). *Direct social work practice: Theory and skills* (6th ed.). Chicago, IL: Dorsey Press.

Herz, M. I, & Marder, S. R. (2002). *Schizophrenia: Comprehensive treatment and management.* New York: Lippincott, Williams & Wilkins.

Hillman, J. L. (2002). *Crisis intervention and trauma: New approaches to evidence-based practice.* New York: Kluwer Academic/Plenum.

Hinden, B. et al. (2002). *Steps toward evidence-based practices for parents with mental illness and their families.* Rockville, MD: Substance Abuse and Mental Health Services Administration.

Hoff, L. (2001). *People in crisis: Clinical and public health perspectives* (5th ed.). San Francisco: Jossey-Bass.

Jobes, D., Berman, A., & Martin, C. (2000). Adolescent suicidality and crisis intervention. In A. R. Roberts (Ed.), *Crisis intervention handbook* (pp. 131–151). New York: Oxford University Press.

Kanel, K. (2003). *A guide to crisis intervention* (2nd ed.). Pacific Grove, CA: Brooks/Cole.

Keitner, G. I., & Miller, I. W. (1990). Family functioning and major depression: An overview. *American Journal of Psychiatry, 147*(9), 1128–1137.

Kidd, S. A. (2003). Street youth: Coping and interventions. *Child Adolescent Social Work Journal,* 20(4), 235–261.

Korkeila, K., Kivela, S.-L., Suominen, S., Vahtera, J, Kivimaki, M., Sundell, J., et al. (2004). Childhood adversities, parent-child relationships and dispositional optimism in adulthood. *Soc Psychiatry Psychiatric Epidemiology, 39,* 286–292.

Kwiatkowska, H. Y. (2001). Family art therapy: Experiments with a new technique. *American Journal of Art Therapy, 40*(1), 27–40.

Lambie, G. W. (2004). Motivational enhancement therapy: A tool for professional school counselors working with adolescents. *Professional School Counseling,* 7(4), 268–277.

Lewinsohn, P. M., & Clarke, G. N. (1999). Psychosocial treatments for adolescent depression. *Clinical Psychology Review, 19,* 329–342.

Lewinsohn, P. M., Rohde, P., Klein, D., & Seely, J. R. (1999). Natural course of adolescent major depressive disorder: I. Continuity into young adulthood. *Journal of the American Academy of Child and Adolescent Psychiatry, 38,* 56–63.

Luthar, S. S. (1993). Annotation: Methodological and conceptual issues in research on childhood resilience. *Journal of Child Psychology and Psychiatry, 34,* 441–453.

Masten, C. A., Best, K., & Garmezy, N. (1990). Resilience and development: Contributions from the study of children who overcome adversity. *Development and Psychopathology, 2,* 425–444.

McGoldrick, M., Gerson, R., & Shellenberger, S. (1999). *Genograms: Assessment and intervention.* New York: Norton.

Morrison, J., & Anders, T. F. (2001). *Interviewing children and adolescents: Skills and strategies for effective DSM-IV diagnosis.* New York: Guilford Press.

Myer, R. A. (2001). *Assessment for crisis intervention: A triage assessment model.* Pacific Grove, CA: Brooks/Cole.

Myer, R. A., Williams, R. C., Ottens, A. J., & Schmidt, A. E. (1992). Crisis assessment: A three-dimensional model for triage. *Journal of Mental Health Counseling, 14,* 137–148.

Nicholson, J., Biebel, K., Hinden, B., Henry, A., & Stier, L. (2002). *Critical issues for parents with mental illness and their families*. Rockville, MD: Center for Mental Health Services, Substance Abuse and Mental Health Services Administration.

Peterson, E. (1995) Communication barriers: 14 tips on teens. The national Parenting Center. Retrieved online August 1, 2004, at http://www.tnpc.com/parentalk/adolescence/teens49.html

Radke-Yarrow, M., McCann, K., DeMulder, E., Belmont, B., Martinez, P. & Richardson, D. T. (1995). Attachment in the context of high-risk conditions. *Development and Psychopathology,* 7(2), 247–265.

Roberts, A. R. (2000). An overview of crisis theory and crisis intervention. In A. R. Roberts (Ed.), *Crisis intervention handbook: Assessment, treatment, and research* (2nd ed., pp. 3–30). New York: Oxford University Press.

Roberts, A. R. (2002). Assessment, crisis intervention, and trauma treatment: The integrative ACT intervention model. *Brief Treatment and Crisis Intervention, 2*(1), 1–22.

Roberts, A. R. (Ed.). (2004). *Crisis intervention handbook: Assessment, treatment, and research* (2nd ed.). New York: Oxford University Press.

Roberts, A. R. (2004). Crisis assessment measures and tools. In A. R. Roberts & K. Yeager (Eds.), *Evidence-based practice manual: Research and outcome measures in health and human services* (pp. 496–503). New York: Oxford University Press.

Rogers, J. R., & Soyka, K. M. (2004). "One size fits all": An existential-constructivist perspective on the crisis intervention approach with suicidal individuals. *Journal of Contemporary Psychotherapy, 34*(1), 8–22.

Roy, E., Boivin, J. F., Haley, N., & Lemire, N. (1998). Mortality among street youth. *Lancet, 352,* 32.

Rudd, D. M, Joiner, T., & Rajab, H. M. (2001). *Treating suicidal behavior: An effective, time-limited approach*. New York: Guilford Press.

Selekman, M. D. (2001). *Living on the razor's edge: Solution-oriented brief family therapy with self-harming adolescents.* New York: Norton.

Silverman, M. M. (1989). Children of psychiatrically ill parents: A prevention perspective. *Hospital and Community Psychiatry, 40*(12), 1257–1265.

Springer, D. W. (2002). Assessment protocols and rapid assessment instruments with troubled adolescents. In A. R. Roberts & G. J. Greene (Eds.), *Social workers' desk reference* (pp. 217–221). New York: Oxford University Press.

Thapar v. Zezulka. (1999). Retrieved August 2, 2004, from http://faculty.smu.edu/tmayo/thapar.htm.

Torrey, E. F. (1988). *Surviving schizophrenia: A family manual.* New York: Harper & Row.

U.S. Public Health Service. (2001). *Report of the Surgeon General's Conference on Children's Mental Health: A national action agenda.* Washington, DC: Department of Health and Human Services; 2000. Retrieved August 2, 2004 from www.surgeongeneral.gov/topics/cmh/childreport.htm.

Votta, E., & Manion, I. (2004). Suicide, high-risk behaviors, and coping style in homeless adolescent males' adjustment. *Journal of Adolescent Health, 34,* 237–243.

Wilmshurst, L. A. (2002). Treatment programs for youth with emotional and behavioral disorders: An outcome study of two alternate approaches. *Mental Health Services Research, 4*(2), 85–96.

16

Crisis Intervention With Early Adolescents Who Have Suffered a Significant Loss

M. SIAN O'HALLORAN
ANN M. INGALA
ELLIS P. COPELAND

This chapter uses three examples to examine crisis intervention with early adolescents. We identify important developmental considerations in assessment, planning, and intervention and apply Roberts's (2000, 2004) seven-stage crisis intervention model in working with significant losses in the lives of youth. The losses we focus on are the death of loved ones, divorce, and the impact of exposure to violence outside the home; however, many of the issues we address can be generalized to other types of crises.

Adolescence is a time of significant physical, social, and psychological change (Weisz & Hawley, 2002). Because change is occurring rapidly during this period of life, writers in the field of adolescent psychology often divide this time into three periods: early adolescence, from about the age of 11 to 14; middle adolescence, from about 15 to 18; and late adolescence, roughly from 18 through 21 (Steinberg, 1996). We focus on the first of these, early adolescence.

Some of the fundamental developmental tasks of adolescents include developing a sense of identity, including clarification of values and a sense of purpose. Erik Erikson (1959, 1963, 1968) wrote extensively on adolescent identity, and the reader is referred to his work on the eight stages of psychosocial development. During a time of already rapid change, the adolescent who is facing a crisis may be more seriously impacted than a person at a different developmental stage. Steinberg and Lerner (2004) refer to the shift in the field of developmental psychology to thinking of adolescence as a period "characterized by dramatic changes in the context, and not simply the content, of development" (p. 49), emphasizing that conflict with parents and siblings, mood disruptions, and engaging in risky behaviors are common to many, though certainly not all, adolescents during this time of change (Steinberg & Sheffield Morris, 2001). It is critical for anyone doing crisis intervention to have an awareness of the distinct cognitive, social, and biological capacities of this age group and to create interventions that bear them in mind.

We include, where pertinent, discussions of techniques drawn from time-limited therapies. Given that we live during a time when brief and solution-focused therapy models are advocated because they are often effective in a short period of time and because many of our clients are unable to pursue the therapy they need due to insurance restrictions, it is important to be aware of these techniques. Fosha (2004) states that in brief therapy, the belief is "Work as if there were no next session" (p. 66), and, indeed, crisis intervention focuses on quickly helping a person in crisis to return to normal functioning.

As part of the increasing focus on evidence-based research (Roberts & Yeager, 2004), there is growing support for particular treatments for adult trauma, as well as studies on treating childhood disorders such as anxiety and depression (Okamoto & LeCroy, 2004). However, there are few empirically supported treatment studies on children and adolescents who are dealing with grief and loss issues. Strategies to help grieving children often use techniques found helpful for children with mood disorders or use adult treatments, modified for children, sometimes without addressing important developmental issues (Cohen, Mannarino, Berliner, & Deblinger, 2000; National Institute of Mental Health [NIMH], 2004). This is changing, as current studies focus on examining specific interventions designed for children and adolescents with particular concerns or disorders. The NIMH Workgroup on Child and Adolescent Mental Health Intervention Development and Deployment recommends that research focus on single disorders as opposed to assuming generalizability of treatment strategies across disorders. Child and adolescent studies possibly most applicable to grief and loss have examined depression (Cohen et al., 2000), natural disasters, and sexual abuse (Goodman, 2004). Based on studies conducted with traumatized children and adolescents, it is conceivable that cognitive-behavioral therapy techniques may be useful when conducting traumatic grief interventions (Goodman, 2004). Much work remains to determine which of several techniques are most effective in cognitive-behavioral therapy, such as relaxation interventions, because most studies have involved a combination of techniques (Cohen et al., 2000).

We use three cases to illustrate issues in crisis intervention with early adolescents.

Jenny, a Caucasian 13-year-old girl, has suffered a series of significant losses. This past year her parents divorced, following several years of progressive deterioration of her father's health due to alcoholism; most recently, her beloved grandmother died. Jenny has become increasingly withdrawn from friends and family, less involved in school activities, and more worried about her appearance, and has lost nearly 10 pounds. Her brothers have noticed that Jenny spends more time alone in her room and has stopped going to their baseball games. Feeling that relationships end in tragedy and that there is little she can control, Jenny avoids closeness and seeks to control her life through rigorous diet and exercise.

The model discussed by Roberts (2000) to help intervene in a crisis situation works very well for Jenny's situation and also demonstrates how time-limited therapies can be helpful in assisting an early adolescent who is forced to cope after a series of losses.

The case of Esperanza permits us to demonstrate the utility of Roberts's model in stabilizing an adolescent in crisis after an unexpected and serious loss, the death of a beloved parent.

Esperanza is a Mexican American girl of 12. Five months ago, her parents were snowmobiling in the mountains when the snowmobile spun out of control and her parents were thrown off. Her mother was hurt, but she recovered quickly. Her father broke his neck and died. Since then, Esperanza has had great difficulty sleeping and concentrating. The academic work she once took great pride in has suffered and her grades have dropped so precipitously that she may not pass seventh grade. She is very depressed and is alternately either very passive or very aggressive at school. She has told several people she is close to that she wants to die.

In this case, special attention had to be paid to the issue of Esperanza's lethality. A lethality assessment, which is the first step in Roberts's model, was combined with the second step, that of relationship building. This case demonstrates how the application of Roberts's model provides a heuristic and sensible approach to assisting an early adolescent after a tragedy.

The case of Peter allows us to examine the utility of Roberts's model following a tragic and catastrophic event where the early adolescent does not perceive that he can ask for help until a later date.

It appeared to be a routine Tuesday morning at Franklin Middle School. Yet, shortly before noon, a call came to the principal's office concerning a shooting at the high school; there were a number of victims. By 1 P.M. enough information had been gathered to confirm that a high school student who had been critically injured had a 12-year-old brother, Peter, who attends Franklin Middle School. The principal asked the school counselor to call Peter's parents, yet the counselor's phone attempts were not successful. The principal was ready to announce to the middle school staff and students that a tragedy had occurred at the nearby high school. Instinct told her that she should isolate Peter and three other students before the announcement was made. By 2 P.M. it was confirmed that Peter's older sister was dead.

Peter's case is one where the counselor will need to convey genuine respect for and acceptance of the client in order to offer the reassurance that Peter can be helped and that his time with the counselor is the appropriate time and place to receive such help.

CRISIS IN THE LIVES OF EARLY ADOLESCENTS

Crises impact the lives of many American youths as a result of experiences as close to home as child abuse and divorce and as distant, for some, as Hurricane Hugo, the massacre at Columbine High School, the terrorist attacks of September 11, 2001, and wars throughout the world. Natural and human-made events precipitate crises in humans; we are exposed to these events daily, either personally or through the media. Terr (1990) distinguishes between Type I crises, in which an acute single event (e.g., the Columbine shootings) precipitates a crisis, and Type II crises, which are responses to seemingly unremitting and prolonged events (e.g., repeated episodes of abuse or family violence). Most discussions of crisis intervention, including ours, focus on the first of these, which Roberts (1996) refers to as an "acute situational crisis" (p. 17):

> A sudden and unpredictable event takes place . . . the individual or family members perceive the event as an imminent threat to their life, psychological well-being, or social functioning; the individual tries to cope, escape the dangerous situation, gain necessary support from a significant other or close relative or friend, and/or adapt by changing one's lifestyle or environment; coping attempts fail and the person's severe emotional state of imbalance escalates into a full-blown crisis. (p. 17)

We discuss immediate, short-term responses to difficult and intense events, including acute psychological crises, acute situational crises, and acute stress disorders (Roberts, 1996). It is important to distinguish this from longer-term psychotherapy; as Hillman (2002), put it, "The goal of crisis intervention is to return individuals to their previous level of functioning; no assumption of previous psychopathology is made" (p. 7). In many cases, crisis intervention may be precisely what is needed to assist an adolescent in crisis, but it is important to remember that, in other situations, more intensive therapy or ongoing support will be needed. It is essential to assess each individual's specific needs carefully and to remember that access to longer-term psychotherapy may be especially important for individuals who have experienced prolonged and repeated crises (Terr's Type II crises). Crisis intervention may be very useful when an early adolescent has experienced a violent episode or if such an event has happened to someone close to him or her, or if personal loss has occurred through the death of a loved one or divorce.

Scope of the Problem and Clinical Considerations

Among early adolescents, crises can take many forms, and the impact of these can vary greatly among individuals. Particular vulnerabilities and risk factors are discussed later; here, it is important to note that no adolescent is protected by gender, culture, or socioeconomic status from the effects of a crisis. Our examples focus on crises due to the impact of violence outside the home, loss due to the death of a loved one, and the divorce of parents. Violence in the home (child abuse or domestic violence) clearly has major impacts on early adolescents, but we do not address this specific topic here, as it is the subject of another chapter in this volume.

Violence is all too common in the lives of youth, whether by direct exposure in their communities, homes, or schools, or through indirect exposure to the media, which often target youth with violent images and other content. Violence claimed the lives of nearly 5,500 young people in the United States in 2001, the second leading cause of death for teenagers, after car accidents (U.S. Census Bureau, 2003). Outside of their homes, American youth regularly experience violence in their communities. Daily, 13 young people under the age of 20 are the victims of homicides, and many of these are killed by firearms (Children's Defense Fund [CDF], 1999). Violence is pervasive in school settings as well: in 2001, almost 13% of ninth-graders reported being threatened or injured with a weapon on school property (U.S. Census Burear, 2003). In 2000, 80,000 male and 62,000 female students reported being victims of nonfatal, nonviolent crimes on school property, and another 33,000 male and 18,000 female students were victims of violent crimes on school property (U.S. Census Bureau, 2003). Tragically, most recently there has been an alarming increase in deadly violence in schools related to gun use (Wilde, 2002).

Other crises are all too common in the lives of early adolescents in this country. In the United States today, there are approximately 41.5 million young people between the ages of 10 and 19; in the 2000 census, over 21 million were between the ages of 10 and 14. Almost half of all marriages of these children's parents end in divorce. Thus, millions of early adolescents are growing up in homes where divorce has occurred, and it is likely that roughly 40% of all children will have parents who divorce (Greene, Anderson, Hetherington, Forgatch, & DeGarmo, 2003). Currently in the United States, 26% of households with children under the age of 18 are single-parent households, which is an increase of 58% from 1970 (Anderson, 2003). Parental divorce can induce a crisis in children, but it does not always do so; recent research indicates that children's responses to divorce are not uniform.

Divorce, though a family crisis, may also be seen as an opportunity for change that is positive. Among some children, there may be little difference on measures of psychosocial adjustment from peers from intact families; some studies actually found higher scores on adjustment measures in children from divorced families. Some of the predictors of positive postdivorce adjustment include good communication and lack of overt conflict between parents, good psychological adjustment of parents, good parenting skills (including displays of warmth and appropriate limit setting), healthy accommodation to the stresses inherent in change, and support from family and friends. However, often related to difficulties in the factors discussed above, estimates are that roughly 20% of children in divorced families, versus 10% from intact families, engage in problem behavior (Greene et al., 2003). For some children the problems continue into adulthood (Laumann-Billings & Emery, 2000).

The death of a parent is one of the most significant and serious losses one can have in a lifetime, especially when the loss is for an early adolescent who is still dependent on the care of a parent. Data indicate that 4% of youth under 18 in the United States live with a widowed parent; the numbers are just slightly lower for those who live with a surviving father than for those who live with a surviving mother (U.S. Census Bureau, 1999). In addition to those who will lose a parent to death, many early adolescents will experience the loss of a sibling, peer, or grandparent. In a recent study of 85 participants age 17–20 reporting on their adolescent years, 70% experienced a loss while in high school; almost 26% of that group had experienced two losses and 14% had experienced three losses during that time (Ringler & Hayden, 2000). The bonds of attachment at this age are very strong; such writers as Bowlby (1980) and Worden (1996) have explored the impact of parental death on children and adolescents in depth. Webb (2002) and others have begun to explore the impact of sibling death, and Ringler and Hayden have studied peer loss among adolescents. Webb lists some warning signs indicating problematic grief in adolescents who have lost a sibling, including social withdrawal, ongoing eating problems, problems with school performance, and continuing aggressiveness or irritability.

Worden (1996) examined the risk factors for high levels of emotional and behavioral problems in bereaved children. Some of the common risk factors evident at four months, one year, and two years after the death include low self-esteem, experiencing a sudden death, the presence of health problems in the surviving parent, depression and fear about the safety of the parent, high levels of family stress and change, and a passive coping style.

ASSESSMENT OF VULNERABILITIES AND RISK FACTORS

It is difficult to predict how a child or adolescent will react to a crisis. As the early adolescent develops, the path of his or her life is marked by thousands of events that vary in the magnitude, duration, and meaning they have for the person. Why individuals react markedly differently to a similar life event is the question at the heart of stress research and is critical to identification of how individuals will react to a crisis event. Unlike adults, children and younger adolescents are subject to many events over which they have little control; therefore, what they perceive as stressful is often different from what an adult might perceive, and is also likely to be different from the perceptions of older adolescents (Brooks-Gunn, 1992). Early adolescence has been viewed as a highly stressful period, specifically in relation to lowered self-esteem, increased conflict with siblings, and early maturing for some (Steinberg & Sheffield Morris, 2001). Additionally, the influence of peer relationships intensifies while family interactions shift (Fuligni, Eccles, Barber, & Clements, 2001). During this period, the early adolescent must cope with many stressors, including puberty, new experiences, increased responsibilities, and devising future-oriented plans and goals. Adding financial hardship of the family, educational disability, illness, and other stressors only increases an early adolescent's vulnerability to a crisis event.

Adolescents cope with stressors in many different ways, and identifying risk factors that predispose individuals to cope in a dysfunctional way in a crisis situation is an important domain of research. The greatest amount of research has focused on internal cognitive or biological factors. The research indicates that individuals' expectations about the world and attributions about the causes of events have particularly important effects on responses to acute stressors. Specific biological and physiological correlates of susceptibility to crisis have also been identified. For example, Seligman (1995) has studied the attributions that children make to both positive and negative events. His results indicate that children who are more vulnerable to crisis tend to make specific and external attributions to positive events (e.g., the teacher gave me a good grade) and global and internal attributions when a negative event occurs (e.g., my inability to act led to the tragedy). Lazarus (1993) also argues that how a child appraises a stressful situation or crisis event is critical to her or his coping process and subsequent adjustment. Wekerle and Wolfe (2003) discuss the importance of one's mood and ability to regulate mode states. Consistent with cognitive theory, what people think will happen when they experience a negative event has important implications for the development of a healthy or unhealthy psychological or physical response. Nader (2001) discusses the interaction of biological disposition and temperament with a child's capacity to cope with a stressful or crisis situation, noting that there can also be environmental influences on temperament over time. Differences have been noted in symmetry of frontal lobe activation related to disposition and responses to the environment; specifically, higher right frontal lobe activation in children is indicative of fearful and negative responses as well as withdrawal from mild stress (Fox, Henderson, Rubin, Calkins, Schmidt, 2001; Rubin, Burgess, Kennedy, & Stewart, 2003). Other styles more reflective of temperament (such as a depressive, stress-reactive, or psychosomatic style) may also reflect the potential for a negative outcome following a crisis event.

At least some aspects of risk factors can also vary with gender. Werner and Smith (2001) found in their longitudinal study that in childhood, boys seem to have more mental health problems, and then the trend is reversed during adolescence, with girls encountering more problems, directly related to stressful life events. Additionally, specific vulnerabilities correlated with gender. Males tended to have increased vulnerability related to parental psychopathology and with substance abuse issues, while females seemed more vulnerable to lasting effects of childhood and adolescent illnesses and problems in relationships with their families, mothers in particular. Keane and Kaloupek (2002) state that gender differences in development of posttraumatic stress disorder may be as a result of biological, psychological, or social differences between the genders, as well as related to differences in types of stressful life events males and females are exposed to.

Other sociocultural factors may also be important. For example, the major focus of adolescent "at risk" research has been on inner-city and urban adolescents, but rural areas represent distinctly different social and economic characteristics. Comparing the health risk behaviors between rural, suburban, and urban adolescents, rural students were at significantly higher risk for smoking, drinking, drug use, teen pregnancy, carrying a weapon other than a gun to school, and carrying a gun at or away from school (Atav & Spencer, 2002).

RESILIENCE AND PROTECTIVE FACTORS

Although research into what makes an individual react in a dysfunctional manner to an acute stressor is important in attempting to understand why some individuals are more susceptible to crisis than others, by itself this research offers a limited view of the process considered here. Recently, work on the other side of this process, how people maintain mental health, has begun to gain greater prominence. Researchers have responded with studies of resilient persons, or children who grew up in aversive environments yet became productive, caring adults. Mash and Dozois (2003) defined the resilient child as one who manages to avoid negative outcomes and/or achieve positive outcomes despite being at significant risk for the development of psychopathology, who displays sustained competence under stress, and who shows recovery from trauma. Resilient individuals are recognized as coping well in spite of great stressors; however, even resilient individuals may become overwhelmed if supports are lost or stressors increase.

Internal psychological and external social or familial forces that contribute to resiliency have been identified. For example, Blocker and Copeland (1994) found that the trait of social responsiveness, including cooperation and participation, most clearly discriminated between resilient and nonresilient high-stressed youths: resilient adolescents were involved in more activities, spent more time on academic pursuits, and spent fewer hours alone than their nonresilient peers. Werner and Smith (2001) found that adolescent males who had realistic educational plans and adolescent females with good self-esteem were the most likely to develop into well-adapted adults. Additional factors for resiliency were positive self-concept and internal locus of control, as well as a source outside the adolescent's family for emotional support (Werner & Smith, 2001). Asby Wills, Sandy, Yaeger, Cleary, and Shinar (2001), in looking at the relationship among coping, stress, and substance abuse with adolescents, noted that behavior coping and engagement had greater protective effects at higher levels of life stress, and disengagement coping increased the risk at high levels of stress. Other protective factors that have been found to contribute to resiliency include an adequate identification figure, a sense of curiosity, a sense of self, social responsiveness, and representational competence (Blocker & Copeland, 1994). The specific factors that may be most important for a given individual can vary with gender (Werner & Smith, 2001) and probably other factors as well.

The ultimate goal in the study of resiliency is to design interventions that better reduce risk factors and/or increase protective factors, and such interventions may have implications for crisis intervention. Sadly, interventions that successfully promote resiliency are less well documented than identification of protective factors that contribute to resiliency. Seligman's (1995) work offers a promising solution to this. Finding that an optimistic attributional style is a hallmark of resiliency, Seligman developed a cognitive training program for children that combats pessimism when faced with adversity or crisis; promotes a temporary, specific, and impersonal explanatory style to negative events and a permanent, pervasive, and personal explanatory style to positive events; teaches disputing and decatastrophizing of adversities; and boosts social skills. Specifically, a child would be trained to attribute negative events to external circumstances that are transitory while crediting successes to personal and stable positive characteristics.

CASE EXAMPLES

We now turn to examine three case studies in light of Roberts's (1996, 2000, 2004) seven-stage model of intervention: (1) assess psychosocial needs, especially lethality, (2) establish rapport, (3) identify major problems, (4) deal with feelings, (5) explore alternatives, (6) generate an action plan to put these alternatives into practice, and (7) follow up.

Jenny: Parental Divorce, Paternal Alcoholism, and Death of Grandmother

Jenny is a White, middle-class, American 13-year-old girl whose parents, Bill and Emily, both age 40, divorced a year ago following several years of progressive deterioration of her father's health and increased absences from home due to alcoholism. For the past two years, her mother has become increasingly involved in her work as an administrator for a health care network and takes complete care of family finances.

Prior to the separation, when her dad seemed to be getting worse, Jenny was able to talk to her mother and grandmother about her sadness for and anger at her father. He had been through several treatment programs but never followed through on aftercare for very long, lapsing again into alcoholism. After the last treatment failure, Emily filed for divorce. Jenny had tried to talk to her mother about her feelings, but Emily had grown bitter about Bill and responded to her daughter, "Your father can't get beyond his problems, but we can do better than that and it is time to move on." Jenny felt she could not talk to her mother and turned to her grandmother, who provided significant emotional support and comfort.

Two months ago, Jenny's beloved grandmother died. Jenny then became increasingly withdrawn from friends and family and less involved in school activities. Although she became quieter and seemed mostly sad, she had several angry outbursts at her mother and her two younger brothers, ages 10 and 8. She frequently woke at night crying and complained to her mother that she was afraid to go to back to sleep for fear the nightmares would return. She dreamed that she was hiking up a mountain with family and friends, but that whenever she turned around, she had lost someone and could not find them and that she was alone on the mountain with the cold night approaching. Over the past month, she has also become increasingly worried about her appearance, and has lost eight pounds. Her mother worried that Jenny was eating less and was spending more time running and swimming than is healthy. Jenny's brothers noticed that Jenny spent more time alone in her room and had stopped going to their baseball games.

Crisis Intervention: Application of Roberts's Seven-Stage Model

Jenny's mother was worried about her and, at the recommendation of the school counselor, Emily set up an appointment for her and her daughter with a counselor in the community. Early in crisis intervention it is essential to assess lethality and establish rapport with a client (Roberts, 2000). Although the counselor encouraged her, Jenny was hesitant to disclose her feelings, saying that there was nothing anyone could do because her grandmother was gone and her dad was too sick to care. Her counselor was quickly able to establish a relationship with Jenny by respecting and acknowledging her hopelessness that anything would change regarding the death of her grandmother, her father's alcoholism, and her parents' divorce. She affirmed the myriad feelings such losses engendered, such as sadness, anger, guilt, and anxiety, and pointed out that sometimes people feel sick and tired and may act out (Worden, 2002), but that such feelings are normal. The counselor encouraged help-seeking behavior and emphasized that others have found it useful to talk about losses in counseling and to develop coping strategies. She also mentioned that she had worked with many people who have suffered losses and that, although each person is different, there are some similar experiences people have when such terrible losses occur and it has helped other people to express their feelings and to begin to develop ways to deal with the losses.

Jenny cried as she told her counselor that her grandmother was "the one person who believed in me, no matter what. My dad checked out a while ago and has not done much with us kids the last couple of years and now my mom has to work so much. I know Mom loves us, but she has so much to do and Gram was always there for me." Jenny feared that the people she loved would leave her through illness or death and thought that maybe it was better to be alone; she reasoned, "Everyone leaves for some reason, and if I don't depend too much on other people, I won't be so sad if something bad happens." Her counselor accurately paraphrased Jenny's concerns and, using open-ended questions, probed further and discovered that Jenny's fear of losing people was part of the reason she had withdrawn from friends.

Jenny said that sometimes she wished she could be with her grandmother. The counselor inquired further and Jenny stated that if she were dead she would be with grandmother. Her counselor asked if Jenny had thought about suicide and Jenny said she had, but that she would never do it because she knew how sad it would make her mother. The counselor conducted a brief assessment asking Jenny of ways she had thought of killing herself. Jenny was vague, saying, "I don't know, maybe a lot of aspirin." The counselor asked Jenny to scale her suicidal ideation from 1 to 10, with 1 being "not at all" and 10 being "very serious" (see Softas-Nall & Francis, 1998). Jenny responded, "It's 1. I could never really do that, it is against my religion, and my Gram would think it was awful. I would never do that to her or my mom." The counselor reflected back that even in death, Grandmother's opinion was very important.

Although the reason for seeking services focused on Jenny's response to her grandmother's death, the counselor was also aware of the divorce and wanted to explore that as well. Webb (2002) notes that in complicated grief like Jenny's, stresses that are superimposed on one another will affect each person differently, but the combined impact of multiple stressors is more likely to lead to greater problems, such as fragmentation of coping abilities. Bowlby (1980) also discusses the increased likelihood of developing disorders under these circumstances.

In the third stage of the crisis intervention model it is important to develop a focus for intervention. The counselor examined the number and significance of the recent losses Jenny experienced and noted that her grandmother's death was the most recent in a series of losses. Roberts (1996) discusses the importance of identifying the precipitating event that leads a client to seek help; this may be the "last straw," but if there are many events that led to the crisis, the problems must be prioritized so that a central focus can be developed. Jenny's counselor asked her to identify the important events she thought led to her being in counseling. Jenny expressed anger that she has had enough to deal with and she is tired of so many bad things happening. Her counselor asked an open-ended question: "What are the losses you are thinking of right now?" Jenny explained about her father's increasing withdrawal from home, the nights spent away from his family, the loss of his job, her mother becoming so busy and preoccupied with work, her parents' divorce, and the humiliation of her family needing to move into a smaller house due to financial problems.

Her counselor acknowledged and further explored Jenny's feelings. Jenny said the divorce was hard on her because her mom was so sad, but that her father had been "missing" for a long time, so it was better than staying married. She had not been able to talk about the divorce much, except with her grandmother, and she still found it hard to believe her parents were not married anymore: "I had such a great childhood and I kept thinking if Daddy could only find a better hospital he could be better and things could be like they were." With this long a list of events, Roberts notes (1996) that it may be helpful to rank them by priority so as to clarify a focus. Jenny identified her grandmother's death and her parents divorce as the most concerning to her at this time.

Once the major problem has been identified, it is important to encourage and explore feelings, as this is the focus of the fourth intervention stage. Throughout counseling, Jenny's counselor used active listening and other basic skills to develop a relationship and to encourage Jenny to express her feelings. The counselor consistently linked past experiences with the present through use of such basic counseling skills as paraphrasing, reflection, and open-ended questions. Although talking was a common vehicle for expression, Jenny loved to paint and write poetry, and these modes of expression were very useful in helping her work through her feelings. The current literature is replete with strategies that can be useful in helping children of different ages work through grief (e.g., see Silverman, 2000; Webb, 2002, 2004; Worden, 2002).

Jenny angrily admitted that she closed herself off to her father and spent less time with him because he yelled a lot and was mean, but that she spent more time with people who were "good' to her, such as her grandmother and friends. Her feelings about moving to a smaller house included embarrassment at having to move from "a big house with a pool where my friends could hang out to a little house with a tiny yard that had so few rooms that my brothers have to share a room. But, even though it is really hard to move, it is better than having to leave my school and friends." Jenny also spent time writing in her journal and doing artwork, which she found relaxing. Although those things helped her to cope in the past, now she worried that she was being "too sad" and that her friends would not want to be around her anymore.

The counselor mentioned that sometimes when young women are distressed and things feel out of control they try to control what is within their own reach, such as weight. Jenny mentioned that her cheerleading coach, trying to be helpful, suggested that exercise was helpful in changing her own mood; thus Jenny, looking for ways to feel better, began to exercise more and more. A few friends had noticed that she looked thinner and complimented her on it, whereupon Jenny thought maybe losing a few pounds by cutting out sweets and dieting might help her lose the few pounds she had gained over the winter.

Although the fourth stage of the crisis intervention model focuses on exploring and expressing feelings, it would be erroneous to think such exploration occurs only at that stage. Throughout the counseling process it is imperative that a counselor be attuned to the child's needs and to respond in an empathic way. In the fifth stage, an emphasis is placed on assessing past coping attempts, developing alternatives, and designing specific solutions. While listening to Jenny, her counselor was particularly attentive to ways Jenny coped effectively so as to reinforce any adaptive behaviors and cognitions. With her counselor's help, Jenny explored how she handled such past stressors as her parents' divorce, the move to a smaller house, and her father's alcoholism. As noted earlier, Jenny found it helpful to spend less time with her father when he was in a bad mood and more time with people who were good to her, such as her grandmother and friends. She had also reframed the move to a smaller house as not so bad because it was better than having to leave her friends and school, and she often wrote in a journal and did art work. Although all these things had been useful, Jenny complained they were not working well any more, and furthermore, she had lost one of her strongest supporters. Roberts (2000) notes that clinicians may need to take the initiative when clients have little insight or if they are emotionally distressed. Jenny felt dismayed that her former coping strategies were either unavailable to her now or that she could not seem to use them effectively.

It can be helpful to hear what other clients have done in the past, and so her counselor asked Jenny if she would like to know something about how other clients coped whose parents were divorced or who had experienced losses. As Jenny seemed interested, her counselor told her about a boy whose favorite uncle, who was also his godfather, had died. The boy talked about feelings as Jenny did, and then he came up with a way to let go of some of the problems he had. One technique was to imagine he was inhaling his anger and his pain deep into his lungs, and then he exhaled all of those feelings into a balloon, which he then took outside and let the feelings go by releasing the balloon into the air. He also wrote a letter to his uncle about many of the wonderful things they had done together and read this to his counselor, and afterward they explored how he felt doing this and what he found helpful. Jenny's counselor then asked Jenny to imagine she was a counselor; what would she recommend, as coping strategies, to a 13- or 14-year-old who was dealing with so many losses? Jenny found this amusing and insisted on sitting in her counselor's chair as she took on the role of a directive list maker. Jenny quickly wrote a list of ideas: spending time with close friends, talking to your family, writing down feelings on sticky-notes and putting them on a wall and making a poem of them, painting feelings and using pictures and words cut from magazines to create a collage of how you feel now and what you want to change to feel better, doing things that are relaxing, taking bubble baths, watching movies that make you laugh, and exercising.

One coping strategy the counselor felt needed to be addressed was exercise and weight loss. She expressed her concern that this strategy might be exacerbating the problem. Jenny felt very good about losing weight and argued that she had felt a bit overweight and that exercise was healthy. As her counselor had worked in the past with clients with eating disorders, she was aware of the futility in arguing about weight. Instead, she focused on the effectiveness or lack thereof in using diet and excessive exercise to feel better about herself. Jenny admitted that she felt tired and had problems concentrating if she did not eat breakfast or lunch and that, though she enjoyed exercise, it was starting to feel all-consuming to her.

Counselor: On a scale of 1 to 10, with 1 being tired and 10 being very energetic, where are you?

Jenny: I'd like to say 8, but I feel like a 4 today.

Counselor: Okay, what would it take to move that to a 5 or 6?

Jenny: Get some sleep!

Counselor: How can you do that today?

Jenny: Hmm. I woke up hungry, so if I ate more and exercised a bit less, I think I would have more energy.

Counselor: What are you willing to do today to move in that direction?

Jenny: I will eat dinner and just go for a short bike ride instead of riding for two hours. That way I will have time to relax before I go to bed.

The focus moved away from weight and food to how to help Jenny feel more energetic. She already had some of the solutions to her own problems.

Jenny and her counselor talked about divorce, depression, eating disorders, loss, and grief. Jenny also read educational material related to these concerns. Through talking, artwork, and writing poetry, Jenny began to understand that many of her feelings of loneliness, anger, sadness, and depression were rooted in the significant losses she had suffered and that it was normal to have difficulties when such things happened. Jenny was encouraged to talk about her feelings in counseling and to think about ways she could reconnect with people who are important to her, especially people whom she saw as "believing in" her. Jenny thought she would like to spend more time with her mom's younger sister and to see her best friends more often.

After Jenny and her counselor spoke with Jenny's mother, aunt, and school counselor, all agreed that Jenny had suffered many losses and that she needed their help. Jenny's aunt arranged her schedule so that she met with Jenny one evening a week, and they spent time together taking hikes, going to movies, or having pizza. Jenny's mother made plans at work to shift responsibilities so she had fewer evening meetings, and she spent that time with her children. Emily was also more sensitive to her daughter's feelings and created opportunities to encourage Jenny to share her thoughts and feelings. Emily also suggested that Jenny speak to one or two of her closest friends so they would know what has been going on. Jenny agreed to do this and found that her friends had been worried about her and were eager to help her. The school counselor, apprised of the cheerleading coach's recommendation, considered ways he could consult with school personnel on helping children with loss and grief.

In the sixth step of the crisis intervention model it is important to move from generating ideas to developing and implementing an action plan. As Jenny began to feel better about herself, felt listened to, and had more energy, she had little trouble in implementing her plans. As noted earlier, she is quite bright and likes to make lists. She began with creating artwork to better express, understand, and manage her feelings. Some of her collages expressed much anger and overwhelming sadness, yet others indicated hope and looking toward the future. She wrote a poem about losses and changes that was later published in a "Young Authors of Colorado" book, and she felt particularly proud of turning her grief and anger into hope and a published work.

In the follow-up stage of crisis intervention, which was at one and two months, Jenny was functioning well and was satisfied that counseling had helped her through a difficult period of her life.

Esperanza: Parental Death

Esperanza is a 12-year-old Mexican American girl. She lives on a small ranch with her family, who raise llamas. She has three older sisters (age 18, 16, 15), a younger brother (age 10), and a horse named Cookie. Her mother, Ana, is 41 and co-owns an insurance business with her sister and brother. Her father, Michael, ran the family business until his tragic death five months ago. Ana and Michael were snowmobiling in the mountains when the snowmobile spun out of control and they were thrown off. Her mother broke her leg and received other minor injuries, but recovered quickly. Her father broke his neck and died.

In the first few months after his death, Esperanza and her siblings openly mourned his loss and took great care of their mother, who alternated between constant weeping and worrying for her children. Due to her injuries, the older children took care of the cleaning, cooking, and ranch work. The eldest, Camille, who was in her first semester of college, decided to take a semester off to help her family; she ran things quite smoothly and was very efficient in helping the children get ready for school and complete their schoolwork and chores. The other sisters, Luisa and Margaret, while devastated by their father's death, spent a lot of time together and decided to begin an ambitious project of gathering together family memorabilia to dedicate to their father's memory. The youngest, Martin, very often distracted and sad, felt his family was very helpful to him and spent a lot of time with his male cousins in his aunt and uncle's house a few miles from home.

After her father's death, Esperanza had great difficulty sleeping and concentrating. She complained of stomach aches to her older sister, who gave her several over-the-counter medications to soothe her stomach and told Esperanza not to bother their mother. The academic work in which she once took great pride suffered; her grades dropped so precipitously that she was in danger of not passing seventh grade. She was alternately very passive or very aggressive at school. She told Luisa that she wanted to die. She thought everyone else was "managing" better than she. Esperanza also told Luisa that she felt responsible for their father's death and that she thought their mother was very angry at her.

Luisa was very alarmed at this, and spoke with Camille and Margaret, who agreed that they needed to speak to their mother, who, though now mostly physically recovered and back at work, seemed very distant at times. Ana immediately went to Esperanza, who denied feeling suicidal. However, Esperanza cried for hours after this and kept repeating that it was her fault her father died. Ana, who is devoutly Catholic, contacted her parish priest, who is a warm and thoughtful person with a reputation for being available during times of crisis. He came to the house and spoke with all of the family about how they were doing; last, he spoke with Esperanza in the presence of her mother. Esperanza was inconsolable and wailed that she wanted to be with her father and that her father might forgive her if she could be with him. No one was able to determine why Esperanza felt so responsible, and at last Father Romero recommended that Ana call a counselor he knew at a university about 30 minutes from their town. He mentioned that this counselor was an expert in working with grieving children. Esperanza and Ana made an appointment and met with the counselor a few days later.

Crisis Intervention: Application of Roberts' Seven-Stage Model

Given the concern expressed by those close to Esperanza (that she was considering suicide and seemingly inconsolable), it was essential for her counselor to quickly establish a relationship with her. This required, of course, empathy, respect, and genuineness (Roberts, 2000; Rogers, 1965). Given that she had expressed a wish to die, it was also critical to assess her lethality. Esperanza is 12 years old and is probably in the third stage of cognitive development, the Formal Operational Stage (Piaget, 1968). At this stage, thinking is logical and children are able to understand abstractions. Of particular relevance here, children of this age can understand that death is not a reversible process (Webb, 2002), and thus her wish to die had to be treated very seriously. Webb also discusses the fact that although it is uncommon for children to express suicidal ideation when a parent dies, their threats must be taken very seriously.

Many writers, Worden (2002) included, are aware that those who care for a child may hesitate in asking about suicidal ideation, fearing that they may suggest ideas to the child. Worden recommends a gentle inquiry to initiate the discussion. Following Roberts (2000), the first stage in crisis intervention is to assess lethality, which includes an assessment of danger to self and others and attending to immediate psychosocial needs. Stage 2 of this model focuses on establishing rapport and rapidly building the relationship. Both steps were attended to in the first half of the counseling session when the counselor made it clear to Esperanza that she knew why those who loved her had referred her to counseling and that other people came to the counselor's office to talk about painful losses. Sensitive to Esperanza's acute sense of loss, the counselor began an assessment of lethality after exploring Esperanza's feelings about being sent to counseling. Bertolino (2003) stresses the importance of counselors working *with* adolescent clients to keep them involved in deciding the direction of therapy and to make it a collaborative venture. Explaining the role of the counselor and participation of parent and child in planning treatment will do much to demystify the process of counseling and give the child and parent a sense of control. This is particularly important in cases like Esperanza's because it is common for bereaved children to feel that they have less control over events than nonbereaved children (Silverman, 2000). To the extent possible, a counselor will want to help children feel they have some control and choice in counseling.

In the second half of the first session, the counselor met with the entire family, except for Martin, who was on a camping trip with his cousins. Each member of the family was asked what they would like changed in their current situation. All emphasized their concern for Esperanza and her expression of suicidal ideation. The counselor chose to use a solution-focused approach to assess Esperanza's suicidal ideation (Softas-Nall & Francis, 1998). It was a surprise to the family that the basis for Esperanza's desire to die was related to her certainty that her mother was angry at her and blamed Esperanza for the death of her husband. Ana was shocked that Esperanza felt responsible, and she reassured her that she was not responsible. She was able to correct Esperanza's misperception that it was she who "made" her parents go snowmobiling on the fateful day. Ana told her that her father had made up his mind that he wanted to go and, as usual, he teased Esperanza that he could not go because he had "so much work to do." Clearing up this misperception did not lessen Esperanza's agony over her father's death, but it did help her to feel that she was not responsible. It was helpful to have the family gathered, as they could provide support for Esperanza that would be important in helping her through this crisis. Esperanza admitted that she had just wanted to die to get away from her painful feelings, but did not have a specific plan for killing herself. After securing a promise that she would not kill herself and did not have a plan or specific means of committing suicide, the session ended with scheduling an appointment to meet again in a few days.

In the next session, after determining once again that Esperanza was not in imminent danger, her counselor began to accomplish the tasks set forth in the third stage of Roberts's model. This stage focuses primarily on identifying the major problem or event that precipitated the crisis. In some cases, it may be helpful to identify problems and to rank them by priority so as to clarify a focus and address potentially harmful aspects of the problem. However, Esperanza made it clear that her crisis was about one problem and one problem only: her father's death.

Discussion about this tremendous loss led naturally into the fourth stage: expression of feelings. Esperanza was assisted in exploring her feelings using the fundamental counseling skills discussed in many elementary counseling skills books, such as Cormier and Nurius (2003) and Egan (2002). The skills used included active and empathic listening, paraphrasing important content, reflecting feelings in the context of events the client is discussing, clarifying confusing or ambiguous statements, and summarizing both content and feelings. Esperanza was also helped by the counselor's use of more direct action skills (Cormier & Nurius, 2003), including gentle confrontation between verbal and nonverbal behaviors. For example, at one point, Esperanza said, "Everyone is handling this better than me. My sisters don't miss him at all." At this, she laughed, while at the same time tears fell from her eyes. Her counselor gently confronted the discrepancy between Esperanza's tears and her laughter. Esperanza admitted that she did not believe her sisters were managing as well as they seemed, but their concentration on a project to memorialize their father made Esperanza feel "left out."

Many techniques designed to help children express their feelings about loss are discussed in the works of prominent writers in the field (e.g., Silverman, 2000; Webb, 1999, 2002, 2004; Worden, 1996). A few techniques that Esperanza found helpful included writing a letter to her father and reading it in session while exploring her feelings, going to the site of the accident and planting a small tree in his memory, and looking at photographs of her family, especially a few special ones of times she spent with her father on the ranch and doing things together at horse fairs. Esperanza is a talented young adolescent, and she said she wanted to create an art collage with color copies of the photographs. She began to work on this with the counselor on a weekly basis because she did not want to take the collage home, fearing that it might upset her mother. In a subsequent family session, Esperanza discussed her project and her mother cried, but, with the counselor's attention to the feelings of both mother and daughter, both felt closer to each other as they were able to talk about how the loss impacted them. Ana asked that Esperanza bring the project home so they could work on it together. Esperanza was excited to do this and to feel that she was doing something special with her mother.

This collage project is an example of what Roberts recommends in the fifth stage of his model, which focuses on generating and exploring adaptive coping strategies in crisis. Very often, a client is too distressed to develop good coping strategies; initially, this was the case with Esperanza. Geldard and Geldard (1999) note that the adolescent who feels suicidal finds coping difficult and is emotionally strained, to the point that suicide is seen as a way of coping. Using the basic counseling skills noted earlier, Esperanza's counselor discussed the fact that many young people who have suffered the death of a parent may go through a time when they cry, feel sad, and have trouble concentrating. Worden (2002) cautions against labeling these symptoms "depression" because they are normal in the first year following parental death and often lessen by the first anniversary; we need to exercise caution in using the term depression to describe a normal response. Esperanza's counselor helped her to see that her responses were normal, but that it was very important to either develop new coping resources or find a way to use the resources that helped her in difficult situations in the past. Esperanza's counselor gave her several examples of children in her age group with whom she had worked and of some of the things they did to help themselves cope. Esperanza was very interested in hearing about what others in her position had done and felt confidence in this counselor, who clearly had experience in working with others who were grieving the loss of a parent.

Esperanza's counselor asked her to describe how she had coped during a time in her past when nothing seemed to be going right or when something bad had happened. Esperanza recalled that when her cousin's parents divorced, it was a very hard time for her, too, because she felt very close to her aunt and uncle. She prayed to God to help her through this time, she focused a lot of attention on helping her cousin, who was very sad, and she rode horses a lot and cleaned the barn. With her counselor's focus on help, Esperanza generated lists of ways she might cope now, one list each for ways of helping herself (1) inside, (2) being with others, and (3) doing things. Both Esperanza and her counselor brainstormed on items they could put under each heading. It helped to put three large pieces of paper on the wall around the room and to use a marker to write ideas as they emerged. Under the heading "Helping myself inside," Esperanza wrote "pray." She has prayed since her father's death, but initially it was for God to make him well, then for God to take her to her father. Now she wrote, "pray to God to help me through this hard time" and "pray to God to give me strength." Her counselor also suggested "listening to the relaxation tape," which she had made at Esperanza's request and which had helped her stomach pains. Esperanza added "drawing and painting in my journal," as she enjoyed artistic expression. Under the second list ("Helping myself by being with others"), there were many items, including spending more time with her little brother, helping her older sister cook, reestablishing riding lessons, arranging outings with one or two friends or cousins at a time, and staying with her godparents for an overnight. Esperanza's counselor took it as a very positive indicator of her progress that Esperanza was willing to spend time with others because, since her father's death, she had been very isolated and withdrawn from those who could offer support. Esperanza was clear that she was not ready to spend time with more than a few people at a time, and her counselor agreed that she was respecting her own limits and taking a step in the right direction. It was the collage of her family and special times with her dad that Esperanza put under the last coping category ("Helping myself by doing things").

It was in the sixth step of Roberts's model, developing an action plan, that Esperanza became stuck. Having ideas, as Esperanza did, is essential, but these ideas need to be planned and executed in the world to help to restore functioning in the client (Roberts, 1996). Initially, Esperanza was excited to begin taking some steps in items related to all three categories. She had no trouble creating goals and developing intermediate steps (Cormier & Nurius, 2003), but, when asked by her counselor which she would do this week, she became stuck in indecision. Outside of counseling, Esperanza sought the advice of her mother and sisters, but did not like any of their suggestions and became surly when she was encouraged to follow her own plan. In counseling, Esperanza pushed her counselor to choose for her. When she refused, Esperanza became annoyed and said people were no longer being helpful to her, and why should she try if everyone else was giving up. This change in mood was remarkable.

Her counselor told her a story of a girl she had worked with whose brother had died; this girl also went through a time of indecision and inaction. Esperanza was relieved to hear that this girl had also found it hard to accept that she had the right to be happy and move on with her life after surviving her brother in a car accident. This client, like Esperanza, was smart and creative, but thought that if she went on with her life she might forget her brother and that having fun would be akin to betraying him. As Roberts (1996) notes, it can be helpful to clients to know that we have worked with others who have had difficulties in executing plans, and it is equally helpful for them to know that these clients ultimately succeeded in overcoming their self-imposed obstacles.

Esperanza did worry that she would begin to forget details from her life with her father, and she still worried at times that if she had not told her parents to go snowmobiling he would be alive. After further clarification and expression of her feelings, Esperanza decided she would focus on completing the collage so that her fear about forgetting her dad could be laid to rest. She also said she wanted to begin praying that day, twice daily, for God to continue giving her strength and to help her believe she did not have anything to do with the accident. Thus, after exploring the difficulty in implementing her plans, Esperanza was able to continue with a course of action more readily.

The last stage of crisis intervention is follow-up. Worden and his colleagues on the Child Bereavement Project (Worden, 1996, 2002; Worden & Silverman, 1996) found that recently bereaved children were no more or less disturbed than the matched nonbereaved controls on a variety of psychological measures. However, when the data were examined one and two years after the death of a parent, there were significant differences between bereaved children and the control group of nonbereaved children. In particular, adolescent boys (age 12–18) who did not show much difference at one year after the death of a parent did indicate that they were more withdrawn and had slightly more social problems than controls. The preadolescent girls had no more problems than the nonbereaved control group at one year past the parental death, but there were significant changes by two years, including more anxiety and depression. This very extensive study has implications for mental health professionals and others who work with children. We must be aware of the long-term effects of losing a parent and know that problems may not appear until one or two years after the death. The professional who is conducting follow-up must bear this information in mind.

Esperanza made very good progress in therapy and after only four months of regularly working together, she and the counselor mutually decided to terminate their regular sessions and moved to periodic check-ins. As her counselor was aware of the research discussed above, she encouraged Esperanza to meet with her every couple of months for a while. The counselor met with Esperanza six times over the next two years and also met with the entire family four times to keep apprised of how everyone else was doing. Nearly 14 months after her father's death, Camille, the eldest, began to develop insomnia and frequent periods of sadness. Having anticipated that one of the other children in the family might later experience more grief over the father's death, Esperanza's counselor encouraged Camille to meet with a counselor at the university Camille attended.

At two years and four months after her father's death, Esperanza felt that she was functioning well. She had good support from family and friends, had earned excellent grades in school, and had won several statewide equestrian events of which she was very proud. She told her former counselor that in the future she might want to come back to counseling, but right now she was too busy having a full and satisfying life, and even periodic follow-up no longer seemed necessary.

Peter: Tragic Death of a Sibling

Peter is a White, upper-middle-class, 12-year-old who comes from an intact family who are active members of their local and church communities. Peter lives with his parents, Judy and Paul, ages 43 and 44, respectively, and his older sister, Cheryl, age 16 years. Judy is part-owner of an interior design company, a business she and two others started nine years ago. Paul is a civil engineer and has been employed by the Army Corps of Engineers for 20 years. Three grandparents all live in the same city. Peter's maternal grandmother died two and a half years ago following surgical complications.

The week following spring break Peter was in his history class. Midway through the class, Peter was called to the principal's office, where he and three other students were told of a tragedy at Southridge High School. Apparently, three students brought weapons into the school and began firing indiscriminately at students and staff shortly before noon. The four students have a brother or sister at the high school who was either known to be wounded or was not accounted for.

The four students exhibited diverse emotions; Peter sat baffled and withdrawn and asked few questions. At 2:30 P.M., Peter's father arrived at school, hugged Peter, and left the building quickly. His parents told Peter of his sister's death at 5 P.M. on the day of the catastrophe.

Three weeks after the tragedy, Peter's parents remain in shock and provide little support for Peter. Peter appeared to be fine and, after a seven-day absence from school, had returned to his classes at Franklin Middle School.

Extended family and neighbors have been very involved with the family, yet Peter had spent most of his time with his granddad, Clay, his mother's father. Peter and Granddad talk a great deal, yet seldom speak directly about Cheryl, as Judy and Paul are obviously not ready to actively deal with the murder of their daughter.

Media attention and focus remains intense. The scale of the tragedy (six students murdered and 14 seriously injured) led to national and international coverage. One positive result is that significant funds were made available for mental health counseling for students, teachers, and their families who were affected by the Southridge tragedy. A month before school was scheduled to end, Judy and Paul were encouraged by a school social worker to take Peter to see a counselor. Peter resisted, yet later consented to please his parents. The counselor reviewed fears, concentration, sleep, safety, and somatic complaints for three sessions. Peter denied any concerns and told his granddad, who had been taking him to the sessions, that he did not want to return for a fourth session. Clay conveyed Peter's desire to Judy and Paul and counseling was terminated by the parents at the end of the school year.

Two months passed, with Judy and Paul beginning to see the benefits of their own mental health counseling. The two took advantage of couple counseling and a grief support group; Judy was engaged in individual therapy. Talk of Cheryl in the household was no longer taboo. As the parents began their recovery, Paul returned to work and Judy increased her hours to 30 a week. Judy's partners, seeing a definite improvement, encouraged Judy to travel on an out-of-state business trip for a four-day period. When Peter was told that his mother would be leaving on a business trip, a tantrum followed and Peter was sick the next day with a fever. Judy rescheduled her trip for three days in the following week and left town without further incident from Peter.

Peter was now reporting somatic concerns and a fear of ghosts to his grandfather, and he was certain that another tragedy was going to follow in the fall. When Clay went in for a medical problem related to blood pressure, Peter became anxious and inconsolable. Judy and Paul decided it was time for Peter to return to a counselor. They selected a new counselor, with crisis expertise, and scheduled an appointment.

Crisis Intervention: Application of Roberts's Seven-Stage Model

Although Judy related the tragedy and Peter's problems of the spring and summer, Peter's presenting problem in counseling was his grandfather's medical problems. He appeared sad and upset and cried briefly. He then stated that what was happening to his grandfather was "not fair." The counselor simply allowed Peter to talk about his grandfather. A consistent issue was that grandfather "has been there for me." After listening attentively and empathetically to Peter's concerns, the counselor began to talk about "problems that we feel we have little control over." The counselor recognized that it took a lot of courage for Peter to come to counseling and that counseling was the appropriate place for him to explore the problems that he could and could not control.

After the counselor conveyed genuine respect for and acceptance of the client (Roberts, 2000), Peter began to relax in the session. He began to talk of his birthday at the end of the month and of going back to school. His increased acceptance of the counseling process enabled the counselor to begin examining the dimensions of the tragedy and the subsequent problems. They began to discuss the tantrum over the summer. In an open manner, consistent with an early adolescent, Peter related that he was mad at his mother for leaving for her trip and that he was saddened by his grandfather's condition. When the counselor asked if he was afraid, he simply said "Maybe" and asked "Why does God make it so hard for people?" This led to further exploration of his spirituality, and Peter seemed to relax more as the counselor openly encouraged him to discuss his beliefs. Many problems faced by clients have a spiritual aspect, especially grief and loss issues. Having a counselor who is willing to explore spirituality and be open to such a discussion facilitates trust in the therapeutic relationship for religious or spiritual clients (Kersting, 2003).

The discussion of God enabled the counselor to explore the death of his sister and any cognition of lethality. Peter noted that his sister is "with God." The two briefly discussed how she died, and the counselor asked if Peter would like to be "with God." Peter said that his time will come and we really don't know when. He spontaneously declared that "death is awful and young kids shouldn't die" and began to cry. The counselor facilitated his emotional expression by being silent and reflecting his feelings. Peter stopped crying and said, "I can't do anything about it anyway," and did not want to discuss his feelings further. The counselor sensed that he was pulling away emotionally and shifted the conversation back to Peter's grandfather, as this seemed like a safer subject. They ended the session by briefly talking about the grandfather and his medical concerns.

Two sessions later, Peter, now 13 years old, was starting eighth grade at the junior high. Judy asked to see the counselor before the session began and explained that Peter was experiencing a difficult start to the school year. On the second day of school, he was sent home for fighting. In the session, Peter readily admitted that he fought with another boy in his class. Peter externalized (Seligman, 1995) the problem and noted that the other boy should not be making jokes about blondes. He then started crying and said that his grandfather had to "go back for more testing. It is just not fair, why us?" He was anxious and agitated and could not see the point. He changed the subject to ask why someone at his sister's funeral said "God works in strange ways." Peter was encouraged to explore his feelings, and he wondered aloud whether or not he wanted to believe in a God who allows such sorrow.

The counselor again asked Peter to explore the role that God has played in his life. The discussion of God enabled Peter to talk about his grandmother's death due to illness, his sister's tragic death, and his grandfather's problems. Peter's eyes were wet as he discussed his grandmother, whom he recalled was a fun and lively woman, and his sister, whom he used to tease with blonde jokes. After a smile came to his face, Peter stated that he was ready to talk about his sister. He began to relate the tragic events of spring as the counselor listened in an empathic and supportive manner.

The counselor examined the coping attempts that worked for Peter in the past and identifed which ones may be adaptive for him in the future. Peter said that he used to be a good problem-solver, that he believed in God, he liked music, and he made friends easily. Over the summer, however, he spent a lot of time alone, playing video games and listening to music. He recalled that, following his sister's death, he simply did not know what to do and felt numb and helpless. He related a recent story about a moment of silence at his school to mark the sixth-month anniversary of the shootings at Southridge High and how he wanted to make contact with another student whose brother was murdered that tragic day. Peter was able to talk to the student after the moment of silence. He felt sad that the boy appeared very isolated, yet Peter remembered how he felt last summer and realized that he was making a choice not to be so isolated. He recalled the summer, when he wanted only to play video games and listen to music. Peter said he still found it hard to talk about things because two of his favorite people to talk with are now dead. The counselor reflected his sadness concerning the intensity of grief Peter has experienced at such a young age.

Peter spent two sessions talking about his sister and the tragic events of Southridge High. The counselor paraphrased important content and encouraged Peter to explore the story and his feelings with greater intensity each session. Peter saw that his mother was benefiting from her own work in therapy and that his father was becoming more open to discussions. His grandfather was still visiting the house a great deal, and Peter could see the relationship between Clay and his father improving. The counselor decided that Peter was ready for Stage 5, generating and exploring adaptive coping strategies.

As Peter gained insight into his thoughts and feelings concerning his sister's death, he began to expand the issues he needed to explore. He discussed an ebb and flow of emotions: one moment he was fine, and the next he was sad. He realized that his concentration in school was "not normal" and that he periodically had trouble sleeping, as some thoughts were intrusive. He was bothered by his mother's trips out of town and he still worried about his grandfather's health. He asked his mother to check in more often when she is out of town and asked his grandfather to be honest with him about his failing health. Peter was now willing to admit he is sometimes fearful of the events he cannot control. He still wanted God "to make it all well," yet the youth director at church helped him to see that God may just want Peter to focus on making himself well. Peter felt that he was doing just that by talking to his counselor and making new friends he can talk with. He decided to lessen his time playing video games and discarded all of his aggressive games; he was proud that he made this decision without the insistence of his parents. He was still having trouble relating to a number of the kids in school, yet he was convinced that being safe is more important than fighting to make a point.

Exploring fears, denial, isolation, worries, emotions, and events he could not control enabled Peter to move to step 6, developing an action plan. He saw the difference between the external events he cannot control and the steps he could take to regain a more realistic perspective. He developed a system to manage his homework and began to again feel that homework was something he could complete on a daily basis. Completing his work helped him to gain a greater sense of control.

Following the one-year anniversary of her death, Judy and Paul turned Cheryl's room into a guest bedroom. Two pictures of Cheryl remained in the room and Peter decided to "take his grieving to the guest room." He related that once a week he went into the room to cry. He noted that sometimes he left the room with a smile on his face. Judy and Paul became more active in church and Peter decided to be a member of the confirmation class. He joined the group a few sessions late, yet was convinced he could keep up with the work required. He renewed his interest in soccer and began to play on weekends with a community team. Peter made the decision to reengage in life.

The final session of crisis intervention finds Peter feeling successful that he was able to mediate a conflict in school, work on homework for an extended period of time, and enjoy his involvement in sports. Through his work in church, he began to thank God for the time he enjoyed with his grandmother and with Cheryl. He realized that the tragedy changed everyone in the community. He understood that his grief for his sister would not end in the near future, yet he was ready to terminate counseling.

One and a half years after counseling was terminated, Peter was ready to enter high school. He decided to attend Southridge, even though a new high school has opened and adolescents in his neighborhood have been given an option. He reported that he misses his sister and still, at times, grieves her death.

Special Considerations

There are many considerations one should bear in mind in working with early adolescents who have suffered a serious loss. Each child is unique, and counselors should expect to find significant individual differences in personality style and temperament that can alter responses to acute stressors. It is important to understand further that all of these are influenced by biopsychosocial, cultural, and familial influences. It is not within the scope of this chapter to explore these in depth, but we wish to highlight the importance of developmental stages, cultural issues, and the differences between youths coping with single episodes and with a series of crises, as well as ethical considerations in working with youth.

First, as noted earlier, adolescence can be divided into three periods. However, the developmental characteristics representative of each period are not always completely consistent with a child's chronological age. For example, a 13-year-old early adolescent eldest child whose parent died may "grow up quickly" as he or she is needed to take on additional responsibilities in the home. This child may have characteristics more similar to an older adolescent of 15 or 16 years. Likewise, a child who has suffered a crisis may regress and seem much younger than his or her chronological age. Intervention in this case may include using approaches that were designed for younger children, such as play therapy. Successful interventions thus need to include careful assessments of each individual's stage of cognitive and emotional development and to design and apply specific techniques in response to this assessment.

Second, cultural differences, which influence myriad behaviors, attitudes, values, and family structures, must also be taken into consideration in working with early adolescents. For example, in our second case, it was clear that Esperanza and Martin's godparents played an important role in their support systems, but this will not be true in all families. In many cases, we must assess, early on, culturally variable definitions of family membership and use the client's definition of family in choosing whom to treat and whom to include in any intervention. It may also be the case that the values of the client's culture conflict with the counselor's. For example, many counselors might view Camille's choice to stay home as "codependent" or "enmeshed"; such a counselor might have suggested that she should return to college to resume her studies rather than take a semester off. However, Camille's family and community do not share this view: they value maintenance of the family and the individual's commitment to the family above a temporary delay in an individual's education. Note that our point is *not* that the counselor should assume a homogeneous, stereotypic set of culturally determined values for any group of people; there is great variation within all groups. Rather, our point is that it is essential to examine one's own cultural assumptions and remain open to the likelihood that these are not appropriate for all people. This will often be particularly important during Roberts's Stages 5 and 6, when counselor and client are working to frame goals and develop plans to implement these goals. The complexity and importance of this issue warrant special consideration by the reader, and we strongly recommend examining the literature focusing more extensively on the relations among adolescents, family, and culture (DeGenova, 1997; Gopaul-McNicol & Thomas-Presswood, 1998; Herring, 1997; McGoldrick & Giordano, 1996; Ponterotto, Casas, Suzuki, & Alexander, 2001; Powell, 1983; Suzuki, Ponterotto, & Meller, 2001; Walsh, 2003).

As discussed earlier, it is also important to acknowledge the differences between clients who present with a single crisis episode, such as Esperanza, and those who present with a series of crises, such as Jenny. In *Helping Bereaved Children,* Webb (2002) discusses a case of two children dealing with the dual losses of parents, who were separated, as well as with the death of a beloved godfather. In complicated bereavement cases such as these, Webb notes that expressions of grief are similar following divorce and death, but that there are differences too that can lead to complex reactions. One difference is the intense anger a child may feel about the divorce, coupled with the self-blame for the failed marriage and often with a hope that parents will reunite. When someone dies, grief reactions will vary greatly, in part due to the degree of closeness one felt with the person who died. In Jenny's case, she was very close to her grandmother and openly grieved more for her than she did when her parents divorced. However, her reaction was complex, perhaps due, in part, to the unresolved grief and mixed feelings she had over her parents' divorce. Worden (1996) also notes that children may feel they need to hide their mourning in a divorce situation because of conflict between parents. This was certainly the case with Jenny, as her mother was not very supportive of her grieving the divorce, but was much more attentive when Jenny's grandmother died.

Last, there are ethical and legal issues specific to work with minor children that must be in the forefront of the counselor's mind. In many cases, minor children are not legally able to give informed consent for treatment. Informed consent means that individuals understand the options available to them, can competently make a decision regarding those options, and agree to the option they chose; legally, this means not only that individuals must be informed and competent, but that their decision is voluntary (Richards, 2003). The age at which children are considered competent to give informed consent varies by state, but in most, though not all, cases, children need the permission and signature of the parents. In divorce situations, this can be complicated by the fact that, if parents have shared custody, both must grant permission for the minor child to be seen in therapy. Thus, the child's ability to receive needed services may be compromised if either parent is unwilling to permit psychological treatment. It is important for counselors to know who the custodial parent or parents are; obtaining proof of custody is recommended (Thompson & Rudolph, 1996). An additional consideration is with regard to releasing information to noncustodial parents. Laws vary by state, and in some states this is a breach of confidentiality (Lawrence & Robinson Kurpius, 2000).

There is also the issue of willingness to participate on the part of the minor child, which can be seriously impacted by the stresses and conflicts that are typical of early adolescent development. For example, an adolescent child (as in the case of Peter) may be referred to therapy, but may not want services and may be resentful about being "forced" into counseling. Furthermore, early in therapy, there must be an explicit discussion among all parties regarding confidentiality, including such issues as what a counselor must report to parents even when a minor is adamant that he or she does not want a parent to be informed (i.e., abuse or a child threatening to do harm to self or another person). There must also be a discussion with parents about permitting a counselor or child not to disclose information to them about counseling sessions. Counselors must be aware of their professional code of ethics and the laws in their state about the age of consent, exceptions to consent, the rights and limits to confidentiality, and the rights to privacy (Richards, 2003). The earlier these issues are addressed, the better for all parties concerned. Addressing these issues early on in an intervention is important not just for ensuring a counselor's compliance with ethical and legal requirements, but also for establishing rapport and trust during the early stages of intervention that makes work in the later stages possible. Adolescents are particularly likely to view unexpected (from their perspective) exposure of information as a fundamental violation of trust, which can compromise any form of intervention.

CONCLUSION

Crisis intervention is a critical and necessary resource for early adolescents. The counselor skilled in crisis intervention can assist in stabilization and intervention to prevent immediate crises from becoming long-standing problems. Crisis intervention is a more cost-effective and time-effective way of dealing with problems than long-term therapy, although it is clear that there are cases where such therapy is necessary.

Counselors working with early adolescents in crisis need to be especially aware of the impacts of developmental issues on individual responses to acute stressors; individuals in this age group vary widely, although it must be assumed that all are struggling with complex and pervasive changes in most aspects of their lives. An awareness of this struggle must be built into any approach to crisis intervention. One important force influencing the course of early adolescent change is an individual's cultural context, and counselors need to be aware of this and of their own cultural preconceptions. Applying Roberts's model of intervention with issues like these in mind has the potential for successful outcomes in many, and perhaps most, instances.

NOTE

Correspondence concerning this chapter should be addressed to M. Sian O'Halloran, Division of Professional Psychology, University of Northern Colorado, Greeley, CO 80639. Electronic mail may be sent to: sianohalloran@hotmail.com.

REFERENCES

Anderson, C. (2003). The diversity, strengths, and challenges of single-parent households. In F. Walsh (Ed.), *Normal family processes: Growing diversity and complexity* (3rd ed., pp. 121–152). New York: Guilford Press.

Ashby Wills, T., Sandy, J. M., Yaeger, A. M., Cleary, S. D., & Shinar, O. (2001). Coping dimensions, life stress, and adolescent substance use: A latent growth analysis. *Journal of Abnormal Psychology, 110*(2), 309–323.

Atav, S., & Spencer, G. A. (2002). Health risk behaviors among adolescents attending rural, suburban, and urban schools: A comparative study. *Family Community Health, 25*(2), 53–64.

Bertolino, B. (2003). *Change-oriented therapy with adolescents and young adults.* New York: Norton.

Blocker, L. S., & Copeland, E. P. (1994). Determinants of resilience in high-stress youth. *High School Journal, 77,* 287–293.

Bowlby, J. (1980). *Attachment and loss: Vol. III.* New York: Basic Books.

Brooks-Gunn, J. (1992). Growing up female: Stressful events and the transition to adolescence. In T. M. Field, P. M. McCabe, & N. Schneiderman (Eds.), *Stress and coping in infancy and childhood* (pp. 119–145). Hillsdale, NJ: Lawrence Erlbaum.

Children's Defense Fund. (1999). *Key facts on youth, crime, and violence.* Washington, DC.

Cohen, J. A., Mannarino, A. P., Berliner, L., & Deblinger, E. (2000). Trauma-focused cognitive behavioral therapy for children and adolescents: An empirical update. *Journal of Interpersonal Violence, 15*(11), 1202–1223.

Cormier, L., & Nurius, P. S. (2003). *Interviewing strategies for helpers (*5th ed.). Pacific Grove, CA: Brooks/Cole.

DeGenova, M. K. (1997). *Families in cultural context.* Mountain View, CA: Mayfield.

Egan, G. (2002). *The skilled helper* (7th ed.). Pacific Grove, CA: Brooks/Cole.

Erikson, E. (1959). Identity and the life cycle. *Psychological Issues, 1,* 1–171.

Erikson. E. (1963). *Childhood and society.* New York: Norton.

Erikson, E. (1968). *Identity: Youth and crisis.* New York: Norton.

Fosha, D. (2004). Brief integrative therapy comes of age: A commentary. *Journal of Psychotherapy Integration, 14*(1), 66–92.

Fox, N. A., Henderson, H. A., Rubin, K. H., Calkins, S. D., & Schmidt, L. A. (2001). Continuity and discontinuity of behavioral inhibition and exuberance: Psychophysiological and behavioral influences across the first four years of life. *Child Development, 72*(1), 1–21.

Fuligni, A. J., Eccles, J. S., Barber, B. L., & Clements, P. (2001). Early adolescent peer orientation and adjustment during high school. *Developmental Psychology, 37*(1), 28–36.

Geldard, K., & Geldard, D. (1999). *Counseling adolescents: The proactive approach*. Thousand Oaks, CA: Sage.

Goodman, R. F. (2004). Treatment of childhood traumatic grief: Application of cognitive-behavioral and client-centered therapies. In N. B. Webb (Ed.), *Mass trauma and violence: Helping families and children cope* (pp. 77–99). New York: Guilford Press.

Gopaul-McNicol, S., & Thomas-Presswood, T. (1998). *Working with linguistically and culturally different children*. Boston: Allyn & Bacon.

Greene, S. M., Anderson, E. R., Hetherington, E. M., Forgatch, M. S., & DeGarmo, D. S. (2003). Risk and resilience after divorce. In F. Walsh (Ed.), *Normal family processes: Growing diversity and complexity* (3rd ed., pp. 96–120). New York: Guilford Press.

Herring, R. D. (1997). *Counseling diverse ethnic youth*. New York: Harcourt Brace.

Hillman, J. L. (2002). *Crisis intervention and trauma: New approaches to evidence-based practice*. New York: Kluwer Academic/Plenum.

Keane, T. M., & Kaloupek, D. G. (2002). Diagnosis, assessment, and monitoring outcomes in PTSD. In R. Yehuda (Ed.), *Treating trauma survivors with PTSD* (pp. 21–42). Washington, DC: American Psychiatric Publishing.

Kersting, K. (2003). Religion and spirituality in the treatment room. *Monitor on Psychology, 34*(11), 40–42.

Laumann-Billings, L., & Emery, R. E. (2000). Distress among young adults from divorced families. *Journal of Family Psychology, 14*(4), 671–687.

Lawrence, G., & Robinson Kurpius, S. E. (2000). Legal and ethical issues involved when counseling minors in nonschool settings. *Journal of Counseling & Development, 78,* 130–136.

Lazarus, R. S. (1993). Coping theory and research: Past, present, and future. *Psychosomatic Medicine, 55,* 234–247.

Mash, E. J., & Dozois, D. J. (2003). Child psychopathology: A developmental-systems perspective. In E. J. Mash & R. A. Barkley (Eds.), *Child psychopathology* (2nd ed., pp. 3–71). New York: Guilford Press.

McGoldrick, M., & Giordano, J. (1996). *Ethnicity and family therapy* (2nd ed.). New York: Guilford Press.

Nader, K. (2001). Treatment methods for childhood trauma. In J. P. Wilson, M. J. Friedman, & J. D. Lindy (Eds.), *Treating psychological trauma and PTSD* (pp. 278–334). New York: Guilford Press.

National Institute of Mental Health. (2004). *The National Advisory Mental Health Council Workgroup on Child and Adolescent Mental Health Intervention Development and Deployment blueprint for change: Research on child and adolescent mental health*. Washington, DC: Government Printing Office.

Okamoto, S. K., & LeCroy, C. W. (2004). Evidence-based practice and manualized treatment with children. In A. R. Roberts & K. R. Yeager (Eds.), *Evidence-based practice manual: Research and outcome measures in health and human services* (pp. 246–252). New York: Oxford University Press.

Piaget, J. (1968). *Six psychological studies*. New York: Vintage Books.

Ponterotto, J. G., Casas, J. M., Suzuki, L. A., & Alexander, C. M. (Eds.). (2001). *Handbook of multicultural counseling*. Thousand Oaks, CA: Sage.

Powell, G. (Ed.). (1983). *The psychological development of minority group children*. New York: Brunner/Mazel.

Richards, D. F. (2003). The central role of informed consent in ethical treatment and research with children. In W. O'Donohue & K. Ferguson (Eds.), *Handbook of professional ethics for psychologists: Issues, questions, and controversies* (pp. 377–389). Thousand Oaks, CA: Sage.

Ringler, L. L., & Hayden, D. C. (2000). Adolescent bereavement and social support: Peer loss compared to other losses. *Journal of Adolescent Research, 15*(2), 209–230.

Roberts, A. R. (1996). Epidemiology and definitions of acute crisis in American society. In A. R. Roberts (Ed.), *Crisis management and brief treatment* (pp. 16–35). Chicago: Nelson-Hall.

Roberts, A. R. (2000). An overview of crisis theory and crisis intervention. In A. R. Roberts (Ed.), *Crisis intervention handbook: Assessment, treatment, and Research* (2nd ed., pp. 3–30). New York: Oxford University Press.

Roberts, A. R. (2004). Crisis assessment measures and tools. In A. R. Roberts & K. Yeager (Eds.), *Evidence-based practice manual: Research and outcome measures in health and human services* (pp. 496–503). New York: Oxford University Press.

Roberts, A. R., & Yeager, K. (2004). Systematic reviews of evidence-based studies and practice-based research: How to search for, develop, and use them. In A. R. Roberts & K. Yeager (Eds.), *Evidence-based practice manual: Research and outcome measures in health and human services* (pp. 3–14). New York: Oxford University Press.

Rogers, C. (1965). *Client-centered therapy: Its current practice, implications, and theory*. Boston: Houghton Mifflin.

Rubin, K. H., Burgess, K. B., Kennedy, A. E., & Stewart, S. L. (2003). Social withdrawal in childhood. In E. J. Mash & R. A. Barkley (Eds.), *Child psychopathology* (2nd ed., pp. 372–406). New York: Guilford Press.

Seligman, M. E. P. (1995). *The optimistic child*. Boston: Houghton Mifflin.

Silverman, P. R. (2000). *Never too young to know: Death in children's lives*. New York: Oxford University Press.

Softas-Nall, L., & Francis, P. C. (1998). A solution-focused approach to a family with a suicidal member. *Family Journal: Counseling and Therapy for Couples and Families, 6*(3), 227–230.

Steinberg, L. (1996). *Adolescence*. New York: McGraw-Hill.

Steinberg, L., & Lerner, R. M. (2004). The scientific study of adolescence: A brief history. *Journal of Early Adolescence, 24*(1), 45–54.

Steinberg, L., & Sheffield Morris, A. (2001). Adolescent development. *Annual Review of Psychology, 52,* 83–110.

Suzuki, L. A., Ponterotto, J. G., & Meller, P. J. (Eds.). (2001). *Handbook of multicultural assessment* (2nd ed.). San Francisco: Jossey-Bass.

Terr, L. (1990). *Too scared to cry.* New York: HarperCollins.

Thompson, C. L., & Rudolph, L. B. (1996). *Counseling children.* Pacific Grove, CA: Brooks/Cole.

U.S. Census Bureau. (1999). *Population profile of the United States: 1999.* Washington, DC: Author.

U.S. Census Bureau. (2003). *Statistical abstract of the United States: 2003* (123rd ed.). Washington, DC: Author.

Walsh, F. (Ed.). (2003). *Normal family process: Growing diversity and complexity* (3rd ed.). New York: Guilford Press.

Webb, N. B. (Ed.). (1999). *Play therapy with children in crisis* (2nd ed.). New York: Guilford Press.

Webb, N. B. (Ed.). (2002). *Helping bereaved children* (2nd ed.). New York: Guilford Press.

Webb, N. B. (Ed.). (2004). *Mass trauma and violence: Helping families and children cope.* New York: Guilford Press.

Weisz, J. R., & Hawley, K. M. (2002). Developmental factors in the treatment of adolescents. *Journal of Counseling and Clinical Psychology, 70*(1), 21–43.

Wekerle, C., & Wolfe, D. A. (2003). Child maltreatment. In E. J. Mash & R. A. Barkley (Eds.), *Child psychopathology* (2nd ed., pp. 632–684). New York: Guilford Press.

Werner, E. E., & Smith, R. S. (2001). *Journeys from childhood to midlife: Risk, resilience, and recovery.* Ithaca, NY: Cornell University Press.

Wilde, J. (2002). *Anger management in schools: Alternatives to student violence.* Lanham, MD: Scarecrow Press.

Worden, J. W. (1996). *Children and grief.* New York: Guilford Press.

Worden, J. W. (2002). *Grief counseling and grief therapy* (3rd ed.). New York: Springer.

Worden, J. W., & Silverman, P. R. (1996). Parental death and the adjustment of school-age children. *Omega: Journal of Death & Dying, 33,* 91–102.

17

Adolescent Suicidality and Crisis Intervention

DAVID A. JOBES
ALAN L. BERMAN
CATHERINE E. MARTIN

Case Scenarios

Tom is a troubled 17-year-old high school senior. Since the divorce of his parents the previous year and a recent breakup with his girlfriend of 3 years, Tom had become increasingly depressed and reckless in his behavior. His attendance at school had become irregular, and his increased use of alcohol, marijuana, and LSD had alarmed some of his close friends. At a recent high school dance Tom was arrested for being drunk and disorderly and for carrying a concealed weapon. Friends reported that Tom had been waving a loaded handgun at his head and placing the muzzle of the gun in his mouth.

Lisa is a 12-year-old seventh grader whose school guidance counselor referred her to a psychologist for an evaluation. Lisa had become quite despondent since the recent death of her beloved grandfather. One of her teachers contacted the guidance counselor after Lisa had turned in a five-page poem entitled "Grandpa and Me in Heaven." The poem depicted a fantastic journey into "sweet death," which culminated in a "heavenly reunion" with her grandfather. When her parents were contacted, they reported that they had recently found a shoe box full of pills and pictures of her grandfather in Lisa's bedroom closet.

Bill, a 20-year-old college junior, was found by a roommate, hanging by a belt in the closet of their dorm room. The roommate (who was supposed to be away for the weekend) entered the room only moments after Bill had begun to hang from the belt, and his immediate intervention probably saved Bill's life. The roommate reported that Bill had become increasingly depressed since he had recently "come out" to his parents about being gay. Bill's parents were enraged by this news and had threatened to disown him if he "did not get such a silly notion out of his head."

The acute suicidal crisis is produced by a unique synergy of intrapersonal, environmental, social, and situational variables. As a response to life crises, suicide and self-destructive behaviors are seen among people of every age, sex, race, religion, and economic and social class. Because patients may respond to life crises with suicidal behaviors, clinicians must be prepared to face the immediate tasks of assessing possible self-harm behavior while concurrently protecting against that possibility. Often these tasks must be accomplished under conditions of incongruent expectations and goals. Suicidal people tend to defy the health professional's expectation that fostering and maintaining life is a shared goal of patient and doctor (Hoff, 1995). Suicidal individuals are typically brought to treatment by others under conditions of acute and volitional threat to life. These are not characteristics of the "good patient"; instead, these qualities bring tension and instability to (and potentially impede) the necessary working alliance with the caregiver (Vlasak, 1994). Thus, working with depressed and suicidal people can be a frightening and difficult undertaking. Indeed, the assessment, treatment, and general management of an acute suicidal crisis are perhaps among the most difficult challenges faced by any mental health professional, despite attempted suicide being one of the most frequently encountered of all mental health emergencies (Roberts, 1991; Schein, 1976).

Completed suicide is a complex and relatively rare (low-base-rate) event. Ideally, clinicians would like to be able to "predict" future occurrences of suicidal behavior and thereby make appropriate interventions. Attempts to construct inventories and use psychological tests to predict suicide (in a statistically valid and reliable manner) have thus far failed. Since completed suicide occurs relatively infrequently, most instruments tend to identify a prohibitive number of "false positives" (i.e., the identification of individuals as suicidal who do not complete suicide). Clinicians are therefore forced to make interventions based on inexact and subjective calculations of potential "suicide risk" (see Berman & Jobes, 1991; Jobes & Berman, 1993).

Nevertheless, clinicians can strengthen their ability to effectively assess and intervene by increasing their understanding of suicidal behaviors. The tragic finality of suicide demands that clinicians develop a knowledge base and a level of competence in suicide risk assessment and intervention. As suicidologists point out, suicidal impulses and behaviors are largely temporal, transient, and situation specific. Suicide intent is state dependent and tends to wax and wane, disappear and return (Berman & Jobes, 1991). Empirical research indicates that most people who kill themselves give some form of prior warning (see Shafii, Carrigan, Whittinghill, & Derrick, 1985) and often desire an outcome other than the termination of their biological existence (Shneidman, 1994). The crisis clinician is thus in a pivotal position. Accurate risk assessment and appropriate interventions can make a life-or-death difference. Making a lifesaving difference is perhaps all the more poignant when the object of assessment and intervention is a young person.

Many hold the view that youthful years should be a carefree time of innocence, play, and exciting exploration. Adolescents are commonly viewed as not yet acquainted with the hardship and responsibility of adulthood (Group for the Advancement of Psychiatry Committee on Adolescence, 1996). This culturally enforced avoidance and denial regarding the nature of adolescence and its connection to suicidal behavior might contribute to the lack of appropriate response to the adolescent suicide attempter (Berman & Jobes, 1991). Crisis clinicians must struggle with the incongruity between this commonly held view and direct evidence that for some youngsters life may be filled with intense turmoil and abject despair.

SCOPE OF THE PROBLEM

In 1996 there were 30,903 certified suicides in the United States. A total of 4,358 of these deaths, or approximately 14%, were of young people between the ages of 15 and 24. The age-specific rate of youthful suicide (12/100,000 for 15- to 24-year-olds) is somewhat lower than rates for adults ages 25 to 44 (15) and 45 to 64 (14.3). However, between 1950 and 1996 the suicide rate for youth aged 15 to 24 increased from 4.5 to 12/100,000 (almost tripled), making suicide the third leading cause of death (behind only accidents and homicide) for young people between the ages of 15 and 24 (National Center for Health Statistics, 1998). Suicide is the second leading cause of death for young people between the ages of 15 and 19 (American Association of Suicidology, 1997).

Over five times more adolescent males than females complete suicide in the United States. In contrast, females are four times as likely to make nonfatal attempts as males. The suicide rate among males between the ages of 15 and 24 has more than tripled since the mid-1950s. The suicide rate for men in this age range remains double the overall rate of suicide in the United States (National Center for Injury Prevention, 1995). (The gender differences in suicidal behaviors observed in adolescents, with some variations, tend to remain fairly consistent across the adult life span. For all ages, completed suicide is a primarily male activity, particularly among the elderly.) Whereas approximately 4,358 American youth between the ages of 15 and 24 completed suicide in 1996, as many as 2 million teenagers may make nonfatal attempts at some point in their teenage lives (Smith & Crawford, 1984). One plausible explanation for these observed sex differences lies in the differential choices of methods employed. In 1996, 62.5% of young people between the ages of 15 and 24 used firearms to complete suicide (National Center for Health Statistics, 1998), a 40% increase above the rate in 1970 (Berman & Jobes, 1995). Whereas the majority of both sexes use guns to complete suicide (in 1996: 65% of males and 47% of females; National Center for Health Statistics, 1998), the overwhelming majority of nonfatal suicidal behaviors consist of ingestion overdoses, better than 80% of which are effected by females. The ingestion of poisons, the lethality of which depends on a number of factors, including the greater chance of rescue and intervention given the time necessary for toxic action, accounted for only 267 suicide deaths in 1990.

Suicidal death among adolescents also is more common among Whites than Blacks, with White males accounting for the majority (71% in 1996) of all youth suicides. However, 15- to 24-year-old Black youth account for a greater proportion of all Black suicides (21% in 1996) than 15- to 24-year-old White youth account for all White suicides (11% in 1996). Although suicide rates among Black adolescents are lower than for White adolescents, for Black males between the ages of 15 and 19 the suicide rate increased 165% between 1980 and 1992 (National Center for Injury Prevention, 1995). For all youth, the highest rates are recorded for youth living in the western, primarily intermountain, states.

CRISIS INTERVENTION: ROBERTS'S SEVEN-STAGE MODEL

Effective intervention and treatment of suicidal people always begins with a thorough assessment and subsequent interventions based on that assessment. Through all phases of working with a suicidal patient, ongoing risk assessment is an imperative. In general practice, clinicians must be prepared to face a range of potential suicidal crisis situations. These crises may range from that of a telephone call from a desperate patient who has just ingested a potentially lethal overdose; to that of a borderline personality in an unstable, intense, and dramatically shifting mood state; to that of a patient in session simply stating vague suicidal ideation and hopelessness, in a context of a history of impulsive acting out.

As described by Roberts (1991), clinicians may effectively respond to an individual in crisis by working through seven stages of intervention: (a) assessing lethality and safety needs, (b) establishing rapport and communication, (c) identifying the major problems, (d) dealing with feelings and providing support, (e) exploring possible alternatives, (f) formulating an action plan, and (g) providing follow-up. Roberts's seven-stage model was developed to apply broadly to a range of crises, but it is clearly applicable to specific interventions with suicidal youth.

Stage 1: Assessing Lethality

An assessment of the overall lethality (i.e., dangerousness) of a crisis situation is the starting point for any crisis intervention effort. The assessment of lethality may perhaps be best understood as a process of psychiatric triage that leads to three treatment options: (1) emergency psychiatric treatment,

(2) outpatient counseling/psychotherapy, and (3) basic emotional support, validation, reassurance, or education. In the case of suicide lethality assessment, clinicians are faced with two primary scenarios—the imminently dangerous situation and the potentially dangerous situation.

Imminent Danger

In some cases, crisis intervention may need to begin with a suicidal patient who has already initiated a suicide attempt. In the imminently dangerous situation, the clinician must be fully prepared to respond to the individual whose suicide attempt may require prompt first aid and/or medical treatment. The patient's level of consciousness and orientation, rationality, and agitation will affect the level of cooperation he or she may give to the immediate assessment of the need for emergency intervention. With appropriate cooperation, questions need to be raised and answered (by the patient or the person making the contact) with regard to the location of the patient, exactly what the patient has done, and the availability of significant others. The clinician's immediate task, to assess the lethality of the attempt, can be aided by the availability of published lethality scales (Smith, Conroy, & Ehler, 1984). Where it is determined that medico-biological danger exists, or where sufficient data for that determination are not available, emergency medical intervention is required. As discussed by Hoff (1995), imminently dangerous situations should be handled by police and rescue squads, which can assure rapid transportation to a hospital emergency room—prompt medical evaluation is crucial. In addition to using lethality scales, one can assess potential lethality by accessing a hospital with a poison control center that can be called for specific overdose information. The exact amount of drug needed to effect a fatal overdose may be difficult to ascertain because the effects vary according to the size of the person, the amount and kind of drug taken, and the person's tolerance for a drug. Generally, sleeping pills, major tranquilizers, tricyclic antidepressants, and aspirin or acetaminophen are dangerous overdose drugs (especially in combination with alcohol). One rule of thumb is that a lethal dose is 10 times the normal dose; in combination with alcohol, only 5 times the normal dose may result in death (Hoff, 1995). It is useful for the clinician to have ready access to emergency phone numbers for the police, emergency rescue squad, hospital emergency rooms, and poison control centers. Needless to say, it is essential to maintain active communication with the client while these procedures are being effected. As part of this communication, the clinician should begin to structure the client's expectations through clear directives about what will happen, thus increasing the chances of establishing a therapeutic alliance with both paramedics and emergency personnel. Future treatment may be facilitated by the presence of the clinician during the medical crisis. Close contact and follow-up after the immediate medical danger is resolved assure that the patient is not simply treated and discharged without a crisis prevention plan in place.

Potential Danger

In contrast to imminently dangerous suicide crises, clinicians more typically encounter suicide crisis situations that are *potentially* dangerous. In these situations clinicians must be prepared to intervene in crises where there is active suicidal ideation but an attempt has not yet been made (but could be made in the near future). In these circumstances, intensive one-to-one clinical contact that fully addresses stages 2 through 6 in Roberts's model is necessary.

Stage 1 lethality assessments of the three initial cases of Tom, Lisa, and Bill reveal three moderately to highly suicidal youth. Bill, who was found hanging in an imminently dangerous situation by his roommate, is obviously the most lethal of the three. However, Tom's depression, reckless behavior, substance abuse, and access to a gun clearly put him at high risk as well. Finally, although Lisa's level of risk is somewhat less extreme, her suicidal preoccupation and her cache of medication for overdosing are distinct causes for concern.

Stage 2: Establishing Rapport and Communication

The importance of the clinical relationship (and the techniques used to enhance it) in the suicidal crisis cannot be overestimated. A number of authors have discussed the difficulties inherent in working with a suicidal individual (Farberow, 1970; Shneidman, 1980; Hendin, 1981). As Shneidman (1980) has observed, working with a highly suicidal person demands a more active and directive kind of involvement. Particularly in a crisis, the ability to make interpersonal contact is critical, and a supportive working relationship must be rapidly established. Hipple and Cimbolic (1979) have noted that suicidal clients must know (and feel) that they are talking with someone who is actively interested in their well-being. Any technique or approach that potentially strengthens the relationship and connectedness should therefore be employed. Eye contact, posture, and other nonverbal cues may be used to express a level of interest, concern, and involvement. Empathic listening, mirroring of feelings, emotional availability, honesty, warmth, and caring can help foster a sense of trust and a willingness to examine possibilities other than self-destruction. Empathy and support are crucial, but it is important to remember that suicidal adolescents often feel out of control. Accordingly, a more active and directive role than would normally be seen in ongoing individual psychotherapy can provide valuable reassurance and structure in a time of crisis.

There are some unique aspects to developing rapport and communication with a suicidal youth. Young people inherently bring to the suicidal crisis a unique set of developmental and emotional issues that may complicate effective assessment and intervention. Adolescence and young adulthood can be a time of tremendous change and turmoil. As Berman (1984) has discussed, adolescents are developmentally caught between childhood and adulthood, which engenders the conflictual task of separating from the world of parents and family, while simultaneously and paradoxically seeking protection from and inclusion within the family system. Accordingly, potential mistrust of adults further complicates the assessment of the young person's emotional status. An example of youthful distrust can be seen when a young person tells a friend about his or her suicidal thoughts with the clear understanding that the peer is not to betray this confidence to an adult. Youthful distrust of adults has been indirectly substantiated in the empirical literature. One recent study of a youthful sample of completed suicides revealed that 83.3% had made suicidal threats in the week prior to their deaths; of these, half made their suicidal intention known *only* to a peer or sibling (Brent et al., 1988).

Other developmental forces also increase the assessment challenge. With limited life experience, youth tend to be more focused on the present rather than the future. When a young person experiences stress, there may be a limited view of future possibilities—momentary and immediate solutions may become appealing (Berman, 1984). Adolescents characteristically have a limited capacity to delay gratification. Plainly stated, if something is wrong, the adolescent may want it fixed immediately. As Cantor (1976) has pointed out, the situation is further complicated by suicidal fantasies that may be common among adolescents. This combination of adolescent impulsivity, poor problem-solving skills, and suicidal fantasies (of escape and relief from pain) can become a recipe for lethal action. Additionally, adolescents are highly vulnerable to peer influence and are often eager to imitate role models as they seek to develop their own sense of identity. It is therefore important to assess and intervene in youthful crises with a keen awareness of the unique developmental issues of the population.

Stage 3: Identify the Major Problems

Identifying the major problems that may underlie a suicidal crisis is best accomplished through a thorough assessment interview. Ideally, an assessment interview should draw upon theory, the strength of the therapeutic relationship, and empirical/clinical knowledge specific to suicidal individuals. Theoretical knowledge provides a conceptual frame and foundation, while the therapeutic relationship (alliance) becomes the vehicle of assessment and treatment. Empirical and clinical knowledge is used to assess key variables that bear on the assessment of suicide risk. In the course of the assessment interview, it is essential for the clinician to listen closely, make direct inquiries, and assess and evaluate key variables.

Clues to Suicide

The clinician must listen carefully for signs, symptoms, or clues that may indicate suicidal intent. Often the clinician is alerted by a patient's direct or indirect comment or nonverbal behavior. The vast majority of suicidal people provide clues to their self-destructive feelings. Close scrutiny of the patient is essential because the clinician must determine whether the youth shares some commonality with those who have acted out their suicidal fantasies (Berman & Jobes, 1991). As Hipple and Cimbolic (1979) have discussed, the suicidal individual may make only veiled or disguised verbal references to suicidal feelings. The clinician must be alert for veiled threats such as "Sometimes it's just not worth it; I feel like giving up"; "I'm so tired, I just want to sleep"; or "People would be a lot happier if I weren't around." As well, other communications (e.g., diaries, journals, school essays, drawings, poems) often contain valuable, nonverbal clues to the adolescent's ideational focus.

Asking About Suicide

The assessment of suicide risk fundamentally requires direct inquiries about suicidal thoughts and feelings. Simply stated, vague suicidal comments should *always* elicit a direct question from the clinician as to whether the patient is thinking about suicide (e.g., "Sometimes when people feel depressed they contemplate suicide. Are you thinking about killing yourself?"; "Do you feel like hurting yourself or ending your life?"; "You sound pretty hopeless. Have you been considering suicide?").

Even for the experienced clinician, asking directly about suicide can be unsettling. Accordingly, there may be a tendency to underestimate the seriousness of the situation and a strong temptation to avoid asking directly about suicide. Frequently, potential helpers fear that a direct inquiry might introduce a dangerous new option not previously considered by the patient (i.e., planting a seed for suicide in the patient's mind).

Avoidance and fear are understandable reactions to suspicions of suicide, but experts in the field strongly support the value of direct inquiry (Hipple & Cimbolic, 1979; Beck, Rush, Shaw, & Emery, 1979; Pope, 1986; Curran, 1987; Alberts, 1988; Berman & Jobes, 1991). Critically, direct inquiry gives the potentially suicidal individual permission to discuss feelings that may have seemed virtually undiscussable. Direct inquiry can bring great relief to the patient—at last the inner battle of life or death can be openly discussed and explored in a safe, supportive, and accepting climate. Moreover, direct inquiry opens the doors for further assessment, potentially bringing out otherwise veiled resistances. The expression of resistances in the therapeutic context may alert the clinician to the distinct possibility of suicidal urges in the client, signaling an interpersonal alienation common to the suicidal character. It is our experience that when clinicians are sensitive and attentive to their suspicions of suicide, they are more often correct than incorrect (i.e., suicide will probably have been at least a consideration for the client).

If the client is genuinely not considering suicide, the dyad can easily move on from the topic of suicide to other areas of inquiry. On the other hand, if the client is considering suicide and the counselor avoids direct inquiry, the client may interpret the counselor's behavior as clear evidence of a lack of caring, therefore confirming his or her sense of both unlovability and the impossibility of receving help. Hopelessness may thus be reinforced, and the risk increases accordingly.

Assuming that the clinician has attended to suicidal clues and the client has affirmed some degree of suicidal thoughts or feelings upon direct inquiry, the clinician must determine whether there is an imminent danger of suicidal behavior at potential risk to the life of the client. The degree and immediacy of suicide risk must be evaluated for both clinical and legal/ethical purposes. When voluntary hospitalization is refused in extreme cases, the law often allows involuntary hospitalization (commitment) when there is evidence of clear and imminent danger to self or others (these considerations being defined by statute in each state). Therefore, the clinician must establish whether the risk of suicide is acute and immediate or chronic and long-term. Is this indeed a crisis situation with a risk of a suicide attempt in the immediate or near future? Is there sufficient upset, agitation, and emotional energy to create an immediately dangerous situation?

Approximately 80% of all suicides occur when the individuals are in a state of acute impulsive crisis. Only a small percentage of suicides are methodical or planned (especially among youthful populations). It can be reassuring to both the client and the clinician to know that most cases are those of *transient* crises. Getting through the crisis phase provides the young person the opportunity to consider more constructive and reversible options for coping. Therefore, one of the most important aspects of suicide assessment, the temporal evaluation of imminent versus long-term risk of self-harm, is essential to further assessment, intervention, and treatment.

The final determination of imminent danger depends on the assessment of key variables or "risk factors" that reflect the degree of suicide risk. It is important to assess the following (not necessarily in the following order): (a) psychological intent, (b) the suicide plan, (c) the history of previous suicidal behavior, and (d) clinical risk variables.

Assessing Psychological Intent

Many attempts have been made to operationally define the concept of suicide (see Jobes, Berman, & Josselson, 1987; Jobes, Casey, Berman, & Wright, 1991; Rosenberg et al., 1988; Shneidman, 1994). Most define suicide as a death that is self-inflicted and intended. By definition, an individual who dies by a self-inflicted accidental death does not intentionally seek the end of his or her life, whereas the aim or purpose of one who completes suicide is escape and/or death.

Clearly, the motive of ending one's existence versus that of receiving more attention from a loved one reflects very different kinds of suicidal intent. It is therefore critical to assess the psychological intention, purpose, motive, or goal of the suicidal individual—what does the option of suicide *mean* to the youth? As Berman and Jobes (1991) have discussed, the stated intent of a suicidal motive in young people is often interpersonal and instrumental. In general, the intended goals of youthful suicidal behavior involve an effort to escape the experience of pain, helplessness, hopelessness, and the emotions and cognitions associated with the suicidal state. For some, this means seeking relief through death; for others, relief may be sought through changes in others' behavior, effected by gambling with life.

Assessing the Suicide Plan

The presence or absence of a plan to attempt suicide is critical to ascertain. The plan reflects both the desired and the expected consequences of suicidal behavior and therefore provides one of the best indicators of what may actually come to pass (Berman & Jobes, 1991). Again, direct inquiry about a potential suicidal plan is necessary. If a plan is acknowledged, it is important to assess its lethality. Suicidal plans generally reveal the relative risk in that the degree of intent is typically related to the lethality of the potential method (e.g., using a gun or hanging infers higher intent, whereas overdosing or cutting infers lower intent).

Empirical research indicates that there tends to be a relationship between level of intent and the lethality of a method identified in the suicidal plan. Indeed, Brent (1987) found that a robust relationship appeared to exist between medical lethality and suicide intent in a study of youthful attempters. In general, lethal plans tend to be concrete and specific and involve dangerous methods. Risk increases when there is evidence of a carefully thought-through and articulated self-harm strategy. Similarly, the availability of lethal means (such as guns or lethal quantities of medications) about which the youngster is knowledgeable also increases the suicide risk. A plan that minimizes the chance of intervention and rescue reflects a greater suicide risk. Conceptually and empirically, the potential for rescue has been found to be central to two well-respected instruments that were constructed specifically to assess the lethality of suicide attempts (see Weissman & Worden, 1972; Smith et al., 1984). Simply put, the less likely that someone will be able to intervene, the greater the risk. Under the heading of rescue, the reversibility of a chosen method and the discoverability of an attempt must be differentially evaluated. A much higher level of suicide intent and lethality is reflected in an attempter who plans to use an irreversible method (e.g., a gun) in a place with little likelihood of discovery (e.g., a remote wooded area). For example, suicide risk may be assessed as low in a case of a vague plan involving the ingestion of pills in front of parents, versus high in a case where an individual has access to a large quantity of barbiturates and plans to ingest them after the parents leave the house.

In summarizing various elements of the assessment of a suicide plan, the clinician must evaluate the lethality and availability of the proposed method and the specificity of the self-harm strategy. Moreover, the clinician must evaluate the probability of postattempt discovery and whether efforts could be made to reverse the impact of the potential suicide act (e.g., pumping the stomach after an overdose).Assessment of the various aspects of a potential plan is perhaps the best means of evaluating suicidal intent and imminent risk of self-harm.

It should be noted that perhaps the majority of suicidal acts by youth are impulsive and unplanned. That does not in any way decrease their potential lethality, particularly if a lethal weapon is accessible at the time of urge and impulse. In the context of the other levels of assessment, the absence of a plan simply means the clinician lacks but one significant source of information.

Assessing Suicide History

Another variable that bears significantly on suicide risk is the presence or absence of a suicidal history. The risk and dangerousness increase significantly when there is *any* previous history of suicidal ideation, gestures, and particularly previous attempts. Risk increases if a previous attempt was recent, if a potentially lethal method was used, or if an effort was made to avoid rescue. Multiple past attempts, particularly if these occurred within the last 12 months and if one or more was potentially lethal, significantly increase the risk of further suicide attempts and of ultimate completion. The clinician should note the contingent reinforcers to prior behaviors to determine what was learned by the client in consequence to these events. In addition, the history of suicidal events in the client's family is an important area of inquiry for assessing the client's level of exposure to suicide and its legacies of possible imitation and modeling and/or possible biological causes to suicidal vulnerability.

Assessing Clinical Risk Variables

It is helpful for the clinician to have a working knowledge of additional risk variables for suicide that have been identified in the empirical literature. Research conducted over the past 25 years has provided practitioners with valuable information concerning various correlates of increased suicide risk (Garland & Zigler, 1993).

As described by Beck and his colleagues (Beck, Resnik, & Lettieri, 1986; Kovacs, Beck, & Weissman, 1975), for example, hopelessness may be one of the single best indicators of suicide risk. A profound sense of hopelessness and helplessness about oneself, others, and the future has been closely linked to depressive conditions and suicide (Rush & Beck, 1978). Other clinical indicators of suicide may include the following: dramatic and inexplicable affective change; affect that is depressed, flat, or blunted; the experience of recent negative environmental changes (losses); feelings of isolation or emptiness; and experience of extreme stress, free-floating rage, agitation, and fatigue.

Young people can be very sensitive to the various interpersonal pressures and expectations of others, including parents, siblings, peers, coaches, teachers, and girlfriends or boyfriends. Murray's (1938) construct of "presses" may be applied to suicidal youth to identify a range of additionally experienced pressures that may be less socioculturally bound, such as genetic factors, physical danger, chance events, alcohol or substance abuse, and psychopathology. As Berman and Jobes (1991) have noted, it is important to examine predisposing conditions, precipitating factors, and psychopathology in the assessment of those forces that may affect the suicidal youth.

Biological and sociocultural forces create a range of predisposing conditions that impinge upon on the suicidal adolescent. The suicidal youth often experiences blows to self-esteem, sense of self, and ability to cope (Berman & Jobes, 1991). These may be the direct result of growing up in a stressful family and having conflictual interpersonal relationships. Research has indicated that the parents of suicidal adolescents have conflictual relationships than do controls, including threats of separation and divorce, additionally the parents have more often experieneced an early loss of one of their parents (Stanley & Barter, 1970; Corder, Shorr, & Corder, 1974; Miller, Chiles, & Barnes, 1982). Further, suicidal youth have more frequent and serious interpersonal problems with peers, are more interpersonally sensitive, and are less likely to have a close confidant (McKenry, Tishler, & Kelley, 1982; Tishler & McKenry, 1982).

Adolescent suicides often are linked to a significant precipitating event, particularly an acute disciplinary crisis or a rejection or humiliation (Shaffer, 1988). It is important to note that such events (e.g., a fight with one's parents, a breakup of a relationship, being teased) are common to the experience of all adolescents and thus must be considered within the broader context of each adolescent's vulnerability to respond with increased suicidality to such stressors. The crisis clinician must be attentive to evidence of psychopathology, because perhaps as many as 90% of adolescent suicide completions involve youth with retrospectively diagnosable mental disorders (cf. Berman & Jobes, 1991; Shaffer, 1988). Empirical research has confirmed that certain types of psychopathology are correlated with suicidal behavior—in particular, mood disorders, especially manic-depressive illness or bipolar spectrum disorders (Garfinkel, Froese, & Hood, 1982; Robbins & Alessi, 1985; Brent et al., 1988); schizophrenia (McIntire, Angle, Wikoff, & Schlicht, 1977); and personality disorders, especially borderline and antisocial (Alessi, McManus, Brickman, & Grapentine, 1984; Berman & Jobes, 1991). Similar to adults, substance abuse disorders (both alcohol and drugs) are often implicated in adolescent suicides and may be comorbid with the preceding disorders (Brent et al., 1988; Garfinkel et al., 1982). The clinician must therefore be particularly sensitive to young people who show any evidence of psychopathology who may be in distress but may not reveal suicidal intention.

Imminent risk for self-harm behavior appears most reactive to conditions that threaten a breakdown in usual coping mechanisms and, consequently, which increase loss of behavioral control. In addition to a variety of psychopathological disorders, as noted earlier, the clinician needs to be alert for significant changes in behavior, particularly if they involve increased reliance on alcohol or drugs. Levels of rage and anxiety also are good measures of the adolescent's ability to maintain control. In addition, behavioral change and/or loss of control often alienate the adolescent from significant others who otherwise could serve to buffer or protect him or her from untoward consequences of thinking designed simply to impulsively end painful affect. Again, hopelessness tends to increase and/or be reinforced under these interactional conditions.

Stage 4: Dealing With Feelings and Providing Support

As Shneidman (1994) has discussed, the suicidal person fundamentally seeks to escape unendurable psychological pain. Critically, the feeling of pain that drives the suicidal situation must be understood idiosyncratically—what is painful to one person may not be painful to the next. Therefore, it is essential that the clinician be empathetically connected to the youth's subjective experience of pain. Connecting with the pain can be achieved through careful and thoughtful listening, emotional availability, and warmth; it may be shown by eye contact, posture, and nonverbal cues that communicate genuine interest, concern, and caring. However, as Curran (1987) has discussed, a suicidal youth may be unwilling or unable to communicate painful feelings. This, of course, is a formidable problem for the accurate assessment of risk. It may be necessary in emergency situations to confer with friends and family who may be aware of the youth's recent emotional status. A teacher or best friend may be able to provide critical information concerning recent behaviors, changes in mood, and potential losses in the young person's life. Whether the information comes directly from the young person or from a friend, parent, or teacher, it is important to try to infer an accurate assessment of the subjective pain. It should be noted, however, that such contacts might adversely affect a therapeutic relationship after the crisis is resolved.

Even though emotional pain is difficult at any age, young people may experience it especially intensely. It is critical that the clinician respect the depth and degree of pain reported by a youth. Self-reports of extreme emotional pain and trauma should not be dismissed as adolescent melodrama. The experience of pain is acute and real to adolescents and potentially life-threatening. As discussed earlier, young people tend to be present oriented and lack the years of life experience that may provide the perspective needed to endure a painful period. It is therefore critical that the clinician appreciate this perhaps limited worldview.

Simply stated, the risk of suicide increases as subjectively perceived psychological pain increases. Accordingly, it may be useful to have the suicidal youth actually rate his or her pain or hopelessness (e.g., ranging from 0 equaling absolutely no pain to 10 equaling absolutely unendurable pain). A subjective rating can be especially useful in helping to understand the young person's degree of pain. It also can help make the suicidal experience more concrete and less abstract for both the youth and the counselor. Moreover, the subjective rating can provide an ongoing barometer of suicide risk, allowing changes and improvements to be tracked beyond the initial crisis and throughout the course of treatment.

Stage 5: Exploring Possible Alternatives

In the course of crisis work it is important to explore possible options and alternative ways of coping (other than suicide). The exploration of possible alternatives typically requires a thorough evaluation of negative forces in the young person's life, as well as positive influences—what are the relative strengths and weaknesses of the individual? Various expectations and pressures can become overwhelming to the young person in the midst of a suicidal crisis, making effective problem solving difficult, if not impossible. The intensity of one particularly salient pressure can potentially outweigh other objective strengths, resources, and abilities. For example, among adolescents who complete suicide, there is a subgroup of seemingly outstanding victims who "seemed to have it all." In such cases various abilities, skills, and strengths may be irrelevant when extraordinarily high standards and an expectation of continued success or perfection rigidly define the individual's self-worth. Such a compulsive demand may defend against an underlying fragile sense of self. Accordingly, an unacceptable performance such as a grade of C on an exam, easily interpreted as the equivalent of an F, could actually precipitate a suicide attempt to thwart the experience of unacceptable feelings. Operationally, the clinician needs to directly ask a youth about the pressures and worries he or she is experiencing and perhaps rank order them to better ascertain their relative importance to the youth. Among these pressures is the adolescent's perceived "fit" within his or her family. Suicidal adolescents often talk of feeling responsible for family problems and conflicts. Some even consider their expendability as a way of freeing their family to move beyond current impasses. Conversely, it is critical to identify and assess the potential strengths, coping skills, and resources available to the young person. Reflecting back strengths and resources to the youth may provide some comfort in the midst of a crisis and underscore alternative means of coping. The risk of suicide is significantly lessened when there is evidence of internal (e.g., cognitive) and external (e.g., interpersonal) resources for coping with conflict and stress (Berman & Jobes, 1991).

The need to explore alternatives in the cases of Tom, Lisa, and Bill is abundantly clear. Tom, a troubled youth reeling out of control, is a suicide waiting to happen. At the time of his arrest, Tom was primarily dealing with his losses and depression by abusing substances and acting out. As an intelligent and generally popular teenager, with friends and family willing to support him, Tom had notable personal and interpersonal resources at his disposal but seemed unable to ask for help. Lisa, struggling to overcome the loss of her beloved grandfather, seemed to be living in a romanticized fantasy world of death and reunion. Her concerned parents were at a loss regarding how to help their daughter work through her grief. Bill, overwhelmed by his parents' hostile reaction to his homosexuality, sought escape from his unbearable feelings. In hindsight, it would seem that Bill, who had only just begun to explore his sexual identity in a gay support group on campus and in psychotherapy at the college counseling center, perhaps came out to his parents prematurely. In each of these three cases, we see individuals suffering through painful losses and debilitating feelings, yet in each case there are resources and potentials for alternative ways of coping.

Stage 6: Formulating an Action Plan

Having thoroughly assessed the risk of suicide, the clinician is in a position to formulate an action (treatment) plan of intervention. As described by Hoff (1995) and others, a series of strategic steps needs to be initiated to ensure the patient's immediate safety and shift the patient's focus from crisis to resolution.

Removing the Means

The first goal should be to immediately reduce the lethality of the situation. This is best accomplished by literally removing the means from the client's access or, at a minimum, delaying access to available means. Pills should be flushed down the toilet or given to others to monitor and dispense; guns and/or other weapons should be removed from the home. Where available, parents or significant others need to be involved in all efforts to safeguard the environment.

Negotiating Safety

One of the clinician's most effective interventive tools involves the negotiation of the patient's safety. Generally, the concrete goal of these negotiations is to ensure the patient's physical safety by establishing that the patient will not hurt him- or herself for a specific period of time. The more concrete and specific the understanding, the better. Typically, the patient will agree to maintain his or her safety until the next clinical contact, at which point a new understanding can be negotiated. The clinician must remember to keep these agreements time limited and renewable. The clinician should also remember that a "contract" with a psychologically wounded (narcissistically injured) teenager does not necessarily guarantee the patient's safety because early wounds may have severely affected the youth's trust and trustability.

Future Linkage

The clinician and the patient must create a crisis game plan that orients the patient toward the future. Long-term goals should be established and operationalized with the patient in short-term steps. This may be accomplished by identifying when the next clinical contacts will occur. Plans for activities and social contacts may be made as well. Scheduling phone contacts to touch base can also be planned. It is critical that the suicidal patient has something to look forward to. Future linkage helps orient the patient to a different and hopefully better future, creating a distance from the immediate crisis.

Decrease Anxiety and Sleep Loss

If the suicidal youth is acutely anxious and/or not able to sleep, the suicidal crisis may become worse. Medication may be indicated as an emergency intervention. However, dosages must be closely monitored and linked to ongoing psychotherapy so that the medication is not used for an overdose. Other symptoms that may exacerbate the patient's ability to benefit from verbal intervention and/or threaten the patient's ability to maintain control must be continuously monitored and treated accordingly.

Decreasing Isolation

The patient must not be left alone in the midst of a suicidal crisis. It is critical that a trustworthy friend or family member remain with the patient through the crisis phase. Efforts must be made to mobilize friends, family, and neighbors, making them aware of the importance of ongoing contact with the suicidal youth. In cases where friends or family are unavailable (or unwilling), hospitalization may be necessary.

Hospitalization

When the risk of suicide remains unabated and high, and the patient is unable to negotiate his or her safety, hospitalization becomes the necessary intervention. Simply stated, stabilization through hospitalization can provide the patient with a safe environment and a chance to remove him- or herself from the environment that produced the suicidal crisis.

Stage 7: Providing Follow-Up

Beyond emergency medical treatment and crisis intervention, after crisis resolution, ongoing counseling and psychotherapy follow-up are essential. In this era of managed care, the prevailing reimbursement structure does not lend itself to providing comprehensive follow-up care following an acute suicidal crisis. In light of the research indicating the importance of follow-up care in treating the suicidal adolescent, these policies should be examined for cost-effectiveness and should be revised accordingly (Brent & Perper, 1995). The absence or amelioration of an immediate crisis is not synonymous with the decision to not provide ongoing psychotherapy. It is important for the clinician to remember that people who have used suicidal behavior to respond to life crises in the past are prone to use such behaviors in future life crises. As the final phase of crisis resolution, the clinician must ensure that follow-up evaluation and treatment are arranged and that a strategic, preventive treatment plan is in place to circumvent potential future suicidal crises.

Various treatment modalities with suicidal clients have been discussed in the literature (see Berman & Jobes, 1991). These modalities range from longer term individual treatment (Hendin, 1981; Jobes, 1995; Toolin, 1962), to shorter term individual models (Beck & Beck, 1978; Getz, Allen, Myers, & Linder, 1983), to group treatment (Comstock & McDermott, 1975; Farberow, 1976; Hipple, 1982). Family therapy may be particularly helpful with youthful populations (Alanen, Rinne, & Paukkonen, 1981; Richman, 1979, 1986). In addition, ongoing pharmacotherapy may be useful in stabilizing mood and intrusive psychopathological symptoms. It is beyond the scope of this chapter to delineate the many aspects and variants of ongoing inpatient and outpatient psychotherapy with the suicidal adolescent. However, it is imperative that the clinician familiarize him- or herself with the increasing array of effective short- and long-term intervention strategies available to treat the depressed and suicidal adolescent, if the alarming increase in suicide among adolescents is to be halted and reversed.

CASE STUDY OUTCOMES

Tom, Lisa, and Bill were three high-risk youth in serious suicidal crises that could have had tragic outcomes. Thankfully, each case received appropriate and effective crisis intervention. Following Tom's arrest, his high school guidance counselor, with the support of his parents, arranged to have him hospitalized. He received intensive psychiatric treatment for his depression and substance abuse, and after 4 weeks he was discharged to the care of an outpatient psychotherapist. After 6 months of therapy and regular attendance at AA and NA meetings, Tom finished his remaining semester of high school and was accepted to a local community college.

After the poem episode, Lisa began to meet with a psychologist in both individual and family sessions. Recognizing her creativity, her therapist used art therapy and encouraged her to continue to write poetry about her feelings. Family therapy was helpful in working through the mourning of the grandfather, since the family had not really dealt with his death. In addition, family work led to an improved relationship between Lisa and her father, who had long been jealous of her special relationship with her grandfather (his father).

Bill was hospitalized for 3 days after his aborted hanging. After discharge, Bill continued to pursue therapy in the counseling center and also continued to attend the gay support group. Bill's parents were horrified by, and felt intensely guilty about, his suicide attempt. Although they continued to disapprove of Bill's lifestyle, they nevertheless refrained from threatening to disown him and avoided discussing the topic with him. About 3 months after his suicide attempt, Bill began dating someone from his support group, and he was markedly less depressed by the end of the school year.

SUMMARY

This chapter has examined the complexities of youthful suicide, a phenomenon that has exhibited dramatic increases over the past 40 years. Although accurate clinical prediction of suicide is virtually impossible, practitioners can nevertheless optimize their capacity to effectively respond to youthful suicide crises by informing themselves of, and developing skills in, suicide risk assessment and interventive strategies. Roberts's (1991) seven-stage model of crisis intervention has been used to illustrate one approach to working with a suicidal youth in crisis. By assessing lethality, establishing rapport, identifying major problems, dealing with feelings, exploring alternatives, formulating an action plan, and providing follow-up, a crisis clinician can make an intervention that may help save the life of a young person in a suicidal crisis.

REFERENCES

Alanen, Y. O., Rinne, R., & Paukkonen, P. (1981). On family dynamics and family therapy in suicidal attempts. *Crisis, 2*, 20–26.

Alberts, F. L. (1988). Psychological assessment. In D. Capuzzi & L. Golden (Eds.), *Preventing adolescent suicide* (pp. 189–211). Muncie, IN: Accelerated Development.

Alessi, N. E., McManus, M., Brickman., A., & Grapentine, L. (1984). Suicidal behavior among serious juvenile offenders. *American Journal of Psychotherapy, 141*, 286–287.

American Association of Suicidology. (1997). *Youth suicide fact sheet.* (Available from the American Association of Suicidology, Suite 408, 4201 Connecticut Avenue, NW, Washington, DC 20008)

Beck, A. J., & Beck, A. T. (1978). Cognitive therapy of depression and suicide. *American Journal of Psychotherapy, 32*, 201–219.

Beck, A. T., Resnick, H. L. P., & Lettieri, D. J. (Eds.), (1986). *The prediction of suicide*, 2nd ed., Bowie, MD: The Charles Press.

Beck, A. T., Rush, A. J., Shaw, B. F., & Emery, G. (1979). *Cognitive therapy of depression.* New York: Guilford.

Berman, A. L. (1984). The problem of teenage suicide. Testimony presented to the United States Senate Committee on the Judiciary Subcommittee on Juvenile Justice.

Berman, A. L. (1986). Adolescent suicide: Issues and challenges. *Seminars in Adolescent Medicine, 2*, 269–277.

Berman, A. L., & Jobes, D. A. (1991). *Adolescent suicide: Assessment and intervention.* Washington, DC: American Psychological Association.

Berman, A. L., & Jobes, D. A. (1995). Suicide prevention in adolescents (age 12–18). *Suicide and Life-Threatening Behavior, 25*(1), 143–154.

Brent, D. A. (1987). Correlates of the medical lethality of suicide attempts in children and adolescents. *Journal of the American Academy of Child and Adolescent Psychiatry, 26*, 87–91.

Brent, D. A., & Perper, J. A. (1995). Research in adolescent suicide: Implications for training, service delivery, and public policy. *Suicide and Life-Threatening Behavior, 25(2)*, 222–230.

Brent, D. A., Perper, J. A., Goldstein, C. E., Kolko, D. J., Allan, M. J., Allman, C. J., & Zelenak, J. P. (1988). Risk factors for adolescent suicide. *Archives of General Psychiatry, 45*, 581–588.

Cantor, P. (1976). Personality characteristics among youthful female suicide attempters. *Journal of Abnormal Psychology, 85*, 324–329.

Comstock, B., & McDermott, M. (1975). Group therapy for patients who attempt suicide. *International Journal of Group Psychotherapy, 25*, 44–49.

Corder, B. F., Shorr, W., & Corder, R. F. (1974). A study of social and psychological characteristics of adolescent suicide attempters in an urban, disadvantaged area. *Adolescence, 9*, 1–16.

Curran, D. K. (1987). *Adolescent suicidal behavior.* Washington, DC: Hemisphere.

Farberow, N. (1970). The suicidal crisis in psychotherapy. In E. Shneidman, N. Farberow, & R. Litman (Eds.), *The psychology of suicide.* New York: Science House.

Farberow, N. L. (1976). Group therapy for self-destructive persons. In J. J. Parad, H. L. P. Resnik, & L. G.

Parad (Eds.), *Emergency and disaster management: A mental health sourcebook*. Bowie, MD: Charles Press.

Garfinkel, B. D., Froese, A., & Hood, J. (1982). Suicide attempts in children and adolescents. *American Journal of Psychiatry, 139*, 1257–1261.

Garland, A. F., & Zigler, E. (1993). Adolescent suicide prevention: Current research and social policy implications. *American Psychologist, 48*(2), 169–182.

Getz, W. L., Allen, D. B., Myers, R. K., & Linder, K. C. (1983). *Brief counseling with suicidal persons*. Lexington, MA: Lexington Books.

Group for the Advancement of Psychiatry Committee on Adolescence. (1996). *Adolescent suicide* (Rep. No. 140). Washington, DC: American Psychiatric Press.

Hendin, H. (1981). Psychotherapy and suicide. *American Journal of Psychotherapy, 35*, 469–480.

Hipple, J. (1982). Group treatment of suicidal clients. *Journal for Specialists in Group Work, 7*, 245–250.

Hipple, J., & Cimbolic, P. (1979). *The counselor and suicidal crisis*. Springfield, IL: Charles C. Thomas.

Hoff, L. A. (1995). *People in crisis*. Menlo Park, CA: Addison-Wesley.

Jobes, D. A. (1995). Psychodynamic treatment of adolescent suicide attempters. In J. Zimmerman & G. Asnis (Eds.), *Treatment approaches with suicidal adolescents*. New York: Wiley.

Jobes, D. A., & Berman, A. L. (1993). Suicide and malpractice liability: Assessing and revising policies, procedures, and practice in outpatient settings. *Professional Psychology: Research and Practice, 24*(1), 91–99.

Jobes, D. A., Berman, A. L., & Josselson, A. R. (1987). Improving the validity and reliability of medicolegal certifications of suicide. *Suicide and Life-Threatening Behavior, 17*, 310–325.

Jobes, D. A., Casey, J. O., Berman, A. L., & Wright, D. G. (1991). Empirical criteria for the determination of suicide manner of death. *Journal of Forensic Sciences, 36*, 244–256.

Kovacs, M., Beck, A. T., & Weissman, A. (1975). The use of suicidal motives in the psychotherapy of attempted suicides. *American Journal of Psychotherapy, 29*, 363–368.

McIntire, M. S., Angle, C. R., Wikoff, R. L., & Schlicht, M. L. (1977). Recurrent adolescent suicidal behavior. *Pediatrics, 60*, 605–608.

McKenry, D., Tishler, C., & Kelley, C. (1982). Adolescent suicide: A comparison of attempters and nonattempters in an emergency room population. *Clinical Pediatrics, 21*, 266–270.

Miller, M. L., Chiles, J. A., & Barnes, V. E. (1982). Suicide attempters within a delinquent population. *Journal of Consulting and Clinical Psychology, 50*, 491–498.

Murray, H. A. (1938). *Explorations in personality*. New York: Oxford University Press.

National Center for Health Statistics. (1998). *Vital statistics of the United States* (Vol. 47, No. 9). Washington, DC: U.S. Government Printing Office.

National Center for Injury Prevention. (1995). *Suicide in the United States: 1980–1992*. Washington, DC: U.S. Government Printing Office.

Pope, K. S. (1986). Assessment and management of suicidal risk: Clinical and legal standards of care. *Independent Practitioner, 6*, 17–23.

Richman, J. (1979). Family therapy of attempted suicide. *Family Process, 18*, 131–142.

Richman, J. (1986). *Family therapy for suicidal people*. New York: Springer.

Robbins, D., & Alessi, N. (1985). Depressive symptoms and suicidal behavior in adolescents. *American Journal of Psychiatry, 142*, 588–592.

Roberts, A. R. (1991). *Contemporary perspectives on crisis intervention and prevention*. Englewood Cliffs, NJ: Prentice Hall.

Rosenberg, M. L., Davidson, L. E., Smith, J. C., Berman, A. L., Buzbee, H., Gantner, G., Gay, G. A., Moore-Lewis, B., Mills, D. H., Murray, D., O'Carroll, P. W., & Jobes, D. (1988). Operational criteria for the determination of suicide. *Journal of Forensic Sciences, 32*, 1445–1455.

Rosenberg, M. L., Smith, J. C., Davidson, L. E., & Conn, J. M. (1987). The emergence of youth suicide: An epidemiological analysis and public health perspective. *Annual Review of Public Health, 8*, 417–440.

Rush, A. J., & Beck, A. T. (1978). Cognitive therapy of depression and suicide. *American Journal of Psychotherapy, 32*, 201–219.

Schein, H. M. (1976). Suicide care: Obstacles in the education of psychiatric residents. *Omega, 7*, 75–82.

Shaffer, D. (1988). The epidemiology of teen suicide: An examination of risk factors. *Journal of Clinical Psychiatry, 49*, 36–41.

Shafii, M., Carrigan, S., Whittinghill, J. R., & Derrick, A. (1985). A psychological autopsy of completed suicide in children and adolescents. *American Journal of Psychiatry, 142*, 1061–1064.

Shneidman, E. S. (1980). Psychotherapy with suicidal patients. In T. B. Karasu & L. Bellak (Eds.), *Specialized techniques in individual psychotherapy*. New York: Brunner/Mazel.

Shneidman, E. S. (1994). *Definition of suicide*. New York: Wiley.

Smith, K., Conroy, R. W., & Ehler, B. D. (1984). Lethality of suicide attempt rating scale. *Suicide and Life-Threatening Behavior, 14*, 215–242.

Smith, K., & Crawford, S. (1984). Suicidal behavior among "normal" high school students. *Suicide and Life-Threatening Behavior, 16*, 313–325.

Stanley, E. J., & Barter, J. J. (1970). Adolescent suicidal behavior. *American Journal of Orthopsychiatry, 40*, 87–96.

Tishler, C., & McKenry, P. (1982). Parental negative self and adolescent suicide attempters. *Journal of the American Academy of Child Psychiatry, 21*, 404–408.

Toolin, J. M. (1962). Suicide and suicide attempts in children and adolescents. *American Journal of Psychiatry, 118*, 719–724.

Vlasak, G. J. (1994). Medical sociology. In S. Perlin (Ed.), *A handbook for the study of suicide* (pp. 131–146). New York: Oxford University Press.

Weissman, A., & Worden, W. (1972). Risk-rescue rating in suicide assessment. *Archives of General Psychiatry, 26*, 553–560.

18

Crisis Intervention at College Counseling Centers

ALLEN J. OTTENS
LINDA L. BLACK
JAMES F. KLEIN

This chapter's focus is on the application of Roberts's (1990, 1996) seven-stage crisis intervention model to the delivery of crisis intervention services at college and university counseling centers. Roberts's model is especially relevant, given several compelling reasons for providing crisis intervention as a therapeutic modality in this setting and with this particular clientele. First, traditional-age (18–24 years old) college students often encounter crises—death of a parent, dating violence, relationship dissolution, and threats to academic performance, to name a few—that threaten their accomplishing critical developmental tasks. These tasks include concretizing personal values, establishing emotional control, acquiring self-confidence, achieving independence, and shaping relationship skills.

Second, college counselors are witnessing the encroachment onto campuses of social problems like sexual violence (Ottens & Hotelling, 2001), the AIDS epidemic, rape trauma, alcohol and drug abuse, suicide, and racism (Fukuyama, 2001). There is also evidence, according to Turner and Berry (2000), that college counseling centers will be challenged by the increasing numbers of students presenting in extreme distress. Findings from a national survey of counseling center directors completed by Gallagher, Gill, and Sysco (2000) indicated that of those directors who participated, 77.1% reported that increases in the severity of psychological problems was a concern for their center. Due to the apparent increases in the severity of traditional-age college student presentations, Benton, Robertson, Tseng, Newton, and Benton (2003) suggest that crisis intervention and trauma debriefing will be important areas of professional development for all facets of college counseling centers.

Furthermore, Ottens and Fisher-McCanne (1990) point out that crisis intervention as a form of brief therapy is highly compatible with both college students' characteristics and institutional needs. According to Fukuyama (2001), time-limited therapy or brief therapy models fit naturally within the quarter or semester structure of most colleges and universities. Furthermore, most clients at college counseling centers meet the criteria suited to brief therapeutic interventions: acute problem onset, previous good adjustment, ability to relate, and high initial motivation (Butcher & Koss, 1978). From an institutional standpoint, crisis intervention, with its brief duration (typically 3 to 13 weeks), makes sense as counseling centers face lengthening waiting lists and set limits on the number of sessions available.

The chapter is organized around two composite case examples of relatively common types of crises encountered by college counselors. We discuss the particulars of each case and present clinical information relevant to the crisis issues. Finally, using the case examples as templates, we guide the reader through the seven stages of the Roberts (1996) model, demonstrating how the model can be adapted for brief, crisis-oriented therapy in the college context.

ACQUAINTANCE RAPE

Tamika

Hesitantly, Tamika, an 18-year-old African American freshman, requests services for problems with concentration and insomnia. She states that she has felt unsettled and "creepy" for the past three weeks. Haltingly, she reports that she is experiencing a vague sense that something awful has happened to her, although she has no distinct memory of any traumatic event. Tamika is concerned that she cannot remember events following a recent sorority-fraternity party. She adds that she remembers going to the party and then waking up naked the next morning, dazed and confused, in an unfamiliar bedroom. She admits to drinking alcohol while at the party but is adamant that she was not drunk. According to Tamika, her sorority sisters told her she left the party around 10 P.M. with a member of the host fraternity. She was not seen after that time.

Trembling, she discloses that she is scared that the fraternity acquaintance, someone she vaguely remembered from her freshman orientation group, may have spiked her drink with "rope," one of the numerous street names for Rohypnol, an illegal tranquilizing drug. She has heard frightening rumors about this crime becoming more frequent at campus parties and local bars. She is at times tearful, angry, and scared. In the absence of any clear memory of the evening's events, she has assumed that she was sexually "taken advantage of" and has no one to blame but herself. She arrived at this conclusion because in the past couple of weeks she heard through the campus grapevine that her fraternity acquaintance has a reputation as a sexual predator.

Since earlier in the week she has found it increasingly difficult to cope with the uncertainty of what happened to her. She is skipping classes, neglecting her grooming, and avoiding friends. She tells the on-call counselor that she feels "tainted" due to being sexually victimized. Compounding the problem, Tamika feels completely isolated, unable to reach out to friends or family for fear of being stigmatized or criticized.

Definitions and Clinical Considerations

When a student like Tamika presents with an acquaintance rape–precipitated crisis, the university counselor needs to consider and incorporate into the intervention plan various facts and implications that are germane to both the general problem of campus acquaintance rape and specifically to its impact on African American women.

Acquaintance rape has been defined as "nonconsensual sex between adults who know each other" (Bechhofer & Parrot, 1991, p. 12). It is contrasted with *date rape,* which is a narrower term that refers to nonconsensual sex between partners who date or who are on a date (Bechhofer & Parrot, 1991). Although these definitions appear straightforward, the campus crisis counselor needs to be aware that it is often difficult to draw distinctions between consensual and nonconsensual sex and who is an acquaintance or a stranger. The definitional distinctions should not obscure the fact that there are important differences in impact and recovery between stranger and acquaintance rape. Research supports the notion that a victim-blaming environment exists for acquaintance rape as opposed to stranger rape (Milburn, Mather, & Conrad, 2000). One's tendency to victim-blame may worsen an already challenging situation and retard the recovery process (Kaly, Heesacker, & Frost, 2002). According to the National Center for Victims of Crime (1998), acquaintance rape victims are less likely to reach out for help because they harbor a sense of distress, humiliation, and fear. Additionally, victims translate this fear to the potential of family, friends, and the public finding out about their victimization, thus creating a sense of futileness (National Center for Victims of Crime, 1998).

In this vignette, the clinical picture and intervention plan are complicated by the apparent use of a "date rape drug" that further traumatizes the victim. Rohypnol and gamma hydroxybutrate (GHB) are two powerful illegal sedatives that have made their way onto some U.S. campuses. Rohypnol, known by such street names as "la rocha," "roachies," and "roofies," is colorless, odorless, and tasteless but has strong amnesiac and disinhibiting effects (Zorza, 2001). Within 30 minutes of ingestion, the victim experiences muscle relaxation and drowsiness. Rohypnol leaves the victim incapacitated and unable to resist sexual exploitation (Zorza, 1998). With Tamika, the counselor must keep in mind that sedative-induced acquaintance rape may require a longer and more painful road to recovery. Unlike rape survivors who were conscious during the assault, those who were drugged simply cannot know how they might have been exploited; as a result, they may experience profound shame or guilt (Zorza, 2001).

Unfortunately, there is a dearth of data on the prevalence of courtship violence for African American college students (Clark, Beckett, Wells, & Dungee-Anderson, 1994). Yet the campus crisis counselor must be aware of several crucial factors. First, the counselor must be alert to any tendency to view forced sexual encounters against African American women as less serious offenses (Foley, Evancic, Karnik, King, & Parks, 1995). Second, as a result of our society's racist and segregationist history, African Americans have tended to be exposed to more violence than White Americans and hence are at greater risk for using or experiencing violence in interpersonal relationships. Finally, any dating or relationship violence among African American students can be viewed as ultimately having a negative impact on the future of the African American family; such violence undermines the positive effects of relationship and family that have been protective buffers against oppression (Clark et al., 1994).

Scope of the Problem

One of the most cited and ambitious studies of sexual victimization among college students was conducted by Koss, Gidycz, and Wisniewski (1987). In their survey of over 6,000 students at 32 U.S. colleges, they found alarmingly high incidence and prevalence rates of sexual violence perpetrated against women respondents. For example, Koss et al. calculated a victimization rate of 83 per 1,000 women who, within just six months preceding the survey, reported a sexual experience that met legal definitions of rape or attempted rape. Perhaps the most distressing finding was that 84% of the women who were raped knew their assailants.

According to Von Steen (2000), forced sexual intercourse among traditional-age college students presents significant risk to one's emotional and physical health. Finley and Corty (1993), at a midwestern university, concluded from their survey results that "by the time they were in junior and senior years, about a third of the women reported having been victims [of forced sexual assault] and about a third of the men reported being perpetrators" (p. 116). On a general level, the U.S. Department of Justice National Crime Survey reported that the highest occurrence of rape and sexual assault in 1997 existed in two age brackets, 16–19-year-olds and 20–24-year-olds (Rennison, 1999). More specifically, estimates cited by researchers of the incidence and prevalence rates for sexual assault at U.S. colleges are in the

15% to 25% range (e.g., Frintner & Rubinson, 1993; Malamuth, Sockloskie, Koss, & Tanaka, 1991; Schwartz & DeKeseredy, 1997).

It was no surprise to the college crisis counselor that Tamika's assailant was known to her, or even that the rape was associated with a fraternity party. Although there is not a definitive answer as to whether fraternity members are more prone to committing rape than other college men (Koss & Cleveland, 1996), student development research, both qualitative and quantitative, suggests that the college crisis counselor should at least be prepared to inquire whether a client's rape and attendance at a fraternity function are connected. For example, Copenhaver and Grauerholz (1991) found that fraternity members resort to the "party method" as a means for sexual exploitation. Fraternity parties are often unsupervised events where the members control the structure of activities and drinking is encouraged. Schwartz and DeKeseredy (1997) have put forth peer-support models suggesting that the bonding, secrecy, shared traditional values toward women, and narrow concepts of masculinity promote sexual victimization of women on campus.

Major Vulnerabilities and Risk Factors

Although not a cause of sexual assault or acquaintance rape per se, alcohol is frequently linked to such aggressive acts. Humphrey, Kitchens, and Patrick (2000) state that violent behavior is linked to substance abuse and that violence associated with alcohol on college campuses is generally directed at property and persons. In a representative study, Muehlenhard and Linton (1987) found that over 50% of the men and over 50% of the women who reported sexual assault on a date had been drinking. It should be kept in mind that alcohol, not illegal sedatives, is the most common date rape drug. However, college crisis workers must absolutely avoid making value judgments about the drinking behavior of an acquaintance rape victim and refrain from blaming the victim, even when the victim, as in Tamika's case, is an underage drinker. The counselor must remember that when a male acquaintance brings a sedative to a party to spike drinks, he is committing a premeditated criminal act. As Abbey, McCauslan, and Ross (1998) have pointed out, the vulnerability resides in the manner in which certain males exploit situational variables:

> A sexually predatory male who has stereotypic beliefs about gender roles and rape is inclined to view women as sexual objects, seek out and exploit all opportunities for sexual encounters, and misperceive friendliness as a sexual come-on because this is what he is hoping to find. He then feels comfortable forcing sex, especially if he feels led on or can attribute his actions to the effects of alcohol. (p. 186)

Indeed, the rape-supportive attitudes and personality characteristics of the male perpetrator are a major consideration in terms of the factors that place college women at risk. The rape-supportive attitudes allow perpetrators to psychologically denigrate women, to provide justification for exploiting women, and to discount the seriousness of their own behavior. In their review of the literature on college men and rape, Berkowitz, Burkhart, and Bourg (1994) pointed out that sexually aggressive men are found to possess hypermasculine and antisocial personality characteristics. Hypermasculine males are likely to harbor callous attitudes toward women and to treat them with anger and rejection; an antisocial orientation has been linked to college men's coercive sexuality. In his interviews with college men who had committed date rape, Kanin (1985) found the men to be constantly on the prowl for sexual partners and willing to use any verbal or physical strategy to get sex.

Another plausible explanation provided by Davis and Liddell (2002) is that in addition to pathological disturbances, date rape can be viewed through the lens of a sociocultural theory of rape. For example, according to Davis and Liddell, sex role socialization via peers and media contribute to the widespread incidence of date rape. These socialized gender roles reveal a culture in which coercive sexuality is normalized, thus creating a rape-supportive environment (Milburn et al., 2000). Furthermore, date rape is viewed as an extreme form of traditionally socialized sexual interactions between males and females (Davis & Liddell, 2002).

The college crisis counselor should be aware that, because Tamika is a freshman student, she is at a higher risk of sexual assault. According to Von Steen (2000), freshmen may experience unhealthy thoughts, feelings, or behaviors that include, but are not limited to, the following: (1) feeling depressed, (2) feeling anxious, (3) drinking or using drugs, (4) withdrawing, or (5) becoming attached to other students who encourage risky behavior. Freshmen women in their first few weeks on campus are especially vulnerable because they have not caught on to the social "rules" (Bohmer & Parrot, 1993). This last point is crucial. College dating relationships are governed by unwritten "scripts" or rules that often reflect a power differential in favor of the male. Therefore, males do not perceive female resistance to sexual encounters as a protest but merely as an extension of the female role in the script (Milburn et al., 2000). Furthermore, Milburn et al. describe rape as an appendage of these traditional sexual scripts.

It is not unusual for young women to enter college with histories of childhood or adolescent sexual assault experiences. The crisis worker should, at some point, very tactfully ascertain whether Tamika's recent acquaintance rape is a revictimization experience. Women with a history of sexual victimization tend to be at a higher risk for being sexually revictimized by a college date or acquaintance (Gidycz, Coble, Latham, & Layman, 1993; Gidycz, Hanson, & Layman, 1995). From a preventive perspective, the crisis counselor should begin considering postvention procedures with Tamika so that she does not become more "victimizable."

Resilience and Protective Factors

After an acquaintance rape on campus, tertiary prevention efforts should be mobilized to limit the damage inflicted by the incident (Benson, Charlton, & Goodhart, 1992). These efforts may involve the college's health center, campus security personnel, residence halls, counseling center, campus ministry office, women's resource center, and judicial affairs office.

Tamika came to the university's counseling center several weeks after the assault. This was an important first step on her part because victims of acquaintance rape may not label their experience as rape or may be too ashamed to seek help. The college crisis worker began brief individual counseling to help Tamika begin the stabilization process and to drain off intense emotions. It is important to consider the gender and value orientation of the crisis worker as factors that will influence recovery (Petretic-Jackson & Jackson, 1990). A male counselor, despite his clinical skill and compassion, may not be trusted. Likewise, the counselor must convey warmth and acceptance and be free of bias toward the victim. The counselor also must be careful about overidentifying with the victim, lest she or he zealously try to rescue the client or take over the recovery (Petretic-Jackson & Jackson, 1990).

The crisis counselor talked with Tamika about possible health consequences of her assault. With the counselor's assistance, Tamika made contact with a physician on the university's health staff who is particularly sensitive to the needs of physically and sexually assaulted women. The physician will perform tests and an examination to check for injuries, possible pregnancy, and sexually transmitted diseases. Confidentiality and respect for the client are essential priorities. The counselor must not divulge information about Tamika's situation without her consent, and the counselor and Tamika must establish a collaborative relationship: the counselor cannot compel her to take any preventive or remedial action, no matter how "good" it might be for her.

Individual counseling may give way to group counseling for survivors of sexual assault. When a college or university offers this counseling service, clients find the healing environment and sense of bonding with other survivors to be especially therapeutic. The group provides an outlet for the expression of feelings and for their validation by other group members, which is important for recovery (Burkhart, 1991).

The residence hall staff can be enlisted to perform important tertiary prevention functions. It may be necessary to provide safer housing for an acquaintance rape victim or to arrange a move to a different residence hall. In Tamika's case, the residence hall staff consulted with her roommate and hall friends to help them respond to Tamika in positive ways and to educate them about how Tamika might feel as she recovers from the assault. The friends were helped to accept Tamika's changed moods and need for personal space and to listen empathically as she disclosed at her own pace.

The college crisis worker should consider the role that spirituality or church involvement might play in recovery and be aware of its particular value for African American clients in crisis (Kanel, 1999). Although Tamika was not comfortable discussing her feelings with the minister of her church back home, she did accept a referral to an African American member of the campus ministry. Some colleges have a women's resource center that may offer alternative therapies and growth activities such as dance, painting, or other expressive arts. Some women (and certainly a small percentage of acquaintance rape victims) may seek redress through the campus judicial affairs office. These officers can counsel students about options available through the code of conduct policies and procedures for handling the case sensitively and appropriately. For some women, the successful prosecution of a case against their assailant brings a powerful sense of empowerment and satisfaction that other women may have been helped.

CRISIS INTERVENTION: APPLICATION OF THE MODEL (TAMIKA)

Stage 1: Establish Rapport and Relationship

Tamika's initial request for a female, African American counselor is honored. The counselor communicates caring and warmth both verbally and nonverbally. In an accepting manner, the counselor allows Tamika to express her feelings and describe the sequence of events. To quell some of Tamika's anxiety, the counselor briefly answers her questions about confidentiality and the effects of date rape drugs like Rohypnol. The counselor allows Tamika to disclose her story through gentle questions and encouragers; she does not sidetrack Tamika by focusing unnecessarily at this point on her academic difficulties.

Stage 2: Conduct a Thorough Assessment, Including Immediate Psychosocial Needs

Given the emerging clinical picture, the Roberts (1996) model suggests assessing for dangerousness to self or others and for the client's immediate psychosocial needs. In this case, the salient issue is to determine immediate psychosocial needs. Rating Tamika across the three dimensions of the Triage Assessment Form (Myer & Ottens, 1994), the counselor arrives at a score of 26, suggesting the need for a more directive counseling approach to help her cope. Health, physical safety, and social support are identified as the three most pressing needs. The counselor assists in facilitating a referral for Tamika to an empathic physician at the university health center. Next, the counselor determines that Tamika is not being harassed or stalked by her assailant and that she is apparently safe remaining in her residence hall room. Social support is found to be available from Tamika's older sister, whom she trusts, and plans are set for the sister to come to campus during the weekend.

Stage 3: Identify Major Problems

The event that precipitated Tamika's visit to the counseling center occurred only three weeks ago. At that time, she felt ready to tell her roommate about the events at the party. The roommate, however, reacted with shock: "How could you have let this happen to you? Don't you know that you've been *raped?*" This insensitive remark shocked Tamika into awareness—finally, someone had provided her with the word that matched her experience.

With a complicated crisis event such as a drug-induced acquaintance rape, the crisis worker can expect a host of problems and issues to emerge. Tamika feels compelled to focus on several concerns that tend to muddle the picture: What should I tell others so they won't think the wrong thing about me? How am I going to make up the schoolwork I've missed? How could I have been so naïve? Among Tamika's expressions of shame, indecision, and worry, the counselor takes note of one that has potential for focusing their work. When Tamika says, "I want to get this mess out of my life and just get on with things," the counselor leans forward and asks the focusing question, "And how would that happen? How can we help you recover?"

Without much difficulty, Tamika puts forth two possibilities: getting a handle on her feelings (e.g., fear, anger, sadness, guilt) and regaining a sense of control over her life. The counselor, who is also concerned about Tamika's withdrawal and disengaging coping choices, adds a third possibility, which is widening the helping net around her.

Toward the close of this counseling session, the counselor and Tamika engage in the following dialogue:

Counselor: Tamika, can you tell me if there was any other time in your life when you felt this way, that is, wanting to get over a terrible mess and get on with things?

Tamika: (pausing to think) Maybe the closest to this is when I was a junior in high school and my favorite teacher, Mrs. Adams, was killed in a car crash. She was my music teacher.

Counselor: That's very sad. . . . How did you manage to carry on after that?

Tamika: Well, eventually I figured God had a plan in this tragedy. I got myself another piano teacher and practiced harder to get better. I wanted to do my best to, you know, to honor her memory.

Counselor: To me that's an indication of exceptional maturity on your part. The way you took a positive meaning from her accident, does that tell us anything about your capacity to do something like that under the present circumstances?

This brief dialogue was a key step in bringing the problem into focus and forging a working alliance between client and counselor.

Stage 4: Deal With Feelings and Emotions

During the early counseling sessions, Tamika is able to ventilate feelings and self-statements. She is fearful of meeting her assailant at some other campus function. She feels simultaneously angry at him and at herself. A number of times, she expresses disgust with herself, such as, "Something must be wrong with me. It's my fault for hanging out in the wrong places." The counselor is aware that, if adhered to, these blaming self-statements could slow Tamika's recovery. Eventually, the responsibility for the assault needs to be placed on the assailant himself. However, during the early sessions, the counselor allows Tamika to express her feelings without being censored. The counselor also helps Tamika to "unpack" or clarify vague emotional sensations, such as her feeling "creepy."

Stage 5: Generate and Explore Alternatives

Fortunately, the college campus and local community contain a number of resources to help Tamika become a survivor of the assault. Initially, the counselor takes a more directive approach given Tamika's isolation, intrusive thoughts, and disengagement. This approach involves suggesting and prioritizing (with input from Tamika) several appropriate resources in order to expand the net of support and caring around her. The student health center, her residence hall staff, and an older, trusted sister are quickly identified. Continued individual counseling is suggested, with referral to a sexual assault supervisors' group in the near future.

A list of helping resources can be generated, and that is often the easiest part. In this case, care must be taken to answer Tamika's ongoing questions about confidentiality. She must be given assurances about the sensitivity of the helping resources. The counselor acts to mobilize helping resources and may serve as an advocate to cut red tape that could unnecessarily delay Tamika's getting medical attention or an appointment with residence hall staff.

Stage 6: Develop and Formulate an Action Plan

Several sessions of individual counseling have helped stabilize Tamika. During the sessions, Tamika has begun telling the narrative of her assault, and this has initiated the process of normalizing her emotional reactions and reframing them as part of the recovery process. One of the important functions of crisis resolution at this stage is to identify and examine self-blaming statements. As healing progresses, there is a shift from recalling and recounting the trauma to exploring the *meaning* of the traumatic event and how it can be incorporated into the self-system (Funderburk, 2001). Journaling, relaxation exercises, and continuing use of her support network (older sister, close friend from home) are part of Tamika's therapeutic adjunctive activities. At the suggestion of a friend and the encouragement of the counselor, Tamika also began kickboxing lessons that were held in the campus recreation center.

Tamika accepts referral into a trauma recovery group that is held in a safe off-campus location. Some group members are students from the campus; about two-thirds are adult women from the local community. In the group, sharing, bonding, and support are important healing factors. The group itself becomes a safe vessel in which the initial meaning attached to the assault is deconstructed and reconstructed. Tamika's perception of herself as "tainted" or stigmatized becomes transformed into "I'm not someone who is 'spoiled' through and through. My recovery and strength give me power over an event that I did not cause. I feel in control when I prevent *him* from winning."

Stage 7: Conduct Follow-up

Recovery from an acquaintance rape, especially a drug-induced one, is an ongoing, difficult process. Group counseling with supportive family and friends and self-empowering extratherapeutic activities (journaling, kickboxing) become part of a multipronged healing strategy. The message that Tamika is internalizing is "Living well is the best revenge."

The crisis intervention with Tamika has proceeded with a focus on the here and now and on the future (Roberts, 1990). Now the crisis counselor schedules occasional check-ins and monitors Tamika's progress and participation in her healing activities. During the check-ins, the counselor performs a brief assessment using the Clinician-Assisted PTSD Scale (Blake et al., 1995) to monitor symptoms. At the follow-up sessions, the counselor inquires into Tamika's current academic, social, spiritual, cognitive, and emotional functioning.

THE IMPOSTER PHENOMENON

Megan, the "Imposter"

Megan, a 20-year-old second-semester sophomore, attends a large public university. She is enrolled in a prelaw curriculum. A serious, high-achieving student (GPA of 3.6 on a 4.0 scale), Megan has set her sights on a lucrative corporate legal career.

Megan presents herself as a walk-in client at her university counseling center. She is in obvious distress, expressing worry that she will fail an important midterm exam. She harbors serious self-doubts about her ability to eventually perform as a lawyer. When the on-call counselor inquires about recent events that might have precipitated her fear, Megan responds:

> I've been worrying about this big exam next week and how I'll mess it up. I couldn't get the worry out of my mind. It just kept building, and I kept telling myself, "You've got to ace it! This is your chance to prove yourself!" I had no confidence in my ability to apply all these complicated principles. After all, if I'm going to be a corporate lawyer, I've got to be able to handle this kind of pressure. Then it dawned on me: I've gotten by all along because courses have been easy, and I've been able to charm my way to good grades. With this test, you either know it or you don't. I'm afraid everybody else will find out I don't have what it takes.

After relating that her academic accomplishments are due to luck and an ingratiating personality, Megan slumps in her chair and sobs quietly. She says she hasn't been sleeping well for the past week in anticipation of this exam; additionally, her racing thoughts seem to have a mind of their own. Because she believes that her academic situation and emotional state are out of her control, she remarks that she doesn't know if she can continue living this way.

She considers a host of impulsive coping options: changing majors, dropping out of school, avoiding her friends on campus, and hatching plans to deceive her parents. Interspersed among Megan's pressured descriptions of these ill-conceived plans are numerous self-deprecating statements, such as "I can't continue fooling myself and others like this" and "I knew eventually others would find out about me."

Definitions and Clinical Considerations

The impostor phenomenon (IP) is described by Clance and Imes (1978) as an internal experience of intellectual phoniness prevalent among a select group of women in clinical and college settings. Leary, Patton, Orlando, and Funk (2000) build on this seminal description by providing the following three constructs central to a sense of impostorism: (1) a feeling of fraudulence as well as believing that others' perceptions are more favorable than warranted, (2) fearing exposure, and (3) engaging in specific behaviors to insulate against information that would certify a sense of worth and competence. The impostor experience persists despite independent, objective, and tangible evidence to the contrary.

Clance and O'Toole (1988) describe the female impostor experience as cyclical. The cycle begins when the student faces an exam, project, or task that involves external evaluation. The individual experiences great self-doubt and fear that, as in Megan's case, may be expressed as generalized anxiety, psychosomatic complaints, or sleep disturbance. It is important for the university crisis counselor to keep in mind that "imposters" are actually high achievers who may attempt to cope by overpreparing or by procrastinating, only to end up in a frenzied rush to catch up. The cycle ends with the impostor likely to have successfully completed the test or project. When she is praised or rewarded for her success, she discounts the recognition, which further feeds into her self-doubt and belief that suffering leads to success. And so the cycle repeats itself.

Imposters tend to be introverted and feel terrorized by failure. The intellectual inauthenticity these women describe often leads to the fear of being publicly unmasked as a fake. This fear led to Megan's choosing impulsive and dysfunctional coping methods.

Scope of the Problem

Clance and Imes (1978) found a higher prevalence of IP among women than among men. Clance and Imes interacted with 150 high-achieving women from a variety of disciplines at both graduate and undergraduate levels. These women all had external evidence of success (degrees, awards, high test scores), yet they felt like impostors. Common clinical symptoms included lack of self-confidence, depression, generalized anxiety, and low frustration tolerance with respect to meeting personal standards (Clance & Imes, 1978; Matthews & Clance, 1985).

The failure to internalize success was initially viewed as unique to females (Clance & Imes, 1978), but college counselors must be aware that IP may be just as prevalent in males (Topping & Kimmel, 1985). The research has been equivocal with regard to gender differences in the expression and prevalence of IP (Thompson, Davis, & Davidson, 1998). King and Cooley (1995), in a study of 127 undergraduates, found that higher levels of IP for females were associated with greater family achievement orientation, higher grade point averages, and more time spent on academic endeavors. However, these results need to be interpreted with caution because of the use of imprecise measures of academic achievement (e.g., GPA) and achievement orientation. The college counselor should bear in mind that when a study uncovers a greater prevalence of IP among females, it may be an artifact of gender-role stereotyping or parental messages regarding scores (King & Cooley, 1995).

Thompson et al. (1998) compared impostors and nonimpostors from a sample of 164 undergraduates. The impostors evidenced higher levels of anxiety, lower self-esteem, and a greater need for perfectionism. One finding of particular relevance for college counselors from this study is the tendency of impostors to overgeneralize, that is, to equate academic failure with failure as a person. Carver and Ganellen (1983) reported this tendency to overgeneralize to be a powerful predictor of depression in college students. Returning to the vignette, if the college counselor has not already assessed for it, he or she should be sure to ask Megan about depressive symptomatology.

Major Vulnerabilities and Risk Factors

Clance and Imes (1978) and Matthews and Clance (1985) suggest that IP develops in the dynamic interactions of the family of origin. Clance (1985) hypothesized that the family context may provide four essential elements in the development of IP. First, in childhood, the imposter believes that her abilities are unique and atypical in her family. Second, the feedback she receives from outside the family system conflicts with feedback from within the system. Third, she is not recognized or praised for accomplishments by family members. Finally, family members communicate that success and intelligence should come with little effort.

The crisis counselor needs to be mindful of the role assigned to the IP sufferer within the family and how that role impacts current thoughts and feelings. Clance and O'Toole (1988) suggested that the IP sufferer has received either of two messages from her family: You are not the bright one, or You are the bright one and success will come easily to you. King and Cooley (1995) considered it possible that IP females in their study received parental messages that implied academic achievement was due to effort rather than talent. Such messages might impress on females that they inherently have less of what it takes.

King and Cooley (1995) presented data that support the hypothesis that a family environment emphasizing achievement is associated with higher levels of IP. They recommended obtaining students' perceptions of the importance of achievement in their families of origin. Miller and Kastburg (1995) interviewed six women employed in higher education settings who came from blue-collar family backgrounds. Although IP was not an issue for all six, for some of the women IP dogged them as a "lifelong charade." This is very preliminary evidence suggesting that socioeconomic status (SES) might impact the degree of IP present.

Crisis counselors should be mindful and inquire about the IP sufferers' perceptions of achievement orientation in their families of origin and recollections of parental messages about achievement and ability. A gauge of the families' SES level might also fill out the clinical picture, as well as ascertaining whether the IP client is the first in the family to attend college.

In addition to the family of origin discussion, a three-pronged study conducted by Leary et al. (2000) with college undergraduates strongly suggests that the behavior of imposters possesses a notable self-presentation element. For example, those research participants who scored high on impostorism and were not likely to be "found out" by audiences were not likely to belittle their accomplishments to the same extent as those who believed their shortcomings may become public. Therefore, the implication for counselors is that one must carefully examine the relationship between an imposter's private self-perception and his or her public self-presentation (Leary et al., 2000).

Resilience and Protective Factors

Megan's request for assistance and support should be viewed by the college crisis worker as an invitation to intervene in the IP cycle. Typically, impostor feelings are not presented in a forthright manner by the client. Persons suffering from IP usually do not seek assistance due to the potential for shame and the embarrassment of being found out. Therefore, it is critical to establish an empathic, nonauthoritarian, therapeutic alliance (Clance & O'Toole, 1988) that allows for identification and emergence of these feelings.

Megan presented at the counseling center with feelings of intense anxiety and a sense of dread prior to her exam. This is significant because the IP sufferer customarily moves away from others who could help. Clance and O'Toole (1988) described this movement away as an attempt to isolate oneself in order to deal with the fear and shame that accompany IP. The alert counselor begins by establishing a supportive and inclusive relationship. The nonjudgmental, accepting relationship reduces Megan's tendency to isolate herself. This relationship may provide the basis for a later referral into a support group.

CRISIS INTERVENTION: APPLICATION OF THE MODEL (MEGAN)

Stage 1: Establish Rapport and Relationship

Megan, a prelaw student, is a walk-in client at her university's counseling center. She is panicking over an upcoming exam. She describes her symptoms, which include an inability to concentrate and spiraling anxiety. "I've got to do well on this test," she repeats, while emphasizing the importance of grades, given her career ambition of becoming a corporate lawyer. During this initial contact, the counselor communicates her concern about Megan's fear of failing by intermittent eye contact, voice tone, and physical proximity. Establishing rapport is crucial, as the counselor surmises that Megan, like other IP clients, may be ashamed to ask for help—an act tantamount to admitting failure. Instead of weakness, she counselor strives to frame Megan's help seeking in terms of hopefulness and strength of character:

Counselor: I'm optimistic about your ability to prevent events from getting out of control. In fact, coming here to talk to someone suggests that you knew this was the right thing to do.

Megan: Well, I felt like I had nowhere else to turn.

Counselor: But isn't there always the option of "toughing it out" in isolated silence? Instead, you seem to be making a more proactive choice.

Stage 2: Conduct a Through Assessment, Including Immediate Psychosocial Needs

The event triggering Megan's panic was the thought that she might not possess the necessary self-confidence for a law career, especially if such a thing as an exam could disquiet her so. She then connected this thought to a realization that there was nothing of intellectual substance to her: she had gotten by through luck and charm. With this information, the counselor establishes the initial clinical impression that Megan presents with the imposter phenomenon. It becomes evident to the counselor that Megan's modal coping style is to overachieve and motivate herself through worrying. Through probes and brief history taking, the counselor defines the scope and duration of the problem. Actually, feeling phony is a long-standing concern for Megan, but it appears now in bold relief given the stressor of the big exam. The nature of IP is such that Megan is likely to struggle to acknowledge previous success and personal strengths despite evidence to the contrary.

The counselor assesses Megan's current functioning utilizing the Triage Assessment Form (TAF; Myer & Ottens, 1994). This assessment reveals most dysfunction in the cognitive domain: the intrusiveness of her self-doubts and how her self-evaluation differs from the reality of her accomplishments. The TAF score of 18 suggests a collaborative approach can be used with Megan at this stage of treatment. The counselor also made note of Megan's offhand comment, "I don't know if I can continue living this way." Later in this initial session, the counselor came back to that comment to unpack its meaning, as it might be an indirect reference to suicidal ideation:

Counselor: Megan, a few minutes ago you said that you didn't know if you can continue living this way. Is that an expression of just how out of control this situation has gotten?

Megan: Absolutely. If this is what important exams are going to do to me, I don't want any more of it. I mean, I can't continue to freak out over every test.

Counselor: I want to be sure I understand exactly what you mean. Are you saying to me that your approach to taking tests has to change—that you don't want to continue freaking out whenever there's a test?

Megan: Yes, that's what I mean.

Counselor: As opposed to saying, "I can't continue living this way" when somebody has plans to hurt themselves?

Megan: (face reddens) You mean suicide? Oh, no, that's not anything I'm even thinking about.

Stage 3: Identify Major Problems

In this case, the precipitating event, the upcoming exam, was quickly established. The problems needing to be addressed were intertwined: how to attenuate the symptoms of anxiety and effectively prepare for the exam.

During this stage, Megan is allowed to express her feelings, which are a mix of catastrophizing about the test outcome and self-doubting personal criticisms. Besides the raw feelings, the counselor also listens for Megan's beliefs about her intellect, work ethic, and attributions for her previous successes. Knowing that IP may have a familial component, the counselor tunes into family messages about success and expectations of Megan's gender.

Stage 4: Deal With Feelings and Emotions

There are two distinct aspects to this component of the crisis intervention model. The counselor strives to allow Megan to freely express her feelings, to experience catharsis, and to tell the story about her current crisis situation. To this end, the counselor relies on standard active listening skills: accurate paraphrasing, minimal encouragers (Egan, 1998), reflecting feelings, summarizing, and reassurances. These complementary counselor responses not only allow the client's dysfunctional style to unfold but also are the basis for establishing a working alliance (Kiesler, 1988). Very cautiously, the counselor at this stage will work "anticomplementary" responses into her dialogue with Megan. Anticomplementary responses include advice giving, interpretations, reframes, and probes. Such responses are designed to begin the process of challenging the client's maladaptive cognitive and behavioral choices (Kiesler, 1988). Such confrontive interventions loosen Megan's maladaptive schemas, help her consider behavioral options, and question her attributions of failure and success. The judicious blending of complementary (supporting or bonding) responses and anticomplementary (challenging or frustrating) responses is thought to constitute an interplay that is fundamental to the therapy process (Hanna & Ottens, 1995). The following is a probing response typical of this stage:

Megan: (emphatically) I can't afford to take this test lightly. I'll try psyching myself up—"You've got to prove yourself on this test! You *can't* screw it up! What if you fail?"

Counselor: Consider this for a moment: Will your success on the test be *because of* or *in spite of* that kind of self-talk?

Stage 5: Generate and Explore Alternatives

The crisis counselor must deal with the immediate concern of how Megan will cope with the upcoming test. Beyond that, the larger questions of dealing with the distorted view of her personal competency and possible familial dynamics may be issues for later counseling work. The counselor is aware that IP clients devalue their opinions and overvalue those of the "authority." Hence, a collaborative approach is used to brainstorm ways to handle the exam. All options are fair game. Eventually, three options are seriously discussed that are the opposite of Megan's initial avoidant, impulsive choices: (1) join a study group with some laid-back friends; (2) provide tutoring for her roommate, who is seriously struggling with prelaw, because one actually learns best by teaching another; and (3) practice a rapid relaxation technique (Ottens, 1984) to lower anxious arousal while studying.

Stage 6: Develop and Formulate an Action Plan

For the short term, that is, to manage the crisis of the upcoming exam, the counselor and Megan adopt a three-pronged approach. First, they draw up a behavioral contract that includes the three coping choices outlined previously. Second, they identify the types of sabotaging self-talk Megan might use to negate the contract (e.g., "Why waste my time helping my roommate?" "This won't work!"). Third, the counselor makes an explicit commitment to be there to help: "Megan, I want you to know that as long as you are committed to working on this contract, I will do all I can to help and support you. This truly is a 50–50 effort on both of our parts."

There are also longer-term considerations, because for the IP client there will always be another test, term paper, or important evaluation that will be cause for self-doubt. Even if Megan excels on the big exam, it will be easy for her to discount her success or to attribute it to external factors. Hence, continued intervention is recommended to target her beliefs around themes of negative self-efficacy, perfectionism, and the use of worry as a self-motivator. She also has the belief that others can somehow see into her and spot her as a phony. In subsequent sessions, the counselor will address these issues, as well as familial achievement expectations. Group counseling is an option, especially if the group is composed of other women who share these IP beliefs.

Stage 7: Conduct Follow-up

Brief, crisis-oriented therapy in this case consisted of 10 individual counseling sessions. Megan elected not to join a group at this time but kept this idea in mind as a later option. The counselor and Megan agreed to schedule a follow-up session during the second week of the next semester.

At that follow-up session, the counselor must note whether Megan has fallen back into the IP cycle. The counselor will want to (1) assess the fluidity or rigidity of Megan's cognitions, (2) discuss future stressors, (3) inquire into how she is rehearsing to handle those stressors, (4) assess her relationships with peers, and (5) learn what evidence she now uses for gauging performance.

CONCLUSION

Several themes emerge from the vignettes of Tamika and Megan. First, the concerns facing both women need to be addressed by the counselor in a sensitive, knowledgeable, and culturally aware manner that demonstrates an understanding of the potential impact that gender, ethnicity, and family history can have on the presentation and maintenance of symptoms. Second, the crisis worker in a college counseling center should be cognizant of the personal context in which these symptoms emerge (e.g., client's potential for self-blame, desire for perfection, cultural expectations—sexually and academically—for young women). Third, the potential for students to isolate from those who could help them needs to be understood in terms of students' developmental needs for autonomy, personal competency, and self-definition. In both vignettes, the potential for isolation was high. The availability of a caring professional allowed each client to engage in a process of stabilization that was facilitated by following the crisis intervention model (Roberts, 1996). Finally, there is the need for ongoing training and education so that counselors can keep abreast of issues facing today's college population. This training builds competency into the counseling staff and makes for more effective service delivery.

Crisis-oriented interventions are a critical and valuable resource for college students. By definition, the college crisis counselor is the initial contact person and stabilization resource that can serve as the conduit to myriad campus and community services. Appropriate crisis intervention and follow-up on the college campus support a student's efforts to balance the academic and emotional demands of college, as well as allowing the counselor an effective strategy to manage a burgeoning caseload.

REFERENCES

Abbey, A., McCauslan, P., & Ross, L. T. (1998). Sexual assault perpetration by college men: The role of alcohol, misperception of sexual intent, and sexual beliefs and experiences. *Journal of Social and Clinical Psychology, 17,* 167–195.

Bechhofer, L., & Parrot, A. (1991). What is acquaintance rape? In A. Parrot & L. Bechhofer (Eds.), *Acquaintance rape: The hidden crime* (pp. 9–25). New York: Wiley.

Benson, D., Charlton, C., & Goodhart, F. (1992). Acquaintance rape on campus: A literature review. *Journal of American College Health, 40,* 157–165.

Benton, S. A., Robertson, J. M., Tseng, W. C., Newton, F. B., & Benton, S. L. (2003). Changes in counseling center client problems across 13 years. *Professional Psychology: Research and Practice, 34,* 66–72.

Berkowitz, A. D., Burkhart, B. R., & Bourg, S. E. (1994). Research on college men and rape. In A. D. Berkowitz (Ed.), *Men and rape: Theory, research, and prevention programs in higher education* (pp. 3–19). New Directions for Student Services, No. 65. San Francisco: Jossey-Bass.

Blake, D., Weathers, F. W., Nagy, L., Kaloupek, D., Klauminzer, G., Charney, D., et al. (1995). The development of a clinician-administered PTSD scale. *Journal of Traumatic Stress, 8,* 75–90.

Bohmer, C., & Parrot, A. (1993). *Sexual assault on campus: The problem and the solution.* New York: Lexington Books.

Burkhart, B. R. (1991). Conceptual and practical analysis of therapy for acquaintance rape victims. In A. Parrot & L. Bechhofer (Eds.), *Acquaintance rape: The hidden crime* (pp. 287–303). New York: Wiley.

Butcher, J. N., & Koss, M. P. (1978). Research on brief and crisis-oriented therapies. In S. L. Garfield & A. E. Bergin (Eds.), *Handbook of psychotherapy and behavior change* (2nd ed., pp. 725–767). New York: Wiley.

Carver, C. S., & Ganellen, R. J. (1983). Depression and components of self-punitiveness: High standards, self-criticism, and overgeneralisation. *Journal of Personality and Social Psychology, 48,* 1097–1111.

Clance, P. R. (1985). *The imposter phenomenon: Overcoming the fear that haunts your success.* Atlanta, GA: Peachtree.

Clance, P. R., & Imes, S. A. (1978). The imposter phenomenon in high-achieving women: Dynamics and therapeutic intervention. *Psychotherapy: Theory, Research, and Practice, 15,* 241–247.

Clance, P. R., & O'Toole, M. A. (1988). The imposter phenomenon: An internal barrier to empowerment and achievement. *Women and Therapy, 6,* 51–64.

Clark, M. L., Beckett, J., Wells, M., & Dungee-Anderson, D. (1994). Courtship violence among African American college students. *Journal of Black Psychology, 20,* 264–281.

Copenhaver, S., & Grauerholz, E. (1991). Sexual victimization among sorority women: Exploring the link between sexual violence and institutional practices. *Sex Roles, 24,* 31–41.

Davis, T. L., & Liddell, D. L. (2002). Getting inside the house: The effectiveness of a rape prevention program for college fraternity men. *Journal of College Student Development, 43,* 35–50.

Egan, G. (1998). *The skilled helper* (6th ed.). Pacific Grove, CA: Brooks/Cole.

Finley, C., & Corty, E. (1993). Rape on campus: The prevalence of sexual assault while enrolled in college. *Journal of College Student Development, 34,* 113–117.

Foley, L. A., Evancic, C., Karnik, K., King, J., & Parks, A. (1995). Date rape: Effects of race of assailant and victim and gender of subjects on perceptions. *Journal of Black Psychology, 21,* 6–18.

Frintner, M. P., & Rubinson, L. (1993). Acquaintance rape: The influence of alcohol, fraternity membership, and sports team membership. *Journal of Sex Education and Therapy, 19,* 272–284.

Fukuyama, M. A. (2001). Counseling in colleges and universities. In D. C. Locke, J. E. Myers, & E. L. Herr (Eds.), *The handbook of counseling* (pp. 319–341). Thousand Oaks, CA: Sage.

Funderburk, J. R. (2001). Group counseling for survivors of sexual assault. In A. J. Ottens & K. Hotelling (Eds.), *Sexual violence on campus in the twenty-first century* (pp. 254–282). New York: Springer.

Gallagher, R. P., Gill, A. M., & Sysco, H. M. (2000). *National survey of counseling center directors 2000.* Alexandria, VA: International Association of Counseling Service.

Gidycz, C. A., Coble, C. N., Latham, L., & Layman, M. J. (1993). A sexual assault experience in adulthood and prior victimization experiences: A prospective analysis. *Psychology of Women Quarterly, 17,* 151–168.

Gidycz, C. A., Hanson, K., & Layman, M. J. (1995). A prospective analysis of the relationships among sexual assault experiences. *Psychology of Women Quarterly, 19,* 5–29.

Hanna, F. J., & Ottens, A. J. (1995). The role of wisdom in psychotherapy. *Journal of Psychotherapy Integration, 5,* 195–219.

Humphrey, K. M., Kitchens, H., & Patrick, J. (2000). Trends in college counseling for the 21st century. In D. C. Davis & K. M. Humphrey (Eds.), *College counseling: Issues and strategies for a new millennium* (pp. 111–131). Alexandria, VA: American Counseling Association.

Kaly, P. W., Heesacker, M., & Frost, H. M. (2002). Collegiate alcohol use and high-risk sexual behavior: A literature review. *Journal of College Student Development, 43*(6), 838–850.

Kanel, K. (1999). *A guide to crisis intervention.* Pacific Grove, CA: Brooks/Cole.

Kanin, E. J. (1985). Date rapists: Differential sexual socialization and relative deprivation. *Archives of Sexual Behavior, 14,* 219–231.

Kiesler, D. J. (1988). *Therapeutic metacommunication.* Palo Alto, CA: Consulting Psychologists Press.

King, J. E., & Cooley, E. L. (1995). Achievement orientation and the imposter phenomenon among college students. *Contemporary Educational Psychology, 20,* 304–312.

Koss, M. P., & Cleveland, H. H. (1996). Athletic participation, fraternity membership, and date rape. *Violence Against Women, 2,* 180–190.

Koss, M. P., Gidycz, C. A., & Wisniewski, N. (1987). The scope of rape: Incidence and prevalence of sexual aggression and victimization in a national sample of higher education students. *Journal of Consulting and Clinical Psychology, 55,* 162–170.

Leary, M. R., Patton, K. M., Orlando, A. E., & Funk, W. W. (2000). The imposter phenomenon: Self-perceptions, reflected appraisals, and interpersonal strategies. *Journal of Personality, 68*(4), 725–756.

Malamuth, N. M., Sockloskie, R. J., Koss, M. P., & Tanaka, J. S. (1991). Characteristics of aggressors against women: Testing a model using a national sample of college students. *Journal of Consulting and Clinical Psychology, 59,* 670–681.

Matthews, G., & Clance, P. R.

(1985). Treatment of the imposter phenomenon in psychotherapy clients. *Psychotherapy in Private Practice, 3,* 71–81.

Milburn, M. A., Mather, R., & Conrad, S. D. (2000). The effects of viewing R-rated movie scenes that objectify women on perceptions of date rape. *Sex Roles, 43*(9–10), 645–664.

Miller, D. G., & Kastberg, S. M. (1995). Of blue collar and ivory: Women from blue-collar backgrounds in higher education. *Roeper Review, 18,* 27–33.

Muehlenhard, C. L., & Linton, M. A. (1987). Date rape and sexual aggression in dating: Incidence and risk factors. *Journal of Counseling Psychology, 34,* 186–196.

Myer, R. A., & Ottens, A. J. (1994). Assessment for crisis intervention on college campuses. *Crisis Intervention, 1,* 31–46.

National Center for Victims of Crime. (1998). *Acquaintance rape.* Retrieved July 4, 2004 from http://www.ncvc.org/ncvc/main.aspx?dbName=DocumentViewer&DocumentID=32306.

Ottens, A. J. (1984). *Coping with academic anxiety.* New York: Rosen.

Ottens, A. J., & Fisher-McCanne, L. (1990). Crisis intervention at the college campus counseling center. In A. R. Roberts (Ed.), *Crisis intervention handbook: Assessment, treatment, and response* (pp. 78–100). Belmont, CA: Wadsworth.

Ottens, A. J., & Hotelling, K. (Eds.). (2001). *Sexual violence on campus in the twenty-first century.* New York: Springer.

Petretic-Jackson, P., & Jackson, T. (1990). Assessment and crisis intervention with rape and incest victims: Strategies, techniques, and case illustrations. In A. R. Roberts (Ed.), *Crisis intervention handbook: Assessment, treatment, and research* (pp. 124–152). Belmont, CA: Wadsworth.

Rennison, C. M. (1999). *National Crime Victim Survey 1998: Changes 1997–1998 with trends 1993–1998* (NCG Publication No. 176353). Washington, DC: U.S. Department of Justice.

Roberts, A. R. (1990). An overview of crisis theory and crisis intervention. In A. R. Roberts (Ed.), *Crisis intervention handbook: Assessment, treatment, and research* (pp. 3–16). Belmont, CA: Wadsworth.

Roberts, A. R. (1996). Epidemiology and definitions of acute crisis in American society. In A. R. Roberts (Ed.), *Crisis management and brief treatment: Theory, technique, and applications* (pp. 16–33). Chicago: Nelson-Hall.

Schwartz, M. D., & DeKeseredy, W. S. (1997). *Sexual assault on the college campus: The role of male peer support.* Thousand Oaks, CA: Sage.

Thompson, T., Davis, H., & Davidson, J. (1998). Attributional and affective responses of impostors to academic success and failure outcomes. *Personality and Individual Differences, 25,* 381–396.

Topping, M. E., & Kimmel, E. B. (1985). The imposter phenomenon: Feeling phony. *Academic Psychology Bulletin, 7,* 213–226.

Turner, A. L., & Berry, T. R. (2000). Counseling center contributions to student retention and graduation: A longitudinal assessment. *Journal of College Student Development, 41,* 627–636.

Von Steen, P. G. (2000). Traditional-age college students. In D. C.

Davis & K. M. Humphrey (Eds.), *College counseling: Issues and strategies for a new millennium* (pp. 111–131). Alexandria, VA: American Counseling Association.

Zorza, J. (1998). Rohypnol and GHB: Terrifying date-rape drugs. *Sexual Assault Report, 2,* 17–30.

Zorza, J. (2001). Drug-facilitated rape. In A. J. Ottens & K. Hotelling (Eds.), *Sexual violence on campus in the twenty-first century* (pp. 53–75). New York: Springer.

IV

CRISIS INTERVENTION AND CRISIS PREVENTION WITH VICTIMS OF VIOLENCE

19

A Comprehensive Model for Crisis Intervention With Battered Women and Their Children

ALBERT R. ROBERTS
BEVERLY SCHENKMAN ROBERTS

Every 9 seconds, somewhere in the United States, a woman is battered by her intimate partner or former partner. Recent estimates indicate that over 8.7 million women are battered annually (Roberts, 2002). Without a better understanding of what constitutes effective crisis intervention, without better-trained personnel staffing 24-hour domestic violence hotlines, and without a much more comprehensive social service delivery system put in place, too many of these women will end up as a statistic in either hospital or homicide records, or at the very least, living out lives ruined by emotional pain, suffering, or permanent injuries. This chapter presents the all too sobering facts about battered women and their children, and suggests the most effective models for crisis intervention, police-based domestic violence units, 24-hour crisis hotlines, and service delivery systems.

Case Scenarios

Sonia was a 20-year-old college student at the time of the interview. She had met Brad the summer after she graduated from high school. Brad was her first boyfriend to take her to expensive restaurants and college fraternity parties. He was very polite to her parents and younger sister when he visited her home to take her on dates. Sonia thought she was very much in love with Brad. Although Sonia was a virgin, six months into the relationship, they had sexual intercourse for the first time. Sonia indicated that Brad was very romantic and the wine she drank that night put her in the mood. Shortly thereafter, Brad thought that Sonia was looking at his friend Tony, and Brad was so jealous that he slapped her for the first time. The next day, Brad apologized, brought Sonia flowers, and blamed his slapping her on the liquor and his love for her. She forgave him. Sonia was completely unprepared for the rapid escalation in violence several months later, when Brad became furiously jealous and violent because of a practical joke from a male coworker of Sonia's. Sonia's lips were bleeding, the inside of her gums were torn up, and she had a swollen face. Sonia indicated that she was in a state of shock and questioned whether she would be able to trust another boyfriend in the future. She obtained a temporary restraining order with the help of her parents. She reported that the police were very helpful by taking photographs of her bruised face and asking her to write down what had happened and sign the police report. The police then went to Brad's house and served him with the restraining order, prohibiting him from having any contact with Sonia or harassing her in any way.

Christy, a 24-year-old college graduate who now manages a restaurant, was physically abused and stalked by a former boyfriend when she was 18, during her freshman year at college. Christy reported that she still has nightmares from time to time in which a current boyfriend (after the batterer) becomes violent toward her. She wonders if the nightmares and lethargy will ever go away. Christy enjoys her job and career and feels that what was most useful to her was the crisis counseling she received soon after the abuse.

Pamela, a 29-year-old teacher and devout Catholic with two young children, initially thought the emotional and physical abuse from her husband was due to the enormous stress associated with his being a medical student. Pamela convinced herself that the abuse would end as soon as her husband completed his residency and had his own medical practice. Pamela endured several years of abuse even years after her husband was established as a respected physician. She permanently left and divorced her husband as a result of the good advice from her priest, crisis intervention, and social support at a group for formerly battered women at the local women's resource center and shelter. Pamela does volunteer work at the local shelter.

Do you know what some women get for their birthdays? A black eye, a punch in the ribs, or a few teeth knocked out. It's so frightening because it doesn't just happen on their birthday. It may be every month, every week, or even every day. It's so frightening because sometimes he abuses the kids, too. Or maybe she's pregnant and he kicks her in the stomach in the same spot where, just a few minutes ago, she felt the baby moving. It's so frightening because the woman doesn't know what to do. She feels so helpless. He's in control. She prays he'll come to his senses and stop. He never does. She prays he won't hurt their kids. He threatens to. She prays he won't kill her. He promises he will. (Haag, undated)

We were married 13 years. It was okay until the past 5 years and he started to hit me to hurt me. He was doing drugs. He was usually high or when he couldn't get drugs, he'd hit me cause he couldn't have it. We'd get in an argument because he'd want money and I'd say no and that's how it would start. He punched and kicked me. Usually I had a black eye and black and blue marks on my legs. He used to steal my money—he stole my Christmas money and my food stamps. He tried to say someone broke into the house, but I knew he had it.

My ex-husband drank every day, especially in the summer. He is very violent. I fear for my life that one day he will get me alone and kill me. He hated my little dog because I spoiled him. He would tell me that he was going to drop kick him (he only weighed 4 pounds). I had to give my dog away because I didn't want him to hurt it. I had to give up my family and friends for the same reason. He broke my nose without even thinking twice. He also tried to strangle me a couple of times and he didn't let go until I faked passing out. I've had to fake a blackout, and that is the only reason I am alive. For all he knew, I could have been dead when he left me lying there on the floor.

The description of the fear, anguish, and physical injuries to which battered women are repeatedly subjected comes from Al Roberts's research files. Case illustrations are included in this chapter to acquaint crisis intervenors, social workers, nurses, psychologists, and counselors with the painful history of the women they will be counseling and assisting. Increasingly, battered women are turning to emergency shelters, telephone crisis intervention services, mental health centers, and support groups for help. Recognition of the need for and actual establishment of crisis intervention services for victims of the battering syndrome has increased dramatically since the 1970s.

The most promising short-term interventions with battered women include 24-hour crisis hotlines, crisis-oriented support groups, shelters for battered women, and/or therapy. Although only a small number of research studies have been conducted on the effectiveness of different types of crisis services for battered women, one research article analyzing 12 outcome studies demonstrated positive outcomes. Tutty, Bidgood, and Rothery (1993) studied outcomes of 76 formerly battered women in Canada after completion of a 10 to 12–session support group. They found significant improvements in self-esteem, locus of control, and decreases in stress and physical abuse 6 months after treatment (Tutty, Bidgood, & Rothery, 1993). Gordon (1996) examined 12 outcome studies on the effectiveness of intervention by community social services, crisis hotlines, women's groups, police, clergy, physicians, psychotherapists, and lawyers. In summary, it seems that battered women consistently found crisis hotlines, women's groups, social workers, and psychotherapists to be very helpful. In sharp contrast, the battered women respondents reported that usually police, clergy, and lawyers are *not* helpful to different types of abused women (Gordon, 1996).

This chapter will examine the alarming prevalence of woman battering, risk factors and vulnerabilities, precursors to crisis episodes, and resilience and protective factors. In addition, the following types of crisis intervention programs will be discussed: early intervention by police-based crisis teams and victim assistance units; assessment and detection in the hospital emergency room; electronic technology to protect battered women in imminent danger; specific intervention techniques used by crisis hotlines and battered women's shelters; and short-term treatment for the victim's children. The chapter will also discuss the importance of referrals.

SCOPE OF THE PROBLEM

Intimate partner abuse is one of the most harmful, traumatic, and life-threatening criminal justice and public health problems in American society. Intimate partner abuse continues to be the single greatest health threat to American women between the ages of 15 and 50. More women sustain injuries as a result of intimate partner abuse than from the combined total of muggings and accidents.

- Every 9 seconds in the United States, a woman is assaulted and battered.
- Each year, 8.7 million women are victims of intimate partner violence.
- Over 90% of the victims of domestic violence are women.
- Every day, four women are murdered by boyfriends, husbands, and former intimate partners.
- Domestic violence is the number one cause of emergency room visits by women.
- Women are most likely to be killed when attempting to leave the abuser.
- The number one cause of women's injuries is abuse at home.
- Approximately one in every four women in the United States has been physically assaulted and/or raped by their intimate partner at some time in their life. (Roberts and Roberts, 2005)

The most accurate statistics on the lifetime prevalence of intimate partner violence comes from the National Violence Against Women Survey conducted by Professors Patricia Tjaden and Nancy Thoennes with grants from the National Institute of Justice and the Centers for Disease Control and Prevention (CDC). This study was based on telephone interviews with a nationally representative sample of 8,000 men and 8,000 women, and indicated that 25% of the women and 7.6% of the men stated that they had been physically battered and/or raped by a spouse, cohabiting partner, or date during their lifetime. These national figures document the high prevalence and consequences of intimate partner abuse. However, in actuality, some women are at much greater risk of becoming victims of intimate partner violence than others. Women at the highest risk of encountering violence from dates and steady boyfriends are high school and college students (Roberts, 1998, 2002).

Date abuse, binge drinking, club drugs, and drug-facilitated sexual assault have been escalating on college campuses and at bars and rave parties frequented by high school students and young adults who are not in school. Female college students, particularly those who are living away from their families during the first year or two of college, are at heightened risk of becoming a victim of dating violence because of the peer pressures to drink or do drugs combined with the lack of supervision and protection often provided by their family (Roberts & Roberts, 2005).

Woman battering is one of the most life-threatening, traumatic, and harmful public health and social problems in American society. Recent estimates indicate that each year approximately 8.7 million women have been victims of some form of assault by their partner (Roberts, 1998; Straus & Gelles, 1991; Tjaden & Thoennes, 1998). Partner violence continues to be the single greatest health threat to American women under the age of 50. On an annual basis, more women sustain injuries as a result of domestic violence than from the combined total of muggings and accidents (Nurius, Hilfrink, & Rafino, 1996).

Women who suffer the most severe injuries require treatment in hospital emergency rooms and hospital trauma centers. It is estimated that 35% of emergency room visits are made by women who need emergency medical care as a result of domestic violence–related injuries (Valentine, Roberts, & Burgess, 1998).

A study published in the *Journal of the American Medical Association* found that up to one in five pregnant women are abused by their partners during pregnancy, with prevalence rates ranging from 0.9 to 20.1% (Gazmararian et al., 1996). Battering during pregnancy endangers both the woman and the fetus, with some of the risks being "miscarriage, preterm labor, chorioamnionitis, low birth weight, fetomaternal hemorrhage, abruptio placentae, and in some cases fetal death or neonatal death" (Carlson & McNutt, 1998, p. 237).

The frequency and duration of violence range from women who are hit once or twice (and make a decision to end the relationship immediately) to women who remain in the relationship and are beaten with increasing frequency for an extended period, which may last for many years (Roberts & Burman, 1998). Petretic-Jackson and Jackson (1996) and Walker (1985) found a strong correlation between women who had suffered chronic abuse and the onset of bipolar disorder, anxiety disorder, posttraumatic stress disorder (PTSD), panic disorder, and/or depression with suicide ideation.

A telephone survey of 16,000 persons from across the nation (8,000 women and 8,000 men) provided research findings on the prevalence, incidence, and consequences of violence against women, including rape and physical assault (Tjaden & Thoennes, 1998). The researchers found that physical battering is widespread among American women of all racial and ethnic groups. The following are Tjaden and Thoennes's major findings:

52% of surveyed women said they were physically assaulted as a child by an adult caretaker and/or as an adult by any type of perpetrator.

1.9% of surveyed women said they were physically assaulted in the previous 12 months.

18% of women surveyed said they experienced a completed or attempted rape at some time in their life, and 0.3% said they experienced a completed or attempted rape in the previous 12 months.

Although there were only 7 emergency shelters for battered women in 1974 (Roberts, 1981), by 1998 there were more than 2,000 shelters and crisis intervention services coast-to-coast for battered women and their children (Roberts, 1998). Through crisis intervention, many women are able to regain control of their lives by identifying current options and goals and by working to attain those goals. The children of battered women may also be in crisis, but their plight has sometimes been overlooked as the domestic violence programs focused their efforts on emergency intervention for the women. The progressive programs now incorporate crisis intervention for children (as well as for the mothers) in the treatment plan.

Battered women are usually subjected to a prolonged pattern of abuse coupled with a recent severe attack; by the time the victim makes contact with a shelter, she is generally in need of both individual crisis intervention and a crisis-oriented support group. Abused women are subjected to an extended period of stress and trauma that results in a continual loss of energy. The woman is in a vulnerable position, and when a particularly severe beating takes place or when other factors occur (e.g., the abuser starting to hurt the children), the woman may be thrust into a state of crisis (Young, 1995).

Effective treatment for battered women and their children in crisis requires an understanding of crisis theory and the techniques of crisis intervention. According to Caplan (1964), Janosik (1984), and Roberts (1996a), a crisis state can occur rapidly when the following four things happen:

1. The victim experiences a precipitating or hazardous incident.
2. The incident is perceived by the woman as threatening to her or her children's safety, and as a result tension and distress intensify.
3. The battered woman attempts to resolve the situation by using customary coping methods and fails.
4. The emotional discomfort and turmoil worsen, and the victim feels that the pain or anguish is unbearable.

At this point of maximum discomfort, when the woman perceives the pain and torment as unbearable, she is in an active crisis state. During this time there is an opportunity for change and growth, and some women are mobilized to seek help from a 24-hour telephone crisis intervention service, the police, the hospital emergency room, or a shelter for battered women.

The emphasis in crisis assessment is on identifying the nature of the precipitating event and the woman's cognitive and affective reaction to it. The five most common precipitating events that lead battered women in crisis to seek the help of a domestic violence program are (a) an acute battering incident resulting in serious physical injury; (b) a major escalation in the degree of violence, for example, from shoving and slapping to attempted strangulation or stab wounds; (c) an impairment in the woman's hearing, sight, or thought process as a direct result of severe batterment; (d) a high-profile story in the news media about a woman who was brutally murdered by her partner after suffering in silence for many years; and (e) a serious abusive injury inflicted on the woman's child. Often the precipitating event is perceived by the woman in crisis as being the final incident, or "last straw," in a long history of violence (Edington, 1987; Podhorin, 1987; Roberts, 1998; Schiller-Ramirez, 1995).

Crisis intervention with battered women needs to be done in an orderly, structured, and humanistic manner. The process is the same for victims of other violent crimes, but it is particularly important to respond quickly to abused women because they may continue to be in danger as long as they remain in a place where the batterer can locate them. Crisis intervention activities can result in the woman either returning to her precrisis state or growing from the crisis intervention so that she learns new coping skills to use in the future (Roberts, 1998).

ZERO TOLERANCE

In a dating, cohabiting, or marital relationship, there is never an excuse, justification, or rationalization that allows a man (or adolescent boy) to hit a woman (or an adolescent girl). The professional literature on domestic violence is replete with citations of the horrendous problems that ensue when women have become involved in long-term relationships in which they are assaulted on a frequent basis. The purpose of this chapter is to educate counselors, social workers, young women, and their families and friends regarding the full spectrum of violent relationships, with the goal of helping them to prevent the likely progression, over time, from the initial incident of being slapped to becoming the victim of severe beatings later on.

One 20-year-old woman who has benefited from a good therapeutic relationship with a psychologist (following her having been hit by a boyfriend when she was 17) now makes it a practice to tell all men she starts to date that she has *zero tolerance* for violence in her dating relationships. She explains that she was slapped around by her first boyfriend, and she will not allow herself to go through that type of disrespect and trauma again. Thus far, her boyfriends have been sensitive to her previous victimization, and she has not been abused again. But her attitude is this: "I need to set forth these boundaries right up front, on the very first date, to reinforce to every guy I date that this isn't going to happen to me ever again. And if, in the future, I meet a guy who is put off by my dating ground rules, then good riddance to him!"

BATTERED WOMEN AT HIGH RISK OF CRISIS EPISODES

For some women, the effects of partner abuse can be short-term, with a quick recovery, while for others the result is chronic dysfunction and mental health disorders. Domestic violence researchers have found that among women who are battered for many years, those who receive the most severe forms of injury seem to have the highest risk for the following difficulties: nightmares and other sleep disturbances, reenactment of trauma, major depression, posttraumatic stress symptoms, substance abuse, self-destructive behavior, psychosexual dysfunction, and/or generalized anxiety disorder. Research studies indicate that, in general, these women's mental health problems were not present early in the relationship but developed as a result of the repeated acts of violence (Gleason, 1993; Woods & Campbell, 1993).

Posttraumatic stress disorder (PTSD) may occur when an individual perceives an event as life-threatening to herself or significant others. Characteristic features of PTSD identified in the clinical literature are as follows:

1. Integration of the traumatic experience by reexperiencing the traumatic event (through recurrent and/or intrusive thoughts, flashbacks, nightmares, or other intense reactions)
2. Management of subsequent stress (increased arousal and hypervigilance)
3. Facilitation of affective expression
4. Determination of the meaning of victimization (Petretic-Jackson & Jackson, 1996, p. 210)

As a result of one or more severe battering incidents, some battered women have had their cognitive schemas or mental maps altered. According to Valentine, under extreme duress, the battered woman's schema is imprinted strongly with a survival message that guides the victim even after the crisis is passed. Victims are then left with the chore of either assimilating that event into their previously existing schemas or altering their schemas to incorporate this terrifying event. She states that "PTSD symptoms consist of intrusive thoughts [nightmares], hypervigilance [i.e., startle responses], and avoidance [i.e., blunted affect to avert all reminders of the incident]" (see chapter 11, this volume).

Crisis intervention and time-limited treatment with battered women must be approached with empathy, sensitivity, and caution. When an abused woman is suffering from PTSD, if the crisis intervenor asks the woman to "reexperience" the violent event, the counselor may inadvertently precipitate a retraumatization rather than the intended therapeutic opportunity (Petretic-Jackson & Jackson, 1996). Before crisis intervention is initiated, it is critically important to create a safe, highly flexible, empowering environment where symptom relief strategies are emphasized. If avoidance, startle overreactions, and nightmares are the primary presenting problems, the crisis intervenor may well facilitate the narrative and storytelling process by utilizing experiential techniques, art therapy, poetry, photographs, and/or police reports.

Stress management techniques can build on the battered woman's inner strengths and potential for positive growth. Examples of these techniques are progressive relaxation, guided imagery, refocusing one's attention on external reality, good nutrition, developing a support system, and using "dosing"—"a technique in which attention is alternately shifted toward and away from the traumatic experience" (Petretic-Jackson & Jackson, 1996, p. 210). Many battered women seem to have developed very limited affective expression as a result of suppressing their emotions. In addition, because battered women generally suppress feelings of anger, they may suddenly express rage a year or two after leaving the batterer.

Many battered women who experienced three or more traumatic and severe battering incidents often take a long time to gain a sense of control of their environment. Their self-esteem, trust in men, and cognitive assumptions are often shattered. The survivor's low self-esteem, weak decision-making skills, intrusive thoughts, and flashbacks often result in a series of acute crisis episodes. The crisis intervenor or counselor needs to help the woman build trust while bolstering her self-esteem. This is done through modeling, reframing, stress inoculation, relaxation techniques, exercise, thought stopping, encouraging journal entries, solution-based therapy, and cognitive restructuring.

TRAUMATIC BATTERING EVENTS, LEGAL ACTION, MEDICAL INJURIES, AND SLEEP DISTURBANCES AS PRECURSORS TO CRISIS EPISODES

Several types of traumatic, life-threatening mental health and legal events or situations often can precipitate a crisis. These include:

- A battered woman sustaining a life-threatening injury (e.g., a concussion, multiple stab wounds, a miscarriage, or strangulation).
- A child being severely physically or psychologically harmed by the batterer.

- The victim obtains a restraining order or files for divorce, and her taking legal action enrages the batterer, resulting in stalking, terroristic threats, and/or a rapid escalation of the battering incidents.
- A battered woman encounters explicit kidnapping or terroristic death threats against herself, her children, and/or her elderly parents.
- The batterer has already made explicit death threats against the formerly battered woman, and he is soon to be released from prison or a residential drug treatment program.

In Roberts's (1996b) study of 210 battered women, the majority of the participants interviewed had experienced one or more severe beatings. The outcomes of these beatings were manifested in anxiety, depression, sleep disturbances, panic attacks, and intrusive thoughts. The following are illustrations of sleep disturbances:

> Somebody chases me or is trying to kill me. I can't remember the last pleasant dream I had.
>
> I have nightmares about him burning up the house. I keep dreaming that the kids and I were trapped in the house with flames all around us and we couldn't get out. I would see his face in the flames, point at us and laughing while we are crying and in pain.
>
> I have the same nightmare a few times a week. I see this guy who looks like my former boyfriend (drug dealer who was shot 3 years ago by the Newark police). He is raising up out of the casket, and he said he loved me and is coming back to stab me to death so I can join him in hell. I wake up screaming, shaking, and sweating. A lot of times I can't fall asleep even though I'm mentally and physically exhausted. The next day at work I'm very jumpy and afraid to talk to any of the men in the office. When my supervisor asks me something, I get this flashback and am reminded of my nightmare and I start crying. I go into the ladies room sometimes for an hour and cry and cry, and then leave work early. I go home and try to calm down by smoking cigarettes and talking with my daughter.

In crisis intervention work with battered women, clinicians must be prepared to understand a range of potential precipitants and precursors. Crisis clinicians need to be aware of the aftermath of traumatic events, common triggering incidents, and precursors to crisis episodes in order to provide battered women with the most appropriate interventions.

RESILIENCE AND PROTECTIVE FACTORS

The previous section examined high-risk groups and trauma, sleep disturbances, and other precursors to crisis episodes. Those groups of individuals with preexisting risk factors and trauma histories have difficulty recovering. In sharp contrast, some abused women have significant inner strengths, also known as *resilience* and *protective factors*, that have been found to mediate and lessen the impact of stress related to battering. The most common protective factors include high self-esteem, a social support network, and cognitive coping skills. One of the most important components of maximizing a battered woman's recovery is accomplished through believing in the client and helping her to realize her strengths. Many battered women feel trapped, socially isolated, and overwhelmed by the physical and emotional pain they have endured. Crisis intervenors and counselors can help the woman to recognize alternative coping strategies.

During the past decade, a growing number of crisis intervenors, counselors, social workers, and psychologists have recognized that a strengths perspective that builds on the resilience of individuals is much more fruitful to helping clients grow and change in positive directions than the previous 50 years of emphasis on pathologizing the client (Saleebey, 1997). The strengths perspective of crisis intervention utilizes empowerment, resilience, healing and wholeness, collaboration, and suspension of disbelief. *Empowerment strategies* create opportunities for individuals and communities (Roberts & Burman, 1998). *Resilience* focuses on accelerating growth and identifying inner capabilities, knowledge, and personal insights. *Healing* refers to the ability of the body and mind to resist disease and chaos. The resilience literature incorporates a strong belief that individuals have self-righting tendencies and a spontaneous inclination toward healing and survival (Saleebey, 1997; Weil, 1995). *Collaboration* refers to clients, counselors, crisis intervenors, and family members all working together to help strengthen the client. *Suspension of disbelief* refers to the ending of pessimism and cynicism and the affirmation of belief, learned optimism, self-protective strategies, a sense of humor, and commitment to change.

An integrated approach to crisis intervention combines Roberts's (1996a) seven-step crisis intervention practice model with solution-based therapy. Gilbert Greene and Mo-Yee Lee, in chapter 3 of this book, provide a detailed discussion with several case applications of an integrated model of solution-based therapy. This practice model emphasizes building on and bolstering one's inner strengths, protective factors, latent coping skills, and positive attributes. It systematically reinforces the importance of realistic goal setting, identifying and explicating the positive exceptions in situations or behavior patterns, and the importance of the dream and miracle questions. We firmly believe that crisis intervention based on enhancing positive coping skills, rediscovering the exceptions and positive alternatives to crisis situations, building on and optimizing the client's bright spots and inner strengths, and seeking partial and full solutions will become common practice during the twenty-first century.

Tedeschi and Calhoun (1995) interviewed over 600 college students who had recently experienced significant stressful life events, including a parent's death, being the victim of a crime, or receiving an accidental injury. The goal of their research was to determine which personality factors might lead to personal growth when an individual is confronted with a crisis situation. The researchers identified the characteristics of extroversion, openness, agreeableness, conscientiousness, and having an "internal locus of control" as benefiting persons in crisis by allowing them to find some positive outcome connected to what might otherwise be viewed as a devastating circumstance. For instance, those who indicated growth from the traumatic experience were more likely to report that they had experienced positive change (i.e., developing a new area of interest, forming a new relationship, or enhancing one's spiritual beliefs).

Some battered women develop positive coping strategies, whereas others develop negative and potentially self-destructive coping strategies. Examples of positive coping strategies include using formal and informal social support networks, seeking informational support, and requesting help from a shelter for battered women. Examples of negative coping mechanisms are dependence on alcohol or drugs or suicide attempts.

Positive coping strategies help women to facilitate their own survival and expedited recovery. The core focus of Lazarus and Folkman's (1984) conceptualization and application of the coping process is based on how an individual makes an appraisal of the stressful event. Appraisal takes place when an individual experiences an event and determines that it is "excessive relative to resources." There are two levels of appraisal related to coping responses:

1. Primary appraisal is viewed as the first level, wherein a person evaluates whether the event has the potential to cause harm (i.e., physical injury), to instill fear, or to interfere with a goal. More specifically, the individual decides whether a particular situation is at risk. The outcome reflects the individual's assessment of the stressful life event and the significance of the event for that individual's well-being.
2. When the event is perceived as harmful or threatening, the individual enters into secondary appraisal, wherein the available resources for coping are examined. When a person is confronted with a circumstance that is perceived as threatening or harmful, the person "enters into secondary appraisal" when she makes efforts to cope with the event (e.g., leaving the violent home immediately and living with a relative or at a shelter). (Lazarus & Folkman, 1984)

Battered women in crisis who are contemplating leaving the violent relationship are confronted by both internal and external barriers. Recent legislation, policy reforms, and federal funding initiatives have resulted in increased funding for transitional housing, job training, and concrete services for battered women. These societal and community-wide changes have empowered and improved the economic status of some battered women who were trapped by poverty, limited welfare checks and food vouchers, no employment skills, a lack of affordable housing, and no affordable child care. However, these policy changes and reforms are not enough.

As noted by Carlson (1997), the following four internal barriers often keep the battered woman trapped in a recurring pattern of acute crisis episodes: "low self-esteem; shame and self-blame for the abuse; poor coping skills; and passivity, depression, and learned helplessness" (p. 292). Carlson (1997) proposed an intervention model grounded in both an ecological perspective and Lazarus and Folkman's (1984) stress and coping paradigm. This practice model should be used by licensed mental health clinicians who are also trained in domestic violence (Carlson, 1997). The intervention is summarized as follows:

- Practice orientation: nonjudgmental acceptance, confidentiality, and a belief in self-determination of the client
- Engagement and developing a collaborative relationship
- Assessment (based on Petretic-Jackson and Jackson [1996], as discussed earlier in this chapter)
- Intervention: development of a safety plan, increasing information, enhancement of coping, enhancement of problem-solving and decision-making skills, and reducing isolation by increasing social support

Unfortunately, although it is important to study the correlation between coping methods in facilitating crisis resolution among battered women, there is a dearth of research in this area. A thorough review of the research related to crime victimization and the connection between cognitive appraisal, attributions, and coping mechanisms indicates no conclusive findings (Wyatt, Notgrass, & Newcomb, 1990; Frieze & Bookwala, 1996; Frazier & Burnett, 1994; Johnson, 1997). Examples of specific strengths are high self-esteem, having a devoted mother, conscientious performance at work or a job training program, or having a social support network.

Much of the professional literature on this topic focuses on the cognitive resources individuals employ when coping with unexpected, stressful life events (Lazarus & Folkman, 1984; Folkman & Lazarus, 1985). Coping has been defined by Folkman (1984) as "cognitive and behavioral efforts to master, reduce, or tolerate the internal and/or external demands that are created by the stressful transaction" (p. 843). These demands include perceptions of potential loss and/or harm, at which time the individual evaluates choices for coping via problem-focused and emotion-focused strategies. Problem-focused strategies are based on the use of problem-solving and action plans, whereas emotion-focused strategies utilize the control of negative or distressing emotions.

SPECIALIZED DOMESTIC VIOLENCE UNITS

In addition to changes in arrest policies and customary practices in domestic cases, many police departments have created specialized domestic violence units to follow up on all domestic-related complaints. Specialized units have the ability to further investigate domestic crimes, make appropriate referrals and arrests, and ensure victim safety long after the patrol officer has left the scene. In some cases, unit members serve as the first responders to domestic calls for service. Units are generally staffed with police investigators or detectives and are often linked with specialized units in a prosecutor's office. They offer an opportunity for personnel to develop specialized knowledge and expertise regarding the investigation and prosecution of domestic crimes. In theory, units create the infrastructure necessary for aggressive, proactive responses to domestic violence rather than the traditional reactive policing approach.

These units also provide an opportunity to link police services with shelter, victim/witness, and batterer programming. Multidisciplinary approaches that integrate the need for both legal and social service interventions are likely to be the most effective in terms of protecting victim safety and ensuring offender accountability. The following police departments are illustrative of the modern police response to domestic violence:

Ann Arbor Police Department: Domestic Violence Enforcement Team in Ann Arbor, Michigan, in partnership with the local battered women's advocacy program, is illustrative of innovative police practice regarding domestic violence. The Enforcement Team was strategically placed in a building adjacent to the SAFE House in an effort to break down the barriers between the police and victim advocacy services and to improve the outcomes for victims. The police unit is able to track the status of cases, cutting through bureaucratic red tape and expediting the serving of bench warrants. Police attend every defendant arraignment and are able to take all domestic cases seriously. Police link with SAFE House staff after an arrest has been made, bringing immediate in-person services to the victim (Littel, Malefyt, Walker, Tucker, & Buel, 1998).

Austin Police Department: Austin/Travis County Family Violence Protection Team in Travis County, Texas, is another example of a collaborative, community response to family violence providing multiple services in one location. Leading the community in a zero-tolerance policy toward family violence, the team, consisting of members of the Austin Police Department, Travis County Sheriff's Office, SafePlace (formerly the Center for Battered Women and Rape Crisis Center), Legal Aid of Central Texas, Women's Advocacy Project (attorneys), and the Travis County Attorney's Office, collaborate to investigate, prosecute, and provide legal and social services for victims. Investigations center around cases of assault, kidnapping, stalking, and protective order violations. Legal services streamlines the process for obtaining emergency or long-term protective orders. The majority of cases are processed by the County Attorney's Office and felonies are handled by the District Attorney's Office. Victim services are provided by victim service counselors from SafePlace, the Austin Police Department, and the Travis County Sheriff's Department. The Austin Child Guidance Center is also available to provide free counseling for children. The team has been in operation since 1997, funded by the Violence Against Women Grants Office (Austin City Connection, 2000).

The Longview Police Department: Domestic Violence Impact Unit in Longview, Washington, six- member team consists of a sergeant, officers, civilian investigator, legal coordinator, crime analyst, and administrative specialist. The unit works to coordinate law enforcement, prosecution, probation, and victim services in domestic violence cases. They provide education and training to police officers, advocates, prosecutors, probation officers, and other community and criminal justice partners. An automated case management system assists the team in tracking offenders and their activities as they are processed through the system.

Not unlike the departments highlighted here, specialized units provide departments with the opportunity to thoroughly investigate misdemeanor level domestic crimes, a function that in the past has been lost to other felony crimes. Following up on high-risk cases is critical to break the cycle of violence before it escalates to the felony level. Creating dialogue between police units, victims' programs, and victims promotes the protection of victims and the opportunity to prevent future acts of violence.

Police departments frequently organize their functions through the creation of specialized departments or units. Division of labor into smaller subunits has been an effective tool for contemporary police departments to manage the variety of tasks required of them. For example, police departments may have investigative units or squads for narcotics, sex crimes, juvenile crimes, fraud, special weapons, arson, and so on. Generally organized around specific crime types, specialized units have afforded police departments the opportunity to attend to the specific dynamics of particular crimes.

Although there are inherent challenges in the specialization of police functions, Peak (1998) identifies several advantages to such specialization. Specialized units place the responsibility of certain tasks with specific individuals, ensuring that the work is completed. In the case of domestic violence, this is especially true. Historically, police investigators followed up only on domestic cases that involved felony-level assaults or homicides. Therefore, the majority of battering incidents were addressed only by patrol officers at the scene. Only the most severe cases of abuse would be transferred to an investigative bureau. Specialized units also provide for the development of expertise and training that ultimately leads to increased efficiency, effectiveness, staff cohesion, and improved morale.

Although the potential is great for specialized units, Susan T. Krumholz (2001) argues that there may be a disjuncture between the image of the Domestic Violence Unit and the reality that some units merely serve a symbolic role. Her research with 169 police departments in Massachusetts revealed a number of issues of concern. First, only 8% of the police departments with Domestic Violence Units reported being supported from a line item in the departments budget, and 11% received partial funding by line item. The majority of departments acknowledge that they were funded solely by grants. This raises serious questions about the stability of such units after the grant period has ended. She also found that departments with such units required on average only two more hours of training per year than police departments without such units. Additionally, she found that the average unit was staffed by two full-time officers, and the majority of units were in operation only during normal business hours.

Further research is needed before we can fully understand the impact of specialized units in the creation of a local community environment where victims can be protected and abusers can be held accountable. Because many police departments find that the majority of their calls for service involve domestic incidents, specialized units may provide the most prudent organizational strategy to taking domestic assault seriously.

THE ROLE OF TECHNOLOGY IN A COORDINATED COMMUNITY RESPONSE

Technology has already begun to revolutionize the police industry. Advanced photographic techniques, computers, DNA profiling, innovations in fingerprinting and forensic techniques, automated crime analysis, computer-aided investigations, computer-aided dispatch, case management systems, simulated training tools, nonlethal weapons, and surveillance technologies are but a few of the many examples of innovative crime-fighting tools. As police departments become more skilled with the uses and advantages of such technologies and communities agree to invest resources in them, police departments are likely to apply such advancements to combat domestic violence in a broad way.

We have already begun to see the potential for technology in protecting battered women from their abusive partners and deterring violent batterers from repeating their abusive and brutal acts. Cellular phones, electronic monitoring systems, and online police services are just a few of the applications of modern technology to policing domestic violence (Roberts, 2002).

Cellular Phones

A national campaign to donate cellular phones for victims of domestic violence is currently under way. Sponsored by the Wireless Foundation (2001), a philanthrophic organization dedicated to utilizing wireless communication for the public good, the Call to Protect program to date has received 30,606 donated cellular phones to provide links to emergency services for victims and their advocates. Established by the Cellular Telecommunications Industry Association (CTIA), the Wireless Foundation coordinates the Call to Protect, a national Donate a Phone campaign. CTIA members, Motorola, Brightpoint, Inc., in partnership with the National Coalition Against Domestic Violence (NCADV) provide free wireless phones and airtime. The phones are preprogrammed to notify authorities at the push of a button. The Donate a Phone Program was started by the Wireless Foundation, Motorola, and the national Coalition Against Domestic Violence. As a result of this national program as well as recent statewide and citywide programs across the United States by Verizon Wireless, more than 2 million cell phones have been collected to help victims of domestic violence.

Victim advocates have also been given donated phones and airtime. This national initiative has involved numerous organizations, clubs, companies, and others to join the fight against domestic violence. Additionally, the Wireless Foundation coordinates the Communities on Phone Patrol (COPP) program, in partnership with Ericsson and CTIA companies, to provide free wireless phone and airtime to volunteer neighborhood watch patrols. On average, 52,000 crimes and emergencies are reported each month in the United States by neighborhood watch groups using wireless phones (Wireless Foundation, 2001).

Electronic Monitoring

Recent developments in electronic monitors, computerized tracking of offenders and victims, and video surveillance have greatly bolstered crime investigations and crime prevention efforts. The goal is to lessen and eventually eliminate violent crime by controlling the physical environment. In the most severe cases, the formerly battered woman agrees to maintain an active restraining order, agrees to testify in court and cooperate with any criminal proceedings against the alleged batterer, has a telephone in her residence, and believes that she is in extreme danger of aggravated assault or attempted murder by the defendant. In these cases, a home electronic monitor (e.g., panic alarm or pendant), also known as the abused woman's active emergency response pendant, can deter the batterer from violating his restraining order.

Private security companies recently began donating and marketing electronic security devices called panic alarms to battered women. The main purpose of these portable alarms, which have a range of about 200 feet from the victim's home, is to provide battered women with an immediate and direct link to their local police in an emergency with just a press of a button. In some jurisdictions in Colorado and New Hampshire, the electronic pendant alarms are coupled with electronic monitoring of batterers through the Juris Monitor ankle bracelet, manufactured by B.I., Inc. If the batterer comes within close proximity of the victim's home, the ankle bracelet sounds a loud alarm in the home and immediately alerts the police. ADT Security has set up electronic pendants for battered women in 30 counties and cities throughout the United States. The women are carefully selected for each program by a screening committee composed of community leaders, including a prosecutor or deputy prosecutor, a supervisor from the local battered women's shelter, and a police administrator. In all cases, the victim has an active restraining order against the batterer and is willing to fully cooperate with the prosecutor's office. One major drawback of these alarms is that the unit will not work if the telephone line is cut or is not working (Roberts, 2002).

Several companies, including T.L.P. Technologies, Inc., Transcience, and B.I. Inc., are currently developing electronic monitors. The alarm system developed by T.L.P. Technologies works even when the phone lines are down and when there is no electric power. In the victim's home, police install the system, which includes a radio transmitter with a battery backup, an antenna, and a remote panic or motion-detector device. T.L.P.'s Visibility Plus Radio Data Alarm System integrates both the alarm system and computer-generated data immediately into the police radio channel instead of using a private security company as an intermediary. This system has been used with hundreds of battered women in both Nassau and Suffolk counties, New York.

The most promising device that pinpoints the location of the victim, whether she is at home, at work, or in the supermarket, was developed by Geo Satellite Positioning Equipment. This advanced technology works by means of a satellite that sends a special signal from a receiver on the ground to the local police computer screen. A street map comes up on the screen and sends a burst of data over the network, including the alarm number and the longitude and latitude of the victim's location within 5 to 10 feet.

Because of the growing awareness of the acute injuries sustained by battered women throughout the Untied States, and the millions of dollars spent on health and mental health care for victims of domestic violence, we predict that the electronic monitoring programs will be expanded to thousands of battered women in every state by the year 2010. Unfortunately, as has been the case with other new legislation, a high-profile crisis situation needs to occur before Congress enacts new legislation.

Online Police Information

Police departments nationwide are beginning to use the World Wide Web as a tool to communicate with the community regarding crime issues. Through

Web pages, police departments have created a vehicle in which information about domestic violence issues can be disseminated to the public at large. Police department Web pages can provide community members with critical information regarding the dynamics of domestic violence, what to do if you are a victim, and where to access community resources.

For example, the Madison Police Department (2000) in Madison, Wisconsin, has a Web page dedicated to Domestic Violence Information. Created by Detective Cindy Murphy, the page provides links to topics such as safety issues to consider when leaving an abusive relationship, a personal safety plan, state laws regarding domestic violence, the cycle of domestic violence, myths and facts about domestic violence, domestic abuse risk assessment, how to obtain a restraining order, and referral to resources and programs available in the Madison area.

Both short-term emergency support and long-term security services are critically needed by battered women and their children. It is important that emergency services, including electronic pendants and cellular phones, be initiated for the thousands of battered women in imminent danger of suffering repeated assaults and being murdered by their former abusive partners. Funding for the new technology should come from both corporate sponsors and government agencies. But first, research needs to be carried out to determine which emergency electronic systems are most effective in protecting battered women. Also, under what conditions does the electronic technology fail to ensure the battered women's safety? *Before new electronic technology is purchased by battered women's shelters and law enforcement agencies, it is critical that comprehensive evaluations and outcome studies be planned and carried out.*

CRISIS INTERVENTION BY POLICE-BASED CRISIS TEAMS AND VICTIM ASSISTANCE UNITS

Surveys of police departments around the United States indicate that approximately 80 to 90% of the police officers' time is spent on service calls, also known as order maintenance activities, for such incidents as assaults among family members, neighbor disputes, bar fights, traffic accidents, and individuals who are drunk and disorderly. The police may have the skills to intervene and resolve a dispute among neighbors, a bar fight, or a traffic accident, but they are rarely skilled in providing crisis intervention and follow-up counseling with victims of domestic violence (Roberts, 1996b, 1990).

In recognition of the large amount of time police spend responding to repeat family violence calls and their lack of clinical skills, a growing number of police departments have developed crisis intervention teams staffed by professional crisis clinicians and/or trained volunteers.

Victims often turn to their local city, county, or township police department when confronted with the unpredictable injuries or life-threatening danger posed by domestic violence. As a result of the *Thurman* case (in which a battered woman was awarded $2.3 million in her lawsuit against the Torrington, Connecticut, police department for its failure to protect her from her violent husband), more police departments have been responsive to calls from domestic violence victims. Police can respond quickly to domestic violence calls and can transport the victim to the local hospital emergency room or the battered women's shelter. In some cities, police receive backup from the crisis team, which arrives at the home or police department shortly after the police transport the victim to police headquarters. The first such crisis team began in 1975 at the Pima County District Attorney's Office in Tucson, Arizona. The acceptance of and growing reliance on this program by the Tucson Police Department is revealed by the significantly increased number of police referrals to the crisis team—there were a total of 840 police referrals in 1977, compared with 4,734 referrals in 1984. It should be noted that these figures reflect referrals for all types of crime victims, but most referrals are for domestic violence cases. Since violence in the home constitutes a considerable percentage of police calls, abused women are frequent beneficiaries of this innovative system.

The following description of the program in Tucson will illustrate the intervention procedures utilized by victim assistance programs:

> The Pima County Victim Witness Program has received national recognition for providing immediate crisis intervention to battered women and other crime victims. It also has served as a model for similar programs in other cities. The program was initiated in 1975 with a grant from the Law Enforcement Assistance Administration (LEAA). The grant-funded program was so successful that, when the grant expired, city and county officials agreed to pay for its continuation. The crisis intervention staff uses two police vehicles (unmarked and radio equipped) to travel to the crime scene. The mobile crisis teams are on patrol every night between 6:00 P.M. and 3:00 A.M. At all other times they are contacted via a beeper system.
>
> Domestic violence cases are potentially the most dangerous for the crisis counselors. The staff members work in pairs, generally in a team of a male and a female. They are given an intensive training program in which they are taught self-defense, escape driving, and how to use a police radio, as well as crisis intervention techniques. (Roberts, 1990)

During the mid-1980s through the 1990s, a small but growing number of police departments developed a program to provide immediate crisis counseling to victims of domestic violence, as well as victims of other violent crimes such as rape. The crisis intervention team provides the following services: crisis counseling, advocacy, transportation to and from medical centers and shelters, and referrals to social service agencies. The majority of clients, over the years, have been battered women.

The crisis intervention team staff are civilian employees, trained volunteers from the community, or clinical social workers (e.g., New York City collaborative programs between Victim Services and NYPD; Austin, Dallas, and Houston Police Departments; Plainfield, New Jersey, Police Department). A crisis team (always working in groups of two) is notified of a crisis situation via the police radio, and the crisis counselors usually meet the police at the crime scene. The police, after determining that the counselors will not be in danger, may leave the home. The clinicians utilize a basic crisis intervention model of assessing the situation, discussing the options, forming a plan of action, and aiding the victim in implementing the plan. The New York and Texas programs have between 3 and 18 full-time staff members and two to four graduate student interns each semester, as well as trained volunteer workers.

The programs are funded by city or state criminal justice grants, city or county general revenue grants, and federal Violence Against Women grants. Initially, all of the budgets came from a combination of state and city grants. In its first year of operation, the Houston crisis intervention program was budgeted at $159,000. The amount had increased to $351,000 by the program's third year of operation.

As of 1998, similar programs had been developed under the auspices of the police departments in many cities, including South Phoenix, Arizona; Santa Ana, San Diego, and Stockton, California; Indianapolis, Indiana; Detroit, Michigan; Omaha, Nebraska; Las Vegas, Nevada; East Windsor, Plainsboro, South Brunswick, and South River, New Jersey; Rochester, New York; Memphis, Tennessee; and Salt Lake City, Utah. However, there are still many communities that have not initiated this type of program. It is hoped that the success of these 24-hour crisis intervention programs will encourage other localities to establish a similar type of service.

VOCATIONAL TRAINING FOR BATTERED WOMEN

Thousands of battered women in large urban areas have been trapped in an intergenerational cycle of poverty, violence, and a dearth of marketable job skills. As part of President Clinton's welfare-to-work initiative, battered women's programs in some cities have developed job training programs specifically for women who were previously abused by their partner. For example, Victim Services in New York City initiated two innovative employment skills training programs. Victim Services' first welfare-to-work training program, Project RISE, began in New York City in late 1997 to help victims of domestic violence who have been recipients of welfare enter the workforce with good-paying jobs. Project RISE provides 6-month training programs to teach formerly battered women word processing computer skills (specifically, Microsoft Word and Excel). The second innovative program, Project Superwomen, assists domestic violence survivors to obtain nontraditional employment in blue-collar positions (which traditionally were held solely by men) that offer a stable income and benefits but do not require advanced training. The women receive 3 months of training to prepare them to work in building maintenance positions, which have the advantage of flexible hours and, often, rent-free housing. The women learn such skills as replacing broken locks; handling light plumbing repairs; and spackling, sanding, and painting apartment walls.

ASSESSMENT AND INTERVENTION IN THE EMERGENCY ROOM

A visit to the emergency room may provide the initial opportunity for some victims to recognize the life-threatening nature of the violent relationship and to begin making important plans to change their situations. At a growing number of large hospitals in urban areas, crisis assessment and intervention are being provided to battered women by emergency room staff.

A recommended way for emergency rooms to handle detection and assessment of batterment is through an adult abuse protocol. Two of the pioneers in the development of these protocols are Karil Klingbeil and Vicky Boyd of Seattle, who in 1976 initiated plans for emergency room intervention with abused women. The social work department of the Harborview Medical Center in Seattle developed an adult abuse protocol that provides specific information on the assessment to be made by the involved staff—the triage nurse, the physician, and the crisis clinician. Using a protocol serves two purposes. First, it alerts the involved hospital staff to provide the appropriate clinical care; second, it documents the violent incident so that if the woman decides to file a legal complaint, "reliable, court-admissible evidence" (including photographs) is available (Klingbeil & Boyd, 1984).

Although this protocol was developed for use by emergency room crisis clinicians, it can easily be adapted for use by other health care personnel. The following case example describes how the adult abuse protocol has been successfully used.

Case Example

Mrs. J was admitted to the emergency room accompanied by her sister. This was the second visit within the month for Mrs. J and the emergency room triage nurse and social worker realized that her physical injuries were much more severe on this second visit. Mrs. J was crying, appeared frightened, and in spite of the pain, she constantly glanced over her shoulder. She indicated that her husband would follow her to the emergency room and that she feared for her life. The social worker immediately notified Security.

Mrs. J indicated that she just wanted to rest briefly and then leave through another entrance. She was four months pregnant and concerned about her unborn child. She reported that this had been the first time Mr. J had struck her in the abdomen. The social worker spent considerable time calming Mrs. J in order to obtain a history of the assaultive event. Consent for photography was obtained and Mrs. J indicated that she *would* press charges. "The attack on my child" seemed to be a turning point in her perception of the gravity of her situation, even though Mr. J had beaten her at least a dozen times over the previous two years.

While the social worker assisted in the history taking, a physician provided emergency medical care: several sutures over the right eye.

With Mrs. J's permission, an interview was conducted with her sister who agreed to let Mrs. J stay with her and also agreed to participate in the police reporting. When Mrs. J felt able, the social worker and sister helped her complete necessary forms for the police who had been called to the emergency room.

Although the physician had carefully explained the procedures and rationale to Mrs. J, the social worker repeated this information and also informed her of the lethality of the battering, tracing from her chart her last three emergency room visits. Mrs. J was quick to minimize the assaults but when the social worker showed her photographs from those visits, documenting bruises around her face and neck, she shook her head and said, "No more, not any more." Her sister provided excellent support and additional family members were on their way to the emergency room to be with Mrs. J. When the police arrived Mrs. J was able to give an accurate report of the day's events. . . . She realized there would be difficult decisions to make and readily accepted a follow-up counseling appointment for a Battered Women's group. (Klingbeil & Boyd, 1984, pp. 16–24)

It should be noted that all cases are not handled as easily as this one. The two aspects of Mrs. J's situation that led to a positive resolution were (a) the immediate involvement of emergency room staff and their discussion with the patient of her history and injuries, and (b) the availability of supportive relatives.

Before the woman leaves the emergency room, the crisis clinician should talk with her about whether to return home or to seek refuge with friends, with family, or at a shelter for abused women. The emergency room staff should be able to provide names and phone numbers of referral sources. It is helpful if the pertinent information is printed on a small business-size card (which is easy to tuck away in a pocket or purse) and given to all abuse victims, as well as to suspected victims (Klingbeil & Boyd, 1984). Even if a woman refuses to acknowledge that her current bruises are the result of batterment, she may decide to keep the card for future use.

Merely having an adult abuse protocol does not ensure that it will be used. A study conducted by Flaherty (1985) at four Philadelphia hospitals found that the protocol was used selectively, mainly for victims who volunteered that they had been battered. The medical staff thus ignored the opportunity to help batterment victims who were not able to volunteer the information. The researchers cited the following reasons for underutilization of the protocol:

1. Some physicians and nurses did not regard battering as a medical problem.
2. Some of the emergency room staff believed that it would be an invasion of privacy to ask a woman questions about how she was injured.
3. Many viewed completing the protocol as an additional burden when they were already overworked.

Of those medical personnel who did recognize batterment as a legitimate problem, the most frequently used intervention technique was the tear-off list of referral sources, which was printed at the bottom of the protocol.

There is a crucial difference between Flaherty et al.'s Philadelphia study and the procedures described previously by Klingbeil and Boyd (1984) in Seattle. The Philadelphia study requested the cooperation of nurses and physicians but did not involve medical crisis clinicians. In contrast, the Harborview Medical Center protocol was created and implemented by the hospital's social work department. It emphasized a multidisciplinary team approach, with the social workers taking the lead role in conducting screening and assessment, often talking to the victim while the physician provided medical treatment.

The information just presented would indicate that the involvement of medical social workers is advisable and perhaps necessary in successfully implementing a crisis assessment and intervention system with battered women in the hospital emergency room.

INTERVENTION TECHNIQUES USED BY TELEPHONE HOTLINES AND BATTERED WOMEN'S SHELTERS

Battered women in crisis may reach out for help in any of a number of ways. The initial contact is generally by telephone, making the phone a lifeline for many women. Violence often occurs late in the evening, on weekends, or on holidays, and shelter staff are usually available 24 hours a day to respond to a crisis call. But a woman in crisis who has just been brutally beaten probably does not know the name or phone number of the local shelter. A frequent scenario is that of a woman and her children hastily escaping from home late in the evening and fleeing to a neighbor's home to make an emergency call for help. Not having the number of the local shelter, these women generally contact the police, a toll-free statewide domestic violence hotline, or the city- or community-wide crisis hotline (which aids people in all types of crisis). If the woman contacts the community-wide hotline, there is generally a brief delay while the worker gathers some basic information and then gives the caller the phone number of the closest shelter. An alternative is for the crisis intervenor to take the caller's phone number and have the shelter worker call her back.

When a battered woman in crisis calls a hotline, it is essential that she be able to talk immediately to a trained crisis clinician—not be put on hold or confronted with an answering machine or voice mail. If she is not able to talk to a caring and knowledgeable crisis intervenor, she may just give up, and a valuable opportunity for intervening in the cycle of violence will have been lost. In these situations time is of the essence; if the violent male is still on the rampage, he is likely to search for her, thereby endangering not only his mate but the neighbor as well.

Hotline workers distinguish between a *crisis call*—one in which the woman is in imminent danger or has just been beaten—and other types of calls in which the individual is not in immediate danger but is anxious or distressed and is seeking information or someone to talk to. The overriding goal of crisis intervention is ensuring the safety of the woman and her children. To determine whether the call is a crisis call, the worker asks such questions as:

- Are you or your children in danger now?
- Is the abuser there now?
- Do you want me to call the police?
- Do you want to leave, and can you do so safely?
- Do you need medical attention?

Programs have different policies regarding transporting women who need refuge but have no way to get there. Although some shelters will send staff to pick up the woman at her home, it is more common for shelter policy to prohibit staff from doing so because of the possibility of the staff member being attacked by the abuser. In cities that have a crisis intervention team affiliated with the police department (e.g., New York City, or Plainsboro and East Windsor, New Jersey), the shelter staff can contact the police, who investigate the situation and radio for the victim advocate or crisis counselor to transport the victim and her children to the shelter. Many times the police themselves are prevailed upon to provide the transportation. Another alternative is for the victim advocate from the shelter to meet the battered woman at the local hospital emergency room.

Once the urgent issues pertaining to the woman's physical safety have been resolved, the crisis intervenor can begin to help the victim talk about her situation and discuss possible courses of action. Throughout this process it is important for the crisis intervenor to remember that he or she can present different alternatives, but the client must make her own final decisions in order to be empowered.

The following is a step-by-step guide to intervention with battered women (originally developed by Jones, 1968), which is included in the training manual prepared by the Abuse Counseling and Treatment (ACT) program in Fort Myers, Florida. It is referred to as the A-B-C process of crisis management—the A referring to "achieving contact," the B to "boiling down the problem," and the C to "coping with the problem."

A. *Achieving contact*
   1. Introduce yourself: name, role, and purpose.
   2. If a phone call, ask the client if she is safe and protected now.
   3. Ask the client how she would like to be addressed: first name, surname, or nickname; this helps the client regain control.
   4. Collect client data; this breaks the ice and allows the client and clinician to get to know each other and develop trust.
   5. Ask the client if she has a clinician or if she is taking any medication.
   6. Identify the client's feelings and ask for a perception check.

B. *Boiling down the problem*
   1. Ask the client to describe briefly what has just happened.
   2. Encourage the client to talk about the here and now.
   3. Ask the client what is the most pressing problem.
   4. Ask the client if it were not for said problems, would she feel better right now.
   5. Ask client if she has been confronted with a similar type of problem before, and if so, how she handled it then. What worked and what didn't?
   6. Review with the client what you heard as the primary problem.

C. *Coping with the problem*
   1. What does the client want to happen?
   2. What is the most important need—the bottom line?
   3. Explore what the client feels is the best solution.
   4. Find out what the client is willing to do to meet her needs.
   5. Help the client formulate a plan of action: resources, activities, time.
   6. Arrange follow-up contact with the client.

Careful recruitment and thorough training of crisis intervention staff is essential to a program's success. It is also necessary for an experienced clinician to be on call at all times for consultation in difficult cases. In addition to knowing what to say, clinicians need to learn about the tone of voice and attitude to be used while handling crisis calls. Crisis clinicians are advised to speak in a steady, calm voice, to ask open-ended questions, and to refrain from being judgmental.

A shelter's policies and procedures manual, should include guidelines for crisis staff. For example, the ACT program in Fort Myers, Florida, has developed a 45-page training manual, which includes sections on shelter policies and procedures, referral procedures, and background information on domestic violence that discusses both the victims and the abusers. The ACT manual explains the wide variation in the emotional reactions of the women who call for help. The client's speaking style may be "fast, slow, hesitant, loud, barely audible, rambling, loss of words, [or] normal." Her emotional reaction may be "angry, highly upset, hysterical, withdrawn, laughing, calm, icy, guilty, or a combination of these" (Houston, 1987, p. 5). No matter what characteristics the caller exhibits, the crisis clinician's task is to try to help the victim cope with the immediate situation. However, the guidelines also advise crisis clinicians to avoid the pitfall of believing they need to provide the caller with immediate, expert solutions to her problems. Crisis clinicians should not subject themselves to guilt feelings if they cannot help an abused woman resolve her situation. If the clinician suspects child abuse or neglect, he or she is required to notify the supervisor and then report the suspected abuse to the appropriate agency (Houston, 1987).

Shelter staff are confronted with a dilemma when the caller is an abused woman who is under the influence of drugs or alcohol or who has psychiatric symptoms. Although such women are victims of batterment, they also have a significant problem which the staff are not trained to treat. Shelter policy generally requires crisis intervenors to screen out battered women who are under the influence of alcohol or drugs, but there are exceptions. At Womanspace (in central New Jersey), women with drug or alcohol problems are accepted provided they are simultaneously enrolled in a drug or alcohol treatment program (Hart, 1999). Likewise, it is the crisis clinician's responsibility to determine whether a woman's behavior is excessively irrational or bizarre or whether she is likely to be a danger to herself or others. If a woman is suspected of having psychiatric problems, she is generally referred to the psychiatric screening unit of a local hospital or to a mental health center for an evaluation.

TELEPHONE LOG

Battered women's shelters usually maintain a written record of all phone calls, whether or not they are crisis calls. In addition to seeking such routine information as name, address, phone number, marital status, and ages of children, the form may include the following: (a) the questions "Are you in immediate danger?" "Do you want me to call the police?" and "How did you get our number?"; (b) action taken by the crisis clinician; and (c) follow-up action (Hart, 1999). Shelters, which are often overcrowded, may also have a section of the form on which the counselor can indicate whether the family is able to be housed immediately, is to be referred to another shelter or safe home, or needs to be put on a waiting list.

Womanspace developed a one-page telephone log form, which on the front asks many of the questions just listed, and on the reverse side contains further screening questions and an explanation of their shelter's policies. An example is the following printed statement, which explains the program's policy on weapons (Hart, 1999):

> We do not allow weapons in the shelter.
> We ask that you not bring a weapon or anything that may be used as a weapon with you.
> Do you own a weapon?
> If yes, do you agree to let us keep it in a safe place for you?

The advantage of printing this and other procedural statements on every telephone form is to ensure that all crisis workers impart the same basic information. At the bottom of each form is a list of nine of the most frequently used telephone numbers, including those of three area police departments. The advantage of having these numbers on every form is that during a crisis, they are always readily available, and valuable time is not lost searching for them.

ART THERAPY

Art therapy has been used effectively with women as well as children who have been subjected to domestic violence. As part of a comprehensive treatment approach in shelters for battered women and their children, art therapy can help victims (including young children) communicate their painful experiences in a nonverbal manner that is less threatening than traditional talk therapy. The goal of art therapy is to deal with the violence that took place, while also empowering the mother and enhancing her parenting skills. It is helpful in initiating the healing process for the mother and her children to have the opportunity to communicate what has occurred through their drawings (Riley, 1994).

Art therapy is also helpful when working with young children who have limited verbal ability. The following illustration shows how art therapy was used in a family session with a battered 23-year-old mother and her 4-year-old son:

> Although this child was not able to draw complete figures and fully describe the reason that brought him to the shelter, he was able to tell a story about the images he created. He said that the figure on the upper right

was sneaking up on the smaller round circle directly to the left of it, which he identified as a "rock star." He said that the first figure bit the rock star in the leg. This very young boy was able to articulate the same story theme that his mother expressed in more detail. His mother explained through her picture that the four-year-old had bitten the abuser's leg when the abuser last attacked the mother. (McGloughlin, 1999, p. 53)

INDIVIDUALIZED TREATMENT FOR CHILDREN

Battered women who seek temporary shelter to escape from the violence at home generally have children who come to the shelter with them. The children often feel confused, afraid, and angry. They miss their father and do not know if or when they will see him again. It is not uncommon for children to be misinformed or uninformed about the reason they were suddenly uprooted from their home, leaving their personal possessions, friends, and school to stay at a crowded shelter. Similarly, the children may not realize that all of the other children have come to the shelter for the same reason.

Moreover, large numbers of these children have at one time or another also been victims of physical abuse. The 1986 Annual Report from the Family Violence Center in Green Bay, Wisconsin, provided data on child abuse committed by the batterer. The center found that close to half (73) of the 148 abusers of the women had on one or more occasions also beaten their children (Prelipp, 1987).

The following is a true story written by Lisa, a 10-year-old girl who came to a shelter after her father's violent attack on her mother.

My Life, by Lisa

One day around two months ago my mom and dad got into a fight. First, my mom and I come home from the mall. We had a really nice time there. But, when we came home our nice time got to be terrible. I knew they were going to get into a fight so I went into my bedroom and did my homework. I knew he was going to talk to her about something, but I didn't know what. Then I heard my mom start screaming and I went to the door and asked what was wrong. My dad said, "Oh, nothing is wrong. Go do your homework." But I knew something was wrong so I went and prayed to God. My dad was really mean that night. I hated him so bad. My mom did not deserve to get hurt. I love her more than anything else in the entire world. Then I heard my mom scream something but I didn't understand what she said because my dad covered her mouth with his hand. Afterward she told me she said call the cops. Anyway, I went back to the door by the bedroom and told my mom I needed help on my homework, but I didn't. I just wanted my mom to come out of the bedroom because I was afraid. Then they both came out. And I hugged my mom and went to bed. Then my dad started to strangle my mom. So I went out and told my dad to stop. He told me to go back to the bedroom and go to sleep. So, I did. But I was so stupid. Then I heard my mom screaming. So I went back into the living room and he was kicking my mom. He wouldn't stop, he kept kicking her in her arm and legs. I told him to stop. He told me to go back to bed but I said, No! Then he took his guitar and was gonna hit her over the head. But I went on top of my mother. He told me to get off. But I said, No. So he put down the guitar, then he got her ice for her arm. Then I went to sleep crying. The next morning I didn't go to school and she didn't go to work. Then he called up the house and talked to her for a while. He threatened to kill her. So we left to go to the shelter. And here I am *now*. (Arbour Disabuse, 1986)

This girl was fortunate in that her mother brought her to the Jersey Battered Women's Service in northern New Jersey, which has a carefully developed counseling program for battered mothers and their children. Sadly, however, there are still a number of shelters that offer only basic child care services; they do not provide the art therapy and crisis counseling needed to help children deal with the turmoil of recent events (Alessi & Hearn, 1998).

Nevertheless, innovative techniques for helping children have been incorporated into the programs of the more progressive shelters. St. Martha's Hall, a shelter in St. Louis, Missouri, provides counseling for the children, and also requires mothers to participate in parenting classes and to meet with the coordinator of the children's program about establishing family goals and meeting the child's individual needs. The program also provides opportunities for mother and child to participate jointly in relaxing recreational activities (Schiller-Ramirez, 1995).

Two other types of intervention—coloring books and groups for children—are used at some shelters.

Coloring Books as Part of an Individualized Treatment Approach

Some shelters utilize specially designed coloring books that discuss domestic violence in terms children can understand. Laura Prato of the Jersey Battered Women's Service in Morristown, New Jersey, has created two coloring books (Prato, undated), one for children aged 3 to 5 entitled *What Is a Shelter?* and another for 6- to 11-year-olds called *Let's Talk It Over.* In addition to the children's books, Prato has written two manuals for shelter workers that serve as a discussion guide for counselors. The books contain realistic, sensitive illustrations that depict the confused, sad, and angry emotions the children are feeling. They are illustrated in black and white so that the children can color the pictures if they wish. Funding for preparation and printing of the books and manuals came from the New Jersey Division of Youth and Family Services. The purpose of the coloring books and the way in which they are to be used are explained in the introduction to the counselors' manuals. The manuals state that the books are used as part of the intake and orientation process for all children who stay at the shelter. The stated objectives of the books are as follows:

- To provide assurances of the child's continued care and safety
- To encourage children to identify and express their feelings
- To provide information needed for children to understand what is happening in their families
- To provide information that will improve each child's ability to adapt to the shelter setting
- To begin to assess the individual child's needs and concerns

The clinicians' manuals stress the importance of how the book is presented to the child, as shown in the following passage:

> The process surrounding the use of the orientation books is extremely important. It is likely to be the initial contact between the counselor and the newly arrived family and one that will set the tone for future interactions. Consistent with the JBWS Children's Program philosophy, this initial meeting communicates respect for mother and child and acceptance of their feelings. (Prato, undated)

Before meeting with the child, the clinician meets privately with the mother to show her the book, explain its purpose, and ask for her permission to read the book to her child. The clinicians are advised to read any available intake information prior to meeting with the child so that they are better able to "anticipate the individual child's special concerns and place the child's responses in a meaningful context" (Prato, undated). The books have been prepared in a way that encourages the child's active participation. Throughout both books there are several places where the child can write his or her thoughts on the page. For example, one of the pages in *Let's Talk It Over* focuses on a child staying at a shelter who misses her father. The caption under the picture states:

> Many children at the shelter think a lot about their fathers, and that's okay. You may not see your father for a while until everyone in your family has a chance to think about things carefully. The little girl in the picture is wondering about her father. . . . What questions do you think she is asking?

There is a place on that page for the child's response to the question. The response could be written by the child or dictated to the counselor, who would write it in the book. On the next page is a large blank space and a caption that reads, "You may use this page to draw a picture of your father." Books such as those developed by the Jersey Battered Women's Service are very appropriate in helping children cope with the crisis that has led to their staying at the shelter.

GROUP TREATMENT FOR CHILDREN

Another way to help children cope is through therapeutic groups such as the approach developed at Haven House, a shelter for battered women and their children in Buffalo, New York. Alessi and Hearn (1998) initiated the group approach when they observed the maladaptive ways in which the children at the shelter reacted to the crisis they were experiencing. The children tended to be aggressive and attempted to resolve problems through hitting. They had considerable anxiety, "biting their fingernails, pulling their hair, and somaticizing feelings as manifested by complaints of headaches and 'tight' stomachs" (Alessi & Hearn, 1998, p. 163). They had ambivalent feelings toward their fathers, loving them as well as hating them.

The two group leaders established a six-session treatment program for children ages 8 to 16 focusing on the following topics: "(1) the identification and expression of feelings; (2) violence; (3) unhealthy ways to solve problems; (4) healthy ways to solve problems; (5) sex, love and sexuality; and (6) termination and saying goodbye" (Alessi & Hearn, 1998, p. 167). To provide an indication of the scope of the group sessions, the following summarizes the content of the session on violence.

The purpose of the session on violence is to give children an opportunity to explore and express feelings about the violence in their families and how it has affected them. This helps children break down their denial and minimization of the problem. It also gives them a chance to learn that other families have similar problems and that many families do not. The following questions are presented to each of the children for reflection and discussion:

1. Why did you come to Haven House?
2. Do you think it's right for a man to hit a woman or a woman to hit a man, and why?
3. Do you think it's right for a parent to hit a child, and why?
4. How do you think you've been affected by the violence in your family?
5. Do you think you'll grow up to be violent or accept violence in intimate relationships?

The children are always given homework to keep the session alive between meetings. For example, after the discussion on violence, they are asked to develop a minidrama on family violence to be presented the next week. Following the session on healthy problem solving, they are asked to prepare a list of healthy ways of coping with their problems (Alessi & Hearn, 1998).

TECHNOLOGY TO PROTECT BATTERED WOMEN

During the 1990s, some battered women in imminent danger seem to have benefited from different types of technology, including alarm/security systems; panic alarms in conjunction with electronic bracelets; cell phones preprogrammed to 911 for an emergency police response; and instant cameras that provide an immediate photographic record documenting the assault and battery.

A few corporations, notably B.I., Inc., T.L.P. Technologies, Inc., ADT Security, and Transcience, have developed electronic monitors to protect women from domestic abuse. T.L.P. Technologies created an alarm system that is fully operational "even when the phone lines are down and when there is no electrical power" (Roberts, 1996c, p. 93). Law enforcement officers install the system in the abused woman's residence. The system includes a radio transmitter with a battery backup, a remote panic or motion-detector device, and an antenna. When the woman is in danger, she transmits an alarm directly to the police radio channel, unlike with other systems, in which a private security company serves as an intermediary (Roberts, 1996c).

ADT established the AWARE Program, which stands for Abused Women's Active Response Emergency Program, in 1992; by 1997 the program was operational in 150 cities across the United States. The women who participate in this program are selected by prosecutors, law enforcement officials, and shelter directors, and they receive an electronic emergency pendant, worn around the neck, donated by ADT. If the batterer is endangering the woman at her home, she activates the pendant, sending a silent alarm to ADT, which notifies the police to respond to the emergency alarm. Each city police department, in collaboration with the prosecutor's office, establishes its own criteria for participation in the AWARE Program, but typically all women who receive the pendant must "(1) be in imminent danger, (2) have a restraining order against the abuser and (3) be willing to prosecute the abuser and testify against him in a court of law, if he is apprehended as a result of the use of the ADT security system" (ADT, 1999). Through the AWARE Program, ADT installs a security system at the woman's residence, and each woman receives a pendant that is operational within a radius of 100 feet from her home system. (Whenever the woman is more than 100 feet from her home, the pendant does not work; therefore, this system offers excellent protection in the home but not at work or other community locations.)

In addition to the ADT pendant system, a number of prosecutors' offices and battered women's shelters have made arrangements with mobile phone companies to provide abused women with preprogrammed cell phones, so that they can press one button to be automatically connected to the 911 police emergency system. This offers women protection when they are away from home. Although no system is foolproof, these electronic devices provide battered women with increased security.

It is the high cost of electronic devices that has prevented *all* battered women who are in danger from having access to enhanced protection through the latest technology. Because of funding limitations (and the fact that the women are generally not financially able to purchase expensive equipment on their own), criminal justice agencies and battered women's shelters are forced to allocate these scarce resources to women whom they determine are at the highest risk for a life-threatening assault. Usually, these devices are reserved for women who are living apart from the batterer and who have obtained a restraining order (also known as an order of protection) from the court. Local battered women's shelters, in cooperation with law enforcement agencies, may be able to contact manufacturers directly and discuss the possibility of donations of some equipment, or a reduced cost if bulk purchases are made. Statewide and community-wide domestic violence coalitions may also target their fund-raising activities toward the acquisition of these electronic devices.

It is vitally important that battered women receive both short-term emergency assistance and long-term security services. Electronic pendants and other electronic technology should be initiated widely to protect the safety of thousands of women who have been severely battered, who have left the violent relationship, and who are still fearful that an abuser will return to harm her again. Funding for these devices should be provided by government agencies and corporate sponsors. Research studies should be conducted to learn which emergency electronic devices provide the most protection for women who have been battered, as well as the drawbacks to particular devices (Roberts, 1996c).

High-intensity Polaroid cameras are being used by police departments and hospital emergency rooms to document the injuries perpetrated by the batterer. Photos that carefully document the woman's injuries are extremely valuable when the case goes to court and may serve to prevent future, more lethal, assaults either because the batterer will be sent to prison on the basis of the indisputable evidence documented in the photographs or because the judge will issue a harsh warning of a prison sentence if he ever assaults the woman again.

Some police officers carry the Spectra instant point-and-shoot camera with them on domestic violence calls, to make a photographic record of the injuries as well as the overall scene at the home (e.g., a knife or gun on the table; children disheveled and crying; damage to doors, walls, or furniture due to the batterer's rampage; a phone cord ripped out of the wall). The advantage of using an instant camera is that the officers can be certain they have accurately photographed the injuries and the disarray at home before leaving the scene.

Similarly, emergency room staff are using these cameras when examining women who admit to being abused or are suspected of being a victim of abuse. Physicians, nurses, or social workers employed in the emergency room are often the first to see the woman following a severe assault. Some abused women with severe injuries go straight to the emergency room without contacting the police. The significant role of medical personnel in identifying victims of domestic violence cannot be overemphasized. Dr. Elaine Alpert, of the Boston University School of Medicine, has stated the importance of hospital personnel taking instant photos of the battered woman's injuries:

> Often, the image, taken on-the-spot, may serve as the only visible evidence that violence has taken place. Cigarette burns, scratches, welts, bite marks, bruises and cuts heal and disappear. But the photo reveals, conclusively, that abuse did take place—and can serve as a crucial piece of incriminating evidence in civil or criminal proceedings against the batterer. (Poremba, 1997, p. 7)

REFERRAL

Knowledge of referral sources is essential when intervening on behalf of abused women in crisis situations. It is just as important for the police, hospitals, and human service agencies to know about and refer to programs helping battered women and their children as it is for staff at domestic violence treatment programs to refer clients to appropriate community resources.

It is frequently determined that the battered woman needs a variety of services, such as job training and placement, low-cost transitional housing, day care, and ongoing counseling; therefore, referral should be made to the appropriate service providers. In its 1995 year-end report, St. Martha's Hall in St. Louis itemized the agencies to which its clients had been referred (Schiller-Ramirez, 1995). Most women were referred to three or more agencies, and several clients were given nine or more referrals, depending on their individual needs. The most frequently used referral sources were as follows:

Legal aid
Medical care
Careers for Homemakers
Job bank
Day care programs
Women in Need (WIN), long-term housing for single women
Alcoholics Anonymous
Women's Self-Help Center, providing counseling and support groups
St. Pat's, a Catholic social service agency that finds low-cost housing and provides classes in budgeting money and other life skills

Examples of other, less frequently used, referral sources were

A shelter in another state	Dental care
Alateen	GED program
Al Anon	Crisis nursery
Literacy Council	Victim Services
Big Brothers	Red Cross

There are two ways in which programs providing crisis intervention services can facilitate the referral process: (a) by publicizing their services to the population at large and to other service providers, and (b) by becoming knowledgeable about community services needed by their clients and in some instances accompanying them to the appropriate agencies.

Publicize the program through the following methods:

1. Print brochures that describe the program's services, and have business cards that provide the program's name and phone number. These materials should be made available in large quantity to police officers, emergency room staff, and other potential sources of referral to the program.
2. Participate in interdisciplinary workshops and seminars on family violence so that the program can become widely known. In addition, this enables the staff to learn about appropriate programs to which their clients can be referred.
3. Attend in-service training programs for police officers, countywide hotline staff, emergency room staff, and others to discuss referral of abused women and to resolve any problems in the referral process which may have occurred.
4. Alert the public through newspaper articles and public service announcements on radio and television, with the program's phone number prominently mentioned.

Become familiar with community resources: Information for crisis clinicians on appropriate referral sources should be available in several ways:

1. The phone number of the most urgently needed agencies—such as the police, victim assistance program, drug/alcohol treatment programs, and psychiatric screening unit—should be readily available, preferably printed on each intake sheet or telephone log form.
2. The program's training manual should contain a section on the most frequently used referral sources. For example, the manual of the ACT program in Fort Myers, Florida, contains eight pages of often-used referral sources, which list the address, phone number, office hours, and services provided for each source.
3. Most major metropolitan areas have a comprehensive resource guide (published by the local United Way or an affiliate such as Call for Action) that provides a comprehensive listing of all of the community ser-

vices in that area. All programs serving abused women and their children should have a copy of and be familiar with their community's resources handbook.

The way in which referrals are made is extremely important, since it may affect the outcome. All too often, victims in crisis do not follow through in making the initial contact with the referral agency. Clinicians and advocates at St. Martha's Hall and other shelters provide support by accompanying the client to the agency in order to demonstrate how to obtain services. This is viewed as a positive alternative to the often intimidating and frustrating experience encountered by women who are given a referral but are expected to fend for themselves.

SUMMARY AND CONCLUSION

A number of important issues and techniques relating to crisis intervention with battered women and their children have been examined in this chapter. Specific methods for crisis intervention in different settings have also been discussed. As increased numbers of women in acute crisis seek help, crisis clinicians and victim advocates must be prepared to respond without delay. Crisis intervention for battered women and their children may do much to alleviate the emotional distress and anguish experienced by those exposed to the trauma of domestic violence. Because of their experience and specialized training, crisis clinicians and medical social workers can play a vital role in assisting women and children in crisis.

Law enforcement officers, victim advocates, hospital emergency room staff, and clinicians at citywide crisis lines and battered women's shelters often come in contact with abused women who are experiencing a crisis. Effective crisis intervention requires an understanding by these service providers of the value and methods of crisis intervention, as well as the community resources to which referrals should be made. Battered women are often motivated to change their lifestyle only during the crisis or postcrisis period. Therefore, it is important for service providers at community agencies to offer immediate assistance to battered women in crisis. With an estimated 8 million couples involved in battering episodes annually, policy makers and program developers should give priority to expanding urgently needed crisis-oriented and follow-up services for battered women and their children.

REFERENCES

ADT (1999). Aware program brochure. Washington, DC.

Alessi, J. J., & Hearn, K. (1998). Group treatment of children in shelters. In A. R. Roberts (Ed.), *Battered women and their families* (2nd ed., pp. 159–173). New York: Springer.

Arbour, D. (1986, December). *Dis-abuse Newsletter*, p. 4. Morristown, NJ: Jersey Battered Women's Service.

Arbour, D. (1987, February 12). Director, Jersey Battered Women's Shelter, Morristown, NJ. Personal communication.

Austin City Connection. (2000). Austin Police Department: Family Violence Protection Team. Available online: www.ci.austin.tx.us/police/afvpt. Retrieved November 9, 2004.

Caplan, G. (1964). *Principles of preventive psychiatry*. New York: Basic Books.

Carlson, B. E. (1997). A stress and coping approach to intervention with abused women. *Family Relations, 46*, 291–298.

Carlson, B. E. & McNutt, L. (1998). Intimate partner violence: Intervention in primary health care settings. In A. R. Roberts (Ed.), *Battered women and their families* (2nd ed., pp. 230–270). New York: Springer.

Dunford, F. W. (1990). The role of arrest in domestic assault: The Omaha Police experiment. *Criminology, 28*, 183–206.

Edington, L. (1987, February 19). Executive Director, *Sojourner*, Indianapolis, IN. Personal communication.

Flaherty, E. W. (1985, February). *Identification and intervention with battered women in the hospital emergency department: Final report*. Philadelphia: Philadelphia Health Management Corp.

Folkman, S. (1984). Personal control, and stress and coping proceses: A theoretical analysis. *Journal of Personality and Social Psychology, 46*, 839–852.

Folkman, S., & Lazarus, R. S. (1985). If it changes it must be a process: Study of emotion and coping during three stages of college examination. *Journal of Personality and Social Psychology, 48*, 150–170.

Frazier, P. A. & Burnett, J. W. (1994). Immediate coping strategies among rape victims. *Journal of Counseling and Development, 72*, 633–639.

Frieze, I., & Bookwala, J. (1996). Coping with unusual stressors: Criminal victimization. In M. Zeidner et al. (Eds.), *Handbook of coping: Theory, research and applications* (pp. 303–321). New York: Wiley.

Gazmararian, J. A., Laxorick, S., Spitz, A. M., Ballard, T. J., Saltzman, L. E., & Marks, J. S. (1996). Prevalence of violence against pregnant women. *Journal of the American Medical Association, 275*, 1915–1920.

Gleason, W. J. (1993). Mental disorders in battered women: An empirical study. *Violence and Victims, 8*, 53–68.

Gordon, J. (1996). Community services available to abused women in crisis: A review of perceived usefulness and efficacy. *Journal of Family Violence. 11(4)*, 315–329.

Greene, G. J., & Lee, M. (1996). Client strengths and crisis intervention: A solution focused approach. *Crisis Intervention and Time-Limited Treatment, 3(1)*, 43–63.

Haag, R. (Undated). The birthday letter. In S. A. Prelipp (Ed.), *Family Violence Center, Inc. Training Manual*. Green Bay, WI: mimeographed.

Hart, P. (June, 1999). Executive Director, Womanspace, Lawrenceville, NJ. Personal communication.

Houston, S. (1987). *Abuse Counseling and Treatment, Inc. (ACT) Manual.* Fort Myers, FL: ACT.

International Association of Chiefs of Police. (2001). *Family Violence Summit recommendations;* IACP Model Domestic Violence Policy, 2004; and Police Chief Magazine. Available online: www.theiacp.org and www.theiacp.org/pubinfo/Research/FamVio or call 1–800-The-IACP. Retrieved November 9, 2004.

Janosik, E. H. (1984). *Crisis counseling.* Belmont, CA: Wadsworth Publishers.

Johnson, K. (1997). Professional help and crime victims. *Social Service Review, 71*, 89–109.

Jones, W. A. (1968). The A-B-C method of crisis management. *Mental Hygiene, 52*, 87–89.

Klingbeil, K. S., & Boyd, V. D. (1984). Emergency room intervention: Detection, assessment and treatment. In A. R. Roberts (Ed.), *Battered women and their families: Intervention strategies and treatment programs* (pp. 7–32). New York: Springer.

Krumholz, S. T. (2001). *Domestic violence units: Effective management or political expedience?* Paper presented at the annual meeting of the Academy of Criminal Justice Sciences, June 2001, Washington, DC.

Lazarus, R. S. & Folkman, S. (1984). *Stress, appraisal and coping.* New York: Springer.

Littel, K., Malefyt, M. B., Walker, A., Tucker, D. D., & Buel, S. M. (1998). *Assessing justice system response to violence against women: A tool for law enforcement, prosecution and the courts to use in developing effective responses.* Violence Against Women Online Resources, Department of Justice, Office of Justice Programs. Available online: www.vaw.umn.edu. Retrieved June 5, 2004.

Madison Police Department. (2000). Domestic violence information. Available online: www.ci.madison.wi.us/police/domestic. Retrieved June 5, 2004.

McGloughlin, M. (May, 1999). *Art therapy with battered women and their children.* M.A. thesis, Eastern Virginia Medical School, Norfolk, Virginia.

Mignon, S. I., & Holmes, W. M. (1995). Police response to mandatory arrest laws. *Crime and Delinquency, 41*(4), 430–442.

Miller, N. (1998). *Domestic violence legislation affecting police and prosecutor responsibilities in the United States: Inferences from a 50-state review of state statutory codes.* Paper presented at the 5th International Family Violence Conference, University of New Hampshire, June 30, 1997. Available online: www.ilj.org/dv/dvvaw. Retrieved June 5, 2004.

Mills, L. (1999). Killing her softly: Intimate abuse and the violence of state intervention. *Harvard Law Review, 113*, 550–613.

New Haven Police Department. (2001). Child Development–Community Policing Program. Available online: www.cityofnewhaven.com/police/cdcp. Retrieved November 9, 2004.

Nurius, P., Hilfrink, M., & Rafino, R. (1996). The single greatest health threat to women: Their partners. In P. Raffoul and C. A. McNeece (Eds.), *Future issues in social work practice* (pp. 159–171). Boston: Allyn and Bacon.

Peak, K. (1998). *Justice administration.* Englewood Cliffs, NJ: Prentice-Hall, Inc.

Pence. E. (1983). The Duluth Domestic Abuse Intervention Project. *Hamline Law Review, 6,* 247–275.

Petretic-Jackson, P., & Jackson, T. (1996). Mental health interventions with battered women. In A. R. Roberts (Ed.), *Helping battered women: New perspectives and remedies* (pp. 188–221). New York: Oxford University Press.

Podhorin, R. (1987, February 12). Director, Womanspace, Inc., Lawrenceville, NJ. Personal communication.

Poremba, B. (Ed.). (Spring 1997). Instant evidence: Break the cycle of family violence. Cambridge, MA: Polaroid Corporation.

Prato, L. (Undated). *What Is a Shelter?; Let's Talk It Over; What Is a Shelter? A ShelterWorker's Manual; Let's Talk It Over: A Shelter Worker's Manual.* Morristown, NJ: Jersey Battered Women's Service.

Prelipp, S. (1987, February 13). Director, Family Violence Center, Green Bay, WI. Personal communication.

Riley, S. (1994). *Integrative approaches to family art therapy.* Chicago: Magnolia Street Publishers.

Roberts, A. R. (1981). *Sheltering battered women: A national study and service guide.* New York: Springer.

Roberts, A. R. (1984). Police intervention. In A. R. Roberts (Ed.), *Battered women and their families: Intervention strategies and treatment programs* (pp. 116–128). New York: Springer.

Roberts, A. R. (1988). Crisis intervention: A practical guide to immediate help for victim families. In A. Horton & J. Williamson (Eds.), *Abuse and religion* (pp. 60–66). Lexington, MA: D. C. Heath.

Roberts, A. R. (1990). *Helping crime victims.* Newbury Park, CA: Sage.

Roberts, A. R. (1996a). Epidemiology and definitions of acute crisis in American society. In A. R. Roberts (Ed.). *Crisis management and brief treatment: Theory, technique and applications* (pp. 16–33). Chicago: Nelson-Hall.

Roberts, A. R. (1996b). A comparative analysis of incarcerated battered women and a community sample of battered women. In A. R. Roberts (Ed.), *Helping battered women: New perspectives and remedies* (pp. 31–43). New York: Oxford University Press.

Roberts, A. R. (1996c). Police responses to battered women. In A. R. Roberts (Ed.), *Helping battered women: New perspectives and remedies* (pp. 85–95). New York: Oxford University Press.

Roberts, A. R. (1998). *Battered women and their families* (2nd ed.). New York: Springer.

Roberts, A. R. & Burman, S. (1998). Crisis intervention and cognitive problem-solving therapy with battered women: A national survey and practice model. In A. R. Roberts (Ed.), *Battered women and their families: Intervention strategies and treatment programs* (2nd ed., pp 3–28). New York: Springer.

Roberts, A. R. (2002). Myths, facts, and realities regarding battered women and their children: An overview. In A. R. Roberts (Ed.), *Handbook of domestic violence intervention strategies: Policies, programs, and legal remedies* (pp. 3–22). New York: Oxford University Press.

Roberts, A. R., & Roberts, B. S. (2005). *Ending intimate abuse: Practical guidelines and survival strategies*. New York: Oxford University Press.

Rosenbaum, M. D. (1998). To break the shell without scrambling the egg: An empirical analysis of the impact of intervention into violent families. *Stanford Law and Policy Review, 9*(2), 409–432.

Saleebey, D. (1997). *The strengths perspective in social work practice* (2nd ed.). White Plains, NY: Longman.

Schiller-Ramirez, M. (1995). *St. Martha's Hall year end report 1994.* St. Louis, MO: St. Martha's Hall.

Sherman, L. W. (1991). From initial deterrence to long-term escalation: Short custody arrest for poverty ghetto domestic violence. *Criminology, 29,* 821–850.

Sherman, L. W., & Berk, R. A. (1984). The specific deterrent effects of arrest for domestic assault. *American Sociological Review, 49,* 261–272.

Sherman, L. W., Schmidt, J., Rogan, D., Smith, D. S., Gartin, P., Cohn, E., et al. (1992). The variable effects of arrest on criminal careers: The Milwaukee Domestic Violence Experiment. *Journal of Criminal Law and Criminology, 83,* 137–169.

Straus, M., & Gelles, R. (1991). *Physical violence in American families.* New Brunswick, NJ: Transaction Books.

Tedeschi, R. G. & Calhoun, L. G. (1995). *Trauma and transformation growing in the aftermath of suffering*. Thousand Oaks, CA: Sage.

Thurman v. City of Torrington, 595 F. Supp. 1521 (D. Conn. 1985).

Tjaden, P., & Thoennes, N. (1998). Battering in America: Findings from the National Violence against Women Survey. *Research in Brief* (60–66). Washington, DC: National Institute of Justice, U.S. Department of Justice.

Tutty, L., Bidgood, B. and Rothery, M. (1993). Support groups for battered women: Research on their efficacy. *Journal of Family Violence, 8*, 325–343.

U.S. Attorney General's Task Force on Family Violence. (1984, September). *Final report.* Washington, DC: Department of Justice.

Valentine, P. V., Roberts, A. R., & Burgess, A. W. (1998). The stress-crisis continuum: Its application to domestic violence. In A. R. Roberts (Ed.), *Battered women and their families* (2nd ed., pp. 29–57). New York: Springer.

Walker, L. E. (1979). *The battered woman.* New York: Harper & Row.

Walker, L. E. (1985). Psychological impact of the criminalization of domestic violence on victims. *Victimology: An International Journal, 10*, 281–300.

Walker, L. E. (1992). Battered woman syndrome and self-defense. *Notre Dame Journal of Law Ethics and Public Policy, 6,* 321–334.

Weil, A. (1995). *Spontaneous healing.* New York: Knopf.

Wireless Foundation. (2004). Donate a wireless phone, help protect domestic violence victims and save lives. Available online: www.wirelessfoundation.org or www.donateaphone.com. Or verizonwireless.com/b2c/aboutus/hopeline.jsp or www.rccwireless.com/zone40/about_us/news. Retrieved November 9, 2004.

Woods, S. J. & Campbell, J. C. (1993). Posttraumatic stress in battered women: Does the diagnosis fit? *Issues in Mental Health Nursing, 14*, 173–186.

Wyatt, G. E., Notgrass, C. M., & Newcomb, M. (1990). Internal and external mediators of women's rape experiences. *Psychology of Women Quarterly, 14*, 153–176.

Young, M. A. (1995). Crisis response teams in the aftermath of disasters. In A. R. Roberts (Ed.), *Crisis intervention and time-limited cognitive treatment* (pp. 151–187). Thousand Oaks, CA: Sage.

20

Crisis Intervention With Stalking Victims

KAREN KNOX
ALBERT R. ROBERTS

Case Scenarios

In April 2004, a University of Texas senior returned home from class to find a male friend in her apartment with a knife. It turned out that her "friend" was also her cyberstalker and rapist. The woman had turned to him for support when the threatening e-mails started, and he even pretended to help her find the cyberstalker, but police found evidence that he had bugged her computer. The woman was violently raped over several hours, and he planned to kill himself in the morning. However, she convinced him to take her to the health clinic, where he was arrested while waiting in the lobby for her.

A woman accused of sending threatening letters to Catherine Zeta-Jones over an 18-month period has been charged with one count of stalking and 24 counts of making criminal threats. The woman was reportedly infatuated with Zeta-Jones's husband, Michael Douglas, who received most of the more than two dozen letters that threatened his wife. The unemployed woman was arrested at her Beverly Hills apartment in June 2004. The female stalker underwent psychiatric tests after a suicide attempt by overdosing on barbiturates while in the county jail, and was found mentally competent to stand trial in August. She has written an apology letter claiming to be a confused woman who was obsessed with Douglas. If convicted, she could face up to 19 years in prison.

Stalking fantasies and obsessions that are only played out at a distance as opposed to psychological stalking as a prelude to physical stalking and murder has been examined by Eric Hickey (2003). For example, some movie star stalkers may fantasize and have delusions about 40 different celebrities, and these types of Hollywood stalkers may each send several hundred to thousands of letters to their fantasy target. These types of stalkers are usually married and have careers. As a result of not wanting to lose their marital partners or careers, they usually confine their stalking to letters, fax messages, e-mails, and telephone calls. Most fantasy, obsessional, and cyber stalkers do not kill their victims. In sharp contrast, stranger power-angry stalkers or a small group of cyberstalkers frequently are dangerous sexual predators or murderers. They usually are single, live alone, and harbor feelings of hatred; have revenge fantasies, low self-esteem, antisocial personalities, and impulse control disorders; are insecure, substance abusers, psychotic, paranoid schizophrenic, and/or reclusive (Hickey, 2003). Because stalking seems to escalate in intensity and frequency over time, and the consequences and trauma can be overwhelming, it is critically important for the victim to be made aware of crisis intervention and legal advocacy options.

Roberts and Dziegielewski (1995) developed a stalking typology and recommended that police social workers and crisis counselors utilize a crisis intervention model to lessen the psychological trauma and fear resulting from stalking victimizations. Spence-Diehl's (2004) recent research demonstrated the effectiveness of crisis intervention and victim advocacy with 36 victims of stalking. Her research indicated an improved sense of well-being and safety among the individuals who received the crisis intervention and advocacy services.

Stalking itself is not new, but legal and clinical responses to its victims and survivors have recently emerged. Stalking victims/survivors need both responses to ensure their safety and well-being—physically, psychologically, and emotionally. Since the first stalking law was passed in 1990 in California, all of the 50 states have passed antistalking laws or modified existing harassment statutes (McCann, 2001; Meloy, 1998; Roberts & Dziegielewski, 1995). Federal antistalking legislation was implemented as part of the Violence Against Women Act in 1996 (Meloy, 1998).

Crisis intervention with stalking victims/survivors has been used primarily in the fields of victim services, sexual assault services, and domestic violence intervention, as the majority of the victims are women who have been acquainted with, known, or had a relationship with their stalker. Results from a national study indicate that women tend to be stalked by a current or former intimate partner (Tjaden & Thoennes, 1998). The above-mentioned fields of practice use crisis intervention and brief time-limited therapy to address the immediate needs of the victims/survivors. However, many survivors continue treatment with support groups or individual therapy.

This chapter provides an overview of the problem of stalking and its impacts on victims/survivors. The major types of stalkers and stalking behaviors and acts are discussed to illustrate how they impact survivors and their treatment needs. An overview of crisis intervention is presented, and case applications are provided using crisis intervention as a model of treatment in working with stalking survivors.

OVERVIEW OF STALKING

Definitions of Stalking

There has been a growing body of research and professional literature on stalking in the past decade, with most studies focusing on incidence and prevalence estimates of stalking, the gender of victims and offenders, and typologies of stalkers and their relationship to the victim (Brewster, 2000, 2002; Cupach & Spitzberg, 1998; Fremouw, Westrup, & Pennypacker, 1996; Kurt, 1995; Logan, Luekefeld, & Walker, 2000; Mechanic, Weaver, & Resnick, 2000; Roberts & Dziegielewski, 1995; Sinclair & Frieze, 2000; Tjaden & Thoennes, 1998). There is also some literature on the impacts and reactions of stalking victims (Emerson, Ferris, & Gardner, 1998; Hall, 1998; Pathe & Mullen, 1997; Tjaden, Thoennes, & Allison, 2000). However, there is a dearth of literature and evidence-based studies focusing on clinical interventions and their effectiveness with stalking victims, survivors, and offenders (Spence-Diehl, 2004).

One of the areas of research concerns definitions of stalking, which include both legal and clinical definitions. The purpose of legal definitions is to define and prosecute criminal behavior. Legal definitions may vary across states, but generally include three elements:

- A pattern of willful, malicious, and repeated behavioral intrusion on another person (the target) that is clearly unwanted and unwelcome.
- An implicit or explicit threat that is evidenced in those behavioral intrusions.
- As a result of those behavioral intrusions, the person who is threatened (the target) experiences reasonable fear. (Meloy, 1998; Tjaden & Thoennes, 1998; Spence-Diehl, 2004)

Clinical definitions differ from legal ones, tending to be more easily operationalized and measurable for research and clinical understanding (Meloy, 1998). These definitions focus on specific types of behaviors and actions that are perceived as harassment by the victim, including unwanted pursuit, threats, surveillance, and intrusive actions. Clinical definitions may include actions or behaviors that are not considered criminal offenses. A recent study by Sheridan, Davies, and Boon (2001) carried out a cluster analysis of 42 stalking behaviors and found two major clusters, one composed of classic stalking behaviors and the other composed of primarily threatening stalking behaviors:

Classic Stalking Behaviors

- Constantly watching/spying/following the target.
- Standing and staring at the target's home or workplace or loitering in the neighborhood.
- Driving by the target's home or workplace and purposefully visiting places the target frequents.
- Telephoning, mailing, sending unwanted gifts after expressly being told not to do so.

Threatening Stalking Behaviors

- Taking and collecting photographs without the target's knowledge.
- Making death threats and threatening suicide.
- Causing criminal damage or vandalism to the target's home or workplace.
- Refusing to accept that a prior relationship with the target is over.
- Sending bizarre or sinister items to the target's home or workplace.
- Confining the target against her or his will.

Prevalence and Incidence

Other research indicates that definitions of stalking affect the reported frequency of stalking. Data from the National Violence Against Women (NVAW) Survey indicate that women reported more stalking victimization than men (8.1% vs. 2.2%); more women (78%) than men are victims, and more men (86%) than women are perpetrators (Tjaden & Thoennes, 1998). However, another study by Spitzberg, Nicastro, and Cousins (1998) indicates no gender differences, which may mean that the same behaviors are appraised differently as a function of gender, so that threatening actions by a man are perceived differently when performed by a woman. Another study suggests that the meaning of violence is different for men and women, with men not feeling threatened or fearful of the same types of behaviors as women (Magdol et al., 1997).

Definitions are only one factor impacting incidence rates of stalking. It is estimated that 1 million adult women and 0.4 million adult men are stalked annually in the United States, with only half of all victims reporting to law enforcement. Of those reported stalking cases, 25% result in arrest and 12% result in criminal prosecution (Meloy, 1998). Another factor concerns victims of domestic violence, where stalking is one of a series of criminal behaviors, including sexual or physical assault, and the criminal reports or charges may not specifically include stalking behaviors.

Characteristics of Stalking

Most individuals who engage in stalking are male (66%–90%), with an average age in the late 30s (McCann, 2001). There has been little research on stalking in children and adolescents. Other demographic characteristics include being unemployed or having unstable work histories, being single with a history of poor attachment, and being better educated and more intelligent than other criminal offenders (McCann, 2001; Meloy & Gothard, 1995; Schwartz-Watts, Morgan, & Barnes, 1997). There are no data currently available on whether or not stalking is more prevalent in a particular social or ethnic group (McCann, 2001; Meloy, 1998).

There is a range of psychiatric disorders that seem to be associated with stalking, with common diagnoses including personality disorders, impulse control disorder, intermittent explosive anger, psychosis, substance abuse, major depression or bipolar disorder, schizophrenia, delusional disorder, and organic mental disorder (Hickey, 2003; McCann, 2001). However, most offenders are not actively psychotic at the time of stalking (Meloy, 1998). Another major factor associated with stalking is a severe disturbance in attachment accompanied by a narcissistic linking fantasy about the relationship with the target. When the offender is rejected, feelings of rage, anger, and humiliation result in obsessive pursuit or stalking behaviors in attempts to control or harm the target (McCann, 2001).

Another critical factor is whether stalking leads to violence; research indicates that the rate of violence in stalking incidents is 25% to 35%, with homicide rates ranging from 2% to 8% (Kienlen, Birmingham, Solberg, O'Regan, & Meloy, 1997; McCann, 2001; Meloy, 1996). Violence is most likely to occur when there has been a prior, intimate relationship between the victim and the offender, when there are more dangerous stalking behaviors present, and when the offender has greater proximity to the target (Hickey, 2003; McCann, 2001; Palerea, Zona, Lane, & Langhinrichsen-Rohling, 1999).

Types of Stalking

A study by Zona, Sharma, and Lane (1993) analyzed the first 74 cases in the Threat Management Unit of the Los Angeles Police Department in an attempt to classify typologies of stalking offenders. Three major types were identified:

Erotomania, which is classified as a delusional disorder subtype where the stalker believes that the target is in love with him or her and goes to great lengths to approach the target.

Love obsessional stalking, when the stalker has a fanatical love and obsession for the target. This type of stalker usually has a primary psychiatric diagnosis, is socially maladjusted, and has poor attachment in relationships (Zona, Palerea, & Lane, 1998).

Simple obsessional stalking, which involves a prior relationship between the target and the stalker. This relationship may be intimate or not, and can vary in terms of intensity and degree of involvement (McCann, 2001).

One other recent and prevalent type of stalking involves the Internet. Cyberstalking allows the offender to gather information on the target for obsessional and pursuit needs and to communicate with the target to threaten or induce fear (Hickey, 2003; Meloy, 1998). Certain factors about e-mail and the Internet facilitate this type of stalking, such as anonymity, which allows the stalker to fantasize and be deceptive without the accompanying social anxiety of face-to-face interactions.

Impacts of Stalking Victimization

Victims of stalking over months or even years experience psychological terrorism, with pervasive fear, anger, and distress at not being able to control their privacy (Davis & Frieze, 2000). The NVAW Survey reported 30% of the women and 20% of the men victims sought counseling, 68% felt their personal safety had gotten worse, 42% were very concerned for their personal safety, and 45% carried something to protect themselves (Tjaden & Thoennes, 1998). Hall (1998) found that stalking victims became more cautious (85%), more paranoid (40%), felt more easily frightened (53%), and became more aggressive (30%). It appears that stalking that is accompanied by assaults and verbal threats is strongly connected to serious emotional consequences for victims (Davis & Frieze, 2000).

Stalking victims also experience psychological trauma and posttraumatic stress disorder (PTSD) symptoms, including recurrent nightmares, problems with sleeping, intrusive thoughts, depression, anxiety, and feeling overwhelmed and vulnerable. Victim reports and research studies of the impact of stalking on mental health and personal safety need to be conducted and analyzed so that a more systematic and refined statement of the impact of stalking victimization can be reached (Davis & Frieze, 2000).

Many stalking victims resort to the same strategies that battered women have used to escape the terror: moving or relocating, quitting jobs, changing their names and appearance, going underground and leaving friends and family behind, becoming more isolated and less trusting. Many survivors still live in fear years after the stalking has ended, afraid that the stalker will reappear, or find them, or be released from prison to return and continue stalking.

Treatment involves interventions that are aimed at symptom reduction of the impact issues, as well as practical issues associated with personal safety and legal responses. Specific theoretical models used with stalking victims include crisis intervention, case management, relaxation training, cognitive-behavioral therapy, and eye movement desensitization and reprocessing (EMDR). This chapter focuses on the use of crisis intervention with stalking victims.

OVERVIEW OF CRISIS INTERVENTION

Theory and Principles

Crisis intervention is an action-oriented model that is present-focused, with the target(s) for intervention being specific to the hazardous event, situation, or problem that precipitated the state of crisis. Therefore, this model focuses on problems in the here and now and addresses past history and psychopathology only as is relevant to the current conditions (Knox & Roberts, 2000; Roberts, 2000).

Crisis theory postulates that most crisis situations are limited to a period of 4 to 6 weeks (Hepworth, Rooney, & Larsen, 1997; Roberts, 2000). Crisis intervention is time-limited in that the goal is to help the client mobilize needed support, resources, and adaptive coping skills to resolve or minimize the disequilibrium experienced by the precipitating event. Once the client has returned to her or his precrisis level of functioning and homeostasis, any further supportive or supplemental services are usually referred to appropriate community agencies and service providers (Knox & Roberts, 2000).

For example, a stalking victim may receive emergency crisis intervention services from a combination of crisis programs over a period of time. Victim advocates and crisis counselors in law enforcement may work with the client through the aftermath of the stalking incident(s) and the reporting and initial investigation and provide short-term crisis counseling. Medical social workers also provide crisis counseling during a medical examination, and in the case of rape, sexual assault crisis programs typically have emergency response services for intervention at the hospital and afterward. Most rape crisis centers and domestic violence shelters provide short-term individual counseling services and time-limited groups. Any further long-term therapy needs would then be referred to other clinical practitioners, support groups, or counseling programs.

Time frames for crisis intervention vary depending on several factors, including the agency mission and services, the client's needs and resources, and the type of crisis or trauma. Crisis intervention can be as brief as one client contact or may require several contacts over a few days of brief treatment, while others may provide ongoing and follow-up services for up to eight weeks. Additional crisis intervention booster sessions may well be needed in the future. For stalking survivors, another critical time for crisis reactions is experienced when any court proceedings are conducted. This may require client involvement or court testimony that triggers memories and feelings about the stalking incident(s), which can produce crisis reactions and revictimization.

Individuals experiencing trauma and crisis need immediate relief and assistance, and the helping process must be adapted to meet those needs as efficiently and effectively as possible. However, clients in an active state of crisis are more amenable to the helping process, and this can facilitate completion of such tasks to meet the rapid response time frame. With a stalking survivor, medical needs must be assessed and intervention initiated immediately. After this, safety issues are addressed. The victim may not feel safe at home if the stalking incident occurred there or if there is concern that the stalker will not be arrested and can find the person there.

Crisis intervention counseling should be implemented simultaneously while addressing these other needs, with the police and/or medical social worker providing multiple crisis services during this first contact. This process could take several hours, depending on the response time by law enforcement and medical professionals and the client's coping skills, level of support, and resources. The crisis worker will need to follow through until the client has stabilized or been contacted by another collateral provider of crisis services.

The crisis worker must be knowledgeable about the appropriate strategies, resources, and other collateral services to initiate timely intervention strategies and meet the goals of treatment. For example, crisis intervention with stalking victims of family violence requires education and training on the dynamics and cycle of battering and abuse, familiarity with the community agencies providing services to this client population, and knowledge about the legal options available to victims.

Another characteristic of crisis intervention models is the use of tasks as a primary change effort. Concrete, basic needs services such as emergency safety, medical needs, food, clothing, and shelter are the first priority in crisis intervention. Mobilizing needed resources may require more direct activity by the social worker in advocating, networking, and brokering for clients, who may not have the knowledge, skills, or capacity to follow through with referrals and collateral contacts at the time of active crisis.

Of course, the emotional and psychological trauma experienced by the client and significant others is an important component for intervention. Ventilation of feelings and reactions to the crisis are essential to the healing process, and the practice skills of reflective communication, active listening, and establishing rapport are essential in developing a relationship and providing supportive counseling for the client.

CRISIS INTERVENTION MODEL

Roberts's (1996, 2000) seven-stage crisis intervention model (Figure 20.1) can be used with a broad range of crises, and can facilitate the assessment

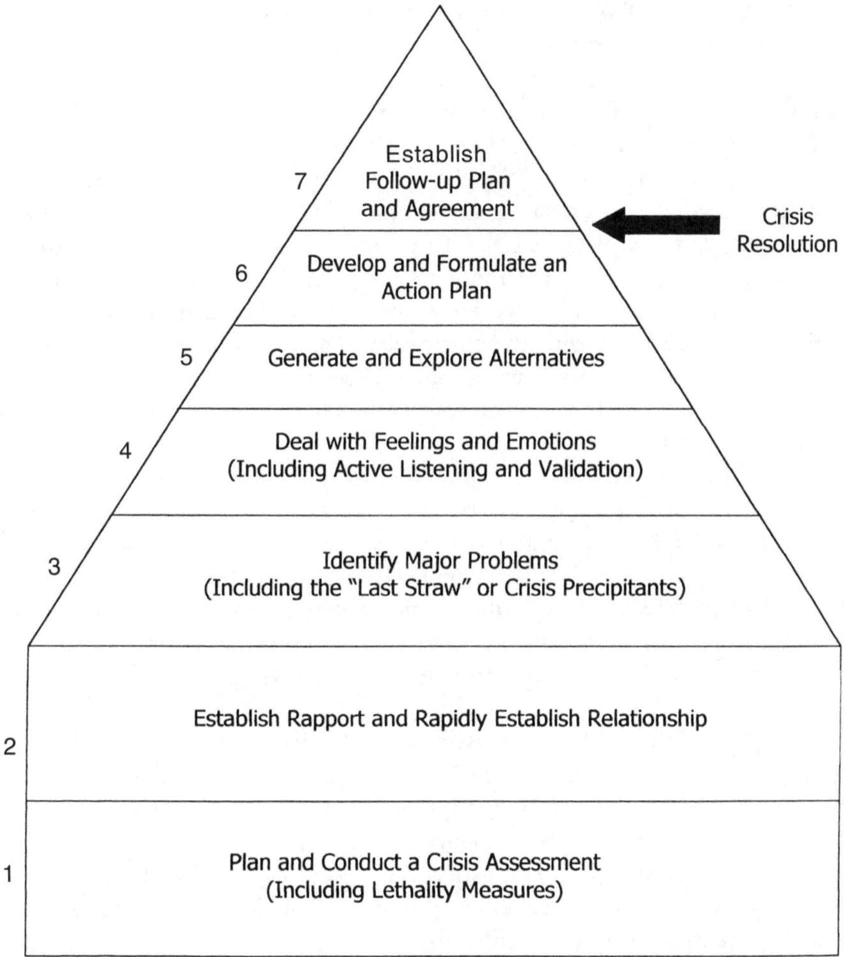

Figure 20.1 Roberts's Seven-Stage Crisis Intervention Model

and helping process for effective crisis intervention across diverse types of clients and trauma situations. This model can be especially useful in working with stalking survivors, as there is such a variety of the types of relationships, behaviors, and actions involved. A discussion and summary of the clinical interventions and goals for each of the seven stages is presented next to allow the reader to understand how crisis intervention can be applied to the stalking case examples.

Stage 1: Assessing Lethality

Assessment in this model is ongoing and critical to effective intervention at all stages, beginning with an assessment of the lethality and safety issues for the client. With stalking survivors it is critical to assess the risk for attempts, plans, or means to harm by the stalker, particularly if the offender is not in legal custody. Although many stalkers are not physically violent, 81% of women stalked by an ex-husband were physically assaulted and 31% were sexually assaulted (Tjaden & Thoennes, 1998).

It is important to assess if the client is in any current danger and to consider future safety concerns in treatment planning. For example, if the stalker is arrested, bail can bring release; if the stalker is incarcerated, the stalking survivor needs to be informed about release dates. In addition to determining lethality and the need for emergency intervention, it is crucial to maintain active communication with the client, either by phone or in person, while emergency procedures are being initiated (Roberts, 2000).

To plan and conduct a thorough assessment, the crisis worker also needs to evaluate the following issues: (1) the severity of the incident or crisis, (2) the client's current emotional state, (3) immediate psychosocial needs, and (4) level of client's current coping skills and resources (Gilliland & James, 1997). In the initial contact, assessment of the client's past or precrisis level of functioning and coping skills is useful; however, past history should not be a focus of assessment unless related directly to the immediate traumatic event. In stalking cases, the relationship is an important factor in the behaviors and actions of the stalker, so gathering this information is useful.

The goals of this stage are assessing and identifying critical areas of intervention, while also recognizing the hazardous event or trauma and acknowledging what has happened. At the same time, the stalking survivor becomes aware of his or her state of vulnerability and initial reactions to the crisis event. It is important that the crisis worker begin to establish a relationship based on respect for and acceptance of the client, while also offering support, empathy, reassurance, and reinforcement that the client has survived and that help is available (Roberts, 2000).

Stage 2: Establishing Rapport and Communication

Survivors of stalking may question their own safety and vulnerability, and trust may be difficult for them to establish at this time. Therefore, active listening and empathic communication skills are essential to establishing rapport and engagement of the client. Even though the need for rapid engagement is essential, the crisis worker should try to let the client set the pace of treatment. Many stalking victims feel out of control or powerless and should not be coerced, confronted, or forced into action; once they have stabilized and dealt with the initial trauma reactions, they will be better able to take action (Knox & Roberts, 2000).

Trauma survivors may require a positive future orientation, with an understanding that they can overcome current problems and hope that change can occur (Roberts, 1996). During this stage, clients need unconditional support, positive regard, concern, and genuineness. Empathic communication skills such as minimal encouragers, reflection of thoughts and feelings, and active listening can reassure the client and help establish trust and rapport. The crisis worker needs to be attentive to the tone and level of the verbal communications to help the client calm down or de-escalate from the initial trauma reactions (Knox & Roberts, 2000).

The crisis worker must also pay attention to his or her body language and facial expressions because stalking survivors may have been violated physically and be hypersensitive to physical space and body movements, which can frighten or startle them. Being observant of the survivor's physical and facial reactions can provide cues to the worker's level of engagement with the client, as well as a gauge to the client's current emotional state. It is also important to remember that delayed reactions or flat affect are common with trauma victims; crisis workers should not assume that these types of reactions mean that the survivor is not in crisis (Knox & Roberts, 2000; Roberts, 1991, 1996).

Stage 3: Identifying the Major Problems

The crisis worker should help the stalking survivor prioritize the most important problems or impacts by identifying these problems in terms of how they affect the survivor's current status. Encouraging the client to ventilate about the precipitating event can lead to problem identification, and some clients have an overwhelming need to talk about the specifics of the stalking situation. This process enables the client to figure out the sequence and context of the event(s), which can facilitate emotional ventilation while providing information to assess and identify major problems to work on. In some stalking cases, the victims may not be aware of the entire sequence of behaviors or actions until the most recent incident, which can precipitate a flood of reactions and emotions when the extent of the stalking is revealed.

Family members and significant others may be important to intervention planning in supportive roles or to ensure the client's safety. However, they may be experiencing their own reactions to the crisis situation, and this should be taken into consideration in contracting and implementing the intervention plan. The crisis worker must ensure that the client system is not overwhelmed during this stage; the focus should be on the most immediate and important problems needing intervention at this time. The first priority in this stage is meeting the basic needs of emotional and physical health and safety. After these have stabilized, other problems can then be addressed (Roberts, 2000).

Stage 4: Dealing With Feelings and Providing Support

It is critical that the crisis worker demonstrate empathy and an anchored understanding of the survivor's experience so that her or his symptoms and reactions are normalized and can be viewed as functional strategies for survival (Roberts, 1996). Many victims blame themselves, and it is important to help them accept that being a victim is not their fault. Many stalking victims blame themselves for being in the relationship or for not being able to predict this type of behavior. Validation and reassurance are especially useful in this stage, because survivors may be experiencing confusing and conflicting feelings.

Many clients follow the grief process when expressing and ventilating their emotions. First, survivors may be in denial about the extent of their emotional reactions and may try to avoid dealing with them in hopes that they will subside. They may be in shock and not be able to access their feelings immediately. However, significant delays in expression and ventilation of feelings can be harmful to the client in processing and resolving the trauma (Roberts, 2000).

Some survivors may express anger and rage about the situation and its effects, which can be healthy as long as these feelings do not escalate out of control. Helping the client calm down and attend to physiological reactions is important in this situation. Other clients may express their grief and sadness, and the crisis worker needs to allow time and space for this reaction without pressuring the client to move along too quickly. Catharsis and ventilation are critical to healthy coping, and throughout this process, the crisis worker must recognize and support the survivor's courage in facing and dealing with these emotional reactions and issues. The crisis worker must also be aware of his or her own emotional reactions and level of comfort in helping the client through this stage (Roberts, 2000).

Stage 5: Exploring Possible Alternatives

In this stage, effective crisis workers help clients recognize and explore a variety of alternatives, such as:

Situational supports, which are people or resources that can be helpful to the client in meeting needs and resolving problems in living as a result of the crisis.

Coping skills, which are behaviors or strategies that promote adaptive responses and help the client reach a precrisis level of functioning.

Positive and constructive thinking patterns, which can lessen the client's levels of anxiety and stress. (Gilliland & James, 1997)

The crisis worker can facilitate healthy coping skills by identifying client strengths and resources. Many survivors feel they do not have a lot of choices, and the crisis worker needs to be familiar with both formal and informal community services to provide referrals. For example, working with a battered woman who is being stalked often requires relocation to a safe place for her and her children. The client may not have the personal resources or financial ability to move, and the crisis worker needs to be informed about the possible alternatives, which may include a shelter program, a protective order, or other emergency housing services.

The crisis worker may need to be more active and directive in this stage if the client has unrealistic expectations or inappropriate coping skills and strategies. Remember that clients are still distressed and in disequilibrium at this stage, and professional expertise and guidance may be necessary to produce positive, realistic alternatives for them. In stalking cases, several areas of the survivor's life can be affected that entail major changes in lifestyle or residence, and effective safety and treatment plans need to be implemented quickly, which requires professional input and experience.

Stage 6: Formulating an Action Plan

In this stage also an active role must be taken by the crisis worker; however, the success of any intervention plan depends on the client's level of involvement, participation, and commitment. The crisis worker must help the client look at both the short-term and long-range impacts in planning intervention. The main goals are to help the client achieve an appropriate level of functioning and maintain adaptive coping skills and resources. It is important to have a manageable treatment plan so that the client can follow through and be successful. Do not overwhelm the client with too many tasks or strategies, which may set the client up for failure (Knox & Roberts, 2000).

Clients must also feel a sense of ownership in the action plan so that they can increase the level of control and autonomy in their lives and to ensure that they not become dependent on other support persons or resources. Obtaining a commitment from the client to follow through with the action plan and any referrals can be maximized by using a mutual process in intervention planning. Ongoing assessment and evaluation are essential to determine whether the intervention plan is appropriate and effective in minimizing or resolving the client's identified problems. During this stage, clients should be processing and reintegrating the crisis impacts to achieve homeostasis and equilibrium in their life.

Termination should begin when the client has achieved the goals of the action plan or has been referred for additional services through other treatment providers. It is important to realize that many stalking survivors may need longer-term therapeutic help in working toward crisis resolution. Stalking sometimes continues over significant time periods, with the average case occurring over 1.8 years (Tjaden & Thoennes, 1998). These survivors may experience PTSD symptoms requiring long-term treatment.

Stage 7: Follow-up Measures

Hopefully, the sixth stage has resulted in significant changes and resolution for the client in regard to his or her postcrisis level of functioning and coping. This last stage should help determine whether these results have been maintained, or if further work remains to be done. Typically, follow-up contacts should be made within four to six weeks after termination. At this stage, the four tasks of crisis resolution should have been addressed:

Physical survival: Maintaining physical health through adaptive coping skills and taking care of oneself through proper nutrition, exercise, sleep, and relaxation.

Expression of feelings: Appropriate emotional expression and ventilation and understanding how emotional reactions affect one's physiological and psychological well-being.

Cognitive mastery: Developing a reality-based understanding of the crisis event, addressing any unfinished business, irrational thoughts, or fears, and adjusting one's self-image in regard to the crisis event and its impacts.

Behavioral/interpersonal adjustments: Adapting to changes in daily life activities, goals, or relationships due to the crisis event and minimizing any long- term negative effects in these areas for the future. (Slaikue, 1984)

It is important to remember that final crisis resolution may take many months or years to achieve, and survivors should be aware that certain events, places, or dates can trigger emotional and physical reactions to the previous trauma. For example, a critical time is at the first anniversary of a crisis event, when clients may reexperience old fears, reactions, or thoughts. This is a normal part of the recovery process, and clients should be prepared to have contingency plans or supportive help through these difficult periods.

REFERENCES

Brewster, M. P. (2000). Stalking by former intimates: Verbal threats and other predictors of physical violence. *Violence and Victims, 15,* 41–54.

Brewster, M. P. (2002). Domestic violence theories, research, and practice implications. In A. R. Roberts (Ed.), *Handbook of domestic violence intervention strategies* (pp. 23–48). New York: Oxford University Press.

Cupach, W. R., & Spitzberg, B. H. (1998). Obsessional relational intrusion and stalking. In B. H. Spitzberg & W. R. Cupach (Eds.), *The dark side of close relationships* (pp. 233–263). Mahwah, NJ: Lawrence Erlbaum.

Davis, K. E., & Frieze, I. H. (2000). Research on stalking: What do we know and where do we go? *Violence and Victims, 15,* 473–487.

Emerson, R. M., Ferris, K. O., & Gardner, C. B. (1998). On being stalked. *Social Problems, 45,* 289–314.

Fremouw, W. J., Westrup, D., & Pennypacker, J. (1997). Stalking on campus: The prevalence and strategies for coping with stalking. *Journal of Forensic Sciences, 42,* 664–667.

Gilliland, B., & James, R. (1997). *Crisis intervention strategies.* Pacific Grove, CA: Brooks/Cole.

Hall, D. M. (1998). The victims of stalking. In J. R. Meloy (Ed.), *The psychology of stalking: Clinical and forensic perspectives* (pp. 113–137). San Diego, CA: Academic Press.

Hepworth, D., Rooney, R., & Larsen, J. (1997). *Direct social work practice: Theory and skills.* Pacific Grove, CA: Brooks/Cole.

Kienlen, K. K., Birmingham, D. L., Solberg, K. B., O'Regan, J. T., & Meloy, J. R. (1997). A comparative study of psychotic and nonpsychotic stalking. *Journal of the American Academy of Psychiatry and the Law, 25,* 317–334.

Knox, K., & Roberts, A. R. (2000). The crisis intervention model. In P. Lehmann & N. Coady (Eds.), *Theoretical perspectives for direct social work practice: A generalist-eclectic approach* (pp. 183–202). New York: Springer.

Kurt, J. L. (1995). Stalking as a variant of domestic violence. *Bulletin of the Academy of Psychiatry and the Law, 23,* 219–223.

Logan, T. K., Luekefeld, C., & Walker, B. (2000). Stalking as a variant of intimate violence: Implications from a young adult sample. *Violence and Victims, 15,* 91–111.

Magdol, L., Moffitt, T. E., Caspi, A., Newman, D. N., Fagan, J., & Silva, P. A. (1997). Gender differences in partner violence in a birth cohort of 21 year olds: Bridging the gap between clinical and epidemiological approaches. *Journal of Consulting and Clinical Psychology, 65,* 68–78.

McCann, J. T. (2001). *Stalking in children and adults: The primitive bond.* Washington, DC: American Psychological Association.

Mechanic, M. B., Weaver, T. L., & Resnick, P. A. (2000). Intimate partner violence and stalking behavior: Explorations of patterns and correlates in a sample of acutely battered women. *Violence and Victims, 15,* 55–72.

Meloy, J. R. (1996). Stalking (obsessional following): A review of some preliminary studies. *Aggression and Violent Behavior, 1,* 147–162.

Meloy, J. R. (1998). The psychology of stalking. In J. R. Meloy (Ed.), *The psychology of stalking: Clinical and forensic perspectives* (pp. 2–27). San Diego, CA: Academic Press.

Meloy, J. R. (1999). Stalking: An old behavior, a new crime. *Psychiatric Clinics of North America, 22,* 85–99.

Meloy, J. R., & Gothard, S. (1995). A demographic and clinical comparison of obsessional followers and offenders with mental disorders. *American Journal of Psychiatry, 152,* 258–263.

Palerea, R. E., Zona, M. A., Lane, J. C., & Langhinrichsen-Rohling, J. (1999). The dangerous nature of intimate relationship stalking: Threats, violence, and associated risk factors. *Behavioral Science and the Law, 17,* 269–283.

Pathe, M., & Mullen, P. E. (1997). The impact of stalkers on their victims. *British Journal of Psychiatry, 170,* 12–17.

Roberts, A. R. (1991). Conceptualizing crisis theory and the crisis intervention model. In A. R. Roberts (Ed.), *Contemporary perspectives on crisis intervention and prevention* (pp. 3–17). Englewood Cliffs, NJ: Prentice-Hall.

Roberts, A. R. (1996). Epidemiology and definitions of acute crisis in American society. In A. R. Roberts (Ed.), *Crisis management and brief treatment: Theory, techniques, and application* (pp. 16–33). Chicago: Nelson-Hall.

Roberts, A. R. (2000). An introduction and overview. In A. R. Roberts (Ed.), *Crisis intervention handbook: Assessment, treatment and research* (2nd ed., pp. 3–21). New York: Oxford University Press.

Roberts, A. R., & Dziegielewski, S. F. (1995). Foundation skills and applications of crisis intervention and cognitive therapy. In A. R. Roberts (Ed.), *Crisis intervention and time-limited cognitive treatment* (pp. 3–27). Thousand Oaks, CA: Sage Publications.

Schwartz-Watts, D., Morgan, D. W, & Barnes, C. J. (1997) Stalkers: The South Carolina experience. *Journal of the American Academy of Psychiatry and the Law, 25,* 541–545.

Sheridan, L., Davies, G., & Boon, J. (2001). Stalking: Perceptions and prevalence. *Journal of Interpersonal Violence, 16*(2), 151–167.

Slaikue, K. (1984). *Crisis intervention: A handbook for practice and research.* Boston: Allyn & Bacon.

Spence-Diehl, E. (2004). Intensive case management for victims of stalking. *Brief Treatment and Crisis Intervention, 4*, 323–341.

Spitzberg, H. C., Nicastro, A. M., & Cousins, A. V. (1998). Exploring the interactional phenomenon of stalking and obsessive relational intrusion. *Communication Report, 11,* 33–47.

Tjaden, P., & Thoennes, N. (1998). *Stalking in America: Findings from the National Violence Against Women Survey* (NCJ Report #169592). Washington DC: National Institute of Justice and Centers for Disease Control and Prevention.

Tjaden, P., Thoennes, N., & Allison, C. J. (2000). Comparing stalking victimization from legal and victim perspectives. *Violence and Victims, 15,* 7–22.

Zona, M. A., Palera, R. E., & Lane, J. C. (1998). Psychiatric diagnosiis and the offender-victim typology of stalking. In J. R. Meloy (Ed.), *The psychology of stalking: Clinical and forensic perspectives* (pp. 69–84). San Diego, CA: Academic Press.

Zona, M. A., Sharma, K. K., & Lane, J. (1993). A comparative study of erotomania and obsessional subjects in a forensic sample. *Journal of Forensic Sciences, 38,* 894–903.

21

School Crisis Intervention, Crisis Prevention, and Crisis Response

SCOTT NEWGASS
DAVID J. SCHONFELD

Vignette 1

A fourth-grade boy is fatally wounded by his cousin while playing with a gun that they find at home. Uncomfortable with addressing the child's death, the school administrators decide not to discuss it with the boy's classmates until after finding someone who can advise them on how to handle such a situation. Several days later, they identify a consultant who can visit the class.

Over the phone, they request that the consultant meet during the upcoming visit with the student who had pulled the trigger to advise them on whether referral for mental health counseling is indicated. They inform the consultant that since the death, the other students have been calling him "murderer," and the school has therefore transferred the boy to another school. Given this limited information, the consultant advises over the phone that referral to mental health counseling is appropriate given the circumstances and suggests that it is not necessary to wait until the visit in a few days in order to assess the child directly.

The consultant arrives at the school about a week after the death has occurred. The child's desk remains unchanged. When the consultant meets several of the students as they return from recess, they explain that they do not wish to discuss what happened and are reluctant to carry on any conversation. Several students begin crying loudly as the consultant is introduced. With some difficulty, the students are encouraged to begin discussing their classmate's death and their reactions to it.

Vignette 2

A school staff member working late on Friday afternoon is notified by a parent that one of the school's third-grade students has just been injured by a gunshot wound to the face. The child's brother, who is in the fourth grade at the school, had been playing with a handgun that accidentally discharged. The principal is notified, and he immediately contacts the other members of the crisis team. The crisis team talks over the phone for the rest of the evening and begins making plans while the principal and the school social worker go to the hospital to offer support to the family. Using the school crisis telephone tree, the entire school staff is contacted over the weekend and notified about an emergency staff meeting on Monday morning prior to the start of the school day.

On Monday morning, the crisis team meets early and discusses its plans; it is joined by consultants from the Regional School Crisis Prevention and Response Program. A staff meeting is held immediately after this meeting, just before the children's arrival. Staff members are encouraged to talk about their reactions to the recent events and are provided advice on how to facilitate discussions within their classrooms. Notification announcements are distributed, and all teachers agree to read the announcement during the homeroom period.

Several children arrive at school with copies of the local newspaper that carries a banner headline story about the tragedy. Rumors are already beginning to surface among the youngsters. Many of the children are just hearing about the situation from their peers as they arrive at school.

During the homeroom period, at a predetermined time, each class is informed of the incident by its teacher, who then facilitates a discussion. Mental health staff join the teacher in leading the discussions in the English and Spanish classes of the two children who were involved in the event. The children are encouraged to express their thoughts and feelings; misinformation is corrected (e.g., according to one rumor the child intentionally shot his sister over a minor disagreement) and concerns answered (e.g., several students volunteer that their parents have advised them to avoid their classmate because he has a gun and may try to kill them). Ultimately, most of the classes decide that they want to do something to show their support for the family. Students begin working on cards, banners, and letters to send to the student in the hospital, as well as cards of support for the student who fired the gun.

Several parents arrive at the school throughout the course of the day because of the impact that this accident has had on the community. A number of these parents do not speak English as their native language. Bilingual staff are available to provide direct support or translation services. A room is identified for parents to come and meet with others so that they have an opportunity to express their upset and concern, as well as to receive some direction on how they can contribute to their children's adjustment during this time. The Child Development–Community Policing Program holds a community meeting at the school to discuss handgun violence.

Over the next several weeks, many staff members talk about their own distress—some because of the recent events, some because the crisis has triggered memories of prior losses. The staff form a mutual support group that continues for several weeks after the crisis. The crisis team provides ongoing evaluation of the needs of students, staff, and parents. The boy who pulled the trigger returns to class the following week and is welcomed back by his classmates. His sister subsequently recovers and is also welcomed back to school. On follow-up, the school staff report that the management of the crisis has led to increased respect for the new principal and has brought them closer as a school community.

Vignette 3

A 14-year-old girl is the unintended victim of a shooting outside her house. One month later, a classmate commits suicide during the school day. Another month passes, and another classmate kills himself during a 3-day weekend.

The first incident presented several obstacles to the school's attempts to provide services; the death took place at the beginning of a week's vacation, and the student, recently transferred into the school, had developed only a small network of friends and acquaintances. When the students returned to school the following week, the staff made announcements in each classroom and offered support services for any students wanting to discuss their reactions to the news or the circumstances of community violence.

When the second student died, several hundred students utilized the support room services over the course of several days. Multiple staff members were assigned from other schools by the coordinator of counseling services of the district crisis team to assist with the interventions. While interventions took place in classrooms and the support rooms, a group within the school initiated by the crisis team began to plan how to reach out to the parents community in an attempt to prevent further suicides. The media coordinator accepted all calls from the press and provided complete information about the interventions taking place, including information on warning signs of suicidality and suggestions for parents on how to discuss this situation with their children. Students began leaving graffiti messages on the locker of the student who had recently died, as well as on the locker of the student who had died a month previously. After discussion with the crisis team about memorialization, the principal announced that messages left on the two students' lockers would be allowed to remain until the following weekend, at which time they would be removed. Parents of children who utilized support room services were contacted directly by telephone concerning the level of intervention their child received and whether or not follow-up with an outside agency for ongoing therapy might be helpful.

Following the third death, another suicide, the school again provided support room services and began to delegate mental health staff to assist in the classroom interventions. Several parents called the school asking them to evaluate their child because of concern about their youngster's suspected suicidality. Only a few students were referred for emergent evaluation off-site, and the parents of those requiring that level of evaluation were asked to come to the school and transport their child. School personnel helped families with inadequate insurance identify mental health services willing to see their children for evaluation and treatment. A meeting was held after the first day of intervention to provide classroom staff with helpful information about screening for suicidal ideation and risk. The press was again contacted to reiterate the suggestions for parents that had been published following the first death by suicide. A community meeting was scheduled for parents and interested community members to hear from experts in crisis intervention, at-risk behaviors among teenagers, and suicide. More than 400 parents attended.

As comparison of the preceding vignettes illustrates, the presence of a preexisting comprehensive crisis response plan will assist a school in anticipating and meeting the needs of its students, staff, and the larger community at the time of crisis. Although crisis can be disruptive to the educational process and be associated with short- and long-term psychological effects, these consequences can often be ameliorated if adequate support is provided at the time of crisis (Kline, Schonfeld, & Lichtenstein, 1995). These support services are more likely to be provided at school if a systematic school crisis response plan is already in place.

Schools have as their principal focus educational goals. Whereas schools are required to have a fire evacuation plan and to conduct regular fire drills, they less commonly have developed and implemented a plan for attending to the psychological and emotional needs of students and staff at the time of crisis. Many within schools (as well as many professionals outside of school systems) view these latter concerns as clinical issues that fall outside the realm of an educational institution. As a result, many schools remain unprepared for a crisis and fail to mobilize optimally the clinical and support resources both within the school and within the broader community to support students and staff when a crisis occurs.

Although schools may attempt to assemble an ad hoc crisis plan and team to address an acute episode, at the time of the crisis many staff members respond to the event in ways that do not allow them to take a thoughtful, broad, and long-term view of the needs of students and staff (Klingman, 1988). An effective crisis response requires prior preparedness and a systematic organizational response that is both flexible enough to be applicable to a broad range of crisis situations and specific enough to provide guidance at the time of a particular crisis.

The plan should address three broad areas: safety and security; obtaining, verifying, and disseminating accurate information to staff, students, parents, and the general public (when appropriate); and the emotional and psychological needs of those involved. All three domains must be addressed concurrently or none will be addressed effectively. This is unlikely to occur in the absence of an organizational school crisis response plan, prior training of school staff, and dedicated response staff and resources within the school.

An effective response should validate typical reactions to traumatic events and provide the mechanisms for students and staff to express and begin to resolve their personal reactions to the event. An organizational plan for systematic school crisis preparedness and response allows schools to remain proactive and ahead of unfolding crises by anticipating needs, assessing developing hazards, and identifying the resources available to respond to a crisis, as well as any service gaps that should be addressed. Relying exclusively on external resources to address a crisis may result in a sense of disempowerment among the staff, may contribute to the public's misperception of the capacity of school personnel to address the psychological and emotional needs of students, and may lead to a failure to anticipate and meet the long-term needs of students and staff subsequent to the initial intervention that may be provided by an external response team. While mental health resources from the community play a vital role in assisting a school in its response to a crisis, primary interventions should be provided by school staff because they already have some history with their students, and they will continue to be with the students—and the school—long after the crisis is over.

THE SCHOOL CRISIS RESPONSE INITIATIVE

In 1991, the School Crisis Response Initiative was formed to address how schools might best prepare for crises. The organizing group, representing the fields of education, pediatric medicine, psychiatry, psychology, social work, and police, included members from Yale University School of Medicine, Department of Pediatrics and Child Study Center, and the Consultation Center; four area school systems; and the New Haven Police Department.

The group set three initial goals: (a) to develop a systematic organizational protocol (Schonfeld, Kline, & Members of the Crisis Intervention Committee, 1994; Lichtenstein, Schonfeld, Kline, & Speese-Linehan, 1995) that would define and anticipate the types of crises that may impact the student body and the local community, identify interventions that would be most effective in reducing long-term trauma, and create a structure to ensure a rapid, reliable, and replicable response mechanism with preliminary definition of personnel and responsibilities; (b) to provide the necessary training to prepare school staff in delivering services based upon the model; and (c) to increase the collaborative relationships between schools and community mental health and social service providers. To date, the program has trained more than 30,000 school and community staff in the use of the model, consulted to more than 2,000 district- and school-level crisis response teams, and provided technical assistance to schools during more than 300 crisis situations. At the Yale Child Study Center, the School Crisis Response Initiative of the National Center for Children Exposed to Violence continues to provide services to school systems across the country.

In the early hours of September 11, 2001, schools throughout the United States were confronted with the overwhelming tasks of assessing risk, managing accessibility to graphic images made available in real time by electronic media, ensuring the safety of their students and staff, providing a stabilizing environment, and assuring parents during those moments of doubt and fear that the school was still safe for their children. Despite enormous chaos and confusion during the initial hours of that autumn morning, schools throughout the country accomplished those tasks with heroic capacity. In the subsequent weeks and months, the perceived need for increased safeguards and preparedness was a focus of resolution, legislation, and program development. Of particular concern was ensuring that an infrastructure for providing security and mobilized response be developed to meet the physical and mechanical needs that arise during a crisis.

With an inexperienced and vulnerable population to serve, schools especially need to develop systems of safety and response to ensure considered and flexible interventions addressing the dangers that they may be exposed to. As a significant component to any crisis plan, schools must also address the psychological and emotional implications of a crisis in their community. Developing the ability to respond to commonly encountered challenges to a school community's sense of well-being allows staff to identify and improve their response capacities, as opposed to preparing only for those most challenging circumstances. This chapter describes a systematic program developed to prepare school personnel to meet the multiple needs arising out of a crisis with a minimum of stress on the individuals involved in the response.

On September 11, the entire country looked to New York City schools with a sense of awe and appreciation due to the remarkable efforts and the professionalism exhibited by all the staff through the long day and into the late night, ensuring that every student returned safely to their home. The New York City Department of Education developed a citywide plan for its 1,200 schools that would provide the mechanisms for a coordinated response. The emotional and physical safety of its students and their families was a significant goal of this plan. In December 2001, the School Crisis Response Initiative began the process of providing integrated training to school-based crisis teams throughout the City of New York. The elements provided in that training are discussed in this chapter.

CRISES BENEFITING FROM A TEAM RESPONSE

Not all crises affecting school children require or benefit from a team response. Generally, circumstances involving issues of privacy and confidentiality, such as child abuse in the home or a sexual assault, are better handled through student assistance teams, unless information about these events has become widely known and generated considerable concern among many members of the school community. Crises that involve significant numbers of students or school staff that typically benefit from a team response include situations involving loss and grief (e.g., the death of a student or staff member); when there is a perceived threat to personal safety (e.g., a school bus accident, an abduction, or a fire); environmental crisis (e.g., a hurricane, a chemical spill on a nearby road, or a gas leak in the school); and when there is a perceived threat to emotional well-being (e.g., a bomb threat, hate-crime graffiti left at the school, or public disclosure of sexual misconduct of staff or students). The organizational model as outlined in this chapter provides a general response plan that is applicable across specific crisis contexts. In special situations, such as suicide postvention (Brent, Etkind, & Carr, 1992; Davidson, Rosenberg, Mercy, Franklin, & Simmons, 1989; Schonfeld et al., 1994), adaptations of the model are indicated in order to address their unique contingencies.

LEVELS OF INTERVENTION

The Regional School Crisis Prevention and Response Program developed its protocols within a hierarchical framework. A regional resource team made up of representatives from mental health, police, academic, school administration, and support agencies meets on a quarterly basis to review program activities, improve mechanisms for training school staff, address service deficits in target areas, and provide support and technical assistance to representatives from the district-level teams. The regional resource team also operates as an information clearinghouse on school crisis prevention and response and related topics.

The next level within the hierarchy is the district-level team, which provides crisis response oversight for the individual school system. This team is generally composed of central office administrators and mental health staff. It establishes relevant districtwide policies and oversees resource allocation, staff training and supervision, and technical assistance for schools within the district at the time of crisis.

The third level in the hierarchy is that of the school-based team, which is generally composed of the school's administrator(s); nursing, social work, psychology, and guidance/counseling staff; classroom staff; and others. Some schools may include a parent representative to assist in contacting parents more rapidly and to provide a liaison between the school and parents. This team is most capable of anticipating the reactions and needs of the students and staff, and is therefore most suited to provide the direct services to students and families at the time of crisis. This team can draw upon additional resources through the district-level team, such as supplemental counseling staff from other schools. Since school-level teams will provide the most direct services to students, they will also experience the greatest level of stress. These teams in particular must have a proactive plan to address the needs of staff providers who may experience vicarious traumatization or compassion fatigue.

The organizational model utilizes a structure of seven roles. Although each role has its own set of tasks and responsibilities, each member of the team should be cross-trained in anticipation of absences. The roles include crisis team chair, assistant team chair, coordinator of counseling services, media coordinator, staff notification coordinator, communication coordinator, and crowd management coordinator (Schonfeld et al., 1994; Lichtenstein et al., 1995). Table 21.1 outlines specific responsibilities for each role.

NOTIFICATION/COMMUNICATION

A team member who is notified of a crisis involving one of its students should immediately notify the chair of the crisis team and inform him or her of what is known to date and whether or not the information has been confirmed. It is preferable that confirmation not be obtained from the family of the victim; rather, the purpose of contact with the family should be to offer condolences and support. Liaison with the local or regional police facilitates timely and accurate confirmation of crisis events, as well as assisting in the coordination of services. A contact person within emergency services, when indicated, should be established to assure that the school system is updated as the event unfolds. The chair will assure that the remaining members of the school and district crisis teams are notified when indicated and decide whether to contact the rest of the school staff before the next school day. The staff notification coordinator will facilitate the contact with all school personnel through the use of a preestablished telephone tree. Before contact is made with the general staff, the crisis team should meet or consult by telephone to determine what initial steps will be taken to meet anticipated needs and will make this information available to the staff notification coordinator. The crisis team chair or designee will make contact with the victim and/or family to offer support and assistance.

Following notification of a crisis, staff should meet, either at the end of the day or prior to the beginning of the next school day, depending on the circumstances and timing. Table 21.2 outlines a sample agenda for this meeting. The crisis team needs to ensure that all information pertinent to the crisis is obtained and disseminated to students and staff in a fashion that facilitates their processing the information and their reactions in the most meaningful way. The school should identify those students closest to the victim(s) and arrange for them to be notified in a quiet and supportive location where their grief can be expressed in private. For the remainder of the

Table 21.1 Roles of Crisis Team Members

Member	Role
Crisis team chair	Chair all meetings of the crisis team and oversee the broad and specific functioning of the team and its members.
Assistant team chair	Assist the chair in all functions and substitute in the event of the unavailability of the chair.
Coordinator of counseling services	Determine the extent and nature of counseling services indicated by a particular crisis and (along with counterpart on District Team) mobilize community resources as needed. Oversee training and supervision of staff providing counseling services. Identify and maintain ongoing liaison with community resources.
Media coordinator	Serve as the sole contact person (along with counterpart on District Team) for all media inquiries. Prepare a brief press release, if indicated, and appropriate statements, in collaboration with other members of the team, for staff, student, and parent notification.
Staff notification coordinator	Establish, coordinate, and initiate a telephone tree for notification of team members and other school staff after school hours.
Communication coordinator	Oversee all direct in-house communication. Screen incoming calls and maintain a log of phone calls related to the crisis. Assist the staff notification coordinator and help maintain an accurate phone directory of community resources and district-level staff.
Crowd management coordinator	In collaboration with local police and fire departments, plan mechanisms for crowd management in the event of various potential crises and directly supervise the movement of students and staff in the event such plans are initiated. A crowd control plan must include arrangements to cordon off areas with physical evidence, to assemble students and faculty for presentations, and, in the event of an actual threat to the physical safety of students, to assure the safe and organized movement of students in order to minimize the risk of harm.

Source: Adapted with permission from Schonfeld, D., Kline, M., & Members of the Crisis Intervention Committee. (1994). School-based crisis intervention: An organizational model. *Crisis Intervention and Time-Limited Treatment, 1*, 158.

student body, announcements should be structured to provide the information to all classes at approximately the same time, thereby reducing the potential problems that may arise should students with different amounts of information meet and compare notes. Rumors and speculation should be corrected as quickly as possible. In general, public address announcements should be avoided because of their depersonalized and disaffected quality and because they cannot anticipate or respond to students' reactions. If it is a staff member who has died, it is best to use a classroom teacher who is already known to the students and has an established relationship with them

Table 21.2 Emergency Staff Meeting Agenda

Share all current information about the crisis event and response, as well as any memorial plans that have already been established.
Provide a forum for teachers and other staff to ask questions, share their own personal reactions or concerns, and offer feedback about reactions they anticipate or have noticed among the student body.
Distribute notification announcements and finalize plans for notifying students and contacting parents (when appropriate).
Inform staff of specific activities to support students, staff, and parents.

to cover the class on a short-term basis. A substitute can be used for this second class but would face enormous challenges if assigned to the grieving classroom.

Notification of parents is usually addressed through printed material sent home with students on the day of notification. In addition to providing information about the crisis event, written material can offer guidance on how parents can help their children deal with their reactions to the crisis and provide information on community mental health resources. Handouts providing suggestions on how to help children of different developmental levels deal with grief, bereavement (Schonfeld, 1993), trauma, or loss, and outlining typical and atypical reactions, as well as guidelines for when to seek additional mental health services, should be prepared prior to any crisis event and placed on file within the school or school district. For those children who are provided individual counseling or services within the support room, contact should be made directly with parents, usually by phone.

If it is likely that media attention will be generated by the event, the media coordinator should contact media representatives and provide them with the appropriate information by way of a press release. Suggestions concerning how the media can best help, and be least disruptive to the students and staff, should be offered. Interviews should be discouraged on school grounds, except those provided by the media coordinator.

MEMORIALIZATION

Teams will need to address both the content and the timing of memorialization. Often, questions regarding memorial activities will be raised within hours of notification of the crisis event. This may divert attention from addressing the acute emotional and psychological needs of the students and staff. The team may need to address early on how best to handle graffiti tags, posters, signs, buttons or T-shirts with a picture of the deceased, and quasi-sanctified memorial areas that draw numbers of students. In some situations, early discussion of memorialization may prompt premature closure of the crisis response.

Spontaneous public displays in hallway shadow boxes or postboards should be discouraged. Rather, students and staff should be given the opportunity to understand and express their needs through more thoughtful interventions. Using school resources and facilities to make multiple copies of newspaper articles, generating buttons commemorating the victim, or other activities that create semipermanent reminders that may persist in the community long after the initial trauma has worn off, should be avoided. For longer term memorial projects, schools should consider that the special acknowledgments of naming permanent objects after the person or dedicating a yearbook may set a precedent that will then be expected when another member of the school community dies. Memorial responses are more successful if they involve an assembled acknowledgment with some ritual content, such as a moment of silence or the lighting of a single candle. When a death involves suicide or another cause of death that bears a stigma (e.g., death by automobile accident while under the influence of alcohol), staff will need to help students acknowledge the loss of the individual student or staff member while taking care not to glamorize the means of death (Schonfeld et al., 1994; Brent et al., 1992).

The team should address how to handle the deceased's desk, locker, personal possessions, assignments hung up for display, and so forth. The team should anticipate that the deceased's locker may be utilized by other students as an informal memorial site, where they will post messages, place flowers, or otherwise acknowledge the loss. These spontaneous expressions should be monitored regularly to detect any unexpected reactions. The team can work with the student's class to help them identify how they would like to deal with the child's empty desk.

The team should remember that it is not the content of the memorial activities that is most important; rather, it is the process of engaging the members of the school community in the planning of a meaningful event. While raising money for a permanent memorial (such as a tree or plaque) may provide staff and students a means of "doing something" to show they care, it is far more helpful to facilitate an ongoing discussion among members of the school community about *how* they care about the deceased and for the survivors and what would be the most meaningful way(s) to express that concern prior to (or in place of) raising such funds.

SUPPORT ROOMS

The school should consider when it is appropriate to set up support rooms for those students requiring more intensive intervention than can be provided by teacher-directed class discussions. The crisis response plan should specify the staffing and location (e.g., in areas without heavy traffic) of support rooms. Support rooms are best for handling limited numbers of students who generally are sharing similar reactions and symptoms. Homogeneous groups of 3 to 6 participants work well, while larger groups of 7 to 10 can generally tolerate more variety in the reactions of participants. When several groups are manifesting different reactions, the school should consider using separate support rooms to meet the distinctive needs of each group. If a number of large groups seek services within the support room(s), more staffing may be required; the coordinator of counseling services should draw on counseling staff from other schools within the district, as well as community mental health resources, if appropriate. He or she should also determine if on-site assistance from community service providers will be necessary or if a direct referral system would work best. In many ways large groups (i.e., more than eight or nine participants) function similarly to classroom groups. If many groups of this size seek assistance through the support rooms, this may indicate that the interventions provided in the classrooms did not sufficiently meet the needs of many students, highlighting the need for further training and support of classroom teachers.

The support room staff, under the guidance of the coordinator of counseling services, should perform an initial assessment, following the principles of mental health triage, of students seeking to utilize the services offered in the support room. Those students with emergent mental health needs demanding immediate action should be referred directly to the appropriate community resources. Extensive evaluations and counseling services in the school setting prior to referral of these students should be avoided. Referring large groups of students to hospital emergency rooms to rule out suicidal risk is not an effective response plan and may only weaken the collaborative relationships between school and community mental health staff. Therefore, the crisis team needs to identify appropriate emergency services in the community that can respond immediately if needed at the time of crisis, as well as urgent services that can be provided within 48 hours for this purpose. Identifying students with needs requiring emergency treatment, such as those assessed as potentially suicidal, is a critical role of the counseling staff. Mental health staff in the support room should be identified as being available for specific, individualized tasks (e.g., one person may have the best assessment skills for suicidality and can be assigned for that purpose, whereas another may have advanced skills around grief work). Evaluations should be brief and goal specific, with the intention of screening students for the most appropriate level of service. The counseling staff should defer more lengthy evaluations and services until a later time, such as the next school day. Youngsters assessed as not requiring emergent mental health services should be offered limited immediate interventions, perhaps in a group setting. Support groups, which might continue to meet on an ongoing basis, may be a useful outcome of the support rooms (Lichtenstein et al., 1995).

Many students who might benefit from additional evaluation and intervention may not request, nor present themselves to support rooms for, these services. School staff may identify students as requiring further evaluation because of the circumstances of the crisis (e.g., if the student was a witness to the crisis or a close friend of the victim) or by their reactions upon notification (e.g., if the student has an extreme or atypical response). As a result, the general classroom staff will need to be able to determine who within their classroom may be at risk, and have a mechanism through which to refer these individuals for additional evaluation and intervention. Table 21.3 outlines risk factors that increase the likelihood that students will require additional services after a crisis event. These factors involve the nature and extent of the student's relationships with the victim, the quality of the student's coping with prior challenges, as well as the current crisis event, and the presence of predisposing factors and concurrent life stressors. Those staff who are part of early identification and intervention programs within the school (e.g., student assistance teams, mental health teams, child study

Table 21.3 Risk Factors for Students

Group affiliation with the victim

School staff should make themselves aware of the formal and informal social networks and the activities that the victim shared with other students: academic, shop, and special classes; afterschool clubs, teams, and extracurricular activities; community and social activities engaged in off-site; the victim's residential neighborhood.

A staff member should consider following the victim's schedule of classes for the first day(s). The crisis team should reach out to the external sites to offer support and guidance to the nonprofessionals who might have regular contact with peers (e.g., the scout leader, little league coach, or dance instructor).

Shared characteristics, interests, or attributes with the victim

Students who perceive themselves as sharing characteristics, interests, or attributes with the victim may be more inclined to have increased anxiety and distress.

Students with prior demonstration of poor coping

Social isolation

History of suicidal ideation/attempts

Prior history of arrests, acting-out behaviors, aggression, or drug/alcohol abuse

Students exhibiting extreme or atypical reactions

Students with grief reactions surpassing those of the general student body that would not be explained by close affiliation with the victim

Students with close relationships with the deceased that exhibit very little reaction to the news

Students with personal history related to the trauma

Former victims of crime or violence

Students who have threatened or acted violently in the past

Students with concurrent adverse personal situations

Family problems

Health problems

Psychiatric history

Significant peer conflicts

teams) should be brought into the crisis response assessment and planning so that they are able to share their prior knowledge of those students who were experiencing difficulties before the crisis.

Individual services should, except on rare occasions, be directed toward either alleviating the dominant features or symptoms that prompted the need for individual attention or for the preliminary assessment regarding the need for referral to community mental health services (e.g., for students with severe suicidal ideation or profound decompensation). Although mental health resources within individual school districts vary greatly in the amount, extent, and nature of counseling services their staff can provide, all school districts need to establish relationships with local community services to provide supplemental or specialized mental health services for crisis situations.

School-based crisis intervention planning and response cannot occur in isolation from the community. A critical component of crisis preparedness planning involves identifying community resources, as well as service gaps, for addressing the emergent mental health needs of students and staff at the time of a crisis. Specific staff should be identified within community social service and mental health agencies to serve as liaisons with the school system. Through effective collaboration between schools and community mental health providers, solutions can be developed to increase the community's capacity to address mental health needs in a timely and effective manner at the time of crisis. Such collaboration and community planning to improve the mental health infrastructure will have clear benefit for members of the school community even outside the context of a crisis event (e.g., when making referrals for students who have non-crisis-related issues that may require ongoing counseling).

CLASSROOM INTERVENTIONS

To meet the emerging needs of students during a school's response to crisis, interventions can be offered in classrooms. Classroom activities will reduce the demands on individual counseling resources, allowing them to target those students requiring more intensive intervention.

Additional in-service training is required to prepare teachers to provide this service. The training should be general enough in nature (e.g., children's developmental understanding of death and their responses to loss; Schonfeld, 1993) that it is clear to teachers (and administrators) that the skills learned can be applied more broadly than just at the time of major crisis events. Teachers may also need additional support and backup by school counseling staff in order to be able to provide this service within their classrooms. A crisis often awakens feelings related to a prior (or concurrent) crisis that may assume a primary focus for a particular child. At these times of stress, given an appropriate opportunity, children may be inclined to disclose a wide range of personal crises (e.g., prior deaths, unresolved issues regarding parent conflict or divorce). Teachers need timely access to appropriate backup services to address these "incidental" concerns (Schonfeld, 1989).

At the time of a crisis, teachers may benefit from additional briefing regarding the types of reactions that they may anticipate in their classrooms and some of the specific behavioral changes that are common following a crisis. Particularly when people are experiencing difficulty in identifying and expressing their feelings, teachers need to be attentive to nonverbal communication. Eye contact, posture, and energy levels may contribute valuable information for directing the flow of the discussion and determining whether a student's needs are being met through classroom interventions.

There are three general categories of classroom activities that can contribute to children's expression of their feelings and thoughts: discussions, written efforts, and art projects. Teachers will be most familiar with the developmental capabilities of their students, as well as their methods for coping with prior stressful situations, and should select the modalities that provide the best match.

Discussions are most effective when led by the teacher. However, if due to his or her personal connection with the crisis event the teacher feels unable to direct the classroom activity, it may be necessary for another staff person to guide the discussion initially while the teacher is allowed to observe and participate. Discussions should attempt to demystify the event and address any magical thinking that may be influencing the students' perceptions through efforts to correct rumors, provide logical explanations of what has transpired wherever possible, and draw out the impressions that students are forming so as to be able to reinforce accurate understanding and redirect mistaken impressions (Newgass & Schonfeld, 1996). Graphic details describing injuries and attendant imagery should be avoided; consideration of the developmental needs and capacities of students can guide how much information they need to process the experience without overwhelming their defensive structures (Yussen & Santrock, 1982).

During these discussions, teachers should not attempt to hide their own feelings and reactions but instead should be encouraged to model meaningful and compassionate ways to talk about feelings. Students will need assistance in focusing on their feelings, as opposed to behaviors or sensations, during these discussions. Teachers should consciously take time for themselves to become aware of their feelings and reactions. Opportunities should be provided for teachers to talk with their peers about how they are reacting to the incident and to their discussions with students.

Written activities are often used as a way of allowing students to express their angst and sorrow. If they are used excessively, or indiscriminately, their impact may be diluted. Entire classes are often assigned the "task" of writing a note or some other exercise, such as a poem or a recollection of a joyful time spent with the victim. However, this activity does not acknowledge the unique relationships that individual students may have or may have had with the victim of a trauma. Whereas some students may have very deep and meaningful relationships with the victim, others' relationships may be more distant or conflicted. An assignment that assumes all relationships are equivalent may reduce the effectiveness for those very students most in need of expressing their loss.

Written activities are most beneficial for students with better developed writing skills. Regardless of the assignment and its purpose (i.e., to be shared within the class, to be sent to the family in an effort to extend emotional support, or as an aid to individual processing of the event), all written assignments associated with responding to a crisis should be reviewed to identify any signs of extreme emotional distress or inappropriate content.

> Following the third death at the school mentioned in vignette 3, several staff worked together with groups of students to produce a notebook of poetry and reflections that might be presented to the parents of the child. When a number of students submitted contributions that reflected their confusion, hurt, and sorrow expressed in a way that may have been painful for the victim's family to read (e.g., "it was cruel of you to do this to us . . . you left us behind with the pain, while you get to escape it"), the staff guided students toward forming themselves into small peer review groups to read and reread each other's work and offer suggestions on alternate ways to express the intended emotional message. As one student commented, "Because we did this, I've found new ways to describe how I feel."

Art projects and manipulatives can also be used to facilitate emotional expression in a classroom setting. These generally take the form of pictures, banners, and temporary memorials. This intervention may be especially helpful for younger children, but all age-groups can use art-related activities to express their inner state. The benefits may expand as multiple sensory experiences are permitted through use of the medium; many students may benefit from finger painting because is employs multiple sensations (i.e., visual, tactile, auditory, and olfactory). Whatever the approach, it is important that the activity be used to elicit emotional responses and not to "diagnose" the students because of the content or structure of their artwork.

> In one of the classrooms at the school responding to the crisis in vignette 3, the art teacher invited students to draw a picture of their feelings. Several media were available for the students' use, including pencils, crayons, tempera, and charcoal. After they had completed their drawings, the teacher asked each student to come forward and describe how the images on the paper illustrated their feelings. Several students became emotional as they talked, and the group spontaneously offered support, encouragement, and validating comments to one another. Several students commented that they were encouraged to hear others describe feelings that they themselves held but hesitated to share.

In adapting these interventions to special education classes, it may be helpful to allow additional "quiet time" and/or to alternate rest with physical activity (Axline, 1983). Music may help students relax so that they are better able to attend to their emotional reaction to a crisis. For some students, concrete methods that provide a framework are most effective, such as the use of a "feelings identification chart" to assist them in better identifying their feelings. Storytelling can also be used. The stories that may be most helpful depend upon the individual class and students. One technique is to tell a story in "rounds," wherein the teacher begins the story and the students take turns contributing elements, while the teacher offers modifications, if necessary. The teacher ultimately brings the story to a close with a straightforward solution that is reality-based yet hopeful.

> In one classroom at the school that responded to the crisis in vignette 2, the individual leading the discussion asked if anyone could think of a story that would show how people can respond to tragedies. One youngster suggested starting the story with "A kid got shot." The facilitator added, "but she went to the hospital, where they are helping her to get better." Another child added, "She nearly died," and the facilitator contributed, "but everyone is pretty sure that she'll be all right in a few weeks." He went on to repeat the story as it had developed to that point: "A kid got shot, but she went to the hospital, where they are helping her to get better. She nearly died, but everyone is pretty sure that she'll be all right in a few weeks." He then asked if anyone wanted to add the next line, to which a girl replied, "And then she'll be able to come back to school." He once again repeated the story, now with a concluding sentence, and was able to use this as a means to examine the children's fears about the violence associated with guns, concerns of death, anxiety about hospitals, and their longing for the girl's return to school. This led to a more directed discussion about the students' worries and techniques to facilitate coping.

FOLLOW-UP AND STAFF SUPPORT

Children and adults grieve and respond to a crisis over time, and long-term reactions to significant events should be expected. Mechanisms need to be in place for referring students and staff for additional counseling outside of the school, if this proves to be necessary. A list of local community agencies, pediatricians, and private mental health providers should be available to staff and parents.

The staff members' responsibility to provide services to students at the time of crisis does not relieve them from experiencing their own reactions to the event. Acute reactions to crisis events among staff members should not be overlooked or discounted; rather, attempts should be made to normalize the distressing reactions that many will experience and provide opportunities for additional support. Unfortunately, mental health services and Employee

Assistance Programs (EAPs) may bear a stigma in the minds of some staff. As part of their crisis protocol, schools should proactively identify any EAP contacts, along with necessary phone numbers and contact names, at the very beginning of a response and encourage staff to make use of their services. Frequent reminders about the service and the guarantee of confidentiality should be given throughout the time that crisis intervention services are offered. Following a crisis, a school system should speak with the EAP to see if its services were adequate to meet the needs of the staff; underutilization of the service may suggest the need for identifying an alternate means of providing staff support at the time of crisis.

Debriefing, a review of activities that has the goal of gaining a better understanding of a team's capacity, should be offered after the team has emerged from the response cycle. Whereas debriefing is intended to focus on the team's activities in executing the crisis plan, there is also an opportunity for team members to express their personal reactions to the event and to identify steps that might relieve stress during future crisis responses. In some cases, a debriefing session may include staff members outside of the crisis team, such as for a teacher whose classroom was most directly impacted by the crisis. The debriefing session will also allow the team to develop plans to evaluate and address ongoing issues, such as the possibility of posttraumatic and anniversary reactions among students and staff.

TRAINING AND TECHNICAL ASSISTANCE

Training of crisis response teams is most effective if it includes all members of the team, which often requires considerable planning. In addition to being most convenient for the trainer (thereby facilitating the involvement of outside consultants), the primary advantage is that team building will develop more predictably when all parties receive training together.

Training for a school crisis team should provide background knowledge on crisis theory and children's developmental understanding of and reactions to death (Schonfeld, 1993); introduce and familiarize the participants with the organizational model (Schonfeld et al., 1994); provide information on classroom interventions; and employ team-building activities. The importance of recognizing and addressing staff needs should be underscored throughout the training.

A vignette activity, wherein team members adopt roles from the model in order to address a school crisis situation, should be used to help the newly developing teams experience the manner of problem solving and decision making that will confront them in a crisis. This vignette should provide the amount of information that might be available to schools at the time of an actual crisis. The subsequent processing of the experience with teams should clarify that there is no "right way" to respond. Rather, the training facilitators should elicit their reasons for making the structural decisions and draw out their rationale for intervention (Gallessich, 1990). The goal is to help the group learn how best to function as a team, and to appreciate both the complexity of responding to a crisis and how an organizational plan can help anticipate many of the issues and provide a mechanism for responding effectively.

It is often helpful to bring together several teams for training off-site (to minimize interruptions that may distract or remove participants from the training) in a full-day (i.e., 5- to 6-hour) workshop. The trainer/consultant can then follow up with individual teams to adapt the practices to the unique issues associated with each team's school. While providing the technical assistance, it is important that the unique cultural, economic, and environmental aspects of the school and its population be considered and that the plan be adapted to meet these unique circumstances. The individual providing technical assistance can also help identify unique vulnerabilities for a school. For example, a school serving a marginalized immigrant population should anticipate the need for increased translation and outreach services at the time of a crisis. Psychological vulnerabilities can also be considered, such as decreased support at home in communities with a high percentage of single-adult-headed households, or increased baseline stressors and decreased resources in disadvantaged communities.

CONCLUSIONS

A school-based crisis intervention team composed predominantly of school-based staff is ideally suited to coordinate crisis prevention activities and to provide intervention services to students at the time of a crisis. This chapter has discussed a systematic crisis intervention model to organize the activities of this team and has highlighted issues to consider in establishing and training school-based crisis teams. If representatives of community social service and mental health agencies are involved in the planning process, it is more likely that their services can be accessed at the time of a crisis for the mutual benefit of the students and the community. Planning for possible contingencies will facilitate optimal performance of the team while ameliorating the negative consequences impacting the students and the service providers, who, as members of the school community, will likely be reacting to the crisis themselves.

ACKNOWLEDGMENTS The authors would like to acknowledge the contributions of the members of the Regional School Crisis Prevention and Response Program, including representatives of the public school systems of East Haven, New Haven, North Haven, and West Haven, Connecticut. We gratefully acknowledge the support of our program from the Community Foundation for

Greater New Haven, the William Caspar Graustein Memorial Fund, the State of Connecticut (Office of Policy and Management), ACES (Area Cooperative Educational Services, Hamden, Connecticut), and the Office for Victims of Crime.

REFERENCES

Axline, V. (1983). *Play therapy*. New York: Ballantine.

Brent, D., Etkind, S., & Carr, W. (1992). Psychiatric effects of exposure to suicide among the friends and acquaintances of adolescent suicide victims. *Journal of the American Academy of Child and Adolescent Psychiatry, 31*, 629–640.

Davidson, L., Rosenberg, M., Mercy, J., Franklin, J., & Simmons, J. (1989). An epidemiologic study of risk factors in two teenage suicide clusters. *Journal of the American Academy of Child and Adolescent Psychiatry, 262*, 2687–2692.

Gallessich, J. (1990). *The profession and practice of consultation*. San Francisco: Jossey-Bass.

Kline, M., Schonfeld, D., & Lichtenstein, R. (1995). Benefits and challenges of school-based crisis response teams. *Journal of School Health, 65*, 245–249.

Klingman, A. (1988). School community in disaster: Planning for intervention. *Journal of Community Psychology, 16*, 205–216.

Lichtenstein, R., Schonfeld, D., Kline, M., & Speese-Linehan, D. (1995). *How to prepare for and respond to a crisis*. Alexandria, VA: Association for Supervision and Curriculum Development.

Marans, S., Adnopoz, J., Berkman, M., Esserman, D., MacDonald, D., Nagler, S., Randall, R., Schaefer, M., & Wearing, M. (1995). *The police–mental health partnership*. New Haven, CT: Yale University Press.

Marans, S., Berkowitz, S., & Cohen, D. (1998). Police and mental health professionals: Collaborative response to the impact of violence on children and families. *Child and Adolescent Psychiatric Clinics of North America, 7*, 635–651.

Newgass, S., & Schonfeld, D. (1996). A crisis in the class: Anticipating and responding to student's needs. *Educational Horizons, 74*, 124–129.

Schonfeld, D. (1989). Crisis intervention for bereavement support: A model of intervention in the children's school. *Clinical Pediatrics, 28*, 27–33.

Schonfeld, D. (1993). Talking with children about death. *Journal of Pediatric Health Care, 7*, 269–274.

Schonfeld, D., Kline, M., & Members of the Crisis Intervention Committee. (1994). School-based crisis intervention: An organizational model. *Crisis Intervention and Time-Limited Treatment, 1*, 155–166.

Yussen, S., & Santrock, J. (1982). *Child development: An introduction*. Dubuque, IA: Wm. C. Brown.

22

Crisis Intervention With Chronic School Violence and Volatile Situations

CHRIS STEWART
GORDON MACNEIL

PRECIPITATING EVENTS RESULTING IN CRISIS SITUATIONS

A ninth-grader is verbally harassed because she doesn't wear "cool" clothes.

A group of "jocks" bully a high school freshman at the bus stop, pushing and tripping him.

The student who informed on another student who ditched classes is beaten up in their subsequent fistfight.

On their way home after a football game, a group of middle school students are beaten up by fans from a rival school.

A high school senior is stabbed for making derogatory comments about another student's girlfriend.

A student is fatally shot when he fails to pay another student for drugs.

Case Studies

John Hanson is a 17-year-old Asian American male. He attends Boca Vista High School, where he is a junior. John is a good student, with an overall grade point average of 3.6. He has had little trouble at school. His greatest transgression was when he was caught skipping school to attend a concert.

He plans to attend college and become an engineer. He has a supportive family and good relationships with both parents and his younger sister.

John is a witness to a tragic event at school. Two days ago, a fellow student, whom John did not know personally but recognized from several shared classes, shot several students and a teacher before committing suicide. One of the students was a close friend of John's. John is experiencing extreme grief and does not feel able to speak with his parents about his feelings.

Jack Fujimoto is a 13-year-old White male attending Prairie View Middle School. Jack has reasonable grades, with an average of 2.5 in all subjects. Jack is small for his age. His parents have been divorced for three years and he currently lives with his mother, who is supportive. He has been the victim of an ongoing campaign by some other students. Several of the school athletes have been bullying Jack for several months because he is a member of the drama club. These students call him "fag" and steal his lunch money on a regular basis. In this last meeting, the boys beat Jack, causing moderate harm, though no bones were broken. Jack is generally a quiet person and likes acting, as it provides him an avenue to express his feelings.

Aretha Jackson is a 16-year-old African American female. She attends Andrew Jackson High School, where she is a sophomore. She attends school regularly and has earned a grade point average of 3.0. She lives with her mother and grandmother. She has one younger brother and one older brother. She receives good support from both her mother and grandmother. Her father left her mother when Aretha was very young, and she has no recollection of him.

Aretha experienced a violent episode when changing classes: another girl threatened her with a box cutter. Aretha had, unknowingly, trespassed into an area that "belonged" to the girl and her friends. Aretha escaped without injury but is upset about the event and fears it may happen again.

In this chapter, we discuss two principal forms of school violence: the first includes acts of violence ranging from bullying, robbery, and simple assaults to homicide; the second includes those catastrophic outbursts against schoolmates and school personnel typified by the shootings in Colorado, Arkansas, and Kentucky. These catastrophic school violence events have a powerful impact on the communities in which they occur. However, we think the more common form of violence, though not garnering the media attention of catastrophic events, is of greater concern due to its chronicity and frequency and the greater numbers of students, teachers, parents, and other school personnel directly impacted by these violent acts in schools nationwide. Both forms of school violence require human service personnel (or trained school personnel) intervention. In particular, comprehensive crisis intervention services should be readily available for those victimized by the violence or exposed to it. This chapter presents a crisis intervention strategy targeting survivors of school violence that employs Roberts's (1991, 1996) crisis intervention model in combination with cognitive therapy.

In this chapter we address school violence in a general sense; we do not identify interventions for specific violent acts (such as rape or aggravated assault) and we have limited our discussion to violence against persons, thus omitting aggression toward property such as vandalism, arson, and bombing school buildings.

DEFINITION OF THE PROBLEM

School violence encompasses a tremendous array of behaviors, ranging from verbally abusing a peer to deliberately bombing persons in a school building and shooting groups of persons with semiautomatic weapons. Despite the diversity of these acts, they are all overt, aggressive acts that result in physical or psychological pain, injury, or death (Fredrick, Middleton, & Butler, 1995). Definitions of school violence have ranged from verbal acts of disrespect to teachers and administrators, theft, and physical assaults (Kelly & Pink, 1982) to the federal government's inclusion of only rape, robbery, and simple and aggravated assaults (Bastian & Taylor, 1992). This more restrictive definition is intended to provide a narrow focus for research studies.

There has also been significant attention given to certain specific aspects of school violence, such as bullying behavior (Dake, Price & Telljohann, 2003). Based on the pioneering work of Olweus (1978), bullying is defined as repeated aggressive behavior intentionally meant to harm another person (Smith, 2000). This definition can be further developed to include specific types of bullying behavior. In general, bullying behavior can be categorized as direct, aimed directly at the victim and including both verbal and physical abuse, or indirect, behavior such as malicious gossiping and exclusion from group participation (Hunter & Boyle, 2002).

Astor (1998) suggests that social workers adopt a definition of violence presented by Straus, Gelles, and Steinmetz (1980): Violence is "an act carried out with the intention, or a perceived intention, of causing physical pain or injury to another person. The physical pain can range from a slight pain such as a slap, to murder" (p. 20). Astor promotes this definition because it includes milder forms of aggression common in elementary schools. He contends that lax rules about aggression, or tolerance for milder forms of aggression in lower grades, fosters more severe aggressive acts in later grades. He points out that changing our definition of violence can lead to increased awareness of the problem, as occurred in the 1970s and 1980s with domestic violence (Astor, 1998). For our discussion, we subscribe to the operational definition that school violence is any intentional verbal or physical act producing pain in the recipient while under the supervision of the school.

SCOPE OF THE PROBLEM

Tragic, catastrophic events have served as vehicles for the popular press to identify school violence as a critical issue. The events in Moses Lake, Washington (1996), Bethel, Alaska (1997), Pearl, Mississippi (1997), Paducah, Kentucky (1997), Jonesboro, Arkansas (1997), Edinboro, Pennsylvania (1998), Springfield, Oregon (1998), Columbine, Colorado (1999), and Conyers, Georgia (1999), have become examples of what might happen in quiet, "good" communities. Had these events occurred in inner-city neighborhoods they might have been no less tragic but perhaps less surprising (Wetzstein, 1998). Consequently, many questions have been raised as to the nature and scope of the school violence issue (Dupper & Meyer-Adams, 2002). Parents and community officials alike are concerned about the perceived level of violence in the nation's schools (Goldstein & Conoley, 1997).

Determining the nature and scope of school violence, as with most complex social phenomena, is not an easy task. Many researchers suggest that the situation is best described from a social-ecological perspective (Espelage & Swearer, 2003; Verlinden, Hersen, & Thomas, 2000), in which individual, family, school, and societal factors all have some influence on creating a violent situation. For example, violence in schools is related to the presence of violence in society; violence exists in society and it leaks into the school environment (Crews & Counts, 1997). As Goldstein and Conoley (1997) write, "High levels of aggression in our homes, our streets, and our mass media rapidly find parallel expression in our schools" (p. 16).

A federal government report in 1993 found that almost 3 million crimes in schools were reported annually, which translates to almost 16,000 crimes per school day (Goldstein & Conoley, 1997). Another report found that 15% of all public schools reported at least one incident of serious violence (including murder, rape, suicide, or physical attack with a weapon) to law enforcement officials in the 1999–2000 school year (U.S. Department of Education, 2004). The report also found that 71% of public schools reported at least one violent incident and 15% of schools experienced at least one serious violent incident during the 1999–2000 school year (U.S. Department of Education, 2004).

The statistics, however, do not present a complete picture. Some researchers claim that statistics can be used by the media to scare concerned parents into watching specific broadcasts (Wetzstein, 1998, p. 2). Some reports have shown that while 3,000 children died from gunfire in 1997, only 40 were actually killed on school property (Schreck, Miller, & Gibson, 2003). Further, the nonfatal assault statistics were stable between 1989 and 1995. In fact, schools have been proven to be safer than their communities (Poland, 1997; Schreck et al., 2003). There is actually evidence to suggest that the total number of school-associated deaths has decreased over the past few years (Verlinden et al., 2000).

To further complicate the matter there is also evidence to suggest that, though shooting deaths may be decreasing, other school violence may be stable or actually increasing. Some reports have demonstrated that although actual numbers of single student death episodes have decreased, the rate of multiple-victim homicide rates has increased significantly (Anderson et al., 2001). Research has also found that 77% of midwestern junior and high school students report being a victim of bullying (Espelage & Swearer, 2003). Further, 64% of schools experienced at least one physical attack or fight and 51% experienced vandalism (U.S. Department of Education, 2004).

Although the implications of these statistics are in question, they do seem to indicate an increase in the number and severity of violence in reported incidents (Agron, 1999; Sheley & Wright, 1998). Such a change in the nature of school violence can be directly linked to the availability of and willingness to use weapons such as guns (Crews & Counts, 1997; Dryfoos, 1998; Sheley & Wright, 1998). It is evident that most students have access to almost any form of weapon they desire, including automatic assault rifles ("When Violence Comes to School," 1998; Crews & Counts, 1997; Goldstein & Conoley, 1997). Most school-related incidents involving guns take place in high schools and most (65%) are intentional shootings (Goldstein & Conoley, 1997). So, although the true scope of school violence remains controversial, the evidence indicating a rise in the type and severity of violence in school settings seems to cause the greatest public concern.

Administrators and students have responded to this perceived fear. Some schools have now included drills that simulate gunfire along with the traditional natural disaster drills (Astor, 1998). Similarly, one report found an increase in the number of students who avoided specific places in school because of fear (Kaufman, et.al., 1998). Another poll found that one in nine teens missed school because of the fear of violence ("When Violence," 1998). This poll also reported that nearly half of the 2,000 sampled teens made some change in their daily activity because of the fear of imminent violence.

RISK AND PROTECTIVE FACTORS

The school violence literature generally prescribes multifactorial, transactional models to explain violent incidences (Espelage & Swearer, 2003; Verlinden et al., 2000). These ecological systems models delineate multiple factors interacting on multiple levels through various developmental stages to explain and maintain violent behavior. So it is possible to have individual characteristics operating in varying family, school, and community environments interacting to create a number of behavioral outcomes. This complex relationship is further complicated by the fact that many characteristics contributing to school violence are comorbid and often are most accurately represented by moderating, mediating, and other indirect relationships.

From a prevention perspective, it is important to understand the factors that may contribute to aggressive and delinquent behavior in a general sense. Several factors have been identified that contribute to participation in aggression and delinquency (Dryfoos, 1998; Kazdin, 1995; Williams, Ayers, & Arthur, 1997). One group of risk factors includes biological and psychosocial characteristics such as an adolescent's degree of impulse control, psychological and emotional problems, the age at which an adolescent first engages in illegal behavior, the age at which an adolescent experiments with drugs or alcohol, an adolescent's family history regarding alcoholism, and the degree to which an adolescent is subject to genetic disorders (Osofsky & Osofsky, 2001; Verlinden et al., 2000). Research with genetics and other biological factors continues to produce promising results despite the current lack of concrete findings.

Also important is the social world of the adolescent, including interpersonal relationships. These factors include higher rates of drug and alcohol use by peers, lack of interest in school on the part of the youth or the youth's parents, and poor academic performance (Dake et al., 2003).

Another set of risk factors encompasses an adolescent's family and community environment and includes such variables as family income level, neighborhood substance use patterns, the local availability of drugs and alcohol, and the degree of neighborhood crime and disorganization (Osofsky & Osofsky, 2001). Authoritarian parental styles and punitive punishment has been linked with bullying behavior, further implicating the harsh home environment as contributing to school violence (Dake et al., 2003).

INTERVENTIONS

Most of the literature related to intervening in school violence focuses on prevention efforts. Prevention is easier, cheaper, and more effective than actually curing the results of violence once it has been perpetrated (Rich, 1992). Many components of school violence prevention models can serve as points of departure for postoccurrence interventions with the perpetrators.

A number of reviews of school violence prevention programs have been published (see Allen-Meares, Washington, & Welsh, 1996; Dryfoos, 1998; Goldstein & Conoley, 1997), and we encourage readers attempting to prevent school violence in their communities to become familiar with the multitude of prevention program options available. One such program is the Stop Bullying Now! campaign sponsored by the U.S. Department of Health and Human Services (www.stopbullyingnow.hrsa.gov). This program provides information for both parents and adolescents to deal with current problems and help prevent future bullying. However, this chapter does not address prevention programs for two reasons: first, such programs focus on the perpetrators of violence, whereas we choose to focus on intervening with the victims of violence. Second, this text focuses on crisis intervention, and while there may be a national crisis with regard to school violence, we are limiting our topic to interventions pertinent to individual victims of violence.

Crisis Intervention Application

School settings provide unique environments for conflict among students. Because the student population in most schools is reasonably small, individuals commonly interact with the same peers repeatedly throughout the day. While this familiarity has positive aspects, it can exacerbate tensions between individuals because some may not be able to avoid those with whom they are having difficulty. Crisis intervention plans necessarily have to address this issue.

Youth in middle and high schools experience intense developmental changes. Not least of these is their creation of a self-identity. During middle school and high school years, youth commonly affiliate with subgroups (such as "brains," "jocks," and "stoners"). The labeling associated with these groups can lead to stigmatization, and individual identity is sometimes subsumed by group identity (Crews & Counts, 1997). There is often tremendous peer pressure to adhere to group norms and members commonly become intolerant of those who do not share their values or beliefs. Consequently, crisis intervention efforts need to assess the victim's self-identify and degree of subgroup assimilation to produce changes consistent with the individual's values. Proposed changes that conflict with the norms of the client's group need to be evaluated with regard to the client's willingness to challenge those norms.

Another factor that can contribute to difficulty in using a crisis intervention model is the common imposition of authority by school faculty and personnel through the use of fear and force. Strict rules and degrading experiences have been associated with violence against teachers as well as school property (Regoli & Hewitt, 1994). It is widely held that adolescents are distrustful of adults. A reckless imposition of authority can result in the youth's unwillingness to take advantage of services provided by adults (Curcio & First, 1993).

Although some trainers or educators adhere to a specific therapeutic model for intervening with crises, the diversity of acts constituting school violence indicates that an array of therapeutic models be considered. Roberts's (1996) seven-step crisis intervention model has garnered wide acceptance in the social work and social service practice community. It is applicable to a broad spectrum of populations and problems. Other chapters of this text present the model in detail, so we direct the reader to those chapters rather than restating its general principles.

It has been our experience that Roberts's crisis intervention model is most useful as an organizing structure or overriding framework in combination with a supplemental therapeutic intervention. Specifically, youth experiencing initial trauma responses to victimization respond well to behavioral interventions followed by cognitive therapy. Those who are not experiencing severe trauma do well with cognitive interventions (Wells & Miller, 1993). Cognitive therapy is one of the most widely used intervention methods in social work practice (Hepworth, Rooney, & Larsen, 1997). It is often used in conjunction with other interventions such as assertiveness training and desensitization (Hepworth et al., 1997). Below is a brief description of the basic principles of cognitive therapy and an illustrative application of the method within the overarching structure of Roberts's crisis intervention model with one of the cases presented at the beginning of the chapter. Included is a brief discussion of special concerns and considerations practitioners should note when applying Roberts's model to victims of school violence.

Cognitive Therapy

Judith Beck (1995) presents a set of 10 principles on which cognitive therapy is based:

Principle 1: Cognitive therapy is based on an ever-evolving formulation of clients and their problems in cognitive terms. The worker is reminded that current thinking is of paramount importance, as it is the present that can be altered. Although precipitating factors and historical developmental events are tremendously important, particularly in the context of school violence, their primary importance is in maintaining thoughts that impede the client from full functioning.

Principle 2: Cognitive therapy requires a sound therapeutic alliance. Consistent with training texts in most social service professions, the therapist-client relationship is of primary importance. Demonstrating empathetic interpersonal skills and requesting feedback concerning the relationship are encouraged. There may be difficulties in establishing a positive alliance due to the role differences between the worker and the adolescent, but our experience suggests that those truly in crisis quickly dismiss their attitudes when they are physically moved from their peers, who can serve as an audience, and when the worker is able to accurately identify their emotional and cognitive state.

Principle 3: Cognitive therapy emphasizes collaboration and active participation by both the worker and the client. Consistent with Principle 6, the therapist may be more active and directive in the initial stages of therapy and allow more freedom and exploration by the client as therapy progresses.

Principle 4: Cognitive therapy is goal-oriented and problem-focused. Many victims of school violence are overwhelmed by the traumatic experience and unable to identify their problem. Using a cognitive approach in conjunction with the crisis intervention model can provide tremendous opportunity to enhance clarity for our clients. Depending on clients' ability to problem-solve, they may need little more assistance than identifying their problem. This is particularly the case when the client identifies a goal of ceasing to ruminate about the event.

Principle 5: Cognitive therapy initially emphasizes the present. Although a significant transgression creates difficulty for clients responding to particular acts of school violence, it is the cognitive processing of those events that serve as an enduring problem. As Beck states, "Resolution and/or a more realistic appraisal of situations that are currently distressing usually lead to symptom reduction" (1995, pp. 6–7).

Principle 6: Cognitive therapy is educative, aims to teach clients to be their own therapist, and emphasizes relapse prevention. In educating clients about the cognitive model, the therapist provides clients a means of helping themselves. Consistent with crisis intervention values, clients are empowered to help themselves rather than becoming dependent on the therapist.

Principle 7: Cognitive therapy aims to be time-limited and posits several goals that are consistent with this aim: provide symptom relief, facilitate a remission of the disorder, help clients resolve their most pressing problems, and teach them tools so that they can help themselves in the future. Given that the precipitating problem for the client is external (interpersonal), cognitive therapy tends to be effective and efficient in relieving distress in adolescent clients. This time-limited structure is congruent with the overarching structure of Roberts's crisis intervention model.

Principle 8: Cognitive therapy sessions are structured. Reviewing the client's progress since the previous meeting, setting an agenda for the session, getting feedback from any homework, discussing agenda items, giving new homework assignments, and summarizing the session are common tasks used in cognitive therapy sessions.

Principle 9: Cognitive therapy teaches patients to identify, evaluate, and respond to their dysfunctional thoughts and beliefs. Through Socratic questioning or guided discovery, therapist and client discover irrational or dysfunctional thoughts that maintain behaviors serving to impede the client from full functioning. By identifying these thoughts and critically evaluating their validity and usefulness, the client is taught to create new schemas that lead to healthier, adaptive behaviors.

Principle 10: Cognitive therapy uses a variety of techniques to change thinking, mood, and behavior. While Socratic questioning and guided discovery are central tools for cognitive therapy, techniques from other therapeutic approaches are employed as well.

These principles are applied through a process in which the therapist assists clients in (1) accepting that their self-statements, assumptions, and beliefs largely mediate their emotional reactions to the precipitating event;

(2) identifying dysfunctional beliefs and patterns of thoughts that underlie their problems; (3) identifying situations that engender dysfunctional cognitions; (4) substituting functional self-statements for self-defeating cognitions; and (5) rewarding themselves for successful coping efforts (Hepworth et al., 1997).

In the case of survivors of school violence, some of the client's thoughts may be rational: there may be real threats of subsequent violence. There may be times when life really is so hard that an appropriate response is to become clinically depressed or anxious. In fact, such a response may be part of a natural grieving process (Moorey, 1996). In either event, a primary problem may be that clients, finding that they are unable to carry out tasks in the same way they had previously, give up and do little more than retreat from life. They generalize their lack of control about one part of their life to all areas of their life. Reversing this pattern becomes the primary goal of cognitive therapy and the crisis intervention. In achieving this goal, the therapist allows the client to accept the negative thoughts (e.g., "When I am around those people I may be in danger"), but either challenges the negative *automatic* thoughts of the client (e.g., "I automatically think that whenever I see them I am in danger. But maybe that isn't so, maybe I'm just worried that I might be in a situation where they could jump me again") or develops strategies to facilitate the client's distracting himself or herself from the negative thoughts and challenging their implications (Moorey, 1996).

APPLICATION OF ROBERTS'S CRISIS INTERVENTION MODEL WITH COGNITVE THERAPY

Assessing Lethality

In assessing the case of Aretha Jackson presented at the beginning of the chapter, we would be concerned that she is safe from further threats of violence. Crisis intervention for persons victimized by school violence should begin with a comprehensive assessment of the incident and persons involved. Ensuring that the victim is safe is of paramount importance. Although the specific perpetrator of the violence may be removed from the scene, members of that person's subgroup may be cause for concern. We would need to know if the girl who threatened Aretha still poses a threat to her. For instance, we would need to find out if she continues to bring a weapon to school. In the case of boxcutters or other weapons, simply disarming the perpetrator of violence may not be sufficient because the weapon can be easily replaced.

Determining if Aretha is a member of an organized group or gang would be important. It is also important to determine if she is a member of informal groups (geeks, brains, etc.). We might make these inquiries by asking about whom Aretha associates with if we are familiar with most of the student population. We also need to assess the client's degree of assimilation into the group at the outset of the first interview.

The client's accounting of pertinent events preceding the altercation should be carefully noted. If possible, the therapist should obtain school information specific to individual students, as intervening after violent events is enhanced by knowledge of the participants, their family situations, specific stressors and strengths, social supports, and so on (Striepling, 1997). In Aretha's case, we would try to access her school records prior to meeting with her. While we value her accounting of the violent event, we try to gather background information so that we can contextualize her comments.

We are concerned with three aspects of potential lethality in Aretha's case. First, how likely is it that she will commit harm to herself as a result of the victimization? Many adolescents are concerned with "saving face" and not losing the respect of their peers. If the individual fears that he or she will be humiliated or disgraced by being victimized, the threat of lethality is increased. We are more concerned with older adolescents in this regard than with early adolescents or younger children. In Aretha's case, we do not think this risk is great, as she readily came for help. Second, what is the threat that Aretha will think about personally redressing the wrong done to her? The common inability of adolescents to think temporally beyond today and delay gratification can often increase the possibility that they will react to "even the score." Aretha's fear that the threat will be repeated suggests that this risk is not great. The third aspect of lethality the therapist should assess is the degree to which there is a viable threat of recrimination by the perpetrator's subgroup. In Aretha's case, we are indeed concerned and will employ the school's administration and security personnel to intervene on her behalf. We will also work with her to identify potential dangerous situations she should avoid.

Establishing Rapport and Communication

As noted, many adolescents have a general distrust of adults. The victim may think that he or she can handle the situation without adult interference. However, it has been our experience that students are willing to trust persons in positions of authority when they are in crisis situations.

We will pay attention to our use of effective interviewing microskills (attentive listening, body language, paraphrasing, etc.) and strive to project an aura of professionalism without being authoritarian with Aretha. Although it does not appear to be the case with Aretha Jackson, it is often the case that the victim played an active part in creating the situation resulting in violence. Nonetheless, the worker should view the client in the victim role for the purposes of crisis intervention. Assuming an authoritarian role will certainly undermine any rapport that has been established between the worker and the client. As noted by Dziegielewski and Resnick (1995), de-emphasizing the term "victim" and instilling the idea that the client is a "survivor" may be helpful.

Identifying Major Problems

Precipitating events must be identified if the client is to successfully process the violent event. This information may be difficult to obtain, particularly if the violent act was an indiscriminate, aggressive act against a representative of a group rather than a specific individual. Many times, the individual unknowingly provokes the attack. In these instances, it is fruitful for therapists to use their professional knowledge to help identify possible causes of the attack. It appears that Aretha unknowingly or unintentionally provoked the threat against her. Helping her understand why the other girl reacted the way she did will help Aretha process the meaning of the threat. If we are unaware of this meaning, we sometimes contact school security personnel or administrators to get their perception of the interaction. While it may be possible to get this information from the perpetrator directly, we have found that the school personnel may have already done so.

A second reason for gathering additional information about the violent act is that adolescents, even when not engaged in a crisis situation, are not known to be particularly good witnesses or reporters of events to which they are a part, so working to gather other views of the event may be helpful in assisting the client to understand what really happened. This understanding may help the client identify or reframe his or her actual problems.

Many violent events are the culmination of a series of negative encounters between the victim and the perpetrator. These bullying situations are similar to a person's being stalked, as the victim may have taken all known steps to avoid an altercation to no avail. As Roberts and Roberts (1990) state, when these steps fail, the client is likely to enter an active crisis state. Although the client is likely to desire answers to the question of why he or she has been targeted, the therapist should remain focused on the nature of the interpersonal behavior pattern, as that is the client's problem.

Entering this active crisis state can provoke a sense of disequilibrium or disorganization, but also is indicative of the client's generating resources to begin overcoming the crisis-provoking event (Roberts & Dziegielewski, 1995). It is at this point that cognitive therapy can be applied, because the victim has begun to make self-statements that may be interfering with normal behaviors. Aretha may be considering her role in the violent interaction as something she should have known about or something she did herself. Her fears may be causing her to become overly cautious.

During the first couple of sessions with Aretha we will work to make sure she is not ruminating about the past event. We will work to identify those problems that impede her ability to function as she did prior to the violence. Specifically, we will help her understand that it is her cognitive responses that restrict her after the violent event.

Dealing With Feelings and Providing Support

Social service providers need to be attentive to social withdrawal of children exposed to traumatic violent events, as inhibition of their normal activity can serve as an indicator of their degree of stress. Children's grief responses are often delayed when compared to adult responses. Still, noting that children are being quiet and polite "angels" may indicate that they are having difficulty adjusting to the aftermath of the precipitating event (Ursano, Fullerton, & Norwood, 1999).

Students typically feel fear, anger, frustration, powerlessness, embarrassment, and shame when they have been victimized by violent aggressors. If they are witness to another's victimization they may also feel guilt that they did not respond more assertively or effectively. Providing attentive, nonjudgmental support allows clients to work through their emotional responses to the event. Normalizing the client's experience facilitates this process. Reconciling the mixture of feelings resulting from being victimized allows clients to move toward applying energy to actively engaging in problem solving.

We will work with Aretha to help her understand that her fearful reaction to being threatened is normal and reasonable. If her emotional vocabulary is limited, we may try to help her develop a broader emotional vocabulary so that she does not fall prey to the common problem of youngsters reporting being only "angry" or "sad" because they have not identified other emotions.

Exploring Possible Alternatives

Once the client's level of emotional distress has been reduced, he or she can begin to generate alternative solutions to the problem(s). Therapists can help clients develop a list of viable alternative responses that will achieve the clients' goals. It is important when working with adolescents to prod them to persist and brainstorm possibilities rather than accepting the first possibility that comes to mind.

It is at this stage that we begin to help clients challenge their irrational cognitions or mediate their emotional reactions to the precipitating event. We work with them to explore if their perceptions are accurate reflections of what is going on in the external world. While we acknowledge the protective function of these thoughts, we help the youth see that there are other ways of thinking about the current situation and that the past is the past. Translating these concepts to young children is sometimes quite challenging, and we often remind ourselves that patience is indeed a virtue.

Formulating an Action Plan

In this step, goals should be clearly formulated. Brower and Nurius (1993) suggest that the goals should be concrete, specific, and measurable. Also, if they are not collaboratively established, there is a risk that the client will not be invested in achieving the stated goals. Providing a mechanism for the client to actively direct treatment goal setting can provide a model for subsequent self-empowerment activity (Roberts & Dziegielewski, 1995).

The therapist is cautioned to remember that school students may lack the cognitive or emotional maturity (or the verbal acumen) to identify the steps necessary to carry out a plan that will achieve their identified goals. We have found that employing a problem-solving model such as the task-centered model (see Epstein, 1992) can provide a structure for articulating this plan. Cognitive-behavioral interventions are compatible with the task-centered model, and the time-limited nature of the model has been amenable to using it in school settings.

Although we have, by this time, already begun our cognitive intervention by challenging the client's self-talk and beliefs, we use this step to direct the client to demonstrate behavioral tasks that indicate that she is achieving her goals. In Aretha's case, we will make sure that she is again doing things that she avoided in the wake of the violent threat. We are very supportive of all efforts (no matter how small) that indicate she is making progress toward overcoming whatever impediments she had immediately following the violent event. We are particularly concerned that Aretha reward herself for her progress, as school victims are often reluctant to acknowledge their progress. We want them to be aware of their progress and how they have overcome their own problems. If our cognitive intervention is to be educational, Aretha needs to be aware of her progress in order to replicate it later.

Follow-up Measures

As in other interventions, the active phase of treatment can vary in duration. By definition, a crisis is time-bound, and there comes a point at which the crisis aspect of the problem diminishes; then, either the intervention has been effective and the client will terminate services, or continued services need to be contracted. Our cognitive intervention, imbedded in Roberts's crisis intervention model, typically focuses on only one or two dysfunctional beliefs or thoughts that are constricting the client from full functioning. However, we recognize that many clients have cognitive or emotional difficulties prior to their victimization that may impede their full recovery. Although successful treatment in crisis intervention is typically defined as the client's return to previous levels of functioning (Roberts & Dziegielewski, 1995), the trauma of being victimized by or exposed to school violence may require treatment beyond the intervention necessary to address the crisis aspect of the problem. In these cases, the client should be referred to service providers for this help. Ethical practice standards indicate that after terminating with the client, the therapist should follow up to ensure that the client is maintaining satisfactory mental health.

Our work with Aretha continued for three weeks while she responded to being threatened by her peer. During that time she overcame her irrational fear of other girls in her school that belonged to organized gangs. While she respected the potential for violence that these girls presented, Aretha also recognized that she was not being singled out as a target for aggression. She no longer avoided public areas of the school. She was able to identify irrational self-talk and challenge these thoughts. As a consequence, Aretha was pleased that she was able to address her own fears and conduct her social activities in the same way she had prior to her violent altercation with her peer. We should note that the perpetrator of the violence had been suspended from school for one week, and that school security personnel had been vigilant in their surveillance of the girls the perpetrator had been hanging out with.

SPECIAL CONSIDERATIONS

The crisis intervention provider should be aware of a few special considerations. First, there are numerous cultural considerations that impact one's successfully engaging clients. It is beyond the scope of this text to elaborate on specific practice techniques for intervening in specific cultures, and the reader is directed to the vast literature emerging in this area (see Cartledge & Johnson, 1997; Castillo, 1997; McGoldrick, Giordano, Pearce, & Giordano, 1996). Second, therapists should be sensitive to gender issues when attempting to provide crisis intervention services. We have found that same-gender relationships are most comfortable for students.

A growing area of concern regards secondary trauma responses on the part of service providers, school personnel, and even parents. Literature emanating from research on posttraumatic stress disorder indicates that those vicariously exposed to the experience of traumatic events are susceptible to experience trauma themselves (Figley, 1995; Hudnall, 1996). The risk of secondary trauma is higher for those repeatedly exposed to persons who have experienced trauma. Therefore, therapists providing crisis intervention services need to take steps to ensure their own health (see Figley, 1995; Hudnall, 1996).

Catastrophic Events

The greatest special consideration in the area of school violence is what we term "catastrophic events." Although, as noted above, the number of catastrophic events is essentially inconsequential in the context of all school violence, the heinous nature of multiple homicides in recent years as well as the impact these events have on entire communities has galvanized the media's attention on this phenomenon.

The media's unwavering attention to the catastrophic homicidal school violence events of the past few years provides a profusion of anecdotal information about the perpetrators, victims, and societal responses to these events, but no systematic research has been presented that provides an understanding of this phenomenon. As in the previous section, our discussion is limited to the crisis intervention aspects of this phenomenon, focusing on the victims of the event rather than the perpetrators. Further, our discussion is limited to postoccurrence interventions. These emanate from literature on disaster relief, but they provide the best information relative to treating survivors of these devastating events.

Assessment and Risk Factors

A primary goal in helping survivors of catastrophic school violence is to restore and promote normative cognitive, emotional, and interpersonal functioning to those adversely affected by trauma and grief (Murphy, Pynoos, & James, 1997). In doing so, service providers should remember that individuals differ in their capacity to adjust to catastrophic events.

Freedy, Resnick, and Kilpatrick (1992) have developed a risk factor model for disaster adjustment. They suggest that workers perform short clinical assessments of factors thought to predict adjustment difficulties in the days and weeks following the disaster. Their identified risk factors include those who have experienced high numbers of negative life events within the past year and individuals with mental health problems prior to the disaster. Experiences during the phenomenon that indicate high risk for poor adjustment include threats of personal injury (including death), personal injury, exposure to grotesque sights, and the loss of a family member or loved one (witnessed or not). Ursano et al. (1999) suggest that the single best predictor of the probability and frequency of postdisaster psychiatric problems is the severity of the disaster, as indicated by the number of injured and the types of their injuries. Having effective cognitive coping skills and a social support network that promotes personal control and competence prior to the disaster are thought to be protective factors that can mediate the risk for poor adjustment to disasters (Freedy et al., 1992).

Postoccurrence Interventions

We are proponents of an integrated model combining Roberts's crisis intervention model and cognitive therapy. However, we recognize that catastrophic events require additional consideration. For instance, the needs of individuals following a disaster can be considered in the context of Maslow's

(1968) hierarchy of needs, suggesting that initial intervention efforts focus on establishing safety and physical health; social and psychological interventions should follow. A crucial intervention component should be to educate members of the community about "normal responses to abnormal events" (Ursano et al., 1999). These responses are physical, cognitive, and emotional in nature. Physical responses usually begin with a sense of shock and disorientation. This commonly triggers a "fight or flight" response which manifests with increased heart rate and breathing and increased sensory perception. As this intense response cannot be maintained for long periods of time, exhaustion follows (Young, 1991, 1995).

Cognitive and emotional responses are similar to the physical responses, with shock and disbelief manifesting initially, perhaps including denial and a sense of suspension of reality. This shock is followed by emotional turmoil as the individual engages emotions such as anger, frustration, guilt, and grief in responding to the losses resulting from the crisis (Young, 1991, 1995). It may take the individual weeks or months to proceed through the shock and emotional turmoil responses, leaving the person mentally and emotionally exhausted. This emotional exhaustion commonly leaves the individual feeling as thought he or she is on an emotional roller coaster, at once overwhelmed by emotion, and the next moment devoid of emotion. Some persons erect defenses to this phenomenon by constricting their range of emotional involvement in the external world (Young, 1991). The goal of crisis intervention can be seen as facilitating the client's journey through this process and emerging as a fully responsive, fully involved person.

It is often appropriate to include family members or friends in counseling sessions, as they can reinforce messages and provide ongoing support. This is the case even if those family members or friends have been traumatized by the event themselves. Peer support groups also provide a valued forum for support in the aftermath of catastrophic events (Young, 1991).

The National Organization of Victim Assistance (NOVA) has been responding to catastrophic school violence events for almost two decades (Young, 1991, 1995). Those administering postevent services will welcome their expertise, particularly the group debriefing process they employ. We refer the reader to chapter 9 in this text detailing this intervention, and note that it is an important mechanism for moving groups of survivors through steps 3 and 4 of Roberts's crisis intervention model (Identifying Major Problems, and Dealing with Feelings and Providing Support).

NOVA's intervention addresses the complicating factor of a whole community's being overwhelmed by the catastrophic event. In these instances, it is important for survivors and their service providers to form a protective barrier against intrusive external forces, including media personnel. Using adults as buffers against external forces is appropriate, provided the adults are not overwhelmed by the trauma themselves. One method of accomplishing this is to facilitate crisis intervention with the adults so that they can then attend to their children. As noted above, the grief response in children is typically delayed (in comparison with adult reactions). This period of shock or denial can be problematic if it lasts for extended periods of time, but does provide a window of time when attention can be focused on adult care providers. Note that we are not suggesting that needed crisis intervention services be withheld from children, and we acknowledge that adults' ability to provide care for their children while they are in the midst of a trauma response should be assessed as well.

In addition to the trauma experienced by those directly exposed to the violent event, the social networks of these victims are also affected by the violence. In particular, parents and siblings of youth are at risk for secondary trauma responses. Social service workers need to be aware of potential interpersonal difficulties manifesting in families exposed to school violence in the weeks and months following the occurrence. Distributing literature offering supportive services can be helpful to those who are not educated about the symptoms of secondary stress reactions, or who have minimized their psychological or social problems subsequent to the violent event.

Finally, social workers and other crisis intervention providers are reminded that persons providing relief services may need psychiatric help as well, particularly police, medical personnel, hotline workers, insurance claims settlers, and community leaders. Special attention should be paid to "heroes," as there is often tremendous pressure to serve as spokespersons for the survivors or relief workers. These heroes may experience conflicting feelings of guilt, satisfaction, and anxiety that their actions do not justify their hero status.

The case of John Hanson exemplifies the need for crisis intervention in a catastrophic event. The assessment of John's situation is of critical importance. The length of time John was exposed to traumatic events and the nature of the events he witnessed will help determine the type and length of his treatment. Those students who witnessed shootings and might be placed in hostage situations will need special consideration and are more likely to exhibit chronic symptomology than those who were present or witnessed peripheral events.

The need for involvement from NOVA would be stressed as well as the need for a group debriefing. Because this event affects the entire community, it would be important to include John's parents and close friends to empower them to help in the healing process. Educating John's parents and other support network members about normal reactions to abnormal situations would be a primary goal, as those closest to John would need to be prepared for these reactions. In working with John directly, we would use a cognitive intervention similar to that described in treating Aretha Jackson. Emphasizing John's fears about his lack of control in the violent situation and the possibility of repeated catastrophic events would require his addressing irrational thoughts that impede his post–traumatic event functioning.

While we work with him to address his cognitive distortions, we also remain supportive of his emotional recovery. Through these interventions it is likely that John will learn to cope with the catastrophic situation.

CONCLUSION AND POLICY RECOMMENDATIONS

While continued efforts and resources need to be devoted to prevention programs directed at creating safe schools, there will always be a need for crisis intervention programs as well. In addition to violence between individuals, tensions between student subgroups in schools have often resulted in aggression between these groups, and crisis interventions with individuals are appropriate for dealing with these skirmishes or transgressions. If these tensions escalate, they can lead to devastating events that traumatize whole schools, if not whole communities. In these instances, disaster-relief models of crisis intervention are most appropriate. School district administrators, as well as social service agency administrators, would be well advised to establish both prevention and postoccurrence plans addressing the issue of school violence.

REFERENCES

Agron, J. (1999). Safe havens: Preventing violence and crime in schools. *American School and University, 71*(6), 18–23.

Allen-Meares, P., Washington, R. O., & Welsh, B. L. (1996). *Social work services in schools* (2nd ed.). Boston: Allyn & Bacon.

Anderson, M., Kaufman, J., Simon, T., Barrios, L., Paulozzi, 1., Ryan, G., et al. (2001). School-associated violent deaths in the United States, 1994–1999. *Journal of the American Medical Association, 286*(21), 2695–2702.

Astor, R. A. (1998). School violence: A blueprint for elementary school interventions. In E. M Freeman, C. G. Franklin, R. Fong, G. L. Shaffer, & E. M. Timberlake (Eds.), *Multisystem skills and interventions in school social work practice* (pp. 281–295). Washington, DC: National Association of Social Workers Press.

Bastian, L. D., & Taylor, B. (1992). School crime. U.S. Department of Justice, Bureau of Justice Statistics. Rockville, MD: U.S. Department of Justice.

Beck, J. S. (1995). *Cognitive therapy: Basics and beyond.* New York: Guilford.

Brower, A. M., & Nurius, P. S. (1993). *Social cognition and individual change: Current theory and counseling guidelines.* Newbury Park, CA: Sage.

Cartledge, G., & Johnson, C. T. (1997). School violence and cultural diversity. In A. P. Goldstein & J. C. Conoley (Eds.), *School violence intervention: Practical handbook* (pp. 391–425). New York: Guilford.

Castillo, R. J. (1997). *Culture and mental illness: A client-centered approach*. Pacific Grove, CA: Brooks/Cole.

Crews, G. A., & Counts, M. R. (1997). *The evolution of school disturbance in America: Colonial times to modern day*. Westport, CT: Praeger.

Curcio, J. L., & First, P. F. (1993). *Violence in the schools: How to proactively prevent and defuse it*. Newbury Park, CA: Sage.

Dake, J., Price, J., & Telljohann, S. (2003). The nature and extent of bullying at school. *Journal of School Health, 73*(5), 173–181.

Dryfoos, J. (1998). *Safe passage: Making it through adolescence in a risky society*. New York: Oxford University Press.

Dupper, D., & Meyer-Adams, N. (2002). Low-level violence, a neglected aspect of school culture. *Urban Education, 37*(3), 350–364.

Dziegielewski, S. F., & Resnick, C. (1995). A model of crisis intervention with adult survivors of incest. *Crisis Intervention and Time-Limited Treatment, 2*(1), 49–55.

Epstein, L. (1992). *Brief treatment and a new look at the task-centered approach*. New York: Macmillan.

Espelage, D., & Swearer, S. (2003). Research on school bullying and victimization: What have we learned and where do we go from here? *School Psychology Review, 32*(3), 365–384.

Figley, C. R. (1995). *Compassion fatigue: Coping with secondary traumatic stress disorder in those who treat the traumatized* (Psychosocial Stress no. 23). New York: Brunner/Mazel.

Frederick, A. D., Middleton, E. J., & Butler, D. (1995). Identification of various levels of school violence. In R. Duhon-Sells (Ed.), *Dealing with youth violence: What schools and communities need to know* (pp. 26–31). Bloomington, IN: National Educational Service.

Freedy, J. R., Resnick, H. S., & Kilpatrick, D. G. (1992). Conceptual framework for evaluating disaster impact: Implications for clinical intervention. In L. S. Austin (Ed.), *Responding to disaster: A guide for mental health professionals* (pp. 3–24). Washington, DC: American Psychiatric Press.

Goldstein, A. P., & Conoley, J. C. (1997). Student aggression: Current status. In A. P. Goldstein & J. C. Conoley (Eds.), *School violence intervention: A practical handbook* (pp. 3–22). New York: Guilford.

Hepworth, D. H., Rooney, R. H., & Larsen, J. A. (1997). *Direct social work practice: Theory and skills* (5th ed.). Pacific Grove, CA: Brooks/Cole.

Hudnall, B. (1996). *Secondary traumatic stress: Self care issues for clinicians, researchers, and educators.* Lutherville, MD: Sidran Press.

Hunter, S., & Boyle, J. (2002). Perceptions of control in the victims of school bullying: The importance of early intervention. *Educational Research, 44*(3), 323–336.

Kaufman, P., Chen, X., Choy, S., Chandler, K. A., Chapman, C. D., Rand, M. R., & Ringel (1998). *Indicators of school crime and safety, 1998*. (U.S. Departments of Education and Justice, NCES 98–251/NCJ 172215). Washington, DC.

Kazdin, A. E. (1995). *Conduct disorders in childhood and adolescence* (2nd ed.) Newbury Park, CA: Sage.

Kelly, D. H., & Pink, W. T. (1982). School crime and individual responsibility: The preparation of a myth? *Urban Review, 14*(1), 47–63.

Larke, P. J., & Carter, N. P. (1995). School violence: Preparing preservice teachers. In R. Duhon-Sells (Ed.), *Dealing with youth violence: What schools and communities need to know* (pp. 45–51). Bloomington, IN: National Educational Service.

Maslow, A. H. (1968). *Toward a psychology of being.* New York: Van Nostrand Reinhold.

McGoldrick, M., Giordano, J., Pearce, J. K., & Giordano, J. (1996). *Ethnicity and family therapy* (2nd ed.). New York: Guilford.

Moorey, S. (1996). When bad things happen to rational people: Cognitive therapy in adverse life circumstances. In P. M. Salkovskis (Ed.), *Frontiers of cognitive therapy* (pp. 450–466). New York: Guilford.

Murphy, L., Pynoos, R. S., & James, C. B. (1997). The trauma/grief focused group psychotherapy module of an elementary school-based violence prevention/intervention program. In J. D. Osofsky (Ed.), *Children in a violent society* (pp. 223–255). New York: Guilford.

Olweus, D. (1978). *Aggression in the schools: Bullies and whipping boys.* Oxford: Blackwell.

Osofsky, H., & Osofsky, J. (2001). Violent and aggressive behaviors in youth: A mental health and prevention perspective. *Psychiatry, 64*(4), 285–295.

Poland, S. (1997). School crisis teams. In A. P. Goldstein & J. C. Conoley (Eds.), *School violence intervention: A practical handbook* (pp. 127–159). New York: Guilford.

Regoli, R. M., & Hewitt, J. D. (1994). *Delinquency in society: A child-centered approach.* New York: McGraw-Hill.

Rich, J. (1992). Predicting and controlling school violence. *Contemporary Education, 64*(1), 35–39.

Roberts, A. R. (1991). Conceptualizing crisis theory and the crisis intervention model. In A. R. Roberts (Ed.), *Contemporary perspectives on crisis intervention and prevention* (pp. 3–17). Englewood Cliffs, NJ: Prentice-Hall.

Roberts, A. R. (1995). *Crisis intervention and time-limited cognitive treatment.* Thousand Oaks, CA: Sage.

Roberts, A. R. (1996). Epidemiology of and definitions of accute crisis in American society. In A. R. Roberts (Ed.), *Crisis management and brief treatment: Theory, technique, and applications* (pp. 16–33). Pacific Grove, CA: Brooks/Cole.

Roberts, A. R., & Dziegielewski, S. F. (1995). Foundation skills and applications of crisis intervention and cognitive therapy. In A. R. Roberts (Ed.), *Crisis intervention and time-limited cognitive treatment* (pp. 3–27). Newbury Park, CA: Sage.

Roberts, A. R., & Roberts, B. (1990). A comprehensive model for crisis intervention with battered women and their children. In A. R. Roberts (Ed.), *Crisis intervention handbook: Assessment, treatment, and research* (pp. 106–123). Belmont, CA: Wadsworth.

Schreck, C., Miller, J. M., & Gibson, C. (2003). Trouble in the school yard: A study of the risk factors of victimization at school. *Crime & Delinquency, 49*(3), 460–484.

Sheley, J. F., & Wright, J. D. (1998, October). *High school youths, weapons, and violence: A national survey.* National Institute of Justice: Research in Brief. Washington, DC: U.S. Government Printing Office.

Smith, P. (2000). Bullying and harassment in schools and the rights of children. *Children and Society, 14,* 294–303.

Straus, M., Gelles, R., & Steinmetz, S. K. (1980). *Behind closed doors: Violence in the American family.* New York: Anchor Press/ Doubleday.

Striepling, S. H. (1997). The low-aggression classroom: A teacher's view. In A. P. Goldstein & J. C. Conoley (Eds.), *School violence intervention: A practical handbook* (pp. 23–45). New York: Guilford.

Ursano, R. J., Fullerton, C. S., & Norwood, A. E. (1999). *Psychiatric dimensions of disaster: Patient care, community consultation and preventive medicine.* American Psychiatric Press Online. Retrieved from www.psych.org/pract_of_psych/disaster.html.

U.S. Department of Education, National Center for Education Statistics. (2004). Crime and safety in America's public schools: Selected findings from the School Survey on Crime and Safety (NCES 2004–370). Washington, DC.

Verlinden, S., Hersen, M., & Thomas, J. (2000). Risk factors in school shootings. *Clinical Psychology Review, 20*(1), 3–56.

Wells, D., & Miller, M. J. (1993). Adolescent affective aggression: An intervention model. *Adolescence, 28,* 781–791.

Wetzstein, C. (1998, July 6). *Make aware or scare? Insight on the News, 14*(25), 37–38.

When violence comes to school. (1998). *Current Health, 24*(8) 6–7.

Williams, J. H., Ayers, C. D., & Arthur, M. W. (1997). Risk and protective factors in the development of delinquency and conduct disorder. In M. W. Fraser (Ed.), *Risk and resilience in childhood: An ecological perspective* (pp. 140–170). Washington, DC: National Association of Social Workers Press.

Young, M. A. (1991). Crisis intervention and the aftermath of disaster. In A. R. Roberts (Ed.), *Contemporary perspectives on crisis intervention and prevention* (pp. 83–103). Englewood Cliffs, NJ: Prentice-Hall.

Young, M. A. (1995). Crisis response teams in the aftermath of disasters. In A. R. Roberts (Ed.), *Crisis intervention and time-limited cognitive treatment* (pp. 151–187). Newbury Park, CA: Sage.

V

CRISIS ASSESSMENT AND CRISIS INTERVENTION IN HEALTH-RELATED AND MENTAL HEALTH–RELATED CRISES

23

Crisis Intervention in the Hospital Emergency Room

MARY BOES
VIRGINIA McDERMOTT

Case 1

When paramedics found Mary Winston, age 68, face down in a pool of blood after answering the call for Code 52, a shooting, they didn't expect to find any signs of life. They had entered the darkened house with flashlights for there was no electricity. Six gunshot wounds had pierced her body: two in her neck, one in both arms, two in her abdomen. As they turned her over from the puddle of thick congealed blood, she slowly took a breath and continued shallow breathing, her eyes wide open. "We can see you're a strong lady, Mary."

Once Mary was in the emergency room, the social worker was called to notify the family. Soon, a large crowd of people of all ages gathered in the ER waiting area. Before Security could be called, two daughters rushed into the trauma room screaming and crying. One rolled over and over on the floor, impeding the medical team's work. The other jumped up and smashed all the windows in the ER door. Mary Winston was the sole matriarch of an extended family. She raised 13 grandchildren as her own. She was the only nurturing presence and figure of stability in a neighborhood where drug lords reigned over the night and poverty and hunger ruled the days.

On hearing "Mary might not make it," 30 people reacted in their joint grief by stampeding through the hospital, banging on patients' doors. One 13-year-old who fainted in the bathroom was assisted by a registered nurse to a stretcher, but when he woke up he punched her in the stomach. "You're killing Grandma," he yelled. He had misinterpreted the emergency procedures the medical staff were doing to her in the ER as signs they were hurting her. While Mary was rushed to surgery, this chaotic crisis enveloped the hospital. The family believed the very foundation of their lives was being threatened.

Case 2

One hectic rainy night, paramedics in Philadelphia were called to the scene of a car crash. By assessing the severe damage of the vehicle, which had rolled over, they realized that any victim would be severely injured, if not dead. They rushed to the side of Chris Jones, age 35, who was covered with blood, screaming "I can't breathe!" and cursing at their struggles to help him. On closer examination they found a deep laceration on the back of his head and blood coming from his left ear. They immobilized his neck and back, in case there were any spinal fractures. Intoxicated and driving at a high rate of speed, he was thrown from the car, smashing head first through the windshield, then banging his head on the pavement.

"Do you remember what happened?" the paramedics asked. "No," he replied. A loss of consciousness at the time of the crash could imply a severe concussion or massive head injury.

Case 3

Mark Smith, a 30-year-old construction worker, had just undergone a highly contested and painful divorce. After drinking one-third of a bottle of Jack Daniels and six beers, he passed out on his sofa. His still smoldering cigarette fell from his fingers onto the cushions. By dawn, the couch ignited, engulfing Mark in flames. He never regained consciousness. The fire spread rapidly throughout the small house. A neighbor on his way to work heard Mark's 9-year-old son, Paul, screaming in panic and terror at the front window. Racing to the porch, the neighbor smashed the glass and pulled the child to safety. The fire company and paramedics had been called by this time and rushed Paul to the ER suffering from severe smoke inhalation and second-degree burns. Some of his clothing and skin were still smoldering.

These three cases portray a type of "quick trajectory" that can occur any time, any place. A person in good health may suddenly become the victim of an automobile accident, a small child may fall into a swimming pool, an "unloaded" gun may discharge, a restaurant patron may choke, a person with a history of heart disease may suffer another attack. These are just some emergency situations that can result in death.

Several types of problems are more likely to arise when there is a life-or-death emergency in a community setting as compared with a health care facility:

Panic: What's happening? What should we do?

Inappropriate action: Let's get him on his feet.

Misinterpreting the situation: Stop whining and go back to bed!

Minimizing the danger: I don't need a doctor. It's just a little indigestion.

Preoccupied by own concerns: I'd better clean this place up before I call anybody.

Glaser and Strauss (1966) are among those who maintain that the American hospital system is well prepared to cope with emergencies. Human and technological resources are mustered most impressively when there is an acute life-or-death crisis. The emergency room, the Intensive Care Unit, and the perpetual readiness of specialists to rush to the scene are life-saving resources that Americans have come to expect from the modern medical center.

Time truly is of the essence when a patient is defined as being on an expected quick trajectory. The staff organizes itself with precision to make the most effective use of the time that remains on the side of life. This contrasts vividly with the more leisurely, almost drifting pattern that surrounds a patient on a lingering trajectory. As staff members devote themselves to the patient's urgent needs, there may be a series of redefinitions in their minds; for example, "He is out of immediate danger but probably will not survive very long" changes to "I think he has passed the crisis point and has the possibility of complete recovery."

The crisis trajectory imposes another condition on both the patient and those concerned. The patient is not in acute danger at the moment, but his or her life might suddenly be threatened at any time. This creates an especially tense situation. It will persist until the patient's condition improves enough so that he or she is out of danger or until the crisis actually arrives and rescue efforts can be made.

Different from all of these is the will-probably-die trajectory. The staff believes that nothing effective can be done. The aim is to keep the patient as comfortable as possible and wait for the end to come, usually within hours or days. This might be the accident victim who is beyond saving or the individual whose suicide attempt failed to end life immediately but did result in a terminal course.

These are not the only types of expected quick trajectories, but they illustrate the range of experience and situations that exist among those who face death in the near future. There are also some common problems that arise in connection with the expected quick trajectory. The family, for example, is likely to be close by the patient. Glaser and Strauss (1966) emphasize the possible disrupting effects of this proximity based on their direct observations. The presence of the family confronts the staff with more demands for interaction and communication. What should those people in the waiting room be told? Who should tell them? Is this the time to prepare them for the bad news, or can it be postponed a little longer? Should all the family be told at once, or is there one person in particular who should be relied on to grasp the situation first? The staff must somehow come to terms with the needs of the family while still carrying out treatment. Obviously, this is a situation to challenge the emergency room social worker's judgment and interpersonal skills.

ER staff traditionally have kept a barrier between the patient and the rest of the family when medical life-saving procedures are under way, sending the family to the waiting room. More enlightened establishments now permit family to be at the bedside and even remain there during the event of a code if they express this wish.

The significance of the interpersonal setting in which dying takes place is emphasized again by the unexpected quick trajectory. Personnel in the emergency room, for example, expect to be called on for immediate life-or-death measures. The experienced ER team adjusts quickly to situations that might immobilize most other people. But in other areas of the same hospital the staff is likely to have a pattern of functioning and a belief system that is less attuned to a sudden turn of events: "The appearance of the unexpected quick trajectory constitutes crisis. On these wards there is no general preparation for quick dying trajectories—at least of certain kinds—and the work and sentimental orders of the ward blow up when they occur" (Glaser & Strauss, 1968, p. 121).

Emergency rooms prime their staff for the sudden onset of medical/surgical distress. Time is of the essence in treatment in order to save lives. Emergency rooms serve as portals for the most vulnerable members of our population. Early identification in the emergency room of individual and family psychosocial stressors, which are often the precipitants to an acute crisis, can lead to crisis stabilization and thereby avert a full-blown crisis at a later stage. Crisis social workers can be integral in helping hospitals develop programs that minimize the chance that victims of abuse or sudden trauma are overlooked (Myer & Hanna, 1996).

This chapter begins with an overview of crisis intervention in the emergency room. Objective data are presented concerning the type and frequency of emergency room visits. Next we consider the subjective reality. A highlight of this chapter is the presentation of a protocol for crisis intervention in the emergency room, a protocol devised from one of the author's eight years of social work experience in an inner-city hospital emergency services department. Throughout this chapter, the focus is on the role of the social worker in situations ranging from moderate to severe crisis.

OVERVIEW

For the purposes of determining the nature of emergency room work today, one of the authors constructed a brief questionnaire which was sent to 25 hospitals across the United States. The nonrandom sample included health care settings as diverse as a 65-bed hospital with one social worker in a town with a population of 9,000 in Caribou, Maine, to Cedar-Sinai Health System in Beverly Hills, California, a 1,200-bed hospital with 30 social workers and 20 case managers. Eleven hospitals responded. Respondents were asked to list the most common urgent and nonurgent problems encountered in the emergency room.

Urgent conditions are those requiring immediate attention within the period of a few hours; there is possible danger to the patient if medically unattended. Disorder is acute. In order of most to least common, hospital staff listed motor vehicle accidents, gunshot wounds, child abuse, domestic violence, and self-inflicted injuries as the most common reasons for coming to an emergency room.

Social Work Staffing

In Caribou, Maine, there is only one social worker assigned to the entire 65-bed hospital. Likewise, there is only one social worker scheduled from 3:00 P.M. to 11:30 P.M. Thursday through Monday in the Emergency Department at University Hospital and Medical Center in Stony Brook, New York. However, the Social Work Services at Stony Brook employs 30 full-time social workers (all MSW level or higher). Twenty-two social workers are assigned Emergency Department rotation to cover on weekdays when the assigned social worker is absent or not scheduled to work. In addition, on-call/re-call coverage is provided by social work staff for overnight coverage to the Emergency Department (and hospitalwide).

The Emergency Department at Stony Brook consists of triage to immediate care (fast track). In the main Emergency Room and Shock-Trauma Departments, all of the nurses have at least an RN degree. The Emergency Department employs an administrative duty nurse and two nurse educators. Nurses assigned to Shock-Trauma are highly trained and exceptionally well-skilled.

In the Shock-Trauma area (the Trauma Centers), the social worker is frequently called on to address issues of grief, bereavement, crisis intervention, locating family of patients, and informing relatives of patients' situations. The Shock-Trauma area receives many traumatic injuries and traumatic illnesses, including motor vehicle accidents, cardiac arrest, burn injuries, overdoses, and falls. Adjacent to the Emergency Department is the Comprehensive Psychiatric Emergency Program (CPEP). CPEP is staffed with five psychiatric social workers and psychiatric nurses. Following medical clearance from the Emergency Department, patients who have inflicted self-harm or experienced altered mental status are evaluated by CPEP staff. CPEP also receives patients from triage who have no medical needs and patients from other psychiatric facilities.

Incidence and Prevalence Estimates

Data from the National Hospital Ambulatory Care Survey for 2002 reveal that falls, being struck by or striking against something, and motor vehicle traffic incidents were the leading causes of injuries presenting to the ER, accounting for about 40% of such visits. Other injuries, poisoning, and adverse effects of medical treatment accounted for 35.5% of ER visits. In nearly 1 out of every 100 ER visits, the patient required immediate attention (e.g., was unconscious or required resuscitation efforts). From 1992 through 2002, the number of ER visits increased from 89.8 million to 110.2 million visits annually (up 23%). This represents an average increase of almost 2 million visits per year. The number of hospital ERs in the United States decreased by about 15% during the same period. The number of injury-related visits for the most recently reported year (2002) was 39.2 million.

Motor vehicle accidents alone kill more than 43,000 people each year and over 4 million car crash victims end up in the emergency room. Burns are one of the most traumatic injuries sustained by the body. Each year in the United States, approximately 2 million burn injuries occur, and half of these require medical attention. Approximately 70,000 of those patients seeking medical attention suffer potentially life-threatening injuries, either from the high percentage of skin area involved or from complications from smoke inhalation and other concomitant injuries. Of the other 1 million people with burns who do not seek medical attention, about 10,000 die at the scene of the accident (Demling & LaLonde, 1989). The rest of the injuries are minor, and treatment with basic first aid at home is adequate.

Burns are the third leading cause of accidental deaths in the United States. The highest risk is among those 18 to 30 years old. Males are twice as likely to be burned as females.

A severe thermal injury can be one of the most devastating physical and psychological injuries a person can suffer. The fire death rate in the United States (57.1 deaths per million population) is the second highest in the world and the highest of all industrialized countries, almost twice that of second-ranking Canada (29.7 deaths per million). Table 23.1 gives a breakdown of general characteristics of persons treated in emergency rooms across the United States. Data are for nonfederal short-stay and general hospitals.

Typically, emergency room patients are prioritized by placing them in one of four categories. The emergent group requires immediate attention and includes cardiac arrest and trauma codes. Urgent and nonurgent cases fall into the intermediate categories. Urgent problems should be treated as soon as possible, generally within one to two hours. These include obvious fractures and acute abdominal pain. Nonurgent problems need to be treated sometime that day but not necessarily in the emergency room, for example, sore throat and simple laceration. The delayed group can be transferred to a walk-in location; these include conditions that don't require emergency room care at all and can be seen at any time, like most rashes or a previous wound that needs checking. Table 23.2 provides a more detailed list of conditions included in each triage category.

Table 23.1 Visits to U.S. Hospital Emergency Departments, 2001

Characteristic	Number of visits (in millions)
All visits	107.5
AGE	
Under 15 years old	22.2
15 to 24 years old	17.4
25 to 44 years old	32.7
45 to 64 years old	19.3
65 to 74 years old	6.6
74 years old and over	9.3
SEX	
Male	50.3
Female	57.2
RACE	
White	82.0
Black	22.2
Asian/Native Hawaiian/Other Pacific Islander	2.1
American Indian/Alaska Native	0.6
More than one race reported	0.1
EXPECTED SOURCE OF PAYMENT	
Private insurance	43.2
Medicare	15.9
Medicaid	18.8
Worker's Compensation	2.7
Self-pay	15.9
No charge	1.0
Other	2.3
Unknown source of payment	7.7

Source: U.S. National Center for Health Statistics, Advance Data, Nos. 335, 337, and 338; June 4, 2003; August 11, 2003; and August 5, 2003.

Social work services in the ER are critical because this is the time when nurses and physicians are being overwhelmed by the traumatic and emergency surgical needs of the patient in the ER. Soon after or at the same time that the person is medically stabilized, the social worker needs to begin the psychosocial protocol. For instance, a greater variety of social issues present to the emergency room. In addition, ER social work demands quick and immediate attention: the time frame for assisting a patient is short and the patient is invariably in a state of crisis. For these reasons, accurate assessment and intervention are essential for effective ER social work.

The following is a protocol used to ensure continuity of social work coverage in one ER of the two hospitals used in a previous study by the author (Boes, 1997). Where locally available resources are provided, social workers would use the resources provided in their own community. Telephone numbers were listed in the protocol, but for this chapter they are deleted.

Table 23.2 Conditions Included in Triage Categories

EMERGENT	URGENT
Cardiac complaints (e.g., chest pains)	Acute abdominal pain
Codes	Acute headache
Conditions associated with airway compromise (e.g., foreign bodies, dystonia, allergic reactions, and angioedema)	Cellulitis
Eye injuries	Major laceration
Falls or jumps of more than 20 feet	Nonurgent complaint in a patient with an underlying medical condition (e.g., diabetes, cancer, hypertension, or AIDS)
Hemodynamic instability	Obvious fracture
Hypo- or hypergycemia	Sexual assault
Inhalation injuries	**NONURGENT**
Limb amputations	Common cold
Respiratory distress	Minor injury
Seizures and postseizure states	Simple laceration
Serious motor vehicle accident cases	Sore throat
Stroke	Sprains or strains
Trauma, including major facial injuries and penetrating injuries to the head, neck, chest, abdomen, axilla, shoulder, groin, or buttocks	Toothache
	DELAYED
	Exams
	Prescription refill
	Rash
	Request for a work slip
	Suture removal
	Wound check

PROTOCOL FOR CRISIS INTERVENTION IN THE EMERGENCY ROOM

Code or Trauma

Assessment

In a code or trauma situation, the assessment will vary according to the patient's medical severity. You will need to monitor the patient's medical condition and intervene accordingly.

Intervention

If the family members are present:

- Your goal is to keep them calm and informed. Obtain any possible medical information on the patient's status (even if it is only "They are running several tests now") to relay to the family for reassurance. Try to keep them calmly in the waiting room. Inform them that a physician or nurse will speak to them as soon as possible.
- It is also helpful to refocus their anxiety. Encouraging them to talk is often helpful. Ask them who they are, what their relationship to the

patient is, what happened, how they got there or learned of it, if there are other family members or clergy who need to be contacted.

If the patient is unidentified or no family or friends are present:

- Check with the ambulance/police/fire rescue who brought in the patient. Inquire where the patient was found, and if anyone at the scene knew the patient.
- Check the hospital's records for any previous admissions that can provide a name, an address, or phone numbers.
- It may be necessary to search the patient's belongings for a piece of information. Use gloves.
- Use the Coles Directory, which provides phone numbers for known addresses. You can then proceed to contact neighbors and others.
- If the patient's address does not have a phone number, it is possible to send a police officer to the home with a message. You need to contact the appropriate district to request this service.

If the code or trauma has resulted in the patient's death:

- Provide emotional support.
- Offer to call any family members or clergy if they desire, or explain that they are free to make unlimited telephone calls. Accompany them.
- If family members wish to view the body, accompany them for support. It is helpful to prepare them for what they may see (e.g., tubes, discoloration) as well as providing tissues, chairs, or anything that might aid with their immediate comfort.
- Explain that they need to contact the funeral home only when they feel able; the funeral home will then locate and retrieve the body from the morgue or the medical examiner's office if they requested an autopsy.
- Make sure that the patient's belongings and valuables are given to the appropriate person.
- If possible, ensure that a spouse or family member does not go home alone or to an empty house.

Abuse

Assessment

Visually assess the patient for the following suspicious injuries:

- Bruises of several colors (indicating they were sustained at different times).
- Bruises that have odd shapes, are clustered, or are located in unusual places for an accident to occur.
- Retinal damage (from being shaken).
- Orbital or facial fractures (if patient was not in a car accident, suspect domestic abuse).

- Rope burns or marks from restraints.
- Signs of hair pulling (bald spots, loose hair, or swollen scalp).
- Fearful behavior (the patient may speak very softly, look around when answering, question the confidentiality of the interview).

Make verbal inquiries:

- Conduct a patient interview without family present, then conduct an interview with the accompanying person to see if there is a conflict of information.
- What were the events that led to the ER admission?
- Who lives in the household (obtain the ages and health of members)?
- Were any family members ever treated for mental health problems?
- What is the patient's past medical history (look for a pattern of "doctor hopping" or similar injuries in the past)?
- How does the patient's caretaker express anger?

Intervention

If child abuse is suspected:

- Patient will be stabilized and transferred to Children's Hospital for further treatment.
- We are required by law to report if abuse is suspected. We also must inform the caretaker that we are doing so. There is no liability for any report made in good faith. Referrals should be made to the state child abuse hotline as well as the local child protective service agency. (Insert child abuse state and city hotline numbers here.)
- Interview the mother privately to ascertain if she is also a victim of abuse.

If spousal abuse is suspected:

- Encourage the victim to file a police report.
- Explain that for his or her own safety, the abuser can be arrested and held in custody and/or the patient take out a Protection Against Abuse order on a 24-hour basis for up to one year.
- Encourage the spouse to call a hotline from the ER. Accompany and assist him or her. (Insert hotline numbers here.)
- Be alert for abuse and neglect in the children.

If elder abuse is suspected:

- Follow the same procedures as you would for spousal abuse and make a referral to elder abuse protective services and a hotline for advocates for the rights of the infirm elderly. (Insert hotline numbers here.)

If the patient alleges rape:

- Patient will be medically stabilized and transferred to a rape crisis treatment center if not available at the hospital. (Insert hotline number here.)

Psychiatric

Assessment

- Is the patient exhibiting behavior that would pose a danger to self or others? If so, contact the nurses to determine if restraints are necessary.
- Review the patient's chart, and consult with accompanying person and with physicians regarding the patient's condition and past mental health history.
- Observe and interview the patient for signs of mental illness (agitation, depression, suicide attempt/overdose, disorientation, etc.).
- Obtain the usual historical information on the presenting problem (symptoms and duration, living situation, precipitating events leading to admission, any history of drugs, alcohol, arrests, medical treatment, etc.).

Intervention

If the patient is medically cleared:

If the patient indicates an acute threat to harm self or others, you *must* call for a psychiatric consult for evaluation.

If psychiatry feels the patient requires inpatient treatment and the patient is willing to enter treatment *voluntarily:*

- If the patient does have insurance, the psychiatrist will arrange for placement.
- If the patient does not have insurance, social work will arrange for placement though the catchment system. The patient's catchment area cannot refuse placement for any reason.
- Provide the patient with a 201 form (voluntary commitment), which he or she is required to sign.

If the psychiatrist has evaluated for inpatient treatment and the patient is resistant, the following procedure is for *involuntary* placement:

- Obtain a 302 form (involuntary commitment).
- The petitioner for placement *must* be the ER physician (if no family member who has witnessed the patient's behavior over the past 30 days is available or willing to petition); the examining physician portion is to be filled out by the psychiatrist. *The social worker is not to fill out any parts of this form.*
- Contact the mental health delegate (insert phone numbers here) to arrange for a receiving facility.
- The patient must be transferred to the facility by ambulance.

If the patient is not medically cleared (admitted):

If the patient is admitted to the hospital *voluntarily:*

- It is only necessary to call a psychiatrist if you, in consult with the ER physicians and nurses, feel suicide precautions are necessary. Psychiatry will then make the ultimate determination if one-on-one companionship is required.

If the patient *refuses* medical admission:

- Contact an administrator. The administrator will need to contact City Hall, which will find a judge on call to issue an Emergency Medical Commitment.

If the patient is homeless with a chronic mental illness:

- You can contact the Mobile Mental Health Unit, which places this population in supervised shelters.

Shelter

Assessment

- First ascertain where the patient stayed the night before or if he or she has friends or family in the area who can provide shelter.
- Ask how long the patient has been without shelter.
- Ask if the patient has ever been to a shelter before; if so, which one?
- Ask if the patient is willing to go to a shelter now if a bed is available. (Patients must be ambulatory for the shelter to accept them.)

Intervention

- If the patient is willing, contact a shelter (a comprehensive listing of shelters is posted in the ER) to see if they have a bed available.
- If there is evidence of a mental health problem, contact the city's Mobile Mental Health Unit (or its equivalent) to arrange for evaluation.
- If there are no beds available anywhere, call the Office of Service to Homeless Adults (OSHA) for outreach (insert phone numbers here). Generally, shelters are available for men only, for women and children, and for families. Referrals for emergency shelter can be made during the evening as well as daytime hours.

Substance Abuse

Assessment

The following questions should be asked during assessment:

- When was the substance last used? What was it? How much was used? What was the method (IV, smoked, snorted, in combination with other substances)?
- How often does the patient use? How long has he or she been drinking or using?
- What are the physical symptoms (e.g., shakes, blackouts, seizures)?
- Has the patient ever been in detoxification or rehabilitation? When, where, and what was the result?
- Is the patient interested in or willing to enter a detoxification or rehabilitation program right now? If so, does he or she want an inpatient or outpatient program?
- What type of insurance does the patient have? Patients must have their insurance card with them as proof of coverage.
- If the patient does not have insurance, contact a referral that will accept him or her.
- Be alert for unsafe environment for children.

Intervention

If the patient is interested in entering a detoxification or rehabilitation program:

- Make sure the patient is medically cleared by the medical staff.
- Make sure that the patient is willing to go immediately from the ER. We will provide a cab voucher if they are unable to pay.
- Contact the patient's insurance company (HMO, Blue Cross, Healthpass, etc.) for precertification. The insurance company will determine where the patient will be referred. The insurance company will call the facility to find a bed and confirm admission; however, this is something we often do to expedite the admission process.

If the patient is uninterested in detoxification or rehabilitation at this time, or would like outpatient help, or it is after hours and facilities are no longer admitting:

- Provide the patient with the pertinent information (the name, address, phone number, and contact person at the agency) and explain the procedure so that he or she can follow up the next day or when ready.

There are assessment and intervention protocols for domestic violence in hospitals and mental health settings (see chapter 19 by Roberts and Roberts in this volume). In addition, for a comprehensive examination of the emerging roles for the emergency room social worker and clinical nurse specialist with battered women, see Boes (1998). For a detailed application of crisis intervention with chemically dependent persons, including polydrug abusers, see chapter 24 by Yeager and Gregiore in this volume.

APPLICATION OF ROBERTS'S SEVEN-STAGE CRISIS INTERVENTION MODEL

Roberts's (1990, p. 42) seven-stage model for crisis intervention provides an excellent guide for crisis workers in hospital emergency departments. In the model, the key element of rapid, accurate assessment is emphasized. Therefore, it is paramount that the emergency room social worker be present from the first moment the crisis presents to the emergency room. The social worker must be considered an integral part of the trauma team; when the words "Trauma Alert" are paged throughout the hospital, the social worker as well as doctors, nurses, respiratory therapists, and lab techs will race to the scene.

Effective intervention with trauma survivors in crisis requires a careful assessment of individual, family, and environmental factors. A crisis by definition is short term and overwhelming. According to Roberts (1990), a crisis can be described as an emotionally distressing change.

Roberts (1991) describes seven stages of working through crisis: (1) assessing lethality and safety needs, (2) establishing rapport and communication,(3) identifying the major problems, (4) dealing with feelings and providing support, (5) exploring possible alternatives, (6) formulating an action plan, and (7) providing follow-up. The seven-stage model applies to a broad range of crises.

Emergency room social workers, however, should recognize that this model is not set up to be rigidly followed in a step-by-step fashion. Instead, the model should be viewed as fluid and adaptable for work in emergency rooms. For example, as new information is made available, such as when a patient's condition is unexpectedly deteriorating, family members and even staff may experience further reactions. Emergency room social workers, therefore, must be attentive to changes in patients and the environment that might influence reactions to the crisis. As the change occurs, the emergency room social worker must be flexible in moving to that part of the model that best corresponds to the current situation. It is important to understand that a key element in crisis intervention is rapid, accurate assessment. This assessment should be holistic, taking into account affective, cognitive, and behavioral reactions (Myer, Williams, Ottens, & Schmidt, 1992).

Assessment also should be continuous, providing the emergency room social workers with information that will facilitate sound clinical judgments (Boes, 1998). Ongoing assessment is essential in determining the needs of patients and their families at that moment. As stated previously, new information may result in emergency room social workers adjusting their approach to match the current state of patients and their families.

Case 1

Use of such a fluid model is invaluable in considering the three case studies presented in this chapter. The case of Mary Winston, gunshot victim, readily lends itself to an application of Roberts's model, beginning with assessing lethality and safety needs. The social worker needs to call Security to manage the safety needs of the woman who smashed all the windows in the ER door. It takes all of the interpersonal skills that a social worker can muster to simultaneously manage the grief of the woman rolling over and over on the floor of the trauma room and also allow for the medical team to continue their work with Mary. The urgency of the present situation may necessitate a call to the nursing supervisor to evaluate the woman to determine if a sedative may be warranted so that the team may continue their efforts. Security again needs to be alerted to the fact that 30 people are stampeding through the hospital banging on patients' doors. A neutral location needs to be established, perhaps the hospital dining room, which can accommodate 30 people at once so that they are removed from the patient floors to assure safety for themselves and patients in the hospital.

The major problem with regard to establishing rapport and communication is that Mary had been such an integral part of so many lives. The level of emotion is so intense and the ability to absorb so many crises simultaneously is indeed a challenge. Once the 30 people are assembled, an immediate priority is that of answering as many concerns as may be addressed. The social worker needs to establish guidelines, for example, that only two people at a time may visit Mary in the trauma room. Before anyone can enter the trauma room, the social worker needs to have the visit approved by the code captain, the physician in charge of running the code and the resuscitation effort. Once this permission is granted, the ER social worker should accompany two people into the trauma room, where chairs should be available should anyone look faint and tissues available for the family's use. In the meantime, the remaining people could be assigned a task such as writing their name, address, phone number, and relationship to Mary. The assigning of a small task may be useful in refocusing attention. While Mary is in surgery, beverages and snacks could be provided to assist with comfort. In establishing rapport, the social worker will encourage the family to tell stories about Mary, to recount how they learned of Mary's tragedy, and will determine who the spokesperson or persons for the family will be.

Mary made it through surgery and was now in the recovery room. The surgeons came to the dining area and informed the family that Mary would be transferred from the recovery room to the intensive care unit. It was explained to the family that only two people could spend the night. Beds were made up for two visitors to stay in the patient lounge, provisions were made for transportation home for the other family members, and consideration was given so that no one would be alone. As the family was about to leave the hospital, Mary died.

Mary's death initiated crisis all over again. One of the girls vomited and the social worker took her to the emergency room for treatment. The family was offered the option of viewing the body, which everyone wished to do. The social worker accompanied two people at a time to the room. An option of calling clergy was also provided by the social worker as well as a discussion of whether or not the family wished for an autopsy. The specifics of what would occur next was explained to the family. If they wanted an autopsy, the body would be transported to the funeral home from the medical examiner's office; if not, it would be picked up from the morgue in the hospital. The social worker offered to call a funeral home and provided the family with telephone use to speak with anyone whom they wished to at that time.

Due to the suddenness of Mary's death, there was extreme shock and anger. One of the boys said that he would be back with a gun. The Philadelphia police were notified and came to the hospital. The major problem appeared to be that Mary was so important to so many people that it seemed she was indispensable. How would the 13 grandchildren whom she had solely raised cope with such a great loss? The emergency room social worker helped the family deal with the immediate crisis and offered her assistance in days to come. Fortunately, the family was large and numerous options were available to them. The social worker dealt with the young boy's feelings who thought that the doctors were killing his grandmother. The social worker explained to the boy that the reason his grandmother's chest had to be cracked was so that the physician could massage her heart back to beating again. Although it looked like the doctor was torturing his grandmother, he was doing his best to save her life.

Many of the situations that confront an ER social worker are extremely complex and complicated. The task, as was true in this case, was to continually prioritize the many crises that were occurring simultaneously. Many alternatives were explored, from providing support, comfort, and privacy to the family during the time they were at the hospital to identifying who would care for whom when they left the hospital.

A very important stage of Roberts's model that can be easily overlooked, especially by an emergency room social worker who is continually dealing with crisis, is that of follow-up. The emotional and physical demands are such that if not given careful consideration, this most important final step can be easily neglected. The family has begun to trust someone who so quickly fades from their lives. Due to this most demanding work, it may be rare that a social worker will take time to attend a funeral, send a sympathy card, or make the crucial follow-up phone calls to assure that the family is safe and to also acknowledge their sadness and assist with referrals and emotional support as needed.

Case 2

For the social worker to intervene effectively, the seven stages of Roberts's crisis intervention model should be followed:

Plan and Conduct a Thorough Assessment for Lethality and Safety Needs

As paramedics exchange with the medical team the status of Chris Jones's condition, "He says he can't breathe," the social worker can help with identification of the client through a search of his belongings. Chris was incoherent and it was difficult to ascertain whether this was due to the effects of intoxication or severe head injury. His orbital area and facial structure were all freely mobile and fractured. A CAT scan revealed that he had swelling in his brain. Chris's condition could quickly deteriorate. One must promptly try to notify next of kin. Chris's wallet only contained the address of his father and that number is unlisted. The social worker used the Coles Directory, a directory organized by address block, to call the next-door neighbor, who agreed to contact the father. Chris has suffered a severe skull fracture and his brain is swelling; he is lapsing into a coma.

Establish Rapport and Communication

The social worker with the doctor meets the family in a private room to describe the dimension of the problem. The social worker uses warmth, acceptance, empathy, caring, and reassurance to provide support and convey the feeling that the social worker is on the family's side and will be a helping person. Crying or angry outbursts are not discouraged but are seen as a positive release of feeling. Only when feelings seem out of control, such as in extreme rage or despondency, should the social worker shift to help the family member concentrate on thinking rather than feeling (Stuart & Sundeen, 1995).

Identify the Major Problems

Helping to ease the impact of the initial wave of shock and grief reaction to the crisis, the social worker escorts the family to the bedside after first warning them that the sight of all the lines and tubes can be distressing. Sensing the family's feeling of powerlessness, she will encourage communication between the family and Chris through nonverbals: handholding and touch. They first are afraid to go near him. Even if he cannot respond, she emphasizes, perhaps he can still hear them, so it is important to talk hopefully and lovingly.

Returning the patient and his family to their previous level of functioning is the goal of crisis intervention. Yet, it is uncertain whether Chris will ever emerge from his coma. Even if he should recover, the rehabilitation process will be long, slow, and difficult. Initially, Chris's mood and affect will be erratic, with many angry outbursts. He might even have some amnesia and permanent change of his personality. All this needs to be explained to the family. He might have to relearn basic skills such as reading, writing, and walking through long months of therapy. His role as breadwinner for the family is threatened for the short term, and perhaps permanently.

During this phase, the clinician should help the family to focus on the most important problem as they see it by having them rank and prioritize several problems and the harmful or potentially threatening aspect of the primary problem. It is important and most productive to help clients ventilate about the precipitating event; this will lead to problem identification (Roberts, 1996).

Dealing With Feelings and Providing Support

This stage involves active listening, communicating with warmth and reassurance, nonjudgmental statements, and validation with accurate empathic statements. The family in crisis might have multiple mood swings throughout the crisis intervention; therefore, Roberts suggests the use of verbal counseling skills to help the clients explore their emotions. These verbal responses include reflecting feelings, restating content, using open-ended questions, summarizing, giving advice and reassurance, interpreting statements, confronting, and using silence.

Throughout this long and uncertain vigil, Chris's parents, wife, and children will need further intervention in dealing with their grief. A referral is made to the in-house social worker for daily contact with the family. The elderly parents remain the most hopeful and are at Chris's bedside daily. They will need encouragement to take turns to rest and to spend time caring for themselves. While the doctors gave a dire prognosis, doubting Chris will ever recover and emerge from his coma, his parents are proven to be ultimately correct. Within two weeks, Chris grasps his father's hand, and after three weeks is able to give a thumbs-up signal.

Generate and Explore Alternatives

Because clients are emotionally distressed and consumed by the aftermath of the crisis episode, it is very useful to have an objective and trained clinician assist them in conceptualizing and discussing adaptive coping responses to the crisis. During this potentially highly productive stage, the social worker and clients collaboratively agree on appropriate alternative coping methods.

Chris's wife lives 200 miles from the hospital. After discussion of options, the social worker arranges for her and the children to stay at the local Ronald McDonald House. The family wants Chris placed in a rehabilitation center near his home. The children need counseling to understand the changes in their dad's personality.

The social worker had quickly assessed the high level of the wife's panic and distress and promptly utilized all the available community resources. This helped allay the wife's fears that the entire family unit would collapse.

Develop and Formulate an Action Plan

This will ultimately restore cognitive functioning for the clients. The precipitating event of Chris's car accident has threatened the family with the loss of a son, husband, and father. Many clients have great difficulty mobilizing themselves and following through on an action plan. It is imperative that clients be encouraged and bolstered so they will follow through. The social worker provides support, an opportunity to freely ventilate their feelings, and and a way to move on to explore their options. The clinician continues to act as a liaison between the family and the medical staff to break down all medical jargon into lay language. The family sits numbly, apparently listening to the doctors, but in their state of anxiety find they can't recall specifics or fully understand. The social worker's action plan will be to support the use of healthy, adaptive defenses, while helping the family take a more active role in exploring solutions of how to best cope. Ultimately, the parents and wife and children decide to band together while Chris recovers in a rehab center in their hometown. This eliminates the wife's panic and worry about how to pay all the bills and feed and care for the children. While still supporting Chris by visiting him, the grandfather will call Chris's job to ascertain his disability coverage and file the necessary papers.

Providing Follow-up

Stage 7 in crisis intervention should involve an informal agreement or formal appointment between the social worker and the family to have another meeting at a designated time, either in person or on the phone, to gauge the family's success in crisis resolution and daily functioning one week, two weeks, or one month later. The family decides to initiate the first phone call in two weeks and report that they are returning to the precrisis level of functioning and continue to rely on support systems while using constructive coping mechanisms.

Case 3

Let us now turn to the case of Paul, the 9-year-old burn and smoke-inhalation victim whose injuries resulted from his father's lit cigarette. First, the ER nurses carefully examine Paul to ensure that all burning has been stopped and cooled. Events within the first hour after injury can make the difference between life and death in a thermally injured patient. During the emergent phase, immediately after injury, medical care focused on the stabilization of the patient's condition. Simultaneously, Roberts's model for crisis intervention provides an excellent guide for crisis workers in the emergency department. Again, the key element of rapid, accurate assessment is emphasized. During the emergent phase of this crisis, the social worker makes the required referrals to the police and child protective services. Then she turns her attention to the grieving and hysterical family members.

In this severe emergency, as in all such crises, the social worker must play a dual role. He or she must gather and record pertinent information about the circumstances that led to the injury and at the same time offer much needed psychological support to prevent traumatization and promote healing at a later stage. By all means, an accusatory demeanor must be avoided. Sometimes in a family crisis such as this, the surviving parent will lash out at his or her troublesome and troubled children. In such a situation, the social worker as an objective arbiter can help enormously to subdue the children's pain and provide an element of calm and caring in a moment of catastrophe. Research shows that the initial encounter between a crisis survivor and a trusted individual, especially one in an authority role, has more impact on his or her eventual recovery than almost anything else (Schwartz & DeKeseredy, 1997; van Wormer & Bartollas, 2000).

RESILIENCY AND THE RESOLUTION OF CRISIS

> [Most crises] call into question the way you love and what's important. This "wake up call" leads to a whole reshifting of values. We suddenly realize that very little is random or trivial, and that life is full of opportunities to love and connect and grow in wisdom. We're not a special group of people here, we're just human beings, frightened, lonely, hurting, and able to grow in response to crisis. (Moyers, 1993)

Feelings of powerlessness awaken panic, which lessens one's powers to effectively cope through a crisis. Panic is like the pessimistic person who turns out all the lights just to see how dark it is. One would never attempt to drive at night down a steep and treacherous cliffside road without headlights. Paradoxically, at the very moment of crisis, when one needs to summon all reservoirs of courage and clear-headed decision making, one can be rendered least capable of doing so.

The social worker's belief in the capacity for growth-oriented change (Saleebey, 1997) is the first step in reestablishing people's faith in their capacity to recover from the crisis event and to return to a precrisis level of functioning. A more ambitious expected outcome is for the patient to recover from the crisis event to a higher than precrisis level of functioning and to an improved quality of life (Stuart & Sundeen, 1995).

The Kennedy family is often alluded to as having great resilience: the ability to bounce back bravely, still vitally immersed in facing life's challenges after suffering so many violent and premature losses of family members. Yet,

> it is not a specific group of individuals who are resilient; rather, each individual has the capacity for resilience, at least potentially. It was formerly thought that resilience was an exclusive property of certain kinds of people blessed with particular genetic/constitutional characteristics, interpersonal relationships, traits and environments. Now the effort is to discover the processes by which anyone might rebound or regenerate following adversity or decline. (Saleebey, 1997)

As Mahrer (1978) explains, "In achieving higher levels of actualization, the aim is to bring into the realm of experiencing the potentials which are present within the person. . . . Sometimes to a very large extent. . . . This calls for guts, courage and hard work."

Before crisis threatens to overwhelm an individual, the social worker, using Roberts's (1990) seven-stage crisis intervention model, alleviates anxiety and supports the emergence of the client's inner strength, for this model facilitates the early identification of crisis precipitants and promotes problem solving and effective crisis resolution. From acknowledging the pain, grief, rage, and confusion stemming from a precipitating crisis through to follow-up, "The purpose is to always look for the seeds of resilience and rebound" (Saleebey, 1997).

CONCLUSION

As emergency rooms increasingly have become the only access to care available, some means is required to identify and alleviate those conditions that produce, precipitate, and perpetuate poor physical and emotional health. One way to achieve early identification and remediation is by crisis intervention, and a hospital emergency room provides one obvious setting for the initiation of this type of service. Yet, because of the volume of patients to be seen and the acute nature of medical treatment, emergency room medical staff are often unable to provide the level of psychosocial care required by patients and their families. Social work coverage and services in emergency rooms are invaluable in meeting patients' long-term as well as short-term needs. Roberts's seven-stage model of crisis intervention is an excellent model for emergency room social workers.

Ponto and Berg (1992) examined 61 patients to determine the cost-benefits of an extended coverage program in an emergency room using master's-level social workers from the community. Results of this study demonstrated that the program operated at only a marginal monetary cost to the hospital; however, the monetary gains for patients, other health professionals, and the hospital were not assessed.

Key to the adoption of evidence-based practice by social work practitioners are the critical thinking and technical skills necessary for identifying and articulating knowledge needs in practice and for efficiently locating and evaluating research evidence relevant to these needs (Cournoyer & Powers, 2002; Howard, McMillan, & Pollio, 2003). The evidence-based practice movement is consistent with social work ethical principles of using the most effective treatments. At the same time, helping practitioners to obtain the latest information and integrate it into their practice presents many challenges. The literature from health care suggests that disseminating information alone is insufficient. Many interventions have been designed to improve practitioners' adherence to evidence-based practice guidelines and are differentially effective. To date, no intervention has demonstrated powerful effects.

Much needs to be learned about how various strategies to supply workers with the latest research knowledge might apply to social work. At the same time, a major lesson from the health field is that multiple strategies are more likely to provide workers with what they need. Social workers' attitudes toward evidence-based practice and barriers to change need to be assessed, and a combination of appropriate interventions to change practice behavior can then be planned and implemented and the progress evaluated. Finally, the hospital emergency room will need to plan for maintenance of workers' gains. Recognizing the difficulties of evidence-based practice may not only help avoid these difficulties but also help overcome cultural beliefs and values held by social workers that challenge the use of evidence-based practice.

REFERENCES

Boes, M. (1997). A typology for establishing social work staffing patterns within an emergency room. *Crisis Intervention, 3,* 171–188.

Boes, M. (1998). Battered women in the emergency room. In A. R. Roberts (Ed.), *Battered women and their families: Intervention strategies and treatment approaches* (2nd ed., pp. 205–229). New York: Springer.

Cournoyer, B. R., & Powers, G. T. (2002). Evidence-based social work: The quiet revolution continues. In A. R. Roberts & G. J. Greene (Eds.), *Social workers' desk reference* (pp. 798–807). New York: Oxford University Press.

Demling, R. H., & LaLonde, C. (1989). *Burn trauma.* New York: Thiene Medical Publishers.

Glaser, B. G., & Strauss, A. (1966). *Awareness of dying.* Chicago: Aldine.

Howard, M. O., McMillan, C. J., & Pollio, D. E. (2003). Teaching evidence-based practice: Toward a new paradigm for social work education. *Research on Social Work Practice 13*, 234–259.

Mahrer, A. (1978). *Experiencing a humanistic theory of psychology and psychiatry.* New York: Brunner/Mazel.

Moyers, B. (1993). *Healing and the mind.* New York: Doubleday.

Myer, R. A., & Hanna, F. J. (1996). Working in hospital emergency departments: Guidelines for crisis intervention workers. In A. R. Roberts (Ed.), *Crisis management and brief treatment: Theory, technique, and applications* (pp. 37–59). Belmont, CA: Wadsworth.

Myer, R. A., Williams, R. C., Ottens, A. J., & Schmidt, A. E. (1992). Crisis assessment: A three-dimensional model for triage. *Journal of Mental Health Counseling, 14*, 137–148.

Ponto, J. M., & Berg, W. (1992). Social work services in the emergency department: A cost-benefit analysis of an extended coverage program. *Health and Social Work, 17*, 66–73.

Roberts, A. R. (1990). An overview of crisis theory and crisis intervention. In A. R. Roberts (Ed.), *Crisis intervention handbook: Assessment, treatment, and research* (pp. 3–16). Belmont, CA: Wadsworth.

Roberts, A. R. (1991). Conceptualizing crisis theory and the crisis intervention model. In A. R. Roberts (Ed.), *Contemporary perspectives on crisis intervention and prevention* (pp. 3–17). Englewood Cliffs, NJ: Prentice-Hall.

Roberts, A. R. (1996). The epidemiology of acute crisis in American society. In A. R. Roberts (Ed.), *Crisis management and brief treatment* (pp. 13–27). Belmont, CA: Wadsworth.

Saleebey, D. (1997). *The strengths perspective in social work practice* (2nd ed.). New York: Longman.

Schwartz, M. D., & DeKeseredy, W. (1997). *Sexual assault on the college campus: The role of male peer support.* Thousand Oaks, CA: Sage.

Stuart, G., & Sundeen, S. (1995). *Principles and practice of psychiatric nursing.* St. Louis: Mosby.

van Wormer, K., & Bartollas, C. (2000). *Women and the criminal justice system: Gender, race, and class.* Boston: Allyn & Bacon.

24

Crisis Intervention Application of Brief Solution-Focused Therapy in Addictions

KENNETH R. YEAGER
THOMAS K. GREGOIRE

Application of Roberts's seven-stage crisis intervention model in substance dependence treatment is presented in this chapter, combined with a strengths perspective and brief solution-focused therapy. Additionally, the authors discuss factors of resilience and methods to capitalize on potential resilience factors within the framework of solution-focused approaches. Application of crisis intervention in addictions encompasses three cases from a direct practice viewpoint, integrating key factors into concise case autopsies utilizing this approach. Finally, the authors provide a brief discussion of evidence-based practice in the field of addiction treatment.

The examples that follow provide a brief outline of the case examples to be detailed throughout this chapter:

Case 1

Dennis is a 41-year-old White male who progresses rapidly through crack cocaine dependence. Consumed by overwhelming cravings for cocaine, Dennis abandons his wife, children, business, and responsibilities. As he seeks comfort in crack cocaine and sex, he progresses into a repetitive cycle of craving, use, and pornography. Having lost all that is important in his life, Dennis presents seeking stabilization from his addiction.

This case demonstrates practical application of Roberts's model as a method to stabilize the individual and how this model can be utilized to develop effective treatment planning within the time constraints of a managed care treatment climate.

The second case of Susan examines Roberts's model in combination with the strengths perspective in addressing opioid addiction in the chronic pain client.

Case 2

Susan's pain is the result of several automobile accidents. Her chronic pain serves as the backdrop for compulsive behaviors rooted in her preoccupation with minimizing her pain while at the same time feeding her addiction. Susan presents in crisis, fearing legal consequences and being cut off from her supply of pain medications.

In this case application, Roberts's model demonstrates effective methods for brief interventions building on the strengths of the addicted chronic pain patient. Application in this case deflects the client's natural defense structures, assisting her to build on her supports rather than remaining entrenched in the agony of her injuries.

Case 3

Scott is a 20-year-old polysubstance-dependent individual who presents in acute withdrawal from several substances, including cocaine, heroin, and methamphetamine. Scott's use began at age 12 and has progressed to complete loss of control. At this point Scott has been asked to leave the university he has been attending and not to return to his parents' home after stealing a large amount of money from his parents. Scott presents in active withdrawal to the treatment center accompanied by his grandfather, who hopes the center can assist his grandson in reclaiming all aspects of his life through the process of recovery.

This case demonstrates how Roberts's model is combined with solution-focused theory to lead the client toward a greater assumption of self-responsibility in the development of a self-directed program of recovery. It demonstrates application of the miracle and exception questions in day-to-day practice as Scott moves through the stages of crisis intervention. Scott's story illustrates the effectiveness of combined solution-focused theory and Roberts's crisis intervention model in addressing issues that reach beyond the issue of dependence to move the patient through the process of recovery.

CRISIS OVERVIEW

The experience of crisis is an inescapable reality. For some, crisis may occur only infrequently. For others, crisis occurs frequently, with one crisis leading to another. Just as crises occur at varying intervals for individuals, there are variances in an individual's ability to cope with crisis (Roberts & Dziegielewski, 1995). Some are able to "work through" their perceptions and reactions to the event with little intervention. For many, however, successful resolution of a crisis event requires skillful intervention to clarify the individual's response to the event (Roberts, 1990).

Crisis intervention consistently occurs when one is addressing substance dependence. Persons presenting for substance dependence treatment frequently find themselves seeking assistance following a crisis or possibly a series of crises. Psychiatrist, psychologist, and social workers functioning within the managed care delivery system have been challenged to provide cost-effective treatment within the least restrictive environment. Professionals practicing in addiction treatments are finding that crisis intervention skills combined with brief solution-focused intervention strategies are effective when applied in today's abbreviated lengths of stay.

Managed care has hastened a fundamental shift in substance abuse treatment delivery. Increasingly, outpatient treatment has supplanted residential treatment, and programs now experience greater variation in both lengths of stay and types of interventions (Book et al., 1995). Cost savings attained in the private sector have led a number of states to implement similar approaches with public programs (Gartner & Mee-Lee, 1995). At least 40 states currently have some type of managed behavioral health care program for public mental health and/or substance abuse, and 5 other states have programs in development (Toff-Bergman, 1998).

However, a number of authors have expressed concern about the consequences of managed care programs for clients. Etheridge, Craddock, Dunteman, and Hubbard (1995) documented substantial declines in treatment services provided over the past decade. Their findings included a considerable increase in the number of clients reporting unmet service needs. Ford (1998) suggested that managed care approaches restrict treatment emphasis to short-term needs. Additional studies of public managed care programs have identified increased levels of client severity (Beinecke, Callahan, Shepard, Cavanaugh, & Larson, 1997) and a reduction in level of care occurring independent of severity (Thompson, Burns, Goldman, & Smith, 1992). Other authors have questioned whether the managed care approach can meet the needs of vulnerable populations (Platt, Widman, Lidz, Rubenstein, & Thompson, 1998; Rivers, 1998; Kusher & Moss, 1995; Wells, Astrachan, Tischler, & Unutzer, 1995). Despite these concerns, many program administrators anticipate making further reductions in the intensity of service because of continuing funding limitations (Rivers, 1998).

Managed care challenges addiction practitioners to rethink treatment strategies. Treating clients in longer term residential settings seems increasingly to be a bygone luxury. Practitioners in the addiction treatment field will continue to experience pressure to provide brief time-limited treatments, and to increase their ability to respond to clients in crisis in a timely, effective manner. In the future, expertise in crisis intervention may become the defining characteristic of the effective addiction counselor.

ESTIMATES OF THE SUBSTANCE DEPENDENCE PROBLEM IN AMERICA

Substance abuse and dependence treatment as a profession continues to adapt to emerging data and facts associated with current prevalence and trends in the United States. For a number of years, the National Household Survey on Drug Abuse (NHSDA) has been considered the gold standard for measuring prevalence of substance abuse and dependence in the United States. This report continues to present estimated treatment need through treatment gap analysis based on estimates of alcohol and drug dependence and abuse.

Estimates of dependence have been included in the survey since 1991 and are based on the criteria established by the American Psychiatric Association (APA) in its *Diagnostic and Statistical Manual of Mental Disorders* (*DSM-III-R* and *DSM-VI-TR;* APA, 1987, 1994), depending on the year of the survey conducted and APA releases. Questions in the 1991–1993 NHSDAs were based on the *DSM-III-R* definition of dependence and abuse. The 1994–2000 NHSDAs were based on the *DSM-IV* definition of dependence and abuse.

Alcohol

About half (51%) of Americans age 12 or older reported being current drinkers of alcohol in the 2002 survey. This translates to an estimated 120 million people. More than one-fifth (22.9%) of persons age 12 or older participated in binge drinking at least once in the 30 days prior to the survey. This translates to about 54 million people.

In 2002, 51% of persons age 12 or older reported being "current" drinkers, having drunk within the prior 30 days. Current drinkers age 12–17 and young adults age 18–25 drank more drinks per day on the days they drank alcohol than adults age 26 or older. Additionally, current drinkers age 18–25 were more likely to drive under the influence of alcohol during the past 30 days than drinkers age 26 or older. Current drinking rates were higher among young adults 18–25 (61%) than adults age 26 or older (54%). A higher percentage of males used alcohol during the past month (57%) than females (45%). Past month alcohol use was higher among Whites

(55%) than American Indians or Alaska Natives (45%), Hispanics (43%), Blacks (40%), or Asians (37%). Heavy drinking was reported by 6.7% of the population age 12 or older, or 15.9 million people (SAMSHA, 2002).

Drugs

In 2002, an estimated 19.5 million Americans age 12 or older were current illicit drug users, meaning they had used an illicit drug during the month prior to the survey interview. This estimate represents 8.3% of the population age 12 years old or older.

Marijuana is the most commonly used illicit drug. In 2002, it was used by 75% of current illicit drug users. Approximately 55% of current illicit drug users used only marijuana, 20% used marijuana and another illicit drug, and the remaining 25% used an illicit drug but not marijuana in the prior month. About 45% of current illicit drug users in 2002 (8.8 million Americans) used illicit drugs other than marijuana and hashish, with or without using marijuana as well.

In 2002, an estimated 2 million persons (0.9%) were current cocaine users, 567,000 of whom used crack during the same period (0.2%). Hallucinogens were used by 1.2 million persons (0.5%), including 676,000 users of Ecstasy (0.3%). There were an estimated 166,000 current heroin users (0.1%). Of the 8.8 million current users of illicit drugs other than marijuana, 6.2 million were current users of psychotherapeutic drugs. This represents 2.6% of the population age 12 or older. Of those who reported current use of any psychotherapeutics, 4.4 million used pain relievers, 1.8 million used tranquilizers, 1.2 million used stimulants, and 0.4 million used sedatives (SAMSHA, 2002).

Treatment Delivery Gap

In 2002, the estimated number of persons age 12 or older needing treatment for an alcohol or illicit drug problem was 22.8 million (9.7% of the total population). Of this population, approximately 2.3 million persons (1% of the total population age 12 or older; 10.3% of those who needed treatment) received treatment at a specialty substance abuse facility in the prior 12 months. More important, 20.5 million persons (8.7% of the total population) did not receive treatment at a specialty substance abuse facility. This trend has remained consistent across the United States, demonstrating a remarkable gap in the substance dependence treatment continuum (NSDUH, 2003).

Prevalence of Severe Mental Illness

In 2002, there were an estimated 17.5 million adults age 18 or older with SMI. This represents 8.3% of all adults. Rates of SMI were highest for persons age 18 to 25 (13.2%) and lowest for persons age 50 or older (4.9%). Among adults, the percentage of females with SMI was higher than the percentage of males (10.5% vs. 6%). Rates were higher for women than men in all age groups (NSDUH, 2004).

Adults who used illicit drugs were more than twice as likely to have SMI as adults who did not use an illicit drug. In 2002, among adults who used illicit drugs in the prior year, 17.1% had SMI; in that year, this rate was 6.9% among adults who did not use an illicit drug. The pattern of higher rates of SMI among illicit drug users has been observed in most demographic subgroups. Additionally, those adults with SMI were more than twice as likely as those without SMI to have used an illicit drug in the prior year.

In the population of persons with SMI, 28.9% used an illicit drug in the prior year, while the rate was 12.7% among those without SMI. Among adults with SMI, the rate of past year cigarette use was 49.3%, while the rate was only 29.9% among adults without SMI. Among adults who were not in the labor force, those with SMI were approximately three times more likely to have used illicit drugs in the prior year (21.2%) as those without SMI (6.9%; NSDUH, 2004).

Substance dependence treatment as a profession is in a state of transition, struggling to develop cost-effective treatment approaches as the prevalence of alcohol and drug use and abuse continues to escalate in the United States. The Substance Abuse and Mental Health Services Administration (SAMHSA) indicates that increasing numbers of individuals are reporting the use of mood-altering substances (SAMHSA, 1998). These reported results are the culmination of the National Household Survey on Drug Abuse, an annual survey that is conducted by SAMHSA and reports estimates of the prevalence of use of a variety of illicit drugs, alcohol, and tobacco. The survey is based on a nationally representative sample of civilian noninstitutionalized persons age 12 years and older.

In 1997, the National Institute on Drug Abuse Survey reported approximately 111 million persons age 12 or over were current alcohol users, which was about 51% of the total population age 12 and older. Approximately, 31.9 million persons (15.3%) engaged in binge drinking, and approximately 11.2 million (5.4% of the population) were heavy drinkers (SAMHSA, 1998).

The National Household Survey estimated that 13.9 million Americans were current users of illicit drugs. The term *current users* was defined as a person who has used an illicit drug sometime in the 30 days prior to the survey interview. Of those identifying as current substance users, nearly 1 in 10 youth age 12 to 17 reported current use of marijuana. The number of youth identifying as marijuana users more than doubled from 1992 to 1997 (SAMHSA, 1998).

There has been an increasing trend in the use of heroin since 1992 as well. Estimates of heroin use ranged from 68,000 persons in 1993 (less than 0.1% of the population) to approximately 325,000 persons in 1997. Estimates of current use of cocaine remain steady, with approximately 1.5 million persons reporting current use. This number represents 0.7% of the population age 12 and older (SAMHSA, 1998).

Additionally, more than half of all youth age 12 to 17 reported that marijuana was easily obtained. Approximately 21% of the same group reported that heroin was easy to obtain. Overall, approximately 15% of the youth population reported being approached by someone offering to sell them drugs within the 30 days prior to the survey (SAMHSA, 1998).

The following list summarizes the prevalence of diagnosis and treatment considerations within the population presenting to the treatment center where these composite case examples were developed:

Substance	Presenting (%)
Alcohol, only	42.0
Polysubstance	58.0
Cocaine	41.6
Opioid	27.2
Sedative hypnotic	14.1
Cannabis	12.5
Other	4.6

These diagnoses were by percentage of Ohio State University Hospitals East Talbot Hall patient population, average of fiscal years 1997 and 1998.

DEFINITIONS OF DEPENDENCE, ACUTE STRESSORS, AND CRISIS EVENT

Crisis events within the substance-dependent population vary somewhat from traditional models of crisis, yet there remains one overwhelming similarity. This is the failure of an individual's coping strategies to ameliorate a current crisis. Frequently, within the substance-dependent population physiological factors work to precipitate crisis as the individual experiences loss of control over his or her use.

Crisis events within the substance-dependent population vary somewhat from the experience of crisis in other disciplines. Persons with addiction problems are highly motivated to maintain the status quo, at least with respect to their substance use. Addicts often make excessive use of denial and other defense mechanisms to avoid crisis and protect their lifestyle. Consequently, practitioners often see clients only in extreme distress and may experience a brief window in which to engage the client. It is at this time that the individual's temporary loss of control creates a willingness to engage in new behaviors to address the crisis event. The applications of brief crisis models, such as that described here, are very advantageous in assisting individuals with an alcohol or other drug problem (Ewing, 1990; Parad & Parad, 1990; Norman, Turner, & Zunz, 1994).

Definitions of substance dependence have varied over the years. For many, the "disease concept" of substance dependence is the primary diagnostic tool. Two examples of diagnostic definitions for substance dependence are those of the World Health Organization and the American Psychiatric Association, which to this day remain the primary diagnostic criteria for substance dependence.

- World Health Organization (1974) A state, psychic and sometimes also physical, resulting from the interaction between a living organism and a drug, characterized by behavioral and other responses that always include a compulsion to take the drug on a continuous or periodic basis in order to experience its psychic effects, and sometimes to avoid the discomfort of its absence.
- The American Psychiatric Association's DSM IV (1994), the accepted diagnostic tool for the profession of social work, defines substance abuse and dependency with varying criteria for each category. It is of interest to note that the DSM-IV separates dependence with physiological dependence from substance dependence without physical dependence. This distinction is an addition to the criteria of dependence. This is likely because of the prevalence of crack cocaine and the recent reemergence of hallucinogenic drugs that do not appear to cause physical dependence. Two components separate abuse from dependence.

A simplistic definition of *substance dependence* is: "If alcohol/drugs are causing problems in your life, . . . then you likely have a problem with alcohol/drugs." This is the case when approaching addiction from a crisis intervention perspective. Persons entering treatment frequently report that the coping mechanisms they used in the past are not working. If the individual could "control" her or his use or life circumstances, there would be no need to seek assistance. Wallace's (1983, 1989), biopsychosocial model of addiction highlights the pervasiveness of alcohol and other drug problems. Crisis for persons with this disorder is just as likely to be precipitated by intrapsychic discomfort, social conflict, or the physiological consequences of continued substance use. Effective evaluation of the crisis mandates that practitioners attend to each area.

APPLICATION OF ROBERTS'S SEVEN-STAGE CRISIS INTERVENTION MODEL AND ANALYSIS OF RISK AND PROTECTIVE FACTORS

Within Roberts's crisis intervention model applied to substance dependence, the social worker must be aware of the delicate balance between stabilization and removal of motivation for treatment. Chemical-dependent persons use maladaptive defense structures combined with numerous irrational beliefs to minimize the extent and severity of their dependence. Crisis intervention often involves addressing the individual's rationalizations, justifications, catastrophizing, and use of negative self-talk to work his or her way out of treatment (Roberts, 1990; Dattilio & Freeman, 1994; Greene, Lee, & Trask, 1996).

To this end, there are differences between the substance-dependent population and the general population seeking assistance. Roberts initially reported the seven-stage model, which identified establishment of rapport as the first stage. In a review of Roberts's work as applied by professionals in clinical practice, one can see the ongoing development of this model. Subsequent publications by Roberts recommend interchanging assessment of lethality (stage 2) with establishment of rapport (stage 1), depending on the presenting problem(s) of the patient (Roberts, 1996).

This is particularly true of cocaine-dependent persons, who experience tremendously intense crises in short periods of time, yet because there is little withdrawal, cocaine-dependent persons may mistake crisis stabilization as an all clear to resume use (Yeager, 1999). The inertia of the recovery environment is extremely powerful; when combined with the powerful cravings frequently associated with crack cocaine, the equation is complete for the relapse process. Second, special emphasis must be placed on examination of the dimensions of the problem (stage 2), exploration of feelings and emotions (stage 3), and exploration of past coping attempts. Emphasis on these steps will assure the substance-dependent individuals of remaining connected with treatment. The following example of crisis intervention with a cocaine-addicted individual demonstrates this process (Roberts, 1990). Table 24.1 provides an overview of Roberts's seven-stage model and compatible solution focused interventions.

Case Study 1: Dennis

Dennis E., Cocaine Dependent

Dennis is a 41-year-old self-employed chemical researcher who presented following "being pattern" episode of cocaine use. Dennis reported being sober for a 10-year period following treatment for alcohol dependence. Dennis eventually began to taper off his attendance of 12-step support meetings as his family and business grew. Dennis is married with two children, age 8 and 11. His younger daughter was diagnosed with leukemia 1 year ago. Dennis reports being very close to his daughters, stating that he reads to them every evening and never misses a doctor's appointment with his younger daughter. Dennis is extremely successful in his work. He reports having secured government contracts for the next 5 years that total millions of dollars of profits for his company. He reports that at this time last year he was receiving an award for "researcher of the year." His plan was to celebrate with a glass of wine.

Table 24.1 Roberts's Seven-Stage Model and Solution-Focused Applications

Stage	Application
Make psychological contact.	Acceptance, Support, Empathy, Mirroring nonverbal communication.
Examine the dimensions of the problem in order to define it.	Scaling, Examination of resilience factors, Empowering the patient, Assess support factors.
Encourage exploration of feelings and emotions.	Acceptance, Support, Empathy.
Explore and assess past coping attempts.	Exception question, Scaling question, Past success.
Generate and explore alternatives and specific solutions.	Miracle question, Exception question, past success, Prediction task, Track current success.
Restore cognitive functioning through implementation of action plan.	Scaling, Empowerment, Exception question, Past success tracking, Track current success.
Follow-up.	Scaling in the form of outcome studies.

Note: This chart is a representation of techniques to use with each stage of Roberts's model. The absence of assessment of lethality as presented in additional publications by Roberts is due to the use of solution-focused therapy as persons progress through the process of recovery. This is not indicative that patients presenting for substance dependence may not experience lethality issues. Work with persons who are substance dependent requires ongoing mental status assessment.

Following this event, there were no apparent consequences. Approximately 1 week later, Dennis drank again, this time at a ball game, to the point of intoxication. Again, there were no consequences. The next day he was extremely tired and was faced with deadlines in his work. He purchased a gram of cocaine, worked 27 hours straight, and completed two projects, including a million-dollar grant application.

Dennis believed he had successfully found the "old Dennis," the one who could work for hours with no breaks. Dennis states, that his relapse was "a major memory event." He reports his thinking instantly reverted to where his thoughts were in his previous addiction to alcohol. His use of cocaine rapidly increased. Within a 1-month period, he was using 3 grams of cocaine daily. In an attempt to save money, he began to smoke crack cocaine.

The introduction of crack cocaine led to isolative patterns of use. Dennis recalls the panic he felt at 3:00 A.M. when he realized that his staff would be returning to work in a few hours, knowing that he would not be able to continue to use cocaine within the confines of his office. Acting on impulse, Dennis removed his computer from his office and drove to a motel with approximately $3,000 of cocaine. With nothing to do in the motel, Dennis began visiting pornographic sites on the Internet. He reports becoming preoccupied with these sites. Caught in a cycle of crack cocaine use, he found that sexual fantasy, paranoia, and isolation began to dominate and control his behaviors. He was particularly occupied with an interactive XXX site; he reports engaging in fantasy, substituting acquaintances for the persons with whom he was interacting. It was not until the supply of cocaine was depleted that the cycle was broken.

Dennis was missing for 4 days before returning home. He had missed two doctor's appointments with his daughter and reports pending separation between him and his wife. Dennis identifies the separation as the precipitating event for seeking treatment. Within the initial contact, he acknowledged hoping his heart would explode so he would not have to face the disappointment of his family following his relapse. He quickly added that death would have been easier to face than having to look at the sadness in his daughter's eyes.

Seeking to understand the severity of Dennis's situation, fears, and feelings led to the rapid establishment of a working relationship (Roberts, 1990). Making psychological contact with Dennis consisted of showing a genuine interest in and respect for him and offering hope. Dennis, like many cocaine addicts, found it easy to share where he had been. What is difficult for many in early recovery is the ability to see a way out of the insanity associated with their cocaine dependence. Letting Dennis know that he was not the first to present with this problem simply did not reduce his anxiety. He was in need of hearing that there are common symptoms associated with cocaine dependence, including physical, mental, and emotional preoccupations with the drug. Although this discussion was helpful, remarkable anxiety remained. There was no significant reduction in tension until discussion of sexual preoccupation occurred. At this point, it became clear that cocaine use had taken Dennis to a place he had not anticipated. Avoiding pushing Dennis away by discussing this issue in detail, the therapist assured him that many authors had discussed the concurrent sexual component with cocaine dependence (Hser, Chou, Yih-ling, Hoffman, Chih-Ping, & Anglin, 1999; Balsheim, Oxman, Van Rooyen, & Girod, 1992). Offering to provide Dennis with information related to this topic, and connecting him with a cocaine-specific group to address this issue seemed to provide a combination of understanding and awareness of resources. This minimized the anxiety carried into the initial session.

The second step in crisis intervention as outlined by Roberts is "examining the dimensions of the problem in order to define it." In this area, a couple of issues required further examination. First was gaining a greater degree of insight into the precipitating event that led Dennis to the treatment center on this date. The therapist used probing questions to expand the information provided initially (Roberts, 1990).

Q: Dennis, you said the pending separation was what led you to seeking help. Can you tell me more about what happened?

A: When I did finally go home, there weren't any questions of "Where were you?" "Are you all right?" or "Thank God you're home!" There was only silence and sadness. When the silence was broken, it was by the sobs of Tiffany. She was trying hard not to . . . but there was no way she could hold back. I knew she was torn between her mother's instructions and her wanting to make sure I was O.K. God just knowing that my daughter . . . after all she had been through . . . was worried

> about me, she was a victim of my use . . . I just couldn't take it. I asked Donna to take me to treatment. There was no answer. Instead, she handed me separation papers and said, "We had an agreement. If you use, we have to leave." I knew she was right, so I got in the car and drove myself. I can't bear the thought of living my life without them.

This account provided much more information and understanding than the previous answer of pending separation. There was greater understanding of the pain Dennis and his family were experiencing. It also provided information surrounding Donna's willingness to do what was best for herself and the children. Dennis knew this was what needed to happen, but he acknowledged that knowing what needed to happen did not make it any less painful (Roberts, 1990; DeJong & Miller, 1995).

Contained within the information provided by Dennis is the third step of Roberts's seven-stage crisis model. While examining the dimensions of the problem, Dennis was encouraged to express his feelings and emotions (stage 3). Dennis clearly expressed the pain associated with the realization that his wife and children had become the victims of his addiction. Further exploration of this issue at this time was not necessary. Dennis had experienced the impact of the feeling, and it was important to encourage him to move beyond this feeling. Dennis noted that it was important for him to stand still and feel this hurt, because it will be necessary to remember this pain when he experiences cravings to use in the future (Roberts, 1990).

Dennis reports that "only the pain associated with the consequences of use is powerful enough to thwart relapse." A basic tenet of solution-focused therapy when applied in crisis intervention is that one does not need to know the cause or function of the problem in order to resolve it (O'Hanlon & Weiner-Davis, 1989). In this case recognizing that Dennis knew best how to cope with his cravings provided a powerful tool for treating his cravings. Because of the respect between the counselor and the patient, and the counselor's willingness to listen, Dennis taught his counselor how to address cravings (Berg & Jaya, 1993).

Clinical Issues/Interventions/ Special Considerations

Since Dennis has been sober previously, the fourth step of Roberts's model, exploring and assessing past coping attempts, became a vital part of the ongoing recovery plan. Assigning specific tasks assisted in reestablishing equilibrium. Dennis was given the assignment to list the right and the wrong ways he had treated his disease in the past. For example, his alarm going off in the morning had provided the opportunity to hit the snooze button four or five times, waking up late and rushing to work. Alternatively, he could get up, fix a healthy breakfast, read his morning meditation books, and begin the day with a plan for recovery. Giving Dennis a clear-cut way to measure coping strategies provided him with a tool to build upon his strengths and to work toward a solution (Fortune, 1985; Levy & Shelton, 1990; Roberts, 1990).

Upon completing the assignment, Dennis identified any specific areas that presented within his recovery environment as high risk. Understanding the reciprocal processes between an individual and his or her recovery environment is crucial for understanding how a patient uses environmental resources in the problem-solving process and how the environment creates challenges for the individual (Pillari, 1998; Zastrow, 1996; Newman & Newman, 1995). Dennis was able to identify three primary areas. First was payday: "It's a very simple equation for me: *Time plus money equal cocaine*." The second area he identified was Internet pornography; and the third was his uncontrollable mood swings.

Dennis was asked to rank the three high-risk situations on a scale of 1 to 10, with 10 being remarkable cravings and 1 being no cravings at all. Scaling provides a clear measure of the problem at hand when working to resolve a crisis (Saleebey, 1996). Dennis rated having money as a 10; his rationale is that there was not a time when he did not experience remarkable cravings when he had money. He rated his Internet pornographic fixation as a 7, stating, "I don't always have to be high to go there." When asked if he felt this required further addressing, Dennis replied, "Absolutely. It's still a very real trigger for my addiction. The third area of mood swings posed more of a problem. Initially Dennis rated this as a 5; after a few minutes of thought, however, he changed it to a 9, reporting, "I never know when it's going to hit. Sometimes it's nothing, other times I'm a raging lunatic." For the sake of argument, it was agreed upon that this would remain a "9." Dennis agreed to address the potential for rage at the worst possible level so as not to minimize the extent and severity of the mood swings.

Following the discussion, the therapist instructed Dennis to list alternatives or possible solution-oriented actions he could take to minimize the impact of each high-risk situation. This took situations previously seen as negative out of the control of the patient and provided the opportunity to assume an active role in minimizing the impact of these issues (Berg, 1994).

Special Considerations of Treatment Planning

Dennis returned with a plan that was simple and applicable in each area. In an effort to control money as a trigger, he agreed to relinquish control of his finances to his business partner. Dennis had contacted with this person, who agreed to take over his checkbook and to manage his finances. Dennis and his partner agreed that he would receive an allowance of $10 per day for lunch and incidentals. A company or bank check would be used for larger transactions.

The issue of the Internet was a bit more complicated because Dennis completed a great deal of his research on the Internet. Two changes were agreed upon. First, Dennis was to move his computer into the main lab, an area that was public and provided sufficient observation to minimize the accessing of Internet sites that contained pornographic material. The second was utilization of a "Net nanny" program that blocked access to pornographic sites. However, all quickly agreed that Dennis was smart enough to work around this if he wanted. The last agreed change was that Dennis would work between the hours of 8:00 A.M. and 6:00 P.M., because there was no real reason for him to be spending excess time in the office. He agreed that the evenings required his focusing on recovery.

The area of mood swings was more abstract and thus required different planning skills. Dennis presented a list of recovering persons whom he agreed to contact daily to minimize the possible occurrences of mood swings. He further agreed to keep this list with him at all times and to contact these persons if he began to experience a mood swing. Dennis noted the need for ongoing treatment and agreed to attend the intensive outpatient program four evenings per week, including a specialized cocaine group one evening per week. Dennis then stated he felt it would be in his best interest to enter a sober living house rather than seeking an apartment on his own, acknowledging that his mood swings occurred primarily when he was alone. Again, the emphasis is placed on the importance of addressing triggers in the person's recovery environment (Pillari, 1998).

In approximately 2½ days, Dennis had stabilized. He developed a plan of action to address the major threats to his recovery and agreed to participate in ongoing outpatient treatment and to move into a sober living arrangement. Treatment had capitalized on Dennis's strengths. He developed the treatment plan and agreed that he was now ready to move ahead with his plan. When asked to report on his level of comfort as scaled on his treatment plan, Dennis reported being extremely comfortable with his recovery plan; he felt ready to move to an intensive outpatient level of care.

Analysis of Risk and Protective Factors (Dennis)

The recovery dimensions outlined by the American Society of Addiction Medicine (Hoffman, Halikas, Mee-Lee, & Weedman, 1991) represent a useful framework for analyzing this case. Such an approach requires the clinician to consider risk and protective factors in each area. Biomedical risks include family history and physical health factors. Relapse potential responses are closely tied to craving or cue reactivity, which are the physiological responses addicts experience when exposed to prior cues for using. The issue of cue reactivity is particularly important when working with persons addicted to cocaine because cues to resume use have been described as "perhaps more powerful than any other drug" (Chiauzzi, 1994). In this case, it would appear that overwork and compensating for becoming intoxicated served as cues for the resumption of cocaine use. Fueled partially by a need to compensate for the physical consequences of his intoxication, and in an effort to increase his energy level, Dennis quickly reverted to a destructive pattern of use.

Psychological or emotional behavioral risk factors include the role of expectations with regard to the perceived positive consequences of further drug use, a lack of effective coping skills, and the presence of psychopathology (Chiauzzi, 1991). Clearly, Dennis approached his first use of cocaine with positive expectations, which initially were rewarded with an increase in his productivity. In describing intrapersonal relapse risk factors, Cummings, Gordon, and Marlatt (1980) noted that both extreme negative and positive emotions might contribute to relapse. Both were operating in Dennis's case. Dennis had been tremendously successful in the workplace, with a growing business that had high profits. In fact, his initial use of alcohol occurred in response to receiving a recognition award. Chiauzzi (1994) noted that the assessment of relapse risk often overlooks the contribution of positive emotions. Just as in extreme negative experiences, extreme highs contribute to upsetting one's equilibrium, often a precipitating event in a crisis. At the same time, Dennis's younger daughter suffered from a potentially fatal illness. By the time Dennis sought help, the paranoia and isolation created by cocaine use and his shame at relapsing had exacerbated his crisis.

Persons in crisis and those in relapse share many characteristics (Chiauzzi, 1994). These include the general loss of equilibrium brought on by extreme emotions, and the consequent compression of one's coping repertoire. At the time of initial consultation, Dennis's ability to contemplate a way out of his crisis was limited to hoping for his own death. However, his affect and mood swings represented an additional psychological risk factor. At presentation, Dennis was extremely depressed. Addressing these mood symptoms was essential to ensuring his ability to remain drug free. Brown et al. (1998) found higher levels of depressive symptoms associated with greater urge to use cocaine, alcohol, and other drugs in high-risk situations.

Social risk factors requiring inquiry included the stability of family relationships, the presence of negative life events, and a lack of supportive social contact (Chiauzzi, 1991). The recent binge by Dennis had led his wife to threaten him with separation. In addition, although he had been tremendously successful at work, his recent crisis had created substantial problems in that setting. The presence of employment and family problems account for a significant amount of variance in posttreatment adjustment (McClellan et al., 1994). In choosing to taper off his attendance at self-help group meetings, Dennis had reduced his contact with the appropriate social support. Havassy, Hall, and Wasserman (1991) found that a lack of social support for a continuing goal of abstinence predicted subsequent relapse.

Case Autopsy: Follow-Up (Dennis)

As planned, Dennis transitioned into a sober living arrangement. He successfully completed a 6-week intensive outpatient treatment consisting of 3 hours of education and group therapy four evenings per week. Dennis again became active in the fellowships of Alcoholics Anonymous (AA) and Cocaine Anonymous (CA). Dennis and his family did reunite; however, his daughter died shortly after his first-year anniversary of recovery. Dennis was able to cope with her death without using mood-altering substances. He reported that the support from his friends in the "program" was tremendous during the time of his loss.

Dennis did experience one relapse after 18 months of remaining clean. At the time, he reported drinking approximately 24 beers at a concert. He reported that being overconfident and eliminating the majority of 12-step support meetings from his schedule contributed to his relapse. Following this use, Dennis presented for one individual session, where he reviewed the plan he had developed to reestablish his recovery. In this session, Dennis worked on stages 2 through 6 of Roberts's model without prompting from the therapist. Using the skills he had learned in previous treatments, Dennis examined the dimensions of the problem; he explored his feelings and emotions, and discussed what he needed to "get back to his program of recovery." Dennis discussed several alternatives and specific plans to resolve issues with Donna should she not accept him back into the home. Upon leaving he successfully implemented this plan. Because of this single self-directed intervention Dennis was able to limit this relapse to a single use episode. At this time, Dennis has been clean for over 2 years. He was elected businessman of the year last year and reports that he is hopeful that he will not return to use.

Case Study 2: Susan

Susan C., Opioid Dependent

Almost 6 years ago to the day, Susan C. brought her brother-in-law to the center for treatment for his cocaine dependence. She was disgusted by his antics, including how he had given up all responsibilities and had placed his family at risk by taking illegal drugs. On this date Susan C. was brought to treatment by the same brother-in-law, who is now 4 years clean and sober. The onetime schoolteacher sat in the assessment office, a mere shadow of herself.

Susan explained: "I was in four car wrecks in a little over 3 years. I have two compressed discs in my spine, which cause a great deal of pain. Initially my physician prescribed Darvocet and Percodan. These worked well for a while. But little by little the pain came back; it always comes back. It may have been the result of sleeping wrong or jerking while stepping down a step;

there always seems to be something to aggravate the pain. For a while I was able to tolerate the pain. Now I can't seem to cope with it. My use of medication has steadily increased. Now I'm using Oxycodone and Oxycotin along with Ultran, Tylenol 3, Percocet, and Darvocet to tolerate the pain.

I've been seeing other doctors and getting prescriptions from them too. It all started out somewhat innocently when I was seeking a second opinion for the pain. I discovered that if I didn't tell them the visit was for a second opinion, they would prescribe the same or similar medications. The next thing I know I'm seeing five or six doctors and all are prescribing similar medications. I used to save them just in case I needed them . . . you know for vacations or whatever. As time progressed I needed more and more pills. Now I'm taking all that are prescribed. It's become a nightmare. I'm having trouble keeping straight in my head what prescription goes with what doctor and what pharmacy. I think my insurance company and the pharmacy are on to me.

Yesterday, one pharmacist refused to fill my prescription without consulting my physician first. He wasn't going to give the prescription back. I raised so much hell he reluctantly gave it to me. I immediately went to another pharmacy in the same chain, and they did fill it. Now I'm scared. I wonder what happens to the prescriptions when they have been filled? Where do they go? Do they go back to the doctor? If they do, I'm in deep trouble. You see, I was so afraid that I wouldn't get the prescription filled that I changed the number from 20 to 50. I know it wasn't right, but I was desperate.

My pain is real . . . and the medication I take comes from doctors. I know I need this medication. If I don't have it, the pain becomes too great to deal with. After all, it was the physicians who got me hooked on them. What I really need is a doctor who will give me something strong enough to deal with the pain I'm experiencing. It's not like I'm some sort of a street bum. I'm not some rum dumb who is just crawling out from under a bridge. I have a genuine problem with pain! They can't send me to jail because I have a legitimate health problem . . . can they?"

Susan's was not an uncommon problem; one study found just fewer than 28% of a pain clinic's patients met three or more criteria for substance abuse (Chabal, Erjavec, Jacobson, Mariano, & Chaney, 1997). Women often use more socially acceptable substances, such as prescription drugs, and often abuse them in medicinal ways (Nichols, 1985). This case will demonstrate the effectiveness of combining both Roberts's crisis intervention model and the strengths perspective approach. In working with Susan, the establishment of psychological contact takes the form of genuine respect for her chronic pain issues, combined with acknowldgement of the need to develop new coping skills to address her pain (Saleebey, 1996; Sullivan & Rapp, 1991; Miller & Berg, 1995). Roberts's first step in crisis intervention and the strengths perspective fit nicely together because they both work to maintain the dignity and integrity of the patient. Both approaches recognize the individual's innate ability to establish recovery and seek to build on previous effective coping skills (Roberts, 1990; Saleebey, 1992, 1996).

In this case, the therapist could assure Susan of the program's ability to address her pain issues. However, there was also the need to caution her that seeking several prescriptions from several different physicians was not legal and that there could be consequences associated with doing this. With that proviso, the therapist assured Susan that the action she was now taking was the single best step she could take to minimize any potential legal consequences.

When combining Roberts's model and the strengths perspective, the initial question was not "Do you believe or think that you might have a drug problem?" Instead, it became "You have been functioning up to now under some very difficult circumstances. What are you doing that has helped you to keep going despite the pain?" This approach moves the client toward an approach that focuses on today rather than on yesterday and all the pain of the past (Roberts, 1990; Rapp, 1992; Saleebey, 1996).

The initial interview should focus on the patient's strengths. For example, instead of asking "what brought you to treatment today," the question becomes "What is it that gave you the courage to ask for help today?" In the case of chronic pain, focusing on pain will only serve to keep the client focused on the perceived need to medicate their pain. A focus on what life could be like if the pain was minimized will eventually lead the client to seek alternative methods for addressing the pain.

Providing the client with an opportunity to examine both coping skills and environmental supports, when combined with the client's strengths, becomes a viable approach within Roberts's second and fourth stage of crisis intervention. The goal was to capitalize on the client's view of her problem as a medical issue rather than as an addiction, which eliminated resistance to entering the recovery process. The desired outcome was to assist the patient in minimizing her dependence on pain medication rather than to force the admission of addiction.

Helpers should assure clients who are entering detoxification from pain medications that they are expected to participate in activities that support pain management through methods other than medication. They should also be informed that medication is given only in response to withdrawal symptoms—for example, elevated pulse, temperature, and blood pressure.

In addition to the limits placed on the client in relation to the use of medication to address pain issues, the therapist asked Susan to develop her personal plan of alternative solutions, step five of Roberts's crisis intervention model. When possible, the client should be encouraged to collaborate with persons in her recovery environment who she has identified as supportive (Benard, 1994; Mclaughlin, Irby, & Langman, 1994). Susan identified several persons as supportive; however, she had little insight as to how these persons could help. In addition, Susan neglected to identify several important persons. To address this, the helper asked Susan to identify persons who she may have omitted from her support person's list and asked her to describe her rationale for omissions from the previous list. There were several false starts before completion of this assignment. Susan's list grew to include her mechanic, plumber, paperboy, and garbage collector; however her physicians, employer, and recovering brother-in-law did not make several of the revised lists. Eventually, Susan resolved to include her physicians, pharmacists, and even her brother-in-law to the list. Susan's list included one brief explanation for the omissions, it read, "OK, OK, I now understand how I am trying to hold on to my old ways!"

Once this task had been completed, Susan was asked to compile a letter to each person on her list, seeking their support for her efforts and requesting suggestions on how she might cope with pain by methods other than medication. Given the possible legal issues involved, the helper cautioned her to provide only vague information related to what prompted this call for assistance. Susan completed 15 letters and agreed to mail 3 per day. The goal was to amplify the patient's individual resilience by increasing awareness of informal networks of support and encouragement (Benard, 1994; Berg & Miller, 1992).

The response was overwhelming. As each letter, card, bouquet of flowers, and telephone call arrived, Susan became less and less defensive. She began to acknowledge how her reliance on the medication as her solitary coping mechanism had led to isolation from the very persons who were the most willing to help her. In addition, Susan became increasingly aware of the sadness, frustration, anger, and fear she was experiencing. Exploration of these feelings, Roberts's third step, led her to becoming the person she felt she was before the accidents and the onset of her problems (Roberts, 1990).

Using the suggestions provided to Susan by her strengths-based support group led to the development of her action plan. Susan incorporated each suggestion into (a) a daily plan for recovery, (b) a list of actions to be taken in high-risk situations, and (c) a medical management plan developed with the assistance of her primary physician and the physician who completed her detoxification.

With this plan in place and demonstration of medical stability, Susan was discharged from the detoxification program 5 days after her initial presentation. She received a prescription for decreasing amounts of Clonopin to ensure successful completion of her detoxification on an outpatient basis and weekly follow-up individual appointments with her counselor on the detoxification unit.

Analysis of Risk and Protective Factors (Susan)

In assessing Susan's case it was important to recognize that physical dependence and tolerance were an expected component of her long-term opioid use for pain. Sees and Clark (1993) noted that determining the existence of dysfunctional behavior is the salient point in the diagnosis of addiction. However, as this case demonstrated, the need for continued pain medication can occur independently of the physical health problem. Ultimately Susan discovered that much of her pain was unrelated to her long-standing injury. This was consistent with Robinson's (1985) suggestion that for some persons pain continues to exist after the physiological process has ameliorated because of the continued reinforcement provided by drug use.

Accessing Susan's social network represented a step toward engaging an important protective factor. Women with addiction problems commonly have fewer social supports than men (Kaufmann, Dore, & Nelson-Zlupko, 1995) and are often more likely to use in isolation. Kail and Litwak (1989) suggested engagement of relatives, and friends contributed to reducing the likelihood of prescription medicine abuse. Other authors have empirically demonstrated the important role of social support in maintaining the benefits of treatment (Bell, Richard, & Feltz, 1996; Havassy et al., 1991).

Perhaps partly because of her brother-in-law's experience, Susan was ambivalent about characterizing her use of drugs as addictive. A strengths-based approach represented an effective mechanism for overcoming the initial denial that might have impeded engagement in substance abuse treatment (Rapp, Kelliher, Fisher, & Hall, 1994). The choice to eschew pressuring Susan to label herself as addicted also contributed to the therapist's ability to create a collaborative relationship. Miller (1995) observed that self-labeling was not an important determinant of subsequent outcomes. Instead, the goal of the initial interview is to "create a salient dissonance or discrepancy between the person's current behavior and important personal goals" (Miller, 1995, p. 95).

Case Autopsy: Follow-Up (Susan)

Following discharge, Susan maintained weekly appointments for a 1-month period. She then began biweekly sessions for a 2-month period and finally finished the remainder of the year with sessions once per month. As time progressed, Susan acknowledged that the symptoms of pain she had experienced were most likely withdrawal from the medication. She noted that she had not used mood-altering substances to address her pain, finding that the nonsteroidal anti-inflammatory medications work extremely well for her.

Following her first drug-free year, with a level of pain that was expected and seen to be reasonable, Susan returned to work. Three years after the crisis, Susan has completed a master's degree in education and is a principal in an inner-city high school. She is an extremely strong advocate of prevention programming to keep teens away from drugs. To this day Susan reports she is not certain if she is an "addict"; however, she quickly acknowledges that her use of medication was the basis of her problems.

Case Study 3: Scott

Scott S., Polysubstance Dependence

Scott presented at the treatment facility accompanied by his grandfather, who reported seeking substance-dependence treatment at this facility 20 years ago and had remained abstinent from all mood-altering chemicals since that time. Scott related to the interviewer that he felt he was "at the end of his rope." His parents have disowned him after he took approximately $4,500 from their business and spent it on a week long binge.

Scott reported using intravenous heroin, alcohol, and cocaine for the past 14 days. His recent binge began when the university he had been attending refused to admit him to classes. Scott returned to campus for the January term only to find he was placed on academic suspension after not meeting the requirements of academic probation from the previous semester. Scott remained on campus with friends rather than returning home to his parents.

Scott's first experience with mood-altering substances was LSD, which he first took at approximately age 12. He remembered being asked if "he wanted to take something that would make him giggle and laugh all night long." He began to smoke pot shortly after this use. Scott reported being an avid "head" throughout high school, having used cannabis daily since age 13. He began to use alcohol on a regular basis at age 14, drinking up to six beers per day in conjunction with one eighth of an ounce of cannabis per day.

Scott said he can best be described as a "garbage head," explaining, "That's a person who has taken about everything." Scott has experimented with sedative hypnotics, amphetamine, and inhalants. His favorites are LSD, cocaine, heroin, and alcohol. Scott had experienced over 200 acid trips, using everything from liquid LSD 25 to four-way windowpane, to designer drugs. The majority of this use occurred between the ages of 14 and 17.

At age 16 Scott began to use powder cocaine. His initial use was limited to weekends; however, it progressed rapidly to near-daily use following graduation from high school. His peak tolerance was $300 of per day intravenous cocaine combined with up to one fifth of alcohol (whiskey). Scott felt his use was out of control, and he wanted to stop the cocaine use. Also during this time Scott was using crystal methamphetamine. He said, "Now that's a drug that will steal your soul." Scott stated this was the only time that he became fearful when he was using. He reported a period of time when he became extremely violent and out of control as a result of his crank use.

Scott said, "The high is so intense, it never seems to end. Once in a while you get a chance to catch your breath, but this doesn't last very long." Scott noted it was during this time that he became involved in stealing and "boosting" in order to support his habit. He indicated that when he was using this drug he just did not care: "The stuff makes you feel invincible. There are a lot of violent and crazy people out there, and the worst are doing crank!"

A friend introduced Scott to heroin when he was following the band Phish. His initial use was intranasal, but he quickly progressed to IV. Scott noted his use has progressed to three $65 bags per day. His liver enzyme tests were all elevated to approximately 10 times normal, indicating possible hepatitis. Scott noted his alcohol consumption had decreased to two 40-ounce beers daily.

He was currently facing legal consequences for "bad checks" and shoplifting. Scott did not expect to be readmitted to the university, which he reported is particularly frustrating to his father, since both he and Scott's grandfather graduated from the school. Scott stated he is becoming dope sick and really doesn't care about the stupid college. He has tried to stop on his own and has failed each time, as the "jones" (withdrawal) becomes more intense.

Scott noted that while driving to the hospital he had seen at least three places where he could cop. He felt that if he was not admitted quickly, he would likely leave and find some dope. He reported that he is not craving, but he is going to have to have something to keep the sickness away or he will find and use heroin. Scott is angry and frustrated that his grandfather has to pay for his admission; however, he acquiesced following his grandfather's insistence that he get help today or walk away from all of the family. The grandfather also reminded Scott that he may well be Scott's last advocate. Scott acknowledged that he has tried everything he knows to establish recovery and had failed. Feeling that he had no other options, Scott agreed to be admitted to the treatment program.

Scott's pattern of use was not atypical of young adults. Use of heroin by American teenagers has increased in recent years. According to the Monitoring the Future Study (Johnston, O'Malley, & Bachman, 1998), the percentage of high school seniors reporting heroin use, while still a small figure, has risen 133% from 1990 to 1997. The pattern of Scott's substance use presented a number of risk factors. Polydependence on alcohol and cocaine has been linked to more acute dependence, an increase in the likelihood of leaving treatment early, and poorer long-term outcomes (Brady, Sonne, Randall, Adinoff, & Malcolm, 1995). Scott's family history of alcoholism and his early age of first use also placed him in a high-risk group for greater psychopathology, increased recidivism, and continued negative consequences (Barbor et al., 1987; Penick et al., 1987).

Scott was not a person who trusted very easily. Therefore, the worker emphasized the process of gaining psychological contact with Scott during assessment. When the worker asked Scott to decide if his grandfather would be involved in the assessment process, Scott chose to "do this on his own." The assessing clinician sought to establish a positive relationship, beginning by examining Scott's resilience factors rather than his problems; resilience factors include skills, abilities, knowledge and insight into what needs to occur to develop a plan for mitigating the crisis (Roberts, 1990). In doing so, the assessor established a relationship with Scott, which led him to feeling a part of the recovery process rather than having a process thrust upon him. Scott requested medication to help with the physical withdrawal he had experienced in the past, but he did not want to take anything that might continue his dependence. He reported a previous methadone detoxification and stated he felt one drug was a substitute for another. Scott asked if there would be a drug detoxification that could minimize the physical symptoms without maintaining his dependence. He was assured that detoxification could be accomplished with a combination of clonidine used as a patch and orally for the extrapyramidal side effects (e.g., anticholinergic effects); Buprinex to minimize cravings and withdrawal symptoms; Bentyl to minimize cramping associated with opioid withdrawal; Motrin to address aches and pains; and Immodium to address diarrhea (Ginther, 1999).

While not pretending to understand the detoxification process, Scott agreed that it seemed to him that his request would be granted, and he entered detoxification with the stipulation that if he felt like a zombie he would leave. Program staff respected and agreed with this stipulation.

In individual meetings with Scott, his social worker sought to further define and examine the parameters of the problem (Roberts, 1990) by eliciting Scott's definition of it. The goal in this case was to assist Scott's awareness of the tensions and conflicts that were present in his life by providing acceptance, empathy, and mirroring nonverbal communication in an environment free from confrontation (Greene et al., 1996). When defining the problem, it is important to allow the patient to explore her or his feelings and emotions surrounding the issues, which is Roberts's third step (Roberts, 1990).

In this case, Scott quickly identified feeling oppressed by his parents, believing that they were trying to force him into a role that he did not want. He spoke of feeling like an abused child:

> Not in the classic sense of abuse. It's like they never listen to my wants and needs, they believe if they give me everything they think I should have, then I will be happy. In all honesty, they could have kept all of the shit they gave me and just listened for a few minutes. That would have really made me happy. Instead they keep throwing things at me that make me; the right clothes, the right club memberships, the right college, what they think I should be instead of hearing what I really want to be!

Scott shared that as he progressed through school toward a business degree, he felt as though he was "selling out" and was being forced to become everything that he hated. He reported feeling conflict between being relieved that he did not have to continue in his classes and the fear of telling his father about his expulsion from school.

Roberts's fourth stage of crisis intervention, exploring past coping attempts (Roberts, 1990) addresses the fine line between solution-focused treatment and sustaining motivation without providing the client with justification for his or her illness. This stage merges well with solution-focused theory because it provides the opportunity to apply the exception question (Koslowski, 1989, Koslowski & Ferrence, 1990; Greene et al., 1996). In this case, the worker asked Scott to examine the right and wrong ways he has treated his disease in the past. This is an inventory of what worked for Scott and what did not when he had attempted to stay sober in the past. Scott was encouraged to develop his list of behaviors that supported his previous attempts at abstinence.

By this point, Scott had progressed into the second day of his detoxification and was quite agitated. He was frustrated and was resistant to examination of strengths or weaknesses. This provided an opportunity to apply scaling questions with the exception questions. The worker used the scaling question to provide Scott with a mechanism to mark his progress. This question asked the client to rank the problem he was experiencing on a scale of 1 to 10, with 10 being the most desirable state and 1 being the least desirable outcome (De Jong & Miller, 1995; Miller & Berg, 1995).

At times it is possible to use the scaling question in combination with the exception question or the miracle question (DeShazer, 1988; De Jong & Miller, 1995; Greene et al., 1996). For example, when meeting in medical rounds, the physician asked Scott:

Physician: On a scale of 1 to10 [as described above] how do you feel today?

Scott: I feel like shit. . . . I'm sick, my head is pounding, my stomach is cramped, my nose is running, I'm either hot or cold and sweating all the time. It could be a little worse, so I'll say I'm about a 3 today.

Physician: When is the last time you felt this lousy and didn't use?

Scott: [Silence] Never!

Physician: You must be doing detox exactly right. If you have never made it beyond this point without using before, you are definitely doing something right! Your addiction is real angry with you, and it is attempting to get you to self-medicate. Just keep doing what you are doing, and we will get you through the worst of the detoxification.

This supportive interaction provided Scott with an opportunity to notice progress that otherwise would have been overlooked. He was also encouraged to learn that, despite feeling poorly, he was doing his detoxification exactly right. Each subsequent interaction with the physician began with the scaling question and follow-up supportive feedback. Roberts's fifth stage, exploring alternatives and specific solutions, provided a format for the miracle question. The miracle question directed Scott to set new and unimagined goals for his recovery (DeShazer, 1988). For example, his social worker asked Scott: "Suppose after this meeting you fell asleep, and while you were sleeping a miracle happened and your problems were suddenly resolved. Because you were asleep, you are not aware that the miracle has happened. What will be the signs that tell you the miracle has occurred?"

From this question, Scott identified three clear indicators. First, "I wouldn't be dope sick. Second, I really wouldn't give a damn what my parents said or did. And third, I would be living my life clean, accomplishing the goals I really wanted." Follow-up questioning attempted to develop a clearer understanding of coping mechanisms and alternative behaviors Scott might apply. Scott indicated that if his parents permitted him to seek education in an area of interest, he would not likely be failing school. If he were not failing and was studying what he wanted, he would be making progress toward his life dream of becoming a marine biologist. From this discussion Scott developed the following goals:

1. Doing whatever he needs to do to finish his detox
2. Telling his parents that he was leaving the school he was attending
3. Making independent living arrangements
4. Enrolling in a college other than where he had been and completing his basic education requirements
5. Seeking acceptance into the University of Florida Marine Biology Program

Using the miracle question to define Scott's goals provided the format for the development and implementation of recovery-specific goals. Shortly after discussing this with his social worker, Scott became an active member in groups. He seemed to have a greater interest in the recovery process. Scott selected a sponsor in the 12-step fellowship of Narcotics Anonymous (NA). He began seeking permission to attend additional NA meetings and to spend time with his sponsor. Scott wrote a letter to his parents explaining his removal from the university. This generated an angry yet predictable response from his father; nevertheless, Scott used his growing sober support system to work his way through this problem. Because of these interactions, over a 4-day period Scott requested placement with a long-term halfway house facility where he could practice independent living skills and from where he could apply to the university.

Scott was now involved in the sixth stage of Roberts's model, the restoration of cognitive functioning. Scott had actively examined the events that contributed to the crisis. He was in the process of developing a clear understanding of the process of addiction and its progression over time. Scott began to verbalize awareness of the overgeneralizations, shoulds, projections, catastrophizing, and self-defeating behaviors that led to his maladaptive dependence on mood-altering substances.

Finally, Scott was replacing his irrational beliefs with new recovery-supported cognitions, using his sponsor and support group to think out his thoughts before turning these into action. Scott reported using the sober support group to increase his awareness of the behaviors that will be required to support his recovery and to facilitate the development of a self-directed program of recovery.

Following a 6-day detoxification and medical stabilization, Scott made the transition to a 3- to 6-month halfway house program. He was developing and implementing his plan for recovery. Scott was "cautiously optimistic" when he left the detoxification center, saying, "This is the first time I've taken the risk to do something out of the shadow of my family. It feels great!"

Analysis of Risk and Protective Factors (Scott)

Among the factors that contributed to Scott's current crisis were the fear of his parents' reaction to his school failure and his general conflict with them over his educational goals. To some extent, Scott's crisis was exacerbated by his need to emancipate from his parents. Paradoxically, his drug and alcohol addiction only further delayed development, including the task of developing his own agenda for his future. Bentler (1992) empirically demonstration that drug and alcohol use by young people impedes many of their important developmental tasks.

The therapist's attention to Scott's cognitive function and negative thought patterns was an important step in helping Scott on the road to recovery. Carroll, Rounsaville, and Gawin (1991) demonstrated that cognitive treatment was highly effective with cocaine-dependent persons, and was particularly beneficial among the more severe cases. Benefits gained from cognitive treatment are maintained over a long time (O'Malley et al., 1994).

Scott's willingness to embrace 12-step groups was a very positive step toward resolving his crisis. The literature is replete with the benefits of these approaches. Weiss et al. (1996) reported a positive association between self-help participation and short-term outcomes among cocaine-dependent patients. Other authors have published similar findings on the general efficacy of 12-step groups when working with alcohol and other drug-dependent clients (Stevens-Smith & Smith, 1998; Johnsen & Herringer, 1993). In fact, Humpreys and Moos (1996) found no significant differences among health outcomes at 1 or 3 years for persons who participated in AA groups only versus those who received outpatient treatment. The benefits of participation in self-help groups seem to have a long-term effect. One study found that ongoing participation in self-help groups was associated with better outcomes even after 3 years (Longabaugh, Wirtz, Zweben, & Stout, 1998).

Participation in self-help groups has also been associated with improvements in other life areas. In addition to finding that participation predicted better posttreatment substance-use outcomes, Morgenstern, Labouvie, McCrady, Kahler, and Frey (1997) determined that 12-step participation was positively associated with increased self-efficacy, motivation to change, and improved coping ability.

Involvement in self-help groups has the potential to influence the social domain as well. Persons who participated in 12-step groups were found to have more close friends, as well as fewer friends who were using alcohol and other drugs (Humphreys & Noke, 1997). Persons participating in an aftercare program had significant reductions in job absenteeism, inpatient hospitalizations, and arrest rates (Miller, Ninonuevo, Klamen, Hoffmann, & Smith, 1997).

Case Autopsy: Follow-Up (Scott)

Scott was discharged from the detoxification level of care and moved into the partial hospitalization program for 10 additional days. During this time, he worked to solidify his self-diagnosis while building his sober support network. Scott developed concrete plans to address high-risk situations, including arranging to enter a sober house near the university. Scott left the treatment center after a total of 16 days in the hospital. He continued his treatment in the intensive outpatient program for 6 weeks, after which he attended aftercare for 3 additional months.

Scott's awareness of the provoking nature of his relationship with his family led to the development of what he called his "family of choice" within the recovery community. He was extremely proud of his involvement in the local recovery fellowships, which provided the opportunity to realize and use his assets and abilities. The input he provided to his peer group complemented his awareness of the need for peer input into his recovery. Scott notes, "My thinking for myself stinks, but my ability to give others feedback is great. I can see exactly what they need. Just as they can see exactly what I need. As a collective, we are doing great things in recovery." Working within the recovery community provided for exponential growth for Scott's recovery from addiction and in his development of mature problem-solving strategies.

Scott applied for, and was accepted into, a marine biology program. He obtained grants and student loans to facilitate his transition. Approximately 6 months after entering detoxification, Scott had realized his goal of studying marine biology. He had also become active in the student union, providing guidance to students who are experiencing problems with substance abuse and dependence. Scott has now been sober for nearly 3 years. Every year Scott visits the treatment center, and last year he and his grandfather attended the 24th anniversary of the treatment center. He continues to communicate with his counselor and peers in recovery by telephone and e-mail.

THE ROLE OF EVIDENCE-BASED PRACTICE IN SUBSTANCE DEPENDENCE TREATMENT

In the early 1990s, a worldwide movement began promoting the adoption of evidence based practice in medicine. This movement emphasized evaluation and utilization of research in decision making as applied to the direct care arenas. The origins of evidence-based practice can be traced to the early 1900s with the work of Mary Richmond and Richard Cabot and may be defined as "the conscientious, explicit and judicious use of current best evidence in making decisions about the care of individual patients" (Roberts & Yeager, 2004, pp. 6, 11).

Evidence-based addiction medicine (EBAM) involves combining clinical expertise with the best available evidence collected from a variety of external sources. The practitioner applying evidence-based approaches seeks to answer questions frequently asked by managed care entities addressing issues of (1) the origin of the treatment approach, (2) the validity of the treatment approach, and (3) the nature of the proposed treatment approach and how the clinician is applying best practice principles. The clinician answers critical questions posed by the managed care entity and provides the highest-quality care as applied to the individual seeking substance dependence treatment.

Challenges arise for practitioners when there is an attempt to weigh the relative effectiveness of the research presented in a manner that tailors the research to an individual treatment need. Unfortunately, scientific research, by nature, doesn't prove anything. Nor will all scientific research apply to each individual treated. However, there is an increasing desire to provide the highest quality of care, which requires the application of valid research and clinical evidence for decision support (Roberts & Yeager, 2004).

Frequently, medical research is biased, written in the form of persuasive communication with the goal of swaying the reader to accept the thinking, research, and findings presented. At the very least, treatment providers are responsible for reviewing and verifying research with a critical eye and to be skillful in ranking the order of research by strength of evidence provided.

In general, the decision making using evidence-based methods is achieved in a series of steps (Gibbs & Gambrill, 2002; Hayward, Wilson, Tunis, & Bass, 1995). The first step is to evaluate the problem to be addressed and formulate answerable questions: What is the best way of assisting an individual with these characteristics who suffers from dependence? Which group treatment method is most effective in reducing recidivism of those addicted to opiates?

The next step is to gather and critically evaluate the evidence available. Evidence is generally ranked hierarchically according to its scientific strength. It is understood that various types of intervention will have been evaluated more frequently and rigorously by virtue of the length of time they have been used and the settings in which they are used. Thus, for newer treatments, only Level 4 evidence may be available (see Table 24.2). In such cases, practitioners should use the method with caution, continue to search for evidence of efficacy, and be prepared to evaluate the efficacy of the method in their own practice. The final steps involve applying the results of the appraisal to practice or policy and then continuously monitoring the outcome (Roberts & Yeager, 2004).

Table 24.2 Levels of Evidence

Level 1	Meta-analysis or replicated randomized controlled treatment (RCT) that includes a placebo condition/control trial or from well-designed cohort or case control analytic study, preferably from more than one center or research group or national consensus panel recommendations based on controlled, randomized studies.
Level 2	At least one RCT with placebo or active comparison condition, evidence obtained from multiple time series with or without intervention, or national consensus panel recommendations based on uncontrolled studies with positive outcomes or based on studies showing dramatic effects of an intervention.
Level 3	Uncontrolled trial with 10 or more subjects, opinions of respected authorities, based on clinical experiences, descriptive studies, or reports of expert consensus.
Level 4	Anecdotal case reports and case studies.

The bottom line is demonstrating an impact on clinical outcome, rating the relative effectiveness or ineffectiveness of a particular approach to treatment, and then asking questions such as How does this approach compare to other, more traditional approaches to treatment? How many patients will achieve better outcomes with this approach?

Critical thinking provides the potential for critical analysis of the evidence and its impact on the individual's treatment. It is important to note that this is not an exact science. Currently, it is an unfortunate truth that there is a lack of randomized controlled studies in the area of addiction treatment. Additionally, there is a need for a greater number of studies supporting evidence-based approaches in addiction treatment. There is a need for the development of stronger levels of evidence, higher-quality research, and research studies reflective of the principles of evidence-based practice and practice-based research.

Those working in the addictions field can support this through application of evidence-based practice and subscribing to evidence-based approaches. Direct care providers can support those entities providing research through adoption of clinical practice guidelines based on high-quality research and by challenging approaches presented in the popular press that lack an evidence-based approach.

Finally, there are always questions pertaining to the best approach for any given patient on any given day. However, as substance dependence treatment grows in sophistication and professionalism, the application of an evidence-based approach will function as a strong foundation for the development of the next generation of research in the treatment of addiction. In doing so, practitioners will be facilitating a transition toward a rational, sensible, clinically complex approach to care of the individual and improving the quality of care provided as well as providing a clinically complex approach to care based on increasingly relevant clinical evidence.

CONCLUSION

The challenge facing social workers in substance-dependence treatment is to balance cost against quality. A completely new dimension of substance-dependence treatment is emerging. This dimension is crisis intervention and brief treatment, designed to stabilize patients as quickly and effectively as possible (Edmunds et al., 1997).

Roberts's crisis intervention model, combined with brief solution-focused therapy and a strengths perspective, provides extremely flexible, practical approaches to intervention with substance-dependent individuals in crisis. The established routes of Roberts's model provide clear guidelines for intervention and progression through detoxification and into a meaningful recovery process. This approach facilitates the development of a self-directed plan of recovery that capitalizes on the individual's strengths rather than taking the approach of more familiar problem-focused models utilized by traditional substance-dependence programs (Day, 1998).

As a result of using the crisis intervention/solution-focused approach, patients experienced rapid normalization and return to their recovery environment. Crisis response in this format sought to place the substance-dependent person in their environment as soon as they are medically stable. The goal was to facilitate greater utilization of the system of community support and relationships that are present in day-to-day life. Keeping the substance-dependent individual in contact with his or her community while participating in outpatient programming provided greater opportunity to address relapse traps and triggers as they occurred.

Links between the crisis and the patient's life history were identified and examined in a manner that maintained the patient's historical and existential continuity. The focus on community supports provided patients the opportunity to reframe what once was perceived as a using environment to an environment where sober support was found. The end result is a treatment process that allows patients to pass through the crisis event while maintaining their dignity, sense of strength, pride, trust, spirituality, and personal identity.

Substance-dependence treatment has traditionally placed a great deal of emphasis on outcome. Meaningful outcome studies have been undertaken to evaluate the effectiveness of treatment modalities for over 25 years. Examination of crisis intervention combined with solution-focused therapy outcomes will need to be examined. It will be important to identify the outcomes that this type of treatment can be expected to bring about, in both short- and long-term goals (e.g., detoxification and stabilization versus maintenance of established recovery goals over extended periods of time). Examination of outcomes within the solution-focused crisis intervention approach will be important for several reasons.

First, emphasis on customer-driven quality improvement may provide the opportunity to respond to what consumers and their families desire in the treatment of substance dependence. Substance dependence, by nature, is disempowering. Many of the systems established for the treatment of substance dependence have resulted in patients experiencing further disempowerment (Day, 1998). It will be important to fully understand how a solution-focused crisis intervention approach impacts outcome.

Second, this model is consistent with policy development and behavioral health care management systems that have been established over the past decade. This model is designed to incorporate individualized treatment planning, utilization of community support, capitalization on consumer strengths, and consumer choice. This model can provide a framework to examine the effectiveness of brief intervention within the recovery environment.

Finally, the model has the potential to accomplish the goals not only of the consumer but also of the payers and system administrators within the public and private sectors. That goal is to reduce the risk and exposure to unplanned increases in costs. Application of the crisis intervention solution-focused approach at this time appears to meet this challenge by (a) reducing hospital days, (b) reducing emergency services, (c) increasing utilization of community support, and (d) reducing relapse potential.

This chapter is not intended to present Roberts's seven-stage model as a replacement for traditional approaches to substance-dependence treatment. The intention is to provide an alternative framework that can be applied within the substance-dependence treatment setting. We hope that this approach will be considered, applied, refined, and researched as a viable alternative when social workers are faced with increasingly complex cases combined with reduced resources.

REFERENCES

American Psychiatric Association. (1994). *Diagnostic and statistical manual of mental disorders* (4th ed.). Washington, DC: Author.

Babor, T., Hoffman, M., DelBoca, F., Hesselbrock, V., Meyer, R., Dolinsky, Z., & Rounsaville, B. (1992). Types of alcoholics, I: Evidence for an empirically derived typology based on indicators of vulnerability and severity. *Archives of General Psychiatry, 49*, 599–608.

Balsheim, K., Oxman, M., Van Rooyen, G., & Girod, D. (1992). Syphilis, sex and crack cocaine: Images of risk and mortality. *Social Science and Medicine, 31*, 147–160.

Barbor, T. F., Korner, P., Wilbur, P., & Good, F. (1987). Screening and early intervention strategies for harmful drinkers: Initial lessons learned from the Amethyst project. *Australian Drug and Alcohol Review, 6*, 325–339.

Beinecke, R., Callahan, J., Shepard, D., Cavanaugh, D., & Larson, M. (1997). The Massachusetts mental health/substance abuse managed care program: The provider's view. *Administration and Policy in Mental Health, 23*, 379–391.

Bell, D., Richard, A., & Feltz, L. (1996). Mediators of drug treatment outcomes. *Addictive Behaviors, 21*, 597–613.

Bentler, P. (1992). Etiologies and consequences of adolescent drug use: Implications for prevention. *Journal of Addictive Diseases, 11*(3), 47–61.

Berg, I. K. (1994). *Family-based services: A solution-focused approach.* New York: Norton.

Berg, I. K., & Jaya, A. (1993). Different and same: Family therapy with Asian-American families. *Journal of Marital and Family Therapy, 19*, 31–38.

Berg, I. K., & Miller, S. D. (1992). *Working with the problem drinker: A solution-focused approach.* New York: Norton.

Blume, S. (1992). Alcohol and other problems in women. In J. Lowinson, P. Ruiz, & R. Millman (Eds.), *Substance abuse* (pp. 794–807). Baltimore: Williams and Wilkins.

Book, J., Harbin, H., Marques, C., Silverman, C., Lizanich-Aro, S., & Lazarus, A. (1995). The ASAM and Green Spring alcohol and drug detoxification and rehabilitation criteria for utilization review. *American Journal on Addictions, 4*, 187–197.

Brady, K., Sonne, E., Randall, C., Adinoff, B., & Malcolm, R. (1995). Features of cocaine dependence with concurrent alcohol abuse. *Drug and Alcohol Dependence, 39*, 69–71.

Brown, R., Monti, P., Myers, M., Martin, R., Rivinus, T., Dubreuil, M., & Rohsenow, D. (1998). Depression among cocaine abusers in treatment: Relation to cocaine and alcohol use and treatment outcome. *American Journal of Psychiatry, 155*, 220–225.

Carroll, K., Rounsaville, B., & Gawin, F. (1991). A comparative trial of psychotherapies for ambulatory cocaine abusers: Relapse prevention and interpersonal psychotherapy. *American Journal of Drug and Alcohol Abuse, 17*, 229–247.

Chabal C., Erjavec, M., Jacobson, L., Mariano, A., & Chaney, E. (1997). Prescription opiate abuse in chronic pain patients: Clinical criteria, incidence, and predictors. *Clinical Journal of Pain, 13*, 150–155.

Chiauzzi, E. (1991). *Preventing relapse in the addictions: A biopsychosocial approach.* New York: Pergamon Press.

Chiauzzi, E. (1994). Turning points: Relapse prevention as crisis intervention. *Crisis Intervention, 1*, 141–154.

Cummings, G., Gordon, J., & Marlatt, G. (1980). Relapse: Prevention and prediction. In W. Miller (Ed.), *Addictive behaviors: Treatment of alcoholism, drug abuse, smoking, and obesity* (pp. 291–321). Oxford: Pergamon Press.

Dattilio, F., & Freeman, A. (1994). *Cognitive-behavioral strategies in crisis intervention.* New York: Guilford.

Day, Stephen L. (1998). Toward consumer focused outcome and performance measurement. In K. M. Coughlin, A. Moore, B. Cooper, & D. Beck, *1998 Behavioral outcomes and guidelines sourcebook: A practical guide to measuring, managing and standardizing mental health and substance abuse treatment* (pp. 179–185). New York: Fulkner and Gray.

DeJong, P., & Miller, S. D. (1995). How to interview for client strengths. *Social Work, 40*, 729–736.

DeShazer, S. (1985). *Keys to solution in brief therapy*. New York: Norton.

DeShazer, S. (1988). *Clues: Investigating solutions in brief therapy*. New York: Norton.

Edmunds, M., Frank, R., Hogan, M., McCarty, D., Robinson-Beale, R., & Weisner, C. (1997). Managing managed care: Quality improvement in behavioral health. In K. M. Coughlin, A. Moore, B. Cooper, & D. Beck, *1998 Behavioral outcomes and guidelines sourcebook: A practical guide to measuring, managing and standardizing mental health and substance abuse treatment* (pp. 134–143). New York: Fulkner and Gray.

Etheridge, R., Craddock, S., Dunteman, G., & Hubbard, R. (1995). Treatment services in two national studies of community-based drug abuse treatment programs. *Journal of Substance Abuse, 7*, 9–26.

Ewing, C. P. (1990). Crisis intervention as brief psychotherapy. In R. A. Wells & V. J. Giannetti (Eds.), *Handbook of brief psychotherapies* (pp. 277–294). New York: Plenum.

Ford, W. (1998). Medical necessity: Its impact in managed mental health care. *Psychiatric Services, 49*, 183–184.

Fortune, A. E. (1985). The task-centered model. In A. E. Fortune (Ed.), *Task-centered practice with families and groups* (pp. 1–30). New York: Springer.

Gartner, L., & Mee-Lee, D. (1995). *The role and status of patient placement criteria in the treatment of substance use disorders*. Publication No. (SMA) 95-3021. Rockville, MD: U.S. Department of Health and Human Service.

Ginther, C. (1999, April). Schuckit addresses state-of-the-art addiction treatments. Special report: Addictive disorders. *Psychiatric Times*, April, 55–57.

Greene, G. J., Lee, Mo-Yee, Trask, R. In addition, Rheinscheld, J. (1996). Client strengths and crisis intervention: A solution focused approach. *Crisis Intervention, 3*, 43–63.

Havassy, B., Hall, S., & Wasserman, D. (1991). Social support and relapse: Commonalties among alcoholics, opiate users, and cigarette smokers. *Addictive Behaviors, 16*, 235–246.

Hoffman, N., Halikas, J., Mee-Lee, D., & Weedman, R. (1991). *Patient placement criteria for the treatment of psychoactive substance use disorders*. Chevy Chase, MD: American Society of Addiction Medicine.

Hser, D., Chou, Yih-ling, Hoffman, Chih-Ping, & Anglin, V. (1999). Cocaine use and high-risk behavior among STD clinic patients. *Sexually Transmitted Diseases, 26*, 82–86.

Humphreys, K., & Moos, R. (1996). Reduced substance-abuse-related health care costs among voluntary participants in Alcoholics Anonymous. *Psychiatric Services, 47*, 709–713.

Humphreys, K., & Noke, J. (1997). The influence of post-treatment mutual help group participation on the friendship networks of substance abuse patients. *American Journal of Community Psychology, 25*, 1–16.

Johnsen, E., & Herringer, L. (1993). A note on the utilization of common support activities and relapse following substance abuse treatment. *Journal of Psychology, 127*, 73–77.

Johnston, L., O'Malley, P., & Bachman, J. (1998). *National survey results on drug use from the Monitoring the Future study, 1975–1997. Vol. 1: Secondary school students.* NIH Publication No. 98-4345. Rockville, MD: National Institute on Drug Abuse.

Kail, B., & Litwak, E. (1989). Family, friends and neighbors: The role of primary groups in preventing the misuse of drugs. *Journal of Drug Issues, 19*, 261–281.

Kaufmann, E., Dore, M., & Nelson-Zlupko, L. (1995). The role of women's therapy groups in the treatment of chemical dependence. *American Journal of Orthopsychiatry, 65*, 355–363.

Koslowski, L. T., & Ferrence, R. G. (1990). Statistical control in research on alcohol and tobacco: An example from research on alcohol and mortality. *British Journal of Addiction, 85*, 271–278.

Koslowski, L. T., Henningfield, R. M., Keenan, R. M., Lei, H., Leigh, G., Jelinek, L. C., Pope, M. A., & Haertzen, C. A. (1993). Patterns of alcohol, cigarette, and caffeine and other drug use in two drug abusing populations. *Journal of Substance Abuse Treatment, 10*, 171–170.

Kusher, J., & Moss, S. (1995). *Purchasing managed care services for alcohol and other drug treatment: Essential elements and policy issues.* Publication No. (SMA) 95-3040. Rockville, MD: U.S. Department of Health and Human Service.

Levy, R. L., & Shelton, J. L. (1990). Tasks in brief therapy. In R. A. Wells & V. J. Gianetti (Eds.), *Handbook of the brief therapies* (pp. 145–163). New York: Plenum.

Longabaugh, R., Wirtz, P., Zweben, A., & Stout, R. (1998). Network support for drinking, Alcoholics Anonymous and long-term matching effects. *Addiction, 93*, 1313–1333.

McClellan, A., Alterman, A., Metzger, D., Grisson, G., Woody, G., Luborsky, L., & O'Brien, C. (1994). Similarity of outcome predictors across opiate, cocaine, and alcohol treatment: Role of treatment services. *Journal of Consulting and Clinical Psychology, 62*, 1141–1158.

Miller, N., Ninonuevo, F., Klamen, D., Hoffmann, N., & Smith, D. (1997). Integration of treatment and post-treatment variables in predicting results of abstinence-based outpatient treatment after one year. *Journal of Psychoactive Drugs, 29*, 239–248.

Miller, S. D., & Berg, I. K. (1995). *The miracle method: A radically new approach to problem drinking.* New York: Norton.

Miller, W. (1995). Increasing motivation for change. In R. Hester & W. Miller (Eds.), *Handbook of alcoholism treatment approaches: Effective alternatives* (2nd ed., pp. 89–104). Boston: Allyn and Bacon.

Morgenstern, J., Labouvie, E., McCrady, B., Kahler, C., & Frey, R. (1997). Affiliation with Alcoholics Anonymous after treatment: A study of its therapeutic effects and mechanisms of action. *Journal of Consulting and Clinical Psychology, 65*, 768–777.

Newman, B. M., & Newman P. R. (1995). *Development through life: A psychological approach* (6th ed.). Pacific Grove, CA: Brooks/Cole.

Nichols, M. (1985). Theoretical concerns in the clinical treatment of substance-abusing women: A feminist analysis. *Alcoholism Treatment Quarterly, 2*, 79–90.

Norman, E., Turner, S., & Zunz, S. (1994). *Substance abuse prevention: A review of the literature.* New York: State Office of Alcohol and Substances Abuse Services.

National Survey of Drug Use by Households (NSDUH). (2003). *Quantity and frequency of alcohol use.* Office of Applied Studies, Substance Abuse and Mental Health Services Administration. Rockville, MD.

National Survey of Drug Use by Households (NSDUH). (2004). *Adults with co-occurring serious mental illness and a substance use disorder.* Office of Applied Studies, Substance Abuse and Mental Health Services Administration. Rockville, MD.

O'Hanlon, W. H., & Weiner-Davis, M. (1989). *In search of solutions: A new direction in psychotherapy.* New York: Norton.

O'Malley, S., Jaffe, A., Chang, G., Rode, S., Shottenfeld, R., Meyer, R., & Rounsaville, B. (1994). Six-month follow-up of naltrexone and coping skills therapy for alcohol dependence. *Archives of General Psychiatry, 53*, 217–224.

Parad, H. J., & Parad, L. G. (1990). Crisis intervention: An introductory overview. In J. J. Parad & L. G. Parad (Eds.), *Crisis intervention book 2: The practitioner's sourcebook for brief therapy* (pp. 3–68). Milwaukee, WI: Family Service America.

Penick, E., Powell, B., Bingham, S., Liskow, V., Miller, M., & Read, M. (1987). A comparative study of familial alcoholism. *Journal of Studies on Alcoholism, 48*, 136–146.

Pillari, V. (1998). *Human behavior in the social environment.* Pacific Grove, CA: Brooks/Cole.

Platt, J., Widman, M., Lidz, V., Rubenstein, D., & Thompson, R. (1998). The case for support services in substance abuse treatment. *American Behavioral Scientist, 41*, 1050–1062.

Rapp, C. A. (1992). The strengths perspective of case management with persons suffering from severe mental illness. In D. Saleebey (Ed.), *The strengths perspective in social work practice* (pp. 45–48). New York: Longman.

Rapp, R., Kelliher, C., Fisher, J., & Hall, F. (1994). Strengths-based case management: A role in addressing denial in substance abuse treatment. *Journal of Case Management, 3*, 139–144.

Rivers, J. (1998). Services for substance abusers in a changing health care system. *American Behavioral Scientist, 41*, 1050–1062.

Roberts, A. R. (1990). Overview of crisis theory and crisis intervention. In A. R. Roberts (Ed.), *Crisis intervention handbook: assessment, treatment, and research* (pp. 3–16). Belmont, CA: Wadsworth.

Roberts, A. R. (1996). Battered women who kill: A comparative study of incarcerated participants with a community sample of battered women. *Journal of Family Violence, 5*, 291–304.

Roberts, A. R., & Dziegielewski, S. F. (1995). Foundation skills and applications of crisis intervention and cognitive therapy. In A. R. Roberts (Ed.), *Crisis intervention and time-limited treatment.* Thousand Oaks, CA: Sage.

Robinson, J. (1985). Prescribing practices for pain in drug dependence: A lesson in ignorance. *Advances in Alcohol and Substance Abuse, 5*, 135–162.

Saleebey, D. (1992). Introduction: Power in the people. In D. Saleebey (Ed.), *The strengths perspective in social work practice* (pp. 3–17). New York: Longman.

Saleebey, D. (1996). The strengths perspective in social work practice: Extensions and cautions. *Social Work, 41*, 296–305.

SAMHSA. (1998). Preliminary results from the 1997 National Household Survey. http://www. Samhas. gov/oas/nhsda97/nhsda976-990.htm.

Sees, K., & Clark, H. (1993). Opioid use in the treatment of chronic pain: Assessment of addiction. *Journal of Pain and Symptom Management, 8*, 257–264.

Stevens-Smith, P., & Smith, R. L. (1998). *Substance abuse counseling: Theory and practice.* Upper Saddle River, NJ: Merrill.

Substance Abuse and Mental Health Services Administration. (2002). Results from the 2001 National Household Survey on Drug Abuse: Volume I. Summary of national findings (DHHS Publication No. SMA 02–3758, NHSDA Series: H-17). Rockville, MD: Author.

Sullivan, W. P., & Rapp, C. A. (1991). Improving clients outcomes: The Kansas technical assistance consultation project. *Community Mental Health Journal, 27*(5), 327–336.

Thompson, J., Burns, B., Goldman, H., & Smith, J. (1992). Initial level of care and clinical status in a managed mental health program. *Hospital and Community Psychiatry, 43*, 599–603.

Toff-Bergman, G. (1998). *Managed behavioral healthcare updates: State and local activity.* SAMHSA Managed Care Tracking Report, 1(1).

Wallace, J. (1983). Alcoholism: Is a shift in paradigm necessary? *Journal of Psychiatric Treatment and Evaluation, 5*, 479–485.

Wallace, J. (1989). A biopsychosocial model of alcoholism. *Social Casework, 70*, 325–332.

Weiss, R., Griffin, M., Najavits, L., Hufford, C., Kogan, J., Thompson, H., Albeck, J., Bishop, S., Daley, D., Mercer, D., & Siqueland, L. (1996). Self-help activities in cocaine dependent patients entering treatment: Results from NIDA collaborative cocaine treatment study. *Drug and Alcohol Dependence, 43*, 79–86.

Wells, K., Astrachan, B., Tischler, G., & Unutzer, J. (1995). Issues and approaches in evaluating managed mental health care. *Milbank Quarterly, 73*, 57–75.

World Health Organization (1981). Nomenclature and classification of drugs and alcohol-related problems: A WHO memorandum. *Bulletin of the World Health Organization, 59*, 225–242.

World Health Organization Expert Committee on Drug Dependence. (1974). *Twentieth report* (Tech. Rep. Series No. 5(51). Geneva, Switzerland: Author.

Yeager, K. R. (in press). The role of intermittent crisis intervention in early recovery from cocaine addiction. *Journal of Crisis Intervention and Time-Limited Treatment, 5.*

Zastrow, C. (1996). *Introduction to social work and social welfare* (6th ed.). Pacific Grove, CA: Brooks/Cole.

25

Mobile Crisis Units: Frontline Community Mental Health Services

JAN LIGON

Gloria

Late Friday afternoon a caseworker from the outpatient mental health center received a call from Gloria, a long-standing client. Gloria was to see the worker and psychiatrist that morning but never came. She was very agitated on the telephone and told her caseworker that she did not intend to return to the mental health center, stating "Don't call me anymore or you might be sorry you did." Gloria's diagnosis is schizophrenia, and she has been hospitalized many times over the years when her symptoms would exacerbate, usually because she had stopped taking her medications. She lives alone in an apartment and receives health benefits, monthly income, rent supplements, and reduced rate passes for public transportation. The outpatient office was closing for the weekend, so the caseworker called the crisis center, to convey what Gloria had said. All clients have access to the crisis center, and caseworkers often call to relate concerns they have about clients who may call or need services after hours. Gloria did call the crisis center about 10:00 P.M. that night and told the hotline worker "I'm telling all of you that if you don't leave me alone somebody's going to get hurt." The hotline worker immediately contacted the mobile crisis unit (MCU) by cellular telephone to relate the details of the telephone call and to provide information maintained on the computer about the client, diagnosis, medications, and treatment history. The MCU proceeded to Gloria's apartment, the last of five calls it would make that shift.

Cindy

It was a hot, humid summer night, when tempers often run short. The Mobile Crisis Unit received a radio call from the county police to advise about a domestic disturbance on an isolated road in the county. The police stated that Cindy, age 19, shot a high-caliber gun into the ceiling of her grandmother's house. The grandmother ran to a neighbor's and called the police. Cindy and her father live in another county. She had not been following curfew rules, and he told her, "You can just go to your grandmother's because I'm done with you here." After a few days with her grandmother, Cindy began to call her father to try to work things out, but he reinforced that he had reached his limit with her. That night, after he hung up on Cindy, she became very upset, grabbed a gun in the house, and shot it into the ceiling several times. The police contacted the Mobile Crisis Unit for assistance, and on arrival there were five police cars and numerous neighbors who had walked over from their modest houses along the road. Cindy's father had been contacted and would arrive soon. Mental health computer records had no previous history to report.

Michael

This evening had been a quiet one for the MCU when a radio communication came in from the county police SWAT team. The team had received a call from Amanda, who advised that her husband, Michael, was in the house with her, armed and threatening to kill himself. Upon arrival, the SWAT team learned that the man had a painful and debilitating physical condition that had become worse. He was very despondent and wanted to die. Amanda stated, "I've talked him down from these states before, but this time things are much worse. He wants to die, but he doesn't want me to be left alone. Our parents are deceased, and we have no children. We're really all each other has." Although the SWAT team was requesting a backup consultation from the Mobile Crisis Unit, the scene quickly became one that required negotiation not only with the client but also with the intervening teams.

As behavioral health services for mental and substance abuse problems have shifted from institutional and inpatient settings to community services and programs, methods for dealing with crisis episodes are changing. In the past, many crisis episodes were addressed by involuntarily transporting clients to an emergency receiving facility such as a psychiatric hospital. However, with the declining influence of institutional inpatient facilities and the growing impact of managed care, it is becoming increasingly likely that crises will now be addressed at the community level. One promising approach to crisis intervention, the MCU, has been utilized in a number of communities to literally intervene at the local level, often in the client's home.

OVERVIEW OF THE PROBLEM

In the United States up to 30% of the population per year may be affected by a mental health or substance abuse problem, and 21% of the population has experienced both problems during their lifetimes. One fourth of the population will experience an anxiety disorder during their lives, 19.3% will experience an affective disorder, and over 2 million people in the United States suffer from schizophrenia. The U.S. Department of Health and Human Services, Substance Abuse and Mental Health Services Administration (SAMHSA) provides extensive information through its annual compilation of statistics (Rouse, 1998) and the Internet <http://www.samhsa.gov>.

Personal and societal costs related to mental health and substance abuse problems exceed $400 billion per year including health care and lost productivity. Although the number of alcohol-related traffic fatalities is declining, 40% of crash-related deaths involve alcohol; for drivers age 21 to 24 the rate is over 50%. Substance abuse is heavily related to crime. For example, of those individuals convicted of burglary, 40% were under the influence of drugs at the time of the crime. Alcohol and other drug use is a factor in over 500,000 emergency room episodes per year and accounts for 11% of the preventable deaths annually. Suicide rates are highest for White and American Indian/Alaskan Native males, while males in the general population who have a psychotic disorder are at almost twice the risk of committing suicide as those having nonpsychotic disorders. Mental disorders are listed as a contributing factor to the cause of death on 7.6% of death certificates (Rouse, 1998).

EXPANSION OF COMMUNITY CRISIS SERVICES

Reding and Raphelson (1995) note that as early as the 1920s psychiatrists in Amsterdam provided home-based psychiatric services with the belief that the care was more effective than that received in an inpatient hospital ward. During that same period, emergency psychiatric services began to appear in the emergency wards of general hospitals as "essentially an on-the-spot adjustment to situational exigencies" (Wellin, Slesinger, & Hollister, 1987, p. 476). Emergency services in urban psychiatric hospitals were begun in the 1930s, followed by community-based services in the 1950s. As documented by Roberts in the overview chapter, crisis services became available in the community following passage of the Community Mental Health Center (CMHC) Act of 1963, which required that all centers receiving federal funds offer 24-hour crisis and emergency services as one of five mandated categories of services.

The CHMC Act focused on moving mental health services from institutional settings to the community, and early intervention was an important component of these programs. With ongoing federal support, these services continued to expand in the 1970s, and the total number of community mental health centers offering emergency services expanded 69% from 1976 to 1981 (Wellin et al., 1987). Between 1969 and 1992, the number of mental health episodes per year doubled, the number of admissions to outpatient and partial care facilities tripled, and the rate of inpatient admissions remained constant. The number of admissions to state and county mental hospitals declined 45% from 1975 to 1992, and the number of admissions to substance abuse treatment facilities receiving public funds remained constant from 1993 to 1996. Over 50% of the funding for substance abuse treatment is from public sources, and 90% of treatment is outpatient (Rouse, 1998).

As an increasing number of clients become covered by various forms of managed care, it is likely that the trend to utilize outpatient and community-based services will expand even further. Community-based crisis intervention presents a unique challenge to both practitioners and administrators of behavioral health services. The need for crisis services continues to grow, while inpatient and institutional supports continue to decline. Therefore, it is essential that community programs develop and implement services that are congruent to community needs. While describing the disappointments and setbacks of federal mental health policy implementation, Kia Bentley (1994) also reports that "cumulative gains have been made, largely because of the family and consumer movements and legislation they helped to create" (p. 288). Georgia is one example of a state in which mental health services have been reformed based on legislation that was primarily driven by consumers of services and their families.

MENTAL HEALTH REFORM IN GEORGIA

In 1993 the Georgia General Assembly passed House Bill 100 (HB100) to reorganize mental health, mental retardation, and substance abuse services in the state into 28 community service boards. The community boards were originally overseen by 19 regional boards; however, the number of regional boards has now been reduced to 13. The law requires that a minimum of 50% of all board members must be consumers of services or their families. The 13 regional boards receive funding, determine needs, contract for the provision of services, and monitor the outcomes of services provided. Additional details about the Georgia reform are available elsewhere (Elliott, 1996). Since the 1993 reform in Georgia, services for residents of DeKalb County, located in metropolitan Atlanta, are now provided by the DeKalb Community Service Board (DCSB), based in Decatur, Georgia. DCSB provides a wide range of services to over 10,000 of the county's 600,000 residents. The county has a long history of committment and advocacy for addressing mental health, mental retardation, and substance abuse issues. Services had previously been provided through outpatient programs, and inpatient treatment was provided through one of the state's eight psychiatric hospitals.

CRISIS SERVICES

Following the passage of HB100, DeKalb County began to offer inpatient services for crisis stabilization in the community. This was consistent with the wishes of consumers and their families that services be provided in the community so that the need for hospitalization could be reduced. The facility's interdisciplinary team of physicians, psychiatrists, nurses, social workers, paraprofessional health workers, dietary workers, and volunteers provide around-the-clock access to assessments, physical examinations, medication, treatment, and case management services. Treatment approaches include individual therapy, 12-step groups, and education groups. In addition, many clients are transported to specialized community programs such as dual diagnosis and day treatment programs or are sent to halfway house and residential programs in the community. The crisis facility also serves as the base of operation for the county's crisis telephone service. In addition, since 1994 a MCU has been in continuous service and provides essential intervention and support services that were not available prior to its inception.

DEVELOPMENT OF MOBILE CRISIS UNITS

Mobile crisis units (MCUs) can be broadly defined as a community-based program, staffed by trained professionals who may be summoned to any location to deliver services. A number of programs have been previously documented in the literature, and early efforts focused on in-home psychiatric services (Chiu & Primeau, 1991). Other programs were specifically intended to avoid hospital admissions (Bengelsdorf & Alden, 1987; Henderson, 1976) and for providing training to psychiatric residents (Zealberg et al., 1990). More recent efforts have included programs that target the homeless mentally ill (Slagg, Lyons, Cook, Wasmer, & Ruth, 1994), with the ability to offer "medications that would otherwise be administered by court order in a hospital" (Reding & Raphelson, 1995, p. 181).

Although the specific features of MCUs vary, Zealberg, Santos, and Fisher (1993) identify a number of advantages offered by mobile crisis units, including increased accessibility of services, the benefit of assessing in the "patient's native environment" (p. 16), and the ability to intervene without delay, to avoid unnecessary arrests or hospitalizations, and to offer crisis training opportunities to mental health professionals. Because police officers are often the first source of contact and response to community crises, the authors also note that MCUs offer the opportunity to collaborate with the law enforcement system.

ROLE OF LAW ENFORCEMENT

Police activities related to mental health and substance abuse are particularly problematic for law enforcement because these calls can be very time-consuming and frequently are not perceived as "real police work" (Olivero & Hansen, 1994, p. 217) compared with activity associated with criminal behavior. Zealberg et al. (1993) note that police officers have little training in mental health issues and "techniques that were developed for use with criminals are often not applicable to nor successful with psychotic patients" (p. 17). This is a significant concern to law enforcement, with Hails and Borum (2003) noting that 7% to 10% of all police calls are related to mental health issues.

Law enforcement agencies and behavioral health care services are systems that may be prone to clash (Kneebone, Roberts, & Hainer, 1995). For example, in the past law enforcement was integrally involved in providing assistance for the involuntary admissions of mental health and substance abuse patients to psychiatric hospitals. However, the current system has become more restrictive concerning involuntary commitments (Olivero & Hansen, 1994) while favoring community-based interventions. Efforts to support community treatment and avoid psychiatric hospitalizations are congruent with the intent of deinstitutionalization However, there has been a corresponding increase in the number of persons with a history of mental problems who are jailed rather than hospitalized, a systemic shift that has been referred to as "transinstitutionalization" (Olivero & Hansen, 1994, p. 217). As noted by Zealberg et al. (1993), "Mobile crisis teams can alleviate the anxiety of law enforcement personnel and can prevent police overreaction" (p. 17). Such was the case in Memphis, when the development of a crisis intervention team came about after the shooting of a mentally ill person by a police officer (Cochran, Deane, & Borum, 2000). The authors note that partnerships between law enforcement and mental health services can be of great benefit in "managing crisis calls in an effective, expedient, and sensitive manner" (p. 1315).

DIFFERENCES IN MCU STAFFING AND SERVICE DELIVERY

MCUs have varied greatly in staffing and service delivery approaches. Gaynor and Hargreaves (1980) note that some mobile units were more likely to use mental health professionals, with psychiatrists available on a consultant basis, whereas Chiu and Primeau (1991) describe a team approach that includes a psychiatrist, a registered nurse, and a social worker. Some MCUs have been positioned as support and consultant services, which are called for assistance by the law enforcement or mental health systems (Bengelsdorf & Alden, 1987; Henderson, 1976; Zealberg, Christie, Puckett, McAlhany, & Durban, 1992). Other programs have been based in vans or other vehicles and offer outreach services to targeted populations (Chiu & Primeau, 1991; Slagg et al., 1994).

Community MCUs differ with respect to staffing and objectives, and the role of law enforcement in these programs also varies. Programs have been described that are designed to increase the knowledge and effectiveness of police officers when working with mental health issues (Dodson-Chaneske, 1988; Tesse & Van Wormer, 1975), as a collaboration with police and psychiatric services (Zealberg et al., 1992), or as a team consisting of police officers and mental health professionals (Lamb, Shaner, Elliott, DeCuir, & Foltz, 1995). On the other hand, many programs have focused on the delivery of services without law enforcement collaboration (Bengelsdorf & Alden, 1987; Chiu & Primeau, 1991; Slagg et al., 1994). Deane, Steadman, Borum, Veysey, and Morrissey (1999) surveyed urban police departments concerning their method of response to situations involving mental health issues and found no significant differences in four approaches to the calls.

MOBILE CRISIS SERVICES IN DEKALB COUNTY, GEORGIA

Prior to 1994, many crises involving mental health and substance abuse problems in DeKalb County were addressed by police department officers who responded to these calls. If necessary, individuals could be arrested, or they could be transported involuntarily by the sheriff's department to the state psychiatric hospital. Community residents, family members, and mental health advocates were very vocal about their displeasure with this arrangment for several reasons. First, the opportunity to resolve the situation at the location of the incident was limited by the expertise of the officer who responded. Second, many arrests and incarcerations were for behavior that was directly related to a mental health issue and were potentially avoidable. Finally, when clients were assessed at the psychiatric hospital, it was not uncommon for the facility to make decisions that conflicted with the judgment and opinions of community providers and family members. With the consumer and family focus of the reform in Georgia, it was now possible for county residents to secure services that were desired, including the MCU.

The MCU operates from 3:00 to 10:30 P.M., 7 days per week, and pairs a uniformed police officer with a mental health professional who operate from a regular marked police car. Each team works 4 days per week, with the operations based at the county's mental health and substance abuse crisis center, which includes the 24-hour crisis telephone service, walk-in services, and inpatient crisis stabilization and detoxification unit. About half of the referrals to the MCU are made by police dispatchers or other officers through the police radio communications system. The other half of the referrals come from the crisis unit or other mental health workers via cellular telephone and pager. Police officers have continuous access to field supervisors, and the mental health worker has direct access to consultation, including administration and staff psychiatrists. In addition, client histories are available through both the law enforcement and the mental health information system. The MCU responds to a wide range of calls that occur in homes, public places, and schools. About half the calls involve a psychotic episode, 25% are related to suicidal individuals, and about one fourth include a substance abuse problem as well. About six calls are completed per shift, which includes a combination of crisis calls and prearranged client and family follow-up calls.

APPLICATIONS OF ROBERTS'S SEVEN-STAGE MODEL

Roberts (1991) provides a highly practical approach to crisis intervention that is consistent with the needs of members of mobile crisis teams. It is important to address each of the seven stages in the model, beginning with stage 1, assessing lethality and safety needs, followed by stage 2, establishing rapport and communication. Stage 3 involves identifying the major problems, followed by stage 4, dealing with feelings and providing support. Possible alternatives are explored in stage 5, followed by the formulation of a plan in stage 6, and follow-up during stage 7. Roberts (1991) aptly stresses the importance of using sound judgment in sequencing the model's stages. For example, an MCU call involving a frightened mental health client could begin with stage 2 to establish rapport, whereas a call concerning an actively suicidal client would begin with assessing lethality, stage 1.

Case Application: Gloria

In the case of Gloria, assessing the lethality of her threats is consistent with stage 1 and began with contacts to the outpatient case manager and the telephone crisis worker. These were both excellent resources to determine from their experience and case records if any history of violence toward self or others was evident. In stage 2 the telephone crisis worker had already spoken with Gloria at her apartment as well as to her neighbor, who was with her and considered a supportive person. In stage 3 it was determined that Gloria's threats were consistent with her not being properly medicated.

In the past this usually resulted in being transported to the psychiatric hospital and involuntarily admitted.

On this call, the team consisted of a uniformed officer and a licensed master's-level social worker, who proceeded to the apartment. In stage 4 the crisis telephone worker had begun the process of offering support to Gloria and her neighbor and provided an opportunity to express feelings. However, given Gloria's level of hostility, this dialogue was of limited benefit, and her neighbor was very relieved to know that the MCU was en route. As the MCU team entered her apartment, Gloria became very fearful about the presence of a uniformed officer. It was now important to go back to stage 1 in order to specifically make sure there were no weapons in the apartment and to assess Gloria's intent to harm herself or someone else. Although a full discussion of assessing suicidal and homicidal intent is beyond the scope of this chapter, a more thorough review of risk factors and assessment techniques is available elsewhere (Sommers-Flanagan & Sommers-Flanagan, 1995).

Continuing to stages 2, 3, and 4, Gloria was calmed by the team and encouraged to relate to it the details of her missing her usual appointment, the status of her medications, her recent appetite and sleep patterns, and any recent events or circumstances that may have impacted her mental status. In stages 5 and 6 it was important to consider the input of both Gloria and her neighbor as well as the previous feedback from the case manager and telephone worker. The team was able to acquire her trust, and she provided helpful input in developing a plan. Gloria had not stopped taking her medications, but she was running low on her supply and attempting to stretch what she had, which led to her decompensation. Although one option was to transport her to the crisis center for further evaluation, her neighbor was willing to stay with her for the night. If there were any difficulties she could contact the telephone crisis line. In stage 7 the neighbor was willing to bring Gloria to the outpatient mental health center for a walk-in meeting with her case worker and the psychiatrist and to replenish her medications at the center pharmacy.

This case illustrates several benefits of the mobile crisis unit. First, the combination of a law enforcement officer and a mental health worker is of tremendous benefit in assessing safety and providing the option of involuntary transportation, if needed. Second, the appearance of a uniformed officer and a plainclothes worker has the effect of balancing the need for authority and empathic support in crisis work. This is not always possible if an officer is working solo and may have to move swiftly to an arrest that could have been avoided. By the same token, it may not be safe for a mental health professional to attempt such a call alone. Finally, there was significant benefit in addressing the crisis from a contextual perspective in Gloria's home. This includes her physical environment and also makes it possible to more accurately assess the viability of her neighbor as an action plan alternative.

There was no further contact until the next morning, when Gloria arrived with her neighbor at the mental health center.

Case Application: Cindy

In the case of Cindy, the assessment of lethality in stage 1 had been addressed by law enforcement officers prior to the arrival and in many cases MCUs. The MCU is not the first responder to police calls but is summoned by officers when appropriate. The MCU was contacted by officers on the scene via police radio. On this shift, the mental health worker was a licensed clinical social worker who had the authority to sign, if necessary, an involuntary order to transport the woman to the psychiatric emergency receiving facility. Although the objective is not to arrest or hospitalize individuals, it is beneficial for the authority to initiate an involuntary intervention to be present. In stage 2, since her father had arrived, team members met separately with Cindy and her father, and in stages 3 and 4 both felt comfortable with sharing their feelings and relating their views of the problems. Options in stage 5 included arrest, involuntary transportation to the psychiatric hospital, or transportation to the crisis center, which is a voluntary status facility. It was agreed that the client would come to the crisis center for further evaluation. Given her age and the lack of any client history, she was admitted for overnight observation, was reevaluated the next morning, and was referred to the outpatient mental health division for both individual and family therapy. For stage 7 a telephone call was placed to the father; it was determined that Cindy had returned home, and she and her father did follow-up with outpatient services.

This case description illustrates several benefits of MCUs reported by Zealberg, Santos, and Fisher (1993). First, the ability to observe and interview on-site "allows for the most complete assessment with the least trauma to the patient" (p. 16). In this case it was also possible to interview Cindy and her father individually and to then converge the information obtained to determine similarities and differences reported. Second, mobile units can respond quickly, prevent situations from escalating, and avoid unnecessary arrests or hospitalizations. Third, a well-executed mobile crisis call "allows for better public education about mental health issues and resources" (p. 17). Fourth, potential cost savings to the county include not only the avoidance of unnecessary arrests or hospitalizations but also the opportunity for "officers to return to duty more quickly" (p. 17).

Case Application: Michael

This evening had been a quiet one for the MCU when a radio communication came in from the county police SWAT team. It had received a call from Amanda, who advised that her husband, Michael, was in the house with her, armed and threatening to kill himself. Upon arrival, the SWAT team learned that the man had a painful and debilitating physical condition that had become worse. He was very despondent and wanted to die. Amanda stated, "I've talked him down from these states before, but this time things are much worse. He wants to die, but he doesn't want me to be left alone. Our parents are deceased, and we have no children. We're really all each other has." Although the SWAT team was requesting a backup consultation from the MCU, the scene quickly became one that required negotiation not only with the client but also with the intervening teams.

The case of Michael points out the importance of stage 1 in assessing both lethality and past experiences with coping behaviors. Although his wife was not being held hostage, this case presented an element of extreme risk and danger to Michael and Amanda and required the use of negotiation skills (Strentz, 1995). On this evening, the team consisted of the uniformed police officer and a registered nurse, and computer records found no criminal or mental health information on Michael. After consultation with the SWAT team, it was agreed that the nurse would, consistent with stage 2, attempt to first establish rapport with Amanda and use her alliance to connect with Michael. The problems (stage 3) were clear, so the predominant effort on this call was to connote empathy and provide support (stage 4). Given the severity of Michael's physical and mental conditions, the only alternative in stages 5 and 6 would be to arrange for his hospitalization. The dialogue between the MCU nurse and the couple went extremely well, and Michael voluntarily surrendered the gun and agreed to go with the MCU to the hospital. A follow-up call to the hospital for stage 7 confirmed that Michael was safe and stabilizing in the hospital.

Although the outcome of this case was positive, it was important to note the difference between this call and others handled by the MCU and SWAT teams. A follow-up meeting was held with the SWAT team and a mobile crisis worker to review the call. The SWAT team members expressed the need for additional training around mental health and substance abuse issues, which was subsequently provided. As noted by Strentz (1995), "The element of danger coexists with the opportunity for successful resolution and personal growth" (p. 147). Therefore, it is also essential to provide cross-training about SWAT team interventions to team members of mobile crisis units.

OUTCOMES OF MCUs

Outcome information about MCUs is limited, and Geller, Fisher, and McDermeit (1995) note that "beliefs about mobile crisis services far outnumber facts" (p. 896). Although Reding and Raphelson (1995) reported a 40% reduction in hospital admissions during a 6-month period, a study by Fisher, Geller, and Wirth-Cauchon (1990) did not "support the numerous claims regarding the ability of mobile crisis intervention to reduce the use of hospitalization" (p. 249). However, Fisher et al. (1990) go on to report that "some mobile crisis teams may be very effective in reducing hospitalizations because they function as part of a system which has other key services available for treatment and diversion" (p. 250).

In addition, Fisher et al. (1990) note that these units often reach people in need of hospitalization, so "that the unnecessary hospitalizations prevented by mobile crisis units are offset by the admission of individuals needing inpatient care who are discovered" (p. 251). Another problem is that "large numbers of persons who have committed minor crimes are taken to jails instead of to hospitals or other psychiatric treatment facilities" (Lamb et al., 1995, p. 1267). Lamb et al. (1995) conducted a follow-up study in Los Angeles of clients having a history of criminal and mental problems who had received outreach services from a police-mental team and found that "remarkably, only two percent of the group were taken to jail" (p. 1269). A study of mental health response models in three law enforcement jurisdictions provides further support that collaborations between police and mental health services can reduce arrests and unnecessary incarcerations of people who have mental health problems (Steadman, Deane, Borum, & Morrissey, 2000).

Dyches, Biegel, Johnsen, Guo, and Min (2002) conducted a matched samples study of those who received mobile crisis services with those receiving services from a hospital. The authors found that consumers were 17% "more likely to receive community-based mental health services after the crisis event than a consumer from the hospital-based intervention cohort" (p. 743). With respect to those who did not have a previous history of mental health services, the authors found that "the hospital-based cohort's likelihood of receiving postcrisis mental health services was 48% less than that of the mobile crisis cohort" (p. 744). Ligon and Thyer (2000) assessed client satisfaction with mobile crisis services in Georgia and found that both mental health clients and their family members reported levels of satisfaction comparable to those for other outpatient services.

INITIATING AND SUSTAINING MCUs

The future of MCUs is dependent on the ability of multiple systems to perceive their value and to then collaborate in a manner that will assure quality services that can be sustained in the community. While it is impossible to document how many MCUs have opened and closed over the years, a number of factors can influence these programs. First, crisis work can be dangerous when interventions occur in neighborhoods and homes with persons who may exhibit or have histories of violent behavior (Zealberg et al., 1993). Second, the behavioral health and law enforcement systems are rife with conflicts between the two systems (Dodson-Chaneske, 1988; Teese & Van Wormer, 1975), so "constant attention must be given to such collaboration" (Zealberg et al., 1992, p. 614). Finally, the larger political and turf factors that exist in any community can, unfortunately, lead to premature cuts despite a program's efficacy (Diamond, 1995; Reding & Raphelson, 1995). Indeed, Hails and Borum (2003) found that only 8% of 84 medium and large law enforcement agencies had access to a mobile crisis unit in their jurisdictions.

The political and organizational environments in which these units operate will no doubt present both obstacles and opportunities. It is also essential to work closely with law enforcement and to include ongoing supervision and training opportunities for police officers and mental health workers. In addition, consumers of services and their families must be involved in the development and refinement of MCUs. As stated by DCSB director, R. Derrill Gay, "Families see Mobile Crisis Units as essential services in community mental health and these are the people who need it, use it, and value it" (personal communication, May 19, 1999). The support of mental health advocacy groups at the national, state, and local levels is also beneficial in the further development of mobile crisis units.

FUTURE OPPORTUNITIES

Although the application and outcomes of mobile crisis units are encouraging, there are a number of opportunities to improve these services and to expand their availability. Zealberg, Hardesty, Meisler, and Santos (1997) identify several key areas of concern that include medical issues and the need for technology to support these units. The authors note that "one of the more frustrating aspects of mobile crisis work involves patients whose presenting symptoms include medical as well as psychiatric diagnoses" (p. 272). Ambulance and EMS services can assist with medical problems, but collaboration with these operations may be problematic due to multiple providers of these services in communities or poor communication capability with MCUs. Because MCUs often address issues related to physical health and medications, the DeKalb unit has found that coupling psychiatrically trained registered nurses with the police officer can be very beneficial. In addition, the DeKalb MCU has added a limited number of antipsychotic and side effects medications, which are carried onboard, ordered by the unit psychiatrist, and administered by the onboard nurse.

Technology offers immense opportunities to improve mobile crisis services. First, equipment is increasingly portable and more affordable, and it is feasible to equip MCUs with computers, cellular telephones, and other emerging products. Second, the ability to merge sources of information is improving, and it is possible for MCUs to determine any criminal and mental health history on clients quickly and efficiently. Finally, technology enables team members of MCUs to enter data and update records without burdensome paperwork and forms. This can include outcome data, new client information, and instructions for other services concerning follow-ups.

Virtually all the MCUs that have been documented are based in urban areas, which is understandable given the concentration of population and availability of resources. However, rural areas are extremely underserved; 21% of all rural counties have no mental health services, compared with only 4% in urban counties. The situation is much worse if overnight care is required; 78% of rural counties have no overnight services, compared with 27% in urban counties (Rouse, 1998). Coupled with the lack of public transportation in rural areas, MCUs offer the potential not only to provide services where needed but also to initiate any follow-up services that may be required.

Although the costs of operating MCUs are a significant concern to communities, Zealberg et al. (1997) note that indirect cost savings must be considered, including the reduced loss of time for police officers, court costs that are avoided when situations are resolved without arrests, and avoidance of high-cost inpatient care in many cases. In addition, behavioral health care is increasingly provided under managed care models. Therefore, managed care organizations are also in a position to gain from such cost savings as avoiding hospitalizations and need to partner with the public sector in developing and supporting MCUs.

MCUs operate across a wide range of geography and sites and encounter very diverse populations. Based on the experience of an MCU based in New York City, Chiu (1994) provides case examples and suggestions on working with Asian, Hispanic, African American, and other diverse groups. In addition, Lyons, Cook, Ruth, Karver, and Slagg (1996) note that the inclusion of consumers of mental health services on MCU teams may be beneficial when responding to calls across a variety of settings, including homes and public places. For example, the authors found that "consumer staff were more likely to do street outreach than were non-consumer staff" (p. 38) and go on to note that consumer experience "can be an advantage for mobile crisis assessment with persons with problems of mental illness and housing instability" (p. 40).

MCUs can be of tremendous benefit to communities when they are carefully staffed and supported by all stakeholders, including consumers of services and their families, law enforcement, and both public and private providers of behavioral health services. However, more research needs to be conducted to determine what combinations of staffing, services, technology, and intervention techniques are most effective and in what settings. It is also important to learn more about working with diverse populations and to investigate the benefits to rural residents through the implementation and evaluation of programs in these underserved areas.

ACKNOWLEDGMENTS The author appreciates the input and support provided by Dr. R. Derrill Gay, Director of the DeKalb Community Service Board, Decatur, Georgia, and to the staff of the Mobile Crisis Unit in the development of this chapter.

REFERENCES

Bengelsdorf, H., & Alden, D. C. (1987). A mobile crisis unit in the psychiatric emergency room. *Hospital and Community Psychiatry, 38*, 662–665.

Chiu, T. L. (1994). The unique challenges faced by psychiatrists and other mental health professionals working in a multicultural setting. *International Journal of Social Psychiatry, 40*, 61–74.

Chiu, T. L., & Primeau, C. (1991). A psychiatric mobile crisis unit in New York City: Description and assessment, with implications for mental health care in the 1990s. *International Journal of Social Psychiatry, 37*, 251–258.

Cochran, S., Deane, M. W., & Borum, R. (2000). Improving police response to mentally ill people. *Psychiatric Services, 51*, 1315–1316.

Deane, M. W., Steadman, H. J., Borum, R., Veysey, B. M., & Morrissey, J. P. (1999). Emerging partnerships between mental health and law enforcement. *Psychiatric Services, 50*, 99–101.

Diamond, R. J. (1995). Some thoughts on: "Around-the-clock mobile psychiatric crisis intervention." *Community Mental Health Journal, 31*, 189–190.

Dodson-Chaneske, D. (1988). Mental health consultation to a police department. *Journal of Human Behavior and Learning, 5*, 35–38.

Elliott, R. L. (1996). Mental health reform in Georgia, 1992–1996. *Psychiatric Services, 47*, 1205–1211.

Fisher, W. H., Geller, J. L., & Wirth-Cauchon, J. (1990). Empirically assessing the impact of mobile crisis capacity on state hospital admissions. *Community Mental Health Journal, 26*, 245–253.

Gaynor, J., & Hargreaves, W. A. (1980). "Emergency room" and "mobile response" models of emergency psychiatric services. *Community Mental Health Journal, 16*, 283–292.

Geller, J. L., Fisher, W. H., & McDermeit, M. (1995). A national survey of mobile crisis services and their evaluation. *Psychiatric Services, 46*, 893–897.

Hails, J., & Borum, R. (2003). Police training and specialized approaches to respond to people with mental illnesses. *Crime and Delinquency, 49*, 52–61.

Henderson, H. E. (1976). Helping families in crisis: Police and social work intervention. *Social Work, 21*, 314–315.

Kneebone, P., Roberts, J., & Hainer, R. J. (1995). Characteristics of police referrals to a psychiatric unit in Australia. *Psychiatric Services, 46*, 620–622.

Lamb, H. R., Shaner, R., Elliott, D. M., DeCuir, W. J., & Foltz, J. T. (1995). Outcome for psychiatric emergency patients seen by an outreach police–mental health team. *Psychiatric Services, 46*, 1267–1271.

Ligon, J. (in press). Client and family satisfaction with brief mental health, substance abuse, and mobile crisis services in an urban setting. *Crisis Intervention and Time-Limited Treatment.*

Ligon, J., & Thyer, B. A. (2000). Client and family satisfaction with brief community menal health, substance abuse, and mobile crisis services in an urban setting. *Crisis Intervention, 6,* 93–99.

Lyons, J. S., Cook, J. A., Ruth, A. R., Karver, M., & Slagg, N. B. (1996). Service delivery using consumer staff in a mobile crisis assessment program. *Community Mental Health Journal, 32,* 33–40.

Olivero, J. M., & Hansen, R. (1994). Linkage agreements between mental health and law: Managing suicidal persons. *Administration and Policy in Mental Health, 21,* 217–225.

Reding, G. R., & Raphelson, M. (1995). Around-the-clock mobile psychiatric crisis intervention: Another effective alternative to psychiatric hospitalization. *Community Mental Health Journal, 31,* 179–187.

Roberts, A. R. (1991). Conceptualizing crisis theory and the crisis intervention model. In A. R. Roberts (Ed.), *Contemporary perspectives on crisis intervention and prevention* (pp. 3–17). Englewood Cliffs, NJ: Prentice-Hall.

Roberts, A. R. (1995). *Crisis intervention and time-limited cognitive treatment.* Thousand Oaks, CA: Sage.

Roberts, A. R. (1996). *Crisis management and brief treatment.* Chicago: Nelson-Hall.

Rouse, B. A. (Ed.). (1998). *Substance abuse and mental health statistics sourcebook.* Washington, DC: U.S. Government Printing Office.

Slagg, N. B., Lyons, J. S., Cook, J. A., Wasmer, D. J., & Ruth, A. (1994). A profile of clients served by a mobile outreach program for homeless mentally ill persons. *Hospital and Community Psychiatry, 45,* 1139–1141.

Sommers-Flanagan, J., & Sommers-Flanagan, R. (1995). Intake interviewing with suicidal patients: A systematic approach. *Professional Psychology: Research and Practice, 26,* 41–47.

Steadman, H. J., Deane, M. W., Borum, R., & Morrissey, J. P. (2000). Comparing outcomes of major models of police responses to mental health emergencies. *Psychiatric Services, 51,* 645–649.

Strentz, T. (1995). Crisis intervention and survival strategies for victims of hostage situations. In A. R. Roberts (Ed.), *Crisis intervention and time-limited cognitive treatment* (pp. 127–147). Thousand Oaks, CA: Sage.

Teese, C. P., & Van Wormer, J. (1975). Mental health training and consultation with suburban police. *Community Mental Health Journal, 11,* 115–121.

Wellin, E., Slesinger, D. P., & Hollister, C. D. (1987). Psychiatric emergency services: Evolution, adaptation, and proliferation. *Social Science and Medicine, 24,* 475–482.

Zealberg, J. J., Christie, S. D., Puckett, J. A., McAlhany, D., & Durban, M. (1992). A mobile crisis program: Collaboration between emergency psychiatric services and police. *Hospital and Community Psychiatry, 43,* 612–615.

Zealberg, J. J., Hardesty, S. J., Meisler, N., & Santos, A. B.

(1997). Mobile psychiatric emergency medical services. In S. W. Henggeler & A. B. Santos (Eds.), *Innovative approaches for difficult-to-treat populations* (pp. 263–274). Washington, DC: American Psychiatric Press.

Zealberg, J. J., Santos, A. B., & Fisher, R. K. (1993). Benefits of mobile crisis programs. *Hospital and Community Psychiatry, 44*, 16–17.

Zealberg, J. J., Santos, A. B., Hiers, T. G., Ballenger, J. C., Puckett, J. A., & Christie, S. D. (1990). From the benches to the trenches: Training residents to provide emergency outreach services: A public/academic project. *Academic Psychiatry, 14*, 211–217.

26

The Comprehensive Crisis Intervention Model of Safe Harbor Behavioral Health Crisis Services

YVONNE M. EATON, LCSW

Safe Harbor Behavioral Health (www.safeharborbh.org) Crisis Services is recognized as a model program by the Pennsylvania State Office of Mental Health. Four types of crisis intervention are available 24 hours per day, 7 days per week, to anyone experiencing a crisis within Erie County, Pennsylvania. A *crisis* is defined very broadly and includes anyone who is experiencing a disturbance of mood, thought, emotion, behavior, or social functioning. Some examples include suicide (ideation, attempts, and completed), psychiatric decompensation, situational stressors, family discord, substance abuse, domestic violence, and bereavement. The structure and functioning of the crisis team results in effective, successful intervention to those in crisis. The four basic services are telephone crisis services, walk-in crisis services, mobile crisis services, and access to crisis residential unit. These services will be discussed using case scenarios to illustrate techniques of crisis intervention.

ORGANIZATIONAL STRUCTURE AND FUNCTIONS

There are 21 crisis services staff scheduled around the clock who have a variety of educational and experiential backgrounds. All staff members complete a month of orientation with subsequent required weekly in-services/ training. Ongoing education is essential in ensuring staff are kept current on clinical intervention strategies and community resources. Training is videotaped for those not on shift at the time it is given. All staff are also certified in Nonviolent Crisis Intervention through the Crisis Prevention Institute, Inc. Staff attend individual clinical supervision sessions twice monthly to review cases and interventions. Field evaluations, in which the clinical supervisor accompanies workers on cases, are conducted frequently to assess clinical and intervention skills, and 24-hour accessibility to a psychiatrist and administrator are provided to all staff. Staff includes 1 intervention specialist, 13 crisis workers, 6 shift supervisors, and 1 director. The intervention specialist provides much of the phone crisis counseling, information, referrals, and telephone triage. They also provide phone support to suicidal callers until the mobile crisis worker arrives on the scene. The intervention specialist is based at the office for the duration of their shift. Crisis workers provide full crisis assessments and face-to-face intervention to individuals and significant others either at the scene of the crisis or on a walk-in basis. These workers utilize techniques of crisis intervention to assist consumers in accessing and utilizing resources to resolve the crisis situation. These workers report to the office but are quickly dispatched to respond to crisis calls by the shift supervisor. Shift supervisors, who also remain in the office, provide clinical and administrative direction to the crisis staff on their shift. They assure all requests for services are responded to in a timely manner as dictated by policy. They conduct documentation reviews and juggle the various demands on their shifts. The director is responsible for the hiring, training, clinical supervision, administrative direction, and discipline of all crisis staff. They are also responsible for the administrative duties of the agency (policies, budget, etc.).

TELEPHONE CRISIS SERVICES

Crisis Services receives more than 2,000 phone calls per month. Crisis calls result in crisis counseling and support, information and referrals, and crisis screening and triage. Crisis staff engage all callers with empathic responses and supportive listening skills. Roberts (1996) offers a comprehensive text for crisis intervention strategies, which includes hotline work. Many callers choose to remain anonymous or, with phone support only, effectively resolve their crises. A screening/triage form is completed for all callers who request further services or face-to-face contact. This essential form addresses both clinical information (such as suicide or homicide risk) and safety issues (such as weapons on the scene and legal history). All calls are assigned an intervention priority code, which allows the shift supervisor to prioritize these multiple requests on a clinical basis. Priority I calls require immediate intervention because of an individual's significant risk of harm to self or others. Some examples of Priority I calls include suicide attempts in progress, police on scene or en route, and suicidal or homicidal ideation with intent and means readily available. Priority II calls require timely intervention because of an inability to cope with current stressors. Risk of harm to self or others is not pressing at the time of contact due to the presence of reliable supports or lack of feasible plan, intent, or method. Some examples include hallucinations, delusions, and suicidal or homicidal ideation with lack of plan or intent. Priority III calls require intervention because of a moderate level of dysfunction. There is no identified risk of harm to self or others. Some examples include impaired ability to meet basic needs (shelter, hygiene), impairment in ability to meet family, educational, or occupational roles, and mood disturbance or other significant vegetative disturbances. Priority IV calls require intervention because of subjective distress and/or mild level of dysfunction or difficulty coping with current stressors. Some examples include minor mood disturbance and relational conflict. Regardless of the intervention priority assigned, all requests for services are addressed as quickly as possible, and every request for service is addressed within 24 hours.

Case Scenario

A phone call was received from an anonymous male caller. This individual was very reluctant to provide information to crisis services. However, it was determined that the consumer had overdosed on 20 Prozac and 20 Ambien. The caller would not provide any demographic or identifying information, and the call had to be traced. While the trace was being completed, the caller became nonresponsive, and the phone was heard dropping to the floor.

Roberts's (1996) seven-stage crisis intervention model was initiated.

Stage 1: Assess Lethality. It was quickly determined via the suicide risk assessment (on the Crisis Services triage form) that the caller had already overdosed on a significant amount of medications, making this a highly lethal/urgent situation.

Stage 2: Establish Rapport. Through the use of rephrasing, paraphrasing, questioning, empathy, and supportive listening, the crisis worker was able to keep the client engaged while the trace was being completed. Establishing rapport with the client was essential because if the client terminated the call, he would likely have died. The triage form utilized by Crisis Services provides workers with structure for questioning, which is particularly helpful in these stressful situations. Some excerpts from the triage appear in Table 26.1.

Stage 3: Identify Major Problem(s). The number one identified problem was a known overdose, which was complicated by the secondary problem of the client's refusal to provide identifying information.

Table 26.1 Sample Triage Questions

Suicidality	Are you/client having thoughts of self harm?	( ) yes	( ) no	( )unknown
	Have you/client done anything to hurt self already?	( ) yes	( ) no	( )unknown
	If yes, describe:			
	How long have you/client had thoughts to hurt self?			
	How might you/client hurt self?			
	Have you/client made any preparations to hurt self?	( ) yes	( ) no	( )unknown
	What keeps you/client from hurting self?			
Homicidality	Are you/client having thoughts to hurt others?	( ) yes	( ) no	( )unknown
	Who do you think about hurting?			
	Have you/client hurt anyone already?	( ) yes	( ) no	( )unknown
	If yes, describe:			
	How long have you/client had thoughts to hurt others?			
	What keeps you/client from hurting others?			

Stage 4: Deal With Feelings. The worker first allowed the client to tell his story about why he felt so bad at this point in his life. The worker began to address those feelings but was unable to do much work in this area because the client became nonresponsive.

Stage 5: Explore Alternatives. Because of the critical nature of the case and the client's unconsciousness, there was no opportunity to explore alternatives or develop an action plan with him in collaboration with Crisis Services.

Stage 6: Develop Action Plan. The crisis worker had to take control of this situation. The following steps were completed:

1. The trace was completed and the address was obtained.
2. A crisis worker and the police were dispatched to the scene.
3. The client was observed through the window lying still on the floor.
4. The police gained entry.
5. The ambulance was called, and the client was transported to the hospital.
6. Because of the client's earlier refusal of crisis assistance and mental health treatment, Crisis Services petitioned for an involuntary commitment, and this was approved.
7. The client was given medical treatment.

Stage 7: Follow-Up. The next morning, a follow-up phone call was made to the hospital, which indicated that the client had been admitted to the mental health unit following his medical stabilization.

WALK-IN CRISIS SERVICES

Any individual may appear at the office for services. Crisis staff will complete a crisis assessment encompassing the evaluation of the individual in crisis, as well as the social context in which the crisis is occurring. The psychosocial format of the evaluation enables the worker to determine the extent and acuity of all reported problem areas, the appropriate therapeutic response for crisis de-escalation, and any referrals indicated for ongoing treatment.

Case Scenario

A 19-year-old male was brought into the office by his parents because he was becoming "bizarre." The consumer was collecting urine in a bottle, collecting used female sanitary products, and making drawings of elaborate machinery. He also began talking about death and harmful effects of heavy metal music and was found burying heavy metal CDs in the backyard. This individual had no previous mental health history.

Roberts's (1996) seven-stage crisis intervention model was initiated.

Stage 1: Assess Lethality. The client's father phoned Crisis Services, expressing concern over bizarre behaviors exhibited by his son. There was no evidence of risk of harm to self or others but obvious evidence of a thought disorder. The father opted to bring his son into the office for a walk-in assessment.

Stage 2: Establish Rapport. Upon the client's arrival, it quickly became apparent that he had not been informed of the purpose of his visit. It was essential that the worker gather the client's perceptions of any difficulties he was having and seek his point of view on the issues mentioned by his father. The use of the worker's empathic communication skills allowed the client to express his thoughts, feelings, and experiences.

Stage 3: Identify Major Problem(s). The assessment of the client included information regarding his mental status. The identified problem was the emergence of a serious thought disorder. It was discovered through the parents' contributions that a diagnosis of mental illness, specifically schizophrenia, existed within the family history.

Stage 4: Deal With Feelings. The crisis worker focused on the thought processes of the client. The client was somewhat insightful at the time of assessment, indicating a realization that others viewed his behaviors as illogical. He, however, explained his delusional beliefs and behavior to the worker. The worker was able to communicate concerns in a nonjudgmental and nonconfrontive way to the client, who was agreeable to seeking inpatient mental health treatment. The client was, however, very fearful. The crisis worker dealt with the client's immediate feelings of fear by explaining the admission process and treatment in detail, as well as offering to accompany the client and family to advocate for their needs. This alliance between the worker and the client was an essential component in getting the client to accept further services.

Stage 5: Explore Alternatives. Various alternative treatment options were discussed with both the client and the family, including two inpatient treatment facilities. The crisis residential unit was also explained as another option if hospitalization was denied.

Stage 6: Develop Action Plan. The crisis worker, client and his parents decided on the following action plan:

1. Hospitalization at one of the inpatient facilities would be pursued.
2. The client was admitted to the inpatient mental health unit.
3. Support group information through AMIECO (Alliance for the Mentally Ill) was provided to the family.
4. Outpatient referrals were given to the client.

Stage 7: Follow-Up. Upon phone follow-up with the client's parents, it was learned that the client had started medications and was responding well. The parents were working actively with the hospital staff to assist in discharge planning.

MOBILE CRISIS SERVICES

Mobile crisis services may be provided by an individual crisis worker or by a team of two crisis staff members at the scene of the crisis. This service shows most clearly the social context in which the crisis is occurring, giving the worker extremely beneficial information and insights. A crisis assessment is completed at the scene, with the goal of quickly determining the most appropriate disposition to meet the individual's needs and obtain relief from distress. Recommendations will include a disposition in the least restrictive setting appropriate for the individual and the presenting crisis.

Case Scenario

Crisis Services received a call from a 30-year-old female who claimed to be calling for someone else. Her speech was slurred, and the information given was inconsistent. The caller did provide an address of the apparent individual in crisis. Because of possible safety issues and unknowns, Crisis Services responded with the police. The consumer was not answering her apartment door, but the landlord assisted us in gaining entry. The consumer was discovered unconscious with a suicide note, an empty bottle of lithium, and 12 serious self-inflicted stab wounds.

Roberts's (1996) seven-stage crisis intervention model was initiated.

Stage 1: Assess Lethality. During the initial phone contact, the client was providing misinformation to Crisis Services, claiming to be calling for a relative in distress. The crisis worker heard various inconsistencies in her story and also noticed the phone number from where the call was originating was also the phone number the caller was claiming to be her "relative's." The caller's slurred speech was another warning sign. The crisis worker did attempt to ask direct questions to assess suicidality, but the caller refused to respond to these questions. The only information gathered about this alleged relative was that she was going to kill herself by overdosing.

Stage 2: Establish Rapport. Through the worker's attentiveness, accurate listening skills, reassurance, and support, the caller was kept engaged and eventually provided an address. While the initial worker was attempting to elicit more information, another worker was able to identify with police assistance that the address provided was in fact the residence that was connected with the incoming phone number; therefore, it was determined that the caller was in fact the one in distress.

Stage 3: Identify Major Problems. Because of various inconsistencies and misinformation provided by the client on the initial phone contact, the major problems were unknown at the time of dispatch. It was not until the crisis worker and the police officer arrived on the scene that the critical nature of the problem was identified. The client would not answer her apartment door, but heavy, labored breathing was heard on the other side. The police forcefully gained entry to find the client naked and unresponsive on the bed with 12 serious self-inflicted stab wounds to her chest area. A suicide note and an empty bottle of lithium were found on the dresser.

Stages 4 and 5: Deal With Feelings and Explore Alternatives. Because of the client's unconscious state and critical condition, the crisis worker was unable to deal with the client's feelings or mutually explore treatment options.

Stage 6: Develop Action Plan. The police officer and crisis worker took control of the situation by doing the following:

1. The police immediately called for an ambulance.
2. The police and crisis worker attempted to stop the bleeding from the client's wounds.
3. The ambulance arrived and transported the client to the hospital.
4. Crisis Services petitioned for an involuntary commitment on an anonymous female (because her true identity was unknown), and this was approved.
5. The client was treated and medically admitted.

Stage 7: Follow-Up. A follow-up phone call was made to the hospital the next day, but the client was still in the intensive care unit (ICU). On day 2 the hospital revealed the client's identity to Crisis Services and reported that the client had eloped from a mental health unit earlier that week. The client was eventually transferred to the original hospital from which she had eloped because her family wanted to assist with her treatment and discharge planning.

Face-to-face contact with individuals in crisis may be provided either by a walk-in or by a mobile service. Crisis Services currently sees more than 350 individuals per month.

ACCESS TO CRISIS RESIDENTIAL UNIT

The crisis residential unit (CRU) provides residential accommodations and continuous, 24-hour supervision for individuals in crisis. This essential resource is another option in providing effective crisis intervention options. CRU is a truly collaborative program between Community Integration Inc, Crisis Services and Stairways (a separate community mental health provider). Crisis Services admits individuals to this unit after a thorough crisis assessment has been conducted and a physician's order from the on-call crisis physician has been obtained. In order to be considered for admission, the individuals must be medically stable, voluntary, and at least 18 years of age, and must present no overt threat to him- or herself or others. The CRU program is an eight-bed facility staffed and run by Stairways, Inc. CRU provides brief treatment (up to 5 days) as an alternative to hospitalization which focuses on problem solving and crisis management.

Services

The following services are provided at CRU (Stairways, 1999):

Assessment: A thorough assessment is conducted to identify and address an individual's emotional needs. In addition, a nursing health assessment is conducted to determine one's physical health needs.

Psychiatric assessment: Each client sees the psychiatric consultant on a daily basis in order to plan and monitor the best course of treatment.

Crisis counseling: Each client receives individual counseling to assist him or her in better understanding the crisis process and ways to effectively cope with the crisis situation. This involves initial problem identification and the development of a rehabilitation plan with a staff member.

Stabilization: The CRU program offers a safe, therapeutic environment in which clients in crisis may feel secure and better able to address their problems with as little stress as possible.

Medication monitoring: CRU offers medication monitoring and education to all clients so that the most appropriate medication regime can be developed.

Programming/psychoeducational groups: The following groups are provided:

1. *Stress reduction:* Reviews the effects of stress on the body and teaches clients to practice one of four techniques to alleviate the symptoms of stress. In addition, assertiveness and goal planning are taught so the clients might feel better able to take control over stressful life events and implement healthy coping strategies during times of stress.
2. *Conflict resolution:* Assists clients in learning how to objectively recognize, evaluate, and execute a healthy course of decision making for daily living. It also helps the client to examine the primary conflict or crisis that resulted in his or her CRU admission so that a prevention plan can be developed.
3. *Symptom management:* Offers suggestions to assist clients in coping with symptoms associated with mental illness. Symptoms covered during this group are modified to meet individual needs.
4. *Recreation:* Aims planned, structured, regular group activities at promoting social interaction and introducing new time-structuring ideas.

Program Steps

Admission

CRU's short-term program utilizes a problem-solving model to resolve crisis situations in the shortest time possible. The maximum stay in most cases will be 5 days; however, the treatment team has the authority to authorize an additional 5 days with clinical rationale. Crisis Services, with a signed release, provides CRU with a copy of the crisis assessment, the safety contract indicating the client's ability to maintain safety, and a verbal report. Crisis Services brings the client, clothes, and medication to the unit. Upon admission, CRU staff count and secure medications, search belongings for weapons or pills, review paperwork, determine the comfort needs of the client (need for food, bath, etc.), and orient the client to the unit and his or her assigned room (Bryan Hickman, personal communication, May 5, 1999).

Treatment Team

The treatment team is run by the director of Crisis Services and includes the supervisor of CRU and an administrative case manager from Case Management Support Services (who authorizes admissions and extensions). A homeless case manager is always in attendance to address the placement needs of the homeless. Additional providers are always welcome to attend to provide their input and recommendations.

The treatment team meets three times per week to review the client's progress, make recommendations for treatment needs, and make plans for discharge. Under certain situations, when there is a clinical need for additional stabilization, an extension of an additional 5 days may be granted by the majority vote of the three main members.

Hospitalization and/or Termination

If it is determined that a client is not making adequate progress at CRU, other accommodations may be necessary. If a client presents an immediate danger to him- or herself or others, Crisis Services will be contacted immediately to pursue hospitalization. Clients who are consistently unable or unwilling to follow the rules at CRU may be discharged after treatment team review and approval (Stairways, 1999).

Discharge

Discharges generally occur when the following conditions exist:

1. Short-term treatment goals are sufficiently met.
2. A client's psychiatric condition or level of functioning has been raised to allow him or her to move to a less restrictive setting.
3. Discharge planning and follow-up are arranged. (Stairways, 1999)

Individuals who choose to leave the unit against clinical advice (ACA) are asked to sign an ACA form. Crisis Services is contacted with every discharge and sent a discharge summary. Crisis Services attempts to follow up on all clients who left ACA.

EMERGENCY PSYCHIATRIC CRISIS STABILIZATION: CASE APPLICATION

Case Scenario

A 35-year-old male with a history of schizophrenia was referred to Crisis Services by another provider after being denied hospitalization. He was very paranoid and delusional, believing that people were attempting to break into his apartment at night. His speech was rapid and tangential, with loose associations. He talked about killing Jeffrey Dahmer and Hannibal Lecter and believed that he was a disciple of Satan. At times he was responding to internal stimuli, whispering to himself and making unusual gestures.

Roberts's (1996) seven-stage crisis intervention model was initiated.

Stage 1: Assess Lethality. By conducting a thorough crisis assessment, it was determined that the client was experiencing nihilistic delusions but was able to contract for safety, indicating he would seek help before acting on any thoughts to hurt himself or others. He had no previous assaultive history nor any current drug or alcohol use. Although psychotic, the client was cooperative and did not appear in danger of impulsively acting out; he did, however, present in a heightened state of anxiety. It seemed that he could benefit from a structured, supervised setting.

Stage 2: Establish Rapport. Understanding and support were two of the most essential skills utilized by the crisis worker in establishing rapport with the client. When intervening with a psychotic client, it is essential to not challenge his or her delusional system or "play along" with it. Challenging this fixed belief system will only create a sense of distrust by the client. Playing along with delusions or hallucinations could incite violence or mistrust when the worker is not aware of or fails to respond to those perceptions that the client is experiencing. The use of attending behavior (Kanel, 1999), such as active listening and supportive posture, were extremely helpful in letting the client know the worker was interested and was there to help.

Stage 3: Identify Major Problem(s). Several problems were identified during the crisis assessment. The client was psychiatrically decompensating. He was not on any medications and was not receiving any outpatient treatment at the time.

Stage 4: Deal With Feelings. The crisis worker, rather than focusing on the delusional beliefs, focused on the client's feelings of anxiety and fear of being alone in his apartment. The worker was able to address these feelings and suggest that together they explore options to make the client feel more comfortable.

Stage 5: Explore Alternatives. Because hospitalization was already denied, other alternative treatment options had to be explored. The CRU was described to the client, who was agreeable to being admitted to this unit. The client also signed a safety contract, indicating his ability to maintain control. The crisis worker received an admission order through the crisis psychiatrist on call, and the client was transported to CRU.

Stage 6: Develop Action Plan. Once the client admitted to CRU, the staff formulated an action plan with him. The following goals were discussed:

1. The client would start medications as prescribed by the CRU consulting psychiatrist.
2. The client would be given an intake appointment for ongoing outpatient services.

3. The client would participate in individual supportive counseling at CRU.

Stage 7: Follow-Up. At the CRU treatment team meeting (2 days after admission), it was determined that the client had started antipsychotic medication, and an intake appointment was scheduled for that day. On the fifth day, the usual day for discharge, the client's progress was discussed, and an extension was granted for an additional 5 days so that the client could get linked up with other mental health services and stabilize further. At the end of the 10-day stay, the client was transferred to a Stairways Group Home (Community Rehabilitation Residence), was on a waiting list for a case manager, was taking psychotropic medication, and had an outpatient follow-up appointment.

CRITICAL INCIDENT STRESS MANAGEMENT FOR CRISIS WORKERS

A "critical incident" is any event that can exert such a stressful impact so as to overwhelm one's usual coping mechanisms (Everly & Mitchell, 1999). Critical Incident Stress Management (CISM) includes a wide variety of techniques and interventions for individuals exposed to life-threatening or traumatic events (Mitchell & Everly, 1993). According to Everly (1995), CISM aims to prevent traumatic stress, mitigate the effects of the critical incident, and maximize recovery. The seven core components of CISM (see chapter 4, pp. 86–90) include the following:

1. *Precrisis preparation:* Educational programs are available on topics of stress, stress reactions, coping strategies, disaster response, and so on, to assist in mental preparedness.
2. *Individual crisis intervention:* Support services and individual crisis intervention.
3. *Large groups:* Large group crisis intervention and demobilization.
4. *Critical Incident Stress Debriefing (CISD):* A group meeting/discussion about a critical incident provided to those directly involved in the incident.
5. *Defusing:* A shortened version of a CISD that takes place about 12 hours after the event.
6. *Family CISM/organizational consultation:* A variety of services and education can be tailored for significant others whose loved one has experienced a critical incident.
7. *Follow-up/referral:* Telephone outreach, station visits, and various referrals can be made.

It is essential that crisis workers exposed to traumatic events be provided with CISM services when appropriate. CISM allows workers the opportunity to discuss the traumatic event, promotes group cohesion, educates them on stress reactions and coping techniques, and shows that the Crisis Services employer cares about the welfare of its employees.

As Maggio and Terenzi (1993) state, administrators must review potential critical incidents and pinpoint particular vulnerabilities of their agency. The following critical incidents have warranted the use of CISM techniques with the crisis workers of Crisis Services:

Nature of Incident	CISM Service
Suicide by gunshot (three times)	CISD
Suicide by hanging (two times)	CISD
Suicide attempt—severe stabbing	CISD
Dead body—several days old	CISD
Threat and assault on crisis worker	CISD
Shooting at crisis worker	Individual consult

Policies indicating response to these critical incidents, as well as aftercare and stress management for the crisis workers, should be in place in all crisis intervention agencies.

REFERENCES

Everly, G. (1995). *Innovations in disaster and trauma psychology: Applications in emergency services and disaster response.* Ellicott City, MD: Chevron.

Everly, G., & Mitchell, J. (1999). *Critical Incident Stress Management—a new era and standard of care in crisis intervention* (2nd ed.). Ellicott City, MD: Chevron.

Gilliland, B., & James, R. (1997). *Crisis intervention strategies* (3rd ed.). Pacific Grove, CA: Brooks/Cole.

Kanel, K. (1999). *A guide to crisis intervention.* Pacific Grove, CA: Brooks/Cole.

Maggio, M., & Terenzi, E. (1993, December). The impact of critical incident stress: Is your office prepared to respond? *Federal Probation, 57,* 10–16.

Mitchell, J., & Everly, G. (1993). *Critical Incident Stress Debriefing: An operations manual for the prevention of traumatic stress among emergency services and disaster workers.* Ellicott City, MD: Chevron.

Roberts, A. (1996). *Crisis management and brief treatment: Theory, technique and applications.* Belmont, CA: Wadsworth.

Stairways. (1999). *Crisis residential unit: A program handbook for clients, their family and friends.* Erie, PA: Author.

27

A Model of Crisis Intervention in Critical and Intensive Care Units of General Hospitals

NORMAN M. SHULMAN
AMY L. SHEWBERT

Historically, when a patient in a medical-surgical hospital is recognized as having a need for psychological support as a result of a medical crisis, the attending physician requests a consultation from a psychiatrist, psychologist, or other mental health professional. Although this professional can provide important diagnostic information on the immediate mental status of the patient, usually little, if any, consideration is given to the patient's ongoing emotional needs. Typically, directives for medication and possibly a referral to another mental health or social service professional are given. Generally, only if a patient becomes a behavior management problem will daily psychological intervention be ordered. When such services are not available, behavior management is frequently left up to nursing, case management, or clerical staff, who often do not have the time or training to attend to these problems, which can be very disruptive. It is thus our assertion that this lack of proper attention to a patient's psychological needs results in an unnecessary burden for the immediate staff and frequently leads to an exacerbation of the patient's crisis. A standing psychological consult available to critical care and other areas of a general hospital would provide the means for giving proper attention to the patients' mind-body experience, while alleviating stressors which the staff is neither trained nor compensated to address. As a result, potential crisis situations can be minimized and in some cases prevented.

DEFINITION AND SCOPE OF MEDICAL CRISIS

Medical crises are an inevitable part of the human experience. Although the definition of a medical crisis is subjective, the drastic change in lifestyle resulting from the crisis is a common theme. Pollin and Kanaan (1995) defined a medical crisis as "a time of unusual emotional distress or disorientation caused by the onset of, or a major change in, the medical condition" (p. 15). Another definition of a medical crisis is the reaction of a person resulting from a substantial variation in experiences differing from the person's usual view of the world (Shulman, 1999). These emergencies create such instability and chaos in the person's life that normality, as the patient previously experienced it, ceases to exist. People in a crisis state demonstrate the following identifiable characteristics (Roberts, 1990):

1. Perception of a meaningful and threatening event
2. Inability to cope with the impact of the event
3. Increased fear, tension, or confusion
4. Subjective discomfort
5. Rapid progression to a state of crisis or disequilibrium

The stress involved with medical crises is typically temporary, yet it can have lifelong effects. The individual's coping skills, cognitive processes, typical affective processes, and history of psychopathology not only determine the degree to which life is affected but also define the medical crisis itself (Roberts, 1996).

The medical crisis generates stress that is universal to all persons in crisis regardless of age, gender, race, and so on. Situational factors, including medical emergencies, life-threatening and chronic illnesses, family health problems, crime, and natural disasters, often incite a medical crisis (Roberts, 1996). Roberts (1996) cites valuable statistics provided by the U.S. Department of Justice establishing the prevalence of medical crises as initiated by medical emergencies. For example, as a result of acute psychiatric or medical emergencies, 254,820 people visit emergency rooms daily; these medical crises also include between 685 and 1,645 suicide attempts per day in a year (Roberts). Regarding life-threatening disease, medical professionals diagnose 3,205 new cancer cases per day, and 140 AIDS patients die each day. Chronic illnesses also account for a great deal of the medical problems experienced by persons in crisis. For instance, a 1991 national health interview survey concludes that some 36 million Americans limit daily activities because of long-term sickness (Pollin & Kanaan, 1995). In addition, 56.5 million individuals suffer problems caused by cardiovascular disease; other chronic illnesses that contribute to the high incidence of medical crises include arthritis, cystic fibrosis, multiple sclerosis, and diabetes mellitus (Pollin

& Kanaan, 1995). Family health problems, consisting of child abuse, drug abuse, domestic violence, and so on, relate directly to the origin of medical crises (as cited in Roberts, 1996). Finally, violent crime estimates also illustrate the high incidence of crises in society today. Data based on the Bureau of Justice statistics indicate that 357 persons are victims of forcible rape every day of the year (Roberts, 1996). Medical crises arbitrarily affect all humans, thus creating a scope of immense proportions.

DIAGNOSTIC DESCRIPTORS OF PATIENTS AND FAMILY

Persons in a crisis state frequently experience similar emotions, reactions, and periods of vulnerability. The medical crisis produces stress for the patient and family. Furthermore, examination of patients in specialized hospital units indicates the same characteristics identifying persons in medical crisis.

Certain characteristics and vulnerabilities identify the patient in crisis. High-risk patients often have suppressed or agitated affect, or "frozen fright," which describes the inability to react entirely (Pollin & Kanaan, 1995). Suicidal ideation combined with depressive symptoms clearly indicates a person with high-risk qualities. Depression is among the most prevalent psychological responses among patients in medical crisis. Goldman and Kimball (1987) report that 25% of patients admitted to critical care units experience symptoms of depression. Four common types of depressed states among special risk patients are: (a) major depressive illness, (b) adjustment disorder, (c) dysthymic disorder, and (d) organic affective disorder (Goldman & Kimball, 1987). A contributory factor to the depression is low self-esteem. Patients report feeling dehumanized by the lack of privacy during treatment times (Rice & Williams, 1997).

Additional common concerns of the patient include quality of life, death, and dying. Other traits of crisis patients consist of inadequate communication with caregivers and inadequate cognitive assimilation of the crisis (Pollin & Kanaan, 1995). Control, self-image, dependency, abandonment, anger, and so on are issues that must be dealt with by the patient in crisis. These descriptors contribute to a patient's vulnerability during the traumatic event. At a time of extreme stress as produced by a medical crisis, patients are susceptible to emotional changes. The degree of vulnerability depends on the "newness, intensity, and duration of the stressful event" (Roberts, 1996 p. 26). Physical and emotional exhaustion, previous crisis experience, and available material resources (Roberts, 1996) are important considerations when determining the risk of the patient in medical crisis.

The family of a person in medical crisis cannot be disregarded when considering the effect on lifestyle change. Family members frequently deny the severity of the situation (Pollin & Kanaan, 1995). A new role as the primary caregiver during hospitalization and after discharge can be an overwhelming responsibility for a family member not properly prepared emotionally. Daily care for people with chronic illness occurs in informal, noninstitutional settings in 70 to 95% of the situations necessitating such activities (as cited in Pollin & Kanaan, 1995). Difficulty with living arrangements and financial commitments create a new burden for all persons involved.

Changes in the family dynamic resulting from differing coping styles in response to the crisis provide an additional stress. Tension between family members can escalate, introducing another problem for the family and patient in crisis that must be resolved. The unpredictability and obscurity of the medical problem are perhaps most difficult for the family. Rice and Williams (1997) describe the exacerbation of family members' fears and anxieties caused by the presence of intimidating equipment and the proximity of critically ill patients. Furthermore, emergency and intensive medical treatment is typically swift and may appear impersonal to a concerned family member. Dealing with life-sustaining issues, life-or-death decisions, and the possibility of death elicit familial emotional complications (Rice & Williams, 1997). The psychological distress of families may also include guilt as a result of the medical crisis.

Specific Intensive Care Unit Symptoms

Patients of specialized intensive care units experience similar symptoms; for example, rehabilitation hospitals provide services for patients with injuries that embody great potential for psychological distress (Bleiberg & Katz, 1991). As a result of medical problems with varying degrees of impairment, disability, and handicap, patients must cope with issues of autonomy, loss, self-concept, and cognitive capacity. Medical intensive care unit (MICU) patients exhibit symptoms of the high-risk patient. Patients diagnosed with cancer experience psychological distress involving matters regarding quality of life, possibilities of disfigurement or disability, pain, and changes in personal relationships (Rozensky, Sweet, & Tovian, 1991). Matus (as cited in Creer, Kotses, & Reynolds, 1991) attests that psychological precipitants (emotional arousal), psychological symptoms (panic), and psychological factors (secondary gain, low self-esteem, etc.) are operants with asthma patients. End-stage renal disease (ESRD) patients, whose treatment often requires up to 12 to 21 hours of dialysis per week, are disturbed by the constant threat of death and increasing dependency.

MICUs are treating increasing numbers of patients with human immunodeficiency virus (HIV) who require psychosocial services for themselves as well as their families and loved ones. Cardiac intensive care units (CICUs) also provide an arena for crisis patients in need of psychological treatment. Thompson (1990) indicates a reduction of anxiety and depression in crisis patients being treated for coronary disease who receive psychological services. Finally, the pediatric intensive care units (PICUs) are the domain of children in crisis coping with a traumatic event. A sense of desperation involved with treating a sick child elicits heartfelt stressors for the staff and families (DeMaso, Koocher, & Meyer, 1996).

A MODEL OF COMPREHENSIVE CARE

This section focuses on how an already established program in a general hospital increases the resilience and reduces the impact of risk factors on patients suffering from a medical crisis. The section will examine how the traditional consult system has proven to be ineffective in helping a patient recover from a crisis. The rationale for a more effective and accessible system will be proposed, followed by a detailed description of the model, including how it interfaces with the rest of the hospital and the social support network.

The Failure of the Traditional Consult System

The traditional consult system continues to fail within most hospitals, and therefore many medical crises that could be prevented are not. For example, in teaching hospitals, where psychiatric residents depend on mental health consults to gain experience, all too frequently several unprepared students respond to a consult and overwhelm an already vulnerable patient. A balance of the patient's emotional needs and the residents' educational needs can be affected with a modicum of sensitivity and forethought, but, unfortunately, this scenario is more the exception than the norm.

The stigma attached to the public's perception of mental illness continues to pervade the general society, and hospitals are no exception. This prejudice creates an indirect negative impact on patient care because hospital staffs often feel that suggesting psychological consultation may be interpreted as an insult by the patient. In fact, this perspective affects staff to the degree that the patient's emotional needs may never by considered. The social stigma attached to mental illness, coupled with the reality of an intense medical perspective of doctors and nurses, facilitates the psychological neglect of patients with psychological needs, especially those in critical care. This phenomenon occurs even when medical conditions are affected by a patient's mental and emotional status. Depression of the chronic type (e.g., dysthymic disorder) can contribute to hostility and behavioral management problems in critical patients.

Finally, physicians' inclinations to divert immediate attention from psychological treatment adversely affect the consult system in a variety of ways. Because physicians in critical care areas are trained specifically to identify and treat medical conditions, a patient's total care tends to remain unaddressed. A physician's professional agenda may also be threatened by a mental health clinician's involvement in the case, especially if it is not asked for, thus resulting in rejections of a psychological consultation. The end result is that all too many patients spend their hospital days without proper psychological help even in intensive care units. This neglect often complicates and exacerbates a patient's existing medical problems to crisis proportions.

Rationale for the Standing Consult

Increasing volumes of evidence demonstrate the efficacy of mental health interventions during a patient's hospital stay for medical or surgical crises. For example, MICUs employ mental health consultants in cancer treatment centers. Rozensky, Sweet and Tovian (1991) describe the therapeutic efficacy of psychological consultation for cancer patients. Assessment of the patient's physical and social environments, psychological strengths and weaknesses, and response to the diagnosis and treatment of cancer, as well as assessment of the patient's personality and coping styles, provide a unique perspective that is integrated into individualized treatment strategies. It is essential that medical professionals realize the value of a holistic approach to treatment as essential within critical care areas, including psychological consultation and ongoing treatment. Such intervention during the patient's hospital stay defies the standard of the "one time only" consult and includes the provision of ongoing supportive and adjustment psychotherapy. This trend to consider a patient's continuing needs includes family therapy, particularly when treatment is compromised by unhealthy family interactions. Additional services include arranging for psychological testing and referrals to related specialists (e.g., neuropsychologists and outpatient aftercare community medical professionals).

Given the traumatic nature of a serious or critical illness or injury and the treatment necessary for patients in these conditions, it seems appropriate to adhere to a comprehensive approach to recovery. The vision of a standing psychological consult embodies the perspective of the mind-body interaction—specifically, that a patient's mental health directly correlates to length of stay and potential for recovery. The model proposed here includes ongoing attention to fluctuations in mental stability as a result of traumatic injury or severe medical conditions.

The following model (see Fig. 27.1) has been established at the Texas Tech University Medical Center in Lubbock, Texas. It includes the burn intensive care unit, transitional care center, rehabilitation, and neonatal and pediatric intensive care units. (The Southwest Cancer Center and the bone marrow transplant unit are covered in a similar fashion by an independent clinician.) The standing consult was approved on these units with the authorization of the acting chief of surgery, John T. Griswold, M.D., of the Texas Tech University Medical School after the model was proposed to him in 1992.

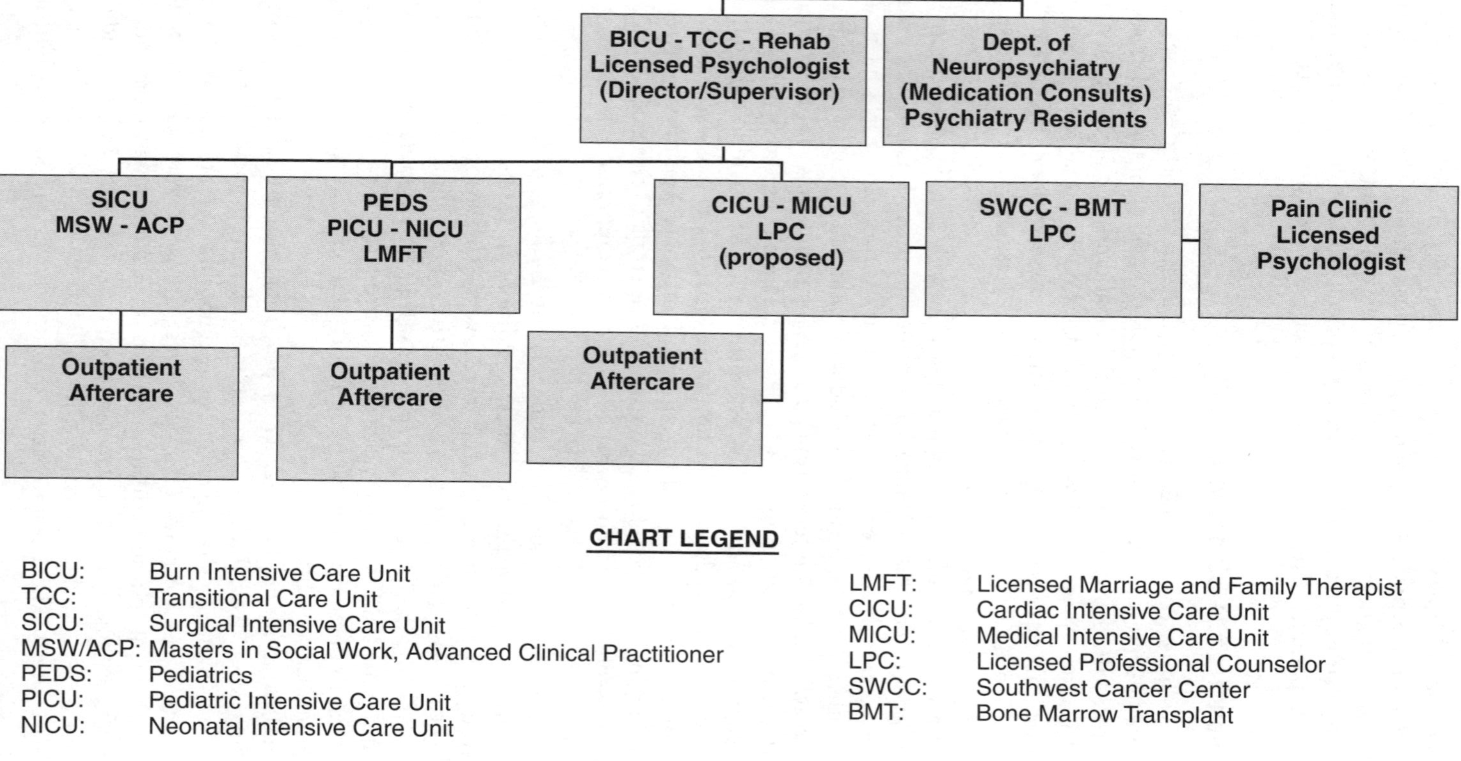

Figure 27.1 Organizational chart of model of comprehensive health care at Texas Tech University Medical Center

Dr. Griswold had been thinking at the time the proposal was made that only half of a patient's needs were attended to at discharge from critical care areas. The Department of Psychiatry, the likely option to turn to regarding the provision of psychological support on these units, did not consider this to be part of its curriculum agenda. Its consultation role had been narrowly defined to include assessment and pharmacotherapy only. On rare occasions, a patient would be followed a few times until discharge, but usually the extent of the consultation ended after one interaction, if a consultation was requested at all. There was also a problem of responsiveness in that frequently a patient would be discharged before a psychiatric resident saw the patient. Unfortunately, when this problem was added to the understandable lack of attention to psychological issues by hospital staff, an inordinate number of patients never had an essential aspect of their treatment attended to.

Traditionally, automatic consults in general hospitals have been limited. Once the resistance to the standing psychological consult was overcome by Dr. Griswold's insistence to the staff of the importance of the program, it was instituted as a component of overall health care. The mental health professional, in this case a licensed psychologist, was able to systematically evaluate every patient admitted to the six-bed burn intensive care unit, the first unit on which it was tried.

The initial assessment included the patient's mental status, internal and external coping resources, degree of family support, and premorbid mental health history. The evaluation included a determination not only of the patient's need for services but also whether the patient and family would accept those services. Psychological interventions were never imposed on a patient (or family), and it was the patient's (or family's) prerogative to terminate the relationship at any time. The attending physician always retained power over the course of treatment, including the option to cancel the intervention.

Rounds were made daily on the burn unit and on weekends when indicated. In addition, the attending physician or staff would call in the clinician at any other time if the situation warranted it. Deference to medical personnel was always given if a procedure was in process or needed to be done at the time of the session. The patient's condition was also taken into consideration in the sense that the patient was never pushed to tolerate more than he or she could handle. As it turned out, the length of the sessions increased as the patient's condition improved. Once a patient stabilized, less time was then required until discharge.

Patient needs were also informally determined by any physician, resident, intern, nurse, therapist, or aide who detected and then passed on important information to the psychologist. Formally, his attendance at weekly staffings provided input regarding the degree and type of interventions. Frequently, the psychologist, with and without his colleagues, would consult with other professionals who might shed more light on a patient's status. The psychologist was in a unique position to subsequently consult a psychiatrist for medication issues, a neuropsychologist, a substance abuse expert, or any other professional who could contribute to the comprehensive care of a patient.

Since a systems approach is utilized, family support was also given on a regular basis, particularly when a patient could not be communicated with directly. The psychologist made it a priority to either convey information himself or encourage physicians working on the case to keep a patient's family updated with concrete and realistic information, even if it was less than positive. Anecdotally, it is safe to say that the overwhelming majority of critical care patients and their families appreciated the consistent presence of a caring mental health professional on an intensive care unit—even in cases where death is imminent. This professional can serve to help a patient maintain dignity with a sense of purpose while facing death. Patients and families were also satisfied with the continuity of psychotherapeutic care made available. They realized that there were times when a patient needed to talk to a neutral party about issues that may not be easily shared with significant others, even clergy.

The unit psychologist was clearly in a unique position to prevent problems from occurring and to be available to respond to occasional conflicts among patients, family members, and professional caregivers, including physicians. Physicians open to the psychologist's role with the treatment team benefited from input not normally made available, as well as from not having to commit valuable time and energy to nonmedical issues. In general, the entire scope of a patient's needs was treated more effectively and efficiently.

While a hospital nonaffiliated psychiatrist was used as a consultant on medication issues, this model suggests the ideal arrangement of pairing a psychiatrist with a psychologist to work in tandem on critical care units. Questions regarding psychiatric medications and follow-up maintenance need not be the concern of the attending and resident physicians alone.

As opposed to the limited consultation offered by existing models, a psychiatric counterpart to the psychologist can also follow a medicated patient daily. Such a professional liaison proves to be efficient for all members of the treatment team. For example, many times issues of drug interactions and the psychologial effects of medication routinely administered to critical care patients can be handled by the specialist most uniquely qualified to address these issues. A psychiatrist experienced in the area of critical care is an invaluable member of the team, allowing other physicians to be free to concentrate on their specific areas of expertise.

At the Texas Tech University Medical Center intensive care and rehabilitation units, the psychological needs of patients are no longer neglected by the absence of integrated treatment. Treatment is now more comprehensive, with issues of compliance, treatment interference, and patient-family-staff conflicts being dealt with quickly and as a function of overall care, since the psychologist is already involved. In this manner, demands on the staff to perform duties outside of their job description are minimized. After discharge, another advantage to the patient is the increased tendency to follow through with outpatient aftercare either with the unit psychologist or with another professional in the community.

The psychologist is also available to staff members whose equilibrium may be disturbed by the extraordinary demands of critical care. Individual and group interventions are useful either for ongoing support or in response to a traumatic event on the unit. As a result, the staff gains a measure of solidarity and security with the knowledge that a trusted professional is readily available to respond to their professional and personal needs.

CASE ILLUSTRATIONS

Case 1

T. is a 35-year-old Hispanic female seen to evaluate her emotional response to traumatic double leg amputations. The patient was injured in an automobile accident, which also involved her 16-year-old son, who was driving and had fallen asleep at the wheel. The patient's son had informed her prior to the accident that he was very tired and that he wanted her to drive. Shortly thereafter, the accident occurred, and the patient's legs were crushed beyond repair. The boy suffered only minor injuries.

The first intervention was agreed to by the patient's husband, who wanted his son seen. This was to allow the boy to see his mother and determine that she was going to live, and to give her an early opportunity to absolve him of any guilt. Once this was accomplished, the patient was talked to daily and encouraged not to give up because her prognosis was good, given current rehabilitation capabilities. These interventions constituted the initial cognitive reframing efforts.

The importance of employing a systems approach is exemplified in this case. As the inpatient psychotherapy progressed (eventually over a course of 65 sessions covering two admissions, over a 5-month period), it came to the therapist's attention that the patient's husband and other son (age 17) were in the midst of their own crises. This information necessitated that family and individual therapy be done with various combinations of family members collaterally with the treatment of the identified patient.

Adjustments and readjustments of coping styles have had to be made over the past several months as minor crises have erupted. For example, the father and one of the sons began drinking more to numb their pain over their loved one's condition. Second, the patient became recurrently depressed during the difficult physical rehabilitation she had to endure. In addition, she was forced to face the hard reality that an above-the-knee amputation posed extremely difficult prosthetic complications. Third, the other son considered dropping out of college, against his mother's wishes, because of his inability to concentrate.

At the time of this writing, the family members are still struggling to balance their respective means of coping. Overall, the situation has been partially reframed successfully in that some positive adaptations have been made. For example, T. returned to graduate school to get a master's degree in counseling so that she can help others. Her husband has stopped drinking, and the boys are being seen individually to facilitate their resolving any residual guilt, resentment, and substance abuse issues.

In the best of all possible circumstances, the family would have accepted the assistance of antidepressant medication, but the patient and her family wanted to work without its potential benefits. They remain committed to working together to complete their collective resolutions and should continue their treatment as outpatients until it is no longer indicated. It is important to note that much of the success of therapy was attributed to the early and consistent interventions provided by the standing consult in place at the time in the surgical intensive care unit where the patient was initially treated. She was then able to be seen subsequently on the regular floor and later as an outpatient, thus ensuring an essential continuity of care.

Case 2

N. is a 43-year-old White male referred for a mental status exam pursuant to several days of unconsciousness caused by a propane explosion. When he was initially seen, the patient had only a sketchy memory of the incident and could remember no details. He was oriented to person but not to place or time. Since one suspected cause of the explosion was a suicide attempt by purposely igniting the propane tank, an assessment of suicidal risk had to be done. However, because of the nature of his mental status, a risk assessment had to be done frequently during the first 2 weeks of his stay in the burn intensive care unit. The patient vehemently denied that he was trying to kill himself, and he never changed his response.

It became imperative that the patient be seen frequently (a total of 32 sessions over a 4-month period) because of his mental health history. Shortly after admission, it became clear from the medications he was taking that he had a premorbid condition of bipolar disorder (depressed). Upon intubation, the patient was unable to receive his psychotropic medications, which included Serzone and Restoril. Therefore, it was feared that when he regained consciousness, he may present behavioral management problems and possible attempt suicide, which he did have a history of.

During the course of his hospitalization, rapport was developed and maintained as a hedge against any disruptive behavior on the floor or suicidal ideation. At times the patient did become agitated and difficult to manage, but with the assistance of psychiatry, a proper administration of his psychotropics restored him to stability. Prior to discharge, contact was made with a physician in his hometown, where treatment (pharmacotherapy and psychotherapy) could continue without interruption.

The standing consult again proved to be invaluable in preventing a crisis from evolving as the patient was seen shortly after admission and regularly after that until discharge. Rather than be treated with heavy sedation alone after becoming a behavior management problem, the patient did not fall between the cracks and his psychological needs were consistently attended to. His mental illness was quickly and properly addressed, and he passed through the hospital with only minimal disturbance to the patient and staff.

APPLICATION OF ROBERTS'S SEVEN-STAGE CRISIS INTERVENTION MODEL IN CRITICAL CARE AREAS

Roberts's (1996) seven-stage crisis intervention model can be applied in hospital settings where initial intervention with health emergencies and other traumatic events naturally occur. However, performing crisis intervention in critical care areas of general hospitals poses unique problems that must be considered. For example, in Case 2, a thorough assessment, including an assessment of lethality, could not be done until well after admission. Since a suicide attempt was suspected, close contact with the medical staff had to be maintained so that this critical assessment could be made as soon after extubation as possible. At this point, if suicidal ideation persisted, the proper suicide prevention protocol could be implemented on the unit, in this case, burn intensive care.

Regarding Case 1, in spite of the fact that a suicide attempt was not the cause of the accident, the patient's despondence in the aftermath of the double amputation had to be considered and a lethality assessment done until it was determined beyond any doubt that T. posed no threat to herself. The "captive audience" reality of the inpatient setting allows for lethality assessments to be made at least daily or, if necessary, multiple times daily by different staff members. Any change in the degree of the lethality is reported to the unit mental health clinician, who would alter the treatment plan as indicated.

Another distinguishing feature of the inpatient crisis intervention is the necessity of establishing rapport (Roberts's, stage 2) with a patient over a sometimes inordinate extended period. Mind-altering pain medications, pain itself, disorientation caused by ICU isolation (resulting in a phenomenon known as *ICU psychosis*), and the difficulty of determining staff identity due to masks and gowns all contribute to a difficult period of rapport building. In addition, frequent interruptions from medical staff for the application of intensive care procedures necessarily shorten time with the patient and interrupt the therapeutic flow.

Both N. and T. were unable to communicate until well after admission. Once the interventions began, rapport was established with both patients piecemeal and over several days. At times, information had to be repeated because of the patients' relatively incoherent mental status early in their medical care. In time (longer with N. than with T. because of mental illness), rapport was successfully established.

In both case examples, identification of the crisis precipitant (stage 3) was readily apparent (i.e., the accidents). Although premorbid issues with both N. and T. certainly affected their individual responses to crisis, it is clear that the interventions were necessitated by the patients' misfortunes. In the cases of most ICU patients, the crisis begins and continues to resolve as their physical condition improves. However, in the case of T., who would suffer numerous physical and family-related emotional setbacks, each new precipitant had to be dealt with aggressively and in a timely manner. The already established rapport with her made subsequent interventions that much easier for her to take advantage of.

The majority of time with both patients was spent dealing with their various feelings about what had happened to them (stage 4). Active listening techniques, as well as conveyance of validation, empathy, warmth, and reassurance, were used to help the patients understand that they were being heard by a caring professional. Basic counseling skills were employed in the course of the supportive psychotherapy to foster their exploration of their emotions about what had happened to them and the potential consequences that awaited them during and after their recoveries. T. required more and longer sessions because of her many concerns about her husband and two children, who complicated her recovery. Their difficulties coping with T.'s amputations and its meaning to them initially created secondary crisis precipitants for her, such as reactive drinking and depression. N.'s adaptations were relatively straightforward and uncomplicated.

In the course of helping T. and N. explore their feelings, various alternatives were generated and explored (stage 5). T. benefited greatly from being aware of the resources available to amputees that would allow her to resume a relatively normal life. The physical rehabilitation protocol for amputees was reviewed with her shortly after she was able to communicate her feelings about the loss of her legs. She received much reassurance from knowing what to expect regarding her physical recovery (which would be done in her hometown), the fitting of prostheses, learning how to walk again, and gradually being able to resume her teaching career. She was also greatly relieved that her family would be worked with individually and collectively to focus on their various problems. This allowed her to focus on her rehabilitation and to spend less time and energy on issues she had no control over.

N. received comfort from learning that the unit was aware of his history of mental illness, was in contact with his treating doctors and family, and therefore would be able to maintain his medication schedule and his stable mental status. In addition, contact with his ex-wife, who remained a valuable source of support in his life, was encouraged and facilitated. This person was especially important because she was N's only nonprofessional support, whereas T. had a multitude of supportive family, friends, and wel-wishers.

As a result of the extended stays of both patients, ample time was available for the development and formulation of their respective action plans (stage 6). Prior to discharge, the hospital assisted in setting up the medical and psychiatric resources that would ensure cognitive and affective stability. With N. several conversations were held with his treating professionals and his ex-wife, who had an investment in assuring that N. would be referred back to his mental health providers upon his return home. The patient participated in developing the discharge plan and knew exactly what was expected of him (i.e., compliance), and what resources were available to him.

T. also had a clear idea of the postdischarge phase of her recovery. The mental health phase was offered to her in the form of aftercare psychotherapy for her and her family members in various combinations. She was pleased with the predictability and availability of the discharge plan and knew she could inquire about it with several different professionals and receive a straight answer.

Both patients agreed to follow-up plans (stage 7). Since T. and her family would return to the hospital where the initial crisis was treated for medical and psychological care, follow-up was easily confirmed. At these times the progress of her medical and emotional rehabilitation was discussed, as well as what she could next expect and have to cope with. N.'s follow-up care, on the other hand, was arranged where he was currently being treated. Phone calls to his providers near his home were made shortly after discharge to ensure follow-through.

Roberts's seven-stage model is well adapted to serving the psychological needs of patients in critical care areas. One can safely assume that crisis intervention with most of these patients is indicated by virtue of their need for intensive care. Although the model's application has to be tempered by the specific demands on units of this kind, the essential elements of the seven stages have universal utility. As a result, patients' crises are alleviated by timely intervention (i.e., as close to the time of the precipitating event as possible). In addition, future crises can be prevented because of the adaptive learning that takes place during the daily, intensive interventions.

CLINICAL CONSIDERATIONS AND IMPLICATIONS

Several special direct service intervention considerations must be taken into account when working with patients in crisis in critical care areas. First, deference to medical staff has to be a priority. Because of the nature of intensive care medical services, there may never be a convenient time for a proper assessment or intervention. It is commonplace for several interruptions to occur during the course of as little as 10 to15 minutes, making the atmosphere less than conducive for crisis management.

At times the therapist has to do his or her best to prioritize the treatment issues and address them in the time available. This becomes especially important when assessing suicidal risk or any other self-destructive behavior that may complicate treatment. In practical terms, this may mean that several brief interventions have to be done before a clear picture of the patient's functioning can be ascertained. The patient's tenuous condition, which can limit the effectiveness of a session, is frequently more of a reason for brief intervention than procedural interruptions.

A second consideration is the indicated emphasis on performing the initial crisis intervention as close to the time of the crisis as possible. As with any crisis, a medical crisis, especially a traumatic event, needs to be processed as early as possible before defenses have the opportunity of reconstituting. This issue becomes most relevant with posttraumatic stress disorder, which if not treated early can fester and manifest its myriad symptoms months or even years later. Therefore, if possible, it is recommended that the patient be seen as soon after admission as possible—for example, shortly after extubation or regaining consciousness.

Another advantage of early intervention is the forging of relationships even when a patient may be initially asymptomatic. Once a bond has been established, the patient will be far more inclined to talk about an emergence of symptoms when they do occur, sometimes well after discharge. It is not unusual for a patient to contact a therapist for issues of PTSD or depression months after the first contact and request outpatient therapy. This, of course, is not as likely to occur without the initial formation of the therapeutic relationship. Creation of this early tie is particularly essential when the impact of heavy sedation, which has the capacity of masking psychopathological symptoms, is considered.

A third consideration is the importance of integrating a family systems model into one's crisis intervention techniques. A critical illness or accident affects an entire family or extended family because these relatives become victims as well. Effective crisis intervention considers the needs of the overall family, which can be used to further the emotional healing of a patient if correctly directed.

When doing critical care crisis intervention, much of the work takes place in the waiting areas or in the corridors of the hospital talking to family members forced to cope with the consequences of a serious illness or accident. Frequently, they become as much or even more in need of crisis services as the patient. Therefore, time and attention should be focused on them in order to maintain family equilibrium for its own sake, as well as for the ultimate recovery of the patient.

A fourth consideration is the potential for burnout of the crisis intervenor performing daily crisis intervention services in repeated life-and-death situations, not to mention with patients who are severely maimed or disfigured. It is imperative that the demands placed on the crisis professional are not excessive and that the intervenor has adequate supervision and emotional support. A high tolerance for stress and multiple available coping resources are prime factors for the crisis professional to have access to while working in a critical care area.

The two case studies presented earlier are informative for crisis intervenors because they are reflective of the ICU patients who are seen as a matter of course. They represent more the rule than the exception. All four of the clinical considerations (i.e., treatment priority given to medical issues, early intervention, a family focus, and staff burnout potential) had to be taken into consideration when working with both patients. In fact, it is unusual to have a patient in critical care when less than all of these intervention themes are present. Occasionally, lack of family involvement becomes a problem. However, the absence of this coping resource usually exacerbates the potential for burnout because the intervenor's role becomes more demanding as involvement with the patient necessarily increases.

Managed Care

Managed care poses unique problems regarding insurance reimbursement for the work performed on the ICUs described earlier. The brunt of inpatient care must be precertified before an insurance carrier is willing to pay for psychotherapeutic services. Unfortunately, the precertification process is often cumbersome, and several days may pass before permission is given. One would think that any patient suffering from severe illness or injury would be automatically certifiable for at least an initial assessment, but this is not the case.

All too often, billing for time spent doing crisis intervention is nonreimbursable because the sessions were not precertified. However, waiting for precertification would be anathema to the maximum efficacy of crisis intervention. Although there is no pat resolution to this issue, professional ethics dictate that the patient must be seen as soon as medically feasible. Hopefully, efforts to retrocertify will be successful on the basis of the logic of the argument. Perhaps someday a limited number of diagnostic evaluation sessions will be automatically precertified for patients victimized by accidents or some other trauma, but until that time comes, struggles with managed care will continue.

Two potential means of reimbursement may be explored to compensate for the denied sessions. One is for the hospital to provide a supplementary stipend to a clinician working in critical care areas. The amount could be based on the average number of nonreimbursable sessions combined with the average number of sessions spent with nonfunded patients. The second alternative is for the facility to apply for grants to foundations specializing in funding innovative medical programs. In fact, both of these options are being explored at University Medical Center in Lubbock, Texas, where the comprehensive, integrated psychological support program mentioned earlier is in the process of being developed in all of its critical care units.

CONCLUSION

It only makes sense for the psychological needs of patients in general hospitals to be attended to along with their physical problems. The general trend in medicine is to recognize this logical, inseparable connection in patients. Although individual physicians and, on a larger scale, certain critical care units integrate treatment successfully, the premise of this chapter is that the successful integration of treatment can be effected in an entire hospital.

If such treatment is properly implemented, patients, families, staff, and the facility should benefit in a variety of ways, not the least important of which is the predicted reduced length of stay (and reduced associated costs). Research soon to be published (Shulman, 1999) should validate this hypothesis, among others, such as the predicted use of less medication, fewer psychological problems, and reduced stress on staff.

Common sense dictates that an essential aspect of health care is the prevention and minimization of potential psychological crises, which complicate and exacerbate ongoing and later treatment. A comprehensive model of crisis intervention in critical and intensive care units is a sensible means of bringing about this necessary improvement in overall health care.

REFERENCES

Bleiberg, R. C., & Katz, B. L. (1991). Psychological components of rehabilitation programs for brain-injured and spinal-cord-injured patients. In R. H. Rozensky, J. J. Sweet, & S. M. Tovian (Eds.), *Handbook of clinical psychology in medical settings* (pp. 375–400). New York: Plenum.

Creer, T. L., Kotses, H., & Reynolds, R. V. (1991). In R. H. Rozensky, J. J. Sweet, & S. M. Tovian (Eds.), *Handbook of clinical psychology in medical settings* (pp. 497–516). New York: Plenum.

DeMaso, D. R., Koocher, G. P., & Meyer, E. C. (1996). Mental health consultation in the pediatric intensive care unit. *Professional Psychology: Research and Practice, 27(2)*, 130–136.

Goldman, L. S., & Kimball, C. P. (1987). Depression in intensive care units. *International Journal of*

Psychiatry in Medicine, 17(3), 201–212.

Pollin, I., & Kanaan, S. B. (1995). *Medical crisis counseling.* New York: Norton.

Rice, D. G., & Williams, C. C. (1997). The intensive care unit: Social work intervention with the families of critically ill patients. *Social Work in Health Care, 2(4),* 391–398.

Roberts, A. R. (1990). Assessment and treatment research. *Crisis intervention handbook.* Belmont, CA: Wadsworth.

Roberts, A. R. (1996). Epidemiology and definitions of acute crisis in American society. In A. R. Roberts (Ed.), *Crisis management and brief treatment: Theory, technique and application* (pp. 16–31). Belmont, CA: Brooks Cole.

Rozensky, R. H., Sweet, J. J., & Tovian, S. M. (1991). *Handbook of clinical psychology in medical settings.* New York: Plenum.

Shulman, N. M. (1999). The relative impact of an open consult system of psychological intervention on burn intensive care patients and staff. Unpublished research data.

Thompson, D. R. (1990). Efficacy of counseling for coronary patients and partners (Doctoral dissertation, Loughborough University of Technology, 1990). *Dissertation Abstracts International, 50.* (50–10B) 4450.

28

The Crisis of Divorce: Cognitive-Behavioral and Constructivist Assessment and Treatment

DONALD K. GRANVOLD

The following are brief examples of separation/divorce-related crises.

- Janet initiated a separation from Terry and has filed for divorce. She and their three children came by the house to pick up some picnic supplies and found Terry lying dead in the backyard next to his shot gun and a bottle of Jack Daniels. A suicide note inside the house detailed that Terry could not stand the thought of another man parenting his children or having sex with the "only woman I have ever loved."
- Lois separated from her husband, Alex, on learning that she has genital herpes, contracted from Alex. The discovery led to Alex's disclosure that he has been having sex with their neighbor.
- Bob returned home early from a business trip to find his wife having sex with two men in the den. Shattered by the violation of trust, Bob filed for divorce.
- Sam has been in and out of several substance abuse treatment programs during the 15 years of his marriage to Toni. Immediately after release from each program he has resumed drinking, stating that he is different from "those alcoholics" because he can control his drinking. After yet another episode when Sam (in a state of inebriation) became physically violent with their 10-year-old son, Toni painfully decided that she could no longer tolerate Sam's alcohol abuse and filed for divorce.
- Norma's 7-year marriage to David has been punctuated by a series of episodes of physical abuse, each one followed by David's expressions of re-

morse, commitment to get help with his jealousy and anger, and assurance that he will never hurt Norma again. Last weekend, in an unprovoked jealous rage, David physically attacked Norma and broke two of her ribs, blackened her eyes, and bruised her arms. After her release from the hospital emergency room, Norma moved out and filed for divorce.

- Carrie understood that Todd, her husband from whom she had separated 6 months earlier, agreed that after the divorce she would maintain managing conservatorship (custody) of their two preschool children. Carrie's attorney called to report that Todd has counterfiled, seeking custody of the children. Carrie suspects that it is related to the fact that she has begun dating. Whatever the motivation, she feels extremely threatened by the action.
- Sue received a letter from the IRS indicating that her ex-husband had failed to file joint income tax returns for the past 3 years. This was information about which she had no prior awareness, as she had signed income tax returns each year with the understanding that her husband forwarded them to the IRS. The IRS letter went on to state that her share of the liability for past taxes, interest, and penalties is $14,000. Her annual income in $19,000.
- Joe has worked hard to overcome the pain of his divorce from Cathy, a woman with whom he wanted to remain married despite his concerns about her stability at times. He has a strong relationship with his 5-year-old daughter and enjoys being a father. He has seen his daughter at every opportunity both during regular visitation and whenever Cathy has allowed it. He received a telephone call from Child Protective Services informing him that he has been charged by Cathy with child sexual abuse of their daughter and an investigation is underway.
- Tommy thought that he had successfully completed the "letting go" process regarding his ex-wife, Mary, who had initiated their divorce a year ago. Tommy has seen Mary infrequently during the past year. Last Saturday night, at a local fund-raiser, he observed Mary romantically engaged with another man. Tommy went into an "emotional tailspin" and reinitiated therapy.

The dissolution of a marital relationship or a similarly committed couple relationship is among the most stressful life circumstances (Bloom, Asher, & White, 1978; Olson & DeFrain, 2000). Divorce is a process characterized by peak periods of stress, extreme loss, pervasive change demands, and markedly altered relationships with significant members of one's personal domain. The challenges to activate robust coping capacities are great. The pain of marital dissolution is extreme for most, regardless of the individual's role in the dissolution decision making. Both those who make the decision to divorce and those who have the decision imposed upon them suffer painful consequences.

Divorce is not a singular event; rather, it is a process characterized both by discrete stressful events and by a cumulative set of losses and adaptation demands. The self system and family system are thrust into an extreme state of disequilibrium as pervasive change demands are realized. Individuals engaged in the divorce process are at risk of crisis in a multitude of ways. Typically, the emotional trauma is highly intense, episodes are repetitive, and crisis opportunities occur not only during the divorce process but long after the divorce is legally final. For some, the intensity of the crisis reaches life-and-death proportions. As evidence of divorce crisis intensity and lethality risk, recently a physician from the East Coast followed his physician ex-wife to Texas, where she traveled to visit his sister. He accosted her on a jogging path, murdered her, and moments later killed himself. His crisis was related to an imminent loss of easy access to his children for visitation. His ex-wife of two years and managing conservator of their two children planned to relocate her practice to Michigan. His recent petition to gain managing conservatorship of his children had been denied by the court.

To effectively treat divorcing/divorced clients, therapists must be skilled in crisis assessment and intervention. This chapter addresses the application of cognitive-behavioral and constructivist crisis intervention procedures to divorce crises. Particular attention is given to the definition of crisis, the types and nature of divorce crises, the psychosocial needs of divorcing individuals, risk assessment, resiliency and strengths assessment, and the application of the Roberts (1990, 1996) intervention model to divorce crisis resolution.

PREVALENCE OF DIVORCE AND MENTAL HEALTH CONSEQUENCES

Divorce is a commonplace phenomenon in the United States and in many countries throughout the world. In the United States, the breakup of the family is a familiar theme resounding across a range of divergent arenas, from political conventions to mental health conferences. The preoccupation with divorce is a reflection, in part, of the pervasive consequences of divorce specifically to the couple and their children, and also to many others in their personal domain. Family members must somehow survive the crisis of the breakup. The paths of their survival often lead to mental health professionals.

Divorce Rates

The U.S. divorce rate spiraled upward during the 1960s and 1970s, reaching a record high in 1981, when 1.21 million people divorced (5.3 per 1,000 population), affecting some 3 million men, women, and children (National Center for Health Statistics, 1986). There were 1,182,000 divorces in the

Table 28.1 International Comparison of Divorce Rates

Country	Year	Divorce Rate per 1,000
Japan*	1997	1.78
United States**	1995	4.44
Germany**	1995	2.07
France**	1996	1.90
Italy**	1994	0.48
United Kingdom**	1994	2.97
Sweden**	1996	2.40

Sources:
*Ministry of Health and Welfare, Statistics and Information Department, Minister's Secretariat. (1999, Feb. 5). *Vital statistics of Japan.* Tokyo.
***United Nations Secretariat,* Department for Economic and Social Information and Policy Analysis, Statistical Division (1998). *Demographic yearbook* (1996 ed.). New York: United Nations.

United States in 1990, 4.7 per 1,000 population, and 20.9 per 100 married women ages 15 and over (Monthly Vital Statistics Report, 1990). According to 1997 provisional data, there were 1,163,000 divorces annually, or 4.3 per 1,000 population. Data released by the U.S. Census Bureau in early 1999 show the U.S. divorce rate at around 50%, up from 43% in 1988. Despite the moderate decline since the 1981 high, divorces continue to occur at a remarkable rate in the United States.

An international comparison of divorce rates shows the United States to have a significantly higher rate than other nations, although the United Kingdom retains a strong second-place standing (4.44 per 1,000 U.S. population, compared with 2.97 per 1,000 population in the United Kingdom; see Table 28.1). These comparative data provide evidence that divorce is occurring at significant rates in many other countries as well, although Italy has a relatively low rate of divorce. Along with a high divorce rate has come a high remarriage rate. A majority of the divorced population remarry (Glick, 1989). Many of these individuals successfully remarry, presumably benefiting from greater maturity as a product of age and learning from "bad" experiences. The divorce rate of remarriages, however, is even higher than that of first marriages (Goldstein, 1999). A notable challenge confronting subsequent marriages is the blending of families. The stresses associated with stepparental and stepsibling relationships compound the already challenging aspects of functioning in a marital relationship (Booth & Edwards, 1992; Halford, 2001).

Factors Influencing the Rise in the Divorce Rate

As I have stated elsewhere (Granvold, 1989), a variety of factors have been identified as influential in the burgeoning failure rate of marriage in the

United States from the 1950s to the present, including the liberalization of divorce laws (no-fault divorce; Katz, 1994; Parkman, 1995); the desacralization of marriage (Weiss, 1975); the shifting roles of women, including their greater economic independence; the greater social acceptance of divorce concomitant with the increasing frequency rate (divorce begets divorce); a shift away from the intrinsic permanence-of-marriage ethic toward a more "pragmatic" view based on internal and external reward-cost factors (Sanchez & Gager, 2000; Scanzoni, 1972); and, perhaps most important, the trend toward greater satisfaction of personal goals, interests, and desires along with higher expectations for marital happiness (Pam & Pearson, 1998; Sanchez & Gager, 2000; Weitzman, 1985). People are no longer willing to remain "long-suffering" in an unrewarding or abusive relationship. For many, the opportunities for success and comfort after divorce are considered to be too great in American society to choose to remain unhappily married.

Divorce and Mental Health

It is well documented that couple relationship problems are among the life stresses most highly associated with psychological disorders (Beach, Sandeen, & O'Leary, 1990; Epstein & Schlesinger, 1994; Halford, 2001; Johnson, 2003; Michelson, 1987; Olson & DeFrain, 2000; Papp, 2003). Divorce is one of the most highly rated risk factors associated with major depression (Anthony & Petronis, 1991; Cozzarelli, Karafa, Collins, & Tagler, 2003; Gallo, Royall, & Anthony, 1993; Kessing, Agerbo, & Mortensen, 2003; McKenry & McKelvey, 2003; Weissman, Bruce, Leaf, Florio, & Holzer, 1991). Furthermore, the presence of a satisfying, committed couple relationship has been found to be associated with low rates of depression (Costello, 1982).

The suicide rate of those separated and divorced is significantly higher than that of their married counterparts (Cantor & Slater, 1995; Kessing et al., 2003; Trovato, 1986). A recent study by the National Institute for Healthcare Research in Rockville, Maryland, found that divorced people in the United States are *three times* as likely to commit suicide as married people. Divorce currently ranks as the number one factor linked with suicide rates in major U.S. cities. In a recent Australian study, separated males were found to commit suicide at 6.2 times the rate of married males, and separated females were found to commit suicide at 1.7 times the rate of married females (Cantor & Slater, 1995). It can be concluded that marital separation and divorce pose significant mental health risks. The consequences are meaningful not only to the divorcing couple, but to their children, extended family, friends, and to society at large.

DEFINITION OF CRISIS

A number of definitions of the term "crisis" have been posited (Bard & Ellison, 1974; Burgess & Holstrom, 1974; Freeman & Dattilio, 1994; Goldenberg, 1983; McCubbin & Patterson, 1983; Olson, 1997; Roberts, 1990; Slaiku, 1990). A crisis can be thought of as consisting of three elements: (1) the presence of a precipitating stressful, life-changing or life-threatening event or circumstance; (2) the individual's perception of the event or circumstance as a significant threat; and (3) the individual's current inability to cope with the threat or to mobilize the psychological or physical resources to facilitate resolution. To consider an event to be crisis-precipitating, the individual must cognitively *appraise* the event as a significant threat to the self system. Consistent with Lazarus (1989), the degree of threat is the consequence of primary and secondary appraisals. *Primary appraisals* establish the relevance of an event to one's well-being or steady state (dynamic homeostasis), and *secondary appraisals* reflect the individual's coping capacities and available resources to meet the demand. Hence, an individual in crisis has experienced a precipitating circumstance that is perceived by the individual as posing a psychosocial accommodation significantly beyond the individual's belief in his or her capacity to cope, adjust, or integrate. The personal consequences of a crisis may take the form of emotional and psychological unrest, as well as physical trauma and detrimental somatic outcomes. And beyond these outcomes, many times personal crises have a detrimental impact on social relationships.

It is noteworthy that a crisis may evolve from an event that many would judge to be positive. Winning the lottery, receiving a promotion, and making a desired move to a new community are events with obvious positive meaning. Curiously, each event may become a crisis for the individual (and family) should the changes associated with it be greater than the individual's (or family's) current capacity to accommodate change. Also, positive life events may occasion opportunities for or stimulate associated challenges that reach crisis proportions. For example, a long-sought promotion may require travel, posing unique changes in family dynamics, division of labor task performance, and child care.

It is also important to acknowledge that a crisis arising from a problematic circumstance has the potential to stimulate extremely positive outcomes (Boss, 1988; Slaiku, 1990). An individual may discover coping abilities and resiliency far beyond precrisis self-views. Meaningful relationships may develop or become strengthened or expanded through crisis resolution. Unforeseen skills and talents may be cultivated and new behaviors learned as the individual lives through the crisis.

Summary

Based on the tripartite definition of crisis delineated here, a stressor becomes a psychological crisis only when the individual experiences a threat to self so intense that his or her *characteristic* capacities to cope and resolve distress are surpassed, or alternatively, the individual's characteristic capacities to cope and resolve distress are so markedly compromised that an otherwise manageable challenge becomes a *crisis*. In either circumstance, the individual's cognitive functioning and the availability of social and instrumental resources play critical roles in distinguishing a manageable stressor from a crisis. Conceptualizing crises in this way lends great viability to the use of cognitive-behavioral and constructivist treatment as a preventive approach for clients in a sea of crisis opportunities and as a means to facilitate a coping repertoire, sense of empowerment, and the proactive mobilization of personal and social resources for those in crisis.

DIVORCE AS CRISIS

The process of divorce may reach crisis status in two ways. The individual may experience a *discrete event* in the couple relationship that results in an extreme perturbation to the self system, or the *cumulative effects* of loss and adaptation demands may limit and impair coping abilities, rendering the individual more likely to experience a stressor as a crisis.

Discrete Event Crises

Discrete stressful events may occur (1) as precipitants of the decision to divorce, (2) during the transition phase of divorce, or (3) well past the finalization of the divorce. Examples of specific life events that *precipitate* the decision to divorce include the discovery of infidelity, an acute escalation of conflict or physical violence, death of a family member (particularly a child) or close friend, evidence of physical or sexual child abuse, disclosure or discovery of gross financial irresponsibility, excessive use of alcohol or prescription drugs, use of illicit drugs, and episodic violation of trust (e.g., dishonesty, deceit, lying).

For many, the crisis of divorce is realized during the transition phase, when resolution of property settlement and child custody or visitation are being sought. This period, after the decision to divorce has been made and before the divorce is legally final, is punctuated by extreme levels of emotion, including acute feelings of loss across many categories (e.g., personal, intimate, moral/ethical, status, lifestyle, financial, physical), rejection and abandonment, hurt, anger, guilt, anxiety, worry, fear, and disappointment. Emotional consequences such as these, coupled with decision making, planning, and the mobilization of environmental and lifestyle change, seriously compromise the coping capacities of divorcing individuals. These individuals are strongly predisposed to psychological crisis.

Subsequent to the decision to divorce and many times well after the divorce is legally final, divorced individuals experience a crisis in relation to the ex-mate. Examples of life events in this category include seeing for the first time the ex-mate with a new mate, learning of predivorce relationship-violating behavior (infidelity; failure to file joint income tax return), acute conflict over parallel parenting (e.g., ex-mate's failure to pick up or return child on time; child not available for scheduled visitation; telephone access to child blocked), failure to receive child support, episodic family and kin side-taking against the individual, and episodic discrimination socially and in the workplace. Although the marital relationship may be over, the ex-mates often remain interconnected in some fashion, particularly when children are involved. The ongoing relationship between ex-mates is typically replete with opportunities for conflict, hurt, and protracted loss.

Cumulative Effect Crises

The second way the divorce process can reach crisis status is as a consequence of the *cumulative effects* of divorce. Divorce thrusts the individual into a state of distress, disorganization, and greater uncertainty about life and the future. Divorcing individuals experience highly meaningful and pervasive losses. Dealing with loss effectively reduces coping ability (Freeman & Dattilio, 1994). Although the experience of loss is a constant in one's ongoing evolution, the loss associated with marital dissolution and the revisioning, restructuring, and reordering of oneself as a single person pose immediate and long-term challenges. Neimeyer (1998) notes that the passing of another from one's life poses an identity challenge in the form of "reinventing" oneself. Inasmuch as one's sense of self is socially embedded, the loss of the mate through divorce results both in a void within and a modification in the nature of one's relationships with all others. One is no longer part of a dyad and therefore sees oneself differently and is seen differently by others. Beyond dealing with loss and identity re-formation, there are other responsibilities of a more practical nature that are physically and emotionally taxing. A change in marital status, for most, poses changes in practical needs (e.g., bank account, charge cards, will) and physical needs (e.g., relocate, replace furnishings). For those who had not been previously employed outside the home, it may require job hunting or academic preparation or training for enhanced entry into the workforce. The very activity of seeking a job may become a crisis given the challenges of job interviewing, mounting economic need during unemployment, and potential rejection inherent in the process, coupled with the individual's depleted coping capacities associated with postdivorce adjustment.

The ultimate consequence of the cumulative effects of the divorce process is that events and circumstances that heretofore would have been effectively met and accommodated may become elevated to crisis status. Many clinical anecdotes could be identified in which relatively minor events or life experiences become crises. An auto accident of fender bender, noninjury proportions, an argument with a family member or friend, a child's failure to call home from camp in a timely manner are all circumstances that require coping and resource mobilization. Events such as these, however, become insurmountable, extraordinary challenges when the divorce process is consuming the individual's emotional and psychological resources.

PSYCHOSOCIAL NEEDS OF DIVORCING/ DIVORCED CLIENTS

A number of stage theorists have collapsed generally common divorce-related experiences into categories (Bohannon, 1971; Brown, 1976; DeFazio & Klenbort, 1975; Everett & Everett, 1994; Fisher, 1973; Froiland & Hozman, 1977; Kaslow, 1984; Kessler, 1975; Kressel, 1980; Rich, 2002; Storm & Sprenkle, 1982; Weiss, 1975). The conceptualization of the divorce process in stages has been criticized as failing to "highlight the complexity of the processes involved in marital dissolution" (Ponzetti & Cate, 1988, p. 3). As I have noted elsewhere (Granvold, 1994), although therapists must be sensitive to the divorcing/divorced client's unique experience, there is facility in broadly subdividing the divorce process to better specify common objectives and tasks associated with a given period in the process. Consistent with Kaslow (1984) and Storm and Sprenkle (1982), divorce is conceptualized as being composed of three overlapping stages, *decision making, transition, and postdivorce recovery*. Each stage has its unique stressors and challenges.

Decision Making

The decision to divorce is not easy for most people. Typically, one or both partners continue their marriage in a state of high dissatisfaction and protracted indecision before ultimately arriving at a decision to divorce. The state of indecision is stressful in itself, characterized by high levels of frustration, anxiety, uncertainty, fear, worry, insecurity, distrust (particularly for the mate who is more greatly committed), hurt, resentment, depression, hopelessness and impending doom, and feelings of disempowerment. There is often an erosion in feelings of love, intimacy, sexual desire, and sexual satisfaction. Individuals who are emotionally fragile, highly dependent on the mate, or lack self-esteem often experience situation-specific crises as the couple move closer to a final decision. This individual, typically more committed and less likely to decide to leave the relationship, is far more vulnerable to crisis responses.

The decision to divorce may *be* the crisis event or, as noted above, a relationship-related crisis may *stimulate* the actual decision to divorce. In either situation, heightened emotion surrounds divorce decision making for most. Whether the decision is unilateral or shared, whether one is the initiator or the one being left, there is pain and disruption associated with the imminent coming apart (Everett & Everett, 1994; Granvold, 1989, 2002; Olson & DeFrain, 2000; Pam & Pearson, 1998; Sprenkle, 1989).

Transition from Married to Single

When the decision is made to divorce, the spouses are thrust into a major life transition. The psychological and emotional responses of the divorcing couple and their children and the behavioral manifestations of these responses during the transition phase may be extreme. A multitude of very significant decisions flow from the decision to divorce (Granvold, 1994, 2002; Olson & DeFrain, 2000; Propst & Fries, 1989; Sprenkle, 1989). During this period, children and family members may be informed of the plan to divorce; often. friends and associates are informed as well. Physical separation must be achieved, which requires the determination of who is going to move, and the location and setting to which the departing mate is to go. The legal system must be accessed either through attorneys or through no-fault unilateral legal actions. The process of filing for a divorce or the experience of being served a divorce petition is commonly unpleasant. These events all too often mark the beginning of an adversarial process punctuated by great acrimony between the divorcing couple. Property settlement and child custody–child visitation determinations are often highly emotionally charged deliberations. Opportunities for interpersonal crises abound at this time.

Postdivorce Recovery

Separation and divorce force the individual to accommodate pervasive change: "Against a backdrop of ambivalence and oscillating emotions, the individual is challenged to integrate: (1) the stress of wholesale change; (2) redefinition of self and object loss trauma; (3) role loss, disorientation, and restructuring; and (4) life-style adjustment" (Granvold, 1989, p. 198). Clients typically struggle with the pain of emotional separation from the mate. Even for those who have experienced an erosion of love, there tends to be a persistence of attachment to the ex-mate which exacerbates the letting-go process (Weiss, 1975). Self-esteem and feelings of self-worth diminish during the entire process of divorce, particularly for the mate who has been rejected. In response to low self-appraisals and feelings such as depression, hurt, loss, and hopelessness, those in recovery often withdraw and become isolated. Loneliness and preoccupation with loss prevail. Common maladaptive coping strategies involve the excessive use of alcohol and drugs (prescribed and illicit), oversleep, overexercise, and overinvestment of time and energy in work. Although grieving is a necessary, adaptive process, and unique from person to person, it may become debilitating to those who allow it to become all-consuming.

One of the greatest challenges during postdivorce recovery is reestablishing one's identity as a single person (Granvold, 2002; Rice, 2003). Compounded by the process of overcoming the loss of the mate, one must formulate a sense of self independent of the ex-spouse. For some, this is appealing.

However, for those who have enjoyed the dyadic identity and connection with the ex-mate, identity re-formation may be a crisis in itself. New roles such as single parent, sole financial provider, and social single contribute to the evolving sense of self as a single person. These new roles facilitate change but are typically stress-provoking.

Divorce does not terminate people's human desires for closeness, intimacy, close relationships with others, and sexual gratification (Schneller, 2003). The world of dating and courtship is one in which skills from the past are once again called into play. Many approach dating with a sense of trepidation, distrust, anxiety, fear, and uncertainty; others find it exciting, rejuvenating, fun, and provocative. Unresolved issues from the dissolved marriage can be stimulated in dating relationships and thrust the individual into crisis. Also, the depletion of coping resources during divorce recovery may render the individual more vulnerable to stressful and crisis responses in newly forming relationships.

Dating naturally leads to opportunities for sexual activity. The loss of one's mate (love object) leaves the individual without partner sexual gratification. The availability of multiple, new sex partners coupled with normal sexual desire is highly likely to lead to sexual activity in dating relationships. Frequently, recently divorced individuals enjoy their sexual freedom by having a series of sexual partners. For some individuals, having sexual relations with several partners across time functions to prevent getting deeply involved with any one person. This pattern is perceived to be a form of self-protection. The obvious risk of having sex with many partners is the possibility of contracting a sexually transmitted disease (STD). Neff and Mantz (1998) suggest that those recently separated or divorced individuals who are dealing with postdivorce recovery issues (loneliness, isolation, depression, or low self-esteem) may fail to adopt rational "safe sex" practices, increasing their risk for disease. They maintain that, in an era in which HIV/AIDS has increasingly become a heterosexual phenomenon (Centers for Disease Control, 1990), the separated and divorced are a possible risk group for HIV infection. I would add to the combination of postdivorce recovery, available multiple sex partners, and the epidemic status of HIV/AIDS and other STDs the disinhibitory effects of alcohol consumption and "recreational" drug use on sexual behavior. While the Neff and Mantz study found inadequate evidence to support the disinhibitory contributions of alcohol use on sexual behavior during marital disruption, they suggest that the lack of evidence is counterintuitive and may be partly explained methodologically. In my clinical experience, alcohol and drug use have often been reported as factors in accounts of indiscriminate and "unprotected" sexual encounters. Despite rational commitments to safe sex practices, substance abuse in combination with the emotional and coping challenges of postdivorce recovery and desires for sexual gratification result in people putting themselves at risk. It can be concluded that, on occasion, attitudes and beliefs are poor predictors of human behavior. Many who profess the wisdom of safe sex practices do not practice it.

RISK ASSESSMENT

As noted, the vulnerabilities of individuals experiencing marital disruption and divorce include low self-esteem, depression, hopelessness, anxiety and fear of the unknown, substance abuse, loneliness, isolation, and sexually transmitted disease. This combination of vulnerabilities coupled with a depletion in coping abilities make this population particularly at risk of suicide. In rare instances, there is risk of homicidal action.

The divorced/divorcing individuals in crisis are at high risk of depression, suicide, and substance abuse. Reinecke (1994) notes that risk assessment should include the identification of risk factors associated with a particular outcome, such as suicide. Risk factors are defined as experiences, events, or propensities that make a particular outcome more likely. Assessment of risk, then, requires exploration of those factors that are known to be associated with a particular outcome.

Depression

Most individuals in the process of divorce or in postdivorce recovery experience some degree of depression; vulnerability to severe clinical depression may be determined by making an assessment of risk factors. Among the relevant risk factors to be assessed are self-esteem level, social involvement/withdrawal, social support from family and friends, history of depression, depression in family of origin, financial problems, parenting problems, substance abuse, and feelings of hopelessness. Both clinical interview and standardized measurement instruments should be used to assess for risk and to determine current status of depression. Recommended self-report instruments for depression include the Beck Depression Inventory–Second Edition (BDI-II; Beck, Steer, & Brown, 1996), the Zung Self-Rated Depression Inventory (Zung, 1965), and the Generalized Contentment Scale (Hudson, 1992). Additionally, the Beck Hopelessness Scale (Beck & Steer, 1988) is highly useful in gaining access to the client's cognitive schemas related to negative expectancy about short- and long-term future. This psychological construct has been found to underlie various mental health disorders (Beck & Steer, 1988). Specifically, hopelessness is a core construct in depression and has been found to be an important mediator of suicide (Beck, 1987; Beck, Rush, Shaw, & Emery, 1979; D. A. Clark, Beck, & Alford, 1999; Reinecke, 1994, 2000).

Lethality

The most critical risk assessment is the determination of lethality. As noted earlier, the likelihood of suicide among separated and divorced men and women is significantly greater than among married individuals. The pain of coping with the loss of love is excruciating for many. Compounding this loss are many change demands that can propel the individual into crisis. Suicide over love loss is a familiar theme. An infrequent but extremely tragic occurrence is murder-suicide among separated and recently divorced couples and couples in extreme marital distress. The separated and divorcing individual is also vulnerable to physical violence, the consequences of which may be extreme physical harm and possibly death (Hardesty, 2002; Logan, Walker, Horvath, & Leukefeld, 2003; Toews, McKenry, & Catlett, 2003). With regard to physical violence and homicidal intention, statements of desire for the estranged or ex-spouse to experience pain or death should be explored regardless of the emotional state of the client at the time. That is to say, expressions made during extreme anger and rage should not be dismissed lightly as anger-driven, misrepresentative, unrealistic, or unintentional statements. Furthermore, when a client expresses fear for his or her safety, the therapist should guide the client in mobilizing protective systems and resources.

Specialized skills are required to recognize a client as suicidal and to assess suicidal risk (Beck et al., 1979; D. C. Clark, 1995; Rudd, Joiner, & Rajab, 2001). Beck and his colleagues recommend that the assessment cover four components: intent, planning, resource availability, and motive. They note that even the mildly depressed individual may commit suicide; thus, our appraisals of intention must be finely discriminating. The therapist must be sensitive to the indicators of suicide in terms of behaviors, emotional states, and verbalizations. The client who suddenly puts his or her affairs in order may actually be preparing for death (e.g., completes a will, organizes and clears desk at work, contacts friends and family with whom he or she has had no recent contact). Other potential indicators of suicidal intent are depression; a sense of overwhelming grief; loss of love, parenting opportunities, and meaning in life (emptiness); hopelessness that life will improve (Beck, 1987); and coldness, hostility, and anger. Clinicians should listen for and explore verbal statements such as the following: "I can't live without her/him"; "I'll never be happy again"; "I can't stand the thought of her/him making love with anyone else"; and "I have to stop this hurt."

Should the client admit to suicidal planning or you surmise it from indicators of intention, make an inquiry into the way the client has considered committing suicide. Following this exploration, determine the resources available to the client to fulfill the plan (e.g., knowledge of lethal levels of drugs, access to firearms). Exploration of motive may expose objectives such as the desire to escape from life or to seek surcease, to retaliate through creating pain in the life of the rejecting ex-mate, and manipulation of significant others through suicidal attempts (Beck et al., 1979).

Reinecke (1994) aptly notes that "if there is a truism in psychology, it is that the best predictor of future behavior is past behavior. So it is with predicting suicidal risk" (p. 75). Accordingly, determine the strength of past suicidal thinking, degree of past planning and mobilization of resources, and actual suicide attempts. Determine whether other family members or close friends have committed or attempted suicide.

Finally, it is important to consider the interactive effects of variables that may contribute to suicide. Substance abuse, depleted coping capacity and intensity of the love loss, social isolation, lack of support system, poverty or financial problems, and history of psychological instability collectively may produce a lethal effect.

The use of self-report instruments may further facilitate suicidal risk assessment, for example, Beck's Scale for Suicide Ideation (Beck et al., 1979). Other relevant instruments may be located in Fischer and Corcoran (1994).

Substance Abuse

Substance abuse is a coping strategy frequently employed by separated and divorced individuals. Alcohol and drugs are effective in reducing stress, assuaging guilt and remorse, and numbing one's emotional pain. Although perhaps effective to these ends, the undesirable consequences of substance abuse are extreme. Depression and suicide, highly associated with substance abuse, are among the major vulnerabilities (Beck, Wright, Newman, & Liese, 1993). On the basis of the above information, it is important to assess the risks of substance abuse among separated and divorced clients. In addition to interview assessment, several viable substance use/abuse assessment instruments are available (Beck et al., 1993; Fischer & Corcoran, 1994).

CLIENT STRENGTHS, RESILIENCE, AND PROTECTIVE STRATEGIES

Before addressing specific strategies that can be implemented in divorce crisis recovery, a statement about philosophy is in order. The intervention model promoted in this chapter is a constructivist approach to human functioning and human change in which individual strengths and assets are emphasized, stimulated, and expanded (Franklin & Nurius, 1998; Granvold, 1996, 2001; Mahoney, 1991, 1995, 2003; Neimeyer & Mahoney, 1995; Saleebey, 1992). Saleebey has identified three essential assumptions that undergird the strengths perspective:

> First, it is assumed every person has an inherent power that may be characterized as life force, transformational capacity, life energy, spirituality, re-

> generative potential, and healing power. . . . Second, a strengths perspective assumes that the power just described is a potent form of knowledge that can guide personal and social transformation. . . . Third, there is a crucial pragmatic presumption about the nature of change . . . that when people's positive capacities are supported, they are more likely to act on their strengths. (p. 24)

Constructivist psychotherapy is optimistically focused on possibilities. Individual strengths (both active and potential), resources, and competencies are collaboratively identified with the client, emphasized, and prompted toward greater activation. Life is viewed as "an ongoing recursion of perturbation and adaptation, disorganization and distress, and emerging complexity and differentiation—a process of evolutionary self-organization" (Granvold, 1996, p. 346). Consistent with this conceptualization of life span development, human disturbance and distress are considered "normal." Problems are construed as opportunities for constructive change. The resiliency and creative potential of all people are emphasized.

Pragmatically, this means that crisis assessment and intervention are focused on the personal, social, and community resources available to the client. An essential personal resource is the client's belief in his or her right and ability to be *empowered* (Freeman & Dattilio, 1994). Client self-efficacy plays a crucial role in empowerment; low self-efficacy impedes empowerment but high self-efficacy effects it. Hence, if lacking, an early goal of therapy is the development of efficacy expectations. Efficacy expectations are not only meaningful in crisis resolution, but they have been found to be associated with postdivorce adjustment (Bould, 1977; Pais, 1978; J. J. White, 1985; Womack, 1987).

Basco and Rush (1996, p. 214) have generated a list of internal resources useful in coping with stress that are worthy of consideration in developing a crisis intervention treatment plan:

Intelligence	Resourcefulness
Practicality	Energy
Analytical-mindedness	Stamina
Common sense	Creativity
Fortitude	Self-esteem
Assertiveness	Money
Sensitivity	Confidence
A sense of humor	Self-perceived competency
Time	Ability to seek out and accept help from others
Personableness	Perserverence
Organizational ability	

Turning now to external coping resources, it has been found that those with active support systems are better adjusted to divorce than those without support (Burrell, 2002; Granvold, Pedler, & Schellie, 1979; Hetherington, 2003; Spanier & Casto, 1979; Wallerstein & Kelly, 1980). It is recommended that individuals in divorce crisis remain active socially through involvement with family and friends, or through participation in interest groups (e.g., Sierra Club) and singles groups. Also, many communities offer psychoeducational seminars focused on postdivorce recovery or grief recovery (Blanton, 1994; Granvold & Welch, 1977; Salts, 1989). Alienation and isolation, feeling disconnected from caring others and social withdrawal, are major contributors to human disturbance and dysfunction. Every effort should be made to promote client involvement in the community.

The client's past history in resolving crises and life dilemmas should be explored as a means of activating coping and adaptive skills and instilling resiliency and to mobilize protective strategies. The risk factors identified above, along with other maladaptive responses to the crisis, should be addressed through the identification of the cognitive, behavioral, and emotional responses that have effectively reduced risk in the past. This may involve the exploration of compensatory actions, the activation of a support system, or the development of novel interests and life goals.

Finally, resilience is represented not only by overt behaviors, but by attitude. The therapist should access the client's self-views regarding his or her capacity to bounce back and return stronger than before. Explorations should be made into self-esteem and self-reliance conceptualizations that support or undermine views of self as resilient. Interventions should be initiated consistent with these findings.

INTERVENTION

In this section, the Roberts (1990, 1996) seven-stage model of crisis intervention is discussed and applied to clients in the process of divorce. Although a client may move in and out of crisis while in counseling during the process of postdivorce adjustment, the intervention highlighted here is crisis-focused.

Velia, a Hispanic woman age 46, presented for therapy shortly after filing for a divorce from her husband of 28 years. The mother of five children ranging in age from 10 to 27, Velia reported extreme unhappiness with the relationship over the past 10 years. She had experienced repeated periods of separation, the last of which began 18 months earlier. During this last separation period, Velia become involved in a sexual relationship with a family friend. The love relationship, now terminated, lasted eight months and ended with an ultimatum from her lover to end the marriage or end the love relationship. Velia, ill-prepared to made a final decision about her marriage at the time, broke off the love relationship. About two months later, immediately prior to presenting for treatment, a family member informed Velia's husband and children of Velia's affair. Velia felt extremely violated by the disclosure. Two of her adult offspring verbally attacked her and subsequently withdrew from her. All four adult children began distancing themselves from her and blamed her for the problems in the marriage. Despite Velia's explanation that her marital unhappiness had lasted over 10 years, the children held their mother solely responsible for the marital distress due to the extramarital relationship. Velia's husband, Jorge, remained willing to "work things out" and actively enlisted the children in trying to convince their mother to remain in the marriage. Velia felt no romantic feelings for Jorge, although she did feel love for him as the father of their children.

While currently committed to the divorce, Velia was concerned with her children's coldness toward her and their strong views that it was their mother's wrongdoing that was accountable for the marital unhappiness. Although not suicidal, Velia experienced extreme depression primarily related to her children's negative judgments of her and her own self-recrimination for allowing herself to love another. She felt a sense of hopelessness and saw her future as empty of possible joy or personal well-being. She felt that she could not go back into the marriage, nor could she gain happiness outside it. *Velia's crisis was the disclosure by her sister and the subsequent loss of respect from her children and their physical and emotional withdrawal from her.*

Engagement and Relationship Formation

Clients who present for therapy in crisis must feel free to express the specific details of the stressful event and their range of emotional responses with a therapist who is open, an active and careful listener, nonjudgmental, talented in Socratic questioning, and an expert in the crisis area. During extreme crises, regardless of the stage of therapy (initial session or much later), clients may evidence an array of thoughts, emotions, and behaviors that are highly uncharacteristic of them when they are not in crisis. For others, the crisis event may serve to activate or amplify characteristic maladaptive responses. Therapists can expect to hear highly irrational thinking ("I'll never recover"); emotionally driven statements ("I'd like to smash his face in"); expressions of extreme and uncontrollable emotion (crying, anger, anxiety, panic); emotionally charged content with flat affect; perseveration—words, phrases, gestures, images ("I'm so bad"); incoherent, disjointed, and spotty accounts of events; and dissociation ("I felt numb; it was as if I was observing someone else"; "I felt nothing, nothing at all as he hit me again and again"). The therapist must be prepared to rapidly assess the client's verbal and nonverbal behavior and to respond with clinical wisdom. Each type of expression enumerated above obligates the therapist to activate strategic responses that complement the client's expression. For example, when a client expresses irrational thoughts during the engagement phase of crisis intervention, it would be inappropriate to attempt cognitive restructuring or cognitive elaboration at that time. It is far more desirable to listen carefully and seek an understanding of the client's thoughts and images, to gain a more global awareness of the crisis situation through Socratic questioning, to elicit feeling states, to reflect content and feelings, to offer strategic empathic expressions, and to display *human emotion* consistent with the nature of the client's crisis. For the client who expresses incoherent, disjointed, and spotty accounts of a stressful circumstance, the therapist may find it effective to use combinations of Socratic questioning, guided imagery, deep muscle relaxation, and repetitive iterations of increasingly complete accounts. In each of these examples, therapist responses complement the client's expressions and function to promote the therapeutic alliance and to further the treatment endeavor.

Although it is highly important to maintain focus on the crisis, the engagement process requires that the therapist ultimately ascertain the client's treatment goals and expectations of the therapist, as well as explicate therapist-held expectations (Garfield, 1998; Granvold, 2001, 2002; Kanfer & Schefft, 1988). Early on, the therapist should act in ways that establish that treatment is a *collaborative* effort between client and therapist. As Freeman and Dattilio (1994) point out, however, "The collaboration is not always 50:50 but may, with the crisis patient, be 30:70 or 90:10, with the therapist providing most of the energy or work within the session or in the therapy more generally" (pp. 6–7). The client should come away from the first session with the understanding that the therapist expects the client to be active in the treatment process and with the awareness that the therapist will actively participate as well. Genuine expressions of empathy, complementary responses to idiosyncratic expressions, structuring the roles of client and therapist, assuming a collaborative stance, and the expression of content about the crisis event and characteristic human responses (therapist knowledge-based expertise) are all meaningful ingredients in establishing a therapeutic alliance and building rapport.

Initial Risk Assessment

When a client presents for treatment in crisis, it is imperative that a risk assessment be completed before ending the session. The therapist should gain an understanding of the crisis situation and establish the severity of the crisis. The next step is to assess the client's strengths, coping capacities, resources (personal, social, financial), and vulnerability to lethal or health-threatening responses. Attention should be given to both suicidal and homicidal ideation, including intent, planning, resource availability, and motive. As noted in the section on risk assessment, a cursory exploration of the client's thoughts about suicide and homicide is inadequate. It is advised that the potential be explored more than once in the session to limit the perfunctory or deceptive denial and to allow greater opportunity to expose indicators of lethality.

Problem Definition

The therapist should seek an understanding of the client's meaning constructions regarding the crisis situation. Recall that a crisis may develop in such challenges as the process of dissolving a marital union; identity re-formation as a single person; assumption of altered role relationships; and return to dating, mate selection, and potential reconstitution of the family with a new mate. These life transitions have unique meanings to each individual. Understanding these meanings may provide the therapist with clinically relevant contextual information useful in crisis intervention. For example, the individual who holds the view that he or she must stay married at all costs (intrinsic permanence view of marriage) is more likely to experience the day when the divorce is final as a greater crisis partly *because* of this view. In a sense, the therapist seeks a determination of *why a crisis is a crisis.*

In recognition of the idiosyncratic nature of meaning constructions, the therapist and client collaborate in generating the meaning of the crisis. The client may have difficulty articulating his or her thoughts about the circumstance. Exploration of the crisis circumstance through Socratic questioning may allow articulation of what took place and expose the client's views of and responses to the event or circumstance. After understanding the client's current thinking, it may be appropriate to guide the elaboration of meanings as a means of extending possibilities. This process is a necessary prerequisite to proceeding to the generation of alternative paths of action.

Constuctivist intervention focuses on the *viability* of meaning constructions. Viability is a function of the *consequences* of the construct to the individual and society, as well as its *coherence* with prevailing personal and social beliefs (Neimeyer, 1993). To clarify, consider the client who states that the divorce is the worst that could happen to him and that he has no reasons to go on living. These meanings, while perhaps consistent with his current thoughts, lack viability for they promote (or at least imply) actions with dire negative consequences to the individual and to society. The clinical objective in this situation is to expand and elaborate possible meanings of the divorce to arrive at meanings that may promote more viable consequences. Merely modifying the view from "It's the worst" to "It's *one* of the worst" achieves greater viability. Other meanings that might be generated with this client include "It hurts so bad"; "I never thought she'd ever leave me"; "I believe in 'love is forever' "; and "Divorce is wrong." All of these views may have unappealing consequences to a degree, but they may be *less* destructive than the client's initial construct. Gaining access to specific beliefs and determining other relevant constructions regarding divorce and the transition to single life may contribute greatly to the formulation of an intervention strategy to meet the crisis.

In the initial interview with Velia, information gathering was focused on formulating the problem specifically through (1) discovering the crisis circumstances and her beliefs that strongly contributed to the crisis, (2) conducting a risk assessment, and (3) gaining a preliminary understanding of her current coping abilities.

On the weekend prior to Velia's coming in for treatment she had seen a family happily interacting at a local park. She longed for the laughter, sharing, and warm interaction visible in that family. She returned home deeply depressed and realized that she must seek help. In defining the problem, I learned that warm family relationships and mutual respect and admiration between children and parents were paramount in Velia's value system. The core meanings of being a mother were to protect her children from pain and discomfort and to always "be there" for them. Her estrangement from her adult children prevented her from fulfilling these roles and threatened her purpose in life. She viewed herself as despicable for her infidelity.

I learned that Velia was a survivor of incest, having been abused by her biological father. She loved her mother dearly, but felt deep hurt over her mother's failure to protect her from her father. She was now confronting her own "failure to protect her children" from the pain of her infidelity and the impending divorce. Velia had demonstrated remarkable coping abilities in the past, but she questioned her current strength. Assessment of additional stressors in her life revealed underemployment and resulting financial hardship. This condition further depleted her coping resources. Velia reported no suicidal ideation now or at any time in her past, and there were no indicators of suicidal intention. She denied any substance abuse or use of prescription drugs. This information, along with the content reported in the introductory vignette, helped define Velia's crisis and gave direction to the intervention.

Explore Emotions and Promote Ongoing Development

Traditional therapeutic approaches have tended to consider emotions such as anger, anxiety, depression, worry, sadness, and the like to be negative, and goals of treatment correspondingly have been to control, alter, or terminate such emotions (Granvold, 1996). Constructivists, social constructionists, and other postmodernists conceptualize emotions as agents of change, adaptation, and self-development (Greenberg & Safran, 1989; Guidano, 1991a, 1991b; Mahoney, 1991,2003; Safran & Greenberg, 1991). I believe that exploring emotions with clients in crisis should be done with the view, consistent with constructivism, that emotions and their expression are crucial to the process of change.

In some circumstances, it is highly appropriate to assist clients in curbing or controlling intense emotion. For example, consider the deeply depressed client whose depression is jeopardizing her job or parenting performance, or there is evidence of strong suicidal ideation or planning. Intervention should focus on protective strategies, behavioral activation, and cognitive changes designed to ensure safety and to prevent incapacitation and dysfunction in fulfilling key responsibilities.

Many contemporary views of emotion emphasize the personal meaning constructions associated with emotionality: "The ways individuals think, feel, speak, and act are integrally tied to the concepts they use to categorize their emotions and make them meaningful" (Nunley & Averill, 1996, p. 226). It is important not only to determine clients' views of the crisis circumstance to which they are emotionally responding, but to gain an understanding of their beliefs about their feelings and emotional expressions. For example, some clients believe themselves to be "seized" by emotion and hold the view that they have little control over their feelings (Nunley & Averill, 1996). Others believe they are "going crazy" or are weak or see themselves as worthless *because* they are experiencing and expressing extreme emotion. Clients may greatly benefit from the view that there is honor in being emotional—that it is "normal" and not necessarily to be considered negative (although extreme and enduring feelings and emotional expressions carry some level of discomfort for most people). Restructuring client views of emotion from negative and undesirable to positive and viable in the process of human change and adaptation will shape client tolerance and appreciation for their emotionality.

As a further means of gleaning what is positive about emotionality, I have found it useful to guide clients in the externalization of their feelings and emotional expressions (M. White & Epston, 1990). This may be accomplished by asking questions such as "What do you think your depression is trying to tell you?" and "If your tears had a voice, what would they be saying?" Questions such as these give rich access to client cognitions and client awareness of behavioral and lifestyle changes that are, truly, in their best interests. Furthermore, the process of externalization reinforces the belief that feelings are useful.

For clients who express flat affect or report little emotional responsivity to crisis events that typically prompt emotional reactions, it is important to employ methods to access feelings and stimulate emotional expressiveness. Experiential techniques have been found to be highly effective with these clients.

> The purpose of these techniques varies, including the stimulation of feelings related to a life event, a preparatory rehearsal of a behavior (e.g., assertive expression), to gain a better understanding of another's thoughts or feelings (e.g., role reversal), and to process negative or ambivalent thoughts or feelings regarding past or more contemporary experiences. (Granvold, 1996, p. 354)

Methods to access affective states and to stimulate emotional arousal include role-playing, psychodrama, behavior rehearsals, imagery and guided discovery, imaginary dialogues (empty-chair technique), and therapeutic rituals. The timely use of techniques such as these may facilitate the arousal and expression of emotions in the divorcing client who, although in crisis, is unemotional.

As established earlier, divorce is about loss—not one loss, but a variety of losses. The accommodation of loss in divorce recovery, as with other traumatic events, requires meaningful expressions of emotion for successful adaptation. Treating the crisis of divorce, therefore, must focus on human emotion as a change process.

Velia: I have been upset since I spoke with Jorge on the phone last weekend.

Don: You say that you've been upset. What feelings make up being upset?

Velia: I feel so guilty . . . and I feel resentment toward him because he's using the children to get me to come home.

Don: So, you're feeling guilty and resentful. Are you feeling any other feelings?

Velia: I guess I am. I'm really angry with Jorge, and overall I just feel depressed. I wish that things were different.

Don: Are there any other feelings here, or do these pretty much cover it?

Velia: I think that's all . . . there's too much here.

Don: It can get a bit overwhelming at times. There's a lot to your situation. . . . Suppose we explore each one of these feelings. Perhaps if we take each one we can arrive at some conclusions that may bring a bit of relief.

Velia: Okay.

Don: You first said that you felt guilty. What was it about the phone call that resulted in your feeling guilty?

Velia: Jorge always tries to make me feel guilty. He tells me how much he loves me and how he can forgive me for what I've done. Then he brings the children into it. He says that we can all be back together as a family. It hurts so much.

Don: So, first there's guilt, followed closely by hurt.

Velia: Yes, that's what usually happens, anyway.

Don: Velia, sometimes people have a tendency to allow guilt to immobilize them. As we've discussed before, if you were to consider guilt as a *motivator*, what actions might you consider taking?

Velia: Well, I could first think that I'm not going to buy into his attempts to make me feel guilty.

Don: That sounds good. So when he makes statements as he did on Saturday night, you will begin telling yourself, "I'm not going to allow him to make me feel guilty."

Velia: Yes, that's what I plan to do. Also, I am going to use the guilt as a *reminder* that I must stay committed to seeing this divorce through, even though Jorge and the children don't want me to do it.

Don: So you are not going to allow feelings of guilt or hurt to deter you from following through with the divorce, an action that you truly believe is best for you.

Explore and Assess Past Coping Attempts

As noted earlier, the divorce-related crisis may be the result of a distinct event or the consequence of the cumulative effects of loss and adaptation demands. In either condition, it is important to assess the coping and adaptation capabilities of the client. Gathering information about loss, coping, and adaptation requires the exploration of the client's developmental history. Goals of this exploration should focus on uncovering client strengths as well as limitations. Often, clients in crisis (and many not in crisis) do not recognize legitimate strengths among their personal resources. They have a tendency to ignore or minimize abilities and to attribute past successes to chance, others' efforts, or the circumstances. Also, clients are inclined to maintain that their talents and their demonstrated coping capacities are uncharacteristic responses; therefore, they are viewed as invalid. Insight into these views will be most helpful to the therapist in promoting greater client self-efficacy.

The therapist may gain an understanding of client coping capacities through interviewing or by means of journaling. Through either means, past successes in problem solving, coping, and adaptation, along with current self-appraisals of coping capacities and resource availability, should be identified and elucidated. During crisis, it can be expected that clients' efficacy expectations become reduced. In response, the therapist should guide explorations into the client's demonstrated and potential coping capacity and resource management. Various means that the client has used to cope in similar crisis situations should be specified and the client queried regarding the possibility of incorporating the same coping measures in the current crisis. Cognitive restructuring, cognitive elaboration, problem solving, and therapist support are all viable approaches in the enhancement of client self-efficacy and in crisis management.

Don: Velia, you have said that coping with your children's reactions to you has been tremendously difficult for you, that you've felt extremely depressed. I understand that you are a *survivor,* that you have suffered terrible abuse but handled it. Do you see yourself as a survivor?

Velia: Yes, I do.

Don: What does that mean to you, that you're a survivor?

Velia: I guess that it means that I haven't let what Dad did to me stop me from being happy, to fall in love, . . . and to pretty much *trust* people.

Don: That says a lot about you, Velia. I'm really pleased for you. Can you see that you must have used tremendous coping skills to get through the abuse and survive as you have?

Velia: I've never really thought about it, but I guess that I have. I'm pretty good, aren't I?!

Don: Yes you are, Velia. I'm impressed, really. Now what do you think would allow you to access those same coping abilities to deal with your current crisis?

Velia: Mmm, good question. I'll have to think about it. But I see where you are headed with this. If I did it before, I can do it again!

Don: Exactly! You have demonstrated that you can cope, and cope well. We will continue to explore your past and uncover the specific strategies you used.

Generate and Explore Alternatives and Solution Seeking

The therapist should promote the view that there is no one way or "right" way to work through a crisis. The task at hand is to generate alternative approaches to the current crisis, with the objective to tailor the solutions specifically to this client at this time. Obviously, the more alternatives generated, the greater the likelihood of creating change strategies that are more appealing to the client and of greater promise in producing effective outcomes. Once alternative strategies are determined, the perceived consequences (viability) of each should be explored. Once again, consider Velia as an illustration of this process.

Velia felt stuck with regard to her relationship with her children. She continued to write to them but received no letters in return. She felt an extreme sense of loss and her deep depression continued. We explored in session many alternative actions that she could take to improve her relationship with her children. Possible consequences of each option were discussed. The alternatives she considered included having a family reunion at her home; appealing to Jorge to talk with the children on her behalf; meeting with each child individually; talking with her daughter Maria, who is least upset with her mother, and enlisting her to accompany Velia in meeting with the other children individually; taking no action and allowing time to heal the hurt; and involving her brother, highly respected by Velia's children, in talking with each of them individually with Velia. The perceived consequences of each action were considered. Velia chose to approach her daughter Maria first. She had in mind asking Maria to go with her when she went to meet individually with her other children. Once this decision was made, the focus of the intervention turned to what Velia hoped to accomplish in face-to-face interactions with her children, the determination of the specific content to be shared and discussed, and the establishment of realistic expectations.

Restore Cognitive Functioning Through Implementation of an Action Plan

Divorce-related crises, like other crises, have the potential of promoting healthy change, empowerment, and creative and novel life experiences. As clients put their change efforts into effect they realize outcomes well beyond the resolution of the current crisis. Successful crisis resolution has the potential of "proving" to the client that relatively rapid and pervasive changes can be accomplished. Additionally, a multitude of cognitive benefits are possible. Several outcomes are likely in the category of self-views. The potential exists that divorced individuals learn to view the process of divorce as having meaningful positive as well as negative consequences. Divorce isn't *all* negative. This contradicts the tendency to all-or-nothing thinking, or dichotomous thinking (Granvold, 1994). The client may develop a sense of greater inner strength and self-reliance. A new or renewed sense of self-confidence and self-efficacy is possible as the individual takes on new responsibilities, fulfills novel roles, and makes independent decisions. Client coping capacities get severely tested during the crisis of divorce. The result is an expansion of coping strategies and an overall increase in coping ability. Many who did not seek the divorce ultimately report a sense of rejuvenation, excitement about life, and joy in experiencing greater novelty both in relationships and in activities.

Another highly significant cognitive outcome is that clients learn the benefits of expanding their meanings about crisis events. They learn that many meanings exist for any event or circumstance in life. Furthermore, they develop *skills in cognitive elaboration* through therapist-guided practice in sessions and self-generated cognitive elaboration in vivo. Journaling, thought records, and verbal accounts in therapy are useful methods in developing these skills.

Another important outcome is that clients learn to view their emotions as instrumental and necessary in the process of change. Rather than viewing feelings of loss, depression, fear, and anxiety as *negative,* these emotional states and their expressions are to be viewed as positive and meaningful in their effects. Emotions are viable agents of change; they serve us well in achieving truly painful transitions. They can be useful guides in activating steps toward healing, renewal, and an evolving self.

Follow-up

Follow-up is one element of relapse prevention, an aspect of intervention that is important in all forms of treatment, including crisis intervention (Granvold & Wodarski, 1994; Greenwald, 1987; Marlatt & Gordon, 1985). Follow-up telephone calls or follow-up cards or letters are appropriate methods to gain information about the client's status following treatment. Useful information may also be gleaned from client feedback with regard to the meaningful aspects of the treatment experience (and aspects of the counseling effort that the client did not find useful). Therapist-initiated three- and six-month follow-up contact is appropriate. At termination, the therapist should make it clear that he or she is always available for future contacts, should the client so desire. It is also important to stress that a booster session may be appropriate and that a follow-up session is not necessarily a sign of dependency or major relapse in recovery.

As I have identified throughout this chapter, in the divorce process there are many opportunities for the individual to experience a crisis. Successful crisis recovery does not protect the individual from encountering future stressful events that may reach crisis proportions. A crisis may actually develop in another aspect of the recovery process well past treatment termination for the original crisis. Recently, a divorcing father who had successfully resolved the crisis of separation and impending divorce was charged by his estranged wife with the sexual abuse of their daughter. The client returned to therapy in crisis regarding the consequences of these allegations. Crisis intervention was implemented as the client was evaluated by social and legal system representatives. Although all parties concluded that the allegations were false, the client was in crisis throughout the entire process.

CONCLUSION

The crisis of divorce has been noticeably absent from the crisis intervention literature. Taking only the suicide rate as an indicator of the *intensity* of the crisis of separation/divorce, and the high divorce rate as representative of the *magnitude* of the problem, one can conclude that mental health professionals should consider this population to be significantly at risk. The crisis intervention strategies and techniques discussed in this chapter, and those detailed elsewhere, should be given strong consideration in meeting the therapeutic needs of the multitudes in our society who are in the throes of coming apart as a couple or a family and attempting to re-vision their lives.

REFERENCES

Anthony, J. C., & Petronis, K. R. (1991). Suspected risk factors for depression among adults 18–44 years old. *Epidemiology, 2,* 123–132.

Bard, M., & Ellison, K. (1974). Crisis intervention and evidence of forcible rape. *The Police Chief, 41,* 68–73.

Basco, M. R., & Rush, A. J. (1996). *Cognitive-behavioral therapy for bipolar disorder.* New York: Guilford.

Beach, S. R. H., Sandeen, E. E., & O'Leary, K. D. (1990). *Depression in marriage.* New York: Guilford.

Beck, A. T. (1987). Hopelessness as a predictor of eventual suicide. *Annals of the New York Academy of Sciences: Psychobiology of Suicidal Behavior, 487,* 90–96.

Beck, A. T., Rush, A. J., Shaw, B. F., & Emery, G. (1979). *Cognitive therapy of depression.* New York: Guilford.

Beck, A. T., & Steer, R. A. (1988). *Beck hopelessness scale manual.* San Antonio: Psychological Corporation.

Beck, A. T., Steer, R. A., & Brown, G. K. (1996). *BDI-II manual.* San Antonio: Psychological Corporation.

Beck, A. T., Wright, F. D., Newman, C. F., & Liese, B. S. (1993). *Cognitive therapy of substance abuse.* New York: Guilford.

Blanton, P. G. (1994). A manual for time-limited group treatment with separated couples. In L. VandeCreek, S. Knapp, et al. (Eds.), *Innovations in clinical practice: A source book* (Vol. 13). Sarasota, FL: Professional Resource Press.

Bloom, B., Asher, J. S., & White, S. W. (1978). Marital disruption as a stressor: A review and analysis. *Psychological Bulletin, 85,* 867–894.

Bohannan, P. (1971). The six stations of divorce. In P. Bohannan (Ed.), *Divorce and after.* New York: Doubleday/Anchor.

Booth, A., & Edwards, J. N. (1992). Starting over: Why remarriages are more unstable. *Journal of Family Issues, 13,* 179–194.

Boss, P. (1988). *Family stress management.* Newbury Park, CA: Sage.

Bould, S. (1977). Female-headed families: Personal fate control and the provider role. *Journal of Marriage and the Family, 39,* 339–349.

Brown, E. (1976). Divorce counseling. In D. H. Olson (Ed.), *Treating relationships.* Lake Mills, IA: Graphic.

Burgess, A., & Holstrom, L. (1974). *Rape: Victims of crisis.* Bowie, MD: Robert J. Brady.

Burrell, N. A. (2002). Divorce: How spouses seek social support. In M. Allen, R. W. Preiss, et al. (Eds.), *Interpersonal communication research: Advances through meta-analysis.* Mahwah, NJ: Lawrence Erlbaum.

Cantor, C. H., & Slater, P. J. (1995). Marital breakdown, parenthood, and suicide. *Journal of Family Studies, 1*(2), 91–104.

Centers for Disease Control. (1990). Update: Acquired immunodefiency syndrome, United States, 1989. *Mortality and Morbidity Weekly Report, 39,* 81–86.

Clark, D. A., Beck, A. T., & Alford, B. A. (1999). *Scientific foundations of cognitive theory and therapy of depression.* New York: Wiley.

Clark, D. C. (1995). Epidemiology, assessment, and management of suicide in depressed patients. In E. E. Beckham & W. R. Leber (Eds.), *Handbook of depression* (2nd ed., pp. 526–538). New York: Guilford.

Costello, C. G. (1982). Social factors associated with depression: A retrospective community study. *Psychological Medicine, 12,* 329–339.

Cozzarelli, C., Karafa, J. A., Collins, N. L., & Tagler, M. J. (2003). Stability and change in adult attachment styles: Association with personal vulnerabilities, life events, and global construals of self and others. *Journal of Social and Clinical Psychology, 22*(3), 315–346.

DeFazio, V. J., & Klenbort, I. (1975). A note on the dynamics of psychotherapy during marital dissolution. *Psychotherapy: Theory Research and Practice, 12,* 101–104.

Epstein, N., & Schlesinger, S. E. (1994). Couples problems. In F. M. Dattilio & A. Freeman (Eds.), *Cognitive-behavioral strategies in crisis intervention* (pp. 258–277). New York: Guilford.

Everett, C., & Everett, S. V. (1994). *Healthy divorce.* San Francisco: Jossey-Bass.

Fischer, J., & Corcoran, K. (1994). *Measures for clinical practice: A source book* (Vol. 2). New York: Free Press.

Fisher, E. O. (1973). A guide to divorce counseling. *The Family Coordinator, 22,* 56–61.

Franklin, C., & Nurius, P. S. (Eds.). (1998). *Constructivism in practice: Methods and challenges.* Milwaukee, WI: Families International.

Freeman, A., & Dattilio, F. M. (1994). Introduction. In F. M. Dattilio & A. Freeman (Eds.), *Cognitive-behavioral strategies in crisis intervention* (pp. 1–22). New York: Guilford.

Froiland, D. J., & Hozman, T. L. (1977). Counseling for constructive divorce. *Personnel and Guidance Journal, 55,* 525–529.

Gallo, J. J., Royall, D. R., & Anthony, J. C. (1993). Risk factors for the onset of depression in middle age and later life. *Social Psychiatry and Psychiatric Epidemiology, 28,* 101–108.

Garfield, S. L. (1998). *The practice of brief psychotherapy* (2nd ed.). New York: Wiley.

Glick, P. C. (1989). Remarried families, stepfamilies and stepchildren: Brief demographic profile. *Family Relations, 38,* 24–27.

Goldenberg, H. (1983). *Contemporary clinical psychology* (2nd ed.). Monterey, CA: Brooks/Cole.

Goldstein, J. R. (1999). The leveling of divorce in the United States. *Demography, 35,* 409–414.

Granvold, D. K. (1989). Postdivorce treatment. In M. Textor (Ed.), *The divorce and divorce therapy handbook* (pp. 197–219). Northvale, NJ: Jason Aronson.

Granvold, D. K. (1994). Cognitive-behavioral divorce therapy. In D. K. Granvold (Ed.), *Cognitive and behavioral treatment: Methods and applications* (pp. 222–246). Pacific Grove, CA: Brooks/Cole.

Granvold, D. K. (1996). Constructivist psychotherapy. *Families in Society: The Journal of Contemporary Human Services, 77*(6), 345–359.

Granvold, D. K. (2001). Constructivist theory. In P. Lehmann & N. Coady (Eds.), *Theoretical perspectives in direct social work practice: An eclectic-generalist approach* (pp. 303–325). New York: Springer.

Granvold, D. K. (2002). Divorce therapy: The application of cognitive-behavioral and constructivist treatment methods. In A. R. Roberts & G. J. Greene (Eds.), *Social workers' desk reference* (pp. 587–590). New York: Oxford University Press.

Granvold, D. K., Pedler, L. M., & Schellie, S. G. (1979). A study of sex role expectancy and female postdivorce adjustment. *Journal of Divorce, 2,* 383–393.

Granvold, D. K., & Welch, G. J. (1977). Intervention for postdivorce adjustment problems: The treatment seminar. *Journal of Divorce, 1,* 82–92.

Granvold, D. K., & Wodarski, J. S. (1994). Cognitive and behavioral treatment: Clinical issues, transfer of training, and relapse prevention. In D. K. Granvold (Ed.), *Cognitive and behavioral treatment: Methods and applications* (pp. 353–375). Pacific Grove, CA: Brooks/Cole.

Greenberg, L. S., & Safran, J. D. (1989). Emotion in psychotherapy. *American Psychologist, 44,* 19–29.

Greenwald, M. A. (1987). Programming treatment generalization. In L. Michelson & L. M. Ascher, (Eds.), *Anxiety and stress disorders* (pp. 583–616). New York: Guilford.

Guidano, V. F. (1991a). Affective change events in a cognitive therapy system approach. In J. D. Safran & L. S. Greenberg (Eds.), *Emotion, psychotherapy, and change* (pp. 50–79). New York: Guilford.

Guidano, V. F. (1991b). *The self in process.* New York: Guilford.

Halford, W. K. (2001). *Brief therapy for couples.* New York: Guilford.

Hardesty, J. L. (2002). Separation assault in the context of postdivorce parenting: An integrative review of the literature. *Violence Against Women, 8*(5), 597–625.

Hetherington, E. M. (2003). Social support and the adjustment of children in divorced and remarried families. *Childhood: A Global Journal of Child Research, 10*(2), 217–236.

Holmes, T. H., & Rahe, R. H. (1967). Social adjustment rating scale. *Journal of Psychosomatic Research, 11,* 213–218.

Hudson, W. W. (1992). *The WALMYR assessment scales scoring manual.* Tempe, AZ: WALMYR Publishing.

Johnson, S. M. (2003). Couples therapy research: Status and directions. In G. P. Sholevar (Ed.), *Textbook of family and couples therapy: Clinical applications* (pp. 797–814). Washington, DC: American Psychiatric Publishing.

Kanfer, F. H., & Schefft, B. K. (1988). *Guiding the process of therapeutic change.* Champaign, IL: Research Press.

Kaslow, F. W. (1984). Divorce: An evolutionary process of change in the family system. *Journal of Divorce, 7,* 21–39.

Katz, S. N. (1994). Historial perspective and current trends in the legal process of divorce. *Future of Children, 4*(1), 44–62.

Kessing, L. V., Agerbo, E., & Mortensen, P. B. (2003). Does the impact of major stressful life events on the risk of developing depression change throughout life? *Psychological Medicine, 33*(7), 1177–1184.

Kessler, S. (1975). *The American way of divorce: Prescriptions for change.* Chicago: Nelson-Hall.

Kressel, K. (1980). Patterns of coping in divorce and some implications for clinical practice. *Family Relations, 29,* 234–240.

Lazarus, R. S. (1989). Constructs of

the mind in mental health and psychotherapy. In A. Freeman, K. M. Simon, L. E. Beutler, & H. Arkowitz (Eds.), *Comprehensive handbook of cognitive therapy* (pp. 99–121). New York: Plenum.

Logan, T. K., Walker, R., Horvath, L. S., & Leukefeld, C. (2003). Divorce, custody, and spousal violence: A random sample of circuit court docket records. *Journal of Family Violence, 18*(5), 269–279.

Mahoney, M. J. (1991). *Human change processes: The scientific foundations of psychotherapy.* New York: Basic Books.

Mahoney, M. J. (Ed.). (1995). *Cognitive and constructive psychotherapies: Theory, research, and practice.* New York: Springer.

Mahoney, M. J. (2003). *Constructive psychotherapy: A practical guide.* New York: Guilford.

Marlatt, G. A., & Gordon, J. R. (Eds.). (1985). *Relapse prevention.* New York: Guilford.

McCubbin, H. I., & Patterson, J. M. (1983). The family stress process: The double ABCX model of adjustment and adaptation. In H. I. McCubbin, M. B. Sussman, & J. M. Patterson (Eds.), *Social stress and the family: Advances and developments in family stress theory and research* (pp. 7–37). New York: Haworth Press.

McKenry, P. C., & McKelvey, M. W. (2003). The psychosocial well-being of Black and White mothers following marital dissolution: A follow-up study. *Psychology of Women Quarterly, 27*(1), 31–36.

Michelson, L. (1987). Cognitive-behavioral assessment and treatment of agoraphobia. In L. Michelson & L. M. Ascher (Eds.), *Anxiety and stress disorders: Cognitive-behavioral assessment and treatment* (pp. 213–279). New York: Guilford.

Monthly Vital Statistics Report. (1990). Vol. 43, no. 9, Supplement.

National Center for Health Statistics. (1986, September 25). Advance report of final divorce statistics. In *1984 Monthly Vital Statistics Report, 35*(6) (Supp. DHS Pub. No. PHS 86–1120). Hyattsville, MD: U.S. Public Health Service.

Neff, J. A., & Mantz, R. J. (1998). Marital status transition, alcohol consumption, and number of sex partners over time in a tri-ethnic sample. *Journal of Divorce & Remarriage, 29*(1), 19–42.

Neimeyer, R. A. (1993). An appraisal of constuctivist psychotherapies. *Journal of Consulting and Clinical Psychology, 61*, 221–234.

Neimeyer, R. A. (1998). *Lessons of loss: A guide to coping.* New York: Primis.

Neimeyer, R. A., & Mahoney, M. J. (Eds.). (1995). *Constructivism in psychotherapy.* Washington, DC: American Psychological Association.

Nunley, E. P., & Averill, J. R. (1996). Emotional creativity: Theoretical and applied aspects. In H. Rosen & K. T. Kuehlwein (Eds.), *Constructing realities: Meaning-making perspectives for psychotherapists* (pp. 223–251). San Francisco: Jossey-Bass.

Olson, D. H. (1997). Family stress and coping: A multi-system perspective. In S. Dreman (Ed.), *The family on the threshold of the 21st century: Trends and implications.* New York: Lawrence Erlbaum.

Olson, D. H., & DeFrain, J. (2000). *Marriage and the family: Diversity and strengths.* Mountain View, CA: Mayfield.

Pais, J. S. (1978). *Social-psychological predictions of adjustment for divorced mothers.* Unpublished doctoral dissertation, University of Tennessee, Knoxville.

Pam, A., & Pearson, J. (1998). *Splitting up: Enmeshment and estrangement in the process of divorce.* New York: Guilford.

Papp, P. (2003). Gender, marriage, and depression. In L. B. Silverstein & T. J. Goodrich (Eds.), *Feminist family therapy: Empowerment in social context* (pp. 211–223). Washington, DC: American Psychological Association.

Parkman, A. M. (1995). The deterioration of the family: A law and economics perspective. In G. B. Melton (Ed.), *Individual, the family, and social good: Personal fulfillment in times of change* (pp. 21–52). Lincoln: University of Nebraska Press.

Ponzetti, J. J., & Cate, R. M. (1988). The divorce process: Toward a typology of marital dissolution. *Journal of Divorce, 11,* 1–20.

Propst, L. R., & Fries, L. (1989). Problems and needs of adults. In M. Textor (Ed.), *The divorce and divorce therapy handbook* (pp. 45–60). Northvale, NJ: Jason Aronson.

Reinecke, M. A. (1994). Suicide and depression. In F. M. Dattilio & A. Freeman (Eds.), *Cognitive-behavioral strategies in crisis intervention* (pp. 67–103). New York: Guilford.

Reinecke, M. A. (2000). Suicide and depression. In F. M. Dattilio & A. Freeman (Eds.), *Cognitive-behavioral strategies in crisis intervention* (2nd ed., pp. 84–126). New York: Guilford.

Rice, J. K. (2003). "I can't go back": Divorce as adaptive resistance. In L. B. Silverstein & T. J. Goodrich (Eds.), *Feminist family therapy: Empowerment in social context* (pp. 51–63). Washington, DC: American Psychological Association.

Rich, P. (2002). *Divorce counseling homework planner.* New York: Wiley.

Roberts, A. R. (1990). An overview of crisis theory and crisis intervention. In A. R. Roberts (Ed.), *Crisis intervention handbook* (pp. 3–16). Belmont, CA: Wadsworth.

Roberts, A. R. (Ed.). (1996). *Crisis management and brief treatment.* Chicago: Nelson-Hall.

Rudd, M. D., Joiner, T., & Rajab, M. H. (2001). *Treating suicidal behavior: An effective, time-limited approach.* New York: Guilford.

Safran, J. D., & Greenberg, L. S. (1991). *Emotion, psychotherapy, and change.* New York: Guilford.

Saleebey, D. (1992). Introduction: Power in the people. In D. Saleebey (Ed.), *The strengths perspective in social work practice* (pp. 3–26). White Plains, NY: Longman.

Salts, C. J. (1989). Group therapy for divorced adults. In M. Textor (Ed.), *The divorce and divorce therapy handbook* (pp. 285–300). Northvale, NJ: Jason Aronson.

Sanchez, L., & Gager, C. T. (2000). Hard living, perceived entitlement to a great marriage, and marital dissolution. *Journal of Marriage and the Family, 62*(3), 708–722.

Scanzoni, J. (1972). *Sexual bargaining.* Englewood Cliffs, NJ: Prentice-Hall.

Schneller, D. P. (2003). *After the breakup: Adult perceptions of post-divorce intimate relationships.* Unpublished doctoral dissertation, Virginia Polytechnic Institute.

Slaiku, K. A. (1990). *Crisis intervention* (2nd ed.). Boston: Allyn & Bacon.

Spanier, G. B., & Casto, R. F. (1979). Adjustment to separation and divorce: An analysis of 50 case studies. *Journal of Divorce, 2,* 241–253.

Sprenkle, D. H. (1989). The clinical practice of divorce therapy. In M. Textor (Ed.), *The divorce and divorce therapy handbook* (pp. 171–195). Northvale, NJ: Jason Aronson.

Storm, C. L., & Sprenkle, D. H. (1982). Individual treatment in divorce therapy: A critique of an assumption. *Journal of Divorce, 6,* 87–98.

Toews, M. L., McKenry, P. C., & Catlett, B. S. (2003). Male-initiated partner abuse during marital separation prior to divorce. *Violence and Victims, 18*(4), 387–404.

Trovato, F. (1986). The relationship between marital dissolution and suicide: The Canadian case. *Journal of Marriage and the Family, 48,* 341–348.

Wallerstein, J. S., & Kelly, J. B. (1980). *Surviving the breakup: How children and parents cope with divorce.* New York: Basic Books.

Weiss, R. S. (1975). *Marital separation.* New York: Basic Books.

Weissman, M. M., Bruce, M., Leaf, P., Florio, L., & Holzer, C. (1991). Affective disorders. In L. Robins & E. Regier (Eds.), *Psychiatric disorders in America* (pp. 53–80). New York: Free Press.

Weitzman, L. J. (1985). *The divorce revolution: The unexpected social and economic consequences for women and children in America.* New York: Free Press.

White, J. J. (1985). *The effect of locus of control on post-divorce adjustment.* Unpublished master's thesis, University of Texas at Arlington.

White, M., & Epston, D. (1990). *Narrative means to therapeutic ends.* New York: Norton.

Womack, C. D. (1987). *The efects of locus of control and lawyer satisfaction on adjustment to divorce.* Unpublished master's thesis, University of Texas at Arlington.

Zung, W. W. K. (1965). A self-rating depression scale. *Archives of General Psychiatry, 12,* 63–70.

29

Crisis Intervention With HIV Positive Women

SARAH J. LEWIS
DIANNE M. HARRISON

This chapter is intended to provide an overview of crisis intervention with women who test positive for the human immunodeficiency virus (HIV) and the many factors that must be considered when working with this population. In order to provide stabilization during a time of crisis, it is necessary for clinicians to have an understanding of not only the emotional and social consequences of being HIV positive, but the physical consequences as well. Because HIV disproportionately affects minority women, it is imperative that clinicians also understand the cultural ramifications of living with HIV as well as cultural coping strategies.

There are several phases of the HIV trajectory in which women typically incur disequilibrium that may require intervention: at the time of HIV positive diagnosis; disclosure of HIV status; deterioration of the immune system; commencement of antiretroviral therapy; application for disability and/or termination of employment; and at the time of a diagnosis of acquired immunodeficiency syndrome (AIDS) (Poindexter, 1997; Brashers, Neidig, Reynolds, & Haas, 1998). The continual uncertainty that results from these events can precipitate situational, developmental, social, or compound crisis states individually or simultaneously (Hoff, 1989; Poindexter, 1997).

As of December 2002 there were 82,764 women with AIDS in the United States. There are disproportionately high rates of infection among African American women (48.6 per 100,000), Latina women (11.3 per 100,000), and American Indian/Alaskan Native women (5.8 per 100,000), compared

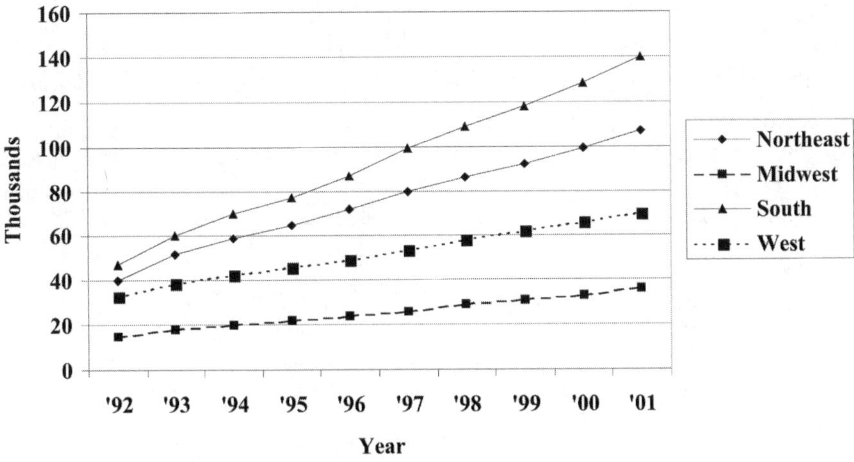

Figure 29.1 Estimated persons living with AIDS by region and year of diagnosis, 1992–2001, United States (CDC, 2002)

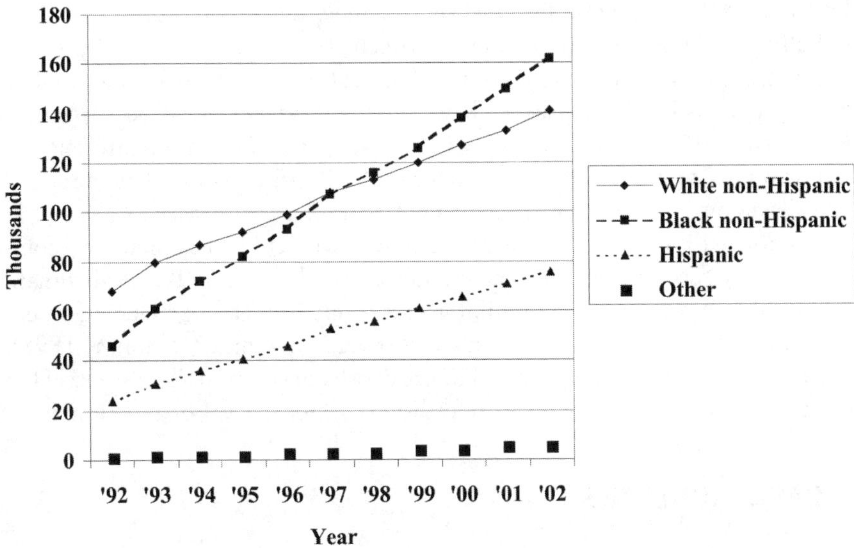

Figure 29.2 Estimated persons living with AIDS by race/ethnicity and year of diagnosis, 1992–2002, United States (CDC, 2002)

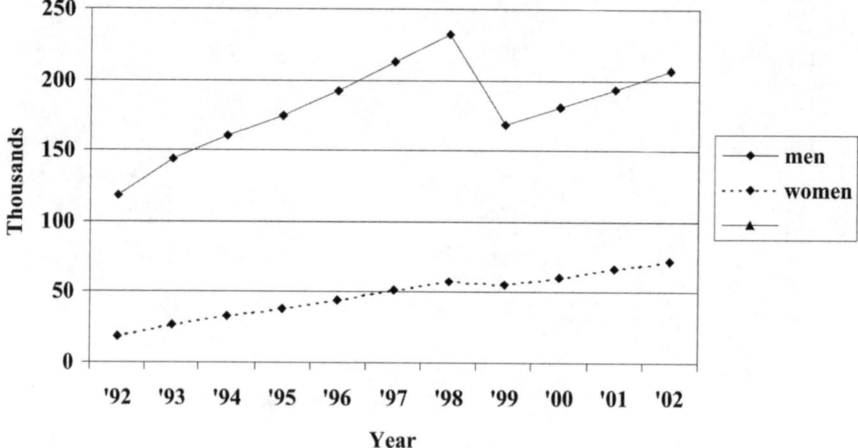

Figure 29.3 Estimated persons living with AIDS by gender and year, 1992–2002, United States (CDC, 2002)

with Caucasian women (2.1 per 100,000). It is important to recognize that that African American and Latina women represent 25% of all women in the United States, yet comprise greater than 82% of all the AIDS cases in women living in the United States (CDC, 2002). Women living within inner cities who are disproportionately affected by poverty and crime are hardest hit by the AIDS crisis (Dodd, Nuehring, Blaney, Blakley, Lizzotte, Potter, & O'Sullivan, 2004). Because of the heterogeneity of the female HIV positive population, it is important to consider the cultural health beliefs as well as historical racism and sexism with which these women have been plagued (Gaskins, 2001). Many of the crises associated with HIV are related not to illness but to contextual factors in which HIV flourishes as well as the social and developmental consequences of HIV, a stigmatized disease.

Clients with HIV often are affected by twin epidemics that are compounded by biopsychosocial factors: substance abuse and HIV (Kalichman, 1998). Substance abuse may inhibit access to medical care, producing a negative impact on quality of life (Israelski, Eversley, Janjus, & Smith, 1998). Social workers must be willing to address substance abuse issues with HIV positive clients so that the client may rise to a higher level of functioning.

CASE VIGNETTES

The following cases are typical of those that face social workers working within a community based AIDS organization that provides case management.

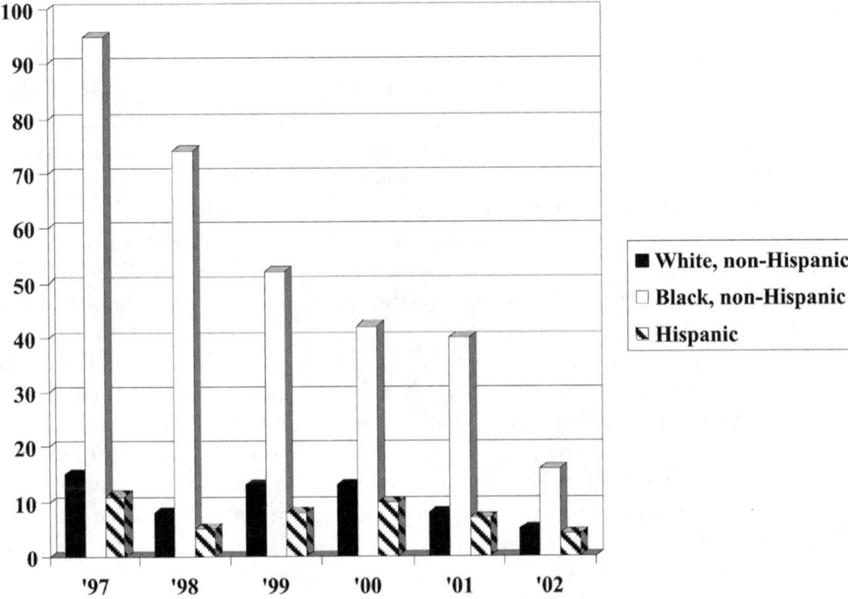

Figure 29.4 Reported cases of HIV/AIDS in infants born to HIV-infected mothers, by year of child's birth and race (CDC, 2002)

Case 1

Mary J., a 22-year-old African American daycare center worker, was referred to a social worker for case management by her OB-GYN after her husband called the doctor and reported that Mary had not gotten out of bed since her last appointment the prior week. At Mary's last appointment with the OB-GYN she had found out that she was HIV positive after routine testing during the first trimester of her pregnancy.

When Mary's physician presented Mary with the consent form for HIV testing, explaining that all pregnant females should be tested, she chuckled and stated, "The HIV test is one test I have worked hard to fail." Mary had participated in no high-risk behavior except for having unprotected sex with her husband. Mary's husband, however, had had several sex partners prior to marriage and had never been tested for HIV.

Mary was not prepared for, and was totally devastated by, the news of her infection and felt as though her world as she knew it had come to an end. She had always believed that if she worked hard and had love in her heart and a strong faith in God, her life would be protected from atrocity. She felt betrayed by her husband and too dirty and infectious to be around the children she worked with, and she didn't know whether to continue carrying the baby that she desperately wanted. When she sat down in the social worker's office she was in shock, unable to comprehend that everything could change in an instant.

Case 2

Linda B. was a 26-year-old White crack cocaine addict. She was arrested while prostituting herself in order to support her drug habit, and the judge presiding over her case ordered that she be tested for HIV. Although Linda had been a sex worker since she left home at age16 because of physical abuse by her parents, she was shocked that she tested HIV positive. Linda told no one of her HIV status for fear of being rejected by her friends who were also sex workers. Linda attempted to stop smoking cocaine but was unsuccessful. Her health began to deteriorate, and a year after her initial diagnosis she collapsed in an alley and was taken to the local hospital with pneumonia and diagnosed with AIDS.

The drug combination that could drastically reduce HIV viral load and strengthen her immune system required strict adherence and monitoring. Linda's doctor believed that Linda would continue using cocaine when she was released and was therefore unwilling to start her on the drug combination. The doctor attempted to explain to Linda that if she could stop using drugs, keep clinic appointments, and regularly take the medication, she could look and feel healthy for several years, but without medication she would probably not live more than 2 years.

When the doctor left the hospital room, Linda called for the nurse to come in. She was afraid of her doctor, but she trusted her nurse. Linda asked the nurse if she would die without the medication, and the nurse confirmed, in a much gentler manner, what the doctor had stated. Linda panicked. She did not want to die, but she did not have the coping skills necessary to live. She was at a turning point. The nurse gave Linda the phone number of a local AIDS case management organization and told her that they might be able to help but that she would have to make the call.

DEFINITION OF CRISIS

Crisis is defined as a "subjective reaction to a stressful life experience that compromises the individual's stability and ability to cope" (Roberts, 1990, p. 328). A defining characteristic of a crisis is that it is time limited, lasting from 4 to 6 weeks; however, HIV positive clients may experience serial crises. Although a stressful or hazardous event precipitates the crisis, it is the perception of the event and the individual's inability to cope with the perceived consequences of the event using previous coping strategies that designate a crisis (Lewis, 2004).

Poindexter (1997) explains that because HIV is a chronic illness that has physical, emotional, social, spiritual, and developmental consequences, an HIV positive person may experience multiple and cumulative crises over time. Crisis states can be the result of developmental, situational, or social conflict (Kanel, 1999; Poindexter, 1997). Each major event throughout the

HIV trajectory may precipitate a crisis in the life of an HIV positive woman. The following are examples of these events:

- Original HIV diagnosis
- Issues related to external and internal stigma
- Issues related to partner infidelity, or other trust issues
- Issues related to role definition (being a woman, partner, mother, etc.)
- The decision to divulge, or not divulge, HIV status to family and peers
- First clinical signs of a compromised immune system
- Issues related to antiretrovirals or other treatment
- Issues related to pregnancy
- AIDS diagnosis

The concept of developmental crisis stems from ego psychology, specifically from Erik Erikson (Pillari, 1998). Erikson proposed eight stages through which a person passes in his or her lifetime. Each stage presents a conflict or crisis that must be mastered in order to successfully develop or move on to the next stage. When an individual faces a chronic or terminal illness in young adulthood, the length of time to master each stage is shortened or otherwise disrupted (Kanel, 1999). The dramatic shift in role perception can also have an impact on developmental tasks.

A situational crisis is not a normal stage of development but an event that is extraordinary. A situational crisis can be precipitated by events such as a violent crime, a sudden death, a natural disaster, or the diagnosis of a chronic or terminal illness. The event can challenge the fundamental assumptions that underlie the individual's worldview (Roberts, 1996). According to Roberts, "A person's vulnerability to a stressful life event is dependent to a certain extent on the newness, intensity, and duration of the stressful event" (1996, p. 22).

Opportunities for situational crises abound throughout the HIV trajectory, resulting in what can be considered a "chain of life stressors" (Roberts, 1996, p. 23). A diagnosis of being HIV positive often changes the way a person imagines his or her world is in the present and will be in the future. Dreams can vanish in an instant, and life plans can suddenly turn into uncertainty. Because HIV positive individuals can have a long asymptomatic period, the first signs of immune system depletion or the diagnosis of an AIDS defining illness can also trigger a crisis. The interpretation of these events by the HIV positive individual is often that death is imminent.

Social crisis is brought about by societal or cultural events or responses (Poindexter, 1997). These events or responses can be racism, sexism, homophobia, or other discriminatory beliefs and their accompanying behaviors. Crisis arises in a cultural sense when cultural identity is challenged. Unfortunately, HIV triggers most of society's negative "isms." Individuals with HIV face a level of discrimination that is far worse than that experienced by individuals with other chronic or terminal diseases (Poindexter, 1999). Even when one does not disclose one's HIV status, one can still be impacted by internalized stigma. Internalized stigma does not require overt mistreatment, but it can occur simply by accepting perceived societal judgment and threat of rejection.

SCOPE OF THE PROBLEM AND PSYCHOSOCIAL VARIABLES

HIV is transmitted through body fluids such as blood, semen, vaginal secretions, and breast milk and leads to suppression of the immune system. Until 1993, a diagnosis of AIDS was given only if an individual was HIV positive and had 1 of 26 opportunistic infections. In January 1993, case definitions were changed to include other clinical markers such as a CD4+ T-lymphocyte count of less than 200 per milliliter of blood or a CD4+ percentage of less than 14, and diagnosis of pulmonary tuberculosis, recurrent pneumonia, or invasive cervical cancer. Opportunistic infections are mostly ubiquitous infections that are generally thought to be benign in individuals with healthy immune systems. However, when depletion of the immune system occurs, these infections take the "opportunity" to propagate and than can be deadly.

Case reporting of surveillance data related to HIV and AIDS has recently gone through several changes. Before 1993, only AIDS cases as defined by the preceding criteria were reported to the Centers for Disease Control (CDC). Immune system depletion to the point of susceptibility to opportunistic infection can take10 years or longer, and because of this the epidemiological picture was quite distorted. Only approximations of HIV infection rates have been available because HIV per se was not reportable; only the outcome of HIV (i.e., AIDS) was reportable.

Since 1994, the CDC has supported uniform HIV surveillance for all 50 states and territories, however, by 1998 only 29 states had implemented HIV reporting making it difficult to analyze trends in HIV infection (CDC, 2002). Because of these unstandardized surveillance requirements, HIV infection surveillance data must be interpreted with caution (CDC, 1998).

In 1997, the death rate for AIDS in the United States was the lowest in a decade—almost two-thirds below rates from just 2 years previous. The decrease is attributed to a new class of drugs known as protease inhibitors. New complex, multi-drug regimes, called highly active antiretroviral therapy, which include a protease inhibitor in combination with one or two other classes of antiretroviral drugs, are capable of lowering viral loads to the point of nondetection, allowing t-cells to resume healthy levels. Another new class of drugs, fusion inhibitors, has just been released. This class of drugs blocks HIV from infecting healthy t-cells. Unfortunately, there are several limitations to aggressive HAART, such as large pill burden, food and

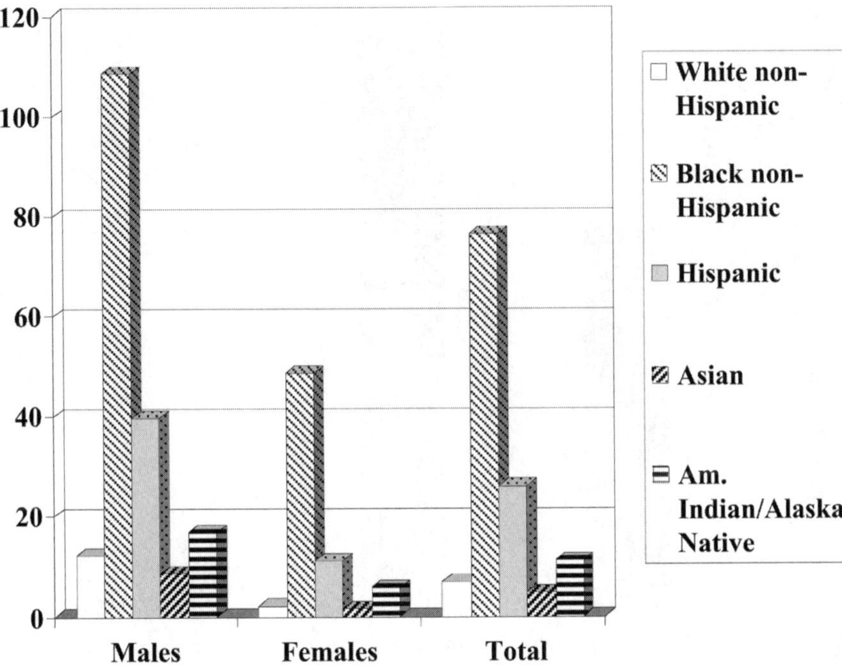

Figure 29.5 AIDS cases and annual rates per 100,000 pop, by race/ethnicity and gender reported in the continental US, 2002 (CDC, 2002)

storage restrictions, severe side effects, and even reduction in quality of life measures. Because of the psychosocial life stressors that many individuals who are HIV face, strict adherence to drug regimens can be quite challenging (Lewis & Abell, 2001).

As of December 2002, there are 82,765 women with living with AIDS, and an additional 199,759 had been reported HIV positive from areas with confidential name-based HIV infection reporting. From 1998 through 2002, the number of AIDS diagnoses increased 7% among women and decreased 5% among men. Women who seek treatment early tend to have the same survival rates as men; however, women have historically been less likely to receive an early diagnosis. Often the impetus for women to get tested is pregnancy.

Pregnancy and HIV

Federal guidelines now require doctors to counsel pregnant women about HIV and encourage them to test voluntarily for HIV. The rationale behind these guidelines is that if women know their HIV status, they can participate in antiretroviral therapy (drugs that fight the virus) during pregnancy and lower HIV transmission risk to the fetus. Vertical transmission rates (from mother to fetus) have dropped dramatically.

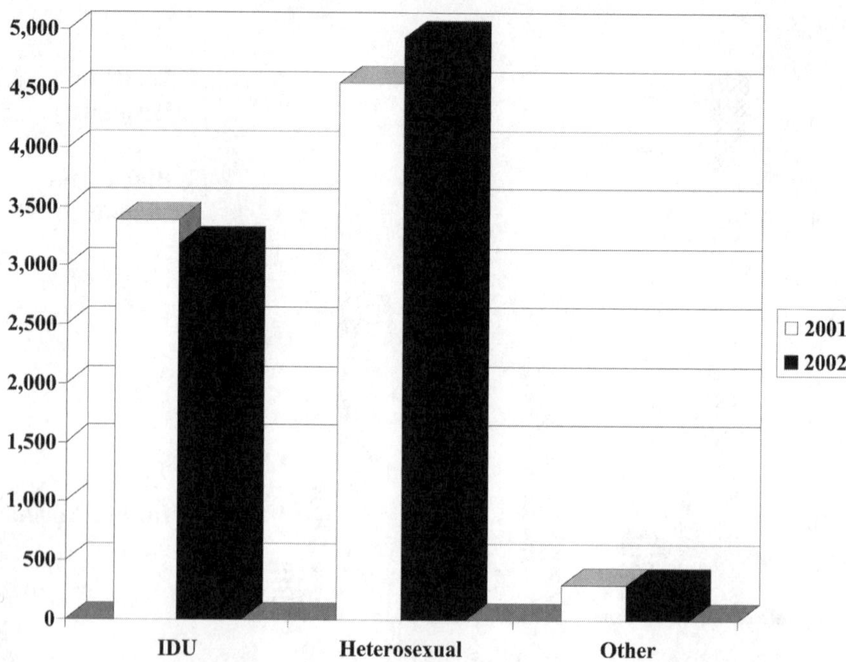

Figure 29.6 Estimated female adult/adolescent AIDS incidence, by exposure category and year of diagnosis, 2001–2002, US

It is estimated that over 6,000 HIV positive women give birth each year. Although each of the babies is born HIV antibody positive, by 18 months, most of them seroconvert to HIV antibody negative after they develop their own immune systems (Siberry, Parson, & Hutton, 2003). Vertical transmission rates have drop at least 80% from 1992 to 2001 and it is now possible to achieve transmission rates as low as 1–2%, compared to 25–30% a decade ago (Anderson, 2001).

It is important to recognize philosophical and cultural perspectives about women and childbirth when considering the topic of women and HIV. The cultural identity associated with motherhood and women's place in society is threatened by the possibility of vertical transmission of the virus. In cultures that place a high value on childbirth, HIV mothers are put in double jeopardy: Have a child and possibly expose it to the virus—making the woman a bad mother; or don't have a child—and have diminished value as a woman.

Recent research has demonstrated that HIV positive pregnant women have higher levels of depression than HIV negative pregnant women (Levine, Aaron, Laquinte, 2003). It is important to note, however, that HIV positive pregnant women had higher levels of depression prior to pregnancy than their HIV-negative counterparts. These findings may be the result of multiple stressors related to HIV, or the contextual stressors that many women with HIV deal with on a daily basis.

Sex Work

Because of the various definitions of prostitution and the often-illegal nature of the trade, it is difficult to estimate the number of persons who are currently involved in sex work. According to Shedlin (1990), there is a social hierarchy of female prostitutes. Escort services or call girl establishments recruit the younger, most attractive women, whereas women who work the street are considered to be the lowest level in the hierarchy.

Studies suggest that HIV transmission is up to four times higher among sex workers who are intravenous drug users (IDUs) as opposed to those who are not IDUs, suggesting that occupational exposure via heterosexual transmission is not the highest reported risk category for sex workers (Cohen, 1994). Sex workers who use crack cocaine tend to have more paying as well as nonpaying sex partners with whom they will have unprotected sex in order to obtain drugs or charge additional money.

Drug Abuse and HIV

Drug abuse and HIV have gone hand and hand since the beginning of the AIDS epidemic in the United States. Surveillance data do not accurately describe the impact of drug abuse on HIV exposure because drug use is a contributing factor in exposure via method of delivery, not a risk factor in and of itself. Intravenous drug use, therefore, is the only reported indicator of the drug abuse/HIV correlation. Although it is impossible to determine exact numbers, studies suggest up to 80% of HIV positive women were infected directly or indirectly through drug use (Ferrando, 1997). Up to 90 % of HIV positive drug abusers have a comorbid psychiatric illness.

Drug abuse and/or psychiatric illness exacerbates psychosocial stresses associated with the HIV disease trajectory and must be considered throughout any intervention. Even though it may seem impossible, it is imperative that treatment of substance abuse and or mental illness be provided concomitantly with medical treatment. If substance abuse and/or psychiatric illness are not addressed initially, sabotage of medical intervention as well as client-worker relationships is likely. Although there are several reasons for addressing these concurrent problems, possibly the most important are the severe individual and societal consequences associated with nonadherence to multidrug regimens.

Consequences of Nonadherence

Nonadherence to protease inhibitors is directly related to the development of antiretroviral drug resistance (Lewis & Abell, 2002). Poor adherence can be a problem with any chronic illness; however, as early as 1996, the issue of nonadherence was recognized as a potential disaster with protease inhibitors (Vanhove et al., 1996).

HIV replicates hundreds of millions of times a day, creating approximately 10 billion viral particles. Every replication is a potential for mutation (Mirken, 1998). When no antiretroviral is being used, these mutations are mostly random natural accidents and make no meaningful difference. When an antiretroviral is stopped and started, as is the case with nonadherence, Darwinian selection pressure is exerted, giving the mutated virus an advantage to survive. The mutations become systematic because the particles that are most drug-susceptible are killed, leaving only drug-resistant particles to replicate.

The strength of the highly active antiretroviral therapy (HAART) is what makes it so susceptible to resistance through viral mutation. A weak regimen like Zidovudine (AZT) monotherapy does not completely halt viral replication, so mutation is not necessary for the virus to survive. When regimens are stronger and completely halt the replication process, only particles that have mutated around the medication survive and replicate. Even though resistance to AZT does happen, it usually takes 18 months to 3 years; resistance to HAART happens much more quickly (Mirken, 1997). There is a serious gap in the literature regarding how much nonadherence is too much nonadherence; however, some believe that less than 95 % adherence is unacceptable. It is interesting to note that new research findings show that viral mutation due to nonadherence follows a bell shaped curve. Individuals who have little adherence (they almost never take their medication) have low levels of viral mutation, individuals with good adherence, but not excellent have high levels of mutation (more than some of the time, but less than 95% of the time), and those with excellent adherence (95% or more) have little viral mutation (Sethi, 2004).

Viral mutation has both personal and societal consequences. The first level is that of increased viral burden in the patient with the mutated virus. The Food and Drug Administration (FDA) have approved only eight protease inhibitors and one fusion inhibitor, and the virus may form resistance to several of the protease inhibitors at one time. This leaves few options for effective regimes.

The societal consequence is a result of an individual who has developed resistance to all available treatments infecting others. The newly infected individuals will acquire the mutated virus, which is resistant to all treatment, leaving them with no treatment options (Mirken, 1997). This new resistant strain of the virus known as a "super virus" is a new phase of the AIDS epidemic.

RESILIENCE AND PROTECTIVE FACTORS

At most AIDS service organizations that provide case management, clinicians attempt to prepare clients for possible future events in order to prevent

Table 29.1 Internet Sites

- http://www.aegis.com
  This site provides information for clients and clinicians. It has an excellent library that is an incredible resource. Site map is easy to navigate and should be a top choice when looking for something quickly.
- http://thebody.com
  This multimedia site, like aegis, can be considered a megasite. The body is updated at least once a day, so outdated information is rare. This site is another excellent site to bookmark.
- http://www.cdc.gov
  This is the site for the Centers for Disease Control. One has to navigate around a bit in order to find information on HIV, but if you are interested in healthcare, it is worth the visit.
- http://www.medscape.com
  This site is a more clinical in nature, but it has the most up-to-date information on new important findings in the medical community.

crisis situations. During the intake, myths are dispelled by educating the client about the disease spectrum, constitutional symptoms, what to do and not to do to stay healthy, and strategies for safer sex. Suggestions for keeping the immune system healthy usually include nutritional facts, information on support groups, hotlines, counselors for stress management and other mental health issues, medication adherence issues, and spiritual support. There are remarkable Internet megasites to help clients and clinicians keep up with new clinical trials, news briefs, as well as the history of the AIDS crisis. (See Table 29.1.)

SEVEN STAGES OF ROBERTS'S CRISIS INTERVENTION MODEL

Roberts's seven-stage model of crisis intervention provides an excellent framework for working with HIV positive individuals who are experiencing a crisis state. The seven stages of intervention are as follows:

- Assessing lethality and safety needs
- Establishing rapport and communication
- Identifying the major problems
- Dealing with feelings and providing support
- Exploring possible alternatives
- Formulating an action plan
- Providing follow-up

It is important for the clinician to remember that what separates a crisis from a difficult situation is the lack of tools and the perception of danger. For example, when a person gets a flat tire in his or her car, if one has the tools, a spare tire, and a safe place to change the tire, the flat is a mere inconvenience. However, if that person is alone on a dark, deserted highway and there is no lug wrench, a feeling of crisis begins to stir. The event, the flat tire, is not the crisis. The perception of danger generated by the lack of tools to ameliorate the situation and the feelings aroused by that perception are the crux of the crisis. The clinician's acknowledgment and assessment of the perceived danger are the starting point for crisis intervention. Roberts's seven-stage model is meant to be a flexible framework for practice, providing guidelines for crisis intervention without rigidity.

Lethality Assessment and Building Rapport

An assessment of suicidal or homicidal ideation should be a part of every crisis intervention even if it is informal and brief. In someone who is newly diagnosed with HIV, the crisis does not usually involve homicidal or suicidal ideation, but instead a strong desire to live. Therefore, the assessment of lethality is usually informal and done within the context of rapport building. If, however, it is suspected that a client could possibly be in immediate danger, a more in-depth lethality assessment is necessary. When danger is suspected, the clinician must ask the client directly whether she has intention to hurt herself or someone else. The directness of this approach may be uncomfortable for the practitioner; however, it gives the client permission to talk about her intentions. The following questions must be answered:

1. Do you want to harm yourself or someone else?
2. Have you ever attempted to harm yourself in the past?
3. Has anyone close to you ever committed suicide or homicide?
4. Do you have a plan? (Clinician must determine if the plan is realistic.)
5. Do you have the (pills, gun, etc.) to carry out the plan?

All agencies and private practitioners should have protocols on safety procedures in place before ever being faced with a homicidal or suicidal client. If the answer to question 1 and any additional question is yes, the clinician must follow through with the aforementioned protocols. Each affirmative answer indicates an increase in the risk of physical harm.

For the most part, crisis intervention with HIV positive women generally begins with the stage of rapport building, or relationship building. The tools or assets that the clinician needs in this stage are a nonjudgmental attitude, the ability to understand verbal and nonverbal communication, sincerity, objectivity, and a sense of humor.

When attempting to build rapport, it is important for the clinician to remember the stigma that is often attached to an HIV positive status. The clinician will be asking the client to reveal very personal actions that are not customarily talked about with anyone, let alone strangers. After working with the HIV positive population for a while, it is easy to forget the discomfort associated with topics such as sex and drug use. These topics become a part of the everyday experience of the practitioner; however, the discomfort may remain for the client. The practitioner must provide a safe and respectful atmosphere for such disclosures; this can be done through modeling a level of comfort with sensitive material often considered taboo.

It is during this stage of assessment that most information gathering will be done. Most agencies have a routine intake form consisting of several pages of questions. These questions are generally used to collect demographic information (place of residence, family size, income, etc.), possible HIV exposure routes, method of payment for medical services, some medical information, and information about the client's family system or other avenues of support. A succession of rapid-fire questions can severely hinder the attempt to build a mutually respectful relationship because there is no give-and-take between parties: The client is doing all the giving. Such one-way communication sets up a dynamic where the clinician is the one with all the power, diminishing the client.

When clinicians are familiar with the intake and assessment process, it is much easier to guide the client to tell his or her story as opposed to giving one-sentence answers to a series of questions. This storytelling provides both a more relaxed atmosphere for the client, as well as an opportunity for the clinician to assess cognitive functioning. A moderately scheduled guide is used to assure the collection of all needed information. The guide does not have to be an actual object (although that may be helpful in the beginning) but instead a way of thinking or arranging the interview. The format of the guide is funnel shaped, meaning the interview starts with very open questions that lead to more direct questions. For example:

- So, Mary, what brings you in to see me today?
- Is this your first pregnancy?
- What are your fears about keeping this baby?

Each question in the preceding sequence gets more focused. There may or may not be several questions between these questions, depending on the depth and breadth of Mary's responses. The guide is moderately scheduled because it gives an outline, not the exact questions or timing of the questions. All the information needed by the agency must be gathered, but it can be gathered in a time frame agreed upon by both the client and the clinician.

Assessment of the Problem

The primary challenge for clinicians working with HIV positive individuals is resisting the urge to become enthralled by the crisis. Because death is so embedded in societal consciousness as the ultimate negative consequence of danger, it is hard to recognize that death is not a crisis. A sign on the wall of the employee lounge in one AIDS service organization reads: "There is no such thing as a crisis." This is to remind clinicians that no matter what the circumstance, when individuals have the tools they need, there is no crisis. The questions and issues that the practitioner needs to identify and assess are shown in Table 29.2 for each of the 2 case illustrations.

When working with HIV positive clients, it is important to always consider possible cognitive impairment of a physiological nature. This is not to imply that the social service clinician should attempt to medically diagnose a client with HIV brain involvement; however, the clinician should be able to recognize telltale signs in order to make immediate medical referrals. These signs may include, but not be limited to, memory impairment, illogical or disorganized thinking, severe headaches, blurred vision, a change in speech, or a change in gait.

Because of the heterogeneity of the HIV positive population, practitioners should take every opportunity to learn about the cultures and customs of the people they serve. For example, many African American members of some fundamentalist religious groups believe that fate and God have a great impact on health (Bekhuis, Cook, Holt, & Scott-Lennox, 1995). African American students have been found to have group-specific thoughts about providers of health services and their own mental health (Millet, Sullivan, Schwebel, & Meyers, 1996). Not all cultures follow or place the same importance on stages of development or life events, and it is important to consider the presenting crisis within the context of the client's cultural identity.

The clinician must assist the client to rank order or prioritize the major problems, as well as the perceived danger that these problems evoke. Although this may seem obvious, it is mentioned as a reminder to the reader of the ease with which projection can occur. The clinician may prioritize the presenting problems differently from the client; however, it is the client who is feeling the distress. If the practitioner believes that groundwork must be laid before

Table 29.2 Type of Danger and Coping Strategies

Aspect of Current Crisis	Positive and Negative Coping Strategies
• What is the perceived danger? ◆ Mary: Not being able to have children. ◆ Linda: Eminent death. • Is the danger physical or emotional? ◆ Mary: Emotional. ◆ Linda: Emotional. • How will the client's life be affected? ◆ Mary: Change in perceived life story. ◆ Linda: Must make a conscious decision to live.	• What strategies (both negative and positive) have been attempted to resolve similar dilemmas in the past? ◆ Mary: Reliance on faith and family. ◆ Linda: Drugs and self-reliance. • What tools are presently necessary to resolve the dilemma? ◆ Mary: Knowledge of vertical transmission risks, faith, and family. ◆ Linda: Knowledge of disease spectrum and adherence issues, trust in someone other than herself, a support system, and drug treatment.

tackling the prioritized problem, he or she is obligated to work through these issues with the client.

For example, Mary identified her main problem as the moral dilemma of keeping her baby and possibly infecting it with HIV, or having an abortion, which was against her religious beliefs. Her cultural identity as a woman was challenged by the belief that she was not fit to bear children, and she was experiencing a tremendous amount of internalized stigma. Although Mary was experiencing several other issues, this was the order of priority that she felt was most important.

In the case of Linda, she needed both medical treatment and drug treatment. Linda recognized that she did not want to die, knew there was some medicine that could give her a chance, but also knew the doctor wouldn't give it to her if she continued using crack. Linda could not imagine life without crack and identified the major problem as the physician who would not prescribe the medicine for her. The clinician's role was to help Linda to understand the true nature of the problem and to assist her in finding a workable solution.

Exploration of Feelings

Women who are newly diagnosed could be experiencing one or more of many feelings:

- Shame: "I caught this disease through drug use or sex."
- Betrayal: "I can't believe that he was cheating on me."
- Anger: "That no good so-and-so gave this to me."
- Loss: "I won't be able to have sex—or a baby—ever again."
- Fear: "I am afraid I am going to die soon."
- Guilt: "I may have given HIV to someone else."

Throughout this chapter perceptions and thoughts have been discussed as the driving force behind crisis. Emotions, according to cognitive theorists, are also driven by cognitions. A primary objective in crisis intervention, therefore, is to provide information to correct distorted ideas and provide better understanding of the precipitating event. This is not to be done in an emotionless vacuum, but instead in a supportive environment that emphasizes the client's strengths.

The clinician must actively listen during this cathartic phase and gently keep the client on track by asking open-ended questions. The clinician's job at this point is to not only actively listen to the client, but to see the client within the client's system. This will provide tools for the next stage where solutions are explored. In order to see the larger client system the practitioner must constantly keep in mind five things: (1) the stage of development of the client (e.g., Ericson or some other developmental theorist);

(2) stage of disease; (3) place in family or support system; (4) cultural norms; and (5) strategies that have worked in the past in similar situations.

In the first case illustration, Mary had several issues to contend with: pregnancy while being HIV positive, internalized stigma, inability to fill a cultural role, and dashed dreams. Mary also had very little knowledge about HIV, and some of her perceptions were formed by misconceptions about the disease. Mary had an amazing support system consisting of both an extended family and the church of which she was an active member. Her feelings were exacerbated by her limited knowledge about the disease spectrum and misinformation that she had about vertical transmission.

Linda had a tremendous amount of fear. She had not trusted anyone since she was 16 years old and left an abusive home to live on the street. She did not have a legal means to support herself, and she did not know how to stop smoking crack cocaine. Linda's fear presented as anger. Anger at the doctor for not giving her the medicine, anger at whoever gave her the virus, anger at cocaine for having a grip on her, and anger at the case manager for not being willing to talk the doctor into prescribing her the medicine.

Exploration of Solutions and Action Plan

Throughout the assessment process, information is gathered in order to explore solutions. By this point in the intervention the clinician has determined whether the client is suicidal or homicidal, has established rapport, investigated the major problem(s), and has explored feelings and thoughts the client is experiencing as a result of the problem(s). Finding a workable solution and developing an action plan are the next two steps. The solution(s) must be tailor made for the client and must take into account the tools with which she has to work. It is also important that the solution provide some immediate relief for the client.

When finding a workable solution, the clinician often has to take an active role. The client, due to the crisis, is experiencing disequilibrium, and is unable to identify tactics or skills to alleviate the situation. The client may not recognize that she has overcome similar or more difficult hurdles in the past, and it is the role of the practitioner to point out these strengths and accomplishments.

The action plan must contain identifiable steps. It is a good idea to take out a piece of paper and write down each step with the client. Draw a line vertically down the paper and on one side of the paper write down the objective or task, and on the other side write down who is to accomplish the task and the timeframe in which it is to be accomplished. The client may only be able to make one phone call a day. This may not seem like much of an accomplishment, but it starts a momentum toward the goal.

In the case of Mary, education about vertical transmission and the HIV disease trajectory was the first step. Although the needed education could begin in the office with the clinician, it was important for Mary to see a physician that specialized in prenatal HIV care. Just the knowledge of available treatments that can greatly reduce the probability of vertical transmission helped to ameliorate much of the crisis state that Mary was experiencing. An appointment was made from the clinician's office for the first prenatal visit with the HIV specialist, and the clinician offered to sit with Mary and her husband when Mary told him about her HIV positive status. The clinician also suggested that Mary make an appointment with her pastor, who had provided her with spiritual counseling since she was a child. The counselor recognized the pastor's name as a member of the local HIV Pastoral Network, and knew that he would provide a great deal of comfort to Mary.

Linda had a completely different set of needs and skills with which to work. She had survived on the streets for many years and had a strong desire to live. She needed a safe and structured environment in order to change her drug abusing lifestyle, but before that she needed someone to explain to her in layperson terms why the doctor could not prescribe medication to her if she could not maintain adherence. Another major issue was that Linda had no legal means of supporting herself and without such, was likely to feel the need to continue her work in the sex trade. Linda's list of things to do was comprised of: (1) application for disability (which would provide income and health insurance); (2) education about disease spectrum and adherence issues; and (3) referral for inpatient drug treatment.

Follow Up

The last step of every action plan should be some form of follow up with the crisis intervention counselor. A set appointment or follow up contact with the clinician gives the client both incentive to accomplish each task on the objective list, and also provides assurance that she does not have to do it all on her own. During the follow up contact the problem and steps taken to overcome the problem are reviewed. If the problem still exists additional possible solutions are investigated. If the problem has been resolved, it is important for the clinician to affirm the client's accomplishment. This affirmation will help to anchor these new found coping strategies for future use.

CONCLUSION

Even though the number of deaths from AIDS-related illnesses have decreased in the recent past, the number of new HIV infections has not slowed. Minority women who are often already marginalized, make up the fastest growing group of new HIV infections. Due to the nature of the virus and the stigma that is associated with it these women may face serial crises.

When working with HIV positive women, crisis intervention clinicians must consider not only psychosocial variables but also physiological complications. It is often the crisis counselor who is the first person to provide factual information to the client in layperson terms. This education helps to form the foundation from which the client can begin to restore cognitive functioning and make informed decisions.

Clinicians must be sensitive to cultural norms including the roles that women tend to play within each culture. The crisis intervention assessment should be within a cultural context that considers the client's system of support. It is important to recognize the strengths of the client and successful coping strategies utilized in the past.

The final word on Mary is a positive one. Mary had her baby and it was HIV antibody positive, but seroconverted to HIV antibody negative at 18 months. Mary discovered that her husband had acquired the virus before he had even met her and the couple decided to stay together. Mary is employed by a women's peer education program through her church where she tells her story to young African American women to help prevent the further spread of HIV. Mary's life is different now than it was before, but according to Mary, it is better.

Linda's story has a positive, yet poignant ending. Linda discontinued her drug use in a treatment center and finally began to trust someone other than herself. She found meaning in life and others who cared a great deal about her. Linda's immune system, however, was unable to recover from the damage done by HIV and years of abuse. Before Linda died, she recognized that healing had taken place and that she had the tools and inner strength to deal with anything.

REFERENCES

Anderson, J. R. (July, 2001). Perinatal transmission and HIV: An unfinished success story. The Hopkins Report.

Bekhuis, T., Cook, H., Holt, K., & Scott-Lennox, J. (1995). Ethnicity, church affiliation, and beliefs about the causal agents of health: A comparative study employing a multivariate analysis of covariance. *Health Education Research* (10): 78–82.

CDC (1998). *HIV/AIDS surveillance report, 10*(1).

Chesney, M. A. (1997). New antiretroviral therapies: Adherence challenges and strategies. *HIV Newsline 3*(3): 65–66.

Cocores, J. A., & Gold, M. S. (1990). Recognition and crisis intervention treatment with cocaine abusers: The Fair Oaks Hospital model. In A. R. Roberts (Ed) *Crisis intervention handbook: Assessment, treatment, and research*. Belmont, CA: Wadsworth Publishing Company.

Ferrando, S. J. (1997). Substance use disorders and HIV illness. *The AIDS Reader, 7*(2): 57–64.

Israelski, R., Eversley,R., Janjua, S., & Smith, S. (1998). Race, HIV symptoms, recovery from drug abuse, and appointment adherence are associated with quality of life (QOL) among HIV infected women. [On-line]. AIDSLINE . Abstract from International Conference for AIDS, 12:1075.

Kanel, K. (1999). *A guide to crisis intervention.* Pacific Grove, CA: Brooks/Cole Publishing Company.

Katz, A. (1996). Gaining a new perspective on life as a consequence of uncertainty in HIV infection. *Journal of the Association of Nurses in AIDS Care,* 7(4): 51–61.

Levine, A. B., Aaron, E., & Laquinte, J. (2003). Prevalence of depression in HIV-infected pregnant women. *American Journal of Obstetrics and Gynecology, 189*(6), Supplement 1.

Lewis, S. J., & Abell, N. (2002). Development and evaluation of the adherence attitude inventory. *Research on Social Work Practice, 12*(1): 107–123

Linn, G. L., Anema, M. G., Hodess, S., Sharpe, C., & Cain, V. A. (1996). Perceived health, HIV illness, and mental distress in African-American clients of AIDS counseling centers. *Journal of Association of Nurses in AIDS Care,* 7(2): 43–52.

Linsk, N. L., & Keigher, S. M. (1997). Of magic bullets and social justice: Emerging challenges of recent advances in AIDS treatment. *Health and Social Work, 22*(1): 70–75.

Millet, P. E., Sullivan, B. F., Schwebel, A. I., & Meyers, L. J. (1996). Black Americans' and white Americans' views of etiology and treatment of mental health problems. *Community Mental Health Journal,* 32: 235–242.

Mirken, B. (1997). How much does it really matter if you take your pills on time? *Bulletin of Experimental Treatments for AIDS.* [on-line] DOCN: BE970902. Available at http://www.sfaf.org

Parad, H. J., & Parad, L. G. (1990). Crisis intervention: An introductory overview. In H. J. Pard & L. G. Parad (Eds.), *Crisis intervention, book 2: The practitioner's sourcebook for brief therapy.* Milwaukee, WI: Family Service America.

Pillari, V. (1998). *Human behavior in the social environment: The developing person in a holistic context.* Pacific Grove, CA: Brooks/Cole Publishing.

Poindexter, C. C. (1997). In the aftermath: Serial crisis intervention for people with HIV. *Health and Social Work, 22*(2): 125–132.

Poindexter, C. C. (1999). HIV-related stigma in a sample of HIV-affected older female African American caregivers. *Social Work, 44*(1): 46–55.

Roberts, A. R., & Burman, S. (1998). Crisis intervention and cognitive problem-solving therapy with battered women: A national survey and practice model. In A. R. Roberts, *Battered women and their families: Intervention strategies and treatment programs* (2nd ed.). New York: Springer Publishing Company, Inc.

Roberts, A. R. (1996). Epidemiology and definitions of acute crisis in American society. In A. R. Roberts (Ed.), *Crisis management and brief treatment: Theory, technique, and applications* (pp. 16–33). Chicago: Nelson-Hall Publishers.

Roberts, A. R. (1990). An overview of crisis theory and crisis intervention. In A. R. Roberts (Ed.), *Crisis intervention handbook: Assess-*

ment, treatment and research. Belmont, CA: Wadsworth Publishing Company.

Sethi, A. K. (January, 2004). Adherence and HIV drug resistance. *The Hopkins HIV Report.*

Siberry, G. K., Parson, G., & Hutton, N. (November, 2003). Management of infants born to HIV infected mothers. *The Hopkins HIV Report.*

Siegel, L., & Korcok, M. (1989). *AIDS: The drug and alcohol connection: What health care professionals need to know*. Center City, MN: Hazelden.

Ungvarski, P. J. (1997). HIV/AIDS: New knowledge, new treatments, and the challenges for nursing. *Journal of the Association of Nurses in AIDS Care, 8*(4): 5–6.

Vanhove, G. F., Schapiro, J. M., Winters, M. A., Merigan, T. C., & Blaschke, T. F. (1996). Patient compliance and drug failure in protease inhibitor monotherapy. *Journal of American Medical Association,* 276: 1955–1956.

Winiarski, M. G. (1991). *AIDS-related psychotherapy*. Boston: Allyn and Bacon.

30

Crisis Intervention With Caregivers

ALLEN J. OTTENS
DONNA KIRKPATRICK PINSON

There is no consensus on a definition of caregiving. A caregiver has been defined simply as "an individual who provides care for another person who, ordinarily, would not require care" (Ilardo & Rothman, 1999, p. 7). Caregivers can be defined more globally as "people who provide tangible, financial, emotional, or informational and coordination support to an impaired family member" (Argüelles, Klausner, Argüelles, & Coon, 2003, p. 101). However defined, family caregiving in the past two decades has become a prominent issue for researchers and clinicians in the field of geropsychology.

With the graying of America—approximately 12% of the U.S. population is over the age of 65 (U.S. Bureau of the Census, 2002)—there is a concomitant increase in the segment of this population requiring care. The majority of disabled older persons are cared for at home (Stone, Cafferata, & Sangl, 1987). Rising up to address this health care challenge is a vast informal (i.e., unpaid) support system of friends and family, and especially among the latter, spouses or daughters or daughters-in-law. These caregivers assist their care recipients in the necessary but demanding activities of daily living (e.g., bathing, dressing, toileting) and often assume responsibility for delivering care previously provided by registered nurses (Hoffman & Mitchell, 1998).

According to a recent survey, 16% of the U.S. population provides unpaid care to a recipient 50 or older, and the typical caregiver is a 46-year-old female who spends over 20 hours per week providing care (National Alliance for Caregiving, 2004). In that survey, older caregivers reported providing care for 10 or more years. Findings such as these led Cavanaugh (1998) to refer to caregiving as a normative "life event challenge." It is predicted that as the 21st century proceeds, the caregiving challenge will grow more complex due to the following factors:

> Long-distance caregiving.
>
> Blended families.
>
> Fewer children to provide care.
>
> Continued increases in the number of working women.
>
> Demands on older adults themselves in caring for their own children (e.g., for grown children with mental illness, developmental disabilities, and long-term illnesses) and possibly grandchildren. (Weiner & Goldberg, 2003, p. 11)

For today's caregivers, tending to disabled older persons may take steep physical, emotional, social, and financial tolls. This is called "caregiver burden." The stresses, for example, of caring for someone with Alzheimer's disease have been vividly chronicled in the popular book *The 36-Hour Day* (Mace & Rabins, 1999). As the burden saps the caregiver's capacity to cope, she or he teeters on the brink of crisis.

What we hope to accomplish in this chapter is to provide a context for understanding and a method for intervening with the crises encountered by caregivers of disabled older persons. Specifically, we begin with a description, in broad brushstrokes, of the caregiving experience. Next, we present a structure for pinpointing caregiver burden and for targeting possible interventions. The third section consists of a case description of a caregiver in crisis. We conclude with a section on the application of Roberts's (1991) seven-stage model to address this crisis.

THE CAREGIVING EXPERIENCE

Providing care for a disabled older person is not necessarily an onerous or debilitating duty. For example, Thompson, Gallagher-Thompson, and Haley (2003) pointed out that longitudinal studies of caregivers of persons with dementing disorders appear to contradict the conventional wisdom that caregiver stress increases as the care recipient's dementing disorder worsens and years of caregiving increase. The notion of caregivers as a uniformly depressed lot can be challenged as well. Schulz, Williamson, Morycz, and Biegel (1993) found that about 45% of their sample of dementia caregivers were consistently "below the threshold" (p. 136) for being at risk of clinical depression at each of four measurement points across their 2-year study. As far as physical health is concerned, 83% of caregivers surveyed recently rated themselves as being in good to excellent health (National Alliance for Caregiving, 2004).

A caregiver may be burdened but still experience an adequate or high level of well-being due to the presence of perceived social support (Chappell & Reid, 2002). Social support serves as a potent protective factor against distress among caregivers. It qualifies as the most effective moderator of caregiver stress (Logsdon & Robinson, 2000). In their review of culturally diverse caregivers, Gallagher-Thompson et al. (2000) suggested that compared to Anglo caregivers, African American caregivers may exhibit less depression, stress, and burden as a result of the strengths of the African American community being brought to bear in support of caregivers and their care receivers. Besides social support, caregivers' well-being has also been found to be associated with a "benign appraisal" of stressors (e.g., perceiving that one has the capacity to manage a problem situation) and problem-focused coping as opposed to avoidance (Goode, Haley, Roth, & Ford, 1998).

A caregiver's subjectively experienced burden may vary based on the type of relationship he or she has with the care recipient. Cicirelli (1993) found that caregivers who felt stronger attachments to their care recipients experienced less subjective burden, whereas stronger obligation to assume the caregiver role was related to greater burden. This attachment versus obligation distinction has been borne out among recently surveyed caregivers who reported that their emotional distress is greater when they feel they had no choice in taking on caregiving responsibilities (National Alliance for Caregiving, 2004).

The quality of the caregiving relationship can undergo improvement. King (1993), in a Canadian qualitative study of daughters caring for aging mothers, found that what began as an overinvolved, conflicted caregiving relationship evolved over time into one in which the daughters learned to balance their mother's needs with their own. The caregiving relationship thus became healthier as the daughters were able to

> (a) make contextual caregiving decisions; (b) set realistic limits on their caregiving activities; (c) accept responsibility for the outcomes of their care decisions; (d) be sensitive to situations that might pose threats to their own needs; and (e) deal rationally with the guilt that necessarily accompanies contextual decisions. (p. 424)

Negative Impacts on Caregivers' Health

When caring for an older disabled person, especially one with progressive dementia, expectations can go awry and challenges can quickly turn into crises. Two types of stressors impinge on caregivers. One type arises from performing direct patient care, such as assisting with the activities of daily living. The second type arises from the patient's behavioral manifestations (e.g., wandering, agitation, lack of cooperation). These behaviors, quite common in dementia caregiving, tend to be more stressful than direct patient care because they occur unpredictably (Goode et al., 1998).

When laboring under these challenging and stressful conditions, caregivers may experience a variety of deleterious social, mental, and physical impacts. Often, these impacts are greatest on those with the heaviest responsibilities, such as the caregivers of persons with dementia. With regard to social impacts of caregiving, dementia caregivers report less time for leisure, more employment complications, and more family conflict than nondementia caregivers (Ory, Hoffman, Yee, Tennstedt, & Schulz, 1999). However, social impacts appear to be more typical than exceptional in the careers of most caregivers regardless of the care recipient's disabling condition. For example, 48% of Hispanic caregivers reported giving up vacations, hobbies, or social activities; 62% of the caregivers who work or once worked had to make adjustments such as arriving late to work or giving up employment entirely; and 22% of African American caregivers say caregiving brought about financial hardship (National Alliance for Caregiving, 2004).

In their exhaustive review of research on the effects of caregiving on health, Bookwala, Yee, and Schulz (2000) noted that over a decade ago, the stresses of caregiving had become solidly linked to detrimental mental health outcomes. In one study, for example, Yee and Schulz (2000) found that compared to men caregivers, women caregivers reported more psychiatric symptomatology (e.g., higher levels of depression and anxiety and lower life satisfaction). Yee and Schulz described a variety of factors that presumably place women at greater risk for psychiatric morbidity. Two such factors are that women are less likely to obtain either formal or informal assistance, and they tend to assume more hands-on roles in personal care tasks.

In another representative study, Haug, Ford, Stange, Noelker, and Gaines (1999) followed a random sample of caregivers over a two-year period. This study is notable in that it utilized a longitudinal design and was not focused on only dementia caregivers. Haug et al. found that at the outset of their study, 40.5% of the caregivers assessed their mental/emotional states as "excellent." At the study's third and final assessment point, only 24.8% made that same claim. Haug et al. noted that a possible factor in this decline was substantial increases in the mean number of instrumental activities of daily living (IADLs) and activities of daily living (ADLs) performed by the caregivers over the course of the study.

The connection between caregiving and poorer physical health is weaker than the link between caregiving and poorer mental health (Bookwala et al., 2000). This may result from the different ways that physical health can be operationalized. Nevertheless, researchers consistently find that caregivers perceive their health to be negatively impacted (Bookwala et al., 2000). In the Haug et al. (1999) study, for example, the caregivers' self-assessed physical health scores declined from 48.7% claiming "very good" or "excellent" health to 32.3% two years later.

There are intriguing studies linking caregiving and more "objective" measures of compromised physical health. Researchers have noted poorer immune system functioning in some caregivers (Vitaliano, Schulz, Kielcot-Glaser, & Grant, 1997) and slow wound healing (Kielcot-Glaser, Marucha, Malarkey, Mercado, & Glaser, 1995). Perhaps most disconcerting is evidence that caregiving is a risk factor for mortality (Schulz & Beach, 1999). Schulz and Beach conducted a prospective population-based cohort study with an average of 4.5 years of follow-up. After adjusting for sociodemographic and certain health factors, they found that those who were providing care and experiencing strain (i.e., mental or emotional strain associated with helping or getting help for each caregiving activity) had mortality risks 63% higher than a control group of noncaregivers.

Summary

Although the social, emotional, and physical impacts of caregiving are not necessarily negative, problems encountered and responsibilities assumed in caregiving can adversely stress the caregiver. The results of that stress are succinctly stated by Bookwala et al. (2000):

> In summary, based on the studies that we have reviewed here, we can conclude that caregivers of both dementia and nondementia patient groups evidence significant psychiatric morbidity compared to noncaregivers or community norms. Caregivers also consistently rate their physical health to be poorer than do noncaregivers and, in some cases, exhibit poorer health-related behaviors, physical disability, and immune and physiological functioning. (p. 127)

Where does caregiver distress come from? What is it about the caregiving experience that can strain the caregivers' capacities to cope? These questions lead us to consider the issue of caregiver burden.

CAREGIVER BURDEN

Montgomery (1989) selected several terms from the literature that target what is meant by burden: stress effects, caregiving consequences, and caregiving impact. For Gottlieb, Thompson, and Bourgeois (2003), burden refers to "the extent to which problems commonly seen in caregiving situations are rated as distressing or troublesome to the caregiver" (p. 42).

A number of instruments have been developed to assess caregiver burden. One commonly used instrument, with reportedly good psychometric properties, is the 24-item Caregiver Burden Inventory (CBI; Novak & Guest, 1989). The CBI has been factor analyzed recently on a U.S. sample by Schwiebert, Giordano, Zhang, and Sealander (1998). The resulting six factors provide some compass points for where to locate burden and for where to target crisis interventions. Each factor is discussed below, and examples are provided from our counseling experience with caregivers that illustrate specific sources of burden.

Factor 1: Time-dependence Burden

Time-dependence burden results from the caregiver's perceived restriction on time. It is commonly experienced by dementia caregivers who are involved in almost continuous and vigilant care. Caregivers' crises may be precipitated by a variety of time-dependence issues.

For example, crises can emanate from a feeling of "role captivity" (Pearlin, Mullan, Semple, & Skaff, 1990). This term aptly captures the demoralizing sense of being tethered to the caregiving site as well as the constant monitoring performed by the caregiver. In our work, we have seen how a sense of role captivity will feed on itself. We recently heard one spouse caregiver's dilemma arising from attending the out-of-town first communion of a granddaughter: "I want to go so bad, but I won't. If I do step out, I'll enjoy the freedom too much, and coming back to this house and him will be more pain than I can bear." Similarly, we have heard a caregiver lament that even a few minutes' trip to the supermarket aroused great agitation in her care receiver: "He panics if I even go to the mailbox!" Moreover, time-dependence burden, not surprisingly, is associated in our experience with an extreme reluctance on the part of the caregiver to request in-home care assistance.

As caregivers' time and space shrink, social isolation increases. Because social isolation is a risk factor for elder abuse (Cooney & Mortimer, 1995), we recommend that crisis workers be alert to or assess for that possibility.

Factor 2: Developmental Burden

This burden arises due to caregivers' feelings of being "off-time" developmentally in comparison to peers. There is a strong sense of being left behind, of missing out on life, and of wishing that current circumstances were different.

For caregivers, developmental burden can be linked with the sacrifices made (e.g., placing career, hobby, or friendships on hold) on behalf of the care recipient. It can be experienced by the daughter who expected that demands on her attention and affection would be coming from adolescent children and husband rather than from a cognitively impaired uncle.

Developmental burden may be experienced in many ways. For one woman of financial means, it came in the form of an existential crisis. As she cared for a husband who was left permanently paralyzed by a stroke, she realized that her image of aging gracefully would never materialize. How often she had pictured herself and her husband bathed in the glow of a southwestern sunset, toasting their love and good fortune as they sat poolside in the company of their old country club friends! Her friends might not yet be in that picture, but never would she.

Factor 3: Physical Burden

Schwiebert et al. (1998) found that three CBI items pertaining to fatigue and care receiver dependence constitute the physical burden factor. With this factor, stress arises due to a feeling that one is on a grueling treadmill: one is exhausted, but the pace never slackens.

"I'm exhausted, but the person is dependent on me" is a caregiver's stance that has crisis potential because it neither allows for easy negotiation nor for a way out. We recommend assessing the caregiver for other rule-bound thinking that closes off his or her options. For example, it is common to hear caregivers argue, "I'm exhausted, but no one can take care of her like I can" or "I'm exhausted, but we must stick to our routine."

Factor 4: Social Burden

Feelings of social burden derive from perceived role conflict. Crises are often precipitated by conflicted relationships with other family members. Caregivers may lash out angrily against the family member who needs to be reminded constantly for the money she or he grudgingly promised to chip in to cover caregiving expenses. We recall the caregiver who endured frequent, intrusive long-distance phone calls from a brother who was highly critical of financial decisions being made in his absence. However, much more common are caregivers' remarks about how little appreciation they receive from family for the work they do.

The conflict is compounded by its emotional aftereffects. Caregivers may consequently worry that their anger drove away potentially valuable support. Or, they may feel shame for saying things in anger that cannot be taken back.

Factor 5: Emotional Burden

The burden caregivers perceive to be due to negative feelings toward their care receivers is defined as emotional burden. This type of burden can lead to a crisis when the caregiver's resentment threatens the caregiving relationship. An overly strained and fatigued caregiver may express her or his resentment as "If it weren't for you, my life would not be a living hell."

Resentment can also run high if there has been a history of abuse in the family. For example, a wife who had endured chronic verbal abuse from her husband might feel especially strained by the demands of caring for him; and we should be alert to any signs of abuse being perpetrated or threatened against the husband. Likewise, caregiving daughters may be emotionally strained in circumstances where their care receiver is a mother who, years earlier, failed to provide protection against a father's abusive advances. In her recent review of risk factors for elder mistreatment in non–African Americans, Benton (1999) concluded that the research is still inconclusive as to whether those who mistreat older adults may have been victims of abuse at a younger age. When faced with a crisis situation as just described, we recommend assessing for the risk of care receiver abuse.

Emotional burden arises also out of feeling embarrassed by the behavior of the care receiver. Should the care recipient become incontinent, the caregiver is often doubly strained due to a reluctance to invite others into the home and by the great difficulty posed by coping with incontinence, an event that often leads to the wrenching decision of nursing home placement (Mittelman, Zeiss, Davies, & Guy, 2003).

With regard to emotional burden, we need also mention the exasperation that many caregivers feel when assisting an "uncooperative" care receiver with his or her ADLs. Bathing, toileting, and physician visits can become tests of whose will shall prevail.

Despite the fact that their emotional burdens fairly cry out for assistance, caregivers increase their risks of experiencing crisis because they are among the most resistant or cautious about seeking support from the social service system. Toseland (1995) commented on the difficulty of recruiting a critical mass of caregivers for a support group: "Making initial contact with a sufficient number of caregivers to begin a group can be difficult. Caregivers tend to be reluctant to ask for help. Seeking help is sometimes perceived as abandoning their responsibility and the person for whom they are caring" (p. 232).

Factor 6: Health Burden

Schwiebert et al. (1998) identified a sixth factor from the CBI that did not appear in Novak and Guest's (1989) original analysis. Consisting of three items, Schwiebert et al. termed it "health burden." These items appear to be reflective of caregivers' perceptions of their own diminishing health.

In our counseling work with caregivers, we have found that they tend to neglect their physical needs. One caregiver living with her 100-year-old mother reported to us that she had relied on gardening for her exercise and that now she and her garden were both "going to pot." Studies such as those by Burton, Newsom, Schulz, Hirsch, and German (1997) bear out that caregivers report getting less physical activity and rest.

Self-care, exercise, good nutrition, and stress management are all components of a wellness-oriented intervention focus for caregivers (Myers, 2003). Yet, as Ilardo and Rothman (1999) point out, caregivers operate out of imperatives that militate against their performing essential self-care. One of these (and the one we most often hear) is "I shouldn't need to take a break. I'm strong" (p. 78). Caregivers continue to put themselves at risk of strain and crisis until such an imperative becomes tempered with a competing awareness: "Good caregiving starts with myself. If I don't look out for me, my care receiver suffers."

Case Study: "Meet Millie"

Millie F. was an 83-year-old living at home with Frank, 82, her spouse of 57 years. They married on November 17, 1945, only a few weeks after he had been discharged from the service. A childless couple, they often talked about how they had "adopted" all the kids on their block and how theirs was the house where all the youngsters liked to hang out. Both maintained lengthy careers, he as a mail fraud investigator with the postal service and she as an interior designer with a large department store chain. With her eye for decoration and color, she always favored splashy, coordinated clothing with jewelry and accessories to match. Frank loved to introduce his vivacious wife at any opportunity. "Here she is. *Meet Millie!*" he would say, beaming. Over the years, fewer and fewer people would catch Frank's little play on words—how he was also referring to *Meet Millie,* a popular TV show of half a century ago that starred Elena Verdugo.

About a year and a half before Millie found herself on the brink of crisis, she noticed some subtle changes in Frank. For example, he seemed to be repeating the same question he had asked just minutes earlier. Then, there was the problem with his temper. He had always been an "ornery cuss," as she described him, but now his orneriness was becoming more intense and personal. Millie wasn't too sure what to make of her observations. After all, Frank seemed his usual self most of the time. However, after the incident with the newspaper delivery boy, she decided to mention the situation to their primary care physician. "Why, he just cursed the boy out because the paper was a little ways down the driveway. I mean, he used language that would have made a sailor blush!"

After a few trips back to the physician with Frank in tow, they received some complicated information, a diagnosis of sorts of Frank's condition, and a prescription for medication that he refused to take. "I thought he told us that Frank had 'old timers' disease," was how she summarized these visits.

As months went by, Millie was becoming increasingly exasperated, angry, and even fearful of Frank. She suspected something was wrong, but she wasn't quite sure to what she should attribute Frank's unpredictable, touchy, and hurtful behavior. Slowly, surely, and almost imperceptibly the situation deteriorated. Millie was beginning to feel like a prisoner in her own home as Frank alienated old friends. Fellowship visits from their church fell off. Frank's anger took the forms of personal criticism bordering on abuse and demands for obedience to his dictates. With the former came a growing depression that began to gnaw at Millie. With the latter came a growing resentment against Frank. His demands failed to take into consideration the fact that Millie was struggling with painful osteoarthritis in her knees and back. He lacked empathy for the efforts she was making to care for him.

The depression and resentment were joined by anxiety. About a week and a half before her referral to a community mental health center, Millie witnessed two events in one day that brought home to her the precarious nature of the situation with Frank. Late that morning Frank had gone out to the mailbox at the end of the driveway. Some minutes later, Millie noticed that Frank had not yet returned inside. After a quick search, she found him in the backyard with a confused look on his face. He made up some excuse to explain why he was standing in the tulip bed. A few hours later, Frank forgot that he had turned on the faucet in a basement washtub. The overflow took two hours to mop up.

Perhaps it was more than coincidence that just two days later Millie made an appointment to speak with a services specialist at the Area Agency on Aging (AAA) in her community. She wanted information about a prescription drug program that she might qualify for. Besides giving Millie the prescription plan information, the services specialist noticed her fatigue and depression. The specialist inquired and learned that Millie was the sole caregiver for an older spouse with suspected Alzheimer's disease and that she had only a tenuous supportive network: a few diehard friends and some nieces and nephews who made irregular phone calls from the East Coast. Considering Millie's strained self-presentation, the specialist tactfully broached the topic of a referral to the local community mental health center (CMHC). Fortunately, the AAA and the CMHC had established a good collaborative arrangement (Lebowitz, Light, & Bailey, 1987) so that the referral could be made swiftly given the risk inherent in this caregiving situation.

Although the offer of a counseling referral took Millie by surprise ("He's the one with the screw loose, and you want *me* to get *my* head examined?"), she agreed to it, and the next day she had a walk-in appointment with the CMHC's on-call crisis counselor. With the referral secured, the AAA's services specialist had done well to apprehend Millie's signs of emotional difficulty and to inquire about her caregiving strain. Furthermore, the specialist was wise to initiate discussion of a referral, as caregivers are notoriously loath to refer themselves to programs that would alleviate their depression. (Gottlieb et al., 2003)

CRISIS INTERVENTION: THE SEVEN-STAGE MODEL

Millie's situation is not yet one in imminent crisis, but there is potential for crisis. One risk is possible mistreatment of the care recipient at the hands of a burdened caregiver, as discussed earlier. A second risk is to the caregiver's health and emotional well-being. Without self-care, caregivers may jeopardize their health, which leads to an earlier and perhaps less appropriate long-term care placement for the care recipient. Roberts's (1991, 2000) model has applicability to caregiving situations that are crises in the offing.

Stage 1: Conduct a Crisis Assessment (Including Lethality)

The crisis counselor noted that Millie had very limited social support. She had not accessed any resources in the community for day care or respite services. Informal support in the form of friends and family came sporadically. Low social support fed into Millie's isolation. She felt, she said, like the Lone Ranger.

Millie's emotional profile was that of someone experiencing depression and anxiety. Certainly her depression was exacerbated by the personal nature of the criticism she received from Frank, by her chronic fatigue and arthritis pain, and by a growing pessimism about how this caregiving situation would resolve. Worries about her health (arthritis and hypertension) featured prominently in her anxiety, and lack of sound information about the disease and what it was doing to Frank added to her uncertainty. There was no indication that Millie had been mistreating Frank, although she was worried that one day he might physically strike out at her.

Administration of the CBI found Millie highest on developmental and emotional burdens. The developmental burden resulted from a combination of a wish to escape her caregiving situation, the emotional drain attached to caregiving, and the role captivity and social isolation into which she felt she was sinking deeper. The emotional burden resulted from the embarrassment she felt when Frank attacked visitors, anger at his verbal criticism of her, and smoldering resentment for performing a difficult yet unappreciated caregiving role.

After the initial walk-in session, the crisis counselor began to conceptualize this caregiving situation. Besides the evident anxiety and depression, the crisis counselor singled out other issues for further exploration:

- Millie failed to request more information and explanations about Frank's dementing condition from their physician.
- Her attempts to reason, argue, or rationalize with Frank over his demands might actually stoke his anger and agitation.
- She eventually bowed to these demands, even when there was no evidence of their reasonableness.
- She neglected her own health needs.
- She lacked knowledge about her community's formal support and assistance programs.

Stage 2: Establish Rapport

After providing a few of the elements of good listening (eye contact, undivided attention, reflecting feelings), the counselor found that Millie was hungry for social contact. Somewhat to her surprise, Millie was really taking to this counselor who had the capacity to understand her point of view.

Initially, the crisis counselor suggested that she and Millie address her obvious stress and exhaustion. Because Millie is from a generation that might be suspicious of counseling, stress and exhaustion, which seem to have a physical basis, appeared to be "safer" topics than anxiety and depression. Millie agreed to this, and that served as the second step toward building a relationship.

The counselor established rapport in several other ways. For example, she was sensitive to some of the jargon and colloquialisms older persons might use. Thus, when Millie got off the elevator for her appointment and promptly got lost trying to find the counselor's office, both could chuckle at Millie's description of herself as a "Wrong-Way Corrigan." If the counselor did not understand Millie's slang, she asked for clarification, as when Millie described feeling the "heebie-jeebies" the day Frank was lost in the tulips.

Many older clients have a capacity for humor, and this can be used in the service of relationship building. It can even be used as a springboard to address counseling topics of substance, as this snippet of dialogue illustrates:

Millie: (laughing) Frank always liked to brag about his service record. And over the years, I must say, he's really embellished that record quite a bit. Now, to hear him tell it, he practically single-handedly chased Mussolini and his henchmen right out of Rome!

Counselor: (laughing along, but then becoming serious) Like that fish that got away that just keeps getting bigger and bigger! But let me ask you this: Is there anything else that he claims that *you* know isn't quite the case?

Millie: Well, come to think of it, a couple of weeks ago my friend Helen came to visit. He told her flat out, and used a few choice words in the process, that he didn't want her coming over anymore, because he said we make too much noise that disturbs him. But he plays the TV so darn loud, he couldn't have heard us over it!

Counselor: So, his reason for forbidding Helen to come over to visit really doesn't hold together. But you abide by it—mainly to keep the peace—and the result is that you feel more isolated. Is that right?

From the very first, it is essential for the counselor to foster a climate of collaboration with the client. By encouraging working *together,* the counselor strongly suggests that something good can be accomplished, and that builds a sense of hope in the client.

Finally, self-disclosure, at the right time, in the right amount, and of an appropriate content, can also help to establish rapport. In a second counseling visit, the counselor disclosed that she had had some deeply personal experience with caregiving herself. The counselor briefly talked about how she had been part of an extended family effort several years earlier on behalf of a physically disabled grandmother.

Stage 3: Identify Major Problems or Crisis Precipitants

Roberts (2000) has pointed out the usefulness of identifying the "last straw" (p. 18), or precipitating event, as well as the client's previous coping methods. In Millie's case, two events—finding Frank in the backyard and the overflowing washtub—seemed to be the turning points in how she viewed her situation. These events could not be easily explained away, and they came to represent the hard truth that something was definitely wrong. They clashed with Millie's wish that all was well and that Frank's old self would prevail.

These two events fit into the counselor's evolving conceptualization of Millie's modal coping style. When faced with threat, especially threat that could overwhelm, Millie's tendency is to cope by using avoidance or hoping that things get better. This is how she had reacted to evidence of Frank's cognitive slippage. When confronted with threat that is less easily bypassed, such as Frank's barrage of verbal criticism or demands for care, Millie adopted an *argue-acquiesce-blame self* coping pattern. That is, she would make a noisy but feeble attempt to argue or reason with him, give in to his demand so as to keep the peace, and then come around to blaming herself for having set him off.

Millie's passive, avoidant, and reactive (as opposed to proactive) coping styles explained her surprising lack of knowledge about Alzheimer's disease and lack of awareness of support services in the community. One question that the counselor posed piqued Millie's curiosity in such a way that she was motivated to learn more about the effect of Alzheimer's disease. At one point, the counselor asked offhandedly, "Frank's anger and cursing at you—do you wonder if this is Frank or the disease doing the talking?"

Stage 4: Encourage Exploration of Feelings

There are two important objectives at Stage 4, as we have found from our work with older clients. One objective is for the client's "story" to be heard. As Mittelman et al. (2003) put it, "We have found that most AD [Alzheimer's disease] caregivers want to tell their stories and they more readily identify problems and solutions when they have been active participants in that process" (p. 79). When clients tell their stories and give us their slant or take on what the problem is, we listen for an overarching theme or title that could be given to that story. In Millie's case, the title that came to the counselor's mind was "I'm a Prisoner in My Own Home." When the counselor shared that title with Millie, her nonverbal reaction was such that the counselor knew it struck home. With regard to identifying problems and solutions from the story, the counselor suggested, "If that's what the title of the story is, could we put our heads together to come up with a workable 'escape plan'?" Put that way, Millie was intrigued to hear more.

A second objective is to validate the client's feelings. Millie's exhaustion, which Frank minimized, was validated: she *is* exhausted, she really is tired. That she felt anger and resentment was understandable. Her perception of the situation was validated. "Maybe," the counselor allowed, "the rules that Frank lays down and his angry outbursts, that you take exception to but then cave into, are not as sound as your perception of the situation." From the extraction of the story title and the validation of feelings and perceptions come possibilities and alternatives.

Stage 5: Generate and Explore Alternatives

The counselor is advised to collaborate, go slowly, and work with a manageable few, but relevant, behavioral alternatives. After putting their heads together and brainstorming, the counselor and Millie came up with these alternatives:

The need for more information: Information needs to be obtained from Frank's physician. What information the physician cannot supply, given his limited time, can be obtained from other sources, such as the local chapter of the Alzheimer's Association.

The need for support: Certainly, it is important for Millie to reconnect with old friends. The counselor also planted the seed for another source of support by saying in a neutral way, "I don't know if you've ever considered becoming a part of a support group that consists of other caregivers who are going through many of the same things you are. It often helps to be with others in the same boat because they can supply an understanding perspective that our well-meaning regular friends just don't have." Not only would a support group, such as are provided through the Alzheimer's Association, provide much needed support, but the group is also a source of useful information about the disease and its insidious progression.

The need for respite: Both Millie and the counselor agreed that both she and Frank could benefit from some time away from each other, although Millie was very skeptical of how Frank would tolerate that. Part of respite also involved some necessary self-care on Millie's own behalf, which could include some recreation and even long-neglected physical therapy for her ailing knee.

The need to resolutely confront the issues: This is a behavioral alternative that was suggested by the counselor. She understood Millie's tendencies to avoid facing issues and to fail to persevere and see a solution through. As this alternative was discussed, Millie saw the importance of "taking the bull by the horns" and not backing off even when the bull began to charge.

Stage Six: Develop and Formulate an Action Plan

The counselor and Millie took each of the above alternatives and worked them into an action plan. To obtain more information, Millie and the counselor role-played how to assertively request information from the physician. Millie learned to write down questions for the physician so she would not forget them in the rush and crush to get Frank to the clinic. Millie was encouraged to make another appointment with the services specialist at AAA to learn about community services and how to join a support group.

At the AAA, Millie learned about a respite program funded by the federal Older Americans Act to pay for a number of respite care hours each year. She learned how to apply and qualify for this service. Perhaps more important, she found out about places offering adult day care in her community where individuals with Alzheimer's disease could socialize and even have lunch. The counselor suggested that Frank attend day care at least twice a week for Millie to derive beneficial respite from it (Zarit, Stephens, Townsend, & Greene, 1998). While Frank was at day care or while the respite worker was in her home, Millie could use this time to visit friends or get therapy for her arthritic knee.

Resolutely confronting the issue was perhaps Millie's toughest challenge. "He's not going to like going to a day care center. It'll be like moving heaven and earth to get him there." In the past, Frank's protestations would be too much for her to bear, and she would back down. This time she promised she would stick to her guns and give the day care and respite care "experiments" a chance to work. To her surprise, Frank began to look forward to day care. He liked the staff, flirted innocently with a couple of the women who attended, and found another veteran of World War II with whom he could share stories.

Stage 7: Follow-up

The counselor and Millie agreed that follow-up (or booster) appointments be scheduled for about three weeks and then stretched to every 6 weeks. These check-in visits would be to take a measure of Millie's current stress level, and the counselor planned to readminister the CBI at each follow-up session. The counselor also looked at these follow-up sessions as an opportunity to assess how well Millie was maintaining her active coping style, as opposed to avoidance. This would come into play over the developmental course of Millie and Frank's caregiving experience, as when, for example, the time came for Millie to consider and research long-term care placement for Frank.

CONCLUSION

The typical challenges of caregiving for an older disabled adult often become burdens that strain the caregiver's capacities to cope. Caregiving can be a rewarding, even a spiritually deep experience, certainly insofar as there is adequate support for the caregiver and a positive attachment to the care recipient. When burden takes a toll, however, there can be numerous untoward emotional and physical effects on the caregivers, and care recipients can experience the rebound effect of these, as in the case of elder abuse.

The caregiver in crisis resorts to maladaptive coping behaviors that often exacerbate an already difficult situation. Also, caregivers feel out of balance socially, emotionally, and physically. This is true for both dementia and non-dementia caregivers. It is important to restore a sense of balance in the lives of caregivers because their focus can be solely on the care recipient to the exclusion of themselves. In this chapter, we illustrated how the stages of a widely adopted crisis intervention model can be utilized to address the burdens of a caregiver and help her find relief from their strain.

REFERENCES

Argüelles, S., Klausner, E. J., Argüelles, T., & Coon, D. W. (2003). Family interventions to address the needs of the caregiving system. In D. W. Coon, D. Gallagher-Thompson, & L. W. Thompson (Eds.), *Innovative interventions to reduce dementia caregiver distress* (pp. 99–118). New York: Springer.

Benton, D. M. (1999). African Americans and elder mistreatment: Targeting information for a high-risk population. In T. Tatara (Ed.), *Understanding elder abuse in minority populations* (pp. 49–64). Philadelphia: Brunner/Mazel.

Bookwala, J., Yee, J. L., & Schulz, R. (2000). Caregiving and detrimental mental and physical health outcomes. In G. M. Williamson, D. R. Shaffer, & P. A. Parmlee (Eds.), *Physical illness and depression in older adults: A handbook of theory, research, and practice* (pp. 93–131). New York: Kluwer Academic/Plenum.

Burton, L. C., Newsom, J. T., Schulz, R., Hirsch, C. H., & German, P. S. (1997). Preventive health behaviors among spousal caregivers. *Preventive Medicine, 26,* 162–169.

Cavanaugh, J. C. (1998). Caregiving to adults: A life event challenge. In I. H. Nordhus, G. R. VandenBos, S. Berg, & P. Fromholt (Eds.), *Clinical geropsychology* (pp. 131–136). Washington, DC: American Psychological Association.

Chappell, N. L., & Reid, R. C. (2002). Burden and well-being among caregivers: Examining the distinction. *The Gerontologist, 42,* 772–780.

Cicirelli, V. G. (1993). Attachment and obligation as daughters' motives for caregiving behavior and subsequent effect on subjective burden. *Psychology and Aging, 8,* 144–155.

Cooney, C., & Mortimer, A. (1995). Elder abuse and dementia: A pilot study. *International Journal of Social Psychiatry, 41,* 276–283.

Gallagher-Thompson, D., Arean, P., Coon, D., Menendez, A., Takaji, K., Haley, W. E., et al. (2000). Development and implementation of intervention strategies for culturally diverse caregiving populations. In R. Schulz (Ed.), *Handbook on dementia caregiving: Evidence-based interventions for family caregivers* (pp. 151–185). New York: Springer.

Goode, K. T., Haley, W. E., Roth, D. L., & Ford, G. R. (1998). Predicting longitudinal changes in caregiver physical and mental health: A stress process model. *Health Psychology, 17,* 190–198.

Gottlieb, B. H., Thompson, L. W., & Bourgeois, M. (2003). Monitoring and evaluating interventions. In D. W. Coon, D. Gallagher-Thompson, & L. W. Thompson (Eds.), *Innovative interventions to reduce dementia caregivers distress* (pp. 28–49). New York: Springer.

Haug, M. R., Ford, A. B., Stange, K. C., Noelker, L. S., & Gaines, A. D. (1999). Effects of giving care on caregivers' health. *Research on Aging, 21,* 515–538.

Hoffman, R. L., & Mitchell, A. M. (1998). Caregiver burden: Historical development. *Nursing Forum, 33,* 5–111.

Ilardo, J. A., & Rothman, C. R. (1999). *I'll take care of you: A practical guide for family caregivers.* Oakland, CA: New Harbinger.

Kielcot-Glaser, J. K., Marucha, P. T., Malarkey, W. B., Mercado, A. M., & Glaser, R. (1995). Slowing of wound healing by psychological stress. *Lancet, 346,* 1194–1196.

King, T. (1993). The experiences of midlife daughters who are caregivers for their mothers. *Health Care for Women International, 14,* 419–426.

Lebowitz, B. D., Light, E., & Bailey, F. (1987). Mental health center services for the elderly: The impact of coordination with area agencies on aging. *The Gerontologist, 27,* 699–702.

Logsdon, M. C., & Robinson, K. (2000). Helping women caregivers obtain support: Barriers and recommendations. *Archives of Psychiatric Nursing, 14,* 244–248.

Mace, N. L., & Rabins, P. V. (1999). *The 36-hour day* (3rd ed.). Baltimore, MD: Johns Hopkins University Press.

Mittelman, M., Zeiss, A., Davies, H., & Guy, D. (2003). Specific stressors of spousal caregivers: Difficult behaviors, loss of sexual intimacy, and incontinence. In D. W. Coon, D. Gallagher-Thompson, & L. W. Thompson (Eds.), *Innovative interventions to reduce caregiver distress* (pp. 77–98). New York: Springer.

Montgomery, R. J. V. (1989). Investigating caregiver burden. In K. S. Markides & C. L. Cooper (Eds.), *Aging, stress, and health* (pp. 201–218). New York: Wiley.

Myers, J. E. (2003). Coping with caregiving stress: A wellness-oriented, strengths-based approach for family counselors. *Family Journal: Counseling and Therapy for Couples and Families, 11,* 153–161.

National Alliance for Caregiving. (2004). *Caregiving in the U.S.* Washington, DC: National Alliance for Caregiving and the American Association of Retired Persons.

Novak, M., & Guest, C. (1989). Application of a multidimensional caregiver burden inventory. *The Gerontologist, 29,* 798–802.

Ory, M. G., Hoffman, R. R., Yee, J. L., Tennstedt, & Schulz, R. (1999). Prevalence and impact of caregiving: A detailed comparison between dementia and nondementia caregivers. *The Gerontologist, 39,* 177–185.

Pearlin, L. I., Mullan, J. T., Semple, S. J., & Skaff, M. M. (1990). Caregiving and the stress process: An overview of concepts and their measures. *The Gerontologist, 30,* 583–594.

Roberts, A. R. (1991). *Contemporary perspectives on crisis intervention and prevention.* Englewood Cliffs, NJ: Prentice Hall.

Roberts, A. R. (2000). An overview of crisis theory and crisis intervention. In A. R. Roberts (Ed.), *Crisis intervention handbook* (2nd ed., pp. 2–30). New York: Oxford University Press.

Schulz, R., & Beach, S. R. (1999). Caregiving as a risk factor for mortality: The caregiver effects study. *Journal of the American Medical Association, 282,* 2215–2219.

Schulz, R., Williamson, G. M., Morycz, R., & Biegel, D. E. (1993). Changes in depression among men and women caring for an Alzheimer's patient. In S. H. Zarit, L. I. Pearlin, & K. W. Schaie (Eds.), *Caregiving systems: Formal and informal helpers* (pp. 119–140). Hillsdale, NJ: Lawrence Erlbaum.

Schwiebert, V. L., Giordano, F. G., Zhang, G., & Sealander, K. A. (1998). Multidimensional measures of caregiver burden: A replication and extension of the Caregiver Burden Inventory. *Journal of Mental Health and Aging, 4,* 47–57.

Stone, R., Cafferata, G. L., & Sangl, L. (1987). Caregivers of the elderly: A national profile. *The Gerontologist, 27,* 616–631.

Thompson, L. W., Gallagher-Thompson, D., & Haley, W. E. (2003). Future directions in dementia caregiving intervention research and practice. In D. W. Coon, D. Gallagher-Thompson, & L. W. Thompson (Eds.), *Innovative interventions to reduce dementia caregiver distress* (pp. 299–311). New York: Springer.

Toseland, R. W. (1995). *Group work with the elderly and family caregivers.* New York: Springer.

U.S. Bureau of the Census, National Center of Health Statistics, and the Bureau of Labor Statistics (2002). Washington, DC: Author.

Vitaliano, P. P., Schulz, R., Kielcot-Glaser, J., & Grant, I. (1997). Research on physiological and physical concomitants of caregiving: Where do we go from here? *Annals of Behavioral Medicine, 19,* 117–123.

Weiner, A., & Goldberg, S. L. (2003). Aging in the new millenium: What the future holds for us. In J. L. Ronch & J. A. Goldfried (Eds.), *Mental wellness in aging: Strengths-based approaches* (pp. 3–14). Baltimore, MD: Health Professions Press.

Yee, J. L., & Schulz, R. (2000). Gender differences in psychiatric morbidity among family caregivers: A review and analysis. *The Gerontologist, 40,* 147–164.

Zarit, S. H., Stephens, M. A. P., Townsend, A., & Greene, R. (1998). Stress reduction for family caregivers: Effects of adult day care use. *Journal of Gerontology: Social Sciences, 53B,* S267–S277.

VI

EVIDENCE-BASED PRACTICE AND RESEARCH

31

The Crisis State Assessment Scale: Development and Psychometrics

SARAH J. LEWIS

Men are disturbed, not by things, but by the principles and notions which they form concerning things.

—Epictetus (c. 55–c. 135), *The Enchiridion*

STATEMENT OF THE PROBLEM

Crisis intervention, based on crisis theory, is one of the most widely used types of brief treatment employed by counselors, social workers, and other mental health professionals working in community settings (Ell, 1995; Roberts, 2000). There is a large body of literature on crisis intervention models and techniques, and a recurring theme in this literature is the importance placed on assessment (Aguilera, 1998; Kanel, 1999; Roberts, 2000; Roberts & Greene, 2002). What is remarkable, however, is the notable lack of standardized instruments with strong psychometric properties available to practitioners. Furthermore, few studies have tested intervention models based on crisis theory (Aguilera, 1998; Janosik, 1994; Roberts, 1996, 2000; Slaikeu, 1984). This may be due to the fact that measurement instruments designed to objectively assess the degree of an individual's crisis state are not available (J. Corcoran & Roberts, 2000). To date, there are few crisis assessment scales with strong psychometric qualities. Of the scales that have been developed, none is capable of measuring the magnitude of a crisis state from the subjective vantage point of the client.

The purpose of this study was to design and test a rapid assessment instrument that measures two constructs: perceived psychological trauma and perceived problems in coping efficacy. These two constructs predict or indicate the magnitude of a crisis state.

Rationale for Measurement

How does a clinician justify treatment for one client and not another? The clinician most likely uses a formula to calculate risk and benefit, though this is typically an informal or even unconscious assessment. By contrast, instrumentation can help a clinician to focus, stay on task, and be conscious of the constructs that he or she is attempting to assess. Measurement tools are not meant to replace the practice wisdom and professional judgment of the clinician, but to enhance them.

Measurement can be defined as the "systematic process of assigning a number to something" (Nunnally, 1978, p. 126). These variables are the client's thoughts or cognitions, behaviors, affect, feelings, or perceptions. The assignment of a number, or the quantification of the variable, allows clinicians to monitor change using a mathematical model (K. J. Corcoran & Fischer, 2000). Standardized measurement is important to the field of crisis intervention because it allows clinicians to understand the comprehensive nature of the client's crisis state with greater accuracy (Nurius & Hudson, 1993).

Accurate measurement is also necessary for gauging the magnitude of the crisis state and for monitoring progress from an objective standpoint. Accurately measuring the severity of different aspects of a crisis state permits the clinician to intervene in the area that is most germane to the current crisis and to use the appropriate degree of intervention. In this way, standardized measures can be used to triangulate: to provide additional information in which to look for congruence of assessment (Nurius & Hudson, 1993).

Focus of This Research

The purpose of this research was the development and validation of a multidimensional rapid assessment instrument (RAI) to assess two constructs associated with a crisis state. The primary goals of the instrument are: (1) standardized measurement of two factors, psychological trauma and problems in perceived coping efficacy, and (2) rapid clinical assessment. The underlying assumptions on which the scale is based are derived from interactional stress theory and crisis theory (James & Gilliland, 2001; Lazarus & Folkman, 1984; Roberts, 2000). These assumptions are as follows:

- A crisis state is a response to a new and intense event that is perceived through primary appraisal to pose a serious threat to either emotional or physical safety (considered to be perceived psychological trauma).

- An individual's crisis response is characterized by the perception through secondary appraisal that he or she is unable to resolve the event due to a dearth of prior experience, lack of resources, and physical and/ or emotional turmoil (considered to be perceived problems in coping efficacy).

LITERATURE REVIEW

Primary Assumptions of Crisis Theory

One confusing aspect of crisis theory is the lexicon used to describe its features. It is often challenging to discern the difference in the literature between discussions of theory and method and between crisis intervention and other approaches.

There is not one crisis theory that encompasses what defines a crisis event (the phenomenon), a crisis response (human response to the phenomenon), or a crisis intervention (the helping process; Gilliland & James, 1993). Instead, there exists a body of literature grounded in the seminal work of Lindemann (1944), Caplan (1964), and Roberts and Grau (1970). A synthesis of ego and cognitive psychology and individual stress theories is also incorporated into crisis theory. A compilation of all of these theories contains the following primary assumptions (Ell, 1995; Parad & Parad, 1990; Roberts, 2000):

- Everyone, at some point in his or her life, will experience acute stress which is not necessarily pathological. Whether or not the stressor is a crisis event is determined by its position in the overall context of the person's life.
- Homeostasis, or balance, is a natural state that all people seek, and when an individual is in a state of emotional disequilibrium, he or she strives to regain emotional balance.
- A period of disequilibrium in which the individual (or family) is vulnerable to further deterioration is present when a stressful event becomes a crisis.
- This disequilibrium makes the individual more amenable to intervention.
- New coping mechanisms are needed to deal with the crisis event.
- The dearth of prior experience with the crisis event creates increased anxiety and struggle, during which the individual often discovers hidden resources.
- The duration of the crisis is somewhat limited, depending on the precipitating event, response patterns, and available resources.
- Certain affective, cognitive, and behavioral tasks must be mastered throughout the crisis phase in order to move to resolution, regardless of the stressor.

The underlying theme here is that a noncrisis state is a state of inner balance, and when that balance is thrown off, the individual strives to regain the balance. Crisis occurs when the individual perceives that he or she does not have the resources necessary to regain balance.

Crisis is aptly defined by Roberts (2000) as follows:

> An acute disruption of psychological homeostasis in which one's usual coping mechanisms fail and there exists evidence of distress and functional impairment. The subjective reaction to a stressful life experience that compromises the individual's stability and ability to cope or function. The main cause of a crisis is an intensely stressful, traumatic, or hazardous event, but two other conditions are also necessary: (1) the individual's perception of the event as the cause of considerable upset and/or disruption; and (2) the individual's inability to resolve the disruption by previously used coping methods. Crisis also refers to "an upset in the steady state." It often has five components: a hazardous or traumatic event, a vulnerable state, a precipitating factor, an active crisis state, and a resolution of the crisis. (p. 516)

Measurement in Crisis Assessment

A major dilemma with the readily available, standardized instruments categorized under crisis assessment is that most focus on the potentiality of suicide or on buffers against suicide (Waters, 1997). The problem is that although lethality assessment is an absolutely critical component of crisis assessment, it is not the only part of the assessment process. That is, not all individuals who are in crisis are either suicidal or homicidal—and yet they are still in crisis.

To assess aspects of a crisis state other than lethality, clinicians generally measure the severity of the event that precipitates the crisis, the stress caused by that event, or the emotional consequences of an unresolved crisis such as depression or anxiety (J. Corcoran & Roberts, 2000). However, measuring the magnitude of a crisis state or the resolution of a crisis state using these variables (precipitating event, stress caused by the event, or emotional consequences of the event) raises several dilemmas. Roberts (1996, 2000), Gilliland and James (1993), and Ell (1995) agree that it is the context in which someone experiences an event and his or her subjective response to the event that determines whether or not an event is a crisis. If this assumption is correct, any event may or may not be experienced as a crisis. More important, it is the subjective response to the event, and not necessarily the event itself, that defines a crisis. In other words, it is the individual who determines whether or not an event or situation is a crisis/tragedy/trauma in his or her subjective experience.

Experts in stress theory such as Lazarus and Folkman (1984), in addition to the previously mentioned experts in crisis theory, claim that stressors are natural. They claim that it is the subjective context of an individual's life circumstances and perception of resources that determines whether or not the stressor induces a crisis state. Here again, it is the individual's perception of his or her available resources in relation to the stressor that leads to a crisis, not the stressor itself. Finally, a crisis state does not equate with pathology, but is instead best viewed as a problem in personal functioning (Ell, 1995; Golan, 1986; Parad & Parad, 1990; Roberts, 2000; Slaikeu, 1984).

"Personal functioning represents the internal events, processes, and experiences of an individual . . . [and] is problematic when an individual's level of distress become[s] large enough to be clinically significant" (Hudson, Mathiesen, & Lewis, 2000, p. 76). To better understand the crisis state as a personal problem, the microtheory of personal and social problems can be employed (Hudson & Faul, 1997). This theory has two fundamental axioms: "Human problems do not exist until someone defines them . . . [and] all human problems are defined in terms of a value base" (p. 49). The first step has already been discussed here: defining a crisis state. The value base has been established in that a crisis state is defined as a problem.

To date, no RAIs measuring the subjective severity of a crisis state from the client's perspective have been developed and psychometrically tested. Clinician-rated crisis-specific scales exist, as do client self-report scales that indirectly tap aspects of the crisis situation (Lewis & Roberts, 2002). These are described in the section to follow.

Crisis/Stress Definitions

Working in the 1950s, Lazarus and his colleagues discovered that the effects of stress were not generalizable or universal; rather, the effects were dependent on individual differences in how people thought about, or appraised, the stressor, and in their motivation to relieve the stress (Lazarus & Eriksen, 1952). The contributions of Lazarus and Folkman (1984) to the study of stress primarily have to do with conceptualizing stress and coping as processes with mediating individual variables. They defined what is now commonly known as the stress process in the following terms: the event (stressor); the cognitions of the event, both primary and secondary (appraisal); and the behaviors that are used to deal with the event (coping).

Social cognitive theory posits that stress is a function of a cognitive appraisal process, or the evaluation of coping self-efficacy in a given situation (Bandura, 1986). When the demands of a situation outweigh an individual's perceived ability to cope, stress is the result (Bandura, 1986; Hill, 1949; Lazarus & Folkman, 1984).

This is where a clarification of terminology becomes imperative. Authors in many fields have defined stress in many different ways; there is no universal definition for stress. Lazarus and Folkman (1984) define psychological stress as "a relationship between the person and the environment that is appraised by the person as taxing or exceeding his or her resources and endangering his or her well-being" (p. 21). This definition of psychological stress closely resembles Roberts's (2000) definition of a crisis: "The subjective reaction to a stressful life experience that compromises the individual's stability and ability to cope or function" (p. 516). This research relates the two concepts of stress and crisis by contending that the degree of a crisis, which is a psychological state, is mediated by thoughts about the magnitude of a stressful life experience (event or situation) and thoughts about whether or not a person can cope with the stressful life event. These thoughts are referred to in stress theory as primary and secondary appraisal.

Primary Appraisal

Primary appraisal is the process of evaluating the threat or strain of an event or situation (Lazarus & Folkman, 1984). During the primary appraisal process, cognitions are concentrated on the magnitude of the threat or strain. According to Lazarus and Folkman, there are three kinds of primary appraisal: irrelevant, benign-positive, and stressful. If an event or situation is appraised as irrelevant, there is "no investment" (p. 32) in the outcome on the part of the individual. When a situation is appraised as benign-positive, it is believed to be solely positive, with no potential negative consequences. This study is concerned with the third type of primary appraisal: stressful. Stress appraisals include harm/loss, threat, and challenge.

Harm/loss appraisals are when the individual believes that he or she has sustained some physical or emotional harm or loss. Examples of this are the death of a loved one, physical injury, financial loss, loss of friendship, diminished self-esteem or sense of worth, and loss of a commitment such as marriage or a business partner. In this type of appraisal, the harm or loss has already happened.

Threat, a form of primary appraisal, is concerned with anticipated harm or loss. Even though an event or situation may have already happened, the individual may anticipate future harm or loss as a result of the event. For example, if a student fails a test, the event has happened (failure of the test). However, the student may still fear the loss of financial support from his or her parents when they find out about the failure.

Challenge appraisals may include threats. These appraisals tend to focus on positive events that contain within them the risk of future negative outcomes. The challenge has to do with mastery of an event or situation; however, there is risk inherent in challenge. For example, a new marriage may be seen as an exciting new challenge: it represents an opportunity to be successful in a relationship. However, it also represents the potential for failure.

Secondary Appraisal

Secondary appraisal is the process of evaluating one's ability to deal with threat or strain. Lazarus and Folkman (1984) claim:

> Secondary appraisal is more than a mere intellectual exercise in spotting what must be done. It is a complex evaluative process that takes into account which coping options are available, the likelihood that a given coping option will accomplish what it is supposed to, and the likelihood that one can apply a particular strategy or set of strategies effectively. (p. 35)

Bandura (1977) further refined Lazarus and Folkman's (1984) theoretical model by adding the important variables of outcome expectancy and efficacy expectations to the concept of secondary appraisal. Outcome expectancy is an individual's belief that certain behaviors will lead to certain outcomes. Efficacy expectation refers to an individual's belief that he or she can effectively carry out the action or behavior necessary to produce the expected outcome.

Basically, Bandura (1977) hypothesized that an individual's belief in his or her ability to handle an event (coping efficacy) mediates his or her stress reaction to that event. Individuals' belief that they can cause a positive outcome is based on their own personal repertoire, or menu, of past successes in similarly stressful situations, rather than on their belief in positive outcomes in general.

Benight and colleagues (Benight, Ironson, Wynings, et al., 1999; Benight, Swift, Sanger, Smith & Zeppelin, 1999) discovered in the aftermath of Hurricane Andrew and Hurricane Opal that higher levels of coping self-efficacy were correlated with lower amounts of psychological distress. After controlling for income, education, gender, age, estimated damage, threat of death, and lost resources, coping self-efficacy accounted for an additional 10% of the variance in the Impact of Events Scale (Benight, Ironson, Wynings, et al., 1999). Benight and colleagues (2000) also found higher levels of perceived coping efficacy to be significantly correlated with a reduction in experiences of distress in a study of the victims following a terrorist bombing in Oklahoma City.

Cozzarelli (1993) showed with a general path model that the effects of self-esteem, optimism, and perceived control were mediated by perceived coping efficacy on both immediate and three-week postabortion psychological adjustment. Cozzarelli claims that feelings of self-efficacy for coping are an important determinant of both coping behavior and adjustment to negative life events.

Gaps in the Literature

In the first place, there are currently no scales that measure the perceived magnitude of a stressor and very few that measure situation-specific coping efficacy. In addition, most studies use a single-item indicator to measure coping efficacy, which creates serious limitations in validity claims. Also, there are currently no RAIs that measure both the perceived magnitude of the event (primary appraisal) and perceived coping efficacy (secondary appraisal).

Second, the scales currently available to measure a crisis do not measure the subjective state of the individual. The researchers who created those crisis scales claim that because an individual is in crisis, he or she is not capable of completing a paper-and-pencil test (Bengelsdorf, Levy, Emerson, & Barile, 1984; Myer, Williams, Ottens, & Schmidt, 1992). This may be true in extreme cases; however, it is not true in all cases. There is no way to determine that an individual is not capable of filling out a paper-and-pencil test until an assessment has been made. To remove the possibility of a standardized objective assessment of a subjective state without any attempt may in fact be a disservice to the individual seeking assistance.

CONCEPTUAL FRAMEWORK FOR THIS RESEARCH

This research focused on the subjective state that a person may experience as a result of a stressor. This state, termed here a crisis state, is an imbalance of internal equilibrium that is the result of a subjective response to a stressor. Internal equilibrium is mental or emotional stability. A stressor can be any event or situation. Coping efficacy is an individual's belief that he or she is capable of dealing with the event or situation considered to be the stressor. Coping efficacy is not equivalent to coping: coping is an action or set of actions that is employed to deal with a stressor.

Lazarus and Folkman (1984) proposed that reactions to a stressor are mediated by cognitive appraisals by the individual. Appraisals, primary and secondary, are simply beliefs about the magnitude of the event or situation as well as beliefs about whether one can handle the event or situation. In primary appraisal, the individual assesses the magnitude of the event or situation considered to be a stressor. For example, he or she may think, "Oh my gosh, this car accident is really bad, the car is not drivable." This perception of the stressor is termed herein *perceived psychological trauma.* Perceived psychological trauma is operationalized as an individual's unique perception of an event or enduring condition that leads the individual to believe that his or her physical life, way of life, or sanity is in jeopardy. The example above relates to financial distress, which potentially jeopardizes way of life.

Secondary appraisal happens immediately following the initial cognition, if not simultaneously, and concerns the individual's thoughts about whether he or she can deal with the situation or event (Lazarus & Folkman, 1984). An example of secondary appraisal that corresponds with the prior example of primary appraisal is, "I can handle this because my insurance will cover the cost to fix the car and a rental car." Or, "I can't handle this because I have no insurance." Coping is the actual action. In this example, coping would be the action of calling the insurance company. Coping efficacy, by contrast, is the belief that one can cope by calling the insurance agency.

These concepts constitute a crisis state. The state is internal and cannot necessarily be determined by indicators such as coping actions. In other words, an individual can be in a crisis state even while using healthy coping behaviors.

There are two main reasons why behavior cannot be used as an indicator of crisis. The first reason is that what may be unhealthy coping in one situation may be healthy coping in another. For example, using denial of imminent death from a terminal disease because one has a project that one wants to continue to work on is beneficial, even though denial is more typically perceived to be a negative coping response. The second reason is that even though a person may appear, through behavioral indicators, to be coping very well, he or she may have the perception of an inability to cope and therefore still have a disruption of equilibrium.

Internal equilibrium (a noncrisis state), referred to in the crisis literature as homeostasis, can be thought of as a playground seesaw that is perfectly balanced. On one side of the fulcrum is one's perception of situations or events (perceived psychological trauma), and on the other, one's perception of ability to cope (coping efficacy) with those situations or events. When the perception of the psychological trauma is greater than the perception of coping efficacy, the seesaw is off balance. The key to determining if an individual is in a crisis state is to measure both sides of the seesaw and compare the two scores: perception of the gravity of the situation and perception of ability to cope in relation to a specific event or situation.

When perceived coping efficacy is viewed from the vantage point of perceived problems in coping efficacy, then both perceived psychological trauma and perceived problems in coping efficacy contribute to disruption in internal equilibrium. One important reason for measuring perceived problems in coping efficacy, as opposed to just perceived coping efficacy, is that clinicians generally focus on problem solving in a therapeutic interaction (Hudson, 1982). The reason for this is that it is not possible to define health except through the relation between healthy and unhealthy. Thus, what indicates health is the lack of markers of ill health. A higher score on either factor indicates a greater problem and will be targeted as the focal point of clinical therapy.

The Crisis State Assessment Scale (CSAS) is the first scale to measure a crisis state defined as perceived psychological trauma and perceived problems in coping efficacy. Moreover, the scale focuses the respondent on a specific event by having him or her specify the event or situation at the top of the instrument. The purpose of this is to help the respondent to focus on that event when responding to each item. In this way, the instrument relies on Bandura's (1997) argument for situation-specific coping efficacy. This idea carries over to perceived psychological trauma. In other words, the scale is also sensitive to an identified problem area.

SCALE PSYCHOMETRICS

Scale Construction

The phenomenon that this scale attempts to capture is a crisis state, defined as an internal disequilibrium resulting from perceived psychological trauma and perceived problems in coping efficacy. These two factors are defined as follows:

Perceived psychological trauma is an individual's unique perception of an event or enduring condition that leads the individual to believe that his or her physical life, way of life, or sanity is in jeopardy.

Perceived problems in coping efficacy is an individual's belief that he or she cannot effectively master the demands of a traumatic condition, threat, or challenge because it exceeds his or her resources.

The tool developed in this study uses a 7-point Likert scale based on presence or absence of the item. The scaling is as follows: 1 = never, 2 = very rarely, 3 = rarely, 4 = sometimes, 5 = often, 6 = almost always, and 7 = always. A single-item indicator of subjective units of psychological distress is also present on the instrument and is scaled with a category partition. The category partition is broken up into equal parts ranging from 1 to 10 in terms of difficulty of the current situation. The partition is anchored with the terms *easy* and *most difficult.*

Subjects

In this study, a convenience sample was used of students 18 years old and older enrolled at two universities, one in the South (University 1), and one in the Northest (University 2), for the spring semester of 2001. A total of 475 data packets were distributed. The return rate at the school in the South was 91.2% and the return rate at the school in the Northeast was 85.14 % (Table 31.1).

RESULTS

Demographics of Subjects

The sample from University 1 (n = 114) was predominately female (87%), and the sample from University 2 (n = 297) was 50% female. The racial/ethnic makeup of the University 1 sample was as follows: 19% African American, 2% Asian, 67% Caucasian, 7% Hispanic, and 5% other. The racial/ethnic makeup of University 2 was 9% African American, 8% Asian, 69% Caucasian, 7% Hispanic, 1% Native American, and 6% other. Figure 31.1 illustrates the gender and racial/ethnic makeup of the combined sample.

Table 31.1 Data Collection Sites and Participant Rates

Location	Packets Distributed	Packets Returned	Percentage Returned	CSAS Completed	Percentage CSAS Completed
University 1	125	114	91	110	88
University 2	350	298	85	292	83
Total	475	412	87	402	85

The mean age of the sample from University 1 was 26.68, with a standard deviation of 8.02. Because of the outliers in this sample, it is important to report that the inner quartile of this sample was between the ages of 21 and 28. The sample from University 2 was younger, with a mean age of 20.72 and a standard deviation of 2.34. The inner quartile for this sample was between the ages of 19 and 21.5.

Reported Crisis Event(s)/Situation(s) on the CSAS

Respondents were asked to write a short description of the crisis event(s) and/or situation(s) to which they would refer while completing the CSAS (see Figure 31.2). The form provided space for three separate events or situations. Table 31.2 describes the crisis event(s) and/or situation(s) and the frequency with which they were reported. Sixteen respondents did not report a crisis event or situation, yet still completed the CSAS. Of those reporting an event, 403 reported one event, 69 reported two events, and 37 reported three events.

Content Validity for the CSAS

Content validity was established via the method purported by Nunnally and Bernstein (1994), in which competent judges determined whether or not each item was a member of the population of items that composed each domain. Three experts in crisis theory judged each item and were in agreement on all items. The original CSAS consisted of 10 to 12 items per domain and had an overall Fleisch-Kincaid grade level index of grade 5.3.

Reliability for the CSAS

There are two distinct scales in the CSAS: perceived psychological trauma and perceived problems in coping efficacy. The alpha and reliability for each of these scales was calculated as well as the global reliability. Listwise deletion was used to remove cases with missing data. Thus, the reliability analyses for the CSAS was 403 (n = 403). The alpha and reliability for each of these scales was found to be good to excellent at 0.85, 0.84 and 0.92, respectively.

A

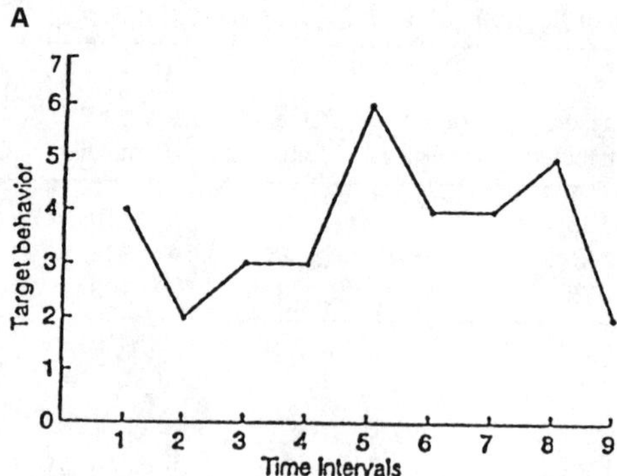

B

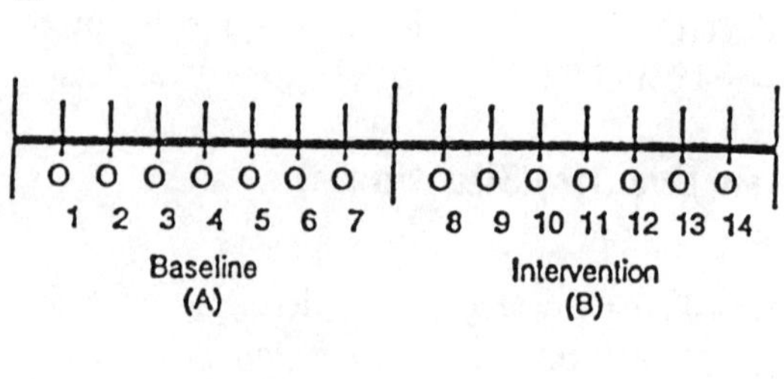

C

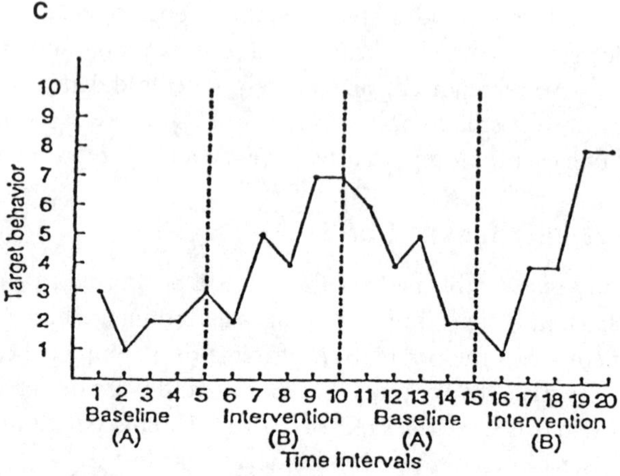

Figure 31.1 Changes in target behavior

Figure 31.2 Crisis State Assessment Scale

This questionnaire is designed to measure the way you feel as a result of a recent traumatic event or situation. Answer each item in relation to the event/situation as carefully and as accurately as you can by placing a number beside each one as follows:

1 = Never 2 = Very rarely 3 = Rarely 4 = Sometimes
5 = Often 6 = Almost always 7 = Always

___ 1. I think about the event/situation when I don't want to.
___ 2. I feel like the event/situation throws my life off balance.
___ 3. I feel like my physical or emotional well-being is threatened by the event/situation.
___ 4. The event/situation is very distressing to me.
___ 5. The event/situation makes me feel like I am going crazy.
___ 6. I feel like I don't have the resources and/or energy to deal with the event/situation.
___ 7. I don't know what to do to make this event/situation manageable.
___ 8. I feel like I cannot handle the event/situation.
___ 9. I don't deal well with events/situations like this one.
___10. I am confident that I can cope with the event/situation.

Imagine that you are facing the easiest situation that you have ever experienced; consider that feeling a 0. Now imagine that you are facing the most difficult situation that you have ever experienced in your lifetime; consider that a 10. On a scale from 1 to 10 indicate the difficulty of the event/situation described above by circling a number below:

Easy : 0 1 2 3 4 5 6 7 8 9 10 : Most difficult

Table 31.2 Crisis Event(s)/Situation(s)

Event	Frequency	Percentage
Trouble with significant other	86	21
Problems with grades/school	53	13
Death of a loved one	48	12
Trouble with parents	36	9
Parents' or grandparents' health problems	30	7
Happy event	30	7
Accident	28	7
Problems with job	25	6
Problems with housing/moving	26	4
Problems with friends	21	5
Personal health	21	5
Graduation	19	5
Financial problems	19	5
Problems with siblings	15	4
Friend's tragedy	10	2
Know or saw someone who died violently	9	2
Rape	7	2
Other (baby, divorce, auto trouble, coming out, happy/sad anniversary, pet, know/saw suicide)	60	15

Respondents could report up to three events, so percentages do not add up to 100.

Factorial Validity

Because each of the subscales in the CSAS was developed according to theoretical propositions, multiple groups confirmatory factor analysis (CFA) was used to establish factorial validity. Correlations between subscale scores and item responses were computed. These correlations were then examined to determine whether items had the highest correlations with their intended subscale.

The CSAS has a strong factor structure, which suggests the presence of distinct factors. The strong correlations observed between the two factors of perceived psychological trauma and perceived problems in coping efficacy are consistent with the theory that these two factors compose another factor, a crisis state. This is also indicated by the strong global reliability coefficient.

Convergent Validity

To establish convergent validity, correlations were found between factors on the CSAS and other indicators of those factors. First, the perceived psychological trauma mean scale score was compared to the mean score of the Index of Clinical Stress. With a sample size of 393, the Pearson's r was 0.536 and was significant at the $p = .001$ level.

Item number CSAS22 was used as the single-item indicator for perceived problems in coping efficacy. The item states: "I am confident that I can cope with the event/situation." Reverse-scoring this item demonstrates problems in perceived coping efficacy. Because the indicator was a member of the final scale item grouping, its influence had to be removed before the correlation was found. The correlation for the four remaining items on problems with perceived coping, and the single-item indicator, was 0.296 and was significant at the $p = .001$ level with a sample size of 403.

Discriminant Validity

Discriminant validity of the CSAS was tested using the background variables ethnicity, age, and academic standing. Table 31.3 illustrates the correlations between mean scale scores for both factors on the CSAS and the background variables.

Table 31.3 Discriminant Validity Correlation Coefficients

	Ethnicity	Age	Academic Standing
Perceived Psychological Trauma	.079	−.013	.059
Perceived Problems in Coping Efficacy	.031	−.093	−.035

*Significant at the $p = .01$ level (2-tailed).

Criterion Validity

Criterion (concurrent) validity was established for perceived psychological trauma by creating two groups, low psychological trauma and high psychological trauma, from the single-item indicator for perceived psychological trauma. Subjects scoring 0–3 (n = 87) on the single-item indicator were placed in the low psychological trauma group, and subjects scoring 4–10 (n = 304) were placed in the high psychological trauma group. Logistic regression was computed to demonstrate the ability of perceived psychological trauma to predict group membership.

There were 389 cases included in the analysis, and after five iterations, the–2 log likelihood was 320.116. The Cox & Snell R square was 0.208 and the Nagelkerke R square was 0.319. Perceived psychological trauma was able to correctly predict group membership into the low psychological trauma group with 41.9% accuracy, and into the high psychological trauma group with 93.1% accuracy. The overall percentage correct was 81.7. The weighting value of B was 1.060, and the standard error was 0.137. The Wald test coefficient was 59.669 and was significant at the $p = .001$ level.

DISCUSSION AND CONCLUSIONS

Crisis intervention has flourished as a therapeutic technique in the field of social work. However, there has been very little research to show whether or not the technique is effective. One of the reasons for this lacuna is that it has been nearly impossible to objectively determine the efficacy of the intervention. To determine effectiveness, one needs to determine the magnitude of the state when the client enters therapy and the magnitude of the state when the client terminates therapy. Never before has there been an instrument to measure the magnitude of a crisis state through the eyes of the client. Although the results of this study are preliminary, the CSAS shows great promise in this area.

Crisis Theory

An interesting finding of this research is that relationships between perceived psychological trauma and specific crisis events were found (chi square = 0.006); however, perceived problems in coping efficacy and crisis events were independent of one another (chi square = 0.261). This finding is consistent with the guiding theory that coping efficacy is independent of the traumatic event and mediates the magnitude of a crisis state. It can be inferred from this finding that some individuals feel they can handle a specific difficult event, and some believe they cannot handle that same event. It is the individual's subjective belief about his or her ability to cope with the event that determines whether or not the individual will enter into a state of crisis.

Clinical Implications

One of the purposes for which the CSAS was developed was to aid clinicians in the assessment of individuals presenting in a crisis state. The CSAS should not be used as the sole determinant of a crisis state, but as an adjunct to other clinical assessment strategies (Lewis & Roberts, 2002).

No instrument until now has attempted to capture the magnitude of a crisis state. Although the CSAS has limitations, such as its correlated measurement error, it is an important first step toward the measurement of the degree to which an individual is in crisis. Crisis intervention has become an increasingly popular therapeutic modality. One of the main reasons for this popularity is that managed care organizations and other insurers will often pay for only a few sessions, which is making longer therapies a thing of the past for all but the affluent. This means that crisis intervention is often used with the most marginalized individuals, those without many health care choices. Social workers have an obligation to ensure that available services to these vulnerable individuals are as effective as possible.

A unique feature of the CSAS is that it allows the client to identify the event or situation that he or she believes is the precipitant of the crisis. The client then has to focus on his or her feelings regarding the magnitude of the event, as well as feelings about whether or not he or she can cope with the event. By requiring the client to focus and complete a pencil-and-paper test, the instrument itself is a part of the intervention, because it begins the process of de-escalation. The CSAS also provides talking points to which the clinician can refer to keep the intervention focused on problem solving in relation to the crisis state (Lewis & Roberts, 2002).

The CSAS can be used in college counseling centers for emergency/crisis sessions, as well as in other facilities. One strategy could be to give the client the scale along with other paperwork that must be completed before the session. Because the CSAS has only five items for each of the two factors, the client burden is not significant. The CSAS is easy to score: the clinician can calculate and interpret the instrument in less than two minutes. The ease of administration and scoring makes it possible to administer the scale at both the beginning and the end of the emergency session to quantify improvement. This suggestion is made with the caution that the score should not be the only indicator of a successful or unsuccessful therapeutic outcome and that the clinician should be cognizant of the measurement error potential of the scale. In other words, there may be something other than perceived psychological trauma and perceived problems in coping efficacy that is causing the variation in the scale score.

Scoring Instructions

Both factors on the final version of the CSAS (see Figure 31.2, p. 735) consist of five items and are based on a 7-point scale. This makes summing and interpreting the scores quick and easy. There are two steps in the scoring process: finding each subscale score and calculating the global score.

To find subscale scores, reverse score item 10 by replacing scores as follows: 1 with 7, 2 with 6, 3 with 5, 4 with 4, 5 with 3, 6 with 2, 7 with 1. Then Find the mean of each subscale by adding all item responses in that subscale and dividing by 5. To find the CSAS global score, add each of the subscale scores (mean scores) together and divide by 2.

Interpretation

The same 7-point Likert scale that is used when responding to CSAS items is used to decipher the scores. If, for example, a person received a 6 on the perceived problems in coping subscale, it can be surmised that he or she "almost always" perceives that he or she is experiencing problems in coping. This may indicate that an intervention is called for to assist the client in finding alternative coping strategies. The global score is meant to be an indicator of the magnitude of a crisis state. Higher scores mean that the individual is in a greater state of crisis.

REFERENCES

Aguilera, D. C. (1998). *Crisis intervention: Theory and methodology*. St. Louis: Mosby-Year Book.

Bandura, A. (1977). Self-efficacy: Toward a unifying theory of behavioral change. *Psychological Review, 84*, 191–215.

Bandura, A. (1986). *Social foundations of thought and action*. Englewood Cliffs, NJ: Prentice-Hall.

Bandura, A. (1997). *Self-efficacy: The exercise of control*. New York: W. H. Freeman.

Bengelsdorf, H., Levy, L. E., Emerson, R. L., & Barile, F. A. (1984). A crisis triage rating scale: Brief dispositional assessment of patients at risk for hospitalization. *Journal of Nervous and Mental Disorders, 172*(7), 424–430.

Benight, C. C., Freyaldenhoven, R. W., Hughes, J., Ruiz, J. M., Zoschke, T. A., & Lovallo, T. (2000). Coping self-efficacy and psychological distress following the Oklahoma City bombing. *Journal of Applied Social Psychology, 30*(7), 1331–1344.

Benight, C. C., Ironson, G., Wynings, C., Klebe, K., Burnett, K., Greenwood, D., et al. (1999). Conservation of resources and coping self-efficacy predicting distress following a natural disaster: A causal model analysis where the environment meets the mind. *Anxiety, Stress, and Coping, 12*, 107–126.

Benight, C. C., Swift, E., Sanger, J., Smith, A., & Zeppelin, D. (1999). Coping self-efficacy as a mediator of distress following a natural disaster. *Journal of Applied Social Psychology, 29*(12), 2443–2464.

Caplan, G. (1964). *Principles of preventive psychiatry*. New York: Basic Books.

Corcoran, J., & Roberts, A. R. (2000). Research on crisis intervention and recommendations for future research. In A. R. Roberts

(Ed.), *Crisis intervention handbook: Assessment, treatment, and research*. New York: Oxford University Press.

Corcoran, K. J., & Fischer, J. (2000). *Measures for clinical practice: A sourcebook* (3rd ed.). New York: Free Press.

Cozzarelli, C. (1993). Personality and self-efficacy as predictors of coping with abortion. *Journal of Personality and Social Psychology, 65*(6), 1224–1236.

Ell, K. (Ed.). (1995). *Crisis intervention*. In R. Edwards (Ed.), *Encyclopedia of social work* (19th ed., Vol. 1). Washington, DC: National Association of Social Workers.

Gilliland, J., & James, J. (1993). *Crisis intervention strategies*. Belmont, CA: Wadsworth.

Golan, N. (Ed.). (1986). *Crisis theory* (3rd ed.). New York: Fress Press.

Hill, R. (1949). *Families under stress, adjustment to the crisis of war, separation, and reunion*. New York: Harper

Hudson, W. W. (1982). *The clinical measurement package: A field manual*. Homewood, IL: Dorsey Press.

Hudson, W. W., & Faul, A. J. (1997). The Index of Drug Involvement: A partial validation. *Social Work, 42*(6), 565–572.

Hudson, W. W., Mathiesen, S. G., & Lewis, S. J. (2000). Personal and social functioning: A pilot study. *Social Service Review, 74*(4), 76–102.

James, R. K., & Gilliland, B. E. (2001). *Crisis intervention strategies* (4th ed.). Belmont, CA: Wadsworth/Thomson Learning.

Kanel, K. (1999). *A guide to crisis intervention*. Pacific Grove, CA: Brooks/Cole.

Lazarus, R. S., & Eriksen, C. W. (1952). Effects of failure stress upon skilled performance. *Journal of Experimental Psychology, 43*, 100–105.

Lazarus, R. S., & Folkman, S. (1984). *Stress, appraisal, and coping*. New York: Springer.

Lewis, S., & Roberts, A. R. (2002). Crisis assessment tools. In A. R. Roberts & G. J. Greene (Eds.), *Social workers' desk reference* (pp. 208–212). New York: Oxford University Press.

Lindemann, E. (1944). Symptomatology and management of acute grief. *American Journal of Psychiatry,* 101, 141–148.

Myer, R. A., Williams, R. C., Ottens, A. J., & Schmidt, A. E. (1992). Crisis assessment: A three-dimensional model for triage. *Journal of Mental Health Counseling, 14*(2), 137–148.

Nunnally, J. C. (1978). *Psychometric theory*. New York: McGraw-Hill.

Nunnally, J. C., & Bernstein, I. H. (1994). *Psychometric theory* (3rd ed.). New York: McGraw-Hill.

Nurius, P. S., & Hudson, W. W. (1993). *Human services: Practice, evaluation, and computers*. Pacific Grove, CA: Brooks/Cole.

Parad, H. J., & Parad, L. G. (1990). *Crisis intervention, book 2: The practitioner's sourcebook for brief therapy*. Milwaukee, WI: Family Service America.

Roberts, A. R. (1996). Epidemiology and definitions of acute crisis in American society. In A. R. Roberts (Ed.), *Crisis management and brief treatment* (pp. 3–17). Chicago: Nelson-Hall.

Roberts, A. R. (2000). An overview of crisis theory and crisis intervention. In A. R. Roberts (Ed.), *Crisis intervention handbook: Assessment, treatment, and research* (2nd ed., pp. 3–30). New York: Oxford University Press.

Roberts, A. R., & Grau, J. J. (1970). Procedures used in crisis intervention by suicide prevention agencies. *Public Health Reports*, Vol. 85 (8): 691–698.

Roberts, A. R., & Greene, G., (Eds.), (2002). *Social workers' desk reference*. New York: Oxford University Press.

Slaikeu, K. A. (1984). *Crisis intervention: A handbook for practice and research*. Boston: Allyn & Bacon.

Waters, D. (1997). *A study of the reliability and validity of the triage assessment scale*. Unpublished doctoral dissertation, University of Memphis, Tennessee.

32

Designs and Procedures for Evaluating Crisis Intervention

SOPHIA F. DZIEGIELEWSKI
GERALD T. POWERS

The overall efficacy, popularity, and necessity of brief, time-limited therapeutic encounters, including crisis intervention approaches used with various types of clients, although well-documented, remains focused on clearly ascertaining the variables that can be linked directly to client change (Auerbach & Kilmann, 1977; Dziegielewski, 2004; Dziegielewski & Roberts, 2004; Dziegielewski, Shields, & Thyer, 1998; Evans, Smith, Hill, Albers, & Neufeld, 1996; Koss & Butcher, 1986;). To date, however, methodological limitations inherent in most forms of time-limited intervention remain, particularly with respect to the paucity of evidence-based practice approaches that support significant differences in the overall effectiveness of and between competing intervention approaches (Monette, Sullivan, & DeJong, 2005; Neimeyer & Pfeffier, 1994; Nugent, Sieppert, & Hudson, 2001). Historically, establishing treatment effectiveness in all areas of counseling has often been met with resistance, especially because client change behavior and the resulting therapeutic gains can be seen as subjective. In fact, Bergin and Suinn (1975) originally suggested that clients are likely to change over time even without any therapeutic intervention.

We recommend that all practitioners make a commitment to evidence-based practice. In other words, all crisis workers and counselors need to thoroughly prepare for intervening on behalf of a large number of different types of persons in crisis. This can be done effectively only if practitioners develop the knowledge base to find out which crisis intervention protocol is most likely to lead to positive outcomes and crisis resolution among clients in crisis (Roberts & Yeager, 2004). Evidence-based practice places necessary emphasis on the crisis clinician's use of empirically validated lethality assessments, intervention protocols, and program evaluation procedures as well as the use of critical thinking in making decisions (Roberts & Yeager, 2004). Professional judgments should be systematically grounded in empirical research, and each client should be carefully assessed to determine the degree to which predicted outcomes have been attained.

This subjectivity makes the task of establishing therapeutic effectiveness and efficiency a complicated one (Dziegielewski & Roberts, 2004). In an effort to formulate the evaluation process, it is useful to first identify two basic assumptions that underlie counseling efforts in the area of crisis management and intervention, and then discuss why they can complicate the measurement of intervention outcomes. First, in time-limited intervention of any type, most counselors agree that the main effect of therapy is not curative, but rather one that directs, facilitates, and accelerates the pace of client progress toward change. Not only is the experience considered noncurative, it must also be time-limited in regard to service delivery. This makes the importance of early and brief intervention a consistent requirement, especially because clients typically remain in treatment fewer than six sessions (Dziegielewski, 1997). Crisis intervention strategies need to support and stabilize clients as well as help them develop new coping strategies that allow them to adjust to the situational experience (Hartman & Sullivan, 1996; Roberts & Dziegielewski, 1995).

Second, crisis is itself a multifaceted phenomenon that does not respond readily to traditional forms of therapeutic measurement and evaluation. In addition, those who encounter them do not uniformly experience crisis situations. The nature, extent, and intensity of any given crisis are, in large measure, a product of the individual's construction of the social reality. The intervention as well as the methods used to evaluate it, often referred to as the blueprint to guide the data collection efforts, must vary accordingly. In the absence of any compelling evidence in support of long-term therapy as a more effective mode of practice, crisis intervention as a unique form of brief, time-limited intervention is often preferred (B. L. Bloom, 1992; Dziegielewski, 2004; Dziegielewski et al., 1998; Koss & Shaing, 1994). Crisis intervention as a time-limited therapy may actually accelerate treatment efficacy as time frames are clearly and openly established and agreed upon between the client and the counselor (Reynolds et al., 1996).

THE IMPORTANCE OF INTEGRATING RESEARCH AND PRACTICE

Helping professionals who routinely work with victims (or survivors) of crises report that there are several factors that seem to be common to virtually all crisis situations. The first of these factors is the acknowledgment that the crisis situation often brings about a time-limited disequilibrium that must be addressed in order for the client to reach a homeostatic balance (Roberts & Dziegielewski, 1995). The disequilibrium associated with crisis serves as a powerful motivational force that can heighten the client's susceptibility to intervention (Dziegielewski, 2004; Koss & Butcher, 1986). Faced with a crisis, the client is often more willing to question previous ways of coping, and thus to explore new or alternative ways of addressing situations that prior to the crisis would not have been considered acceptable. This renders the client more open to trying new courses of action for therapeutic intervention that can facilitate the planning of concrete goals and objectives. All of this is entirely consistent with the so-called strengths perspective in which clients are believed to already possess the resources necessary to address stressful situations. They simply are not using them, are underutilizing them, or are currently unaware of how to best use them on their own behalf (see Greene, Lee, Trask, & Rheinscheld in this volume for a detailed discussion of how to integrate the strengths perspective and solution-focused treatment with crisis intervention).

By nature, a crisis situation and the attendant reaction is self-limiting (Dziegielewski & Resnick, 1996; Roberts, 1990; Slaikeu, 1984). Beginning with Lindemann's (1944) initial formulation of crisis intervention in his now classic study of the Coconut Grove Nightclub disaster, crises have been characterized as time-limited phenomena that inevitably get resolved one way or another (with or without professional help) in a relatively brief period. The client's pressing need to resolve the crisis and thus alleviate the associated pain appears to heighten motivation, so much so that nominal levels of therapeutic intervention provided during the crisis period tend to produce positive and sometimes dramatic therapeutic results (Parad et al., 1990).

Given this narrow window of vulnerability to change, it is considered essential that clients who experience crisis must be provided immediate assistance to maximize the potential for constructive growth. Some authors, particularly those in the domestic violence field, believe that immediate intervention is so important that the postponement of appropriate help for more than 11 days places the client at greater risk of repeat victimization (Davis & Taylor, 1997).

According to Roberts and Dziegielewski (1995), Gilliland and James (2003), and other professionals in the area, positive life changes can be achieved following a crisis. Furthermore, the way a client handles a present crisis may have a profound and lasting impact, not only on the individual's current adjustment, but also on his or her capacity to cope with future crisis situations. From a research perspective, this suggests that practitioners should seek to understand and accurately explain the intervention approach being implemented. In addition, it is important to accurately identify the expected impact of the intervention and the anticipated adaptive responses. Unless outcome measures are clearly defined in operational terms, it is difficult to determine whether the intervention goals and objectives have been attained. The goals and objectives, in turn, must clearly be linked to positive life changes and methods of coping that enhance continued client functioning. Consequently, the central task of outcome-based research is to measure the presence and magnitude of both immediate and long-term changes that result from the counseling process (Lambert & Hill, 1994).

THE ROLE OF THE PRACTITIONER IN EMPIRICAL PRACTICE

From a clinical perspective, some of the important limitations associated with many of the studies that have traditionally compared short- and long-term intervention methods remain. In establishing an empirical basis for crisis intervention, similar to other forms of practice, one primary limitation rests in the fact that the independent variable cannot be adequately addressed in a homogeneous fashion alone. For example, when evaluating crisis intervention programs in particular, Neimeyer and Pfeiffer (1994) report that many researchers operate on the assumption that there are no important individual differences among clinicians with respect to what goes on during the therapeutic encounter. Limited attention is often given to ensuring that those who provide crisis intervention services have been adequately trained. It is assumed that all practitioners have the same effect on client progress. This lack of attention to measuring the relative effectiveness of the social worker can lead to myths that support some sort of global and homogeneous index of client improvement. These "uniformity myths," as Kiesler (1966) originally coined them, deflect attention from possible important individual differences both within and between groups of clients and therapists who treat them. Several studies clearly provide ample evidence in support of the relative effectiveness of time-limited crisis intervention strategies (Davis & Taylor, 1997; Hartman & Sullivan, 1996; Mezzina & Vidoni, 1995; Neimeyer & Pfeiffer, 1994; Rudd, Joiner, & Rajab, 1995). Equally apparent, however, is the relative absence of any clear-cut preferences regarding the "impact of alternative treatments, on alternative clinical problems with clients of varying characteristics and other manifold conditions that may mediate treatment" (Kazdin, 1994, p. 20). Simply stated, the critical issues to be addressed are essentially no different now than they were when Paul first issued his now famous dictum in 1966: "What treatment, by whom, is most effective for this individual with that specific problem, and under which set of circumstances?" (p. 111).

The purpose of this chapter is to present clinically grounded research models that are relevant for those in crisis situations and that remain sensitive to the three major variables of the therapeutic paradigm: the client, the social worker as a researcher/practitioner, and the outcome. Against a general background of group design, or nomothetic, research, we consider several different evaluation models, all of which emphasize what Chassan (1967) and others have referred to as "intensive" or "idiographic" designs. When used alone, none of them is foolproof. Together, however, they provide a useful set of assessment tools that can help social workers evaluate the efficacy of their practice and improve the quality of the services they provide.

MACRO AND MICRO ANALYSES IN CRISIS INTERVENTION

Over the years, a variety of measurement strategies have been employed in an effort to assess various dimensions of the crisis intervention process. When viewed as a whole, they provide an intriguing array of designs ranging from macro to micro levels of analysis. For example, in an attempt to assess the process and outcome of crisis intervention in terms of suicide interventions, Neimeyer and Pfeiffer (1994) attempted to chronicle the relative effectiveness of various suicide intervention strategies and how such strategies actually contributed to the therapeutic relationship. When effectiveness was measured from a macro perspective, these methods focused primarily on epidemiological data collected by local, regional, and national organizations. Some studies compared suicide rates before and after the implementation of a particular intervention program. Other studies employed quasi-experimental designs in which similar populations of treated and untreated suicide attempters were compared. In still other studies, cohorts of treated clients were compared with population parameters based on data derived from the National Center for Health and Statistics in the United States. There are serious methodological problems inherent in the use of extant data, however, especially with respect to threats to internal validity as well as comparability across idiosyncratic samples. In an effort to address some of these apparent weaknesses, client or caller satisfaction methods are sometimes used to help validate client perceptions and support the intrinsic worth of the study. Based on these macro types of analyses, many suicide programs and crisis intervention services have failed to gather the kinds of information necessary to adequately establish program effectiveness (Neimeyer & Pfeiffer, 1994). Without such information, it is impossible to determine whether negative findings are the result of inadequacies in the practice theory or liabilities in the research methodology. For questions like this, there are no easy answers.

The fact that a crisis is itself a dynamic and multifaceted phenomenon can also complicate the measurement process, particularly when it is done on an aggregate basis, or when primarily relying on secondary sources. Studies that rely exclusively on self-report can also be problematic. For example, when looking specifically at rural adolescents at risk of suicide, Evans et al.

(1996) clearly established a relationship between characteristics such as the respondent's family dynamics and whether there was a history of abuse. Regardless of how data are collected (via a database, support lines, or self-report) crisis intervention strategies represent multifaceted perspectives that consistently pose challenging assessment problems for the professional practitioner.

Some practitioners have argued that the most effective way to assess the efficacy of practice interventions at the micro level is to focus the evaluation lens on the idiosyncratic interactions that take place between the worker and the client (M. Bloom, Fischer, & Orme, 2003). The approach typically combines both quantitative and qualitative methods that rely heavily on the client's personal constructions of the crisis experience. Such methods tend to minimize threats to internal validity, but they raise serious questions with respect to generalizability. In focusing on the rich detail of the client-worker transactions and subsequent outcomes, the search for scientifically objective generalizations is abandoned in favor of in-depth insights that can be attained only by exploring the individual case as it is subjectively experienced. Toward this end, the worker can employ a variety of evaluation strategies. It is generally agreed that no single measure can adequately capture all the relevant subtleties of the crisis intervention process. As a result, Denzin (1970) and others encourage the use of multiple measures. Through an evaluation strategy referred to as "triangulation," it is believed workers can arrive at a reasonably accurate approximation of what is actually going on in the intervention process.

When addressing service effectiveness on a much smaller scale or with a more individualized focus, the micro level of *intervention* becomes the primary locus of attention. For example, from a micro perspective, issues such as individual worker influences and the subsequent treatment effectiveness that results become paramount. To highlight this perspective, skills are sometimes measured through simulated calling experiences or formalized role-plays. In an attempt to quantify this more micro perspective, Neimeyer and Pfeiffer (1994) discuss the potential value of using specific measurement instruments designed to directly measure the skill of the worker. When dealing with suicide prevention, these authors also suggest that one such instrument that may be utilized is the Suicide Intervention Response Inventory (SIRI-2), designed to measure forced responses of the professional helper in the crisis intervention setting. In fact, a variety of useful rapid assessment instruments have been designed and tested for use in crisis situations, including indices that measure life stress, negative expectations, depression, problem-solving behaviors and attitudes, personality characteristics, and other, similar traits associated with psychiatric conditions, as well as other relevant crisis-related phenomena (see Buros, 1978, Corcoran & Fischer, 1999a, 1999b). The micro approach not only invites the use of these indices for the measurement of crisis behaviors, it virtually mandates it. However, the authors of these instruments recommend caution in their use. They recognize that the evaluation of a crisis situation is a multifaceted undertaking that cannot be adequately assessed if one relies solely on a single instrument or focuses on a single dimension such as the worker's effectiveness. Overall, these authors warn that there is a paucity of literature from both a macro and a micro perspective. Very few studies address outcome-based measurement involving the evaluation of crisis intervention in general or suicide prevention services in particular (Neimeyer & Pfeiffer, 1994).

PREREQUISITES TO EFFECTIVE EVALUATION

Each of the chapters in this handbook discusses the application of crisis intervention strategies with a different population at risk. While sharing much in common with respect to many of the technical characteristics of the crisis intervention process, it is clear that there is wide variability regarding various dimensions of the short-term therapeutic experience. Crisis experiences can vary in terms of the identified problem, the client's reaction, the social worker's handling of the situation, the surrounding circumstances, and the expected outcome. Although some researchers have utilized the classical pretest-posttest design to measure practice effectiveness (Dziegielewski, 1991), other researchers have concluded that such attempts at utilizing group designs remain problematic (Bergin, 1971). Similarly, Kazdin (1986, 1994) noted that investigations that involve groups and conclusions about average client performance can either misrepresent or under- or overrepresent the effects of intervention on the individuals being served.

In discussing the need for specificity in conducting outcome research, Bergin (1971) cautioned that "it is essential that the entire therapeutic enterprise be broken down into specific sets of measures and operations, or in other words, be dimensionalized" (p. 253). This ideal is still supported and considered essential in crisis intervention, as evidenced in the more recent work of Neimeyer and Pfeiffer (1994). This concept, however, remains complicated because in the measurement of crisis intervention, techniques that evaluate crisis situations require an intimate understanding between the crisis counselor and the individual in crisis. The resulting assessment must also reflect the multifaceted assessment process that will be initiated (Dziegielewski & Roberts, 1994). In viewing crisis intervention from an empirical standpoint, the various dimensions of the intervention experience need to be treated as a complex network of functional relationships within which there occurs a series of interactions among the primary factors (i.e., the independent and dependent variables). Simply stated, in any functional relationship, the independent variables operate as presumed causes and the dependent variables operate as the presumed effects. Therefore, in crisis intervention, an important first step in the evaluation process is to sort out what are believed to be the causal connections operating in any given crisis situation. This involves identifying a series of interdependent problem-solving steps that logically flow from the presenting problem (Powers, Meenaghan, & Toomey, 1985). Embedded in the logic of this problem-solving process is an implied hypothesis, the calculus of which can be stated as follows:

> *In crisis situations, if X (e.g., suicide prevention service) is employed as an intervention strategy (i.e., the independent variable), then it is expected that Y (i.e., a return to previous functioning level) will be the predicted outcome (i.e., the dependent variable).*

Crisis intervention is no different from any other form of intervention. Inevitably, it involves, in one way or another, the testing of this implied hypothesis. For example, when it is believed that residential crisis services can serve as a supportive measure for those in crisis, thereby limiting hospitalization and increasing stabilization, specific steps to outline a plan of action become necessary. Teague, Trabin, and Ray (2004) recently identified and discussed key concepts and common performance indicators and measures that should lead to accountability in behavioral health care. The Adult Mental Health Workgroup (AMHW) is a nationally representative group jointly sponsored by the Carter Center in Atlanta and SAMHSA's Center for Mental Health Services and SAMHSA's Center for Substance Abuse treatment. Based on the consensus of five work groups, they recently developed measures and outcomes for key aspects of quality and appropriate behavioral treatment. Examples of performance indicators are:

> Treatment duration—Mean length of service during the reporting period for persons receiving services in each of three levels of care: inpatient/24-hour, day/night structured outpatient programs, and ambulatory; and
>
> Follow-up after hospitalization—Percent of persons discharged from 24-hour mental health inpatient care who receive follow-up ambulatory or day/night mental health treatment with 7 days. (Teague, Rabin, & Ray, 2004, p. 59)

Empirical practice requires that the clinician-researcher specify clearly what it is he or she intends to do with or on behalf of the client, as well as the expected consequences of those actions. To do this, both the intervention and the outcome must be defined in operational or measurable terms. To say that emotional support will result in enhanced client self-esteem, or that ventilation will reduce depression, although on the surface both may appear very important in practice, they simply are not adequate statements of testable hypotheses. As is true in all time-limited interventions, counseling and social work clinicians are expected to state exactly what is meant by concepts such as "emotional support" and "ventilation," as well as what changes are expected to occur as a result of their use (Dziegielewski, 1996, 1997; Roberts, 1990).

Based on this premise, Hartman and Sullivan (1996) clearly established specific objectives for center staff working in residential crisis services. They maintain that the key objectives include stabilizing crisis situations efficiently by reducing presenting symptoms; maintaining or reducing the frequency of hospitalizations or preadmission levels; helping consumers return to previous levels of satisfaction and service, such as housing and vocational status; and attaining high levels of consumer satisfaction with services.

Although the task of operationally defining concepts is not an easy one, most researchers concur that it is essential to the effective evaluation of empirically based practice, regardless of one's theoretical orientation (Bisman & Hardcastle, 1999; M. Bloom et al., 2003; Monette et al., 2005). Furthermore, the value and subsequent recognition of our clinical practice efforts will prove to be only as good as the empirical observations on which they are based.

MEASURING GOALS AND OBJECTIVES

The brief and time-limited nature of crisis intervention presents some interesting challenges for the clinician who wishes to evaluate his or her practice. From the very outset, clients in crisis need to be convinced that change is possible and that they are capable of contributing to the change process. In so doing, they gain confidence and competence, attributes that should be mirrored in the behavior of the helping professional. The development of this mutual respect and confidence in one another's abilities provides the necessary foundation for both practice and its evaluation. Basically, no matter what evaluation strategy one employs, it is likely to be meaningful only if it is initiated early and brought to closure fairly quickly. In addition, the methodology itself should not be experienced by the client as being in any way intrusive to the helping process. Ideally, the purposes of both the intervention and the evaluation should be compatible and mutually supportive.

This mutuality of purpose can be facilitated by the social work professional not only by helping the client to participate in the development of appropriate treatment goals, but also by enabling the client to stay task-oriented in regard to pursuing them. The social work professional can facilitate this process by helping the client establish specific and limited goals (Dziegielewski, 2004). Simply stated, a goal may be defined as the desirable objective that is to be achieved as a result of treatment. Well-stated goals permit the practitioner to determine whether he or she has the skills and desire to work with the client (Cormier & Cormier, 1991).

Brower and Nurius (1993) suggest two key *characteristics* to be considered when designing effective intervention goals. First, goals need to be as clear and as behaviorally specific as possible. The more precisely they are defined in measurable terms, the easier it is to verify if and when they are achieved. Once defined, the goals may be further refined in terms of more specific immediate, intermediate, and long-term objectives. Second, both the helping professional and the client should mutually agree on all goals and objectives. This may seem difficult during times of crisis, particularly when the helping professional is required to assume a very active role to help the client meet his or her own needs. This role, however, should always be one of facilitation in which the client is helped to achieve what he or she has deemed essential to regain an enhanced homeostatic balance (Dziegielewski, 1997). Only the client can determine whether the goals and objectives sought are consistent with his or her own culture and values. It is up to the social worker to help the client structure and establish the intervention strategy; however, emphasis on mutuality is central to the development of goals and objectives.

Social workers have long realized the value of goal setting as a means of facilitating the intervention process. With the advent of managed care, however, pressures from both within and outside the profession have heightened awareness of the importance of documenting outcomes. A new performance standard has been established, one that requires practitioners to have mastered the technical skills necessary to evaluate the efficacy of their interventive strategies. For empirically based practice to be meaningful, social workers must be capable of establishing the kind of practice climate in which programmatic goals, and the specific objectives designed to meet them, are viewed as realistic, obtainable, and measurable. Given the complexities of contemporary practice, however, no one methodological approach is likely to prove appropriate for all types of crisis situations. The research challenge for crisis workers, as it is inevitably for practice in general, is to fit the method to the problem, and not vice versa. This requires a thoughtful selection of research strategies, the various threads of which can be creatively woven throughout the broader fabric of the overall intervention plan.

Goal Attainment Scaling

One evaluation model that has historically gained and continues to receive widespread attention and use is Goal Attainment Scaling (GAS; Lambert & Hill, 1994). This type of scaling was originally introduced by Kiresuk and Sherman (1968) as a way of measuring programmatic outcomes for community mental health services and appears to be adaptable to a wide range of crisis intervention situations. It is discussed here as an example of an evaluation model that combines a number of very useful idiographic as well as nomothetic methodological features.

GAS employs a client-specific technique designed to provide outcome information regarding the attainment of individualized clinical and social goals. Several researchers support the belief that in today's practice environment, insight-oriented intervention strategy is limited (Bellak & Small, 1978; Dziegielewski, 1997, 1998; Fischer, 1976; Koss & Butcher, 1986;). Therefore, these types of highly structured scaling methods, with their clear conceptualization and methodology, remain popular and necessary for practice survival in today's managed care environment. The structured nature of crisis intervention, organized around the attainment of limited goals with concretely specified objectives, articulates especially well with the methodological requisites of standardized measures such as the GAS.

The GAS requires that a number of individually tailored intervention goals and objectives be specified in relation to a set of graded scale points ranging from the *least* to the *most* favorable outcomes considered likely. It is suggested that at least two of the five points comprising the Likert-type scale be defined with sufficient specificity to permit reliable judgments with respect to whether the client's behavior falls at, above, or below a given point. Numeric values are then assigned to each point, with the least favorable outcome scored –2, the most favorable outcome scored +2, and the outcome considered most likely assigned a value of 0. The net result of this scaling procedure is a transformation of each outcome into an approximate random variable, thus allowing the overall attainment of specific goals to be treated as standard scores, a feature that becomes important when GAS is used for program evaluation purposes.

This process is operationalized in the form of a Goal Attainment Guide. For example, the intervention objectives for a particular suicidal client may include (1) the elimination of suicidal ideation, (2) the alleviation of depression, and (3) the enhancement of self-esteem. Table 32.1 illustrates how these goals might be defined in terms of expected outcomes that are relevant to a specific client. Although goals can be tailored to each client's needs, a *Dictionary of Goal Attainment Scaling* is available to assist clinicians in their efforts to operationally define goals and construct Goal Attainment Guides (Garwick & Lampman, 1973).

Although somewhat dated, the definitions contained in the Goal Attainment Guide continue to be relevant to today's behaviorally based, outcome-focused practice environment, structured as it is with a specific time frame in mind. The definitions for the expected level of success (i.e., the midpoint of the 5-point scale) represent clinical predictions concerning client performance at some predetermined future date (e.g., four or six weeks following the formulations of the goals; Lambert & Hill, 1994). The amount and direction of goal attainment can then be measured by comparing baseline functioning with the level of functioning recorded on the identified target date. A checkmark is used to record the initial performance level and an asterisk (*) is used to record performance at the point of follow-up. The guide can be revised at follow-up to reflect new goals or anticipated changes in the performance levels of existing goals. While goals and objectives are some-

Table 32.1 Sample Goal Attainment Guide Illustrating Scaling Procedure for Hypothetical Suicidal Client

	Goals		
Levels of expected attainment	Suicide Weight: 40	Depression Weight: 20	Self-esteem Weight: 10
Least favorable outcome thought likely (−2)	Commits suicide or makes additional suicidal attempt(s).		
Less than expected success (−1)	Preoccupied with thoughts of suicide as a possible solution to personal problems; says "life is not worth living."	Complains of being very depressed all the time; eating and sleeping patterns irregular; cries daily; not working.	Considers self a "bad person"; criticizes self; feels people would be better off without him or her.
Expected level of success (0)	Occasionally thinks about suicide, but is able to consider alternative solutions to personal problems.	Complains of being depressed all the time; eats at least two meals a day; sleeps at least six hours a night; cries occasionally; misses work occasionally.	Doesn't verbally criticize self, but says he or she is not very happy.
More than expected success (+1)		Only occasional feelings of depression; eating and sleeping regularly; no longer crying; working regularly.	
Most favorable outcome thought likely (+2)	No longer considers suicide a viable solution to personal problems; talks of future plans.		Reports he or she likes self and way of living and/or reports being "reasonably happy."

times used synonymously in treatment records, in the context of GAS, they function as benchmarks in relation to which the outcome variables are identified and measured. Specific weights can also be assigned to each goal or objective as a way of reflecting its relative importance or priority in the overall intervention plan. Because weighting represents a relative rather than an absolute indicator of importance, however, the sum need not equal 100 or any other fixed total. The actual numerical value of the assigned weight is of significance only when GAS is used as a basis for comparing the relative effectiveness of alternative intervention approaches within or between programs.

The computing of GAS scores can be a simple or a complex matter, depending on the purposes for which the evaluation methodology is to be used. When employed as a program evaluation technique, which relies on the availability of aggregate data, it is appropriate that composite standardized scores be derived. This is a fairly complex process requiring some statistical sophistication. When used as a framework for the evaluation of a single case (e.g., individual, family, or group), however, the process is much less complicated. In fact, the only meaningful determination is whether or to what extent the predicted goals have been attained. For those who prefer to quantify such judgments, it is possible to derive a composite score by determining the amount and direction of change occurring in relation to each goal and then summing their respective contributions. An average attainment score can be calculated simply by dividing the composite score by the total number of goals. This makes it possible to compare attainment levels across clients while controlling for the number of goals.

Any number of goals may be specified for a particular client and any subject area may be included as an appropriate goal. Even the same goal can be defined in more than one way. For example, the goal of alleviating depression may be scaled in relation to self-report or in relation to specific cutoff points on a standardized instrument such as the Beck Depression Inventory (Beck, 1967). It is essential, however, that all goals be defined in terms of a graded series of verifiable expectations in ways that are relevant to the idiosyncrasies of the particular case.

It should be emphasized that the use of GAS as a framework for the intensive study of a single case does not warrant inferences concerning causal relationships between intervention and outcome. In fact, by stressing the importance of outcome factors, it tends to deflect attention away from concern for issues directly involving interventions. Although it cannot be concluded that the identified intervention is necessarily responsible for the attainment of goals, when expected goals are not realized it does raise serious questions concerning the efficacy of the intervention strategy. In addition, the construction of a Goal Attainment Guide can serve as a useful rallying point around which practitioners and clients can negotiate the particulars of an intervention contract, including the formulation of objectives, the establishment of priorities, and the assignment of responsibilities. In summary, the GAS is an example of how goal and objective attainment can be specified in order to monitor, organize, and aid as a means for collecting information on the assessment process to establish empirically based practice (Hart, 1978).

GAS suffers from many of the same limitations as other systems of measurement that are designed to treat data that are inherently ordinal in nature as if it possessed the characteristics of an interval or ratio scale. Researchers have modified the original version of GAS to fit local conditions. Therefore, any consideration of it as a single system of measurement would be misleading (Lambert & Hill, 1994). Nevertheless, measurement vehicles such as the GAS can provide a systematic yet flexible practice evaluation model that can help bridge the methodological gap between clinical and administrative interests.

USING MEASUREMENT INSTRUMENTS

Once the goals and objectives of intervention have been established, the difficult task of evaluating the clinical intervention in standardized or operationally based terms can be addressed. This task is simplified greatly when problems are articulated in terms of realistic goals and operationally defined objectives rather than in vague and nebulous language. Terms such as "stress," "anxiety," and "depression" are often used to describe important facets of a client's social-psychological functioning. Although commonplace in our professional jargon, such terms tend to carry rather subjective connotations. This semantic elusiveness makes it very difficult to establish reliable measures of change.

Measuring practice effectiveness, as stated earlier, typically involves a process designed to determine whether or to what extent mutually negotiated goals and objectives have been met. Change is documented through some type of concrete measurement that is indicative of client progress. Dziegielewski (2002, 2004) suggests that this process can be greatly facilitated by establishing clear-cut contracts with clients, who, in turn, provide a viable foundation for a variety of individual or group evaluation designs. Once the contract is in place, standardized instruments can be used as repeated measures to gather consistent data from baseline through termination and follow-up. It is the responsibility of the social work professional, of course, to select, implement, and evaluate the appropriateness of the measurement instruments. Most professionals agree that standardized scales (i.e., those that have been assessed for reliability and validity) are generally preferred.

In recent years, social workers have begun to rely more heavily on standardized instruments in an effort to achieve greater accuracy and objectivity in their attempts to measure some of the more commonly encountered clinical problems. The most notable development in this regard has been the emergence of numerous brief pencil-and-paper assessment devices known as rapid assessment instruments (RAIs). As standardized measures, RAIs share a number of characteristics in common. They are brief, are relatively easy to administer, score, and interpret, and they require very little knowledge of testing procedures on the part of the clinician. For the most part, they are self-report measures that can be completed by the client, usually within 15 minutes. They are independent of any particular theoretical orientation, and as such can be used with a variety of interventive methods. Because they provide a systematic overview of the client's problem, they often tend to stimulate discussion related to the information elicited by the instrument itself. The score that is generated provides an operational index of the frequency, duration, or intensity of the problem. Most RAIs can be used as repeated measures, and thus are adaptable to the methodological requirements of both research design and goal assessment purposes. In addition to providing a standardized means by which change can be monitored over time with a single client, RAIs can also be used to make equivalent comparisons across clients experiencing a common problem (e.g., marital conflict).

One of the major advantages of standardized RAIs is the availability of information concerning reliability and validity. Reliability refers to the stability of a measure; in other words, do the questions that compose the instrument mean the same thing to the individual answering them at different times, and would different individuals interpret those same questions in a similar manner? Unless an instrument yields consistent data, it is impossible for it to be valid. But even highly reliable instruments are of little value unless their validity can also be demonstrated. Validity speaks to the general question of whether an instrument does in fact measure what it purports to measure.

There are several different approaches to establishing validity (Chen, 1997; Cone, 1998; Powers et al., 1985; Schutte & Malouff, 1995), each of which is designed to provide information regarding how much confidence we can have in the instrument as an accurate indicator of the problem under consideration. Levels of reliability and validity vary greatly among available instruments, and it is very helpful to the social work professional to know in advance the extent to which these issues have been addressed. Information concerning reliability and validity, as well as other factors related to the standardization process (e.g., the procedures for administering, scoring, and interpreting the instrument), can help the professional make informed judgments concerning the appropriateness of any given instrument.

The key to selecting the best instrument for the intervention is knowing where and how to access the relevant information concerning potentially useful measures. Fortunately, there are a number of excellent sources available to the clinician to help facilitate this process. One such compilation of standardized measures is *Measures of Clinical Practice* by Corcoran and Fischer (1999a, 1999b) and another is *Sourcebook of Adult Assessment Strategies* by Schutte and Malouff (1995). These reference texts can serve as valuable resources for identifying useful RAIs suited for the kinds of problems most commonly encountered in clinical social work practice. Corcoran and Fischer have done an excellent job, not only in identifying and evaluating a viable cross-section of useful clinically grounded instruments, but also in discussing a number of issues critical to their use. Schutte and Malouff provide a list of mental health–related measures for adults and guidelines for their use with different types of practice-related problems. In addition to an introduction to the basic principles of measurement, these books discuss various types of measurement tools, including the advantages and disadvantages of RAIs. Corcoran and Fischer also provide some useful guidelines for locating, selecting, evaluating, and administering prospective measures. Further, the instruments are provided in two volumes in relation to their appropriateness for use with one of three target populations: adults, children, or couples and families. They are also cross-indexed by problem area, which makes the selection process very easy. The availability of these as well as numerous other similar references related to special interest areas greatly enhances the social work professional's options with respect to monitoring and evaluation practice (Buros, 1978; Mitchell, 1983a, 1983b).

Overall, the RAIs can serve as valuable adjuncts for the social work professional's evaluation efforts. In crisis intervention, however, more emphasis on their utility is needed. To date, the reviews and acceptance of this type of assessment tool have been mixed. For example, in the area of suicide risk, Jobes, Eyman, and Yufit (1995) found that most professionals familiar with such instruments tended to use them only infrequently. Many of these same professionals believed that, when specifically used to quantify behaviors and feelings in times of crisis, their utility was limited. Until these perceived shortcomings have been resolved, RAIs should probably be employed only as one aspect of a more comprehensively triangulated evaluation strategy.

One of the more notable deficits cited in the evaluation literature related to crisis intervention is the paucity of studies that look directly at social work practitioner effectiveness. It should be noted that there are a variety of tools available that can help the social worker to measure his or her own perceived effectiveness (Fischer, 1976). This type of introspective practice assessment is intentionally designed to provide social workers with the kinds of timely feedback they need to enable them to modify and refine their techniques and strategies for future use in similar cases. Several scales and other concrete measurement indices have been designed to assist the social worker to do this (Corcoran & Fischer, 1999a, 1999b).

Last, to further enhance the measurement of practice effectiveness, many social workers are feeling pressured to incorporate additional forms of measurement as part of the treatment plan (Dziegielewski, 1997). The pressure to incorporate individual, family, and social rankings is becoming more common. This requires a procedure capable of monitoring a client's functioning level that can be clearly measured and documented. To provide this additional form of measurement, an increasing number of professionals are turning to the *DSM-IV* and providing Axis V (Generalized Assessment of Functioning [GAF]) rating scores for each client served. In this method, ratings of a client's functioning are assigned at the outset of therapy and again on discharge. The scales allow for the assignment of a number that represents a client's behaviors. The scales are designed to enable the worker to differentially rank identified behaviors from 0 to 100, with higher ratings indicating higher overall functioning and coping levels. By rating the highest level of functioning a client has attained over the past year and then comparing it to his or her current level of functioning, helpful comparisons can be made. This process can help social workers to both quantify client problems and document observable changes that may be attributable to the counseling relationship. This allows the worker to track performance variations across behaviors relative to client functioning. See the *DSM-IV* (American Psychiatric Association, 2000) for scale rankings for the above. Also, in the *DSM-IV-TR* "Criteria Sets and Axes Provided for Further Study," there are two scales that are not required for diagnosis yet can provide a format for ranking function that might be particularly helpful to social work professionals. The first of these optional scales is the relational functioning scale termed the Global Assessment of Relational Functioning (GARF). This index is used to address the status of family or other ongoing relationships on a hypothetical continuum from *competent* to *dysfunctional* (American Psychiatric Association, 2000). The second index is the Social and Occupational Functioning Assessment Scale (SOFAS). With this scale the individual's level of social and occupational functioning can be addressed (American Psychiatric Association, 2000). The complementary nature of these scales in identifying and assessing client problems is evident in the fact that all three scales, GARF, GAF, and SOFAS, use the same rating system. The rankings for each scale range from 0 to 100, with the lower numbers representing more severe problems. The use of all three of these tools has been encouraging for obvious reasons. Collectively, they provide a viable framework within which social workers can apply concrete measures to a wide variety of practice situations. They also provide a multidimensional perspective that permits workers to document variations in levels of functioning across system sizes, including the individual (GAF), family (GARF), and social (SOFAS) perspective.

In summary, it is obvious that the helping relationship is a complex one that cannot be measured completely through the use of standardized scales or social worker assessment measures. To facilitate measurement of effectiveness, specific concrete goals and objectives must incorporate a number of direct behavioral observation techniques, self-anchored rating scales, client logs, projective tests, Q-sort techniques, unobtrusive measures, and personality tests as well as a variety of mechanical devices for monitoring physiological functioning. Together, these methods can provide a range of qualitative and quantitative measures for evaluating practice. Several of them are especially well suited for the assessment of practice based on the more phenomenological and existentially grounded theories. Space limitations do not permit a discussion of these methods in this chapter; however, there are a number of excellent sources available that discuss in detail the kinds of information one would need to make informed decisions regarding their selection and application to specific cases (M. Bloom et al., 2003; Powers et al., 1985; Rubin & Babbie, 1993).

CASE-RELATED OR MICRO DESIGNS IN CRISIS INTERVENTION

As a specific type of micro-level design, intensive is distinguished from extensive models of research because it is primarily concerned with the study of single cases (i.e., N = 1). In this chapter, the terms single-system (M. Bloom et al., 2003), single-subject, and single-case designs (Bisman & Hardcastle, 1999) are used more or less interchangeably. Preference is noted, however, for the term single-system and single-case designs as they allow for a broader definition of the case under study rather than simply referring directly to one specific client as a subject.

We have chosen to highlight the single-system or case designs in crisis intervention, even though it has been argued that they add little to the confirmatory process that leads to scientific generalizations. The reason for this focus is simple: they are of enormous value to the scientifically oriented clinician interested in evaluating the effectiveness of his or her own practice interventions (M. Bloom et al., 2003). These intensive designs provide the means by which clinicians can evaluate the idiosyncratic aspects of their practice, while at the same time allowing for the generation of practice-relevant hypotheses suitable for testing via the more traditional extensive research approaches.

Further, it is important to note that the distinction between extensive and intensive models of research relate directly to the long-standing controversy regarding the relative merits of nomothetic versus idiographic research as originally differentiated by Allport (1962). Advocates of the nomothetic approaches emphasize the primacy of the confirmatory aspect of scientific activity, in which the ultimate goal is to discover the laws that apply to individuals in general. These researchers believe that the aggregate is of greater importance than are the individuals who compose it. As a result, nomothetists devote their time to the study of groups in an effort to confirm or disprove hypothetical statements and thus arrive at scientific generalizations concerning some aspect of the empirical world. In contrast, advocates of the idiographic approach tend to be more interested in the study of individuals as individuals. Rather than focusing their attention on the discovery of general propositions, they prefer to investigate the rich and intricate details of specific cases, including the deviant cases that prove to be exceptions to the rule. In crisis intervention, the acknowledgment of both approaches appears relevant and both contribute to the cushion of knowledge that informs our practice. One should not be seen as superior to the other, and with some overlap they can prove to be complementary.

The intensive or idiographic models of research are emphasized here simply because they lend themselves more directly to the primary purposes of the clinician, that is, the assessment of the social worker's own practice on a case-by-case basis. There is no intent to discount the importance of the extensive or nomothetic approaches. In fact, the probability of success in practice is likely to increase to the extent that more social workers can participate in studies that involve controlled observation and systematic verification. In this sense, the two approaches are indeed complementary, one generating scientific generalizations under controlled circumstances and the other applying and evaluating their utility in the idiosyncratic crucible of practice.

Ideally, in measuring the effectiveness of any time-limited crisis situation, the clinician-researcher needs to be able to identify with confidence a causal relationship between the independent variable (i.e., the intervention) and the dependent variable (i.e., the target behavior). For the social worker it is problematic when extraneous variables (those not directly related to the intervention) occur and cannot be clearly identified and controlled during the therapeutic process. These extraneous variables represent competing hypotheses that could be conceived as possible causes of change in the target behavior. To the extent that this occurs, it raises serious questions with respect to the internal validity of the intervention, thus reducing the level of confidence warranted by any causal inferences that might be drawn.

The classic work by Campbell and Stanley (1966) clearly describes a number of possible design weaknesses that pose threats to internal validity. For social workers engaging in empirically based practice, knowledge of these factors is essential for measuring effective and efficient services. It is important to remember that when a practice design can effectively control the influences and subsequent contamination from outside (extraneous) variables, it is said to be valid. Single-case designs can offer the practitioner a means for measuring practice effectiveness; however, as Barlow and Hersen (1984) and other researchers (Bisman & Hardcastle, 1999; M. Bloom et al., 2003) openly point out, single-case study designs vary widely with respect to their ability to accomplish this goal.

TIME-SERIES DESIGNS

The prototype for the intensive/idiographic model of practice research is the time-series design (Fischer, 1976). The process involves the measurement of change in some target behavior (usually the identified problem) at given intervals over a more or less extended period of time (M. Bloom et al., 2003). In this case, the successive observations made during the course of therapeutic intervention enable the clinician to systematically monitor the nature and extent of change in a target behavior. The actual observations and the recording of those observations may be done by the social worker, the client, or any other willing mediator with whom the client interacts on a regular basis, including, for instance, a family member, a friend, or a teacher.

Once a target behavior has been identified and an appropriate observational approach selected, it is a relatively simple matter to record any changes that occur during the course of intervention. The amount and direction of changes are usually portrayed in the form of a two-dimensional graph, as illustrated in Figure 32.1.

A

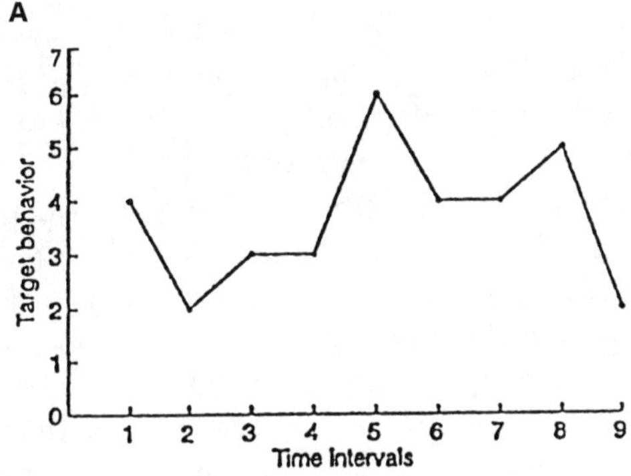

B

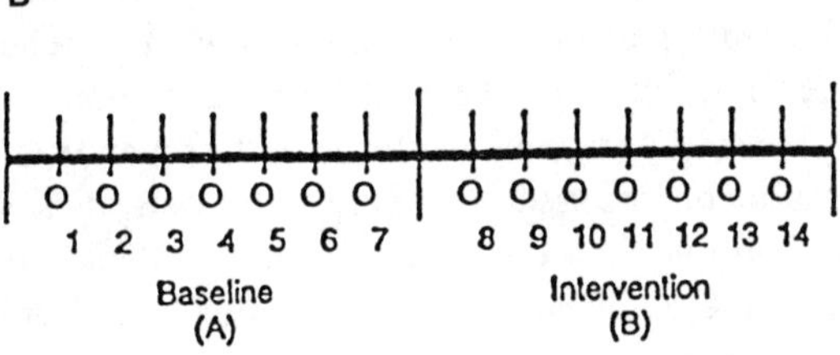

C

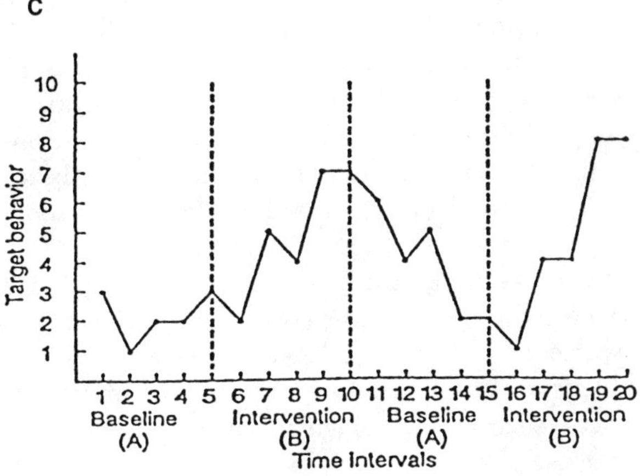

Figure 32.1 Changes in target behavior

Basically, the practitioner identifies the target behavior and plots it in relation to gradations (in frequency, duration, or intensity) arranged along the vertical axis. Successive observations are similarly recorded at regular time intervals, as indicated along the horizontal axis. The points are then joined in a continuous line that reflects the pattern of behavioral change that has occurred over the intervention time period.

This type of graph creates a visual presentation of information that facilitates the display of client behavior change. For example, a client reports an inability or lack of desire to handle his or her own affairs after the death of a loved one. When charting client responses, it would be expected that frustration and the actual inability to handle everyday affairs would decrease when given a subsequent intervention. Conversely, if the intent were to increase activities of daily living and eventually eliminate any dysfunctional crisis-related behaviors, we would expect the observed pattern to go in the opposite direction in response to intervention.

In all single-subject designs, the preintervention observation phase is referred to as the baseline period and generally labeled A. The intent of the baseline is to determine whether the pattern of behavior observed during the baseline (i.e., Phase A) changes in the expected direction following the introduction of treatment (the treatment is referred to as Phase B). If changes occur during intervention, then the social worker has some basis on which to infer that the treatment may have had something to do with it.

In working with clients in crisis, however, collecting baseline data in advance of treatment may not be practical, as the necessity of an immediate intervention may negate the luxury of advance data collection.In most crisis situations, delays in the initiation of treatment are not only likely to be viewed as theoretically questionable, but also may pose serious ethical implications (Kazdin & Wilson, 1978). In crisis, often the best one can expect with respect to the collection of baseline information may be a retrospective reconstruction of relevant data as reported by the client or some other available informant.

In some instances, as in the case of a suicidal individual, reliable preintervention data concerning the target behavior (i.e., desire to commit suicide) may not be possible. In such cases, preintervention data of a historical nature may be available from family members or friends or from archival records. In other instances, such as those involving work with AIDS patients and their families, the use of available data can prove to be a potentially valuable and reliable resource for the systematic reconstruction of important baseline information concerning the history of prior difficulties.

For example, Christ, Moynihan, and Gallo-Silver (1995) describe the assessment process with someone who has recently been diagnosed with HIV infection. They define a specific protocol to assist in gathering an expeditious and comprehensive assessment. The purpose of such a protocol is intended, in part, to document the incidences of current sexual activities and relationships as well as to use the information gathered to address past, current, or future potential for high-risk behaviors. To the extent that such "hard data" are systematically gathered and recorded in relation to specific high-risk behaviors, it may be possible to selectively exploit such information to create useful baseline measures. With some modifications, this strategy for collecting baseline information can be adopted by virtually any service delivery system that regularly interacts with clients who may subsequently be seen in a crisis situation.

It is apparent that the more rigorous the design, the more confidence one can have that threats to internal validity can be effectively ruled out. Unfortunately, the most rigorous designs require the use of baseline measures. Despite the limitations already noted, it is useful to understand some of the more sophisticated derivations of the time-series design. Although they may not always prove to be of practical value in the evaluation of particular crisis situations, they do provide useful models against which to compare the rigor of alternative approaches.

Two of the most commonly encountered variants of the basic time-series design are the reversal design and the multiple baseline approach (M. Bloom et al., 2003). In the reversal design, intervention is introduced for a prescribed period of time and then abruptly withdrawn, with the resulting circumstances essentially approximating preintervention or baseline conditions. In the absence of intervention, certain types of client behaviors might be expected to move in the direction of preintervention levels. When this occurs, it is generally considered to support a causal relationship, especially when treatment is subsequently reinstated (A_1-B_1-A_2-B_2) with concomitant improvements in the client's functioning.

Suppose, for example, a clinician were employing cognitive therapy as a means of reducing anxiety associated with the inability to control violent tendencies. The theory supporting the use of this intervention assumes that the inability to control one's temper is escalated by irrational thoughts, which in turn inhibit self-control and justify violence as a course of action. The clinician employs cognitive techniques and observes an improvement in the client's self-control during the intervention phase (B_1). The techniques are subsequently withdrawn and the client returns to his former state of irrational thinking during the second baseline period (A_2), with a concomitant increase in anxiety and potential fear over loss of control. This return to baseline conditions and ultimately to a second intervention phase provides the rationale for naming the process a reversal design. As can be seen by this example, reversal designs can be problematic, especially when the behavior one is exhibiting is dangerous to self or others. In this case, once the client's locus of control becomes questionable, immediate reinitiation of the treatment phase is warranted.

In a second type of design, the multiple baseline approach, like its A-B-A-B counterpart, is also used to minimize the possibility of behavior change due to chance. Unlike the reversal design, however, there is no withdrawal of intervention. Instead, baseline data are collected either on more than one target behavior, on the same target behavior but in more than one setting, or on more than one but similar clients. Intervention techniques are applied in a sequential manner so that once a change in the initial target behavior is observed, the intervention is systematically introduced with the next target behavior or in an alternative setting (Bisman & Hardcastle, 1999; M. Bloom et al., 2003; Fischer, 1976).

The sequential nature of the multiple baseline approach is especially useful in client interventions where more than one problem must be addressed or there is more than one target behavior that is expected to be affected by the intervention. This is true in most crisis situations where the precipitating events typically affect various aspects of the client's overall social-psychological functioning. It is important to keep in mind, however, that the validity of any multiple baseline approach is based on the assumption that the selected target behaviors are themselves independent of one another. If changes in one behavior were somehow functionally interdependent, use of the multiple baseline approach would be discouraged.

Both the A-B-A-B design and the multiple baseline approach begin to approximate the level of confidence achieved in what Campbell and Stanley (1966) refer to as true experiments. However, they are the most difficult to implement and, with respect to the evaluation of crisis intervention, have only limited utility for the practical, ethical, and methodological reasons cited earlier.

A final note is in order before we conclude our discussion of the time-series designs. In most instances, it is possible to determine whether meaningful change has occurred by means of simple visual inspection of the two-dimensional graph. Sometimes, however, it is impossible to determine from visual inspection alone whether the shift that occurs between the baseline and the intervention phases is dramatic enough to constitute a significant change. This is due to the fact that time-series data tend to be serially dependent (Gottman & Leiblum, 1974). In cases in which the observed changes may be due to serial dependence, the worker can apply some fairly simple statistical procedures (referred to as autocorrelation) to help resolve the issue (M. Bloom et al., 2003).

ALTERNATIVE MODELS

Thus far, we have discussed a number of basic time-series designs as prototype examples of intensive, idiographic, or micro-based models of practice research in crisis situations. In light of the identified limitations, a number of recommendations have emerged recently involving adaptations of the single-system model. When viewed collectively, they provide added flexibility with respect to the evaluation process. When used alone, they are not as methodologically rigorous as some of the more controlled designs. However, they do represent marked improvements over the methodologically soft or vague assessment techniques that typically characterize most efforts to evaluate social work practice. Most of the research strategies discussed here can be used in conjunction with various components of the more rigorous designs, thus providing a repertoire of techniques that can be used selectively in response to the idiosyncratic demands of a particular case. In addition, it is sometimes possible to employ several of the proposed evaluation strategies simultaneously within or across client systems. When this is done intentionally, it is referred to as triangulation, a process that enables the clinician to use each strategy as a means of cross-validating the findings generated by alternative strategies (Denzin, 1970).

In most crisis situations, there is a need for immediate clinical intervention. This inevitably makes the task of gathering relevant baseline data and the application of empirically based measures very difficult. Although direct observations of the client's preintervention or baseline functioning can be very useful, caution needs to be exercised to avoid the drawing of unwarranted conclusions. As Bisman and Hardcastle (1999) remind us, it is inappropriate to infer that any observed changes, which rely solely on the sample recording of repeated measures, are necessarily attributable to the social worker's intervention. Although positive (or negative) changes may occur concurrently with intervention, this approach does not permit us to rule out the possibility that other factors may be responsible for the observed change.

To address this limitation, a number of useful suggestions appear in the literature, including careful replication as a means of increasing causal validity (Bisman & Hardcastle, 1999) to variations on the basic time-series design, including the use of baseline measures (Barlow & Hersen, 1984). In such models, the series of observations used to monitor change in the target behavior begins prior to the introduction of any formal treatment and relies on an extended baseline with continuous measurements of the target behavior (Bisman & Hardcastle, 1999). It is worth noting, however, that extended baselines should not be relied on to control for many of the threats to causal validity. Only careful replication under controlled conditions can adequately address this limitation.

INTERVENTION AND EVALUATION: INTEGRATING THE TWO

The process of integrating our social work interventions with appropriate evaluation strategies requires that the two functions complement one another in a seamless and synergistic manner. For many social workers, this requirement has been both frustrating and confusing. Social work practitioners are increasingly being expected to operationalize the target behaviors they wish to change in clients as part of the assessment process (Dziegielewski, 1996). Yet the link between their actual practice behaviors and the strategies required to effectively assess them has proven to be elusive.

For example, in case planning, empirically based practice dictates that the problem statement, the behaviorally based goals and objectives, and the accompanying intervention plan be clearly identified. To effectively implement such a plan in an informed and sensitive manner, the social worker should be well versed in the following procedures. Initially, it is essential that the worker create a positive and supportive relationship with the client. This process is greatly facilitated by the articulation of a set of mutually negotiated, realistic, and specific time-limited goals and objectives. These goals and objectives should be clearly outlined in relation to the client's identified needs and capacities. Further, the social worker must be well aware of the personal, cultural, and environmental dynamics that surround the crisis situation as well as how these dynamics may impact the problem-solving process. The social worker's role is one of action and direction, particularly when individuals are in the early phases of the crisis experience. It is essential to realize that for individuals in crisis, the usual methods of coping do not always appear to be working. At times, clients may feel as though they are losing control and, as a result, seek the active direction and involvement of the social worker.

Second, the social worker must also be aware of the unique set of characteristics embedded in the crisis situation and how those characteristics can personally affect the social worker. The use of standardized methods, such as RAIs, are essential in helping to quantify subjective aspects of the intervention; however, they should not be viewed as all-inclusive. They are often limited in utility by the very nature of the crisis situation itself. For example, an RAI designed to measure depression may in fact prove quite reliable in measuring the symptoms associated with chronic depression. In crisis situations, however, the development of depressive symptomology might indeed be functional for a grieving widower or widow. The most appropriate approach may be to allow the experience of losing a loved one to progress naturally. In this instance, the dynamics that surround the crisis situation are somewhat atypical. Stated simply, the person who is depressed following a crisis (e.g., the loss of a loved one) may need to be treated very differently from the individual who is experiencing depression based on a specific mental health problem. As a situational factor, a reactive depression might actually prove to be a positive step in the client's overall adjustment to the crisis situation. Issues such as these, which are somewhat unique to crisis situations, can complicate the use of RAIs. This ambiguity has encouraged social workers to strive for other modes of formalized measurement. This has increased the usage of methods that require the client to rate stress and feelings of discontent on instruments such as self-anchored rating scales. To further supplement these efforts, scales such as the GAF, GARF, and SOFAS have also been used to assist in behaviorally based outcome measures. Overall, social workers are well advised to develop a range of measurement techniques that will enable them to operationally define the various dimensions of their practice.

Finally, if our goal is one of establishing empirically based practice, the importance of applying practice wisdom that is informed by theory cannot be overestimated. This requires that social workers not only be aware of what is likely to work for a particular client, but also that they possess the theoretical knowledge necessary to justify the selection and application of appropriate interventive techniques. Theory informs practice by providing a plausible framework within which critical intervention and evaluation issues can be simultaneously raised and interpreted. The more we know about the theoretical underpinnings of any given problem-solving-focused counseling strategy, the better informed we will be in our efforts to predict and explain the possible consequences of the entire intervention process. As stated earlier, practice wisdom often dictates how best to proceed in helping a client, given the specific nature of the crisis situation and the surrounding circumstances. It can also help the practitioner decide when to apply or withdraw the various components of the treatment package throughout the course of the intervention process. Counseling and social work professionals are increasingly being called on to balance practice skills with empirical techniques, techniques that in the end will yield more efficient and effective modes of service. For the crisis intervention worker, the use of measurement devices, such as structured questionnaires and psychometric instruments, needs to be supplemented with practice wisdom, theory, and, in the final analysis, life experience (Corcoran & Fischer, 1999a; Rittner, Smyth, & Wodarski, 1995).

SUMMARY

The efficacy of crisis intervention as a viable alternative to the more traditional long-term models of therapy has been well documented. The question is no longer whether crisis intervention or short-term therapeutic measures work, but rather, what techniques work best with what kinds of clients and problems and under what set of circumstances (Dziegielewski et al., 1998). Managed care presents a type of service delivery never before experienced. Social workers must show that the time-limited, brief services they provide are necessary and effective. This challenge has been a particularly vigorous one for crisis intervention advocates because of the fluctuating nature inherent in any crisis response. In this arena, however, effectiveness must extend beyond merely helping the client. Ultimately, the process of validating the effectiveness of our practice dictates that we be able to demonstrate that the greatest concrete and identifiable therapeutic gain has been achieved, in the quickest amount of time, and with the least expenditure of financial and professional resources. This means that not only should the treatment that social workers provide be therapeutically necessary and effective, but also that it should be delivered in a manner that is professionally competitive with other disciplines that claim similar treatment strategies and techniques.

Professional interest in the various forms of time-limited, brief therapy has increased greatly and will most probably continue to increase in the coming years. Social work practice that operates within a framework of a planned, time-limited, brief intervention format appears to be both a viable and essential practice modality, especially in today's managed care environment. Health maintenance organizations and employee assistance programs generally favor highly structured, brief forms of therapy, and as they continue to grow, so, too, will use of the time-limited models they support (Dziegielewski, 2004). Further, insight-oriented intervention strategies and cure-focused therapeutic approaches seem to have given way to more pragmatically grounded practice strategies.

Social workers, like their physician counterparts, rarely "cure" client problems; nor should they be expected to do so. What should be expected, however, is that we help clients utilize their own potential to help diminish or alleviate symptoms and states of being that cause discomfort. The prevailing emphasis on client individuality and time-limited, concrete changes is not only accepted as a reasonable professional expectation, but these elements are now generally recognized as essential to state-of-the-art practice (Dziegielewski, 2002, 2004).

Throughout this chapter, it has been argued that the best way to evaluate the relative effectiveness of our crisis intervention strategies is through the creative use of various intensive research designs. In recent years, a range of quantitative and qualitative research methods has evolved (Dziegielewski & Roberts, 2004). These idiographically grounded methods are of particular value to the social work and counseling professional because they are specially designed for use in clinical practice situations where the primary unit of attention is a single-client system (i.e., an individual, a family, a couple, or a group). For the most part, they are relatively simple, straightforward evaluation strategies that can be unobtrusively incorporated into the helping professional's daily practice routines. When used appropriately, they not only provide useful evaluative feedback, but also enhance the overall quality of the intervention itself.

The micro or intensive designs of research make no pretense with respect to their contribution to scientific generalizations (Baumgartner, Strong, & Hensley, 2002). They do, however, enable the crisis clinician to test the utility of scientific generalizations in the crucible of practice. The time-limited nature of most crises is such that both the intervention and the evaluation must be initiated quickly. In many instances, it is necessary to proceed under less than optimal circumstances. The clinician is inescapably faced with the issue of somehow balancing the requirements of evaluation with those of practice, and of course, in any apparent conflict between the two, the interests of the latter must always be accorded primary consideration. It is not surprising, therefore, that methodological purists may at times be critical of our evaluation efforts. But the methodological rigor of any research endeavor is inevitably a relative rather than an absolute condition. Each evaluation effort represents an imperfect attempt to arrive at a closer approximation of the truth. As such, research provides no guarantee of certitude. It simply helps us reduce the probability of error in the face of uncertainty. If we can tolerate its limitations and exploit its possibilities, we can almost certainly improve the quality of the services we provide our clients.

One final observation before we conclude our discussion. The delivery of any human service, regardless of its form, never takes place in an ethical and political vacuum. Professional actions should always be guided by an unequivocal set of professional values. All professional codes of ethics speak to the paramount importance of client rights, including self-determination and confidentiality—rights that are believed to play a critical role in the helping process. However, practice also takes place in an administrative context that is driven, in part at least, by accountability issues that are of central concern to the profession, to the agencies that deliver services, and to the vendors that reimburse them (Dziegielewski, 2004). These opposing forces may, at times, cause tension between ideological and administrative considerations, particularly as the worker struggles to satisfy the conflicting expectations of multiple constituencies.

Issues of this type are never easily resolved. They require an uncanny ability to understand and balance multiple personal and organizational demands in ways that ultimately serve the best interests of our clients. Assuming that we are not immobilized by the magnitude of such moral and political dilemmas, we can take some solace in the words of the late John Cardinal Newman (1902): "Nothing would ever be accomplished if a person waited so long as to do it so well that no other person could find fault with it."

REFERENCES

Allport, G. W. (1962). The general and the unique in psychological science. *Journal of Personality, 30,* 405–422.

American Psychiatric Association. (2000). *Diagnostic and statistical manual of mental disorders–text revision* (4th ed.). Washington, DC: Author.

Auerbach, S. M., & Kilmann, P. R. (1977). Crisis intervention: A review of outcome research. *Psychological Bulletin, 84,* 1189–1217.

Barlow, D. H., & Hersen, M. (1984). *Single-case experimental designs: Strategies for studying behavior change* (2nd ed.). New York: Pergamon Press.

Baumgartner, T. A., Strong, C. H., & Hensley, L. D. (2002). Conducting and reading research in health performance (3rd ed.). New York: McGraw-Hill.

Beck, A. T. (1967). *Depression: Clinical, experimental and theoretical aspects.* New York: Harper & Row.

Bellak, L., & Small, L. (1978). *Emergency psychotherapy and brief psychotherapy.* New York: Grune & Stratton.

Bergin, A. E. (1971). The evaluation of therapeutic outcomes. In A. E. Bergin & S. L. Garfield (Eds.), *Handbook of psychotherapy and behavior change* (pp. 217–270). New York: Wiley.

Bergin, A. E. & Suinn, R. M. (1975). Individual psychotherapy and behavior therapy. *Annual Review of Psychology,* 26, 509–555.

Bisman, C. D., & Hardcastle, D. A. (1999). *Integrating research into practice.* Belmont, CA: Brooks/Cole and Wadsworth.

Bloom, B. L. (1992). *Planned short-term psychotherapy: A clinical handbook.* Boston: Allyn & Bacon.

Bloom, M., Fischer, J. & Orme, J. (2003). *Evaluating practice: Guidelines for the accountable professional* (4th ed.). Boston: Allyn & Bacon.

Brower, A. M., & Nurius, P. S. (1993). *Social cognitions and individual change: Current theory and counseling guidelines.* Newbury Park, CA: Sage.

Buros, O. K. (Ed.). (1978). *The eighth mental measurements yearbook* (2 vols.). Highland Park, NJ: Gryphon Press.

Campbell, D. T., & Stanley, J. C. (1966). *Experimental and quasi-experimental designs for research and teaching.* Chicago: Rand McNally.

Chassan, J. B. (1967). *Research designs in clinical psychology and psychiatry.* New York: Appleton-Century-Crofts.

Chen, S. (1997). *Measurement and analysis in psychosocial research.* Brookfield, VT: Avebury.

Christ, G. H., Moynihan, R. T., & Gallo-Silver, L. (1995). Crisis intervention with AIDS patients and their families. In A. R. Roberts (Ed.), *Crisis intervention and time-limited cognitive treatment.* Thousand Oaks, CA: Sage.

Cone, J. D. (1998). Psychometric considerations: Concepts, contents and methods. In A. S. Bellack & M. Hersen (Eds.), *Behavioral assessment: A practical handbook* (4th ed., pp. 22–46), Boston: Allyn & Bacon.

Corcoran, K., & Fischer, J. (1999a). *Measures of clinical practice: A sourcebook. Vol. 1. Couples, families, and children* (3rd ed.). New York: Free Press.

Corcoran, K., & Fischer, J. (1999b). *Measures of clinical practice: A sourcebook. Vol. 2. Adults* (3rd ed.). New York: Free Press.

Cormier, W. H., & Cormier, L. S. (1991). *Interviewing strategies for helpers* (3rd ed.). Pacific Grove, CA: Brooks/Cole.

Davis, R. C., & Taylor, B. G. (1997). A proactive response to family violence: The results of a randomized experiment. *Criminology, 35*(2), 307–333.

Denzin, N. (1970). *The research act.* Chicago: Aldine.

Dziegielewski, S. F. (1991). Social group work with family members who have a relative suffering from dementia: A controlled evaluation. *Research on Social Work Practice, 1*(4), 358–370.

Dziegielewski, S. F. (1996). Managed

care principles: The need for social work in the health care environment. *Crisis Intervention and Time Limited Therapy, 3*(2), 97–110.

Dziegielewski, S. F. (1997). Time limited brief therapy: The state of practice. *Crisis Intervention and Time Limited Treatment, 3*(3), 217–228.

Dziegielewski, S. (1998). *The many faces of health social work.* New York: Springer.

Dziegielewski, S. F. (2002). *DSM-IV-TR in action.* New York: Wiley.

Dziegielewski, S. F. (2004). *The changing face of health care social work: Professional practice in managed behavioral health care* (2nd ed.). New York: Springer.

Dziegielewski, S. F., & Resnick, C. A. (1996). A model of crisis intervention with adult survivors of incest. *Crisis Intervention and Time-Limited Treatment, 2*(1), 49–56.

Dziegielewski, S. F., & Roberts, A. R. (2004). Health care evidence-based practice: A product of political and cultural times. In A. R. Roberts & K. R. Yeager (Eds.), *Handbook of practice-focused research and evaluation* (pp. 200–204). New York: Oxford University Press.

Dziegielewski, S. F., Shields, J. P., & Thyer, B. A. (1998). Short-term treatment: Models, methods, and research. In J. B. Williams & K. Ell (Eds.), *Advances in mental health research: Implications for practice* (pp. 287–308). Washington, DC: NASW Press.

Evans, W., Smith, M., Hill, G., Albers, E., & Neufeld, J. (1996). Rural adolescent views of risk and protective factors associated with suicide. *Crisis Intervention and Time-Limited Treatment, 3*(1), 1–13.

Fischer, J. (1976). *Effective casework practice: An eclectic approach.* New York: McGraw-Hill.

Garwick, G., & Lampman, S. (1973). *Dictionary of goal attainment scaling.* Minneapolis: Program Evaluation Project.

Gilliland, B. E., & James, R. K. (2003). *Crisis intervention strategies* (4th ed.). Pacific Grove, CA: Brooks/Cole.

Gottman, J. M., & Leiblum, S. R. (1974). *How to do psychotherapy and how to evaluate it.* New York: Holt, Rinehart and Winston.

Hart, R. R. (1978). Therapeutic effectiveness of setting and monitoring goals. *Journal of Consulting and Clinical Psychology, 46,* 1242–1245.

Hartman, D. J., & Sullivan, W. P. (1996, October). Residential crisis services as an alternative to inpatient care. *Families in Society: The Journal of Contemporary Human Services,* 496–501.

Jobes, D., Eyman, T., & Yufit, X. (1995). How clinicians assess suicide risk in adolescents. *Crisis intervention and time-limited treatment,* 2, 1–12.

Kazdin, A. E. (1986). The evaluation of psychotherapy: Research designs and methodology. In S. L. Garfield & A. E. Bergin (Eds.), *Handbook of psychotherapy and behavior change* (pp. 23–68). New York: Wiley.

Kazdin, A. E. (1994). Methodology, design and evaluation in psychotherapy research. In S. L. Garfield & A. E. Bergin (Eds.), *Handbook of psychotherapy and behavior change* (4th ed., pp. 19–71). New York: Wiley.

Kazdin, A. E., & Wilson, G. T. (1978). *Evaluation of behavior therapy: Issues, evidence and re-*

search strategies. Cambridge, MA: Ballinger.

Kiesler, D. J. (1966). Some myths of psychotherapy research and the search for a paradigm. *Psychological Bulletin, 65,* 110–136.

Kiresuk, T. J., & Sherman, R. E. (1968). Goal attainment scaling: A general method for evaluating comprehensive community mental health programs. *Community Mental Health Journal, 4,* 443–453.

Koss, M. P., & Butcher, J. N. (1986). Research on brief psychotherapy. In S. L. Garfield & A. E. Bergin (Eds.), *Handbook of psychotherapy and behavior change* (pp. 627–670). New York: Wiley.

Koss, M. P., & Shaing, J. (1994). Research in brief therapy. In A. E. Bergin & S. L. Garfield (Eds.), *Handbook of psychotherapy and behavior change* (4th ed., pp. 664–700). New York: Wiley.

Lambert, M. J., & Hill, C. E. (1994). Assessing psychotherapy outcomes and process. In S. L. Garfield & A. E. Bergin (Eds.), *Handbook of psychotherapy and behavior change* (4th ed., pp. 72–113). New York: Wiley.

Lindemann, E. (1944). Symptomatology and management of acute grief. *American Journal of Psychiatry, 101,* 141–148.

Mezzina, R., & Vidoni, D. (1995). Beyond the mental hospital: Crisis intervention and continuity of care in Trieste. A four-year follow-up study in a community mental health centre. *International Journal of Social Psychiatry, 41,* 1–20.

Mitchell, J. V. (1983a). *Ninth mental measurement yearbook.* Lincoln: University of Nebraska Press.

Mitchell, J. V. (1983b). *Tests in print III.* Lincoln: University of Nebraska Press.

Monette, D. R., Sullivan, T. J., & DeJong, C. R. (2005). *Applied social research: A tool for human services.* Belmont, CA: Books/Cole-Thompson Learning.

Neimeyer, R. A., & Pfeiffer, A. M. (1994). Evaluation of suicide intervention effectiveness. *Death Studies, 18,* 131–166.

Nugent, W. R., Sieppert, J. D., & Hudson, W. W. (2001). *Practice evaluation for the 21st century.* Belmont, CA: Brooks/Cole-Thomson Learning.

Parad, H., et al. (1990). *Crisis intervention: The practitioner's sourcebook for brief therapy.* Milwaukee, WI: Family Service Association of America.

Paul, G. L. (1966). *Insight versus desensitization in psychotherapy.* Stanford, CA: Stanford University Press.

Powers, G. T., Meenaghan, T., & Toomey, B. (1985). *Practice-focused research.* Englewood Cliffs, NJ: Prentice-Hall.

Reynolds, S., Stiles, W. B., Barkman, M., et al. (1996). Acceleration of changes in impact during contrasting time-limited psychotherapies. *Journal of Consulting and Clinical Psychology,* 64, 577–586.

Rittner, B., Smyth, N. J., & Wodarski, J. (1995). Assessment and crisis intervention strategies with suicidal clients. *Crisis Intervention and Time-Limited Treatment, 2*(1), 71–84.

Roberts, A. R. (1990). *Crisis intervention handbook: Assessment, treatment and research.* Belmont, CA: Wadsworth.

Roberts, A. R., & Dziegielewski, S. F. (1995). Foundation skills and applications of crisis intervention and cognitive therapy. In A. R. Roberts (Ed.), *Crisis intervention and time-*

limited cognitive treatment (pp. 3–27). Thousand Oaks, CA: Sage.

Roberts, A. R., & Yeager, K. (2004). Systematic reviews of evidence-based studies and practice-based research: How to search for, develop, and use them. In A. R. Roberts & K. R. Yeager (Eds.), *Evidence-based practice manual: Research and outcome measures in health and human services* (pp. 3–14). New York: Oxford University Press.

Rubin, A., & Babbie, E. (1993). *Research methods for social work* (2nd ed.). Pacific Grove, CA: Brooks/Cole.

Rudd, M. D., Joiner, T. E., & Rajab, M. H. (1995). Help negotiation after acute suicidal crisis. *Journal of Counseling and Clinical Psychology, 63*(3), 499–503.

Schutte, N. S., & Malouff, J. M. (1995). *Sourcebook of adult assessment strategies.* New York: Plenum Press.

Slaikeu, K. A. (1984). *Crisis intervention: A handbook for practice and research.* Boston: Allyn & Bacon.

Teague, G. B., Trabin, T., & Ray, C. (2004). Toward common performance indicators and measures for accountability in behavioral health care. In A. R. Roberts & K. R. Yeager (Eds.), *Evidence-based practice manual: Research and outcome measures in health and human services* (pp. 46–61). New York: Oxford University Press.

Glossary

A-B-C model of crisis management: A three-stage sequential model for intervening with persons in crisis. The "A" refers to "achieving contact," the "B" to "boiling down the problem," and the "C" to "coping." (See chapter 19.)

Acquaintance rape: Nonconsensual sex between adults who know each other. (See chapter 18.)

Adolescence: Transitional period between childhood and adulthood, typically commencing with the onset of puberty, during which youth develop the physical, social, emotional, and intellectual skills necessary for adult functioning. (See chapter 16.)

Adolescent school subgroups: Naturally formed groups within school populations, commonly identified by ethnicity, activity, or year in school. Individuals may be associated with multiple groups. Examples include "jocks," "brains," "druggies," "homeboys," or "seniors." (See chapter 22.)

Adult abuse protocol: A detailed assessment and intervention guide for the abused adult, based on assessments made by multidisciplinary staff, such as a triage nurse, a physician, and a social worker. Using this protocol accomplishes two purposes: (1) It alerts the involved hospital staff to provide the appropriate clinical care, and (2) it documents the violent incident, so that if the victim decides to file a legal complaint, reliable, court-admissible evidence (including photographs) is available. (See chapter 23.)

Affective disorders: Affective disorders affect moods and are commonly called *mood disorders.* They comprise a wide spectrum of emotions, from elation to depression to mania, with depression dominating the clinical picture. Affective disorders also manifest themselves in physical symptoms, self-destructive behavior, loss of social functioning, and impaired reality testing. The frequency, intensity, and duration of the moods distinguish affective disorders from common, everyday moods. (See chapters 25 and 26.)

Aggression: Acting with intent to dominate or behave destructively; physical or verbal force directed toward the environment, another person, or oneself. (See chapter 10.)

AIDS service organization (ASO): A not-for-profit or for-profit community organization that may or may not provide health services. ASOs are generally funded through federal, state, and/or local dollars to provide psychosocial services to people with HIV and/or AIDS. (See chapter 29.)

Anticholinergic: An agent that blocks parasympathetic nerve impulses. Associated with medications utilized to minimize the discomfort associated with opioid withdrawal. (See chapter 24.)

Anticomplementary counselor responses: Counselor responses such as interpretations, reframes, and probes that are designed to "loosen" client's maladaptive cognitions or challenge dysfunctional behavioral choices. (See chapter 7.)

Antiretroviral therapy or antiviral therapy: Medication that slows, stops, or alters the production of viral particles. There are currently three classes of antiretroviral drugs: nonnucleoside reverse transcriptase inhibitors (NNRTI), nucleoside reverse transcriptase inhibitors (NRTI), and protease inhibitors. (See chapter 14.)

Baseline period: The period during a pre-intervention phase when a series of observations are made to monitor subsequent changes in the client's target behavior. It provides a basis on which to determine whether the behavior observed during baseline (i.e., phase A) changes in the expected direction following the introduction of treatment (i.e., phase B). (See chapters 20 and 21.)

Battered women's hotlines and shelters: The primary focus of these services is to ensure women's safety through crisis telephone counseling or provision of short-term housing at a safe residential shelter. Many shelters provide not only safe lodging but also peer counseling, support groups, information on women's legal rights, and referral to social service agencies. In some communities, emergency services for battered women have expanded further to include parenting education workshops, assistance in finding transitional and permanent housing, employment counseling and job placement, and group counseling for batterers. These crisis intervention and housing placements for battered women and their children exist in every state and in many large metropolitan areas in the United States. (See chapters 1 and 8.)

Bereavement: See "Normal bereavement" and "Uncomplicated bereavement."

Binge: A prolonged episode of continuous alcohol or drug use extending over a period greater than 24 hours. (See chapter 24.)

Bioterrorism: The use of biological weapons by terrorists that produce pathogens, organic biocides, and/or disease-producing microorganisms that inflict death, disease outbreaks, and injuries. (See chapter 11).

Brief therapy: A type of intervention based on the premise that a system in crisis is more open to change, and that certain and often brief intervention into the unstable system can result in lasting changes in how the system functions. (See chapters 1, 3, and 24.)

Buprinex: A medication used in opioid detoxification that binds with opiate receptors in the central nervous system, altering both perception of and emotional response to pain through an unknown mechanism. (See chapter 24.)

Catastrophic events: Acute, localized violent occurrences producing widespread trauma in those experiencing or exposed to the event. These incidents commonly directly victimize groups of people and frequently include multiple fatal assaults. (See chapters 5, 6–11, 14, 16, and 22.)

Code: Word used to alert the medical team to start resuscitation efforts (CPR) to revive a victim of cardiac and pulmonary arrest. Combined with different words to designate different types of emergencies at hospitals and broadcast over the PA system. Examples: CODE Blue for victim of cardiac arrest; CODE Red for fire. (See chapter 23.)

Cognitive elaboration: The generation of alternative conceptualizations of a given event, phenomenon, or stimulus condition. This process is completed in recognition that multiple meanings exist for all human experience. (See chapter 28.)

Completed suicide: See Suicide. *Suicide* and *completed suicide* are interchangeable terms. (See chapter 2.)

Constructive: A term associated with "constructivism" or "constructive metatheory" in psychology, a tradition emphasizing the active participation of each person in his or her own life organization and development. (See chapter 28.)

Coping questions: Coping questions ask clients to talk about how they manage to survive and endure their problems. Coping questions help clients to notice their resources and strengths despite adversities. (See chapters 1–4.)

Counterterrorism: This is a diplomatic, strategic, law enforcement intelligence offensive operation that uses specially trained personnel and resources to discover, disrupt, or destroy terrorist capabilities, plans, and networks. (See chapters 7 and 11.)

Cravings: A term defined in various ways related to drug use. Typically it refers to an intense desire to obtain and use a drug. (See chapter 24.)

Crisis: An acute disruption of psychological homeostasis in which one's usual coping mechanisms fail and there exists evidence of distress and functional impairment. The subjective reaction to a stressful life experience that compromises the individual's stability and ability to cope or function. The main cause of a crisis is an intensely stressful, traumatic, or hazardous event, but two other conditions are also necessary: (1) the individual's perception of the event as the cause of considerable upset and/or disruption; and (2) the individual's inability to resolve the disruption by previously used coping methods. *Crisis* also refers to "an upset in the steady state." It often has five components: a hazardous or traumatic event, a vulnerable state, a precipitating factor, an active crisis state, and the resolution of the crisis. (See chapters 1–4.)

Crisis call to domestic violence hotline: A telephone call to a hotline in which the caller is in imminent danger or has just been abused or battered by an intimate partner. (See chapters 1 and 19.)

Crisis intervention: The first stage of crisis intervention, also known as emotional "first aid," focuses on establishing rapport, making a rapid assessment, and stabilizing and reducing the person's symptoms of distress and the impact of a crisis. The next stages utilize crisis intervention strategies (e.g., active listening, ventilation, reflection of feeling, storytelling, reframing, and exploring alternative solutions) while assisting the individual in crisis to return to a state of adaptive functioning, crisis resolution, and cognitive mastery. This type of timely intervention focuses on helping to mobilize the resources of those differentially affected. Crisis intervention may be given over the telephone or in person. (See chapters 1 and 2.) For in-depth case applications of Roberts's seven-stage crisis intervention model to a range of urgent and acute crisis episodes. (See chapters 1–5 and 16–30.)

Crisis intervention service: These services provide a person in crisis with the phone numbers of local hotlines, community crisis centers, crisis intervention units at the local community mental health center, rape crisis centers, battered women's shelters, and family crisis intervention programs, which then provide follow-up and home-based crisis services. Crisis intervention services are available 24 hours a day, seven days a week, and are usually staffed by crisis clinicians, counselors, social workers, hospital emergency room staff, and trained volunteers. (See chapters 1, 2, and 23–30.)

Crisis-oriented treatments: Treatment approaches that apply to all practice models and techniques, which are focused on resolving immediate crisis situations and emotionally volatile conflicts with a minimum number of contacts (usually one to six), and are characterized as time-limited and goal-directed. (See chapter 1.)

Crisis residential unit: A 24-hour supervised setting for individuals experiencing any type of crisis who are 18 years of age or older, medically stable and no overt threat to themselves or others. This brief stay (up to 5 days) focuses on problem solving and crisis management through individual supportive counseling, group treatment, psychiatric and nursing services, as well as appropriate referrals. (See chapter 20.)

Crisis resolution: The goal of interventions given by trained volunteers and professionals to persons in crisis. Resolution involves the restoration of equilibrium, cognitive mastery of the situation, and the development of new coping methods. An effective crisis resolution removes vulnerabilities from the individual's past and bolsters the individual with an increased repertoire of coping skills that serve as a buffer against similar situations in the future. (See chapters 1 through 5.)

Critical incident: An event that has the potential to overwhelm one's usual coping mechanisms, resulting in psychological distress and an impairment of normal adaptive functioning. (See chapters 6, 8, and 9.)

Critical Incident Stress Debriefing: A seven-stage structured group meeting or discussion in which personnel who have been affected by a traumatic event given a chance to discuss their thoughts and emotions in a controlled manner usually, 1 to 10 days after an acute crisis and 3 to 4 weeks after a mass disaster. (See chapter 9.)

Critical Incident Stress Management (CISM): An integrated and comprehensive multicomponent program for providing crisis and disaster mental health services. A variety of stress management techniques/intervention provided to emergency services personnel, police, and/or firefighters who are exposed to life-threatening or traumatic incidents. This model was developed by Jeffrey Mitchell and George Everly (authors of chapter 9 and cofounders of the International Critical Incident Stress Foundation). (See chapters 8 and 9.)

Date rape: Nonconsensual sex between partners who date or are on a date. (See chapter 18.)

Date rape drugs: Sedative-type drugs, some of which are illegal substances, that render victims unable to defend themselves against sexual exploitation; alcohol, Rohypenol, and Ectasy are three of the most common date rape drugs. (See chapter 18.)

Debriefing at school: A meeting held soon after a crisis event to review the activities of a school crisis intervention team during a recent crisis response with the primary goal of supporting team members and ultimately improving the future functioning of the team as a whole and the quality of the interventions offered. (See chapter 21.)

Decompensation: Person having a chronic mental condition may periodically experience worsening symptoms such as depression or psychosis. This general decline in condition is called *decompensation.* (See chapters 15, 25, and 28.)

Defusing: An approximately 1-hour, three-phase, structured small-group discussion provided within hours of a crisis for purposes of assessment, triaging, and acute symptom mitigation. (See chapters 8 and 9.)

Deinstitutionalization: The Community Mental Health Centers Act of 1963 required that mental health services be moved from inpatient institutions to community-based services. This transition is referred to as *deinstitutionalization,* and one of the services mandated by the act is crisis services. (See chapters 25 and 26.)

Delayed: Group that can be transferred to a "walk-in" location. These include conditions that do not require emergency room care at all and can be seen at any time, like most rashes or a previous wound that needs checking. (See chapter 23.)

Dependent variables: Variables that represent the presumed effect in any functional relationship. (See chapter 32.)

Disequilibrium: An emotional state that may be characterized by confusing emotions, somatic complaints, and erratic behavior. The severe emotional discomfort experienced by the person in crisis propels him or her toward action that will reduce the subjective discomfort. Crisis intervention usually alleviates the early symptoms of disequilibrium within the first 6 weeks of treatment, and hopefully soon restores equilibrium. (See chapters 1, 2, and 5.)

Dismantling treatment strategy: A strategy involving the orderly removal of one or more components of the treatment package, accompanied by careful recording of the apparent effects. This systematic elimination, or isolation, enables the clinician to "determine the necessary and sufficient components for therapeutic change." (See chapter 35.)

District-level crisis intervention team: A school crisis intervention team composed of staff from the school district's central office to provide oversight, resources, and administrative support to school-based crisis intervention teams. (See chapter 21.)

Ego fragmentation: Ego fragmentations, sometimes referred to as *dissociative disorders,* are characterized by disturbances in normally integrated functions of memory, identity, or consciousness. They are found in diagnoses such as posttraumatic stress disorder, acute stress disorder, and somatization disorder. Harsh psychosocial stressors such as physical threat, wartime, and disasters predispose susceptible persons to ego fragmentations. (See chapters 5 and 8.)

Emergency room: A department in a hospital open 24 hours a day to victims of emergent and urgent situations. Treatment is provided by a medical team of doctors, nurses, respiratory therapists, lab technicians, and social workers. (See chapter 23.)

Emergent: Group that requires immediate attention and includes cardiac arrest and trauma codes. (See chapter 23.)

Exception questions: Questions that inquire about times when the problem is either absent, less intense, or dealt with in a manner that is acceptable to the client. (See chapter 3.)

Excitatory toxicity: Massive release of neurotransmitters that in high enough concentrations may damage or destroy the neural substrates they serve. (See chapter 5.)

Extensive designs of research: Designs that emphasize the primacy of the confirmatory aspect of scientific activity. The goal of these designs is to discover laws that apply to aggregates of individuals rather than to the individuals who constitute the aggregate. In this approach, the ultimate goal is to discover scientific generalization under controlled circumstances. (See chapter 32.)

Goal Attainment Scaling (GAS): This evaluation method measures intervention outcomes in which a number of individually tailored treatment goals are specified in relation to a set of graded scale points ranging from the least favorable to the most favorable outcomes considered likely. It is suggested that at least five points comprising a Likert-type scale is assigned with the "least favorable outcome" scored –2, the "most favorable outcome" scored +2, and the "most likely outcome" assigned a value of zero. (See chapter 32.)

HIV trajectory: The stages of HIV infection and the symptoms that accompany those stages. (See chapter 29.)

HIV viral load: The amount of viral particles per milliliter of blood (scientifically "quantitative plasma HIV RNA"). The viral load is an indication of prognosis, with a high load indicating that the virus is progressing rapidly. (See chapter 29.)

Idiographic research: This approach focuses on the study of individuals as individuals, rather than on the discovery of general propositions. Idiographic research investigates the rich and intricate detail of specific cases, including deviant cases that prove to be exceptions to the general rule. (See chapter 32.)

Imposter phenomenon: An internal experience of intellectual phoniness that persists despite independent, objective, and tangible evidence to the contrary. (See chapter 18.)

Independent variables: Variables that represent the presumed cause of any functional relationship. (See chapter 32.)

Information and referral (I and R) services: The goals of I and R services are to facilitate access to community human services and to overcome the many barriers that may obstruct a person's entry to needed community resources. (See chapter 1.)

Intensive designs of research: Designs primarily concerned with the study of single cases. They provide the means by which clinicians can evaluate the idiosyncratic aspects of their practice. Intensive research models can serve to generate relevant hypotheses suitable for testing by the more traditional extensive research approaches. (See chapter 32.)

Internal validity: The level of confidence warranted by any causal inference. The designs that effectively control contamination from outside variables are said to be internally valid. (See chapter 32.)

Intervention period: The period of time, typically referred to as the B phase, in any time-series design during which treatment is purposefully administered. (See chapter 32.)

Intervention priority code: Method of prioritizing crisis requests on a clinical basis. Priorities range from I to IV, depending on clinical symptoms and presenting problems of the individual. These priorities dictate in which order cases should be responded to and in what time frame. (See chapters 6 and 26.)

IOP Intensive outpatient program: Outpatient substance dependence treatment, usually offered three evenings per week, 3 hours each evening. (See chapter 12.)

Lethality: Measuring the degree to which a person is capable of causing death. Assessing for lethality entails asking about suicidal ideation, prior suicide attempts, homicidal thoughts, and feasibility of carrying out suicidal ideation or homicide. (See chapters 1, 2, 6, and 17.)

LSD (Lysergic acid diethylamide): A class of drugs referred to as the *serotonergic hallucinogens.* (See chapter 24.)

Maladaptive reaction: A codependent's tendency to continue investing time and energy to control a substance abuser's actions and behaviors despite repetitive adverse consequences. (See chapter 24.)

Nonurgent: Problems that need to be treated sometime today and not necessarily in the emergency room (e.g., sore throat or simple laceration). (See chapter 27.)

Nonviolent crisis intervention: Variety of prevention and intervention techniques proven effective in resolving potentially violent crises. This model is taught by the CPI Crisis Prevention Institute, Inc. (See chapter 22.)

Normal bereavement: The reactions to loss of a significant person, which may not be immediate, but which rarely occurs after the first 2 to 3 months after the loss. Normal bereavement involves feelings of depression that the person regards as "normal," although professional help may be sought for associated symptoms, such as insomnia or weight loss. Bereavement varies considerably among people of different ages and cultural groups. (See chapters 1 and 12.)

Objectified case studies: Studies that attempt to relate the process of intervention (what the worker does) to the outcome of that intervention (whether what the worker does can be concluded to be effective). (See chapter 32.)

Outcome evaluation: A process aimed at establishing whether a program or intervention is achieving its objectives and whether the results are due to the interventions provided. (See chapter 32.)

Parametric treatment strategies: Strategies that attempt to determine in what quantity and/or in what sequence the components of a treatment package are likely to have their most beneficial impact. By systematically manipulating one or more of the components of a treatment package, it is possible to monitor the differential effects. (See chapter 32.)

Perturbation: A state of system disequilibrium characterized by disorganization and distress, resulting in adaptation and emerging complexity and differentiation. (See chapter 31.)

Postmodernism: Refers to philosophical reflection in which a conception of reality independent of the observer is replaced with notions of language actually constituting the structures of a perspectival social reality. (See chapter 3.)

Posttraumatic stress disorder (PTSD): A diagnosis given to people who experience symptoms of intrusion, avoidance, or hyperarousal after experiencing or observing serious injury, threat, or death of a close associate (after experiencing any event that is extremely traumatic and terrifying, and that provokes feelings of helplessness). PTSD occurs when a person perceives an event as life-threatening and/or when the experience challenges his or her notions of fairness and justice. (See chapters 4 and 6.)

Postvention: Activities that take place in the aftermath of a crisis event to review the crisis response to date, with the primary goal of identifying ongoing needs of students and staff, as well as steps that can be taken to prevent the occurrence of comparable events (e.g., in suicide postvention, case finding for additional students at risk of suicide). (See chapter 21.)

Prevention: Efforts designed to avert inappropriate and antisocial behaviors prior to their occurrence. (See chapter 21.)

Primary adolescent suicide prevention: Programs offered in schools, churches, and recreational and social organizations, designed to serve as a deterrent to a suicidal crisis. These programs focus on education, peer counseling, and other prevention methods. Teaching about the prevention and identification of possible suicide attemptors may be part of these programs. (See chapters 17 and 18.)

Protocol: The step-by-step or sequential plan of a treatment. (See chapters 8 and 17.)

Psychosocial crises: Crises that are characterized primarily by psychosocial problems such as homelessness, extreme social isolation, and unmet primary care needs, and that may contribute to physical and psychological trauma and illness. (See chapter 1.)

Rape crisis programs: Programs that include specialized protocols for rape victims and that have been established by medical centers, community mental health centers, women's counseling centers, crisis clinics, and victim assistance centers. The protocol in these crisis intervention services generally begins with an initial visit from a social worker, victim advocate, or nurse while the victim is being examined in the hospital emergency room. Follow-up is often handled through telephone contact and in-person counseling sessions for 1 to 10 weeks following the rape. (See chapters 1 and 5.)

Rape-supportive attitudes: Stereotypic beliefs or societal "myths" about rape that result in the following: women being portrayed as sexual objects, discounting the impact of rape as a traumatically violent act, and absolving the perpetrator of full responsibility for committing rape. (See chapter 18.)

Rape victim: A person who reports having experienced a sexual assault that meets the legal criteria for rape. Forcible rape is unwanted and coerced sexual penetration of another person. (See chapters 18 and 20.)

Rapid assessment instruments (RAIs): Evaluation instruments that refer to any one of numerous assessment devices that are relatively easy to administer, score, and interpret and can be used to measure one or more dimensions of a client's target behavior. RAIs require very little knowledge of testing procedures on the part of the practitioner. The score that is generated provides an operational index of the fre-

Steady state: A total condition of the system in which it is in balance both internally and with its environment, but which is in change; a moving balance or dynamic homeostasis. (See chapter 11.)

Strengths perspective: A practice perspective that looks at individuals, families, and communities in light of their capacities, strengths, talents, competencies, possibilities, and resources. (See chapter 3.)

Stress inoculation training (SIT): A useful treatment package for clients who have resolved many assault-related problems but continue to exhibit severe fear responses. A cognitively and behaviorally based anxiety management approach, SIT is designed to assist the client in actively coping with target-specific, assault-related anxiety. (See chapters 1, 7, and 20.)

Student developmental tasks: Predictable challenges facing late adolescent college students that require some measure of successful resolution or adaptation. Typical age-related tasks include coordinating apparent contradictory aspects of self, managing emotions, achieving greater cognitive complexity, and forming mutually satisfying relationships characterized by autonomous interdependence. (See chapter 21.)

Suicidal behavior: Potentially self-injurious behavior for which there is evidence that the person intended at some level to kill herself or himself or wished to use the appearance of such an intention to obtain some other end. (See chapter 2.)

Suicidal ideation: Any self-reported thoughts of engaging in suicidal behavior. (See chapter 2.)

Suicidal intent: One's motive for engaging in suicidal behavior. (See chapters 4 and 5.)

Suicide: Death where there is evidence that the injury was self-inflicted and that the person intended to kill herself or himself. (See chapter 2 and 16.)

Suicide attempt: A potentially self-injurious behavior with a nonfatal outcome, for which there is evidence that the person intended at some level to kill herself or himself. (See chapter 2.)

Suicide prevention and crisis centers: Centers that provide immediate assessment and crisis intervention to suicidal and depressed callers. The first prototype for these centers was established in London in 1906 when the Salvation Army opened an antisuicide bureau aimed at helping suicide attemptors. The first federally funded suicide prevention center was established in 1958 in Los Angeles. The Los Angeles Suicide Prevention Center, codirected by Edwin Schneidman and Norman Farberow, provided comprehensive training to medical interns, psychiatric residents, and graduate students in psychology, social work and counseling. (See chapters 1 and 6.)

Suicidologists: Researchers who study suicidal behavior and suicide-related phenomena. The founder of the term *suicidology* was Edwin Schneidman. (See chapters 1, 2, and 5.)

Surveillance data: Reports produced by the Centers for Disease Control (CDC) or state departments of health on the number of HIV and/or AIDS cases and the routes of transmission, age, race, and gender of those cases. (See chapter 28.)

SWAT team: Special weapons and tactics teams are units based within police departments that receive focused training to deal with hostage situations. SWAT usually use state-of-the art equipment and communications technology, and team members are trained in hostage negotiation skills. (See chapters 19 and 20.)

Telephone crisis services: Crisis counseling, crisis stabilization, screening, information, and referrals provided to any individual calling in crisis or any significant other calling for someone else. (See chapters 1 and 25.)

Time-series designs: Research designs that involve the measurement of change in some target behavior (usually the identified problem) at given intervals over a more or less extended period of time. Successive observations made during the course of therapeutic intervention enable the practitioner to systematically monitor the nature and extent of change in a target behavior. Typically, the phases of the time-series are referred to as baseline (A) and intervention (B). (See chapter 32.)

Transdermal infusion system: A method of delivering medicine by placing it in a special gel-like matrix "patch" that is applied to the skin. The medicine is absorbed through the skin at a fixed rate. (See chapter 29.)

Transinstitutionalization: Movement of clients back and forth between systems. For example, it is common for people to move between the mental health and criminal justice systems. (See chapter 26.)

Treatment package strategy: A treatment evaluation strategy in which the impact of intervention is assessed as a total entity. In order to rule out potential threats to internal validity, such as changes attributable to motivation, spontaneous remission, intervening historical events, and the like, some sort of control or comparison condition must be incorporated into the research design. (See chapter 32.)

Triangulation: A process involving the use of several evaluation strategies simultaneously within or across client systems. When done intentionally, triangulation enables the clinician to use each strategy as a means of cross-validating the findings generated by alternative strategies. (See chapter 28.)

Trigger: A term used to describe environmental cues that lead the substance-dependent person to crave his or her drug of choice. (See chapter 24.)

Directory of Suicide Prevention and Crisis Intervention Internet Resources and 24-Hour Hotlines

PREPARED BY
DAVID AURISANO
JONATHON SINGER
ALBERT R. ROBERTS

SUICIDE PREVENTION WEBSITES

Organizations

- *American Association of Suicidology (AAS)*: The American Association of Suicidology is a national organization devoted to understanding and preventing suicide through promoting research, training professionals and volunteers, and working to raise public awareness. AAS offers a credentialing program both for crisis centers and for individual crisis workers. http://www.suicidology.org. Dr. Alan L. Berman and Dr. David A. Jobes, co-authors of Chapter 17 in this book, are Executive Director of AAS, and former president of AAS respectively.
- *American Foundation for Suicide Prevention*: This organization is committed to advancing knowledge and prevention of suicide. It provides statistics, articles on suicide, and information and services for survivors. http://www.afsp.org/home.htm.
- *Befrienders International*: Befrienders International provides free, non-judgmental counseling services for people in crisis. The website contains statistics and articles on suicide, and information on depression, self-harm, homosexuality, and anti-bullying. http://www.befrienders.org.
- *Kristin Brooks Hope Center*: The Kristin Brooks Hope Center runs the international 1–800-SUICIDE hotline system. The website provides information on crisis centers and hotlines, suicide and advocacy. http://www.hopeline.com.

tion of professionals that aims to advance the treatment of trauma, emergency services, and forensic mental health. This organization works to identify expertise and provide standards and training for professionals who provide trauma services. They publish and disseminate to their members monographs and info sheets of traumatic stress response protocols for emergency responders and violence prevention protocols. The 10-step Trauma Response Protocol developed by Dr. Mark D. Lerner (President of the Academy) and Dr. Raymond Shelton (Director of Professional Development at the Academy) and their associates is highlighted in chapter 6 in this book. http://www.aaets.org.

- *National Organization of Victim's Assistance:* The National Organization of Victim Assistance is a professional organization devoted to the recognition of victim's rights and the delivery of victim services. NOVA offers training in group crisis intervention throughout North America and maintains a national crisis response team. http://www.trynova.org
- *International Critical Incident Stress Foundation (ICISF):* The ICISF is a foundation dedicated to understanding and ameliorating the stress reactions that occur following a critical and emergency incident. The foundation offers training in multi-component Critical Incident Stress Management and Critical Incident Stress Debriefing every month in different parts of the United States. This foundation is well-known for training and certifying critical incident and disaster response teams throughout the world. Two of the authors of Chapter 9 in this book, Dr. George S. Everly, Jr. and Dr. Jeffrey T. Mitchell are co-founders of the ICISF, and Dr. Victor Welzant is the Director of Training at ICISF and co-author of chapter 8 in this book. Every two years, ICISF convenes a World Congress on Crisis Intervention, Emergency Preparedness, and Critical Incident Stress Debriefing with 1,200–1,500 participants in attendance. The next Congress is scheduled for March 2007 in Baltimore, Maryland. http://www.icisf.org
- *National Clearinghouse on Child Abuse and Neglect Information:* This website offers a manual on crisis intervention in child abuse and neglect. This manual is designed to assist caseworkers is responding to families in crisis. It presents information on crisis theory, a 9-step model of intervention, and examines specific approaches to crisis intervention. http://nccanch.acf.hhs.gov/pubs/usermanuals/crisis/index.cfm
- *National Domestic Violence Hotline:* The National Domestic Violence Hotline is a national hotline provided for by the Violence against Women Act of 1994. In addition to information about the hotline, the website contains information on domestic violence, teens and dating violence, domestic violence in the workplace, information for victims and survivors of domestic violence, and information for abusers. http://www.ndvh.org/.

CHILD ABUSE AND NEGLECT

- *National Clearinghouse on Child Abuse and Neglect Information (NCCANCH):* A service of the U.S. Department of Health and Human Services, Administration for Children and Families, Children's Bureau.

The purpose of NCCANCH is to provide the most current information on child maltreatment to researchers, service providers, consumers, and the media. Services include telephone staff (non-hotline), publications (free for download, hardcopy, or CD orders), and online databases. http://nccanch.acf.hhs.gov/

- *ChildhelpUSA: Treatment and Prevention of Child Abuse:* Childhelp-USA is a private non-profit organization founded in 1959 with programs in Arizona, California, New York, and Virginia. ChildhelpUSA services include counseling, residential treatment, group homes, foster care, professional training, educational programs, community outreach, and public awareness. ChildhelpUSA sponsors the ChildhelpUSA® National Child Abuse Hotline, 1–800-4-A-CHILD® which provides toll-free 24 hour crisis counseling, referrals to local agencies and adult survivor groups throughout the United States and Canada. http://www.childhelpusa.org/
- *National Data Archive on Child Abuse and Neglect (NDACAN):* The purpose of NDACAN is to improve and expand the use of data collected by researchers. Based out of Cornell University, NDACAN acquires microdata from researchers and national data collection efforts and makes these datasets available to the research community for secondary analysis. http://www.ndacan.cornell.edu/
- *The Child Abuse Prevention Network:* The target audience of CAPN is professionals in the field of child abuse and neglect. CAPN serves as a clearinghouse of websites related to child abuse prevention. http://child-abuse.com/

DEATH OF A LOVED ONE

- *HealthyPlace.com:* Provides basic information about grief and loss. Three online videos discuss how to prepare for the death of a loved one, how to cope with the loss of a parent, and how to help your child through a death in the family. http://www.healthyplace.com/communities/depression/related/loss_grief_3.asp
- *AARP:* A clearinghouse of resources on grief and loss, including links to community resources, articles on grief and loss over the lifespan, financial preparation, and remembrance rituals. http://www.aarp.org/life/griefandloss/
- *Alive Alone, Inc:* Resources for parents who have lost a child. Includes a bi-monthly newsletter and information on self-help support groups. http://www.alivealone.org
- *Bereaved Parents of the USA:* Non-profit self-help group for parents who have lost a loved one, including children, pets, parents, etc. Includes an excellent resource page with information on grief and loss, medical information and financial resources. http://www.bereavedparentsusa.org/
- *Parents of Murdered Children:* PMOC, originally only for parents of murdered children, has an expanded focus to include support for all survivors of loved ones who have been murdered. Services include

- *Al-Anon/Alateen:* Information on one of the largest and oldest support groups for people who live with alcoholics. National Hotline: 800–344-2666. http://www.al-anon.org/
- *American Council on Alcoholism:* Resource for the public on the effects of alcoholism. Provides information about treatment resources. National Hotline: 800–527-5344. http://www.aca-usa.org/

RUNAWAY YOUTH

- *National Runaway Switchboard:* A service of the Family and Youth Service Bureaus. NRS provides a 24-hour hotline for runaway youth. State-sponsored hotlines (e.g. Texas and Florida) are connected to the NRS's national hotline. The hotline provides crisis intervention, referrals to local services, and education on ways to return home. The site also provides information for parents, educators, social service providers, and law enforcement officials. 1–800-RUNAWAY. http://www.nrscrisisline.org/kids.asp
- *Focus Adolescent Services:* Designed for consumers, FAS provides an annotated list of internet resources about runaway youth. http://www.focusas.com/Runaways.html

ADOLESCENT AND YOUNG ADULT MENTAL ILLNESS

- *Substance Abuse and Mental Health Services Administration (SAMHSA):* SAMHSA provides information on Child and Adolescent Mental Health for consumers, service providers and researchers. The child and adolescent section provides information on national programs which address the various issues associated with children's mental health. http://www.mentalhealth.org/child/childhealth.asp
- *Youth and Mental Illness:* A self-help booklet produced by the Canadian Psychiatric Association. http://www.cpa-apc.org/MIAW/pamphlets/Youth.asp

SEPARATION AND DIVORCE

- *Canadian Mental Health Association:* Provides information for consumers on separation and divorce. http://www.cmha.ca/english/info_centre/mh_pamphlets/mh_pamphlet_08.htm
- *Divorce Anonymous:* This is a 12-step self-help group designed to help participants manage their feelings of loss, confusion, loneliness, anger, and/or grieve related to separation and divorce, and to help participants to learn new coping skills in support of new relationships. http://www.divorceanonymous.org/blog/index.php

Index